The **Rough Guide** to

Malaysia, Singapore and Brunei

written and researched by

Charles de Ledesma, Mark Lewis,

Richard Lim and Steven Martin

with additional research by

Anette Dal Jensen

ROUGH GUIDES

www.roughguides.com

Contents

Malay life colour
section following p.218

Visiting a longhouse
colour section following
p.440

◄◄ Shadow puppets ◄ Malaysian rainforest

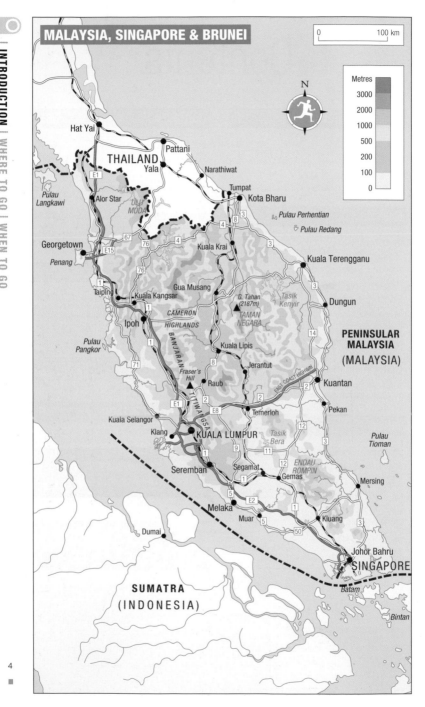

MALAYSIA, SINGAPORE & BRUNEI

0   100 km

N

Metres
3000
2000
1000
500
200
100
0

Hat Yai

Pattani

THAILAND
Yala

Narathiwat

Pulau
Langkawi

Alor Star

ULU
MUDA

Tumpat

Kota Bharu

Pulau Perhentian

Pulau Redang

Georgetown

Penang

Kuala Krai

Kuala Terengganu

Taiping

Kuala Kangsar

Gua Musang

G. Tahan
(2187m)

Tasik
Kenyir

Dungun

CAMERON
HIGHLANDS

TAMAN
NEGARA

Ipoh

PENINSULAR
MALAYSIA
(MALAYSIA)

Pulau
Pangkor

BANJARAN

Kuala Lipis

Fraser's
Hill

Jerantut

Raub

TITIWANGSA

EAST COAST HIGHWAY

Kuantan

Kuala Selangor

Temerloh

Pekan

Klang

KUALA LUMPUR

Tasik
Bera

Pulau
Tioman

Seremban

Segamat

ENDAU
ROMPIN

Gemas

Mersing

Melaka

Muar

Kluang

Dumai

Johor Bahru

SINGAPORE

SUMATRA
(INDONESIA)

Batam

Bintan

4

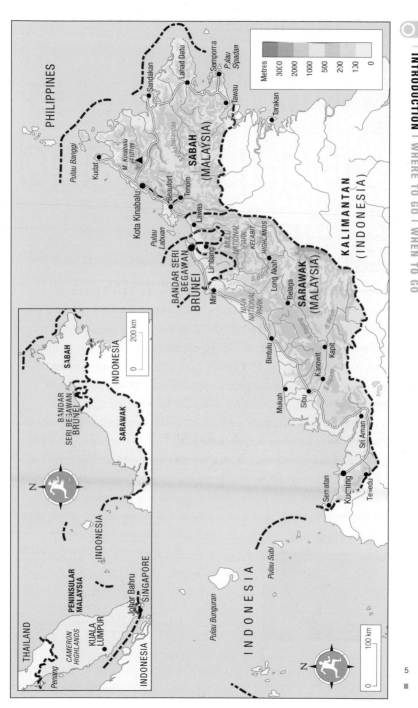

Malaysia, Singapore and Brunei

Though Malaysia, Singapore and Brunei don't possess the grand ancient ruins of neighbouring Thailand, they do boast a rich cultural heritage that's readily apparent to visitors. Populated by a blend of Malays, Chinese, Indians and – in the case of Malaysia and Brunei – indigenous groups, the three countries rejoice in a huge variety of annual festivals as well as wonderful cuisines, while traditional architecture and crafts still thrive in rural areas. There's astonishing natural beauty to take in, including gorgeous beaches and some of the world's oldest tropical rainforest, much of which is surprisingly accessible. Malaysia's national parks are superb for trekking and wildlife-watching, and sometimes for cave exploration and river rafting too.

Malaysia, Singapore and Brunei are part of the Malay archipelago, stretching from Indonesia to the Philippines, and as such share not only similarities in their ethnic make-up but also part of their **history**. Each became an important port of call on the trade route between India and China, the two great markets of the early world, and later formed the linchpins of the Portuguese, Dutch and British empires. Malaysia has only existed in its present form since 1963, when the federation of the

Fact file

• With 28 million inhabitants, Malaysia is divided into two distinct regions. Peninsular Malaysia, where the capital, Kuala Lumpur, is situated, is separated by more than 600km of the South China Sea from East Malaysia, comprising the states of Sabah and Sarawak on the island of Borneo.

• At just 700 square kilometres in size, Singapore is a crowded nation of nearly 5 million people, its main island linked to the southern tip of Peninsular Malaysia by two bridges.

• Made up of two enclaves in eastern Sarawak, Brunei is nearly ten times the size of Singapore, but has less than one-tenth the population.

• Both Malaysia and Singapore are British-style parliamentary democracies, the former with a ceremonial head of state known as the Yang di Pertuan Agung (the post rotates among the sultans from each state of the federation). Brunei is ruled by its sultan.

• Malaysia's economy, historically dominated by agriculture and mining, now features a healthy manufacturing sector, as does Singapore, where shipping and financial services are also key industries. Brunei profits handsomely from its reserves of oil and gas.

eleven Peninsula states was joined by Singapore and the two Bornean territories of Sarawak and Sabah. Singapore left the union and became an independent country in 1965; Brunei, always content to be its own enclave in Borneo, only lost its British colonial status in 1984.

Since then, Malaysia, Singapore and Brunei have been united in their **economic predominance** among Southeast Asian nations. While Brunei is locked into a paternalistic regime, using its considerable oil wealth to guarantee its citizens an enviable standard of living, the city-state of Singapore has long been a model of free-market profiteering, having transformed from a port with no natural resources into a giant in commerce. Malaysia is pursuing a similarly ambitious goal by aiming to achieve First World

Shophouses

A standard feature of local townscapes is rows of **shophouses** – two- or three-storey buildings traditionally containing a shop at street level, with residential quarters behind and above. For visitors, their most striking feature is that at ground level the front wall is usually set back from the street. This creates a so-called **"five-foot way"** overhung by the upper part of the house, which shelters pedestrians from the sun and pelting rain.

Shophouses were fusion architecture: facades have **Western** features such as shuttered windows and gables, while inside there might be an area open to the sky, in the manner of **Chinese** courtyard houses. Some, especially from the early part of the last century, are bedecked with columns, floral plaster motifs and beautiful tilework, while later properties feature simpler Art Deco touches. Sadly, shophouses ceased to be built after the 1960s and many have been demolished to make way for modern complexes, though some have won a new lease of life as swanky restaurants and boutiques.

status by 2020, to which end the country is investing heavily in new infrastructure, from highways to ports and factories.

Today, the dominant cultural force in the region is undoubtedly **Islam**, adopted by the Malays in the fourteenth century, though in Chinese-dominated Singapore, **Buddhism** and **Taoism** together hold sway among half the population. But it's the religious plurality – there are also sizeable Christian and Hindu minorities – that is so attractive, often providing surprising juxtapositions of mosques, temples and churches. Add to this the colour and chutzpah evident in Chinese temples and street fairs, Indian

> Malaysia and Singapore have something to teach the rest of the world when it comes to building successful multicultural societies.

festival days and everyday life in Malay kampungs (villages), plus the indigenous traditions of Borneo, and it's easy to see why visitors are drawn into a vibrant celebration of ethnic diversity; indeed, despite some issues, both Malaysia and Singapore have something to teach the rest of the world when it comes to building successful multicultural societies.

Where to go

Malaysia's capital, **Kuala Lumpur** (usually referred to as KL), is the social and economic driving force of a nation eager to better itself, a fact reflected in the relentless growth in air-conditioned shopping malls and designer bars and restaurants in the city, and in the continuing sprawl of suburbia and industry around it. But this is also a city firmly rooted in tradition, where the same Malay executives who wear suits to work dress in traditional clothes at festival times, and markets and food stalls are crowded in among high-rise hotels and bank towers, especially in older areas such as Chinatown and Little India.

Just a couple of hours' drive south of the capital lies the birthplace of Malay civilization, **Melaka**, its historical architecture and mellow atmosphere making it a must on anybody's itinerary. Much further up the **west coast** is the island of **Penang**, site of the first British settlement in Malaysia. Its capital, **Georgetown**, still features some beautifully restored colonial buildings and a vibrant Chinatown district, and is, together with Melaka, a UNESCO World Heritage Site recognized for its cultural and architectural diversity. For a taste of Old England, head for the hill stations of **Fraser's Hill** and the **Cameron Highlands**, where cooler temperatures and lush countryside provide ample opportunities for walks, birdwatching, rounds of golf and cream teas. North of Penang, Malay, rather than Chinese, traditions

◄ Longhouse

9

▼ Coconut palms, Terengganu

hold sway at **Alor Star**, the last major town before the Thai border. This far north, the premier tourist destination is **Pulau Langkawi**, an island with world-class resorts and picture-postcard beaches.

The Peninsula's **east coast** is much more rural and relaxing, peppered with rustic villages and stunning islands such as **Pulau Perhentian** and **Pulau Tioman**, busy with backpackers and package tourists alike. The state capitals of **Kota Bharu**, near the northeastern Thai border, and **Kuala Terengganu**, further south, are showcases for the best of Malay traditions, craft production and performing arts.

Crossing the Peninsula's mountainous **interior** by road or rail allows you to venture into the majestic tropical rainforests of **Taman Negara**. The national park's four thousand square kilometres have enough to keep you occupied for days: trails, salt-lick hides for animal-watching, aerial forest-canopy walkways, limestone caves and waterfalls. Here you may well also come across the **Orang Asli**, the Peninsula's indigenous peoples, a few of whom cling to a semi-nomadic lifestyle within the park.

> The ideal time to visit most of the region is between March and early October, when you will avoid the worst of the rains and there is less humidity

Across the sea from the Peninsula are the east Malaysian states of Sarawak and Sabah. For most travellers, their first taste of **Sarawak** is **Kuching**, the old colonial capital, and then the Iban **longhouses** of the Batang Ai river system. **Sibu**, much further to the north on the Rejang River, is the starting point for trips to less touristed Iban, Kayan and Kenyah longhouses.

In the north of the state, **Gunung Mulu National Park** is the principal destination, its extraordinary razor-sharp limestone needles providing demanding climbing, while within the park's mountains lay vast chambers and deep, snaking caves. More remote still are the rarely explored **Kelabit Highlands,** further to the east, where the mountain air is refreshingly cool and flora and fauna abundant.

The main reason for a trip to **Sabah** is to conquer the 4101m granite peak of **Mount Kinabalu**, which is set in its own national park, though the lively modern capital **Kota Kinabalu** and its idyllic offshore islands, Gaya and Manukan, have their appeal, too. Beyond this, Sabah is worth a visit for its **wildlife**: turtles, orang-utans, proboscis monkeys and hornbills are just a few of the exotic residents of the jungle and plentiful islands. Marine attractions feature in the far east at **Pulau Sipadan**, pointing out towards the southern Philippines, which has a host of sharks, other fish and turtles, while neighbouring **Pulau Mabul** contains hip, but often pricey, diving resorts.

An ideal starting-point for first-time visitors to Southeast Asia, **Singapore** scarcely comes across as much more populous and crowded than KL, thanks to Western standards of organization and hygiene – though prices that are likewise at Western levels do make an impression. The island has fascinating Chinese and Indian quarters, excellent historical museums and a smattering of colonial architecture as well as great shopping, all of which will keep you occupied for several days. Singapore also rightly holds a reputation as Asia's **gastronomic capital**, a place where you can just as readily savour fantastic snacks at simple hawker stalls or an exquisite Chinese banquet in a swanky restaurant.

For those who venture into the tiny kingdom of **Brunei**, sandwiched between Sarawak's two most northerly divisions, there are few more stirring sights than the spectacle of

Cave, Gunung Mulu National Park

INTRODUCTION | WHERE TO GO | WHEN TO GO

the main mosque in the capital **Bandar Seri Begawan**, close to Kampung Ayer water village. In the sparsely populated Temburong district, you can visit unspoiled rainforest at the **Ulu Temburong National Park** where abundant wildlife roams and the rivers are clear.

When to go

Temperatures vary little in Malaysia, Singapore and Brunei, hovering constantly at or just above 30°C by day, while humidity is high year-round. Showers occur year-round too, often in the mid-afternoon, though these short, sheeting downpours clear up as quickly as they arrive. The major distinction in the seasons is marked by the arrival of the northeast monsoon (ushering in what is locally called the **rainy season**). This particularly affects the east coast of Peninsular Malaysia and the western end of Sarawak, with late November to mid-February seeing the heaviest rainfall. On the Peninsula's west coast and in Sabah, September and October are the wettest months. Monsoonal downpours can be heavy and prolonged, sometimes lasting two or three hours and prohibiting more or less all activity for the duration; boats to most of the islands in affected areas will not attempt the sea swell during the height of the rainy season. In mountainous areas like the Cameron Highlands, the Kelabit Highlands and in the hill stations and upland national parks, you may experience more frequent rain as the high peaks gather clouds more or less permanently.

The **ideal time** to visit most of the region is between March and early October, when you will avoid the worst of the rains and there is less humidity, though note that both ends of this period can be characterized by a stifling lack of breezes. Despite the rains, the months of January and

Wildlife

Although development strategies and environmental and ecological changes have all made their mark in hindering wildlife-spotting opportunities, Peninsular Malaysia, Borneo and Singapore remain a paradise for lovers of the natural world, harbouring over 600 types of birds and more than 200 mammal species. The national parks of Peninsular Malaysia are home to Asian elephants, sun bears, cloud leopards and tigers, as well as tapirs, barking deer, macaques and gibbons. Hornbills and eagles can be spied overhead, while back at ground level pythons and cobras can grow up to nine metres long. Travellers to some of Borneo's forests and parks stand a good chance of seeing the elusive **proboscis monkey**, so-called because of its bulbous, drooping nose. The island is also one of only two habitats in the world (the other is Sumatra) for **orang-utans** in the wild – indeed, the name is Malay for "man of the forest".

The region's **marine life** is equally diverse: divers off the east coast of Sabah can swim with white-tip sharks, clown fish and barracuda, while along the coasts of the Peninsula, as well as northeast Sabah, green and hawksbill **turtles** drag themselves ashore in season to lay their eggs by night. Even cosmopolitan Singapore maintains a pocket of primary rainforest that's home to long-tailed macaques and snakes.

February are rewarding, with a number of significant **festivals**, notably Chinese New Year and the Hindu celebration of Thaipusam, taking place. Visiting just after the rainy season can afford the best of all worlds, with verdant countryside and bountiful waterfalls, though there is still a clammy quality to the air. Arrive in Sabah a little later, in May, and you'll be able to take in the Sabah Fest, a week-long celebration of Sabahan culture, while in Sarawak, June's Gawai Festival is well worth attending, when longhouse doors are flung open for two days of rice-harvest merry-making, with dancing, eating, drinking and music.

◀ Sunrise, Perhentian Islands

Average daily temperatures and rainfall

	Jan	Feb	Mar	Apr	May	Jun	Jul	Aug	Sep	Oct	Nov	Dec
Cameron Highlands												
Max/min °C	21/14	22/14	23/14	23/15	23/15	23/15	22/14	22/15	22/15	22/15	22/15	21/15
Rain (mm)	120	111	198	277	273	137	165	172	241	334	305	202
Kota Bharu												
Max/min °C	29/22	30/23	31/23	32/24	33/24	32/24	32/23	32/23	32/23	31/23	29/23	29/23
Rain (mm)	163	60	99	81	114	132	157	168	195	286	651	603
Kota Kinabalu												
Max/min °C	30/23	30/23	31/23	32/24	32/24	31/24	31/24	31/24	31/23	31/23	31/23	31/23
Rain (mm)	153	63	71	124	218	311	277	256	314	334	296	241
Kuala Lumpur												
Max/min °C	32/22	33/22	33/23	33/23	33/23	32/23	32/23	32/23	32/23	32/23	31/23	31/23
Rain (mm)	159	154	223	276	182	119	120	133	173	258	263	223
Kuching												
Max/min °C	30/23	30/23	31/23	32/23	33/23	33/23	32/23	33/23	32/23	32/23	31/23	31/23
Rain (mm)	683	522	339	286	253	199	199	211	271	326	343	465
Penang												
Max/min °C	32/23	32/23	32/24	32/24	31/24	31/24	31/23	31/23	31/23	31/23	31/23	31/23
Rain (mm)	70	93	141	214	240	170	208	235	341	380	246	107
Singapore												
Max/min °C	32/23	32/23	32/24	32/24	31/24	31/24	31/23	31/23	31/23	31/23	31/23	31/23
Rain (mm)	70	93	141	214	240	170	208	235	341	380	246	107

26

things not to miss

It's not possible to see everything that Malaysia, Singapore and Brunei have to offer in one trip – and we don't suggest you try. What follows is a selective taste, in no particular order, of the countries' highlights: natural wonders, stunning buildings and a colourful heritage. They're arranged in five colour-coded categories, which you can browse through to find the very best things to see and experience. All highlights have a page reference to take you straight into the Guide, where you can find out more.

01 **The Perhentian Islands** Page **285** • A popular pair of islands off the east coast, with beautiful beaches, great snorkelling and accommodation for all budgets.

02 Little India, Singapore Page **631** • On Serangoon Road you can almost believe you're in downtown Chennai – the area has all the sights, sounds and smells of the Indian subcontinent.

04 Traditional crafts Page **62** • Malaysia boasts a wide range of crafts, from batik and *songket* (brocade) to rattan baskets and *labu*, gourd-shaped ceramic jugs.

03 Adventure tourism Page **59** • White-water rafting, caving and paragliding, among other activities, are becoming more widely available in Malaysia.

05 **Ulu Temburong Park** Page **574** • A beautiful approach by longboat brings you to Brunei's only national park; treks and a canopy walkway will keep you busy during your stay.

06 **Omar Ali Saifuddien Mosque** Page **564** • The centre of Brunei's capital is dominated by the magnificent Omar Ali Saifuddien Mosque.

08 **Sungai Kinabatangan** Page **540** • Cruise through pristine jungle along this spectacular river, spotting proboscis monkeys and, occasionally, orang-utans.

07 **Taman Negara** Page **228** • Malaysia's premier national park, Taman Negara, is one of the world's oldest rainforests, with hides for wildlife-spotting, treetop walkways and treks lasting from an hour to a whole week.

09 **Shopping in KL** Page **128** • Malaysia's capital boasts a host of excellent malls, as well as vibrant street markets where bargaining is de rigueur.

10 **Georgetown** Page **180** • A bustling Chinese-dominated haven with elaborate temples, colonial-era mansions and beaches galore.

11 **Kuching** Page **395** • Sarawak's capital is a laid-back place with an excellent historical museum, decent restaurants and a convivial waterfront.

12 **Singapore's arts scene** Page **675** • As befits the largest city in the region, Singapore hosts a dynamic range of artistic activity – catch anything from Chinese street opera to indie rock gigs.

13 **Proboscis monkeys, Bako** Page **415** • These odd-looking creatures roam *kerangas* forest and mangrove swamps in the national park, not far from Kuching.

14 **Rainforest Music Festival** Page **415** • Held annually near Kuching, this world-music festival is an opportunity to see indigenous performers alongside musicians from across the globe.

15 **Malay entertainments** Page **279** & *Malay life* colour section • Ranging from shadow-puppet plays to top-spinning, Malay pastimes and traditional arts can be among the most enthralling events to witness.

17 Cameron Highlands Page **148** • Misty tea plantations, afternoon tea and jungle trails in cool mountain air.

16 Melaka Page **338** • The city's complex historical heritage is evident in its Portuguese, Dutch and British buildings and Peranakan ancestral homes.

18 Mount Kinabalu Page **519** • Watch dawn over Borneo from the summit of Southeast Asia's highest mountain.

19 Gunung Mulu National Park Page **465** • A sea of razor-sharp limestone pinnacles reward the challenging haul up Gunung Api, and the park also boasts underground caves which teem with wildlife.

20 Kampung Ayer Page **564** • Bandar Seri Begawan's colourful water village is reached by boats whose shape means they are sometimes called "flying coffins".

21 Langkawi Page **208** • Luxurious resorts on sublime beaches pretty much sums up these west-coast islands, close to the border with Thailand.

22 **Kelabit Highlands** Page **474** • These remote uplands offer some excellent walks and hikes plus encounters with friendly tribal communities along the way.

23 **The Petronas Towers** Page **107** • These iconic towers in KL not only hold your gaze from all angles but also house one of the city's best shopping malls.

24 **Food** Page **47** • Simple stalls in markets and malls and on the street serve up mouthwatering noodles, snacks and desserts.

23

25 **Diving at Pulau Sipadan** Page **545** • The spectacular islands off Sabah offer the thrill of swimming with sharks and turtles.

26 **Longhouses in Sarawak** Page **46** & *Visiting a longhouse* colour section • These vast communal dwellings, home to members of indigenous tribes, are found along rivers and in remote mountain locations.

Basics

Basics

Getting there

Located at the heart of Southeast Asia, and on the busy aviation corridor between Europe and Australasia, Malaysia and Singapore enjoy excellent international air links. Malaysia naturally has sited its chief international airport in the Kuala Lumpur (KL) area, but also has international airports in Johor Bahru, Kuching, Kota Kinabalu, Langkawi and Penang; note, however, that for the most part these handle flights within East Asia only. If you're flying long-haul to east Malaysia or, for that matter, Brunei, you may well find yourself having to transit in Kuala Lumpur or Singapore.

Singapore and Bangkok are very much the **regional air hubs**, and fares to these two airports are especially competitive. If your focus is Malaysia, you could look for a good fare to Singapore or perhaps Bangkok, then head to Malaysia overland or on one of the region's **budget flights**. If you do pay slightly more to fly into **KL**, you recoup this by not allotting additional time and expense to onward journeys or overnight stays elsewhere, notably pricey Singapore.

The **peak seasons** for fares to Southeast Asia are the Christmas/New Year period, typically from mid-December until early January, and July and August. Fares during these periods can be up to twice the price at other times of year, unless you book well in advance. Note that fares can also rise at weekends and around major local festivals, such as Islamic holidays and the Chinese New Year. Sample fares given throughout include taxes and any fuel surcharges at the time of writing.

From the UK and Ireland

London Heathrow has daily **nonstop** flights to KL (with Malaysia Airlines) and to Singapore (British Airways, Qantas and Singapore Airlines), taking around thirteen hours. It's also possible to fly nonstop to KL from **London Stansted** with the budget carrier AirAsia X, and to Singapore from **Manchester** with Singapore Airlines. Flying with any other airline will involve a change of plane in Europe or the Middle East, and possibly an additional stopover elsewhere. If you're starting from the **Ireland**, you'll have to change planes at

London Heathrow or Manchester or at a hub elsewhere in Europe. The very best **fares** to KL or Singapore are around the £400/€450 mark outside high season, either on full-cost airlines operating indirect flights or on AirAsia.

From the US and Canada

In most cases the trip from North America, including a stopover, will take at least twenty hours if you fly the **transatlantic** route from the eastern seaboard, or nineteen hours minimum if you cross **the Pacific** from the west coast. These two routes aren't necessarily the most economical choices however – it can sometimes be cheaper to fly westwards from the east coast, stopping off in Northeast Asia en route. **Fares** start at around US$900 or Can$1500 if you're flying from a major US or Canadian airport on either coast.

If you're in a rush, you could take advantage of Singapore Airlines' **nonstop flights** from Los Angeles (17hr) or New York (18hr) to Singapore. Malaysia Airlines also operates direct to KL from the same two cities.

Otherwise, plenty of airlines operate to East Asia from major North American cities. If your target is Borneo, it's worth investigating the possibility of connecting with Malaysia Airlines or Royal Brunei Airlines, which fly from Hong Kong to Kota Kinabalu and Bandar Seri Begawan respectively.

From Australia and New Zealand

There's a particularly good range of flights from Australia and New Zealand into

27

Six steps to a better kind of travel

At Rough Guides we are passionately committed to travel. We feel strongly that only through travelling do we truly come to understand the world we live in and the people we share it with – plus tourism has brought a great deal of **benefit** to developing economies around the world over the last few decades. But the extraordinary growth in tourism has also damaged some places irreparably, and of course **climate change** is exacerbated by most forms of transport, especially flying. This means that now more than ever it's important to **travel thoughtfully** and **responsibly**, with respect for the cultures you're visiting – not only to derive the most benefit from your trip but also to preserve the best bits of the planet for everyone to enjoy. At Rough Guides we feel there are six main areas in which you can make a difference:

- Consider what you're contributing to the **local economy**, and how much the services you use do the same, whether it's through employing local workers and guides or sourcing locally grown produce and local services.
- Consider the **environment** on holiday as well as at home. Water is scarce in many developing destinations, and the biodiversity of local flora and fauna can be adversely affected by tourism. Try to patronize businesses that take account of this.
- Travel with a purpose, not just to tick off experiences. Consider **spending longer** in a place, and getting to know it and its people.
- Give thought to how often you **fly**. Try to avoid short hops by air and more harmful night flights.
- Consider **alternatives to flying**, travelling instead by bus, train, boat and even by bike or on foot where possible.
- Make your trips **"climate neutral"** via a reputable carbon offset scheme. All Rough Guide flights are offset, and every year we donate money to a variety of charities devoted to combating the effects of climate change.

Malaysia, Singapore and Brunei, including several direct connections into **Borneo** with Royal Brunei Airlines, plus **budget flights** from Australia to KL with AirAsia X and to Singapore with Tiger Airways and Jetstar.

If you're flying from Darwin to Singapore, **fares** are as little as A$120 return in low season with Tiger Airways, while Melbourne to KL with AirAsia will set you back at least A$350. Auckland to Singapore generally starts at NZ$1500 return on full-cost airlines.

From South Africa

The quickest way to reach Malaysia or Singapore from South Africa is to fly with **Malaysia Airlines** or **Singapore Airlines**, both of which offer nonstop flights to their home countries from Johannesburg, with connections from Cape Town. Reckon on around ten hours' flying time with either airline. **Fares** from South Africa to Malaysia

or Singapore aren't cheap, starting at around R7200 return, including taxes.

From elsewhere in Southeast Asia

It's both a cliché and a fact: **budget air travel** has taken off in a big way in Asia. If you plan it right, you can easily take in Malaysia, Singapore or Brunei as part of a general meander through the region, taking advantage of efficient, cheap air connections with many Southeast Asian capitals and provincial cities, and with a minimum of backtracking.

The most useful no-frills carriers for the three countries covered in this book are the Malaysia's **AirAsia** and **Firefly**, and Singapore's **Jetstar** and **Tiger Airways**. Though fuel surcharges and taxes do take some of the shine off the fares, prices can still be keen, especially if you book well in advance of your journey: on AirAsia, for example, Bali to Johor Bahru one way starts at £12/$18 all-in, while Chiang Mai to KL starts at around £55/$80.

You can, of course, reach Malaysia or Singapore from their immediate neighbours by means other than flying. There are **road** connections from Thailand and from Kalimantan (Indonesian Borneo), **ferries** from the Indonesian island of Sumatra and from the southern Philippines, and **trains** from Thailand. Below is a round-up of the most popular routes.

From Thailand

There are two daily **rail** services between Thailand and Malaysia, supplemented by the luxurious Eastern and Oriental Express, which runs all the way to Singapore (see box below). The two ordinary rail services comprise an express run between the southern Thai city of **Hat Yai** and **KL**, run by the Malaysian rail company KTM (ⓦwww.ktmb.com.my), and an express between **Bangkok** and the Malaysian west-coast city of **Butterworth** (close to Penang island), run by State Railway of Thailand (ⓦwww.railway.co.th). The KTM service leaves Hat Yai at 2.50pm, taking sixteen hours to reach KL; the Bangkok train leaves Hualamphong Station at around 2pm, stopping ten times en route (notably at Hua Hin, Surat Thani, Hat Yai and Alor Star in Kedah), and arriving in Butterworth 24 hours later. Also useful is the Thai rail service from Hat Yai, which is on the west coast of southern Thailand, across to **Sungai Golok** on the east coast, close to the Malaysian border crossing at Rantau Panjang, from where buses run to Kota Bharu.

Hat Yai–KL **fares** start at RM44 in an ordinary seat, rising to RM57 in a lower-berth sleeper. For more on the Malaysian rail network, see p.38.

As regards **flights**, there are plenty of services connecting Bangkok and Chiang Mai with KL and Singapore. Some of the less obvious connections include Bangkok to Penang (AirAsia); Ko Samui to KL (Berjaya Air), Penang (Firefly) and Singapore (Bangkok Airways); and Phuket to KL (AirAsia), Penang (Firefly) and Singapore (Tiger Airways). Note that Bangkok Airways (ⓦwww.bangkokair.com) and Berjaya Air (ⓦwww.berjaya-air.com) are not budget operators.

A few scheduled **ferry** services sail from the most southwesterly Thai town of Satun to the Malaysian west-coast town of Kuala Perlis (30min) and to Pulau Langkawi (1hr 30min). Departing from Thailand by sea for Malaysia, ensure your passport is stamped at the immigration office at the pier to avoid problems with the Malaysian immigration officials when you arrive. Another option is the ferry from the southern Thai town of Ban Taba to the Malaysian town of Pengkalan Kubor, where frequent buses run to Kota Bharu, 20km away. There are buses to Ban

The Eastern & Oriental Express

Unlike some luxury trains in other parts of the world, the **Eastern & Oriental Express** isn't a re-creation of a classic colonial-era rail journey, but a sort of fantasy realization of how such a service might have looked had it existed in the Far East. Employing 1970s Japanese rolling stock, given an elegant old-world cladding with wooden inlay work and featuring Thai and Malay motifs, the train departs from Bangkok on certain Sundays bound for Singapore, returning on Thursdays. En route there are extended stops at Kanchanaburi for a visit to the infamous bridge over the **River Kwai**, and at Butterworth, where there's time for a half-day tour of **Georgetown**. An observation deck at the rear of the train makes the most of the passing scenery.

The trip takes four days and three nights (three days and two nights if done from Singapore) and costs around £1200/US$1750 per person in swish, en-suite Pullman accommodation, including meals of Eurasian fusion food, though alcohol costs extra. On the southbound leg, leaving the train at KL is not a bad idea, as this eliminates the third night of the journey and brings the fare down to £1000/US$1500. For **bookings** contacts in various countries and more details of the trip, see ⓦwww.orient-express.com.

Taba from the provincial capital, Narathiwat (1hr 30min).

The easiest road access from Thailand is via Hat Yai, from where **buses** and shared taxis run regularly to Butterworth (4hr) and nearby Georgetown on Penang island. From the interior Thai town of Betong, there's a road across the border to the Malaysian town of **Keroh**, from where Route 67 leads west to meet Route 1 at Sungai Petani; shared taxis run along the route. You can also get a taxi from Ban Taba for the few kilometres south to Kota Bharu.

From Indonesia

There are plenty of budget flights from Indonesia to Malaysia and Singapore. **From Java**, AirAsia operates flights to KL from Bandung, Jakarta, Surabaya and Yogyakarta, while there are flights to Singapore from Jakarta and Surabaya with Jetstar. You can reach northern Borneo from Jakarta and Surabaya with Royal Brunei Airways into Bandar Seri Begawan. **From Sumatra**, AirAsia operates from Medan, Padang and Pekanbaru to KL, as well as from Medan to Penang (also served by Firefly) and Johor Bahru; there are also flights to Singapore from Medan and Palembang (with Singapore Airlines subsidiary **SilkAir**, not a budget carrier; ⓦwww.silkair.com), and from Padang (Tiger Airways). There are also flights **from Bali** to Bandar Seri Begawan (Royal Brunei), Johor Bahru and KL (AirAsia) and Singapore (Jetstar); and **from Lombok** to Singapore (SilkAir). Surprisingly there aren't any flights **from Kalimantan** to Malaysian Borneo, though AirAsia does operate from Balikpapan to KL.

It's possible to reach Sarawak from Kalimantan on just one road route, through the border town of Entikong and onwards to Kuching. The bus trip from the western city of Pontianak to Entikong takes seven hours, crossing to the Sarawak border town of Tebedu; you can stay on the same bus for another three hours to reach Kuching.

As for **ferries**, a service operates from Medan in northern Sumatra to Penang (4hr) and, from Dumai further south, there's a daily service to Melaka (2hr), with more sailings from Dumai and Tanjong Balai to Port Klang near KL (3hr). There are also a few services from Bintan and Batam islands in the Riau archipelago (accessible by plane or boat from Sumatra or Jakarta) to Johor Bahru (30min) or Singapore (30min); and a minor ferry crossing from Tanjung Balai to Kukup (45min) just to the southwest of Johor Bahru. Over in Borneo, there are daily ferries to Tawau in Sabah from Nunakan in Kalimantan (1hr).

From the Philippines

Despite the proximity of Sabah to the southern Philippines, there aren't many transport links between the two, though a ferry service operates between Zamboanga and Sandakan. As for **flights**, there are low-cost options from Manila to KL (AirAsia), Kota Kinabalu (AirAsia) and Singapore (Jetstar and Tiger Airways). Full-cost flights on Philippine Airlines (ⓦwww .philippineairlines.com) include Cebu to KL and to Kota Kinabalu, and Manila to Bandar Seri Begawan.

Airlines, agents and operators

Online booking

A selection of good online booking websites is listed below.

ⓦwww.ebookers.com (in UK), ⓦwww .ebookers.ie (in Ireland)
ⓦwww.expedia.co.uk (in UK), ⓦwww.expedia .com (in US), ⓦwww.expedia.ca (in Canada)
ⓦwww.lastminute.com (in UK)
ⓦwww.opodo.co.uk (in UK)
ⓦwww.orbitz.com (in US)
ⓦwww.travel.co.za (in South Africa)
ⓦwww.travelocity.co.uk (in UK), ⓦwww .travelocity.com (in US), ⓦwww.travelocity.ca (in Canada), ⓦwww.travelocity.co.nz (in New Zealand)
ⓦwww.travelonline.co.za (in South Africa)
ⓦwww.zuji.com.au (in Australia)

Airlines

AirAsia ⓦwww.airasia.com. Budget flights to KL from Southeast Asia, plus long-haul from Australia and London Stansted via its sister company AirAsia X; also Bangkok, Phuket and Pekanbaru to Singapore.
Air France ⓦwww.airfrance.com. Paris to Singapore, with connections from UK and Irish airports.

Air India ⓦ www.airindia.com. Flights to KL and to Singapore via Bombay, Delhi or Madras.

British Airways ⓦ www.ba.com. Nonstop from London Heathrow and Sydney to Singapore. Connections available from North America.

Cathay Pacific ⓦ www.cathaypacific.com. London Heathrow to Hong Kong, with onward connections to KL, Penang and Singapore. Connections available from North America.

China Airlines ⓦ www.china-airlines.com. From several North American cities to Taipei, with onward connections to KL, Penang and Singapore.

Emirates ⓦ www.emirates.com. Auckland to Singapore via Brisbane, and Melbourne to Singapore; Jo'burg, New York and various UK airports to KL and Singapore via Dubai.

Etihad ⓦ www.etihadairways.com. London to Singapore via Abu Dhabi.

EVA Air ⓦ www.evaair.com. To Singapore and KL, via Taipei, from North American cities.

Firefly ⓦ www.fireflyz.com.my. Malaysia Airlines subsidiary with low-cost flights to Penang and KL from Thailand and Indonesia.

Gulf Air ⓦ www.gulfairco.com. London Heathrow to KL via Bahrain.

Japan Airlines ⓦ www.japanair.com. From North America to KL and Singapore, via Tokyo.

Jetstar ⓦ www.jetstar.com. Low-cost flights to Singapore from the main Australian cities.

KLM ⓦ www.klm.com. Daily flights via Amsterdam to both KL and Singapore; connections from UK and Irish airports.

Korean Airlines ⓦ www.koreanair.com. From several major North American cities to Seoul, with onward flights to Singapore.

Lufthansa ⓦ www.lufthansa.com. Frankfurt to Singapore nonstop and to KL, with connections from UK and Irish airports.

Malaysia Airlines (MAS) ⓦ www.mas.com.my. Nonstop to KL from London Heathrow, Auckland and several Australian cities; LA and New York to KL via Taipei and Stockholm respectively; Cape Town to KL via Jo'burg.

Northwest ⓦ www.nwa.com. Flights to Singapore from its Asian hub in Tokyo, with connections from North American cities.

Qantas ⓦ www.qantas.com.au. Adelaide, Brisbane, London, Melbourne, Perth and Sydney nonstop to Singapore.

Qatar Airways ⓦ www.qatarairways.com. London Gatwick, Heathrow and Manchester to KL and Singapore, via Doha.

Royal Brunei Airlines ⓦ www.bruneiair.com. Auckland, Brisbane, London and Perth to Bandar Seri Begawan.

Singapore Airlines (SIA) ⓦ www.singaporeair .com. To Singapore from the main Australian cities plus Auckland and Christchurch, as well as Cape Town, Johannesburg, LA, London Heathrow, Manchester and New York; most of these flights are nonstop. Also San Francisco to Singapore via Hong Kong.

Thai Airways ⓦ www.thaiair.com. Daily nonstop to Bangkok from London Heathrow and LA, with onward connections to Bandar Seri Begawan, KL, Penang and Singapore.

Tiger Airways ⓦ www.tigerairways.com. Singapore budget airline with flights from Australian cities and a few Southeast Asian countries too.

United Airlines ⓦ www.united.com. Washington DC and Chicago to Singapore, via Tokyo and Hong Kong respectively.

Agents and operators

Adventure Center US ☎ 1-800/228-8747, ⓦ www.adventurecenter.com. Offers a good range of packages, mainly focused on east Malaysia.

Adventure World Australia ☎ 02/8913 0755, ⓦ www.adventureworld.com.au; New Zealand ☎ 0800/238368, ⓦ www.adventureworld.co.nz. A range of East Malaysia and Brunei options, with mid-range or upmarket accommodation.

Allways Dive Expedition Australia ☎ 1800/338 239, ⓦ www.allwaysdive.com.au. Dive holidays to the prime dive sites of Sabah.

Asialuxe Holidays US ☎ 1-800/742-3133, ⓦ www .asialuxeholidays.com. Deluxe packages from the US featuring Langkawi and east Malaysia, plus two-centre holidays featuring Singapore and one other destination.

Asian Pacific Adventures US ☎ 1-800/825-1680, ⓦ www.asianpacificadventures.com. A handful of Malaysia packages, dominated by Borneo.

Bales Worldwide UK ☎ 0845/057 1819, ⓦ www .balesworldwide.com. Upmarket packages featuring several mix-and-match Borneo tours.

Bestway Tours US & Canada ☎ 1-800/663-0844, ⓦ www.bestway.com. A handful of cultural tours featuring Malaysia and Singapore.

Borneo Lifestyles US ☎ 310/672-9473, ⓦ www .borneolifestyles.com. A limited range of east Malaysia tours, but with the possibility of adding on customized trips.

Borneo Tour Specialists Australia ☎ 07/3221 5777, ⓦ www.borneo.com.au. Small-group, customizable tours of all of Borneo, covering nature, wildlife, trekking and tribal culture.

Deep Discoveries US & Canada ☎ 1-800/667-5362, ⓦ www.deepdiscoveries.com. Sabah dive packages with optional extensions to wildlife sites on land.

Dive Adventures Australia ☎1800/222234, ⓦ www.deepdiscoveries.com. Sabah and Labuan dive packages.

Eastravel UK ☎01473/214305, ⓦ www.eastravel .co.uk. A small range of Malaysia and Singapore trips.

Educational Travel Center US ☎1-800/747-5551, ⓦ www.edtrav.com. Student/youth discount agent.

eMalaysiaTravel.com US ☎618/529-8033, ⓦ www.emalaysiatravel.com. Various Malaysia offerings – KL city breaks, diving off Sabah, Taman Negara trips and so forth.

Emerald Global UK ☎020/7312 1708, ⓦ www .etours-online.com. Malaysia packages based in cities or resorts; Singapore too.

Exodus UK ☎0845/863 9600, ⓦ www.exodus .co.uk. A small number of adventure-slanted packages covering Malaysia and Singapore.

Explore Worldwide UK ☎0845/013 1539, ⓦ www.exploreworldwide.com. Adventure trips to Malaysia, plus Singapore.

Explorient US ☎1-800/785-1233, ⓦ www .explorient.com. A range of short tours, focused on major cities and with a cultural emphasis, which can be combined with one another.

Flight Centre US ☎1-866/967-5351, Canada ☎1-877/967-5302, UK ☎0870/499 0040, Australia ☎133 133, New Zealand ☎0800/243544, South Africa ☎0860/400 727; ⓦ www.flightcentre .com. Budget travel specialist with a few Malaysia packages as well as flights.

Gala Tours US ☎562/692-5000, ⓦ www.galatour .com. A range of short breaks taking in KL plus Penang, Kuching or Kota Kinabalu.

Golden Days in Malaysia UK ☎020/8893 1781, ⓦ www.goldendays.co.uk. A good range of Malaysia itineraries, with the option of taking in Singapore and Brunei too.

Intrepid Travel US ☎1-800/970-7299, Canada ☎1-866/360-1151, UK ☎020/3147 7777, Australia ☎1300/364 512, New Zealand ☎0800/600 610; ⓦ www.intrepidtravel.com. Several Malaysia offerings, mainly focused on Borneo, to suit different budgets and tastes.

Kumuka US & Canada ☎1-800/517-0867, UK ☎0800/092 9595, Ireland ☎1800/946843, Australia ☎1300/667277, New Zealand ☎0800/440499; ⓦ www.kumuka.com. Small-group east Malaysia packages.

Lee Travel Ireland ☎021/427 7111, ⓦ www .leetravel.ie. Flights worldwide.

Lee's Travel UK ☎0871/855 33 88, ⓦ www .leestravel.com. Far Eastern travel deals, including discounted Malaysia and Singapore Airlines tickets.

LTI Tours US & Canada ☎1-888/962-6111, ⓦ www.ltitours.com. A good range of Malaysia and Singapore packages.

Malaysia Experience UK ☎01249/467164, ⓦ www.malaysiaexperience.co.uk. Upmarket resort- and city-based packages.

North South Travel UK ☎&℻01245/608 291, ⓦ www.northsouthtravel.co.uk. Discounted fares worldwide; profits are used to support projects in the developing world.

Pandaw Cruises US 1-800/798-4223, UK ☎0131/514 5035; ⓦ www.pandaw.com. Luxury cruises up the Rejang River in Sarawak.

Pentravel South Africa ☎0860/106264, ⓦ www .pentravel.co.za. Budget flights plus KL-, Penang- and Singapore-based holidays.

Peregrine Adventures UK ☎0844/736 0170, Australia ☎03/8601 4444; ⓦ www .peregrineadventures.com. Experienced operator with a handful of east Malaysia packages.

Premier Holidays UK ☎0844/493 7080, ⓦ www .premierholidays.co.uk. Tours of east Malaysia and Brunei, plus resort-centred holidays in Peninsular Malaysia and Singapore.

Ramblers Worldwide Holidays UK ☎01707/331133, ⓦ www.ramblersholidays .co.uk. Two-week walking holidays in Sabah, covering Kinabalu and the usual wildlife spots.

Reef & Rainforest US ☎1-800/794-9767, ⓦ www.reefrainforest.com. Sabah dive packages based in resorts or a liveaboard.

Rex Air UK ☎020/7439 1898, ⓦ www.rexair .co.uk. Specialist in discounted flights to the Far East, with a few package tours to boot.

Scott Dunn World UK ☎020/8682 5000, ⓦ www .scottdunn.com. Top-end package holidays centred on Malaysia's island and beach resorts.

Silverbird UK ☎020/8875 9090, ⓦ www .silverbird.co.uk. Far East travel specialist, all of whose tours are individually customized.

Skedaddle ☎0191/265 1110, ⓦ www.skedaddle .co.uk. Cycling tours worldwide including itineraries around east Malaysia, using specialist knowledge of suitable routes.

STA Travel US ☎1-800/781-4040, ⓦ www .statravel.com; UK ☎0871/230 0040, ⓦ www .statravel.co.uk; Australia ☎134 782, ⓦ www .statravel.com.au; New Zealand ☎0800/474 400, ⓦ www.statravel.co.nz; South Africa ☎0861/781 781, ⓦ www.statravel.co.za. Worldwide specialists in low-cost flights for students and under-26s; other customers also welcome.

Symbiosis US ☎1-866/723 7903, UK ☎0845/123 2844; ⓦ www.symbiosis-travel.com. Cycling, diving, trekking and other adventure activities in various Malaysian locations, plus a few resort-based holidays.

Thompsons Tours South Africa ☎0861/846677, ⓦ www.thompsons.co.za. Flights and various packages to Southeast Asia.

Tour East Canada ☎1-877/578-8888, ⓦwww
.toureast.com. Packages combining Singapore with
another Southeast Asian attraction.
Trailfinders UK ☎0845/058 5858, ⓦwww
.trailfinders.com; Ireland ☎01/677 7888, ⓦwww
.trailfinders.ie; Australia ☎1300/780 212, ⓦwww
.trailfinders.com.au. Efficient agent selling flights and
a variety of Malaysia tours.
Transindus ☎020/8566 2729, ⓦwww.transindus
.co.uk. Peninsular and east Malaysia packages, with
the option of visiting Singapore.
Travel Bag UK ☎0871/703 4700, ⓦwww.travelbag
.co.uk. Far Eastern packages and discount flights.
Travel Clearance Australia ☎1300/900 800,
ⓦwww.travelclearance.com.au. Discounted deals
on flights and holidays.

Travel Cuts Canada ☎1-866/246-9762, US
☎1-800/592-2887; ⓦwww.travelcuts.com.
Canadian student-travel organization.
Travel Masters US ☎512/323-6961, ⓦwww
.travel-masters.net. Dive packages at Sipadan plus
side trips in Sabah.
Travelmood UK ☎0800/011 1945, ⓦwww
.travelmood.com. Discount flights plus resort-based
Malaysia packages.
Trips Tailormade UK ☎0117/311 6050, ⓦwww
.tripsworldwide.co.uk. Luxury Malaysia trips, with
plenty of Borneo offerings.
USIT Ireland ☎01/602 1904, ⓦwww.usit.ie.
Student and youth travel.

Health

No inoculations are required for visiting Malaysia, Singapore or Brunei, although
the immigration authorities may require a yellow-fever vaccination certificate if
you have transited an endemic area, normally Africa or South America, within the
preceding six days.

It's a wise precaution to visit your doctor no
less than two months before you leave to
check that you are up to date with your
polio, typhoid, tetanus and hepatitis inoculations. **Tap water** is drinkable throughout
Malaysia, Singapore and Brunei, although in
rural areas it's best to buy bottled water,
which is widely available.

Medical resources for travellers

US and Canada

CDC ☎1-800/311-3435, ⓦwww.cdc.gov/travel.
Official US government travel health site.
Canadian Society for International Health
ⓦwww.csih.org. Extensive list of travel health
centres.
International Society for Travel Medicine
☎1-770/736-7060, ⓦwww.istm.org. Has a full list
of travel health clinics.

Australia, New Zealand and
South Africa

Travellers' Medical and Vaccination Centre
☎1300/658 844, ⓦwww.tmvc.com.au. Lists travel
clinics in Australia, New Zealand and South Africa.

UK and Ireland

Hospital for Tropical Diseases Travel Clinic
☎020/7387 4411 or 0845/155 5000, ⓦwww
.thehtd.org.
**MASTA (Medical Advisory Service for
Travellers Abroad)** ☎0870/606 2782, ⓦwww
.masta.org for the nearest clinic.
Travel Medicine Services ☎028/9031 5220.
Tropical Medical Bureau Ireland ☎1850/487
674, ⓦwww.tmb.ie.

Medical problems

The levels of hygiene and medical care in
Malaysia, Singapore and Brunei are higher

33
■

than in much of the rest of Southeast Asia; with any luck, the most serious thing you'll go down with is an upset stomach or insect or leech bites.

Heat problems

Travellers unused to tropical climates periodically suffer from sunburn and **dehydration**. The easiest way to avoid this is to restrict your exposure to the midday sun, use high-factor sun screens, wear sunglasses and a hat. You should also drink plenty of water and, if you do become dehydrated, keep up a regular intake of fluids. Rehydration preparations such as Dioralyte are handy; the DIY version is a handful of sugar with a good pinch of salt added to a litre of bottled water, which creates roughly the right mineral balance. **Heat stroke** is more serious and can require hospitalization: its onset is indicated by a high temperature, dry red skin and a fast pulse.

Stomach problems

The most common complaint is a stomach problem, which can range from a mild dose of diarrhoea to full-blown dysentery. The majority of stomach bugs may be unpleasant, but are unthreatening; however, if you notice blood or mucus in your stools, then you may have amoebic or bacillary dysentery, in which case you should seek medical help.

Since stomach bugs are usually transmitted by contaminated food and water, steer clear of raw vegetables and shellfish, always wash unpeeled fruit, and stick to freshly cooked foods, avoiding anything reheated. But however careful you are, food that's spicy or just different can sometimes upset your system, in which case, try to stick to relatively bland dishes and avoid fried food.

Dengue fever and malaria

The main mosquito-borne disease to be aware of – and the chief reason to take measures to avoid mosquito bites (see p.36) – is **dengue fever**. The disease is caused by a virus spread by the *Aedes aegypti* mosquito, which has distinctive white marks on its legs, and flares up periodically, not just in rural areas but also in the major cities.

Symptoms include severe headaches, pain in the bones (especially of the back), fever and often a fine, red rash over the body. There's no specific treatment, just plenty of rest, an adequate fluid intake and painkillers when required.

Although the risk of catching **malaria** is extremely low, if you think you might be staying in remote areas for some time then you should consider protection against it. Most doctors will advise the use of antimalarial tablets which, though not completely effective in protecting against the disease, do considerably lessen the risk and can help reduce the symptoms should you develop the disease. Bear in mind you have to start taking the tablets before you arrive in a malaria zone, and continue taking them after you return – ask your doctor for the latest advice.

Altitude sickness

Altitude sickness (or acute mountain sickness) is a potentially life-threatening illness affecting people who ascend above around 3500m. Symptoms include dizziness, headache, shortness of breath, nausea; in severe cases it can lead to a swelling of the brain and lungs which can prove fatal. In Malaysia it's only likely to be relevant to those climbing **Mount Kinabalu** (4101m), and most people report only mild symptoms at this altitude. If you're affected, there's little you can do apart from descending to lower altitude, although there are prescription drugs which may temporarily control the symptoms.

Cuts, bites and stings

Wearing protective clothing when swimming, snorkelling or diving can help avoid sunburn and protect against any sea stings. **Sea lice**, minute creatures that cause painful though harmless bites are the most common hazard; more dangerous are **jellyfish**, whose stings must be doused with vinegar to deactivate the poison before you seek medical help.

Coral can also cause nasty cuts and grazes; any wounds should be cleaned and kept as dry as possible until properly healed. The only way to avoid well-camouflaged sea urchins and stone fish is by not stepping on the seabed: even thick-soled shoes don't provide total protection against their long, sharp spines, which can be removed by softening the skin by holding it over a steaming pan of water.

As for **mosquitoes**, you can best avoid being bitten by covering up as much as is practical, and applying repellent to exposed flesh. Note that most locally sold repellent is based on **citronella**; if you want a concentrated repellent containing **DEET**, which some say is more effective, it's best to buy it at home. Rural or beachside accommodation often features **mosquito nets**, and some places also provide slow-burning **mosquito coils** which generate a little bit of smoke that apparently deters the insects.

For many people, the ubiquitous **leech** – whose bite is not actually harmful or painful – is the most irritating aspect to jungle trekking. Whenever there's been rainfall, you can rely upon the leeches to come out. Always tuck your trousers into your socks and tie your bootlaces tight. The best anti-leech socks are made from calico and available in specialist stores. If you find the leeches are getting through, the best remedy is to soak the outside of your socks and your boots in insect repellent, or dampen tobacco and apply it in between your socks and shoes.

Poisonous **snakes** are rare, but if you are bitten you must remain absolutely still and calm until help arrives. Meanwhile, get someone to clean and disinfect the wound thoroughly (alcohol will do if nothing else can be found), and apply a bandage with gentle pressure to the affected area.

Pharmacies, clinics and hospitals

Medical services in Malaysia, Singapore and Brunei are excellent, with staff almost everywhere speaking English and using up-to-date treatments. Details of pharmacies and hospitals are in the "Listings" sections of the Guide for cities and major towns.

Pharmacies stock a wide range of medicines and health-related items, from contraceptives to contact lens solution; opening hours are the same as for other shops. Pharmacists can recommend products for skin complaints or simple stomach problems, though it always pays to get a proper diagnosis.

Private **clinics** are found even in the smallest towns – your hotel or the local tourist office will be able to recommend a good English-speaking doctor. A consultation costs around RM30, not including the cost of any prescribed medication; don't forget to keep the receipts for insurance-claim purposes. Finally, the emergency department of each town's general hospital will see foreigners for a small fee, though obviously costs rise rapidly if continued treatment or overnight stays are necessary.

Getting around

Public transport in Malaysia, Singapore and Brunei is reliable, though not as cheap as in other Southeast Asian countries. Much of your travelling, particularly in Peninsular Malaysia, will be by bus, minivan or, less often, long-distance taxi. Budget flights are a great option for making hops within the Peninsula or around the region, especially in view of the fact that there are no ferries between Peninsular and east Malaysia. The Malaysian train system, limited to the Peninsula (apart from a small stretch of rail line in Sabah), has to a degree been superseded by fast highways which ensure buses actually outpace the trains, though it still has its uses, particularly in the interior and on the express run north from Butterworth to Bangkok.

Sabah and **Sarawak** have their own travel peculiarities – in Sarawak, for instance, you're reliant on boats, and occasionally planes, for some long-distance travel. **Brunei**'s bus service, covering routes through the main towns, is supplemented by boats in remote areas such as the Temburong district. The chapters on Sarawak, Sabah, Brunei and Singapore contain detailed information on their respective transport systems; the emphasis in the rest of this section is largely on Peninsular Malaysia.

Note that the transport system is subject to heavy pressure whenever there's a nation-wide **public holiday** – particularly during Muslim festivals, the Chinese New Year, Deepavali, Christmas and New Year. A day or two before each festival, whole communities embark upon what's called **balik kampung**, which literally means returning to their home villages (and towns) to be with family. You should make bus, train or flight reservations at least **one week in advance** to travel at these times; if you're driving, steel yourself for more than the usual number of jams.

For a run-down of public transport routes in each region covered by this book, see the "Travel details" sections at the end of each Guide chapter.

Buses

The national **bus network** is generally the easiest, quickest and cheapest way of getting around Malaysia, with regular services between all major Peninsular cities and towns. Besides intercity services, which operate largely on an **express** basis, there are also **local buses** that run to destinations up to 100km away, though being stopping services they may well take up to three hours to cover this relatively short distance. For more on local buses, see p.44.

The chief difficulty you might experience in using buses is simply the sheer profusion of options, for the network is about as far from being integrated as it's possible to get. Any major bus station in Malaysia feels not unlike a traditional street market; turn up and you'll find a zillion and one vendors with broadly similar offerings at similar prices. While all this might seem like a recipe for chaos, in practice things do work reasonably well. Finding out about available bus connections is usually straightforward, but if not, local tourist offices should be able to help. In any case, on the main routes (in practice, along the major highways), the plethora of bus companies means departures are pretty **frequent** (in practice, hourly or every other hour during daylight hours). Much of the time you can just turn up and get a ticket for the next available bus.

For intercity journeys, you'll often find yourself relying on a handful of well-established bus companies. The largest of these is **Transnasional** (ⓦ www.transnasional.com .my), whose services have the entire Peninsula pretty well covered. Their website has a useful timetable search facility which allows you to establish likely departure and journey times, with fares, for a large number of routes. Other major bus companies include **Plusliner** (Ⓦwww.plusliner.com) and **Konsortium Bas Ekspres** (Ⓦwww.kbes.com.my). Complementing these outifts are numerous small-scale intercity operators which generally focus on services between their home state and one or two adjacent states.

Whichever bus company you travel with, you'll find that practically all intercity buses are reasonably comfortable, with **air conditioning** and curtains to help screen out the blazing tropical sun, though on the down side, the way seats are packed together can make things awkward for taller travellers. The buses generally don't have toilets, but on the longer journeys there'll be an extended rest stop every couple of hours or so, and there's often a half-hour meal stopover at lunchtime or dinnertime as well. On a few plum routes, notably KL–Singapore and KL–Penang, there are additional **luxury** or "executive" coaches to choose from, charging double the regular fares and featuring greater legroom and on-board TVs and toilets.

All intercity **fares** are eminently reasonable (see box, p.41), but note that if you want to leave the bus at a small town en route, you may be charged the full fare or the fare until the next major town. Local buses, where available, are more cost-effective for such journeys, though they take much longer.

Finally, note that express and local buses usually operate from separate stations; the local bus station is often fairly central, the express-bus station a little further out. In some towns, buses may call at both stations before terminating.

Various buses ply the long-distance routes across **Sabah**, but they are heavily outnumbered by the minivans that buzz around the state, which generally leave from the same terminals. Faster and slightly more expensive than the scheduled bus services, minivans only leave when jam-packed and are often very uncomfortable as a result. Also prevalent in Sabah are four-wheel-drives (4X4s), usually Toyota Land Cruisers, which take only eight passengers and whose fares are at least twenty percent higher than going by minivan.

In **Sarawak**, modern air-conditioned buses ply the trans-state coastal road between Kuching and the Brunei border, serving Sibu, Bintulu and Miri en route. Again, fares are very reasonable: the fifteen-hour trip from Kuching to Miri costs around RM80, for example. In addition, local buses serve the satellite towns and villages around the state's main settlements. These buses are particularly useful when exploring southwestern Sarawak and for the cross-border trip to Pontianak in Indonesian Kalimantan. Four-wheel-drives are being used for navigating the logging tracks that have opened up remote inland areas; details of routes are given in the Guide.

Trains

The Peninsula's intercity train service, operated by **KTM** (short for "Keretapi Tanah Melayu" or Malay Land Trains; Ⓦwww.ktmb .com.my), is limited to a network shaped roughly like a Y, the arms of which, for historical reasons, don't intersect at KL, but an annoying 170km further south at Gemas, close to the Negeri Sembilan/Johor boundary. One arm goes from Gemas up to Thailand, another down to Singapore; the remaining branch cuts its way through the jungled interior up to Tumpat, on the east coast near the Thai border. KTM also runs the Komuter rail service in KL and its environs, for details of which, see p.89.

There are two main classes of train: **express** services, which call mostly at major stations and are generally modern, fully air-conditioned and well maintained; and **local** ("Mel" on timetables) trains, often not air-conditioned and of variable quality, which operate on various segments between Singapore and Tumpat and call at every town, village and hamlet en route.

Unfortunately, not even the express trains can keep up with buses where modern highways exist alongside. The 370-kilometre journey from KL to Johor Bahru, for example, takes the train five and a half hours at best; on a good day on the roads, buses are roughly an hour quicker. Until the rail tracks themselves and the infrastructure attending them are modernized, you're unlikely to be heavily reliant on the trains for journeys along the west coast and in the south.

The rail system does, however, retain a couple of advantages. **Sleeper services** –

between KL and Singapore, between KL and Hat Yai, and between Singapore and Tumpat, not to mention the international service from Butterworth to Bangkok – can save on a night's accommodation. Express trains also remain the quickest way to reach some parts of the forested **interior**, and local trains through the interior can also be handy for reaching certain small settlements; for more on the interior's rail service, see the box on the "Jungle Railway", p.227. Moreover, there's still a certain thrill in arriving at some of the splendidly solid colonial stations, built when the train was the prime means of transport.

Ticket types

Many **express** trains run by night and so offer the option of **sleeper berths**, which come in **superior** and **premier** class, while the seats divide into **economy** and **superior** versions. The chief distinction between these labels boils down to nothing more complex than how many berths or seats are packed into each carriage. Superior seats are less crammed together than their economy counterparts and come with minor extras like aircraft-style trays on seat backs and the odd TV screen.

There are exceptions to this picture, notably on the Senandung Malam KL–Singapore service, which has an additional tier of comfort in the form of a **premier deluxe** carriage, featuring six en-suite cabins each containing two berths; lone travellers can pay a supplement to have the whole cabin to themselves. As for the two **daytime express** services which run between KL and Singapore, they have **superior** and **premier seats**, the latter smarter and offering more legroom.

Local trains, plus the Ekonomi Siang Singapore–Gemas service, feature economy-class seats only. Note, however, that these trains are older and scruffier than their express counterparts (some Gua Musang–Tumpat services are positively dilapidated).

For sample **fares**, see the box on p.41. Note that premier berths cost double relative to superior ones, while premier deluxe berths cost three times as much. At the other end of the scale, tickets on local trains are very cheap; the longest possible local train

THE MALAYSIAN RAIL NETWORK

BANGKOK (International Express)
Hat Yai (Thailand)
Padang Besar
Arau
Alor Setar
Gurun
Sungai Petani
Bukit Mertajam
Butterworth
Nibong Tebal
Parit Buntar
Bagan Serai
Taiping
Kuala Kangsar
Sungai Siput
Ipoh
Batu Gajah
Kampar
Tapah Road
Sungkai
Slim River
Tanjung Malim
Rawang
Sungai Buloh
KL SENTRAL
Kajang
Seremban
Rembau
Tampin
Batang Melaka
Gemas
Segamat
Labis
Paloh
Kluang
Kulai
Kempas Bahru
Johor Bahru
SINGAPORE (Singapura)

Tumpat (Kelantan coast)
Wakaf Bharu (for Kota Bharu)
Pasir Mas
Tanah Merah
Kuala Krai
Dabong
Gua Musang
Kuala Lipis
Jerantut
Kuala Krau
Mentakab
Triang
Bahau

See 'KL Transport' map, Chapter 1

Malaysian long-distance rail services

Express
Kuala Lumpur–Butterworth
Kuala Lumpur–Ipoh (weekends)
Kuala Lumpur–Tumpat
Kuala Lumpur–Hat Yai (Thailand)
Butterworth–Bangkok (International Express)
Singapore–Butterworth
Singapore–Tumpat

Local
Gemas–Kuala Lipis
Kuala Lipis–Tumpat
Gua Musang–Tumpat
Singapore–Kluang (Tebrau Express)

Local trains call at virtually every station on the network. This map shows only stations served by most express trains.

journey, Kuala Lipis–Tumpat (7hr 30min, compared to 5hr 30min by express train), costs RM11 as compared to RM19 for a superior-class seat on an express train.

Buying tickets

While tickets can be **bought in advance** for any train, it's only on express trains that seat and berth reservations can be made. Reserving a day or two in advance is certainly recommended, particularly if you want a berth. Bookings can be made at major stations, by phone on ☎03/2267 1200 for collection at your starting station the next day, and online at KTM's website. **Timetables** are usually available at major train stations and, depending on the state of KTM's website, may be available for download along with fare tables.

Long-distance taxis

Most towns in Malaysia have a **long-distance taxi** rank, usually close to or in the express bus station. The taxis run between cities and towns throughout the country, and can be a lot quicker than the buses. The snag is that they operate on a **shared** basis, meaning you have to wait for enough people show up to fill the four passenger seats in the vehicle, but in most major towns this shouldn't take more than thirty minutes, especially to set off before 10am; afternoon journeys can involve a bit of thumb-twiddling. **Fares** usually work out to be two to three times the corresponding fare in an express bus; see the table opposite for sample prices. Note that long-distance taxi fares, in particular, may be subject to jumps when fuel prices are rising rapidly.

For many visitors travelling in small groups, the real advantage of these taxis is that you can **charter** one for your journey, the price for which is the same as paying for all four passenger places. Not only does this mean you'll set off immediately, but it also allows you to access destinations that may not be served directly by buses or, indeed, by shared taxis. There's no danger of being ripped off: charter prices to a large number of destinations, both the popular and the obscure, are set by the authorities and are usually chalked up on a board in the taxi office or listed on a laminated tariff card (*senarai tambang*), which you can ask to see.

Some taxi operators assume any tourist who shows up will want to charter a taxi; if you want to use the taxi on a shared basis, say *"nak kongsi dengan orang lain."*

Ferries and boats

Ferries sail to all the major islands off Peninsular Malaysia's east and west coasts. The traditional *penambang* (sometimes called "bumboats"), compact motorized craft originally used for fishing, are rapidly being replaced by larger, sleeker express models. On most ferries, you buy your ticket in advance from booths at the jetty (on some you can pay on the boat as well); details are given in the text. Barring rainy-season storms, there are daily services from the mainland to Tioman and the Perhentian islands (other east-coast islands are hard to reach off-season).

Within **Sarawak**, the most common form of public transport, buses aside, are the long, low and narrow express boats which ply the state's river systems. A lifeline for the inhabitants of the interior, these craft run to a regular timetable; buy your ticket on board, preferably half an hour before departure, and reserve a seat. On the smaller tributaries, travel is by longboat.

Sabah has no express-boat river services, though regular ferries connect Pulau Labuan with Kota Kinabalu, Sipitang and Menumbok, all on the west coast; details are given in the text. In **Brunei**, there are some useful boat services, including the speedboat service from Bandar Seri Begawan to Bangar for Temburong Park, and the regular boats from Bandar to Lawas or Limbang in Sarawak and Pulau Labuan in Sabah.

Planes

With the advent of Far Eastern low-cost airlines, **flying** around the region is now within the reach of all but the most thrifty of backpackers. Malaysian domestic flights are operated by Malaysia Airlines (**MAS**) and the budget carriers **AirAsia** and **Firefly**. From Singapore, **Singapore Airlines** and the budget companies **Tiger Airways** and **Jetstar** offer a range of connections to the major Peninsular and east Malaysian cities, while **Royal Brunei Airlines** operates from

Bandar Seri Begawan to Kuching, Kota Kinabalu and KL.

If you're flying within Malaysia, note that many connections between regional airports require a change of plane in KL, making flying much less of a time-saver than it might appear at first sight. Note also that flights between Malaysia and Singapore or Brunei are more expensive than the distances involved would suggest, as these count as international services.

Airfares throughout this section are for one-way tickets (return fares are usually double the cost) and include taxes and any fuel surcharges.

MAS and Firefly

MAS (Malaysia ☎1300/883000, ⊛www.malaysiaairlines.com) flies from KL to most of the state capitals as well as Langkawi and Labuan. It also operates flights within East Malaysia through its subsidiary **MASwings** (⊛www.MASwings.com.my), some of whose services use tiny propeller-driven Twin Otter planes that are something of a lifeline for rural communities. To take on AirAsia, MAS even has a budget subsidiary called **Firefly** (⊛www.fireflyz.com.my) with the added attraction that it operates mainly out of Penang rather than

KL, though it also has flights out of KL's small Subang airport.

Short hops within the Peninsula start at around RM120 on MAS; going with Firefly can halve fares if they operate on the same route. As for Borneo flights, MASwings' fare for Kuching to Kinabalu is around RM170 if booked early. Note that **booking online** is becoming the norm; many Malaysian cities no longer have a downtown MAS office.

AirAsia

The no-frills carrier **AirAsia** (☎03/2171 9333, ⊛www.airasia.com) offers a network of internal flights rivalling those of MAS and is reasonably efficient, though delays of up to an hour aren't uncommon. Most of its flights are to and from KL airport's low-cost-carrier terminal, though conveniently it also has services between Senai airport near **Johor Bahru** and Penang, Kuching, Miri, Sibu and Kota Kinabalu.

Despite the inevitable fuel surcharges and taxes, AirAsia's prices are attractive – fares for short hops within the Peninsula are as low as RM40 all-in, while the very longest domestic route offered, from KL to Kota Kinabalu in eastern Sabah (2hr 30min), weighs in at around RM170 one way if booked early enough. Note, however, that

Fare comparisons

Journey	By bus	By shared taxi	By rail (superior class, upper berth/seat)	By air (including any taxes and fuel surcharges)
KL–Johor Bahru	RM32; 4hr 30min	RM80; 4hr	RM33 (seat only, daytime express); 5hr 30min	RM120 (MAS); from RM40 (AirAsia); 40min
KL–Penang	RM35 (RM55 executive coach); 5hr 30min	RM110; 4hr 30min	RM38/30; 9hr 30min	from RM125 (MAS); from RM50 (AirAsia); 45min
KL–Kota Bharu	RM40; 8hr 30min	RM115; 8hr	RM51/46; 12hr 30min to Wakaf Bharu, then a short bus/taxi ride	from RM125 (MAS); from RM40 (AirAsia); 50min
Johor Bahru–Kota Bharu	RM64; 12hr	–	RM48/RM35; 11hr 30min	from RM80 (two AirAsia single tickets via KL); 1hr

41
■

hefty surcharges apply if your checked-in baggage weighs more than 15kg, and that the lowest fares are hard to come by for travel on or close to public holidays, and during the school holidays.

Other airlines

Singapore Airlines (Singapore ☎6223 8888, Malaysia ☎03/2692 3122, Brunei ☎02/244901; ⊛www.singaporeair.com) and its subsidiary **SilkAir** (Singapore ☎6223 8888, Malaysia 03/2698 7033; ⊛www.silkair.com) between them fly from Singapore to several key Malaysian destinations, including KL, Kota Kinabalu, Kuching, Langkawi and Penang, plus Brunei. Expect to pay around S$250 to Penang, S$270 to Kuching, S$470 to Kota Kinabalu. Similar prices are charged by **Royal Brunei Airways** (Brunei ☎02/212222, Malaysia ☎03/2070 7166, Singapore ☎6235 4672; ⊛www.bruneiair.com), which flies to KL, Singapore and Kota Kinabalu from Brunei. Much cheaper are **Jetstar** (Singapore ☎800/616 1977, ⊛www.jetstar.com) and **Tiger Airways** (Singapore ☎6538 4437, ⊛www.tigerairways.com), on which it's sometimes possible to turn up Singapore–Kota Kinabalu tickets for as little as S$65.

It's no accident that three Malaysian resort islands, **Pangkor**, **Redang** and **Tioman**, have airstrips served by **Berjaya Air** (Malaysia ☎03/2141 0088, Singapore ☎6227 3688; ⊛www.berjaya-air.com), for all play host to resorts owned by the Malaysian conglomerate Berjaya Corporation. Berjaya Air flies to all three from KL, and to Redang and Tioman from Singapore. Unsurprisingly, prices are distinctly elevated – for example, RM250 to Pangkor from KL, S$180 to Redang from Singapore.

Driving and vehicle rental

The **roads** in **Peninsular Malaysia** are generally excellent, making driving there a viable prospect for tourists. It's mostly the same story in **Sarawak** and **Brunei**, though **Sabah** is the odd one out; a sizeable minority of roads there are rough, unpaved and highly susceptible to flash flooding. **Singapore** is another tale altogether, boasting modern highways with a built-in road-use charging system that talks to a black-box gizmo fitted in every car.

Despite these disparities, the three countries do share certain rules of the road. All use the UK system of **driving on the left**. It's compulsory to wear seat belts in the front of the vehicle (and in the back too, in Singapore). To **rent a vehicle**, you must be 23 or over and have held a clean driving licence for at least a year; a national driving licence, particularly if written in English, is sufficient, though there's no harm in acquiring an International Driving Licence.

Because of Singapore's unique road-pricing technology, and the fact that some car rental outlets don't allow their cars to be driven between Malaysia and Singapore, the rest of this section concentrates on Malaysia. For information on driving in Singapore and Brunei, see the respective chapters.

Malaysian roads

Malaysian highways – called **expressways** and usually referred to by a number prefixed "E" – are a pleasure to drive; they're wide and efficient, and feature convenient **rest stops** with toilets, shops and small food courts. In contrast, the streets of major cities can be a pain, regularly traffic-snarled, with patchy signposting and confusing one-way systems to boot. At least most cities and towns do boast a liberal sprinkling of **car parks**, and even where you can't find one, there's usually no problem with parking in a lane or side street.

Speed limits are 110kph on expressways, 90kph on the narrower trunk and state roads (prefixed "route" in this book, though on signage you tend to see just the road number, sometimes preceded by a letter specific to the state – for example D for Kelantan), and 50kph in built-up areas. For intercity journeys, expressways are almost always quicker than using a trunk road, even if the latter passes through the town where you're starting out while the expressway is a little way away. Whatever road you're on, it's wise to stick religiously to the speed limit as speed traps are commonplace and fines hefty. In the event you are pulled up for a traffic offence, note that it's not unknown for Malaysian police to ask for a bribe, which will set you back less than the fine. Never offer

Malay vocabulary for drivers

The following list should help decipher road signage in Peninsular Malaysia and parts of Brunei, much of which is in Malay.

Utara	North	**Kawasan rehat**	Highway rest stop
Selatan	South		
Barat	West	**Kurangkan laju**	Reduce speed
Timur	East	**Lebuhraya**	Expressway/ highway
Di belakang	Behind		
Di hadapan	Ahead	**Lencongan**	Detour
Awas	Caution	**Pembinaan di**	Road works ahead
Berhenti	Stop	**hadapan**	
Beri laluan	Give way	**Pusat bandar/**	Town/city centre
Dilarang meletak	No parking	**bandaraya**	
kereta		**Simpang ke...**	Junction/ turning for...
Dilarang memotong	No overtaking		
Had laju/jam	Speed limit/ per hour	**Zon had laju**	Zone where speed limit applies
Ikut kiri/kanan	Keep left/right		
Jalan sehala	One-way street		

to bribe a police officer and think carefully before you give in to an invitation to do so.

All expressways are built and run by private concessions and as such attract **tolls**, generally at a rate of around RM20 per 100km, though on some roads a flat fee is levied. At toll points (signed "Tol Plaza"), you can pay in cash (there are cashiers on hand to dispense change) or by waving a stored-value **Touch 'n Go** card in front of a sensor; see Ⓦwww.touchngo.com.my for a list of card vendors. Get in the appropriate lane as you approach the toll points: some lanes are for certain types of vehicle only, some (signed "Touch 'n Go sahaja") require card payments.

Once out on the roads, you'll rapidly become aware of the behaviour of quite a few Malaysian motorists, which their compatriots might term *gila* (Malay for "insane"). Swerving from lane to lane in the thick of the traffic, overtaking close to blind corners and careering down hill roads are not uncommon, as are tragic stories in the press of pile-ups and road fatalities. Not for nothing does the exhortation *"pandu cermat"* (drive safely) appear on numerous highway signboards, though the message still isn't getting through.

If you're new to driving in Malaysia, the best approach is to take all of this with equanimity and drive conservatively; concede the right of way if you're not quite sure of the intentions of others. One confusing habit that some local drivers have is that they flash their headlights to claim the right of way rather than concede it.

Car and bike rental

Car rental rates begin at around RM220 per day for rental of a basic 1.5-litre Proton, including unlimited mileage and collision damage waiver insurance. The excess can be RM1500 or more but this can be reduced or set to zero by paying a surcharge of up to ten percent on the daily rental rate. The cost of **fuel** is held down by a national subsidy and was at RM2 per litre at the time of writing, though the price has been known to spike if oil soars on global markets.

Motorbike rental is much more informal, usually offered by Malaysian guesthouses and shops in more touristy areas. Officially, you must be over 21 and have an appropriate driving licence, though it's unlikely you'll have to show the latter; you'll probably need to leave your passport as a deposit, however. Wearing helmets is compulsory. The cost of rental is around RM25 per day, while **bicycles**, which can be useful in rural areas, can be rented for a few ringgit a day.

Car rental agencies

Avis ☏1800/881 054, Ⓦwww.avis.com.my. Offices in KL, KL airport, Johor Bahru, Kuantan and Penang.

Hawk ☎03/5631 6488, ⓦwww.hawkrentacar
.com.my. KL, KL airport, Johor Bahru, Melaka, Kota
Bharu, Kuantan and Penang.

Hertz ☎03/2148 6433, ⓦwww.hertz.com.
Locations include KL, Alor Star, Johor Bahru, Kuantan,
Kuching, Kota Kinabalu and Penang.

Mayflower ☎1800/881 688, ⓦwww
.mayflowercarrental.com. KL, Johor Bahru, Kota
Kinabalu, Kuantan, Kuching and Langkawi.

Orix ☎03/9284 7799, ⓦwww.orixcarrentals.com
.my. KL, KL airport, Johor Bahru, Kuantan and Penang.

City and local transport

Most Malaysian cities and towns have some
kind of **bus service** serving both urban
areas and hinterland; details are given in the
text wherever appropriate. Fares are always
very low even if some of the bus networks –
in places like KL and Georgetown – appear
absolutely unfathomable to visitors (and to
some locals); journeys of up to an hour
often cost no more than a couple of ringgit.
As a result, fares for local buses are given in
the text only where they exceed RM3. In
KL, there are also the Komuter train and
metro-style light rail and monorail systems,
which are fairly efficient.

Taxis are always metered, but you may
find that taxi drivers would prefer to turn off
the meter and negotiate a fare, which isn't
legal. If you want to charter a vehicle for a
specific itinerary (if not a taxi, your accommodation can usually find you a car with a
driver), spending several hours meandering
around town and out to the surrounding
countryside, reckon on paying at least RM30
per hour.

Trishaws (bicycle rickshaws), seating two
people, are seen less and less these days,
but they're still very much part of the tourist
scene in places like Melaka, Penang and
Singapore. Taking a trishaw tour can be a
useful, atmospheric introduction to the town
and some drivers provide interesting,
anecdotal information. In most cases, they
aren't much cheaper than taking a taxi –
bargain hard to fix the price in advance. You
can expect to pay a minimum of RM3 for a
short journey, while chartering by the hour
can cost as much as RM25.

Accommodation

While accommodation in Malaysia is not the cheapest in Southeast Asia, it is
often still possible to find basic double rooms for under RM40 (£7.50/US$11),
while mid-range en-suite rooms can go for as little as RM100 (£20/US$30),
including breakfast. With a little shopping around, you may well turn up a room in
a plush four-star hotel for RM200 (£35/US$55). This section focuses mainly on
accommodation across Malaysia; for more on Singapore and Brunei, where
prices are significantly higher, see p.596 and p.558 respectively.

The very cheapest form of accommodation is
a **dormitory** at a backpacker hostel, guesthouse or lodge. These generally exist in well-
touristed spots – Kuala Lumpur, Georgetown,
Kota Bharu, Cherating, Kuching, Miri, Kota
Kinabalu and Sandakan, to name a few
popular locations. At the other end of the
scale, the region's luxury hotels offer a level of
comfort and style to rank with any in the
world. What's more, many mid-range and
top-bracket hotels offer **promotional**
discounts which can slash twenty percent or
more off the rack rate; it's worth seeking out
such deals online or if you turn up
somewhere without a reservation. It's also
worth seeking a discount if you're staying for
a couple of weeks in one place.

Reservations a week or two in advance
are essential to be sure of getting a budget
or mid-range room during a major festival
(including Chinese New Year, Hari Raya and
Deepavali – see p.70 for dates) or the school

holidays (see p.70). Rates remain relatively stable throughout the year, rising slightly during the major holiday periods.

At the budget end of the market you'll have to **share a bathroom**, which in most cases will feature a shower and Western-style toilet. **Air-conditioning** is standard in most hotels, and is becoming increasingly common at the budget end of the market. Note that a single room may contain a double bed, while a double can have a double bed, two single beds or even two double beds; a triple will usually have three doubles or a combination or doubles and singles. Baby cots are usually available only in more expensive places.

Guesthouses, hostels and chalets

The mainstay of the travellers' scene in Malaysia (and Singapore) are the **guesthouses** or, as they are sometimes called, B&Bs or **backpackers**, located in popular tourist areas. These can range from simple affairs in renovated shophouses to modern multistorey buildings complete with satellite TV, DVD players and internet. Their advantage for travellers on a tight budget is that almost all offer dorm beds, costing anywhere between RM10 and RM30. There are usually basic double rooms available, too, with a fan and possibly a mosquito net at the cheaper end of the market, from RM20 upwards. Malaysia also has a handful of internationally affiliated youth hostels, but these are often hopelessly far-flung and no cheaper than guesthouses; rare exceptions are noted in the text.

In national parks, islands and in resort-style compounds you'll often come across accommodation in so-called **chalets**, ranging from simple A-frame huts to luxury affairs with a veranda, sitting area, TV, mini-bar, etc. The cheapest chalets cost the same as a basic double in a guesthouse, while at the top end you could pay upwards of RM1000 for a two-night chalet package at the dive resorts off Sabah's east coast.

Hotels

The **cheapest hotels** in Malaysia tend to cater for a local clientele and seldom need to be booked in advance: just go to the next place around the corner if your first choice is full. Rooms are usually divided from one another by thin partitions and contain a washbasin, table and ceiling fan, though never a mosquito net. In the better places – often old converted mansions – you may also be treated to polished wooden floors and antique furniture. That said, showers and toilets are often shared and can be pretty basic. Another consideration is the noise level, which can be considerable since most places are on main streets. A word of warning: some of the hotels at the cheaper end of the scale also function as brothels, especially those described using the Malay term *rumah persinggahan* or *rumah tumpangan*, or those which allow rooms to be paid for by the hour.

Mid-range hotels are often the only alternative in smaller towns, though they're rarely better value than a well-kept budget place.

Accommodation price codes

Accommodation in the Malaysia chapters of this book has been categorized according to the following price codes, reflecting the price of the **cheapest double room** (for Singapore and Brunei price codes see p.596 & p.558 respectively). In view of the fact that many Malaysian hotels offer frequent promotional discounts, the price codes represent discounted rates if these are likely to be available most of the year; otherwise the published rates are used. **Promotional rates** become much harder to come by during major festivals or during the school holidays. **Taxes** – ten percent service charge and five percent government tax, often signified by "++" after the rate – are levied by expensive and the better mid-range hotels, and have been factored into the price codes where they apply. **Breakfast** isn't usually included in the rate, unless otherwise stated.

① RM25 and under	④ RM76–100	⑦ RM221–300
② RM26–50	⑤ RM101–150	⑧ RM301–400
③ RM51–75	⑥ RM151–220	⑨ RM401 and over

The big difference is in the comfort of the mattress – nearly always sprung – and getting your own Western-style, but cramped, bathroom. Prices start at around RM60, for which you can expect air-conditioning, en-suite facilities and, relatively decent furnishings and, sometimes, a telephone and refrigerator. In these places, too, a genuine distinction is made between single rooms and doubles.

The **high-end** hotels are as comfortable as you might expect, and many have state-of-the-art facilities, including a swimming pool, spa and gym. Some may add a touch of class by incorporating kampung-style archi-tecture, such as saddle-shaped roofs with woodcarving. While rates can be as low as RM200 per night, in popular destinations such as Penang and Kota Kinabalu they can rocket above the RM300 mark, though this is obviously still great value compared to equivalent hotels in Western cities. Note that many five-star hotels adjust their rates on a daily basis depending on their occupancy level; the latest rates can usually be looked up on their website.

Camping

Despite the rural nature of much of Malaysia, there are few official opportunities for camping, perhaps because guesthouses and hotels are so reasonable, and because the heat and humidity, not to mention the generous supply of insects, make camping something that only strange foreigners willingly do. Where there are **campsites**, typically in nature parks, they are either free to use or charge around RM10 per person per night; facilities are basic and may not be well maintained. A few lodges and camps have sturdy A-frame tents for hire.

If you go trekking in more remote regions, for example in Endau Rompin National Park in Peninsular Malaysia and parts of the Kelabit Highlands in Sabah, camping is about your only option. Often, visitors find it easier to go on package trips organized by specialist tour operators who will provide tents and equipment, if necessary.

Longhouses

Staying in a longhouse is *de rigueur* for many travellers visiting Sarawak, and offers the chance to try activities such as weaving and cooking, even using a blowpipe. It used to be that visitors would simply turn up at a longhouse and would be granted a place to stay by the headman, paying only for meals and offering some gifts as an additional token of thanks for the community's hospitality. These days, however, visits are invariably arranged through a **tour operator**.

The cheaper packages (costing around RM150 a night, including transport and meals) generally have you sleeping on mats rather than beds, either in a large communal room or on the veranda, and the main washing facilities may well be the nearest river. For meals the party will be divided up into smaller groups, each of which will eat wilth a different family. At the pricier end of the scale (expect to pay at least RM200 a night), visitors may sleep six to a room on proper beds, have access to washing facilities in a modern block with hot water and eat separately from the host community, with more Western-style food available.

Note that while it might seem a fantastic idea to visit a longhouse during a **festival** and witness traditional celebrations, the place may be so crowded that people end up sleeping sardine-fashion in the communal areas; in fact many tour operators will advise that it's impractical to try anything more ambitious than a day-trip during a festival. For more background on longhouses, including information on etiquette to observe during your stay, see the *Visiting a longhouse* colour section.

Homestays

In certain areas **homestay programmes** are available, whereby you stay with a Malaysian family, paying for your bed and board. Though facilities are likely to be modest, homestays can be a good way of sampling home cooking and culture. Tourist offices can usually furnish a list of local homestays if requested; the main things to ask about are whether a special programme will be laid on for you – not necessarily a good thing if you simply want to be left to relax – and whether your hosts are able to speak English, without which you may find yourself somewhat cut off from them and the community.

Food and drink

One of the best reasons to come to Malaysia and Singapore (even Brunei, to a lesser extent) is the food, comprising two of the world's most venerated cuisines – Chinese and Indian – and one of the most underrated – Malay. Even if you think you know two out of the three pretty well, be prepared to be surprised: Chinese food here boasts a lot of the provincial diversity that you just don't find in the West's Cantonese-dominated Chinese restaurants, while Indian fare is predominantly southern Indian, lighter and spicier than northern food.

Furthermore, each of the three cuisines has learnt more than a few tricks off the other two – the Chinese here do curries, for example – giving rise to some distinctive fusion food. Add to this cross-fertilization the existence of a range of regional variations and specialities, plus excellent seafood and unusual tropical produce, and the result is – if you dare to order enterprisingly – a dazzling gastronomic experience.

None of this need come at great expense. From the ubiquitous food stalls and cheap street diners called **kedai kopis**, the standard of cooking is high and food everywhere is remarkably good value. Basic noodle- or rice-based one-plate meals at a stall or *kedai kopi* rarely come to more than a few ringgit or Singapore dollars. Even a full meal with drinks in a fancy restaurant seldom runs to more than RM50 a head in Malaysia, though expect to pay Western prices at quite a few places in Singapore. The most renowned culinary centres are Singapore, Georgetown, KL, Melaka and Kota Bharu, although other towns have their own distinctive dishes too.

Places to eat

One myth to bust immediately is the notion that you will get food poisoning eating at street stalls and cheap diners. Standards of hygiene are usually good, and as most food is cooked to order (or, in the case of rice-with-toppings spreads, only on display for a few hours), it's generally pretty safe.

Food stalls and food courts

Some of the cheapest and most delicious food available in Malaysia and Singapore comes from **food stalls**, traditionally wooden pushcarts on the roadside, surrounded by a few wobbly tables with stools to sit at. Most stalls serve one or a few standard **noodle** and **rice dishes** or specialize in certain delicacies, from oyster omelettes to squid curry. Particularly in Singapore and KL, you'll even come across stalls selling burgers and steak, or even Japanese and Korean food. There's usually a drinks stall on hand too.

For many visitors, however, there is a psychological barrier to having a meal by the roadside. To ease yourself into the *modus*

Eating etiquette

Malays and Indians often eat with the **right hand**, using the palm as a scoop and the thumb to help push food into the mouth. **Chopsticks** are, of course, used for Chinese food, though note that a spoon is always used to help with rice, gravies and slippery fare such as mushrooms or tofu, and that you don't attempt to pick up rice with chopsticks (unless you've a rice bowl, in which case you lift the bowl to your mouth and use the chopsticks as a sort of shovel). If you can't face either local style of eating, note that **cutlery** is universally available – for local fare, always a fork and spoon, the fork serving to push food on to the spoon.

operandi of stalls, take advantage of the fact that many are nowadays assembled into user-friendly **medan selera** (literally "appetite square") or **food courts**, also known as **hawker centres** in Singapore. Usually taking up a floor of an office building or shopping mall, or housed beneath pavilions, food courts conveniently feature stall lots with menus displayed and fixed tables, plus toilets. You don't have to sit close to the stall you're patronizing: find a free table, and the vendor will track you down when your food is ready (some Singapore food centres have tables with numbers that must be quoted when ordering). You generally pay when your food is delivered, though payment is sometimes asked for when you order.

Stalls open at various times from morning to evening, with most closing well before midnight except in the big cities. During the Muslim fasting month of **Ramadan**, however, Muslim-run stalls don't open until mid-afternoon, though this is also when you can take advantage of the **pasar Ramadan**, afternoon food markets at which stalls sell masses of savouries and sweet treats to take away; tourist offices can tell you where one is taking place. Ramadan is also the time to stuff yourself at the massive fast-breaking buffets which most major hotels lay on throughout the month.

The kedai kopi

Few downtown streets are without a **kedai kopi**, sometimes known as a *kopitiam* in Hokkien Chinese. Both terms literally mean "coffee shop", but despite the name, a *kedai kopi* is actually an inexpensive diner rather than a café. Most serve noodle and rice dishes all day, often with a *campur*-style spread (see below) at lunchtime, sometimes in the evening too. Some *kedai kopis* function as miniature food markets, housing a handful of vendors – perhaps one offering curries and griddle breads, another doing a particular Chinese noodle dish, and so on. Menus, where available, are often written up on a board, though a few of the slicker places have printed menus of meat and seafood dishes.

Most *kedai kopis* open at 8am to serve breakfast, and don't shut until the early evening, a few staying open as late as 10pm.

Culinary standards are seldom spectacular but are satisfying all the same, and you're unlikely to spend more than small change for a filling one-plate meal. It's worth noting that in some Malaysian towns, particularly on the east coast, the Chinese-run *kedai kopis* are often the only places where you'll be able to get **alcohol**.

Restaurants, cafés and bakeries

More sophisticated restaurants only exist in the big cities. Some are simply upmarket versions of *kedai kopis*, serving a more diverse list of local favourites in slick surroundings. Don't expect a stiffly formal ambience in these places, however – while some places can be sedate, the Chinese, in particular, prefer restaurants to be noisy, sociable affairs.

Where the pricier restaurants come into their own is for **international fare** – anything from Vietnamese to Tex-Mex. KL, Singapore and Georgetown all have dynamic restaurant scenes, and the five-star hotels usually boast a top-flight restaurant of their own. The chief letdown is that the service can be amateurish, reflecting how novel this sort of dining experience is for many of the staff.

Most large Malaysian towns feature a few attempts at Western **cafés**, serving passable fries, sandwiches, burgers, shakes and so forth. It's also easy to find **bakeries**, which can represent a welcome change from the local rice-based diet – though don't be surprised to find chilli sardine buns and other Asian/Western hybrids, or cakes with decidedly artificial fillings and colourings. For anything really decent in the café or bakery line, you'll need to be in one of the big cities.

Phone numbers are included in our restaurant reviews where it's advisable to make reservations. Note that **tipping** is not expected in restaurants where bills include a service charge (as they usually do).

The cuisines

A convenient and inexpensive way to get acquainted with a variety of local dishes is to sample the food spreads available at many of the *kedai kopis*, particularly at lunchtime. The concept is pretty much summed up by the Malay name for such spreads, **nasi** campur ("mixed rice"), though Chinese and Indian *kedai kopis*, too, offer these arrays of stir fries, curries and other savouries, set out in metal trays or plates. As in a cafeteria, you simply tell the person behind the counter which items appeal to you, and a helping of each will be piled atop a largish serving of rice. If the plainness of the rice soon palls, ask for it to be doused with a scoopful of gravy (*kuah* in Malay) from any stew or stir fry on display, for which you'll be charged little extra (if anything).

Campur food is not haute cuisine – and that's precisely the attraction. Whether you have, say, *ikan kembong* (mackerel) deep fried and served whole, or chicken pieces braised in soy sauce, or bean sprouts stir-fried with salted fish or shrimp, any *campur* spread is much closer to **home cooking** than anything served in formal restaurants.

Nasi campur and noodle dishes are meals in themselves, but otherwise eating is generally a **shared** experience – stir fries and other dishes arrive in quick succession and everyone present helps themselves to several servings of each, eaten with rice, as the meal progresses.

Breakfast can present a conundrum in small towns, where the rice and noodle dishes that locals enjoy at all times of day may be all that's easily available. If you can't get used to the likes of rice porridge at dawn, try to find a stall or *kedai kopi* offering *roti bakar*, toast served with butter and **kaya**. The latter is a scrumptious sweet spread not unlike English lemon curd in that it's made with eggs, though creamed coconut is the magic ingredient that accounts for most of the flavour. *Kaya* is often an orangey colour, but don't fret if you're served some that's a murky green thanks to the aromatic pandan leaf having been added to the mixture during cooking.

Malay food

In its influences, Malay cuisine looks to the north and east, most obviously to China in the use of noodles and soy sauce, but also to neighbouring Thailand, with which it shares an affinity for ingredients such as lemon grass, the ginger-like galingale and fermented fish sauce (the Malay version, *budu*, is made from anchovies). But Malay fare also draws on Indian and Middle East cooking in the use of spices, and in dishes such as *biriyani* rice. The resulting cuisine is characterized by being both spicy and a little sweet. Naturally there's a particular emphasis on **local ingredients**: *santan* (coconut milk) lends a sweet, creamy undertone to many stews and curries, while *belacan*, a pungent fermented prawn paste (something of an acquired taste), is found in chilli condiments and sauces. A range of unusual **herbs**, including curry, kaffir lime and turmeric leaves, also play a prominent role.

The cuisine of the southern part of the Peninsula tends to be more *lemak* (rich) than further north, where the Thai influence is strongest and where you'll thus find many a *tom yam* stew – spicy and sour (the latter by dint of lemon grass) – on offer. The most famous Malay dish is arguably **satay** (see box, p.50), though this can be hard to find outside the big cities; another classic, and this time ubiquitous, is *nasi lemak* (see box, p.50), standard breakfast fare. Also quintessentially Malay is **rendang**, a dryish curry made by slow-cooking meat (usually beef) in coconut milk flavoured with galingale and a variety of herbs and spices.

For many visitors, one of the most striking things about Malay food is the bewildering array of **kuih-muih** (or just *kuih*), or sweetmeats, on display at markets at street stalls. Often featuring coconut and sometimes *gula melaka* (palm-sugar molasses), *kuih* come in all shapes and sizes, and in as many colours (often artificial nowadays) as you find in a paints catalogue – rainbow-hued layer cakes of rice flour are about the most extreme example.

Chinese food

The range of Chinese cooking available in Malaysia and Singapore represents a mouthwatering sweep through China's southeastern seaboard, reflecting the historical pattern of emigration from **Fujian**, **Guangzhou** and **Hainan Island** provinces. This diversity is evident in popular dishes served at any collection of stalls or *kopitiams*. Cantonese *char siew* (roast pork, given a reddish honey-based marinade) is frequently served over plain rice as a meal in itself, or as a garnish in noodle dishes such as

Six of the best

The culinary highlights listed below are mostly fairly easy to find, and many of these foods cut across racial boundaries as well, with each ethnic group modifying the dish slightly to suit its own cooking style. For more local dishes see pp.749–755.

Nasi lemak Rice fragrantly cooked in coconut milk and served with fried peanuts, tiny fried anchovies, cucumber, boiled egg and spicy *sambal*.

Roti canai Called *roti prata* in Singapore, this Indian-inspired griddle bread comes with a thin curry sauce. The most ubiquitous of a long list of rotis, it's served by Malay and Indian *kedai kopis* and stalls.

Nasi goreng Literally, fried rice, though not as in Chinese restaurants; Malay and Indian versions feature a little spice and chilli, along with the usual mix of vegetables plus shrimp, chicken and/or egg bits.

Char kuay teow A Hokkien Chinese dish of fried tagliatelle-style rice noodles rendered dark by soy sauce and garnished with egg, pork and prawns. The Singapore version is decidedly sweet. Malay *kuay teow goreng* is also available and tends to be plainer, though also spicier.

Satay A Malay dish of chicken, mutton or beef kebabed on bamboo sticks, marinaded and barbecued. The meat is accompanied by cucumber, raw onion and *ketupat*, which is sticky-rice cubes steamed in a wrap of woven leaves. All these are meant to be dipped in a spicy peanut sauce. Chinese satay featuring pork also exists.

Laksa A spicy seafood noodle soup, Nonya in origin. Singapore *laksa*, served with fishcake dumplings and beansprouts, is rich and a little sweet thanks to copious use of coconut milk, while Penang's *asam laksa* features flaked fish and a sour flavour from tamarind.

wonton mee (*wonton* being Cantonese pork dumplings); also very common is Hainanese chicken rice, comprising steamed chicken accompanied by savoury rice cooked in chicken stock. Fujian province contributes dishes such as *hae mee*, yellow noodles in a rich prawn broth; *yong tau foo*, from the Hakka ethnic group on the border with Guangzhou, and comprising bean curd, fishball dumplings and assorted vegetables, poached and served with broth and sweet dipping sauces; and *mee pok*, a Teochew (Chaozhou) dish featuring ribbon-like noodles with fishball dumplings and a spicy dressing.

Restaurant dining, on the other hand, is dominated by **Cantonese** food. Menus are sometimes predictable – including standbys such as sweet-and-sour pork, lemon chicken, steamed sea bass, Yangzhou fried rice, claypot rice (rice cooked in an earthenware pot with sweet *lap cheong* pork sausage) and so forth – but the quality of cooking is usually very high.

Many Cantonese places offer great **dim sum** lunches, at which small servings of numerous savouries such as *siu mai*

dumplings (of pork and prawn), crispy yam puffs and *chee cheong fun* (rice-flour rolls stuffed with pork and dredged in sweet sauce) are consumed. Traditionally, they're all served in bamboo steamers and ordered off trolleys wheeled around by waitresses, though these days you might well make your selection from a menu, with the food arriving directly from the kitchen.

Where available, take the opportunity to try **specialities** such as steamboat, a sort of fondue involving the dunking of raw vegetables, meat and seafood into boiling stock to cook (the stock itself is drunk as part of the meal), or chilli crab (served at some seafood places), in which crab pieces are served up in a spicy tomato sauce. It's also worth sampling humdrum but very commonplace stomach-fillers such as **rice porridge** – either plain, with salted fish and omelette strips added for flavour, or already flavoured by being cooked with chicken or fish – and **pow**, steamed buns containing a savoury filling of *char siew* or chicken, or sometimes a sweet filling of red bean paste. Both porridge and *pow* are widely available as breakfast fare, while *pow* is sold throughout the day as a snack.

Nonya food

Named after the word used to describe womenfolk of the Peranakan communities (see p.712), Nonya food is to Penang, Melaka and Singapore as Creole food is to Louisiana, a product of the melding of cultures. In the case of Nonya food, the blend is of Chinese and Malay (and also Indonesian) cuisines and can seem more Malay than Chinese thanks to its use of spices, except that pork is widely used.

Nonya **popiah** (spring rolls) is one of the standard dishes: rather than being fried, the rolls are assembled by coating a steamed wrap with a sweet sauce made of palm sugar, then stuffed mainly with stir-fried *bangkwang*, a crunchy turnip-like vegetable. Another classic is **laksa**, noodles in a spicy soup flavoured in part by *daun kesom* – a herb fittingly referred to in English as laksa leaf (see box opposite). Other well-known Nonya dishes include **kuih pai tee**, not unlike fried spring rolls in texture but shaped like cup cakes, with the filling spooned in; **asam fish**, a spicy, tangy fish stew featuring tamarind (the *asam* of the name); and **otak-otak**, fish mashed with coconut milk and chilli paste, then put in a narrow banana-leaf envelope and steamed or barbecued.

As with Malay food, the very best Nonya cooking is prepared in the home, these days often by elderly matriarchs, though a younger generation of cooks is perpetuating the tradition. The best places to find Nonya restaurants are KL, Penang, Melaka and Singapore.

Indian food

The classic **southern Indian** dish is the *dosai* or *thosai*, a thin rice-flour pancake, often stuffed with a vegetable mixture. It's usually served accompanied by *sambar*, a coconut chutney; *rasam*, a tamarind broth; and perhaps a few small helpings of vegetable or dhal curries. Also very common are a range of roti griddle breads, plus the more substantial *murtabak*, thicker than a roti and stuffed with egg, onion and minced meat, with sweet banana versions sometimes available. At lunchtime many South Indian cafés turn to serving *daun pisang* (literally, banana leaf), a meal comprising rice heaped on a banana-leaf "platter" and small, replenishable heaps of various curries placed alongside. In some restaurants you'll find more substantial dishes such as the popular fish-head curry (don't be put off by the idea – the "cheeks" between the mouth and gills are packed with tasty flesh).

A notable aspect of the Indian eating scene in Malaysia is the "**mamak**" *kedai kopi*, run by Muslims of Indian descent. With Malay restaurants not that common, *mamak* establishments have become de facto meeting places for all creeds, being halal and open late. Foodwise, they're very similar to other South Indian places, though there's perhaps more of an emphasis on meat in *mamak* joints. Tamil and *mamak* eating places aren't hard to tell apart, as the former display pictures of Hindu gods, while the latter have framed Arabic inscriptions on the walls. There are also a few Indian Muslim coffee shops in Singapore, particularly in Little India and the Arab quarter, but the term *mamak* is little used there.

The food served in **northern Indian** restaurants (only found in big cities), is richer, less fiery and more reliant on mutton and chicken. The most famous style of **north Indian** cooking is *tandoori* – named after the clay oven in which the food is cooked; you'll commonly come across *tandoori* chicken marinated in yoghurt and spices and then baked. Breads such as nan also tend to feature rather than rice, though just about every restaurant has a version of biriyani.

Borneo cuisine

Much of the diet of the indigenous groups living in settled communities in **east Malaysia** tends to revolve around standard Malay and Chinese dishes. But in the remoter regions, or at festival times, you may have an opportunity to sample indigenous cuisine. In **Sabah**'s Klias Peninsula and in **Brunei**, villagers still produce *ambuyat*, a glue-like, sago-starch porridge that's dipped in sauce; then there's the Murut speciality of *jaruk* – raw wild boar, fermented in a bamboo

Special diets

Malay food is, unfortunately, a tough nut to crack for **vegetarians**, as meat and seafood are well integrated into the cuisine. Among the standard savoury dishes, it's really only *sayur lodeh* (a rich mixed-vegetable curry made with coconut milk), *tauhu goreng* (deep-fried tofu with a peanut dressing similar to satay sauce) and *acar* (pickles) that veggies can handle. Eating places run by the **Chinese** and **Indian** communities are the best bets, as these groups have some familarity with vegetarianism thanks to the cultural influence of Buddhism and Hinduism. Chinese restaurants can always whip up veg stir fries to order and many places now feature **Chinese vegetarian** cuisine, featuring the use of textured veg protein and gluten mock meats, often uncannily like the real thing, and delicious when done right.

If you're a strict vegetarian, you'll want to avoid **seafood derivatives** commonly used in cooking. This means eschewing dishes like *rojak* (containing fermented prawn paste) and the chilli dip called *sambal belacan* (containing *belacan*, the Malay answer to prawn paste) – though for some visitors, vegetarian or not, the pungency of prawn paste is enough of a deterrent. Oyster sauce, used in Chinese stir fries, is omitted for vegetarian purposes in favour of soy sauce or just salt. Note also that the delicious gravy that accompanies **roti canai** is only likely to be suitable for veggies if you spot telltale lentils.

If you need to **explain in Malay** that you're vegetarian, try *saya hanya makan sayuran* ("I only eat vegetables"). Even if the person taking your order speaks English, it can be useful to list the things you don't eat (in Malay you'd say, for example, *saya tak mahu ayam dan ikan dan udang* for "I don't want chicken or fish or prawn" – see p.749 for more terms). Expect a few misunderstandings. The cook may leave out one thing on your proscribed list, only to substitute another; certain ingredients, such as dried shrimp, are so commonplace that the cook will mechanically add them without realizing it.

Halal food

Halal fare doesn't just feature at Malay and *mamak* restaurants and stalls. The catering at mid-range and top-tier Malaysian hotels is in fact mostly halal, or at least **"pork-free"** and even the Chinese dishes served at top hotel restaurants have their pork content replaced with something else. Of course, the pork-free billing doesn't equate to being halal, but many local Muslims are prepared to overlook this grey area or get round it by ordering seafood.

In **Singapore**, most hawker centres have a row or two of Muslim stalls, and in areas where the great majority of the population is Muslim, such as **Kelantan** and **Terengganu**, halal or pork-free food is the norm, even at Chinese and Indian restaurants.

tube and definitely an acquired taste. Among the most famous of Sabah's dishes is *hinava*, raw fish pickled in lime juice. In **Sarawak**, you may be able to sample wild boar when eating with Iban or Kelabit communities. Wild boar is in fact most prized and is cooked on a spit or stewed, and served with rice (perhaps *lemang* – glutinous rice cooked in bamboo) and jungle ferns. River fish is a longhouse basic; the most easily available, tilapia, is usually grilled with pepper and herbs, or steamed in bamboo cylinders.

In the main Borneo cities there are ample opportunities to encounter examples of river fish, ferns and spices (Sarawak pepper is world-renowned) being given a transnational twist in fusion cooking. Many of the boldest examples can be found in buffets at top-flight hotels.

Tropical fruit

Markets feature a delightful range of locally grown **fruit**, though modern agricultural practices are leading to a decline in some varieties. Below are some of the more unusual fruits to watch out for.

Bananas (pisang) Look out for the delicious *pisang mas*, small, straight, thin-skinned and aromatically sweet; *pisang rastali*, slightly bigger, with dark blotches on the skin and not quite so sweet; plus green- and even red-skinned varieties.

Chempedak This smaller version of the *nangka* (see jackfruit below) is normally deep-fried, enabling the seed, not unlike new potato, to be eaten too.

Ciku Looks like an apple; varies from yellow to pinkish brown when ripe, with a soft, pulpy flesh.

Durian One of the most popular fruits in Southeast Asia, durians are also, for many visitors, the most repugnant thanks to their unpleasant smell. In season (March–Aug & Nov–Feb), they're the size of soccer balls and have a thick green skin covered with sharp spikes. Inside, rows of large seeds are coated with squidgy yellow-white flesh, whose flavour has been likened to vomit-flavoured custard.

Guava Has a green, textured skin and flesh with five times the vitamin C content of oranges.

Jackfruit Like some kind of giant grenade, the jackfruit (*nangka*) grows up to 40cm long and has a coarse greenish-yellow exterior, enclosing large seeds whose sweet flesh has a powerful odour, vaguely like overripe pineapple.

Langsat Together with its sister fruit, the *duku*, this looks like a small, round potato, with juicy, segmented white flesh containing small, bitter seeds.

Longan Not unlike the lychee, this stone fruit has sweet, juicy translucent flesh inside a thin brown skin.

Mangosteen Available from June–Aug & Nov–Jan, mangosteens have a segmented white flesh with a sweet, slightly tart flavour. Be warned: the thick purple rind contains juice that stains clothes indelibly.

Pomelo Much grown around Ipoh, this pale green citrus fruit is slightly smaller than a soccer ball and, at its best, is juicier and sweeter than grapefruit. Slice away the rind with a knife, then separate and peel the giant segments with your hands.

Rambutan Rambutans are the shape and size of hen's eggs, with a soft, spiny exterior (the redder, the riper) that gives them their name – *rambut* means "hair" in Malay. To get at the sweet translucent white flesh coating the stone inside, simply make a small tear in the peel with your nails and twist open.

Salak Teardrop-shaped, the *salak* has a skin like a snake's and a bitter taste.

Soursop Inside the bumpy, muddy-green skin of this fruit is smooth white flesh like blancmange. Margaret Brooke, wife of Sarawak's second rajah, Charles, described it as "tasting like cotton wool dipped in vinegar and sugar".

Star fruit This waxy, pale green fruit, star-shaped in cross-section, is said to be good for high blood pressure. The yellower the fruit, the sweeter its flesh – though it can be rather insipid.

Desserts

Appropriately, given the steamy climate, stalls offer a range of desserts that often revolve around **ice** milled down to something resembling slush. More jarringly, desserts often include ingredients such as **pulses**, **sticky rice** or even **yam** and **sweet potato**, all of which can be turned into a sweet stew or porridge.

At their best, local desserts are certainly a lot more interesting than most ice-cream sundaes ever get. Easy to find and worth trying is **eis kacang** (also known as *air batu campur* – "mixed ice" – or ABC), comprising a small helping of aduki beans, sweetcorn and bits of jelly, covered with a snowy mound doused in colourful syrups. Even better, though high in cholesterol, is **cendol**, luscious coconut milk sweetened with *gula melaka* and mixed with green fragments of mung-bean-flour jelly. You'll even find delicious red-bean ice cream on sale, its flavour dominated by coconut milk rather than the beans.

Drinks

Bottled water is widely available at around RM2 a litre, while among the freshly squeezed **juices**, watermelon, orange and carrot are pretty common, as is the faintly sappy but invigorating sugar cane, extracted by pressing the canes through mangles. Some street stalls also do a range of cordial-based drinks, nowhere near as good. Rather better are lychee and longan drinks, made with diluted tinned juices and served with some of the fruit at the bottom. The usual range of **soft drinks** is available everywhere for around RM1.50 a can/carton, with the F&N and Yeo companies providing more unusual flavours. Sweetened soya milk in cartons or – much tastier – freshly made at stalls is another popular local choice, as is the refreshing, sweet *chin chow*, which looks like cola but is in fact made from a seaweed and comes with strands of seaweed jelly.

Tea (*teh*) and **coffee** (*kopi*) are as much national drinks as they are in the West. If ordered with milk, they'll come with a generous amount of the sweetened condensed variety or sometimes evaporated milk (only large hotels and smarter Western-style cafés have regular milk). If you don't have a sweet tooth, either ask for your drink *kurang manis* (literally "lacking in sweetness"), in which case less condensed milk will be added, or have it black (use the suffix "o", eg *kopi o* for black coffee); there's more on the complexities of ordering drinks on p.754.

Locals adore their tea or coffee **tarik**, literally "pulled", which in practice means frothing the drink by repeatedly pouring it out of a container in one hand to another container in the other hand, and back. Occasionally this can be quite an entertaining feat, the drink being poured from head height with scarcely a drop being spilt.

Alcohol

Alcohol is generally not hard to find in **Malaysia** and **Singapore**. Most of the big cities have a bar scenes, though in the towns drinking is limited to a few non-Muslim restaurants, drinks stalls at food courts (which usually serve beer and perhaps stout), Chinese *kedai kopis* and Chinese-style bars – often no better than tarted-up *kedai kopis*, the walls perhaps plastered with posters of Hong Kong showbiz poppets. However, in the strongly Muslim areas, particularly Kelantan and Terengganu, only a small

number of establishments, usually Chinese *kedai kopis* and stalls, are licensed. **Brunei** is officially dry, though non-Muslim visitors may bring alcohol into the country for their own consumption (see p.67).

Anchor and Tiger **beer** (lager) are locally produced and easily available, though you can also get Western and Thai beers as well as the Chinese Tsingtao and a variety of **stouts**, including Guinness and the Singaporean ABC. Locally produced **whisky** and **rum** are cheap enough, too, though they're pretty rough and benefit from being mixed with Coke. **Brandy**, which is what the local Chinese drink, tends to be better. The more upmarket restaurants and bars serve beer on draught, cocktails and (generally pricey) imported **wine**. In the longhouses of Sabah and Sarawak, you might be invited to sample *tuak*, a rice wine about the same strength as beer.

Where bars exist in numbers, fierce competition ensures **happy hours** are a regular feature (usually daily 5–7pm), bringing the beer price down to around RM8 a glass, though spirits still remain pricey. While some bars open from lunchtime till late, most tend to open from early evening until the small hours.

The media

Both Malaysia and Singapore boast plenty of newspapers, TV channels and radio stations serving up lively reportage of events, sports and entertainment, though don't expect to come across hard-hitting or healthily sceptical coverage of domestic politics. The major media organizations in each country are at least partly owned by the government in question; in Singapore, most newspapers have actually been herded into a conglomerate in which the state has a major stake.

Furthermore, the media are kept on their toes by a legal requirement that they must periodically renew their licence to publish. Thus it was that the *Sarawak Tribune* was suspended indefinitely in 2006 after it reproduced the controversial Danish cartoons of the Prophet Muhammad; the

paper subsequently elected to shut down for good.

Given all these circumstances, it's no surprise that in the 2008 World Press Freedom Index, issued by the pressure group Reporters Without Borders, Malaysia and Singapore were far down the rankings at no. 132 and no. 144 respectively – below much poorer nations not exactly noted for being exemplars of free speech, such as Tajikistan and Albania. Brunei's media are both much less diverse and no more outspoken than in Malaysia and Singapore.

A wide range of **foreign newspapers** and magazines are sold in the main cities, and international TV channels are available via satellite and cable, though any coverage of domestic stories they may run is often viewed with suspicion by the powers that be. There are occasional bans on issues of foreign magazines containing pieces that displease the authorities, while Singapore's leaders have a long history of winning defamation suits against foreign publications in the island's courts.

If this all seems an unremittingly bleak picture, it should be said that coverage of Malaysia's opposition parties has increased after they took power in several states in the country's 2008 general election. Furthermore, the advent of **independent news websites** and **blogs** has been a breath of fresh air in recent years – to the extent that in the run-up to the 2006 general elections in Singapore, the government there attempted to ban blogging by opposition politicians or indeed anyone writing about political matters. Elsewhere in cyberspace, it's possible to turn up various **Youtube** clips of discussion forums and interviews with activists, offering an alternative take on local issues.

Newspapers, magazines and online news

Malaysia and Singapore both have English, Malay, Chinese and Tamil newspapers, while Brunei's papers appear in English and Malay. Though Malaysia's national dailies are available in towns in east Malaysia, locally published English-language papers such as the *Borneo Post* in Sarawak (Ⓦ www .theborneopost.com) and the *Daily Express* in Sabah (Ⓦ www.dailyexpress.com.my) are more popular there.

Malaysia

Aliran Monthly Ⓦ www.aliran.com. Campaining magazine with an avowed pro-human-rights stance.
Malaysia Insider Ⓦ www.themalaysiainsider.com. Considered more moderate than some of its online counterparts, the *Insider* provides intelligent news and commentary in English and Malay.
Malaysia Today Ⓦ www.malaysia-today.net. This news website and blog was thrust into the international spotlight after the man behind it, Raja Petra Kamaruddin, was interned under Malaysia's Internal Security Act for two months in 2008. At the time of writing, Malaysian ISPs were still restricting access to the site on government orders.
Malaysiakini (Malaysia Now) Ⓦ www .malaysiakini.com. Invigorating reportage and opinion with an anti-establishment slant.
New Straits Times Ⓦ www.nst.com.my. Closely linked to the UMNO party is this offshoot of Singapore's *Straits Times*, created after the island separated from the Federation. A tabloid, it offers a broad range of news, sports and arts coverage.
The Nut Graph Ⓦ thenutgraph.com. Thoughtful analysis of Malaysian affairs with an emphasis on the links between politics and culture. Among their awkward-squad columinists are film director Amir Muhammad and Marina Mahathir, daughter of the former PM (she is also to be found in *The Star*).
Rengah Sarawak Ⓦ www.rengah.c2o.org. Admirable website offering stories pertinent to Sarawak's indigenous communities and their concerns.
The Star Ⓦ www.thestar.com.my. Founded by the MCA party, *The Star* is Malaysia's best-selling English daily and offers some perceptive analysis of domestic politics. Ironically, its Insight Down South column is more probing of Singapore affairs than most stuff in the island state's own papers.
The Sun Ⓦ www.sun2surf.com. More independent-minded than the other national English dailies, though rather populist; free.

Singapore

Straits Times Ⓦ www.straitstimes.com. This venerable broadsheet was founded in 1845, though sadly its pedigree isn't matched by the candour of its journalism; not bad on foreign news, however.
Talking Cock Ⓦ www.talkingcock.com. Satirical website which takes a sardonic look at local news and aspects of Singapore society.
Today Ⓦ www.todayonline.com. A free paper from the state-owned broadcaster Mediacorp, *Today* is generally less bland than the *Straits Times* and carries worthwhile arts reviews at the weekend.
Wayang Party Club Ⓦ wayangparty.com. Escaping official censure or worse thus far, this audacious website delivers insightful analysis of political machinations in Singapore, plus some coverage of events in Malaysia.

Brunei

Borneo Bulletin ⓦ www.brunet.bn/news/bb. The main paper in Brunei, the *Bulletin* has limited news content, but its letters page does allow topics seldom discussed in this strict state to get an airing.

Television and radio

TV and radio in Malaysia, Singapore and Brunei are dominated by the state-owned broadcasters **RTM**, **Mediacorp** and **RTB** respectively, putting out programmes in several languages. Terrestrial **television** features an unexceptional mix of news, documentaries and dramas made locally and abroad, cookery and talk shows, Islamic discussions and so forth; **radio** is even less original and tends to be dominated by pop music and talk shows. A variety of foreign TV channels, including CNN, BBC World, National Geographic, ESPN Sports, Aljazeera (which has its Far Eastern base in KL) and so forth are available on cable and satellite in Malaysia, and on cable in Singapore (where ownership of satellite dishes is banned). Note that Malaysian TV is easily picked up in Singapore and Singapore TV in southern Johor.

Malaysia

Capital FM ⓦ www.capitalfm.com.my. One of the country's more progressive music stations, transcending chart hits to include some indie, house and jazz among its offerings. Only audible in the KL area (88.9FM) at the time of writing.
Cats FM ⓦ www.catsfm.com. Kuching-based FM station offering music plus Sarawakian news; see the website for frequencies around the state.

RTM1 & RTM2 ⓦ www.rtm.gov.my. Malaysia's staple state-owned TV channels, with some programming in English, Chinese and Tamil. News in English is broadcast on RTM2 at 8pm daily.
Traxxfm ⓦ www.traxxfm.net. Established RTM station with a mix of news and music in English, available on various frequencies around the Peninsula.
TV3 ⓦ www.tv3.com.my. English and Malay news, drama and documentaries, plus some Chinese programmes. Along with the youth-oriented channels NTV7, 8TV and TV9, it's part of the same conglomerate as the *New Straits Times*.
XFresh ⓦ www.xfresh.com. A great station for homegrown pop and rock music in Malay and English, though the patter is in Malay only. Audible in cities nationwide.

Singapore

BBC World Service ⓦ www.bbcworldservice.com. 88.9FM, 24hr.
Channel News Asia ⓦ www.channelnewsasia .com. Mediacorp's CNN-like diet of rolling TV news, via cable.
Channel 5 ⓦ 5.mediacorptv.sg. The main terrestrial channel for English programming, with plenty of imported shows.
Mediacorp Radio ⓦ www.mediacorpradio.sg. Several English-language radio stations, including the speech-based 938 LIve (93.8FM) and Symphony (92.4FM) for classical music.

Brunei

Radio and Television Brunei (RTB) ⓦ www .rtb.gov.bn. RTB derives a noticeable chunk of its programming from Malaysia.

Festivals

With so many ethnic groups and religions represented in Malaysia, Singapore and Brunei, you'll be unlucky if your trip doesn't coincide with some sort of festival. Religious celebrations range from exuberant, family-oriented pageants to blood-curdlingly gory displays of devotion. Chinese religious festivals – in particular, the Festival of the Hungry Ghosts – are the best times to catch a free performance of a Chinese opera, or *wayang*, featuring crashing cymbals, clanging gongs and stylized singing. Secular events might comprise a parade with a cast of thousands, or just a local market with a few cultural demonstrations laid on.

Bear in mind that the major festival periods may play havoc with even the best-planned travel itineraries. Some festivals are also public holidays; check the lists on p.70 for those.

A festival and events calendar

The dates of many festivals change annually according to the lunar calendar. The Islamic calendar shifts forward relative to the Gregorian calendar by about ten days each year, so that, for example, a Muslim festival that happens in mid-April one year will be nearer the beginning of April the following year. We've listed rough timings, but specific dates for each year are listed on various websites.

January & February

Ponggal A Tamil harvest and New Year festival held at the start of the Tamil month of Thai. Ponggal translates as "overflow", and the festival is celebrated by boiling sugar, rice and milk together in a new claypot over a wood fire till the mixture spills over, symbolizing prosperity and plenty (mid-Jan).
Thaipusam Entranced Hindu penitents carry elaborate steel arches (*kavadi*), attached to their skin by hooks and skewers, to honour Lord Subramaniam. The biggest processions are at Kuala Lumpur's Batu Caves and from Singapore's Sri Srinivasa Perumal Temple to the Chettiar Hindu Temple (late Jan/early Feb).
Chinese New Year At which Chinese communities settle debts, visit friends and relatives and give children red envelopes (*hong bao/ang pao*) containing money; Chinese operas and lion- and dragon-dance troupes perform in the streets, while markets sell sausages and waxed ducks, pussy willow, chrysanthemums and mandarin oranges. Singapore and the major towns of west-coast Malaysia see Chingay parades, featuring stilt-walkers, lion dancers and floats (late Jan/early to mid-Feb).
Chap Goh Mei The fifteenth and climactic night of the Chinese New Year period (known as *Guan Hsiao Chieh* in Sarawak), and a time for more feasting and firecrackers; women who throw an orange into the sea at this time are supposed to be granted a good husband (Feb).
Brunei National Day The sultan and tens of thousands of Bruneians watch parades and fireworks at the Sultan Hassanal Bolkiah National Stadium, just outside Bandar Seri Begawan (Feb 23).

March–May

Easter Candlelit processions are held on Good Friday at churches such as St Peter's in Melaka and St Joseph's in Singapore (March/April).
Qing Ming Ancestral graves are cleaned and restored, and offerings made by Chinese families at the beginning of the third lunar month, signifying the beginning of spring and a new farming year (April).
Vesak Day Saffron-robed monks chant prayers at packed Buddhist temples, and devotees release caged birds to commemorate the Buddha's birth, enlightenment and the attainment of Nirvana (May).
Sabah Fest A week of events in Kota Kinabalu, offering a chance to experience Sabah's food, handicrafts, dance and music; right at the end comes *Rumah Terbuka Malaysia Tadau Kaamatan*, a harvest festival in Kota Kinabalu (late May).

June–August

Yang di-Pertuan Agong's Birthday Festivities are held in KL to celebrate the birthday of Malaysia's king, elected every five years by the country's nine sultans or rajahs from among their number (June).

57

Gawai Dayak Sarawak's Iban and Bidayuh peoples celebrate the end of harvesting with extravagant longhouse feasts. Aim to be in a longhouse on the Rejang or Batang Ai rivers, or on dry land around Serian or Bau (June).

Feast of St Peter Melaka's Eurasian community decorate their boats to honour the patron saint of fishermen (June 24).

Dragon Boat Festival Rowing boats, bearing a dragon's head and tail, race in Penang, Melaka, Singapore and Kota Kinabalu, to commemorate a Chinese scholar who drowned himself in protest against political corruption (June/July).

Sultan of Brunei's Birthday Starting with a speech by the sultan on the padang, celebrations continue for two weeks with parades, lantern processions, traditional sports competitions and fireworks (July 15).

Sarawak Extravaganza Kuching hosts a month of arts and crafts shows, street parades, food fairs and traditional games, all celebrating the culture of Sarawak (Aug).

Singapore National Day Singapore's independence is celebrated with a huge show at the National Stadium, featuring military parades and fireworks (Aug 9).

Festival of the Hungry Ghosts Held to appease the souls of the dead released from purgatory during the seventh lunar month, when Chinese street operas are held, and joss sticks, red candles and paper money are burnt outside Chinese homes (late Aug).

Ramadan Muslims spend the ninth month of the Islamic calendar fasting in the daytime, and breaking their fasts nightly with delicious Malay sweetmeats served at stalls outside mosques (starts around Aug 21 in 2009).

Malaysia National Day Parades in KL's Merdeka Square and other cities mark the formation of the state of Malaysia (Aug 31).

September–December

Moon Cake Festival Also known as the Mid-Autumn Festival, this is when Chinese people eat and exchange moon cakes, made from sesame and lotus seeds and sometimes stuffed with a duck egg. Essentially a harvest festival (Sept).

Hari Raya Puasa/Aidilfitri The end of Ramadan which Muslims celebrate by feasting, and by visiting family and friends; this is the only time the region's royal palaces are open to the public (falls in Sept in 2009).

Navarathiri Hindu temples devote nine nights to classical dance and music in honour of the consorts of the Hindu gods, Shiva, Vishnu and Brahman (Sept–Oct).

Thimithi Hindu firewalking ceremony in which devotees prove the strength of their faith by running across a pit of hot coals; best seen at the Sri Mariamman Temple in Singapore (Oct/Nov).

Deepavali Also known as *Divali*, this Hindu festival celebrates the victory of Light over Dark: oil lamps are lit outside homes to attract Lakshmi, the goddess of prosperity, and prayers are offered at all temples (Oct/Nov).

Hari Raya Haji/Aidiladha Muslims gather at mosques to honour those who have completed the hajj, or pilgrimage to Mecca; goats are sacrificed and their meat given to the needy (late Nov in 2009.)

Christmas Shopping centres in major cities compete to create the most spectacular Christmas decorations (Dec 25).

Sports and outdoor activities

With some of the oldest tropical rainforest in the world and countless beaches and islands, trekking, snorkelling and scuba diving are common pursuits in Malaysia. The more established resorts on the islands of Penang, Langkawi and Tioman offer more elaborate sports such as jet skiing and paragliding, while Cherating (the budget-travellers' centre on the east coast), with its exposed, windy bay, is a hot spot for windsurfers.

If you intend to take up any of the pursuits below, check that they are covered by your insurance policy.

Snorkelling, diving and windsurfing

The crystal-clear waters of Malaysia and its abundance of tropical fish and coral make snorkelling and diving a must for any under-water enthusiast. This is particularly true of Sabah's **Sipidan Island Marine Reserve** and the Peninsula's east coast, with islands like the **Perhentians**, **Redang**, **Kapas** and **Tioman**. Sabah's Kota Kinabalu and Sarawak's Miri also have dive schools offering PADI (Professional Association of Diving Instructors) courses with access to nearby dive sites.

Dive shops offer courses ranging from a beginner's open-water course, at around RM800, right through to the dive-master certificate, a fourteen-day course costing from RM1800. All equipment should be included in the price, and make sure that the shop is registered with PADI or SSI (Scuba Schools International). Most beachside guesthouses have **snorkelling** equipment for rent at no more than RM20 per day.

In some popular **snorkelling** areas there are lanes for motorboats clearly marked with buoy lines – always stay on the correct side of the line or you risk a nasty accident. If you're not sure in which areas it is safe to swim or snorkel, always seek local advice. However tempting the **coral** looks, you should never touch it as this can cause irrep-arable damage to the reefs and upset the delicate underwater ecosystem.

Windsurfing has yet to take off in all but the most expensive resorts in Malaysia, with

the notable exception of Cherating. Its large, open bay and shallow waters provide near-perfect conditions for the sport during the northeast monsoon season.

White-water rafting

White-water rafting has become a highly popular activity near the Sabah capital Kota Kinabalu. Two hours' drive south lies **Sungai Padas**, a grade 3 river which, at its northern end, runs through the spectacular Padas Gorge. Most specialist operators (see p.499), provide a day's rafting there for around RM150, including equipment. Opportunities for rafting in **Peninsular Malaysia** tend to be in out-of-the-way spots in the interior; it's best to go with an operator such as Nomad Adventure (Ⓦwww .nomadadventure.com) or Khersonese Expedition (Ⓦwww.thepaddlerz.com).

Trekking

The majority of treks in Malaysia require some forethought and preparation. As well as the fierce sun, the tropical climate can unleash torrential rain without any warning, which rapidly affects the condition of trails or the height of a river – what started out as a ten-hour trip can end up taking twice as long. That said, the time of year is not a hugely significant factor when planning a trek. Although the rainy season (Nov–Feb) undoubtedly slows your progress on some of the trails, conditions are less humid then, and the parks and adventure tours are not oversubscribed.

Treks in national parks almost always require that you go in a group with a **guide**, although it's quite possible to go to most parks on your own and then join a group once there. Costs

Checklist of trekking equipment

The list below assumes you'll be spending the night in a hostel or lodge; you will also need a tent if you plan to camp.

Essentials
Backpack
Sleeping bag
Mosquito net
Water bottle
Toiletries and toilet paper
Torch (and/or head torch)
Sewing kit
Pocket knife
Sunglasses (UV protective)
Sun block and lip balm
Insect repellent
Compass
Clothing and footwear
Breathable shirts/T-shirts

Lightweight, quick-drying trousers
Rainproof coat or poncho
Cotton hat with brim
Fleece jacket
Trekking boots
Cotton and woollen socks
Anti-leech socks

Other useful items
Plastic bag (to rainproof your pack)
Emergency snack food
Spare bootlaces
Small towel
Insulation mat
Basic first-aid kit

and conditions vary among the parks; each park account in the Guide contains details, and tour operators in Kuala Lumpur, Kuching, Miri and Kota Kinabalu (listed throughout the Guide) can also furnish information on conditions and options in the parks.

For inexperienced trekkers, **Taman Negara** is probably the best place to start, boasting the greatest variety of walks, many of which can be done without a guide, while **Bako National Park** in southwest Sarawak offers fairly easy, day-long hikes, and is a

haven for birdlife. For the more experienced, other parks in Sarawak, especially **Gunung Mulu**, should offer sufficient challenges for most tastes while Sabah's **Maliau Basin** is at the very demanding end of the scale. The largely inaccessible Endau-Rompin Park in the south of Peninsular Malaysia is for serious expedition fiends only. **Mount Kinabalu** Park in Sabah is in a class of its own, the hike to the top of the mountain a demanding but highly rewarding combination of trekking and climbing.

Culture and etiquette

Despite the obvious openness to influences from around the globe, and the urbanity of Kuala Lumpur, Singapore, Penang and Kuching, society in Malaysia, Singapore and Brunei remains fairly conservative and conformist. Behaviour that departs from established cultural and behavioural norms – basically, anything that draws attention to the individuals concerned – can create a bit of a scene and become problematic. These norms are well worth noting, being both tricky for outsiders to discern and widely applicable elsewhere in Asia.

Though allowances are made for foreigners, until you acquire some familiarity with where

the limits lie, it's best to err on the side of caution. Get the balance right and you'll find locals helpful and welcoming, while respectful of your need for some privacy.

Dress

For both men and women, exposing lots of bare flesh is generally a no-no in this part of Asia, and the minimum degree to which you should **cover up** can seem surprisingly prim. Islamic tradition suffuses the dress code for locals, Muslim or otherwise, and dictates that both men and women should keep torsos covered; shirt sleeves, if short, should come down to the elbow (vests are thus not OK, and for women, long-sleeved tops are preferable), while shorts (or skirts) should extend down to the knee (long trousers are ideal). Figure-hugging clothes are often frowned upon, particularly for women.

Of course dress codes are more liberal in most cities (Singapore and Kota Kinabalu in particular), on the beach and when pursuing sporting activities, but it's surprising how often the minimum standards mentioned above are complied with. Also, remember that in Muslim tradition, the soles of shoes are considered unclean, having been in contact with the dirt of the street. Thus before entering any home (Muslim or otherwise), it's almost universal practice to remove footwear at the threshold or before stepping onto any carpeted or matted area.

Discretion and body language

Given the fairly conformist nature of society, discretion should be your watchword. **Canoodling** in public will not win you any friends and could make you the subject of unwanted attention. In a situation where you need to make a **complaint**, the most effective approach is not to raise your voice but to go out of your way to be reasonable while stating your case. Drinking **alcohol** in public is not acceptable away from restaurants, bars and street dining areas.

In relation to body language, note that **touching someone's head**, be they Muslim or otherwise, must be avoided, as the head is considered sacred in Eastern culture. Handshakes are fairly commonplace when meeting someone; Muslims often follow this by touching the palm of the right hand to their own chest. Some Muslims may be reluctant to shake hands with the opposite sex; however, in this case a smile, nod and the right-hand-palm gesture mentioned above will suffice.

Visiting places of worship

It's not uncommon to see various temples and mosques happily existing side by side, each providing a social as well as a religious focal point for the corresponding community. Architectural traditions mean that the Chinese and Indian temples, built out of brick, have long outlasted the timber Malay mosque, and some are among the oldest structures you're likely to see in the region. Many of these buildings are worth a look around, though only at the largest temples might you get a little tour, courtesy of the caretaker.

When **visiting mosques** men should wear long trousers and a shirt or top with sleeves coming down to the elbows (long sleeves are even better); women will also have to don a long cloak and headdress, which is provided by most mosques. You'll be required to remove your shoes before entering. No non-Muslim is allowed to enter a mosque during prayer time or go into the prayer hall at any time, although it's possible to stand just outside and look in.

Most Chinese and Hindu temples are open from early morning to early evening; devotees go in when they like, to make offerings or to pray. At Hindu temples, as with mosques, you're expected to remove your shoes before entering.

Women travellers

Women who respect local customs and exercise common sense should have few problems travelling alone or with other women. A basic rule is not to do things you wouldn't do at home, so hitch-hiking, for example, is best avoided.

Some Western women have been known to find the atmosphere in largely Muslim areas, such as Kelantan or Terengganu, off-putting. Arriving there from Thailand or from a more cosmopolitan part of Malaysia, some women travellers go out of their way to observe the dress code mentioned earlier, yet an unlucky few still find themselves being

The status of Malay women

Malay women are among the most emancipated in the Islamic world. They often attain prominent roles in business, academia and other areas of public life, and are not lacking in confidence or social skills, as a visit to any Malay-run shop, hotel or market stall will attest. Malay women are also very much the linchpin of the family, and husbands often give way to their wives in domestic matters.

The more conservative tide running through the Islamic world has had little impact on this situation, although many Malay women now wear a *tudung* (**headscarf**) whereas a generation or two ago they were often content not to wear one. Sometimes this is merely indicative of an acceptance of the trappings of the religion or possibly a desire to please parents – it's not unusual to see Malay women at a club partying away in the unlikely combination of headscarf, skimpy T-shirt and tight jeans.

All of this is not to say that the outlook for Malay women is without struggle. Recent amendments to Malaysia's Islamic family law, which were passed in the face of disquiet among the government's own women senators, were criticized by women's rights groups as weakening the rights of Muslim women. Campaigning has led to more liberal revisions to the law, which were being debated at the time of writing.

stared at or subjected to wolf-whistles or lewd gestures. This is all the more annoying if you spot local Chinese women wandering around in skimpy tops without anyone batting an eyelid. Though it's no consolation, it's worthwhile to note that the ground rules are different for locals; the Malay, Chinese and Indian communities, having lived together for generations, have an unspoken understanding as to how the respective communities can behave in public.

Shopping and souvenirs

Southeast Asia offers real shopping bargains, with electrical equipment, cameras, clothes, fabrics, tapes and CDs all selling at highly competitive prices. What's more, the region's ethnic diversity means you'll be spoilt for choice when it comes to souvenirs and handicrafts. Throughout the Guide, good buys and bargains are picked out and there are features on the best things to buy in specific regions.

Unless you're in a department store, prices are negotiable, so be prepared to **haggle**. If you're planning to buy something pricey – a camera, say – it's a good idea to pay a visit to a fixed-price store to check the correct retail price; this way, you'll know if you're being ripped off. Asking for the "best price" is always a good start to negotiations; from there, it's a question of technique, but be realistic – shopkeepers will soon lose interest if you offer an unreasonably low price. If you

do buy any electrical goods, make sure you get an international guarantee, and that it is endorsed by the shop.

Malaysian pastimes throw up some interesting purchases: wayang kulit (shadow play) **puppets**, portraying characters from Hindu legend, are attractive and light to carry; equally colourful but completely impractical if you have to carry them around are the Malay **kites**, which can be several metres long. There's a round-up below of the other main souvenir items you might want to bring back.

In east Malaysia, the craft shops of Kota Kinabalu in Sabah have a wide variety of ethnic handicrafts native to the state. Most colourful of these are the **tudong duang**, a multicoloured cover, meant to keep flies off food, that looks like a conical hat. Sarawak's peoples also produce a wide range of **handicrafts** using raw materials from the forest, with designs that are inspired by animist beliefs. In longhouses, you may see blowpipes and tools being made. Kuching is also renowned for its **pottery**, ceramic vases and bowls bearing Iban and Bidayuh native designs.

Fabrics

The art of producing batik cloth originated in Indonesia, but today batik is available across Southeast Asia and supports a thriving industry in Malaysia. To make batik, hot wax is applied to a piece of cloth with either a pen or a copper stamp; when the cloth is dyed, the wax resists the dye and a pattern appears, a process that can be repeated many times to build up colours. Note that some vendors try to pass off printed cloth as batik. Make sure the brightness of the pattern is equal on both sides – if it's obviously lighter on one side, it is likely the cloth is printed.

Batik is used to create shirts, skirts, bags and hats, as well as traditional **sarongs** – rectangular lengths of cloth wrapped around the waist and legs to form a sort of skirt worn by both males and females. These start at around RM20 and are more expensive, depending on how complex and colourful the design is.

The exquisite style of fabric known as **songket** is a big step up in price from batik;

made by hand-weaving gold and silver thread into plain cloth, songket is used to make sarongs, headscarves and the like. Expect to pay at least RM120 for a sarong-length of cloth, and RM300–400 for the most decorative pieces. The other thing you'll be able to buy in Indian enclaves everywhere is primary-coloured silk **sarees** – look in Little India in Singapore and the Jalan TAR in Kuala Lumpur for the best bargains.

Unique to Sarawak is **pua kumbu** (in Iban, "blanket"), a textile whose complex designs are created using the *ikat* method of weaving (see p.425 for more). The cloth is best picked up in the bazaar towns or longhouses along the state's many rivers.

Metalwork and woodcarving

Of the wealth of metalwork on offer, **silverware** from Kelantan is among the finest and most intricately designed; it's commonly used to make earrings, brooches and pendants, as well as more substantial pieces. Selangor State is known for its **pewter** – a refined blend of tin, antimony and copper, which makes elegant vases, tankards and ornaments.

Over in Brunei, the speciality is **brassware** – kettles (called *kiri*) and gongs – decorated with elaborate Islamic motifs. Brunei brassware, however, is substantially more expensive than similarly sized Malaysian pewter articles.

Natural resources from the forest have traditionally been put to good use, with rattan, cane, bamboo and *mengkuang* (pandanus) used to make baskets, bird cages, mats, hats and shoulder bags. **Woodcarving** skills, once employed to decorate the palaces and public buildings of the early sultans, are today used to make

Duty-free goods

Malaysia has no duty on cameras, watches, cosmetics, perfumes or cigarettes. Pulau Labuan, Pulau Langkawi and Pulau Tioman are duty-free islands, which in practice means that goods there (including alcohol) can be forty percent cheaper than on the Malaysian mainland, though it's not as though a particularly impressive range of products is on sale. Duty-free products in Singapore include electronic and electrical goods, cosmetics, cameras, clocks, watches, jewellery, precious stones and metals.

less exotic articles such as mirror frames. However, it's still possible to see statues and masks created by the Orang Asli. As animists, Orang Asli artists draw upon the natural world – animals, trees, fish, as well as more abstract elements like fire and water – for their imagery. Of particular interest are the carvings of the Mah Meri of Selangor, which are improvisations on the theme of *moyang*, literally "ancestor", which is the generic name for all spirit images.

Travel essentials

Costs

Those entering Malaysia from Thailand will find that costs are slightly higher – both food and accommodation are more expensive – whereas travellers arriving from Indonesia will find prices a little lower overall. Travelling in a group naturally helps keep accommodation and eating costs down. The region affords some savings for senior citizens, and an ISIC student card might occasionally pay dividends.

Note that **bargaining** is routine throughout Malaysia and Singapore when buying stuff in markets or small shops, though you don't haggle for meals or accommodation.

Malaysia

In **Peninsular Malaysia** you can scrape by on £12/US$18 per day staying in dorms, eating at hawker stalls and getting around by bus. Double that and you'll be able to exist in relative comfort and not have to think too hard about occasionally treating yourself. Over in **east Malaysia** the minimum daily outlay is a little higher at £15/US$22, as accommodation and tours tend to cost a little more here.

Singapore and Brunei

For the cost of a dorm bed in **Singapore**, you could easily get a private room in a KL guesthouse, which only goes to show how much pricier Singapore is than Malaysia. As a rule of thumb, whatever the cost of something in Malaysian ringgit, you'll pay roughly the same number of Singapore dollars for it across the Causeway – and a Singapore dollar happens to be worth more than 2 ringgit.

Surviving in Singapore thus requires a minimum budget of £20/US$30 a day. Upgrading your lodgings to a private room in a guesthouse, eating one of your daily meals in a cheap restaurant and having a beer or two could require £35/US$50 a day.

Costs in **Brunei** are even higher than in Singapore as there is little In the way of budget accommodation; furthermore, you are going to be largely dependent on taxis to see anything outside the capital, as the public transport network is still minimal. As a result, the minimum daily outlay is likely to be around £40/US$60.

Crime and personal safety

If you lose something in Malaysia, Singapore or Brunei, you're more likely to have someone running after you with it than running away. Nevertheless, you shouldn't become complacent: pickpockets and **snatch-thieves** are on the prowl in Malaysia's more touristed cities, and theft from dormitories by other tourists is a common complaint. If you have to report a crime, be sure to get a copy of the police report for insurance purposes.

Sensible **precautions** include carrying your passport, traveller's cheques and other valuables in a concealed money belt, and making use of the safety deposit box that many guesthouses and hotels have. It's

Emergency numbers

Malaysia
Police ☎999
Fire Brigade/Ambulance ☎994

Singapore
Police ☎999
Fire Brigade/Ambulance ☎995

Brunei
Police ☎993
Ambulance ☎991
Fire Brigade ☎995

worth taking a photocopy of the relevant pages of your passport, too, in case it's lost or stolen. If you use traveller's cheques, keep a separate record of the serial numbers, together with a note of which ones you've cashed.

It's worth repeating here that it is very unwise to have anything to do with illegal drugs of any description in Malaysia, Singapore and Brunei (see box, p.66).

Malaysia

If you do need to report a crime in Malaysia, head for the nearest police station, where there'll invariably be someone who speaks English. In many major tourist spots, there are specific tourist police stations geared up to problems faced by foreign travellers.

Restrictions on contact between people of the opposite sex (such as the offence of *khalwat*, or "close proximity") and eating in public during daylight hours in the Ramadan month apply to Muslims only.

Singapore

Singapore is known locally as a "fine city" – there are substantial **fines** for misdemeanours including littering, jaywalking – here defined as crossing a main road within 50m of a designated pedestrian crossing – and so forth, though these penalties are seldom enforced as the populace has become compliant over the years. One thing to bear in mind is that **chewing gum** is outlawed in Singapore on the grounds that used gum can foul the streets.

Singapore's police, who wear dark-blue uniforms, keep a fairly low profile, but are polite and helpful when approached; see p.683 for contact details.

Electricity

Mains voltage in Malaysia, Singapore and Brunei is **230 volts**, so any equipment using 110 volts will need a converter. The plugs in all three countries have three square prongs like British ones.

Entry requirements

Nationals of the UK, Ireland, the US, Canada, Australia, New Zealand and South Africa don't need visas in advance to stay in Malaysia, Singapore or Brunei, and it's straightforward to extend your permission to stay. That said, it's always a good idea to check with the relevant embassy or consulate, as the rules on visas are complex and subject to change. Ensure that your passport is valid for at least six months from the date of your trip, and has several blank pages for entry stamps.

Malaysia

Upon arrival in Malaysia, citizens of Australia, Canada, the UK, Ireland, US, New Zealand and South Africa are given a passport stamp entitling them to a **three-month stay**. Visitors who enter via Sarawak, however, receive a one-month stamp (see below). It's a straightforward matter to extend this permit by applying at the Immigration Department, who have offices (listed in the Guide) in Kuala Lumpur and major towns. Visitors from the above countries can also cross into Singapore or Thailand and back to be granted a fresh Malaysia entry stamp. Visa requirements for various nationalities are listed on ⓦ www.kln.gov.my.

Tourists travelling from the Peninsula to east Malaysia (Sarawak and Sabah) must be cleared again by immigration; visitors to Sabah can remain as long as their original entry stamp is valid, but arriving in Sarawak from whichever territory generates a new thirty-day stamp, which can be easily renewed.

When you arrive, you will normally be given a lengthy landing card to complete; note that you need to hang onto the small **departure**

Drugs: a warning

In Malaysia, Singapore and Brunei, the possession of **illegal drugs** – hard or soft – carries a hefty prison sentence or even the death penalty. If you are arrested for drugs offences you can expect no mercy from the authorities and little help from your consular representatives. The simple advice, therefore, is not to have anything to do with drugs in any of these countries, and never agree to carry anything through customs for a third party.

portion of the card for when you leave Malaysia.

Malaysian embassies and consulates

Australia 7 Perth Ave, Yarralumla, Canberra, ACT 6000 ☎02/6273 1543.
Brunei No. 61, Simpang 336, Kg Sungai Akar, Jalan Kebangsaan, P.O. Box 2826, Bandar Seri Begawan ☎02/381095.
Canada 60 Boteler St, Ottawa, ON K1N 8Y7 ☎613/241-5182.
Indonesia Jalan H.R. Rasuna Said, Kav. X/6, No. 1-3 Kuningan, Jakarta Selatan 12950 ☎021/5224947.
Ireland Shelbourne House, Level 3A-5A, Ballsbridge, Dublin 4 ☎01/667 7280.
New Zealand 10 Washington Ave, Brooklyn, Wellington ☎04/801385 2439.
Singapore 301 Jervois Rd ☎6325 0111.
South Africa 1007 Schoeman St, Arcadia, Pretoria 0083 ☎012/342 5990.
Thailand 35 South Sathorn Rd, Bangkok 10120 ☎02/629 6800.
UK 45 Belgrave Square, London SW1X 8QT ☎020/7919 0251.
US 3516 International Court, NW Washington, DC 20008 ☎202/572-9700; 313 East 43rd St, New York ☎212/490-1420; 550 South Hope St, Suite 400, Los Angeles 90071 ☎213/892-1238.

Singapore

Upon arrival in Singapore, citizens of the UK, Ireland, the US, Canada, Australia, New Zealand and South Africa are normally stamped in for fourteen days, though a month's stay can be granted if requested. Extending your stay for up to three months is possible but extensions beyond this are rare. If you have any problems extending your stay, there's always the option of taking a bus up to Johor Bahru just inside Malaysia, then returning to Singapore, whereupon you're given a new entry stamp.

Singaporean embassies and consulates

Australia 17 Forster Crescent, Yarralumla, Canberra, ACT 2600 ☎02/6271 0700.
Canada Suite 1820, 999 Hastings St, Vancouver, BC V6C 2W2 ☎604/669 5115.
Indonesia Block X/4 Kav No. 2, Jalan H.R. Rasuna Said, Kuningan, Jakarta ☎021/2995 0400.
Ireland 2 Ely Place Upper, Dublin 2 ☎01/669 1700.
Malaysia 209 Jalan Tun Razak, Kuala Lumpur 50400 ☎03/2161 6404.
New Zealand 17 Kabul St, Khandallah, Wellington ☎04/470 0850.
South Africa 980 Schoeman St, Arcadia, Pretoria 0083 ☎012/430 6035.
Thailand 129 South Sathorn Rd, Bangkok 10120 ☎02/286-2111.
UK 9 Wilton Crescent, Belgravia, London SW1X 8SP ☎020/7235 8315.
US 3501 International Place NW, Washington, DC 20008 ☎202/537-3100.

Brunei

US nationals can visit Brunei for up to ninety days without a visa, while British and New Zealand passport holders are granted thirty days, and Canadians, Australians and South Africans fourteen. Once you're in Brunei, extending your permission to stay is usually a formality; apply at the Immigration Department in Bandar Seri Begawan.

Bruneian embassies and consulates

Australia 10 Beale Crescent, Deakin, ACT 2600 Canberra ☎02/6285 4500.
Canada 395 Laurier Ave, Ottawa, ON, KIN 6R4 ☎613/234-5656.
Indonesia Jalan Teuku Umar 9, Menteng, Jakarta ☎021/3190 6080.
Ireland No office; contact their UK representation.
Malaysia No. 19-10, 19th floor, Menara Tan & Tan, Jalan Tun Razak, Kuala Lumpur 50400 ☎03/2161 2800.

New Zealand No office; contact their Australia representation.
Singapore 325 Tanglin Rd ☎6733 9055.
South Africa see the Singapore embassy.
Thailand 3, Ekamai 8, 63 Sukhumvit Rd Bangkok 10110 ☎02/7147387.
UK 19/20 Belgrave Square, London SW1X 8PG ☎0207/581 0521.
US 3520 International Court NW, Washington, DC 20008 ☎202/237-1838.

Customs allowances

Malaysia's duty-free allowances let you bring in 200 cigarettes or 225g of tobacco, and up to a litre of wine, spirits or liquor. There's no customs clearance for passengers travelling from Singapore or Peninsular Malaysia to East Malaysia, nor for people passing between Sabah and Sarawak.

Entering **Singapore** from anywhere other than Malaysia (with which there are no duty-free restrictions), you can bring in one litre each of spirits, wine and beer duty-free; duty is payable on all tobacco.

Visitors to **Brunei** may bring in 200 cigarettes, 50 cigars or 250g of tobacco, and 60ml of perfume; non-Muslims over 17 can also import two quarts of liquor and twelve cans of beer for personal consumption (any alcohol brought into the country must be declared upon arrival).

Gay and lesbian travellers

Though Malaysia's largest cities, plus Singapore, have long had a discreet gay scene, the public profile of gays and lesbians was until recently still summed up by the old "don't ask, don't tell" maxim. However, cyberspace has helped galvanize gay people in both countries, providing a virtual refuge within which to socialize and campaign. Hitherto strait-laced **Singapore** is now the home of an excellent gay news and lifestyle website (Ⓦwww.fridae.com), permits exploration of gay themes in the arts and for a time even played host to outdoor gay rave parties, which drew major international participation. While the environment in **Malaysia** is always going to be more conservative – illustrated by the fact that *Brokeback Mountain* failed to be screened there, and by occasional raids on gay saunas

– the Malaysian government has no obvious Islamically inspired appetite to clamp down on the existing, limited gay nightlife.

For all the general loosening up over the years, it's very much a case of two steps forward and one step back. In 2007, following an extraordinary parliamentary debate, Singapore MPs finally agreed to repeal **colonial-era laws** criminalizing anal and oral sex, though they retained the injunction on such activity between men. Speaking in the debate, Prime Minister Lee Hsien Loong noted that public opinion on gay matters was divided, though he reiterated that government would continue not to enforce the law against gay sex and had no intention of compelling gay venues to "go underground". The same colonial legislation remains on the statute book in Malaysia, and while a few gay-friendly bars do thrive there, any gay-related campaigning that exists tends to be channelled into the relatively uncontentious issue of HIV/AIDS. Meanwhile, Singapore has consistently declined to give official recognition to its **gay lobby** group, People Like Us (Ⓦwww.plu.sg). Needless to say, all this makes legal recognition of gay partnerships a distant prospect in either country.

This mixed picture shouldn't deter gay visitors from getting to know and enjoy the local scene, such as it is. A small number of gay establishments are reviewed in this guide, and more listings are available on Ⓦwww.fridae.com and the Bangkok-based Ⓦwww.utopia-asia.com.

Insurance

A typical travel insurance policy usually provides cover for the loss of bags, tickets and – up to a certain limit – cash or cheques, as well as cancellation or curtailment of your journey. Some policy premiums now include so-called dangerous sports; in Malaysia, for example, this can mean scuba diving, white-water rafting or trekking (notably in the Maliau Basin of Sabah). Always ascertain whether medical coverage will be paid out as treatment proceeds or only after return home, and whether there is a 24-hour medical emergency number. When securing baggage cover, make sure that the per-article limit will cover your most valuable possession. If you need to make a claim, you should keep receipts for medicines and medical treatment, and in the event you have anything stolen, you must obtain an official statement from the police.

Internet

Internet cafés and shops can be found in all Malaysian cities and large towns, often in malls or in upstairs premises along central streets. While many may serve the odd coffee or Coke, the emphasis often isn't on beverages or even getting online, but on networked gaming, the terminals swamped by kids playing noisy shoot-em-ups late into the night. Periodic crackdowns temporarily compel the internet cafés to keep sensible hours and, it's hoped, the youths in their beds. At least the cafés do provide reliable internet access, costing RM3–6 per hour in practically all cases. In small towns, access may be available in guesthouses that see foreign travellers, or mobile-phone shops, both charging standard rates.

Likewise, it's not hard to get online in Brunei or Singapore; for details, see the respective chapters.

Laundry

Most Malaysian towns have laundries (*dobi*) where you can have clothes washed cheaply and quickly, according to weight, picking them up later in the day or early the next day. In addition, some hostels and guesthouses have washing machines available for guests to use for a small charge. Small sachets of soap powder are readily available from general stores if you prefer to handwash. Dry-cleaning services are less common, though any hotel of a decent standard will be able to oblige.

Living in Malaysia and Singapore

Opportunities for non-residents to find short-term employment in Malaysia and Singapore are few and far between. On an unofficial basis, helpers are often required in guesthouses; the wages you'll get for these tasks are low, but board and lodging are often included. On a more formal level, both Singapore and KL in particular have large communities of skilled expats with work permits, secured by their employer. In Malaysia expats can still expect elevated salaries, but this perk is increasingly rare in Singapore, where living standards are high enough as it is.

English-language-teaching qualifications are in demand by language schools in both countries, while in Malaysia it's also possible to find work if you are a qualified diving instructor. There are also a few volunteer schemes mainly focusing on nature conservation fieldwork, though note that they are seldom cheap to join.

Study and work programmes

AFS Intercultural Programs US ☎1-800/AFS-INFO, Canada ☎1-800/361-7248, UK ☎0113/242 6136, Australia ☎1300/131 736, NZ ☎0800/600 300, SA ☎011/447 2673; ⊛www.afs.org. Community service schemes in Malaysia.

Earthwatch Institute US & Canada ☎1-800/776-0188, UK ☎01865/318 831, Australia ☎03/9682 6828; ⊛www.earthwatch.org. Offers a range of nature-conservation projects; past projects include bat conservation and climate-change studies in Malaysia.

Fulbright Program US ☎212/984-5487, ⊛us.fulbright.org. Regular opportunities for US citizens to spend several months teaching English in rural Malaysia, without requiring teaching experience.

W-O-X UK ☎0845/371 3070, ⊛www .orangutanproject.com. Orang-utan conservation in Malaysia, mostly at rehabilitation centres or upriver locations in Borneo.

Mail

Malaysia has a well-organized postal service operated by Pos Malaysia (☎1300/300 300, ⊛www.pos.com.my), whose website gives details of postage rates, express mail and courier ("PosLaju") services and so forth. For airmail letters, **aerogrammes** are cost-effective at 50 sen apiece, as compared to RM1.50 to airmail the lightest letters to Australasia; expect delivery to take one to two weeks depending on the destination. **Surface mail** – which can be useful as a relatively cheap way to send parcels – takes at least four weeks. Usual post office opening hours are Monday to Saturday 8am to 6pm.

Each Malaysian town has a **General Post Office** (GPO) with a **poste restante** section, where mail will be held for two months. If you're having mail sent this way, tell the sender to underline your surname or put it in capitals, and to address the letter as follows: name, Poste Restante, GPO, town or city, state. When picking up mail, be sure to have staff check under first names as well as family names – misfiling of letters is common.

In **Brunei**, post offices are open Monday to Thursday between 8am and 4.30pm, and on Friday and Saturday from 8am till noon. For details of postal services in **Singapore**, see p.683.

Maps

Most Malaysian tourist offices have free maps of the local area, of decidedly variable quality and offering little that the maps in this book don't already include. You're only likely to need additional maps if you want to **drive** around the country, in which case Rough Guides' Malaysia map, printed on tearproof plastic, should more than suffice. The best maps published inside Malaysia are the city and regional maps from the Johor Bahru-based World Express Mapping, sold in all bookshops. Whichever maps you use, one thing to be aware of is that the high rate of highway construction and road alterations in countryside and city alike means that inaccuracies plague most maps almost as soon as they appear. For details of Singapore maps, see p.590.

Money

Malaysia's unit of currency is the **ringgit** (pronounced *ring-git* and written "RM" before the price), divided into 100 sen. Notes come in RM1, RM2, RM5, RM10, RM50 and RM100 denominations, though the RM2 notes had practically vanished from circulation at the time of writing. Coins are minted in 1 sen, 5 sen, 10 sen, 20 sen and 50 sen denominations; don't allow people to palm off RM1 coins on you, as these are no longer legal tender. Note that you will sometimes hear the word "dollar" used informally to refer the ringgit.

At the time of writing, the **exchange rate** was around RM3.6 to US$1 and RM5.30 to £1. Rates are posted daily in banks and exchange kiosks, and published in the press. The maximum amount of rinngit you can

take into or out of the country is RM1000. There is no limit on the amount of foreign currency you can take with you into the country, although you are supposed to declare it at customs, and in theory you cannot take out more foreign currency than you declared on the way in.

Singapore's currency is the **Singapore dollar**, written simply as $ (or S$ in this book to distinguish it from other dollars) and divided into 100 cents. Notes are issued in denominations of $2, $5, $10, $20, $50 and $100, with a couple of larger bills, rarely seen; coins come in denominations of 1, 5, 10, 20 and 50 cents, and $1. At the time of writing, the **exchange rate** was around S$1.50 to US$1, S$2.20 to £1.

Brunei's currency is the **Brunei dollar**, which is divided into 100 cents; you'll see it written as B$, or simply as $. The Brunei dollar has parity with the Singapore dollar and both are legal tender in either country. Notes come in $1, $5, $10, $50, $100, $500 and $1000 denominations; coins come in denominations of 1, 5, 10, 20 and 50 cents.

Note that while most town centres have **ATMs** where you can withdraw cash using a credit or debit card, you won't be able to use plastic to settle bills in budget hotels and *kedai kopis*.

Banks

Major banks in **Malaysia** include Maybank, HSBC, Citibank, Standard Chartered, RHB Bank and Bank Bumiputra Commerce. Banking hours are generally Monday to Friday 9.30am to 4pm and Saturday 9.30 to 11.30am (closed on every first and third Sat of the month), though in the largely Muslim states of Kedah, Kelantan and Terengganu, Friday is a holiday and Sunday a working day. Licensed **moneychangers'** kiosks, found in bigger towns all over the country, tend to open later, until around 6pm, with some opening at weekends and until 9pm, too; some hotels will exchange money at all hours. Exchange rates tend to be more generous at moneychangers. It's not generally difficult to change money in Sabah or Sarawak, though if you are travelling along a river in the interior for any length of time, it's a wise idea to carry a fair amount of cash, in smallish denominations.

For details of Singapore banks, see p.682. Brunei **banking hours** are Monday to Friday 9am to 3pm and Saturday 9am to 11am. Banks represented in Brunei include the International Bank of Brunei, Citibank, Standard Chartered Bank and the Overseas Union Bank.

Opening hours and public holidays

In **Malaysia**, shops are open daily from 9.30am to 7pm, while shopping centres are typically open daily from 10am to 10pm. Government offices tend to work Monday to Friday from 8am to 4.15pm or 9am to 5pm, with an hour off for lunch, except on Friday when the break lasts from 12.15pm to 2.45pm to allow Muslims to attend prayers. Note that in the states of Kedah, Kelantan and Terengganu, the working week runs from Sunday to Thursday, with Friday and Saturday being days off.

In **Singapore**, shopping centres open daily 10am to 10pm. Offices generally work Monday to Friday 8.30am to 5pm and sometimes on Saturday mornings. Government offices in **Brunei** are open from 7.45am to 12.15pm and from 1.30pm to 4.30pm, except on Friday and Sunday; shopping centres open daily from 10am to 10pm.

Opening hours for temples and mosques are given in the text where applicable. For banking hours, see p.69.

Public and school holidays

As a guide, public holiday dates for **2009** are given below (the relevant government websites issue new lists for each year a few months in advance). Note that Muslim holidays (marked with an asterisk) move earlier by ten or eleven days each year, and that each Malaysian state has its own additional holidays, which could be to do with the sultan's birthday or an Islamic event (in states with a largely Muslim population) or tribal, such as Gawai in June in Sarawak. For an explanation of the festivities associated with some of the holidays below, see p.57.

It pays to be aware of not just public holidays but also the local **school holidays**, as Malaysian accommodation can be hard to come by during these periods. In

Malaysia, schools get a week off in mid-March and late August, and two weeks off at the start of June, with a long break from mid-November to the end of the year. Singapore school breaks are almost identical, except that the June holiday lasts the whole month, and kids get a week off in early September rather than late August.

Malaysian public holidays

January 1 New Year's Day
January 26 Chinese New Year
March 9 Birthday of the Prophet Muhammad*
May 1 Labour Day
May 9 Vesak Day
June 6 Yang Dipertuan Agong's Birthday
August 31 National Day
September 20 & 21 Hari Raya Puasa*
October 17 Deepavali
November 27 Hari Raya Haji (or Korban)*
December 18 Maal Hijrah (the Muslim New Year)*
December 25 Christmas Day

Singaporean public holidays

January 1 New Year's Day
January 26 & 27 Chinese New Year
April 10 Good Friday
May 1 Labour Day
May 9 Vesak Day
August 9 National Day
September 20 Hari Raya Puasa*
October 17 Deepavali
November 27 Hari Raya Haji*
December 25 Christmas Day

Brunei public holidays

January 1 New Year's Day
January 26 Chinese New Year
February 23 National Day
March 9 Birthday of the Prophet Muhammad*
May 31 Armed Forces' Day
July 15 Sultan's Birthday
July 20 Israk Mikraj (the night when the Prophet ascended to heaven)*
August 21 First day of Ramadan*
September 15 Anniversary of Revelation of the Koran*
September 20 Hari Raya Aidilfitri*
November 27 Hari Raya Aidiladha*
December 18 Maal Hijrah (the Muslim New Year)*
December 25 Christmas Day

Phones

Coin- and card-operated phones aren't hard to find in Malaysia, Singapore and Brunei,

International calls

Io make international calls to any of the countries below, dial your international access code (⑦00 in Malaysia and Brunei, most often ⑦001 in Singapore) then the relevant country code from the list, then the number (including any area code, but excluding any initial zero). However, note that it is still possible to dial a Singapore number from Malaysia using ⑦02 (the area code for Singapore from the days it was part of Malaysia), then the number. From Singapore, you can call Malaysia by dialling ⑦020, then the area code (omitting the initial zero), then the number.

IDD country codes

Australia ⑦61	Malaysia ⑦60	South Africa ⑦27
Brunei ⑦673	New Zealand ⑦64	UK ⑦44
Ireland ⑦353	Singapore ⑦65	US & Canada ⑦1

and calls can be made from many internet cafés as well. If you want to use your **mobile/cell phone**, bear in mind that for roaming to work, your phone must be **GSM/ triband** (older North American phones may not satisfy this). The same condition applies if you want to use a prepaid **local SIM card**, which is a much cheaper option than roaming, though do also ensure your phone isn't locked to your current network. Outlets specializing in "hand phones" (as mobile phones are referred to locally) are easily found, even in small towns.

Malaysia

There are public phones in most Malaysian towns. Local calls are very cheap at just 10 sen for three minutes, but for long-distance calls, it can be more convenient to buy a **phonecard**. Your best bet is to use a card such as iTalk (@www.i-talk.com.my; from RM10) which enables you to make discounted calls from the line in your hotel room as well as from payphones. Phone-cards are available from Shell and Petronas service stations, 7-Eleven outlets and newsagents.

There are two big players in the **mobile phone** market, namely Hotlink/Maxis (@www .hotlink.com.my) and Celcom (@www .celcom.com.my), with the smaller DiGi (@www.digi.com.my) bringing up the rear. On the Peninsula you'll usually get a signal on both coasts, along highways and major roads, and on touristy islands. In the forested interior, as a rule your phone will work in any town large enough to be served by express trains (as well as at the Taman Negara

headquarters). Sabah and Sarawak coverage is much patchier, focusing on cities and the populated river valleys, though even in the Kelabit Highlands mobile calls are possible.

In general, a **prepaid SIM card** will cost up to RM20, including a certain amount of call time. Mobile tariffs can be complex, though you can expect calls made to other Malaysian numbers to cost no more than RM0.50 per minute.

Singapore

Payphones are easy to find in Singapore, though many take **phonecards** rather than coins; the cards (S$5/10) are available from post offices, 7-Elevens and retail outlets of the phone company, Singtel (@www.singtel .com). Both Singtel and its rival Starhub (@www.starhub.com) also offer phonecards that are geared to international calls (from S$10), with their own international access codes; details of these cards, sold by the same outlets as regular phonecards, are available from both company's websites. The same two firms dominate the mobile phone market in Singapore; their **SIM cards** (S$18) are available from post offices and 7-Eleven stores, though note that your passport will be scanned as a form of registration of any SIM purchase.

Local calls cost 10¢ for three minutes if made from a payphone, or 10¢ per minute from a mobile. The island has no area codes – the only time you'll punch more than eight digits for a local number is if you're dialling a toll-free (⑦1800) or special-rate (eg ⑦1900) number. For directory enquiries, call ⑦100 (⑦104 for international enquiries).

Operator and directory services

Malaysia
Local directory enquiries: ☏103
Operator-assisted calls (including international collect/reverse charge): ☏101
Business number online searches: ⓦwww.yellowpages.com.my

Singapore
Local directory enquiries: ☏100
Operator-assisted international calls: ☏104
Business number online searches: ⓦwww.yellowpages.com.sg

Brunei
Local directory enquiries: ☏113

Brunei

International calls can be made in booths at the Telekom office in the capital (see p.571) or from cardphones; if you want to call collect, substitute ☏01 for the usual ☏00 international code, then dial the number as though making an ordinary international call; this brings the number up on the operator's system. **Phonecards** start at $10 and can be bought from the Telekom office and post offices. **SIM cards** can be obtained from outlets of the mobile provider DST Communications (ⓦwww.dst-group.com).

Time

For administrative convenience, Malaysia, Singapore and Brunei are all eight hours ahead of Universal Time (GMT), all year. This close to the equator, you can rely on dawn being around 6.30am in the Peninsula and Singapore, dusk at around 7.30pm; in Borneo both happen roughly an hour earlier. Not taking into account daylight saving time elsewhere, the three countries are two hours behind Sydney, thirteen hours ahead of US Eastern Standard Time and sixteen hours ahead of US Pacific Standard Time.

Tipping

Tipping is seldom necessary in Malaysia, Singapore and Brunei. When eating out at a proper restaurant, it's customary to tip if a service charge isn't included, though note that you are never required to tip in *kedai kopis* or *kopitiams*. It's not necessary to tip taxi drivers either, unless they have gone out of their way to be helpful. Otherwise you might want to offer a modest tip to a hotel porter or hairdresser, or a tour guide if they have been exceptional.

Tourist information

There are two official sources of tourist information in Malaysia. The first is the country's tourism board, **Tourism Malaysia** (ⓦwww .tourismmalaysia.gov.my), which has offices in most of the state capitals. They're complemented by tourist offices, sometimes called **Tourism Information Centres**, run by the state governments and again to be found in most of the state capitals. As a rule, all these offices are more than happy to furnish you with glossy brochures and leaflets, though note that tourist literature and websites can feature quite a few inaccuracies – unfortunately the people who manage the attractions, transport companies and tourist offices don't update one another or their output nearly enough. Tourist-office staff are not likely to have personal experience of off-the-beaten-track destinations, but can usually provide some nitty-gritty information on matters like bus travel or contact details for accommodation throughout their area of coverage. If you want to make further enquiries, phoning the attraction or resort concerned is often the best way to do so, as emails and faxes can be slow to elicit responses.

Singapore is another proposition altogether, with a huge amount of generally reliable information on everything from bus times to museum exhibitions available in print and on line. Tourist information is put out by the **Singapore Tourism Board**

(@www.visitsingapore.com), which has an incredibly thorough website and operates several downtown **Visitor Centres** (see p.590 for details). Brunei's official tourism website is @www.tourismbrunei.com.

Official information sources aside, there are plenty of **websites** concerned with Malaysia tourism. Many are thinly disguised fronts for travel agencies intent on marketing their packages, but the best of these sites boast in-depth accounts of the more off-the-beaten-track towns and sights, and sometimes reportage on tourism-related issues too, though don't assume the information is up to date.

Tourism Malaysia offices abroad

Australia Level 2, 171 Clarence St, Sydney ☎02/9299 4441, ⓔmptb.sydney@tourism.gov.my.
Canada 1590-1111 West Georgia St, Vancouver ☎604/689-8899, ⓔmtpb.vancouver@tourism .gov.my.
Singapore #01-01B/C/D 80 Robinson Rd ☎6532 6321, ⓔmtpb.singapore@tourism.gov.my.
South Africa First floor, Building 5, Commerce Square, 39 Rivonia Rd, Sandhurst, Johannesburg ☎011/268 0292, ⓔmtpb.johannesburg@tourism .gov.my.
UK 57 Trafalgar Square, London ☎020/7930 7932, ⓔmptb.london@tourism.gov.my.
US 120 East 56th St, Suite 810, New York ☎212/754 1113, ⓔmptb.ny@tourism.gov.my; 818 West 7th St, Suite 970, Los Angeles ☎213/689 9702, ⓔmptb.la@tourism.gov.my.

Malaysian state tourism contacts

Johor ☎07/223 4935, @www.tourismjohor.com.
Kedah ☎04/735 1030, @www.visitkedah.com.my.
Kelantan ☎09/748 5534, @www.tic.kelantan .gov.my
Labuan ☎087/422622, @www.labuantourism .com.my.
Melaka ☎06/281 4803, @www.melaka.gov.my.
Negeri Sembilan ☎06/763 5388, @www.ns.gov .my/tourism.
Pahang ☎09/516 1007, @www.pahangtourism .com.my.
Penang ☎04/262 0202, @www.tourismpenang .gov.my.
Sabah ☎088/212 121, @www.sabahtourism.com.
Sarawak ☎082/423 600, @www .sarawaktourism.com.
Selangor ☎03/5511 1122, @www .selangortourism.com.

Terengganu ☎09/622 1553, @www.tourism .terengganu.gov.my.

Singapore Tourism Board offices abroad

Australia Level 11, AWA Building, 47 York St, Sydney ☎02/9290 2888, ⓔstb-syd@stb-syd .org.au.
Malaysia Ground floor, Menara Keck Seng (next to the *Westin Hotel*), 203 Jalan Bukit Bintang, KL ☎03/2142 7133, ⓔinfo@stb.org.my.
New Zealand c/o Vivaldi World Limited, 1340C Glenbrook Rd, RD1, Waiuku, Auckland ☎0800/608 506, ⓔstbnz@stb-syd.org.au.
UK Grand Buildlings, 1–3 Strand, London ☎020/7484 2710, ⓔstb_london@stb.gov.sg.
US 1156 Avenue of the Americas, Suite 702, New York ☎212/302 4861; 5670 Wiltshire Blvd #1550, Los Angeles ☎323/677 0808, @www .visitsingapore-usa.com.

Other tourist information sources

@www.allmalaysia.info Excellent tourism compendium put together by *The Star* newspaper, featuring travel-related news stories, state-by-state accounts of sights and background articles on culture and events.
@www.virtualmalaysia.com The tourism portal of Malaysia's Ministry of Tourism, with coverage of various sights, tourism-related directories and assorted packages on sale.
@www.wildasia.net Dedicated to sustainable and responsible tourism, this Malaysia-based site features numerous articles on Southeast Asia with plenty on Malaysia itself, of course, including descriptions of forest reserves and dive sites, plus a list of the more environmentally aware resorts.

Travellers with disabilities

Of the three countries covered in this book, **Singapore** is the most accessible to travellers with disabilities; hefty tax incentives are provided for developers who include access features for the disabled in new buildings. In contrast, Malaysia and Brunei make few provisions, if any.

Across the region, life is made a lot easier if you can afford the more upmarket hotels, which usually have disabled provision, and to shell out for taxis and the odd domestic flight. Similarly, the more expensive international airlines tend to be better equipped to get you there in the first place: MAS, British Airways, KLM, Singapore and Qantas all carry aisle wheelchairs and have at least one toilet adapted for disabled passengers. However, few, if any, tour operators offering holidays in the region accommodate the needs of those with disabilities.

Singapore is certainly making a concerted effort to improve disabled provision: the **MRT** metro system has lifts on most, if not all, of its stations, and there are about two dozen bus routes with wheelchair-accessible vehicles, though these operate only at certain times of day (see ⓦ www.sbstransit .com.sg for details). Most of the major **taxi** companies have accessible vehicles available to book, too.

In Malaysia, wheelchair-users will have a hard time negotiating the uneven pavements in most towns and cities, and will find it difficult to board buses, trains, ferries and the LRT metro system in Kuala Lumpur, none of which has been adapted for wheelchairs. The situation is similar if not worse in east Malaysia and Brunei, with little provision for disabled travellers.

Contacts for travellers with disabilities

Malaysian Confederation of the Disabled
☎ 03/7956 2300, ⓔ mcd_dpimalaysia@yahoo .com. A member of Disabled Peoples International, working for equal opportunities for disabled people in Malaysia.

Disabled People's Association Singapore
☎ 6899 1220, ⓦ www.dpa.org.sg. Non-profit organization whose website has information on transport and other material to do with access.

Travelling with children

Malaysia, Singapore and Brunei are very child-friendly countries in which to travel. Disposable nappies and powdered milk are easy to find (fresh milk is sold in super-markets), and bland Chinese soups and rice dishes, or bakery fare, are ideal for systems unaccustomed to spicy food. Many restaurants and the slicker *kedai kopis* have high chairs, though only upmarket hotels provide baby cots or a baby-sitting service. However, rooms in the cheaper hotels can usually be booked with an extra bed for little extra cost. Children under 12 get into many attractions for half-price and enjoy discounts on buses and trains.

Guide

Guide

Kuala Lumpur
and around

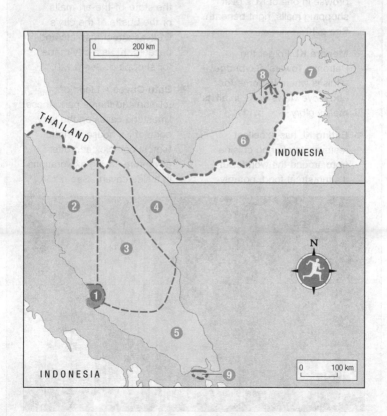

CHAPTER 1   # Highlights

* **Islamic Arts Museum** One of the most sophisticated museums in the capital, documenting Muslim cultures through arts and crafts. See p.104

* **Petronas Towers** Come to gawp at these surprisingly serene twin structures, then browse in one of KL's best shopping malls, right beneath. See p.107

* **Menara KL** Forget the Petronas Towers' Skybridge – this is where to come for bird's-eye views of KL in all its messy glory. See p.111

* **Eating** KL has excellent restaurants offering cuisine from around the world, but it's the street food, notably at Jalan Alor, that's often the most memorable dining experience. See p.116

* **Clubbing** KL is definitely Malaysia's party capital, home to some exceptional clubs that draw big-name DJs. See p.124

* **Shopping** Whether you prefer the bright lights of the state-of-the-art malls or the bustle of the city's endless street markets and bazaars, KL is a city made for shopping. See p.128

* **Batu Caves** A blend of religion and theme park, these limestone caves on the very edge of KL house a Hindu temple complex and offer adventure caving explorations in a side cavern. See p.134

▲ Petronas Towers

Kuala Lumpur
and around

ounded in the mid-nineteenth century, **KUALA LUMPUR** – or **KL** as it's known to residents and visitors alike – has never had a coherent style, a situation only aggravated by the fact that the city has changed almost beyond recognition over the last thirty years. The first grand buildings around Merdeka Square, dating from the 1890s, were eccentric mishmashes themselves, the result of British engineers and architects fusing, or perhaps confusing, influences from around the empire and the world – Moghul, Malay, Moorish and Victorian. Today, those colonial buildings that remain are overshadowed by towering modern buildings – most notably the Petronas Towers – that wouldn't be out of place in Hong Kong or New York, reflecting the fact that this, the youngest of Southeast Asia's capitals, is also the most economically successful after Singapore. A sociable and safe place, KL has a real buzz to it, with good nightlife and enough interesting monuments to keep visitors busy for a few days at least. The ethnic and cultural mix of Malays, Chinese and Indians makes itself felt throughout: in conversations on the street, in the sheer variety of food for sale and in the profusion of mosques, Buddhist temples and Hindu shrines.

Yet many visitors, as well as some Malaysians, have mixed feelings about KL. Malaysia's former prime minister, Abdullah Badawi, has spoken of the country being able to afford first-class infrastructure while retaining a third-world mentality, lagging behind when it comes to understanding planning, maintenance and service. You'll see ample evidence of this in KL, where it's also clear that untrammelled development has given the city more than its share of featureless buildings and follies, plus terrible traffic snarl-ups. For some locals, the capital is only worth tolerating as a place to acquire good money and experience before returning to a cherished provincial village; others say that KL has been their salvation, the only city in the country big and broad-minded enough to allow them to explore their true artistic or spiritual identity.

For the many travellers who visit both KL and Singapore, it's hard not to conclude that if only KL took some of Singapore's ability to organize systematically and transparently, while Singapore had some of KL's pleasingly organic qualities and didn't take itself quite so seriously, then both cities would genuinely be enriched. As things stand, they remain rivals, competing in their own way for investment and recognition while grudgingly admiring each other.

A stay of a few days is enough to appreciate the best of KL's **attractions**, including the colonial core around **Merdeka Square** and the adjacent enclaves of **Chinatown** and **Little India**, plus, to the east, the restaurants, shops and nightlife of the so-called **Golden Triangle**, the modern sector of downtown KL. It can be equally rewarding just strolling and taking in KL's street life, in particular its boisterous **markets**, ranging from fish and produce markets stuffed into alleyways, to stalls selling cooked food of every shape and description, or inexpensive clothes and accessories. KL's hinterland isn't devoid of genuinely worthwhile sights either, among them the rugged limestone **Batu Caves**, which contain the country's most sacred Hindu shrine, showcasing the lifestyle and culture of the Peninsula's indigenous peoples; the **Forest Research Institute of Malaysia**, with a treetop canopy walkway for a quick taste of the rainforest; and **Kuala Selangor**, home to numerous fireflies that magically flash in unison.

Some history

KL was founded in 1857 when the ruler of Selangor State, Rajah Abdullah, sent a party of Chinese prospectors to search for **tin** deposits in the area of the confluence of the Gombak and Klang rivers. The pioneers had their reward in the discovery of rich deposits 6km from the confluence, near **Ampang**, which grew into a staging post for Chinese labourers who arrived to work in the mines. Settlements at confluences were commonplace in the Peninsula, but uncommonly this particular village acquired the name Kuala Lumpur ("muddy confluence" in Malay) rather than, as convention dictated, being named after the lesser of the two fusing rivers (KL should, by rights, have been called Kuala Gombak).

Until the 1880s KL was little more than a wooden shantytown; small steamers could get within 30km of it along Sungai Klang, but the rest of the trip was either by shallow boat or through the jungle. Yet people were drawn to the town like bees to honey; early British investors, Malay farmers, Chinese *towkays* and workers all arrived looking for work, whether it was in the mines, on surrounding rubber estates or, later, on roads and railway construction. The first Chinese *towkays* (merchants) set up two secret societies in Ampang, and fierce competition between them for the economic spoils soon developed. Until the 1870s, this rivalry effectively restrained the growth of Ampang (which, though the initial nucleus of KL, lies to the east of the present-day city). The arrival of an influential Chinese merchant, **Yap Ah Loy**, helped unify the divergent groups. Ah Loy's career symbolized the Eldorado lifestyle of KL's early years. Having left China with hardly a penny to his name, he became KL's Kapitan Cina, or Chinese headman, by the time he was 30. He is reputed to have brought law and order to the frontier town by ruthlessly making an example of criminals, parading them through the streets on a first offence and, if they re-offended twice, executing them. He led the rebuilding of KL after it was razed during the Selangor Civil War (1867–73) and personally bore much of the cost of a second rebuilding after another devastating fire in 1881.

The British Resident of Selangor State, **Frank Swettenham**, had most of KL's wooden huts demolished in the 1880s and imported **British architects** from India to design solid, grand edifices suitable for a new capital. By 1887 the city had five hundred brick buildings, and eight times that number in the early 1900s, by which time KL had also become capital of the Federated Malay States.

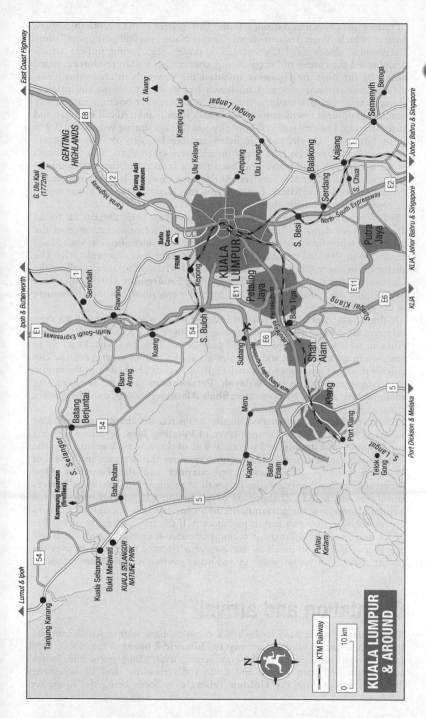

KUALA LUMPUR & AROUND

KTM Railway

0   10 km

N

East Coast Highway ▲

G. Nuang ▲

GENTING HIGHLANDS

E8

Semenyih

Beroga

Kampung Lui

Sungai Langat

Johor Bahru & Singapore ▼

G. Ulu Kali (1772m) ▲

Karak Highway

Orang Asli Museum

2

Ulu Kelang

Ampang

Ulu Langat

Balakong

Kajang

Serdang

S. Chua

KLIA, Johor Bahru & Singapore ▼

Batu Caves

FRIM

KUALA LUMPUR

Kepong

S. Besi

Putra Jaya

North–South Expressway

E2

Petaling Jaya

Batu Tiga

E11

E6

KLIA, Johor Bahru & Singapore ▼

Ipoh & Butterworth ▲

Serendah

Rawang

1

S. Buloh

54

Kuang

Subang

Lebuhraya Persekutuan

Shah Alam

Sungai Klang

KLIA ▼

North–South Expressway

E1

Baru Arang

Meru

New Klang Valley Expressway

E6

Klang

5

Port Dickson & Melaka ▼

Batang Berjuntai

54

Batu Rotan

S. Selangor

Kapar

Batu Enam

Port Klang

Telok Gong

S. Langat

Lumut & Ipoh ▲

Tanjung Karang

54

Kuala Selangor

Bukit Melawati

KUALA SELANGOR NATURE PARK

Kampung Kuantan (fireflies)

5

Pulau Ketam

Development continued steadily in the first quarter of the twentieth century, during which time Indians from Tamil Nadu swelled the population. Catastrophic floods in 1926 inspired a major engineering project which straightened the course of Sungai Klang, confining it within reinforced, raised banks. By the time the **Japanese invaded** the Peninsula in December 1941, the commercial zone around Chinatown had grown to eclipse the original colonial area, and the *towkays*, enriched by the rubber boom, were already installed in opulent townhouses along today's Jalan Tuanku Abdul Rahman and Jalan Ampang. The city suffered little physical damage during World War II, but as in Singapore, the Japanese inflicted terrible brutality on their historic enemies, the Chinese (at least five thousand were killed in the first few weeks of the occupation alone), and sent thousands of Indians to Burma to build the infamous railway; very few survived. At the same time, the Japanese ingratiated themselves with some Malays by suggesting that loyalty to the occupiers would be rewarded with independence after the war.

Following the **Japanese surrender** in September 1945, the British found that nationalist demands had replaced the Malays' former acceptance of the colonizers, while for some of the Chinese population, identification with Mao's revolution in 1949 led to a desire to see Malaya become a communist state. The alienation of many Chinese was heightened by Malay reluctance to allow the Chinese full rights of citizenship. The ensuing **Emergency** (1948–60), which stopped just short of civil war, left KL relatively unscathed, but the atmosphere in the city remained tense.

Malaysia was twelve years into its independence when simmering rivalries between the Malays and the Chinese spilled over into KL's May 1969 **race riots**, in which at least two hundred people lost their lives. Thanks partly to pragmatism on both sides, and the imposition of a state of emergency, the city quickly managed to return to normal. In 1974 KL was plucked from the bosom of Selangor and designated **Wilayah Persekutuan** (Federal Territory), an administrative zone in its own right; **Shah Alam**, west along the Klang Valley, replaced KL as Selangor's capital.

After a period of consolidation, in the 1990s KL and the rest of the Klang Valley, including KL's satellite new town of **Petaling Jaya**, became a thriving conurbation. That decade, and the early part of the new millennium, saw the realization of several huge infrastructural ventures that are part and parcel of local life today – KL's international **airport** and the **Formula One racetrack**, both at Sepang in the far south of Selangor; the **Petronas Towers** and the attendant **KLCC** shopping development; **KL Sentral**, the new rail hub; and **Putrajaya**, the government's administrative hub (though KL remains the legislative centre and seat of parliament). If the transformation of swathes of KL and much of Selangor is taking place less dramatically today, it is still proceeding apace – so much so that concerns are now being voiced over the potential strain on water resources and other environmental repercussions.

Orientation and arrival

Many visitors find it hard to discern a distinct centre within Kuala Lumpur. Indeed, there are two hubs of activity: the **historical heart** of the city, centred on the now-no-longer-muddy confluence, with Chinatown, the Jamek mosque, the old train station and Little India close by; and an altogether different modern core, the **Golden Triangle**, its focus being the upmarket hotels, restaurants and malls of **Bukit Bintang**, just 2km east of the old centre. Most points of interest lie within the loop comprising Jalan Tun Razak, Lebuhraya Mahameru, Jalan Damansara and so forth along its length. Inside this circuit are the **Lake Gardens** and their attendant museums and specialist parks, which lie just to the west of the historical zone, while on the north-eastern fringe of the Golden Triangle lies the stretch of prime real estate known as **KLCC** (confusingly, standing for Kuala Lumpur City Centre), home to the **Petronas Towers**.

Arrival

The only arrival points that aren't fairly central are KL's airports, in particular the massive Kuala Lumpur International Airport at Sepang, near the coast on the southern edge of Selangor. For more on using the various KL transport options mentioned below, see the section on p.88.

By air

KLIA, as KL's main airport is usually known (ⓦ www.klia.com.my), is divided into two separate terminal complexes, both reachable off the E6 highway. The **main terminal**, used by most airlines except budget carriers, is some 50km south of KL as the crow flies, and actually closer to Seremban than KL. The arrivals hall is broadly divided into international and domestic sections, the former containing a **tourist office** (daily 6am–midnight; ⓣ 03/8776 5651) and 24-hour bureau de change operated by the RHB bank, with various ATMs and other exchange facilities dotted around both sections. There are also plenty of desks representing the main car rental outlets and KL's pricier hotels; the airport also has a five-star hotel of its own, the overpriced *Pan Pacific* (ⓣ 03/8787 3333, ⓦ klairport.panpacific.com; ⓽). Malaysia Airlines has a sales counter on level 3 of arrivals.

Various trains and buses connect the main terminal with other parts of the country. For many visitors heading to downtown KL, the most convenient option is to use one of the two light rail links (sometimes labelled ERL on route maps; ⓦ www.kliaekspres.com) from level 1: either the **KLIA Ekspres** (daily 5am–midnight; every 15–20min; 28min) or the fractionally slower **KLIA Transit** (every 30min 6am–1am), which calls at three stops outside KL en route. Fares to KL on each service are RM35 one way. Both services terminate at KL Sentral, the downtown rail hub; see p.86 for onward transport details from KL Sentral.

Airport **buses**, leaving from the main terminal's bus station (signed from level 2), are much cheaper and slower than the trains. Among the KL departures are services to Nilai station (for Komuter trains; every 30min 7am–11.30pm; RM2.50) and KL Sentral (hourly 6.30am–12.30am; RM10), run by Airport Coach; and services operated by Star Shuttle (ⓦ www.starwira.com) to Puduraya bus station in Chinatown (at least hourly 5.30am–11.15pm; 1hr 15min; RM12) and to certain downtown hotels (hourly 7am–12.30am; 1hr 30min; RM15). There are also several buses a day north to Ipoh (RM42). For details of transport to Seremban, see p.303.

Taxis to KL are quite a reasonable option: the hour-long drive to downtown KL starts at around RM70 for up to three passengers, with fares varying according to your destination and the type of vehicle used. To avoid getting ensnared in tricky bargaining with touts, buy a fixed-fare ticket for your journey from the counter near the arrivals exit.

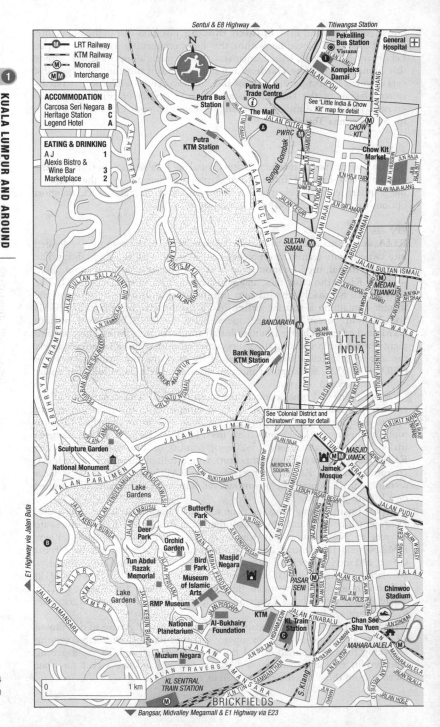

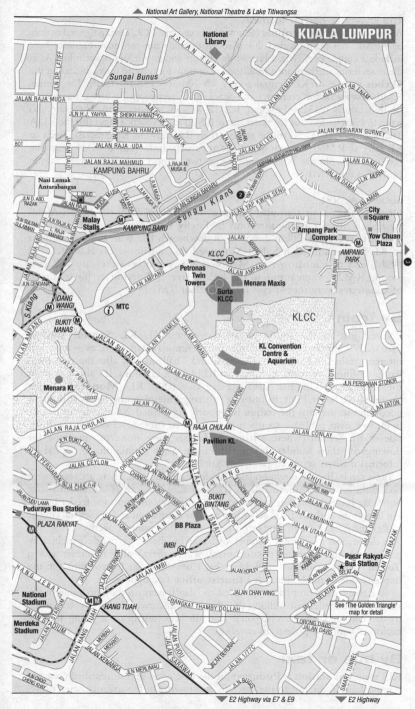

▲ National Art Gallery, National Theatre & Lake Titiwangsa

KUALA LUMPUR

National Library

JALAN TUN RAZAK

JLN DR. LATIFF

Sungai Bunus

JALAN RAJA MUDA

JLN H.J. YAHYA

JALAN SEMARAK

JLN MAKTAB ENAM

SHEIKH AHMAD

JALAN HAMZAH

JALAN PESIARAN GURNEY

JALAN RAJA UDA

JALAN DAMAI

JALAN RAJA MAHMUD

KAMPUNG BAHRU

JALAN DAMAI

JLN MURNI

Nasi Lemak Antarabangsa

JALAN AMAN

JLN D. ABD RAZAK

JALAN RAJA

Sungai Klang

City Square

Malay Stalls

KAMPUNG BARU

KLCC

Ampang Park Complex

Yow Chuan Plaza

JALAN AMPANG

AMPANG PARK

DANG WANGI

Petronas Twin Towers

Menara Maxis

BUKIT NANAS

MTC

Suria KLCC

KLCC

JALAN SULTAN ISMAIL

JALAN P. RAMLEE

JALAN PINANG

KL Convention Centre & Aquarium

Menara KL

JALAN PERAK

JLN PERSIARAN STONOR

JALAN TENGAH

JALAN EATON

JALAN RAJA CHULAN

RAJA CHULAN

JALAN CONLAY

JLN BUKIT CEYLON

Pavilion KL

JALAN CEYLON

BINTANG

JALAN RAJA CHULAN

LORONG CEYLON

Puduraya Bus Station

BUKIT BINTANG

PLAZA RAKYAT

J A L A N   B U K I T

BB Plaza

IMBI

Pasar Rakyat Bus Station

JALAN IMBI

JALAN HORLEY

HANG JEBAT

National Stadium

JALAN CHAN WING

See 'The Golden Triangle' map for detail

HANG TUAH

Merdeka Stadium

CHANGKAT THAMBY DOLLAH

LORONG DAVIS

JALAN DAVIS

JLN CHOO CHENG KHAY

SMART TUNNEL

JLN BUGIS

▼ E2 Highway via E7 & E9   ▼ E2 Highway

The low-cost-carrier terminal

A **low-cost-carrier terminal** (Ⓦwww.klia.com.my/LCCTerminal), used mainly by AirAsia, has been created 20km south of the main terminal. Facilities here include a couple of ATMs, a bureau de change and an AirAsia ticket office. As at the main terminal, there are a multitude of options for onward travel, including the **Skybus** service to KL Sentral (every 15–30min 7.15am–1.15am; 1hr 15min; RM9; Ⓦwww.skybus.com.my) and Starshuttle's service to Puduraya bus station (at least hourly 6.45am–11.45pm; RM12; Ⓦwww.starwira.com). There are also buses to Nilai station (for Komuter trains; RM2) and to Salak Tinggi (for the KLIA Transit service; RM1.50 to the station, then RM12.50 to KL Sentral). **Taxis** to KL start at RM60 depending on the type of vehicle (buy a ticket from the taxi counter). Shuttle buses connect the two airport terminals (every 20min 6am–12.30am; RM1.50).

Subang airport

Once KL's main air terminal, **Subang airport** (officially the Sultan Abdul Aziz Shah airport) is now used only by Firefly, Tiger Airways and Berjaya Air. The airport is some 20km due west of downtown KL, with bus connections to KL Sentral and Jalan Sultan Mohamed in Chinatown on RapidKL bus #U81, and to Chinatown on Metrobus #9. A taxi into the city will cost around RM25, whereas one to the Kelana Jaya LRT terminus, just a couple of kilometres away, should cost no more than RM10.

By train

Located just to the southwest of downtown KL, **KL Sentral station** (☎03/2279 8699) is the hub for the Peninsula's rail services – not just intercity trains to Singapore, Kelantan and Thailand, but also the two local Komuter lines (see p.89) and the two KLIA light rail links. It's also a stop on the Kelana Jaya–Gombak **LRT** service (see p.88). KL's **Monorail** service begins at KL Sentral but, in just one of many little planning lapses that you'll encounter in the city, the station is a poorly signposted 200m away in Brick-fields (see map, p.115) – to reach it, descend to street level on the southeast side of KL Sentral (where a handful of buses leave, none of much use for downtown), then wander through the open space (sometimes occupied by informal market) across to Jalan Tun Sambanthan.

Taxis can be flagged down on Jalan Tun Sambanthan itself. There are convenient taxi ranks on the northern side of KL Sentral, where the *Hilton* and *Meridien* hotels are located, and also on the south side (follow the signs for feeder buses), but fares from both are fixed according to your destination and are several ringgit higher than the metered fare; buy a ticket from the counters nearby.

In the station itself are a number of banks on the western side (reached by passageways from the main concourse), where there's also an outlet selling **Touch 'n Go cards** (see p.88; Mon–Fri 10am–8pm, Sat 10am–3pm). On the opposite side of the building is a **tourist office** (see opposite).

Note that there's no pedestrian access to Jalan Travers on the north side of the station, which rules out walking the 2km to Chinatown – even if you manage to descend to Jalan Travers, you'll find the trek northeast is along frenetic highways with few pedestrian crossings.

By bus or taxi

KL's main **bus station** is **Puduraya**, at the base of an undistinguished concrete box on Jalan Pudu, just to the east of Chinatown. On the main passenger level of the station (where the ticket booths are located), you'll find a moneychanger (hidden amid the kiosks at the opposite end from the food stalls) and a couple of ATMs, with a bank upstairs. Close to the back of the station is the Plaza Rakyat LRT station (an unsigned exit at the back of the Puduraya's passenger concourse gives onto a lane leading to the LRT). There are several backpacker hostels opposite and around the station, while Chinatown is within easy walking distance, and the guesthouses on Tengkat Tong Shin are also not hard to reach on foot. Alternatively, for Bukit Bintang, take any of the RapidKL buses #U27, #U31, #U32, #U44, #U45, #U46, #U47 or #U48, which head east along Jalan Pudu and Jalan Imbi, then north up Jalan Sultan Ismail to the Lot 10 Shopping Centre.

Buses from the east coast (Kelantan and Terengganu, especially) end up at **Putra bus station**, a smaller, more modern terminus to the northwest of the city centre, close to the Putra World Trade Centre. Around 500m east is the PWTC LRT station. Fractionally closer to the south is Putra station, served by Komuter trains to the old Kuala Lumpur station (on the edge of Chinatown) and KL Sentral. About 1km northeast of the Putra bus station is **Pekeliling bus station** on Jalan Tun Razak, used by buses from the interior and some services from Kuantan. Conveniently, the separate Titiwangsa stations on the Monorail and the LRT are very close at hand, just to the north.

Some buses from Singapore use the **Pasar Rakyat bus station**, in a non-descript area close to the eastern section of Jalan Tun Razak. Head 500m north up any of the quiet lanes here and you're on the eastern section of Jalan Bukit Bintang, with the bright lights of Bukit Bintang 1km uphill to the west; taxis aren't hard to find at the bus station itself. Back in Chinatown, the **Klang bus station**, at the south end of Jalan Sultan Mohammed is used by Klang Valley buses to and from Port Klang and towns along the way; virtually next door is an LRT stop, Pasar Seni.

Finally, most **long-distance taxis** end up on the upper floors of Puduraya bus station, though a few use Putra or Pekeliling stations depending on where they started out.

Information and city transport

Of KL's three tourist offices, the biggest is the **Malaysia Tourism Centre** at 109 Jalan Ampang (MTC; daily 8am–10pm; ℡03/9235 4800, ⓦwww.mtc .gov.my), not far from the Bukit Nanas Monorail stop; you can also get here on bus #B105 from Central Market in Chinatown. Like its two smaller counterparts, which are located at **KL Sentral** (head past the busy AirAsia office on level 1 to find it hidden away on the east side of the building; daily 9am–6pm; ℡03/2272 5823) and at the **Putra World Trade Centre** (level 2; Mon–Fri 9am–6pm; ℡03/2615 8540), the MTC is mainly of use for leaflets and free city **maps**, though staff at all three offices can offer good general advice. The MTC also houses exchange facilities and payphones, plus a **travel agent** (℡03/2163 0162) which can arrange trips to Taman Negara and other attractions.

If you want to keep an ear to the ground on happenings around town then, besides scanning the newspapers, you should seek out the monthly **listings** magazines *Klue* (ⓦwww.klue.com.my) and *Time Out KL* (ⓦwww.timeoutkl .com). Also worth a look is ⓦwww.visionkl.com, a handy repository of sights, restaurants, clubs and events. The most detailed **map** of the city and the

Touch 'n Go cards

With KL only toddling towards a properly integrated transport system, you'll find you need to line up to buy a ticket every time you change from one service to another – if you transfer from the LRT to the Monorail, for example. It soon becomes a drag, one which can be avoided by having a stored-value **Touch 'n Go card** (ⓦ www.touchngo.com.my), though they only become worthwhile if you're spending a lot of time in KL or driving around the Peninsula. The cards can be used at LRT, Monorail and KTM stations (look for ticket gates bearing the card's logo) and by machines on some buses; simply press the card against the sensor to have the fare deducted. The card itself costs RM10 and is available in several denominations starting from a stored value of RM20, with a minimum top-up of RM10 subsequently. The snag is that only a few downtown stations sell the cards – at the time of writing, KL Sentral, KLCC, Masjid Jamek, Dang Wangi and KTM's MidValley – and these are also the only stations where you can buy new credit. It's also possible to add credit at a handful of small outlets (convenience stores, pharmacies, etc – see the website for details), at ATMs (you may find that only Malaysian bank cards are accepted) and at highway toll points.

surrounding conurbation, handy for drivers, is the enormous *The Big Atlas of Klang Valley and Beyond*, published by World Express Mapping and available at many bookshops (RM37). One thing to bear in mind is that given the chaotic nature of KL city planning – or lack thereof – maps and listings tend to go out of date fairly quickly; don't be surprised if roads, venues and buildings have sprung into existence or ceased to be.

City transport

Downtown KL isn't that large, so it's tempting to do a lot of your exploring **on foot**, but many pedestrians soon find themselves wilting thanks to the combined effects of humidity and traffic fumes from the vehicle-choked roads. Thankfully, the two light rail transit (LRT) lines and the Monorail, along with KTM's Komuter train services and taxis, are reasonably efficient and inexpensive. However, the various transport lines, having been created piecemeal, don't coordinate well with one another – interchanges may involve inconvenient walks and network-wide tickets don't exist. The main body attempting to coordinate all this is **RapidKL** (ⓣ03/7625 6999, ⓦ www.rapidkl.com.my), which runs both the LRT lines and many of the city's buses; its website includes network maps and details of monthly transport passes.

The LRT and the Monorail

The **Light Rail Transit** (**LRT**; every 5–10min 6am–midnight, or until 11.30pm on Sun) is a metro network comprising two, mostly elevated, lines, with a convenient central **interchange** at Masjid Jamek near Little India. The **Kelana Jaya** line (often known by its old name, **Putra**), is the more useful of the two, passing through KL Sentral, Chinatown and the old colonial district (Pasar Seni/Masjid Jamek stations) and KLCC. The other line, officially called **Ampang and Sri Petaling** (its old name, **Star**, is still used), has two branches which join at Chan Sow Lin station and continue up to Sentul Timur in the north of the city. For visitors, it's mainly of use for travel between Chinatown (Plaza Rakyat station) and Little India (Masjid Jamek or Bandaraya stations) and Chow Kit Market (Sultan Ismail station). **Fares** start at RM0.70 and climb in small steps up to RM2.50.

The LRT is complemented by the privately run **Monorail** (every 5–10min 6am–midnight; ⓦwww.monorail.com.my), an elevated rail system with a noticeable tilt as it cambers around bends, and with a different commercial sponsor shamelessly associated with each station. From its KL Sentral terminus (200m from the KL Sentral rail hub), the line at first heads east, through Brickfields and the southern edge of Chinatown, then swings north and west through Bukit Bintang and along Jalan Sultan Ismail, nearly reaching Jalan TAR before heading north through Chow Kit to terminate at Titiwangsa station on Jalan Tun Razak. There are interchanges with the LRT at Bukit Nanas (requiring a five-minute walk to Dang Wangi station) and at Hang Tuah. **Fares** range from RM1.20 for a trip of a couple of stops, up to RM2.50 to ride the line end to end.

The LRT and Monorail together take care of most journeys visitors need to make within downtown KL, with the notable exception of Chinatown/Masjid Jamek to Bukit Bintang. The Monorail just about covers this, if you're prepared to trudge south to Maharajalela station; otherwise, you could brave KL's bus system or steel your lungs for the trudge east along busy Jalan Pudu and Jalan Bukit Bintang.

Komuter trains

Modern **Komuter** trains, run by national rail operator KTM (☎03/2267 1200, ⓦwww.ktmb.com.my) travel on two lines – one from Seremban, the capital of Negeri Sembilan, northwest to Rawang (where an extension continues to Kuala Kubu Bharu, close to Fraser's Hill) and the other from the northern suburb of Sentul west to Port Klang. Both connect at four downtown stations, namely Putra, near the Putra World Trade Centre; Bank Negara, near Little India; the old Kuala Lumpur train station, in the colonial district; and KL Sentral. The trains run at every fifteen to twenty minutes during the day, but only every half-hour after 8pm. **Tickets** (RM1–9), can be purchased from the stations and automatic machines at the stops; return tickets cost double the one-way fare. Weekly and monthly passes for designated journeys are also available.

Buses

Though KL's **bus** services are reasonable, most visitors avoid them as they seem impossible to fathom. The small grid of streets around Puduraya and Central Market is very much the **hub** of the network, but there are no proper terminuses – you just have to check out the numerous bus stops, which don't always display the numbers of buses which pass by. Buildings with key stops close by, including the Sinarkota Building, the Kotaraya Building and the Bangkok Bank, appear on the Chinatown map on p.99.

A handful of companies operate city buses, notably **RapidKL** and **Metrobus** (☎03/5635 7897). Metrobus services have regular numbers, while RapidKL bus numbers are prefixed B, E, T and U, respectively denoting city services (operating downtown only), express buses, local services (for short hops from residential areas to bus or train stations) and trunk buses (for travel into and out of the centre). Services start up around 6am and begin winding down from 10pm onwards. Given KL's frequent traffic snarl-ups, do allow plenty of time for your journey.

Fares are low. RapidKL operates an unusual day-pass system, where any ticket entitles you to make additional journeys on the same route the rest of the day; fares are RM2, RM5, RM1 and RM2 for B, E, T and U services respectively. Metrobus and other companies use a zonal fare system, with fares starting at under RM1 downtown and rising to RM2.50 for journeys to the

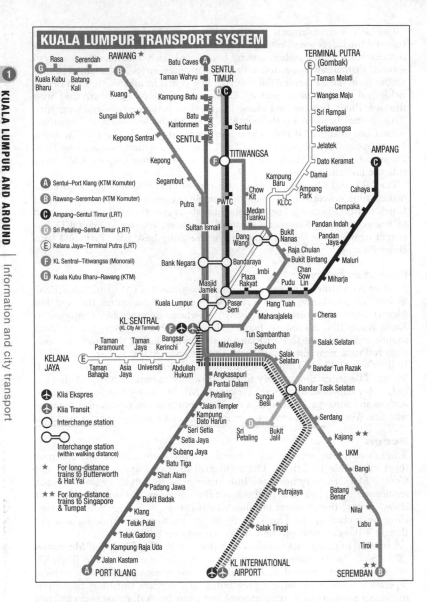

KUALA LUMPUR TRANSPORT SYSTEM

RAWANG ★

Rasa   Serendah
Kuala Kubu   Batang
Bharu   Kali
Kuang
Sungai Buloh ★
Kepong Sentral
Kepong
Segambut
Putra
Sultan Ismail

Batu Caves **A**
SENTUL
TIMUR
Taman Wahyu
Kampung Batu
Batu
Kantonmen
Sentul
SENTUL
TITIWANGSA
PWTC

TERMINAL PUTRA
(Gombak) **E**
Taman Melati
Wangsa Maju
Sri Rampai
Setiawangsa
Jelatek
Dato Keramat
Damai

A Sentul–Port Klang (KTM Komuter)
B Rawang–Seremban (KTM Komuter)
C Ampang–Sentul Timur (LRT)
D Sri Petaling–Sentul Timur (LRT)
E Kelana Jaya–Terminal Putra (LRT)
F KL Sentral–Titiwangsa (Monorail)
G Kuala Kubu Bharu–Rawang (KTM)

Kampung
Baru
Chow
Kit
Medan
Tuanku
Dang
Wangi
Bukit
Nanas
Raja Chulan
Bukit Bintang
Imbi
Plaza
Rakyat
Pudu
Hang Tuah
Maharajalela

Ampang
Park
KLCC
Chan
Sow
Lin

AMPANG
C
Cahaya
Cempaka
Pandan Indah
Pandan
Jaya
Maluri
Miharja

Bank Negara
Masjid
Jamek
Kuala Lumpur
KL SENTRAL
(KL City Air Terminal)
Bangsar
Kerinchi
Bandaraya
Pasar
Seni
Tun Sambanthan
Midvalley
Seputeh

Cheras
Salak Selatan
Bandar Tun Razak

KELANA
JAYA **E**
Taman
Paramount
Taman
Bahagia
Taman
Jaya
Asia
Jaya
Universiti
Abdullah
Hukum

Salak
Selatan
Angkasapuri
Pantai Dalam
Petaling
Jalan Templer
Kampung
Dato Harun
Seri Setia
Setia Jaya
Subang Jaya
Batu Tiga
Shah Alam
Padang Jawa
Bukit Badak
Klang
Teluk Pulai
Teluk Gadong
Kampung Raja Uda
Jalan Kastam

Sungai
Besi
Sri
Petaling
Bukit
Jalil

Bandar Tasik Selatan
Serdang
Kajang ★★
UKM
Bangi

D

Putrajaya
Batang
Benar
Nilai
Labu
Tiroi

A PORT KLANG

Salak Tinggi

KL INTERNATIONAL
AIRPORT

SEREMBAN **B** ★★

✈ Klia Ekspres
✈ Klia Transit
○ Interchange station
⊂⊃ Interchange station
(within walking distance)
★ For long-distance
trains to Butterworth
& Hat Yai
★★ For long-distance
trains to Singapore
& Tumpat

---

city limits. On some buses you pay the conductor; on others you pay the driver or drop the money into a machine close to the driver (in which case change isn't given).

Finally, you'll notice open-top double-decker tourist buses plying around Chinatown, Bukit Bintang and other parts of downtown, offering a hop-on, hop-off **city tour** (Ⓦwww.myhoponhopoff.com) – rather pricey at RM38 for unlimited use on any one day, and prone to getting delayed in the sludge-like traffic.

Taxis

Though cheap and convenient, KL taxis are also the bane of many a visitor to the city as the drivers are notorious for trying to rip people off by not using the meter. Instead they try to negotiate an inflated price for journeys, asking you how much you're willing to pay for the ride or naming a fee on the spot. The only way to avoid this sort of situation is to check if the driver switches on the meter as he is required by law to do when accepting your custom; if he doesn't, insist that he do so, failing which, ask to be set down and wait for another taxi to come along.

Taxis themselves come in several **classes**. Ordinary taxis are painted in various colours, but always display the words "Teksi Bermeter" on a sign on the roof; slightly smarter vehicles, usually in yellow, display "Teksi Premier" instead. At night, these roof signs are lit to indicate the taxi is available (though some drivers have a habit of leaving the light on even when they already have a passenger). A third class of taxis comprises posh, high-sided Enviro 2000 vehicles powered by natural gas, though these tend not to ply the streets looking for custom but instead cluster around upmarket hotels.

Metered **fares** are low: in regular taxis the flagfall is RM2, and the tariff is 10 sen for every 150m travelled. This translates into just RM4–5 for a typical journey between Bukit Bintang and Chinatown, or RM6–7 for Bukit Bintang to KL Sentral, or Chinatown to KLCC. Expect to pay a few ringgit more for downtown journeys in the smarter taxis.

There are numerous taxi **ranks** around the city, usually situated close to bus stops and outside shopping malls. Some drivers don't speak much English, so you may want to have the address of your destination written down in Malay, or mention a well-known landmark nearby.

There are plenty of companies you can call to book a taxi, among them Comfort Taxi (☎03/8024 2727), Radio Taxi (☎03/9221 7600), Sunlight (☎03/9058 9986), Supercab (☎03/2095 3399) and SW Taxis (☎03/2693 6211); you'll be charged an extra couple of ringgit for the booking. E-Smartcab has premier taxis fitted with **wheelchair** ramps (☎03/5192 2773 or 5192 1775, Ⓦwww.cabcharge.com.my).

Accommodation

There's a wide range of accommodation available in KL, and though rates are higher here than anywhere else in the country, they remain reasonable thanks to an oversupply of rooms at many times of year. As elsewhere in Malaysia, many hotels offer **promotional rates** – which are well worth asking about (or checking on their websites). Additionally, a few places have discounts outside weekends (price codes below correspond to weekend rates). Even without a discount, it's usually not hard to find a simple double in a guesthouse with shared facilities for RM60 a night, while a good mid-range hotel room can be had for around RM150; anything costing above RM250 a night will certainly be pretty luxurious.

Historically, it's been **Chinatown**, very close to Puduraya bus station, that's been the draw for KL's budget travellers. These days, however, it's in danger of being usurped as a travellers' haunt by the more sedate **Bukit Bintang**, fifteen minutes' walk to the east. Here, just a few streets from the fancy hotels and malls which dominate the area, and close to the celebrated Chinese food stalls of Jalan Alor, you'll find plenty of excellent guesthouses on and around

Tengkat Tong Shin. Though more expensive than the hostels of Chinatown, these guesthouses are often better value – less cramped and noisy, with slicker facilities and self-service breakfasts included in the rate.

Slightly further afield, there are more upscale hotels along **Jalan Sultan Ismail** and **Jalan Ampang**, which, together with Bukit Bintang, form part of KL's so-called **Golden Triangle**. All other parts of KL pale as regards accommodation, though **Little India** and nearby **Chow Kit**, linked by the fiendishly busy **Jalan Tuanku Abdul Rahman**, feature a number of mid-range hotels, while **Brickfields**, convenient for KL Sentral, has a couple of places worth considering.

During busy periods – July, August, November and December, plus school and public holidays – it's advisable to **book** your accommodation in advance. If you prefer to book **online**, try ⓦwww.hostelworld.com or www.hostelz.com for up-to-date lists of hostels and guesthouses, or the many KL hotel-booking websites which can be found on the Net – though note that it's always worth comparing their deals with any promotional rate the hotel may be offering.

Chinatown and around

Old-style Chinese flophouses are now rather scarce in Chinatown, having been edged out by backpacker-oriented places, not to mention hotels. The most mundane establishments tend to be clustered around the bus station; if it's inexpensive accommodation you're after, you'd do better to pay a bit more to stay close to the popular Petaling Street market. Hardly any hotels in the area have swimming pools, though there is an ageing public pool nearby at the Chinwoo Stadium (see p.133).

Note that some budget hotels, including even well-run ones, have rates for hourly use, a telltale sign that locals take advantage of them for a bit of hanky-panky. The cheap places reviewed here are currently free of this. Except where noted, the locations of the places below are shown on the map on p.99.

Hostels and guesthouses

Anuja Backpackers Inn 28 Jalan Pudu ☏03/2026 6479, ⓔanujainn@sgsmc.com. Boxy and rather bare rooms, though reasonably kept, some with a/c (as do the dorms) but all sharing facilities. The tiny lounge has a TV and internet access. Dorms RM10, ❷.

Backpacker's Travellers Inn Second floor, 60b Jalan Sultan ☏03/2078 2473, ⓦwww.backpackerskl.com. Well-established place where the narrow corridors are lined with louvred windows belonging to rather plain rooms. Some rooms and the dorms have a/c; a few rooms also have attached bathrooms. The chief attractions are the cool rooftop bar with affordable beers, and the fact that they have a travel agency offering a variety of trips – the Kuala Selangor fireflies and FRIM being the most obvious prospects. Breakfast available for a few ringgit extra. Dorm beds RM11, ❷.

Backpacker's Travellers Lodge First floor, 158 Jalan Tun H.S. Lee ☏03/2031 0889, ⓕ2078 1128. Slightly more spartan than the *Backpacker's Travellers Inn* – its sister operation – and featuring unadorned, somewhat cell-like rooms and dorms

with tiled floors and small shared bathrooms. A few rooms have a/c and en-suite facilities. Simple breakfasts can be ordered. Internet access. Dorm beds RM10, ❷.

Kameleon Travellers Lodge 35–37 Jalan Pudu Lama ☏03/2070 7770, ⓔkameleontravellerslodge@hotmail.com. Simple Indian-run guesthouse with spacious rooms, sharing facilities, and the option of a/c in a few doubles. Internet access is available and there's a small terrace with cane furniture to sit out on. A better choice than many of the places on Jalan Pudu itself. ❷.

Le Village Guesthouse 99a Jalan Tun H.S. Lee ☏03/2026 6737, ⓔdwahashim@yahoo.com. The abstract paintings in the entrance stairway set the tone at this chillled-out place above the *Kamal Curry House*, in a building which was one of the grandest shophouses in KL when it was built in the 1910s. Inside there's more artwork on multicoloured walls, and simple rooms and three-bed dorms with sliding doors. All rooms have fan (the windowless ones can still be stuffy, though) and share facilities; there's also a simple kitchen.

All floors have a sitting area. Good choice. Dorms RM12, ②.

Matahari Lodge 58-1 Jalan Hang Kasturi ☎03/2070 5570, ⊛www.mataharilodge .com. Immaculate guesthouse with gleaming white corridors and spotless showers and toilets. There's a/c in the common areas, and the cool air is sucked into the rooms – pleasantly if simply kitted out, with floral bedlinen and the odd fancy lamp – by extractor fans in the walls. Complimentary self-service breakfast, coin-operated washing machines, satellite TV, free wi-fi and a couple of terminals for net access, too. Not the place if you want a funky vibe, but ever so relaxed. Small surcharges at weekends. ③

Oasis Guesthouse 125 Jalan Petaling ☎03/2031 0188, ⓔoasiskl@yahoo.com. It may not quite be the "backpackers' Eden" it styles itself as, but it's friendly and pleasant enough, with tidy rooms in pastel colour schemes, reasonable shared facilities and the option of a/c. Dorms RM12, ②.

Pudu Hostel Third floor, Wisma Lai Choon, 10 Jalan Pudu ☎03/2078 9600, ⊛www.puduhostel .com. It's prominently signed at the start of Jalan Pudu, but this place is a bit of a let-down, as institutional as hostels get and just a little tatty throughout. Still, they do have a/c, pool and snooker tables in the lounge and net access. Dorms RM12, ②.

Red Dragon Hostel 80 Jalan Sultan ☎03/2078 9366, ⓔhostelrd@yahoo.com. A labyrinthine affair and a bit joyless on account of its scale, though reasonably run. There are over thirty rooms, some with a/c, plus an enormous lounge and a café open to the hubbub of Jalan Sultan. Internet access and bigscreen TV available. Dorms RM18, ②.

Serai Inn Second floor, 62 Jalan Hang Lekiu ☎03/2070 4728, ⊛www.seraiinn.com. Entered via an alley off Jalan Hang Lekiu, this excellent little backpackers' place offers dorms and a range of rooms, all with a/c, plus free wi-fi and simple breakfasts. Dorm beds RM25, ③.

YWCA 12 Jalan Hang Jebat ☎&ⓕ03/2031 7753. Cosily removed from the din of Chinatown but a little staid, the *YWCA* lets its rooms only to women, couples and families. The older block has simple rooms with fan and shared facilities, while the newer blue-and-white block has en-suite rooms with the option of a/c in some. Weekly and monthly rates available. ③

Hotels

Ancasa Jalan Tun Tan Cheng Lock ☎03/2026 6060, ⊛www.ancasa-hotel.com. Slick hotel with decent-sized and comfortably furnished rooms. There's also a pricey spa for massages, aromatherapy and other treatments, plus a decent restaurant and bar, though breakfast isn't included in the rate. Prices rise by ten percent at weekends. ⑥

China Town 2 70–72 Jalan Petaling ☎03/2072 9933, ⊛www.hotelchinatown2.com. Pretty much identical in concept and feel to the *Chinatown Inn* (perhaps no surprise as the respective owners are brothers), though with slightly smarter rooms, including some singles, crammed deep into a building which runs all the way to Jalan Sultan. Internet access and wi-fi in the lobby. ④

Chinatown Inn 52–54 Jalan Petaling ☎03/2070 4008, ⊛www.chinatowninn.com. Reached by an unobtrusive doorway behind the market stalls, this is a little haven in the heart of Chinatown. The rooms are bland but spacious enough; all have TV and attached bathroom, and most have a/c – which is just as well, as many are windowless. Internet access available, and free wi-fi in the lobby. ③

Citin 38 Jalan Pudu ☎03/2031 7777, ⊛www .citinhotels.com. A cheerful, modern hotel, recently refurbished though already a bit tatty in places. Still, rooms have flatscreen TV and attached bathroom, and there's free internet access during the day (on their own terminals or your laptop via wi-fi). Rate includes breakfast. ⑤

D'Oriental Inn 82 & 84 Jalan Petaling ☎03/2026 8181, ⊛www.dorientalinn.com. Nicely located in the thick of the market, but the rooms are bland, though they are en suite and come with TV. Wi-fi is free but breakfast costs extra. ⑥

Heritage Station Kuala Lumpur Station, Jalan Sultan Hishamuddin ☎03/2272 1688, ⊛www .heritagehotelmalaysia.com; see map, pp.84–85. The city's finest hotel during the colonial era, now trading on past glories and beset by a sleepy ennui. The attraction is, of course, the building itself, though it's not nearly as atmospheric as you might hope; the rooms are very spacious but blandly furnished. Amenities are limited to a humdrum bar-restaurant. Free wi-fi in the lobby. Rate includes breakfast. ⑤

Malaya Jalan Hang Lekir ☎03/2072 7722, ⊛www.hotelmalaya.com.my. An old faithful of a hotel, with a dreary 1970s facade to prove it. Rooms – all a/c and en suite, with proper bathtubs – are comfortable if unremarkable, and the place isn't as slick as some other mid-range hotels, but it does have a great location bordering on the thick of the Petaling Street action. Rate includes breakfast. Be sure to ask about promotional discounts. ⑤

Mandarin Pacific 2–8 Jalan Sultan ☎03/2070 3000, ⊛www.mandpac.com.my. Not unlike the *Malaya*, with an unappealing exterior and decent en-suite rooms, but a bit dull, for which it compensates by being slightly cheaper. Breakfast included. ⑤

Puduraya Above Puduraya bus station ☎03/2072 1000, ⓕ2070 5567. A functional hotel which, despite rather dated rooms, is pretty efficient and insulated from the clamour of Jalan Pudu. Some rooms boast good views of the Maybank Tower and other KL landmarks. Ten-percent discounts outside weekends; rate includes an Asian buffet breakfast. ❺

Stayorange.com 16 Jalan Petaling ☎03/2070 2208, ⓦwww.stayorange.com. Done out in the colour scheme of a big-name European budget airline, and likewise featuring ridiculously cheap prices if you book way ahead. Rooms are en suite but are cramped despite containing a minimum of furniture; there are also boxy rooms with two-bunk beds and sharing facilities. Best rate ❶, but more generally ❸.

Swiss Inn 62 Jalan Sultan ☎03/2072 3333, ⓦwww.swissinnkualalumpur.com. From the same stable as the *Swiss Garden* (see p.96), this well-liked hotel has been extended into the adjacent property to include whole set of new rooms with minimalist decor and flatscreen TVs; rooms in the original part are slightly larger and also come with fridge. The coffee house affords a good view of the Petaling Street market. Rate includes breakfast. ❻

The Golden Triangle, including Bukit Bintang

Many of Bukit Bintang's guesthouses occupy nicely restored old **shophouses**, with small, comfortable rooms separated from one another using simple partitions of plywood or other material. It's hard to go wrong with any of these, just as it's difficult to be badly disappointed with any of the Golden Triangle's upmarket hotels. The area also boasts excellent serviced **apartments** offering a lot more space than you'd get in a similarly priced hotel room. For the locations of the places reviewed below, see the map on pp.108–109.

Guesthouses

Anjung Guesthouse 4 Tengkat Tong Shin ☎03/2148 6812, ⓦwww.anjungkl.com. Unpretentious place offering a range of rooms including singles and triples, and an eight-bed dorm, all with nice tiled floors, a/c and sharing facilities. You can relax to satellite TV in the lounge or sit at tables out front. There's free wi-fi and a book exchange too. Rate includes breakfast. Discounts outside weekends. Dorms RM30, ❹.

Classic Inn 52 Lorong 1/77A, Changkat Thambi Dollah ☎03/2148 8648, ⓦwww.classicinn.com .my. Nicely run guesthouse: rooms are en suite and have a/c and TV; there's also a lounge kitted out with stylish wooden furniture and featuring satellite TV. They also serve up a Western breakfast, included in the rate, or can order up local favourites like *roti canai* if you prefer. ❺

🏃 **Green Hut** 48 Tengkat Tong Shin ☎03/2142 3339, ⓦwww.thegreenhut.com. Easily spotted thanks to its lime-green exterior, with more bright multicoloured walls and a suitably romantic jungle mural within, *Green Hut* is a relaxed place boasting simple a/c rooms sharing spotless facilities (a few rooms are en suite). The cosy lounge has internet terminals and satellite TV. Rate includes breakfast. Dorms RM25, ❸.

The Haven Guesthouse 3 Jalan Bukit Bintang ☎03/2142 5313, ⓦwwwthehavenkl.com. Bravely housed in one of the last remaining shophouses on Jalan Bukit Bintang, this is packed with timber walls and partitions everywhere, giving the impression of being inside a very elaborate tree-house. The dorms and most rooms have a/c, and a few have their own shower. Self-service coffee, tea and toast available all day. Free wi-fi. Dorm beds from RM28, ❹.

🏃 **Number Eight Guesthouse** 8–10 Tengkat Tong Shin ☎03/2144 2050, ⓦwww .numbereight.com.my. A sleek setup that broke the mould by infusing designer chic into shophouse surroundings, evident right away in the stylish furnishings in the two lounges and permeating every room. All rooms have a/c and marble-topped sinks, though only a few are en suite (and these also have TV/DVD systems). Rate includes a self-service breakfast of toast, fruit and coffee/tea. Dorms RM30, ❹.

Pondok Lodge 20-2c Changkat Bukit Bintang ☎03/2142 8449, ⓦwww.pondoklodge.com. One of the longest-established guesthouses in the area, with simply furnished, somewhat boxy rooms, plus a four-bed dorm. All have a/c but share bathrooms. Satellite TV and internet access are available in the lounge, and a simple breakfast is included in the rate. Dorms RM25, ❸.

Pujangga Homestay 21 Jalan Berangan ☎03/2141 4243, ⓦwww.pujangga-homestay.com. A couple of adjacent 1970s terraced houses have been combined here to produce a sprawling guest-house with single and double rooms and dorms. There are also a couple of lounges with satellite TV, a kitchen and internet terminals (plus free wi-fi). Rates include breakfast. Dorm beds from RM25, ❸.

Red Palm 5 Tengkat Tong Shin ☏ 03/2143 1279, Ⓦ www.redpalm-kl.com. Bizarrely unsigned – look for it opposite the *Number Eight Guesthouse* – is this well-regarded, informal establishment with just three rooms and a dorm upstairs, all sharing facilities. Downstairs is a spacious lounge with a number of internet terminals and TV. Rates include breakfast. Reservations advised. Dorm beds RM25, ❸.

🏃 **Travellers Palm Lodge** 10 Jalan Rembia ☏ 03/2145 4745, Ⓦ www.travellerspalm -kl.com. Down a lane off Tengkat Tong Shin is this delightful guesthouse fronted by two travellers' palms in the tiny front garden. Inside the house is dotted with interesting paintings, and bits of old furniture are scattered around the lovely, spacious lounge. There's a range of rooms – all with a/c except the lone single – and an eight-bed a/c dorm; all share facilities. Snug and secure; rate includes breakfast. Dorm beds RM25, ❸.

Hotels

Alpha Genesis 45 Tengkat Tong Shin ☏ 03/2141 2000, Ⓦ www.alphagenesis.com. Modern business-oriented hotel that has the distinction of being a little cosier than many others in the same price bracket. Rate includes breakfast. ❻

Comfort Inn 65 Changkat Bukit Bintang ☏ 03/2141 3636, Ⓦ www.hotelcomfort.biz. Behind the ugly concrete exterior is a tiny hotel offering smallish, plain a/c rooms with TV and a boxy attached bathroom. Still, this ranks among the cheapest hotels in the area and staff are friendly. Up to 20min free internet use on their PCs and there's free wi-fi in the reception area. ❹

🏃 **Corus** Jalan Ampang ☏ 03/2161 8888, Ⓦ www.corushotelkl.com. A tried-and-tested mid-1980s hotel that's maturing well despite an ill-advised exterior makeover involving lots of pale orange paint. Thankfully, decor in the plush rooms is suitably muted. Amenities include Chinese and Japanese restaurants, a swimming pool and sauna. ❼

Equatorial Jalan Sultan Ismail ☏ 03/2161 7777, Ⓦ www.equatorial.com. Vast five-star hotel with tastefully decorated rooms, a swimming pool, wireless internet access and some good restaurants and cafés. ❽

🏃 **Federal** 35 Jalan Bukit Bintang ☏ 03/2148 9166, Ⓦ www.fhihotels.com. Venerable hotel dating from the year of Malaysia's independence and nicely updated over the decades, the current incarnation sporting a beautiful marbled lobby. Facilities include a pool, bowling alley and the revolving *Bintang* restaurant which, like some of the rooms, offers views over the concrete jungle of malls that dominate Bukit Bintang. ❼

Impiana KLCC 13 Jalan Pinang ☏ 03/2147 1111, Ⓦ www.impiana.com. This tastefully decorated hotel offers subdued but stylish rooms with slick bathroom fittings. Ideally placed for both Bintang Walk and KLCC, it also boasts a swimming pool and spa, and keener rates than other hotels in its class. ❽

Mandarin Oriental KLCC ☏ 03/2380 8888, Ⓦ www.mandarinoriental.com. Enormous hotel (it only looks small by virtue of being conveniently next to the Twin Towers) and as sumptuous as they come, with its own luxury spa, swimming pools, tennis courts and some tip-top restaurants. All this doesn't come cheap: the lowest regularly available rate is around RM760 a night. ❾

Marriott 183 Jalan Bukit Bintang ☏ 03/2715 9000, Ⓦ www.marriott.com. Among the crème de la crème of KL hotels, with top-notch rooms and facilities including the obligatory pool, spa and gym, plus several good restaurants. Watch for exceptional discounts that are available from time to time. ❾

🏃 **Maya** 138 Jalan Ampang ☏ 03/2711 8866, Ⓦ www.hotelmaya.com.my. This stunning boutique hotel has two hundred rooms arranged around a vast, futuristic central atrium and is distinguished by chic designer furnishings throughout. Each grade of room has its own design quirks; in the cheapest studio rooms, for example, the bathrooms have glass walls (with privacy curtains) so you can watch the big-screen TV while soaking in the bath. Room safes have built-in power points for your gadgets and every room has net access. The hotel also boasts a range of spa treatments and restaurants, plus free transfers to and from the airport. Rack rates start at RM700, though you can often get one-third off online, with breakfast included. ❾

Nikko 165 Jalan Ampang ☏ 03/2161 1111, Ⓦ www .hotelnikko.com.my. Swanky Japanese-owned five-star affair with a great range of restaurants – including, naturally, Japanese – plus a pool and spa. It caters mainly to business travellers, so rates fall at weekends – though in general staying is only worthwhile if you get a promotional deal (typically under RM500 for a double), as the rack rate is extortionate. ❾

Piccolo 101 Jalan Bukit Bintang ☏ 03/2303 8000, Ⓦ www.thepiccolohotel.com. They brag that they're a "hip boutique hotel" and indeed try to take a leaf out of the *Maya*'s book, with modish designer touches everywhere, plus an Italian restaurant and a Japanese-style spa. Good rates for the location. ❽

Radius 51a Changkat Bukit Bintang ☏ 03/2715 3888, Ⓦ www.radius-international.com. Substantial hotel with reasonable rooms, a restaurant and café, and a terrace swimming pool with views of Menara

❶

KL and the Maybank Tower. Promotional rates, with breakfast thrown in, often apply. **6**

Renaissance Junction of Jalan Sultan Ismail and Jalan Ampang ☎03/2162 2233, ⓦwww.renaissance -kul.com. Part of the Marriott group, and featuring an excellent outdoor swimming pool, gym and restaurants. The east wing is around twenty percent cheaper. Rates exclude breakfast. **8**

🏃 **Seasons View** 61 Jalan Alor ☎03/2145 7577, ⓦwww.seasonsview.com. On one level, a mundane, smallish, lower-mid-range hotel – but it's competently run, has modern en-suite rooms, a good location amid the culinary splendour of Jalan Alor and great rates (which include breakfast). **5**

Swiss Garden 117 Jalan Pudu ☎03/2141 3333, ⓦwww.swissgarden.com. This substantial modern hotel is conveniently located at the edge of Bukit Bintang and halfway to Chinatown. Facilities include satellite TV, a couple of restaurants plus a pool, gym and spa. **7**

Serviced apartments

🏃 **KL Plaza Suites** 179 Jalan Bukit Bintang ☎03/2145 6988,

ⓦwww.berjayaresorts.com.my. Great-value serviced apartments, including some sleeping up to six, with their own pleasant lounge, optional kitchenette, plus use of swimming pool. Parking is available. **7**

Pacific Regency Menara Panglobal, Jalan Puncak, off Jalan P. Ramlee ☎03/2332 7777, ⓦwww .pacific-regency.com. Luxury apartments complete with kitchenette, huge bathroom, satellite TV, free wireless internet access and, on the roof, a swimming pool and the excellent *Luna* bar (see p.124). Ample parking too. The location at the foot of Bukit Nanas isn't near any stations – though if you can afford the rates, taxi fares won't trouble you in the least. **8**

Somerset 8 Lorong Ceylon ☎03/2055 8888, ⓦwww.somerset.com. Popular with executive types, these immaculate one- and two-bed apartments in a brand-new tower block are equipped with swish furnishings, satellite TV/DVD systems and wired internet access. On the fourth floor are a sauna, gym, a swimming pool with good views and a poolside café, open only for breakfast (included in the rate). **9**

Little India, Chow Kit and the Putra World Trade Centre

The places reviewed below appear on the map on p.106, except for the *Legend* which appears on the map on pp.84–85.

Coliseum Hotel 98–100 Jalan TAR ☎03/2692 6270. A famous survivor dating from the 1920s, though now caught in a dreary time warp; much of the place looks like it hasn't been updated since the 1960s. The lobby and bar are moderately atmospheric, but don't make up for the plain rooms (with fan – there's no a/c), ancient and unexciting furniture and shared bathrooms which are a little frayed at the edges. **3**

Garden City Hotel 214 Jalan Bunus, off Jalan Masjid India ☎03/2711 7777, ⓦwww.garden-city -hotel.net. Trying to reinforce the horticultural connection in its name, this place has a dark green exterior bizarrely festooned with window boxes packed with plastic tulips. Thankfully the interior is free of such kitsch, housing serviceable, modern en-suite rooms. Rate includes breakfast. **5**

Hotel Champagne 141 Jalan Bunus, off Jalan Masjid India ☎03/2698 6333. Budget place with rooms set around a central well. The decor is dull in the extreme and the bathrooms are dated, but it's a decent option nonetheless and not too noisy given the location. **4**

Hostel Cosmopolitan fourth floor, 73 & 75 Jalan Haji Hussein ☎012/268 9305, ⓦwww .hostelcosmopolitan.blogspot.com. The management

here runs a tight ship and their hostel does just fine for itself, despite the unpromising location on the edge of Chow Kit market (look for the big sign at the top of their building). There are just four rooms plus a fourteen-bed women's dorm and an eighteen-bed mixed dorm, all with bright bed linen and sharing facilities, including internet terminals, free wi-fi and a kitchen. There really could be more showers and toilets, though. Dorm beds from RM20, **3**.

Legend Hotel Putra Place, 100 Jalan Putra, across from the Putra World Trade Centre ☎03/4042 9888, ⓦwww.legendsgroup.com. Above the Mall shopping development, this luxury hotel boasts a rooftop pool and several restaurants and bars. Unusually, they have a range of serviced apart-ments which can offer better value than the rooms, whose chief distinction is that they all have a PC for internet access. **8**

Maytower Hotel 7 Jalan Munshi Abdullah ☎03/2692 9298, ⓦwww.maytower.com.my. Yet another hotel with a choice of rooms or apartments, though in this case the rooms are much better value, stylishly appointed in earthy tones and equipped with flatscreen TV and safe. Good value, even though breakfast costs extra. Rooms **6**, apartments **9**.

Palace 46-1 Jalan Masjid India ☎03/2698 6122, ⓦwww.palacehotel.com.my. Reasonable hotel with modern a/c rooms (though bathrooms are dated) in the thick of the night market. No breakfast though. ❺–❻

Tune Hotel 316 Jalan TAR ☎03/7962 5888, ⓦwww.tunehotel.com. The first of what will be a host of AirAsia-supported no-frills hotels across the country, with airline-like rates – cheap if you book very early. Rooms and bathrooms are small and functional in the extreme; at least the window glass is nice and thick, given the frenetic traffic on Jalan TAR. All rooms have fans but you can pay extra for a/c (around RM14 for 12hr). Lobby facilities, such as they are, amount to a couple of fast-food outlets and a convenience store. ❶ possible, but typically ❸.

Brickfields and KL Sentral
The places reviewed below appear on the map on p.115.

Florida 71–73 Jalan Thambypillai ☎03/2260 1333, ⓕ2274 9107. A functional hotel lacking the seediness that taints many lodgings in the area. En-suite rooms with a/c and TV. ❸

Hilton 3 Jalan Stesen Sentral ☎03/2264 2264, ⓦwww.kuala-lumpur.hilton.com. Lavish hotel whose lobby wouldn't look out of place fronting a modern art museum and with rooms straight out of the style magazines. Rates vary throughout the year, but reckon on at least RM500 a night. ❾

Le Meridien 2 Jalan Stesen Sentral ☎03/2263 7888, ⓦkualalumpur.lemeridien.com. Not quite as opulent as the *Hilton* next door, but grand by anyone else's standards, with a pool and spa, and a fancy Lebanese restaurant. As at the *Hilton*, rates wander all over the place, although don't expect rooms any cheaper than RM450 a night. ❾

YMCA 95 Jalan Padang Belia ☎03/2274 1439, ⓦwww.ymcakl.com. A well-maintained place reminiscent of campus accommodation, and open to male and female guests. Rooms, all with a/c and TV, range from singles to quads, with the option of attached bathrooms with the singles and doubles. Facilities include a café, laundry, barber's and tennis courts (you'll need your own gear, though). Good value, particularly as breakfast is included. ❹

Further out

Carcosa Seri Negara Taman Tasik Perdana ☎03/2295 0888, ⓦwww.ghmhotels.com. See map, pp.84–85. Set in its own grounds just west of the Lake Gardens, these two colonial mansions containing thirteen suites are without doubt the most exclusive place to stay in KL – the management can truthfully boast "Queen Elizabeth slept here." For more, see p.113. Occasional promotions shave only small amounts off the rack rate, which starts at RM1250 including breakfast. ❾

The City

Most visitors divide their time equally between old and new KL, which is probably the best strategy for seeing the city. Very close to the historic "muddy confluence", **Merdeka Square**, with its colonial-era courthouses and administrative buildings, is pretty much on everyone's list, as is **Chinatown** to the southeast; in between lie the city's old **Jamek Mosque** and **Pasar Seni**, one of KL's main crafts markets. Worthwhile forays can be made north to **Little India** (and, if you're so inclined, on up to **Chow Kit Market**); south to the **old train station**, **Masjid Negara** (the National Mosque) and the adjacent **Islamic Arts Museum**; further south to the **National Museum** and the **Brickfields** district, both close to KL Sentral; and west to the **Lake Gardens**, one of surprisingly few green lungs in this tropical city.

All the while, you'll probably be shuttling across to the **Golden Triangle**. Not actually a triangle, it takes in the **Menara KL** communications tower, with amazing views over the city, as well as the numerous hotels, malls, restaurants and clubs of **Bukit Bintang**, focused on Jalan Bukit Bintang, Jalan Imbi and

Jalan Sultan Ismail. The Golden Triangle is bounded on its northern edge by **Jalan Ampang**, one of the first streets to be developed as a residential area for rich tin *towkays* and colonial administrators at the start of the twentieth century, and which still retains a few mansions, some now housing embassies. Close to the junction of Jalan Ampang and Jalan Tun Razak are the **Petronas Towers**. If you've a particular interest in KL's architectural heritage, it's worth arranging a **walking tour** (see p.133).

The colonial quarter

The small **colonial quarter**, which developed around the confluence of the Gombak and Klang rivers in the 1880s, is the area of KL that arguably best retains its historic character, with an eccentric fusion of building styles, including practically all of the city's Moorish-style buildings. At its heart on the west bank of the Klang is a beautifully tended English cricket ground and padang (field), revered for its place in Malaysian history, for it was here that on August 31, 1957, Malaysia's first prime minister, Tunku Abdul Rahman, declared *merdeka*, or independence. Subsequently, the space was renamed Dataran Merdeka, or **Merdeka Square**.

On the western side of the square, the **Royal Selangor Club** was the British elite's favourite watering hole. The club itself was founded in the 1880s, though the present clubhouse, a low, black-and-white mock Tudor structure, is a 1970s rebuilding of a structure built by A.B. Hubbock in 1910, after the original was badly damaged by fire. Colonial wags used to refer to the building as "the Spotted Dog", supposedly in memory of the club mascot, a Dalmatian, which a former member used to tie up at the steps. To the north, the Anglican **St Mary's Cathedral** (1894), usually open in the daytime, welcomed the city's European inhabitants every Sunday before they repaired to the club.

The 95-metre **flagpole** just south of the square is supposedly the tallest in the world. Locals flock here on weekend evenings to parade beside the fairy lights of the **Sultan Abdul Samad Building**, across Jalan Sultan Hishamuddin from here. With a two-storey grey-and-red brick facade dominated by a forty-metre-high clock tower, and curved colonnades topped with impressive copper cupolas, it was completed in 1897 and ranks among the earliest of the

The Hash House Harriers

Dotty Englishmen took their dottiness with them all around the empire. Among them was one A.S. Gispert who joined a club in Melaka, the Springgit Harriers, which indulged in a version of the English running game Hare and Hounds. The game is simple: a runner or "hare" sets a paper trail for a group – the "hounds" – that later sets off in pursuit. The trail, often through stretches of woodland, might periodically break or veer off in a different direction, requiring the "hounds" to fan out and try and pick it up. In 1938 Gispert managed to enthuse some of his fellow drinkers who peopled the *Hash House*, as the dining room of the Royal Selangor Club was known, into taking part in the game. The group became known as the **Hash House Harriers**, and its members would run on Mondays after their weekly training session for the Malay States Volunteer Reserves.

Gispert was killed helping to defend Singapore in early 1942, but after the war the other members revived the tradition, and the Hash House Harriers went on to become an international running club. The original KL group, respectfully regarded as the mother of all hashing groups, is still in existence (Ⓦwww.motherhash.org).

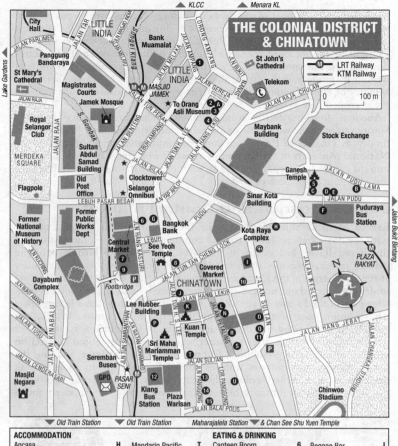

THE COLONIAL DISTRICT & CHINATOWN

M — LRT Railway
KTM Railway

0   100 m

ACCOMMODATION				EATING & DRINKING			
Ancasa	H	Mandarin Pacific	T	Canteen Room	6	Reggae Bar	J
Anuja Backpackers Inn	D	Matahari Lodge	P	Five Plus Two Maju	4	Santa	2
Backpacker's Travellers Inn	Q	Oasis Guesthouse	U	Hameeds Café	12	Seng Kee	11
Boolipaolipr'o Travollers Lodge	J	Pudu Hostel	C	Ikopi	13	Speakeasy	1
China Town 2	R	Puduraya	F	Lai Foong	0	Sri Bariuou	5
Chinatown Inn	N	Red Dragon Hostel	I	Mangrove Food Court	7	Tang City Food Court	10
Citin	E	Serai Inn	A	O Kawan	3	Wan Fo Yuan	14
D'Orientala	S	Stayorange.com	L	Old China Café	15		
Kameleon Travellers Lodge	B	Swiss Inn	0	Precious Old China	9		
Le Village Guesthouse	G	YWCA	M	Purple Cane Tea House	13		
Malaya	K						

capital's **Moorish-style buildings**, characterized by onion domes, cupolas, colonnades, arched windows and wedding-cake plasterwork. One man was largely responsible for this original urban fabric – Charles Edwin Spooner, the state engineer in the 1890s. Under his guidance, architect Anthony Norman (also responsible for St Mary's) came up with an initial design for the Sultan Abdul Samad Building – in the Neoclassical Renaissance style, which was then the general standard for government buildings throughout the British Empire. But Spooner argued that the symbols of the Federated Malay States, a protectorate rather than a colony, should reflect the Islamic sensibilities of the Malay rulers. So a more "Eastern" design was eventually used, though one not based on traditional Malay timber buildings but imported from colonial India. Subsequent buildings by Norman in this mould include the old Post Office next door and the former Public Works Department further south.

Originally the Sultan Abdul Samad Building housed the colonial administration's offices, and until recently it was home to the High Court. At the time of writing its future was uncertain, though part of it may eventually house the Ministry of Unity, Culture, Arts and Heritage, with the possibility of a museum being created here as well.

Also in a Moorish style, the cream-coloured building to the south of Merdeka Square was once the workplace of former British prime minister John Major in his days as a banker. In 1996 it was converted from government offices into the **National Museum of History**, now closed. The exhibits have been integrated into the National Museum (see p.114), but the future status of the building itself was uncertain at the time of writing.

Jamek Mosque and Central Market

East of Merdeka Square, Lebuh Pasar Besar connects the colonial quarter with the more frenetic life of the old commercial district on the east side of the Klang River. Just north of the river bridge is the **Jamek Mosque** (Masjid Jamek; open to visitors outside prayer times; free), on a promontory at the confluence of the Klang and Gombak rivers. It was here – on a section of dry land carved out from the enveloping forest – that tin prospectors from Klang established a base in the 1850s, which soon turned into a boom town. The mosque, part of the second great period of expansion in KL, was completed in 1909 by the British architect A.B. Hubbock, who took over from Anthony Norman after the latter was compulsorily retired in 1903 on grounds of inefficiency. Hubbock had previously lived in India, and thus the Jamek Mosque incorporates features copied from Mogul mosques – pink brick walls and arched colonnades, topped by oval cupolas and squat minarets. There's an intimacy here that isn't obvious at the modern, much

▲ Jamek Mosque

larger national mosque to the south, and the grounds, bordered by palms, are a pleasant place to sit and rest. The main entrance is on Jalan Tun Perak.

Head south off Lebuh Pasar Besar and you reach the Art Deco **Central Market** (daily 9am–10pm). Backing onto the Klang River, this large pastel-coloured brick hangar was built in the 1920s as the capital's wet market, though the butchers and fishmongers have long since left for places like Chow Kit and the back alleys of nearby Chinatown. In the mid-1980s the market was converted into what's known as **Pasar Seni**, meaning "art market", though most of the shops within actually sell **crafts** and souvenirs – anything from models of the Petronas Towers to T-shirts. It was once hoped that Pasar Seni would follow in the footsteps of London's famous Covent Garden Market and become a major tourist draw, but despite a recent revamp aimed at taking the place upmarket, there's still a distinctly dowdy feel to it, and for every worth-while outlet showcasing *songket* or silverware, there's a mundane shop selling watches or magazines. Still, the market is definitely worth a browse, and is a lively meeting point at weekends and most evenings, when a few buskers outside entertain the kids with Malay pop covers. The streets to the east and north are worth a stroll, featuring a sprinkling of Neoclassical and Art Deco shophouses and an unfussy Art Deco clock tower on Lebuh Ampang.

Chinatown

Spreading out east from Central Market is **Chinatown**, once KL's commercial kernel, dating from the arrival of the first traders in the 1860s. Bordered by Jalan Sultan to the east, Jalan Tun Perak to the north and Jalan Maharajalela to the south, the area had adopted its current extent by the late nineteenth century, with southern-Chinese shophouses, coffee shops and temples springing up along narrow streets such as Jalan Tun H.S. Lee (formerly Main St) and Jalan Petaling. Though the shophouses today are fairly workaday, unlike those in Melaka's Jonkers Walk area or around Penang's Lebuh Chulia, it is encouraging that a few of the period buildings are being refurbished despite the threat of redevelopment constantly hanging over the area.

For locals and visitors alike, **Jalan Petaling** (still often called **Petaling St**) is very much the main draw. Home to brothels and gambling dens in KL's early years, these days it's the haunt of market traders who, under a modern blue glass roof, do a roaring trade in fake watches and handbags and pirated DVDs, from late morning until well into the evening. The buzz spills over into neighbouring streets, which feature shops and hawkers selling all manner of foodstuffs, from *ba kwa* (slices of pork, given a sweet marinade and grilled) to local fruits and molasses-like herbal brews in tureens. The Chinese restaurants and stalls in the vicinity are among the most popular eating places in KL, some staying open into the small hours.

See Yeoh and Chan See Shu Yuen temples

Just past the junction of Jalan Tun H.S. Lee and Jalan Cheng Lock is the **See Yeoh Temple**, founded in 1883 by Yap Ah Loy, KL's early Chinese headman, who funded its construction; a photograph of him is often prominently displayed on one of the altars. The temple is atmospheric but not particularly interesting, though it comes to life on festival days. You're better off heading to the very southern end of Jalan Petaling to visit the area's largest temple, **Chan See Shu Yuen**, a clan temple covering Chinese with the very common name of Chan (also transliterated Chen and Tan). From outside, you can see the intri-cately carved roof, its images depicting more monumental events in Chinese history and mythology; the inner shrine is covered in scenes of lions, dragons

▲ Southern gateway to the Petaling Street market

and mythical creatures battling with warriors. Most engaging of all, however, are the two gentleman figurines on the altar representing ancestors of the clan or possibly their servants – and wearing Western top hats to indicate their link with the colonial past.

Sri Maha Mariamman Temple

Oddly perhaps, one of KL's main Hindu shrines, the **Sri Maha Mariamman Temple**, is also located in the heart of Chinatown, on Jalan Tun H.S. Lee (where you can also pause to take a look at the nearby **Kuan Ti Temple**, an attractively restored Taoist affair dating back to the late nineteenth century). The earliest shrine on the Sri Maha Mariamman site was built in 1873 by Tamil immigrants and named after the Hindu deity, Mariamman, whose intercession was sought to provide protection against sickness and "unholy incidents". In the case of the Tamils, who had arrived to build the railways or work on the plantations, they needed all the solace they could find from the appalling rigours of their working life.

Significant rebuilding of the temple took place in the 1960s, when sculptors from India were commissioned to design idols to adorn the five tiers of the gate tower – these now shine with gold embellishments, precious stones and exquisite Spanish and Italian tiles. Garland-makers sell their wares outside the entrance, while above it is a hectic profusion of Hindu gods, frozen in dozens of scenes from the *Ramayana*.

During the Hindu **Thaipusam** festival, the temple's golden chariot is paraded through the streets on its route to the Batu Caves, on the northern edge of the city (see p.136). The rest of the year, the chariot is kept in a large room in the temple; you might be able to persuade an attendant to unlock the door and let you have a peek.

The temple is always open to the public and is free to visit, although you may want to contribute a ringgit or two towards its upkeep. Visitors must leave their shoes at a rack situated to the left of the entrance.

Chinatown's eastern edge

Chinatown's main west–east thoroughfares, Jalan Tun Perak and Jalan Tun Tan Cheng Lock (the latter the route of the original rail line through KL) converge at the Puduraya intersection, just off which stands the **Maybank Building**. Built in the late 1980s by Hijjas Kasturi, it's a structure typical of the new KL, designed with Islamic principles of purity in mind. Unlike many of the other modern skyscrapers here, there's actually a reason to venture inside – to visit either the small art gallery or the **Numismatic Museum** (Mon–Sat 10am–6pm; free), both on the main lobby floor. The latter is an unusually interesting collection, arranged chronologically, starting with tin ingots, gold dust and bars of silver or, for what the caption describes as "ordinary people", cowrie shells, rice and beads – all of which were once used for transactions in the region. Coins were gradually introduced with the arrival of the various colonizing powers; early sixteenth-century Portuguese coins on display are delicately engraved with miniatures of the Malay Peninsula and tiny kites billowing in the air. The first mass-produced coins, issued by the British East India Company, bore the company's coat of arms – a practice echoed later by timber and rubber companies, who until the late eighteenth century minted tokens to pay their expanding labour pool. During the Japanese invasion, the occupying administration produced its own bank notes which, after the Japanese surrender, the British diligently collected and stamped "not legal tender".

East of here, a little street, Jalan Pudu Lama, is the location of KL's second most important Hindu shrine, the **Court Hill Ganesh Temple** (free), a small and often crowded place, with stalls outside selling garlands, incense, sweetmeats and charms. This was a favoured stop for visitors on their way to KL's original law courts, once sited nearby. Supplicants prayed to the chief deity, Lord Ganesh, who specializes in the removal of all obstacles to prosperity, peace and success.

The old train station and around

One the city's best-known colonial buildings, the old **Kuala Lumpur train station** now feels distinctly unloved and cut off from its peers. It ought to be easy enough to reach from Merdeka Square, but Jalan Sultan Hishamuddin here becomes a broad, feverishly busy highway, with hardly any designated crossings. It's easier to head southwest from Central Market, across the bridge and down along the western side of the river, past the Dayabumi Complex and the modern General Post Office; eventually you'll come to a small gate opening onto newer platforms at the far northern end of the station. Alternatively, take a Komuter train to the station; if you're on a service which happens to arrive on one of the atmospheric older platforms, you immediately get to take in the arched ceilings, so evocative of those at the main stations in London.

The station was completed in 1911 by A.B. Hubbock and, as with his Jamek Mosque, reflects his inspiration from North Indian Islamic architecture in its meshing spires, minarets and arches. For the best view of the facade, you'll need to get across to the western side of Jalan Sultan Hishamuddin; conveniently, a pedestrian subway links the station with KTM's headquarters opposite – itself an attractive Moorish structure designed by Hubbock, finished around the same time as the station and actually more imposing than its counterpart.

Masjid Negara

Once at the KTM building, you can easily take the opportunity to walk to a few attractions on the fringes of the Lake Gardens, beginning with the **Masjid Negara** (National Mosque; daily 9am–6pm except Fri 2.45–6pm). Opened in

KL's new architecture

The explosion of giant-scale **architecture** projects in and around KL began in the 1970s, when KL's first construction boom gave room for inventive architects to expand on themes suited to its tropical climate. The resulting buildings saw traditional elements interacting with innovative architectural expressions, often to striking effect. One of the earliest examples of this is the **Dayabumi Complex** just south of Merdeka Square. Malay architect Nik Mohammed took modern mosque architecture as his model and produced this tower, whose high-vaulted entrance arches and glistening white open fretwork have become characteristic of progressive Malaysian city architecture.

The architect who best demonstrates the fusing of essentially religious motifs with new design is **Hijjas Kasturi**. His most impressive work is perhaps the **Maybank Building**, where the predominance of white denotes purity, while its great height, sleekness and grandeur are reminiscent of a minaret. In his **Tabung Haji Building**, close to the intersection of Jalan Ampang and Jalan Tun Abdul Razak (and very near the *Nikko* hotel, which he also designed), the five columns supporting the bottle-like structure represent the five pillars of Islam, the single tower unity with God; appropriately, the building is the headquarters of the Pilgrims Fund, which provides Islamic banking services and coordinates matters to do with the Hajj. A more recent and equally striking design of his is the **Telekom Malaysia** headquarters, close to Jalan Klang Lama south of Brickfields, which, from certain angles, resembles a shark's fin slicing through the sky.

These themes were developed throughout the 1990s, during which a trio of buildings, the **National Library**, **Art Gallery** and **Theatre**, on Jalan Tun Razak, have reinterpreted traditional Malay forms. The library, designed by Shamsuddin Mohammed, has a gleaming roof covered in large blue ceramic tiles, the grandeur of which contrasts with the interior's incorporation of everyday cultural symbols: sculpture that utilizes the shapes of traditional earthenware pots, and walls bearing the patterns of the traditional woven *songket* cloth. Another modern take on traditional Malay building styles, the **Bank Muamalat Building**, can be seen on Jalan Melaka, near Masjid Jamek LRT station. Of course, the manic expansion of KL in the 1990s also gave rise to Malaysia's one world-famous icon, with its own Islamic touches, in the **Petronas Twin Towers** (see p.107).

1965, it's starting to look rather dated, but does feature impressive rectangles of white marble bisected by pools of water, and a hall that can hold up to ten thousand worshippers. In the prayer hall, size gives way to decorative prowess, the dome adorned with eighteen points signifying the five pillars of Islam and the thirteen states of Malaysia. To enter as a visitor (between prayers only), you need to be properly dressed: robes can be borrowed (free) from the desk at the mosque entrance.

The Islamic Arts Museum

Just up Jalan Lembah Perdana from the mosque is the ultramodern **Islamic Arts Museum** (daily 10am–6pm; RM10, or RM12 if there are temporary exhibitions; ⓦ www.iamm.org.my). In a city that's frankly lacking in good museums, this well-documented collection is a real standout, housed in an open-plan building with gleaming marble floors; allow around ninety minutes to do it justice. Note that if you're arriving by taxi, you may find that the driver will know only its Malay name, Muzium Kesenian Islam (and if that doesn't work, just ask for the Masjid Negara).

Things begin rather unpromisingly on **level 1** with a mundane collection of dioramas of Muslim holy places. Most interesting of these is the Great Mosque of Xi'an in central China, looking for all the world like a Chinese temple; it's the first of a number of exhibits that give deserved attention to the often neglected subject of Islam in the Far East, a theme continued elsewhere on this level in the India, China and Malay galleries. In the India gallery, devoted to the Moguls, look out in particular for an intricately carved wooden locking mechanism, designed to cloister the harem away from the rest of the world; the China gallery boasts some good examples of porcelain bearing Arabic calligraphy, and yet more Arabic script in scroll paintings on the far wall. Best of all here is the Malay gallery, featuring, among other items, an impressive three-metre-high archway, once part of a house belonging to an Indonesian notable, with black, red and gold lacquering and a trelliswork of leaves as its main motif. Below it is displayed an equally fine trunk that was used as a travelling box by Terengganu royalty. Built of the much-prized *cengal* hardwood, it's decorated in red and gold and bears the names of Islam's revered first four caliphs.

On **level 2**, there are some good displays of richly embroidered textiles and marquetry, as well as some unusual examples of Western European ceramic crockery, influenced by the Islamic world in their design and in some cases actually produced for that market. But what's likely to excite your interest most here is the terrace containing the museum's main **dome**, a blue-and-white affair with floral ornamentation. Built by Iranian craftsmen, it's just one of several gorgeous domes in the building, but the only one that's meant to illustrate the exterior of a grand mosque. Finally, look out for the bizarre reversed dome ceiling, bulging downwards from above – it's the last thing you see as you make your way back to the foyer from the area containing the **gift shop** and Arab **restaurant** (closed Mon), both excellent.

The RMP Museum

Beyond the Islamic Arts Museum, the **RMP Museum** (Tues–Sun 10am–6pm, Fri closed noon–3pm; free), on Jalan Perdana, covers the vivid history of the Malaysian police force. Among the photographs are some fascinating images (c.1900), including a shot of British officers and their local charges on patrol on buffaloes. The museum also has a variety of weapons confiscated from the communists during the Emergency, including a vicious assortment of *parangs* and a curved, bladed implement known as a Sarawak or Iban axe. Once you've had a look around, you can, if you're feeling energetic, continue up Jalan Perdana into the Lake Gardens (see p.112) or head up the flight of steps opposite the museum to the hill where the National Planetarium is located (see p.113).

Little India to Chow Kit Market

Just to the north of Chinatown is **Little India**, still something of a commercial centre for KL's Indian community, though these days it is being eclipsed in that by Brickfields (see p.114). More compact than Chinatown, though equally fascinating, Little India is traditionally the main area in the city for buying garments, especially saris and *songkets*, as well as jewellery.

If you approach from Chinatown, you'll notice Indian restaurants and shops beginning to figure as soon as you head north from Jalan Tun Perak. Only a few steps north from the Masjid Jamek LRT station is **Jalan Melayu**, its name indicative of the former Malay community here; these days it's home to quite a few Indian stores, some selling excellent *burfi* and other sweet confections. Approaching **Jalan Masjid India**, you encounter a popular covered market smaller than the one in Chinatown's Petaling Street, but otherwise not that dissimilar, and selling a few fake accessories too. Further up is **Masjid India**

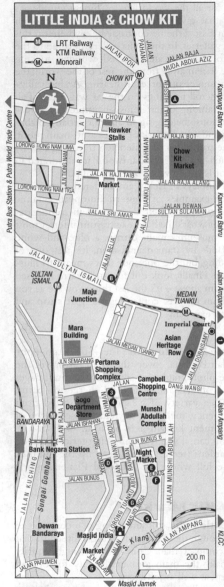

LITTLE INDIA & CHOW KIT

Ⓜ LRT Railway
Ⓜ KTM Railway
Ⓜ Monorail

itself, a reddish-brown Indian-influenced affair dating from the 1960s and now disconcertingly slick after a recent renovation; the first mosque on the site, a mere hut, was built one hundred years earlier. If you continue a few minutes further along the street you come to a little square, to the right (east) of which you'll find plenty of *kedai kopis* and, come evening, street vendors selling food; turn off to the left and you come to Lorong Tuanku Abdul Rahman, whose northern end is dominated by a **night market**, busiest at weekends. Mainly Malay-run, the stalls sell both food and an eclectic range of bits and pieces, from T-shirts to trinkets.

Along Jalan TAR to Chow Kit

Chow Kit Market, most easily reached by Monorail, is some 1500m north of Little India, along **Jalan Tuanku Abdul Rahman** (or **Jalan TAR** as it's always known). If you want to save yourself the walk from Little India, head west to Jalan Raja Laut, where virtually any bus will take you north to Chow Kit (Jalan TAR carries southbound traffic only). The walk along Jalan TAR does, however, offer occasional glimpses of Neoclassical and Art Deco buildings and shops, in various states of repair, as some compensation for the furious traffic. The best-known example of one of these period pieces is the modest **Coliseum Hotel** (at no. 98), where the British owners of the rubber plantations once met to sink tumblers of whisky and water and eat steak. Dating from the 1920s (the adjacent Coliseum Cinema is of the same vintage), it has a rather bare facade for a Neoclassical structure, but the

EATING & DRINKING		ACCOMMODATION	
Capital Café	4	Coliseum	D
Coliseum Café	D	Garden City Hotel	F
Jai Hind	6	Hostel Cosmopolitan	A
The Loft	2	Hotel Champagne	E
Maison	1	Maytower	C
Saravanaa Bhavan	5	Palace	G
Sithique Nasi Kandar	3	Tune	B

interior is genuinely atmospheric – it scarcely seems to have changed for decades. Come here for a cold beer rather than the food, which can be very ordinary.

At the northern end of Jalan TAR, **Chow Kit** has a noticeable Indonesian presence; you'll come across Indonesian music and snacks on sale among the stalls in the sprawling produce and goods **market** that permeates the back alleys east of Jalan TAR, though more prominent are numerous vendors offering more usual items such as sandals, satay or *songkoks* (black caps resembling flattish fezzes, worn by Malay men). Chow Kit has a reputation as a good place to buy **secondhand clothes** (sometimes called "*baju* bundle"), but most clothes outlets offer mundane new items. To track down second-hand garments, you may need to head out of the main market and across to Jalan Haji Taib on the west side of Jalan TAR; here you may chance upon items like Levi's 501s in reasonable condition and at prices that are almost too reasonable to be true – starting from RM20 a pair. The market operates much of the day and into the evening, but note that some locals prefer to give Chow Kit a wide berth after dark, as it's also something of a red-light area.

If you've time on your hands and enjoy a wander, you could head 1km east from Chow Kit (along either Jalan Raja Bot or Jalan Raja Alang) into **Kampung Bahru**, a designated Malay reserve area (there are others throughout the Peninsula) – land that only people whose ID defines them as ethnic Malays can own, and indeed with its own status in law, not under the direct control of the KL city council. Once the area had a distinct village feel but these days it is rapidly modernizing, though Jalan Raja Muda Musa here still features some of the best Malay **food stalls** in the city. Hidden away off a side road to the south is the Kampung Baru LRT station.

The Golden Triangle

The heart of modern KL, the **Golden Triangle** has two main focal points. Many visitors make a bee-line for the huge development that is **KLCC** (Kuala Lumpur City Centre; Ⓦ www.klcc.com.my), which occupies a site once home to the Selangor Turf Club. The chief attraction here is the **Petronas Towers**, soaring above one of KL's best malls, **Suria KLCC**; also here is the city's glossy **aquarium**. But often it's **Bukit Bintang** ("Star Hill"), home to many of KL's best hotels and restaurants, that makes a deeper impression.

The Petronas Towers and the aquarium aside, there are few specific sights in the Golden Triangle, though you may want to head east from Bukit Bintang to **Komploko Budaya Kraf**, the city's largest handicrafts gallery, or – if you've a head for heights – northwest to Bukit Nanas, which affords great views of the city from the communications tower, **Menara KL**. Just to the south of Bukit Bintang, the disused **Pudu Jail** is a perverse sight of sorts, looking like a nightmarish concentration camp, its yellowing walls overlooked by grim watchtowers; you get a bird's-eye view from the Monorail as it swings past. Sections of the exterior wall are still covered with what's claimed to be the longest mural in the world, depicting lush jungles and lazy beaches – the work of the prisoners, who used their hands to apply the paint. Somehow this piece of prime real estate has escaped redevelopment for more than a decade, though the city's draft 2020 development plan has earmarked it for conversion into the same bland mixture of hotels, malls and apartments that characterizes the rest of the area, with only the jail's mosque being preserved.

The Petronas Towers

Much of KLCC is taken up by a mundane park, but there's no mistaking the grandiosity of the **Petronas Towers**, in the northwest of the site, at the

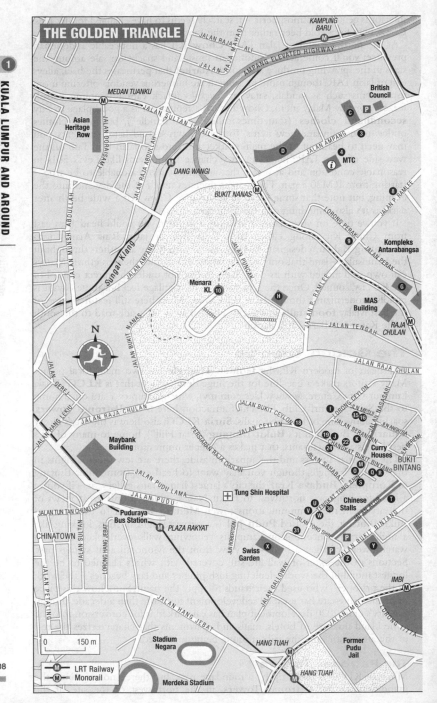

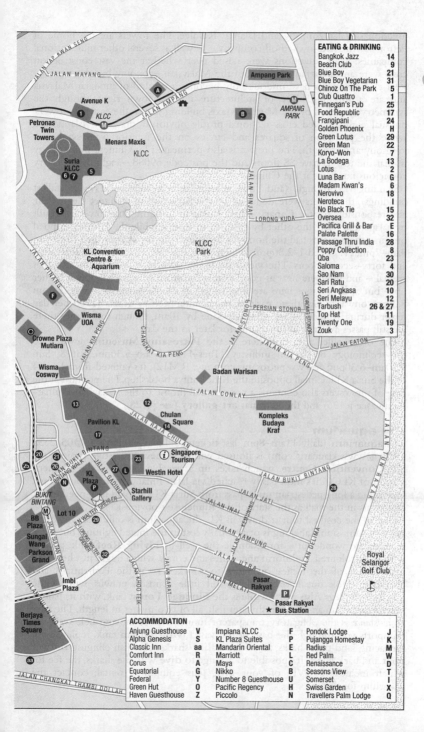

EATING & DRINKING

Bangkok Jazz	14
Beach Club	9
Blue Boy	21
Blue Boy Vegetarian	31
Chinoz On The Park	5
Club Quattro	1
Finnegan's Pub	25
Food Republic	17
Frangipani	24
Golden Phoenix	H
Green Lotus	29
Green Man	22
Koryo-Won	7
La Bodega	13
Lotus	2
Luna Bar	G
Madam Kwan's	6
Nerovivo	18
Neroteca	I
No Black Tie	15
Oversea	32
Pacifica Grill & Bar	E
Palate Palette	16
Passage Thru India	28
Poppy Collection	8
Qba	23
Saloma	4
Sao Nam	30
Sari Ratu	20
Seri Angkasa	10
Seri Melayu	12
Tarbush	26 & 27
Top Hat	11
Twenty One	19
Zouk	3

ACCOMMODATION

Anjung Guesthouse	V	Impiana KLCC	F	Pondok Lodge	J
Alpha Genesis	S	KL Plaza Suites	P	Pujangga Homestay	K
Classic Inn	aa	Mandarin Oriental	E	Radius	M
Comfort Inn	R	Marriott	L	Red Palm	W
Corus	A	Maya	C	Renaissance	D
Equatorial	G	Nikko	B	Seasons View	T
Federal	Y	Number 8 Guesthouse	U	Somerset	I
Green Hut	O	Pacific Regency	H	Swiss Garden	X
Haven Guesthouse	Z	Piccolo	N	Travellers Palm Lodge	Q

junction of Jalan Ampang and Jalan P. Ramlee. The towers are the home of Petronas – the state-owned oil company – as well as several other multinational companies. Many questions were raised over whether the vast construction costs were an unwarranted drain on the Malaysian economy, but the tapering steel-clad structures have undoubtedly become a symbol of modern Malaysia and are a stunning piece of architecture in their own right, though the symmetry is spoiled by the Menara Maxis building just to the east. The towers' unusual eight-pointed cross-sectional profile obviously draws on Islamic art, while the profusion of squares and circles on the interior walls symbolize harmony and strength. The project is also permeated by Chinese numerology in that the towers have 88 floors and the postcode 59088 – eight being a very auspicious number for the Chinese.

Standing 452m high (and still ranking among the world's very tallest buildings), the towers were designed by the Argentinean architect Cesar Pelli, also responsible for the Canary Wharf Tower in London. One tower was built by a Japanese team, the other by rivals from Korea; while the Japanese topped out first, the Koreans had the honour of engineering the **skybridge** (Tues–Sun 9am–7pm, Fri closed 1–2.30pm), which joins the towers at both the forty-first and forty-second floors. The views from the skybridge are actually not that special – and nowhere near as good as those as from Menara KL, much higher up – but at least passes here are free, issued in the basement of tower 2 from 8.30am onwards. Get there early if you're interested as tickets (1700 per day, fewer during Ramadan) are often all gone by 10am, though sometimes there are still passes available at lunchtime for later in the day.

The other chief attraction here is the **Petrosains Museum**, devoted to the technology of the oil industry (Tues–Fri 9.30am–5.30pm, Sat & Sun 9.30am–6.30pm; Ⓦ www.petrosains.com.my; RM12); it's entered from level 4 of the Suria KLCC mall opposite the Kinokuniya bookshop. The podium at the base of the towers also contains a concert hall (home to the Malaysian Philharmonic; see p.126) and the Petronas **art gallery** (see p.128).

The aquarium

KL's **aquarium** (daily 11am–8pm, last tickets sold at 7pm; RM38; ☎03/2333 1888, Ⓦ www.klaquaria.com) is housed within its newest prestige project, the **KL Convention Centre**, which takes up a sizeable chunk of the southern section of KLCC. It's most easily reached via Jalan Pinang, though you can get here using a long pedestrian underpass from Suria KLCC (you may need to ask directions in the mall as the start of the tunnel isn't obvious).

One of the costliest tourist draws in KL, the aquarium is only just worth the price of admission. Labelling is occasionally lost in the muted lighting, but some sections are wonderful – for example the well-lit **Living Reef** tank, packed with multicoloured, multiform anemones and corals, which might just help you make sense of the riches on view to snorkellers at the Perhentians and elsewhere; look out here for delightful little crimson prawns with white tentacles and legs. Also worthwhile is the **Flooded Forest** tank, with its pair of hefty Amazonian arapaima freshwater fish, all of two metres in length. The *pièce de résistance* is the obligatory transparent tunnel, whose moving-belt walkway transports you through the base of the vast **Living Ocean** tank, replete with menacing sand tiger sharks, all with parasitic sharksucker fish clinging to their front and back edges. It's possible to arrange to **dive** with the sharks, the fee for which includes a DVD of your dive, plus equipment rental; contact the aquarium for details.

Bukit Bintang

Even if you're on a tight budget, you'll probably spend a fair amount of your time wandering – as many locals do – the area around the junction of Jalan Bukit Bintang and Jalan Sultan Ismail. A profusion of largely modest malls here offer plenty of affordable **shopping** (the notable exception is the gigantic Pavilion KL mall, packed with designer outlets), while the pavement around the Lot 10 Mall, east of the junction, has evolved into **Bintang Walk**, home to a parade of smart cafés, not to mention debonair locals. By night the centre of attention, at least as regards dining, switches to nearby **Jalan Alor**, which boasts some of the best Chinese eating in the city; close by on Changkat Bukit Bintang and Tengkat Tong Shin are more excellent restaurants, serving up a variety of cuisines. A little further to the north, the junction of Jalan Sultan Ismail and **Jalan P. Ramlee** features some of the slickest **clubs** in the city.

Menara KL and Bukit Nanas

The area north of the western stretch of Jalan Raja Chulan is dominated by forested **Bukit Nanas**, on which stands the **Menara KL** communications tower (daily 9am–10pm, last tickets 9.30pm; RM20; Ⓦwww.menarakl.com .my). At 421m, the tower offers vistas east across the Petronas Towers to the blue peaks of the Titiwangsa range that marks the start of the Peninsula's interior, and west along the unmitigated urban sprawl of the Klang Valley; dusk is an especially worthwhile time to come, as the city lights up. Though free audio guides describe what can be seen in each direction, it's probably best to hold off visiting until you've explored KL enough to have some familiarity with the city's layout.

You might also find it worthwhile to combine a visit with tea or a meal at the revolving *Seri Angkasa* restaurant at the top (see p.120), though most people head to the tower's **observation deck** just below. Both are contained in the bulbous portion of the tower, which was designed in the shape of a *gasing*, the Malay spinning top. Fixed binoculars (free) on the observation deck allow you to espy city life in minute detail, even picking out pedestrians narrowly avoiding being run over they scurry across the streets of Chinatown.

To the west of the tower's base, on Jalan Bukit Nanas, are a fine collection of **colonial school buildings**, including the St John's Institution (1904) and Bukit Nanas Convent School, which remain among KL's top schools. If you're admiring the tower at night, note that the lights around the tower's crown change colour for special occasions – green for Muslim festivals, purple for Deepavali and red for the Chinese New Year.

The usual **approach** to the tower is via Jalan Puncak, to the south; bus #B110 from Central Market or #B113 from Jalan Sultan Ismail in Bukit Bintang will drop you close by at the junction of Jalan Raja Chulan and Jalan P. Ramlee, or you could walk from the Raja Chulan Monorail station. With a couple of flights of steps as shortcuts, it only takes ten minutes to walk from the foot of the hill to the tower, though there are also free shuttles every fifteen minutes from the start of the access road. On the way up you pass the **Flying Fox** (daily 10am–7pm; RM30; Ⓣ03/2020 5444), run by the New Zealand bungee-jump specialist A.J. Hackett, on which participants are strapped into a harness on a steel hawser and then allowed to glide gently along the hillside. One other attraction bears mention: free guided **nature walks** through the jungle of Bukit Nanas, leaving from the base of the tower at 11am, 12.30pm, 2.30pm and 4.30pm. Despite what it says on the literature, you don't have to have a Menara KL ticket to join in.

Kompleks Budaya Kraf and Badan Warisan

Just south of KLCC, Jalan Conlay has two places worth making time for. Most people who come this way are bound for **Kompleks Budaya Kraf** (daily 9am–6pm; free), devoted to the country's wide range of arts and crafts, including silver-, pewter- and brass-ware, batik, woodcarvings and ceramics. This is a good opportunity to see excellent examples of Malaysia's crafts in one place, and to do some serious souvenir shopping. There's also a small **crafts museum** within the complex (RM3).

If you're heading this way, it would be a shame not to pop into **Badan Warisan** at 2 Jalan Stonor (Mon–Sat 10am–5.30pm; free; ⓦ www.badanwarisan .org.my). This is Malaysia's architecture conservation trust, campaigning to preserve the rich heritage of shophouses, temples and colonial buildings that developers and many municipal authorities seem intent on destroying. It's housed in a 1925 colonial mansion which contains a gift shop, good for books on local architecture, and hosts occasional temporary exhibitions, focusing on anything from colonial furniture to restoration work. Also in the grounds is the beautifully restored **Rumah Penghulu Abu Seman**, a traditional timber house that once belonged to a Malay chieftain. Moved here from Kedah, it can only be visited on a guided tour (11am & 3pm; RM5).

The Lake Gardens

West of the colonial quarter, the **Lake Gardens** (aka Taman Tasik Perdana), are an expanse of close-cropped lawns, gardens and hills, originally laid out in the 1890s by the British state treasurer to Malaya, Alfred Venning, though much of the landscaping has been carried out in the last 25 years. The park, spread around a lake, incorporates a number of sights – including the National Monument, the Butterfly Park and Bird Park and the National Planetarium – while just 1km west of the National Monument is Malaysia's Parliament House.

Most people enter the gardens either from the north, along **Jalan Parlimen**, or from the south using **Jalan Lembah Perdana** (where Masjid Negara and the Islamic Arts Museum are located) or **Jalan Damansara** (site of the National Museum; a footbridge connects the museum with the planetarium). Note that both Jalan Parlimen and Jalan Damansara are busy highways, and that many of the gardens' attractions are a little way from the main road; it's easiest to get here by taxi or bus (Jalan Parlimen is served by Metrobus service #6 from Jalan Tun Perak in Chinatown).

In the gardens

Opposite the main entrance, off Jalan Parlimen, is the **National Monument**, a great bronze sculpture designed by Felix de Weldon, better known for his work on the Iwo Jima Memorial in Washington DC. The monument was constructed in 1966 to commemorate the nation's heroes, yet strangely the seven military figures protruding from it appear European rather than from any of the various Malaysian ethnic groups who fought in World War II and during the Emergency. Reached by a path leading up from the car park, the monument stands in a tranquil spot surrounded by a moat with fountains and ornamental pewter water lilies. Back at the car park is the **Taman ASEAN Sculpture Garden**, to which neighbouring countries have contributed abstract works in marble, iron, wood and bamboo.

Five minutes' walk south of the National Monument is the **Butterfly Park** (daily 9am–6pm; RM17), an unexpected delight featuring a large collection of amazingly colourful butterflies – some with fifteen-centimetre wing spans

– flitting around a pretty garden under netting; just as impressive are the giant koi carp in the garden's ponds. Also worth seeing is the **Bird Park**, which bills itself as the world's largest covered bird park (daily 9am–6pm; RM39; Ⓦwww.klbirdpark.com); retrace your steps from the Butterfly Park to Jalan Cenderawasih and turn left uphill, following the road for 200m to the Bird Park entrance. Within, walkways loop around streams and pools taking in the enclosures of indigenous species such as hornbills, the brahminy kite and the hawk eagle, and specimens of the largest pheasant in the world, the argus pheasant, not to mention parrots, toucans, flamingoes and birds of prey. If you're into tropical plants, you'll love the **Orchid** and **Hibiscus** (*bunga raya*) **Gardens** (daily 9am–6pm; Sat & Sun RM1, otherwise free), just north of the Bird Park, where hundreds of plants are grown and sold.

The main road through the gardens then weaves down past a field of deer, to the **Tun Abdul Razak Memorial**, a house built for the second Malaysian prime minister, who is commemorated by a collection of memorabilia inside, while his motorboat and golf trolley are ceremonially positioned outside. From here, you're only twenty minutes from the southern entrance. Beyond is the **lake** itself, which takes nearly an hour to walk around.

The planetarium

On a hill to the east of the lake and reachable on foot using the steps opposite the RMP Museum (see p.105) is yet another public edifice with obligatory Islamic-influenced architecture, the **National Planetarium** (daily except Mon 9.30am–4.15pm; RM1). A rather unconvincing evocation of a teleport chamber at the front entrance gives onto a series of halls containing two planetariums (RM2) plus a Space Theatre showing wide-screen IMAX films, not necessarily about space (RM6). Those with cast-iron stomachs might care to experience the Space Ball (closed noon–2pm; RM2), a human-sized gyroscopic device that spins volunteers around to the amusement of onlookers. Finally, there's a weird UV-lit lift labelled Galeri Pemandangan, which takes you up a minaret-like tower to a viewing gallery. From here there are panoramic views over the planetarium's blue onion dome and the surrounding Lake Gardens, as well across to KL Sentral and the rest of downtown. Having taken your fill of the planetarium, you could take the pedestrian bridge south to the National Museum (see p.114).

The Carcosa Seri Negara

The **Carcosa Seri Negara** is KL's most exclusive hotel, secluded up a winding hill road to the west of the lake. This former colonial residence of the British governor of the Malay States comprises two elegant whitewashed mansions with Neoclassical touches – the "Carcosa", built in 1904 for Sir Frank Swettenham; and the "Seri Negara", formerly called the "King's House", which was used for guests. At independence, Malaysia's first prime minister, Tunku Abdul Rahman, gifted the buildings to Britain who used them as the official residence of the British high commissioner. Abdul Rahman's successor, Dr Mahathir, secured the return of the buildings, and in 1989, after an inaugural visit by Queen Elizabeth II, the mansion and guest-house became a hotel.

The hotel's oh-so-English **cream tea** is a fitting reward for a hot day's wander around the Lake Gardens – as long as you don't mind paying RM70 a head for the privilege. Just don't turn up looking sweaty and dishevelled, as you will be if you attempt to tramp up here along Persiaran Mahameru, which starts on Jalan Damansara south of the Lake Gardens; it's much better to take a taxi.

The National Museum

Built in 1963, the **National Museum** (Muzium Negara; daily 9am–6pm; RM2; Ⓦ www.museum.gov.my) has a sweeping roof characteristic of northern Malay architecture, which somehow sets the tone for the ethnographic exhibits for which the museum was best known. But following the recent closure of the National Museum of History, the role of showcasing Malaysia through a historical prism has fallen on the National Museum, requiring a wholesale revamp that saw many of the ethnographic items being locked away. Still, the four new galleries are reasonably entertaining and worth at least an hour's browse. The museum is best reached by taxi; ironically, it's impossible to get to it from KL Sentral – diagonally across on Jalan Travers – because of the lack of a northern exit from the station.

The main entrance gives onto the **first floor**, where you turn right to reach **Gallery A**, packed with rather dry prehistoric artefacts – Paleolithic and Neolithic stone tools and axe-heads, Bronze Age drums and bells, plus some burial urns from East Malaysia, and so forth. **Gallery B** is devoted to the early Malay kingdoms, in particular the Melaka Sultanate, with a particularly good collection of *keris* and items recovered from sunken trading ships.

The pace picks up on the **second floor**, where **Gallery C** covers the colonial era, beginning with the Portuguese in Melaka. Amid the reconstructions of Portuguese fortifications and specimens of matchlocks and cannonballs, look out for a fine seventeenth-century German Bellarmine jug depicting a bearded face – characteristic of such jugs – on the neck of the vessel. There are more examples of munitions left subsequently by the Dutch, and then some exploration of the British "occupation" of the Straits Settlements (Singapore, Melaka and Penang) and "interference" in all the Malay States. The signing of the Pangkor treaty in Perak, which established a legal blueprint for the Resident system (see p.171), is depicted in a diorama; not far away is a good example of a *bunga mas*, a sort of gold miniature tree that the northern Malay states once sent as tribute to Thailand. Another metal, namely tin, dominates the final part of the gallery, which focuses on the growth of the commodity-based industries that still matter hugely to the Malaysian economy today; in the large section on tin-mining, look out for some ridiculous animal-shaped coinage – including a thirty-centimetre crocodile – supposedly used in Selangor and Perak in the eighteenth century.

Still on the second floor, **Gallery D** wraps things up with a rather bland look at how modern Malaysia came to be. Here you can learn about the nation's founding fathers, of various races, whose names you see on street signs in Chinatown and elsewhere downtown, though there's only cursory coverage of the Emergency or the reasons behind Singapore's exit from the Federation in 1965.

Exiting the **ground floor**, where the **gift shop** is located, turn right to reach the footbridge to the planetarium (see p.113) and a pink annexe housing the **Malay World** gallery (free), covering the Malay-speaking peoples of Southeast Asia and further afield, with some nice examples of *songket* and batik. Below it is the most interesting thing here, though, an excellent little museum of **Orang Asli woodcarving** (free), containing not only an edifying run-down of all the indigenous groups in the Peninsula but also some fantastic totem-pole-like objects and grotesque face masks such as the one-fanged *moyang melor*, which were used in rites of ancestor worship.

Brickfields and KL Sentral

Located 2km south of the city centre, the **Brickfields** district was first settled by Tamils employed to build the railways, and named after the brickworks which lined the rail tracks. Even today, the area retains a strong South Indian presence, particularly noticeable along Jalan Tun Sambanthan – the main thoroughfare – especially on the western stretch beyond Jalan Travers. Brickfields remains largely a laid-back residential neighbourhood, though with the creation of **KL Sentral** station and its two attendant five-star hotels, the area shows signs of slowly going upmarket. Still, a wander through the streets south of Jalan Tun Sambanthan reveals a profusion of old mission schools, churches and temples, as well as a few good places to eat (see p.121). Arriving by Monorail at KL Sentral puts you right on Jalan Tun Sambanthan, along which the original rail line once ran.

One of the most interesting shrines is the Hindu **Kandaswamy Temple** on Jalan Scott, right at the eastern edge of Brickfields and with the Monorail curling around the back. Reminiscent of Chinatown's Sri Maha Mariamman Temple, it was originally built by the Sri Lankan Tamil community in the 1900s, though the present structure was consecrated in 1997. It's all the more appealing for being little visited by tourists; just don't expect to find anyone on hand who can explain the layout, which includes, in the far right corner of the entrance wall, a collection of nine garlanded deities representing the planets. Not far away on Jalan Scott is one of several independent visual arts venues in KL, the Wei-ling Gallery (see p.128).

It's also worth heading to the **Maha Vihara Temple** on Jalan Berhala. A serene affair with a prominent white stupa, it is the headquarters of Sinhalese Buddhism in Malaysia. Close by is the **Temple of Fine Arts**, a substantial Indian cultural centre featuring a crafts shop, a terrific vegetarian restaurant (see p.121) and concerts of Indian music and dance. North up Jalan Berhala and around the corner is another tranquil place of worship, **Zion Cathedral**, a church funded and built by Lutheran Tamils in the 1920s and featuring period pews and the original 1927 German-made church bell – though it cracked a few years ago and is now displayed in the grounds.

Eating

Food is without doubt one of the highlights of any visit to KL. There are simply many more opportunities to enjoy high-calibre cooking here, in a variety of local and international styles, than anywhere else in the country, and whether you dine in a chic bistro-style restaurant or at a humble roadside stall, prices are almost always very reasonable.

Despite plenty of scope for cosmopolitan, upmarket dining, for many locals eating is still fundamentally about Malay, Chinese and Indian **street food**. The best-known food stalls are held in the same kind of reverence as a top-flight restaurant might be in a Western city, and people will travel across KL just to seek out a stall whose take on a particular dish is said to be better than anyone else's. If you find customers lining up to partake of some stall's spring rolls or *laksa*, it's a sure-fire indicator of quality. Stalls, whether on the street or collected into **food courts** (found in or close to major office blocks and shopping malls), are your best bets for inexpensive, satisfying meals, as are **kedai kopis**, also very common though a little thin on the ground in the Golden Triangle.

KL's **restaurants**, ranging from characterful little affairs in beautifully refurbished shophouses to banqueting halls in five-star hotels, are an equally vital part of the food experience. Be aware, however, that price and decor are not a watertight indicator of consistency or quality, and that service can be hesitant even in big hotels.

Chinatown and around

There are some superb food **stalls** in Chinatown, serving up everything from rich yet subtle *bak kut teh* (pork-rib consommé, flavoured with herbs) to cooling sweet treats like *cendol*. The stalls here aren't always that easy for foreign visitors to get to grips with, however, particularly when some of the best lurk in the market alleys between Jalan Tun H.S. Lee and Jalan Petaling, and may be signed

▲ Fruit-seller in Chinatown

only in Chinese or not at all. Still, you can get an excellent taster of how stalls operate, and of street food, in the *Tang City Food Court* (see p.118).

Otherwise, the area has plenty of *kedai kopis* and a few cheap or mid-priced **restaurants**, with a few particularly touristy places at the eastern end of Jalan Hang Lekir. You're not limited to Chinese food either, since the fringes of Chinatown, especially the zone north of Jalan Hang Lekir and around the Central Market, feature plenty of **Indian** and **mamak** places.

Canteen Room 8 Jalan Hang Kasturi. This attempt at a stylish modern café is best visited in the morning, when it serves up a range of cooked Western breakfasts (around RM7), though unfortunately the coffee is instant. A mixture of Asian and Western light meals is on offer the rest of the day. Mon–Sat 7am–7pm.

Five Plus Two Maju Jalan Hang Lekiu. The unusual name (*maju* means "progress") apparently came during a moment of prayer to someone associated with this Indian *kedai kopi*. While the food may not be divinely inspired, it does feature reliable *nasi campur*, and some days there's also fish-head curry and South Indian *apam* pancakes. Noodles can be fried to order. Closed evenings and all day Sun.

Hameeds Café Klang bus station. Busy *kedai kopi* serving tandoori chicken, curries and rice dishes; fish-head curry is the house speciality. Open till late.

Ikopi first floor, 6 Jalan Panggong. Smart café with modern decor and parquet flooring, serving up a range of pricey speciality coffees (from RM14) plus more affordable lattes, macchiatos and so forth (around RM5). A few local and Western snacks available. If they're not busy, staff can tell you about their brewing techniques and the unusual gadgets involved. Daily except Tues noon–10pm.

Lai Foong Corner of Jalan Tun Tan Cheng Lock and Jalan Tun H S Lee. One of the most popular *kedai kopis* in Chinatown, to which locals flock for its noodle and rice dishes – in particular the Hainanese beef noodle, flavoured with herbs and served with not just beef slices but also tripe, should you want it. Mon–Sat 7.30am–5pm.

Mangrove Food Court Central Market. The outlets here, specializing in food from different corners of the Peninsula, can be indifferent, but the Rasa Kelantan stall is outstanding, serving east-coast specialities like *nasi kerabu* and *nasi dagang*, plus a range of curries and unusual stir-fries such as *pucuk paku* (edible fern). For dessert, the *Thai Corner* stall is as good a place as any to try to get to grips with Malay sweets (*kuih, bubur pulut hitam*, and so forth).

O Kawan 58 Jalan Hang Lekiu. A small, pleasant Chinese-run café offering local breakfasts – softboiled eggs, toast with *kaya* – plus home-made cake and, for lunch, staple fare like *nasi lemak* and *laksa*. Mon–Fri 8.30am–6pm, Sat 9.30am–2pm.

Old China Café 11 Jalan Balai Polis ☎03/2072 5915, ⊛www.oldchina.com.my. Nonya restaurant atmospherically housed in a 1920s shophouse which was once home to KL's laundry guild; much of the decor, including the saloon-style swing doors at the entrance, is original and lovingly preserved. Among must-trys are classic dishes such as *itek tim*, duck soup; *babi pong teh*, pork cooked with soy sauce and preserved soybeans; *chap chye*, the classic Nonya veg stir-fry; and desserts such as *bubur cha cha* or sago with *gula melaka*. Not expensive either – RM50 is ample to feed two. Daily 11.30am–11pm.

Precious Old China Upstairs in the southwestern corner of Central Market ☎03/2273 7372. A much posher version of *Old China Café*, packed with artwork and antique furniture, though not as atmospheric as the original. The menu is virtually the same except no pork is served. Daily 11.30am–9.30pm.

Purple Cane Tea House Third floor (lift access only), 6 Jalan Panggong. Chinese tea shop where you can appreciate a variety of speciality teas, from relatively mundane green tea to varieties such as *pu'er*, reddish-brown like some of Malaysia's jungle rivers and imbued with a strong smoky flavour. They also do bizarre concoctions of tea, egg and various fruit flavours – actually pretty palatable – plus some rice and noodle snacks. Their teas are available to buy in leaf form from their shop around the corner at 11 Jalan Sultan. Daily 11am–7pm; shop daily except Tues 10am–10pm.

Santa 7 Jalan Tun H.S. Lee. Maintain a healthy dietary fibre intake at this otherwise unremarkable Indian *kedai kopi* which, unusually, offers freshly made chapatis and chickpea curry, plus other, more commonly found curries and rice dishes.

Seng Kee 50 Jalan Sultan. Frenetically busy, quintessentially Chinese restaurant serving up great Cantonese fare – everything from standards like beef with *kai lan* to occasional river-fish dishes, depending on supply. The house speciality, however, is *loh shee fun*, which unappetizingly translates as mouse noodles but is actually fantastic: stubby lengths of noodle fried with soy sauce, served in a clay pot and topped with pork crackling and a raw egg. Daily 10.30am till late.

Sri Ganesa Next to the Court Hill Ganesh Temple. You can't site an Indian restaurant next to a major Hindu shrine without it thriving. This one is indeed frequently packed and boasts as many as two dozen offerings in its vast *nasi campur* spread, including fried spicy cauliflower, green egg curry and other meaty and veggie options.

🏃 Tang City Food Court Jalan Hang Lekir. A fine collection of fairly priced, tourist-friendly stalls, all recommended, from the Economy Mixed Rice *campur*-type spread at the front onwards. This is a great place to try prawn *mee* (available from the Lim Kee stall) or *yong tau foo* (available at a couple of other stalls – scan the signs). For afters, try the whimsically named

Summer Shala'la stall at the front on the left, which does souped-up versions of local desserts, such *as batu campur* augmented with various fruit toppings.

Wan Fo Yuan Vegetarian Restaurant Jalan Panggong. Tip-top though unprepossessing a/c place, lurking behind dark glass doors. The extensive picture menu features teppenyaki ribs, fried goose rice and other "meaty" treats – all made with soya – or gluten-based substitutes or occasionally yam, and often boasting depths of smoky flavour that seem miraculous considering the vegetarian ingredients. Most dishes cost around RM10 (rice or noodle one-plate meals RM6) and servings are generous. Daily 10am–10pm.

The Golden Triangle and Kampung Bahru

Besides numerous upmarket restaurants, the Golden Triangle also boasts some of the best Chinese food stalls in KL, along **Jalan Alor**. The street actually has a double layer of food outlets, being lined with mid-priced, open-air Chinese restaurants which have stalls and tables arranged in front of them. It's all pretty informal: even if you're in one of the restaurants you can order from the stalls outside, as long as you can explain where your table is. A few places open around lunchtime, but things really gets going from late afternoon onwards, and the stalls stay open right into the small hours.

As for the food, KL Chinese absolutely swear by the Hokkien noodles (*fu-kien meen* in Cantonese), comprising egg noodles fried in lard, seasoned with dark soy sauce and garnished with prawn, pork and fish-cake slices, and greens; look for a popular stall serving it near the Changkat Bukit Bintang end of the road. For the really daring, there are at least two stalls serving up frog porridge: rice gruel containing, well, bits of frog, actually hard to distinguish from chicken.

As for inexpensive eats elsewhere in the Golden Triangle, there are convenient stalls on the fourth floor of the Sungai Wang Plaza, close to the junction of Jalan Sultan Ismail and Jalan Imbi, and also plenty of stalls in the food courts at Suria KLCC. Close to Jalan Alor, there are a number of *mamak* places on Jalan Nagasari.

On the northern fringes of the Golden Triangle, **Kampung Bahru** is noteworthy for hosting one of KL's most extensive collections of Malay stalls, on and around Jalan Raja Muda Musa; they're easily reached using the Kampung Baru LRT stop. Among these is the *Nasi Lemak Antarabangsa* outlet, which devotees say does the best *nasi lemak* breakfast in the city. The stall shuts by 11am, but many of the other stalls are open late into the evening.

Blue Boy Vegetarian On an unnamed lane off Jalan Tong Shin. Occupying the ground floor of an apartment block is this collection of stalls serving veggie versions of street food – everything from chicken rice to *asam laksa*. Daily 7.30am–9.30pm.

🏃 Chinoz On The Park G47, Suria KLCC ℡03/2166 8277. Smart, convivial café-restaurant with generally Mediterranean-slanted food, from Lebanese lamb wraps to various pizzas (some of the best in town, from RM25), plus a good range of cocktails. The icing on the cake is the

great location facing KLCC's kitsch musical fountains. Daily 8am–midnight.

Food Republic Level 1, Pavilion KL mall. A spin-off of the Singapore chain of branded food courts, this expansive, slick place features some 25 outlets specializing in food from around the Peninsula or East Asia in general, with several proper restaurants on the fringes – including a franchise of the British chain Yo! Sushi plus a member of the Singapore-based chain Crystal Jade Kitchen, serving Hong Kong-style noodles and *dim sum*. Always busy.

Golden Phoenix *Hotel Equatorial*, Jalan Sultan Ismail ☏03/2161 7777. Top-flight non-halal Cantonese restaurant (with a touch of Sichuan) serving up good seafood dishes. The *belacan* pomfret (decidedly not mainland Chinese fare) is worth tackling – if you've never had pungent *belacan* before, you'll either adore it or decide you'll never touch the stuff again. Daily noon–2.30pm & 6.30–10.30pm.

Green Lotus Café Jalan Walter Grenier ☏03/2141 3007. Nestling anonymously behind a tiny oriental garden is this place with amusingly chichi decor – red drapes, a wall-mounted moose's head and faux Baroque mirror – and something of a gay Chinese hangout. The menu features a good pan-East Asian mix with dishes from RM10; portions are generous. Mon–Sat 5–11pm, Sun 4–11pm.

Koryo-Won Fourth floor, Suria KLCC mall ☏03/2171 2189; Starhill Gallery ☏03/2143 2189. Halal Korean restaurant specializing in good old Korean barbecues, done to a turn at your table. Not cheap: prices start at RM65 per person, excluding rice. Daily 10am–10pm.

La Bodega Lot C3.06.00, Level 3, in the side Connection block at Pavilion KL mall ☏03/2148 8018, ⊛www.bodega.com.my. Like the original setup in Bangsar, this serves up tapas plus deli food (including all-day breakfasts and great sandwiches and cakes) and modern European fare. Daily 8am–2am.

Lotus 2 Jalan Binjai. Phenomenal 24hr *mamak* joint, the size of a supermarket, that's a major social hub by evening and into the post-clubbing hours. They do all the usual South Indian favourites plus *nasi kandar*, with some of the food laid out in self-service spreads.

Madam Kwan's Lot 420/421, Level 4, Suria KLCC mall ☏03/2026 2297. If street stalls and *kedai kopis* don't appeal, come here to try Madam Kwan's elaborate takes on classic local fare, from *nasi lemak* to chicken rice, though naturally at elevated prices: main courses start at RM10. Daily 11am–10.30pm.

Neroteca Ground floor, Somerset Apartments, 8 Lorong Ceylon ☏03/2070 0530. Relaxed sister restaurant to *Nerovivo* just up the hill, and cheaper too, serving deli food, including sandwiches and (unlike its pork-free sibling) parma ham. Daily 9.30am–midnight, though Tues from 6.30pm.

Nerovivo 3a Jalan Ceylon ☏03/2070 3120. This upmarket restaurant is among the best Italian places in KL, with chic modern decor and an extensive menu including plenty of meat and seafood options. Though they can be a little inconsistent, they do generally produce great pizzas. Not cheap – pizzas and pasta start at RM25, while main courses start

around the RM55 mark – and not great for an intimate meal either, as both the background music and conversation can be pretty loud. Daily noon till late, except Sat closed lunchtime.

🏃 **Oversea** 84–88 Jalan Imbi ☏03/2148 7567. Established and much-loved Cantonese restaurant, well known for excellent roast meats such as *char siew*, plus *dim sum* at lunchtime and great seafood, including its trademark (non-Cantonese) *asam* fish head. Daily 11.30am–2.30pm & 5.30–10.30pm.

Pacifica Grill & Bar *Mandarin Oriental*, KLCC ☏03/2179 8882. Specializing in pricey modern European cuisine with Asian influences, this place is particularly strong on fish and steaks. Mon–Fri noon–2.30pm & 7–11pm, Sat 7–11pm, Sun (brunch) 11.30am–3.30pm.

🏃 **Palate Palette** 21 Jalan Mesui ☏03/2142 2148, ⊛www.palatepalette .com. You couldn't wish for a friendlier and more unpretentious venue despite the lofty aims of combining creativity in cuisine and the visual arts, as the snazzy decor attests. The menu encompasses a wide range of fare with fusion touches – everything from Thai roast beef sandwich to lamb chops with black bean sauce. Mains from RM20, with cheaper sandwiches, soups and salads available, and a vast range of cocktails; portions tend to be small. Daily except Mon noon till late.

Passage Thru India 4 Jalan Delima, close to the junction of Jalan Bukit Bintang and Jalan Tun Razak ☏03/2145 0366. Well-regarded place drawing its menu from every part of the subcontinent. Prices are reasonable – tandoori chicken will set you back around RM18. Daily 11.30am–2.30pm & 6.30–11pm.

Qba *Westin Hotel*, 199 Jalan Bukit Bintang ☏03/2731 8333. Latin American-themed restaurant with generous portions and a cosy ambience, though on the pricey side – plenty on the menu is around the RM50 mark. Put together your own grill platters featuring steak, chicken or seafood (charged by weight) or go for lighter tapas or other options. Daily from 5pm till late.

🏃 **Sao Nam** 21 Tengkat Tong Shin ☏03/2144 1225, ⊛www.saonam.com.my. You don't have to be mad about Vietnamese food to warm to this unpretentious restaurant. Beneath wall posters extolling the collectivist life, definitive beef *pho* noodles are served up, alongside delightful mangosteen salad – a house speciality – and, to wash it down afterwards, Vietnamese drip-style coffee, brewed in a filter placed over your cup. Good-value weekday set lunches too (RM20). Tues–Sun 12.30–2.30pm & 7–10.30pm.

Sari Ratu 42–4 Jalan Sultan Ismail ⊤03/2141 1811. Indonesian restaurant serving good-value food from around the archipelago, including *nasi padang*. Daily 11am–11pm.

Seri Angkasa Revolving atop Menara KL ⊤03/2020 5055. The buffets, which are what most customers end up going for (lunch RM70, tea RM40, dinner RM150), aren't that spectacular – but the views are. Smart casual dress required (no shorts, sleeveless tops or sandals). Daily: lunch noon–3pm, tea 3.30–5.30pm, dinner 6.30–11.30pm; Sat & Sun additional brunch (11.30am–3pm; RM80) and high tea (3.30–5.30pm; RM50) options.

Tarbush LG16, Starhill Gallery ⊤03/2144 6393; 138 Jalan Bukit Bintang ⊤03/2142 8558. A classy Lebanese par excellence, with a particularly elegant feel at the Starhill Gallery. There's plenty for carnivores, including classic *shish tawook* (grilled chicken breast) plus a best-of-everything mixed grill at around RM35, as well as loads for veggies if you order up meze (selections, all at around RM12,

include hummus, stuffed vine leaves and tabbouleh). The fruity milkshakes are as luscious as anything sold on the streets of Beirut. Daily 11am till late.

Top Hat 7 Jalan Kia Peng ⊤03/2142 8611. Classy restaurant based in a renovated 1930s mansion. Nonya food dominates proceedings, from the *kuih pai tee* appetizers (their signature dish, thanks to the resemblance to top hats) to mainstays like *laksa*, but there's a fair amount of Western and fusion fare as well. Desserts, mainly gateaux, are particularly sinful. A wide range of three-course set meals can be good value. Daily 11.30am–10.45pm.

Twenty One 21 Changkat Bukit Bintang ⊤03/2142 0021, ⊛www.twentyone.com.my. A breakaway from *La Bodega*, this trendy restaurant specializes in clever fusion cuisine – almond-crusted rack of lamb, for example, with more straightforward risottos, salads and plenty of cakes for dessert. Quality varies but is reliable by and large; mains from RM30. Reserve at weekends. Daily noon till late.

Little India, Chow Kit and beyond

Little India is a good area for both Indian and Malay food – there are a number of inexpensive Indian restaurants and sweetmeat shops along Jalan Melayu, while in and around Lorong TAR's *pasar malam* are quite a few Malay food stalls and Indian *kedai kopis*. There's also a useful food court opposite the *Palace Hotel* that stays open late. A few truly venerable *kedai kopis*, some housed in equally venerable shophouses, can be found along hectic Jalan TAR, while there are more stalls, Malay and even Indonesian, around Chow Kit Market.

The only upmarket eating in the area is at the so-called **Asian Heritage Row** on Jalan Doraisamy, close to Medan Tuanku Monorail station and the *Imperial* hotel. A terrace of refurbished 1920s shophouses, it's home to a string of smart restaurants, bars and clubs, though unfortunately the quality is very patchy. Unless otherwise noted, the locations of the places are on the map on p.106.

A J Kompleks Damai, 50 Jalan Lumut, off Jalan Ipoh ⊤03/4044 8888; see map, pp.84–85. A Malay diner like no other, with funky modern decor on the walls and a soundtrack of world music or vintage Malay tunes. They do amazing buffet spreads, good value at RM10–15 depending on what you have, which feature several fish curries and the likes of *ayam kicap* (chicken and potatoes cooked in soy sauce), *tempeh goreng* (fried fermented bean cakes) and *ulam* (Malay salad). The place is just a few minutes' walk south from Titiwangsa station; head through Pekeliling bus station and past the *Vistana* hotel, then turn left. Mon–Sat 7.45am till late; shorter hours in Ramadan.

Capital Café 213 Jalan TAR. Housed in a Neoclassical block, this endearing

kedai kopi is something of a period piece itself, looking as though little has been altered since it first opened in the 1950s. The halal food caters to all tastes: there's *nasi lemak* in the morning, *rojak* and *nasi padang* during the day and excellent satay in the evenings, plus Chinese rice and noodle dishes cooked to order throughout. Daily 7am–8pm.

Coliseum Café 98 Jalan TAR. Colonial-era hotel restaurant known for bland meat-and-two-veg meals, once served up by Hainanese chefs who emulated English cooking to please their colonial masters. The restaurant still serves up steaks and fish and chips today, of distinctly variable quality; you may be better off sticking to the rice and noodle offerings. Service can be shambolic, but the atmosphere partly makes amends. Daily 8am–10pm.

Jai Hind 11–15 Jalan Melayu. Friendly Sikh-run
kedai kopi which, besides an impressively wide-
ranging *campur*-type spread of curries and stir-fries,
also has an extensive menu of North Indian
savouries and sweets, as good as you'll get in much
posher restaurants but at half the price. Mon–Sat
8am–9pm, Sun 10am–7pm.
Saravanaa Bhavan Jalan Masjid India.
Member of a slightly eccentric Madras-based
chain of vegetarian restaurants that's spread its
tentacles as far afield as London and New York.
The menu features all the usual South Indian
delights – *thosai*, *idli*, *uthapam*, and so forth –
plus a few supposedly Chinese aberrations,
to be avoided. Be warned that spicing can be
incendiary even by South Indian standards.
Inexpensive, with main courses under RM10.
Daily 8am–10pm.
Sithique Nasi Kandar 233 Jalan TAR. One of a
handful of popular *kedai kopis* on Jalan TAR
serving Penang-style variations on *mamak* fare,
with an impressive range of fiery curries, including
fish head as well as cuttlefish. Daily
7.30am–7.30pm.

Brickfields

Naturally enough, **Indian food** dominates the Brickfields eating scene; the
restaurants reviewed are shown on the map on p.115.

Annalakshmi Temple of Fine Arts,
114–116 Jalan Berhala ☎03/2274 0799.
Community-run South Indian vegetarian restaurant
with a stupendous eat-all-you-want buffet,
featuring terrific home cooking. You actually pay
what you feel the meal is worth to you, and the
profits go to support the work of the Temple of Fine
Arts (see p.115), among other projects. Daily
except Mon 11.30am–3pm & 6.30–10pm.
Gem 124 Jalan Tun Sambanthan, Brickfields
☎03/2260 1373. Reliable a/c restaurant serving
up South Indian chicken, mutton and seafood
curries from RM10 and up. The *thali* platters make
for a good deal, costing around RM10. Conveniently
close to the Monorail station. Daily 11.30am–3pm
& 6–11pm.
Ghandhi's Ground floor, Scott Sentral Service
Suite, Jalan Padang Belia. Once this was housed in
shack by a car park, but success has enabled them
to move into a sterile cafeteria-style place below
an apartment block. Still, they cook to order a
range of delicious if oddly named Indian vegetarian
dishes (Y2K Chicken, and so forth), making use of
soya chunks and other meat substitutes. Friendly
and inexpensive. Daily 7–11am, 11.30am–2pm &
5pm till late.
Lai Fatt Ikan Bakar Jalan Thambypillai.
Kedai kopi doing delicious *ikan bakar* and
barbecued stingray, covered in spices and served
on banana leaves.
Sri Devi Jalan Travers. Widely reckoned to sell
some of Brickfields' best Indian food, this little
place does excellent banana-leaf curries from
midday onwards and wonderful *dosai* all day.
The *masala dosai* is particularly fine. Inexpensive.

Bangsar

Of the handful of suburbs to have enjoyed a mushrooming of upmarket
restaurants and bars, **Bangsar** is the closest to downtown KL. Just four
kilometres' southwest from Chinatown is the epicentre of the area's thriving
eating and drinking scene, the small grid of streets known as **Bangsar Baru**,
beginning pretty much at the junction of Jalan Maarof and the southern part
of Jalan Ara. Altogether the area is very much an expat ghetto as well as
catering to well-heeled local professionals, though these days there's less of a
reason to trek here as many places that cut their teeth in Bangsar have
sprouted branches downtown. Bangsar also boasts a great *mamak*, *Devi's
Corner*, that's crammed most nights, and a heaving Sunday **pasar malam**
that's one of the city's best markets for takeaway cooked food, with some fresh
produce also available. A little incongruous here are a smattering of Tamil
clubs, a spillover from Brickfields just to the east.

Bus #U87 travels to Bangsar Baru from the Sultan Mohamed terminal in
Chinatown, via KL Sentral. The LRT isn't convenient for Bangsar Baru,
however, as Bangsar station is some way downhill from Bangsar Baru with busy

BANGSAR BARU

EATING & DRINKING

Alexis Bistro	**8**
Country Farm Organic	**14**
Daily Grind	**15**
Delicious	**10**
Devi's Corner	**9**
Finnegan's	**1**
House Frankfurt	**2**
La Bodega	**5**
Madam Kwan's	**13**
Planter Jim's	**4**
Reunion	**12**
Ronnie Q's	**7**
Saravanaa Bhavan	**6**
The Social	**11**
Telawi Street Bistro	**3**

0 — 100 m

JALAN TELAWI 6
JALAN TELAWI 5
JALAN TELAWI 3
JALAN TELAWI
JALAN MAAROF
LORONG MAAROF
JALAN TELAWI 4
JALAN TELAWI 2
JALAN TELAWI 1
JALAN TERASEK 4
JALAN TERASEK
JALAN ARA
JALAN MAAROF

Sunday Market

Bangsar Village II

Food Centre

Silverfish Books

Bangsar Seafood Village

Bangsar Village

★ Bus Stop

Brickfields ▼

highways to cross in between. A **taxi** to Bangsar Baru from Chinatown shouldn't cost more than RM6.

Alexis Bistro 29 Jalan Telawi 3 ☎03/2284 2880, ⓦwww.alexis.com.my. The de facto clubhouse of Kuala Lumpur's movers and shakers – you'll see newspaper editors, academics, film-makers and politicos chewing the fat and putting Malaysia to rights here. Both local and Western fare is served, so don't be surprised that slick noodle and pasta dishes feature on the menu. There's also a formidable gateau counter. Main courses from around RM15. Daily 9am till late.

Country Farm Organics Lower ground level, Bangsar Village mall ☎03/2284 2094, ⓦwww .countryfarmorganics.com. Bravely blazing a trail for organic products in Malaysia, this supermarket has its own small restaurant serving mainly noodles and rice dishes, plus veggie spaghetti and sandwiches, made with organic produce. They also do a good range of smoothies and juices. Daily 10am–9.30pm.

Daily Grind Lower ground level, Bangsar Village mall ☎03/2287 6708, ⓦwww.thedailygrind .my. Gourmet burger joint with not just beef patties but also burgers of salmon, crab, chicken and lamb, plus a great range of side orders and their own range of relishes. Not cheap though – most burgers cost RM25–40. Daily 11am–11pm.

Delicious Ground floor, Bangsar Village II mall ☎03/2288 1554, ⓦwww.delicous .com.my. Once upon a time, a store selling clothes for the larger woman decided to branch out into health-conscious catering – and this superb café-restaurant was the result. The food's not actually starved of fat, sugar and salt, but is expertly prepared and reasonably priced – sandwiches, quiches, pastas and salads start at RM20. The deep-dish pies, if available (the menu changes regularly; RM20), are recommended, as are the

luscious cakes, which probably boost their clothing sales. Breakfasts (cooked or featuring French toast or waffles) available at weekends until 6pm. Mon–Fri 11am–1am, Sat & Sun 9am–1am.
House Frankfurt 12 Jalan Telawi 5 ⓣ03/2284 1624. If the pork-free nature of a lot of KL dining is getting you down, come to this agreeable bar-restaurant to enjoy *schweinfleisch* – as grilled pork knuckle, *wurst* or schnitzel. They also do classic southern German *spätzle*, little pasta bits with cheese and bacon. A great place for a drink too (see p.124). Daily noon–midnight.
La Bodega 16 Jalan Telawi 2 ⓣ03/2287 8318, ⓦwww.bodega.com.my. Basically a tapas bar augmented by a bistro and deli; see review on p.119. There's also a lounge with cosy armchairs, cocktails and yet more tapas. Deli daily 8am–10pm; rest of the place Mon–Fri noon till late, Sat & Sun 10am till late.
Madam Kwan's 65 Jalan Telawi 3 ⓣ03/2284 2297. See review on p.119. Daily 11.30am till late.
Planter Jim's 6–8 Jalan Telawi 2 ⓣ03/2282 4084. Consistently good Thai food with an eclectic twist. Good desserts too, including a Thai-style *air batu campur* with jackfruit and water chestnut. Moderately priced. Daily noon till late.

Reunion Level 2, Bangsar Village II mall ⓣ03/2287 3770. From the same stable as *Delicious*, this excellent Chinese restaurant really draws the punters with its elegant decor and classic Cantonese fare, including *dim sum* during the day at weekends. Mon–Fri noon–3pm & 6–10.30pm, Sat & Sun 10.30am–3pm & 6–10.30pm.
Saravanaa Bhavan 52 Jalan Maarof. See review on p.121. Daily 8am–10pm.
The Social 57–59 Jalan Telawi 3. Convivial bar-restaurant with a mix of Asian and Western fare, plus football matches on satellite TV. Set lunches at RM25 are good value. Best of all, the terrace tables offer a superb view of the hectic Sunday *pasar malam*. Daily noon–2am.
Telawi Street Bistro 1 Jalan Telawi 3 ⓣ03/2284 3168, ⓦwww.telawi.com.my. The decor is modern, the food influenced by Western bistros – so modern continental European and Mediterranean flavours predominate. Very strong on pizza, not just in its traditional form but also in pocket (stuffed, à la calzone) and plank (long rectangular crusts with up to four toppings) varieties. Daily noon–midnight.

Drinking, nightlife and entertainment

The most fashionable of KL's **bars** and **clubs** are concentrated in the Golden Triangle, with Bangsar also playing host to a few slick bars. If the drinking scene seems to tick over healthily enough, KL's **clubbing** appears surprisingly buoyant for the size of the city. It's only during Ramadan that both the bars and clubs are distinctly quiet.

The local **performing arts** scene is modest, and furthermore is split between KL and its satellite town Petaling Jaya, which, with its complex system of numbered roads which even residents don't understand, is best accessed by taxi. **Theatre** is probably the strongest suit, and throughout the year there are concerts, musicals and so forth, by local as well as visiting international performers and troupes. There's also a dedicated community of people working in the **visual arts**. For event **listings**, check the national press and also the monthly magazines **Klue** (ⓦwww.klue.com.my) and **Time Out** (ⓦwww.timeoutkl.com). In a similar spirit, ⓦwww.kakiseni.com is worth consulting not only for listings but also for an intelligent look at how the performing arts can reach a *modus vivendi* with the multicultural Asian and Muslim values that hold sway in Malaysia.

Bars and pubs

Bar **hours** vary from one venue to the next, but most places are open from mid-afternoon till midnight, at least. Beer in KL costs around RM12 a pint (when available on draught; bottles and cans are more common), a couple of ringgit less during the happy hours which most places offer.

Coliseum Hotel 98 Jalan TAR; see map, p.106. Endearingly antiquated, the bar here has a rich history and relaxed atmosphere, though some of the cocktails are a bit iffy. Sip a chilled beer and imagine the planters and colonial administrators of yesteryear gathering to quench their thirst. Daily 10am–10pm.

Finnegan's Pub 51 Jalan Sultan Ismail, Bukit Bintang; 6 Jalan Telawi 5, Bangsar; see maps, pp.108–109 & 122. This chain bills itself as "Malaysia's leading Irish pubs", which isn't saying much, though the venues are pleasant enough. Guinness, Kilkenny and Strongbow cider on tap, plus a menu of generic pub food – ploughman's lunches, pies – as well as pricier steaks and the obligatory Irish stew. Also good for football on satellite TV.

Frangipani 25 Changkat Bukit Bintang; see map, pp.108–109. Behind the impressive Art Deco-style facade is a bar with sleek minimalist decor, excellent cocktails, pumping house sounds and a beautiful straight and gay clientele, almost as pretty as the downstairs restaurant's pricey nouvelle cuisine. Tues–Sun: bar from 6pm till late, restaurant 7.30–10.30pm.

The Green Man 40 Changkat Bukit Bintang; see map, pp.108–109. Small, likeable pub serving reasonably priced local and imported beer and bacon and cheese toasties. Particularly busy when there's football or rugby on TV (there's also a pool table). Mon–Thurs 4pm till late, Fri–Sun noon till late.

House Frankfurt 12 Jalan Telawi 5, Bangsar; see map, p.122. Relaxed venue with amicable management and walls lined with vintage photos of German movie stars. They offer a terrific range of Pilseners and German dark beers and *weissbier*, plus *schnapps* and German wines. Daily noon–midnight.

Luna Bar Level 34, *Pacific Regency Hotel Apartments*, Menara Panglobal, Jalan Puncak; see map, pp.108–109. If you've only time to take in a couple of bars while in KL, you could do far worse than drop by this gorgeous rooftop poolside venue, with loungey sounds and breathtaking views of KL's skyline.

Reggae Bar 158 Jalan Tun H.S. Lee, Chinatown; see map, p.99. No-frills bar below a hostel and thus very popular with backpackers, though a few locals drop by too. The wall are plastered with Bob Marley memorabilia, though the DJs do recognize that other reggae artistes are available. Daily 5pm till late.

Ronnie Q's 32 Jalan Telawi 2, Bangsar; see map, p.122. Plenty of bars feature football matches on satellite TV, but at *Ronnie Q's* the focus is very much on sport – not just soccer but also cricket and rugby. The closest thing KL has to a Western sports bar.

Speakeasy 9 Jalan Ampang; see map, p.99. A rare example of its species in the Chinatown area, this bar-restaurant does Tiger on draught plus Heineken, as well as a menu of light meals and snacks. Pool tables available. Mon–Fri 10am–11pm.

Clubs and live music

KL's clubland is largely focused around the junction of **Jalan Sultan Ismail** and **Jalan P. Ramlee** in the Golden Triangle; there are also a number of venues springing up around **Asian Heritage Row** on Jalan Doraisamy, close to Medan Tuanku station on the Monorail. The music policy at any venue can change as often as KL experiences a thunderstorm, but as a general rule weekends tend to feature more hardcore dance sounds, while during the week retro hits and fairly accessible R&B take over. To keep up with happenings, including which big-name DJs might be in town, check out the Friday club listings in the *Star* newspaper, the free *Juice* magazine (available at bars and clubs, or at Ⓦ www.juiceonline.com) or the clubs' own websites, though don't be surprised if some haven't been updated in a while. Most clubs get going late and don't wind down until 3am or so; a **cover charge** of RM20–40 often applies (more if well-known DJs are playing), though women get in free at some venues during mid-week. Post-clubbing, you could do worse than join locals for food or a *teh tarik* nightcap down Jalan Alor (see p.118) or at one of several 24-hour restaurants (such as the *Lotus*, p.124, or one of a couple of *mamak* places on Jalan Nagasari, downhill from Jalan Alor).

Unfortunately, **live music** in KL isn't much to write home about. With Malaysia a recognized centre for music piracy, it's simply uneconomic for most international bands to show up, and the fact that religious conservatives have kicked up a huge stink when the likes of Avril Lavigne and Gwen Stefani have decided to perform here certainly doesn't help. Ultimately most of the concerts that take place are by very safe big-name pop, soul or country artists, plus occasional indie bands (many more of whom show up in Singapore). That said, KL has a few small venues where local singer-songwriters and bands performing in English get to strut their stuff, and there are sometimes shows by Malay pop-stars and old-school rockers, which are publicized in the press.

Clubs

Beach Club 97 Jalan P. Ramlee, Golden Triangle; see map, pp.108–109 Established venue with a somewhat clichéd thatched tropical-hut theme; definitely something of a meat market. Still, the mix of commercial chart and house sounds does pull in the punters.

Club Quattro Avenue K mall, 156 Jalan Ampang; see map, pp.108–109. One of the most welcome recent additions to the scene, with four spaces themed after the four seasons – totally perverse in the tropics, but with a diverse range of sounds on offer too, there's something to please everyone.

The Loft/Cynna Asian Heritage Row, Jalan Doraisamy ☎03/2691 5668; see map, p.106. A mixture of house (more hardcore at *Cynna*), R&B and retro sounds at this sleek and surprisingly spacious venue.

Maison Jalan Yap Ah Shak, behind the *Sheraton* and very close to Asian Heritage Row ⓦwww.maison .com.my; see map, p.106. An impressive conversion of colonial-era property, retaining the period facade but all minimalist decor within. Nightly except Mon.

Poppy Collection 18-1 Jalan P. Ramlee ⓦwww .poppy-collection.com; see map, pp.108–109. Swanky designer venue, spinning soul and R&B downstairs in the *Poppy Garden*, with largely unadulterated house sounds above in the *Passion* lounge. No cover charge except during special events.

Zouk 113 Jalan Ampang, Golden Triangle ⓦwww .zoukclub.com.my; see map, pp.108–109. Operating out of its own hypermodern building, this offshoot of one of Singapore's top clubs has rapidly become a mainstay of the KL scene too. There are several venues within, spinning an eclectic range of music, including a smidgen of indie. Tues–Sat evenings.

Live venues

Alexis Bistro & Wine Bar Ground floor, Great Eastern mall, 303 Jalan Ampang ☎03/4260 2288, ⓦwww.alexis.com.my; see map, pp.84–85. Smart venue with occasional live jazz or blues sets by local or low-key international groups. Worth the trek – it's 2km east of the Ampang Park LRT stop.

Bangkok Jazz Chulan Square, Jalan Raja Chulan, Bukit Bintang ☎03/2145 8708; see map, pp.108–109. Below a Thai restaurant is this smart space with different live jazz combos Wed–Sat evenings. Daily 5pm till late.

No Black Tie 17 Jalan Mesui, Bukit Bintang ☎03/2142 3737; see map, pp.108–109. Occasional music venue, gorgeously done out in tropical timbers. It majors on jazz but takes pride in putting on left-field performers from various musical genres – here you just might stumble upon the likes of satirical songwriter Rafique Rashid. Sadly it tends to keep its events hush-hush, so either call to find out what's on or turn up on spec.

Gay KL

KL's gay community is fairly discreet, though the smart cafés of fashionable **Bintang Walk** – the stretch of Jalan Bukit Bintang just east of Jalan Sultan Ismail – have a noticeably gay clientele at weekends. The chief gay downtown venue proper is *Blue Boy*, 50 Jalan Sultan Ismail, actually in a dingy lane off the main drag. It attracts a local and foreign crowd, though beware the odd hustler. Much more agreeable but a little far out is *Marketplace* at 4a Lorong Yap Kwan Seng, fifteen minutes' walk from the KLCC LRT station (see map, pp.84–85; it's really best reached by taxi). Nestling a short distance off the road itself, this swanky bar-restaurant attracts a largely gay crowd on Saturdays after about 11.30pm. More centrally, both *Frangipani* (see opposite) and the *Green Lotus Café* (see p.119) are also gay hangouts, and if you see mainstream clubs advertising what are euphemistically called "boys' nights", you'll know you can head there too. For more on gay venues and social events in the city, try the website ⓦwww.mylpg.net.

Theatre and classical music

Most prominent among KL's **theatre** companies is the Actors Studio. Based in Bangsar, it mounts several productions each year, ranging from Malaysianized versions of foreign classics to work by local playwrights, and has been instrumental in the creation and running of one of the city's more impressive independent arts centres, KLPac (see below). Other drama companies worth making time for include the Five Arts Centre (ⓦ www.fiveartscentre.org), the Straits Theatre Company and the satirical Instant Café.

There are two home-grown **orchestras** to choose from, namely the Malaysian Philharmonic Orchestra (ⓦ www.malaysianphilharmonic.com) and the Dama Orchestra (ⓦ www.damaorchestra.com), the latter specializing in Chinese classical music and musicals. Watch the press for news of international recitals.

Theatres, performance spaces and concert halls

Besides the **venues** listed here, you'll find that there are occasional concerts at the KL Convention Centre and also at out-of-town resorts such as Genting Highlands; check the press for details.

Dewan Philharmonik Petronas Twin Towers, KLCC ☎ 03/2051 7007. The home of the Malaysian Philharmonic, it also hosts concerts by other performers, not just in the classical domain. Box office is on the ground floor, Tower 2 (Mon–Sat 10am–6pm).

Istana Budaya (National Theatre) Jalan Tun Razak, east of the junction with Jalan Pahang and south of Titiwangsa Gardens ☎ 03/4026 5558, ⓦ www.istanabudaya.gov.my. Besides providing a spacious modern home for the National Theatre Company and the National Symphony Orchestra, this venue sees performances by visiting international orchestras as well as staging pop concerts, plays and ballets. Just over 1km from Titiwangsa (LRT/Monorail) or Chow Kit (Monorail) stations.

KLPac Jalan Strachan, off Jalan Ipoh ☎ 03/4047 9000, ⓦ www.klpac.com. A joint project of the stalwart Actors Studio company and the construction conglomerate which is redeveloping the area, the KL Performing Arts Centre is housed in a former rail depot revamped to look like something Frank Lloyd Wright could have doodled. It hosts jazz, indie and dance events plus, of course, plays by various companies. The location couldn't be more awkward, in the depths of the old Sentul Raya Golf Club and cut off from the nearby Sentul Komuter station by the rail line, which you can't cross safely without a big detour. Get here by taxi; just pray that the driver is a culture vulture or remembers the golf course. As for heading back, be prepared for a trudge out to Jalan Ipoh, where you can pick up a taxi.

Panggung Bandaraya Corner of Jalan Sultan Hishamuddin and Jalan Tun Perak ⓦ www.dbkl .gov.my/panggung. Occasional performances of Malay drama (*bangsawan*) take place in this historic theatre with a Moorish facade.

Film

Cinema in KL is something of a let-down. Hollywood blockbusters are easy enough to find, though expect the censor's scissors to have excised any unusually torrid bits. However, more adventurous international films are thin on the ground, and local independent productions, which often hold a mirror up to taboo or sensitive social issues, don't get the popular acclaim they deserve. Still, it's worth looking out for screenings of films by the likes of Yasmin Ahmad, whose *Sepet* (2004) dealt amusingly yet touchingly with a Chinese–Malay love affair; its sequel *Gubra* (2006) sees the Malay woman of the romance plunged into a complex tale whose main theme is betrayal. Also worth keeping an eye out for is the work of opinionated writer and director Amir Muhammad. His latest film at the time of writing, *Lelaki Komunis Terakhir* (*The Last Communist*; 2006), was banned by the government just as it was about to open, apparently because it dealt with the awkward subject of Chin Peng, the ringleader behind the violent Emergency of the 1950s.

The two main **cinema chains**, both with online booking facilities, are Golden Screen Cinemas (ⓦ www.gsc.com.my) and TGV (ⓦ www.tgv.com.my). GSC's screens at Mid Valley Megamall (☎ 03/8312 3456) are your best bet for occasional art-house films from abroad; TGV has a conveniently located multiplex at Suria KLCC (☎03/7492 2929). Also worth a look-in for its local cachet – even if the Indian and Cantonese action flicks it has specialized in for generations aren't your thing – is the Coliseum Cinema on Jalan TAR. Finally, there's also the DiGi IMAX cinema on level 10 of the Berjaya Times Square mall, Jalan Imbi (☎03/2117 3046).

Cultural shows

Traditional dance can be seen at the **cultural shows** put on by the MTC and by a couple of restaurants for diners, though what's on offer is a little touristy. Indian dance is better catered for, thanks to the Temple of Fine Arts. Traditional festivals may see more authentic performances being staged; check the press or ask at MTC for details.

Malaysia Tourism Centre (MTC) 109 Jalan Ampang ☎03/2164 3929, ⓦwww.mtc.gov.my. Half-hour dance shows, featuring performers from Borneo as well as the Peninsula, are held on Mondays and Tuesday from 3pm. More interesting are occasional music sessions featuring *dikir barat*, improvised Malay folk music from the east coast; check the website for details.

Saloma Next to MTC, Jalan Ampang ☎03/2161 0122, ⓦwww.saloma.com.my. Similar in concept to the better-established *Seri Melayu*, this offers set meals and à la carte fare at lunchtime, and an evening buffet (RM70) with a performance of traditional dance, supposedly focusing on different

states of the Federation each night. Daily noon–2.30pm & 6.30–10.30pm.
Seri Melayu Jalan Conlay ☎03/2145 1833. In a traditional Malay-style house, this restaurant serves up Malay buffets (evenings RM70) and does nightly traditional dance shows. Smartish dress required (avoid shorts and sleeveless tops). Daily noon–3pm & 6.30pm till late.
Temple of Fine Arts 114–116 Jalan Berhala, Brickfields ☎03/2274 3709. Community-run cultural centre set up to preserve Tamil culture by promoting dance, theatre, folk, classical music and craft-making. Probably the best place in KL to see traditional Indian dance – call to check their programme.

Visual arts

KL has been developing a strong visual arts scene over the years. At first artists were mainly reliant on the support of state- or corporate-funded galleries, but with standards of living rising all the time, artists are increasingly autonomous and audacious, sustained by interest from private buyers and by showings at a number of excellent independent galleries. Painting is the dominant medium and, despite an extended flirtation with Expressionism, these days it's **figurative art** that's making the strongest impression.

As for names to look out for, the older generation of Malaysian **artists** includes the likes of Latif Mohidin and Jolly Koh, both colourful abstract painters; Ibrahim Hussein, specializing in design-based pop art; and Redza Piyadasa, whose work ranges from conceptual art to mixed-media studies with more of an obvious social conscience. Also worth checking out are Sylvia Lee Goh from Penang, whose oils often reflect her Baba-Nonya background; and Loh Ek Sem and Anuar Dan, both of whom focus on Malaysia's vanishing rural life. Among the new wave of artists, keep an eye out for the **Matahati** group, young Malay artists led by Sabah-born Bayu Utomo Radjikin, whose works, exploring issues of identity in modern Malaysia, have a distinctively Malay sensibility; you're also likely to come across work by Wong Hoy Cheong and Jalaini Abu Hassan, both making big waves at the moment. **Sculpture** and installations are a worthwhile minority interest, and one of the more challenging practitioners is Abdul Multhalib Musa, whose creations resemble giant abstract combs or slinky springs.

Art Folio M28, Avenue K mall, 156 Jalan Ampang ☎03/2162 3339. Stacks of watercolours, oil paintings and ceramics, at high prices; gives a reasonable picture of current trends. Mon–Sat 10.30am–7pm.

Art House Second floor, Wisma Cosway, Jalan Raja Chulan (close to the junction with Jalan Perak), Golden Triangle ☎03/2148 2283. Specializes in high-quality brush paintings and ceramics from China, and represents a few local Chinese artists. Mon–Sat 10am–7.30pm.

Artists' Colony Kompleks Budaya Kraf, Jalan Conlay, Golden Triangle. Around the edges of the crafts complex are a bunch of cottages rented out as inexpensive studios to up-and-coming artists, mainly Malay, whom you can watch at work. It's all very down to earth and they charge reasonable prices if you're buying. Sunday is the best day to turn up, as most of the artists are around then.

Galeri Petronas Level 3, Suria KLCC mall, KLCC ☎03/2051 7090, ⓦwww.galeripetronas.com.my. Large space with interesting temporary exhibitions, though perhaps not quite as cutting-edge as it once was. Tues–Sun 10am–8pm.

National Art Gallery (Balai Seni Lukis Negara) Jalan Tun Razak ☎03/4025 4990, ⓦwww .artgallery.gov.my. A striking, vaguely pyramidal building whose interior has shades of New York's Guggenheim about it, but the quality of the exhibitions varies. Best reached by taxi; Jalan Tun Razak is too busy to make the 1km walk from Titiwangsa station worthwhile. Daily 10am–6pm.

Rimbun Dahan Kilometer 27, Jalan Kuang, Kuang ☎03/6038 3690, ⓦwww.rimbundahan.org. The estate of renowned Malaysian architect Hijjas Kasturi is also a key centre for artistic endeavour, supporting several artist residencies every year. Exhibitions are held twice a year (usually Feb & May; call for details), at which you can not only get acquainted with the artists and their work but also take in the splendid architecture of the estate. To get here, take the Komuter train to Sungai Buloh, then get a taxi from the main station exit (not from the road by the platform where you are set down; RM10); you may need to ask for "*rumah Hijjas Kasturi*".

Starhill Gallery Next to the *Marriott*, Bintang Walk ⓦwww.starhillgallery.com. Amid all the designer outlets here are a few actual galleries, slightly too fashionable for their own good, though a few gems pop up for sale occasionally.

Valentine Willie Fine Art First floor, 17 Jalan Telawi 3, Bangsar Baru ⓦwww.vwfa.net. Specializing in modern Southeast Asian artists, particularly from Thailand and Indonesia, and of course home-grown talent. Mon–Fri noon–8pm, Sat noon–6pm.

Wei-Ling Gallery 8 Jalan Scott, Brickfields (just a little northeast of the *YMCA*) ☎03/2260 1106, ⓦwww.weiling-gallery.com. A great venue in an old shophouse, showcasing the most interesting of the new wave of artists plus established names. Mon–Fri noon–7pm, Sat 10am–5pm.

Shopping

There's no city in Malaysia where consumerism is as widespread and in-your-face as KL. The malls of the Golden Triangle are big haunts for youths and yuppies alike, while **street markets** remain a draw for everyone, offering a gregarious atmosphere and goods of all sorts. Jalan Petaling in Chinatown (see p.101) is, of course a big draw day and night, particularly for fake watches and leather goods; some of these have started to creep into the covered market on Jalan Masjid India and the nearby Lorong Tuanku Abdul Rahman *pasar malam* (see p.106), but their mainstays remain Malay- and Indian-style clothes and fabrics, plus a few eccentricities such as herbal tonics and various charms alleged to improve male vigour. Chow Kit Market (see p.107) has some clothing bargains but little else of interest. A great just-out-of-town market for knick-knacks and general bric-a-brac happens every weekend inside the **Amcorp Mall** in Petaling Jaya, close to Taman Jaya station on the LRT.

If no specific **business hours** are given in the shop listings that follow, then the establishment keeps the usual Malaysian shopping hours, opening by mid-morning and shutting at 8pm (an hour or two later in the case of outlets within malls), six or seven days a week.

Handicrafts

Malaysian crafts tend to be available a little more cheaply in the provincial areas where they originate. Nevertheless, KL is a good place to bone up on handicrafts – there's an excellent range on sale, though note that many of the items are made in other Southeast Asian countries.

Central Market (Pasar Seni) Jalan Hang Kasturi, Chinatown. The selection of wares here is all a bit *rojak*, as locals would say – like the Malaysian salad, a bit of a jumble, including batik clothing, *songket*, silverware and Malay kites, plus irrelevances like sunglasses. The recent reorganization of part of the ground floor into separate lanes for Malay, Chinese and other local ethnic wares hasn't done the presentation much good. Look out for Asli Kraf on the ground floor, an Orang Asli-run shop mainly selling woven bamboo, *mengkuang* and rattan items made by Orang Asli communities, including tubular fish traps that make great light fittings. There's also a branch here of Native Gallery (see below).

Janji 303a, level 3, Suria KLCC ☎03/2161 5880. Small outfit selling indigenous handicrafts, with proceeds going back to the communities that made them. Here you'll find Terengganu batik (unusually, in tastefully muted colours), Kelantan silverware and Sarawak rattan baskets, plus some nontraditional items – fun asymmetrical teapots from Perak, for example. Daily 10am–10pm.

Karyaneka Kompleks Budaya Kraf, Jalan Conlay ☎03/2164 9907. There's a bit of everything at this crafts emporium – Kelantan kites in silver filigree (RM60 buys a small ornamental example, while for one 30cm across you could pay RM2000); baskets and bags of woven *mengkuang* (pandanus) leaves, sometimes with attractive designs; and so forth. For a taster, visit their much smaller shop on the lower ground level of BB Plaza, Jalan Bukit Bintang. Daily 10am–8pm.

Lavanya Arts Temple of Fine Arts, 114–116 Jalan Berhala, Brickfields. If you've an interest in Indian handicrafts, this small outlet is the place to come. Tues–Sat 10am–8pm, Sun 10am–2pm.

Native Gallery 10–12 Jalan Hang Lekir ☎03/2070 4567. Best for *pua kumbu* weaving and wooden kitchenware, both from Sarawak.

Peter Hoe Second floor, Lee Rubber Building, corner of Jalan Tun H.S. Lee and Jalan Hang Lekir, and also at 2 Jalan Hang Lekir. The latter outlet specializes in batik, made in Indonesia to their own designs and in less garish colours than usual. Their main shop (reached by the side entrance of the Lee Rubber Building) is much larger and sells a variety of soft furnishings, knick-knacks, textile bags and so forth, mostly imported from around the region. Daily 10am–7pm.

Pucuk Rebung 302a, level 3, Suria KLCC ☎03/2162 0069. One of the most upmarket crafts outlets in Suria KLCC, stocking items that reflect Malay culture, including batik, *songkets* and silverware, plus some Nonya items and Sarawak beadwork. There's even a mini-museum at the back featuring many not-for-sale pieces. Pricey. Daily 10am–10pm.

Royal Selangor Pewter Factory 4 Jalan Usahawan Lima, Setapak Industrial Area ⓦvisitorcentre.royalselangor.com. For years pewter was something of a souvenir cliché in Malaysia, though pewter platters, mugs and other objects can be elegant. The Royal Selangor factory has a visitor centre (daily 9am–5pm) offering guided tours (free) and, of course, the opportunity to buy their products. The factory is at least 5km northeast of Chow Kit, and 2km west of the Wangsa Maju LRT stop; best to take a taxi from the latter. They also have stores at Suria KLCC, the Lot 10 Shopping Centre in Bukit Bintang and the Gardens mall in Mid Valley.

Books and CDs

The larger KL **bookshops** are pretty impressive, carrying a range of English publications similar in scope to what you'll find at a good bookshop in the West, though in less depth. You'll also find a very good range of literature on Malaysia and the rest of Southeast Asia – everything from historical monographs to coffee-table books about local architecture. Unfortunately, in this country of rampant piracy, **music** shops are nothing to write home about.

Borders Berjaya Times Square, Bukit Bintang. One of the world's largest examples of the chain, on two expansive floors. Fantastic for books, not so great for CDs. Daily 9am–11pm.

Kinokuniya Level 4, Suria KLCC. Efficient Japanese chain with plenty of English publications, including a decent travel section; a pleasure to use.

MPH Unit JA1, ground floor, Mid Valley Megamall; smaller outlets on the ground floor at BB Plaza, Bukit Bintang; level 1, KL Sentral; and in Bangsar Baru at the Bangsar Village mall; ⓦ www.mph.com. my. This veteran survivor of the local book trade is resting on its laurels somewhat, though it still carries a decent mix of novels and non-fiction titles.
Rock Corner First floor, Bangsar Village mall ⓣ 03/2284 6062. Bravely independent retailer, good for hard-to-find rock and indie CDs.

Silverfish Books 67-1 Jalan Telawi 3, Bangsar, next to *Madam Kwan's* ⓣ 03/2284 4837. Not just a bookshop but an independent publisher to boot, and good for material on Malaysia.
Times Bookstore Level 6, Pavilion KL mall ⓦ www.timesbookstores.com.my. Reasonably well organized member of the Singapore-based chain.

Malls

Locals and visitors alike come to KL's **shopping malls** to seek refuge from the heat as much as to shop; for local young people, the malls are also important places to socialize. Mostly located outside the old centre, particularly in the Golden Triangle, the malls divide into two categories – gargantuan affairs in the manner of Western malls and featuring international chains and designer names, and smaller, denser Southeast Asian-style complexes, basically indoor bazaars with row upon row of tiny independent retailers. Ironically, the simpler malls tend to be much more popular than their more sophisticated, pricier counterparts, and can be atmospheric places to wander. Many malls, of whatever type, house a **supermarket** or department store of one sort or another.

Bukit Bintang

BB Plaza Jalan Bukit Bintang, just west of Jalan Sultan Ismail. Teeming local-style mall with good deals on cameras and electronic equipment.
Berjaya Times Square Jalan Imbi, right opposite the Monorail's Imbi stop ⓦ www .timessquarekl.com. Enormous mall with indoor theme park rides and an IMAX cinema. It also houses the UK chain store Debenhams, a huge Borders and the Shasta supermarket. Not as buzzing as it should be, however.
Pavilion KL Between Jalan Bukit Bintang and Jalan Raja Chulan ⓦ www.pavilion-kl.com. One of the very largest malls in the city – and that's saying something – with a parade of big-name designer outlets on Jalan Bukit Bintang and branches of Singapore's Tangs department store and Malaysia's Parkson chain, present here in an especially upmarket version. There's also a Times bookshop, GSC cinema, a great food court (see p.118) and a plethora of eating and nightlife outlets in the western connection annexe plus yet more, often overpriced, boutiques and restaurants tucked away on the upper levels.
Lot 10 Shopping Centre Bintang Walk. Specializes in designer clothes and accessories, as well as playing host to the Japanese department store Isetan.
Starhill Gallery Next to the *Marriott*, Bintang Walk ⓦ www.starhillgallery.com. More designer names than is healthy, orbiting a suitably grand atrium.

Just as noteworthy is the maze of top-notch restaurants at the base of the building.
Sungai Wang Plaza Jalan Sultan Ismail ⓦ www .Sungaiwang.com. Joined onto BB Plaza and just as popular as its neighbour, KL's first mall offers everything from clothes to consumer electronics. Generally keenly priced.

KLCC

Avenue K 156 Jalan Ampang, just across from the Petronas Twin Towers and over KLCC LRT station. Worth a look if you're into designer outlets, but a bit staid.
Suria KLCC At the base of the Petronas Twin Towers ⓦ www.suriaklcc.com.my. A mall so large it's subdivided into sub-malls for ease of reference, Suria KLCC's oval atriums are home to UK department store Marks & Spencer, Isetan and Cold Storage supermarkets, plus numerous restaurants and a TGV multiplex cinema.

Bangsar and Mid Valley

Bangsar Shopping Centre 285 Jalan Maarof, Bangsar. Upmarket affair, a good place to have a suit made, buy gifts or just find some food from home that you miss. Plenty of restaurants and coffee shops to boot.
Bangsar Village and Village II Bangsar Baru ⓦ bangsarvillage.com. The boutiques tend to play second fiddle to the restaurants in these two malls, joined by a bridge above street level. Shopping

highlights include an MPH bookshop and the Country Farm Organics supermarket, selling organic produce and even eco-friendly detergent – the likes of which you'll hardly see on sale anywhere else in the country.

Mid Valley Megamall/Gardens Mall Off Jalan Syed Putra, 2km south of Brickfields ⓦ www .midvalley.com.my. The sprawling Mid Valley mall certainly gives Suria KLCC a run for its money;

come here for the Carrefour hypermarket, the Jusco and Metrojaya department stores, the MPH bookshop, the GSC cinema and the usual plethora of outlets selling everything from cosmetics to computers. Recently a new, more upmarket mall called Gardens has sprung up alongside, home to designer labels and the Singapore-based department store Robinsons. Both malls are easy to reach as the KTM Mid Valley Komuter station is close by.

Listings

Airlines For details of MAS, AirAsia and Berjaya Air offices, see p.132. International airlines with offices in KL include: Air France/KLM, *Parkroyal Hotel*, Jalan Sultan Ismail ☎03/7712 4555; Air Mauritius, Central Plaza, Jalan Sultan Ismail ☎03/2142 9161; Austrian Airlines, Central Plaza, Jalan Sultan Ismail ☎03/2148 8033; British Airways, c/o Qantas; Cathay Pacific, Menara IMC, Jalan Sultan Ismail ☎03/2078 3377; China Airlines, Amoda Building, 22 Jalan Imbi ☎03/2142 7344; Emirates, UBN Tower, Jalan P. Ramlee ☎03/2058 5888; Garuda, Menara Citibank, Jalan Ampang ☎03/2162 2811; Gulf Air, Central Plaza, Jalan Sultan Ismail ☎03/2141 2676; Japan Airlines, Menara Citibank, Jalan Ampang ☎1800/813366; KLM, see Air France; Korean Air, Mui Plaza, Jalan P. Ramlee ☎03/2142 8311; Qantas, Menara IMC, Jalan Sultan Ismail ☎03/6279 5033; Royal Brunei, UBN Tower, Jalan P. Ramlee ☎03/2070 7166; Singapore Airlines, Menara Multi-Purpose, Jalan Munshi Abdullah ☎03/2692 3122; SilkAir ☎03/2698 7033; South African Airways, c/o Pacific World Travel, Angkasa-raya Building, Jalan Ampang ☎03/2141 7456; SriLankan Airlines, Kompleks Antarabangsa, Jalan Sultan Ismail ☎03/2143 3353; Swiss Airlines, Kenanga International building, Jalan Sultan Ismail ☎03/2163 5885; Thai Airways, Wisma Goldhill, Jalan Raja Chulan ☎03/2031 2363.

Banks and exchange There are banks with ATMs throughout KL; Maybank is usually your best bet for foreign exchange. You may get better rates from official moneychangers, which can be found in shopping malls and in and around transport hubs.

Buses For intercity bus enquiries, the following numbers may come in handy. KL Sentral: Transnasional ☎03/2273 6473. Pasar Rakyat bus station: Transtar ☎03/2141 1771 (luxury buses to Singapore). Pekeliling: Plusliner ☎03/4042 1256. Puduraya: Konsortium Bas Ekspres ☎03/2070 9410 (Penang/Kedah), ☎03/2070 1321 (JB/Singapore);

Plusliner ☎03/2070 2617; Transnasional ☎03/2070 3300; Utama Ekspres ☎03/2070 3940. Putra: Ekspres Mutiara ☎03/4045 2122; Transnasional ☎03/4042 9530; Triton ☎03/4044 6591; Utama Ekspres ☎03/4045 2122. Old Railway Station: Plusliner/Nice ☎03/2272 1586 (luxury buses to Penang & Singapore).

Casino KL has long had a casino at Genting Highlands (ⓦ www.genting.com.my), which also attracts vacationing locals as it features several fairly pricey resorts, a theme park, shopping malls and so forth. It's 30km out of town, best reached via the Karak Highway (E8); express buses head there from Puduraya, Pekeliling and Pasar Rakyat bus stations, and there are also shared taxis from Puduraya.

Cultural centres Alliance Française, 15 Lorong Gurney ☎03/2694 7880; British Council, West Block, Wisma Selangor Dredging, Jalan Ampang (next to the *Maya* hotel) ☎03/2723 7900; Goethe-Institut, sixth floor, 374 Jalan Tun Razak ☎03/2164 2011.

Embassies and consulates Australia, 6 Jalan Yap Kwan Seng ☎03/2146 5555; Brunei, nineteenth floor, Menara Tan & Tan, 207 Jalan Tun Razak ☎03/2161 2800; Cambodia, 46 Jalan U Thant ☎03/4257 1150; Canada, seventeenth floor, Menara Tan & Tan, 207 Jalan Tun Razak ☎03/2718 3333; China, 229 Jalan Ampang ☎03/2163 6815; India, 2 Jalan Taman Duta ☎03/2093 3504; Indonesia, 233 Jalan Tun Razak ☎03/2145 2011; Ireland, The Amp Walk, 218 Jalan Ampang ☎03/2161 2963; Japan, 11 Persiaran Stonor ☎03/2143 1739; Laos, 25 Jalan Damai ☎03/2141 8662; Netherlands, seventh floor, The Amp Walk, 218 Jalan Ampang ☎03/2168 6200; New Zealand, level 21, Menara IMC, Jalan Sultan Ismail ☎03/2078 2533; Philip-pines, 1 Changkat Kia Peng ☎03/2148 9989; Singapore, 209 Jalan Tun Razak ☎03/2161 6277; South Africa, 12 Lorong Titiwangsa 12 ☎03/4026 5700; South Korea, Jalan Nipah ☎03/4251 2336; Thailand, 206 Jalan Ampang ☎03/2148 8222;

Destinations in the Peninsula are easily reached by bus or train, but low-cost flights do speed up the journey to Kota Bharu or Kuala Terengganu. **Driving** around the Peninsula is quite feasible (see p.43 for car-rental agencies); the main hurdle is how to reach the highways from downtown KL, with its confusing road signage, one-way systems and countless express bypasses. The **E1** (North–South Expressway northbound) is signed from Jalan Duta, which branches off Middle Ring Road I west of the Lake Gardens; the **E2** (North–South Expressway southbound) starts at Sungai Besi 2km south of Chinatown, and is most quickly reached using the long underground **SMART** tunnel on the eastern section of Jalan Tun Razak. For the **E8** (linked to the **East Coast Highway** to Kuantan, and **Route 8** into the interior), get onto Jalan Tun Razak (or use Jalan Raja Laut if starting from Chinatown) and head northwest to Jalan Ipoh; proceed up this for a short distance, then turn right onto Jalan Sentul and follow signs for the highway.

By bus or long-distance taxi

Most long-distance buses and taxis leave from the **Puduraya bus station**. From street level, various staircases lead up to the main concourse where at least seventy bus companies are represented. Most routes are served by more than one operator, meaning there are several departures a day for most destinations. Also split into two groups are the 23 flights of steps leading down to the bus bays on the ground floor; make sure to ask which bay your bus leaves from. **Long-distance taxis** leave from the car parks on the upper floors; fares per vehicle are, for example, around RM260 to Cameron Highlands, RM380 to Kuala Tahan (the main Taman Negara entrance) and RM460 to Kota Bharu or Kuala Terengganu.

Some buses to **Kuantan** leave from Puduraya, but others, along with buses to the **interior**, use the small **Pekeliling bus station**, very close to Titiwangsa station on the Monorail and LRT. For buses to coastal **Kelantan** and **Terengganu** (including Kota Bharu and Kuala Terengganu), as well as yet more services to Kuantan, go to the **Putra bus station**, by the Putra World Trade Centre (and a short walk from the PWTC LRT or the KTM Putra station). For buses west to Port Klang, Klang and Shah Alam, use the **Klang bus station** in Chinatown. While there are plenty of buses from Puduraya to Singapore, some luxury services leave from the **Pasar Rakyat bus station** and from the **old train station**.

As usual, there are no central enquiry numbers for the bus stations; to buy tickets, it's best to turn up and speak to the various bus companies directly. Numbers for a few of the larger companies are listed on p.131.

By air

Malaysia Airlines (MAS; ☏1300/883000, ⊛www.mas.com.my) and its **Firefly** subsidiary (☏03/7845 4543, ⊛www.fireflyz.com.my) have a ticket office at KL Sentral (near the KLIA Express departure area; ☏03/2272 4248; daily 4.30am–midnight). You can also buy tickets at the MAS Building, Jalan Sultan Ismail (☏03/2165 5319). **AirAsia** (☏03/8775 4000, ⊛www.airasia.com.my) also has an office at KL Sentral (near *McDonalds*; ☏03/2274 2714; daily 8am–10pm). **Berjaya Air** is on level 6 of KL Plaza, Bukit Bintang (☏03/2141 0088, ⊛berjaya-air.com). International airlines are listed on p.131. For **flight information**, check ⊛www.klia.com.my, or call ☏03/8776 2000 (KLIA main terminal), 03/8777 6777 (KLIA low-cost-carrier terminal) or 03/7845 3245 (Subang).

By train and ferry

For timetables and ticket reservations for **express trains** to Singapore, Tumpat (via the interior) and Hat Yai in Thailand (via Butterworth and the west coast), call KTM on ☏03/2267 1200, or check ⊛www.ktmb.com.my. The only **ferries** from the vicinity of KL are those to Sumatra from Port Klang (see p.140), reachable by Komuter train.

UK, 185 Jalan Ampang ☏03/2170 2200; US, 376 Jalan Tun Razak ☏03/2168 5000; Vietnam, 4 Persiaran Stonor ☏03/2148 4036.

Formula 1 Check ⊛www.malaysiangp.com.my for details of the Sepang circuit, ticketing and special buses that run from Nilai station during the event. There are a few hotels in the vicinity, such as the *Concorde* (⊛www.concorde.net /sepang) and *Empress* (⊛www .empresshotelsepang.com), but trains make commuting from downtown KL fairly quick.

Hospitals and clinics General Hospital, Jalan Pahang ☏03/2692 1044; Gleneagles Hospital, Jalan Ampang ☏03/4257 1300; Pantai Medical Centre, Jalan Bukit Pantai, not far from Kerinchi LRT station ☏03/2296 0888; Tung Shin Hospital, Jalan Pudu ☏03/2072 1655.

internet access Chinatown has a couple of internet places along Jalan Sultan, close to Jalan Tun Tan Cheng Lock. In Bukit Bintang, there's a 24hr cybercafé on Tengkat Tong Shin, and there are several more internet cafés on the stretch of Jalan Bukit Bintang just west of the junction with Jalan Sultan Ismail. The usual charges apply (RM3–6 per hr), with Bukit Bintang rates tending to be more expensive.

Left luggage Luggage can be stored for a few ringgit per day at KL Sentral station and Puduraya bus station (look out for a couple of counters at the back of the passenger level). At KLIA, the service costs RM10–30 per day depending on the size of the bags; see the "Facilities" section of ⊛www.klia.com.my for more.

Police KL has its own Tourist Police station, where you can report stolen property for insurance claims. Useful locations include at MTC, 109 Jalan Ampang (☏03/2163 3657), and at Puduraya bus station.

Post office The General Post Office is just south of the Dayabumi Complex (Mon–Fri 8am–4pm, Sat 8am–2pm); poste restante/general delivery mail comes here. In Chinatown, there's a post office upstairs at the Puduraya bus station; a post office with extended hours can be found at Suria KLCC (daily 10am–6pm).

Sports facilities Sports facilities open to the public in downtown KL are surprisingly limited. One of the most conveniently located is the swimming pool in Chinatown; to find it, take the unnamed road at the western end of Jalan Hang Jebat up to the hilltop Chinwoo Stadium, a striking circular Modernist building built in the 1950s, then continue down the steps on the

south side of the hill to where the pool is hidden away (Mon–Fri 2–8pm; Sat & Sun 9am–8pm; RM4). The pool is well maintained but the showers and changing facilities are basic, and they have an odd rule that baggy swimwear is not allowed (they'll sell you appropriate swimming trunks if required). There's also a sports complex at Jalan Terasek 3 (just west of Bangsar Baru; ☏03/2284 6065) with badminton and tennis courts, and a pool. Private health clubs with gyms and aerobics programmes, and perhaps also a sauna and a swimming pool, aren't hard to find. Fitness First (⊛www .fitnessfirst.com.my) and California Fitness (⊛www.californiafitness.com.my) both have convenient locations at 22 Jalan Sultan Ismail and in the Lot 10 Shopping Centre respectively; Fitness First is also in the Menara Maxis, next to Suria KLCC. For a round of golf, try the KL Golf and Country Club at Bukit Kiara, just west of Bangsar (take a taxi); non-members can usually get in on weekdays (book in advance on ☏03/2093 1111), but be prepared to show proof of your handicap.

Travel agents and tour operators International flights and tours can be booked through, among others, Holiday Tours & Travel, fifth floor, Wisma UOA II, Jalan Pinang (☏03/2719 1818, ⊛www .holidaytours.com.my), and next to Tourism Malaysia on level 1 of KL Sentral (☏03/2273 2200); Reliance Tours, third floor, Sungai Wang Plaza, Bukit Bintang (☏03/2148 6022, ⊛www.tourworld.com.my); or STA, fifth floor, Magnum Plaza, 128 Jalan Pudu (☏03/2148 9800, ⊛www.statravel.com.my). For packages within Malaysia, you could try Angel Tours, 148a Jalan Bukit Bintang (☏03/2148 8288); Discovery Overland, Block B, Megan Avenue II, 12 Jalan Yap Kwan Seng (☏03/2164 8113, ⊛www .discoveryoverland.com); Holiday Tours, listed above; Jet Asia, Pudu Plaza, Jalan Landak (near the Pudu LRT station; ☏03/2142 1911, ⊛www .jetasiatravel.com); or Malaysian Travel Business, at the MTC tourist office (☏03/2163 0162).

Visa extensions The Immigration Office is at Block 1, Pusat Bandar Damansara (☏03/2095 5077), just beyond the Bangsar Shopping Centre; Metrobus #6 from Chinatown or Rapid KL bus #U82 from KL Sentral will get you there.

Walking tours Malaysian Tourist Guides Council (✉mtgc@streamyx.net) runs three-hour guided walks; they typically start from Merdeka Square and cost RM200 for up to ten people.

Around Kuala Lumpur

With the reckless urbanization of the Klang Valley proceeding apace, pickings are increasingly slim as regards excursions from KL. The most obvious attractions are to the north, where limestone peaks rise up out of the forest and the roads narrow as you pass through small kampungs. There is dramatic scenery as close as 13km from the city, where the Hindu shrine at the **Batu Caves** attracts enough visitors to make it one of Malaysia's main tourist attractions. Nearby, the **Forest Institute of Malaysia** encompasses the portion of primary rainforest nearest to the capital.

A day-trip northwest of KL is the quiet town of **Kuala Selangor** which offers the chance to observe the nightly dance of **fireflies**. But the most surreal day-trip you can make from KL is to the very Chinese fishing village on **Pulau Ketam**, off the coast near Port Klang, which will have you thinking you've fetched up somewhere like Taiwan.

As some of the sights mentioned in this section can be a bit of a slog to get to by public transport, you may want to take advantage of excursions offered by some travel agents, for example at the *Backpacker's Travellers Inn* (see p.92) or MTC (see p.133).

FRIM, Batu Caves and the Orang Asli Museum

Malaysia's **Forest Research Institute** (FRIM), the **Orang Asli Museum** and – one of the most popular attractions around KL – the **Batu Caves** lie to the north of the capital, along or off the so-called Middle Ring Road II, which is called Jalan Batu Caves in the vicinity of the caves themselves. Their proximity to this road makes it feasible to visit all three in a circuit, if you're driving. There are two routes out here: either take the **E8 Highway**, which intersects Jalan Batu Caves, or use **Jalan Ipoh**, which starts at Chow Kit and meets Jalan Batu Caves 4km west of the E8. FRIM is west of Jalan Ipoh, the Orang Asli Museum close to the E8, and the caves are in between the two. Inconveniently, it's largely impossible to go from one sight to the next by bus.

FRIM

If you can't make it out to Taman Negara and its forest-canopy walkway, you can instead stroll through the treetops at the **Forest Research Institute of Malaysia (FRIM)** (Mon–Fri 8am–5.30pm, Sat & Sun 9am–4pm; RM5; ☎03/6279 7525, ⓦwww.frim.gov.my). The canopy walkway here (Tues–Thurs, Sat & Sun 9am–1.30pm; RM5) provides a unique view of KL's skyscrapers through the trees. The fifteen-square-kilometre park also has several worthwhile trails, for which you should bring along drinking water and insect repellent, and wear shoes rather than sandals. For those who wish to learn more about Malaysia's ecological heritage, there's also a museum containing details of the institute's research, an arboretum and an eclectic range of wood-based antiques and implements, including an intricately carved boat, treasure chests and a four-poster bed.

FRIM is signposted 4km west of the junction of Jalan Ipoh and Middle Ring Road II. The best way to get there by public transport is to catch a Komuter **train** to Kepong station, 2km from the site, to which you can continue by taxi.

Batu Caves

Long before you reach the entrance to the **Batu Caves**, you'll see them ahead: small, black holes in the vast limestone thumbs which comprise a ridge of hills in Gombak, on the very fringes of greater KL. In 1891, ten years after the caves were noticed by the American explorer William Hornaby, local Indian dignitaries convinced the British colonial authorities that the caves were ideal places in which to worship (probably because their spectacular geography was thought reminiscent of the sacred Himalayas). Soon ever-increasing numbers of devotees were visiting the caves to pray at the shrine established here to Lord Muruga, also known as **Lord Subramaniam**; later the temple complex was expanded to include a shrine to the elephant-headed deity **Ganesh**. The caves are always

▲ Batu Caves

packed with visitors, but the numbers most days are nothing compared to the thousands upon thousands of devotees who descend here during the annual three-day **Thaipusam festival**.

Arriving at the site, you're immediately struck by the immense staircase leading up into the limestone crags, with a gigantic, recently erected golden statue of **Lord Murugan**, the Hindu god of war, to one side; it's claimed to be the tallest such statue in the world. There are a number of minor temples at ground level, but for many the most tempting thing is to head straight up the 272 individually numbered steps to the caves, pausing only to catch their breath or take photos of the marauding macaques who make their presence all too obvious on the steps and in the caves themselves.

The caves

Three-quarters of the way up the steps – at step 204, to be precise – a turning on the left leads to a vast side cavern known as the **Dark Caves**, which can only be visited on a guided tour (see "Practicalities" opposite). Here a two-kilometre passageway gives onto five chambers populated by a large variety of insects and at least three types of **bats**, which can be distinguished by their faces and calls. The caves also house a variety of interesting limestone formations, including several towering **flow stones**, so called because they have a continuous sheet of water running down them.

Thaipusam at the Batu Caves

The most important festival in the Malaysian Hindu calendar (along with *Deepavali*), **Thaipusam** honours the Hindu deity Lord Subramaniam. It's a day of penance and celebration, held during full moon in the month of "Thai" (relative to the Gregorian calendar, it always falls between mid-Jan and mid-Feb), when huge crowds arrive at the Batu Caves. What was originally intended to be a day of penance for past sins has now become a major tourist attraction, with both Malaysians and foreigners flocking to the festival every year.

The start of *Thaipusam* is marked by the departure at dawn, from KL's Sri Maha Mariamman Temple, of a golden chariot bearing a statue of Subramaniam. Thousands of devotees follow on foot as it makes its seven-hour procession to the caves. As part of their penance – and in a trance-like state – the devotees carry numerous types of **kavadi** ("burdens" in Tamil), the most popular being milk jugs decorated with peacock feathers placed on top of the head, which are connected to the penitents' flesh by hooks. Others wear wooden frames with sharp spikes protruding from them which are carried on the back and hooked into the skin; trident-shaped skewers are placed through some devotees' tongues and cheeks. This rather grisly procession has its origins in India, where most of Lord Subramaniam's temples were sited on high ridges which pilgrims would walk up, carrying heavy pitchers or pots to honour the deity. At Batu Caves, the 272-step climb up to the main chamber expresses the idea that you cannot reach God without expending effort.

Once at the caves, the Subramaniam statue is placed in a tent before being carried up to the temple cave, where devotees participate in ceremonies and rituals to Subramaniam and Ganesh. Things climax with a celebration for Rama, when milk from the *kavadi* vessel can be spilt as an offering; incense and camphor are burned as the bearers unload their devotional burdens.

Extra buses run to the caves during *Thaipusam*. It's advisable to get there early (say 7am) for a good view of the proceedings. Although there are numerous vendors selling food and drink at the caves, it's a good idea to take water and snacks with you, as the size of the crowd is horrendous.

At the top of the main staircase, there's a clear view through to the **Subramaniam Swamy Temple** (daily 8am–7pm), set deep in a cave around 100m high and 80m long, the cave walls lined with idols representing the six lives of Lord Subramaniam. The temple, illuminated via the huge void in the cave ceiling beyond another set of steps far inside the caves, has an entrance guarded by two statues, their index fingers pointing upwards towards the light. Within the temple, devoted to Lord Subramaniam and another deity, Rama, a dome is densely sculpted with more scenes from the scriptures. In a chamber at the back of the temple is a statue of Rama, who watches over the well-being of all immigrants, adorned with silver jewellery and a silk sarong. If you want to look closely at this inner sanctum, the temple staff will mark a small red dot on your forehead, giving you a spiritual right to enter.

Back at ground level, turn right from the main staircase to reach the so-called **Cave Villa** (daily 8.30am–8pm; RM15) a newly established complex incorporating the **Art Gallery Cave**, which contains dozens of striking multicoloured statues of deities, portraying scenes from the Hindu scriptures. There's also a large pond packed with koi carp with a walkway across it for close-up views, though frankly you can get a good look from outside the perimeter railings. It's worth taking a short stroll past the Cave Villa to reach a small side temple fronted by an endearing, bright green statue of **Hanuman**, the monkey god and a central character in the *Ramayana* epic, stories of which are depicted using more statuary in the **Ramayana Cave** beyond (free).

Practicalities

The caves are on Jalan Batu Caves, roughly midway between the junctions with Jalan Ipoh and the E8. The Komuter **rail** service which presently terminates at Sentul is supposed to be extended to Batu Caves by 2010. In the meantime, you can get here on Metrobus #11 from the Bangkok Bank building in Chinatown (hourly; 1hr) or from Jalan Raja Laut in Chow Kit; it's also possible to hop on the LRT to the Gombak terminus, then get a taxi the rest of the way (RM7.50).

There are two tours to the **Dark Caves** (www.darkcave.com.my). The education tour is simply a guided walk around the caves (30min; RM35), on which various creatures and rock formations are pointed out. Much more memorable is the adventure tour (3–4hr; RM80 per person for a group of five or more), on which you get to clamber up, down and through some of the more interesting nooks and crannies of the system. This tour needs to be booked at least two days in advance (through the website or by calling ☎03/6189 6682 or 012 247 5610); boots, helmets and headlamps are provided, but it's best to bring a change of clothes and a towel for freshening up later.

The Orang Asli Museum

Run by the government's Department for Orang Asli Affairs, the **Orang Asli Museum** (daily except Fri 9am–5pm; free), holds a certain interest if this is as far into rural Malaysia as you're going to get. Located about 20km northeast of KL as the crow flies, the museum aims to present a portrait of the various groups of Orang Asli, once nomadic hunter-gatherers in the jungle, though now largely resident in rural settlements.

The foyer contains a large map of the Peninsula making clear that the Orang Asli are found, in varying numbers, in just about every state, a fact that surprises some visitors, who see little sign of them during their travels. Besides collections of the fishing nets, guns and blowpipes the Orang Asli use to eke out their traditional existence, the museum also has photographs of Orang

Asli press-ganged by the Malay and British military to fight the communist guerrillas in the 1950s (see p.697). Other displays describe the changes forced on the Orang Asli over the past thirty years – some positive, like the development of health and school networks, others less encouraging, like the erosion of the family system as young men drift off to look for seasonal work.

Particularly interesting, hidden in an annexe to the rear of the building, are examples of traditional handicrafts, including the **head carvings** made by the Mah Meri tribe from the swampy region on the borders of Selangor and Negeri Sembilan, and the Jah Hut from the slopes of Gunung Benom in central Pehang. The carvings, around 50cm high, show stylized, fierce facial expressions, and are fashioned from a particularly strong, heavy hardwood. They still have religious significance – the most common image used, the animist deity Moyang, represents the spirit of the ancestors.

Practicalities

The Orang Asli Museum is off Jalan Gombak, some 5km east of Batu Caves. The #174 **bus**, operated by either Len Seng or Permata Kiara and signed "Gombak Batu 12", heads here from Lebuh Ampang in Chinatown (around RM3). Ask the driver to tell you when you've arrived, as it's not obvious; leaving the bus, cross to the east side of the road and head 50m further up, where a steep side road leads to the museum. Arriving by **car**, turn east off the E8 onto Jalan Batu Caves and you'll come to Jalan Gombak after 1km; turn left (north) up this and continue another 2km or so to reach the site.

Kuala Selangor and around

KUALA SELANGOR lies close to the coast on Route 5, some 70km northwest of KL, on the banks of Sungai Selangor. A former royal town, today it's a small, sleepy affair; the chief reason a stream of visitors continue to come here is to see the river's **fireflies**, which glow spectacularly in the early evening. But until recently, this natural spectacle looked to be in terminal decline: the fireflies' mangrove habitat was rapidly being cleared, and the river becoming increasingly polluted. Belatedly, the authorities have stepped in with public education programmes to ensure better waste management, and there's talk of setting aside part of the river as a reserve. For the moment, things appear to have stabilized, and you stand a reasonable chance of enjoying a decent light show, weather permitting. It's possible to visit the town on a long day-trip from KL, taking in the town's forts and nature park by day. Just pray there isn't an outbreak of **rain**, as the fireflies don't perform in wet conditions.

All that remains of Kuala Selangor's more glorious past are the remnants of two forts overlooking the town, the largest of which, **Fort Altingberg** (daily 9am–4.30pm; free), recalls a period in Malaysian history when this part of the country changed hands, bloodily, on several occasions. Originally called Fort Melawati, Altingberg was built by local people during the reign of Sultan Ibrahim of Selangor in the eighteenth century, and was later captured by the Dutch (who renamed it) as part of an attempt to wrestle the tin trade from the sultans. The fortress was partly destroyed during local skirmishes in the Selangor Civil War (1867–73). Within its grounds is a cannon, reputed to be from the Dutch era, and a rock used for executions. **Bukit Melawati**, the hill on which the fort is based, also has a lighthouse and a resthouse built during the British colonial period. At weekends the road from the town up to the fort is closed to traffic and all visitors ascend by way of a trolley car (RM2).

Kuala Selangor Nature Park

Its edges lying directly below the fort, the **Kuala Selangor Nature Park** (daily 9am–5.30pm) encompasses mudflats, mangroves and a small patch of forest with clearly marked trails. The area is host to around 150 species of birds, with thirty more migratory species passing through, as well as silverleaf monkeys, which live in the forest, and a variety of crabs and fish in the mangroves.

The park is a five-hundred-metre walk from Bukit Melawati (follow signs for "Taman Alam"). You can also get here on the **buses** which run up Route 5 from Klang; ask to be let off at the park, and you'll be dropped at a petrol station, from where the park is 200m up Jalan Klinik.

Firefly trips

Boats leave on firefly-spotting trips from two locations several kilometres from town: **Bukit Belimbing**, on the north bank across the river bridge; and at **Kampung Kuantan**, on the south bank. At Bukit Belimbing, trips are run by the **Firefly Park Resort**, from whose jetty motorized boats set out on half-hour trips (daily 7.45–10pm; RM12 per person); boats from Kampung Kuantan's jetty operate to a similar schedule and at similar prices. There are no buses to either of the jetties, so taxis from Kuala Selangor get away with pretty steep prices – expect a ride to the resort to cost at least RM15. It's important to remain quiet when watching the firefly display and not to take flash photographs, as such behaviour scares the insects away.

Practicalities

Kuala Selangor is very close to the junction of Route 5 and Route 54, which leads here from KL via Sungai Buloh. The **drive** from KL takes at least an hour depending on traffic and your starting point; take the E1 northbound from KL (as described on p.132) and turn off onto Route 54 at the Sungai Buloh exit. If you're heading for Kampung Kuantan, look out for a signed turning on the right as you near Kuala Selangor.

Red-and-white Selangor Omnibus **buses** (#141; RM5.50; 2hr) head to Kuala Selangor roughly hourly, either from bay 23 in Puduraya station or from just outside the station; you can also pick up the service from the clock tower in Chinatown and in the Chow Kit area. Note that the last bus back to KL leaves around 8pm, so if you want to see the fireflies, you'll have to overnight in Kuala Selangor unless you come on a tour from KL (for example, the RM180 fireflies trip offered by Malaysian Travel Business, see p.133) or have your own transport. The town has a **bus station** along Route 5, about 2km south of the centre. Local buses leave here bound for the centre, which is a

Fireflies

There are more than a hundred species of firefly, among which those found in Southeast Asia give some of the most striking displays. The **fireflies** of the kind found in Kuala Selangor, known as *kelip-kelip* in Malay, are actually six-millimetre-long beetles which belong to the *Lampyridae* family, and can be found in a belt stretching from India to Papua New Guinea.

During the day, the fireflies rest on blades of grass or in palm trees behind the river's mangrove swamps. After sunset they move to the mangroves themselves, the males attracting mates with **synchronized flashes** of light at a rate of three per second (scientists are still trying to work out exactly why the males flash in this manner). Females flash back at males to indicate interest and initiate mating. The most successful males are apparently those which flash most brightly and fly fastest.

nondescript square, but you'll probably find that buses pass through the station and terminate at the square itself, very close to Bukit Melawati.

The only **hotel** in town itself is the *Kuala Selangor*, on the central square (☎03/3289 2709; ❷). A simple, homely place, it has a variety of rooms, including some with air-conditioning and en-suite facilities. Basic chalets with fan and bathroom are available in the Nature Park (☎03/3289 2294, ⓔksnaturepark@yahoo.com; ❷), for which you'll generally need to reserve at weekends. As there's nowhere to get food here, you may want to bring your own provisions. The slickest accommodation in the area is at the *Firefly Park Resort* (☎03/3289 1208, ⓦwww.fireflypark.com; Mon–Thurs ❺, otherwise ❼), where chalets have all mod cons. The resort has its own café (rates include breakfast), but for food, it's a better idea to try one of the **seafood restaurants** at Pasir Penambang, on the north bank of the Selangor River 5km from Kuala Selangor; make your way across the river bridge, turn left and it's signed down a turning on the left.

Port Klang and Pulau Ketam

Eight kilometres west of Klang is **PORT KLANG**, from where ferries run to Indonesia and to nearby **Pulau Ketam**, home to an old Chinese fishing village with temples, seafood restaurants and a relaxed feel. Port Klang itself has little of interest, but has some good **seafood restaurants** of its own nearby at Teluk Gong, easily reached by taxi.

The best way to get here is by Komuter train; the **train station** is opposite the **ferry terminal**, with bus passengers disembarking 100m further along the road from here. From the terminal, comfortable air-conditioned boats leave for Sumatra, bound for either **Dumai** (2 daily; RM110) or **Tanjung Balai** (2 daily; RM120); to find out the latest schedules, call the boat operators on ☎03/3165 7501 or 3165 3073.

Pulau Ketam

Small, narrow **ferries** kitted out like aircraft cabins also depart from the Port Klang ferry terminal for **PULAU KETAM** (roughly daily 8.30am–6.30pm: Mon–Fri hourly, Sat & Sun every 45min; RM7), taking up to 45 minutes to reach the island. The moment you set foot inside one of the vessels, you're in a kind of parallel universe: this is Chinese day-tripper land, with videos of Chinese karaoke clips or soap operas blaring from the on-board video screens. The boats may call en route at another island where there's a rustic fishing village called **Sungai Lima**, merely a foretaste of the village on Pulau Ketam itself, where every house is built on pilings above the sand, and practically every street is a concrete walkway or boardwalk raised up in the same fashion.

Close to the jetty is a friendly travel agency (ⓦwww.greenway2u.com) which sells a colourful but rather schematic **map** of the village (you won't need it as it's hard to get lost) as well as arranging walking **tours** of the island and its fish farms (around RM15 per person). The island's mosque is just a short walk on from the jetty on Jalan Merdeka, the main thoroughfare, but in truth most of the island's five thousand inhabitants are Buddhist Teochew and Hokkien Chinese. The road soon veers left and is lined with grocers and other shops, and **restaurants** serving seafood including, of course, crab (as the Malay word *ketam* translates) – some of the poor creatures are tied up in buckets, eyes twitching on stalks, as they await customers selecting them for the pot. Beyond a shop selling Buddhist paraphernalia is a sort of central square where you'll find the **Hock Leng Temple**, as well as a small grotto

▲ Pulau Ketam

containing a representation of Kwan Yin, the Goddess of Mercy, looking decidedly Madonna-like with a halo of red electric lights.

From here, you can wander around as you please. If you backtrack a little and take a turning on the left, you reach a bridge over a creek lined with houses with sampans moored below; continue on from here to enter a largely Teochew residential neighbourhood. If you move on from the central square, you come to yet another residential area of concrete and wooden houses, nearly all with their front doors left wide open. There's plenty of refuse littering the mudflats beneath, unfortunately, but more endearingly you'll also see shrines outside many homes and occasional collections of pans made of netting containing seafood products being left out to dry. Do heed cries of "Ding! Ding!" uttered by schoolkids racing up behind you on bicycles with no bells.

There are a number of inexpensive **hotels** where you can overnight, including the *Hotel Sea Lion* (☎03/3110 4121; ❸) and the *Pulau Ketam Inn* (☎03/3110 5206; ❷) on Jalan Merdeka.

Travel details

Trains

KL to: Alor Star (daily; 11hr 45min); Butterworth (3 daily; 9hr); Dabong (daily; 11hr); Gemas (4 daily; 3hr 30min); Gua Musang (daily; 9hr 30min); Jerantut (daily; 7hr); Hat Yai (Thailand; daily; 14hr 30min); Ipoh (3 daily; 3hr 30min); Johor Bahru (3 daily; 6hr 30min); Kuala Kangsar (3 daily; 5hr 45min); Kuala Lipis (daily; 8hr); Port Klang (frequent; 1hr); Seremban (frequent; 1hr–1hr 30min); Singapore (3 daily; 8hr); Sungai Petani (daily; 10hr 45min); Taiping (3 daily; 6hr 45min); Wakaf Bharu (for Kota Bharu; daily; 13hr 15min).

Buses

Buses depart from KL for major destinations around the Peninsula frequently, typically hourly or every two hours throughout the day, with additional night-time departures on the longest routes. Frequencies are given below only where there are significant departures from this pattern.

Pasar Rakyat station to: Singapore (several daily; 6hr).

Pekeliling station to: Jerantut (4 daily; 3hr 30min); Kuala Lipis (6 daily; 4hr 30min); Kuala Terengganu (several daily; 7hr); Kuantan (3hr 30min); Temerloh (2hr 30min); Triang (several daily; 4hr).

Pudu Raya station to: Alor Star (8hr); Butterworth (5hr 30min); Cameron Highlands (4hr 30min); Genting Highlands (1hr); Georgetown (6hr); Hat Yai (Thailand; several daily; 9hr); Ipoh (4hr); Johor Bahru (5hr); Kuantan (4hr); Lumut (4hr); Melaka (2hr); Mersing (at least 5 daily; 6hr); Seremban (1hr); Singapore (6hr); Taiping (4hr 30min).

Putra station to: Gua Musang (several daily; 5hr); Kota Bharu (9hr); Kuala Besut (for the Perhentians; 1–2 daily; 8hr); Kuala Terengganu (several daily; 7hr); Kuantan (3 daily; 3hr 30min); Tasik Kenyir (2 daily; 8hr).

Ferries

Port Klang to: Dumai (Sumatra; 2 daily; 2hr 45min); Pulau Ketam (every 45min–1hr; 45min); Tanjung Balai (Sumatra; 2 daily; 3hr 30min).

Flights

Besides the flights listed below, there are also several flights a day with Singapore Airlines and Tiger Airways to Singapore, and with Royal Brunei Airways to Bandar Seri Begawan.

MAS

KLIA to: Alor Star (2 daily; 50min); Bandar Seri Begawan (daily; 2hr 20min); Bintulu (2 daily; 2hr 15min); Johor Bahru (5 daily; 45min); Kota Bharu (5 daily; 55min); Kota Kinabalu (9 daily; 2hr 30min); Kuala Terengganu (3 daily; 45min); Kuantan (5 daily; 40min); Kuching (at least 10 daily; 1hr 45min); Labuan (2 daily; 2hr 25min); Langkawi (5 daily; 55min); Miri (5 daily; 2hr 15min); Penang (at least 10 daily; 45min); Sibu (1 daily; 2hr); Singapore (at least 12 daily; 55min); Tawau (daily; 2hr 45min)

AirAsia

KLIA Low-Cost-Carrier Terminal to: Alor Star (daily; 55min); Bintulu (2 daily; 2hr); Johor Bahru (daily; 50min); Kota Bharu (3 daily; 55min); Kota Kinabalu (7 daily; 2hr 30min); Kuala Terengganu (2 daily; 55min); Kuantan (daily; 30min); Kuching (7 daily; 1hr 40min); Labuan (2 daily; 2hr 25min); Langkawi (5 daily; 1hr); Miri (3 daily; 2hr 15min); Penang (3 daily; 40min); Sandakan (3 daily; 2hr 45min); Sibu (3 daily; 1hr 45min); Singapore (5 daily; 55min); Tawau (3 daily; 2hr 45min).

Berjaya Air

Subang Airport to: Pulau Pangkor (5 weekly; 40min); Pulau Redang (March–Oct 2 daily; 45min); Pulau Tioman (2 daily; 1hr).

Firefly

Subang Airport to: Johor Bahru (2 daily; 45min); Kuala Terengganu (2 daily; 55min); Kota Bharu (3 daily; 55min); Langkawi (daily; 55min); Penang (5 daily; 45min).

2

The west coast

CHAPTER 2   # Highlights

* **Cameron Highlands**
  Cool down amidst the tea
  plantations and jungle trails
  of this colonial hill station.
  See p.148

* **Kellie's Castle** A never-
  completed picturesque 1920s
  Scottish mansion set in the
  hills near Ipoh. See p.163

* **Pulau Pangkor** Laid-back
  tropical island with some of
  the best beaches on the west
  coast. See p.164

* **Kuala Kangsar** Sleepy but
  charming royal capital with a
  splendid mosque and sultan's
  palace. See p.170

* **Taiping** Bustling traditional
  town with tranquil gardens
  and a mini hill station
  as well as Malaysia's
  largest Mangrove Reserve
  nearby. See p.172

* **Georgetown** Bustling
  Chinese-dominated haven
  with elaborate temples,
  colonial mansions and
  beaches galore. See p.180

* **Ulu Muda Forest Reserve**
  West Malaysia's unexplored
  nature reserve with over
  500 square kilometres of
  preserved rainforest.
  See p.207

* **Langkawi** Perfect
  beaches and exotic resorts
  characterize these islands
  close to Thailand.
  See p.208

▲ Kellie's Castle

2

The west coast

The **west coast** of Peninsular Malaysia, from Kuala Lumpur north to the Thai border, is the most industrialized and densely populated – not to mention cosmopolitan – part of the whole country. Its considerable natural resources have long brought eager traders and entrepreneurs here, but it was the demand for the region's tin in the late nineteenth century that spearheaded Malaysia's phenomenal economic rise. Immigrant workers, most of whom settled in the region for good, bestowed a permanent legacy here – the predominantly Chinese towns that punctuate the route north. **Perak State** (*perak* meaning "silver") once boasted the richest single tin field in the world. When the light industry surrounding Malaysia's other major commodity, rubber, took over from the dying tin trade in the 1950s, the essentially agricultural nature of much of the region wasn't quite obliterated. The states of **Kedah** and **Perlis**, the latter tucked into the northern border, share the distinction of being the historical *jelapang padi*, or "rice bowl", of Malaysia, where rich, emerald-green paddy fields and jutting limestone outcrops form the Peninsula's most dramatic scenery, also hosting the peaceful **Perlis State Park**, a great place for caving. More adventurous nature trekking is on offer in the stunning **Ulu Muda Forest Reserve**, which borders Kedah and Thailand, and is a great, unexplored and vast expanse of rainforest and several salt licks, home to much wildlife, including white elephants, tapirs and panthers. It is also possible to go tubing down shallow river rapids and camp overnight in the jungle here.

Most visitors are too intent on the beckoning delights of Thailand to bother stopping at anything other than the major destinations. But nowhere are the rural delights of the country more apparent than at the **hill stations** north of the capital, once cool refuges for colonial administrators. The largest of these, the **Cameron Highlands**, some 150km north of KL, is one of the country's most significant tourist spots, a locally popular mountain retreat with opportunities for forest treks and indulgence in the traditional British comforts of crackling log fires and cream teas.

Due west of here, tiny and tranquil **Pulau Pangkor**, though not as idyllic as the islands of the Peninsula's east coast, is an increasingly visited resort, with the best beaches in the area. However, the fastest development is on its far northern rival, **Pulau Langkawi**, the largest island in the glittering and largely unpopulated Langkawi archipelago. Most travellers wisely have little time for the mainland port of **Butterworth**, just using it for access to the UNESCO World Heritage site and holiday island of **Penang**, whose vibrant capital, **Georgetown**, combines modern shopping malls with ancient Chinese shophouses.

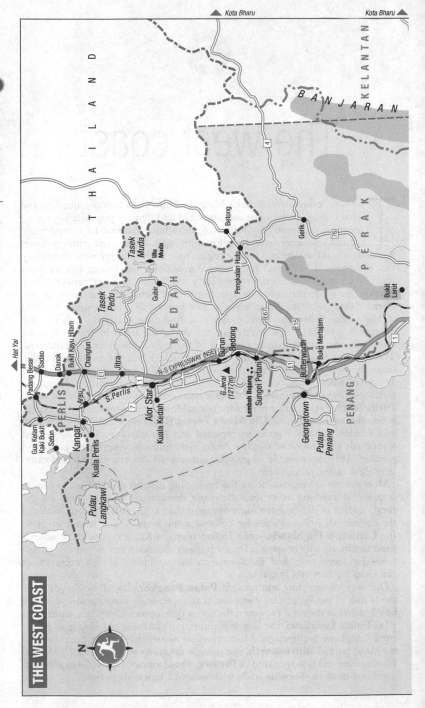

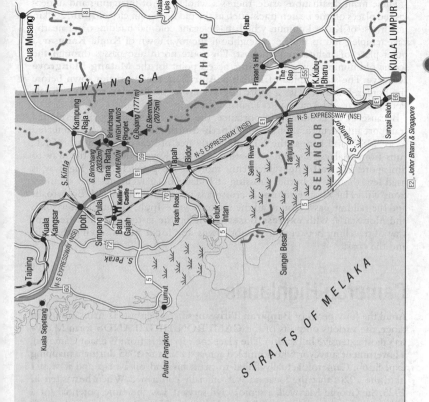

These main destinations aside, there's a whole host of intriguing and under-visited places off the beaten track, such as the old tin-boom city of **Ipoh**, 200km northwest of Kuala Lumpur, which has elegant colonial buildings and nearby cave temples, and its northern neighbour the royal town of **Kuala Kangsar**, a quiet place of architectural interest. The route north also passes through the scenic old mining town of **Taiping**, access point for the **Matang Mangrove Reserve**. The state capital of Kedah is **Alor Star**, the last major town before the border. From here it's a short hop via any of the **border towns** – Kuala Perlis, Kangar and Arau – into Thailand itself.

Because of its economic importance, the west coast has a well-developed transport infrastructure. The wide **North–South Expressway** (also referred to as "NSE" and here as the **E1**), pleasantly free of heavy traffic north of KL, runs from Malaysia's northern border at Bukit Kayu Hitam all the way to Singapore. The **rail line**, which runs more or less parallel to the highway, is used less, though its border crossing at Padang Besar facilitates easy connections with Hat Yai, the transport crossroads of southern Thailand. Both roads and the rail line pass through all the major towns – Ipoh, Taiping, Butterworth and Alor Star – with **express buses** providing the fastest and most frequent way of travelling between the major towns, and **local buses** serving the hills and the coast.

Cameron Highlands

Amid the lofty peaks of **Banjaran Titiwangsa**, the Peninsula's main mountain range, the various outposts of the **CAMERON HIGHLANDS** form Malaysia's most extensive hill station. The place took its name from William Cameron, a government surveyor who stumbled across the area in 1885 during a mapping expedition. Cameron actually failed to mark his find on a map, and it wasn't until the 1920s that the location was officially confirmed. When he visited in 1925, Sir George Maxwell, a senior civil servant, saw the same potential for a hill station here as he'd seen at Fraser's Hill (see p.252). Others, too, were quick to see the benefits of the region. Tea planters migrating from India were followed by Chinese vegetable farmers and wealthy landowners in search of a weekend retreat; the Highlands' subsequent development culminated in today's hotels and luxury apartments. The "Ye Olde English" atmosphere really does feel contrived at times, but there is no denying that the locals get a kick out of it. Despite the crowds and crassness – especially during the March to May hot-season school holidays – there are some leisurely nature walks up here, and if you have been in the lowlands of Malaysia or Southeast Asia for some time, the Highlands are a good place to cool off and clear out your lungs, sample the locally produced strawberries or relax with tea and scones.

The highlands encompass three small towns: **Ringlet**, a rich agricultural area and site of the famous tea plantations; 13km beyond and 300m higher, **Tanah Rata**, the principal settlement of the highlands; and 5km further north, **Brinchang**, renowned for the fruit and vegetable farms to the north of the town. The best **accommodation** is in Tanah Rata and Brinchang. Accommodation **prices** soar at peak holiday times (Christmas, Easter, Hari Raya and Deepavali) when you can expect the price of an ordinary room to double; book ahead to ensure a place. A useful website with more on accommodation plus other aspects of visiting the Highlands is ⓦ www.cameronhighlands.com.

Tours of the whole region, which take around three hours, can be arranged by any of the hotels or hostels and depart from your place of accommodation

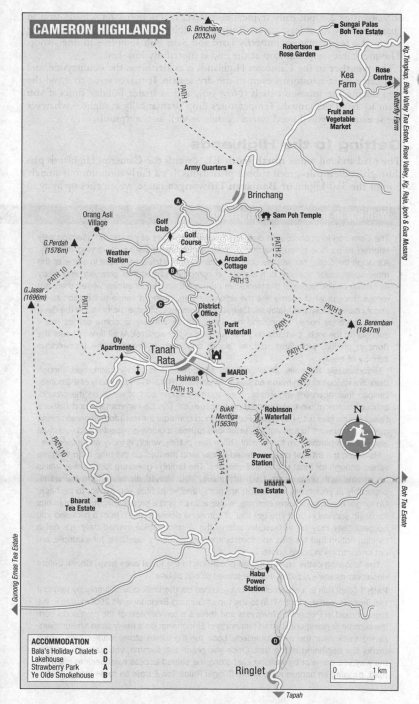

CAMERON HIGHLANDS

G. Brinchang (2032m)

Sungai Palas Boh Tea Estate

Robertson Rose Garden

Kea Farm

Rose Centre

Fruit and Vegetable Market

Army Quarters

Brinchang

Sam Poh Temple

Orang Asli Village

Golf Club

Golf Course

G. Perdah (1576m)

Weather Station

Arcadia Cottage

G. Jasar (1696m)

District Office

Parit Waterfall

G. Bereman (1847m)

Oly Apartments

Tanah Rata

Haiwan

MARDI

Bukit Mentiga (1563m)

Robinson Waterfall

Power Station

Bharat Tea Estate

Bharat Tea Estate

Gunong Emas Tea Estate

Habu Power Station

Ringlet

Tapah

PATH 1
PATH 2
PATH 3
PATH 3
PATH 4
PATH 5
PATH 7
PATH 8
PATH 9
PATH 9A
PATH 10
PATH 11
PATH 10
PATH 13
PATH 14

N

0   1 km

ACCOMMODATION
Bala's Holiday Chalets   C
Lakehouse   D
Strawberry Park   A
Ye Olde Smokehouse   B

Kg. Tringkap, Blue Valley Tea Estate, Rose Valley, Kg. Raja, Ipoh & Gua Musang

Butterfly Farm

Boh Tea Estate

at 9.30am or 2.30pm daily (typical cost RM25). Though a bit whistle-stop in character, they do at least cover all the main sights and destinations – including a stop at a tea plantation, butterfly farm and Sam Poh Temple – in one swoop. The inevitable shopping stop at the end is mercifully low-key.

The **weather** in the Cameron Highlands is as British as the countryside, and you can expect rainstorms even in the dry season. It makes sense to avoid the area during the monsoon itself (Nov–Jan), and at major holiday times if you want to avoid the crowds. Temperatures drop dramatically at night – whatever the season – so you'll need warm clothes, as well as waterproofs.

Getting to the Highlands

The road and rail routes **north from KL** towards the Cameron Highlands pass through endless pale-green rubber plantations. It's a fairly monotonous stretch, but for the 350-kilometre **Banjaran Titiwangsa** range, which rises up away to

---

Walking in the Cameron Highlands

The Cameron Highlands, with over ten thousand species of plants and affectionately referred to as "the green pharmacy", offer a number of **walks** of varying difficulty. Although the forest sometimes obscures the view, the trails here take in some of the most spectacular scenery in Malaysia, encompassing textured greenery and misty mountain peaks. Some of the walks are no more than casual strolls, while others are romps through what seems like the wild unknown, giving a sense of isolation rarely encountered in lowland Malaysia. Despite the presence of large mammals in the deep forest, such as honey bears and monkeys, you're unlikely to come across many animals on the trails, perhaps only the odd wild pig or squirrel. At all times of year the **flora** is prolific, with ferns, pitcher plants and orchids amongst the tremendous canopy of trees.

Unfortunately, the trails are often badly signposted and poorly maintained, though there are various sketch **maps** on sale in Tanah Rata (RM3–4) and at many of the hotels. Despite their apparent vagueness, they do make some sort of sense on the ground, although some of the trails marked no longer exist. The *Cameronian Inn* and *Father's Guest House* (see p.154) in Tanah Rata are good contacts for trail information and hiring guides. If you want to attempt any **unofficial routes**, a guide is essential and you must also obtain a permit from the District Office (see p.156), which is tricky and expensive.

However, the **official trails**, detailed below (and marked on the map on p.149) are varied enough for most tastes and energies. The timings given are for one-way walks for people with an average level of fitness. You should always inform someone, preferably at your hotel, where you are going and what time you expect to be back. On longer hikes, take warm clothing, water, a torch and a cigarette lighter or matches for basic survival should you get lost. If someone doesn't return from a hike and you suspect they may be in **trouble**, inform the District Office immediately. It's not a fanciful notion that the hills and forests are dangerous – mudslides, for example, are not uncommon in some spots.

The following paths are numbered according to the **local area map**. Check before departing as several paths may be closed or out of use.

Path 1 (2hr) This is a steep climb, but you can do the walk downhill only by taking a taxi (from Brinchang for RM15) to the top of Gunung Brinchang. At 2000m, this is the highest road in Peninsular Malaysia and there's a terrific view of the highlands from the summit. If going uphill, start just north of Brinchang, on a rarely used and unmaintained track near the army quarters. Look for the white stone marker 1/48 which marks the beginning of the trail. Once you reach the summit, you can either return the way you came or by walking east along the sealed access road back to the main road, passing an access road to the Sungai Palas Tea Estate en route (see p.158).

the east. Hardly more than a crossroads, **Tapah** lies about 40km to the southwest of the Highlands along Route 59 (a long and winding road providing a scenic, but dizzying journey). Tapah is the main train stop for the Cameron Highlands, but faster buses now travel directly to Tanah Rata. There is also a new road to the Highlands from the town of Simpang Pulai (Exit 137), on the North–South Expressway just south of Ipoh. Although not quite as scenic as the old road, most public transport now uses this route. From Simpang Pulai, the gateway town of Kampung Raja is reached in less than an hour.

If you're **driving from KL**, you may want to go via Tapah, but continue your journey north via the new road through Kampung Raja rather than doubling back on Route 59. If you have time to spare and want to get off the main highways, a less direct but more interesting route is the coastal Route 5, running through low-lying marshland almost all the way to **Teluk Intan**, 157km northwest of the capital. Here you can stop off at the leaning

Path 2 (1hr 30min) Begins just before the Sam Poh Temple below Brinchang – not clearly marked, and often a bit of a scramble, you'll need to be reasonably fit and well prepared for this option. The route undulates severely and eventually merges with Path 3.

Path 3 (2hr 30min) Starts at *Arcadia Cottage* to the southeast of the golf course, crossing streams and climbing quite steeply to reach the peak of Gunung Beremban (1841m). Once at the top, you can retrace your steps, or head down Path 5, 7 or 8.

Path 4 (20min) Paved in stretches, this walk starts south of the golf course and goes past Parit Waterfall, leading on to a watchtower with good views over Brinchang. The last stop is the Forest Department HQ from where a sealed path leads back to the main road.

Path 5 (1hr) Branches off from Path 3 and ends up at the Malaysian Agriculture Research and Development Institute (MARDI). It's an easy walk through peaceful woodland, after which you can cut back up the road to Tanah Rata.

Path 7 (2hr) Starts near MARDI and climbs steeply to Gunung Beremban; an arduous and very overgrown hike best recommended as a descent route from Path 3.

Path 8 (3hr) Another route to Gunung Beremban, a tough approach from Robinson Waterfall; more taxing than Path 7.

Path 9 and **9A** (1hr) The descent from Robinson Waterfall to the power station is steep and strenuous; the station caretaker will let you through to the road to Boh. Path 9A, an easier downhill grade than Path 9, branches off from the main route and emerges in a vegetable farm on the Boh road.

Path 10 (2hr 30min) Starts just behind the *Oly Apartments* and involves a fairly strenuous climb to Gunung Jasar (1696m). It then drops down to the Orang Asli village, where you join a small road leading back to the main road.

Path 11 (2hr) Takes you up to Gunung Perdah (1576m), a slightly shorter and less challenging route than Path 10. Again, you come out at the Orang Asli village and take the small road back into town.

Path 13 (1hr) An alternate access to Path 14, its starting point is a half-hour's walk southwest of the *Cameronian Holiday Inn* in Tanah Rata.

Path 14 (3hr) This is a tricky and initially steep route via Bukit Mentiga (1563m), with great views. It begins at Haiwan (a veterinary centre) and continues south, becoming very hard to make out until it joins the road 8km from Tanah Rata. Best not to do this one alone.

▲ Cameron Highlands

pagoda-like clock tower and grab a bowl of noodles, before taking the minor back roads to **Bidor**, 14km south of Tapah, to connect with the North–South Expressway and Route 1. If you're coming from the **east coast** via motorbike or four-wheel drive, you can take the rather rough road from Gua Musang to Brinchang (90km).

There are five express buses a day **from KL** (4hr; RM35 directly to Tanah Rata) to the Highlands (the last one leaves at 3.30pm). Tour operators offer daily direct connections from Taman Negara and the Perhentians, too.

Ringlet and the Boh Tea Estate

There's not much to **RINGLET**, the first settlement you reach in the Cameron Highlands, 47km from Tapah. There are several **tea plantations** in the area; one of the most worthwhile to visit is the **Boh Tea Estate** (Tues–Sun 11am–3pm), 8km northeast of town. There's a free tour on which you'll see the whole production process – from the picking to the packing of the tea, which you cannot do at the estate's more frequented **Palas** division, north of Brinchang (see p.158). There are buses from Ringlet to Habu daily at approximately hourly intervals from 8am to 5.30pm. From here, it's another 10km on a hilly and winding road to the estate. The quickest way to get to the tea estate is to take a taxi (RM30 one way) from Tanah Rata. **Buses** from Tapah stop on the main road in Ringlet before moving on to Tanah Ratah, from where there are buses eight times a day back to Ringlet starting at 8am, with the last service at 5.30pm. Although this is a rather isolated place to base yourself, there is one deluxe **place to stay**, the *Lakehouse* (T05/495 6152, Wwww.lakehouse -cameron.com; O), an elegant Tudor-style mansion with a lounge, games room, and restaurant serving traditional English food.

Tanah Rata

The tidy town of **TANAH RATA** is the Highlands' most developed settlement, a bustling place festooned with hotels, white-balustraded buildings, flowers and parks. It comprises little more than one street (officially called Jalan

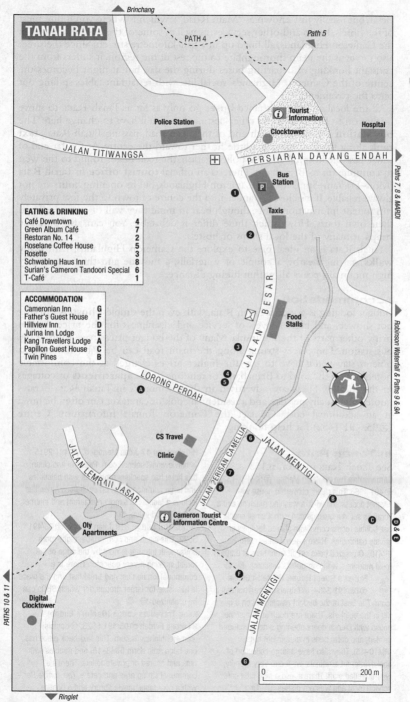

TANAH RATA

Brinchang

PATH 4

Path 5

Police Station

Tourist Information

Clocktower

Hospital

JALAN TITIWANGSA

PERSIARAN DAYANG ENDAH

Paths 7, 8 & MARDI

Bus Station

Taxis

1

2

EATING & DRINKING

Café Downtown	4
Green Album Café	7
Restoran No. 14	2
Roselane Coffee House	5
Rosette	3
Schwabing Haus Inn	8
Surian's Cameron Tandoori Special	6
T-Café	1

ACCOMMODATION

Cameronian Inn	G
Father's Guest House	F
Hillview Inn	D
Jurina Inn Lodge	E
Kang Travellers Lodge	A
Papillon Guest House	C
Twin Pines	B

JALAN BESAR

Food Stalls

Robinson Waterfall & Paths 9 & 9A

3

LORONG PERDAH

4

5

A

N

CS Travel

Clinic

6

JALAN MENTIGI

JALAN PERSIAN CAMELIA

7

8

JALAN LEMRAII JASAR

Oly Apartments

Cameron Tourist Information Centre

B

C

D & E

F

JALAN MENTIGI

PATHS 10 & 11

Digital Clocktower

G

0	200 m

Ringlet

Besar, but usually just known as "Main Road"), which is where you'll find most of the hotels, banks and other services, as well as some of the best restaurants in the Cameron Highlands, all lined up in a half-kilometre stretch. Since the street also serves as the main thoroughfare to the rest of the region, it suffers from the constant honking of departing buses during the day, but at night becomes the centre of the Cameron Highlands' social life, with restaurant tables spilling out onto the pavement.

All the local and long-distance **buses** go only as far as Tanah Rata; to move further on to Brinchang and other destinations you'll have to change here. The **bus station** is near the north end of the main road, passing Tanah Rata's **taxi rank** along the way, located a little further toward the centre. At the far end of town, past the hospital and the police station, the road bends round to the west to continue on to Brinchang. There is an official **tourist office** in Tanah Rata (Mon–Fri 9am–5pm) for the Cameron Highlands, but its opening hours are not always reliable. If it's closed, wander into the centre of town to the few privately run tourist information spots, though bear in mind they will of course sell you their own tours. How much these differ is debatable. You can also purchase **maps** at many of the local shops or hostels.

Tanah Rata is an ideal base to explore the Cameron Highlands, with many **walks** starting nearby, a couple of waterfalls, a mosque and three reasonably high mountain peaks all within hiking distance.

Accommodation

Budget lodging is good in Tanah Rata, with even the simplest **hostels** offering hot showers and higher levels of service and cleanliness for the price than in many other parts of the Peninsula. Many of the budget places have touts at the bus station. The places strung along the main road can be a bit noisy; for a quieter stay you'll have to pay the higher prices charged at the comfortable hotels out on the road to Brinchang, or rent one of the **apartments** or cottages in the locality. These are advertised in shop windows in Tanah Rata – rates quoted are usually per day, and a residential cook or caretaker can often be hired at an additional cost. Contact the Cameron Tourist Information Centre (℡05/491 1452) for help booking.

In Tanah Rata

See Tanah Rata map on p.153.

Cameronian Inn 16 Jalan Mentigi ℡05/491 1327, ℻491 4966. This clean, converted house with internet access and wi-fi, a washing machine and a library is set in a quiet garden with a small snack bar. Double rooms come with shared facilities or private bathrooms. There's also a small dorm (RM10). Organized treks set off from here at 9.30am most mornings, with non-guests welcome. ❷–❹

Father's Guest House Off Jalan Gereja ℡05/491 2484, ℮fathersonline@hotmail .com. The best of the budget places, set on a quiet hill in the outskirts. There are doubles in a stone house with French doors opening onto a secluded garden, and dorm beds in aluminium huts (RM10–15). They also have a large collection of books, internet terminals, wi-fi and very friendly, well-travelled staff. There's also a nice little café serving local and Western dishes. ❷–❹

Hillview Inn 17 Jalan Mentigi ℡05/491 2915, ℮hillviewinn@hotmail.com. Peaceful and clean, this hotel has spacious rooms, all with balconies and large common areas on each floor. Amenities include a laundry, a simple restaurant and internet access. Good value. ❸

Jurina Hill Lodge 819 Jalan Mentigi ℡05/491 5522. This clean and comfortable eight-room house with internet is right by the edge of the forest, making it very peaceful. There is a communal kitchen serving breakfast and the place is available for larger groups, for which BBQs can be organized. ❸–❹

Kang Travellers Lodge (Daniel's Lodge) 9 Lorong Perdah ℡05/491 5823, ℗daniels .cameronhighlands.com. This laid-back place has one huge attic dorm (RM8–15) and doubles with fans and shared or private toilets. There's a communal sitting area and café – The Jungle Bar – with a pool table, movie library and a bonfire (weather permitting) though some of the furniture could do with a good scrub. Tours can also be organized. ❷

Papillon Guest House 8 Jalan Mentigi ☎013/301 8535. Very friendly family house with dorms (RM12) and en-suite doubles. There's a kitchen, laundry facilities and a lounge. Though it is pretty basic, the owner guarantees no bedbugs along with offering free reiki. Rates include a light breakfast. ❷

Twin Pines 2 Jalan Mentigi ☎05/491 2169, ⊛twinpines.cameronhighlands.com. Set back from the road with a blue roof, this laid-back place is popular with travellers and has well-informed and friendly staff, though it can be noisy due to the thin-walled rooms. There's an attractive patio garden, a café and online facilities. Dorms are RM12 and rooms are with shared or private bath. ❶–❸

On the road to Brinchang

See Cameron Highlands map on p.149.

Bala's Holiday Chalets ☎05/491 1660, ⊛www.balaschalet.com. A kilometre or so towards

Brinchang, this lovingly refurbished colonial-era boarding school has a variety of tastefully furnished rooms. There's a lounge, dining rooms and a log fire plus beautiful gardens, which are a great spot for afternoon tea. Internet service and free shuttle pick-up from Tanah Rata. ❺–❻

Strawberry Park ☎05/491 1166, ℱ05/491 1949. A modern apartment-style hotel in a great location at the top of a hill, making it rather inaccessible, though a hotel minibus leaves on request. There's an indoor swimming pool and sauna, which are also available to non-guests for day-use. Tennis courts along with a golf course and a discotheque make up for the rather over-priced rooms. ❾

Ye Olde Smokehouse Hotel ☎05/491 1215, ⊛www.thesmokehouse.com.my. Midway along the Tanah Rata–Brinchang road. Twelve suites, most with four-poster beds, and a faint smoky aroma throughout. The hotel was built in 1937 and its colonial-era pedigree is what you pay for. Leaded windows and wooden beams give a country-pub feel. Rates include English breakfast. ❾

Eating and drinking

The local Highlands speciality is Chinese **steamboat**. It's similar to a meat fondue, and involves cooking your food at the table on a burner. You get vegetables, meat and prawns, which you dip in a boiling pot filled with stock. The Malay **food stalls** along the main road are open in the evening and serve satay, *tom yam* (spicy Thai soup) and the usual rice and noodle combinations, for about RM4 per dish.

Café Downtown 41 Jalan Besar. This is a good spot for breakfast and lunch. Does tasty pastries and cakes as well as set meals of noodles and rice.

Green Album Café 58b Jalan Perisan Camellia. Upstairs above the shops parallel to Jalan Besar, this delightful little café with friendly staff offers local teas and coffees, fresh smoothies, fruit juices as well as Thai and Chinese food.

Restoran No. 14 Jalan Besar, across from the petrol station. This popular banana-leaf restaurant serves cheap and tasty *masala dosai* and good early-morning breakfast roti.

Roselane Coffee House 44 Jalan Besar. The various set menus and low-price meat grills here make up for the twee decor. Local and English dishes are on the menu.

Rosette Jalan Besar. Along with wi-fi, this reasonably priced place has a curiously diverse menu of ramen, set breakfasts, steamboat and scones.

Schwabing Haus Inn 57b Jalan Perisan Camellia. Almost next door to the *Green Album Café*, this

Swiss-German restaurant is slightly overpriced, but a good choice if you are hungry for Western food. The mushroom soup is good.

Surian's Cameron Tandoori Special Corner of Jalan Perisan Camellia and Jalan Mentigi. As the name might suggest, this place has great tandoori dishes and excellent naan breads.

T-Café Jalan Besar. This place has the Highland's best baked goodies, as well as an excellent selection of vegetarian dishes. The apple pie is a house speciality. Not to be confused with the fast-food place next door – the entrance is at the side of the building.

Ye Olde Smokehouse On the Tanah Rata–Brinchang road ☎05/491 1215. The eponymous hotel opens its restaurant to non-guests, but enforces a formal (given the decor) dress code. Unless you're absolutely dying for a traditional English roast – and are ready to pay dearly for it – it's probably better to wait until you get home.

Listings

Banks There is a branch of HSBC on Jalan Besar, north of the post office, and a Maybank with an ATM on the northern branch of Jalan Mentigi.
District office 39007 Tanah Rata ☎ 05/491 1066, ⓕ 491 1843 (Mon–Thurs 8am–1pm & 2–4.30pm, Fri 8am–12.15pm & 2.45–4.30pm, Sat 8am–12.15pm). Contact them immediately if you suspect someone has got lost on a walk. Also call here to obtain permits for unofficial trails.
Hospital Jalan Besar, opposite the park ☎ 05/491 1966. There's also a clinic at 48 Main Rd (8.30am–12.30pm, 2–5.30pm & 8–10pm). Ring doorbell after clinic hours in emergencies.
Internet access Many hotels offer internet access and there are places along Jalan Besar, too.
Laundry There are numerous places along Jalan Besar, plus most hostels have laundry services.

Police station Jalan Besar, opposite the *New Garden Inn* ☎ 05/491 1222.
Post office Jalan Besar ☎ 05/491 1051.
Service station There are service stations in both Tanah Rata and Brinchang.
Sport Cameron Highlands Golf Club has an 18-hole course (RM53 on weekdays, RM84 on weekends and holidays), caddy fees and equipment rental extra; ☎ 05/491 1126; there's a strict dress code (no collarless shirts, shorts or flip-flops).
Taxi rank Jalan Besar ☎ 05/491 2355.
Travel agent CS Travel, 47 Jalan Besar ☎ 05/491 1200, ⓦ www.cstravel.com or Cameron Tourist Information Centre, Jalan Besar ☎ 05/491 1452. They can help with express bus tickets from Tapah to all major destinations and will also book Highlands tours.

Brinchang and around

BRINCHANG, 5km or so further north, sprawls around a central square and the main road – Jalan Besar. Some say it lacks the charm of its neighbour, but most visitors will find there is little difference between the two settlements. Brinchang has a lively **night market** from 4pm on Fridays, Saturdays and daily on school holidays (end Nov to early Jan). In peak periods, you may have to resort to Brinchang as an alternative to Tanah Rata in order to find a room – not a disaster, since Walks 1 to 3 are easily approached from here, and reaching the **farms** and **tea estates** to the north is quicker from here too. A more challenging alternative to the local trails is to hike to the summit of **Gunung Brinchang** (2032m), the highest peak in Malaysia accessible by road. This takes two to three hours from Brinchang and although the road there is sealed, it's an extremely steep and exhausting climb. On a clear day though, the views back down the broad valley are wonderful. You can also walk to the **Sam Poh Temple**, 1km southeast of Brinchang, a gaudy modern place with a monastery that was built in 1965.

Arrival

Buses leave Tanah Rata for Brinchang and Kampung Raja every hour or so between 6.30am and 6.30pm, from the **bus stop** just south of the square. A **taxi** from Tanah Rata to Brinchang costs around RM7.

Accommodation

Most of the **hotels** in Brinchang line the east and west sides of the central square, and are uniformly overpriced. Brinchang has only a few budget options and sees very little of the backpacker scene. The standard high-season price hikes apply.

Flora De Cottage 18 Jalan Angsana ☎ 05/490 1700, ⓔ flora.enquiry@gmail.com. With a cute, flowery entrance opposite the new row of stalls in the west side of town, this is ideal for visiting the night market and has clean rooms with TVs and hot showers. ❸

Kowloon 34–35 Jalan Besar ☎ 05/491 1366, ⓕ 491 1803. Above the Chinese restaurant of the same name, this place has small, comfortable rooms with TVs and bathrooms. ❹–❺
Hotel Sentosa 38 Jalan Besar ☎ 05/491 5492. With wooden floors throughout, this is a good-value

option, where further discounts can be negotiated; call to check the rates of the day. ②

Hotel Titiwangsa 187–188 Jalan Besar ☎05/491 1188/1189. A new hotel, just at the beginning of town, with non-smoking rooms and a lift for weary feet after a day's walking. ⑤

Parkland 45 Jalan Besar ☎05/491 1299, ℱ491 1803. In a five-storey shophouse with the obligatory mock-Tudor gables, the *Parkland* is run by the same management as the *Kowloon* with similar standards but larger rooms. They also offer apartments futher up the hill at various sizes and prices. ⑤

Rosa Passadena 1 Bandar Baru Brinchang ☎05/491 2288. Large, modern, professionally run hotel offering rooms with safe deposit boxes, mini-bars and TVs. ⑥

Silverstar 10 Jalan Besar ☎05/491 1387. Fifteen clean and fair-sized rooms with *mandi*-style bath. The Chinese restaurant on the ground floor is very popular. ②

🏃 **Tudor Home Inn** 10a Jalan Angsana ☎05/490 1353, ℮ronny@tudorhomeinn .com.my. With colourful hallways, basic yet clean rooms and wi-fi, this friendly family-run hotel is great value. ③

Eating and drinking

As well as the Malay **food stalls** in the central square, the following cafés and restaurants are worth a try.

Jew May Yen Jalan Besar, west side of square. Good busy Chinese restaurant, which is popular with the locals. Steamboat and tasty soups.

Sakaya Jalan Besar. This inexpensive Chinese eating house does buffet lunches, costing from RM5 for three dishes, including rice.

Strawberry Moment 23–24 Jalan Angsana. Using strawberries and vegetables from their own farm, this bright, new restaurant offers a mulitude of strawberry dishes, including cream cakes, ice cream, strawberry club sandwiches and even spaghetti.

North of Brinchang

All over the Cameron Highlands – but especially north of Brinchang – you'll pass small sheds or greenhouses by the roadside, selling cabbages, leeks, cauliflowers, mushrooms and strawberries. These are the produce of the area's various fruit and vegetable **farms**, where narrow plots are cut out of the sheer hillsides to increase the surface area for planting, forming giant steps all the way up the slopes. However, terrace farming poses a problem for the transporting of the harvested crop, since the paths between the terraces are only wide enough for one nimble-footed person. This has been solved by the introduction of a **cable system**, initially operated by brute force but now powered by diesel engines, which hoists the large baskets of vegetables from the terraces to trucks waiting by the roadside high above, from where they are taken to market – over forty percent of the produce is for export to Singapore, Brunei and Hong Kong.

A couple of more specific targets might entice you out into the countryside north of Brinchang. There's a **Butterfly Farm** and a **Butterfly Garden** (daily 8am–6pm;

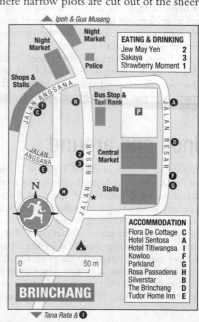

RM5), 5km to the north at Kea Farm. The two establishments are very similar and just a hundred metres away from each other. Both have hundreds of butterflies of various species flitting among the flowers and ponds; the Kampung Raja bus from Brinchang passes both places, or you can get a taxi from Tanah Rata for about RM15. Flower lovers are well served by the **Rose Centre** at Kea Farm (daily 8am–5pm; RM3), which has a spectacular view of the surrounding valleys from its summit, crowned in surreal fashion by a colourful Mother-Hubbard-like boot. The sculptures here, of which the boot is one, were created by Burmese craftsmen and do a lot to liven up a potentially dull attraction. Besides roses, there are also other temperate-climate flowers – rare and expensive in tropical Southeast Asia – being cultivated here.

The Sungai Palas Tea Estate

Set high in the hills north of Brinchang, the **Sungai Palas Tea Estate** (Tues–Sun 9am–4.30pm, tours roughly every 10min; free) is a great visit for tea lovers. Despite the romantic imagery used on tea packaging, handpicking – though the best method for producing the highest-quality tea – is now far too labour-intensive to be economical. Instead, the small, green leaves are picked with shears. Once in the factory, the full baskets are emptied into large wire vats where the leaves are withered by alternate blasts of hot and cold air for sixteen to eighteen hours; this removes around fifty percent of their moisture. They are then sifted of dust and impurities and rolled by ancient, bulky machines. This breaks up the leaves and releases the moisture for the all-important process of **fermentation**. Following ninety minutes' grinding, the soggy mass is fired at 90°C to halt the fermentation process, and the leaves turn black. After being sorted into grades, the tea matures for three to six months before being packaged and transported to market.

How much you glean of this process from your guide is variable, as the noise in parts of the factory is so deafening that all sound save the roar of the dryers is obliterated. Some areas of the building are also made extremely dusty by the tea impurities, so take a handkerchief to cover your mouth and nose. There's a pleasant **café** and garden on the premises where you can enjoy a cup of tea before or after the tour.

Six **buses** run back and forth from Tanah Rata to the estate from Brinchang's bus station between 6.30am and 6.30pm. To return, it is also possible to walk the 6km or so along the road back to Brinchang, though the hilliness of the route may put you off. From Tanah Rata a taxi should cost around RM25.

Ipoh and around

Eighty kilometres north of Tapah in the Kinta Valley is **IPOH**, the state capital of Perak and third-biggest city in Malaysia. It grew rich on the tin trade, which transformed it within the space of forty years at the end of the nineteenth century from a tiny kampung in a landscape dominated by dramatic limestone outcrops to a sprawling boom town. Now a metropolis of over half a million people, Ipoh (the name comes from that of the *upas* tree which thrived in the area, and whose sap was used by the Orang Asli for blowpipe dart poison) is a far cry from the original village on this site. With the discovery of a major field in 1880, it became a prime destination for pioneers, merchants and fortune-seekers from all over the world, and a cosmopolitan city, something reflected in the broad mix of cultures today. To accommodate the rapidly increasing

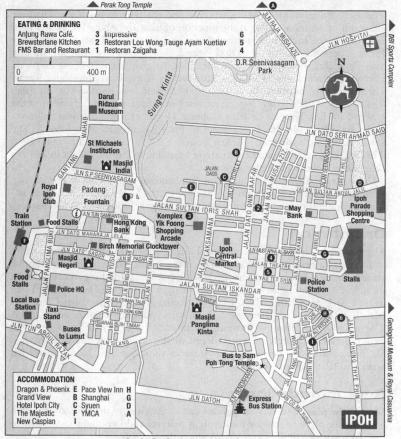

EATING & DRINKING

Anjung Rawa Café.	3	Impressive	6
Brewsterlane Kitchen	2	Restoran Lou Wong Tauge Ayam Kuetiav	5
FMS Bar and Restaurant	1	Restoran Zaigaha	4

ACCOMMODATION

Dragon & Phoenix	E	Pace View Inn	H
Grand View	B	Shanghai	G
Hotel Ipoh City	C	Syuen	D
The Majestic	F	YMCA	A
New Caspian	I		

Sam Poh Tong Temple, Airport & Medan Gopeng Express Bus Station ▼

population, between 1905 and 1914 the city expanded across Sungai Kinta into a "new town" area, its economic good fortune reflected in a multitude of **colonial buildings** and Chinese mansions.

Yet despite its historical significance and present-day administrative importance, Ipoh's new town doesn't have much to offer the visitor. Although the colonial architecture around the padang is certainly worth a look, the main reason people stop here is to visit Ipoh's outlying attractions – the Chinese cave temples of **Sam Poh Tong** and **Perak Tong**, the anachronistic ruin of **Kellie's Castle** and the unique development at the **Tambun Hot Springs**. To do these sights justice, you're likely to have to spend at least one night in the city.

Arrival and information

Both the North–South Expressway and Route 1 pass through Ipoh, which is also a major stop for express buses and trains between Butterworth and KL. The **train station** is on Jalan Panglima Bukit Gantang Wahab (more simply Jalan Panglima), west of the old town, with daily services to KL (RM18) and two evening services to Butterworth (RM17), which is also the train to Hat Yai in Thailand. Just south of the train station, at the junction of Jalan Tun Abdul Razak and Jalan Panglima, is the **local bus station** (buses to Taiping and Kuala Kangsar every 15min), opposite which is a **taxi stand**. Local buses to **Lumut** (hourly 6am–7pm; 2hr), the departure point for Pulau Pangkor (see p.164), use a separate forecourt, beside a row of shops, a little further along Jalan Tun Abdul Razak. There are two **express bus** stations: one near the roundabout on Jalan Bendahara and the Medan Gopeng express bus station, 4km out of town (on the way to Sam Poh Temple) on Jalan Gopeng. The latter is the one you will most likely use, which also has buses direct to both KL airports (4hr; RM42). The Sultan Azlan Shah **airport** is 15km from the city; a taxi into the centre costs RM25, though you are unlikely to arrive here, due to the only flight in and out being twice a week to Medan, Sumatra.

The **tourist office** is on Jalan Tun Sambanthan at the end of the padang, close to the train station (Mon–Fri 8am–5pm; ☏05/241 2959); besides assistance on Ipoh, it can provide information on travel throughout Perak State.

Orientation

The **layout** of central Ipoh is reasonably straightforward, since the roads more or less form a grid system. What is confusing is that some of the old colonial **street names** have been changed in favour of something more Islamic, though the street signs haven't always caught up; hence, Jalan C.M. Yusuf instead of Jalan Chamberlain, Jalan Mustapha Al-Bakri for Jalan Clare and Jalan Bandar Timar for Jalan Leech. In practice, people recognize either name. The muddy and lethargic **Sungai Kinta** cuts the centre of Ipoh neatly in two; most of the hotels are situated east of the river, while the **old town** is on the opposite side between the two major thoroughfares, Jalan Sultan Idris Shah and Jalan Sultan Iskander.

Accommodation

Most of the **places to stay** in Ipoh are east of the river, in the new town, which is the better place to stay for funky night markets and late-night restaurants, as the old town practically closes down when the sun sets.

Dragon & Phoenix 23–25 Jalan Toh Puan Chah ☏05/253 4661, ℱ253 5096. A relatively quiet and friendly hotel set back from the main road with clean rooms. ❸

Grand View Hotel 36 Jalan Horley ☏05/243 1488, ℱ243 1811. Although a bit out of the way, this well-run hotel has clean bright rooms and a good view from the side and back (the front rooms look onto a parking garage). All rooms are en suite, with a/c, TV and kettle. ❹

Hotel Ipoh City 18 Jalan Dass ☏05/241 8282. Smart new hotel with wi-fi, a/c, fridge, hairdryer and tea- and coffee-making facilities in all rooms. There is a Western and Chinese restaurant on the ground floor. ❺

The Majestic Above the train station, set back a little from Jalan Panglima ☏05/255 5605, ℱ255 3393. Probably only worth stopping at if you are getting the train and are short on time, as the

rooms in this colonial-era hotel are in a dire need of some TLC. An extra RM25 will get you a room off of the huge tiled veranda, which is worth a brief look even if you're not staying here. Breakfast is included. ❹

New Caspian Hotel 20–26 Jalan Ali Pitchay ☏05/243 9254, ℱ243 9258. With an uncanny resemblance to its sister hotel on Jalan Jubilee with the same name, this friendly place has en-suite rooms that come with a/c, though they are a little worn. ❸

Pace View Inn 3–9 Jalan Ali Pitchay ☏05/241 3644, ⊛www.paceview.blogspot.com. Efficiently run with clean bathrooms, a kettle, TV, wi-fi and a/c, this hotel is good value for this price bracket. ❸

🏃 **Shanghai** 85 Jalan Mustapha Al-Bakri ☏05/241 2070. This is the best value in town, with some older fan rooms, all having private bathrooms and wi-fi. There are also new rooms with a/c for an extra RM10–20 depending on double or twin beds. Friendly owner and a good location for restaurants and night markets. ❷

Syuen 88 Jalan Sultan Abdul Jalil ☎05/253 8889, ℻253 3335, ℮syhotel@streamyx.com. The top hotel in Ipoh. Of international standard with all the trimmings, including a stately lobby and a rooftop swimming pool. ❻–❼

YMCA 311 Jalan Raja Musa Aziz ☎05/254 0809. Located about a kilometre north of the town centre in a leafy suburb, the local Y has clean rooms and excellent security, although not the cheapest rates in town. ❸

The City

Although most of Ipoh's attractions are on the outskirts, there are a few buildings in the centre that make a leisurely stroll through the old town worthwhile. The most prominent reminder of Ipoh's economic heyday is the **train station**, built in 1917 at the height of the tin boom. With its Moorish turrets and domes, and a veranda that runs the entire two-hundred-metre length of the building, it's a typical example of the British conception of "East meets West".

From the train station, it's a short walk northeast past the tourist office, to the **padang**, around which there are several interesting colonial-era buildings including, on the north side, St Michael's School (opened in 1912 and still running today) built in Neo-Gothic style, which was used as the Japanese army administration and medical centre during World War II. Next door is the **Masjid India** (1908), which was built in the Chettiar style by a sheikh who migrated from South India; today, it serves the Indian Muslim community. Walking south away from the **padang**, you'll come to the modern **Masjid Negeri** on Jalan Sultan Iskandar. This is one of the more conspicuous landmarks in the centre of town, all tacky 1960s cladding, with a minaret that rises over 40m above its mosaic-tiled domes. Directly opposite the mosque, on the parallel Jalan Dato' Sagor, stands the **Birch Memorial Clock Tower**, a square, white tower incorporating a portrait bust of J.W.W. Birch, the first British Resident of Perak, who was murdered after his abruptness offended the local sultan. Another interesting mosque is the **Masjid Panglima Kinta**, on Jalan Masjid just off Jalan Sultan Iskandar. It was the first mosque in Ipoh as well as the site of the first madrasah (Islamic school) and has unusual Moorish-style arches.

The **Darul Ridzuan Museum** (daily 9am–5pm; free), along Jalan Panglima Bukit Gantang Wahab, is housed in an elegant, former tin-miner's mansion, only a short walk north from the station. Covering two floors, the museum has evocative photos of Ipoh's glory days during the tin boom, but otherwise the displays lack imagination.

Eating and drinking

Ipoh is an excellent place to sample both local Chinese and Malay dishes. At lunchtime, regional specialities are available at most Chinese **restaurants** and **cafés**, including *sar hor fun*. On Jalan Pitchay, near the *New Caspian Hotel*, is the clean and bright *Impressive* hawker centre, a good choice for cheap Chinese stir-fry and Indian sweets. Many of Ipoh's old town restaurants close in the evenings, so you may have to turn to the new town or the **food stalls**, some of which lie near the train station and at the top of Jalan C. M. Yusuf. The best stalls, however, are at the southern end of Jalan Greenhill, east of the *Shanghai Hotel*, where nearly a hundred stay open well into the night (some to around 3am), serving just about anything you care to name. There are also often great night markets in the main stretch. Gerbang Malam, reaching down Jalan Dato Tahwil Azar, sells funky T-shirts and much more, with a nice vibe. On Jalan Sultan Abdul Jalil you'll also find some very good-quality Indian stalls.

Anjung Rawa Kafé Jalan Sultan Idris Shah. This relaxing, friendly and family-run café serves good Malay food and fresh juices.

Brewsterlane Kitchen 140 Jalan Sultan Idris Shah. This almost European-looking place does good tempura and claypot dishes alongside mashed potato croquettes with salmon – and friendly service.

FMS Bar and Restaurant At the far end of the padang and though closed for refurbishment at the time of writing, this colonial-era building overlooking the padang is said to be Malaysia's oldest bar, dating back to 1906.

Restoran Lou Wong Tauge Ayam Kuetiav On the corner of Jalan Yau Tet Shin and Jalan Raja Musa Aziz. This busy place does excellent chicken with beansprouts as well as many other great dishes and is very popular with the locals.

Restoran Zaiqaha On the corner of Jalan Mustapha Al-Bakri and Jalan Raja Musa Aziz, with "AK Tom Yam" above the doorway. This cheap-as-chips place does good roti, *tom yam* seafood and rice and noodle dishes. Opens late afternoon.

Listings

Airport ☎05/312 2460 for flight information to Medan.

Banks Maybank and Bank Bumiputra are on Jalan Sultan Idris Shah.

Buses Tickets for Lumut buses can be bought from Perak Roadways, under the advertising hoardings on Jalan Tun Abdul Razak, opposite the express bus station.

Car rental No main international rental companies due to the airport practically being shut, but try the reliable C.M. Yusof on ☎05/255 5510.

Cinemas Fourth floor of the Ipoh Parade shopping complex, Jalan Sultan Abdul Jalil, just east of the *Syuen Hotel*.

Hospital On Jalan Hospital ☎05/253 3333.

Internet access There are several places around the Kompleks Yik Foong shopping arcade on Jalan Laksamana.

Police On Jalan Panglima between the bus and train stations ☎05/245 1500.

Post office The GPO is practically next door to the train station, on Jalan Panglima.

Taxis There's a taxi stand at the bus station. To phone for a cab, call Teksi Ipoh on ☎05/253 4188 or 05/241 1388. If taking a taxi to the attractions outside town, it's worth booking.

Trains ☎05/254 0481 for information.

Travel agents Aidil Travel on Jalan Lim Bo Seng (☎05/255 0303), and Keris Tour on Jalan Ali Pitchay (☎05/241 7100).

Visa extensions The Immigration Office is over halfway to Kuala Kangsar on Jalan Bandar Meru Raya (☎05/501 7100).

Around Ipoh

Much of Ipoh's striking surroundings have been marred by unsightly manufacturing industries. Nevertheless, it's not long before you escape the industrialization and find yourself in the heart of extensive rubber plantations, typical of so much of this part of the country. To the north and south of Ipoh are craggy **limestone peaks**; those nearest to the city are riddled with caves where Ipoh's immigrant workers established **Buddhist temples**, now popular pilgrimage centres, particularly during the Chinese New Year celebrations. **Kellie's Castle** and the **Tambun Hot Springs** also make interesting excursions.

The Perak Tong and Sam Poh Tong temples

The **Perak Tong Temple** (daily 8am–5pm; free), 6km north of Ipoh, is the more impressive of the two Chinese cave temples just outside the city, situated in dramatic surroundings and doubling as a centre for Chinese art; to get here, take the #141 Kuala Kangsar bus from the local bus station (20min). The gaudiness of the temple's exterior – bright red-and-yellow pavilions flanked by feathery willows and lotus ponds – gives no hint of the eerie atmosphere inside, where darkened cavern upon cavern honeycombs up into the rock formation. The huge first chamber is dominated by a fifteen-metre-high golden statue of the Buddha flanked by two startled-looking companions dancing and playing instruments. A massive bell, believed to be more than a century old, fills the chamber with booming echoes from time to time – it's rung by visiting devotees to draw attention to the donation they've just offered. Walking past the bell into the next chamber, as your eyes become more accustomed to the gloom, you'll notice the decorated walls, covered with complex calligraphy and delicate flower paintings. Towards the back of this musty hollow, a steep flight of 385 crudely fashioned steps climbs up and out of the cave to a sort of balcony, with views of great limestone outcrops and ugly factory buildings.

The **Sam Poh Tong Temple** (daily 8am–4.30pm; free), just south of the city, is also a popular place of pilgrimage for Chinese Buddhists. Built into a rock face, the huge limestone caverns open towards the rear to give more impressive views over the surrounding suburbs and hills. Unfortunately, the upkeep of the temple leaves a lot to be desired; the place is covered with litter and graffiti. There's an expensive bar nearby and a good Chinese vegetarian restaurant. A visit to the temple makes an easy half-day trip: catch the green "Kinta" bus #66 or #73 (to Kampar) from the local **bus** station; it's about a ten-minute journey and buses come about every half-hour.

Kellie's Castle

If you only have time for one trip from Ipoh, make it **Kellie's Castle**, a mansion situated in the Kinta Kelas Rubber Estate, 12km south of Ipoh. It stands as a symbol of the prosperity achieved by many enterprising foreigners who capitalized on the potential of the rubber market in the early 1900s. The mansion, with a weighty rectangular tower and apricot-coloured bricks, was to be the second home of William Kellie Smith, a Scottish entrepreneur, who settled here in order to make his fortune. Designed with splendour in mind, there were even plans for a lift to be installed, the first in Malaysia. However, during the mansion's construction in the 1920s, an epidemic of Spanish influenza broke out, killing many of the Tamil workers. In an act of appeasement, Smith had a Hindu temple built near the house; among the deities represented on the temple roof is a figure dressed in a white suit and pith helmet, presumably Smith himself. While work resumed on the "castle", Smith left on a trip to England in 1925; however, he fell ill and died in Portugal and the castle was never completed. Whether he really is haunting the castle to this day remains debatable, but adds to the general air of abandoned mystery of this otherwise peaceful place. There's also a tree that looks like a bear.

Getting to the castle from Ipoh is best done by taxi (about RM20 one way if you book with Teksi Ipoh, see opposite; or RM50 return including a wait while you look around). For a cheaper but more complicated transport option you can take bus #36 or #37 from the local bus station to Batu Gajah (departures every 1hr 30min; 30min), from where you can walk the remaining 4km on the A8 road (clearly signposted), or catch bus #67 to Kampar (not passing Sam Poh Tong Temple), which passes the castle fairly frequently, or take a taxi from the main road (around RM5).

Tambun Hot Springs and Gua Tambun

Eight kilometres northeast of Ipoh, at the **Tambun Hot Springs** (daily 3pm–midnight; RM5), you can indulge in mineral-rich soaks in the two thermal swimming pools, one cooler than the other, which are fed by hot springs. All around you, steaming slimy water breaks through the surface of the earth; you can even crawl into the corner of a nearby limestone cave for a natural sauna (not for the claustrophobic). Another of the surrounding caves, once inhabited by Japanese monks, was later home to Japanese soldiers hiding out during World War II; they left painted characters on some of the cave walls.

In the 1930s, evidence of a prehistoric civilization dating back 10,000 years was discovered at the nearby **Gua Tambun** (Tambun Cave). Drawings on the cave walls and limestone cliffs include that of a large meat-eating fish, the *degong*.

To get there, take the Tambun **bus** from Ipoh's local bus station for about thirty minutes until you see the signpost for "Resort Air Panas", off to the right of the main road; the springs are a further kilometre down a dirt track.

Lumut

LUMUT is a quiet coastal town, about 80km southwest of Ipoh. Most people come here to take a ferry across to Pulau Pangkor (although it's also possible to fly there, see p.166). Once a relatively obscure fishing village, Lumut has become the main base of the Royal Malaysian Navy, whose towering apartment buildings dominate the coastline from the sea. In an attempt to cash in on the success of Pulau Pangkor, Lumut too has seen its own spate of development, though this is still low-key. The town manages to retain some charm, with multicoloured fishing boats bobbing about in the tiny marina, and stores specializing in shell and coral handicrafts.

Practicalities

Buses run roughly every hour from Ipoh (daily 9.30am–7.50pm; 2hr; RM9), once a day from Taiping (2hr; RM7), four times a day from Butterworth (3hr; RM16), every hour from KL (8am–midnight; 4hr; RM24) and once a day from Singapore (12hr; RM56). The **bus station** is on the road out to Ipoh, a minute's walk south of the **jetty** from where the boats to Pangkor depart; all boat tickets can be bought at the jetty itself. The **tourist information** office (☏05/683 4057) is located between the bus station and the jetty. Walking north from the bus station takes you to a filling station at the junction with both the shore road (Jalan Iskandar Shah/Jalan Titi Panjang) and another inland road (Jalan Sultan Idris Shah), which leads off to your left. If you need to **change money**, it's better to do so here, as it can be hard to change traveller's cheques in Pangkor Town; most of Lumut's several moneychangers and banks are on Jalan Sultan Idris Shah.

Although most people continue straight on to the island, if you need to spend the night in Lumut, there are a few **places to stay**. Further down Jalan Sultan Idris Shah there's the *Orient Setar* (☏05/683 4199, ℻683 4223; ❻). It's the top spot in town, very pleasantly situated on the beach. Along the same road is the *Galaxy Inn* (☏05/683 8731; ℻683 8723; ❸), the quietest of the mid-range choices. Lumut's least expensive option is the clean and basic *Phin Lum Hooi*, 93 Jalan Titi Panjang (☏05/683 5641; ❷) – to get there, walk to the service station, and turn right onto the shore road.

Pulau Pangkor

With some of the best beaches on this side of the Malay Peninsula, **PULAU PANGKOR** is one of the west coast's more appealing islands. It's also one of the most accessible – just a forty-minute ferry ride from the port of **Lumut** (see above). This fact has turned Pangkor into an increasingly popular though very chilled weekend resort, with a small airport and an international-standard hotel. These facilities are disproportionate to Pangkor's small size and at odds with its quiet, almost genteel, atmosphere, though most places to stay are

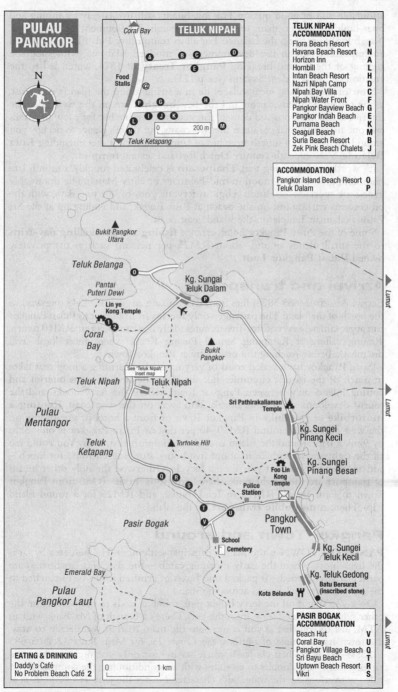

PULAU PANGKOR

N

TELUK NIPAH

Coral Bay

Food Stalls

@

0   200 m

Teluk Ketapang

TELUK NIPAH ACCOMMODATION

Flora Beach Resort	I
Havana Beach Resort	N
Horizon Inn	A
Hornbill	L
Intan Beach Resort	H
Nazri Nipah Camp	D
Nipah Bay Villa	C
Nipah Water Front	F
Pangkor Bayview Beach	G
Pangkor Indah Beach	E
Purnama Beach	K
Seagull Beach	M
Suria Beach Resort	B
Zek Pink Beach Chalets	J

ACCOMMODATION

Pangkor Island Beach Resort	O
Teluk Dalam	P

Bukit Pangkor Utara

Teluk Belanga

Pantai Puteri Dewi

Lin ye Kong Temple

Coral Bay

Kg. Sungai Teluk Dalam

Bukit Pangkor

Lumut

See 'Teluk Nipah' inset map

Teluk Nipah

Teluk Nipah

Pulau Mentangor

Sri Pathirakaliaman Temple

Kg. Sungei Pinang Kecil

Teluk Ketapang

Tortoise Hill

Kg. Sungei Pinang Besar

Lumut

Foo Lin Kong Temple

Police Station

Pasir Bogak

Pangkor Town

Kg. Sungei Teluk Kecil

School

Cemetery

Emerald Bay

Kg. Teluk Gedong

Pulau Pangkor Laut

Kota Belanda

Batu Bersurat (inscribed stone)

Lumut

PASIR BOGAK ACCOMMODATION

Beach Hut	V
Coral Bay	U
Pangkor Village Beach	Q
Sri Bayu Beach	T
Uptown Beach Resort	R
Vikri	S

EATING & DRINKING

Daddy's Café	1
No Problem Beach Café	2

0   1 km

affordable and of good quality. The inhabitants still live largely by fishing and boat-building rather than tourism – although development around Teluk Nipah looks set to tip the balance. For all its tranquillity, Pulau Pangkor played an important part in the development of modern Malaysia, witnessing the signing of the ground-breaking **Pangkor Treaty** of 1874, which led to the creation of the Resident System (see p.171).

Most of the thriving local villages lie in a string along the island's east coast, while tourist accommodation and the best **beaches** are on the west side. The interior is mountainous and densely forested, inaccessible but for a few tiny trails and one main road that connects the two coasts, but there's plenty to occupy you around the rim, from superb stretches of sand to historical sites, including **Kota Belanda**, a seventeenth-century Dutch fort and several **temples**.

It's worth remembering that **Thaipusam** is celebrated roughly a month late here, falling on the full moon in mid-February or early March. The unmissably gruesome spectacle of Hindu religious fervour goes on for two days, with the processions starting out on the beach at Pasir Bogak, and ending up at the Sri Pathirakaliaman Temple on the island's east coast.

Some of the Pulau Pangkor hotels arrange **fishing** and **snorkelling day-trips** to the small islands around (about RM25 per person) such as the privately owned **Pulau Pangkor Laut**.

Arrival and transport

Berjaya Air (☎05/685 5828) flies from KL's Subang airport (RM248 one way) to the north of the island. The passenger-only **ferries** from Lumut to Pulau Pangkor run approximately every forty-five minutes (daily 6.30am–8.30pm; RM10 return; 40min), calling at Kampung Sungai Pinang Kecil, where most locals will disembark, before reaching the main jetty at Pangkor Town.

Pulau Pangkor has a sealed **road** of varying quality forming a loop that takes in much of the island's circumference, avoiding the mountainous interior and cutting inland only between Pangkor Town, where the ferry docks, and the tourist developments at Pasir Bogak, 2km away on the west coast. **Renting a motorbike** or **pushbike** in Pangkor Town or from a hotel or guesthouse on the west coast costs around RM30–40 per day. As Pulau Pangkor is only 3km by 9km, a trip around the island is easily accomplished in a day. You could see all the sights by motorbike in about five hours, stopping en route for lunch – add another few hours if you're on a bicycle. Otherwise the only other means of transport are the bright pink, shared **minibus taxis** (RM6 from Pangkor Town to Pasir Bogak, RM12 to Teluk Nipah and RM25 for a round-island trip). There is **no public transport** on the island.

Pangkor Town and around

PANGKOR TOWN is the island's principal settlement. The best area by far is the lively port, where the early-morning catch – the *ikan bilis* (anchovies) are particularly renowned – is packed into boxes of crushed ice to be dispatched to the mainland as well as sold across the island.

Once you've got off the ferry, bright pink minibus **taxis** to the beaches on the other side of the island leave from the jetty. There's a branch of Maybank with an **ATM**, just to your left as you come onto the main road. If you decide **to stay**, the town has a couple of options: the *Chuan Fu*, 60 Main Rd (☎&℉05/685 1123; ❶–❷), is the best choice if you're staying for only one night, with rooms ranging from basic doubles to en suites with air-conditioning; the communal rear balcony overlooking the water adds character. Nearer the jetty, *Hotel Min Lian* at

▲ Pulau Pangkor beach

no. 1a (☎05/685 1294; ❹) charges more, but the rooms are of a better quality. Around the *Chuan Fu* are a number of Chinese **restaurants** and an off-licence. The best hawker stalls are in the T-junction across the street from the jetty.

South to Teluk Gedong

Following the coastal road south out of town, after 1.5km you come to pretty **KAMPUNG TELUK GEDONG**, a gathering of traditional wooden stilted houses named after the bay in which they are cradled. Here, set back from the road on the right, is the **Kota Belanda**, or Dutch fort, originally built in 1670 to store tin supplies from Perak and keep a check on piracy in the Straits, but destroyed in 1690 by the Malays, who were discontent with Dutch rule. The fort was rebuilt in 1743 but only remained in use for a further five years, when the Dutch finally withdrew after being subjected to several more attacks. The abandoned site was left to decay, and the disappointing half-built structure that you see today is a recent reconstruction.

A few metres further along the road, on the left, lies the **Batu Bersurat**, a huge boulder under a canopy. On the rock, the year 1743 is inscribed beside a drawing which – with the use of some imagination – depicts a tiger mauling a child, a grisly memorial to a Dutch child who disappeared while playing nearby. A more plausible account of the incident is that the infant was kidnapped by the Malays, in retribution for the continuing Dutch presence.

West to Pasir Bogak and Teluk Ketapang

A two-kilometre road connects the east and west coasts of Pulau Pangkor, terminating in the west at the holiday village of **PASIR BOGAK**, the biggest and most upmarket development on the island, though it does, in parts, have an air of days gone by about it.

Better beaches are to be found about 2km further north at **TELUK KETAPANG** ("Turtle Bay"), named for the sometime, yet no more, resident – the increasingly rare giant **leatherback turtle**. The creatures used to swim thousands of miles to lay their eggs on this beach, but the population has been forced to move due to the busy seas on Malaysia's west coast, though rare sightings do still occur. Instead, take the opportunity to stretch out on the white-sand beaches – edged by palm trees – which are slightly less crowded than Pasir Bogak's, and much wider and cleaner. There's no accommodation at Teluk Ketapang; you'll have to stay either in Pasir Bogak or a few kilometres further north in Teluk Nipah. Whereas Teluk Nipah boasts nicer beaches, Pasir Bogak is a quieter place to stay, as the hotels and resorts are further spread out. Most of the hotels in Pasir Bogak have **restaurants** attached and there are some food stalls scattered in the streets. Otherwise, the food in town is generally overpriced.

Accommodation

Hotels in Pasir Bogak arrange their prices into three categories: low (weekdays), high (weekends) and peak (holidays), with peak prices being around fifty percent higher than low season. Prices listed below are for double rooms during low season.

Beach Hut Hotel ⊕&ⓕ05/685 1159. Almost ghost town resort with chalets and rooms reminiscent of former glory days, not really compensated for by its great location on the beach. ❹–❺

Coral Bay ⊕05/685 5111. This high-rise hotel has high-quality though rather bland rooms at a reasonable rate. There is a pool and a fitness centre and full-board packages are also on offer. Breakfast included. ❻

Pangkor Village Beach ⊕05/685 2227, ⓕ685 3787. Has a wide choice of accommodation from dorms at RM18 and tents at RM8 during weekdays (excluding tent hire) to chalets set in a pleasant garden just off the beach. There's a restaurant and breakfast is included. Great location with watersports facilities right next door. ❺

Sri Bayu Beach ⊕05/685 1929. The spacious lobby leads onto a well-landscaped garden and deluxe chalets. The rooms themselves though, while comfortable enough, aren't quite up to the whopping price tag. ❼

Uptown Beach Resort ⊕05/685 4510, ⓕ685 2832. Large complex of doubles perched on the hillside with great views, though rooms are nothing special. The hotel offers various activities, ranging from round-island tours at RM10 per person to fishing trips at RM100 per person, to karaoke for groups at RM350. ❺

Vikri ⊕05/685 4258. A-frame huts (❷), as well as new chalets (❹) shaded by tall trees, across the road from the beach. Restaurant serving banana-leaf curries for lunch and dinner.

Teluk Nipah

TELUK NIPAH has become something of a travellers' hangout mainly because of its good beaches and laid-back atmosphere. It's nigh impossible not to switch off here, though the roar of the friendly local youths' motorbikes can be off-putting. **Coral Bay** at the north end is the best beach – a perfect cove with smooth, white sand, backed by dense jungle climbing steeply to Bukit Pangkor, one of the island's three peaks. It's easy to get to by walking north out of town and round the bend past the new development and the smelly bins. This is the best spot on the island for **snorkelling**, and most of the hostels here rent out masks, snorkels and fins for about RM20 a day.

There are **food stalls** lined up along the beach in between the two roads into the kampung, and a few **restaurants** across the road, along with an **internet café** and **convenience stores**. Wandering north out of town to Coral Bay, the friendly and laid-back *No Problem Beach Café* serves rice (try the 'Punkcore Special') and noodle dishes as well as burgers and soups and is a good place for an evening beer. A little further along the beach is the more expensive *Daddy's Café*, which is an excellent choice for a romantic dinner with wine. At the far end of the beach is the small and charming **Lin Ye Kong** temple, which is well worth a visit, in particular for the view as well as the giant toadstools and fairytale doors. Crossing the bridge behind the temple and following the path at the edge of the forest or climbing the rocks, takes you to a very small, secluded beach, hidden amongst large boulders. The island across Coral Bay is accessible by foot during low tide in February, though best done wearing sandals.

Accommodation

Much of the recent development on the island has focused on Teluk Nipah because of its beaches. There are new places opening all the time, but the atmosphere is still quiet and informal. Seasonal price categories are the same as at Pasir Bogak.

Inexpensive

Flora Beach Resort ☎05/685 3878, ⓦwww .florabeachresort.com. A welcoming and busy place with fifteen wooden chalets with private bathrooms, TVs and a/c. Good value. ❸

Intan Beach Resort ☎013/454 3823. This very friendly, family-run place has very simple chalets with clean sheets (no top sheets) in a small garden as well as two A-frames at half the cost. There are bicycles on loan for free as well as laundry service and the owner can organize fishing trips. ❶–❷

Nazri Nipah Camp ☎05/685 2014. Very popular with travellers and well laid out with chalets and simple A-frames around a lovely communal garden area, perfect for socializing. There is a little café serving breakfast and coffees. ❷

Seagull Beach ☎05/685 2878, ⓕ685 2857. A larger complex with rooms, chalets and even cheaper A-frames. This place has a restaurant, launderette, internet access and wi-fi as well as motorbike hire, though the owner is fairly eccentric. ❸

Suria Beach Resort ☎05/685 3922. This friendly and well-run resort hosts lots of groups and is a good option out of peak season. The rooms are nothing special, but they are clean and come with balconies. ❸

Moderate and expensive

Havana Beach Resort ☎05/685 3333, ⓔinfo@havana.com.my. This is the first place reached on the coast road from Teluk Katapang with spacious chalets set in a well-kept garden across the road from the beach. ❻

Horizon Inn ☎05/685 3398, ⓕ05/685 3339. This two-storey building sits at the north end of the coast road and has nice sea-view rooms and a restaurant. ❺

Hornbill ☎05/685 2005, ⓕ685 2006. All the rooms in this two-storey building boast wooden floors, balconies and a view of the beach. You can, however, get a similarly equipped chalet at one of the inland places for less. Breakfast included. ❺

Nipah Bay Villa ☎05/685 2198. There are many types of chalets available, from doubles to family rooms housing eight people. All rooms have a/c, satellite TV and hot water in good, clean bathrooms. Cheaper dorms are also available for RM25–40. There's a restaurant plus internet access. ❺

Nipah Water Front ☎012/517 3855. As the name suggests, these chalets are facing the beach; it's cheaper for a side view than a sea view and all come with a/c, hot showers and TVs. ❺

Pangkor Bayview Beach Resort ☎05/685 3540. Family-friendly large resort with a pool and a restaurant. All rooms have a/c, and full-board packages for groups are available. ❻

Pangkor Indah Beach ☎05/685 2107. These pleasant wooden chalets have a/c and TVs and are kept in OK condition. ❹

Purnama Beach ☎&ⓕ05/685 3530. Large development with a good range of options, from comfortable doubles with shared bath to newer brick "villas". There's a restaurant, plus laundry service and free internet. ❹

Zek Pink Beach Chalets ☎&ⓕ05/685 3529. These pink-painted chalets live up to their name; even the furniture is in rosy shades. ❹

The north coast

The road cuts inland from Teluk Nipah and crosses to the northeastern tip of the island, where it branches off west to the high-class *Pangkor Island Beach Resort* (☎05/685 1091, ⓕ685 2390; ❾), situated in secluded **TELUK BELANGA** and with its own golf course and private beach.

Doubling back to the junction with the main road, you'll pass the airport and come to the government-owned *Teluk Dalam Resort* (☎05/685 5000, ⓕ685 4000; ❽), with large chalets set around a quiet bay, with a couple of restaurants. After continuing up the steep hill and craggy headland, the road descends into the first bay on the east coast. There's not much to see on this side of the island for the next 3km until you reach the **Sri Pathirakaliaman** Hindu temple, overlooking the sea. Only worth a cursory glance, it lies just north of **Kampung Sungai Pinang Kecil**, little more than a few straggling dwellings by the roadside, and the first stop for the ferry from Lumut. One kilometre further north of the more substantial Kampung Sungai Pinang Besar is the **Foo Lin Kong Temple**, a cross between a place of worship and a theme park. Inside the dim, rather spooky room that houses the shrine are some authentic-looking shrunken heads designed to ward off evil spirits. Surrounding the temple itself is a miniature Great Wall of China spreading up the hillside and a small children's playground. Apart from a number of enormous fish in the small pond (look out for the huge grey ones), it is also worth noticing the twelve rooftop sculptures of the temple, each representing an animal in the Chinese zodiac. Pangkor Town is just 1km or so south from here along the main road.

Kuala Kangsar

While Ipoh is the state administrative capital of Perak, **KUALA KANGSAR** – 50km to the northwest – is its royal town, home to the sultans of Perak since the fifteenth century, with monuments to match. Built at a grandiose sweep of Sungai Perak, it's a neat, attractive town of green parks and flowers, little-visited by tourists.

Several places of interest are within easy walking distance of the town centre. Heading east from the clock tower in the centre of town, follow Jalan Istana as it curves around the fast-moving river, passing through the ornamental gateway that straddles the street. After about 2km, as the gentle gradient of Bukit Chandan begins, you'll reach the **Masjid Ubudiah**, whose large, gold, onion domes soar skywards; non-Muslims should ask permission before entering.

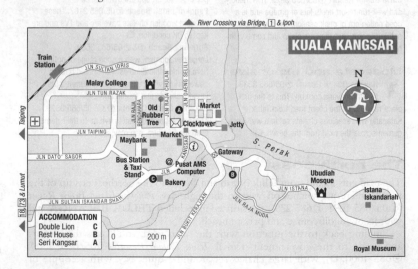

The Resident system

Late in 1873, Rajah Abdullah of Perak invited the new Governor of the Straits Settlements, Andrew Clarke, to appoint a **Resident** (colonial officer) to Perak, in exchange for Abdullah being recognized as the Sultan of Perak instead of his rival. This held some appeal for the British, whose involvement in Malay affairs had hitherto been unofficial, and would facilitate economic progress in the region. So on January 20, 1874, the **Pangkor Treaty** was signed by Clarke and Abdullah; the idea was that the Resident – each state would have its own – would play an advisory role in Malay affairs of state in return for taking a sympathetic attitude to Malay customs and rituals.

It is doubtful that the Malays had any idea of the long-term consequences of the treaty, whose original version indicated that the decision-making process would be collective, much like the Malays' own courts; more significantly, the distinction between the political and the religious was from the start a nonsensical concept for the Malays, for whom all action was dictated by the laws of Islam. The interpretation of the newly created post was in the hands of **Hugh Low** (1824–1905), whose jurisdiction of Perak (1877–89) was based in Kuala Kangsar. The personable Low lived modestly by British standards and his linguistic skills won him favour with the local chiefs, with whom he could soon converse fluently, and whose practices he quickly understood. Having spent nearly thirty years in Borneo, Low had become great friends with Charles and James Brooke (see p.393), and sought to emulate their relatively benign system of government.

The approval of the Malay nobility – by no means guaranteed – was vital to the success of the Residency scheme, and was secured principally by compensating them for the income they had lost from taxes and property. This suited the sultans well; they not only obtained financial security for themselves by virtue of their healthy stipends, but also got protection from other rivals. As time went on, lesser figures were given positions within the bureaucracy, thus weaving the Malays into the fabric of the administration, of which the cornerstone was the **State Council**. Although the sultan was its ceremonial head, the Resident chose the constituent members and set the political agenda, in consultation with his deputies – the district officers – and the governor.

The increasing power of central government soon began to diminish the consultative side of the Resident's role, and by the 1890s fewer and fewer meetings of the council were being held. Even in religious matters, the goalposts were often moved to suit British purposes. Furthermore, there were few Residents as talented and sympathetic as Hugh Low and so, predictably, the involvement of the British in Malay affairs became less advisory and more reformatory. Sultan Abdullah, bent on acquiring local power and status, thereby inadvertently provided a foot in the door for the British, an act which ultimately led to their full political intervention in the Peninsula.

A five-minute walk onward up the same road brings you to the imposing white marble **Istana Iskandariah**, the sultan's ultramodern official palace. It's closed to the public, though a stroll round to the left of the huge gates gives a good view down the river. Close by, off to the left as you circle the palace to rejoin the road, the **Royal Museum of Perak** (Mon–Thurs, Sat & Sun 10am–5pm; Fri 9am–12.15pm & 3–5pm; free) is of greater architectural significance. This former royal residence, the erstwhile Istana Kenangan, is a traditional stilted wooden structure built without the use of nails and decorated with intricate friezes and geometric-patterned wall panels. Inside, the museum displays a collection of royal artefacts (medals, costumes and so on), although its photographs of past and present royalty in Perak are of more interest.

Back in town, the most evocative memory of colonial days is provided by the **Malay College** on Jalan Tun Razak, its elegant columns and porticoes visible as you approach the centre from the train station. Founded in January 1905, it was conceived by British administrators as a training ground for the sons of Malay nobility, an "Eton of the East", where discipline and tradition was more English than in England – although the schoolboys were required to wear formal Malay dress, as they still do today.

The jetty is situated close to the clock tower, from which you turn right down the hill towards the river. Here, you can catch boats (30 sen) to the other side to visit **Sayong**, a village where the *labu* is made from smooth river clay and finished in traditional kilns; this gourd-shaped vessel is renowned for keeping liquids cool even in the blazing midday sun and is one of the most common handicrafts in Malaysia. You can also get there by taxi (RM50), should the hour-long walk to the village on the other side of the river not appeal. However, bicycles can be rented from the *Double Lion* for RM5, making it possible to cycle, using the new and rather grand bridge in the north end of town and then doubling back south on the other side. There are also **river cruises** (20min; RM10) from the jetty.

Practicalities

Kuala Kangsar lies on Route 1 and on the main west-coast train line. The **train station** is on the northwestern outskirts of town, a twenty-minute walk from the clock tower in the centre. Buses from Ipoh, Butterworth and Taiping pull up at the **bus station** at the bottom of Jalan Raja Bendahara, close to the river, behind which there is a Maybank. The **tourist information** office (℡05/777 7717, Ⓦwww.visitkualakangsar.com) is by the clock tower. There are a couple of **places to stay** including the simple but friendly *Double Lion* at 74 Jalan Kangsar (℡05/776 1010), just south of the bus station, with clean rooms, ranging from fan singles with shared bath (❷) to en-suite air-conditioned rooms with TV (❹). In the middle of town near the clock tower, the *Seri Kangsar*, at 33 Jalan Daeng Selili (℡05/777 7301, Ⓕ777 7101; ❹), has simple en-suite rooms also with air-conditioning and TV. A quieter option is the *Rest House* (℡05/776 4262; ❹), along Jalan Istana, half a kilometre southeast of the clock tower. Although it's a bit run down, this is a friendly place with a raised location, overlooking the river. There's **internet** access at Pusat AMS Computer, second floor, 86 Jalan Kangsar (℡05/777 6320), which is close to most of the town's **restaurants** serving the usual fare.

Taiping and around

Set against the backdrop of the mist-laden Bintang Hills, **TAIPING** – like so many places in Perak – has its origins in the discovery of tin here in the first decades of the nineteenth century. As a mining centre, overrun by enthusiastic prospectors, it had an unsurprisingly turbulent early history. Yet despite shaky beginnings, Taiping was thriving by the late nineteenth century. Its growing prosperity helped fund many firsts at a time when Kuala Lumpur was barely on the map: the first rail line in the country (built to facilitate the export of the tin); the first English-language school in 1878; the first museum in 1883; and the first English-language newspaper (the *Perak Pioneer*) in 1894. With the establishment of the nearby hill station of **Bukit Larut** (formerly Maxwell Hill) as a retreat for its administrators, Taiping was, with the tin trade as its life force, firmly at the forefront of the colonial development of the Federated Malay States. Then, in the mid-twentieth century, Taiping became the headquarters of the Japanese military administration of Malaya and Sumatra during World War II.

Map labels:

TAIPING

N

0   100 m

Kamunting Express Bus Station

Ling Nam Temple
Perak Museum
Prison
All Saints' Church
JLN BEREK LILANG
JLN TAMING SARI
JLN AIR TERJUN
Zoo
Taman Tasik
JLN PADANG BOLA
JLN SULTAN MANSOR
JALAN KELAB LAMA
Telekom
Police Station
Padang
JLN RESIDEN
District Office
JLN ISTANA LABUT
JLN MUZIUM HULU
JLN KEMUNING
LORONG KING EDWARD
King Edward School
Central Market
JLN STESEN
JLN BEREK
JLN PASAR
JLN KELAB LAMA
JLN PASAR SULTAN ABDULLAH
JALAN TUPAI
Clock tower
Food Markets
JLN MAHARAJA LELA
JLN SLENGKUNGAN CIRCULAR ROAD
Train Station
JLN TAMING SARI
JLN CHUNG THYE PIN
JLN KOTA
JLN ISLAM
JLN PASAR
Netsurfer
Central Market
JALAN TUPAI
JALAN TUPAI
JLN PANGGUNG WAYANG
Long Distance Taxi Stand
Food Stalls
JLN IDRIS
JLN MASJID
Popular Bookstore
Local Bus Station & Taxis
JLN STEPHENS
JLN CONVENT
Mosque

Penang & Ipoh

ACCOMMODATION
Aun Chuan   D
Casuarina Inn   A
Cherry Inn   C
Fuliyean   B
Furama   E
Legend Inn   F

EATING & DRINKING
Annapoorna   2
Nasi Kandar D Mutiara   1

Nowadays, bypassed by the North–South Expressway and replaced in administrative importance by Ipoh, Taiping itself is declining gracefully, its tattered two-storey shopfronts indicative of the run-down atmosphere that pervades the town. Taiping is also the entry point for the **Matang Mangrove Reserve**, the largest of its kind in Peninsular Malaysia, stretching 52km along the coastline. Although the main reason people visit is to relax at Bukit Larut or explore the mangrove reserve, allow yourself at least a day to explore the sights of Taiping – the **Taiping Lake Gardens**, **Perak Museum** and the fine buildings which line the wide roads.

Arrival and information

The **train station** is on Jalan Stesen behind the hospital, just over a kilometre west of the centre of Taiping. An inconvenient 7km taxi ride (RM10) north of the centre is the Kamunting **express bus station**, at which it is most likely you will arrive. The **local bus station** is on Jalan Panggung Wayang, and the friendly **visitors' information centre** (Mon–Fri 8.30am–5.30pm, Sat 8.30am–3pm; often closed for an hour at noon), where you can get a good heritage tour **map** of Taiping, is located in the old clock tower on Jalan Tupai.

Accommodation

For a town of its size, Taiping has a remarkable number of **hotels**, which is just as well because in high season it often has to cater for the overspill from Bukit Larut. It's worth noting that the striking Peranakan-style *Peace Hotel* on Jalan Panggung Wayang is not a regular hotel at all but a brothel, as has been reported about the *Peking Hotel* on Jalan Idris.

Aun Chuan 25 Jalan Kota ☎05/807 5322, on the junction with Jalan Halaman Pasar, above KFC. The least expensive option in town with fan rooms and shared facilites ❶, as well as en-suite rooms with a/c and wooden floors throughout. ❷

Casuarina Inn Taman Tasik ☎05/804 1339, ℱ804 1337. Standing on the site of the former official quarters of the British Resident in Perak State, overlooking the lake gardens, this friendly hotel offers huge, though slightly worn, en-suite rooms. ❸

🏃 **Cherry Inn** 17 Jalan Stesen ☎05/805 2223. New and shiny with an interesing sitting room, this well-run place offers fan rooms with shared facilities, and another RM40 will get you an en suite and a/c. There is also a family wing with two rooms and a sitting area available at extra cost. ❹

Fuliyean 14 Jalan Berek ☎05/806 8648, ℱ807 0648. At the lower end of this price bracket, this place has spotless rooms with TVs and en-suite bathrooms. ❸

🏃 **Furama** 30 Jalan Peng Long ☎05/807 1077, ⓦwww.hotelfurama.com.my. This clean, bright hotel is located between the Lake Garden and one of the large hawker centres. The well-maintained en-suite rooms come with a/c, TV, kettle and wi-fi. Laundry service is available. Good value. ❹

Legend Inn Corner of Jalan Convent and Jalan Masjid ☎05/806 0000, ⓦwww.legendinn.com. Conveniently located near the bus station and with its own coffee house. Late checkouts can be arranged. ❹–❺

The Town

Taiping is easily walkable, and since the central streets are laid out on a grid system, there's no problem finding your way around. The four main streets, which run parallel to each other, are Jalan Taming Sari, Jalan Pasar, Jalan Kota and Jalan Panggung Wayang. Up Jalan Pasar are the **padang** and the sparkling-white **District Office**, which marks the northern limit of the Chinese district. The gardens – Taman Tasik – spread to the northeast of here, close to the foot of Bukit Larut, with the museum a little to the northwest; on the opposite side of town, on its southwestern outskirts, are three **temples** for the Hindu, Chinese and Muslim communities respectively.

A wander around the shop-lined streets surrounding Taiping's **central market** does little to detract from its reputation as a murky old mining town, though Taiping's numerous, lively **night markets** (see opposite) bring welcome splashes of colour and life. North of here up Jalan Taming Sari is **All Saints' Church**, founded in 1887. The oldest church in Malaysia cuts a forlorn figure these days: termites are slowly destroying the wooden structure, and there's talk of completely demolishing and rebuilding the church. In some ways, the tiny churchyard is more interesting, containing the graves of the earliest British and Australian settlers, many of whom died at an early age; others, after many years of service to the Malay States, failed to obtain a pension to allow them to return home.

Another hundred metres further on, the **Perak Museum** (daily 9.30am–5pm; closed Fri noon–2.45pm; free; ⓦwww.museumperak.gov.my), housed in a cool and spacious colonial building, boasted as many as thirteen thousand exhibits when it opened in 1883. There are three major collections, all designed to portray Malaysia's wide cultural and natural heritage embracing anthropology, zoology and local history with displays of stuffed local fauna as well as an extensive collection of ancient weapons and Orang Asli implements and ornaments. Next door

▲ Taiping Lake Gardens

to the museum, the **Ling Nam Temple** is one of Taiping's main Chinese centres of worship, while opposite the museum is a **prison**, built in 1879 and subsequently used by the Japanese during World War II – today it's where some of the executions of Malaysia's drug offenders are carried out. The prison has a little shop selling handicrafts made by the inmates.

Backtracking down Jalan Taming Sari takes you to the padang, from where it's a ten-minute stroll east to **Taiping Lake Gardens**, the extensive lake gardens which are landscaped around two former tin-mining pools. At the height of the industry's success, large areas of countryside were being laid waste, creating unsightly muddy heaps and stagnant pools. In Taiping, at least, the Resident retained a colonial sense of propriety and turned this area into a park in 1880. It's still immaculately kept, with a gazebo, freshwater fish in the lakes and a profusion of flowers. There's also a nine-hole golf course and even a small zoo, popular with local tourists (daily 8:30am–6pm; RM12 and night tours 8–11pm; RM16; Ⓦ www.zootaiping.gov.my).

A few minutes' walk to the northeast of the park, past the lotus pond, is the **Commonwealth War Cemetery**, a serene memorial to the casualties of World War II, containing the graves of 866 men, many of whom could not be identified. Split in two by the road to Bukit Larut, the cemetery is divided between Hindu and Muslim Indians on one side and Christian British and Australians on the other. Close by are the **Burmese Pools**, a series of natural rock pools that are not nearly as inviting as they sound. A much better bet for a cool dip are the more traditional **Coronation Pools** (RM1), just at the base of Bukit Larut, where the chlorine-free water comes straight from the hills.

Eating and drinking

The most atmospheric meals in town are those at Taiping's numerous **food markets**, which are located on almost every street. The largest is along Jalan Chung Thye Phin (Cross Street), while the eastern side of the food market on Jalan Tupai is great for ice-cream sundaes and fruit salads, as well as all manner of main courses. On Jalan Idris Taiping is another large row of stalls, where you can get a burger or seafood. *Restoran Annapoorna* on the corner at 164 Jalan Taming Sari is recommended for its good-value and tasty Indian food. On Jalan Stesen is *Nasi Kandar D Mutiara*, which serves a wide variety of good Indian food.

Bukit Larut (Maxwell Hill)

BUKIT LARUT (formerly Maxwell Hill) – 12km northeast of Taiping – is Malaysia's smallest (and oldest) hill station. Named after the first Assistant Resident of Perak, George Maxwell, the name changed back to Bukit Larut in 1979 as part of a general trend to return to local rather than English place names. At approximately 1035m above sea level, the climate is wonderfully cool, and on a clear day there are spectacular views down to the west coast. Unfortunately its status as reputedly the wettest place in Malaysia, with 5m of rainfall annually, also means that it's frequently quite cloudy at the top, which can be very atmospheric. Bukit Larut is great for birdwatching, and local guides can be hired at the bottom of the hill. There are a few tame forest **walks** here too; most walkers stick to the main road winding up the mountain. The climb to The Cottage – a stone bungalow built in the 1880s for British officialdom – leads through groves of evergreens and the largest variety of flowers in the country, to the only accessible **summit**. Protect yourself against leeches, which can be a problem in the forest (particularly just after rainfall), by wearing long trousers, and socks and shoes, rather than sandals.

The narrow road up to the hill station twists and turns round some terrifying bends and is accessible only by government Land Rover or on foot; private vehicles are not allowed up. The service (hourly 8am–4pm; 35min; RM7 round trip) begins at the foot of the hill, twenty minutes' walk from the Lake Gardens in Taiping, and these seats are on a first-come, first-served basis. The last jeep down is at 5pm; be sure to be there at least fifteen minutes before.

Many people prefer to **walk** up from Taiping instead, which takes from two and a half to three hours; the marked path starts at the Land Rover pick-up point. You'll need to be quite fit, but this way you get more time to take in the views and can still make it down again by early evening. About midway to the summit is the Tea Garden House, little more than a shelter now, though once part of an extensive tea estate. It's an ideal place to stop for a rest, as the view at this point is superb, with the town of Taiping and the mirror-like waters of the gardens visible below.

Practicalities

The choice for **accommodation** on Bukit Larut is between resthouses and bungalows. Standards are pretty uniform, with most places offering hot water, kitchen facilities and spacious rooms. As there's only room for a total of 53 people, you'll need to **book in advance** at the office at the foot of the hill (⊤05/807 7241 or 807 7243), where guides also can be hired for birdwatching. Bungalow prices are for the whole building (sleeping six), while the resthouses rent out individual rooms. **Food** is available at each of the resthouses, while at the bungalows, the caretaker can arrange for food to be prepared for you, or you can do your own cooking – buy your provisions in Taiping.

The Land Rover stops right next to the *Rumah Beringin* bungalow (RM200), not quite as quiet as the other places as day-trippers often come here for a couple of hours before heading back down. All the other places to stay are of an equally basic standard and dotted around the hills within a mile of the drop-off point; the driver will take you to your door if you ask. A few minutes' walk up from the Land Rover stop brings you to the *Rumah Angkasa* (❻). A quarter of a mile uphill from the Land Rover stop, there's a junction to the left where there are the *Rumah Cendana* (🄾), *Rumah Tempinis* (🄾) and the VIP-class *Sri Kayangan* (🄿) bungalows, all spaced well away from each other; taking a right leads, after about 400m, to the *Rumah Rehat Gunung Hijau* resthouse, which is the most secluded accommodation option up here (🄾) with four rooms in one bungalow, sleeping up to ten people.

Matang Mangrove Reserve

Around 16km west of Taiping is the **Matang Mangrove Forest Reserve** (daily 9am–5pm; free; ☎05/858 1762), Peninsular Malaysia's largest, with several species of mangrove and an excellent place for birdwatching. The mangrove rivers are sometimes visited by large porpoises and otters, as well as the more frequent wild boars, macaques, monitor lizards, mangrove pit vipers and mudskippers. It is possible to book bungalows (RM30–50) in the forest by calling in advance using the above number.

Getting there from Taiping, take Route 74 going west and follow the signs for Matang, looking out for signs toward Kuala Sepetang. Alternatively, get local bus #77 (daily 6am–7pm; hourly) to **Kuala Sepetang**, which is not much of a town bar a few dusty streets and a large number of Chinese birds' nest houses. A good place to stop for lunch is the *Salleh Stall* on Jalan Truma, which serves great *mee udang* (RM7).

Though it's free to enter through the official park entrance about a kilometre out of town, a guide is needed for river tours. **Tours** are sometimes available from the forest office as well as local nature guides (☎012/619 5432, 🖥www .geocities.com/greenvillagemalaysia; RM200 or RM50 per person for four people or more; add an extra RM100 to your party to include transport from Taiping); these incorporate the mangroves, a local charcoal factory (an additional RM6 per person) and a fishing village. It is also possible to book tours for firefly and crocodile night safaris and an Orang Asli archeological burial site.

Penang

North of Taiping, towards the coast, the landscape becomes increasingly flat and arid as the road eases away from the backbone of mountains that dominate the western seaboard. Sitting 94km north of Taiping is the dusty, industrial port town of **Butterworth**, part of **PENANG**, a confusing amalgam of state and island. Everything of interest in Penang State is on **Pulau Pinang** ("Betel Nut Island" in Malay) – a large island, 285 square kilometres in area, upon which the first British settlement on the Malay Peninsula was sited. The confusion gets worse, as the island's city (Malaysia's second largest), the likeable **Georgetown**, is also often referred to as "Penang". With Melaka, Penang was listed as a UNESCO World Heritage site in 2008, a reflection of the cultural heritage so visible here, and this will undoubtedly affect the already bustling tourist industry. Where more high-rise hotel complexes might have been built, the city is looking to restore more of its older colonial buildings in a move to preserve the UNESCO status that a decade of lobbying fought so hard to get.

Georgetown is likely to be your base during a stay on Pulau Pinang, but some visitors also make trips out to the beaches at **Batu Ferringhi** or the much quieter **Teluk Bahang** along the north coast. Better beaches are found in the

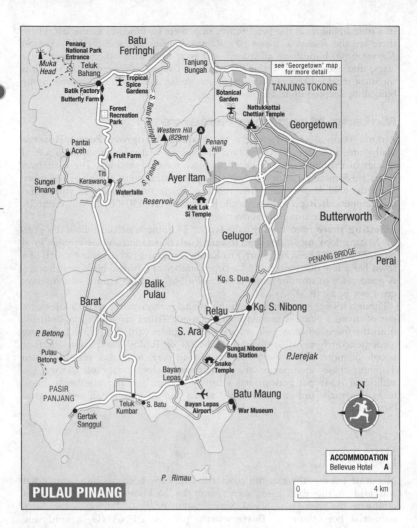

Penang National Park
Batu Ferringhi
Penang National Park Entrance
Muka Head
Teluk Bahang
Tropical Spice Gardens
Batik Factory
Butterfly Farm
Forest Recreation Park
Pantai Aceh
Fruit Farm
Titi Kerawang
Sungei Pinang
Waterfalls
S. Batu Ferringhi
S. Pinang
Tanjung Bungah
Western Hill (829m)
Penang Hill
Ayer Itam
Reservoir
Kek Lok Si Temple
see 'Georgetown' map for more detail
TANJUNG TOKONG
Botanical Garden
Nattukkottai Chettiar Temple
Georgetown
Butterworth
Gelugor
PENANG BRIDGE
Perai
Kg. S. Dua
Balik Pulau
Barat
Relau
S. Ara
Kg. S. Nibong
P. Betong
Pulau Betong
Sungai Nibong Bus Station
Snake Temple
P.Jerejak
PASIR PANJANG
Gertak Sanggul
Teluk Kumbar
S. Batu
Bayan Lepas
Bayan Lepas Airport
Batu Maung
War Museum
P. Rimau
N

PULAU PINANG

ACCOMMODATION
Bellevue Hotel A

0   4 km

newly opened **Penang National Park** on Muka Head, where an hour's walk through the jungle rewards with somewhat cleaner water, turtle hatching sites and camping facilities.

The island is the focus of several important **festivals** and events throughout the year, starting with Thaipusam. Perhaps the best known of the rest is the Penang Bridge Run held in May, when thousands of competitors hurtle across the bridge to Butterworth at dawn as part of a half-marathon. June is also a busy month, witnessing the International Dragonboat Race, the Equestrian Carnival and, on the northern coast, a beach volleyball tournament. In July, Georgetown's flower festival and Grand Parade provide colour, while the Cultural Festival provides a showcase for Penang's Malays, Chinese and Indians. In November, Batu Ferrenghi becomes host to the Penang Jazz Festival.

Some history

Pulau Pinang was ruled by the **sultans of Kedah** until the late eighteenth century. In the wake of years of harassment by Kedah's enemies, the sultan, Mohammed J'wa Mu'Azzam Shah II, was prepared to afford trade facilities to any nation that would provide him with military protection. Enter the charming and diplomatic **Francis Light** in 1771 in search of a regional trading base with China for both his company and the **East India Company** - quickly gaining the honorary title of "Deva Rajah" (God-king) with the sultan taking him into his confidence.

After failed negotiations between the sultan and the EIC's own agent, Edward Moncton, it was another twelve years before an agreement was reached with the new Sultan Abdullah and Light. The French had a regional foothold in Sumatra and the Dutch controlled Melaka, the foremost trading port in the region, and a deal was made between Light and Abdullah for RM30,000 a year, along with protection for the sultan from the Burmese and Siamese. However, the EIC's new governor-general, Charles Cornwallis, refused to be party to these plans and Light, concealing the facts from both parties, formally **established a port** at Penang on August 11, 1786 on his own initiative. For the next five years, Light adopted stalling tactics with the sultan, assuring him that the matter of protection was being referred to authorities in London. The sultan eventually caught on, but was unable to drive the British out and settled on an annual payment of only RM6000, and no role in the future government of the island.

So it was that Penang, then inhabited by fewer than a hundred indigenous fishermen, became the **first British settlement** in the Malay Peninsula. After an initial, late-eighteenth-century influx of mainly Chinese immigrants, attracted by the possibilities of new commerce, Penang quickly became a major colonial administrative centre; within two years, four hundred acres were under cultivation and the population had reached ten thousand. Francis Light was made superintendent and declared the island a free port, renaming it "Prince of Wales Island" after the British heir apparent. Georgetown took its name after the British king at that time, George III, and has retained its colonial name even though the island's name has reverted to Penang.

For a time, all looked rosy for Penang, with Georgetown proclaimed as capital of the newly established **Straits Settlements** (incorporating Melaka and Singapore) in 1826. But the founding of Singapore in 1819 was the beginning of the end for Georgetown, as the new colony overtook its predecessor in every respect. In retrospect, this had one beneficial effect: with Georgetown stuck in the economic doldrums for a century or more, there was no significant development within the city, and consequently many of its colonial and early Chinese buildings survive to this day. Although Penang was occupied by the Japanese during World War II, the strategic significance of Singapore once more proved to be Penang's saving grace, and there was very little bomb damage to the island.

Butterworth

Realistically, the only reason to spend any time at all in **BUTTERWORTH**, 370km from KL, is to sort out your transport to Penang island – which can usually be done within half an hour of arrival. The **bus station**, **ferry pier**, long-distance-**taxi stand** and **train station** are all next door to each other, lying right on the quayside, so you shouldn't have to venture any further.

There are plenty of **places to stay**, although the decent hotels are a fair way from the port; none of the nearby options are particularly appealing. If you get stuck, the closest place to the front is the *Beach Garden Hotel* (☏04/332 2845; ❸) at 4835 Jalan Pantai, which, although there's neither a beach nor a garden, is friendly enough.

The passenger and car **ferry service to Georgetown** takes fifteen minutes (passengers 1.20 sen, motorbikes RM2, cars RM7.70; you only pay for the inbound journey to the island, leaving again is free) and runs from 6am until 12.30am. When you have disembarked from the train you will soon be approached by taxi drivers who will offer to take you to Penang. The ferry is faster and cheaper, so keep on walking over the signposted causeway to the ferry ticketing booth.

The **Penang Bridge**, the longest in Asia at 13.5km, crosses from just 1.5km south of Butterworth – turn west off Route 1 for the bridge – to the east coast of the island, 8km south of Georgetown (a **toll** of RM7 is payable only on the journey out from the mainland); if you are coming over by **long-distance taxi** from any point on the Peninsula, check whether the toll is included in the fare.

Georgetown

Visiting **GEORGETOWN** in 1879, stalwart Victorian traveller Isabella Bird called it "a brilliant place under a brilliant sky", a simple statement on which it's hard to improve – Malaysia's most fascinating city retains more of its cultural history than virtually anywhere else in the country. Fort Cornwallis, St George's Church and the many buildings on and around Lebuh Pantai all survive from the earliest colonial days, and the communities of Chinatown and Little India have contributed some fine temples. Later Thai and Burmese arrivals left their mark on the city, but its predominant feature are the rows of peeling two-storey **Chinese shophouses**, their shutters painted in pastel colours, with bright-red Chinese lettering covering their colonnades and cheerfully designed awnings to shield the goods from the glaring sun. While the confusion of rickshaws, buses, lorries and scooters make parts of Georgetown as frenetic and polluted as most other places in the region, life in the slow lane has changed very little over the years. The rituals of worship, eating out at a roadside stall and the running of the family business, have all continued with little concern for Georgetown's contemporary technological development. It may no longer be a sleepy backwater – most of the island's one-million strong population now lives here – but the city's soul is firmly rooted in the past.

Nowadays, parts of downtown Georgetown sparkle with the state-of-the-art hotels and air-conditioned shopping malls familiar to much of modern Malaysia. But perhaps more than any other place in the country Georgetown is a magnet for budget travellers – the city is something of a hangout, a place not only to renew Thai visas, but also to relax and observe street life from a pavement café and stock up on luxuries that beach life may not provide.

Arrival and information

Passenger and car **ferries from Butterworth** dock at the centrally located terminal on **Pengkalan Weld** in Georgetown; those **from Medan** (Indonesia) and **Langkawi** dock at **Swettenham Pier**, a few hundred metres north along the dockside. The main local **bus station** and **taxi stand** is by the ferry terminal on Pengkalan Weld and most buses also stop at the KOMTAR building, a short walk from the hotels and major amenities. The Penang Bridge brings **drivers** into the island on Jalan Udini, 8km south of Georgetown on the east coast. Driving into the city is not for the traffic-shy, though the major routes are well signposted. It's easiest to park in the KOMTAR building on Jalan

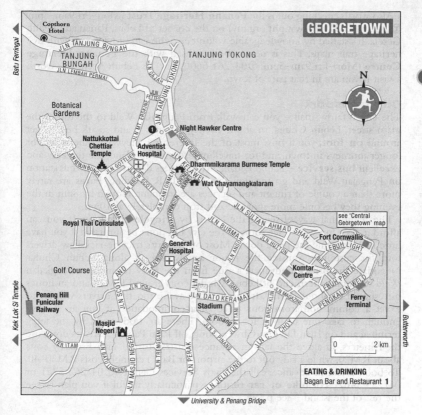

GEORGETOWN

Copthorn Hotel

TANJUNG BUNGAH

TANJUNG TOKONG

N

Botanical Gardens

Night Hawker Centre

Nattukkottai Chettiar Temple

Adventist Hospital

Dharmmikarama Burmese Temple

Wat Chayamangkalaram

Royal Thai Consulate

see 'Central Georgetown' map

General Hospital

Fort Cornwallis

LEBUH LIGHT

Golf Course

Komtar Centre

PENGKALAN WELD

Penang Hill Funicular Railway

Ferry Terminal

JLN DATO KERAMAT

Stadium

S. Pinang

Masjid Negeri

0   2 km

EATING & DRINKING
Bagan Bar and Restaurant **1**

Batu Ferringhi

Kek Lok Si Temple

Butterworth

University & Penang Bridge

Penang, which is within easy walking distance of the hotel area (mid-range and above hotels usually have private car parks). The **express bus** station on the island, Sungai Nibong, is about 5km south of the centre, close to the Snake Temple. As all buses either to or from here will pass through Butterworth, you are better off going to Butterworth as the transport links there are more frequent. The **airport** is at Bayan Lepas on the southeastern tip of the island. The local bus system is called Rapid Penang, and bus #401 (roughly hourly 6am–9pm; RM2) takes about 45 minutes to run into Georgetown from the airport, stopping at the KOMTAR building and subsequently at the Pengkalan Weld bus station; a taxi into the city costs RM35 – buy a coupon beforehand from inside the terminal building.

If you arrive by ferry, the most convenient tourist office is the **Penang Tourist Centre** (Mon–Sat 10am–6pm; ☎04/261 6663), Pesera King Edward. A couple of doors down at no. 10 is **Tourism Malaysia** (Mon–Fri 8am–5pm; ☎04/262 0066), which is more helpful. They can sell you a **tourist newspaper** (RM3; it's also available free at some hotels), which provides a map and general information. Half-day **tours** of the city and the island (around RM45) can be booked at most hotels and agents and are not a bad way to see Penang if your time is limited.

Also worth checking out is the **Penang Heritage Trust** (Mon–Fri 9am–5pm; ☏04/264 2631, ⓦwww.pht.org.my) on the corner of Lebuh Pantai and Lebuh Gereja. It's staffed by knowledgeable volunteers who can provide you with free heritage trail maps. This is not to be confused with the **Penang Heritage Centre** (Mon–Fri 9am–5pm; ☏04/261 6606) on 118 Lebuh Aceh, also worth a visit if you are in that part of town.

City transport

The city is fairly small – you can walk from Pengkalan Weld to the top of the main street, Lebuh Chulia, in about twenty minutes – and so it's best to get around **on foot**; you'll miss most of the interesting alleyways otherwise. For longer journeys in town, and for travelling around the island, use the easy and excellent **bus service** – Rapid Penang. Most routes depart from the bus station on Pengalan Weld and go through the KOMTAR building. **Fares** are rarely more than a couple of ringgit and services are frequent, though by 8pm in the evening they become more sporadic and stop completely at 10pm.

The traditional way of seeing the city is by **tricycle-rickshaw**. If you can afford it, it's a fun way to see some of the city, but don't be surprised if you have little luck haggling the price down. Most of the city's tricycle-rickshaw drivers tout for customers outside the major hotels and all along Lebuh Chulia. Negotiate the price in advance; a ride from the ferry terminal at Pengkalan Weld to the northern end of Lebuh Chulia costs around RM10 and an hour's hire should be about RM30. It's good to be aware too, that drivers will try to exact a commission from your place of accommodation if you are foolish enough to take one to look for a room. There are **taxi** stands by the ferry terminal and on Jalan Dr. Lim Chwee Long, off Jalan Penang. Drivers don't use their meters, so agree the fare in advance – a trip to the Thai Embassy costs about RM20, while a ride out to the airport or Batu Ferringhi costs RM30–40. To book a taxi in advance, call the Taxis Services Centre (☏04/262 5721 or 04/229 9467). For **bike or car rental** – particularly useful if you plan to see the rest of the island – see p.195.

Accommodation

Georgetown has a profusion of hotels and guesthouses, with plenty of choice at the budget end of the scale. The budget places, mostly on and around **Lebuh Chulia**, are usually within ramshackle wooden-shuttered mansions, often with courtyards and elegant internal staircases. Most have dorm beds as well as private

---

Street names in Georgetown

The most confusing thing about finding your way around Georgetown is understanding the **street names**, which all used to reflect the city's colonial past; however, the current political climate encourages either a Malay translation of an existing name (Penang Rd has become Jalan Penang, Penang St is Lebuh Penang, Weld Quay has become Pengkalan Weld, Church St is Lebuh Gereja and Beach St is now Lebuh Pantai) or complete renaming. This would be relatively straightforward were it not for the fact that the new names have not always been popularly accepted – Lorong Cinta, for example, is almost universally known as Love Lane – and even on official maps you'll sometimes see either name used. The most awkward of the new names is Jalan Masjid Kapitan Kling for the erstwhile Pitt Street, which more often than not is referred to simply as Lebuh Pitt. Several street names are also used repeatedly, such as Lorong Chulia and Lebuh Chulia, Lorong Penang and Lebuh Penang; also, don't confuse Lorong Cinta with Lebuh Cintra.

rooms, and offer other useful services, such as selling bus tickets to Thailand and obtaining Thai visas. The two official **youth hostels** are a long way from the city centre: the *YMCA* is at 211 Jalan Macalister, 4km west from the KOMTAR building (T04/229 2349; ❹), and the *YWCA* is 7km southwest of the centre at 8 Jalan Masjid Negeri (T04/828 1855; ❸).

Budget on Lebuh Chulia & Jalan Penang

Ai Goh 465 Jalan Penang T04/262 9922, F263 2922. On the corner of Jalan Penang and Lebuh Kimberly, this very basic, and a little shabby, hotel has fan cubicle rooms with shared as well as private showers. It's relatively quiet, as it's set back from the street. ❶–❷

Banana Guest House 355 Lebuh Chulia T04/262 6171, Einfo@banananewguesthouse.com. This new place is right on the T junction of Love Lane and Lebuh Chulia and has cheap, basic rooms of the usual ranges. The café-bar is something of a travellers' hangout with internet terminals and wi-fi. ❶–❷

Blue Diamond Hotel 422 Lebuh Chulia T04/261 1089. Large, atmospheric building with simple rooms. The cheapest are with fans and shared bathrooms; the rooms are huge and the sheets are clean. There is a courtyard with a bar and live music to the early hours out the front. Dorms RM10, ❶–❷ .

Hang Chow 511 Lebuh Chulia T04/261 0810. Clean and tidy fan rooms. A few ringgit more will get you your own shower (all are hot); and a few more will buy a/c. There's a nice *kopitiam* restaurant downstairs, serving local and continental food, including pizza. ❷

Jim's Place 431 Lebuh Chulia T016/653 6963. This very small place has only four basic upstairs rooms, all with shared bathroom. The sign outside has a tag-line saying "anything you need, Jim'll fix it" and he probably will. ❶

Oasies Hotel (formerly Swiss Hotel) 431f Lebuh Chulia T04/262 2345. Good-value, clean and functional hostel with sturdier walls than most. It's set back from the road (the sign above the entrance still reads *Swiss Hotel*), with parking as well as an airy café with wi-fi. ❷

Olive Spring 300 302 Lebuh Chulia T04/261 4641. Friendly place with somewhat old-school singles and doubles. The upstairs rooms at the back near the balcony are the most popular as they're quieter. All rooms have shared facilities. The adjoined *Rainforest* bakery next door supplies freshly made bread and cakes for the downstairs café. ❶

Tourist Guest House 425 Lebuh Chulia T012/504 6582, Etouristguesthouse@hotmail.com. Good sturdy doors and either shared or private bathrooms and fans or a/c, makes this place great value. The usual transfers, visas motorbike hire and so on, can be arranged. ❶–❷

White House 72 Jalan Penang T04/263 2385. Very clean, large rooms, with hot showers and optional a/c, for half what you'd pay elsewhere. Though pretty soulless, this place offers some of the best-value rooms in town. ❷

Budget elsewhere

These places are off the main drags of Chulia and Penang and so tend to be quieter.

75 Traveller's Lodge 75 Jalan Muntri T04/262 3378, E75lodge@gmail.com. With free wi-fi and hot showers, this place is an old favourite with travellers, though the rooms are the standard cubicles. There is a good common area for socializing. ❶–❷

Broadway Hostel 35f Jalan Masjid Kapitan Kling T04/262 8550, F262 8560. In a modern building, this friendly place has small and very basic but tidy fan rooms with thin walls and a/c rooms with two double beds. All rooms have shared facilities. ❷–❸

D'Budget Hostel 9 Lebuh Gereja T04/263 4794. Conveniently close to the ferry terminals, this friendly Indian-run place has spartan but clean and secure rooms. There's a large roof patio plus internet access, laundry facilities and a TV room. ❷

Love Lane Inn 54 Lorong Cinta T016/419 8409, Eocean008@hotmail.com. The rooms are spartan and clean, but rather sterile; the more expensive en suite and a/c rooms are by far the best. Nice touch with free tea and coffee as well as wi-fi and very knowledgeable staff. ❶–❷

Modern 179c Lebuh Muntri T04/263 5424. On the corner of Lebuh Leith, this basic place has a variety of rooms: fan or a/c, en suite or shared showers – all in need of some modernization. The nicest rooms are the large doubles with large, private balconies, so ask to view before you check in. ❷

Noble 36 Lorong Pasar T04/261 2372, F263 2372. Tucked away on a quiet side street, this friendly place has fan rooms with wood floors. The en-suite rooms are especially good value. Spacious common area with drinks and a kettle. ❶

Old Penang Guest House 53 Lorong Cinta T04/263 8805, Eoldpenang@gmail.com. This wonderfully restored house with twelve rooms, wooden floors and a dorm at RM15 is the best value in the area. The sheets are crisp and clean, there is a beautiful common room with free wi-fi and a plasma screen showing movies. Light breakfast included. ❶

Oriental Guest House 81 Lebuh Muntri ☏ 04/261 3378, Ⓕ 263 3378. With a great downstairs communal area, these cubicle rooms have high ceilings and the ones downstairs have original tile floors. All fan rooms with shared facilities. ❶

SD Guest House 28 Lebuh Muntri ☏ 04/261 6102, Ⓦ www.sdguesthouse.com.my. With a sister hotel on Lorong Cinta, this relatively new place is very clean, though spartan, with fan rooms (❶), en-suite and a/c rooms (❷).

Star Lodge 39 Lebuh Muntri ☏ 04/262 6378, Ⓔ 75lodge@gmail.com. Run by the same management as the *75 Traveller's Lodge* a few doors away, the rooms come with either fan, a/c and shared or private facilities with new bathrooms. ❷

Moderate

🏃 **Cathay** 15 Lebuh Leith ☏ 04/262 6271, Ⓕ 263 9300. Stylish colonial mansion dating from 1910 and used in the film *Beyond Rangoon*, with fan or a/c rooms with own bathrooms and a courtyard fountain, making for a tranquil environment. Some of the rooms are a bit small and the bathrooms could do with a makeover, so ask to see before you check in. ❹

Hong Ping 273b Lebuh Chulia ☏ 04/262 5243, Ⓕ 262 3270. This hotel above a massage spa, is the only mid-range option on Lebuh Chulia; it's clean and well run and all rooms have a/c, TVs and hot showers and there is a lift. Good value. ❸–❹

Malaysia 7 Jalan Penang ☏ 04/263 3311, Ⓦ www.hotelmalaysia.com.my. Best of the hotels along this strip. The smartly decorated rooms have kettles and fridges and there's a health centre and hairdressing salon, too. ❺

Merchant 55 Jalan Penang ☏ 04/263 2828, Ⓕ 262 5511. Smartish place; all rooms have bathtubs and fridges. Continental breakfast included. ❺

Oriental 105 Jalan Penang ☏ 04/263 4211, Ⓔ hostpg@pd.jaring.my. Reasonable rooms with helpful, professional staff. There's a North Indian restaurant in the basement as well as a Japanese karaoke lounge. ❹

Peking 50a Jalan Penang ☏ 04/263 6191. Large, clean rooms with nice tile floors, but the walls could use a lick of paint. All rooms are en suite, with a/c and TV. ❹

Expensive

🏃 **Cheong Fatt Tze Mansion** 14 Lebuh Leith ☏ 04/262 0006, Ⓦ www.cheongfatttzemansion.com. Hyperbole aside, this is the best accommodation in all of Malaysia. This huge, century-old Chinese mansion with fifteen stylish en-suite rooms was used as a set for the movie *Indochine*. Guests have the run of the place – there are no roped-off areas or "staff only" signs here. Besides the reading and TV room, there is a games room with ping-pong table and free internet access, as well as a stunning courtyard open to the sky, where you can while away the day sipping beer and admiring the intricately carved Chinese scrollwork. If you're really lucky you'll be in the courtyard during a cloudburst and experience the house being naturally cooled by the rain as the architects intended. Rate includes breakfast. Book ahead. ❽

Cititel 66 Jalan Penang ☏ 04/370 1188, Ⓦ www.cititelhotel.com. Large new business hotel with well-appointed but smallish rooms. There's a large jacuzzi and three restaurants: Japanese, Chinese, and a 24-hour café. Rate includes breakfast. ❼

City Bayview 25a Lebuh Farquhar ☏ 04/263 3161, Ⓔ cbvpg@tm.net.my. Modern luxury high-rise close to the sea, with its own pool and fantastic views over the bay from the revolving rooftop restaurant. ❼

Eastern & Oriental (E&O) Hotel 10 Lebuh Farquhar ☏ 04/222 2000, Ⓦ www.e-o-hotel.com. This atmospheric colonial hotel is a landmark in Penang – all rooms have been converted into beautifully appointed suites and there are several upscale restaurants to choose from. If you can't afford to stay here, have a beer in the bar. This will give you an excuse to stand under the huge domed ceiling in the lobby and listen to a most remarkable echo. ❾

The city centre

The main area of interest in Georgetown is the central square-kilometre or so bordered by Jalan Penang, Jalan Magazine and the sharply curving coast. The most prominent, if not most aesthetically pleasing, landmark is the Komplex Tun Abdul Razak (or KOMTAR), a huge high-rise of shops and offices towering over the western corner of the city centre. You can visit the **viewing deck** (RM5), on the fifty-eighth floor of the KOMTAR building, which affords fantastic views of the harbour, Penang Hill, temples and other sites within the city. You will need to obtain a pass to enter the lifts by leaving your passport on the second floor.

The entire centre of Georgetown could effectively be termed **Chinatown**, since it is dominated by shuttered two-storey shophouses and a liberal scattering of *kongsi*s (clan associations) that have stood here in various forms since the late eighteenth century. In the thick of it is tiny **Little India**, between Lebuh King and Lebuh Queen, while the remnants of the city's **colonial** past – Fort Cornwallis, St George's Church and the building housing the Penang Museum – are all clustered relatively close together at the northeastern end of town, not far from Swettenham Docks. For a reminder of Penang's past economic success, the area around **Lebuh Leith**, west of the central area, is worth exploring. It's typified by the mansions of "millionaires' row" and the *Eastern and Oriental (E&O) Hotel*, built in 1885 by the Armenian Sarkies brothers (who also ran Singapore's *Raffles Hotel*); former guests include Somerset Maugham and Noel Coward. Even if you can't afford to stay here, stroll through the grand lobby with its cool marble floors and high dome.

Fort Cornwallis and the waterfront

The site of **Fort Cornwallis** (Mon–Sat 9am–6.30pm; RM3) on the north-eastern tip of Pulau Pinang marks the spot where the British fleet, under Captain Francis Light, landed on July 16, 1786. A fort fronting the blustery north channel was hastily thrown up to provide barracks for Light and his men, and was named after Lord Charles Cornwallis, Governor-General of India. The present structure dates from around twenty years after, but for all its significance, little remains to excite the senses, apart from a horse living on the roof and the seventeenth-century **Sri Rambai cannon**, sited in the northwest corner of the citadel; the latter considered a living entity with mystical powers – local belief being that barren women can conceive by laying flowers on its barrel.

Right by the entrance to the fort, and previously hosted by Penang Museum, stands a statue of Francis Light, cast in 1936 for the 150th anniversary of the founding of Penang. As there was no image available, Sir Francis's features were copied from a portrait of his son, Colonel William Light, founder of Adelaide in Australia.

The large expanse of green that borders the fort, the **Padang Kota Lama**, was once the favourite promenade of the island's colonial administrators and thronged with rickshaws and carriages. On the south side, opposite the grand sweep of the **Esplanade**, now used for sports and other public events, the padang is bordered by some superb examples of Anglo-Victorian architecture: the **Dewan Undangan Negeri** (State Legislative Building) with its weighty portico and ornate gables, and the **Dewan Seri Pinang** (town hall), of equal aesthetic if not political merit, the city's affairs now being conducted from the KOMTAR building. At the back of the town hall is the **Penang Art Gallery** on Lebuh Duke (daily except Fri and Sun 9am–5pm; free).

There's a Moorish-style **clock tower** on the southeast corner of the padang, at the junction of Lebuh Light and Lebuh Pantai. Presented to the town in 1897 to mark Queen Victoria's Diamond Jubilee, it is sixty feet (20m) high, each foot representing a year of her reign. A bomb dropped during World War II caused the tower to tilt slightly.

Jalan Masjid Kapitan Kling and Lebuh Chulia

On the western side of Lebuh Pantai you're in Chinatown. A leisurely five-minute stroll from here, along Lebuh Chulia or down any of the parallel side streets running northwest, brings you to Jalan Masjid Kapitan Kling (or Lebuh

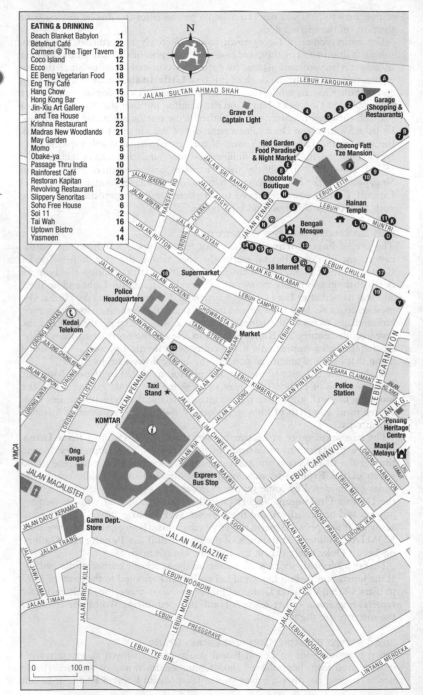

EATING & DRINKING

Beach Blanket Babylon	1
Betelnut Café	22
Carmen @ The Tiger Tavern	B
Coco Island	12
Ecco	13
EE Beng Vegetarian Food	18
Eng Thy Café	17
Hang Chow	15
Hong Kong Bar	19
Jin-Xiu Art Gallery and Tea House	11
Krishna Restaurant	23
Madras New Woodlands	21
May Garden	8
Momo	5
Obake-ya	9
Passage Thru India	10
Rainforest Café	20
Restoran Kapitan	24
Revolving Restaurant	7
Slippery Senoritas	3
Soho Free House	6
Soi 11	2
Tai Wah	16
Uptown Bistro	4
Yasmeen	14

N

LEBUH FARQUHAR

JALAN SULTAN AHMAD SHAH

Garage (Shopping & Restaurants)

Grave of Captain Light

Red Garden Food Paradise & Night Market

Cheong Fatt Tze Mansion

JALAN SRI BAHARI

Chocolate Boutique

JALAN SEKERAT

JALAN ARIFFIN

TRANSFER RD

JALAN ARGYLL

LORONG CLARKE

JALAN D. KOYAH

JALAN PENANG

LEBUH LEITH

Hainan Temple

LEBUH MUNTRI

JALAN HUTTON

Bengali Mosque

JALAN KEDAH

JALAN DICKENS

Supermarket

18 Internet

LEBUH CHULIA

Police Headquarters

LEBUH CAMPBELL

CHOWRASTA ST

TAMIL STREET

LEBUH CINTRA

Market

LORONG MADRAS

Kedai Telekom

JLN ONG CHONG KENG

LORONG KINTA

JALAN TALIPON

LORONG KINTA

JALAN KINTA

KENG KWEE ST

JALAN KUALA KANGSAR

LEBUH KIMBERLEY

JALAN PINTAL TALI (ROPE WALK)

PESARA CLAIMANT

LEBUH CARNAVON

JALAN KG. KAKA

Police Station

JALAN MACALISTER

JALAN PENANG

Taxi Stand ★

JALAN DR. LIM CHWEE LONG

JALAN S. UJONG

Penang Heritage Centre

Masjid Melayu

JALAN KG.

KOMTAR

Ong Kongsi

JALAN RIA

JALAN MAXWELL

LEBUH CARNAVON

LORONG CARNAVON

LEBUH MELAYU

LORONG PRANGIN

LORONG IKAN

YMCA

JALAN DATO' KERAMAT

Gama Dept. Store

Express Bus Stop

LEBUH TEK SOON

JALAN MAGAZINE

JALAN PRANGIN

JALAN TRANG

JALAN JAWA LAMA

JALAN BRICK KILN

LEBUH NOORDIN

JALAN C. Y. CHOY

JALAN TIMAH

LEBUH MCNAIR

LEBUH NOORDIN

LEBUH PRESSGRAVE

LEBUH TYE SIN

LINTANG MERDEKA

0   100 m

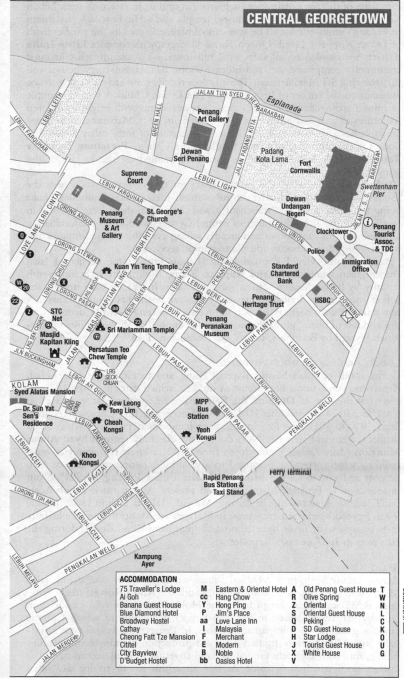

CENTRAL GEORGETOWN

JALAN LEITH
LEBUH LEITH
LEBUH FARQUHAR
GREEN HALL
JALAN TUN SYED SHEIKH BARAKBAH
Esplanade

Penang
Art Gallery

Dewan
Seri Penang

JALAN PADANG KOTA

Padang
Kota Lama

Fort
Cornwallis

JALAN T.S.S. BARAKBAH

Supreme
Court

LEBUH FARQUHAR

LEBUH LIGHT

Swettenham
Pier

LOVE LANE (LRG CINTA)

LORONG ARGUS

Penang
Museum
& Art
Gallery

St. George's
Church

Dewan
Undangan
Negeri

LORONG STEWART

(LEBUH PITT)

LEBUH UNION

Clocktower

Police

Penang
Tourist
Assoc.
& TDC

LORONG CHULIA

Kuan Yin Teng Temple

LEBUH KING

LEBUH BISHOP

PENANG STREET

Standard
Chartered
Bank

Immigration
Office

LEBUH CHULIA

LORONG PASAR

LEBOH MUDA

LEBUH QUEEN

LEBUH GEREJA

LEBUH DOWNING

STC
Net

LRG SEK CHUAN

MASJID KAPITAN KLING

LEBUH CHINA

21

Penang
Heritage Trust

HSBC

Masjid
Kapitan Kling

Sri Mariamman Temple

23

Penang
Peranakan
Museum

bb

LEBUH PANTAI

JLN BUCKINGHAM

Persatuan Teo
Chew Temple

LEBUH PASAR

LEBUH GEREJA

KOLAM

LRG SECK CHUAN

24

LEBUH CHINA

Syed Alatas Mansion

LEBUH AH QUEE

JALAN

Dr. Sun Yat
Sen's
Residence

Kew Leong
Tong Lim

LEBUH

MPP
Bus
Station

PENGKALAN WELD

LEBUH ARMENIAN

Cheah
Kongsi

Yeoh
Kongsi

LEBUH ACHEH

Khoo
Kongsi

LEBUH PASAR

LORONG TOH AKA

LEBUH PANTAI

CHULIA

Rapid Penang
Bus Station &
Taxi Stand

Ferry Terminal

LEBUH VICTORIA

LEBUH ARMENIAN

LEBUH ACEH

PENGKALAN WELD

LEBUH MELAYU

Kampung
Ayer

JALAN MERDEKA

Butterworth ▶

187

ACCOMMODATION

75 Traveller's Lodge	**M**	Eastern & Oriental Hotel	**A**	Old Penang Guest House	**T**
Ai Goh	**cc**	Hang Chow	**R**	Olive Spring	**W**
Banana Guest House	**Y**	Hong Ping	**Z**	Oriental	**N**
Blue Diamond Hotel	**P**	Jim's Place	**S**	Oriental Guest House	**L**
Broadway Hostel	**aa**	Love Lane Inn	**I**	Peking	**C**
Cathay	**F**	Malaysia	**D**	SD Guest House	**K**
Cheong Fatt Tze Mansion	**E**	Merchant	**H**	Star Lodge	**O**
Cititel	**B**	Modern	**J**	Tourist Guest House	**U**
City Bayview	**bb**	Noble	**X**	White House	**G**
D'Budget Hostel		Oasiss Hotel	**V**		

Pitt), one of the city's main thoroughfares. Around its intersection with Lebuh Chulia you'll find a mosque, a Chinese temple and a Hindu temple, testament to Penang's multi-ethnicity. The area east of here, enclosed by the parallel roads of Lebuh King and Lebuh Queen, forms Georgetown's compact **Little India** district. Surrounded on all sides by Chinatown, it's a vibrant, self-contained community comprising sari and incense shops, banana-leaf-curry houses and the towering **Sri Mariamman Temple** (open daily from early morning to late evening) on the corner of Lebuh Queen and Lebuh Chulia. A typical example of Hindu architecture, the lofty entrance tower teems with brightly coloured sculptures of gods and swans devoted to the main deity, Mariamman; the inner sanctum has a nine-metre-high dome, with statues of forty other deities and lions. On the other side of Lebuh Chulia is the Chinese **Persatuan Teochew Temple**, which features fearsome guardians painted on the insides of the temple doors.

Lebuh Chulia itself – the central artery of Chinatown – was where the southern Indian immigrants chose to establish their earliest businesses (*chulia* being the Tamil word for "merchant"), and the Indian shops here still deal in textiles. But the area (like much of central Georgetown) looks predominantly Chinese with its shophouses and arcades selling everything from antiques and bamboo furniture to books and photographic services.

Back on Jalan Masjid Kapitan Kling (Lebuh Pitt), at the corner of Jalan Buckingham, stands the **Masjid Kapitan Kling**. Built in the early nineteenth century by Indian Muslim settlers (originally East India Company troops), the yellow mosque is in Indian-influenced Islamic style and has a single minaret. A few minutes' walk north you reach the **Kuan Yin Teng Temple**, dedicated to the goddess of mercy, probably the most worshipped of all the Chinese deities much revered by Buddhists, Taoists and Confucians alike.

Lebuh Aceh and Lebuh Armenian

Going south on Jalan Masjid Kapitan Kling and turning right into Lebuh Armenian, you'll find a blue house at no. 120, which dates from the 1870s. It served as the base of **Dr Sun Yat Sen** (make an appointment with Mr Yap ☏04/262 0123 for viewing; RM3), president of the first Chinese Republic, from 1910 to 1911. The interior has been handsomely preserved with carved timber screens and air wells. Next door is the elegantly restored **Syed Alatas Mansion** (daily 9am–5.30pm, closed Tues; RM3), a lovely two-storey colonial building which originally belonged to a wealthy Achenese merchant of Arab descent and now hosts the **Muzium Islam Pulau Pinang**, a well-laid-out introduction to Penang's Islamic past and present. As you reach Lebuh Aceh, you'll see the oldest mosque in Penang, **Masjid Melayu**, built in 1808, unusual for its Egyptian-style minaret – most in Malaysia are Moorish. The hole halfway up was supposedly made by a cannonball fired from Khoo Kongsi during the clan riots in 1867 (see box opposite).

Khoo Kongsi

Across Lebuh Aceh, in a secluded square on an alleyway connecting Jalan Masjid Kapitan Kling and Lebuh Pantai, stands the **Khoo Kongsi** (daily 9am–5pm; RM5 admission), *kongsi* being the Hokkien term for (clan) association (and by extension applied to the clan house), a building in which Chinese families gather to worship their ancestors. In Penang, the *kongsi*s were originally formed to provide mutual help and protection for nineteenth-century immigrants, who naturally tended to band together in clans according to the district from which they came. At one time this led to rivalry and often violence between the different Chinese communities, though these days the *kongsi*s have reverted to their supportive role, helping with the education of members' children, settling disputes between clan members or advancing loans. Consequently, they are an important means of preserving solidarity, although traditionally women have been excluded from many of the functions and are rarely represented in the hierarchy. Many of the *kongsi*s in Penang are excellent examples of traditional Chinese architecture, well over a hundred years old. There is generally a spacious courtyard in front of the clan house, opposite which is a stage for theatrical performances, and two halls in the main building itself, one for the shrine of the clan deity, the other for the display of the ancestral tablets (the equivalent of gravestones).

Completed in 1894, the Khoo Kongsi was an ambitious and extensive project with a roof styled in the manner of a grand palace; it took eight years to complete but was immediately gutted in a mysterious fire. Suspecting sabotage, the clan members rebuilt the house on a lesser scale, making the excuse that the previous design had been too noble to house the ancestral tablets of ordinary mortals. The resulting structure, meticulously crafted by experts from China, has a saddle-shaped roof that reputedly weighs 25 tonnes. Its central hall is dark with heavy, intricately carved beams and pillars and bulky mother-of-pearl inlaid furniture; an Art Deco grandfather clock stands somewhat incongruously in the corner. Behind this is a separate chamber, with delicate black-and-white line drawings depicting scenes of courtly life. The hall on the left is a richly decorated shrine to **Tua Peh Kong**, the god of prosperity; the right-hand hall contains the gilded ancestral tablets. Connecting all three halls is a balcony minutely decorated in bas-relief, whose carvings depict episodes from folk tales – even the bars on the windows have been carved into bamboo sticks.

The Penang Riots

Chinese immigrants in Penang brought their traditions with them, including the establishment of **triads** (secret societies), branches of organizations that had evolved in China during the eighteenth century as a means of overthrowing Manchu rule. Once in Penang, the societies provided mutual aid and protection for the Chinese community, their position later bolstered by alliances with Malay religious groups originally established to assist members with funerals and marriages.

As the societies grew in wealth and power, gang warfare and extortion rackets became commonplace. The newly appointed governor-general, Sir Harry Ord, and his inefficient police force (largely composed of non-Chinese) proved ineffective in preventing the increasing turmoil. In 1867, matters came to a head in the series of events known subsequently as the **Penang Riots**. For nine days Georgetown was shaken by fighting between the Tua Peh Kong society, supported by the Malay Red Flag, and the Ghee Hin, allied with the Malay White Flag. Police intervention resulted in a temporary truce, but a major clash seemed inevitable when, on August 1, 1867, the headman of the Tua Peh Kong falsely charged the Ghee Hin and the White Flag societies with stealing cloth belonging to Tua Peh Kong dyers. All hell broke loose, and fighting raged around Lebuhs Armenian, Church and Chulia. Barricades were erected around the Khoo Kongsi, where much of the fiercest fighting took place, and you can still find bullet holes in the surrounding shops and houses.

The fighting was eventually quelled by **sepoys** (Indian troops) brought in from Singapore by the governor-general, but by then hundreds had been killed and scores of houses burned. As compensation for the devastation suffered by the city, a penalty of RM5000 was levied on each of the secret societies, some of which was later used to finance the building of four police stations to deal with any future trouble.

Exiting the compound and turning back into Lebuh Armenian you'll come across **Cheah Kongsi** (daily 9am–5pm; free). Like its more illustrious cousin, this clan house stands in a large compound, only accessible through a narrow entrance from the street. Not as grand as the nearby Khoo Kongsi, Cheah Kongsi gets fewer tourists, making it more serene, with a pleasant shaded balcony where old Chinese men play chess in the long hot afternoons.

Lebuh Farquhar, Lebuh Gereja and Lebuh Leith

Near the northern end of Jalan Masjid Kapitan Kling, opposite the junction with Lebuh Bishop, is the Anglican **St George's Church** (daily 9am–5pm; free). One of the oldest buildings in Penang, and as simple and unpretentious as anything built in the Greek style in Asia can be, it was constructed in 1817–19 by the East India Company using convict labour; its cool, pastel-blue interior must have been a welcome retreat from the heat for the new congregation. In 1886, on the centenary of the founding of Penang, a memorial to Francis Light was built in front of the church in the form of a Greek temple.

A side street to Jalan Masjid Kapitan Kling, is Lebuh Gereja (Church Street), where half-way down lies **Pinang Peranakan Mansion** (Mon–Fri 9.30am–5pm, Sat 9.30am–3pm; RM10; ⓦ www.pinangperanakanmansion.com.my), the now privately owned and beautifully restored 1890s mansion once belonging to Kapitan Cina Chung Keng Kwee, a Penang personality and "secret society" leader. It is partly a museum of cultural artefacts and antiques, while also an efficient glimpse into how a rich Peranakan (Baba-Nyonya) once lived; the word "peranakan" means "local born". The Baba-Nyonya are a perfect example of Malaysia's rich cultural heritage as the unique marriage between Chinese settlers and Malay women resulted in an identity of their own (see p.712).

Doubling back to the church along **Lebuh Farquhar** (which takes its name from a former lieutenant-governor of the settlement), you come to the **Penang Museum** (daily except Fri 9am–5pm; RM1), housed in a building dating from 1821 that was originally the first English-medium public school in the east. It has an excellent collection of memorabilia: rickshaws, Peranakan furniture, clothing and ceramics, faded black-and-white photographs of early Penang's Chinese millionaires and a panoramic photograph of Georgetown taken in the 1870s – note just how many buildings still survive. With downstairs centred on the people and cultures living in Penang and upstairs focused on its political past, it is an interesting introduction to life on the island.

Continuing west underneath a footbridge and turning left on **Lebuh Leith**, you'll soon reach the stunning **Cheong Fatt Tze Mansion** at no. 14 (☎04/262 0006, ⓦ www.cheongfatttzemansion.com), whose outer walls are painted a striking indigo blue. Built by Thio Thiaw Siat, a Cantonese businessman, it's the best example of eclectic nineteenth-century Peranakan architecture in Penang. The mansion, with its elaborate ceremonial halls, bedrooms and libraries, separated by cobbled courtyards, small gardens and heavy wooden doors, has been magnificently restored. The interior can only be seen by joining an hour-long guided tour (daily 11am & 3pm), which is well worth the RM12 entrance fee. The mansion is also a hotel (see p.184).

Turning back north on Lebuh Leith and then left on Lebuh Farquhar, you'll find the legendary **Eastern & Oriental Hotel**, once part of the Sarkies brothers' select chain of colonial retreats (as was the *Raffles* in Singapore; see p.609). Rudyard Kipling and Somerset Maugham both stayed here, taking tiffin on the terrace and enjoying the cooling sea breeze. Opposite, on Upper Penang Road (where the main clubs and bars are situated) the **Little Penang Street Market** takes place on the last Sunday of each month, with arts and crafts, book

▲ Cheong Fatt Tze Mansion

readings, exhibitions and children's activities. About five minutes' walk west along Lebuh Farquhar, the road merges with sea-facing Jalan Sultan Ahmad Shah, across which you'll find the overgrown churchyard where Francis Light is buried.

Eating

Georgetown's status as Malaysia's second city means there is no shortage of cafés and restaurants, and there's a wide choice of Malay, Chinese and South Indian food as well as North Indian and Nonya specialities. **Hawker stalls** dish out the cheapest meals and are located either in permanent sites, in which case they're open all day and evening, or by the roadsides and down alleyways, when they spring up at meal times only. In addition, a roving **pasar malam** (night market), with stalls selling all manner of food, is held every two weeks at various venues around town – any of the tourist offices will have the details.

Of the **cafés** (usually open 8am–11pm), the ubiquitous **Chinese** *kedai kopi*s serve reliable rice and noodle standards, with many also specializing in fine Hainan chicken rice. The other local favourite is Penang *laksa*, noodles in thick fish soup, garnished with vegetables, pineapple and *belacan* (shrimp paste). The **South Indian** *kedai kopi*s on Lebuh Penang (the eastern edge of Little India) offer *murtabak*, roti and biriyani as well as a bewildering array of vegetarian banana-leaf curries; none serves alcohol. The main travellers' hangouts are dotted on or around Lebuh Chulia, often little more than hole-in-the-wall joints serving **Western breakfasts**, banana pancakes and milk shakes at reasonable prices. These tend to open from around 9am to 5pm (the exceptions are noted below). For more **upmarket restaurants**, head to Gurney Drive, where some good seafood places housed in old villas with outdoor tables facing the sea make for an atmospheric treat.

Hawker stalls

Chinatown Lebuh Kimberley and Lebuh Cintra. Open late into the night, stalls prepare every sort of noodle and rice dish, each for just a few ringgit.

Food Court KOMTAR building. On the ground floor and on the roof. The atmosphere's a little sterile, but there's a good range of Chinese, Malay and Indian food.

Jalan Tun Syed Shah Barakah Near Fort Cornwallis, at the west end of the esplanade. Most of the stalls serve Chinese food, though a few do Malay fare too. The fruit juices here are particularly good.

Pesiaran Gurney (Gurney Drive) 3km northwest along the coast before Tanjung Tokong (take any bus going to Batu Ferringhi). This area with many hawker-style restaurants specializing in seafood becomes very lively at night, when the locals come out to stroll along the promenade.

Red Garden Food Paradise and Night Market Entrances on Penang Road and Leith Street, covering the area between the two parallel streets. There is practically everything on offer here; Chinese, Italian, the usual Western fare, Malay, Indian, Thai, Japanese and a great waffle stall along with entertainment such as karaoke. Each dish will set you back around RM5–10. The bar is run separately and rather pushy waiters will come to your table.

Cafés

Coco Island 422 Lebuh Chulia. In the courtyard of the *Blue Diamond Hotel*, this place is worth going to, just for the good Mexican stall in the corner with the grumpy owner. The café itself also serves the usual mix of local and Western food with beer to wash down the live music entertainment.

Ecco Café 402 Lebuh Chulia. The best pizzeria in the area, also serving other Mediterranean dishes, including delicious handmade pasta dishes.

EE Beng Vegetarian Food Lebuh Dickens. Opposite the police HQ, two-thirds down the road. The excellent Chinese vegetarian buffet is cheap and delicious with many fake meat dishes and vegetable curries. 6am–9.30pm.

Eng Thy Café 340 Lebuh Chulia. Popular with travellers, this place serves good fruit shakes and Western breakfasts as well as a large variety of inexpensive snacks. Movie screenings in the evenings make for a noisy dinner. Daily 8am–midnight.

Krishna Restaurant 75 Lebuh Pasar. Excellent banana-leaf-curry house with rock-bottom prices. Try their *dosai*. Daily 7am–9.30pm (closed one Wed each month). Recommended.

Madras New Woodlands 60 Lebuh Penang. Excellent South and North Indian veggie food at cheap prices – RM5–7 for tasty lunchtime *thalis* – an array of spicy dishes with crispy pancakes.

Rainforest Café 300–302 Lebuh Chulia. Connected to the *Olive Spring Guest House*, this bakery serves a wide choice of breads and cakes. Great cheese on toast and Earl Grey tea on offer, too.

Restoran Kapitan Corner of Lebuh Chulia and Lebuh Queen. The best chicken biriyani in town is served at this busy and cheap Indian place.

Yasmeen Jalan Penang. Delicious and cheap halal Indian food, including lots of spicy, cumin-coloured vegetables and curries to dip your roti into. The tandoori chicken is good too.

Restaurants

Jin-Xiu Art Gallery and Tea House 58 Muntri St. Gorgeous little gem serving rice and noodle dishes and teas with local artwork adorning the walls. Kitchen closed 4–6pm.

May Garden 70 Jalan Penang. Plush but affordable Cantonese restaurant with excellent food. Very popular with tourists from the nearby high-rise hotels.

Obake-ya 10 Lebuh Leith. If you are hungry for Japanese food, including sushi and tasty ramen at reasonable prices, this is the place to go.

Passage Thru India 11a Lebuh Leith. Next door to *Obake-ya* and opposite the Cheong Fatt Tze Mansion, this is a good place the to go for lunch with set deals of North and South Indian food at around RM13.

Revolving Restaurant Fourteenth floor, *City Bayview Hotel*, Lebuh Farquhar. Serves Western and Asian dishes, with a colourful all-you-can-eat dinner buffet (RM57) featuring live music.

Drinking, nightlife and entertainment

Most of Georgetown's **bars** are comfortable places in which to hang out. With the periodic arrival of the Malaysian navy, though, a good many turn into rowdy meat markets, and a place that may have been fine the night before can become unpleasant for women visitors. Usual opening hours are 6pm to 2am with happy hours often running from 6pm to 8pm. If there's live music, it usually starts at 10.30pm. In Georgetown's **discos**, which stay open until the early hours (a cover charge of around RM50 usually applies), you're more likely to hear local pop music than the latest Western club sounds.

Other entertainment is thin on the ground: the Rex (Jalan Burma) **cinemas** show recent releases of English-language movies; check the *New Straits Times* and other Penang listings.

Bars

Bagan Bar and Restaurant 18 Jalan Bagan Jermal. Often with live bands, this trendy bar is the place to be seen. Gay-friendly and with an interesting, though pricey, menu (tomato soup with gin, for starters), wine and cocktail list. Open till 1am weekdays and 2am weekends.

Betelnut Café 360 Lebuh Chulia. Very popular with travellers, with tables spilling onto the pavement. Limited choice of spirits on offer as well as beer and a snack menu.

Hong Kong Bar Lebuh Chulia. A classic liberty-port dive with command plaques and photos of warships adorning the walls – although if you happen to be here when the Australian fleet is in port, give this place a wide berth. Open daily 5pm till late.

Soho Free House Jalan Penang. English pub-style place with a fitting menu (including shepherd's pie) and Guinness on draught. There's a pool table and free wi-fi.

Tai Wah Lebuh Chulia. This daytime café turns into a lively bar full of Indonesian guest workers in the evening; serves some of the cheapest beer in town.

Clubs

Beach Blanket Babylon The Garage, Upper Jalan Penang. Classy decor in a renovated colonial building. Something for everyone with live pop music nightly (except Sun), sports on TV, a well-stocked bar and a small menu.

Carmen @ The Tiger Tavern Basement, *City Bayview Hotel*, 25a Lebuh Farquhar. Open till 3am every night except Sunday with live bands and DJs from 9.30pm.

Momo The Bungalow, Upper Jl Penang. Big and dark with local DJs spinning R&B and hip-hop to a large dancefloor. Gay-friendly.

Slippery Señoritas Garage, 2 Jalan Penang. A Latin-themed disco of the kind that has popped up all over Asia in the last half decade. Except for half the name, there's really nothing Latin about it, but this is the island's most lively pick-up joint.

Soi 11 Upper Jl Penang. Nicely set up, this is a good alternative to the bigger clubs, if you want to be able to have a relatively audible conversation as well as a dance over a cocktail or beer.

Uptown Bistro 20 Jalan Sultan Ahmad Shah. This stand-alone building is hard to miss. There's a nightly live band (Chinese pop) indoors as well as a beer garden in the courtyard.

Out from the city centre

There are several sights on the western and northern **outskirts** of Georgetown that are worth exploring, most of which provide a welcome break from the frenetic city. In particular, trips to **Penang Hill**, the **Botanical Gardens** and **Ayer Itam**, with its sprawling **Kek Lok Si Temple**, are a cool alternative to heading for the northern beaches for the day. For true temple buffs, there are three more worth visiting: the Thai **Wat Chayamangkalarm**, the Burmese **Dharmmikarama Temple**, and the **Nattukottai Chettiar Temple**. **Buses** run to all the destinations from the Rapid Penang bus station or the station at the KOMTAR building.

Three temples and the Botanical Gardens

A fifteen-minute bus ride (take Rapid Penang bus #101 or #103) towards Batu Ferringhi brings you to **Wat Chayamangkalaram** on Lorong Burma, a Thai temple painted in yellow and blue and flanked by two statues, whose fierce grimaces and weighty swords are designed to ward off unwanted visitors. Inside, a 33-metre-long statue of the Reclining Buddha is surrounded by other, elaborately decorated Buddha images covered with gold leaf. The Burmese **Dharmmikarama Temple** across the road is less spectacular, although the white-stone elephants at the entrance are attractive and the temple's two stupas are lit to good effect at night. Both temples are open between sunrise and sunset (free).

Further west on Jalan Kebun Bunga is the **Nattukottai Chettiar Temple**, a seven-kilometre bus ride from the city centre on either Rapid Penang bus #101 or #102; ask to be dropped off at *The Waterfall Hotel*, from where the temple is a five-minute walk north. This is the focus of the Hindu **Thaipusam** festival in February, in honour of Lord Subramanian, when thousands of devotees walk through the streets bearing *kavadi*s (sacred yokes) fixed to their bodies by hooks and spikes spearing their flesh. The biggest such event in Malaysia is at Kuala Lumpur's Batu Caves (see p.136); the festivities in Georgetown are a similar blend of hypnotic frenzy and celebration. At other times of the year, you're free to concentrate on the temple itself, in which an unusual wooden colonnaded walkway with exquisite pictorial tiles leads up to the inner sanctum, where a life-sized solid-silver peacock – the birds crop up throughout the temple – bows its head to the deity, Lord Subramanian.

Just five more minutes further up Jalan Kebun Bunga (formerly Waterfall Rd) from the temple lie the **Botanical Gardens** (daily 5am–9pm; free) in a lush valley. They are a good place to escape the city and enjoy some fresh air. Unfortunately, the waterfall that gave the road its name, and supplies water to the city, has been cordoned off, and can't be easily seen from a distance either, though within the gardens there is access to the stream below the fall.

Ayer Itam and the Kek Lok Si Temple

A thirty-minute bus ride west (take Rapid Penang bus #203 or #204), **Ayer Itam** is an appealing wooded hilly area, spread around the Ayer Itam Dam. As you approach Ayer Itam, the sprawling, fairytale complex of **Kek Lok Si Temple** (open morning to late evening; free) makes an intriguing sight, the tips of its colourful towers peeking cheekily through the treetops. Supposedly the largest Buddhist temple in Malaysia, it's a serious place of worship as well as being a major tourist spot, with fantastic shrines and pagodas, linked by hundreds of steps, and bedecked with flags, lanterns and statues. The abbot of the Kuan Yin Temple on Lebuh Pitt arrived from China in 1885 and chose this site because the landscape around Ayer Itam reminded him of his homeland. He raised money from rich Chinese merchants to fund the construction of the huge temple, set across twelve hectares and modelled on Fok San Monastery in Fuzhou (Foochow), China. The entrance to the complex is approached through a line of trinket stalls, their awnings forming a tunnel stretching a few hundred metres uphill. On the way up is a pond for turtles, which represent eternity. The seven-tier Ban Po, or "Million Buddhas Precious Pagoda" is the most prominent feature of the compound and is built in three different styles. The lower section of simple Chinese saddle-shaped eaves represents the goddess of mercy; the central levels represent the laughing Buddha and have elaborate Thai arched windows; at the top is a golden Burmese stupa, representing the historical Buddha. It costs RM4 to climb the 193 steps to the top, where there is a great **view** of Georgetown and the bay.

Penang Hill

Just on the outskirts of Georgetown is the small hill station of **Penang Hill** (Bukit Bendera), an 821-metre-high dome of tropical forest due west of the city. It was the first colonial hill station in Peninsular Malaysia and once the retreat for the colony's wealthiest administrators. Nowadays it's a popular excursion for the locals and can get quite crowded at weekends. The cooler climate (the average temperature is 5 degrees lower than Georgetown) benefits flowering trees and shrubs, and there are several gentle, well-marked walks through areas whose names (Tiger Hill, Strawberry Hill) hark back to colonial days. You can also walk down to the Botanical Gardens, a steep descent that takes about an hour.

To get to the hill, take Rapid Penang bus #204, which terminates at the base of Penang Hill. Note that the last bus back into town departs at 10pm. The last part of the journey is made by **funicular railway** (daily 6.30am–9.30pm, till 11.15pm on Sat; every half-hour; 30min; RM4 return), which deposits you at the top of the hill. A taxi to Penang Hill will set you back around RM25. At the top there's a temple, a mosque, a post office, a police station, a few restaurants and food stalls and a **hotel**, the *Bellevue* (℡04/829 9500, ℻829 2052; ●), with large rooms and a terrace affording superb views over Georgetown; a drink or a meal here is perfect at sunset when the city's lights flicker on in the distance, though the menu is rather uninspiring. If you can afford it, *David Brown's Restaurant and Tea Terraces* is far superior, with sandwiches, afternoon tea, expensive roasts for dinner and an excellent wine list, but it will set you back significantly, a roast being around RM50. Alternatively, down on the ground at the other end of Jalan Stesen Bukit Bendera (which is the road leading up to the funicular) there is a 24-hour food market, *Asia Café*, which gets busy at night. Also worth a peek is the "bat cave temple", **Tua Pek Kong**; follow the yellow signs down Jalan Pokok Ceri around the bend and then up the hill, passing or stopping **Thni Kong Thua Temple** at a crossroad along the way. The tiny temple is home to one of the gods of luck as well as a number of bats, living in the cave at the back of the temple.

Listings

Airlines AirAsia, 332 Lebuh Chulia ℡04/250 0020; Cathay Pacific, Unit 3.05, Menara Boustead, Jalan Sultan Ahmed Shah ℡04/226 0411; Firefly, ground floor, KOMTAR building, Jalan Penang ℡04/250 2000; Malaysia Airlines, ground floor, KOMTAR building, Jalan Penang ℡04/250 2000; Singapore Airlines, Wisma Penang Gardens, Jalan Sultan Ahmed Shah ℡04/226 3201; Thai International, level 3, Burmah Place, Burmah Rd ℡04/226 7000.

Airport ℡04/643 4411 for flight information.

Banks and exchange Major banks (Mon–Fri 9.30am–3pm, Sat 9.30–11.30am) are along Lebuh Pantai, including Standard Chartered and HSBC Bank, but since they charge a hefty commission, the licensed moneychangers on Lebuh Pantai, Lebuh Chulia and Jalan Masjid Kapitan Kling (daily 8.30am–6pm) are preferable – they charge no commission and their rates are often better.

Bike rental Outlets on Lebuh Chulia rent out motorbikes (RM35 a day) and bicycles (RM10 a day). Try Tanjung Mutiara Mini Market at no. 417b or Sam Bookstore at no. 473.

Bookshops United Books Ltd, Jalan Penang, has a large selection of English-language books. There are several bookshops in the KOMTAR building, including Popular Books on the second floor. Times Books in the nearby Lifestyle department store also has a good selection. In addition, there are a few secondhand bookshops on Lebuh Chulia, the best of which is Sam Bookstore at no. 473 (the friendly and enterprising owner also rents bikes, books tickets, handles Thai visas and stores luggage).

Car rental Avis, at the airport ℡04/643 9633; Hertz, 38 Lebuh Farquhar ℡04/643 0208 and at the airport ℡04/643 0208; Orix, at the airport ℡04/644 4772.

Consulates Australia, c/o 1c Lorong Hutton ℡04/263 3320; Indonesia, 467 Jalan Burma ℡04/227 4686; Thailand, 1 Jalan Tunku Abdul Rahman ℡04/262 8029; UK, 2 Weld Quay ℡04/263 0330. There is no representation here for citizens of the US, Canada, Ireland or New Zealand – KL has the nearest offices (see p.131).

Hospitals Adventist Hospital, Jalan Burma (℡04/226 1133; to get there, take Rapid Penang bus #101 or #102); General Hospital, Jalan Utama (℡04/229 3333).

Internet access As well as a few places in the KOMTAR building, you'll find no shortage of internet terminals on and around Lebuh Chulia. The going rate is around RM2 for half an hour, and many guesthouses have free wi-fi.

Pharmacy There are several along Jalan Penang (10am–6pm).

Police The police headquarters is on Jalan Penang; in emergencies call ℡999.

Post office The General Post Office is on Lebuh Downing (Mon–Fri 8.30am–5pm, Sat 8.30am–4pm). The efficient poste restante/general delivery office is here; a parcel-wrapping service is available at book and stationery shops on Lebuh Chulia.

Sport You can play golf at Bukit Jambul Country Club, 2 Jalan Bukit Jambul (☏04/644 2255; green fee RM74), or the Penang Turf Club Golf (☏04/226 6701; green fee RM84). There's racing at the Penang Turf Club, Jalan Batu Gantung (☏04/226 6701) – see the local paper for fixtures. You can swim at the Pertama Sports Complex, Paya Terubong, near Ayer Itam (daily 9–11am & 4–9pm; RM4).

Telephone offices For international calls you can buy a phonecard or use the Telekom office at the GPO on Lebuh Downing, open 24hr.

Travel agents Try MSL Travel in the *Angora Hotel*, 202 Jalan Macalister, for student and youth travel. There are a large number of other agencies along Lebuh Chulia.

Visa extensions Pejabat Imigresen, Lebuh Pantai, on the corner of Lebuh Light (☏04/261 5122). For on-the-spot visa extensions.

The northern coast

The narrow strip, about 15km in length, along Pulau Pinang's **north coast** has been aggressively marketed since the early days of package tourism. Hemmed in by the densely forested interior, this stretch of coast is punctuated by a series of bays and beaches, linked by a twisting road lined with resort hotels which advertise themselves as being part of the "Pearl of the Orient". However, the filthy ocean rather detracts from this image, and there's nothing here to touch the east coast waters of the Peninsula. There are three main developments strung out along the northern coast: Tanjung Bungah, Batu Ferringhi and Teluk Bahang. The first two have arisen purely to serve the needs of tourism. Occupied for the most part by a string of deluxe resorts, **Batu Ferringhi** is the biggest of the three, and has gone a fair way towards establishing a community and spirit of its own, while **Teluk Bahang** is the only place to maintain its fishing-village roots. If you want to stay at any of the beaches, it's wise to ring the hotels and guesthouses first to check on space, especially during Christmas, Easter and *Hari Raya*. Between Teluk Bahang and Batu Ferrenghi lies the peaceful **Tropical Spice Garden** (9am–6pm daily; RM13; bus #101 or 105 from Georgetown), eight acres of the exotic herbs, spices and flora that brought so many traders to these shores during colonial times. Guided tours (RM20) available thrice daily, all starting before lunch.

Batu Ferringhi

BATU FERRINGHI ("White Man's Rock"), a twenty-minute bus ride from Georgetown on Rapid Penang bus #101 or #103, is dominated by high-rises towering all along the far-from-pristine beach, as well as expensive restaurants and shops. If your main interest is swimming or snorkelling, or if you've spent some time at one of the beaches on the east coast and are looking for more of the same, you'll be sorely disappointed. The sea, simply put, is dirty.

Orientation is very simple: the road – along which all the hotels and restaurants are lined up – runs more or less straight along the coast for 3km. The centre, such as it is, lies between two bridges a couple of kilometres apart and has a Telekom office, post office and police station, almost opposite which are a mosque and a clinic; the bus from Georgetown stops here, and will take you wherever you want along the main road if you ask. There are several **internet** cafés and **moneychangers** along the main road. Happily for visitors with money, every major hotel has a pool. During the day the trinket stalls, tailors' shops and street hawkers remain fairly unobtrusive, but when the sun goes down the road comes alive with brightly lit stalls selling batik, T-shirts and fake designer watches.

BATU FERRINGHI

Food Stalls

Taxi Stand

Clinic

Police

N

0   200 m

EATING & DRINKING

Bocadillo	1
Eden Seafood Village	4
Ferringhi Garden	2
Jewel of the North	7
The Net	6
The Palace	3
The Ship	5

ACCOMMODATION

Ah Beng	B
Ah Kang Guest House	M
Ali's	D
Baba's	F
Bayview	A
D' Ferringhi	I
E.T. Budget Guest House	C
Holiday Inn	H
Ismail's Beach Guest House	K
Lone Pine	J
Park Royal	G
Rasa Sayang	L
Shalini's Guest House	E

Accommodation

Towards the western end of Batu Ferringhi there's a small enclave of **budget guesthouses** facing the beach, reached by the road next to the *Guan Guan Café*. The standards tend to be lower than in Georgetown and the prices higher. If you come here by taxi, just have the taxi drop you on the main road (near the post office), as they will charge you commission if they take you directly to a guesthouse. Independent travellers don't get particularly good deals in the expensive **hotels**, most of whose business is with tour groups, but it's definitely worth enquiring about discounts by phoning in advance, as there are often special offers of up to fifty percent off the advertised rate during non-peak times.

Budget

Ah Beng ☏ 04/881 1036. A serene, family-run place with polished wood floors, a communal balcony overlooking the sea, and a washing machine. Fan rooms ❷; en suite with a/c in new extension ❹.

Ah Kang Guest House ☏ 04/881 1308. A handful of rooms set around the house courtyard. The fan rooms are fairly shabby with shared bathroom (cold showers) ❶; the newer en suites with a/c are in much better condition ❸.

Ali's ☏ 04/881 1316, ⓔ alisguesthouse_pg @yahoo.com. This very popular place has a relaxing open-air café and garden, and a pleasant wooden veranda. A five-bed dorm is available for RM150 per night. Fan rooms have either shared or private bathrooms. ❸

Baba's ☏ 04/881 1686. A spotless and friendly guesthouse with wi-fi and a sea-view communal balcony. Fan rooms have shared bathrooms ❷; en suite with a/c ❸

E.T. Budget Guest House ☏ 04/881 1553. Same management as *Baba's* and with similar standards. Fan rooms with shared bathrooms ❷; en suite (either cold or hot showers) with a/c ❸.

Shalini's Guest House ☏ 04/881 1859. This somewhat eccentric family residence (the entrance is through their living room) and guesthouse also hires out apartments. Clean fan or a/c rooms with shared bathrooms ❷; en suite with fan or a/c ❸–❹.

Moderate and expensive

Bayview ☏ 04/881 2123, ⓔ bbr@po.jaring.my. This is grander than most, with a ballroom and glass lifts, but no more expensive than some of its neighbours. ❾

D'Ferringhi Hotel and Restaurant ☏ 04/881 9000, ⓕ 881 9002. This new and airy place is a good option if you are looking for a little moderate comfort, though there are no extra facilities, apart from a restaurant. ❻

197

Holiday Inn ℡04/881 1601, ⊛www.penang
.holiday-inn.com. Well-appointed rooms, some with
parquet flooring. Their kids' club makes this a good
option for families. ❾

Ismail's Beach Guest House ℡04/881 2569,
©cabinkdn@yahoo.com. Tastefully furnished, all
rooms with a/c and fridges, this is the best
mid-range option. The most expensive room is right
on the beach, but the others are not far off. ❺

Lone Pine ℡04/881 1511, ⊛www.lonepinehotel
.com. Established in 1948, this boutique hotel
situated around a colonial-era bungalow was the first

in Batu Ferringhi. It's now been refurbished along
clean modern lines. Its seaside *Bungalow Restaurant*
serves Hainanese and Western cuisine. ❽

Park Royal ℡04/881 1133, ℱ881 2233. This
medium-rise hotel boasts an elegant colonial-style
Indonesian restaurant, *Tiffins*. There's also a
Japanese restaurant. ❾

Rasa Sayang Resort & Spa ℡04/881 1811,
⊛www.shangri-la.com. This classy low-rise hotel
boasts traditional Malay architecture with its
Minangkabau-style roofs and is the most expensive
resort here. ❾

Eating and drinking

There are some budget **restaurants** in Batu Ferringhi, but most places are
overpriced, catering for the overspill from the large hotels, all of which have
several restaurants of their own. By the beach are some cheap food stalls and
cafes. There are also some good (but pricey) seafood restaurants. There's a
hawker centre called the *Matahari Food and Beer Garden* near the first bridge.

Bocadillo Woodfired oven pizzas, right on the
beach, at around RM15–20 along with juices, fruit
shakes, teas and coffees.

Eden Seafood Village The boast at this huge
beachfront place is "Anything that swims, we cook
it". A cultural show accompanies the evening
meal, but you'll pay a hefty price, at around RM30
a dish.

Ferringhi Garden Expensive, but well-appointed
place set in a garden with a charcoal BBQ, steaks,
seafood and a resident dessert chef. It boasts an
award for the cleanest and most pleasant restaurant in Penang, though it doesn't say from whom.

Jewel of the North Located east of the
stream, this place has tasty North Indian food

at around RM20–25 per dish. Open for lunch and
dinner.

The Net Inexpensive banana-leaf curries served
10.30am–2.30pm, as well as other South Indian
meals at lunchtime and evenings.

The Palace Across from the mosque, this colour-
fully decorated restaurant serves Western as well
as Indian food at RM5–12 per dish. Open for lunch
and dinner.

The Ship It's a ship that's a restaurant, so fairly hard
to miss. The staff wear nautical clothes and serve
steaks at high prices, each dish being somewhere
between RM25–50, but the food is good and it's a
fun, though very touristy, place to visit.

Teluk Bahang

Five kilometres west of Batu Ferringhi, the small fishing kampung of **TELUK
BAHANG** is the place to come to escape the development. Towards the
western end of the village, the long spindly pier, with its multitude of fishing
boats, is the focus of daily life. Teluk Bahang is also the entry point to **Penang
National Park** (℡04/881 3530, ©tnpp@wildlife.gov.my), encompassing
Muka Head, a rocky headland with better beaches than both Teluk Bahang
and Batu Ferringhi. The park is an accessible way to experience a jungle walk,
if you are short of time. There are two major walks in the forest, each only
lasting around an hour and culminating in beaches. Camping is possible on the
beach on the west side, Pantai Keracut, close to a lake as well as being a landing
area for two turtle species; green turtles from April to August and Olive Ridley
turtles between September and February – camping equipment can be hired by
the main entrance of the park and you must register before entering the park,
whether you are camping or not. Should you be lucky to see any of the turtles,
there are guidelines of conduct to be observed (as well as your own common
sense), so your presence has less impact on the creatures. For a Day Visitor pass,
you can just show up, but for camping it is advisable to check availability prior

to arrival as the park can only hold up to 110 campers per night. The Pasir Panjang beach right on the southwestern tip is the best bet for a good clean stretch of sand and sea.

Just to the south of Teluk Bahang are the Butterfly Farm and Forest Recreation Park and Museum (see p.201).

Practicalities
Accommodation in Teluk Bahang is limited. At the roundabout, there is the standard *Hotbay Motel* (℡04/881 9555; ❸), which offer air-conditioned rooms with hot showers. Add an extra RM20 in peak season. Along the beach past the bridge is the *Fisherman's Village* (❶), with very simple rooms in a Malay family home. It is not possible to book.

Teluk Bahang's real attraction is its plethora of inexpensive **places to eat** on the little stretch of main road, including an excellent seafood restaurant, *The End of the World* (daily 6–10pm), just by the pier. Off the northeast corner of the roundabout is *Restoran Khaleel*, which serves tasty and inexpensive *nasi campur*, banana rotis and ice cream.

The rest of the island

Given that all the accommodation on Penang island is either in Georgetown, near the airport or on the north coast, seeing the **rest of the island** generally means making day-trips. Public transport takes in most of the points of interest picked out below. However, getting around by bus rather misses the point, which is to get away from the main road and explore the jungle, beaches and kampungs at leisure. It's much better to **rent a motorbike**, or even a **bicycle**, from one of the outlets on Lebuh Chulia – the circuit is a seventy-kilometre round trip, so you have to be fairly fit to accomplish it using pedal-power, especially since some parts of the road are very steep. Once clear of the outskirts of Georgetown the traffic eases up; the interior is blissfully free of traffic, though it can get busy along the northern and eastern shore roads.

South from Georgetown to Gertak Sanggul
The road south from Pengkalan Weld in Georgetown heads past the university to the **Snake Temple**, 12km from the city (reachable on Rapid Penang bus #401). This is a major attraction for Asian bus-tour groups and the usual souvenir and food stalls clutter the otherwise impressive entrance which is guarded by two stone lions. The temple was founded in memory of Chor Soo King, a monk who arrived from China over a hundred years ago and gained local fame as a healer. Inside, draped lazily over parts of the altar, are a handful of poisonous green snakes (mostly Wagler's pit vipers) which, legend has it, mysteriously appeared upon completion of the temple in 1850 and have made the temple their refuge ever since. The snakes seem rather lethargic and the temple caretaker says that their fangs have been pulled out. He also claims that it's safe to have your photograph taken with the snakes curled around your neck and shoulders, and he'll charge you RM30 if you choose to do so. Don't, however, come crying to us if you try this and get bitten.

Continuing south, the road leads past the airport at Bayan Lepas to **Batu Maung**, 7km from the Snake Temple, which can also be reached directly on Rapid Penang bus #302 and #307. Apart from the pretty coastal scenery, the only other reason to come here is to visit the **Penang War Museum** (daily 9am–7pm), located on the site of a British military fortress built in the 1930s. Situated on twenty acres of land, the fort was blasted and dug into the hill by

Moving on from Penang island

Most journeys from Penang island involve changing in Butterworth, where you can pick up long-distance buses and trains to destinations in the Peninsula and on to Hat Yai, Surat Thani and Bangkok in Thailand (although you can also catch many buses directly from Penang). The Sungai Nibong Bus Terminal, in the outskirts of Georgetown, also serves many destinations, but all buses from here stop in Butterworth en route.

By air

Among the direct international **flights** from Georgetown are services to **Medan** in Sumatra, **Bangkok, Koh Samui** and **Phuket** in Thailand and **Singapore**. To get to Bayan Lepas International Airport, take bus #401 (hourly 6am–9pm; 45min; RM2) from Pengkalan Weld or the KOMTAR building.

By ferry

The passenger and car **ferry** from the Pengkalan Weld terminal is free on the leg to **Butterworth**, a fifteen-minute journey (daily 6am–12.30am, every 20min). Express ferries to **Medan** (Sumatra, Indonesia; 4hr) and **Langkawi** (2hr 30min) depart daily from Swettenham Pier. The ferry to Langkawi departs from Penang at 8.15am and 8.30am (RM60 one way); the return trip departs from Langkawi at 2.30pm and 5.15pm. Tickets for both Langkawi and Sumatra can be purchased in advance from the office next to the Penang Tourist Centre. Tickets for Langkawi are sold by the Kuala Perlis–Langkawi Ferry Service (☎04/262 5630) and Langkawi Ferry Service (☎04/264 2088), both at the Penang Port Commission building; the travel agencies on Lebuh Chulia, as well as many guesthouses, will also book tickets for you.

local labourers. It includes underground tunnels, an observation tower, a cook house and an infirmary.

West of here, the four-kilometre stretch of road along the south coast towards **Gertak Sanggul** is one of the most attractive parts of the island, gently winding and tree-lined, with the odd tantalizing glimpse of glittering ocean. The road ends at a scenic bay where you can watch the local fishing boats at work. It's possible to reach Gertak Sanggul directly from Georgetown on Rapid Penang bus #401.

North to Teluk Bahang

Just to the east of Teluk Kumbar, the road north winds steeply up to the village of **Barat**, where you have the choice of heading northeast to **Balik Pulau** or southwest to **Pulau Betong**. Neither are particularly enthralling, though there's something attractive in the quiet pace of life and the friendliness of the local people. Balik Pulau is probably the better choice, simply because of the string of good cafés along the main road.

Back on the main road, the route climbs very steeply as it winds round the jungle-clad hillside, offering the occasional view over the flat, forested plain which stretches toward the sea. A couple of kilometres from the turning for Sungai Pinang are the disappointing **Titi Kerawang Waterfalls**, outside the rainy season little more than a dismal, rubbish-strewn trickle; however, they're worth a stop to buy fresh fruit from the roadside stalls. Continue 1km further to the **Tropical Fruit Farm** (daily 9am–6pm; ☎04/866 5168; bus #501 from Georgetown), where over two hundred varieties of tropical and sub-tropical fruits are grown on 25 hectares. A tour of the farm, which includes a fresh fruit platter, costs RM20. They also run their own buses to several hotels in town, but this will almost double the cost.

By bus

All **long-distance buses** stop at or depart from Butterworth, wherever they are heading. Some buses, including several to Thailand, also depart from the Sungai Nibong Bus Terminal, located 5km out of town. There is a shuttle bus from the KOMTAR building for Sungai Nibong. Buses leave for many destinations on the Peninsula (including KL, Kota Bharu, Kuala Terengganu and the Cameron Highlands), as well as Singapore and Thailand, but they can get busy, so it is advisable to book ahead, either at your hotel, with the many agents around Jalan Chulia or on the ground floor of the KOMTAR building. There are more services from the terminal at Butterworth, which are so numerous that you can just turn up without booking beforehand.

By train

The nearest **train station** is in Butterworth (℡04/323 7962); there is a booking office in the Pengkalan Weld bus station, where you can reserve tickets to anywhere on the Peninsula as well as for the International Express to Bangkok (20hr).

By taxi

Taxis from the Pengkalan Weld ferry terminal charge about RM80 per vehicle to **Butterworth** station, so you're much better off taking the ferry, which is faster and free in this direction. Long-distance taxis to **Hat Yai** in Thailand (RM350 for up to four passengers) depart from several hostels on Lebuh Chulia.

The road then levels and straightens out for the next 4km before reaching the **Forest Recreation Park** (Tues–Sun 9am–5pm; free) on the east side of the road. The museum here (RM1) introduces visitors to the different types of forest on Penang, and there are several well-marked forest trails and a children's playground nearby. They also run guided jungle discovery tours (2–5 hr; RM13–33). If you're joining a tour, you can be picked up from various hotels in town (transport RM5–10 extra). Another kilometre further along the road to Teluk Bahang is the **Butterfly Farm** (Mon–Fri 9am–5pm, Sat & Sun 9am–6pm; RM4; bus #101 from Georgetown). This is home to all manner of creepy-crawlies, including frogs, snakes, stick insects and scorpions, as well as four thousand butterflies of around 120 different species. Also nearby is a **batik factory** (9am–6pm; free) where you can watch Malaysian-style batik being made and buy the finished product. Less than 1km further north is the roundabout at Teluk Bahang.

Sungai Petani and around

From Butterworth, the train line and highways run north, into the state of **Kedah** and through the small town of **Sungai Petani**, 35km away. Few people stop here, but those who do are drawn by two fairly specialist attractions: the **archeological remains** at Lembah Bujang (Bujang Valley), 10km further northwest, and **Gunung Jerai** (Kedah Peak), 9km north of the valley.

Sungai Petani

SUNGAI PETANI is the nearest point from which to reach both the Bujang Valley and Kedah Peak. If you plan to visit both Lembah Bujang and Gunung

A short history of Kedah

Kedah's history is a sad catalogue of invasion and subjugation, mainly by the Thais, lasting more or less up until the beginning of the twentieth century. The state has long been noted for its **independent spirit**: an eleventh-century Chola-dynasty tablet inscription mentions "Kadaram [Kedah] of fierce strength". By the thirteenth century, Kedah was already asserting its own economic superiority over the Srivijaya Empire (see p.688) by sending ships to India to trade jungle products for such exotic goods as Arabian glass and Chinese porcelain. Despite becoming a vassal state of **Ayuthaya** – the mighty Thai kingdom – during the mid-seventeenth century, Kedah still managed to express its defiance. For decades, the Malay states had been left to get on with their own affairs, provided they sent monetary tributes to Thailand from time to time. But when, in 1645, the Kedah ruler was summoned to appear at the Thai court in person – an unprecedented request – he refused point-blank, claiming that it was beneath the dignity of a sultan to prostrate himself before another ruler. In a climb-down, the king of Ayuthaya sent a statue of himself to Kedah, instructing the court, rather hopefully, to pay homage to it twice a day. At the beginning of the nineteenth century, Kedah's relationship with its Thai conquerors degenerated into a **jihad**, or holy war, led by Sultan Ahmad. The strength of religious feeling frightened the Bangkok government, who deposed Ahmad, but in 1842 the British, anxious to see peace in the region and realizing the strength of Ahmad's hold over his people, forced the sultan's reinstatement. Even this gesture had little effect on stubborn Kedah: as recently as the beginning of the twentieth century, when Kedah was transferred by the Thais to British control, it adamantly refused to become part of the Federated Malay States.

Jerai in one day, you'll need to stay overnight at one of Sungai Petani's few **hotels**, which are close to the centre; otherwise, you can just make a short detour from Sungai Petani and continue on from there to your next destination, as there's no particular reason to stay in the town itself.

A clock tower dominates Jalan Ibrahim, the main north–south road through town; from here, a side road directly to the east leads to the **train station**. One block south of the clock tower, another side road branching east, Jalan Kuala Ketil, crosses over the tracks and leads to the **express bus stop** – little more than a yard and some food stalls. A further block south and to the west is Jalan Petri, which continues west past the local bus station, taxi stand and budget **hotels**.

West along Jalan Petri from the local bus station, at no. 7 is the *Duta* (☎04/421 2040; ❸), with large, colourful and comfortable en-suite rooms with either fans or air-conditioning. A nice pool and a little more luxury awaits at the *Sungai Petani Inn* (☎04/421 3411, ⓕ421 2423; ❺), at 427 Jalan Kolam Air, a short taxi ride from the station. For good cheap Malay and Indian **food**, try *Restauran Lih Pin*, across from the *Duta* hotel. Further west along Jalan Petri, the *Restauran Bee Ah Ton*, is a more traditional *kopitiam*. For Chinese food, there's a restaurant at the *Lucky Hotel* on the other side of Jalan Petri doing good soups, and a small but lively **night market** one block north on Jalan Dewa – the street leading north from the local bus station.

Lembah Bujang

Ten kilometres northwest of Sungai Petani, on the banks of Sungai Bujang and in the shadow of Gunung Jerai, lies Malaysia's most important archeological site, **Lembah Bujang**, proving the existence of a significant Hindu-Buddhist kingdom here as far back as the fourth century. The kingdom had trading ties with the Khmers of Cambodia and was visited by the Chinese monk I-Tsing in 671. By the seventh century the Lembah Bujang kingdom was part of the large Srivijaya Empire of Sumatra, reaching its architectural peak in the ninth and tenth centuries (contemporaneous with Borobodur in Java). In 1025, Lembuh Bujang was attacked by the Chola kingdom of India, but later formed an alliance with the Cholas against the waning Srivijaya Empire. Trading continued, but by the fourteenth century Lembah Bujang's significance had faded, and with the rise of Islam the temples were left to the jungle.

The on-site **archeological museum** (Mon–Sun 9am–5pm; free) displays photographs of some of the finds *in situ*, as well as a number of relocated carved stone pillars, pots and jewels. Behind the museum, eight *candis* (including Candi Bukit Batu Pahat) have been reconstructed using original materials. There's a snackshop on the premises.

Getting there from Sungai Petani's local bus station is quite straightforward with a local bus (hourly; 45min; RM3) for Merbok or Tanjung Dawai. Ask the bus driver to let you off in Merbok, a small village with one main road; follow the signpost for the museum for 2km through fruit orchards. To catch the bus back to Sungai Petani, you need to flag it down – locals can show you where. **Accommodation** is available at the nearby *Damai Park Resort* (signposted off the road from Merbok; ☎04/457 3340; fan ❸, a/c ❺), which has several clean en-suite chalets dotted around a shady park planted with fruit trees. There's a large clean dorm up a hill where RM15 gets you a mattress on the floor; kitchen facilities are available. It's a lovely quiet retreat during the week – all you hear are the sounds of the nearby stream; that said, it can get busy at weekends, when advance **reservations** are often necessary.

Gunung Jerai

Dominating the landscape, **Gunung Jerai** (1200m) is a massive limestone outcrop 9km north of Lembah Bujang as the crow flies. It's the highest peak in Kedah, and on clear days offers panoramic views over the rolling rice fields stretching up to Perlis in the north, and along the coastline from Penang to Langkawi. Gunung Jerai is replete with history and legend; tales abound of the infamous **Rajah Bersiong** ("the king with fangs") who once held court over the ancient kingdom of Langkasuka, and archeological digs here have revealed the existence of a water temple (Candi Telaga Sembilan) which many believe was the private pool of Rajah Bersiong. A few hours is enough to stroll around the **Sungai Teroi Forest Recreation Park** halfway up the mountain, with its rare orchids and wildlife including the lesser mouse deer and the long-tailed macaque, for which the conservation area is renowned. At the top of the path leading to the recreation park is a **Museum of Forestry** (daily 9am–3pm; free), which is of limited interest.

The jumping-off point for Gunung Jerai is just north of the town of **Gurun**, on Route 1. Local bus #2 from Sungai Petani (every 45min; 30min) drops you at the bottom of the mountain, from where you can drive or walk up to the summit (a gentle 2hr climb) or get one of the **minibuses** that make the journey up every 45 minutes (daily 8.30am–5pm; RM5 return).

Alor Star and around

The tidy state capital of Kedah, **Alor Star**, is a city keen to preserve its heritage, a fact attested to by its many royal buildings and museums. Though little visited by tourists, it has enough architectural and cultural interest to make it a good place to stop and relax on your way to or from Thailand, Ulu

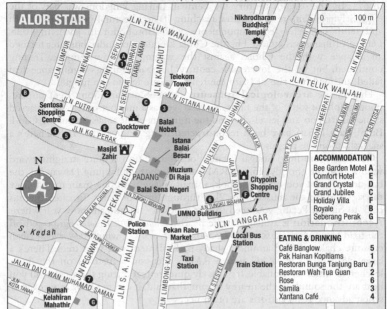

Muda Forest Reserve (see p.207) or the ferry to Langkawi. Something of Kedah's past (see box, p.202) is evidenced by the many Thais still living in Alor Star today, worshipping in the splendidly restored Thai temple and running businesses and restaurants. For all that, Alor Star is one of the most Malay towns you'll find on the west coast, sustained in part by the predominance of Islam which, throughout the years of external domination, played an important part in the maintenance of traditional Malay values. It's a fact worth keeping in mind for women just returning from Thailand or Langkawi: shorts and sleeveless tops are better left for the beach, as is advised for most non-beach destinations.

Arrival and information

Located close to the E1 and the main west-coast train line, Alor Star is something of a **transport hub**, with connections to Thailand and Singapore, as well as most cities on the Peninsula. Alor Star's huge Shahab Perdana **express bus station** is located 5km north of the centre. Shahab Perdana is well connected to the city by municipal buses (RM1.20) and taxis (RM10). Buses coming from the south usually stop in town first, so if you're staying in Alor Star, get off in front of the large UMNO Building on Jalan Tungku Ibrahim. If you miss the stop, you can easily catch a local bus back into town from Shahab Perdana. Buses leave Shahab Perdana every fifteen minutes for the twelve-kilometre journey to the jetty at **Kuala Kedah**, from where ferries depart for **Pulau Langkawi**. A taxi ride is around RM20 to the jetty from town. Shahab Perdana is also a departure point for buses to Kangar, from where there's a connecting service to the Langkawi jetty at **Kuala Perlis** (however, from Alor Star it's more convenient to take the ferry via Kuala Kedah). Buses to **Thailand** only go as far as the border, where you'll have to change to a Thai bus bound for Hat Yai or Bangkok. The **local bus station** also connects with Shahab Perdana as well as local destinations, such as Naka (4 daily) for the Ulu Muda Forest Reserve. These buses also stop opposite the Pekan Rabu market on Jalan Tunku Ibrahim, across from the UMNO building, where you'll find a **taxi rank**.

The **train** station, unsurprisingly on Jalan Stesyen, is just a minute's walk east of the local bus station. Alor Star is a principal station on the west-coast route and a place to pick up the express train to Hat Yai and Bangkok as well as southbound for Butterworth, Ipoh and Kuala Lumpur. You can also take a **taxi** from the taxi station south of the Pekan Rabu market to the Thai border (RM50 per person; 2hr), then transfer to a Thai taxi for the onward journey to Hat Yai (60km). The domestic **airport** (MAS office ☎04/721 1186), 11km north of town, is accessible by the hourly Kepala Batas bus from Shahab Perdana, or by taxi (around RM25); AirAsia has offices here too.

Most of the major **banks** are on the square by or in the UMNO building. There are many **internet cafés** in the Citypoint shopping centre.

Accommodation

Most of Alor Star's hotels are in the mid-range category and they are generally well run with friendly staff.

Bee Garden Motel Lebuhraya Darul Aman ☎04/733 5355, ✉beegardenmotel@gmail.com. Newly opened and well appointed, this is the best-value accommodation in town with clean sheets and private bathrooms. Free wi-fi. Recommended. ❸

Comfort Motel 2c Jalan Kampung Perak ☎04/734 4866, ℻733 9788. Clean and cheap, this small motel with shared bathrooms is friendly, though bring earplugs as the nightguard likes watching TV. ❷

Grand Crystal 40 Jalan Kampung Perak ☎04/731 3333, ✉crystal@ghihotels.com.my. Reasonable business-class hotel with a pool. Rates include breakfast. ❺

Grand Jubilee 429 Jalan Kanchut ☎&℻04/733 0055. Friendly place with simple en-suite fan and a/c rooms. ❸

Holiday Villa Southeast corner of the Citypoint shopping centre, Jalan Tunku Ibrahim ☎04/734 9999, ⊛www.holidayvilla.com.my. By far the most luxurious hotel in town, with tastefully appointed rooms, a classy lobby and nice views from the upper floors. Amenities include a pool and fitness centre. ❼

Royale 97 Jalan Putra ☎04/733 0921, ℻733 0925. This clean and bright hotel with well-equipped rooms has a quiet riverside location and friendly staff. Good value. ❺

Hotel Seberang Perak Lorong Kilang Ais, Jalan Dato Wan Muhamad Saman ☎04/772 2288, ✉ibsoew@pd.jaring.my. Right behind the Ruhmah Kelahiran Mahathir, this friendly family-run hotel has small, pink-painted, basic but clean rooms with a/c and attached (Asian) toilets and shower. ❸

The Town

The rather murky Sungai Kedah runs along the western and southern outskirts of Alor Star. There are a few canals in the city, all fairly polluted. The main sights are located in the west of the town around the old padang. The area just to the west is dominated by impressive **Masjid Zahir**, claimed to be the oldest in Malaysia. Facing the mosque, the elegant **Istana Balai Besar** (Royal Audience Hall) – the principal official building during the eighteenth century – stands serene on the grounds of the padang. The present two-storey, open-colonnaded structure dates back only to 1904, when the original hall was rebuilt to host the marriages of Sultan Abdul Hamid's five eldest children. So grand was the refurbishment and so lavish the ceremony that the state was nearly bankrupted.

Just behind the Balai Besar, the old royal palace now serves as the **Muzium Di Raja** (daily 9am–5pm, closed Fri noon–2pm; free), an excellent way of preserving this dainty little 1930s building. The museum has its fair share of eulogistic memorabilia – medals and fond recollections of the current sultan's salad days – and some of the rooms have been kept exactly as they were used by the sultan and his family.

Across the way stands a curious octagonal tower, the **Balai Nobat**, housing the sacred instruments of the royal orchestra; unfortunately, the tower and its contents are not open for public view, as they are considered the most treasured part of the sultan's regalia and played only during royal ceremonies.

On the padang's south side, stands the grandiose, white-stucco **Balai Seni Negeri** (Mon–Sat 9am–5pm, Sun 8am–3pm; free), a former courthouse and the first modern structure in Alor Star. It is now an art gallery showing local artists, some of better quality than others. Most interesting are woodcarvings complete with a model of a traditional Malay house. South of the padang, across the Sungai Kedah, is **Rumah Kelahiran Mahathir** (Tues–Sun 9am–5pm, closed Fri noon–3pm; free), at 18 Lorong Kilang Ais, the birthplace and family home of Dr Mahathir Mohamad. It's now a museum, documenting the life of the local doctor who became the most powerful Malaysian prime minister of modern times. Even if you're not interested in Mahathir himself, it's worth taking a glimpse inside his former house to get an idea of what traditional middle-class Malay houses looked like in the 1950s.

Just north of the padang on Jalan Kanchut is the **Telekom Tower** (daily 10am–10pm; RM10), the most modern sight in Alor Star. A mini-version of the one in KL, it has a fast-food restaurant and viewing gallery, peacefully popular with courting couples at sunset. Continue north from here and then east along Jalan Telok Wanjah and you'll come to the **Nikhrodharam Buddhist Temple**, just beside the roundabout. The building of this glittering temple complex, decorated with many colourful statues, mosaics and paintings, began in the 1950s and was only finished in 1995. A match for many in Thailand, it is a testimony to the continuing influence of Thai culture in the city.

For a glimpse of contemporary culture, head for the **Pekan Rabu**, a daily market running from morning to midnight. Situated in a large building on Jalan Tunku Ibrahim, it comprises a large collection of stalls selling everything from handicrafts to local farm produce. It's a good place to sample traditional Kedah food like *dodol durian*, a sweet cake made from the notoriously pungent durian fruit.

Hop on any bus heading north from Jalan Penak Melayu, adjacent to the padang, and after about 1500m you'll pass the **Muzium Negeri** (Tues–Sun 10am–6pm, closed Fri noon–3pm; free). On Jalan Lebuhraya Darulaman, it contains some background information on the archeological finds at Lembah Bujang (see p.202). Close to the entrance, there's a delicate silver tree, known as the *bunga mas dan perak* ("the gold and silver flowers"). The name refers to a practice, established in the seventeenth century, of honouring the ruling government of Thailand by a triennial presentation of two small trees of gold and silver, about 1m in height, meticulously detailed even down to the birds nesting in their branches

Eating

Despite Alor Star's Malay overtones, its restaurant sector seems to be predominantly Chinese. Chinatown is around the veritable restaurant row of Jalan Putera to the east of the padang, where there are also lots of hawkers to choose from. You'd also do well to sample some Thai cuisine while in town.

Café Banglow Jalan Kampung Perak. Popular with a young Chinese crowd, this place has lovely little huts scattered around a somewhat untidy garden with fairylights and lanterns. There's a seafood BBQ and an indoor bar, doubling as a karaoke nightclub.

Pak Hainan Kopitiams Right next to the *Bee Garden Motel*, this modern coffee house has noodle and rice dishes along with teas, coffees and cakes.

Restoran Bunga Tanjung Baru On the corner of Jalan Pegawai and Jalan Dato Wan Muhamad Saman, near the Rumah Kelahiran Mahatir, you'll find this eatery offering South Indian fare.

Restoran Wah Tua Guan On Jalan Pintu Sepuluh. Interesting herb and tea shop with dishes containing ginseng, delicious soups and a fridge full of unidentifiable foodstuffs and medicines.

Rose Restaurant On Jalan Sultan Badlishah, this place has decent South Indian food.

Samila Hotel Restaurant On the northwest corner of the padang. Head here if you're in the mood for Western food.

Xantana Café Opposite the *Grand Crystal*, this bar and café with a friendly owner, has a good lunch selection of Chinese and Thai food as well as a popular BBQ outside at night.

Ulu Muda Forest Reserve

Perhaps the most exciting destination inland on the west coast is the **Ulu Muda Forest Reserve**. A vast expanse of rainforest jungle, bordering with and crossing over to Thailand, this is the ideal place to go trekking and tubing in still unspoilt nature (guide obligatory). The man-made dam within the reserve forms large freshwater lakes and supplies water to most of Penang, Kedah and Perlis states; a result of this is that many dead trees are waterlogged, their spindly tops acting as resting places for much birdlife, including the grey-headed fish eagle and the blue-banded kingfisher. The park is also home to white elephants, Sumatran rhinoceros, sun bears, tapirs, deers and tigers as well as several species of monkeys, insects and reptiles.

The reserve is rich with salt licks, some of the largest in the country, and hot springs, which many animals visit early in the morning or at night, when the temperatures drop. There are observation huts, where you can sit tight and hope for visits until the early hours. Within the forest, there are various streams excellent for tubing; starting with a gentle trek, you carry a rubber tube to the

▲ Tapir

top of the stream. The tube will carry you down mild rapids – then go back and do it again.

To get there, the best set-off point is Alor Star, taking Route K8 through Naka and heading on to Gubir – about an hour and a half drive. From Butterworth, take the North-South Expressway and exit at Gurun, taking route K10 to Sik, where you turn onto Route K13 to Gubir.

Using public transport, you can also get a bus from Alor Star to Naka (4 daily; 2hr; RM4), from where you will have to take a taxi. Alternatively, from Butterworth, take a local bus to Sik and then further to Gubir.

Good, sturdy **chalets** are available at the government-run *Mada Resort* (☎04/752 1779; ❹) in Gubir, the nearest town to Ulu Muda. You can only get to base camp within the forest from the jetty in small boats with a guide (about 1hr, depending on water levels); **camping** is possible, though trips are costly at about RM250–450, depending on what you want to do. Ron's Adventures (☎04/977 7578, ✉ronsadventures@hotmail.com) is an excellent choice with tailored treks, and Ron will organize permissions for you as well as lend you the all-important leech socks. At the time of writing, a wildlife office, tourist information and a small number of chalets were being built respectively at the jetty and at base camp. August to December can see heavy rainfall, but the park is still accessible. Upon entry it is best to note down everything you bring in – and check that it is brought back out on exit.

Pulau Langkawi

Situated 30km off the coast, at the very northwestern tip of the Peninsula, is a cluster of 104 tropical islands known collectively as **LANGKAWI**. The archipelago's beauty has fostered many traditional stories, so much so that Langkawi has become known as the "Islands of Legends". In true Malay fashion, almost every major landmark here has a myth associated with it, each story hijacked by the tourist authorities to promote the islands. Only three are inhabited, including the largest of the group, **Pulau Langkawi** (around 500 square kilometres), once a haven for pirates, now a sought-after refuge for wealthy tourists as well as new developments catering for the more modest budgets. Pulau Langkawi has in recent years seen unparalleled development, enhanced by its duty-free status, making it Malaysia's premier island retreat. Some of the country's most luxurious hotels are here, and an airport has been built to cope with the increasing number of visitors, with flights landing daily from Singapore, KL and Penang. Langkawi is not a budget destination, though more budget places are surfacing; to appreciate all the islands have to offer, you need to spend quite a bit of money, though you could scrape by on RM40–50 a day, if all you do is sit on the beach. In high season, it is advisable to book.

Pulau Langkawi's natural attractions – a mountainous interior, white sands, limestone outcrops and lush vegetation – have remained relatively unspoilt. The island's charms consist largely of lazing around on beaches and enjoying the sunshine, although you can also visit the splendid **Telaga Tujuh** waterfall and the **Telaga Air Panas** hot springs, or the most popular attraction – the **Langkawi Cable Car**, to the top of **Gunung Mat Cincang**.

The principal town on the island is **Kuah**, a boom town of hotels and shops in the southeast, where you'll find most of the duty-free bargains. The main tourist development has taken place around two bays on the western side of the island, at **Pantai Tengah** and **Pantai Cenang**. The former is the more

PULAU LANGKAWI

Kuala Perlis ▲   Kuala Kedah ▲   Penang ▲

Satun ▲

0   5 km

N

THE WEST COAST

209

Cave of Legends

Gua Cerita

117m ▲

Tanjung Rhu

Pulau Pasir

Pulau Gasing

Galeria Ferdana

Telaga Air Panas

Durian Perangin Waterfall

Pulau Laggun

285m ▲

Cave of Bats

Kilim Geoforest Jetty

S.K.Isap

Teluk Apau

Pulau Tanjung Dendang

P. Chorong

Pulau Payar Marine Park ▼

Kisap

420m ▲

Palau Timon

372m ▲

Pulau Tiloi

Pulau Bumbun

Kg. Penerah

G

Kuah   Jetty

P. Tuba

Padang Lalang

Air Hangat Village

Teluk pasir Hitam

Teluk Ewa

G. Raya (881m) ▲

Lubuk Semilang

Kg. Ulu Melaka

Makam Mahsuri ▼

Hospital ✚

Langkawi Golf Club

Pulau Dayang Bunting

283m ▲

Pasir Tengorak

S. China

Crocodile Adventure

Langkawi Golf Club

708m ▲

Pantai Datai

Telaga Tujuh

Langkawi Cable Car

Oriental Village

Pantai Kok

S. Petang

Padang Matsirat

Kuala Teriang

Kedewang

Temonyong

Underwater World

New Runway & Breakwater

Pantai Cenang

Pantai Tengah

see 'Pantai Tengah & Pantai Cenang' map for more detail

Pulau Tepor

Pulau Rebak

Pulau Singa Besar ▼

Pulau Dunung

ACCOMMODATION

Andaman   B
Berjaya Resort   E
Datai   C
Langkasuka Resort   D
Tanjung Sanctuary   A
The Four Seasons   F
Westin Langkawi   G

commercialized, whereas the latter is popular with travellers and has more budget accommodation. More recent building work has taken place at two beaches on the north coast, **Pantai Datai** and **Tanjung Rhu**, where accommodation is limited to top-class resorts.

There is basically one circular route around the island, with the other main road cutting the island in two, connecting north and south; even the minor roads are well surfaced and signposted. **Public transport** around the island is limited to **taxis**. A trip from the Kuah jetty to Pantai Cenang costs RM25, while a four-hour taxi tour of the island runs to around RM100 per vehicle for up to four people. If you think you can handle the local driving habits, which are not at all in the same league as, say Penang, it's definitely worthwhile to **rent a car** (from RM50–80) or **motorbike** (RM25) for the day, and see the island at your own pace. There are plenty of rental opportunities at the Kuah jetty, in Kuah town or Pantai Cenang. Some places also rent **bicycles** for RM20 per day.

On the neighbouring islands of **Pulau Dayang Bunting** and **Pulau Tuba**, designated **geoforest parks** provide a little extra interest, as do snorkelling trips to **Pulau Singa Besar** and **Pulau Payer**. You can also dive and snorkel further south in the **Pulau Payar Marine Park**, though the only way to do this is by taking an expensive day-trip. There's a **website** (ⓦ www.langkawi-online.com) which offers general information on the island as well as bookings. It is possible, though not advisable, to **camp** on Pasir Tengorak beach, but you must obtain permission first from the Forest Department (ⓣ 04/966 6835) and be prepared for many inquisitive (and sometimes hostile) monkeys.

Getting to Langkawi

There are ferries every day from two points on the mainland, one from **Kuala Perlis** (see p.220; 1hr; RM18 one way), close to the Thai border, and the other from **Kuala Kedah** (see p.204; 1hr 30min; RM23 one way), 51km to the south, just 8km from Alor Star. Ferries depart at least hourly (8am–7pm) from both jetties; there's no need to book tickets in advance. All ferry services run to the **Kuah jetty** on the southeastern tip of the island, about five minutes' drive from Kuah itself. Two daily passenger boats sail here from **Penang** (departing at 8.30am and 8.45am; 2hr 30min; RM60 one way; the return trips depart at 2.30pm and 5.30pm), it is advised to book tickets in advance. There are also ferry services from **Thailand**: three times daily from Satun, on the border (1hr 30min; RM30) as well as daily boats from Koh Lipe. You can leave **luggage** at the ferry terminal for RM2. There are **flights** to Pulau Langkawi from KL, Penang and Singapore.

Kuah

Lining a large sweep of bay in the southeastern corner of the island, **KUAH**, with a population of thirteen thousand, is easily the largest town on Langkawi. The centre has been greatly developed in recent years, with a new ferry terminal, hotels and shopping complexes popping up all along the bay. Beside the ferry terminal is **Dataran Lang** (Eagle Square), graced by an enormous sculpture of an eagle (Langkawi means "red eagle" and you're likely to spot several brahminy kites and white-bellied fishing eagles during your stay here). Next to the square is **Lagenda Langkawi Dalan Taman** (daily 9am–7pm; free), a theme park based around the legends of the islands, its landscaped gardens punctuated by more giant sculptures. There are vantage points over the bay and surroundings, but no shade or place to buy refreshments. Most of the hotels and shopping complexes are further around the bay.

Arrival and information

Ferries run to the jetty on the southeastern tip of the island, about five minutes' drive from Kuah itself. A taxi from the jetty into Kuah costs around RM6. The **airport** (☎04/955 1311) is 20km west of Kuah, near Pantai Cenang. A taxi from the airport to Pantai Cenang is RM18 and RM30 gets you to Tanjung Rhu. A ride from Kuah to the airport costs around RM25. There's a MAS office (☎04/966 6622), an AirAsia office (☎04/966 7750) and a Firefly office (☎04/955 6332) in the airport.

The Langkawi **tourist office** (daily 9am–5pm; ☎04/966 7789) located on Jalan Persiaran Putera (the route into Kuah from the jetty) next to the mosque, has very helpful staff; there's also an information booth at the airport, open in the evenings (9–11pm). As well as the numerous duty-free shops along the main road, selling everything from hooch to handbags, you'll find the **post office** (daily except Fri 9am–5pm), **police station** (☎04/966 6222) and a little further out of town, towards Pantai Cenang, is the **hospital** (☎04/966 3333). Behind the MAYA shopping complex, also on the main road, are three parallel streets where all the **banks** (virtually the only places to change money on the island) and the **Telekom centre** are located. There are **internet cafés** at 1 Jalan Pandak Maya and 3 Jalan Pandak Maya.

Accommodation

There's little in the way of budget **accommodation** in Kuah, so you're better off heading to Pantai Cenang. If you absolutely need to stay here, just about a kilometre from the jetty, on Jalan Persiaran Putera, past the giant Lada Complex on the right, there's the *Asia Hotel* (☎04/966 6216; ❸) with good-value clean and comfortable rooms. After crossing a bridge, you'll see the high-rise *City Bayview* up a small hill (☎04/966 1818, ⓦwww.bayviewintl.com; ❼). It's the top hotel along this strip, though not really worth paying more for, unless you want a pool. Two kilometres southeast down the main road from the ferry terminal is the *Westin Langkawi Resort & Spa*, Jalan Pantai Dato' Syed Omar (☎04/966 8888, ⓕ966 3097; ❾). Set in landscaped grounds, with a private beach, sports facilities and several swimming pools, this hotel commands a spectacular view of island-dotted Langkawi Bay.

Eating

Kuah has numerous eating places of various standards, from the **hawker stalls** – past the post office heading towards the jetty – to the pricier seafood **restaurants**. Despite the ready availability of fresh fish, these places are fairly expensive, each dish setting you back at least RM15–20, and there are better places elsewhere on the island. There is a large mixed (seafood, Malay, Western, Thai) restaurant, *Jai Island Café*, just by the bridge, with reliable dishes around RM8–10.

Makam Mahsuri

Taking the main road west out of Kuah, just past the Langkawi Golf Club, about 10km from town, you see a signpost for **Makam Mahsuri** (the tomb of Mahsuri; daily 8am–6pm; RM10). In **Kampung Mawat**, a couple of kilometres off the main road west of Kuah, the tomb is enshrined in Langkawi's most famous legend, which tells of a young woman named Mahsuri, born over two hundred years ago. Her beauty was such that it inspired a vengeful accusation of adultery from a spurned suitor – or, as some versions have it, a jealous mother-in-law – while her husband was away fighting the invading Siamese. Mahsuri protested her innocence but was found guilty by the village elders,

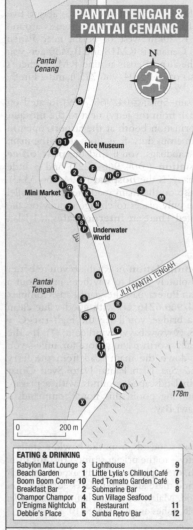

▲ Langkasuka Resort

PANTAI TENGAH & PANTAI CENANG

Pantai Cenang

N

Rice Museum

Mini Market

Underwater World

JLN PANTAI TENGAH

Pantai Tengah

▲ 178m

0   200 m

EATING & DRINKING

Babylon Mat Lounge	3	Lighthouse	9
Beach Garden	1	Little Lylia's Chillout Café	7
Boom Boom Corner	10	Red Tomato Garden Café	6
Breakfast Bar	2	Submarine Bar	8
Champor Champor	4	Sun Village Seafood	
D'Enigma Nightclub	R	Restaurant	11
Debbie's Place	5	Sunba Retro Bar	12

ACCOMMODATION

Amzar Motel	K	Pelangi Beach Resort	B
Aseania Resort	R	Rainbow Lodge	M
Beach Garden Resort	D	Shirin Restaurant	
Bon Ton Resort	A	and Guest House	N
Casa del Mar	C	Sunset Beach Resort	Q
Charlie Motel	S	Sweet Inn	H
Daddy's Guest House	F	The Palms	J
Delta Motel	P	Tropical Resort	U
Frangipani Langkawi		Vistar Travel Lodge	T
Resort and Spa	V	Zackry Guest House	W
Gecko	G		
Grand Beach	E		
Langkapuri Beach Resort	O		
Langkawi Holiday Villa	X		
Malibest Resort	L		
Melati Tanjung Motel	I		

who sentenced her to death. She was tied to a stake, and as the ceremonial dagger was plunged into her, began to bleed white blood, a sign that proved her innocence. With her dying breath, Mahsuri muttered a curse on Langkawi's prosperity, to last seven generations – judging by the island's increasing income in recent years, this must be starting to wear off.

Pantai Tengah and Pantai Cenang

Back on the main road, heading west, you travel a further 8km to a junction from where the first of the island's western beaches, **PANTAI TENGAH**, 6km away, is clearly signposted. It's a sleepy stretch, less crowded and catering more to package holidays than **PANTAI CENANG**, the next beach development and more of a town, hosting most of the island's budget accommodation and traveller vibe. Although Pantai Cenang is more developed, the buildings at both beaches are unobtrusive, mainly because of the government's requirement that beachfront accommodation doesn't exceed the height of a coconut tree. The beach at Tengah is a quiet stretch of crunchy sand, whereas Cenang boasts a wider and cleaner beach. There are sometimes jellyfish in the water at both beaches, so take local advice before you swim. During the months of September and October, the waves can get as high as 4m, but usually the sea is tranquil.

To the north, at Underwater World, there's a rocky outcrop which separates the bays of Pantai Tengah and Pantai Cenang. The bay at Pantai Cenang forms a large sweep of wide beach with sugary sand. Plenty of places on the beach offer **water sports** and **boat rental**, one of the more organized centres being Langkawi Marine

Sports (☎04/955 1389). Its prices are negotiable and vary with the time of year – during low season (weekdays, non-holidays) expect to pay around RM240 per boat (for up to eight people) for a round-the-island boat tour, RM200 for half a day's fishing or RM50 for fifteen minutes' waterskiing, or thirty minutes on a jet ski. Also, for waterskiing, parasailing and canoeing, try Cabana Watersport (☎012/470 5325).

Along the coast road, you'll find no shortage of **mini-markets** selling general provisions; most also provide **internet** terminals. There is an excellent wi-fi system, Winet, which is available through many of the guesthouses and hotels and the signal often stretches to places not officially carrying it. You'll need to buy a card with access codes from a hotel on the system (RM10 per 24hr). There are also plenty of outfits **renting cars, motorbikes and bicycles** as well as shops selling clothes and a few spas offering treatments.

The main attraction on the west coast, besides the beach, is **Underwater World** (daily 10am–6pm; RM38), boasting the largest aquarium in Asia; it houses over five thousand marine and freshwater fish. Although the attached duty-free shopping complex seems like the main reason for the operation, the fish are well presented, the highlight being a walk-through aquarium where sharks, turtles and hundreds of other sea creatures swim around and above boggle-eyed visitors in a transparent tunnel. There's also a touch pool where you can get feely with starfish, sea slugs and sea cucumbers.

At the northern end of Pantai Cenang is a rather deserted **rice museum** (10am–6pm; free), although you may be able to get a personal tour which provides a hands-on experience with traditional planting equipment and even gives you the opportunity to get your feet wet in a paddy field.

Accommodation

There are dozens of places to stay, but even the budget options start at RM40, though a few places offer dorm beds, too – and more are likely to develop. You'll get better rates at the luxury resorts by booking a package deal through a travel agent. Accommodation is a little sparser on Pantai Tengah than on Pantai Cenang.

Inexpensive

Amzar Motel ☎04/955 1354. Though "beach view chalets" are advertised, there is no view of the beach, it being on the other side of the road. However, these basic chalets are good value with own bathrooms. ❷

Daddy's Guest House ☎017/585 6686. At the back of the *Sweet Inn* is a colourful row of guest rooms with hammocks outside. The fan rooms are great value and there are also a couple of well-equipped, self-catering apartments with delightfully kitsch decor. ❷

Gecko ☎019/428 3801, ✉rebeccafiott @hotmail.com. This is the best traveller's place on the island with rooms and chalets set in a garden around a café, serving breakfasts and lunches, and doubling up as a chilled-out bar. During peak times, it is essential to book. Dorm beds at RM15. ❷

Grand Beach ☎04/955 1457, ℻955 3846. Almost right on the beach, these clean bungalows with fans ❷ or a/c ❺ are priced more reasonably than others of equal standard. There is also a room sleeping five people for RM150 with a/c.

Rainbow Lodge ☎04/955 5991, ✉rainbow_lodge69@yahoo.com. Set beside a paddy field, about a 5min walk from the beach, this peaceful and friendly place offers excellent-value rooms with bathrooms and either fan or a/c. There is a little café with a bar for socializing. Internet access available. ❷

Shirin Restaurant and Guest House ☎04/955 5991. All with shared showers, these fan or a/c rooms are basic, but good value. English, French, Italian, Japanese and Persian are spoken. Look out for the sign as it's set just back from the road. ❷

Vistar Travel Lodge ☎04/955 3952, ✉info@vistartravellodge.com. Also on Pantai Tengah and newly renovated with good clean bathrooms. Rooms are set around a communal garden with tables and a tree with festoon lights. The restaurant next door serves Malay and Thai food. Dorm beds RM20. ❷

Zackry Guest House ✉zackryghouse@gmail.com. On Pantai Tengah, this true backpacker place is a short wander from the beach. There's an honesty bar, kitchen for guest use, free tea and coffee and a communal fridge. There is also free wi-fi and dorms are available at RM20. ❷

Moderate

Aseania Resort ☎04/955 2020, ⓦwww.langkawi-resorts.com/aseaniaresort. Although the pink palace exterior may be off-putting, the rooms themselves are nicely appointed and there's a 150m long pool with a waterfall and slides. The *D'Enigma Nightclub* entrance is on the ground floor in the lobby. ❻

Charlie Motel ☎04/955 1200, ✉charlie.motel @yahoo.com.my. This beachfront place in a garden setting has wooden A-frame chalets sleeping up to three. There's also a decent restaurant on the premises as well as wi-fi. ❹

Delta Motel ☎04/955 2253, ⓕ953 1307. Closely spaced, large wooden chalets in a shady garden right by the beach. The restaurant serves local food (no alcohol allowed). It is on the slip-road just by Underwater World with a budget option for RM25 per person for six people sharing. ❹

Malibest Resort ☎04/955 8222, ✉malibestlgk @yahoo.com.my. Large resort on the beach with nicely appointed chalets and rooms with a/c and hot showers and a good restaurant. There are five luxury treetop chalets at RM200. ❺

Langkapuri Beach Resort ☎04/955 1202, ⓕ955 1959. A range of concrete chalets on a leafy patch of beach. All the rooms have a/c, fridge and hot showers. ❹

🏃 Melati Tanjung Motel ☎04/955 1099. Newly built rooms right on the beach with a/c, fridge and excellent bathrooms. There is a restaurant next door serving Indian and Malay food. ❹

Sunset Beach Resort ☎04/955 1751, ⓦwww.sunsetbeachresort.com. An intimate alternative to the big resorts, the tastefully decorated rooms surround a central courtyard with a lush garden. Friendly service. ❻

Sweet Inn ☎04/955 8864. Newly built and just before *Gecko*, this 22-room complex is great value with a/c, fridge, hot showers, wi-fi and TVs. The courtyard café serves excellent soups and chicken satay at decent prices. ❹

The Palms ☎017/631 0121, ✉sue_arnold @yahoo.co.uk. Lovely and quiet guesthouse run by a friendly couple. There is a little café as well as a toaster and kettle for guest use. Good value. ❹

Tropical Resort ☎04/955 4075, ⓕ955 1959. A German-Malay run resort with two rows of very clean chalets and on-site shoplet and spa. The beach is accessible via a row of trees at the back. ❹

Expensive

Beach Garden Resort ☎04/955 1363, ⓦwww.beachgardenresort.com. More intimate than the large resorts, this place has tastefully decorated rooms surrounding a leafy courtyard. There's a small swimming pool and a restaurant on the beach. ❼

Casa del Mar ☎04/955 2388, ⓦwww.casadelmar-langkawi.com. This German-managed boutique hotel's exterior and lobby have a colonial Mexican flavour. The rooms are tastefully decorated and there's a spa and small pool. ❾

Frangipani Langkawi Resort and Spa ☎04/952 0000, ⓦwww.frangipanilangkawi.com. Pleasant, kampung-style resort in a garden setting. The accommodation is in well-designed, two-storey chalets with all the trimmings. There's a pool and a seaside restaurant. ❾

Langkawi Holiday Villa ☎04/955 1701, ⓦwww.holidayvillahotels.com. Large luxury resort with a spa and choice of restaurants, including Italian and Japanese. Extensive lawn and large pool, but the rooms are slightly worn. Has a good range of water sports open to non-guests. ❽

Pelangi Beach Resort ☎04/952 8888, ⓦwww.pelangibeachresort.com. Pantai Cenang's finest accommodation; an impressive five-star development of two-storey timber chalets, echoing traditional Malay architecture. All the luxuries you'd expect for the price. ❾

Eating and drinking

The large resorts all have attached **restaurants**, where the emphasis is on Westernized Asian dishes. The smaller establishments tend to have restaurants right on the beach serving simpler local fare. Although there's more choice at Pantai Cenang, Pantai Tengah has a few good establishments and is usually less crowded.

Babylon Mat Lounge A popular beachfront bar and café, serving snacks, burgers and cocktails with downbeat music. It's a great place to watch the sunset and Cabana Watersports next door often has a good BBQ in the evening.

Beach Garden A pretty beachside operation serving Western food including pizza and pasta with beer to wash it down.

Boom Boom Corner Serves tasty and inexpensive Pakistani food.

Breakfast Bar Friendly place serving sandwiches and good Western breakfasts from 7am to 10pm. This is the best breakfast place in town.

Champor Champor Its name meaning "mix mix", this small bar and restaurant, in a leafy, secluded spot, serves tasty if slightly pricey fusion cuisine, and the owner is a character.

Debbie's Place Irish Pub The most Irish thing about this friendly place, apart from the Guinness, is the four-leaf-clover sign above the door.

D'Enigma Nightclub This crazy place is inside the *Aseania Resort* at the end of Pantai Cenang. With live bands and DJs every night, it's where to let loose.

Lighthouse At the end of Jalan Pantai Tengah, this stylish restaurant has an extensive drinks list and is a good place to enjoy a cocktail at sunset. The menu consists of Mediterranean and Malaysian cuisine served in an elegantly modern setting. Daily 11am–2am.

Little Lylia's Chillout Café On the beach and sometimes with live music, this place has a diverse menu, mainly serving Western food, sometimes with a BBQ in the evening. The salads are particularly good. Try the Langkawi Sunset cocktail.

Red Tomato Garden Café Popular with travellers for its free wi-fi and good food, this place serves Western breakfasts and home-made bread as well as some pricier pasta and main dishes for lunch and dinner. Try their pizzas from a wood-fired oven. No alcohol.

Submarine Bar At the far end of the beach, this place is a little less atmospheric and the hanging flags can be a little off-putting, but the cocktail list is the biggest on the island and if you like rock music, they often have it on full blast.

Sun Village Seafood Restaurant In a wooden Malay-style building, this place has an extensive wine list and serves a variety of grilled seafood as well as less expensive curries.

Sunba Retro Bar A more intimate affair than *D'Enigma* and also open late. The DJs generally play easy listening or softer dance music and there's sometimes a live reggae band, though it can get crowded.

North to Pantai Kok

Heading north 5km, a right turn after the airport brings you to the **Padang Matsirat** (literally, "Field of Burnt Rice"). Shortly after Mahsuri's death, the Siamese conquered Kedah and prepared to attack Langkawi. In order to halt the advance of the invaders, the island's inhabitants set fire to their staple crop and poisoned their wells. To this day, so the legend goes, traces of burnt rice resurface in the area after a heavy downfall of rain.

Just past the *Sheraton* complex is the beach of **PANTAI KOK**, which lies on the far western stretch of Langkawi. Previously considered Langkawi's most beautiful beach, it has now unfortunately been ruined by the construction of a marina. From here, you're only 2km from the splendid falls at Telaga Tujuh, just to the north (see p.216) and 4km from the Langkawi Cable Car.

Accommodation and eating

Unfortunately, the budget **accommodation** on the beach has been bulldozed to make way for a golf course, so pricier complexes are the only option. On the shore road north of Pantai Cenang, the beautiful *Bon Ton Resort* (℡04/955 6787; ⑨) has seven preserved Malay houses on stilts, set among palm trees. There is a pool and direct access to the beach. The restaurant is worth visiting for its well-presented local food and home-made cakes, though pricey. Further up the coast is the *Langkasuka Resort* (℡04/955 6888; ⑦–⑨), a luxurious place on a lovely beach, with promotional discounts of up to fifty percent. A couple of kilometres uphill along the coast road, near the junction with the road leading inland is the stylish *Tanjung Sanctuary Langkawi* (℡04/955 2977, ⓦwww.tanjung-sanctuary-langkawi.com; ⑧), with lavish accommodation in natural surroundings. It's on a forested rocky headland and has its own private beach, plus a swimming pool and a restaurant built on stilts over the water. Another 4km west at the end of the road, is the luxurious *Berjaya Langkawi Beach and Spa Resort* (℡04/959 1888, Ⓦwww.berjayaresorts.com.my; ⑨); the decor is somewhat kitsch, but the Japanese massages, facials and forest spa are its real attraction.

Telaga Tujuh and the Langkawi Cable Car

The road beyond the turn-off to the *Berjaya Resort*, leads to a car park, from where a dirt track heads up to the island's most wonderful natural attraction, **Telaga Tujuh** (literally, "Seven Pools"), a cascading freshwater stream that has pounded large recesses into the rock, forming several pools down a slope. During the rainy season, the slipperiness of the moss covering the rock in between the pools enables you to slide rapidly from one pool to another, before the fast-flowing water disappears over the cliff to form the ninety-metre **waterfall** you can see from below – it's only the depth of the water in the last pool that prevents you from shooting off the end too. This being Langkawi, there's an associated legend, suggesting the spot is the playground of mountain fairies. They're believed to have left behind a special kind of lime and the *sintuk* (a climbing plant with enormous pods), which grow around these pools; the locals use them as a hair wash, which is thought to rinse away bad luck.

The walk to the pools from the turning near the *Berjaya Resort* takes about 45 minutes, the last stage of which involves a steep two-hundred-metre climb up from the inevitable cluster of souvenir stalls at the base of the hill. Look out for the long-tailed macaques that bound around the trail; they are playful, but can display aggression if provoked or if you are (or look like you are) carrying food.

Heading back toward Pantai Kok about a kilometre, turn right and inside the otherwise fairly pointless (unless you like shopping) **Oriental Village** is the best man-made attraction the island has to offer. With a 42-degree incline, the **Langkawi Cable Car** (℡04/959 4225; Mon–Thurs 10am–6pm, Fri–Sun & public hols 10am–7pm; RM25) is not only the steepest in the world, it also boasts the longest free span for a mono-cable car; a thrilling 950m long, great for eagle spotting. There is a superb **canopy walkway** 700 metres above sea-level on the top of Gunung Mat Cinang, overlooking the forest treetops with a spectacular view over the Andaman Sea; on a clear day you can see several Thai islands in the distance.

Crocodile Adventure and The Datai

From Pantai Kok, the main road north heads to Pulau Langkawi's **north coast**. On the way, after about 7km, you'll pass **Crocodile Adventure** (daily 9am–6pm; RM15), Malaysia's largest crocodile farm where you can view some 1500 saltwater crocodiles (*Crocodilus porosus*) at various stages of their development. There are also the usual shows that feature "crocodile wrestling" and the like. More interesting perhaps are the feedings that take place before each show. Ten kilometres further on, there's a road off to the left that leads a further 12km to **The Datai** (℡04/959 2500, Ⓔdatai@ghmhotels.com; ⑨), the quintessential rainforest resort. Volcanic rock and wood have been used to stunning effect, creating architecture that's in harmony with the surrounding forest. The views across the bay to Thailand are stunning, as is the price. The restaurant is open to non-guests, but none of the facilities are. Under the same management is the *Andaman* (℡04/959 1088, Ⓦwww.theandaman.com; ⑨), which shares the beach at Datai Bay.

Malay life

The Malays once led a largely rural existence as farmers and fisherfolk. Many have now settled in the cities, and the urban Malays you meet may well be keener on, say, Western music than doing folk dances. Yet something of the old way of life can be glimpsed in villages, and you'll come across traditional pastimes and art forms in cultural centres and during festivals.

Kite-maker at work ▲

Top-spinning ▼

Satay being barbecued ▼

Pastimes and sports

Some village **pastimes** have become competitive affairs, and it's well worth taking in a contest or demonstration if you can.

Kite-flying is fun to watch as the kites are sizeable (up to 2m in length), bear gaudy floral motifs and come in various elaborate shapes, most strikingly that of the *wau bulan*, a stylized outline of which is used as Malaysia Airlines' logo. Enthusiasts formerly coated the strings with ground glass to try to cut their rivals' kites adrift, but nowadays competitions (there's one in Kelantan most years) focus on kite-handling skills or on how melodiously the rattan strip on a kite hums in the wind.

Top-spinning is also taken seriously; people compete to knock out one another's tops or to see whose top spins the longest. Players launch the tops from shoulder height rather like a shot put – no mean feat with the bigger tops intended for endurance spinning, as they can weigh several kilos and keep going for over an hour.

Food

Both spicy and sweet, Malay cooking draws on Chinese, Thai and Indian influences and makes use of unusual herbs. Desserts are temptingly colourful if sometimes a bit weird. Must-try dishes include:

Nasi lemak – rice cooked in coconut milk and served with egg and spicy anchovies.

Satay – little kebabs with a peanut-sauce dip.

Singapore mee rebus – yellow egg noodles in a thick, spicy gravy.

Cendol – iced coconut milk with palm molasses, mung-bean flour bits and aduki beans.

Music and dance

Like Malay cooking, Malay music and dance show influences from elsewhere in Asia and the Muslim world, and sometimes further afield.

Among the many traditional musical genres, the hip-hop-like wordplay of **dikir barat** makes it the one to look out for, even if you don't understand Malay; shows are sometimes advertised on flyposters. A performance is led by a *tukang karut* who improvises rhyming couplets, reprised by a male chorus over an accompaniment of percussion and the oboe-like serunai. *Dikir barat* is often staged in a competitive atmosphere, with two contingents trying to outshine each other in wit and sometimes taking verbal potshots at each other too.

The most common Malay folk **dance** is the **joget**, a lively affair danced by couples and thought to be derived from dance forms introduced by the Portuguese in Melaka. You may come across it if you're invited to a Malay function, and it also features at touristy dance shows, with audience participation encouraged – though should you get involved, don't take your partner by the hand. In *joget*, men and women alternately dance face-to-face or side-by-side, but they never touch.

If there is one must-see piece of Malay entertainment, it's **wayang kulit**, the name meaning "skin show", as it features puppets made of hide. The audience sees only their silhouettes on a screen, though these may be brightly coloured if the puppets are painted. Sadly, *wayang kulit* is banned in its heartland, Kelantan, but tourists have special privileges to view shows in the state capital, Kota Bharu; for more on the genre see p.279.

▲ Rebana drums

▼ Puppet-maker shows off his creations

Kampung house ▲

Men wearing the baju Melayu and samping ▼

Kampung houses

One of the most charming sights in rural areas are **kampung houses**. They are generally made of timber (though plaited bamboo strips may be used for the walls), and are shaded by coconut palms and raised on posts as protection against floods and wild animals. Roofs are made of traditional *atap* (palm thatch) or corrugated iron, and each region has its own distinctive style: curved, tiered roofs are typical on the east coast, while elsewhere you may see hipped roofs or, in Negeri Sembilan, even Minangkabau-style saddle-shaped affairs.

Malay carpenters excel at decorative woodcarving, and fancier houses may feature patterned fanlights, veranda railings with tracery and repeated fretwork motifs at the edges of roofs. Inside, the principal living space adjoins the bedrooms, which are concealed by screens or drapes. Houses were traditionally put together using an elaborate jointing system rather than nails, allowing a property to be dismantled and reassembled elsewhere. Unfortunately, the effects of the elements and termites mean that it's rare to find kampung houses over two hundred years old.

Traditional dress

You'll often come across Malays in traditional attire – the **baju Melayu** for men, and the **baju kurung** for women. Accessories for men include the **songkok**, a flattish oval cap of stiff card lined with black velvet, and the **samping**, a knee-length sarong, sometimes worn over trousers. The finest *sampings*, worn on special occasions, are made of *songket*, hand-woven brocade featuring beautiful geometrical patterns in gold thread. Women may wear a **tudung** (headscarf) or sometimes a **selendang** (shawl).

Tanjung Rhu and around

Returning to the main north coast road and continuing 10km east you reach the inaccessible **Pantai Pasir Hitam** ("Black Sand Beach"). Five kilometres east, the road intersects with the main north–south route across the island at the village of **Padang Lalang**. Turn left, and a couple of kilometres along is **TANJUNG RHU**, also known as "Casuarina Beach" because of the profusion of these pine-like trees here. The only developments here are the *Tanjung Rhu Resort* (⊕04/959 1033, ⓦwww.tanjungrhu.com.my; ❾), which is almost as luxurious as the *Four Seasons Resort Langkawi* (⊕04/950 8899, ⓦwww.fourseasons.com /langkawi; ❾) next door, a good place to go for a sunset cocktail, if you want to treat yourself. It's within walking distance of a beautiful public beach with boat hire shacks for day-trips as well as some food stalls. The sea here, sheltered by the curve of the bay, is unusually tranquil. The tide goes out far enough for you to walk out to the nearby islands of **PULAU PASIR** and **PULAU GASING**, perfect for a bit of secluded sunbathing. On a promontory accessible only by boat from Tanjung Rhu (RM100), you'll find the isolated **Gua Cerita** or "Cave of Tales", facing the Thai coastline. Despite the profusion of bat droppings, it's worth having a close look inside the cave, as you can make out ancient lettering on the walls – verses of the Koran.

South of Tanjung Rhu

Back at the crossroads at Padang Lalang, you can either head for the interior to **Gunung Raya** or continue east to the site of **Telaga Air Panas**. To reach the top of Gunung Raya (881m), the tallest mountain on the island, take the curvy road, which branches east after about 7km. As you climb higher through the jungle, the view on a clear day becomes ever more spectacular. The other option is to continue past the crossroads another 2km east to the site of Telaga Air Panas ("Hot Springs"), the result of another Langkawi legend: the area was reputedly formed during a quarrel between the island's two leading families over a rejected offer of marriage. Household items were flung about in the fight: the spot where gravy splashed from the pots became known as Kuah ("gravy"), and here, where the jugs of boiling water landed, hot springs spouted. There's not much to see and what there is has been subsumed within the **Air Hangat Village** (daily 9am–6pm; free; ⊕04/959 1357), which encompasses the hot springs and an arts pavilion, designed in traditional Malay kampung style; demonstrations of folk and classical dance, kick boxing and *silat* are put on here at various times of the day. There's also an expensive **restaurant** that puts on a cultural show every evening, inevitably catering to tour groups.

Further on is the turn-off for **Durian Perangin**, a waterfall reached along a difficult and rocky path, and fairly disappointing unless you happen to catch it during the wet season when the water level is high. Shortly after this, the road curves to the south for the remaining 10km to Kuah. Next along the road is the **Galeria Perdana** (daily 8.30am–5.30pm; RM10), which contains over ten thousand state gifts and awards presented to former PM Mahathir – an eclectic collection ranging from African woodcarvings to Japanese ceramics. Taking the north road up from here, you reach the **Kilim Geoforest jetty** (⊕04/959 4967; daily 9am–6pm; RM150 for a one-hour boat trip/RM250 for a three-hour trip; up to 8 people in a boat, so you can spread the cost by waiting for others to show up), one of Langkawi's newer attractions – a mangrove forest covering over 100 sq km. It is thanks to the mangroves that Langkawi escaped relatively unscathed by the tsunami of 2004, due to their massive root systems protecting against erosion. Tours will take you through the mangrove swamps using designated river paths, stopping at **Gua Kelawar**, or "Cave of Bats", where hundreds of bats rest during the day, only interrupted by gawping tourists, though no flash photography is allowed. Along with visiting a **floating fish farm**, there is also a stop for **eagle feeding**. Chicken skin and guts are dropped in the river to be picked up by fish eagles circling above. Whether these trips have an effect on the eagles' lives and upbringing of their young has yet to be seen.

Other Langkawi islands

Day-trips to some of the nearer islands to Pulau Langkawi are organized by various hotels at Pantai Tengah or Pantai Cenang and by a couple of local firms. These excursions are great if you're into diving, snorkelling and fishing, but otherwise provide little incentive to leave the main island. It's also possible to get to some islands independently, taking the island-hopping boat which visits – among others – Pulau Singa Besar and Pulau Dayang Bunting; it leaves from the Marble Beach jetty, two minutes' walk southeast of the Kuah jetty (daily 9am & 2.30pm; RM30–55); the tourist office in Kuah also has details of the current route and trips.

Pulau Dayang Bunting (literally, "Island of the Pregnant Maiden") is the second largest island in the archipelago, about fifteen minutes' boat ride from Marble Beach jetty. It's the exception to the rule in having at least a couple of specific points of interest, but you'll have to visit on a day-trip as there's nowhere to stay. A large and tranquil freshwater lake, **Tasik Dayang Bunting**, is believed to have magical properties making barren women fertile. Legend also has it that the lake is inhabited by a large white crocodile, but don't let that stop you from going for a swim in this lovely green lake surrounded by massive, densely forested limestone outcrops. The entire island is dotted with these, which are at their most dramatic around the **Gua Langsir** ("Cave of the Banshee"), a towering 91-metre-high cave on the island's west coast, which is said to be haunted – probably because of the sounds of the thousands of bats which live inside. The island-hopping boat drops you at a jetty near the lake before continuing to the cave, 8km to the north. Day-trips will also do a stop on **Pulau Singa Besar**, a wildlife sanctuary 3km off the southern tip of Pantai Tengah, good for snorkelling.

Mountainous **Pulau Tuba**, 5km south of Langkawi, is the only other island with accommodation – just the one option, the *Sunrise Beach Resort* (T04/966 9752, @putri51@hotmail.com; @), with its own swimming pool. There's barely enough space around the rim of the island for the dirt track which encircles it, though it does take in some deserted beaches. It's awkward to get to Tuba – a matter of hanging round the Marble Beach jetty until someone offers to take you across in one of the small speedboats, so best to call the resort and ask for advice when you pre-book.

Pulau Payar Marine Park has great schools of tropical fish, including black-finned sharks. South of the island, 13km west of the Peninsula, lies a coral garden supporting the largest number of coral species in the country. A few companies organize day-trips to the marine park, including Langkawi Coral, which has an office at Kuah ferry terminal (T04/966 7318, @www .langkawicoral.com). Prices range around RM240 and usually include hotel pick-ups, lunch and all snorkelling equipment, although it's worth shopping around (there are also operators in Pantai Cenang) as some smaller outfits charge less for the same trip.

North to the Thai border

The tiny state of **Perlis** – at 800 square km, the smallest in Malaysia – lies at the northwestern tip of the Peninsula, bordering Thailand. Together with neighbouring Kedah, it's traditionally been viewed as the country's agricultural heartland, something reflected in the landscape which is dominated by lustrous, bright-green paddy fields. The only real reason to stop here is to visit the **Perlis State Park**, a good place for caving as well as several designated jungle treks.

Kangar, Arau and Kaki Bukit

KANGAR, the state capital of Perlis, is an unremarkable modern town. The central **bus station** is where you change buses for the **Thai border** (see box, p.220) or to **Kuala Perlis** in order to take the ferry to Langkawi. The nearest **train station** is 10km to the east at **ARAU**, the least interesting of all Malaysia's royal towns – its Royal Palace (closed to the public) on the main road looks like little more than a comfortable mansion. The town is only really handy for the daily morning train making the two-hour journey to Hat Yai, Thailand or the International Express from Butterworth to Bangkok, a journey of nineteen hours (check the latest train schedule: ⓦ www.ktmb.com .my). A morning southbound train departs from Arau for the two-and-a-half hour journey to Butterworth; another southbound train departs from Arau in the evening and terminates in Kuala Lumpur the following morning (again, check the latest timetable).

Perlis State Park and Gua Kelam
Kaki Bukit

Bordering Thailand is the large **Perlis State Park**, home to the stump-tail macaque and the white-handed gibbon, black panthers, rich birdlife and at least 85 caves, along with several trails for trekking. You will need to obtain a permit before entering the park, which is easily done from the park office and most treks or caving trips require hiring a guide. It's possible to climb to the highest peak (533m above sea level) in the park in one day (3hr journey up, 2hr down), worth the trip for the magnificent views.

You can visit **Gua Kelam Kaki Bukit** (literally, "a cave of darkness at the foot of a hill") without a permit, a 370 metre long limestone cave that was once part of a working tin mine. The stream that runs through the cavern was formerly used to carry away excavated tin ore to the processing plant near the cave's entrance. Access through the cave is by way of a suspended wooden walkway, also used by locals – and their motorbikes – as a means of getting to the other side of the valley, though for visitors the walkway's attraction is that it allows them to look down into the former mine. The cave is 1km north of **Kaki Bukit**, a small town on the Thai border. There is a daily market close to the park entrance and border with hawker stalls, which gets custom from both Malays and Thais, the latter being allowed to cross the border for a few hours to shop.

To reach the park, from the North–South Expressway, head toward Kangar, using Route 7 and continue towards Padang Besar. Take the turning toward Kaki Bukit, where the sign says "Gua Kelam 8.5 km" and head towards Kaki Bukit from where you turn right onto Route R15 until you reach the Kampung Wang Kelian. Take a right turn and proceed for 3km to the *Perlis*

State Park Visitor Centre (℡04/977 7578: ❹–❺) on your right, where chalets, dorms and camping can be booked. The excellent chalets are set by a small stream just inside the forest. There are no cooking facilities in the chalets, apart from a kettle, so you will either need to bring provisions or organise pre-planned food with the visitor centre. You can also reach Kaki Bukit by a local bus from Kangar, 41km away, which has daily connections to Ipoh, Kuala Lumpur and Melaka.

Kuala Perlis

Though it's the second largest settlement in the state, the little town of **KUALA PERLIS**, 45km north of Alor Star, has only two streets. There's no real reason to come here other than to catch the ferry to Langkawi or Satun in Thailand; buses drop you at an unmarked stand adjacent to the jetty, from where a wooden footbridge connects with the older, more interesting part of town, a ramshackle collection of buildings on stilts. Though you can reserve tickets at the Kuala Perlis–Langkawi Ferry Service's jetty office (℡04/985 4494), it's just as easy to turn up and board, with departures on the hour (7am–7pm), plus 9.30am, 3.30pm and 5.30pm (1hr; RM12).

There are two **banks** in the main part of town, near the jetty. The town also has a couple of **hotels** in case you decide to stay. Close to the jetty is the *Kuala Perlis Seaview Hotel* (℡04/985 2171; ❺), with spacious and clean rooms (but no sea view). In the budget category, it's best to avoid the grimy options across from the ferry terminal and walk about a kilometre down the main road to the outskirts of town; opposite the mosque is a right turn from where the *Asia Hotel*, 18 Taman Sentosa (℡04/985 5392; ❷), is signposted. It has a better-than-average Chinese **restaurant** downstairs.

You can reach Satun in **Thailand** directly from Kuala Perlis: small boats from Langkawi stop here en route, leaving from the jetty four times a day (45min; RM30). There are also connections to Phuket, Koh Lanta and Koh Phi Phi, though these are combined boat and bus tickets, so can also be done independently.

Crossing the Malaysia/Thailand border

There are two border crossings, both open from 6am to 10pm, one on the train line at the village of **Padang Besar** and another, 20km southeast on Route 1, at **Bukit Kayu Hitam**. Make sure that your passport is stamped by the border police upon entry in either direction, or you can be fined for entering illegally when you leave the country.

There are regular **bus** connections from both border crossings to **Hat Yai**, southern Thailand's transport hub, 60km away. If travelling by bus or taxi via Padang Besar, you'll have to get off before the border and cross the 2km of no-man's land on foot or get a taxi (RM30–50 each way). Taking a direct bus to Hat Yai is the easiest option.

The **train** comes to a halt at the border crossing of **Padang Besar**, where a very long platform connects the Malaysian service with its Thai counterpart. You don't change trains here, although you must get off and go through customs at the station. There are only two northbound trains a day, one terminating in Hat Yai and the other via Hat Yai to Bangkok. Due to heightened security on this line, the railway timetable is often at odds with actual arrival and departure times. If you plan on getting on a north- or south-bound train at Padang Besar, it's best to check the timetable posted at the station for the latest estimated arrival and departure times.

Travel details

Trains

Alor Star to: Arau (daily; 45min); Bangkok (Thailand; daily; 20hr); Butterworth (daily; 2hr 45min); Hat Yai (Thailand; daily; 2hr 20min); Ipoh (daily; 8hr); Kuala Kangsar (daily; 6hr); Kuala Lumpur (daily; 12hr); Sungai Petani (daily; 1hr); Taiping (daily; 5hr 20min); Tapah Road (daily; 9hr).

Butterworth to: Alor Star (daily; 2hr 45min); Bangkok (Thailand; daily; 22hr); Hat Yai (Thailand; daily – note that ferries from George-town to Butterworth start at 4.45am; 4hr 45min); Ipoh (2 daily; 5hr); Kuala Kangsar (daily; 4hr); Kuala Lumpur (3 daily; 9hr); Sungai Petani (daily; 1hr); Taiping (daily; 3hr 15min); Tapah Road (daily; 6hr 45min).

Ipoh to: Alor Star (daily; 7hr 20min); Butterworth (2 daily; 5hr); Kuala Kangsar (daily; 2hr); Kuala Lumpur (3 daily; 3hr 30min); Sungai Petani (daily; 6hr 15min); Taiping (2 daily; 2hr); Tapah Road (5 daily; 1hr 30min).

Kuala Kangsar to: Alor Star (daily; 6hr); Butter-worth (daily; 4hr); Ipoh (2 daily; 2hr); Kuala Lumpur (3 daily; 6hr); Sungai Petani (daily; 5hr); Taiping (2 daily; 1hr); Tapah Road (2 daily; 3hr).

Taiping to: Alor Star (daily; 5hr 20min); Butter-worth (2 daily; 3hr 15min); Ipoh (2 daily; 2hr); Kuala Kangsar (2 daily; 1hr); Kuala Lumpur (3 daily; 7hr); Sungai Petani (daily; 4hr 20min); Tapah Road (2 daily; 4hr).

Tapah to: Alor Star (daily; 9hr); Butterworth (2 daily; 6hr 45min); Ipoh (5 daily; 1hr 30min); Kuala Kangsar (2 daily; 3hr); Kuala Lumpur (5 daily; 4hr); Sungai Petani (daily; 8hr); Taiping (2 daily; 4hr).

Buses

Alor Star to: Butterworth (every 30min; 2hr); Ipoh (4 daily; 4hr); Johor Bahru (3 daily; 12hr); Kangar (hourly; 1hr 15min); Kota Bahru (2 daily; 8hr); Kuala Kedah (every 15min; 15min); Kuala Lumpur (every 30min; 8hr); Kuala Terengganu (2 daily; 9hr); Kuantan (2 daily; 9hr); Melaka (2 daily; 9hr); Seremban (3 daily; 7hr); Singapore (3 daily; 13hr); Sungai Petani (every 30min; 1hr 15min).

Butterworth to: Alor Star (every 30min; 1hr 30min); Cameron Highlands (3 daily; 4hr); Hat Yai (Thailand; 4 daily; 3hr); Ipoh (9 daily; 2hr 30min); Johor Bahru (10 daily; 10hr); Kangar (hourly; 2hr 15min); Kota Bharu (3 daily; 6hr); Kuala Kangsar (2 daily; 2hr 45min); Kuala Lumpur (hourly 8am–12.30am; 5hr);

Kuala Terengganu (1 daily; 8hr); Kuantan (2 daily; 9hr); Lumut (7 daily; 3hr); Melaka (2 daily; 8hr); Seremban (9 daily; 6hr); Singapore (at least 2 daily; 10hr); Sungai Petani (every 45min; 40min); Taiping (hourly; 2hr 15min).

Cameron Highlands to: Butterworth (5 daily; 4hr); Ipoh (4 daily; 2hr); Kuala Lumpur (9 daily; 4hr); Melaka (1 daily; 5hr 30min); Singapore (1 daily; 10hr).

Ipoh to: Alor Star (4 daily; 4hr); Butterworth (3 daily; 3hr); Cameron Highlands (4 daily; 2hr); Johor Bahru (2 daily; 7hr 30min); Kangar (3 daily; 4hr); KLIA and LCCT Airports (6 daily; 3hr); Kota Bahru (2 daily; 8hr); Kuala Kangsar (every 45min; 1hr); Kuala Lumpur (hourly; 3hr 30min); Kuala Perlis (1 daily; 5hr); Kuala Terengganu (2 daily; 11hr); Kuantan (1 daily; 8hr); Lumut (8 daily; 2hr); Melaka (1 daily; 6hr); Penang (hourly; 2hr 30min); Seremban (2 daily; 5hr); Singapore (4 daily; 9hr).

Kangar to: Alor Star (7 daily; 1hr 15min); Butter-worth (10 daily; 2hr 30min); Ipoh (6 daily; 6hr); Kota Bahru (2 daily; 8hr); Kuala Lumpur (6 daily; 8hr); Kuala Perlis (every 45min; 30min); Melaka (2 daily; 9hr); Seremban (2 daily; 8hr).

Lumut to: Butterworth (6 daily; 3hr); Ipoh (hourly; 1hr 45min); Johor Bahru (3 daily; 8hr 30min); Kota Bharu (daily; 7hr 30 min); Kuala Kangsar (2 daily; 1hr 30min); Kuala Lumpur (hourly; 4hr); Taiping (4 daily; 1hr 10min); Singapore (daily; 10hr).

Tapah to: Butterworth (4 daily; 3hr 30min); Ipoh (8 daily; 1hr); Kuala Lumpur (hourly; 2hr); Kuala Terengganu (daily; 6hr); Kuantan (2 daily; 6hr); Lumut (daily; 2hr); Melaka (daily; 5hr 30min); Singapore (daily; 10hr).

Ferries

Butterworth to: Georgetown (every 20min–1hr, 6am–12.30am; 20min).

Georgetown to: Butterworth (every 20min–1hr, 5.45am–12.30am; 20min); Langkawi (2 daily; 2hr 30min); Medan (Indonesia; daily; 4hr).

Kuala Kedah to: Langkawi (20 daily, 7am–7pm; 1hr 45min).

Kuala Perlis to: Langkawi (16 daily, 7am–7pm; 1hr 15min); Satun (Thailand; 3 daily; 30min).

Langkawi to: Kuala Kedah (20 daily, 7am–7pm; 1hr 45min); Kuala Perlis (16 daily, 7am–7pm; 1hr); Penang (2 daily; 2hr 30min).

Lumut to: Pangkor (every 30min, 7am–8.30pm; 45min).

Flights

Alor Star to: Kuala Lumpur (3 daily; 1hr).
Georgetown to: Johor Bahru (2 daily; 1hr);
Kota Bharu (daily; 1hr); Kota Kinabalu (daily; 2hr);
Kuala Lumpur (at least 13 daily; 45min); Kuala

Terengganu (daily; 1hr 15min); Kuching (daily; 2hr);
Langkawi (2 daily; 45min); Singapore (at least 4
daily; 1hr 25min).
Langkawi to: Kuala Lumpur (at least 10 daily;
1hr); Penang (2 daily; 45min); Singapore (daily;
1hr 30min).

3

The interior

CHAPTER 3

Highlights

✳ **Taman Negara via Kuala Tahan** The Peninsula's largest and oldest nature reserve offers river trips, hikes and wildlife-spotting amid a vast tract of ancient rainforest, best visited via the park headquarters at Kuala Tahan. See p.234

✳ **Taman Negara via Kuala Koh** Though difficult to reach, Kuala Koh is worth the effort: this is Kuala Tahan in miniature, rewarding visitors with trails, river excursions and a canopy walkway. See p.249

✳ **Fraser's Hill** This relaxing hill station makes for a great overnight break, with short nature trails to tackle and varied birdlife. See p.252

✳ **Kenong Rimba** A little-developed reserve adjoining Taman Negara, offering its own trekking and wildlife-spotting opportunities. See p.260

✳ **Stong State Park** In the interior of Kelantan State, Stong boasts a picturesque waterfall, good trekking up a mountainside and a marvellous jungle camp. See p.265

▲ Cruising down the river at Kuala Koh, Taman Negara

The interior

The peaks of the **Banjaran Titiwangsa**, the Peninsula's spine, form the western boundary of the **interior**; to their east is an H-shaped range of steep, sandstone peaks with knife-edge ridges and luxuriant valleys where small towns and kampungs nestle. The rivers which flow from these mountains – the Pahang, Tembeling, Lebir and Nenggiri, among many others – once provided the northern interior's indigenous peoples, the Negritos and Senoi, with their main means of transport. Visitors, too, can travel by river, to reach **Taman Negara**, the country's first national park, straddling the borders of Pahang, Kelantan and Terengganu states. Other worthwhile stops include **Kuala Lipis**, the former capital of Pahang; the **Kenong Rimba** and **Stong** state parks; and the hill station of **Fraser's Hill**, 75km north of Kuala Lumpur, which affords good **birdwatching** and relaxing walks in temperatures a pleasant 5°C or so cooler than in the lowlands.

Route 8 is the interior's main artery, running from Bentong near KL northeast to Kota Bharu. Taking around eight hours to drive in its entirety, it's not the wide conduit that the more recent highways are, so expect to be periodically slowed behind ponderous lorries. The quickest way to reach Route 8 from KL is the **E8** (the **Karak Highway**), a multilane rollercoaster of a road that careers through the foothills of the Genting Highlands to link with Route 8 just south of Bentong. Expect a few thrilling, cambered descents on this road – and be warned that there are often nasty accidents on it, too. The E8 also connects onto the **East Coast Highway** running east across the interior to Kuantan. Another new road slices across the northern part of the interior, from just north of Gua Musang west to the Cameron Highlands and Ipoh, and, eventually, east to Kuala Berang near Tasik Kenyir. Bus services along these routes are reasonably efficient, but unless you're in a real hurry to get from one coast to the other, consider a trip on the **jungle railway** (see box, p.227), serving most of the interior's attractions except Fraser's Hill.

Some history

The interior comprises much of Pahang and Kelantan, which were the last regions of Peninsular Malaysia to excite the interest of the British colonial authorities. Until the 1880s the Bendahara (Prince) of Pahang, Wan Ahmed, ran his state as a private fiefdom, unvisited by outsiders except for a hundred or so Chinese and European gold prospectors who had established contacts with some remote Malay villages and Orang Asli settlements. When explorer and colonial administrator **Sir Hugh Clifford** visited, he noted that the region "did not boast a mile of road and…was smothered in deep, damp forest, threaded across a network of streams and rivers…flecked here and there by little splashes

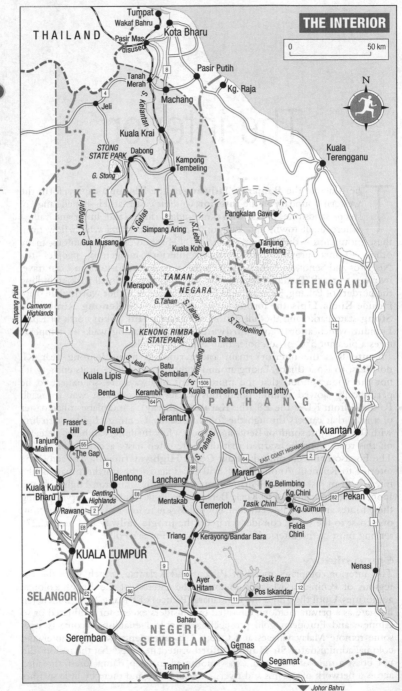

THE INTERIOR

0   50 km

N

THAILAND

Tumpat
Wakaf Bharu
Pasir Mas disused   Kota Bharu

Pasir Putih

Tanah Merah   Kg. Raja
Jeli   Machang

Kuala Krai   Kuala Terengganu

STONG STATE PARK   Dabong
G. Stong   Kampong Tembeling

K E L A N T A N

S. Nenggiri   S. Galas   Pangkalan Gawi
S. Lebir
Simpang Aring
Gua Musang   Kuala Koh   Tanjung Mentong

TAMAN NEGARA   TERENGGANU

Merapoh
G. Tahan   S. Tahan

KENONG RIMBA STATE PARK   S. Tembeling
Kuala Tahan
S. Jelai   Batu Sembilan   S. Tembeling
Kuala Lipis
Benta   Kerambit   Kuala Tembeling (Tembeling jetty)
P A H A N G
Jerantut
Fraser's Hill   Raub   S. Pahang   Kuantan
Tanjung Malim
The Gap   EAST COAST HIGHWAY
Kuala Kubu Bharu   Bentong   Lanchang   Maran
Genting Highlands   Kg.Belimbing   Kg.Chini   Pekan
Rawang   Mentakab   Temerloh   Tasik Chini   Kg.Gumum
Triang   Kerayong/Bandar Bara   Felda Chini

KUALA LUMPUR

Ayer Hitam   Tasik Bera   Nenasi
Pos Iskandar
SELANGOR

Bahau
NEGERI SEMBILAN
Seremban   Gemas   Segamat
Tampin

Johor Bahru

of sunlight." What Clifford also noted – and indeed the reason for his visit – was that Pahang was "wonderfully rich in minerals". Wan Ahmed gave the British mining and planting rights, in exchange for military protection against the incursions of the Siamese and Kelantanese.

First to arrive were British officials, followed by tin and gold prospectors, then investors in rubber and other plantation enterprises. The new arrivals initially

The jungle railway

It took indentured Tamil labourers eight years to achieve the remarkable feat of building the five-hundred-kilometre jungle railway from **Gemas**, southeast of KL, to **Tumpat** on the northeast coast. The first section from Gemas to Kuala Lipis opened in 1920, with the full extent of the line following in 1931. Initially it was used exclusively for freight – for tin and rubber, and later oil palm – before a passenger service, originally known as the "Golden Blowpipe", opened in 1938. Today the route is served by trains from both **KL** and **Singapore**.

By dint of its very existence, the line doesn't pass through virgin jungle; instead much of the route is flanked by *belukar*-type woodland, and the line often dips through cuttings below ferny embankments, or skirts the backs of kampung gardens, within eyeshot of bougainvillea and fruiting rambutan and mango trees. None of this is to detract from the fact that as a way of encountering **rural life**, a ride on the jungle train can't be beaten, giving you the chance to take in backwater scenery in the company of cheroot-smoking old men in sarongs, and fast-talking women hauling kids, poultry and vegetables to and from the nearest market.

For the unadulterated jungle railway experience, you need to be on one of the slow **local trains** (usually denoted "Mel" in timetables), which call at just about every obscure hamlet on the route, some with Orang Asli names. Their much more efficient express counterparts have relatively modern, charmless rolling stock, and their air-conditioning insulates you from the onrushing countryside; moreover, the schedules mean that they tend to do their run through the interior by night. The most atmospheric of the local services are those running in **Kelantan**, between Gua Musang and Tumpat on the coast. So dilapidated are these trains, with broken seats, non-functioning fans and fused lights (you may be plunged into pitch darkness on the several occasions when the train enters a tunnel), that it feels as though they must date from the colonial era. In fact, they were acquired in the 1980s, and should finally be replaced in the next few years, so ride them while they're still around; you'll be too absorbed in the whole experience to notice minor discomforts. The local service between Gemas and Gua Musang or Tumpat uses rather better-maintained rolling stock of about the same vintage, and takes you through the best stretch for actual **jungle vistas**, in Pahang south of Gua Musang, where hill after hill is blanketed in rainforest. Wherever you are, don't be tempted to rest your elbow on the window rim or, worse, stick your head out for a better look – lineside shrubbery packs a sharp punch when brushed past at speed. The open windows on some trains act in effect as mobile hedge trimmers, slicing away twigs and leaves, which end up all over the carriages.

Timetables are to be taken with a pinch of salt, as delays on the line aren't uncommon, and it's not unknown for trains to show up early either; even if you've bought tickets in advance (not usually necessary except for express services), be at the station fifteen minutes ahead of the scheduled departure. Occasionally you may find that the time on the ticket doesn't match the timetable, in which case ask station staff for clarification. Even if everything appears to be going to schedule, note that there's only one set of tracks on long stretches of the route: delays elsewhere may mean your train being held at a siding or even reversing for an extended period to let an oncoming train pass.

used the rivers to get around, though the larger companies soon began to clear tracks – the forerunners of the area's roads – into the valleys and along the mountain ridges, and development was made easier again when the railway opened in the 1920s. Slowly, small towns like **Temerloh**, **Raub** and **Kuala Lipis** grew in size and importance, while new settlements like Gua Musang were established to cater for the influx of Chinese merchants and workers.

Since the 1980s, when the **Route 8 highway** into the interior was completed, much of the region has been transformed, and the primeval landscape tamed to a large extent, providing economic incentives for people from both coasts to move into these areas. The spread of the timber, rubber and palm-oil industries has had a huge impact, in particular upon the **Orang Asli**. Since the Emergency, when many Orang Asli were forcibly resettled into villages (see p.697), their lifestyle has been gradually diluted. Back in the 1970s an expert on the Orang Asli, Iskandar Carey, wrote: "there are groups of Senoi [one of the three main Orang Asli peoples] in the deep jungle who have never seen a road, although they are familiar with helicopters, a word for which has been incorporated into their language." These days many indigenous people have made their way into the cash economy and the fringes, at least, of mainstream society, a transition steered in large part by the government's Department of Orang Asli Affairs. However, three-quarters of the Orang Asli remain below the poverty line (compared to less than a tenth of the population as a whole), a fact which makes it all the harder for them to confront the many forces – from planning agencies to Christian and Muslim groups – seeking to influence their destiny. The issue of **land rights** is among the gravest of their problems, for while the country's Aboriginal People's Act has led to the creation of Orang Asli reserves, at the same time many Asli traditional areas have been gazetted as state land, rendering the inhabitants there, at best, tolerated guests of the government.

Taman Negara

Two hundred and fifty kilometres northeast of KL is Peninsular Malaysia's largest and most important protected area, **TAMAN NEGARA** (literally "national park"; headquarters; ⊕09/266 1122). Spread over 4343 square kilometres, the park comprises dense lowland forest, higher altitude cloudforest (enveloping the Peninsula's highest peak, **Gunung Tahan**), numerous hills, Orang Asli settlements, hides, campsites and an upmarket jungle retreat. From the streams that snake down from the mountains and feed fierce waterfalls, to the lush flora and fauna, the park experience (as the tourist brochures never tire of telling you) is second to none.

Every trek into the forest has its fascinations. If you've never been inside tropical rainforest before, just listening to the bird, insect and animal sounds, marvelling at the sheer size of dipterocarp trees and peering into the forest canopy is a memorable experience. There are a myriad of entrancing sights: flowering lianas, giant bamboo stands with fungi which glow in the dark and chattering macaque monkeys rattling across the treetops. If you're not a hardcore wildlife spotter (see box, p.235), you can take advantage of opportunities for a

TAMAN NEGARA

Dungun ▲

0   10 km

S. Dungun

Kuala Berang ◄

760m ▲

580m ▲

742m ▲

G. Padang
(1320m) ▲

G. Gajah Terum
(1557m) ▲

G. Mandi Angin
(G. Chelah) (1480m) ▲

Tanjung
Mentong ⊠

Tasik Kenyir

S. Pertang

G. Bewek
(947m) ▲

G. Gagu
(1376m) ▲

G. Belalai
(854m) ▲

J. Aur

Kuala
Chamir

Kuala
Klapor

S. Tembeling

S. Melimau

G. Penumpu
(1096m) ▲

Kepayang
Besar ◉
Perkai Lodge

Kuala Keniam

G. Dulang
(1063m) ▲

Kuala Lanchang ◄

Kg. Lanchang

S. Lebir

Kuala
Koh

S. Koh

G. Kemara G. Perlis
(1279m) ▲

S. Keniam

Padang   S. Keniam

Kuala Trenggan

▲ Abai Waterfall

G. Warisan ⚶

Nusa Holiday
Village

Park HQ

Kuala
Tahan

Sungei Tiang Airstrip

S. Tekai

S. Aring

Kota Bharu ◄

S. Relai

Kg. Geno

S. Chihu

Four Steps
Waterfall ⚶

S. Trenggan

Kuala
Teku

Puteh
Camp

S. Tahan

S. Tahan Trail

Lata
Berkoh

Gua Telinga

Kuala Atok

1508 ▶

64 ▶

G. Timan
(215m) ▲

G. Gedong
(205m) ▲

G. Lubi

G. Kechau (946m) ▲

Wray's Camp

Gua
Timpat

Melantai Camp

S. Tenor

Bukit Guling
Gendang (570m) ▲

Simpang Aring ◄

G. Rabong
Sinting (1539m) ▲

Bukit Peningat ▲

Gua Siput

Batu
Lompat

S. Tenor

773m ▲

S. Atok

TENTS TEMOR TRAIL

Tembeling Jetty ▶

Kota Bharu ◄

Kg.
Toh

Bukit Tujoh
(867m) ▲

S. Kechau

KENONG RIMBA

S. Kesong
(580m) ▲

S. Jelai

Jerantut ▶

Gua Musang ◄

Merapoh ⊠

S. Tanum

Kuala Lipis

Padang Tengku ▶

N

Dabong ◄

Cameron Highlands ▲

river swim or even angling. On the other hand, if you're simply keen to glimpse something of primary rainforest, it's much easier to give Taman Negara a miss and instead make for FRIM on the outskirts of KL (see p.134), or the Bukit Timah Nature Reserve in Singapore (see p.644).

Planning a visit

The **best time** to visit the park is between February and mid-October when the weather is less likely to be wet, though note that from May to August is the park's busiest period. During this time it makes sense to book ahead, particularly for budget accommodation; at other times, discounted rates are often available. Between mid-November and mid-January in particular, a visit may well turn into a rather sodden experience – not just on the trails either, as the cheaper chalet accommodation can be leak-prone – and for your pains you may discover that movement within the park is restricted by the conditions.

Most of the park's trails don't require anything beyond an average level of fitness. Unless you're undertaking extended treks, you won't need special **gear**: T-shirts, long trousers and sturdy sports shoes are adequate (though think seriously about hiking boots, which cope much better with muddy conditions). Though you'll be screened by the forest canopy much of the time, do have a sun hat and water to hand. It's a good idea to take **binoculars** to get the best possible look at birds from the jungle floor, while a **magnifying glass** can open up a whole new world of insects and leaf and bark formations. More mundanely, you'll need mosquito **repellent** and a good **torch**.

To **budget** for your trip, a useful rule of thumb is that for any trek involving overnighting in the forest (other than in a hide close to a park office or accessible by boat), you're likely to want to hire a guide. The charge for this may seem steep, and the cost of boat excursions can also mount up (see box, p.239), but these are the only substantial outlays that you'll face, as inexpensive accommodation, eating and transport options are generally easy to find. Many visitors never do any serious trekking and stay for just two or three nights, enough to get a reasonable flavour of the park.

Access to the park

Though there are four entry points to Taman Negara, only one figures in the schemes of the vast majority of visitors – **Kuala Tahan** – the location of the **park headquarters** (most of the coverage here is dedicated to this entry point). Tourist facilities spill across from here to the opposite bank of the Tembeling River, where the once-sleepy Kuala Tahan **village** positively brims with chalet developments. If you want a relatively solitary, at-one-with-nature experience, you may well not take to Kuala Tahan, but it does have convenience as its trump card: it boasts reasonable transport connections, simple shops and restaurants, and even cell-phone coverage, though **no banks** or ATMs.

The other three park entrances, covered at the end of this account on pp.248–251, are awkward to get to and have limited facilities – which means that if you put in the extra preparation needed to take advantage of any of them, you may well find you have the park largely to yourself. Whichever entrance you use, upon arrival you will need to pay the nominal park **fees**, tabled on p.239, at the local office of the Wildlife Department.

Tourist transfers to the park headquarters are available from KL and elsewhere (see box, p.233), but if you want to reach Kuala Tahan by **public transport**, you'll almost certainly pass through **Jerantut**, just over 50km from Kuala Tahan. **Kuala Lipis** (see p.256) is also a potential jumping-off point for the park, and it has some surviving colonial architecture to help while away any spare time you may have.

Jerantut

Hemmed in by ridges to the west and south, busy **JERANTUT** used to be busier not so long ago, when the town centre sat right on the Raub–Maran road. These days a modern bypass just to the south takes most of the through traffic. Furthermore, with the completion of Route 1508 to Kuala Tahan, Jerantut's status as gateway to Taman Negara is somewhat diminished. An accommodation shakeout has ensued, though the town remains a very reasonable place to overnight.

The town is served by **express trains** from KL, Singapore and Kota Bharu (unfortunately, most of these arrive in the small hours). You can also get there by **bus**: from KL, SE Express (℡03/4043 4690) operates to Jerantut from the Pekeliling bus station (daily at 8.45am, 10.45am, 2.45pm & 4pm; RM15), and there are both express and local buses to Jerantut from Kuantan.

The part of the centre of interest to visitors is shaped like an inverted L, which has the **train station** and **bus station** at its northern end, and which is lined by most of the town's amenities, including a couple of **banks** at the eastern end of Jalan Tahan. An unofficial though helpful **information** kiosk (really an agency providing tours and so forth) is just a little way west of the bus station and the Aktif **supermarket**, one of the best places to stock up on supplies for the park. Close by, signed near the *Sri Kim Yen* hotel, is Green Park Adventure (℡09/266 1503, http://my-greenpark.blogspot.com), an excellent **tour operator** offering not just Taman Negara packages but also trips further afield to sites such as Kenong Rimba (see p.260), Kuala Gandah, the Taman Negara Kuala Koh entrance (see p.249) and the Stong State Park (see p.265). The best of a couple of **internet** places in town, AZM, is close to the train station.

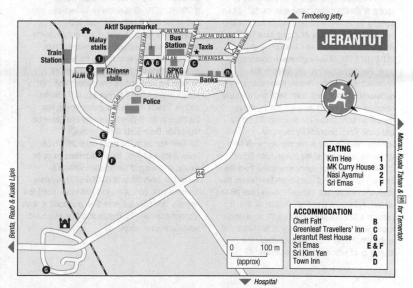

The Kuala Gandah elephant sanctuary

The southern part of the interior has one attraction worth making a diversion for, the **Kuala Gandah National Elephant Conservation Centre** (daily roughly 9am–1pm & 2–5pm except Fri closed from 12.30–2.45pm; donations appreciated; ☏09/279 0391), run by the Wildlife Department. Here they care for elephants being relocated to reserves from areas of habitat destruction, or which had to be subdued while *mengamuk* – a Malay term that would be untranslatable were it not the source of the English word "amok". The best time to turn up is 2pm (2.45pm on Fri), when for a couple of hours visitors have the chance to get hands-on with the elephants, riding, feeding or even bathing with them (bring a change of clothes).

Driving the East Coast Highway, turn north at Lanchang, 70km northeast of KL, for the twenty-minute drive to the sanctuary. Without your own transport, you can arrange a trip **from Jerantut** with the Green Park Adventure agency there (see p.231), which charges around RM160 per person for a group of four, including lunch and transfers, making it easy to visit the sanctuary before or after a trip to Taman Negara. It's also possible to do an organized day-trip from KL; contact the travel agent at MTC (see p.133), which charges RM190 per person, or ask around at backpacker guesthouses.

The bus station has a little kiosk advertising bus tickets for Kuala Tahan, but in fact you pay the driver on board. Next door, shared taxis run not only to surrounding towns but also quite a few east–coast destinations, though expect to pay at least RM200 to Kuantan, much more if you want to head all the way to Kota Bharu. Tickets for boats run by **SPKG** from Tembeling jetty to Kuala Tahan (and on to their *Nusa Holiday Village* accommodation further upriver) can be bought from their office at 16 Jalan Diwangsa (☏09/266 2369, ✉spkg@tm.net.my).

Accommodation

Chett Fatt Jalan Diwangsa ☏09/266 5805. A choice of double rooms, some with a/c but not en suite, or larger rooms (sleeping up to four), some with attached bathroom. All rooms have TV. ❶

Greenleaf Travellers' Inn Jalan Diwangsa ☏09/267 2131, ✇www.greenleaf-tamannegara .com. Perhaps unsurprisingly, green is the dominant colour at this homely if unexciting backpackers' place, with dorm beds and a variety of rooms. Some rooms have a/c and TV, though none is en suite. Unlike the *Sri Emas*, it's pretty laid-back. Dorm beds RM10, rooms ❶.

Jerantut Rest House A few minutes' walk from the centre, just south of the end of Jalan Besar ☏09/266 3619. Once serenely removed from the centre, this complex of colonial-era bungalows now abuts the new bypass, and renovations have diluted whatever character it had left. Despite all this, it remains a pleasant place to stay, with en-suite a/c rooms with TV and a large lounge in lurid pink and white. When busy, it can feel appealingly like staying in an extended Malay household. ❸

Sri Emas In two locations on Jalan Besar ☏09/260 1770, ✇www.taman-negara-nks.com. Part of the NKS Travel juggernaut, with backpackers being shipped in and out every day as though on a conveyor belt. Besides dorms, there's a wide variety of rooms, for two to four people, with fan or a/c, and with or without en-suite facilities and TV. Everything's well run; there's also a laundry service and fast internet access. Tickets are sold for their morning bus transfers to the Perhentian islands and Cameron Highlands. Dorm beds RM8, rooms ❶.

Sri Kim Yen Jalan Diwangsa ☏09/266 2168. Reasonably well-kept, simply furnished en-suite rooms, with a/c and TV. Excellent value. ❷

Town Inn Jalan Tahan ☏09/266 6811, ✇www .towninn-hotel.com. A friendly mid-range hotel, the rooms a little boxy but more than presentable, with a/c, bathroom and TV. There's also free wired and wireless internet access. ❸

Eating

The most obvious – and justifiably popular – place to eat in Jerantut is the large open-air **food court** east of the train station. Largely Malay-run, the stalls do an unusually good range of rice and noodle dishes. A smattering of Chinese stalls and restaurants can be found close to the station; among these is the *Kim Hee kedai kopi*, which does tasty dim sum for breakfast, and the daytime-only *Nasi Ayamui* which, as the name suggests, specializes in chicken rice. South along Jalan Besar, the *MK Curry House* serves good *murtabak*, decent curries and mediocre *biriyani*, while the more southerly of the two Sri Emas premises has a large open-air café serving Western and local fare, and is open till late.

Travel to Kuala Tahan

There's only one road to Kuala Tahan, **Route 1508**, branching north off Route 64 10km east of Jerantut. **Driving** from KL, leave the East Coast Highway at Temerloh, heading up Route 98 for Jerantut, then pick up Route 64 eastwards for the Kuala Tahan road. Starting from Kuantan, pick up Route 64 at Maran.

Jerantut is the only town with direct links to Kuala Tahan – a very convenient local **bus** departs for the village at 5.30am, 8am, 1.30pm & 5.15pm (RM6; 1hr 30min), as well as **shared taxis** (RM75).

Much more alluring than reaching the park by road is **boating** up to Kuala Tahan on the muddy **Tembeling River**, taking in the age-old rainforest swathing both banks. For most visitors the ride, in motorized ten-seater sampans, is an essential part of the Taman Negara experience, though not necessarily

---

Tourist transfers and packages

Though the bus from Jerantut to Kuala Tahan makes reaching Taman Negara straightforward, many visitors prefer to book themselves a tourist transfer or package trip, with KL the most popular starting point. From the **Bukit Bintang** area, there is a bus to the Tembeling jetty leaving from the *Crowne Plaza Mutiara Hotel* on Jalan Sultan Ismail (departures every morning at around 8.30am; RM60–70 one way); tickets can be bought from the travel agent based at the MTC tourist office in KL (℡03/2163 0162). There are also buses daily at 8am from the *Radius* hotel on Changkat Bukit Bintang, operated by **Han Travel** (℡03/2031 0899, ⓦwww.taman-negara.com; RM40). The same firm operates buses at 8.30am from its offices at Kompleks Selangor on Jalan Sultan in **Chinatown**, from where the rival **NKS Travel** (℡03/2072 0336, ⓦwww.taman-negara-nks.com) operates its own jetty buses from the *Mandarin Pacific Hotel* (daily 8.30am; RM40). Han Travel also runs transfers from Kuala Besut (the departure point for the Perhentian islands) and from the Cameron Highlands to Jerantut (RM60), while NKS does the same routes but will take you the park itself (RM90).

All these companies also offer Taman Negara **package trips**, usually comprising two or three nights at Kuala Tahan with a range of accommodation and meal options, and possibly activities such as walks and boat excursions as well. While they're undoubtedly convenient and give you enough time to get a reasonable flavour of the park, you may well prefer the flexibility of an independent visit, eating where you please and organizing activities of your own choosing – which almost always works out cheaper. For details of the packages at the *Taman Negara Resort*, see p.236.

If you do want to make your own arrangements at the park, note that despite what you may be told, there's no need to book your accommodation through, for example, the agent who arranges your transport to the park; simply shop around once you've arrived or call ahead.

worth doing in both directions (you may prefer to save the trip for the finale: the ride back from Kuala Tahan is downriver and thus quicker by about half an hour). The **jetty** for the boat trips (daily 9am & 2pm except Fri 9am & 2.30pm; RM35 one way, RM70 return; 3hr upriver) is at **Kuala Tembeling**, the access road for which leaves Route 64 just east of Jerantut; local buses to Kuala Lipis will drop you close to the jetty, while a taxi to the jetty will cost RM24 from town. Boat **tickets** can be bought at the jetty (which has *kedai kopi*s for a bite while you await your sailing) or in advance from NKS Travel or Han Travel (see box, p.233) or SPKG in Jerantut.

The park

The area now called Taman Negara was first protected by state legislation in 1925, when 1300 square kilometres were designated as the Gunung Tahan Game Reserve; thirteen years later it became the King George V National Park. At independence, the park was renamed Taman Negara and extended to its current boundaries. Today the park, managed by the government's Department of Wildlife and National Parks (more simply known as the Wildlife Department; Ⓦ www .wildlife.gov.my) forms by far the largest undivided tract of rainforest in Peninsular Malaysia; indeed it contains some of the **oldest rainforest** in the world – older than the Congo or Amazon – which has evolved over 130 million years. Some of the Peninsula's one thousand **Batek** Orang Asli, a subgroup of the Negritos, remain in the area; most are hunter-gatherers (the park authorities generally turn a blind eye to their hunting game here). You may pass their vine-and-forest-brush

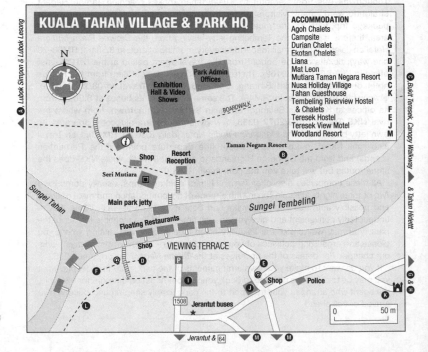

Park wildlife

Although for many visitors the chance of seeing sizeable mammals, especially **elephants**, is one of the park's big draws, bear in mind that success generally means making a three- or four-day trek into the forest, requiring the services of a guide. But stay overnight in the hides – tree houses positioned beside salt licks – and you might spot **mouse deer**, **tapir** and **seladang** (wild ox), especially during the rainy season, while **wild pigs** have been known to forage right in the midst of the park headquarters itself. **Birdlife** is ever present; the park has over three hundred species, many quite easy to spot with good binoculars and some patience. For a run-down of the park habitats and denizens, see p.721.

Unfortunately, the undoubted success of Taman Negara, with over sixty thousand visitors a year, brings its own problems. According to some local environmentalists, the increasing number of visitors is having an impact on the park's ecosystem: the popular trail to Gunung Tahan is suffering accelerated **erosion** and some littering due to the large number of hikers. Also of concern is the effect on the food chain of the drift of large mammals away from the much-touristed Kuala Tahan area.

shelters, built to stand only for a few days before their inhabitants move on again, and you can even take a discreet look at a couple of semi-permanent settlements in the vicinity of Kuala Tahan.

Arrival and information

Arriving by **boat**, you will be deposited either at the park jetty, with steps leading up to the sprawling *Mutiara Taman Negara Resort* and the **park headquarters** (⊤09/266 1122, ⑤266 4110), or on the opposite (village) bank, above which the road into the park headquarters ends in a small car park and viewing terrace. **Buses** drop you just short of the car park, at the start of the road leading up to the *Teresek View Motel*. An office at the car park has "Information" signage outside, but it's really an agency selling trekking packages and so forth.

The park headquarters' **information desk** (daily 8am–10pm, except Ramadan until 6.30pm) should be your first port of call: here you can pay the nominal park entry fees, buy any licences you may need, book **hides** and **activity packages**, charter **boats** or hire **guides**. There is a **left luggage** service, costing roughly RM5 per item per day, with a deposit sometimes required. It's worth putting any questions you have about the park to the staff, many of whom are guides and may be local to the area. For a list of park fees and charges, see p.239. Close by is a pricey **convenience store**.

The Wildlife Department puts on a free **video screening** about the park in the Interpretive Centre nearby (daily 9.30am, 3pm & 8.45pm). It's informative and worth attending if you're at a loose end – even if everyone does snigger when **tigers** get mentioned: they're down to around two hundred within the park and seldom spotted, though droppings or prints are sometimes seen.

KUALA TAHAN village has a few basic shops and stalls scattered about: there's a reasonably priced **convenience store** opposite the *Teresek View Motel*, and near this is one of a couple of places offering **internet** access at a premium rate (RM6 per hr). The **tour operators** SPKG and NKS each have an office in and among the restaurants; look out for their logos on the restaurant signs. You should take a torch with you to wander around the village in the evening, as the **electricity** can be flaky.

Accommodation

It's in the village of Kuala Tahan that you'll find practically all the budget and mid-range places to stay in the vicinity (except for *Mutiara Taman Negara Resort*, and a couple of places upriver on the village side). The *Mutiara Taman Negara Resort* runs a **campsite**, which is signposted uphill from the information desk, at the start of the trail to Lubok Lesong. Unfortunately it was closed at the time of writing, supposedly because of "too many wild pigs" roaming around the park HQ, but if it reopens charges should be fairly low: it used to cost RM5 per person to stay here, with rental of a two-person tent for RM14 per day. There are toilets and showers on site.

Agoh Chalets ⓣ&ⓕ 09/266 9570. A range of two- and four-person en-suite chalets, all with a timber-effect cladding and a/c, arranged around a pleasant garden. Serviceable if uninspired. ❸

Durian Chalet ⓣ 09/266 8940. Delightful, rustic chalets of woven bamboo, clustered around a pretty garden with a teeming fish pond. They're all reasonably maintained and have shack-like bathrooms attached. There's also a separate brick "family house" (RM50), which can be rented out as a four-person dorm. A great place to get away from it all. It's a 5min walk from the *Teresek View*, down a steep hill and through a small stand of rubber trees. Dorm beds RM10, chalets ❷

Ekotan Chalets ⓣ 09/266 9897. Substantial a/c chalets with larger bathrooms than most, plus dorms, some with a/c, for five to eight people. Dorm beds RM13 (RM20 with a/c), chalets ❹

Liana ⓣ 09/266 9322. A barracks of a building with four-bed dorms but thankfully not the rigours of boot camp; rooms are pleasant and the shared facilities reasonably well kept. The management, when you can find them, are friendly. Dorm beds RM10.

Mat Leon Perched on the steep river bank a short way up from Kuala Tahan ⓣ 013/998 9517, ⓦwww.matleon.com. Metal-roofed bamboo chalets with simple furnishings and somewhat cell-like attached bathrooms, plus a dorm with shared facilities. This far from the village, it makes sense that there's a small canteen too. The place is a 10min walk beyond the *Tahan Guesthouse*, but don't try it with luggage: the road undulates steeply and there's a short jungle trail to navigate right at the end. The easiest way to get here is by boat from the signed platform among the floating restaurants. Dorm beds RM15, chalets ❹

Mutiara Taman Negara Resort At the park entrance ⓣ 09/266 2200 or 3500, ⓦwww.mutiarahotels.com. Though pricey, this three-star resort can be busy, and it's worth booking a couple of months ahead to stay during the peak season or local school holidays. The cheapest, though limited, rooms are in a guesthouse block; most of the accommodation comprises much pricier a/c chalets, with a spacious bathroom, woven bamboo walls and cane furniture. They also have institutional eight-bed dorms with bunk beds (at an astounding RM60). There are two- or three-night packages available, but these are worthwhile mainly for the convenience: a three-day, two-night Explorer deal, with some meals and guided activities thrown in, costs around RM1800 for two people – much more than the sum of its parts. Transfers to and from the park can be arranged for an additional premium. ❼

Nusa Holiday Village Around 15min away by boat ⓣ 09/266 2369, ⓦwww.tamannegara-nusaholiday.com.my. Though not vast, this resort, run by SPKG, does have quite a collection of accommodation. Cheapest are the six- or eight-bed dorms, decent enough, with facilities in a separate block, and the slightly threadbare, en-suite A-frame chalets. Best, at around double the rate for the A-frames, are the so-called "Malay houses", with cane furniture, mosquito nets, a tiled bathroom, fan and a/c; similar are the fractionally cheaper "Malay cottages", lacking a/c but probably the best value here. The restaurant serves up simple fare. Budget a few ringgit extra per day for shuttling to and from the park HQ on SPKG's boats. If you want to hike outside the park from here, you could walk to the Abai Waterfall in about 1hr, or up the nearby peak of Gunung Warisan, 2hr away. Dorm beds RM15, rooms ❸

Tahan Guesthouse ⓣ 09/266 7752, ⓔjungletreker@gmail.com. This two-storey affair is like a kindergarten gone native, painted in bright colours and decorated with wildlife-related murals. Accommodation comprises four-bed dorms and en-suite rooms, all with fan. The place is well kept and the amicable female proprietor speaks excellent English. A good choice; small discounts available when things are quiet. ❸

Tembeling Riverview Hostel & Chalets ⓣ&ⓕ 09/266 6766. Simple, slightly shabby en-suite timber chalets with thatched roofs, plus some four- and eight-bed dorms. Dorm beds RM12, chalets ❷

▲ Taman Negara Resort

Teresek Hostel ☎013/276 7032. Eight- and ten-bed dorms featuring bunk beds and pastel colour schemes. Showers and toilets are clean enough. Dorm beds RM10.

Teresek View Motel ☎&℉09/266 9744. Once a modest array of chalets, but now transformed into a large pale-pink building with comfy en-suite rooms (pricier ones have a/c) on two floors, plus a café below. It's well run too; you won't envy staff persevering with the task of keeping the place free of muddy footprints. Dorm beds RM10, rooms ❸

Woodland Resort Reached not off the main road but by heading a short distance southeast from the

Teresek View ☎09/2661111, ⓦwww.woodland .com.my. One of a handful of substantial tourist developments just south of the village, this is not so much characterless as just plain incongruous, with chalet units somewhere in between kampung house and alpine hut, surrounded by a rubber plantation. The rooms are utterly bland but do pack in the creature comforts – a/c, TV, fridge and modern bathroom. The indigo-tiled swimming pool is probably the best feature. Rate includes breakfast. ❺

Eating

A few accommodation options have their own **restaurants**, but most visitors eat in the row of floating, glorified *kedai kopis* moored beside the shingle beach. Little **"umbrella boats"** shuttle on demand between the tiny park jetty and the closest floating restaurants opposite on the village side (daily roughly 7am–11pm; deposit the RM1 fare in the boatman's tin). Opening up daily around 8am for breakfast and staying open until 11pm, the restaurants offer the usual rice and noodle dishes, sometimes *roti canai*, plus Western travellers' fare such as pancakes, sandwiches and milk shakes. The *Family* restaurant (the names are generally signed on the village side only) has a slight edge over the rest in terms of ambience, with fancy lighting, bamboo roll-up blinds and potted orchids. Wherever you're staying, the resort's *Seri Mutiara* **restaurant** is worth a splurge, serving mouthwatering fare at eyewatering prices – around RM20 for noodles, for example. Still, the lunch and dinner buffets can be good value, starting at RM40. This is also the only spot in Kuala Tahan where alcohol can be consumed.

Note that environmental compliance at some restaurants leaves something to be desired: if you witness scraps going straight in the river, you may want to raise the matter with the park authorities.

Leaving the park headquarters

The **Jerantut bus** leaves from Kuala Tahan's main road daily at 7.30am, 10am, 3.30pm and 7pm; pay the driver the RM6 fare. **Boats** downriver to the Tembeling jetty leave daily at 9am and 2pm, or 9am and 2.30pm on Fridays (RM35). If you didn't buy a return ticket when you came, reserve your ticket the day before your journey, at the SPKG or NKS platforms among the floating restaurants. You can arrange the onward trip to Jerantut with them, or try to find a shared taxi once at Tembeling jetty (around RM20 per person). If you intend to use one of the afternoon boats, note that in low season some of these departures may be curtailed; to avoid any nasty surprises, double-check with the boat operator the day before your journey.

Treks and other activities

The account of the park below is divided into three sections: **day-trips** that you can make from Kuala Tahan, trips made from the **upriver sites** at Trenggan and Keniam and **longer trails** – the Rentis Tenor and Gunung Tahan – which require a certain commitment. Getting well away from the park headquarters to boost your wildlife-spotting prospects is worth the time and expense; you'll never forget the first time you see an elephant in the forest. For some treks you'll require specific equipment and resources, which are detailed where appropriate. None of the trails themselves, however, requires any special skills, nor do they demand anything beyond an average level of fitness. There's a **map** showing the area around Kuala Tahan on p.241 and a map of the whole park on p.229.

Most people in the park for just a few days also sign up for one or two of the little **activity packages** offered by the *Mutiara Taman Negara Resort* (their bookings counter is next to the resort's reception) and by some of the Kuala Tahan accommodation. The prices charged by each are broadly similar, as are the activities: the resort has a night jungle walk (1hr–1hr 30min; RM35) and night safari (2hr; RM40), plus cave exploration (2hr; RM50) and "rapids-shooting" trips (1hr; RM50). The **night jungle walks** are fun if you like insects and flora – the park staff escort a chain of groups of about ten on a spooky hike, pointing out the odd scorpion, luminous worm and medicinal plant on a circuit of the area around the resort. The **night safaris** actually take place outside the park; you're driven around a plantation in a 4X4, and may get to see leopard cats or the occasional snake. Neither the cave exploration or rapids trips are especially challenging; they're designed to appeal to families and can be good fun.

Beyond these possibilities, you can think about doing a guided forest walk, or spending a night in one of several **hides**. These are positioned deep in the jungle overlooking salt licks, where you can espy animals drinking the brackish water, or indulge in a spot of **birdwatching** at dawn. Ardent twitchers will want to get hold of a decent birding guide, such as *Birds of Taman Negara* by Morten Strange and Dennis Yong, published by Draco in Singapore.

If you're into **fishing** (and in case you're wondering, any fish caught must be returned to the water), a good bet is the Sungai Keniam, northeast of Kuala Tahan, where you might hope to catch catfish or snakehead. You may also want to ask about the community-run *ikan kelah* sanctuary at Lubok Tenor, a short boat ride upstream from Kuala Tahan. Day-trips on which you can fish for the sizeable kelah, also called golden mahseer (zoological name *Tor tambroides*) must be arranged in advance and cost at least RM400 for two people, including boat transfers from Kuala Tahan, lunch and equipment rental (enquiries on ☎012 483 2006 or 09/266 3070).

To get into truly undisturbed forest you really need to stay for a week or more. On a week's visit, you could start with the thirty-kilometre **Rentis Tenor trail**, a lasso-shaped trek leading west from Kuala Tahan to Gua Telinga, then northwest into deep forest to the campsite at Sungai Tenor. Having returned to Kuala Tahan, you could then go upriver to Kuala Keniam, walk along the wild **Keniam trail** (where elephants are sometimes spotted), and spend the night in a hide before taking a sampan from Kuala Trenggan back to park headquarters. Unless the park is very busy, you're unlikely to see more than a handful of people on these trails. The most challenging thing you could do in a week is the 55-kilometre trek northwest to **Gunung Tahan** (a shorter, quicker approach is from Merapoh; see p.249); allow a day extra either side of the trek to sort out arrangements.

If you have a **specialist interest**, in particular types of fauna, for example, it's worth calling the park headquarters a week in advance of your visit to see if a guide with matching knowledge can be arranged. Being trained by the Wildlife Department, the guides are in fact generally much better on fauna than flora, though many guides are experts on neither, as the most important component of their training is a knowledge of the trails. This also means that some have been known to fall short when it comes to more general skills – for example offering support in the event of a mishap.

Leeches can be a serious problem after rain; see p.36 for general advice in keeping them at bay. Many of the park guides prefer to wear shorts as they say it's easier to deal with leeches if you can see them – but this approach requires an advanced jungle temperament. If you're truly leech-phobic, you might want to take a chance on a tactic some guides swear by, spraying shoes and socks with a potent insecticide on sale in Kuala Tahan.

Except on the very simplest day hikes, you should **inform park staff** of your plans so they know where to look if you get into difficulty. You won't

Taman Negara fees and charges

Park entry	RM1 per person
Camping permit	RM1 per person per night
Camera licence	RM5
Fishing licence	RM10
Use of fishing lodges	RM8 per person
Hides	RM5 per person
Guide hire	Around RM150 per day, plus RM100 for overnighting

Boat excursions

The sample prices below are to charter a four-seater boat to your destination and back (ten-seater boats may be available on request). The boatman may wait for you at the destination or, more likely, return to collect you at an arranged time.

Destination	Cost
Canopy walkway	RM40
Gua Telinga	RM40
Kuala Keniam	RM180
Kuala Keniam Kecil	RM300
Kuala Perkai (for *Perkai Lodge*)	RM280
Kuala Trenggan	RM90
Lata Berkoh	RM120
Lubok Lesong	RM80
Tabing/Cegar Anjing hides	RM40

Spending a night in one of the park's six **hides** (known as *bumbuns*) doesn't guarantee sightings of large mammals, especially in the dry season when the **salt licks** – where plant-eating animals come to supplement their mineral intake – are often so waterless that there's little reason for deer, tapir, elephant, leopard or *seladang* to visit, but it's an experience you're unlikely to forget.

The hides are basic, featuring only wooden beds without mattresses, and a simple chemical toilet; bring sleeping bags, food that doesn't require heating, and water. As well as a torch, take rain gear, hat and sleeping bag, and all the food and drink you will need – and bring all your rubbish back for proper disposal at the resort. It's best to go in a group and take turns keeping watch, listening hard and occasionally shining the **torch** (these can be rented at the park information desk) at the salt lick – if an animal is present its eyes will reflect brightly in the beam. Many people leave scraps of food below the hide, although environmentalists disapprove of this, as it interferes with the animals' naturally balanced diet.

There are four hides north of the *Taman Negara Resort* and two to the south. Of the northern ones, the closest is **Bumbun Tahan**, which is situated just south of the junction with the Bukit Teresek trail. Deeper in the park and thus more promising are **Bumbun Tabing**, on the east bank of Sungai Tahan (see p.243 for directions), and **Bumbun Cegar Anjing**, an hour further and slightly to the south, on the west bank of Sungai Tahan, beside an old airstrip. It's reached by fording the river, but in the wet season is only accessible by boat, as the river's too powerful to wade across. The most distant hide to the north of the resort is the **Bumbun Kumbang**, which can be a good place to catch sight of animals such as elephants. It's an eleven-kilometre walk from Kuala Tahan, but can be reached by taking a boat to Kuala Trenggan (45min from the resort), followed by a 45-minute hike

To the south, **Bumbun Blau** is on the Gua Telinga trail, and beyond the cave, **Bumbun Yong**, at either of which there's only a small chance of spotting wildlife as the hides are quite close both to the traffic on Sungai Tembeling and the resort's vast electricity generator.

You have to **book** your bunk in the hide at the Wildlife Department office. All the hides sleep twelve people, except for Bumbun Tabing, which sleeps eight. Although you don't need to book to use the park's various **campsites**, check with the Wildlife Department as to which are open and their current condition. All the campsites, with the exception of the one at Kuala Tahan, have no facilities whatsoever, though most are close to rivers where you can wash.

be able to phone for help, as the cell-phone signal dies out just a little way from Kuala Tahan. If you do get lost and night is about to close in, it's best to make your way down to either of the Tahan or Tembeling rivers; there is boat traffic on both into the evening, and if you are unlucky enough not to be spotted, you may be able to find a dry section of bank where you can spend the night.

Boats can be chartered like a taxi service to get around the park, and are useful for day-trips as well as longer treks if you're short on time; book boats at the Wildlife Department's information desk (see box, p.239 for fares). It can be cheaper to use SPKG's **river bus** service, on which fares are per passenger; their boats run at fixed times to a few key locations around the park, for example to Kuala Trenggan (2 daily; RM30 one way or RM50 return). For more details and tickets, ask at the SPKG office moored among the floating restaurants.

Day-treks

Popular and easy places to visit close to the park headquarters are **Bukit Teresek**; the **canopy walkway**, where you might be able to observe treetop jungle life close up; the large limestone **Telinga** cave; and the **Berkoh Falls** (the first part of the trail there is a good way to kill a couple of spare hours). You could feasibly tackle two, perhaps three, of these in a day.

Bukit Teresek

Although it's the most heavily used trail in the park, the route to **Bukit Teresek** is an excellent starter trek, taking about an hour in each direction. If you're staying at the *Resort*, you can access the trail va the path right at the eastern end of the chalet compound, but everyone else uses the extended stretch of boardwalk which begins east of the interpretive centre. The trail proper, heading northeast away from the river, is mostly just a mass of plaited tree roots. Note the impressive stand of giant bamboo early on (described on one of many display boards here that feature some of the most common plants and animals in the park) and occasional clumps of feathery, blue-green *paku merah* or peacock fern (likewise featured).

Most of the last 800m of the trail, taking you up Bukit Teresek (342m) itself, involves a steeply rising series of steps; if somehow you haven't already noticed the sauna-like conditions, you will now, and it would self-flagellating not to pause at least once to catch your breath. The clanking of your shoes against the steps (made out of the same material as the earlier boardwalk – fibreglass-reinforced plastic, park officials proudly say) is enough to scare off most wildlife, so content yourself with the prospect of the views from the top – though initially you'll be disappointed that the clearing at the top of the steps is largely screened by trees. From here, you'll need to continue another ten or fifteen minutes north to reach the so-called second view, where on clear days you can get marvellous

DAY-TRIPS & SHORT TRAILS

▲ Giant bamboo lining the Bukit Teresek trail

vistas north over the valley to Gunung Tahan (2187m) and Gunung Perlis (1279m) are marvellous. Back at the base of the hill, the canopy walkway is just 300m to the south along a clearly marked, springy path crisscrossed by slippery tree roots.

The canopy walkway and the Bukit Indah trail

About thirty minutes' walk northeast from the resort, along the riverside Bukit Indah trail, is the **canopy walkway** (take the second turning, signed, to the left; daily 9am–3pm, except Fri until noon; RM5). At any one time only a small group of people can gain access to the walkway, so you're likely to have to wait at the start. Taking around thirty minutes to negotiate, the walkway is a five-hundred-metre-long swaying bridge made from aluminium ladders bound by rope, supported at twenty- to sixty-metre intervals by 250-year-old *tualang* trees. Set 30m above the ground, it's reached by climbing a sturdy wooden tower; you return to terra firma by another wooden stairwell at the end of the third section. Once you've got used to the walkway's swaying, you can take in the views of Sungai Tembeling and, if you're lucky, observe the geckos, cicadas, crickets and grasshoppers which live at this height. Other species you may see include the grey-banded leaf monkey, with a call that sounds like a rattling tin can, and the white-eyed dusky leaf monkey, with its deep, nasal "ha-haw" cry; both lope about in groups of six to eight.

Past the canopy the route divides, with one branch leading north and slightly uphill to the Tabing hide, another 1km further on. The other goes northeast, heading marginally downhill and cutting back towards Sungai Tembeling along the lovely **Bukit Indah trail**. Initially, this follows the river bank and you're bound to see monkeys, plenty of birdlife, squirrels, shrews, a multitude of insects and (if it's early or late in the day) perhaps tapir or *seladang* (wild ox). The path to Bukit Indah itself leaves the main riverside trail (which continues to Kuala Trenggan, 6km away) and climbs at a slight gradient for 200m; the top of the hill offers a lovely view over Sungai Tembeling. It's a three-kilometre, three-hour return trip from the resort office.

Gua Telinga and Kemah Keladong

Another major trail leads south not far from Sungai Tembeling, with branches off to the limestone outcrop of Gua Telinga, the Blau and Yong hides, and the campsite at Kemah Keladong. The quickest way to tackle this is by chartering a boat five minutes downriver to the jetty more or less due east of the cave. A short, steep path leads up from here to the top of the river bank, where the trail levels out and veers right almost immediately. Close by you may come across a semi-permanent **Batek settlement**, comprising several *atap*-thatch shelters around a clearing. You may spy women cooking meals in little woks and plenty of children at play, but be discreet about photography; the headman speaks some English and may ask you to pay a small sum for the privilege.

Continuing along the trail, you'll find what looks like a side trail on your left after just a few minutes. Take this and after twenty or thirty minutes you'll come to a rope bridge over a stream and, another fifteen minutes from here, a signpost for Gua Telinga, now just 500m away, and Bumbun Blau. To reach the cave, simply carry on in the direction signed, ignoring a side trail that soon presents itself. **Gua Telinga** looks small and unassuming, but it's deceptively deep – something you only discover when you slide through it. Although in theory it's possible to follow a guide rope through the eighty-metre cave, in practice only small adults or children will be able to tug themselves through the narrow cavities – most people will have to crawl along dark narrow passages in places and negotiate areas of deep, squishy guano. Thousands of tiny roundleaf and fruit bats reside in the cave, as well as giant toads, black-striped frogs and whip spiders (which aren't poisonous). You're most likely to see the roundleaf bats, so called because of the shape of the "leaves" of skin around their nostrils, which help direct the sound signals transmitted to assist the bat in navigation.

Back at the signpost, it's another 1km to the Blau hide through beautiful tall forest, and another kilometre to that at Yong, where the trail divides, north to Kemah Rentis (see p.248) and southeast to the tranquil **Kemah Keladong campsite**, 500m further on, on the terraced bank of Sungai Yong. With an early start, it's quite possible to reach this point, have a swim in the river and get back to the resort before dusk.

There's an alternative, longer approach to Gua Telinga, starting from the Sungai Tahan just across from the park headquarters. Having crossed the river by sampan (ask staff at the information desk to arrange this), on the opposite bank you follow the trail through a small kampung into the trees. The undulating trail ultimately leads to the jetty east of the cave, but you'll need to turn off to the right after 2km or so, for Gua Telinga and Blau.

Lata Berkoh

Most people visit the "roaring rapids" of **Lata Berkoh** by boat, as it's an eight-kilometre, three-hour trip on foot. You could, however, walk the trail there and arrange for a boat to pick you up for the return journey – or vice versa – getting the best of both worlds. While it's possible to hike all the way to Lata Berkoh, if water levels are high you're likely to face a swim across the river close to the end; it's best to ask the Wildlife Department about current conditions. If you only have a morning left to fill, you could walk the trail as far as Lubok Simpon, where there's a popular swimming spot, then turn back.

Sampans to the rapids head upstream on Sungai Tahan, the busiest of the park's tributaries. The jetty at the other end is just 100m from the simple **Berkoh Lodge**, a small shelter with toilets, set back from the river in a clearing; there's also a **campsite** here.

The **waterfall** itself is 50m north of the lodge. There's a deep pool with surprisingly clear water for swimming (tread carefully around the large rocks on the river bed) and you can picnic here too, overlooking the swirling water. If you ask the boatman to cut his engine, you'll improve your chances of hearing the sounds of the forest and of seeing kingfishers with their yellow-and-red wings and white beaks, large grey-and-green fish eagles, melodious bulbul birds and, on the rocks, camouflaged monitor lizards.

The **trail** from the resort to Lata Berkoh starts at the park headquarters' campsite and leads gently downhill, past the turning for the Tabing hide to the east. After around 3km you reach the campsite at **Lubok Simpon**, just to the left of which there's a broad, pebbled beach leading down to a deep pool in Sungai Tahan. The route to the waterfall veers west from the main trail around thirty minutes' walk beyond the campsite, crossing gullies and steep ridges before reaching the river, which must be forded. The final part of the trail runs north along the west side of Sungai Tahan before reaching the falls.

Kuala Trenggan, Kuala Keniam and the Perkai Lodge

Two sites up the Sungai Tembeling from the park headquarters, Kuala Trenggan and Kuala Keniam, offer interesting day hikes. **KUALA TRENGGAN**, 11km up the Sungai Tembeling from the park headquarters, can be reached either by boat, which takes less than an hour, or by one of two trails, which take between six and eight hours. The shorter and more direct trail (9km) runs alongside Sungai Tembeling and can be quite hard going as sections of it are narrow or steep, and there are several shallow streams to ford; the easier inland route (12km) runs north past the campsite at Lubok Lesong, bearing right into dense forest where elephant tracks may be seen, and then crosses the narrow Sungai Trenggan 500m to the north. Whichever route you choose, your target will be the **Kumbang hide**, 45 minutes on from Kuala Trenggan.

A further 20km up Sungai Tembeling is **KUALA KENIAM** (2hr by boat from Kuala Tahan). From here, you could hike two hours down the **Perkai trail** alongside Sungai Perkai (which cuts away from Sungai Tembeling 200m north of the lodge). The trail, which runs roughly parallel to the river, leads to the **Perkai Lodge** (also reachable by boat from Kuala Tahan), a popular spot for fishing and bird-spotting; in places it's possible to leave the main path and find a way down to the water. This far from Kuala Tahan, the region is rich in **wildlife**, including banded and dusky leaf monkeys, long-tailed macaques and white-handed gibbons, all of which are relatively easy to spot, especially with binoculars. As for big mammals, elephants certainly roam in these parts; smaller animals like tapirs, civets and deer are best seen at night or early in the morning. The lodge itself is a basic shelter with beds but no mattresses (bring sleeping bags), toilets and simple cooking facilities. The water supply can be a problem, in which case you'll need to wash with river water, which is clear here and fine for cooking with, too. There's also a space to **camp** nearby.

The Keniam–Trenggan trail

Hiking the 13km between Kuala Keniam and Kuala Trenggan is a great highlight of the park, combining the possibility of seeing elephants with visits to three caves, one of which is big enough for an army to camp in. The trail is a tough one, with innumerable streams to wade through, hills to circumvent and trees blocking the path. Usually a full day's hike in dry conditions, it can be covered in around six hours and you should probably hire a guide. Some people take two days instead, overnighting either in the Kepayang Besar cave (conveniently, no tent is needed here), in one of the caves en route or on a stretch of clear ground near a stream.

The trail cuts southwest from Kuala Keniam along a narrow, winding path through dense forest dominated by huge *meranti* trees with red-brown fissured bark. It's two hours before you enter limestone-cave country, first reaching **Gua Luas** which, though it doesn't have a large internal cavity, is impressive nonetheless. One hundred metres south is **Gua Daun Menari** ("Cave of the Dancing Leaves"), which does have a large chamber through which the wind blows leaves and other jungle debris. Climb up the side of the cave and you'll see small dark holes leading into the cave chamber where, in the pitch darkness, thousands of roundleaf bats live.

To regain the main trail, go back 50m towards Gua Luas and look for an indistinct path on the left; follow this for another 30m, at which point you should see the main trail ahead. Bear left here – the third cave, **Kepayang Besar**, is around ten minutes' walk further on. This has a very large chamber at the eastern side of the outcrop, which is easy to enter and an excellent place to spend the night. The fourth cave, **Kepayang Kecil**, is the last limestone outcrop on the trail. Here, a line of fig trees drops a curtain of roots down the rock, behind which lies a small chamber, with a slightly larger one to the right, containing stalactites and stalagmites.

After passing Kepayang Kecil you're about halfway along the trail, but there are plenty more streams to cross, with armies of ants, flies and leeches. The trail is illuminated in places by patches of sunlight highlighting tropical fungi on the trees and plants, though you're soon back in the gloom again. Parts of the path are wide and easy to follow, while other sections are far narrower, passing through tunnels of bamboo. The final two hours comprise more boggy crossings as the trail descends slightly to Kuala Trenggan. Rather than be collected by boat and heading back to Kuala Tahan, you can prolong the excursion by overnighting near here in the **Kumbang hide**.

Longer trails

The two main long trails in the park are the trek to **Gunung Tahan** and back, requiring a week, and the four-day, circular **Rentis Tenor**, a trail which reaches the beautiful Sungai Tenor before dipping back east. For either, you'll need loose-fitting, lightweight cotton clothing with long sleeves, long trousers to keep insects at bay, a raincoat or waterproof poncho and a litre bottle of water (plus water-purifying equipment or tablets). Also take a tent, a powerful torch, cooking equipment and a compass, all of which can be rented from the Wildlife Department, from whom you can also buy spare batteries; check with your guide or the resort office as to how much food you'll need to take. For Gunung Tahan you also need a sleeping bag for the two nights spent at a high-altitude camp.

Perhaps the most important advice on all long-distance trails is to know your limitations and not run out of time. Slipping and sliding along in the dark is no fun and can be dangerous – it's easy to fall at night and impossible to spot snakes or other forest-floor creatures that might be on the path.

The Gunung Tahan trail

To the Batek Orang Asli, **Gunung Tahan** is the Forbidden Mountain, its summit the home of a vast monkey, who stands guard over magic stones. The Batek venture to the foothills on hunting expeditions but rarely head further up the mountain, because of this belief. Reaching the summit, Peninsular Malaysia's highest peak at 2187m, is the highlight of any adventurous visitor's stay in Taman Negara. Although in high season hundreds of people trudge along the trail every week, the sense of individual achievement after fording Sungai Tahan dozens of times, hauling yourself up and down innumerable hills and camping out every night – let alone the arduous ascent – is supreme. Not for nothing do successful hikers proudly display their "I climbed Gunung Tahan" T-shirts.

One of the chief thrills of the route is that it passes through various types of terrain, from lowland jungle to cloudforest, before reaching the summit. Attaining the summit involves following precarious ridges which weave around the back of the mountain, since the most obvious approach from Sungai Tahan would mean scaling the almost sheer one-thousand-metre-high Teku Gorge – which the first expedition to attempt this route, organized by the Sultan of Pahang, tried and failed to do in 1863. The summit was finally reached in 1905 by a combined British–Malay team, led by the explorer Leonard Wray.

The Gunung Tahan trail must be booked one month in advance, and is the only one in the park on which you must be accompanied by a **guide** (for which a flat fee of RM500 applies, for a group of up to twelve). The first day involves an easy six-hour walk to **Melantai**, the campsite on the east bank of Sungai Tahan, across the river from Lata Berkoh. On the second day more ground is covered, the route taking eight hours and crossing 27 hills, including a long trudge up Bukit Malang ("Unlucky Hill"). This section culminates at **Gunung Rajah** (576m), before descending to Sungai Puteh, a tiny tributary of the Tahan. Before the campsite at **Kuala Teku** you'll ford the Tahan half a dozen times – if the river's high, extra time and energy is spent following paths along the edge of the river, crossing at shallower spots.

On the third day you climb from 168m to 1100m in seven hours of steady, unrelenting trekking, which takes you up onto a ridge. Prominent among the large trees along the ridge is *seraya*, with a reddish-brown trunk, as well as oaks and conifers, but the *seraya* thin out when the ridge turns to the west. Here, the character of the landscape changes dramatically to montane oak forest, where elephant tracks are common. Park experts believe that elephants live around this point, where the forest is more open and less dense than lower down, but still rich enough in foliage to provide food. The night is spent at the Gunung Tahan base camp, **Wray's Camp**, named after Leonard Wray.

The fourth day's trek consists of six hours of hard climbing along steep gullies, ending up at **Padang Camp**, on the Tangga Lima Belas Ridge, sited on a plateau sheltered by tall trees. The summit is now only two and a half hours away, through open, hilly ground with knee-high plants, exposed rocks and peaty streams, which support thick shrubs and small trees. Weather conditions up the mountain can't be relied upon: the moss forest, which ranges from 1500m to 2000m, is often shrouded in cloud, which can be present even at the top. The trail follows a ridge into the moss forest and soon reaches the **summit** where, provided it's clear, there's a stupendous view, around 50km in all directions. It's a pristine environment: pitcher plants, orchids and other rare plants grow in the crevices and gullies of the summit.

On the return trip, the fifth night is spent back at the padang, the sixth at Sungai Puteh, and by the end of day seven you're back at Kuala Tahan. If you don't fancy retracing your steps, you can continue more quickly westwards and exit the park at **Merapoh**.

Four-Steps Waterfall

The seven-day (50km) trail to **Four-Steps Waterfall**, east of Gunung Tahan, follows the same route as that described above for the first three days. At **Kuala Teku**, hikers take the right fork instead, which after eight hours of following the course of the Sungai Tahan reaches the foot of the falls. Although the falls are only 30m high, their gorgeous setting makes the trek worthwhile: flat stones by the path are a good point to rest, listen to the sound of the water and look out for birds and monkeys. You can camp below the falls at **Pasir Panjang**, which can be reached in around three hours along a clear path to the right of the falls.

Rentis Tenor

The other major long-distance trail is the four-day, thirty-kilometre, circular **Rentis Tenor**, which leads south to Sungai Yong, then northwest to the campsite at Kemah Rentis and southeast back to Kuala Tahan. A guide isn't compulsory, but in practice hardly anyone goes without hiring one.

The initial route is the same as that to Gua Telinga, bearing north at the Yong hide (2hr from the resort), before following the course of Sungai Yong and reaching the campsite at **Kemah Yong**, just under 10km from the resort. Two hundred metres south of the campsite a side trail leads off to the left to **Bukit Guling Gendang** (570m), a steep, ninety-minute climb best undertaken in the morning, after a good night's rest. From the top, there's a lovely view north to Gunung Tahan, west to Gua Siput and beyond that to Bukit Penyengat (713m), the highest limestone outcrop in Peninsular Malaysia. Towards the summit the terrain changes from lowland tropical to montane forest, where tall conifer trees allow light to penetrate to the forest floor and **squirrels** predominate, with the black giant and cream giant the main species. Both are as big as a domestic cat, their call varying from a grunt to a machine-gun burst of small squeaks.

On day three the main trail continues on into the upper catchment of Sungai Yong, then over a low saddle into the catchment of Sungai Rentis. The path narrows through thick forest alongside the river, crossing it several times, until it joins Sungai Tenor three hours later. Here there is a remote and beautiful clearing, **Kemah Rentis**, beside the river, where you camp. It's a fifteen-kilometre hike back to the resort from here; some trekkers take it easy and spend a fourth night at **Kemah Lameh** (4km from Kemah Rentis) or the **Lubok Lesong** campsite (8km from Kemah Rentis) on Sungai Tahan.

As for the trail itself from Sungai Tenor, follow the river downstream through undulating terrain to the rapids at **Lata Keitiah** (which takes around 1hr), beyond which another tributary stream, Sungai Lameh, enters the Tenor. You're now in lowland open forest where walking is fairly easy; after four hours the trail leads to **Bumbun Cegar Anjing** (another possible overnight stop) from where it's 3km back to the resort.

Alternative entrances to Taman Negara

Taman Negara's occasional billing as Malaysia's tri-state park is realized in the northern part of the interior, where it's possible to enter the park at **Merapoh** in Pahang, **Kuala Koh** in Kelantan and at **Tanjung Mentong** in Terengganu. Visiting any of these is a matter of balancing various pros and cons. It's preferable to rent a car to reach Kuala Koh or Merapoh, because of the lack of transport to the former and because the latter is best explored with your own wheels; nonetheless both can be visited using public transport if you're prepared to pay to be collected and driven around at certain points.

If you are visiting Taman Negara via any of the three entrances covered here, be sure to read the general practical advice on p.230.

Merapoh (Sungai Relau)

Taman Negara's northern Pahang entrance is officially called **Sungai Relau** after the river that runs close to the park accommodation, but most people refer to it as **MERAPOH**, the name of the nearest town, 7km west on the jungle railway. This is the only part of Taman Negara with a proper road running deep into the park from the entrance, and it's this that gives access to the trails – most famously, that to **Gunung Tahan** (see p.246) – and other attractions.

Just before the park gates is the oversized **interpretive centre**, whose displays are worth a quick look if you're at a loose end (you may need to get someone to unlock the building if it's quiet). Beyond, the park accommodation and offices have a certain colonial air, comprising an old-fashioned collection of bungalows around a field; look out for the signboard here with a **map** of the park's layout.

Head east from this area via a small bridge over the Sungai Relau, and you're at the start of 14km of road undulating through the jungle. Several trails lead off the initial few kilometres, including the Rentis Gajah ("elephant trail"), leading to Gua Gajah ("elephant cave"). A few kilometres on is a short trail north off the road that leads down in a matter of minutes to the park's sleek new **hide**, **Bumbun Rimau**, close to a salt lick. Drive another few kilometres on from here and you come to the red Menara Bukit Seraya, an **observation tower** with views of forested ridges and valleys to the north in Kelantan, and, on a clear day, east to Gunung Tahan.

The road ends at Kuala Juram, a picturesque spot with trees overhanging the limpid Juram river, a stretch of which teems with *kelah* (mahseer) fish; unlike at Lubok Tenor near Kuala Tahan, fishing isn't allowed at this particular sanctuary. If you came to Merapoh to take on the challenge of Gunung Tahan, the suspension bridge over the river here is the gateway to your exertions on the mountain trail.

Practicalities

Merapoh is easy to get to thanks to express and local **rail** services, though note that at the time of writing the only express trains calling here were those to and from Singapore. The road to the park branches off the main road pretty much opposite the train station; to get to the park entrance without your own car, contact the friendly Relau agency (☎017/915 3034, ⓦwww.relauriver.com .my). Besides ferrying visitors between station and park by prior arrangement (RM5 per person), they also furnish transport within the park – going from the park accommodation all the way to Kuala Juram will cost around RM50 for two people, for example. Their drivers tend to speak little English, but park staff should be able to smooth communication once you've arrived.

Merapoh is the only part of Taman Negara with **accommodation** managed by the Wildlife Department (☎&ⓕ09/912 4894). Most of it is in the form of two large dorms (RM10), though there are a few chalets (❷) and three-bed rooms available, plus a campsite by the Relau river. Reservations can also be made through Relau, whose website details various packages ("Pakej" in Malay) that include lodging, guided activities and transfers; package trips may also be available from Kiara Holidays in Kuala Lipis (see p.261). To visit during public or school holidays, it's wise to book early.

One major hassle of visiting Merapoh is that there is **no catering** available at the park. You will either have to bring provisions and your own utensils to make use of the kitchens on site, or else eat in Merapoh town. If you're intending to tackle **Gunung Tahan**, bring all the gear you need except perhaps tents, which can be rented from the Wildlife Department, and be sure to book a guide well in advance (around RM950 for the four days).

Kuala Koh

In many ways **KUALA KOH** is the most appealing of the alternative entrances to Taman Negara, offering much of what you get at Kuala Tahan but within a much smaller area and – unless you happen to encounter a student party – without the crowds. A suspension bridge from the park accommodation leads over the Lebir River straight into the park proper; turn left once across to reach the circular **canopy walkway** after just a few minutes. Though lower down and shorter than the one at Kuala Tahan, it's fun to traverse all the same and offers impressive views, particularly of the massive trees to which it's attached – note in particular the enormous, stout *tualang* tree midway along, with its whitish bark. The path to the walkway also gives access to various **trails**, including the **Bulatan Ara**, a well-signed one-hour loop, and the trail to the **Impian hide**. A branch trail off the latter leads to a **Rafflesia site** where you may be lucky enough to spot a few of these bizarre stinky blooms. **Wildlife** in the area includes wild boar, tapir, mousedeer and occasionally elephant.

A pleasant **river trip** is to head up the Lebir for half an hour to Kuala Pertang (a negotiable RM70 return per four-person boat, including a wait), passing a few sandy banks where you can camp, swim or fish; the river is home to *ikan kelah* amongst other freshwater denizens. The ride takes you under the overhanging boughs of leaning *neram* trees, some hung with the leafy tresses of **tiger orchids**, one of the world's largest types of orchid. You can also go **tubing** along the river (RM15), being carried downstream inside or on an inflated rubber ring.

Practicalities

If you don't have transport, you might be able to arrange a trip here from Gua Musang with the management of the park accommodation (see below). Driving, turn off Route 8 at **Simpang Aring** (signed about half an hour north of Gua Musang) and follow signs along the winding road through the extensive Felda Aring oil-palm plantation to reach the entrance after about an hour. Here the park offices sit atop a small hill close to the confluence of the Lebir and Koh rivers; the **jetty** for boat trips is at the base of the hill, while next door to the park offices is a simple **restaurant**.

Round the side of the hill, on the way to the suspension bridge, is the park's **accommodation**. At the time of writing it was marketed as the *Taman Negara Kuala Koh Resort* (☎012 965 4788, ⓦwww.taman-negara-koh .blogspot.com), but note that the name and the concession for this may change hands in 2010, in which case you may need to contact the Wildlife Department in Kuala Tahan to discover who is taking over bookings. In the meantime, the present management does an excellent job of running the large dorm (beds RM12), campsite (RM2 per person) and handful of chalets (❷), which are substantial affairs with attached bathroom but no air-conditioning or mosquito nets. The management can also arrange boat trips, tent rental, night walks etc; check their website for details of prices and of various packages that include not just activities but also **transport** from and to Gua Musang (which, if arranged separately, will cost you RM70 there and back, for a minimum of two people – rather less than getting a taxi). Note that to confirm a booking, you will need to make a down-payment to them at any Malaysian bank once you arrive in the country. Packages with transfers from Jerantut or Cameron Highlands can also be arranged with Green Park Adventure in Jerantut (see p.231).

Tanjung Mentong

It's at **TANJUNG MENTONG**, on the southern shores of Tasik Kenyir, that the cons will probably outweigh the advantages for most independent travellers. As with the rest of the lake, access is by boat from the Gawi jetty (see p.306) – and boat charter is usually expensive (eg RM600 per day for a six-seater). Accommodation comprises eight chalets, a dorm and campsite; prices were being revised at the time of writing, but will be in line with those at Kuala Koh and Merapoh. For current details and more advice on practicalities, contact the Wildlife Department's Kuala Terengganu office (⊕09/622 1460), though it's easier to book a package with the Ping Anchorage agency (see p.305). Fishing is one of the chief draws, plus there's a straightforward two-day hike to Gunung Gagau, and you can explore Gua Bewah and Gua Taat, caves just outside the park perimeter. It's also possible to spot *Rafflesia* blooms in certain areas.

From KL northeast to Dabong

Two routes cut across the interior from KL to the northeast coast: the jungle railway and Route 8. The main points of interest are **Fraser's Hill**, 100km north of KL; **Kuala Lipis**, the former tin-mining town and erstwhile capital of Pahang, 170km northeast of KL; the state park at **Kenong Rimba**; the caves at **Gua Musang**; and **Stong State Park**. But the chief reason for making the trip to the northeast coast is to spend time in the region's forests and limestone hills, an environment even now somewhat removed from the economic expansion of much of the rest of the Peninsula.

In this lush and rugged region, **Senoi** Orang Asli still lead semi-nomadic lives along inaccessible river basins and in the wide catchment area of the ponderous **jungle railway**. The lifestyles of the two main groups, the Temiar and the Semiar, revolve around a combination of shifting cultivation (where there is still enough accessible land left for this to be feasible), the trading of forest products, fishing and animal trapping. The Temiar are mountain dwellers, though the Temiar of southern Kelantan sometimes raft timber down Sungai Kelantan to sell the wood on to Chinese middlemen. Although the Temiar are increasingly exploiting the forest for timber, their logging practices are marginal compared to those of the State Forestry Department. The **Semiar**, in contrast, prefer to live in lowland jungle or flat open country, and there are several Semiar communities close to Merapoh, at the northern edge of Pahang.

On the final section of the jungle railway, the geography changes from mountainous, river-gashed jungle to plantations of rubber, pepper and oil palm. This is also **cattle country**, where cows grazing along the track sidings are a constant problem for train drivers; there are occasional collisions. For Kota Bharu, get off at the penultimate stop, Wakaf Bharu, 7km away.

Fraser's Hill (Bukit Fraser)

The development at **FRASER'S HILL** (actually seven hills), 1500m up in the Titiwangsa mountain range, was built to provide welcome relief for the British expatriate community from the humidity of Kuala Lumpur, 75km to the south as the crow flies. The hills were originally known as Ulu Tras, until the arrival in the 1890s of a solitary British pioneer, called James Fraser. An accountant by profession, he travelled to Australia at the peak of its gold rush and then came to Malaya. Although gold wasn't found in any quantity in the hills here, Fraser did find plentiful **tin** deposits. The tin was excavated by Chinese miners and hauled by mule along a perilous hill route down through thick jungle, to the nearest town, Raub, where Fraser set up a camp and a gambling den for his workers. After 25 years, Fraser mysteriously disappeared, and when a search party trekked up into the area to look for him in 1917, the camp and mines were deserted. However, the excellent location recommended itself to the party, who soon convinced the British authorities that it would make a perfect **hill station**.

During the Emergency in the 1950s, the surrounding mountainous jungle provided perfect cover for some of the communist guerrillas' secret camps, from where they launched strikes on British-owned plantations and neighbouring towns. If you approach Fraser's Hill via Kuala Kubu Bharu, due north of KL, roughly halfway up you'll see a sign, "Emergency Historical Site", marking the spot where Sir Henry Gurney, the British High Commissioner for Malaya at the height of the communist insurgency in 1951, was ambushed and killed. The guerrillas hadn't known how important their quarry was: their aim had been only to steal guns, ammunition and food, but when Gurney strode towards them demanding that they put down their weapons, they opened fire.

Just on the Pahang side of the Pahang/Selangor border, Fraser's Hill was never as popular as the much larger Cameron Highlands to the north, and its fortunes have taken a dip with the recent suspension of buses to the hill. The place remains well tended, though, its streets planted with flowering rhododendrons, ageratums and daylilies. The chief attraction is the chance to tackle a network of nature **trails** in relatively cool conditions, but **birdwatching** is also a draw, with long-tailed sibias and silver-eared mesias among the birds potentially on view. Every June, the Fraser's Hill International Bird Race has teams competing to sight as many species of bird as they can. While there's nothing especially compelling about the place, Fraser's makes a good getaway from the heat and hubbub of KL, and at weekends (when accommodation prices shoot up) it draws families from there and as far away as Singapore. A day-trip from KL is feasible only with a car; in any case, it's far preferable to spend a restful night at the hill station.

Arrival and information

Fraser's Hill lies on the road between **Kuala Kubu Bharu** (KKB), on Route 1 (the old north–south main road on the Peninsula), and **Raub** on Route 8. If you're driving from KL, it's best to head there via KKB, either using Route 1 itself or the North–South Expressway initially, which you leave at the Rawang exit. A bus used to run to the hill en route between KKB and Raub, but this has been suspended with little likelihood of being reinstated, and talk of starting a daily bus from KL has so far come to nothing; for now, the only way to reach

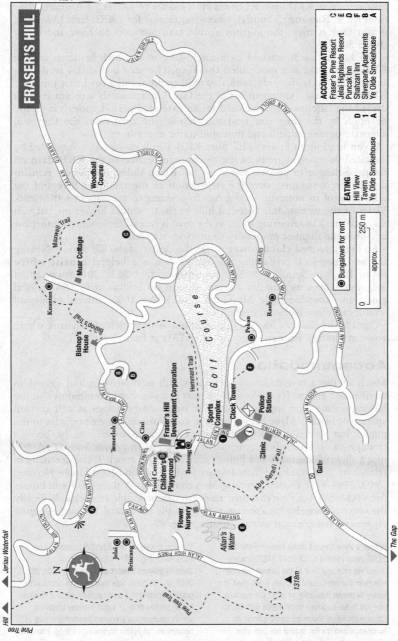

FRASER'S HILL

▲ The Gap (new route)

JALAN GIRDLE

JALAN GIRDLE

JALAN GIRDLE

JALAN QUARRY

Woodball Course

Maxwell Trail

Muar Cottage

Kuantan

Bishop's House

Bishop's Trail

C

Tanneroh

Cini

B

B

Fraser's Hill Development Corporation

Hemmant Trail

JALAN MAXWELL

JALAN LADY MAXWELL

JALAN PINOK PINE

Food Centre

Children's Playground

Bentong

Sports Complex

JALAN GENTING

Clock Tower

Police Station

i

Clinic

JALAN RICHMOND

JALAN LEMARO

JALAN VALLEY

Golf Course

Ranib

Pekan

F

JALAN GENTING GOLF

JALAN MAGOR

JALAN GENTING

Gate

JALAN GAR

The Gap

JALAN SEMANTAN

A

JALAN SHAH

PAHANG

Flower Nursery

JALAN AMPANG

Abu Seradi Hill

E

Allan's Water

JALAN HIGH PINES

JALAN TERLING

JALAN JERIAU

Jelai

Brincang

N

Pine Tree Trail

1318m

▲ Jeriau Waterfall

◀ Hill

Pine Tree ◀ ◀

ACCOMMODATION

Fraser's Pine Resort	C
Jelai Highlands Resort	E
Puncak Inn	D
Shahzan Inn	F
Silverpark Apartments	B
Ye Olde Smokehouse	A

| | Bungalows for rent |

EATING

Hill View	D
Tavern	1
Ye Olde Smokehouse	A

0 — 250 m
approx.

Fraser's Hill without a car is by chartering a taxi from KKB (around RM60). At least getting to KKB from KL is simply a matter of catching a Komuter train from KL to **Rawang** (3 hourly), where you change for a KKB train (2 hourly); if you time it right, the journey should take just over an hour and a half (RM5.50).

The hill station is reached by a single-lane road which branches off the KKB–Raub road at a spot called **the Gap**. The idea is that this road takes summit-bound traffic only, with downhill traffic using a road that joins the KKB–Raub road 1km northeast of the Gap. Unfortunately a recent landslip caused the latter road to be closed for an extended period, though it should be open by the time you read this. If not, the road from the Gap will alternate between uphill and downhill traffic every hour.

If you head up to Fraser's Hill from KKB, you'll pass a lake surrounded by denuded slopes – the result of the recent construction of the **KKB dam** on Sungai Selangor to provide water for the Klang Valley; the project remains dogged by controversy over the destruction of the rainforest here and the relocation of its nomadic Orang Asli inhabitants to permanent settlements. Vistas of the surrounding forested hills begin to unfold higher up, but you may not feel like savouring them as the road is one of those which somehow amplifies the slightest propensity to motion sickness.

An old-fashioned **clock tower** marks the centre of the hill station. Nearby, in the large block containing the *Puncak Inn*, is a helpful **tourist office** (Mon–Fri 8am–5pm, Sat & Sun 8am–10pm; ℡09/362 2201, ⓦwww.pkbf .org.my), whose website has a useful section on birdlife at Fraser's. A local guide, the knowledgeable Mr Durai (℡013/983 1633, Ⓔdurefh@hotmail .com), can often be found here.

Outside the *Shahzan Inn* (see opposite) is a small branch of Maybank where you can **change money** (there are no ATMs at Fraser's Hill).

Accommodation

Much of the accommodation in Fraser's Hill is motel-like, and geared to families and groups. It's also possible to stay in a number of **bungalows** (at the hill station the term applies to detached single-storey houses as well as small apartment blocks). Many belong to large corporations and are rarely let to the public, but several (including *Bentong*, *Cini* and *Kuantan*) can be booked through the tourist office (apartments and rooms in houses from ❺). A few, much slicker bungalows and houses with a hint of mock Tudor about them (*Brinchang, Jelai, Raub* and *Temerloh*) are let by Highland Rest House Holding (℡03/2164 8937, ⓦwww.hrhbungalows.com; rooms ❻, three-bedroom houses from RM450), but note that their rates can nearly double at weekends. Finally, the tourist office also has a few units to let in the substantial, modern *Silverpark Apartments* complex, crowning a nearby ridge (❺).

Fraser's Pine Resort Jalan Quarry ℡09/362 2122, reservations ℡03/7804 3422, ⓦwww .thepines.com.my. One of the largest developments in the area, unobtrusively positioned in a valley between two hills; on offer are modern one- to three-bedroom apartments with basic kitchen facilities. Rates go stratospheric at weekends and during school holidays (the "Calendar" section of the website lists variations through the year). Breakfast is included. Low season ❺, high ❼.

Jelai Highlands Resort Jalan Ampang ℡09/362 2600, Ⓕ362 2604. Spacious en-suite rooms with green carpets and a small amount of cane furniture, but all slightly tatty. The rate includes breakfast, which, unusually, is a cooked Western one (rice or noodles are an option on weekends only). Prices rise by twenty percent at weekends. Weekdays ❹.

Puncak Inn Jalan Genting; bookings through the tourist office. This place occupies a decidedly institutional block, though rooms are in reasonable condition, having been recently upgraded, and have their own bathroom with hot water. ❹

Shahzan Inn Jalan Lady Guillemard ☎09/362 2300, ✉shahzan8@tm.net.my. Located next to the golf course, this hotel comprises tiers of rooms ascending a terraced hillside. It's largely bland and modern, but everything's in good shape; rooms are en suite and have satellite TV. Breakfast is included. Good value during the week; at weekends, rates rise by a third. Weekdays ❺.

Ye Olde Smokehouse Jalan Semantan ☎09/362 2226, ✇www.thesmokehouse .com.my/fh.htm. The most characterful lodging in Fraser's Hill by a mile, quaintly decorated throughout in the style of a stereotypical English country inn. You can lounge by the fire in the evenings and then retire to your room's four-poster bed, guaranteed to make the cool nights pass all the more blissfully; rooms are very spacious and the bathrooms have been sympathetically renovated. The restaurant serves some of the most delightful (non-spicy) food you might have in Malaysia. Rates (it doesn't hurt to ask about weekday discounts) include a full English breakfast. ❽

The hill station

As is apparent the moment you arrive, the hill station comprises several wooded hills, with named trails snaking off on all sides. If you don't fancy wandering through the undergrowth, you can enjoy some pleasant walks just by following the roads, which are seldom steep. The easiest target is a small lake, **Allan's Water**, along Jalan Ampang, where you can rent a rowing boat (RM6 for 15min). Another possibility is to head to **Jeriau Waterfall**, around 4km north of the clock tower on foot; on the way you'll pass *Ye Olde Smokehouse*, where the **cream teas** (daily 3.30–6pm) are a very strong inducement to pause for a breather. Another reason to drop by is to survey the reasonably convincing English country decor – some of which might have rubbed off from its origins, in 1924, as a sort of club for British personnel in Malaya who'd fought in World War I. Yet another good walk involves taking Jalan Lady Guillemard east to the loop road, Jalan Girdle; this leads to the most remote section of the hill station, bordering **Ulu Tramin Forest Reserve**. Completing the circle, all the way round and back to the tourist office, takes around ninety minutes.

Most of the **trails** can be covered in less than two hours (indeed it would only take a couple of days to cover them all), and signage has been improved after a couple of major scares in recent years when a British biologist and some unsupervised boys from Singapore separately got lost up here for days. Both incidents were highly atypical, so you shouldn't be paranoid about losing your way, but it doesn't hurt to talk through your route with the tourist office before you set out, and you may want to engage Mr Durai as a guide. The trails can get quite slippery in wet weather, so be sure to wear proper footgear and take the standard precautions against leeches (see p.36).

The **Abu Suradi trail** begins on Jalan Genting close to the mosque, and takes about twenty minutes to reach its southern end, also on Jalan Genting, near the clinic. The **Hemmant trail** also starts from near the mosque and snakes along the edge of the golf course just within the jungle. At the far end of the trail, you can turn left and either walk on to Jalan Lady Maxwell, or continue as far as the Bishop's House, where you can pick up the **Bishop's trail**. Along here is a birdwatching tower, about which the tourist office can provide details. After about 45 minutes, this route joins the **Maxwell trail**, at which point you can either leave the trail by turning right up the hill and returning to town via Jalan Lady Maxwell, or continue another hour on the

Maxwell trail until it reaches Jalan Quarry. Here there's a course for **woodball** – a hybrid of croquet and golf, played with long mallets – with equipment available to rent. The longest trail is the **Pine Tree trail** (4km), which starts at the end of Jalan High Pines and winds up to Pine Tree Hill.

Eating and drinking

Culinary pride of place on Fraser's Hill goes to the **restaurant** at *Ye Olde Smokehouse*. It's pricey (main courses start at RM40), but is well worth the expense for a slap-up meal: the classic English fare – beef Wellington, oxtail stew with dumplings, bread-and-butter pudding and the like – is pretty convincing, and the service suitably reserved and unhurried. They also do **cream teas** (daily 3.30–6pm), as well as a good range of beers and whiskeys, plus shandy, all of which go down especially well in the country-pub-style lounge. Things are fairly informal during the day, but don't turn up in a T-shirt and shorts in the evening.

By the time you read this, many of the cheaper restaurants should have moved to a new food centre at the children's playground as part of a general remodelling of the hill station. It's worth checking out the *Hill View* here, which serves Chinese food. Back at the clock tower is the *Tavern*, for American breakfasts, steaks and burgers, as well as pricey scones. Both the *Tavern* and the *Hill View* serve alcohol.

Kuala Lipis

It's hard to believe that **KUALA LIPIS**, about 100km northeast of Fraser's Hill by road, was the state capital of Pahang from 1898 to 1955. Today, it's a sleepy, inconsequential place, situated at the confluence of Sungai Lipis and Sungai Jelai (a tributary of the Pahang), dwarfed by steep hills and surrounded by forest and plantations, though a certain frontier-town charm still lingers.

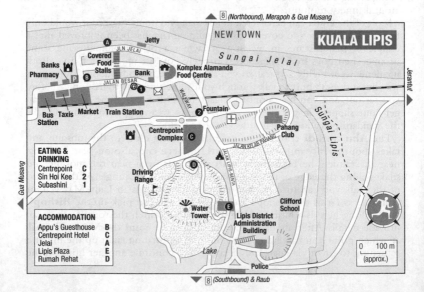

Kuala Lipis started life as a small riverside settlement in the early nineteenth century; the population grew from a few dozen to around two thousand by the 1890s. By then it was a **trading centre** for *gaharu* (a fragrant aloe wood used to make joss sticks) and other jungle products, collected by the Semiar and traded with Chinese *towkays*. Until the first road was built from Kuala Lumpur in the 1890s – allowing the 170-kilometre journey here from the capital to be made by bullock cart – the river was the only means of transport; the trip from Singapore by ship and then sampan upriver took over two weeks. Nevertheless, because of its central geographical position and early importance as a transit point on Sungai Pahang for locally mined tin, Kuala Lipis was where the colonial government set up its state administrative headquarters. However, the tin deposits soon evaporated, and while today Kuala Lipis benefits to a degree from nearby gold-mining, it has long since been eclipsed by the rise of Kuantan on the east coast.

For a town whose main street is only a few hundred metres long, Kuala Lipis boasts an unusual number of colonial-era buildings, which makes the town a reasonable place to stop over en route to Taman Negara at Kuala Tahan or even Merapoh. Also nearby is the **Kenong Rimba State Park** (see p.260), promising rainforest hikes without the crowds that pack Taman Negara's headquarters.

Arrival and information

Both **train and bus stations** are on the old town's main street, Jalan Besar, though it is possible that the bus station will be moved across the river to the new town springing up there. The KTM ticket office is only open sporadically by day (roughly 10–11.30am, 12.30–3pm & 5.30–7pm) but stays open from 9.30pm until 4am, during which time the express trains trundle through. There is no official **tourist office** in town; the establishment of that name in the train station is really a travel agency.

Jalan Besar is also where you'll find a few **banks**, the post office and a couple of pharmacies. There's also a reliable internet café here, located upstairs a few doors from the *Subashini* restaurant. For general supplies, head to the Aktif **supermarket** on the ground floor of the Centrepoint Complex – intended to be a grand shopping development but in reality several floors of dreary stores around a central courtyard dominated by wheeling swiftlets at night.

The easiest way to reach the **Taman Negara** headquarters (see p.234) from Kuala Lipis is to charter a taxi to the Tembeling jetty (around RM50), though it's also possible to get a local bus to Jerantut, getting off at Tembeling where boats head to Kuala Tahan. Alternatively, hop on a train for Jerantut and get the Kuala Tahan bus from there.

Accommodation

There are plenty of budget and mid-range places to stay, though avoid the cheapest places you'll see in the centre, as they tend to be seedy.

Appu's Guesthouse 63 Jalan Besar ☎09/312 2619, ✉jungleappu@yahoo.com. Appu leads trips to Kenong Rimba and has put his affection for the forest into the jungle mural that adorns one wall here. His guesthouse is a homely affair, with a range of basic rooms (including a quad room with a/c) which share facilities. The sign outside reads *Lipis Guest House*. Dorm beds RM10, rooms ❶.

Centrepoint Hotel ☎09/312 2688, ✉centrepointhotel@gmail.com. The Centrepoint Complex's saving grace, this hotel boasts a vast

range of rooms in "regular" and "executive" grades. All have a/c, satellite TV and tiled bathrooms; the regular rooms are rather poky and often windowless, but they're good value nonetheless. Be sure to ask about promotional rates, which apply most of the year. There's a decent restaurant too (rates include buffet breakfast). Wi-fi available. Reception is on level 5. ❸
Jelai 44 Jalan Jelai ☏09/312 1192, ✉hjelai @streamyx.com. First impressions here aren't promising: the receptionists are barricaded behind glass like bank tellers, and the corridors are bare. Somehow, though, the rooms are immaculate – spotless, with a/c, bathroom and TV, and there's wi-fi too. They have a second hotel near the Centrepoint Complex but it's nowhere near as good. ❸

Lipis Plaza Komplex Taipan, Jalan Benta–Lipis ☏09/312 5588, ✉info@lipisplaza.com. Spacious but rather plain rooms in a modern complex nestled at the base of Bukit Residen. Rates include breakfast. ❹
Rumah Rehat (Government Rest House) Bukit Residen ☏09/312 2784, ℻312 3953. Not to be confused with the *Rumah Rehat* to the south of town, Clifford's former home has been jazzed up with a coat of scarlet paint, but the interior is rather bland. Still, the rooms – all with a/c and TV – are well kept if dull, and the attached bathrooms are large, dwarfing rooms in many cheap hotels. Inconveniently, the café isn't open for breakfast. A taxi from town will cost around RM6. ❸

The Town

The old core of Kuala Lipis comprises just a few streets of quaint shophouses, some given a nice new lick of paint, squeezed into a sliver of land between the train line and the Jelai River. The tracks form a divide in more ways than one, for south of the line is an altogether different landscape of wooded hillsides and playing fields, nestled among which are the town's surviving colonial buildings. An elevated pedestrian walkway and a road bridge are practically all that connect the old centre with the town's hinterland, which is small enough to cover on foot in two or three hours.

From the complex traffic intersection by the Centrepoint development, a road leads east along a small ridge, past the town's hospital, to the **Pahang Club** (1867). Though once the archetypal colonial club in the tropics, it's not at all grand – indeed there's something of the English rural train station about the building, all white wooden slats and grilles. The club was the first building constructed by the British in the town, later serving as a temporary residence for Pahang's most famous Resident, Hugh Clifford. It's now a meeting place and sports venue for the town's small business community, and is restricted to members, though if you ask nicely you may be allowed to look around.

The buildings you can see across the fields to the south of the Pahang Club belong to the town's historic Clifford School. Don't head across the fields to get there, but instead take the road that descends southwest from the club, joining the town's north–south artery close to an Indian temple, where you turn left. Further on, just before the major T-junction, you'll spot a flight of steps up to the top of a hillock crowned by the town's largest colonial structure, the crimson-and-white **Lipis District Administration Building**. Dating from 1919, it's been beautifully maintained and now serves as the local law court. Below here is the access road for **Clifford School**, built in 1913 and part-funded by Hugh Clifford; the original buildings are at the far end of the compound. The school is still one of a select group where the country's leaders and royalty are educated – though these days it's perhaps equally known for having been attended by Malaysia's biggest-selling pop songstress, Siti Nurhaliza. There's not a lot to see, but you may be able to have a discreet look around.

▲ Kuala Lipis administration building

Hugh Clifford lived in a graceful two-storey house atop one of the town's highest hills, now called **Bukit Residen**, the access road for which coils upwards from just south of the *Lipis Plaza* hotel and near a colourful **Hindu temple** that's worth a brief look. It's a pleasant, none too taxing stroll to the top, but the rewards are slim: the building is now the somewhat disappointing *Government Rest House*, which curiously has its own mini-ethnographic museum downstairs, and the marvellous views of the Pahang jungles the hill once offered have been largely obscured by trees.

A vibrant **pasar malam** takes place around the bus station every Friday night. Stalls sell everything from cleaning utensils and digital watches to comb honey, edible ferns and river fish (some produce may have been brought by Orang Asli from as far away as Kelantan), while hawkers prepare satay, noodles and snacks,

Eating and drinking

The best place to **eat** in town is the lively *Sin Hoi Kee*, just across from the Centrepoint Complex, with a wide-ranging Chinese menu at reasonable prices. The restaurant at the *Centrepoint Hotel* comes a close second, offering a great seafood platter with chips and tartare sauce, plus steaks and sandwiches. For an inexpensive meal, head along Jalan Besar to *Subashini*, a terrific, friendly Tamil curry house with the usual spread of fiery fare as well as *nasi lemak* and *mee goreng* at breakfast; get there early if you want dinner, as it can be shut around 8pm. Otherwise, there are plenty of **food stalls** in the Alamanda food centre and Centrepoint Complex for Malay and Chinese fare, while the alley connecting Jalan Besar and Jalan Jelai has a collection of Chinese *kedai kopis* and bakeries. For a drink, there are a few somewhat tacky Chinese **beer gardens** in the lanes around the Centrepoint Complex.

Kenong Rimba State Park

Coupled with a visit to Kuala Lipis, **Kenong Rimba State Park** makes for a nicely varied three- to five-day stop-off en route from KL to Kota Bharu. Rimba's main attraction is that it offers a compact version of the Taman Negara experience – jungle trails, riverside camping, mammal-spotting and excellent birdwatching – at much reduced prices and without the hype which characterizes the larger park on its northeastern border. One-tenth of the size of Taman Negara, Kenong Rimba stretches over 128 square kilometres of the Kenong Valley, east of Banjaran Titiwangsa. It's dotted with limestone hills, which are riddled with caves of varying sizes, and crossed by trails that snake

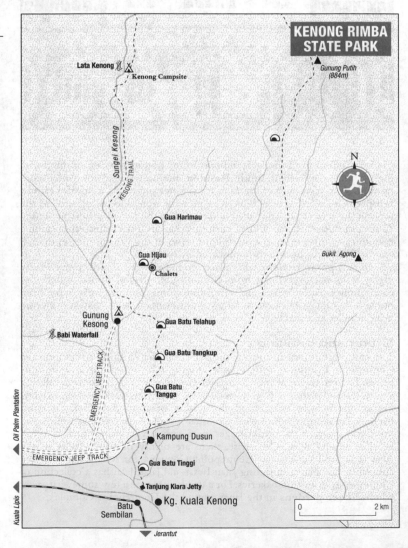

along the forest floor. The park is also a promising place to spot big mammals, though it's still unlikely you'll catch sight of a tiger or elephant.

As Rimba is small, you can see most of its main sights within **four days**. You could check out the caves for a day, spend another trekking to the waterfall, and two or three days walking back through the jungle, where you may chance upon a village of the nomadic Batek people. The main trail in the park, the nine-kilometre Kesong trail, heads north from park headquarters along the Sungai Kesong to the Lata Kenong ("Seven Steps Waterfall"). Here you are surrounded by lowland forest, through which little sunlight penetrates. Over the years, the Batek have cleared portions of forest around this trail for agricultural purposes, which could account for the jungle's impenetrability – secondary forest tends to grow back more thickly than primary. Returning on the south-eastern loop of the trail takes longer and is harder going as it traverses several small hills – Gunung Putih (884m) is the largest. If you only have time for a brief visit to the park, you could make straight for the waterfall and camp there for a night, leaving the park by the same route the next day.

The caves

The first of the six **caves** in Rimba is outside the park proper, close to the Tanjung Kiara jetty. About ten minutes' walk from the jetty along the road, look out for a path on your left which leads west to **Gua Batu Tinggi**, a small cave just big enough to clamber into. Inside, there's a surprising variety of plant life, including orchids and fig trees.

Gua Batu Tangga ("Cave of Rock Steps") is a twenty-minute walk direct from the camp at Gunung Kesong, though you can also get there from the Batu Tinggi cave by returning along the trail leading to it and crossing the road, following the path to the left of a house – a sign points to the cave, which lies twenty minutes' walk further on. Shaped like an inverted wok, the large limestone cave has a wide, deep chamber, in whose northwest corner a row of rocks forms ledges or steps, which give the cave its name. The cave is sometimes occupied by elephants – the trail through it narrows between rocks rubbed smooth over time, probably by the passage of the great creatures – but you're more likely to catch sight of mousedeer or porcupine scurrying away. Two smaller caves, **Gua Batu Tangkup** and **Gua Batu Telahup**, are just a few hundred metres beyond Tangga on the same trail.

Two more caves lie close to the park headquarters: **Gua Hijau** ("Green Cave"), just five minutes' walk east over two bridges, is home to thousands of bats, while **Gua Harimau** ("Tiger Cave"), a little further along on the right, is scarcely more than an overhang and reputedly the lair of tigers.

Practicalities

As there's no scheduled transport to the park, it's best to go on a **package** trip or hire a guide who can make the necessary arrangements. The most straight-forward option is to go with Kiara Holidays, an agency based on level 4 of the Centrepoint Complex in Kuala Lipis (℡09/312 2777, ⊛www.kiaraholidays .com); you may also be available to find their staff in the *Centrepoint Hotel*. They offer a range of packages that include transfers, meals at the park's café and use of the park chalets and dorms, which they currently hold the concession to run; a two-day trip, for example, costs RM250 per person if you have a group of at least three. Packages are also available from Green Park Adventure in Jerantut (see p.231). Appu at *Appu's Guesthouse* has done plenty of Kenong Rimba treks in his time, and charges RM80 per person per day (minimum group size four) including food, plus RM150 return per group to cover transport. His trips, which offer a range of routes, usually involve camping (incurring a park fee of RM5 per person per night), though he can arrange to use the park accommodation if you so wish.

No special **equipment** is needed in the park, but be sure to bring decent walking shoes and plenty of drinking water on the trails. Mosquito repellent is also worth having on hand, and make sure to take precautions against leeches (see p.36). It's also worth bringing a torch, swimsuit, sandals (for wading through streams), a rain poncho and a change of clothing.

Gua Musang

As you head north by train or on Route 8 you'll find the jungle landscape altering near Merapoh, 80km north of Kuala Lipis, where there's a predominance of large, round limestone hills. From here, it's another half-hour by local train to **GUA MUSANG**, just off Route 8 and a few kilometres south of the recently built road from Simpang Pulai near the Cameron Highlands. As in Kuala Lipis, there's a distinct frontier spirit here, but that's about the only parallel. Being in Kelantan, Gua Musang has noticably fewer Malaysians of Indian extraction than towns in Pahang; the Malay used here shows signs of the distinctive Kelantanese twang – and alcohol is practically unavailable. For more on Kelantan society and politics, see p.272. After the arrival of Route 8, Gua Musang expanded quickly as logging money flowed in, the new road having made remote tracts of forest accessible to the timber saws. While logging appears to have tailed off, Gua Musang's development is proceeding apace, and a **new town** is springing up a couple of kilometres south of the original settlement.

Gua Musang is fairly close to the Taman Negara entrances at Merapoh (see p.248) and Kuala Koh (see p.249), but the main reason visitors stop off is to explore the **caves** that riddle the mass of limestone above the town. Both the caves and the town are named after a small creature, the *musang*, which looks like a civet and used to live up in the caves; it's now almost extinct.

Arrival and information

Gua Musang's **train station** is at the northern end of the old town. The station master may agree to let you leave **luggage** at your own risk in his office at the train station – if so you do, it's worth having a quick glance at the antiquated signalling equipment still in use. The main **bus station** is 2km to the south in the new town; buses to and from points north still call at the old bus station along Jalan Pulai, though they start

Map labels:
Bank KFC
Train Station
JALAN BESAR
Caves
Food Stalls
JALAN PEKAN LAMA
GM Skynet
JALAN PULAI
Supermarket
Police
Old Bus Station

EATING
GM Food Garden — 2
Kedai Makan Mana Lagi — 1
Restoran Haji Sulaiman — D

ACCOMMODATION
Evergreen — B
Fully Inn — C
Gua Musang — F
Gunung Emas — A
Kesedar Inn — E
Usaha — D

0 — 100 m

GUA MUSANG

New Town, **F** & **8**

and end their journeys in the new town. A taxi ride between the two will cost around RM5. Both bus stations have taxis available to charter for destinations such as Kuala Besut (for the Perhentians), Kuala Lipis and Kota Bharu (prices for these three are roughly RM100 per car), or even the Cameron Highlands (RM120).

There are a few **banks** in the old town on Jalan Besar, close to the train station. Jalan Pulai, the road leading towards the new town, has a couple of **internet** cafés along it and a **supermarket** close to the **post office**.

Accommodation

Considering how small Gua Musang is, it's surprising that it has several decent places to stay, mostly used by local tourists, travelling salesmen and the like.

Evergreen 57 Jalan Besar ☎09/912 2273. Justifiably popular for its reasonably priced rooms with a/c, TV and attached bathroom, though they are very plain. ❷

Fully Inn 75 Jalan Pekan Lama ☎09/912 3311, ☏912 3322. Chinese-run hotel that's the grandest in town, with a thing for ostentatious marble stairways. Rooms are slickly furnished, with satellite TV, a/c and bathroom. The restaurant serves largely Asian fare with a few Western dishes thrown in, at slightly inflated places. Rates include breakfast. ❹

Gua Musang In the new town, close to the bus station ☎09/912 2121. A decent hotel with a/c en-suite rooms. ❸

Gunung Emas 20 Jalan Besar ☎09/912 6843. Fine for a night, with a/c rooms, some en suite, others – somewhat shabbier – with shared facilities. ❷

Kesedar Inn 400m west of the Jalan Pulai Mosque ☎09/912 1229, ✉kes_inn@streamyx .com. Quite a contrast to the long lane on which it lies, lined with wooden stilt houses and fruit trees, the *Kesedar Inn* is a complex of largely new buildings with hints of colonial styling. Most rooms have mod cons and modern furnishings, though the cheapest ones are quite old-fashioned. Breakfast is included. It's worth calling ahead if you want to stay, if only because part or all of the hotel may be converted into a hospitality college in the years to come. ❸

Usaha 187 Jalan Pulai, across from the old bus station ☎09/912 4003, ☏912 4002. A friendly Malay-run hotel with a popular restaurant below. Not quite as well kept as it should be, but the simple rooms, en suite with TV and a/c, are more than acceptable. ❸

The caves

To get to the caves, cross the rail track at the station and walk through the small kampung in the shadow of the rock behind the station. Here you'll have to ask one of the villagers to guide you (it's usual to pay around RM10 for this); it is possible to reach the caves on your own, but the trail – which is directly at the back of the huts – is difficult to negotiate after rain, when it's likely to be extremely slippery. Wear strong shoes and take a torch to use inside the cave. Once you've climbed steeply up 20m of rock face you'll see a narrow ledge; turn left and edge carefully along until you see a long slit in the rock which leads into a cave – you'll need to be fairly thin to negotiate this. The inside of the cave is enormous, 60m long and 30m high in places, and well lit by sunlight from holes above. The main cave leads to lesser ones, which have rock formations jutting out from the walls and ceilings. The only way out is by the same route, which you'll need to take very carefully, especially the near-vertical descent off the ledge and back down to the kampung.

Eating

One of the few eating places in town really to advertise its presence is *Kedai Makan Mana Lagi*, a converted open-air food court on Jalan Besar that's festooned with coloured lights in the evening. This simple, lively Malay restaurant serves food with a Thai twist, as is often the case in Kelantan; even the humble fried *kangkung* with squid has a lemongrass kick to it. They have a good range of *tom yam* and *kerabu*-style dishes, plus quite a lot of seafood, including *ikan tiga rasa*, one of the house specialities – though none of the staff can explain what the three flavours of the name derive from. *Restoran Haji Sulaiman*, below the *Usaha* hotel, is also a good bet, busy well into the night and serving both Malay and Chinese food. Otherwise, for Chinese food, there's the rather spartan pavilion of the *GM Food Garden* on Jalan Pulai, and plenty of stalls and *kedai kopis* on and around Jalan Pekan Lama.

Dabong and around

Around 55km north of Gua Musang, **DABONG** is a Malay village sited on the east bank of the wide Sungai Galas and surrounded by flat-topped limestone peaks and dark-green forest. The main reason to come here is to visit the excellent **Stong State Park** (often referred to by its old name, **Jelawang Park**) around Gunung Stong to the south of town, where you can overnight on the mountainside for magical sunrise views, and enjoy hiking close to a series of waterfalls and plunge pools.

Bypassed by Route 8, Dabong itself has been very much a backwater, its main links to the outside world being the river, the rail line (Dabong is an express-train stop) and the Gua Musang–Jeli road, which passes to the west of the village. Until recently villagers had to get a boat west across the Galas to the access road for Stong State Park and the Gua Musang road, but a major new bridge has put paid to this hassle. There's also a minor road west to Dabong from Kampung Tembeling on Route 8.

Dabong is not quite the classic kampung these days, its older, wooden houses now overshadowed by brick and concrete constructions. There's only one **place to stay** here, *Rumah Rehat Dabong* (℡019/960 6789; ❷), run by the friendly Din, who speaks some English (ask around for "Abang Din" if he's not there when you arrive). To reach it from the **train station**, head along the station road, past the school on the right, and immediately turn left into Jalan Pejabat; the resthouse is the long, largely yellow bungalow 50m further along on the right. The building looks a little dilapidated on the outside, but the rooms (some with a/c) are totally serviceable, with a *mandi* and a squat toilet. The walls are thin though, and with the mosque just across the road, interrupted sleep is a distinct possibility. For **food**, there's nothing more than a *kedai kopi* or two and a couple of shops on the station road.

Gua Ikan

A minor attraction near Dabong is **Gua Ikan**, one of several limestone caves a little way south of the village. It's an hour's walk away along a modern road lined with monotonous *belukar*: from the station, cross the rail track, turn right (south), and continue for 4km. Better is to try to ask around for a taxi or pay one of the locals to give you a ride there on the back of a motorbike. The caves are clearly signposted off to the right of the road, set in a small, unmaintained park. In the main cave, 40m long and 20m high, you can follow the course of a stream which runs along the cave floor; make sure to bring a torch and sturdy sandals (the rocks are too slippery to go barefoot and the stream may be knee-high at times, making shoes impractical). Any locals present may be able to point out a few rock formations, including a structure shaped vaguely like an upright piano, which people like to say would be suitable for *bersanding* – that part of the Malay wedding ceremony during which bride and groom are presented on a dais to the guests. The stream leads out to the other side of the cave to a small rock-enclosed area, a lovely spot to rest and listen to the birds and monkeys.

Stong State Park

Stong State Park is an off-the-beaten-track gem, offering the prospect of hiking through lush forest and then alongside Peninsular Malaysia's highest waterfall (variously called Lata Jelawang or Air Terjun Stong), eventually ending up at the top of **Gunung Stong**, one of Kelantan's highest peaks at over 1400m. Just as big an incentive is overnighting halfway up the mountain at the atmospheric *Baha's Camp*, a rustic collection of a ten or so wood and bamboo huts sited close to a cliff over which one tier of the waterfall plunges. The huts are very clammy at night because of the high humidity, but you'll soon find yourself being lulled into sleep by the constant babbling of flowing water nearby. There's a pool here that's great for a nocturnal swim, though make sure to get a good night's rest as you will want to be up at dawn to watch the sunrise, when you may well be treated to the sight of a golden orb rising over a sea of cottonwool clouds blanketing the plains.

From the camp you can set off on the three-hour **Seven Waterfalls** circuit, which takes you up the west side of the waterfall to a simple campsite, then heads down the east side. The uphill part of the trek takes around ninety minutes and is fairly gruelling, involving some sheer, muddy sections, though rocks at the side of the trail allow you to rest and look back over the forest. The **Elephant trek**, the longer of the two trails here, follows the main path up the mountain for two hours to the top of Gunung Stong, before winding along the ridge and crossing over onto neighbouring Gunung Ayam. Although it's possible to return to the waterfall campsite the same day on this trek, it's preferable to camp for the night at a clearing along the trail, near a small stream – you'll need some warm clothing and a sleeping bag. Elephants are sometimes seen here, and there's a chance of encountering **tapir** and **deer** in the early morning or early evening. Of course, you don't have to attempt anything as arduous as either of these treks: much more relaxing is to take a gentle stroll up by the various tiers of the waterfall and swim in the plunge pools as the fancy takes you.

Practicalities

The easiest way to visit the park is to book a **package** with a guesthouse in Kota Bharu (see p.276). A two-day package, including train tickets and three meals which will be cooked and eaten in the camp's kitchen – nothing more than a large open-sided shelter (and a great place to enjoy the staff's campfire-style renditions of Malay pop tunes on battered guitars after dinner) – will cost around RM170 per person for a group of four; three-day packages are also available for around RM300 per person. It is possible to make your own arrangements to stay at *Baha's Camp* (☎019/959 1020); accommodation costs a nominal amount, around RM15 per person, but you will also need to agree on the cost of meals (unless you want to lug food up) and transfers from and back to Dabong. If you just turn up in Dabong on spec, Din at the *Rumah Rehat* there may be able to help contact the camp and arrange a visit, including transport to the base of Gunung Stong, which is over an hour's walk away via a modern road with little shade.

At the foot of the mountain are the sturdy chalets of the *Stong Hill Resort*, which has sadly been closed for a while, though the state tourist office in Kota Bharu may be able to say if it has reopened. Until then, its only interest is as a place to store most of your luggage in order to ease the trek up to the camp. If you aren't accompanied by a guide from Kota Bharu or met by someone from the camp, cross the bridge at the base of the falls, head past the last few chalets on the far side and take the narrow track that continues steeply up through the forest for about half an hour before levelling out; altogether it takes around 45 minutes to reach the camp.

Travel details

Trains

Express services through the interior run once daily in each direction between KL and Tumpat near Kota Bharu, and between Singapore and Tumpat. They're supplemented by a stopping service between Singapore and Tumpat, and by local services (calling at almost every minor station, and denoted "Mel" on timetables) on various stretches of the line between Gemas and Tumpat. While combined frequencies are given here, the journey times are for express services; local trains take roughly half as long again.
Gua Musang to: Dabong (6 daily; 1hr); Gemas (3 daily; 6hr 30min); Jerantut (3 daily; 2hr 45min); Johor Bahru (2 daily; 11hr); Kota Bharu (Wakaf Bharu station; 6 daily; 3hr 30min); Kuala Lipis (4 daily; 1hr 45min); Kuala Lumpur (1 daily; 9hr 30min); Merapoh (3 daily; 30min); Seremban (1 daily; 8hr); Singapore (2 daily; 12hr).
Jerantut to: Dabong (3 daily; 3hr 45min); Gemas (4 daily; 4hr); Gua Musang (3 daily; 2hr 45min); Johor Bahru (2 daily; 7hr 30min); Kota Bharu (Wakaf Bharu station; 3 daily; 6hr); Kuala Lipis (4 daily; 1hr); Kuala Lumpur (1 daily; 7hr 30min); Merapoh (2 daily; 3hr 30min); Seremban (1 daily; 6hr); Singapore (2 daily; 9hr).

Buses

Most intercity journeys depart during daylight hours.
Gua Musang to: Kota Bharu (several daily; 4hr); Kuala Lipis (2 daily; 2hr 30min); Kuala Lumpur (4 daily; 6hr).
Jerantut to: Kuala Lipis (hourly; 1hr 30min); Kuala Tahan (4 daily; 1hr 45min); Kuantan (7 daily; 3hr express or 4hr local); Tembeling jetty (hourly; 40min); Temerloh (10 daily; 1hr).
Kuala Lipis to: Gua Musang (2 daily; 2hr); Kuala Lumpur (6 daily; 4hr); Kuantan (2 daily; 6hr); Raub (several daily; 1hr 30min).

Boats

Kuala Tembeling jetty to: Kuala Tahan (daily at 9am & 2pm except Fri 9am & 2.30pm; 2hr 30min–3hr).

The east coast

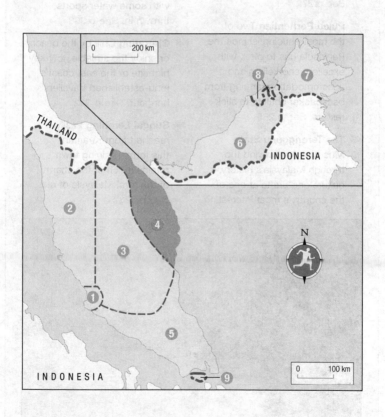

CHAPTER 4 # Highlights

✳ **Kota Bharu** One of the Peninsula's most appealing cities, offering a glimpse of Kelantanese Malay culture; come here to see traditional crafts being made and traditional art forms staged. See p.272

✳ **Pulau Perhentian** Two of the most enticing islands the Peninsula has to offer, with excellent snorkelling and accommodation ranging from backpacker chalets to slick resorts. See p.285

✳ **The Terengganu State Museum** A whirlwind trip through Malaysia's history, culture and crafts at one of the country's most interesting cultural complexes, in Kuala Terengganu. See p.303

✳ **Pulau Kapas** A small island with some decent sands and opportunities for snorkelling and kayaking – perfect for a couple of days' relaxation, with some water sports thrown in. See p.308

✳ **Cherating** Chill by the beach or enjoy the amiable, low-key nightlife at the east coast's long-established travellers' hangout. See p.312

✳ **Sungai Lembing** Easily reached from Kuantan, this former mining town retains much of the charm of the rural Malaysia of old. See p.323

▲ Beach on the west shore of Pulau Perhentian Besar

The east coast

The four-hundred-kilometre stretch from the northeastern corner of the Peninsula to Kuantan, roughly halfway down the east coast, draws visitors for two major reasons: the many **beaches and islands**, especially in Terengganu, and traditional **Malay culture**. The greatest appeal arguably lies in the casuarina-fringed beaches and coral reefs of **Pulau Perhentian**, **Pulau Redang** and **Pulau Kapas**, some of the most beautiful islands in the South China Sea, all three with great opportunities for diving and snorkelling. Further south along the coast, the backpackers' enclave of **Cherating** is a deservedly popular place to simply chill out for a few days. All along the east coast, there are a handful of beaches where, between May and September, it's possible to view marine **turtles** coming ashore to lay their eggs. Among the cities, it's vibrant **Kota Bharu**, close to the Thai border, that stands out for its opportunities to glimpse the gradually disappearing worlds of Malay crafts and performing arts. **Kuala Terengganu**, 140km to the south, is more downbeat, though it does have an atmospheric old Chinese quarter, a traditional boat-building industry and an excellent museum. Both are infinitely preferable to the sheer mundanity of **Kuantan**, which is partly redeemed by a few good beaches and restaurants.

Flights to Kota Bharu or Kuala Terengganu can be useful time-savers, but road access to the east coast has really opened up with the completion of the **East Coast Highway**. This links up with the E8 Highway from KL to Karak in the interior, and arrives on the coast just north of Kuantan, reducing the drive from KL to the east coast to a three-hour whizz. The highway's impact will soon be felt even more directly when phase two, north to Kuala Terengganu, is completed in the next few years. Meanwhile, the backbone roads through the region remain the coast road (called Route 3 between Kuala Terengganu and Kuantan) and its shadow, running 10 to 20km inland (Route 14 south of Kuala Terengganu, Route 3 to the north). Unsurprisingly, it's the coastal road that's the more interesting, connecting a string of laid-back small towns and fishing kampungs. The only **rail** service is the atmospheric one through the interior (see box, p.227) to Tumpat, near Kota Bharu.

Some history

The east coast displays a quite different cultural legacy from the more populous, commercial western seaboard. For hundreds of years, the Malay rulers of the northern states of **Kelantan** and **Terengganu** were vassals of the Thai kingdom of **Ayuthaya**, suffering repeated invasions as well as the unruly squabbles of their own princes. Nevertheless, the Malays enjoyed a great deal of autonomy, and both states remained free of British control until 1909, thus escaping the

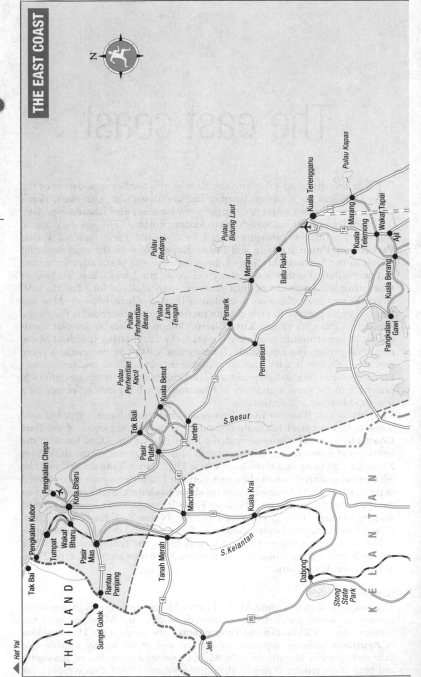

THE EAST COAST

Pulau Kapas

Kuala Terengganu

Marang

Pulau Bidung Laut

Wakaf Tapai

Kuala
Telemong

Ajil

Pulau Redang

Merang

Batu Rakit

Kuala Berang

Penarik

Pangkalan
Gawi

*Pulau Perhentian
Besar*

Pulau Lang Tengah

Permaisuri

*Pulau Perhentian
Kecil*

Kuala Besut

S.Besut

Tok Bali

Jerteh

Pengkalan Chepa

Pasir
Puteh

Kota Bharu

Machang

Kuala Krai

Pengkalan Kubor

Wakaf
Bharu

Tumpat

Pasir
Mas

Tanah Merah

S.Kelantan

Tak Bai

Pengkalan Kubor

Rantau
Panjang

THAILAND

Sungei Golok

Jeli

Dabong

Stong
State
Park

K E L A N T A N

Hat Yai

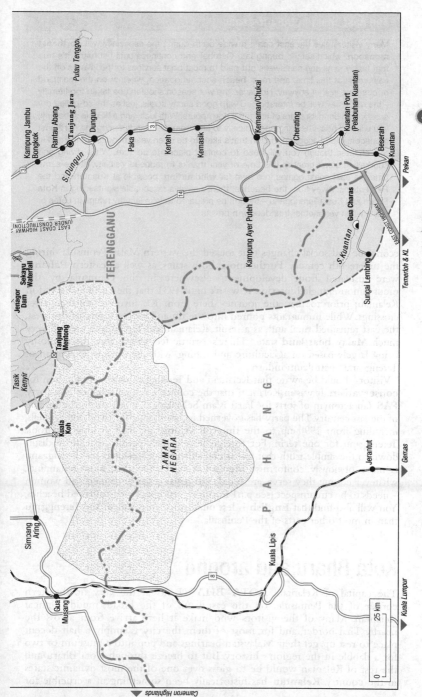

Many visitors give the east coast a wide berth during the especially wet **northeast monsoon**, which sets in during late October and continues until February. It's true that heavy rains and sea swells put paid to most boat services to the islands off the east coast at this time, and most beach accommodation, whether on the mainland or offshore, is shut anyway. However, the wet season shouldn't be taken too literally – the rains may well be interspersed with good sunny spells, just as the so-called dry season can bring its share of torrential downpours. With luck, and a flexible schedule, you will find boats heading sporadically to and from the islands during the northeast monsoon; island accommodation that's likely to be open year-round is highlighted in this chapter, though you will need to contact places to be sure. While diving and snorkelling aren't great at this time of year thanks to reduced visibility, at the same time the east coast comes into own for **windsurfing**, possible at Kuantan and the Perhentians. Away from the beaches, there's always reasonable sightseeing in Kota Bharu and Kuala Terengganu – though be prepared to take lengthy refuge in cafés or malls when yet another thunderstorm breaks.

economic and social changes that rocked the western Malay Peninsula during the nineteenth century. Furthermore, both states, as well as eastern **Pahang**, were insulated from developments elsewhere in the Peninsula by the mountainous, jungled interior. It wasn't until 1931 that the rail line arrived in Kelantan; prior to that, the journey here from KL involved thirteen river crossings. While immigrants poured into the tin and rubber towns of the west, the east remained rural and, as a result, Kelantan and Terengganu are still very much **Malay heartland** states. There's a rustic feel to the area, the economy being largely based on agriculture and fishing, with the obvious exception of Terengganu's petroleum industry.

Visitors should be aware that Kelantan and Terengganu have a reputation for **conservatism**. It was in Kelantan that the country's religious opposition party, **PAS** (an acronym of sorts for Parti Islam SeMalaysia), was born in the middle of the last century. The party has governed its home state for two lengthy spells, including from 1990 up to the time of writing, and not so long ago took Terengganu for one term. For foreign visitors, this political backdrop distils down to the simple truth that the **social climate** of Kelantan and Terengganu is more obviously conformist: **alcohol** is hard to obtain; most restaurants, whatever cuisine they serve, are **halal**; and **dress** – for both men and women – needs to be circumspect (see p.61 for more), except at well-touristed beaches. You will also find that **English** is less understood in Kelantan and Terengganu than in most other parts of the Peninsula.

Kota Bharu and around

The capital of Kelantan, **KOTA BHARU** sits at the very northeastern corner of the Peninsula, on the east bank of the broad, muddy Sungai Kelantan. Many of the visitors who make it here arrive from across the nearby Thai border, and for most of them the city is simply a half-decent place to rest up, get their Malaysian bearings and pop into a museum or two for a dabble in the region's history. But to breeze through Kota Bharu and the rest of Kelantan would be to gloss over one of the most dynamic states in the country. **Kelantan** has historically been something of a crucible for

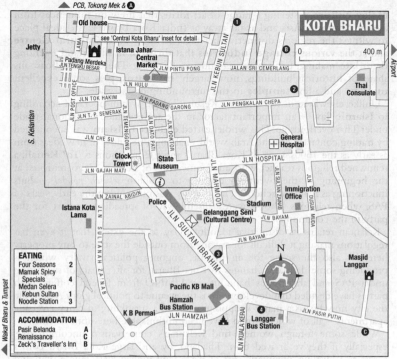

ACCOMMODATION

Bunga Raya Backpacker Lodge	**L**	Grand Riverview	**O**	KB Backpackers Lodge	**N**	Rumah Rakit Nik Ismail	**Q**
Crystal Lodge	**P**	Ideal Traveller's House	**H**	Pesona Inn	**M**	Royal Guesthouse	**F**
Flora Place	**I**	Indah	**H**	Ridel	**G**	Temenggong	**J**
		KB Backpackers Inn	**K**				

Malay culture, fostering a range of art forms that drew on influences from around Southeast Asia and as far away as India. Kota Bharu is the ideal place to witness the region's distinctive heritage, on show at its **Cultural Centre** and at the various **cottage industries** that thrive in its hinterland – among them kite-making, batik printing and woodcarving. The city also boasts its share of historical buildings, now largely **museums**, plus some excellent **markets** and a few **temples** in the surrounding countryside.

Unlike elsewhere in the country, Kelantan's legal system operated according to **Islamic law** – an important factor in the maintenance of national pride under Thai overlordship. This wholehearted embrace of **Islam** was encouraged by trading contacts with the Arab world, enabling a free flow of new ideas from as early as the 1600s. One of Kota Bharu's most famous sons is **To' Kenali**, a renowned religious teacher who, after some years of study in Cairo, returned at the beginning of the twentieth century to establish *sekolah pondok* – huts functioning as religious schools. This strategy was mirrored in the early years of PAS, when religious schools were a useful way of spreading support for the party in the community.

Kelantan retains its distinctive identity today, to the extent that it even has regulations making it difficult for anyone from outside the state to buy property here. It's also the scene for an intense, ongoing political rivalry which is producing some dramatic changes in Kota Bharu, for after years of stagnation under PAS and abstemious handouts by UMNO from federal coffers, both parties have decided that development is the avenue to political glory. As a result, the city now boasts a major shopping mall and a sprinkling of fancy riverside apartments – all of which would have been unthinkable here until recently.

While some foreign women find Kelantan's conservatism uncomfortable, especially if they've arrived from Thailand, by and large Kota Bharu comes across as a bustling, pragmatic sort of place (and indeed Kelantanese men and women alike have a reputation in Malaysia for entrepreneurial talent). One additional thing that strikes those visitors with some knowledge of Malay is the unique **dialect** (*kecek Kelate*) heard in Kota Bharu and all over the state. So odd it's confusing even to many Malays, broad Kelantanese will have your head spinning: it's about as singsong as Malay gets; features various contractions, changes to consonant clusters and twists to word endings, such as the conversion of *-an* to *-ay* (Kelantan is actually rendered here as "Kelatay"); and boasts a few words all of its own, such as *gwano* instead of *bagaimana* for "how", and – worth noting – **ria** sometimes instead of ringgit.

Arrival, information and transport

Long-distance **buses** arrive at one of the two bus stations, inconveniently situated on the southern outskirts of the city: the state bus company, SKMK, operates out of the **Langgar bus station** on Jalan Pasir Puteh, as do Transnasional and MARA; other companies use the **Hamzah bus station**, 600m west. A taxi into the centre should cost around RM7; unlicensed taxis (basically, private cars) charge double that and may be all you can find, particularly at night. Many long-distance services call at the **local bus station**, off Jalan Padang Garong in the centre, on their way to one of the other stations. **Long-distance taxis** park up in various spaces on Jalan Doktor, south of the local bus station.

The nearest **train station** is 7km west at **Wakaf Bharu**. From here it's a twenty-minute ride into town on bus #19, which runs between 7am and 6pm or so to the local bus station; a taxi into town will cost around RM15. The **airport** is 9km northeast of the centre, from where a taxi into town costs

RM20 – buy a coupon from the airport's taxi counter. A couple of agencies with desks at the airport operate transport to the Perhentians.

The state **tourist office** (TIC; Mon–Thurs & Sun 8am–4.45pm; T09/748 5534), close to the clock tower on Jalan Sultan Ibrahim, is helpful and has useful leaflets on local food and customs; **tours** of various local craft workshops, cookery courses and homestays can be booked here. They can also tell you about various **cultural festivals** held throughout the year, celebrating traditional kites or drumming, or other facets of local life. Open practically identical hours is the **Tourism Malaysia** office (T09/747 7554) at the Kampung Kraftangan, northwest of the central market.

Local taxis (book on T09/744 7104) operate from the same general area as long-distance taxis. Handy for getting around the city environs are SKMK's red **Cityliner** buses, many of which are air-conditioned. The city also has a few **trishaws**, which can be found along the roads around the local bus station. The fare for a journey around the centre is around RM5; make sure you agree the price beforehand.

Accommodation

For a fairly small city, Kota Bharu has an excellent range of accommodation. Budget travellers will appreciate the choice of good-value **guesthouses**, many of which can arrange tickets for onward travel and offer packages to Stong State Park (aka Jelawang; see p.265) and sometimes to Taman Negara via Kuala Koh (see p.249). Roselan Hanafiah at the tourist office runs a **homestay programme** offering the chance to stay with a family, often expert in a particular craft which you can be taught; for a minimum of two people staying for two nights, expect to pay around RM320 per person, including all meals and craft materials.

Hotels

Crystal Lodge 124 Jalan Che Su T09/747 0888, W www.crystallodge.com .my. Two enormous Chinese porcelain vases in the lobby set the tone at this sleek mid-range hotel. Facilities include a café-restaurant, parking next door and plenty of satellite TV channels. A good deal, with keen rates for single rooms, and breakfast included. ④

Flora Place Jalan Kebun Sultan T09/747 7888, E flora888@streamyx.com. This is a well-run modern affair with satellite TV and a small fridge in the rooms. The views from the rooftop restaurant are disappointing though – most of what you see is urban sprawl – and rates are arguably slightly too high, despite breakfast being included. ⑤

Grand Riverview Jalan Post Office Lama T09/743 9988, W www.grh.com.my. The river views aren't anything to write home about, but still, this substantial hotel is modern and comfortable, and the rooms are spacious, en suite and offer a/c and satellite TV. There's wi-fi in the lobby and a pool too. Not a terrible option if they stick to the rack rate, but discounts are available most of the time. Rates include breakfast. ⑥

Indah 236a & b Jalan Tengku Besar T09/748 5081, F748 2788. A simple hotel that's really showing its age, but more than tolerable. The rooms, arranged around a shabby rectangular shaft, all have a/c, TV and bathroom. ③

Renaissance Jalan Sultan Yahya Petra T09/746 2233, W www.marriott.com. The only five-star hotel in Kota Bharu, as locals invariably describe it – and a bargain. There's a range of rooms, some with great views over the city, and all featuring a bathroom with an actual bath and plenty of marble, plus a fridge and satellite TV. Among the amenities are a couple of restaurants, a gorgeous blue-tiled pool, a gym and, at the time of writing, the only hotel bar in the city with alcohol. Breakfast included. ⑦

Ridel At the northern end of the Pelangi mall, with its entrance facing the river T09/747 7000, W www.ridelhotel.com.my. The owner has a thing about fish – so every room has fish paintings to enliven what is otherwise rather minimalist decor, with one wall in red, black or blue, the rest in white. Pleasant enough, but lacks that reassuring well-managed feel. Rates include breakfast. ⑤

Royal Guesthouse Jalan Hilir Kota T09/743 0008, E royalgh@streamyx.com. There's nothing regal about the bland exterior of this misnamed hotel, but the rooms are a bit more stylish than many others in this price bracket. There's also a restaurant serving Thai and other Southeast Asian fare. Breakfast included. ⑤

Temenggong Jalan Tok Hakim ⓣ09/748 3844, ⓕ744 1481. Rather dull a/c en-suite rooms, in need of refreshing, with TV and fridge. If they're full, they may steer you to their sister establishment nearby, the *Suria*, but it isn't as good. ④

Guesthouses

Bunga Raya Backpacker Lodge North side of Jalan Padang Garong ⓣ09/748 9866. Simple fan rooms and dorms, mostly windowless; bathrooms are bigger than in some competing establishments. There's a small lounge with TV and a couple of terminals for free internet access. Dorm beds RM10, rooms ②.

🏃 **Ideal Travellers' House** 3954f & g Jalan Kebun Sultan ⓣ09/744 2246, ⓦwww .ugoideal.com. At the end of a quiet lane off Jalan Kebun Sultan, this excellent guesthouse is just like staying in a middle-class Chinese home dating back around thirty years – because that's exactly what it is. There's a range of fan rooms; one is especially spacious, with its own bathroom and a balcony for views of the garden, dominated by a mature *jambu* fruit tree. Transport ticket bookings and internet access available. ②

KB Backpacker Inn 171–181 Jalan Padang Garong ⓣ09/744 4944, ⓕ744 7955. A slightly scruffy establishment with acceptable rooms and dorms, sharing facilities, plus a TV lounge. Trips to Stong State Park available. Dorm beds RM10, rooms ②.

🏃 **KB Backpackers Lodge** First floor, 1872d Jalan Padang Garong ⓣ09/748 8841, ⓔbackpackerslodge2@yahoo.co.uk. A friendly travellers' haunt, with the customary facilities – rooms, some nicely decorated with handicrafts, an eight-bed dorm, lounge, roof garden, internet access, transfers to the Perhentians and packages to Stong State Park. Some rooms have a/c, though all share bathrooms. Dorm beds RM10, rooms ②.

Pasir Belanda In the rural Banggol district on Jalan PCB, around 4km north of the city ⓣ09/747 7046, ⓦwww.pasirbelanda.com. This Dutch-run establishment boasts several superb traditionally styled chalets, equipped with all mod cons, in a leafy compound sandwiched between a residential area and a jungly creek. Activities such as batik painting and boating are available, as are tours and bike rental. You can get here on the #10 bus, disembarking after Banggol mosque, from where you follow the signs 1500m east to the site, or take a taxi (around RM15). ⑥

Pesona Inn North side of Jalan Padang Garong ⓣ&ⓕ09/747 0085. Well kept, with various types of room, from so-called backpacker rooms with fan and sharing facilities to rooms with a/c, TV and the option of an en-suite bathroom. There's no lounge, but it does have free coffee and tea, and a laundry service. ②

🏃 **Rumah Rakit Nik Ismail** On the Sungai Kelantan, close to the *Grand Riverview Hotel* ⓣ09/747 5794, ⓕ712 9294. Pretty much unique in Malaysia is this accommodation on a floating platform (hence *rumah rakit*, "raft house"), featuring a cosy lounge kitted out with antique furniture, a veranda that's great for views of the sunset across the river, and just four rooms, with four-poster beds and sharing three bathrooms. Simply one of the most characterful places to stay on the east coast; to find it, head west along Jalan Che Su and walk down the path just before the Goodyear garage, then veer right to reach steps heading down to river, where the smart Malay-style timber bungalow is unmistakable. Reservations essential. ⑤

Zeck's Travellers' Inn On a lane off Jalan Sri Cemerlang ⓣ09/743 1613, ⓔzecktravellers @yahoo.com. Friendly, family-run Malay guesthouse occupying two adjacent properties and slightly marooned in a residential area. There are dorms and a large selection of rooms with fan or a/c, including some pairs of rooms with a bathroom shared between them, plus a smart four-person family room with parquet flooring and en suite. Ticket reservations and Perhentians transfers on offer. Dorm beds RM10, rooms ②.

The City and around

To wander around Kota Bharu is to be at the heart of PAS's fiefdom: images of the party's turbanned leader – and Kelantan chief minister – Nik Aziz bin Nik Mat are commonplace, and banners proclaim Kota Bharu an "**Islamic City**". The reality, though, is that Kota Bharu is a multi-ethnic jigsaw like every other Malaysian city, with plenty of Chinese and a few Indian businesses on show in the centre.

The city centre is compact and easily negotiated on foot. Useful **reference points** include the curious rocket-like clock tower marking the junction of the town's three major roads, Jalan Hospital, Jalan Sultan Ibrahim and Jalan Temenggong; the towering radio mast off Jalan Doktor, a handy landmark when it's illuminated at night; and, in the south of town, the gleaming Pacific KB Mall complex. Most of the city's **markets** and many of the **banks** and the biggest stores lie between Jalan Hospital and Jalan Pintu Pong, a few blocks to the north.

While there's plenty in Kota Bharu itself to keep you occupied for a couple of days, the surrounding areas offer **craft workshops** and a few **temples**. There's also the possibility of an excursion down the Kelantan River to **Pulau Suri**, and relaxation at a **beach** east of town.

Around Padang Merdeka

West of the markets, and close to the river, the quiet oasis of **Padang Merdeka** marks Kota Bharu's historical centre. It was here that the British displayed the body of the defeated Tok Janggut (Father Long Beard), a peasant spiritual leader who spearheaded a revolt against the colonial system of land taxes and tenancy regulations in 1915, one of the few specifically anti-colonial incidents to occur on the east coast. The four **museums** that occupy the vicinity today are open daily, except on Friday, between 8.45am and 4.45pm.

Dominating the eastern end of the square is the immense **Sultan Ismail Petra Arch**, built to mark Kota Bharu being declared a showcase for Malay culture. To the east of the arch, and half-hidden behind high walls and entrance gates, the single-storey **Istana Balai Besar** dates from 1844; containing the Throne Room and State Legislative Assembly, it's now used primarily for ceremonial functions and is closed to the public. To the right of its gates is the former Kelantan **State Treasury Bank**, whose presence gave the square its unofficial name of "Padang Bank". An unobtrusive stone bunker no more than two metres high, it remained in use until well into the twentieth century.

However, it's the **Istana Jahar**, to the north of the arch, that really draws your attention, an impressively styled traditional structure built in 1887, with a timber portico and polished decorative panels adorning the exterior. Extensive renovations carried out by Sultan Mohammed IV in 1911 added an Italian marble floor, which cools the interior, and two wrought-iron spiral staircases. The palace is now a museum housing an exhibition on **royal ceremonies** (RM2), which can be seen in an hour. In fact, many of the ceremonies in question – depicted using life-sized dioramas – would have been practised by commoners as well, though obviously not with the same level of opulence. The ground floor is given over to displays concerning weddings, including a bridal suite boasting a striking four-poster with linen and canopy, all in royal golden yellow. Exhibits upstairs illustrate how infants had to undergo rites prior to the most mundane of life experiences, such as the *istiadat naik endoi*, a ritual haircut before their first doze in a cradle.

A stone's throw further north is the yellow **Istana Batu** (RM2), an incongruous 1930s villa built as the sultan's residence. One of the first concrete constructions in the state (its name means "stone palace"), it's now the Kelantan Royal Museum, the rooms furnished largely as they would have been originally. A brief wander through is worthwhile if only to survey the tat which royals the world over seem to feel obliged to accumulate – here including stacks of crystal glassware and English crockery. Directly opposite to the east is the **Kampung Kraftangan** or "Handicraft Village" (same times as the museums), a collection of variable gift shops selling silverware, rattan baskets etc, with one outlet offering batik classes (RM50 at Zecsman Design, though note that not much English is spoken). It's also home to the excellent *Cikgu* restaurant (see p.283).

The padang is bordered on its northern side by the white **Masjid Negeri**, completed in 1925. Also called the Mohammadi mosque, it's been referred to as Serambi Mekah, "veranda of Mecca", because of its prominent role in the spread of Islam throughout Kelantan. If you pop in for a look, note the enormous drum once used to summon the faithful to prayer. Close by, west along Jalan Sultan, is the **Islamic Museum** (free), of interest only for the building itself, a pastel blue-green echo of the Istana Jahar, built in the 1910s as a residence for the chief minister.

The adjacent **Second World War Memorial** (RM2), a squat, pale yellow building, was originally the Mercantile Bank of India, but became known locally as *bank kerapu*, literally "frequent bank", for the odd reason that there are numerous bumps and pits on the roughly rendered exterior. The war museum inside is pertinent; it was Kelantan's beaches where Japanese troops first set foot in Malaya, capturing all of the state in December 1941, with Singapore falling just two months later – during the occupation, the bank became the local base for the Japanese secret police. While the war artefacts are largely desultory (bits of old ordnance, ration pouches and the like), the commentaries give some useful insight into the swiftness of the Japanese advance and the British collapse.

It's worth taking a little detour up Jalan Post Office Lama, the road leading north from the war museum: just a couple of minutes' walk away, on the left, is a **traditional house**, one of the oldest in the city, with stone finials and wooden carvings in the fanlight windows. Resembling a subdued, compact version of the Istana Jahar, it was once the residence of a court official; nowadays it's in private hands and isn't open to the public.

The markets

Just east of the historical centre is Kota Bharu's humming **central market** (aka Pasar Besar Siti Khadijah; daily roughly 8am–6pm), one of the focal points of the city. The main building, an octagonal hall, has a perspex roof casting a soft light over the multicoloured patchwork filling most of the main trading floor – a mass of vegetables, dried goods and, sadly, turtle eggs (on sale all down the east coast, and laid by the moderately threatened green turtle). The whole scene is worth contemplating at length from one of the upper floors – the vantage point of many a tourist-brochure snap. Trading continues east of here in a new extension to the market, with more stalls spilling out onto the surrounding pavements.

Though lacking in atmosphere, the **Bazaar Buluh Kubu**, a couple of minutes' walk west of the central market, does have a good range of batik items, *songket*s and other crafts on sale. A few blocks to the south is the still more humdrum **Pasar MPKB**, a municipal-run mix of wet market and food stalls.

More exciting than any of these is the informal, morning-only **Friday market** which, accompanied by a major Islamic gathering and sermon, sets up in the streets just south of Pasar MPKB. A visit here is to witness the rustic heart of Kelantan laid bare, as traders and shoppers pour in from the surrounding kampungs on their weekend day out in the city. Amid the mundane household merchandise you may spot oddities such eel oil, intended to aid male performance and sold with coils of dried, varnished-looking eels alongside as an attention-grabber. Most striking of all is the emphasis on folk remedies and general quackery, ranging from herbal products whose labels proclaim them beneficial to both men and women, to little blue pills dispensed – invariably to

THE EAST COAST | Kota Bharu and around

elderly men in traditional garb – by youths in baseball caps and jeans, who don surgical gloves to count out the required quantity.

The State Museum and the Cultural Centre

Situated on the corner of Jalan Hospital and Jalan Sultan Ibrahim, the dreary **State Museum** (Thurs–Sat 8am–4.45pm; RM2) houses an odd collection including romantic rural Malay paintings and lots of earthenware pots. Better is the collection of musical instruments on the first floor, among which is the *kertok*, a large coconut with its top sliced off and a piece of wood fastened across the opening to form a sounding board. Decorated with colourful pennants and hit with a cloth beater, it's one of the percussion instruments peculiar to Kelantan.

You can see these in action (and possibly try your hand at them), and watch many other Malay artistic and recreational activities, at the excellent

---

The performing arts in Kelantan

Kelantan has one of the richest artistic traditions of any state in Peninsular Malaysia, boasting two costumed dance/drama forms, **mak yong** and the Thai-influenced **menora**, as well as **wayang kulit**, or shadow puppetry, which, for visitors lucky enough to see a performance, is one of the most striking entertainments available in Malaysia. Traditionally, *wayang kulit* is staged on a dais screened from the audience by a large cloth sheet, illuminated from behind by a dangling light bulb. The cast is a set of stencils made of hide and formed into the shapes of the various characters, which are manipulated against the screen by a sole puppeteer, who also improvises and voices all the dialogue. Reflecting the long history of Indian influence in the region, the tales enacted are taken from the Hindu epic, the *Ramayana*; in the past, *wayang kulit* would function as a sort of kampung soap opera, serializing *Ramayana* instalments nightly during the months after the rice harvest. Performances are gripping affairs, as the puppets (comprising royalty, demons, clowns and a monkey god, often painted in translucent colours which come through on the screen) inveigle, romance and fight to a hypnotic soundtrack provided by an ensemble of drums, gongs and the oboe-like *serunai*, seated behind the puppeteer.

Sadly, all three of the above traditional art forms were **banned** in Kelantan by the PAS-led state government in the 1990s. PAS has cited issues of public morality – which could mean they object to the fact that both *mak yong* and *menora* can involve an element of cross-dressing, the male lead in *mak yong* traditionally being played by a woman, while a *menora* troupe usually consists of three men, who take female roles as necessary. PAS also objects to the non-Islamic nature of these performances, since they involve folk tales or, in the case of *wayang kulit*, Hindu mythology. Finally, the party also has a problem with the **spiritualism** permeating these arts. A *wayang kulit* performance always begins with a *buka panggung* ceremony, in which the puppeteer readies the stage by reciting mantras and making offerings of food to the spirits; while *mak yong* can be staged for an individual as part of a folk-healing tradition called *main puteri*, in which the performers enter a trance to remove a spirit believed to be affecting that person.

Whatever the reasons for the ban, the effect has been akin to cultural hara-kiri, depriving a generation of Kelantanese of their own cultural traditions. Dozens of *wayang kulit* troupes have been reduced to a mere handful, performing largely outside Kelantan or, thanks to one concession from PAS, for the benefit of the mainly tourist audience at Kota Bharu's Cultural Centre. On a brighter note, all three forms mentioned here are being passed on to a new generation, and sometimes staged, at the National Arts Academy in KL (✆www.ask.edu.my).

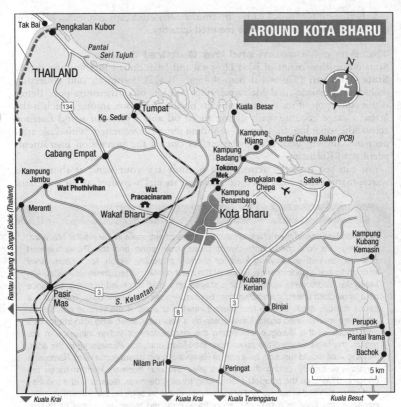

Cultural Centre (Gelanggang Seni; open Feb–Oct except during Ramadan) on Jalan Mahmood, southeast of the museum. Free demonstrations here (Mon, Wed & Sat; check times with the tourist office) feature many of the traditional **pastimes** of the Peninsula, such as *gasing* (spinning tops) and *congkak* (a mancala game like those found in West Africa and the Middle East, involving the strategic movement of seeds around the holes on a wooden board). Best of all, on Wednesday evenings there are *wayang kulit* (shadow puppetry) performances from 9pm until around midnight, though the action doesn't begin until around 9.30pm when the instrumental prelude is over.

The craft workshops

Most of Kota Bharu's craft workshops lie on the road to **PCB**, the uninspiring beach 11km north of the city, but there are also a handful in the city centre. Some guesthouses offer **tours** of the craft workshops, and Roselan Hanefiah at the state tourist office can arrange customized half-day craft-centred tours, with an interpreter, some demonstrations and lunch thrown in, for around RM85 per person.

Kelantanese **silverware** is well known throughout the Peninsula, and an excellent place to view silversmiths at work is K.B. Permai, southwest of the centre on Jalan Sultanah Zainab, close to the intersection with Jalan Hamzah. At their workshop you can watch artisans shaping silver wire into fine filigree, as well as producing items such as embossed gongs and jewellery, and there's an opportunity to buy at much keener prices than in Kuala Lumpur.

It's also possible to observe the making of **gasing** (spinning tops), resembling a discus except for a short steel spike inserted in one side. There's a *gasing* workshop very close to Kampung Kraftangan: head north up the road on the east side of the complex until you see the school bearing the name "Sek. Menengah Zainab (2)" on the right. Opposite is a lane, Jalan Tok Semian, where you will find the Kalimi Enterprise workshop, run by two brothers who speak some English, one specializing in *gasing*, the other in traditional kites (for more on which, see the *Malay life* colour section).

A *wayang kulit* **puppeteer** who also makes the tools of his trade, Pak Eusoff, can be visited in Kampung Laut, a village on the west side of Sungai Kelantan; you can get a boat there (around RM1) from the jetty signed "Bot penambang ke Kg Laut" close to the *Ridel* hotel. Inside his workshop, very close to the pier on the far side, are examples of his distinctively translucent puppets. Eusoff offers one-day taster courses in puppet-making but doesn't speak much English, so it's best to visit with a Malay speaker.

As for workshops on the PCB road, there are several outlets specializing in **batik** and *songket*s here, including Pantas Batek (℡09/744 1616) in Kampung Penambang, just over 4km from Kota Bharu, and Sabihah Batek (℡09/774 2350), close to Kampung Kijang, 8km from town. You can see **kites** being made at the Sapi'e Wau workshop (no phone) in Kampung Pauh Badang (between Penambang and Kijang villages); the little building is opposite Balai Polis Badang, the police post. Each kite craftsman has his own style of decoration, although tradition dictates that leaf patterns and a pair of birds are the principal motifs. The most unusual aspect of the kite is the long projection above its head, supporting a large bow that hums when the kite is airborne.

Finally, one of the most impressive examples of artisanship in the Kota Bharu area is the **woodcarving** at May Kris (℡09/747 3760) in Banggol, just before Kampung Pauh Badang. Here, in a workshop within his home, Rosman bin Ramli turns out some stunning examples of hilts and scabbards in *kemuning* wood for the *kris*, the traditional Malay dagger. The hilts feature

▲ Batik printing

stylized birds' heads, usually fiendishly detailed; simple, abstract versions are available to buy with blades or as paperweights for around RM150, while the ornate versions will set you back at least ten times as much. Visits are by appointment only, and you'll need to ask directions as Rosman's house is a little way off the main road.

Temples

Northwest of the city centre is **Tokong Mek**, a Chinese temple dating to the late eighteenth century, testament to the long Chinese presence in Kelantan. The community here identifies only weakly with their heritage, and the very use of Malay to categorize themselves underlines the fact that local Chinese are proudly integrated. The temple itself, featuring a multi-tiered pagoda and some gaudy ornamental gateways, is a 1500m walk from the Padang Merdeka: head north up Jalan Post Office Lama and its continuation Jalan Atas Banggol, which meets the east–west Jalan Wakaf Mek Zainab; turn left here and continue to the roundabout where you turn right onto Jalan PCB. After another 200m you will see the temple signed on the left.

Several Thai temples out of town can be visited on buses #27 or #43 bound for the stretch of beach called Pantai Seri Tujuh. One of the most glamorous is **Wat Pracacinaram**, easily spotted just outside Wakaf Bharu, on the road to Cabang Empat. It's a brand-new building, with an elaborate triple-layered roof decorated in gold, sapphire and red. **Wakaf Bharu** itself is home to the nearest train station to Kota Bharu, but is otherwise a nondescript little town.

At the **Wat Phothivihan**, 15km west of Kota Bharu, a forty-metre-long Reclining Buddha is said to be the second largest in the world (not a unique claim in these parts). The colossal, if rather insipid, plaster statue contains ashes of the deceased, laid to rest here according to custom. You can reach Wat Phothivihan on the #19 or #27 **bus**; get off at Cabang Empat, from where the temple is a three-and-a-half-kilometre walk or a short taxi ride away.

Pulau Suri

If the idea of screaming down the wide tea-coloured Kelantan River in a motorized sampan sounds appealing, then consider an excursion to **Pulau Suri**, one of many small riverine islands north of Kota Bharu. Getting there is more than half the fun, though the island itself has a boatyard and some pleasant paths for walking.

The journey proper begins at **Jeti Kok Majid**, a pier on the west bank of the river, which can be reached in about an hour on the #43 bus. Driving, head south out of town and west across the bridge towards Wakaf Bharu; once at the roundabout on the far side, head right (northeast) on the Tumpat road, following signs for Palekbang, then Kok Majid. After bargaining, you can expect to pay something like RM50 for the trip to the island and back, including a wait, though don't be surprised if the boatman allows on a few local passengers laden with sacks of rice and other provisions.

The boat ride lasts about half an hour, taking you past various rustic islands with the odd modern school building poking out. Be sure to bring a hat and plenty of sun cream as there is no absolutely shade. Bankside **vegetation** along the way includes clumps of yellow-blossomed sea hibiscus, half-submerged nipah palms with strange ball-like fruits, and crinkly-leaved acanthus; you may also spot monitor lizards and kingfishers, and perhaps trained macaques being used by locals to harvest coconuts.

Arriving at Pulau Suri, you'll spot a boatyard next to the jetty where they mend (but no longer build) traditional wooden boats. From here you can head inland along a path lined with coconut trees. There's a simple **café** or two for refreshments and also plenty of houses offering **homestays**; if you're interested, make arrangements beforehand through guesthouses in Kota Bharu or the state tourist office.

Pantai Irama

Compared to what's on offer in Terengganu, the sands in Kelantan are nothing special, and some of the best beaches lie some way south of Kota Bharu, close to the border with Terengganu itself. That said, if you're continuing to the interior, a seaside outing here makes a nice prelude to the jungles. Of nearby beaches, **Pantai Irama** ("Rhythm Beach") is the best, a quiet, tree-fringed stretch of white sand 20km east of Kota Bharu. Unless you visit on a Friday, you should have the place to yourself, though the prevailing conservatism may not be conducive to relaxed sunbathing. To get there, take the #23 or #39 **bus** (every 30min; 45min) to **Bachok** from Kota Bharu's local bus station; the beach is about 500m north of the bus terminus.

Eating and drinking

Kota Bharu has a few Malay restaurants dotted around the centre, but for many locals, the Malay culinary scene in the city is dominated by the outdoor **night food market** (aka *Medan Selera MPKB*), on the nondescript northern fringes of the centre. Note that the market may be moved in the near future, so you may have to ask around for its location. Other than the expected Malay specialities, such as excellent **nasi kerabu** (quintessentially Kelantanese rice, tinted blue using flower petals – though these days additives may be used instead – and typically served with fish curry), the few dozen stalls here also offer a great range of *murtabaks*; just watching the sellers stretch, fold and flip the dough on their griddles is mouthwatering. You might want to wash your meal down with *sup ekor* (essentially oxtail soup) or *sup tulang* (made from beef bones), or round it off by sampling the colourful *kuihs*, including *jala emas*, which look like saffron-coloured vermicelli. The whole thing gets going daily around 6pm and stays open till midnight, with a brief break around 8pm for the *maghrib* prayer. Chinese street food is on offer at the cavernous *Medan Selera Kebun Sultan* on Jalan Kebun Sultan.

For another very Malaysian eating experience, join the throngs at the humble pushcart operation signed *Nasi Kukus Kebun Sultan*, also on Jalan Kebun Sultan. Part of a small row of Malay stalls, this attracts locals of all creeds with its freshly prepared *sambal* fish, okra curry, *ikan bakar* (grilled fish) and the like. Point at your preferred toppings and they will be poured over the rice, on a banana leaf, which is then folded into a pyramid shape and wrapped up in newspaper for you to take away.

This brilliant street food apart, the city has a decent selection of low-key **restaurants**. The Chinese eating places on Jalan Kebun Sultan are among the few that aren't halal, and these are also your best bet for **alcohol**, along with the swish bar at the *Renaissance* hotel. To combine eating with shopping, head to the **Pacific KB Mall**: aside from a couple of Western cafés, it has a handy food court on the top floor.

Restaurants and kedai kopis

Cikgu Kampung Kraftangan. This self-service place offers the chance to try the classic Malay meal called *nasi ulam*. Dishes like fried chicken, vegetable curry and *asam pedas* *ikan patin* (catfish in a spicy tamarind sauce) are laid out in trays along with rice and the *ulam*, a Malay salad featuring blanched vegetables and a variety of greens and herbs, some incredibly bitter, such as *daun ketereh* (cashew-nut leaves). It's probably best to stick to okra, aubergine and *pucuk paku* (curly-tipped edible fronds) when assembling your *ulam*. If you're feeling brave, have the dip made of *tempoyak* (fermented durian) and *budu* (fermented fish sauce). You can eat well for under RM10 per head. Daily except Fri 11.30am–4.30pm.

Four Seasons Jalan Dusun Raja ☎09/743 6666. A modern Chinese restaurant with a varied menu, particularly strong on seafood, including reliable winners like steamed fish in soya sauce. Their oyster omelette and steamboat are also recommended. Meals are priced according to the amount ordered – almost any four dishes from the menu, plus rice, Chinese tea and fresh fruit for dessert, will come to around RM50. Packed at weekends. Daily noon–2.30pm & 6–10pm.

Golden City Jalan Padang Garong. Lively, brightly lit *kedai kopi* serving decent Chinese food, including *curry mee* and other spicy noodle dishes for around RM5. Along with the upstairs drinking area, it stays open until 11pm.

Hayaki Jalan Pintu Pong. As close as the centre gets to a Western-style café, and one of very few venues in Kota Bharu where 20-somethings can chill out. The menu features both Western and Asian snacks and light meals, plus a range of ice-cream desserts.

Mamak Spicy Specials Jalan Sultan Yahya Petra. The usual *mamak* favourites in modern surroundings, well placed for both long-distance bus stations and the Pacific KB Mall. A popular meeting place well into the evening.

 Muhibah Jalan Pintu Pong. Excellent, inexpensive Chinese-owned vegetarian establishment with plenty of Malay staff and patrons, as befits a place whose name means "harmony". Downstairs comprises a bakery and café, serving local and Western pastries and ice-blended shakes; upstairs is a small restaurant with a great spread of stir-fries and stew toppings for rice, featuring the usual mock meats. You don't have to be veggie to enjoy it, and it's a haven on hot days – both floors have a/c. Daily early until 9pm or so.

Noodle Station Jalan Ismail, with a branch at the Pacific KB Mall. A small restaurant serving up numerous tasty wonton noodle permutations – fried or in soup, with prawn or chicken in various guises, costing up to RM5. There's a culinary gear change after the main course, when a range of sorbets and coffees become the chief temptations. Daily 8am till late.

Sri Devi Jalan Kebun Sultan. Top-notch South Indian *kedai kopi* with excellent *mee goreng* and banana-leaf curries. Daily roughly 7.30am–8.30pm.

White House Jalan Sultanah Zainab. No grand mansion, but a tiny bungalow housing the most mundane-looking *kedai kopi* which is in fact a city institution and social nexus, attracting Malay worshippers at the Masjid Negeri opposite as well as Chinese professionals. The trademark dish is humble *telur setengah masak* – softboiled eggs cracked into a saucer, seasoned with soy sauce and white pepper, and delicious scooped up with buttered toast, all washed down with *teh* or *kopi tarek*. A great place for breakfast or a late snack. Daily roughly 8am–1pm & 9pm–1am.

Listings

Banks and exchange There are several banks in and around the rectangle bounded by Jalan Pintu Pong, Jalan Padang Garong and Jalan Kebun Sultan. Maybank operates a convenient foreign exchange office on the corner of Jalan Pintu Pong and Jalan Parit Dalam (daily 9.30am–5.30pm).

Bookshops The Pacific KB mall has a branch of the Popular bookstore, while on Jalan Padang Garong, next to the *Suria* hotel, you'll find the Muda Osman bookshop.

Car rental Hawk, a little way north of the *Sri Devi* restaurant on Jalan Kebun Sultan (☎09/773 3824).

Hospital Jalan Hospital ☎09/748 5533.

Internet access Quite a few small internet cafés lurk, usually in upstairs premises, on the lanes between Jalan Pintu Pong and Jalan Padang Garong.

Left luggage At the bus station on Jalan Hamzah (daily 8am–10pm).

Pharmacies There are several centrally located pharmacies, including a Guardian pharmacy on Jalan Padang Garong and another Guardian, plus a Watsons, in the Pacific KB Mall.

Police Headquarters on Jalan Sultan Ibrahim (☎09/748 5522).

Post office The GPO is on Jalan Sultan Ibrahim; there's also a convenient branch post office on the lane just south of Jalan Pintu Pong.

Shopping For general requirements (as opposed to crafts), try the Pacific KB Mall, which houses the huge Pacific supermarket and plenty of other shops. More centrally, on Jalan Pintu Pong there's a Mydin supermarket and the old-fashioned Pantai Timur shopping complex. The night market on Jalan Parit Dalam, east of the central market, is worth a browse.

Thai visas Many nationalities can get a one-month visa stamped in at the border. Visas can be obtained in advance from the Thai Consulate,

For most **long-distance buses**, you simply need to turn up at Hamzah or Langgar bus stations, as both serve a variety of destinations. However, Transnasional buses to Kuala Terengganu and Kuantan, plus SKMK buses to places within or just outside Kelantan – notably Wakaf Bharu (for trains), Rantau Panjang (to cross into Thailand) and **Kuala Besut** (for the Perhentians; RM5) – operate from the **local bus station**. SKMK has an information counter here (daily 8am–9pm, closed Fri 12.45–2pm; ℡09/744 0114). Long-distance taxi fares are around RM40 per vehicle to Kuala Besut, RM100 to Kuala Terengganu; the taxi stand on Jalan Doktor (℡09/744 7104) can give fares for other destinations.

The **express train** to KL leaves Wakaf Bharu station (℡09/719 6986) in the early part of the evening, with the Singapore-bound express following several hours later. Heading to the station in the late afternoon, do allow for rush-hour congestion on roads out of Kota Bharu.

Both **MAS** (℡09/771 4700) and **AirAsia** (℡09/743 7000) fly to KL only, while **Firefly** flies to KL and Penang.

Crossing the Thai border

There are two designated crossings into Thailand near Kota Bharu, one inland, the other at the mouth of the Golok River. Both of these **border posts** are open daily between 6am and 10pm – but remember that Thailand is one hour behind Malaysia, and that the **security situation** in southern Thailand has been precarious in recent years. **Visas** for Thailand can be obtained from the consulate in Kota Bharu (see "Listings" below).

The more popular crossing is at **Rantau Panjang**, 30km southwest of Kota Bharu. Bus #29 departs from the local bus station in Kota Bharu every thirty minutes (6.45am–6.30pm; RM5) for the 45-minute trip there, or you can take a shared taxi from Kota Bharu for RM4 per person. Once at Rantau Panjang, it's a short walk across the border to **Sungai Golok** on the Thai side. Trains from here to Bangkok (22hr), via Hat Yai and Surat Thani, leave at 11.30am and 1.35pm (timetables on ⊛www.railway.co.th), and buses to Hat Yai (4hr) are frequent. The coastal crossing is at **Pengkalan Kubor**, 20km northwest of Kota Bharu, which connects with the small town of Tak Bai on the Thai side. Take bus #27 from the local bus station for the thirty-minute journey, then the car ferry. On the Thai side, the closest large town to either crossing is **Narathiwat**, from where there are buses to other parts of southern Thailand, plus flights to Bangkok.

4426 Jalan Pengkalan Chepa (℡09/748 2545; Mon–Thurs & Sun 9am–noon & 2–3.30pm); note that they have been known to refuse entry to people in shorts, so dress smartly.
Travel agents Kota Bharu has a dearth of good travel agents, though the city's guesthouses help plug the gap by arranging trips to the most obvious nearby attractions, the Perhentians and Stong State Park. Otherwise, try Ping Anchorage, the very

efficient Kuala Terengganu-based tour operator, which has a branch office on Jalan Padang Garong (℡09/744 2020), or KB Backpackers, at the *Ridel* hotel (℡013/744 2125, ⊛www.kb-backpackers .com.my).
Visa extensions At the Immigration Department, second floor, Wisma Persekutuan, Jalan Bayam (Mon–Wed & Sun 8am–4pm, Thurs 8am–12.45pm; ℡09/748 2120).

Pulau Perhentian

The name **Pulau Perhentian** actually covers two islands, **Perhentian Besar** and **Perhentian Kecil** (their names meaning large and small stopping places, respectively; Big Island and Small Island are sometimes used instead), both textbook tropical paradises. Despite an increasing number of visitors, they retain

Snorkelling and diving around the Perhentians

Outside the monsoon, conditions in the waters around the Perhentians are superb: currents are gentle, and visibility is up to 20m (although the sea lice can be a problem, inflicting an unpleasant but harmless sting not unlike that of a jellyfish). A **snorkelling** foray around the rocks at the ends of most bays turns up an astonishing array of brightly coloured fish, including blacktip reef sharks, and live coral. For the more adventurous still, there are some spectacular **dive sites** a short boat ride offshore, including a couple of wreck dives open to those with Advanced Open Water qualifications.

Snorkelling trips to undeveloped coves around either island, with five stops, cost around RM30 per person; your accommodation can either charter you a boat or tell you where to join one of these trips. At a few places, including the *Arwana Resort* and *Mama's Chalet* on Besar, you can also arrange a snorkelling trip further afield, southeast to Pulau Lang Tengah, for around RM60 per person in a group of ten or so. Snorkel, mask and fins can be rented from a **dive shop** – every Perhentians beach has several of these, and also offer a variety of **PADI courses**, including Open Water and the introductory Discover Scuba; a couple also offer specialist facilities such as Nitrox. A single dive for qualified divers starts at around RM90, Open Water costs RM900 and up, and Advanced Open Water RM800. Among the many operators worth talking to are Flora Bay Divers (Flora Bay; Ⓦwww.florabaydivers.com), Steffen Sea Sports (Coral Bay; Ⓦwww.steffen-sea-sports.com); Turtle Bay Divers (Long Beach, west shore of Besar and at *D'Lagoon*; Ⓦwww.turtlebaydivers.com); and Watercolours Dive Centre (west shore of Besar; Ⓦwww.watercoloursworld.com). The last of these is unique in offering a four-day **Eco Diver** course (RM750), qualifying you to take part in international marine-life surveys organized by Reef Check (Ⓦreefcheck.org). They also organize a weekly **talk** on the state of the Perhentians' reefs.

A number of operators offer diving trips to Pulau Lang Tengah or Pulau Redang, for a surcharge of around RM60 or RM100 per person respectively over the cost of the same number of dives at the Perhentians. For a few do's and don'ts of snorkelling and diving, see p.288.

considerable appeal, and the essentials of any idyllic island holiday – fantastic sandy beaches, and great **snorkelling** and **diving** – are all in place. Away from the beach and marine pursuits, both islands have jungly hills in their interior, with a few paths for some **walks** and opportunities to spot flying foxes, monkeys and monitor lizards. All this is capped by a laid-back atmosphere both rare and refreshing among popular island destinations, thanks partly, it must be said, to the austere attitude towards alcohol here in Terengganu.

Much of the **accommodation** on the islands comprises low-priced chalets and resorts, the most basic of which are pretty rustic; a few places still use hurricane lamps, and even those with regular lighting may only have electricity in the evenings. Perhentian Kecil caters more to the backpacker scene, epitomized by **Long Beach**, while Besar, the more developed of the two, has most of the mid-range accommodation and is popular with families, package tourists and better-heeled independent travellers. **Peak season** is roughly June until the end of August, outside which rates fall by at least 25 percent. Many resorts begin closing in late October, sometimes earlier, and don't open again until the following February or March, but it is possible to find a few places to stay during the northeast monsoon for a truly isolated island experience.

It's well worth **booking** in advance for the peak season. Accommodation here is a fast-moving target as places can change hands – and their phone numbers – from one season to the next, so talk to travel agents, particularly those at Kuala

Besut (see p.288) for advice. Most of the mid-range places do their own full-board **packages**, typically for three days and two nights, and include boat transfers and some snorkelling (pricier diving packages are also available).

Many resorts run a **restaurant**, open to all-comers. A handful of these serve up moderately elaborate Asian cuisine, or a range of pizzas, steaks and pasta, but the vast majority offer the usual rice and noodle variations, plus simple Western fare such as omelettes, pancakes and occasionally even baked potatoes; seafood, unsurprisingly, also features.

While PAS was in charge of Terengganu not so long ago, the party's lukewarm attitude to commercialization helped keep large-scale development on the Perhentians to a minimum. This was just as well, given that both islands are home to several **turtle nesting** sites (some resorts may offer nighttime turtle-spotting trips during the season), and that the impact of the existing resorts on the environment isn't negligible, with shortages of **water** (much of which comes from wells) a hassle during the tourist peak. Things have loosened up slightly with UMNO back in the driving seat: a couple of major resorts have since been completed, and **alcohol** is sold openly these days at a handful of restaurants.

There's no problem with using **cell phones** on both islands, and you may well prefer texting to getting **on line** at the lunatic rates here – at least RM3 for fifteen minutes.

ACCOMMODATION

Abdul's	bb	Fauna Beach	dd	Perhentian Island Resort	T
Arwana	hh	Flora Bay	cc	Petani Beach House	R
Aur Bay	M	Flora Bay 2	ee	Reef Chalets	V
Bayu Dive Lodge	ff	Lemon Grass	I	Samudra Beach Cottages	gg
Bintang View	G	Mama's Chalet	X	Senja Bay Resort	P
Bubbles	ii	Matahari	F	Shari-La Island Resort	K
Bubu Resort	C	Maya Guesthouse	O	Simfony	D
Cempaka	H	Mira's Place	Q	Teratak Amelia	N
Coral View	U	Mohsin Chalets	J	Tunabay Island Resort	aa
D'Ayumni House	Z	Moonlight Chalets	B	Watercolours Impiani Resort	S
D'Lagoon	A	New Cocohut	Y	Watercolours Paradise	
Fatimah	L	Panorama	E	Resort	W

Turtle Beach

Wind Turbines

Coral Bay (Teluk Aur)

Lazy Buoy

Long Beach (Pasir Panjang)

Rock Garden

Perhentian Kecil

Butterfly

Kampung Pasir Hantu

Tanjung Basi

Three Coves Bay

Perhentian Besar

Marine Park Offices

Flora Bay (Teluk Dalam)

N

Shark Point

PULAU PERHENTIAN

0   1 km

Kuala Besut

Travel to and around the Perhentians

Perhentians boats depart from the little town of **Kuala Besut** on the northern Terengganu coast, off Route 3. Several agencies have desks just outside arrivals at Kota Bharu airport, where you can arrange taxis to Kuala Besut (RM80 for four people) and boat tickets. Note that visiting the Perhentians incurs a marine parks **conservation fee** of RM5, valid for three days' stay, which you pay at the jetty before setting off (keep the ticket/receipt in case you need to produce it later).

Kuala Besut

KUALA BESUT is easily reached by chartering a **taxi** from Kota Bharu (RM40), Kota Bharu airport (RM80) or Kuala Terengganu (RM60). There is also transport here from Taman Negara/Jerantut and the Cameron Highlands, run by Taman Negara specialist agencies (see p.233), and a nighttime bus from KL's Putra bus station (RM31). **Local buses** operated by S.P. Bumi run to Kuala Besut from Kuala Terengganu around three times daily (RM8.50). Travelling by bus from Kota Bharu, catch bus #3 for the hour's ride to Pasir Puteh, from where bus #96 (every 30min) makes the remaining half-hour journey to Kuala Besut.

Kuala Besut itself is practically a one-street affair, the street in question running past the **boat terminal** (on the right as you arrive) and terminating just beyond the **bus and taxi station**, which is just a few seconds' drive further on. Several **agents** selling boat tickets and Perhentians packages can be found in the lanes along this street or in the boat terminal; the best include Anjung Holidays (℡09/697 4095, ⓦwww.anjungholidays.com) in the boat terminal and Perhentian Trans Holiday (℡09/690 3269, ⓦwww.perhentiantrans.com) on the lane opposite the ferry terminal.

Should you happen to get stuck in Kuala Besut, you can stay at the *Nan Hotel* (℡09/697 4892; ❷) on the lane directly opposite the boat terminal; the rooms are decent, including a few with air-conditioning and TV.

Around the boat terminal are a number of decent stalls and restaurants with a particular emphasis on **seafood**, including the Chinese-run *Sakura*, practically opposite the terminal. For Malay food, head for *Unjang*, next to the bus station;

Perhentians do's and don'ts

- Do bring more than enough **cash** to last the duration of your trip – there are no banks or ATMs on the islands. Plastic can be used to pay for accommodation and food only at some mid-range places, and using it incurs a small surcharge.
- Do bring **mosquito repellent**.
- Don't leave **valuables**, even clothes, on the beach – whether crowded or deserted – and then go off swimming or snorkelling, even if you've asked someone to keep an eye on your possessions. Thieves have been known to appear seemingly from nowhere on snatch-and-grab raids.
- Do **swim with care**: look out for **boat lanes**, marked by strings of buoys, and stay on the correct side of them to avoid being wiped out by a speedboat. Note also on that on Long Beach there can be a dangerous **undertow** from February to April and in October; a few people get swept out every year and have to be rescued.
- Do be mindful of sharp-pronged boat **anchors** sticking out of the sand as you walk along the beach at night – particularly if you're looking up at the stars.
- As always, don't touch the **coral** when you snorkel or dive.

the most humble of *kedai kopis*, in the popularity stakes it nonetheless wipes the floor with the competition thanks to its brilliant self-service *nasi campur* spread, which often feature *ayam bakar* and a rich *sayur lodeh*, plus more unusual concoctions, such as a pineapple curry.

Perhentians boats

Boats (RM35 one way; 40min) set off for the Perhentians several times a day. All boats drop you at the bay of your choice, though at those bays without a jetty (notably Long Beach), you'll transfer to a smaller boat to get ashore (RM2). **Return tickets** are available for the price of two one-way tickets, and you don't need to know exactly when or from which bit of the islands you're going to come back from; the day before your departure, show your ticket to staff at your accommodation, and they'll arrange for you to be picked up at the required time (boats typically depart at 8am, noon and also at 4pm if there's demand). Note that the boat service is regular only between March and October; at other times sailings are much reduced thanks to the harsh northeast monsoon, although there is usually at least one boat a day to the fishing village on Perhentian Kecil.

A so-called **water taxi** service operates around the Perhentians, provided by plenty of small speedboats. **Fares** start at a few ringgit per person for a journey between adjacent bays (walking is often not an option thanks to rocky obstructions), rising to RM25 to travel from one side of Besar to the other, or from one island to the other. When you need a boat taxi, just inform the management of the accommodation or restaurant where you happen to be, and they'll usually be able to rustle up one of the boatmen within a few minutes. The exception to this is after dark, when the water taxis can become scarce and you may have to pay double the usual fare if there are few others to share the ride. If you simply need to get across either island, you may be able to use one of the **footpaths** instead (after dark a **torch** is essential for these, and handy for beach walks too).

Perhentian Kecil

For many visitors, it's the east-facing **Long Beach**, boasting a wide stretch of glistening-white, deep, soft sand, that's the prime attraction of **Perhentian Kecil**. It does lack a view of the sunset, which is lost behind the island's hilly spine, but somehow that really doesn't matter: the light gently fades away, leaving the illumination from the beach restaurants and their CDs of Bob Marley or pumping house to dominate the senses. There's a genuinely infectious buzz about the place; during the peak season there are fairly frequent **beach parties** that can be enormous fun. Things can be a bit too intense at the height of the season, when you might prefer to stay on the quieter west-facing coves, such as **Coral Bay**, which has sheltered waters (which make it a better bet than Long Beach during the northeast monsoon), good snorkelling and sunset views, though its character has been somewhat spoilt by the building of a huge, incongruously modern jetty. As Coral Bay and Long Beach are only a ten-minute walk apart via a footpath through the woods, shuttling between them to sample different hangouts is straightforward (remember to bring a torch at night).

The only village – the spookily named **Kampung Pasir Hantu** (meaning "Sand of Ghosts") – is in the southeast of the island; there's no reason to go there unless you need a clinic or the police station. You're more likely to attempt a foray up through the woods over the spine of the island where a couple of **wind turbines** and solar panels have been installed. It takes around half an hour to reach the turbines using the track from the southern part of Long Beach, and another half-hour to descend to the *D'Lagoon* resort at the northern part of the island.

Internet access is available at Lazy Buoy and the Gen Mini Mart, in the middle of Long Beach. The latter also changes traveller's cheques, while the former offers a range of **water sports** during the northeast monsoon, including windsurfing and bodyboarding.

Accommodation

Western shore, including Coral Bay

Aur Bay ☎013/995 0817. Fairly basic but popular chalets with fan, mosquito nets and private facilities. They also have a veranda, but each faces the chalet opposite rather than the beach. Rates drop by a third outside the peak season. ❸

Fatimah ☎09/691 1560. Rooms here are two to a chalet, and hardly sophisticated, with fan and plasticky floor lining, but the en-suite facilities are quite reasonable. As at the adjacent *Aur Beach*, of which this is an offshoot, the chalets face each other. Not bad for the price. ❷

Maya Guesthouse ☎019/970 4426, ✉mayaguesthouse@yahoo.com.my. A range of en-suite fan chalets around a garden compound, with a café. Good discounts outside the peak season. ❸

Mira's Place ☎019/967 2349. A small cluster of charmingly rustic chalets on their own immaculate cove, a half-hour walk south of Coral Bay. The friendly woman proprietor speaks some English. A great choice for that Robinson Crusoe experience you always wanted. Open all year. ❷

🏃 **Petani Beach House** ☎09/691 1642, ⓦwww.perhentian-beach.com. Five airy en-suite chalets with a certain Zen-like simplicity to their decor and with driftwood tables on each veranda. They're all set in a leafy beachfront garden with hammocks to laze in. The restaurant boasts vistas of glorious blue sea and excellent meals prepared to order by the Malay-South African couple who run the place. You get free use of canoes too. *Petani* is secluded on its own cove, from where it's a rough 45min hike up and over the headland to the adjacent beach and *Mira's Place*; water taxis are a much better way to get around. Open all year. Room-only ❺

Senja Bay Resort ☎09/691 1799, ⓦwww.senjabay.com. This complex of en-suite chalets, built up a hillside and connected by decking, contains quite spacious, well-maintained rooms, if rather simply furnished. There's also a restaurant and dive shop; diving and snorkelling packages are available. ❺

Shari-La Island Resort ☎09/691 1500, ⓦwww.shari-la.com. Dozens of chalets shoehorned in above the ugly jetty at the northern end of the bay, and still too new to feel like anything but a blot on the landscape. It's comfortable enough, though, with a/c in every room. As at its sister resort, the well-established *Coral View* on Besar, rooms feature plenty of wood panelling. Has a restaurant, plus internet access. ❻

Teratak Amelia ☎019/913 0742. Behind the beachfront *Amelia Café* are these simple, tidy en-suite chalets with colourful floral bed linen and a hammock on every veranda. ❸

Watercolours Impiani Resort ☎09/691 1852, ⓦwww.impiani.com. A range of fancy a/c en-suite chalets in a wooded setting, with a restaurant serving mainly Western fare with BBQs every few nights. Diving and snorkelling can be arranged through the dive shop at their sister resort on Besar, to which free transfers are available. A sound choice. ❻

Eastern shore, including Long Beach

🏃 **Bintang View** ☎013/997 1563 or 019/935 3574. Not the fanciest of chalets but well kept and very homely, with toilets and showers in two separate blocks. There are also simple rooms in one block, and a café. Run by a friendly Malay-Irish couple, the place is somewhat removed from the noise of the beach though only a couple of minutes' walk away. ❷

Bubu Resort ☎03/2142 6688 or 09/697 8888, ⓦwww.buburesort.com.my. Catering mainly for package holidaymakers is this motel-like complex of en-suite a/c rooms, with its own restaurant and bar. All perfectly decent, but jars on unassuming Long Beach, and there could be more of the same to come as they may be setting up a second operation next to *Cempaka*. ❽

Cempaka ☎013/946 6791. A mishmash of A-frames, a tad run-down, and rather better en-suite chalets in a longhouse-type block. ❷

D'Lagoon ☎019/985 7089, ⓦwww.geocities.com/d_lagoon_my. Nestling in the trees on an isolated cove at the northeastern tip of the island, this place offers unremarkable en-suite chalets as well as rooms with shared facilities, plus a restaurant. Its trump card is that it presides over good snorkelling and diving, with a fantastic coral garden offshore. Across the narrow neck of the island is a turtle-spotting beach on the western shore. ❷

Lemon Grass ☎012/956 2393 or 019/938 3893. Simple, sound chalets with fan and mosquito net; toilets and showers are in a separate shack. Good views from the restaurant compensate for the less-than-wonderful facilities. ❸

Matahari ☎09/691 1740 or 014/836 2863. Set a little way back from the beach and reached via a concrete walkway, this is a jumble of wooden chalets and A-frames with faded blue roofs – generally a little rough around the edges, but pretty good value and popular, and almost all en suite. Prices vary widely; the rate for a/c accommodation is four times what the most basic room costs. ❷

🏃 **Mohsin Chalets** ☎09/691 1580, @www .mohsinperhentian.com.my. Four tiers of longhouse-style wooden buildings on a hillside behind Long Beach. Rooms are en suite, and many have a/c as well. The elevated restaurant enjoys views over the beach just a few minutes' walk away, and is a great spot to watch international football matches on big-screen TV. Rates rise with the quality of the view – basically, the higher up you are. Packages available. Open year-round. Dorms RM30, rooms ❺.

Moonlight Chalets ☎09/691 1777. A wide range of chalets set at the northern end of the beach, ranging from dirt-cheap A-frames to en-suite doubles (the best deal), with the option of a/c and hot showers in some. The restaurant has a good view across the beach. A-frames ❷, rooms ❸.

Panorama ☎09/691 1590, @www.malaysia -panorama.com. Set back from the beach in the shady jungle, this place has some simple chalets with fan and plusher en-suite ones, including pricey rooms with a/c. There are also family chalets with two double beds, hot water and the option of a/c. The restaurant does a wide range of mainly Western fare, including pizzas and tacos. ❷

Simfony No phone. Nothing but metal-roofed A-frames, including some larger ones with bathrooms and even some sleeping four. It's all pretty basic, though the place is smack in the heart of Long Beach. ❷

Eating and drinking

For **eating**, standouts include *Rumours* at *Mohsin Chalets*, which serves pricey assorted fajitas, burgers, pasta dishes and some Malay food, with movie screenings in the evenings, while *Panorama* is popular for its pizzas in the evening. Restaurants around the Lazy Buoy shop, in particular *Family*, also offers an evening meat and seafood **barbecue** (around RM15) featuring a choice of barracuda, squid, prawns, etc, cooked and served up with various sauces plus salad and potatoes.

Perhentian Besar

The beaches on the **western shore** of Perhentian Besar and at **Flora Bay** on the southern shore remain relaxed, despite a nearly continuous string of resorts. Flora Bay (aka Teluk Dalam) is less cramped but also tends to be slightly institutional in feel, whereas the western shore is packed in a pleasingly organic way; the latter also has a good vibe after dark when the restaurants get very busy, though the sunset is predictably lost behind Kecil. From the western shore, a steep **trail** (45min) to the western end of Flora Bay begins just past the second jetty south of *Abdul's*, behind some villas intended for visiting politicians. Another trail links Flora Bay with the *Perhentian Island Resort* (30min), passing the island's waterworks close to the bay. The easiest trail is that between *New Cocohut* and *Mama's Chalet*, a fifteen-minute hike over the wooded headland; poorly signed, it starts with steps leading uphill just behind *New Cocohut* and not at the beachfront steps, which lead to a viewing platform.

For the finest beaches on Besar, get a water taxi to **Three Coves Bay** on the north of the island, a stunning conglomeration of three beaches separated from the western shore by rocky outcrops. This area also provides a secluded haven between May and September for green and hawksbill turtles to lay their eggs.

Internet access is available at the *Perhentian Island Resort* and *Flora Bay*, among others.

Accommodation

Western shore

Abdul's ☎09/691 1610 or 019/912 7303. Sturdy en-suite chalets in "semi-detached" pairs, the better, roomier (and much pricier) ones fronting the beach, some with a/c. They're a little sparsely furnished but not a bad choice. ❸

Coral View ☎09/697 4943 or 7427, ℱ09/690 2600. A range of modern rooms, mainly in smart, steep-roofed chalets with small attached bathrooms. They're all connected by various walkways taking you through a pleasant garden that's magical at night, when subtle lighting comes into play. There's a restaurant and dive shop too. The management could be sharper, and the fan chalets are certainly a good deal (a/c comes at a premium). ❺

🏃 **D'Ayumni House** ☎09/691 1680 or 019 436 4463, ⓦwww.d-ayumnihouse.blogspot .com. Discreetly signed behind Seahorse Divers in between *New Coconut* and the *Tunabay* resort, this comprises a "longhouse" block containing a general shop, internet café and family room sleeping four, plus three semi-detached chalets on the opposite side of a small garden, two containing dorms and the third housing double rooms. It's friendly and well run; all accommodation has pleasant tiled bathrooms and there is free cable internet access in the rooms if you brought a laptop. Dorm beds RM40, rooms ❺.

Mama's Chalet ☎019/985 3359, ⓦwww .mamaschalet.com. Prim, very decent chalets, including a few seafacing ones with fanlights of multicoloured glass. All rooms have private facilities, and there's a popular restaurant, too. ❸

New Cocohut ☎09/691 1810 or 697 4982 (bookings), ⓦwww.perhentianislandcocohut.com. Chinese-run establishment with reasonable en-suite a/c rooms and chalets. Cheapest are the rooms in two-storey blocks; the chalets have the bonus of TV, hot water and fridge. The popular restaurant scores points too. Rates include breakfast. ❺

Perhentian Island Resort ☎09/691 1112 or 03/2144 8350, ⓦwww.perhentianresort.com.my. A veritable campus of bungalows and chalets containing various grades of room, all spacious and boasting modern furnishings and verandas. Well-placed wooden wind chimes add atmosphere, but staff can seem out of their depth; all in all, you'd expect better for the price. ❼

Reef Chalets ☎09/691 1762 or 013/981 6762, ⓔthereefpp@hotmail.com. A semicircle of chalets

with hints of traditional Malay architecture, largish bathrooms and a choice of fan or a/c. With rather plain decor, they are slightly overpriced, though the garden setting is undeniably lush. ❺

🏃 **Tunabay Island Resort** ☎09/691 1800 or 690 2902, ⓦwww.tunabay.com.my. This well-managed collection of chalets gets it just right, combining the comforts of a mid-range city hotel with a cool informality that's perfect for a laid-back beach holiday. The restaurant and bar are deservedly popular, and breakfast is included in the rate. ❻

Watercolours Paradise Resort ☎019/981 1852, ⓦwww.watercoloursworld.com. Simply furnished en-suite chalet rooms with fan and a small veranda, some with a seaview and a/c. There's also a well-run dive shop and a busy restaurant. Open year-round. ❸

Flora Bay and other southern shore

Arwana ☎09/752 1741, ⓦwww .arwanaperhentian.com.my. This sizeable resort sits behind the only bit of indifferent pebbly sand on Flora Bay. The nicest rooms are in the row of chalets with verandas facing the beach, but most rooms are in three-storey blocks built around the enticing swimming pool. The large restaurant serves buffet meals and has football on satellite TV plus karaoke nights; the resort also has its own dive shop. It's not as well run as the facilities deserve, but packages can be good value. ❻

🏃 **Bayu Dive Lodge** ☎09/691 1650, ⓦwww .alualudivers.com. You don't have to be a diver to take advantage of this slick new accommodation, which grew out of the Alu-Alu dive shop here. There's a vast range of options, including pricey seaview cottages, slightly cheaper chalets further back and longhouse rooms, all set in a neat garden. Depending on the room category, decor may include sparkling white tiled floors and swish modern lighting, while bathrooms may boast designer fittings; hot water and a/c available in some rooms. A restaurant may be open by the time you read this. ❸

Bubbles ☎012/983 8038, ⓦwww.bubblesdc .com. A boat ride from Flora Bay is the *Bubbles Resort and Dive Centre*, concealed behind a row of beachfront trees at Tanjung Tukas in the southeast of the island. Accommodation mostly comprises three rows of stark white A-frames at the back, which wouldn't look amiss on a Pink Floyd album cover, though there are also more conventional-looking chalets with the option of a/c. Own restaurant. ❸

Fauna Beach ☎ 09/691 1607, ⓕ 691 1600. Pleasant, unremarkable chalets with fan (plus a couple with a/c), facing the beach and set in a neat garden. ❸

Flora Bay & Flora Bay 2 ☎ 09/691 1666, ⓦ www.florabayresort.com. A huge range of options, from inexpensive rooms with fan, to beachfront chalets, including some overpriced units with a/c. All rooms are en suite. *Flora Bay*, with its garden of frangipanis and oleanders, is marginally preferable to its counterpart, which features rather institutional two-storey blocks. Own dive shop. ❸

Samudra Beach Cottages ☎ 09/697 7608 or 019/969 0957. Fairly standard chalets, three rooms to a unit, plus cheaper A-frames. Not bad at all, though fraying a little at the edges. ❷

Eating and drinking

The best **eating** on the island is on the western shore. Here, the restaurant at *Tunabay Resort* serves a range of pasta dishes, salads and seafood, with evening barbecues. Also worth a look is the atmospheric restaurant at *Coral View*, with a variety of "sizzlings" (basically grills – choose from fish or mixed seafood or meat), plus a range of non-alcoholic "mocktails". Otherwise, you can't go far wrong at *New Cocohut* for Chinese fare, *Mama's Chalet* for Malay food or *Watercolours* for pizzas. The food at Flora Bay is much of a muchness, with a few open-air restaurants serving up a mix of Western and Asian standards, plus the odd barbecue.

Merang, Pulau Redang and Pulau Lang Tengah

A tiny coastal kampung some 35km northwest of Kuala Terengganu, **Merang** (not to be confused with Marang, south of Kuala Terengganu) is the departure point for the one-hour boat trip out to **Pulau Redang** (also served by flights from KL and Singapore) or **Pulau Lang Tengah**, both of which have great snorkelling and diving, though hardly any inexpensive accommodation. Practically all visitors to these islands arrive on resort-based package trips, but if it's chiefly the underwater attractions that tempt you, then you may be able to arrange a side trip here with one of the dive operators on the Perhentians (see p.286). Note that the resorts on both islands shut up shop during the northeast monsoon.

Merang

Most travellers who make it to **MERANG**, along the coastal road just south of the Sungai Merang creek, only glimpse the back of the village as the road swings past. The beach, which can be reached along a couple of side roads, is not exceptional, the sand strewn in places with sea morning glories. Still, the village is usually quiet, there's reasonable swimming, and the beach gives a memorable view of the quartet of islands offshore – from left to right, the Perhentians, Lang Tengah, Redang and finally Bidung Laut, once the site of a refugee camp for Vietnamese boat people.

S.P. Bumi operates a daytime **bus** service between Kuala Besut and Kuala Terengganu via Merang, with around three departures daily in each direction; fares to Merang from either starting point are around RM5. Chartering a taxi here costs around RM60 from Kuala Besut, or RM40 from Kuala Terengganu. The buses stop at or opposite Merang's school, where a turning off the coast road leads to the riverside, ten minutes' walk away, and a succession of **jetties** for the islands. Most jetties serve specific resorts, so you may need to ask around to find the boat you want; tickets (around RM45 one way to either Redang or Lang Tengah) are available from booths or from the boatmen, though most people on packages have their transfers included.

Merang has a limited amount of beachfront **accommodation**. Head down the side road from the bus stop on the east (southbound) side of the road, and you come to a T-junction; turn right here to reach the best of the budget places, the friendly *Kembara Resort* (℡09/653 1770, ⓦkembararesort.tripod .com; dorm beds RM10, rooms ❷), set in a large garden with tables shaded by palms. They have a variety of rooms (a few with a/c), cooking facilities – handy as there are only basic dining-out options in Merang – and internet access, and can arrange all-day snorkelling trips to Redang (RM100 per person). A little further along is *Aryani* (℡09/653 2111, ⓦwww.thearyani .com; ❾), an immaculate Malay-styled spa resort of just seventeen luxurious rooms and suites, most of which have a sunken outdoor bath to lounge in. Besides a range of treatments, many of which are derived from tropical herbs and flowers, there's a sumptuous pool and fine local and Western fare in the slick restaurant. For a mere RM1055 per night, you can sleep in their Heritage Suite, a century-old Malay stilt house which once belonged to a Terengganu sultan – it was moved here piece by piece.

Pulau Redang

Just 5km by 8km in size, **PULAU REDANG** is very much a resort enclave, with more than fifteen establishments having set up here over the past few years, and a few more on the way. For most visitors, the chief attraction is the abundant marine life, sustained by the **coral reefs** that thrive around the island. The house reefs have had to endure a lot over recent decades – a large-scale attack by the crown-of-thorns starfish in the mid-1970s and, more recently, silt deposition caused by development all over the island. Forests have been felled and hillsides levelled to make way for a **golf course**; new roads and a freshwater pipeline from the mainland have been laid; a kampung has been built inland for the two-thousand-strong fishing community who used to live in a traditional floating village, removed to make way for a jetty and even more tourist development.

Thankfully, coral reefs have remarkable properties of self-renewal, and Redang's marine environment appears to have stabilized in a reasonable state. Conservation has certainly been helped by Redang's designation as one of Malaysia's **marine parks**, and by the regulation of certain activities, such as spear-fishing, trawling and water sports, in the vicinity. The best **snorkelling** is off the southern coast around the islets of Pulau Pinang and Pulau Ekor Tibu, while most of the **dive sites** are located off Redang's eastern shore, which, as it happens, is where almost all the resorts are located (most have their own dive shops). Among the most common fish are batfish, angel fish, box fish and butterfly fish, which feed off the many anemone, sponges and bivalves to be found around the rocks. The highlight of the island's social calendar is arguably the **candat sotong** festival in April, celebrating a pastime popular all along the east coast, involving the catching of squid by dipping small hand-held lures with hooks on one end into the sea.

Arrival and information

There's regular transport to Redang from March to October only, when the resorts are open. Almost all **boats** to Redang depart from Merang (RM95 return), except for those to the *Berjaya Beach* and *Redang Beach* resorts, which use Kuala

Terengganu's Shahbandar jetty (RM100 return). In addition, Berjaya Air (W berjaya-air.com) operates daily **flights** to Redang's airstrip from KL (Subang airport; RM570 return) and Singapore (Seletar airport; S$380), with boats ferrying arrivals from the airstrip to the various resorts. Note that visitors to Redang are, in theory, liable to pay a RM5 marine parks **conservation fee** covering three days' stay, though in practice you may find it's levied only if you're on a snorkelling or diving package; your accommodation may collect the fee just before taking you to one of the most popular snorkelling areas, around Pulau Pinang just south of Redang (which, as it happens, is also the site of the Marine Park Centre, which administers the park).

The best source for the latest **information** on Redang is W www.redang.org, run by a Singapore-based couple who are passionate about the island. Their website includes sections on all the practical aspects of visiting Redang, plus coverage of dive sites and conservation.

It's usually cheaper to book a **package** to Redang than to visit independently. Standard packages typically include accommodation, boat transfers, some or all meals and at least one snorkelling excursion (but normally exclude equipment rental); some resorts also offer diving packages. Packages are available through travel agents or the resorts themselves – practically all of them have booking offices in Kuala Terengganu, and a few have offices in KL as well.

Accommodation

Most **accommodation** on Redang is located on the island's eastern shore, either on **Pasir Panjang** (Long Beach) and the adjacent Shark Bay, or just to the south at another bay, **Teluk Kalung**. Pasir Panjang features a particularly gorgeous stretch of fine white sand that, appropriately, seems to go on forever; Teluk Kalung's beach is narrower and pebbly in places, but is largely inviting nonetheless. The beaches on the north of the island, at **Teluk Dalam**, home of the *Berjaya Beach* resort, rival those at Pasir Panjang. The resorts have en-suite, air-conditioned rooms and their own **restaurants**.

Given the predominance of packages at Redang, and the fact that some resorts don't have accommodation-only rates, some reviews include the price *per night* of a basic three-day, two-night **package** for two people (indicated by "FBP", for full-board package). Where rates rise during the height of the season (July & Aug) or at weekends, the prices or codes apply to the higher rate; look out for good discounts at the start or end of season. "B&B" denotes a room-only rate, with breakfast included; "KT" next to a phone number indicates a sales office in Kuala Terengganu.

Southern Redang
Redang Kalong Teluk Kalung, reservations T 03/7960 7163, W www.redangkalong.com. A single-storey timber development comprising rather sparsely furnished a/c rooms, with its own dive shop. FBP RM410.

Pasir Panjang/Shark Bay
Coral Redang T 09/630 7110 or (KT) 623 6200, W www.coralredang.com.my. A bit more characterful than most places on Redang, with rooms boasting cane furniture, a veranda, bamboo matting on the walls and a touch of marble in the bathroom. There's also a small swimming pool with a poolside bar. FBP from RM550, B&B ❸.

Laguna Redang T 09/630 7888 or (KT) T 631 0888, W www.lagunaredang.com.my. One of the largest and slickest establishments on Redang, with over two hundred rooms all set around the enormous freeform pool. Rooms are very cosy and have their own fridge and a safe. Internet access available at a premium. FBP RM550, B&B ❾.

Redang Beach (KT) T 09/623 8188, W www .redang.com.my. A sizeable collection of two-storey blocks with tiled roofs and comfortable, modern rooms. FBP including two snorkelling trips RM500, B&B ❽.

Redang Lagoon (KT) T 09/666 5020, W www .redanglagoon.com. Along with *Redang Reef*, one of the best-value places on the island, though the vaguely Malay-themed chalets aren't anything special. FBP RM335, room only ⑤.

Redang Pelangi ℡09/624 2158, ⓦwww .redangpelangi.com. Unremarkable two- and four-bed rooms, each with their own safe. Rates fall by at least fifteen percent outside peak season. FBP RM380.

Redang Reef ℡09/630 2181 or (KT) 622 6181, ⓦwww.redangreefresort.com.my. Perched on the headland at the southern end of Shark Bay, and reached by a long wooden walkway, this has simply furnished rooms and may offer discounts early and late in the season. FBP410.

Teluk Dalam

Berjaya Beach ℡09/697 3988 or (KT) 630 8866, ⓦwww.berjayaresorts.com.my. A cut above most of the rest, with its own swimming pool and tennis facilities. In addition to snorkelling, offered on their packages, they also have optional round-island boat trips on which you can snorkel and feed the fish by hand, and can organize jungle walks. Standard packages are half-board and include one snorkelling trip for RM470, B&B ⑨.

Pulau Lang Tengah

A chip off the old Redang block, **Lang Tengah** island offers a much more low-key version of the Redang experience, being only a fraction the size of its near neighbour and with just a handful of places to stay. As at Redang, there's a RM5 **conservation charge** to pay, and **packages** are the most common way to visit. Arguably the best accommodation here is at *D'Coconut Lagoon* (℡03/4252 6686, ⓦwww.dcoconutlagoon.com; bed and breakfast from ❼ plus RM95 per person for boat transfers from Merang). The budget rooms are perhaps a little too packed together, but all accommodation is very comfy, with air conditioner and hot water; service is friendly and there's a competent dive shop too.

Kuala Terengganu

Only thirty years ago, **KUALA TERENGGANU**, 140km southeast of Kota Bharu and 170km north of Kuantan, was little more than an oversized fishing village that just happened to be the capital of Terengganu and the seat of its sultanate, which was founded in the early eighteenth century by Zainal Abidin of the royal house of Johor. The town enjoyed a long spell as an important port, exporting gold and pepper to China, but by the late nineteenth century it had been eclipsed by the rise of Singapore and other new ports in the Melaka Straits.

Following the transfer of Terengganu from Siamese to British control in the early twentieth century, the state became the last in the Peninsula to take a British Adviser, in 1919. However, Terengganu continued to languish as a rural state with, unusually, most of its settlements at river mouths – a pattern that can still be discerned today – rather than on the lower reaches of rivers, as elsewhere in Peninsular Malaysia. Over fifty years on, the discovery of **oil** off the coast dramatically altered the outlook; thanks to petroleum and the attendant petrochemicals industry, Terengganu's economy now rivals that of Penang, as is hinted at everywhere in major infrastructure projects.

For the visitor, however, this activity is belied by a certain **austerity** about Terengganu that's most noticeable in Kuala Terengganu itself, which lacks the commercial buzz of Kuantan or even Kota Bharu. This is partly because oil revenues haven't much trickled down to the man or woman in the street, but is also down to the fact that Terengganu is in some ways more conservative and inward-looking than neighbouring Kelantan. It was in Terengganu that the only rebellion in the Peninsula led by religious scholars occurred, in the 1920s, and

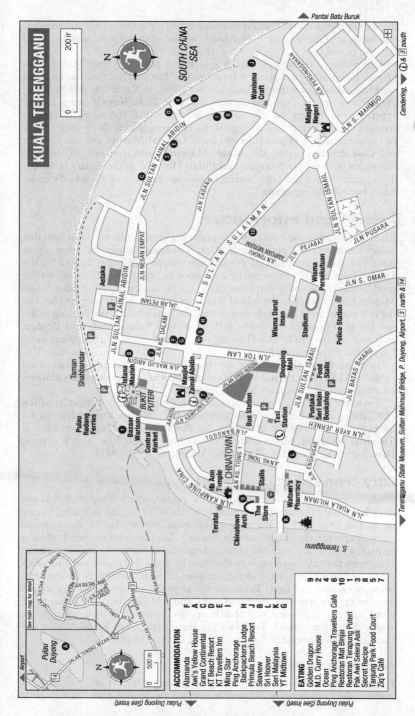

KUALA TERENGGANU

200 m

0

N

SOUTH CHINA
SEA

▲ Pantai Batu Buruk

Wanisma
Craft

Masjid
Negeri

Cendering, ▼ ① & ③ south

► Terengganu State Museum, Sultan Mahmud Bridge, P. Duyong, Airport, ③ north & ⑭

JLN PERSINGGAHAN

JLN S. MAHMUD

JLN SULTAN ISMAIL

JLN PUSARA

JLN SULTAN ZAINAL ABIDIN

JLN LADANG

Astaka

JLN NESAN EMPAT

JLN SULTAN ZAINAL ABIDIN

JALAN PETANI

JLN PEJABAT

JLN TENGKU
TAMPUAN MERIAM

Wisma
Persekutuan

JLN S. OMAR

Wisma Darul
Iman

Stadium

Police Station

JLN KG. DALAM

Masjid
Zainal Abidin

Istana
Maziah

JLN MASJID ABIDIN

Taman
Shahbandar

Pulau
Redang
Ferries

Bazaar
Warisan

BUKIT
PUTERI

JLN KOTA

JLN KAMPUNG DAIK

JALAN SYED HUSSIN

JLN TOK LAM

Shopping
Mall

Bus Station

Taxi
Station

Pustaka
Seri Intan
Bookshop

JLN SULTAN ISMAIL

JLN BATAS B.BARU

Food
Stalls

Central
Market

JLN BANGGOL

JLN KG. TIONG 1

JLN KG. TIONG 2

CHINATOWN

Hb Ann
Temple

JLN KAMPUNG CINA

Chinatown
Arch

The
Store

Stalls

Watson's
Pharmacy

Teratai

S. Terengganu

JLN AYER JERNEH

JLN ENGPUSAR

JLN KUALA HILIRAN

▼ Pulau Duyong (See inset)   ▲ Pulau Duyong (See inset)

ACCOMMODATION

Alamanda	F
Awi's Yellow House	A
Grand Continental	C
KT Beach Resort	D
KT Travellers Inn	E
Ming Star	I
Ping Anchorage	H
Backpackers Lodge	J
Primula Beach Resort	B
Seaview	L
Sri Hoover	K
Seri Malaysia	K
YT Midtown	G

EATING

Golden Dragon	9
M.D. Curry House	2
Ocean	4
Ping Anchorage Travellers Café	6
Restoran Mat Binjai	10
Restoran Terapung Puteri	1
Pak Awi Selera Asli	3
Secret Recipe	8
Tanjung Park Food Court	5
Ziq's Café	7

See main map for detail

JALAN SULTAN ISMAIL

JALAN S. OMAR

JLN TENGKU CENDERA

③

JALAN SULTAN MOHAMMAD

JALAN IBRAHIM

JLN KEMAJUAN

JALAN TENGKU MIZAN

Pulau
Duyong

④

Airport

⑭

N

500 m

0

Cendering (See Inset)

the state's present-day Islamic credentials are proclaimed by a huge hillside sign, translating as "God protect Terengganu", on the main western approach road into the capital.

Many visitors use the city simply as a transit point for Terengganu's best-known attractions – the pleasant **beaches** that line most of the coastline, and sparkling **islands**, from the Perhentians (see p.285) to Kapas (see p.308). Using the city as a base, you can also venture inland to **Tasik Kenyir** (see p.306) to experience something of the outdoor life for which the state's interior is renowned. However, there's enough in Kuala Terengganu itself to reward a day or two's sightseeing, in particular the lively **Central Market** and the adjacent old **Chinatown** quarter; the **State Museum**, which is one of the best complexes of its type in Malaysia; and **Pulau Duyong**, in the estuary of Sungai Terengganu, where the city's maritime heritage survives in the island's traditional **boat-building trade**.

Arrival and information

Kuala Terengganu's compact centre is built on a semicircular parcel of land that bulges north into the very mouth of the Terengganu River, the river which flows past the western half of the city, the eastern half being flanked by the South China Sea. If you arrive by road from any of the coastal towns to the south, chances are you'll enter the city from the southeast, along Jalan Sultan Mahmud; but if you use the inland Route 14 from Kuantan, your approach to the city may be from the southwest along Jalan Sultan Mohamad. Feeding traffic into this road from the northwest is the impressive **Sultan Mahmud Bridge**, built over the river and Pulau Duyong; you'll use this approach if arriving along Route 3 from points north.

The **airport** lies 18km north of the city; a taxi into the centre from here costs around RM20. Intercity and local buses use the spacious, modern **bus station**, smack in the centre on Jalan Masjid Abidin.

Next to the post office on Jalan Sultan Zainal Abidin is the state **tourist office** (TIC; daily except Fri 8am–5pm; ℡09/622 1553, Ⓦwww.tourism.terengganu .gov.my), with a range of brochures. An alternative source of information is **Tourism Malaysia**, whose office is just a little way south on Jalan Kampung Daik (Sun–Wed 8am–5pm, Thurs 8am–3.30pm; ℡09/630 9433).

City transport

Kuala Terengganu is small enough to walk around, which is just as well as the city's **bus** service (*bas bandar*) is limited to a handful of vehicles operating hourly or so. The brainchild of the state government, they're clad in wood motifs resembling what you might see in a Malay palace, though the overall effect is to make them look rather like vintage American streetcars. At least two routes exist, from the city centre west to the State Museum in Losong and also south to the craft workshops of Cendering; enquire at the tourist offices for the latest routes, schedules and fares. **Taxis** are found easily enough at the taxi station close to the bus station, and around the Central Market, but you'd have to be pretty lucky to flag one down. Hotels can usually summon up a taxi or a car with a driver, if requested. **Trishaws** ply along Jalan Sultan Zainal Abidin, and there are often a couple parked up near the Central Market.

Accommodation

Kuala Terengganu has a reasonable range of places to stay, including a couple of hotels slightly out from the centre overlooking the South China Sea, though at the time of writing the merits of a seaside location were somewhat negated by an ongoing municipal project to remould several kilometres of beach from the city centre southwards. There's also a decent backpackers' **hostel**, run by the city's largest travel agency. With your own transport, and a taste for pricey, traditionally styled accommodation, you could consider basing yourself out of town at the *Aryani* in Merang (see p.294).

Alamanda 28 & 28a Jalan Tok Lam ☏09/622 8888, ℱ623 8899. The tacky waterfall feature in the tiny lobby sets the tone at this budget hotel, well located near the bus station. Rooms all have a/c and bathroom, though the cheapest ones are poky, windowless and can be a bit shabby; you may prefer to pay a little bit more for the superior-class rooms. ❸

Awi's Yellow House Pulau Duyong ☏09/622 2080 or 017 984 0337. A delightful timber complex built on stilts over the water on the island's eastern shore. Accommodation is mostly in huts (not actually yellow) with walls of matted bamboo and thatched roofs, and a solitary ceiling light. Rooms all have mosquito nets and their own shower and toilet – a square hole in the floor. There's also a kitchen and canoes available to rent. The only snags are that getting back by public transport can seem a little forbidding after dark (ask Awi if he can arrange a taxi or collect you), and that the place is occasionally booked by student groups, which can make it a little more lively than you'd like. The best way to reach *Awi's* is to arrive by boat, then follow the track south from the jetty for around 5min (you may need to ask directions); for more on transport to Duyong and the island itself, see p.302. ❷

Grand Continental Jalan Sultan Zainal Abidin ☏09/625 1888, ℗www.ghihotels.com. The biggest and best place in town, part of a national chain. Predictably modern, with slick rooms, marbled bathrooms, satellite TV, a swimming pool and a coffee house licensed to serve beer. Rate includes breakfast. ❻

KT Beach Resort 548e Jalan Sultan Zainal Abidin ☏09/631 5555, ℱ631 6666. A motel-like complex on a desultory stretch of public beach, with appealing Chinese-style wooden benches and vases in the reception area, and jumbo-sized TVs in the rooms. They also manage some worthwhile, fully furnished apartments, nicely suited to families, in the ugly concrete block across from the *Tian Kee* restaurant. ❹

KT Travellers Inn First floor, 201 Jalan Sultan Zainal Abidin ☏09/622 3666, ℱ623 2692. A blandly modern place that isn't particularly geared towards backpackers, despite the name. Rooms tend to be boxy but come with a/c, TV and their own clean, tiled bathroom. ❹

Ming Star Eastern section of Jalan Sultan Zainal Abidin ☏09/622 8666, ℗mingstarhotel.com. Competently run hotel with modern en-suite rooms, including fancy glass shower stalls in the bathrooms, its own restaurant and free wi-fi on the ground floor; rate includes breakfast. ❺

Ping Anchorage Backpackers Lodge 77a Jalan Sultan Sulaiman ☏09/626 2020, ℗www .pinganchorage.com.my. A range of basic rooms, mostly with fan, louvred internal windows, cement flooring and shared facilities, though some rooms have their own bathroom and/or a/c. There's also a rooftop garden to lounge in and use of a washing machine, and the management – the travel agency with premises below – also runs a great café with satellite TV a couple of doors away. Dorm beds RM9, rooms ❶

Primula Beach Resort Jalan Persinggahan ☏09/622 2100, ℗www.primulahotels.com. Behind the ugly ochre and peach facade is a well-kept hotel complete with swimming pool, gym and two restaurants, including the poolside *Mumbai* – basically a glorified *mamak* joint. Rooms are spacious, with TV and a/c, and the bathrooms have proper bathtubs. The beach is nice, but swimming is often not possible because of the undertow. Ample parking. Rate includes breakfast. ❻

Seaview 18a Jalan Masjid Abidin ☏09/622 1911, ℱ631 3118. This ageing hotel has comfortable if very dull a/c rooms with largish bathrooms. The sea views are not going to be etched into memory; more appealingly, west-facing rooms look out on the Istana and Bukit Puteri. Free wi-fi. ❹

Seri Hoover 49 Jalan Sultan Ismail ☏09/623 3833, ℱ622 5975. Rooms are adequate for the price, with TV, a/c and bathroom, though fraying slightly at the edges; there's also free parking, but no breakfast. ❸

Seri Malaysia Jalan Hiliran, on the riverside ☏09/623 6454, ℗www.serimalaysia.com.my. Unexciting but sound chain hotel with views of Pulau Duyong from some rooms, though what appear to be balconies are in fact just parapets masking the a/c units. Rate includes breakfast. ❺

YT Midtown 30 Jalan Tok Lam ☏09/622 3088, ℮ythotel@streamyx.com. In a city not noted for bustling efficiency, this slick multi-storey hotel, with some 140 rooms, actually hits the right note. All rooms have functional modern fittings and decor, plus TV and bathroom. The central location is a bonus, as is the buffet breakfast included in the rate. You might want to enquire about their sister hotel next to the *KT Beach Resort*, which should be completed by the time you read this. ⑤

The City

As a brief foray around town will bear out, Kuala Terengganu is even more of a hotchpotch than most Malaysian cities, sprinkled with a range of oil-funded showpieces of varying degrees of success. At the time of writing the city was also undergoing a giddy **revamp** aimed at transforming it into the east coast's tourism hub.

The main artery through the commercial sector is Jalan Sultan Ismail, where you'll find the banks and government offices; the **old town**, including **Chinatown**, is the sector west of Jalan Masjid Abidin and probably the most attractive place to wander. The outskirts hold various **craft workshops** and the **Terengganu State Museum**, while only 500m west across Sungai Terengganu from the centre are the boatyards of **Pulau Duyong**.

The old town

Behind railings on Jalan Sultan Zainal Abidin, the neat and precise **Istana Maziah** (closed to the public) is one of the city's few historic monuments. Now used only for royal functions, it's vaguely reminiscent of a French chateau but with Malay touches in some of the roofs and pediments.

Just beyond to the west is a white tower, still serving as a lighthouse. It crowns the steep hillock of **Bukit Puteri** ("Princess Hill"; daily except Fri 9am–5pm; RM1), now a lovely little park with mature trees and chirruping cicadas. There are good views from here over town – including of the blindingly white **Masjid Zainal Abidin** just to the south, with its bell-shaped roofs – and the Terengganu River. Relics of the hill's time as a stronghold during the early nineteenth century, when the sultans Mohammed and Umar were fighting each other for the Terengganu throne, include a fort, supposedly built using honey to bind the bricks, and several cannons imported from Spain and Portugal. Note in particular one large and one small cannon side by side, together called Meriam Beranak or "mother and daughter cannon"; they must once have menaced ships sailing upriver, but now seem to be taking aim at the white elephant that is the *Ri-Yaz Resort* at the northern end of Pulau Duyong (see p.302). What looks like a crashed flying saucer that's half-buried itself in the river's far shore is in fact part of a lavish sports complex.

You can ascend Bukit Puteri using either the long flight of steps starting near the state tourist office or, more easily, the escalators at the new **Bazaar Warisan** next door, whose uppermost floor is just a few steps short of the hilltop. The "bazaar" itself, grandly intended to blend Turkish and Malay influences, has turned out to be a lacklustre collection of batik shops and jewellers.

A bit further on and much more rewarding is Terengganu's **Central Market** (aka Pasar Payang; daily 6am–6pm), an airy, modern multistorey building backing onto the river. The ground floor is taken up by a thriving wet market, plus plenty of stalls selling a marvellous range of Malay confections in just about every conceivable hue. The upper floors comprise a maze of food stalls and outlets where you can seek out batik, *songkets* and brassware.

Heading south from the market takes you along Jalan Kampung Cina (aka Jalan Bandar), which, true to its name, gives access to **Chinatown**, established as long ago as the eighteenth century when the trading links between Terengganu and China drew Chinese to settle here. Many of the shophouses have recently enjoyed a new lick of paint courtesy of the state government, and while the colours are gaudy and not necessarily historically accurate, the whole area looks cheery. While you're in the vicinity, it's worth taking a look at the photogenic **Ho Ann Temple** and, a short distance away, the ornamental gateway that marks the southern entrance to Chinatown.

Arts and crafts workshops

Local artisans have long been known for their **brassware**, working in an alloy called "white brass", unique to the state. Formerly the preserve of the sultans, white brass – containing at least forty percent zinc, with added nickel to make the colour less yellow – is now used to make decorative articles such as candlesticks. At **Wanisma Craft** (daily: shop 9am–6.30pm, workshop until 4pm), close to the junction of Jalan Sultan Zainal Abidin and Jalan Ladang in the east of the centre, you can observe the traditional "lost wax" technique, whereby a wax maquette is covered with clay, then fired in a kiln to melt the wax and leave behind a mould into which to pour molten brass. When the metal solidifies, the clay is chipped off. There's also a **batik workshop** where you can watch cloth being handprinted. Both batik garments and brass items such as betel-nut sets and small gongs can be bought in their shop, though note that the workshop may not have anyone who can explain the procedures in English.

The weaving of *mengkuang* (pandanus) can be seen at Ky Enterprises, about 3km due south of the centre on Jalan Panji Alam, where women fashion the long, slender leaves into delicate but functional items like bags and floor mats. You can get here on the S.P. Bumi local bus bound for neighbouring Pasir Panjang. Perhaps the most famous of several workshops in Pasir Panjang itself, about 500m west of Jalan Panji Alam, is that belonging to Abu Bakar bin Mohammed Amin, a **kris** maker on Lorong Saga (call to make an appointment; ☏09/622 7968). Here you can watch the two-edged dagger and its wooden sheath being decorated. Arriving by bus, ask to be let off at the nearby school, Sekolah Kebangsaan Pasir Panjang.

Close to the coast 7km south of the city, one of Malaysia's largest **batik** producers, Noor Arfa, stays close to its Kuala Terengganu roots by maintaining a factory and showroom (daily except Fri 9am–5pm; ⓦwww.noor-arfa.com .my). Here you can watch batik artists at work and shop for garments and fabrics, including *songkets* (from RM120) and psychedelic rainbowy shirts (from

The kris

The **kris** occupies a treasured position in Malay culture, a symbol of manhood and honour believed to harbour protective spirits. Traditionally, all young men crossing the barrier of puberty receive one, which remains with them for the rest of their lives, tucked into the folds of a sarong; for an enemy to relieve someone of a *kris* is tantamount to stripping him of his virility.

The weapon itself is intended to deliver a horizontal thrust rather than the more usual downward stab. When a sultan executed a treacherous subject, he did so by sliding a long *kris* through his windpipe, just above the collar bone, thereby inflicting a swift – though bloody – death. The distinguishing feature of the dagger is the hilt, shaped like the butt of a gun to facilitate a sure grip. The hilt can be used to inflict a damaging blow to the head in combat, especially if there isn't time to unsheath the weapon.

The daggers can be highly decorative: the iron blade is often embellished with fingerprint patterns or the body of a snake, while the hilt can be made from ivory, wood or metal; the designs are usually based on the theme of a bird's head.

RM80). The factory is in the Cendering Industrial Area along Route 3, beyond the Kuala Ibai bridge and just north of the coastal village of **Cendering**; ask at the tourist office about *bas bandar* services here. If you're driving out there along the coast road, it's worth pausing briefly en route at the unmistakable **Tengku Tengah Zaharah Mosque**, built on piles just above the surface of an artificial lake, hence its local epithet, the "Floating Mosque".

Pulau Duyong

Pulau Duyong ("Mermaid Island") is the largest of the islets dotting the Terengganu estuary. For now the island remains largely tranquil, though it hasn't escaped development: what were once two islets have been joined by reclamation to form what you see today, and the northern section of Duyong was levelled in double-quick time to build a prestige yacht club for the annual **Monsoon Cup** race (@www.monsooncup.com.my), staged in November as the northeast monsoon gets going. The rest of the island, however, still features a rustic kampung, a great place for an hour's stroll. The island is also the proud home of a venerable **boat-building** tradition, which you can observe from the sidelines at any of the boatyards.

The easiest way to reach Duyong is by **boat**; they run sporadically by day from the moorings next to the Central Market (RM1/1.50 depending on the vessel). Occasionally there are also boats from the jetty behind the *Seri Malaysia* hotel, but most appear to operate on a triangular route, from the market to the island, then back across the river to the hotel, and downriver to the market. If you turn right once on the island, you'll eventually come to the yacht club and the lavish *Ri-Yaz Resort*, miserably empty outside the Monsoon Cup period. Much more interesting is to head left on the road from the jetty, which swings a little inland after a minute, close to a school; take a left here and follow the road/track (while keeping close to the shore) and you pass a couple of **boatyards**. The one with the two-storey blue facade has a series of displays and press clippings, some in English, on their work.

Continue, and after a few minutes you come to *Awi's Yellow House* (see p.299; its tiny sign beneath a thatched awning is easily missed). Around ten minutes

Boat-building on Pulau Duyong

The shipwrights of Pulau Duyong work mostly from memory rather than set plans. For hulls, their preferred material is **cengal**, a wood whose toughness and imperviousness to termite attack make it prized not only for boats but also the best kampung houses. The hull planking is fastened with strong hardwood pegs, and then a special sealant – derived from swampland trees, and resistant to rot – is applied. Unusually, the frame is fitted afterwards, giving the whole structure strength and flexibility. As construction takes place in **dry docks**, the finished boats have to be manoeuvred on rollers into the water, an effort that often requires local villagers to pitch in en masse.

Historically, the boatyards produced a variety of **schooners**, from humble fishing craft to the hulking *perahu besar*, which could be up to 30m in length. These days however, motorized, modern alternatives to the old-fashioned wooden boats, the increasing cost of timber, plus the lure of other careers in Malaysia's modernizing economy, have all contributed to a steep decline in boat-building on the island. Today fewer than five boatyards are still engaged in the business, compared to more than three dozen twenty years ago. With the fall in local demand for working boats of the traditional kind, any salvation for Duyong's boat-building looks to lie in clients from around the world, who have been placing orders for all manner of bespoke craft.

▲ Boatyard at Pulau Duyong

from the jetty and close to the Sultan Mahmud bridge is another boatyard, attractively sited amid a stand of impossibly tall coconut trees. Here you can get a good view of the islet to the south that is home to **Taman Tamadun Islam**, much promoted locally as a sort of Islamic theme park, though the reality is that it contains dismal scaled-down reconstructions of some of the world's greatest mosques.

The Terengganu State Museum

Arriving at the **Terengganu State Museum** (daily 9am–5pm, closed Fri noon–3pm; RM5; ☏09/622 1444 for information on special exhibitions), 5km west of the town centre, you might think you've chanced upon an *Alice in Wonderland* realm. Confronting you here are a series of proud buildings modelled on the archetypal Terengganu village house, but absolutely gargantuan in scale. Somehow the dislocation in size is fitting though, for at its best the museum far outstrips most of its provincial counterparts in the quality and extent of its exhibits. The museum can be reached by the *bas bandar* service from the city centre.

The main building, **Bangunan Utama**, houses displays of exquisite fabrics at its lowest level, while the second floor has displays on various crafts and the third details the history of Terengganu. In the attached building to the left is the **Petronas Oil Gallery**, and behind this the **Islamic Gallery**, with fine examples of Koranic calligraphy, sometimes executed on local artefacts – copper jars, trays and so forth. Beside the river are two examples of the **sailing boats** for which Kuala Terengganu is famed – unique blends, which you can climb into, of European ships and Chinese junks. A small **Maritime Museum** is close by, as is an outdoor gallery of smaller, beautifully decorated fishing boats.

The landscaped gardens feature imposing modern interpretations of the triple-roofed houses common to the area. Also within the grounds are ancient timber palaces, which have been rebuilt, the supreme example being the **Istana Tengku Long**, originally built in 1888 entirely without nails (to Malays, these signify death, because of their use in coffins). Like the majority of traditional east-coast houses, the hardwood rectangular building has a high, pointed roof and a pair of slightly curved wooden gables at either end. Each gable is fitted with twenty gilded screens, intricately carved with verses from the Koran and designed to not only admit air but also provide protection from driving rain.

Eating and drinking

Like Kelantan, Terengganu has its own signature rice dish, **nasi dagang**, which, like Kelantan's *nasi kerabu*, is usually served with a fish curry. There the resemblance ends, for while *nasi kerabu* is essentially ordinary rice tinted unusual colours with flower petals, *nasi dagang* is a slightly sticky rice, steamed with a little coconut milk and chopped shallots, and often eaten for breakfast.

There are a couple of decent Malay restaurants in town, and the Malay stalls at the Central Market are worth trying, as are those just south of the junction of Jalan Sultan Ismail and Jalan Tok Lam. Chinatown is the obvious focus for **Chinese fare**, with a bunch of busy food stalls along Jalan Kampung Tiong 1 (where there's also a little row of Malay stalls) and several excellent restaurants on the main street, though the two seaside places close to the *KT Beach Resort* are also worthwhile.

It's no surprise that Kuala Terengganu is largely dry; your best bets for **alcohol** are the Chinese restaurants and stalls, the coffee house at the *Grand Continental* hotel, which serves beer, the travellers' café run by Ping Anchorage, and what passes for a beer garden at the Tanjung Park Food Court, at the end of the lane containing the *Ocean* restaurant.

Golden Dragon Jalan Kampung Cina ℡ 09/622 3034. One of the best-established restaurants in Chinatown, with reliable seafood (the steamed fish is worth trying) and other Cantonese fare. Daily 10.30am–3pm & 6.15–9.30pm.

M.D. Curry House Jalan Kampung Dalam. Tiny, humble South Indian *kedai kopi* run by a friendly Tamil guy from Penang. There's a range of rotis, noodles and *idli* in the morning, *nasi campur* plus *biriyani* at lunchtime, and a bit of everything in the evening. A few non-Indian standbys keep the multi-cultural clientele happy, such as Chinese-style chicken in soy sauce and good *acar* (pickles) for the Malays.

Ocean Just along from the *KT Beach Resort*, on Jalan Sultan Zainal Abidin. Well-regarded Chinese restaurant specializing in seafood, with steamboats another popular choice. The adjacent *Tian Kee* (evenings only) is just as good and pork-free. Daily noon–2.30pm & 5.30–11.30pm.

🏃 **Pak Awi Selera Asli** Jalan Sultan Zainal Abidin. A busy diner offering *nasi lemak* and noodles for breakfast, and self-service *nasi campur* from around 10am till close of play. Unusually, the emphasis isn't on east-coast food but on fare from around the Peninsula; the friendly owner, who hails from Penang, can explain the various dishes to you. Daily except Fri 8am–5pm.

Ping Anchorage Travellers Café Jalan Sultan Sulaiman. The backpackers' favourite, serving Western café food with some local dishes thrown in. There's also satellite TV with live football matches and good films, and beer. Daily 7am–11pm.

Restoran Mat Binjai Jalan Sultan Sulaiman. Established place specializing in Terengganu fare, and nicely complementing *Pak Awi*. Come here for dishes like *sotong bakar* (barbecued squid), kampung-style fried chicken and *sayur golok* (vegetables stewed with coconut milk). Daily except Fri 8am–7pm.

Restoran Terapung Puteri Jalan Sultan Zainal Abidin. Not actually floating as its name translates, but built on stanchions at the waterfront, this is in essence a very smartly turned-out *kedai kopi*, popular with Malay families on an evening out. While the food's not spectacular, at least there's plenty of choice, from *ayam bakar* (grilled chicken) to tangy mango *kerabu* – unripe mango shreds laced with dried shrimp and some fiery green chilli. Also worth trying is the Pattani-style *nasi goreng*, in which the rice is parcelled up inside a square omelette. Daily 11am–late.

Secret Recipe Eastern part of Jalan Sultan Zainal Abidin ℡ 09/622 5909. This a/c chain restaurant hardly grabs the attention in KL or Singapore, but

Transport options from Kuala Terengganu are uncomplicated. MAS (☏ 09/662 6600) and AirAsia (☏ 09/667 2267), both with offices at the airport, **fly** to KL, as does Firefly, which also serves Penang. For flight information, call ☏ 09/667 0080.

From the **bus** station, there are express departures to major destinations on the Peninsula as well as local services to towns within Terengganu as far afield as Kemaman/Chukai. Long-distance **taxis** park up just to the south of the local bus station, and can be chartered to destinations across the Peninsula, including Kota Bharu (RM100) and Kuantan (RM140).

The **Shahbandar jetty** on the seafront is used by a couple of resort boats to Pulau Redang. You could, in principle, use these to head to Redang independently (RM100 return), but might well then have to charter another boat to reach the resort of your choice; in any case, package trips to Redang – which are the best way to visit – usually include boat transfers in the price.

it's just about the best place in Kuala Terengganu for a dose of Western food, serving grills, salads, smoothies and an extensive range of cheesecakes.

Ziq's Cafe Jalan Kampung Daik. Conveniently located across from the bus station is this surprisingly smart café offering a mix of Western and local fare, including passable pizzas (from RM7), plus a Western set breakfast. Daily except Fri 8.30am–late.

Listings

Banks and exchange All the major banks have offices on Jalan Sultan Ismail, west of the junction with Jalan Tok Lam; the Maybank here is your best bet for changing money.

Bookshops The best bookshop is Pustaka Seri Intan, on the south side of Jalan Sultan Ismail (opposite the Maybank); it only has a limited range of English novels, but carries a good selection of magazines.

Car rental You can arrange this through Ping Anchorage (see below) either at their counter at the airport or by contacting their city-centre office.

Hospitals and clinics The state hospital is on Jalan Sultan Mahmud (☏ 09/623 3355 or 621 2121), 1km southeast of the centre. There are plenty of privately run walk-in clinics and the odd dentist's surgery along Jalan Tok Lam, some staying open well into the evening.

Internet access There are a few internet cafés round town, including an efficient place a couple of doors down from the *Ping Anchorage Travellers Café*, and Neo.Net on Jalan Kampung Tiong 1 in Chinatown.

Left luggage Available at the express bus station on Jalan Sultan Zainal Abidin and at the local bus station on Jalan Masjid Abidin (both RM1 a day).

Pharmacy There's a branch of Watson's on Jalan Sultan Ismail.

Police The main police station is on Jalan Sultan Ismail (☏ 09/624 6222).

Post office The GPO on Jalan Sultan Zainal Abidin has poste restante.

Shopping For everyday purchases, try the small Astaka shopping complex next to the long-distance bus station or the Store, a general emporium and supermarket in Chinatown. The city's first attempt at a modern mall is on Jalan Tok Lam next to the bus station, but this had largely failed to find tenants at the time of writing. As Chinatown shows signs of gentrification, a few boutiques and souvenir shops are taking root on Jalan Kampung Cina, of which the longest established is Teratai at no. 151. Camera shops cluster on Jalan Syed Hussin, just north of the local bus station.

Travel agents Ping Anchorage Travel and Tours, 77a Jalan Sultan Sulalman (☏ 09/626 2020, ⓦ www.pinganchorage.com.my), is one of the country's most successful travel agents; efficient and well organized, they offer numerous packages and plenty of information on sights throughout the east coast and the interior.

Visa extensions The Immigration Department is in Wisma Persekutuan on Jalan Sultan Ismail (Sun–Thurs 8am–5pm; ☏ 09/622 1424).

Tasik Kenyir

More than three hundred square kilometres in area, **Tasik Kenyir** was created in the 1980s when the Kenyir hydroelectric dam across Sungai Terengganu was completed. The whole site was once lush jungle, and with bare tree trunks still to be seen jutting out of the clear waters, it can be hard to blot out the thought that the lake somehow isn't quite meant to exist.

Tasik Kenyir is much touted as a back-to-nature experience, though it's a bit of a half-baked proposition thanks to poor transport connections, not to mention the fact that the attractions are scattered around, making exploration difficult when boat charter is as expensive as it is here. That said, the lake offers scope for **fishing**, waterborne excursions and wildlife-spotting – there's a reasonable chance of glimpsing **elephants** on the shore from time to time. On the lake periphery are many **waterfalls** where it's possible to swim, and in the hills to the south of the lake you can visit the limestone **Bewah and Taat caves**. The lake is also Terengganu's gateway to **Taman Negara**, thanks to the park entrance at Tanjung Mentong at the southern end of the lake (see p.250).

Getting there

Pangkalan Gawi, the jetty in the northeast of the lake, can be reached by road and thus serves as the focal point for arrivals. A **taxi** to the jetty costs around RM70 from Kuala Terengganu. There are no **buses** to the lake from here, but ironically there is a bus service all the way from KL, the Tasik Kenyir Express (℡03/4044 4276; RM44), which leaves from Putra bus station (daily 9am & 9pm; 8hr). You can drive to the lake using **Route 3** west of Kuala Terengganu (accessible from Jertih, not far southwest of Kota Bharu, or from Kuala Terengganu via the Sultan Mahmud Bridge), following signs for the lake; alternatively, if on **Route 14**, turn off 30km from Kuala Terengganu at Ajil, heading west along Route 106 for **Kuala Berang**, then northwest, all the while following intermittent signage for the lake. It will soon also be possible to reach the jetty from the interior, by turning off **Route 8** at Simpang Aring onto Route 1742, which serves the Taman Negara entrance at Kuala Koh; instead of turning right midway for the park entrance, stay on the main road – nearly completed at the time of writing – and you will eventually skirt around the northern edge of the lake. The drive from Gua Musang to the jetty will take around ninety minutes.

Information and accommodation

One of the Terengganu state government's websites (🆆www.ketengah.gov.my/kenyir) has useful general **information** for visitors and lists accommodation around the lake, though it may not be kept up to date. There's a **tourist office** at the Gawi jetty itself (daily 8am–5pm; ℡09/626 7788).

A few **chalets** and **rafthouses** around the lake offer modest comforts at modest rates. The problem is that they are presently only accessible by boat from the Gawi jetty – and chartering a standard six-seater vessel can cost several hundred ringgit a day. The good news is that it will be possible to drive to some of the northern shore accommodation once the new road from the interior is finished. If you're not travelling in a group, you can avoid the expense of boat charter by staying at the Gawi jetty, though the only accommodation here is the swankiest place of all, the *Lake Kenyir Resort* (℡09/666 8888 or 03/2052 7766, 🆆www.lakekenyir.com; ❽), an elegant collection of buildings with Terengganu-style pitched roofs, steep at the top and gently sloping below. It's probably best to arrive on one of their full-board packages, some of which include a lake excursion, or book through Ping Anchorage (W www.pinganchorage.com.my), which offers a good discount on the ridiculous rack rate. The company also has packages for rafthouse or houseboat stays, starting at RM260 per person if you can assemble a group of ten, and including a lake cruise plus transfers from Kuala Terengganu. Finally, they also offer a day-trip to the lake from Kuala Terengganu (from RM200 per person), starting with a look at the dam, followed by a cruise to the Lasir Waterfall.

Marang

The coastal village of **MARANG**, 17km south of Kuala Terengganu (and not to be confused with Merang, the transit point for Pulau Redang, north of Kuala Terengganu), was once nicknamed "cowboy town" because of its dusty one-horse feel, with ramshackle wooden shops and houses. In those days Marang drew a steady stream of foreign visitors, attracted by the promise of rustic Malaysia. Then the town suffered death by a thousand modernizations: many residents have now been relocated to a new settlement just inland, while at the waterfront a jetty complex and landscaped parks have been built. The sanitized result has neither slickness nor old-fashioned charm, and only remains a target for tourists as it is the departure point for the delightful **Pulau Kapas** and **Pulau Gemia** (see p.308), just 6km offshore.

Practicalities

There are local **buses** at least hourly between Kuala Terengganu and Marang during the daytime, or you could charter a **taxi** for the journey (around RM30). It's also possible to reach Marang on the long-distance Kuantan–Kuala Terengganu buses that travel the coast road, via Cherating, Dungun and Rantau Abang. To move on from Marang, you can either flag down local buses (note that southbound services go no further than Dungun or Kemaman; see p.311) or arrange pick-up by an express bus; tickets for Transnasional services should be available at the **petrol station** to the south of the Marang River (T 09/618 2606). Amid the shops on the main road is a bank with an **ATM**.

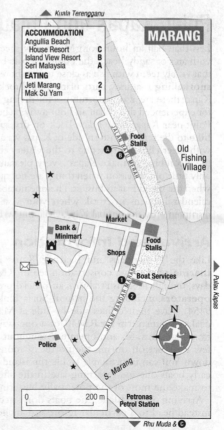

Kuala Terengganu

MARANG

ACCOMMODATION
Angullia Beach
  House Resort   C
Island View Resort   B
Seri Malaysia   A
EATING
Jeti Marang   2
Mak Su Yam   1

Old Fishing Village

Food Stalls

JALAN PHAH MERAH

Market

Bank & Minimart

Food Stalls

Shops

Boat Services

JALAN BANDAR MARANG

N

Police

S. Marang

0   200 m

Petronas Petrol Station

Pulau Kapas

Rhu Muda & C

You're unlikely to get stuck in Marang, but there's decent **accommodation** here should you need it; most of the places to stay are on or around the hillock north of the jetty area, no more than ten minutes' walk from the jetty or the main road. Among the establishments are the *Island View Resort* (T09/618 2006; ❸), a sort of cross between beach chalets and a tiny motel, its rooms old-fangled but with attached bathroom and air-conditioning, and the mid-range *Seri Malaysia* (T09/618 2889, Wwww.serimalaysia.com.my; ❺), with a swimming pool and restaurant, though it's overpriced unless discounts happen to be available. On a nice stretch of beach at **Rhu Muda**, 2km to the south (at the 20km marker out of Kuala Terengganu), a homely if slightly frayed choice is the *Angullia Beach House Resort* (T&F09/618 1322, Wwww.angulliaresort.com; ❸), with a vast range of en-suite chalets, a restaurant, well-tended grounds and good views of Kapas. They organize fun trips up the Marang River (RM40 per person), on which you get to see monkeys and lizards, and glimpse village activities like the making of *atap* thatch and palm sugar.

As for **food**, there are plenty of stalls around town, plus a large, reasonable seafood restaurant, the *Jeti Marang* (open irregularly from late afternoon), opposite which there's *Mak Su Yam*, a simple place with inexpensive rice and noodle dishes.

Pulau Kapas and Pulau Gemia

Less than half an hour from Marang by speedboat is diminutive **Pulau Kapas**, with arcs of sandy beach the colour of pale brown sugar, and aquamarine waters that visibly teem with fish as close to the shore as at the island's sole jetty. Naturally, **snorkelling** is a draw, particularly round rocky **Pulau Gemia**, just northwest of Kapas; there are also opportunities for **diving**, with a Japanese wreck dive suitable for experienced divers half an hour away by boat, and black reeftip sharks at Shark Point near *Kapas Turtle Valley*. Back on dry land, it's possible to take a 45-minute **hike** to the remote eastern side of Kapas via a track that leads back from the jetty, with sheer cliffs plummeting to the water's edge making for a dramatic walk. All these combine to make Kapas a very pleasant island to retreat to for a spell; the only time of the season when things are not quite so idyllic is from June to August, when the island is at its busiest. The one notable highlight in the island's slim social calendar happens in April, when your visit might be enlivened – or slightly disrupted – by the annual Kapas–Marang **swimathon**.

Arrival and information

Like the Perhentians and Redang, Kapas is one of Terengganu's designated **marine parks**, so a conservation fee of RM5 applies for a stay of up to three days, though there isn't always an official present to collect it. The Kapas **boat operators**, including the helpful Suria Link (T&F09/618 3754 or 019 983 9454), have their offices side-by-side at Marang's jetty, and all offer the same deal of a return trip for RM40, or a one-way trip for RM20. Boats usually run from 9am onwards and operate throughout the day, leaving when full, though few boats set off during the northeast monsoon when the island nearly shuts down. You can in principle tackle the island as a **day-trip**, catching one of the early boats out and returning late in the afternoon, but this does entail having to make the most of the potentially blistering heat of midday.

Arriving on the island, the boats don't necessarily use the sole jetty and may instead head to a particular resort and anchor in the shallows metres from the beach, to which you'll have to wade. Given the small size of the island, you don't need to worry about exactly where the boats arrive, unless you've tons of luggage.

Most places to stay on Kapas can arrange **snorkelling** – either just rental of gear (from RM10), or with a boat trip out to a choice site (from RM30). There's one **dive shop** on the island, namely Aqua-Sport (☎019/983 5879, ⓦwww.divekapas .com), offering PADI Open Water and Discover Scuba courses (RM980 and RM200 respectively), as well as regular dives (RM110 for one, with slightly cheaper rates for multiple dives). They also have **kayaks** available for an invigorating but none too strenuous paddle around the coves (RM15 per hr).

Accommodation and eating

For such a tiny island, Kapas has a surprising range of **accommodation** options, including a basic **campsite**, *Harmony* (☎&ⓕ09/618 6179; RM10 per person per night, RM15 for tent rental), though it's used mainly by locals and can be noisy. All the places to stay are on the western shore, facing the mainland.

Some mid-range places levy **surcharges** of twenty percent or more at weekends and during public and school holidays; rates indicated here are for weekdays. All the resorts have their own **restaurants**, of varying degrees of sophistication.

PULAU KAPAS

Pulau Gemia

Snorkelling

Pulau Kapas

Snorkelling

Solar Power Plant

Kapas View Point

Aqua-Sport Dive Shop

N

0   400 m

ACCOMMODATION
Duta Puri Island Resort	H
Gem Island Resort and Spa	A
Harmony Campsite	B
Kapas Beach Chalet	F
Kapas Coral Beach	D
Kapas Island Resort	G
Kapas Turtle Valley	J
Mak Cik Gemuk Beach Resort	E
Qimi Chalet	C
Rumah Panjang Captain	I

Duta Puri Island Resort ☎09/624 6090, ⓦwww .dutaresorts.com. A large complex with a range of en-suite rooms and chalets connected by board-walks. They're showing their age a bit and are simply furnished, but most have a/c and are quite pleasant, as is the pavilion restaurant. Weekend and holiday surcharges of RM20. **⑤**

Kapas Beach Chalet ☎017/936 0750. Malay/ Dutch-run establishment with nine decent A-frame chalets, plus more basic rooms in a long bungalow; all are en suite. Popular – actually a little too busy during peak periods. The food can be a little overpriced. Rooms **②**, chalets **③**.

Kapas Coral Beach ☎09/618 1976. A handful of chalets, spacious enough though nothing fancy. Recent renovations may make the asking prices seem more sensible. **③**

Kapas Island Resort ☎09/631 6468, ⓦwww .kapasislandresort.com. Neat Malay-style a/c

bungalows, all en suite, are set in a large garden. Western and Malay food is served in an airy restaurant, diving and snorkelling can be arranged, and kayaks and fishing gear are available to rent. The place also boasts its own swimming pool. Rates include breakfast, and rise by RM30 at weekends and holidays. **④**

Kapas Turtle Valley ☎013/354 3650, ⓦwww.kapasturtlevalley.com. Marvellous, low-key affair on its own secluded cove, with half a dozen chalets featuring four-poster beds and swish bathrooms, though no a/c. The Dutch couple who run the place also have larger family chalets, and serve up fare ranging from Malaysian to Mediterranean. Boat transfers can be arranged through Surla Link to save you the steep walk over the wooded headland from the western shore. Rate includes breakfast. **⑤**

Mak Cik Gemuk Beach Resort ☎09/624 5120. A cluster of en-suite chalets painted a vibrant

309

orange, with the option of a/c in some. There are also much cheaper rooms in a long, low block, with tolerable toilets and showers in a separate building. Institutional, but popular with locals in particular. Rooms ②, chalets ④.

🏃 **Qimi Chalet** ℡019/648 1714, ⓦwww .qimichaletkapas.com. Comfortable chalets with sea-facing balcony and open-air bathroom. Top of the line – and costing three times as much to stay in – is the Kemboja unit, on a par with a decent KL apartment, boasting a/c, a proper bath in the bathroom and good views from its perch up a slope. There's also a beachfront restaurant housed in a simple pavilion. It's possible to arrange to stay during the northeast monsoon, when you may have the island virtually to yourself. ④

Rumah Panjang Captain ℡012/377 0214 or 017 988 9046. Sometimes known by its old name,

Lighthouse, this is a rustic elevated longhouse of dark timber, with rooms and a large dorm with rugs and a row of ten regular beds. The lounge at the front is comfy, with bamboo furniture and nice cushions. All facilities are shared. Not the most sophisticated of places, but the chilled-out atmosphere compensates, as does the cool beach-hut bar festooned with vinyl records. Dorm beds RM25, rooms ③.

Pula Gemia

Gem Island Resort and Spa ℡09/612 5110, ⓦwww.gem-travel.com.my/gemisland. A well-designed place with all the chalets built on stilts at the water's edge. It offers a variety of packages, such as three-day, two-night deals for RM700 per person, including meals and transfers.

Southern Terengganu

The stretch of Terengganu between Marang and the Pahang border offers fairly slim pickings for travellers. Pleasant **beaches** are the main draw, any of which make for a great way to break a drive along the coast road, though facilities at most amount to a mere straggle of food stalls. One stretch of beach with accommodation lies some 40km south of Marang at the village of **Rantau Abang**, where a Turtle Information Centre serves as a somewhat forlorn reminder of the importance of Malaysia's east coast as a nesting site for many of the world's threatened marine turtles. The only other place of note is the very upmarket resort at Tanjung Jara.

Rantau Abang

No more than a handful of guesthouses strung out along a couple of kilometres of dusty road, **RANTAU ABANG** used to reap a rich reward from its status as one of a handful of places in the world where the giant **leatherback turtle** comes to lay its eggs. The village retains a small **Turtle Information Centre** (hours variable but open at least Sun–Thurs 8am–4pm; free), with informative displays on turtle biology and conservation, but with the collapse in leatherback turtle populations in the Pacific Ocean at least, Rantau Abang has drifted into relative obscurity. It's still a pleasant way station though, offering a beach with fine sand and, being on a straight stretch of coast, superb 180-degree views of blue-green sea. If you want to spot turtles, your best bets are elsewhere along the east coast; see the box on pp.316–317 for more on marine turtles and their conservation.

Practicalities

Local **buses** from Kuala Terengganu and Marang run at least hourly during daylight hours to Rantau Abang. Coming by local bus from the south, you have to change at Dungun, 13km away (see opposite), from where you can easily get another local bus for the remainder of the journey. Buses can drop you on the main road close to the Petronas petrol station, just a short walk from the Turtle Information Centre and the **accommodation**, all close to the beach. Prices rise a little when the turtles might theoretically arrive to nest (May–Sept), though they're not high to begin with; the price codes in this section refer to the high-season rate. Close to the information centre are two well-kept places: the friendly, long-established *Awang's* (☎09/844 3500; ❸), with a variety of simple en-suite rooms, some overpriced air-conditioned chalets and an amazing caged myna chirruping incessantly in Malay; and *Turtles De' Village Inn* (☎09/845 6001, ℱ848 3210; ❸), where all the rooms are spacious affairs with two beds, air-conditioning, a bathroom and a small veranda. Around a kilometre south of the information centre, *Dahimah's Guesthouse* (☎09/845 2843, ℰdahimahs@hotmail.com; ❷) is slightly back from the beach and has a wide range of accommodation, from simple doubles with fan to family rooms with TV, air-conditioning and a proper bath (RM120).

Awang's has a simple **restaurant**, but by far the best eating in the area is at the venerable *C.B. Wee*, close to the *Tanjong Jara Resort*; either guesthouse should be able to arrange a taxi there if requested.

Tanjung Jara

The contrast between the unprepossessing guesthouses of Rantau Abang and the super-luxurious **Tanjong Jara Resort** (☎09/845 1100 or 03/2783 1000, ⓦwww.tanjongjararesort.com; ❾) could not be greater. Four kilometres south of Rantau Abang and north of Dungun, this is one of the priciest resorts on the east coast, a Malay-themed spa complex of timber pavilions and houses fit for a sultan, where doubles start at over R1000 a night. The expected range of traditional treatments are on offer, there's a diving and water-sports centre on site (the reefs of the **Pulau Tenggul** marine park are only a short boat ride offshore), and when your system has been suitably reinvigorated by expert pampering or marine exertions, you can assuage your appetite at their *Nelayan* seafood restaurant, at which there's no menu – the chef cooks everything to order in consultation with guests. The resort also offers a range of activities and hikes, from waterfall treks led by their very own intrepid naturalist, Captain Mok, to demonstrations of traditional Malay pastimes.

On the west (northbound) side of the coast road, just south of the signed turning for the resort, a sense of normality is restored at the excellent *C.B. Wee* (daily 9am–3pm & 6–10pm; ☎09/844 3515), a halal Chinese restaurant that's a popular port of call for drivers, tour-group buses and even resort guests. Seafood, including great butter prawns, is the natural thing to go for, but they also do a limited range of Western fare, including steak and chips, and whatever you order, it'll be freshly prepared and worth the wait.

Dungun to the Pahang border

The backwater town of **Dungun**, a little further south of Tanjung Jara, is predominantly Chinese, with a handful of shophouses and a night market each Thursday; there's no reason to spend much time here, though. The **local bus station** (for services to Rantau Abang or south to Kemaman/Chukai) is on the west side of the padang; if you're arriving by local bus and need to change for a long-distance service, ask the driver for "Kaunter Transnasional", and you should be let off the bus at the start of the access road for Dungun, where there's an office selling tickets for Transnasional and several other long-distance operators.

South of Dungun, the highway swerves suddenly inland, bypassing a small promontory, before rejoining the coast at **Paka**, where a veritable forest of gleaming metal towers and piping marks the nucleus of Terengganu's petrochemicals industry. Just to the south is the town of **KERTEH**, one of whose quiet beaches is home to the **Ma'Daerah Turtle Sanctuary** (May–Aug; Ⓦmadaerah.org). Here you can get hands-on experience of turtle conservation by taking part in the three-day Weekend with Turtles volunteer programme, on which you might be involved in anything from patrolling the beach to moving eggs into the hatchery. The fee (RM250; it's best to sign up a month in advance) covers dorm accommodation at the sanctuary, a rustic-looking collection of timber buildings, on Friday and Saturday night, and meals; staff will collect you from the main road in Kerteh, which is served by express buses plying the Kuantan–Kuala Terengganu route.

Another 20km to the south is **KEMASIK**, a fishing village with a decent stretch of beach sliced in two by a small creek. A couple of steep rocky outcrops, standing sentinel at the front of the beach, offer a good panorama if you make the climb, though you may find that picking your way back down is a lot trickier than clambering up.

Kemaman/Chukai

More or less midway between Dungun and Kuantan, the southernmost settlement of significance in Terengganu is the nondescript fusion of **Kemaman** and neighbouring **Chukai**, no longer distinguishable as separate towns; you'll probably need to change buses here if you're using local services in either direction. This is also where you'll find the closest **banks** to Cherating – Maybank, best for foreign exchange, is five minutes' walk from the bus station in the direction of the river – and one of the best **cafés** on the east coast, in the shape of 🎋 *Hai Peng*, 3753 Jalan Sulaimani (daily except Fri 6.30am–6.30pm; ☏09/859 7810). Determinedly kept going by Elaine, whose father started the business in 1940, this Hainanese coffee shop roasts its own delicious coffee, using Indonesian beans. Besides fantastic ice-blended coffees, they do various lattes and a good range of snacks – peanut-butter-and-banana sandwiches, *kuih*, great *roti kahwin* (buttered toast spread with *kaya*), curry puffs and so forth. It's a popular hangout for locals of all creeds, who come here to chat around the old-fashioned marble-topped tables, beneath walls plastered with vintage film posters and photographs. The only snag is finding the place – Jalan Sulaimani runs roughly parallel to Sungai Kemaman, with Maybank at the southeastern end, and *Hai Peng* is in a unremarkable four-storey building around ten minutes' walk away to the northwest, close to the traffic lights.

Cherating

At first it can be hard to discern the appeal of **CHERATING**, a laid-back village of sorts, dominated by a strip of tourist accommodation, 45km north of Kuantan. Many of the locals have long since moved out, to a new settlement a little way to the south, and the beach, hugging the northern end of a windswept bay, is pleasant but pebbly in places. Nevertheless, at its best, Cherating is an outstanding little travellers' community, chilled out yet warm-spirited, a place to share quality time with old companions and, chances are, to end up with a whole bunch of new acquaintances too.

Arrival and information

Any express **bus** plying the coast road between Kuala Terengganu and Kuantan will drop you off at Cherating (RM15 from Kuala Terengganu), either in **Cherating Lama** (the old village, where the backpacker accommodation is located) or in the new settlement at **Cherating Baru**. If you're starting out in Kuantan, it makes more sense to use one of the red-and-white Sihat or brown-and-white Mira local buses terminating at Kemaman, since discounts aren't given for short hops on the express services; to be let off in Cherating Lama (RM3.50; 1hr 30min), press the buzzer when you see the 168-kilometre marker on the left. Chartering a **taxi** here from Kuantan is worth considering, at RM70. If you're driving here from KL, simply follow the East Coast Highway all the way to Pelabuhan Kuantan, the port 25km north of Kuantan, where you pick up the coast road.

Tourism Malaysia operates a **tourist office** (Mon–Fri 9am–5pm; no phone) at the eastern end of the road into Cherating Lama. On the main drag itself are a few agencies for bus-ticket bookings and other travel arrangements, such as

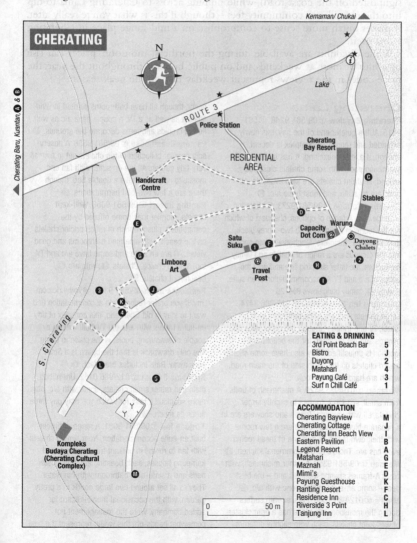

CHERATING

EATING & DRINKING	
3rd Point Beach Bar	5
Bistro	J
Duyong	2
Matahari	4
Payung Café	3
Surf n Chill Café	1

ACCOMMODATION	
Cherating Bayview	M
Cherating Cottage	J
Cherating Inn Beach View	I
Eastern Pavilion	B
Legend Resort	A
Matahari	G
Maznah	E
Mimi's	D
Payung Guesthouse	K
Ranting Resort	F
Residence Inn	C
Riverside 3 Point	H
Tanjung Inn	L

transfers to Taman Negara or islands off the east coast. Among these are Travelpost and Capacity Dot Com, both of which also sell tickets for Cherating River trips (RM25 per person) and have **internet access** and **bike rental** (RM5 per hr); additionally, Capacity Dot Com runs a useful little **library** and book exchange. With no banks or ATMs in Cherating, if you run short of ringgit, you'll have to change **cash** (rates won't be great) with either of these agencies, or make the short trip north to Kemaman/Chukai (see p.312) to use the banks there.

Accommodation

With your own transport, you could consider staying in Cherating Baru, which boasts several modern, family-oriented resort developments (all signposted off the coast road), while nipping across to Cherating Lama to dip into the old village's community feel – though if this is what you're really after, it makes much more sense to compromise on a mid-range place in Cherating Lama itself.

While discounts are available during the northeast monsoon, prices can rise by a fifth or more at weekends and on public holidays throughout the year; the price codes in the reviews represent weekday rates in the peak season.

Cherating Lama

Cherating Bayview ☏ 09/581 9248, ℻ 581 9415. At the quieter end of the bay, this newly extended and renovated complex is decent enough, if a little unexciting. It has its own swimming pool, with some chalets clustered around; seafront chalets are also available. All units are en suite, and most have a/c. ❺

Cherating Cottage ☏ 09/581 9273, ⓦ cherating -cottage.com. A range of options, cheapest of which are the rooms in a slightly drab two-storey block, their so-called "travellers' longhouse". Also packed into the grounds are a range of chalets and family bungalows, the latter sleeping five and with the bonus of a/c and TV. All accommodation is en suite. Rooms ❸, family bungalows RM120.

Cherating Inn Beach View ☏ 019/986 3474. Large chalets with a/c, slick bathroom with hot water, TV and fridge – though the decor wins no awards and the premium for the beachfront location is unjustified. They also have some slightly frayed chalets on the north side of the main road, which are hardly worth a look. ❻

Matahari ☏ 019/935 9420. A mishmash of units, from small, spartan A-frames to slightly larger chalets, all with veranda. Toilets and showers are in a separate block, though there are a few rooms with their own facilities, and one of these rooms even has a/c. There's also a communal kitchen. ❶

Maznah ☏ 09/581 9359. Another mishmash, with basic A-frames sharing facilities and – the best deal – some en-suite chalets, one with a/c. ❷

Mimi's ☏ 012/985 1669. Popular with surfers during the monsoon, this place has a tight cluster of well-kept chalets, each with slightly different decor, though all have bathrooms painted in vivid shades as well as a TV; a couple have a/c as well. Potted orchids and ferns decorate the grounds. ❸

Payung Guesthouse ☏ 09/581 9658. A deserv- edly popular collection of ten chalets set in a small, very tidy garden. All are en suite, with fan and mosquito net; most have a double bed, though there are a few two-bed permutations. ❷

Ranting Resort ☏ 09/581 9068. Well-kept chalets, roomier than some offered by the competition, plus a bunch of much pricier chalets on the beach, with nice tiled bathrooms and good views. All are en suite and some have a/c and TV too. A good choice. Chalets ❸, with a/c ❹, beachfront chalets ❺.

Residence Inn ☏ 09/581 9333, ⓦ www.ric.com .my. If you prefer resort-style accommodation and want to stay in old Cherating, this complex of tidy en-suite rooms with a/c and TV, built around a couple of swimming pools, is the place to come. The only drawback is that the beach is a 5min walk away. Rate includes breakfast. ❻

Riverside 3 Point ☏ 012/986 0162. Unexciting, plain and rather small chalets, some with a/c, plus more spacious affairs for which you may pay three times as much. ❷

Tanjung Inn ☏ 09/581 9081. A range of timber- built en-suite accommodation, from simple chalets with fan to rooms in brilliant traditionally styled kampung houses, each boasting a/c, four-poster beds and a slate-tiled bathroom with hot water. They're all set around two large ponds in a pretty garden, with the occasional monitor lizard for added company. Were the management not somewhat hands-off, this would represent the best value in Cherating. Fan chalets ❸, a/c rooms ❺, four-bed family units RM150.

Cherating Baru

Eastern Pavilion ☎09/581 9500, reservations ☎03/2162 2922, ⊛www.holidayvillacherating .com. Each of the twelve "villas" here is actually a luxurious elaboration of the kampung house, supposedly deriving from every state of the Federation. They all come with one or two beautifully appointed bedrooms, a lounge and a small outdoor pool and jacuzzi, discreetly screened from prying eyes – a great place to pamper yourself. By comparison, the neighbouring *Holiday Villa*, sharing the same management, is pretty mundane. Rates (from RM700) include breakfast. ❾

Legend Resort ☎09/581 9818, ⊛www .legendsgroup.com. A series of interlinked pools with a central waterfall feature lies at the heart of this sprawling, popular development, which also adjoins a stretch of (public) beach. The expansive central lounge and lobby area has a small stage where karaoke and a house band provide the evening entertainment; otherwise, pool tables and squash courts should help keep you occupied. The rooms themselves are modern and unremarkable. ❼

Activities

Part of the attraction here is the range of **activities** away from the beach, all of which are conducive both to unwinding and to socializing. In the village itself, it's possible to take a **batik** class at which you learn how to slap your own designs onto fabric or T-shirts, perhaps mixing the dyes yourself to achieve the hues you want. Classes (RM25–35) are conducted at Limbong Art on the main road. There's also a **handicrafts centre** showcasing the art of *mengkuang* (pandanus) weaving, while at the **Kompleks Budaya** you can take in a Malay cultural show (schedule available at the tourist office), featuring dancing, traditional hobbies such as top-spinning and, for a bit of a diversion, trained monkeys retrieving coconuts from the tops of the palms.

For a back-to-nature experience, some guesthouses and chalets offer Sungai Cherating **boat trips**, on which you have a chance to spot long-tailed macaques (admittedly, hard to miss in the village itself), black-and-white hornbills, plus otters, tree snakes and, just possibly, the odd crocodile. Nighttime trips are also available, with fireflies the main attraction. A couple of kilometres from the village, around the rocky headland at the eastern end of the bay, and close to the exclusive *Club Med* development at Chendor beach, Cherating has its own **turtle sanctuary** (daily 9am–6pm & 9pm–5am; ☎09/581 9078), where hatchlings are released into the sea nightly at 10.30pm, and where you can see green turtles come ashore during the egg-laying season.

The beach

Of course a trip here wouldn't be complete without some time spent on the **beach**. While the sands range from off-white to a weird orange, at least the shelter of the bay here ensures calm waters, suitable for children. If you want a swim, it's best to avoid low tide, when the sea recedes 100m or more, requiring you to plod over soft, wet sand to reach it, still further to get deep enough to swim. The headland obliterates any sunrise views, but in good weather it's still worth taking a dawn stroll on the beach, when the headland looms darkly against a glowing eastern sky, and the only activity to disturb the stillness is a few fishing boats. For something rather more stimulating, try some **horse-riding** at Penn stables (✉pennendu@streamyx.com) near the *Duyong* restaurant; they do beginner's lessons (RM10) or half-hour canters on the beach (RM50). During the northeast monsoon **surfing** becomes a real attraction, with the best waves crashing in from December to February. Talk to the guys at the Satu Suku Surf School, on the main road (Nov–March daily 9am–9pm; ✉satusuku@gmail.com), who will advise on the best surfing in the area; they sell boards as well as rent them (RM70 per day) and do lessons

While four types of marine turtle lay their eggs on Malaysia's east coast, for years it was the sight of the largest of these, the giant **leatherbacks**, with their unusual black, rubbery skin, that was the star attraction, drawing visitors from far and wide to Rantau Abang in Terengganu. This has made the survival of the endangered leatherback turtle a particularly emotive cause for concern, but in fact all other kinds of marine turtle – **green** (Malaysian nesting sites include the Perhentians; Pulau Redang; Cherating; Ma'Daerah, see p.312; and the Turtle Islands National Park in Sabah, see p.534), **hawksbill** (Pulau Redang; Paka, south of Dungun; Penarik, north of Merang; Turtle Islands National Park; and Padang Kemunting near Melaka, see p.357), **Olive Ridley** (Paka and Penarik), and **Kemp's Ridley** and **loggerhead** (neither of which nest in Malaysia) – are also at risk. Harmful fishing methods, such as the use of **trawl nets**, are responsible for the deaths of thousands of marine turtles each year, which helps to explain the dramatic reduction in leatherbacks nesting on the Terengganu coast. In 1956, more than ten thousand were recorded; in 2000, just three; in 2002, there were no sightings of leatherbacks in Rantau Abang for the first time since records began; in 2005, leatherback, hawksbill and Olive Ridley's statistics in Terengganu were all at zero, and green turtle figures were significantly down. Even allowing for the fact that nesting turtle numbers vary cyclically, these statistics could hardly be more disheartening. On the rare occasions when leatherback eggs are turned up, they often fail to hatch, probably because of the increasing rarity of male–female turtle encounters.

With a survival rate of only fifty percent among hatchlings under ordinary conditions, any human pressure on turtle populations has drastic consequences for their survival. For Chinese in Malaysia and Singapore, turtle soup is a classic delicacy, and while Malays eschew turtle meat, they do consume **turtle eggs**, which are on sale at markets throughout the east coast. The eggs, which look not unlike ping-pong balls, are laid by the green turtle and their collection is licensed at certain sites, though there's no guarantee that what is sold was collected legally. There appears to be no political will to outlaw this traditional food, a sad irony given Malaysia's general turtle conservation efforts. At least the deliberate slaughter of turtles for their shells, once fashioned into bowls and earrings, primarily for the Japanese market, has been banned since 1992.

The leatherback life cycle

Among leatherback turtles, only the female – measuring 150cm in length and weighing 400kg on average – comes ashore. She heaves herself out of the water at night with her enormous front flippers until she reaches dry sand; she then uses her rear flippers to make digging movements, creating a narrow hole 50–80cm deep in which she deposits up to a hundred eggs. The turtle then covers the hole with her hind flippers while disguising the whole nest site by churning up more sand with the front ones.

Although a female never lays in consecutive seasons, she can nest three or four times within the same season at two-weekly intervals. The eggs incubate for around sixty days, after which the hatchlings, no more than a hand-span in length, crawl to the surface. The first few hours of a hatchling's life are particularly hazardous, for it can be picked off by crabs, birds and other predators before even reaching the sea. Usually emerging under cover of night, hatchlings instinctively seem to know in which direction the sea lies, even if it can't be seen from where they hatched, and propel

(RM100 for a single session or RM270 for three, including use of equipment). **Kayaks** can be rented from the *3rd Point Beach Bar* (RM30 per hr).

Eating and drinking

The old village boasts a string of inexpensive **restaurants**, all much of a muchness, emphasizing seafood – including the oddly named *lala*, a sort of clam, themselves rapidly towards the water. Years later, the mature females perform another baffling feat: swimming in waters as far away as South America, they somehow manage to find their way back to nest on the very Malaysian beach where they themselves hatched.

Turtle-spotting and conservation

Turtle-spotting was once something of a sport, with participants taking outrageous liberties such as riding the creatures for the sake of a photograph. Nowadays, humans are excluded from various designated **sanctuaries** for nesting turtles, including stretches of mainland beach, as well as locations on the Perhentian islands and Pulau Redang. At these sites the eggs are dug up immediately after the turtle has laid them and reburied in sealed-off **hatcheries** on the beach. Burying the eggs in sand of the correct temperature is crucial as warm sand produces more females, while cooler sand favours males. When the hatchlings emerge, they are released at the top of the beach and their scurry to the sea is supervised to ensure their safe progress.

Cherating on the east coast is one of few sites where the public is allowed to watch the nesting turtles under the supervision of rangers. Observers are asked to keep at least 5m away and refrain from making noise and using torches or camera flashes (unfortunately, not everyone obeys the rules). Elsewhere, it's possible to volunteer for turtle-conservation programmes at Ma'Daerah (see p.312) and at the Talang-Satang National Park near Kuching (see p.422).

▲ Turtles eggs on sale at an east-coast market

which turns up in a variety of sauces – but there are also a couple of places for decent Western food, and just about everywhere does a few Western snacks. The *kedai kopis* across from the *Payung Café* both serve reasonable Malay cuisine, as do the *kedai kopis* opposite *Matahari*, with *roti canai* in the morning and *nasi campur* later in the day. Several restaurants serve **alcohol**, which can lead to some gentle carousing well into the night, as does the *3rd Point Beach Bar*, which pumps out rave and reggae sounds into the evening. Make the most of Cherating if you're intending to continue into Terengganu and Kelantan; opportunities to sample relatively unformulaic Western fare and quaff beer are few and far between further north.

Bistro At the *Cherating Cottage*. A combination of Asian and Western fare, with decent pizzas the most notable offering.

Duyong An old faithful, this large, airy place overlooking the eastern end of the beach offers an excellent range of Chinese and Thai dishes, plus a few Western standbys such as fish and chips, and steak. Veggie dishes can be cooked to order. Beer – including that Thai favourite, Chang – and stout are served. Daily 10am till late.

Payung Café Despite red, gold and green lights on the approach path and other reggae-associated touches, it's Italian food that grabs the attention – pizzas (RM15) and pasta dishes (from RM7) and so

forth. The ambience is at its best after dark, when you can dine by candelight in the main pavilion or at the riverside tables under dimly lit coconut palms. Wi-fi available. Daily except Tues 9am till late.

Surf n Chill Café One of the nicest places to chill out in Cherating, spinning music as diverse as Manu Chao, the Rolling Stones and Jack Johnson, with red PVC sofas to relax on plus some tables out front under a thatched awning. The food is a mix of Western and Asian, with a particular emphasis on high-class burgers (starting at RM15), and mocktails are available, though no alcohol. There's a pool table, too. Daily except Tues 5pm till late (but open seven days a week in July & Aug).

Kuantan

KUANTAN is one of those Malaysian cities that offer little to capture the imagination. The state capital of **Pahang** since the 1955, the city is an undistinguished agglomeration of concrete buildings around an older core of shophouses close to Sungai Kuantan. While there's very little by way of historical or cultural interest in the city itself, Kuantan can be a breath of fresh air after a sojourn in Kelantan or Terengganu – it's closer in feel to the cities of the west coast than to Kuala Terengganu or Kota Bharu, and still offers better shopping and eating prospects than either of its counterparts further north. If you're arriving from elsewhere in the country, however, Kuantan can seem mundane. With the creation of the **East Coast Highway** to Pelabuhan Kuantan, the port 40km north of the city, it's straightforward to bypass Kuantan altogether if you're travelling between KL and the east coast.

If you do hang around in the city for a night or two, it's worth considering a day-trip to the nearby cave temple of **Gua Charas** (see p.323) or, just slightly further afield, the former mining town of **Sungai Lembing** (see p.324), which remains largely untouched by modern development. You might also want to head south to **Pekan** (see p.325), the former capital of the state, which retains a cultural heritage that Kuantan so obviously lacks.

Arrival and information

If Kuantan has a focus of sorts, it's the **padang**, between which and the river are the oldest streets in the city, where you'll also find quite a few of the hotels and restaurants. However, plenty of the city's amenities are scattered in all directions from the padang, including the **express bus station**, several blocks to the north close to Jalan Tun Ismail. The **bus station** amounts to little more than a car park on Jalan Besar, close to the river. **Taxis** can be found between Jalan Besar and Jalan Mahkota, whereas long-distance taxis arrive at the express bus station. A taxi to the centre from the Sultan Ahmad Shah **airport**, 15km west of town, costs RM30.

Tourism Malaysia has a **tourist office** at street level in the Mahkota Square business complex, south of the padang (Mon–Fri 9am–5pm; ☏09/517 7111).

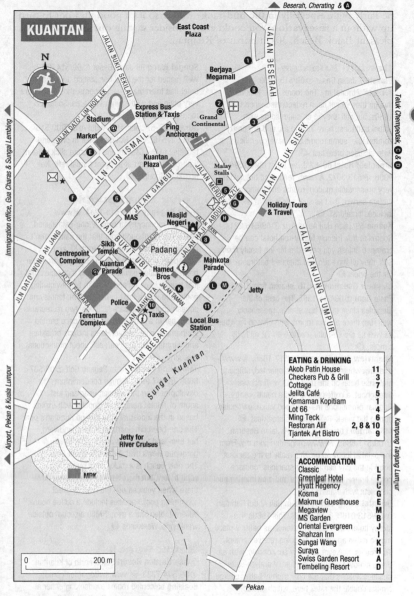

Beserah, Cherating & **A**

KUANTAN

N

East Coast Plaza

Berjaya Megamall

Express Bus Station & Taxis

Grand Continental

Ping Anchorage

Stadium

Market

Kuantan Plaza

Malay Stalls

MAS

Masjid Negeri

Holiday Tours & Travel

Sikh Temple

Centrepoint Complex

Kuantan @ Parade

Padang

Hamed Bros

Mahkota Parade

Jetty

Police

Terentum Complex

Local Bus Station

Taxis

Sungai Kuantan

Jetty for River Cruises

MPK

0   200 m

Pekan

JALAN BESERAH

Teluk Chempedak, C & D

THE EAST COAST | Kuantan

4

Immigration office, Gua Charas & Sungai Lembing

JALAN SUKIT SEKILAU

JALAN DATO' LIM HOE LEK

JLN TUN ISMAIL

JALAN GAMBUT

JALAN BUKIT UBI

JALAN DATO' WONG AH JANG

JALAN PETMAHA

JALAN TELUK SISEK

JALAN MERDEKA

JALAN ABDUL AZIZ

JALAN MASJID

JALAN HAJI

JALAN PARIT

JALAN TANJUNG LUMPUR

JALAN TAMAN

JALAN MAHKOTA

Airport, Pekan & Kuala Lumpur

Kampung Tanjung Lumpur

EATING & DRINKING

Akob Patin House	11
Checkers Pub & Grill	3
Cottage	7
Jelita Café	5
Kemaman Kopitiam	1
Lot 66	4
Ming Teck	6
Restoran Alif	2, 8 & 10
Tjantek Art Bistro	9

ACCOMMODATION

Classic	L
Greenleaf Hotel	F
Hyatt Regency	G
Kosma	U
Makmur Guesthouse	E
Megaview	M
MS Garden	B
Oriental Evergreen	J
Shahzan Inn	I
Sungai Wang	K
Suraya	H
Swiss Garden Resort	A
Tembeling Resort	D

Pahang Tourism, the state's tourism promotion body (℡09/516 1007, ⊛www .pahangtourism.com.my), runs a helpful tourist office of their own on Jalan Mahkota.

Accommodation

There's no shortage of places to stay in Kuantan, so much so that many establishments offer **discounts** off their published prices – yet occupancy rates can be fairly high, especially in the mid-range hotels, so it's a good idea not to turn up without a **reservation**. You could even consider staying **out of town** at the pleasant Balok Beach, 30km north of Kuantan.

Central Kuantan

Classic 7 Jalan Besar ℡ 09/516 4599, Ⓔ chotel@tm.net.my. The rooms here look as though they've not been redecorated since the 1980s, but still, they're en suite (some with actual bathtubs), have TV and a/c and are pretty comfortable; some rooms also have river views. Rate includes breakfast. ❹

Greenleaf Hotel 60–62 Jalan Bukit Ubi ℡ 09/515 9966, Ⓕ 513 3072. A newly renovated hotel with very presentable modern rooms and bathrooms, though service isn't as sharp as it could be. Rate includes breakfast. ❹

Kosma 59 Jalan Haji Abdul Aziz ℡ 09/516 2214. Rooms at this friendly Malay-run hotel can be cramped unless you pay extra for the family rooms. Still, they all have a/c and attached bathroom. OK for the price. ❸

Makmur Guesthouse B16, second floor, Jalan Pasar Baru ℡ 09/514 1363. The best of the cheapies close to the bus station, reasonably well run; there are fan rooms with shared facilities as well as a/c en-suite rooms with TV, all fairly simple. ❷

Megaview Jalan Besar ℡ 09/517 1888, Ⓦ www .megaviewhotel.com. Business-oriented, efficient high-rise hotel on the river, with wi-fi access throughout, a coffee house and a health centre. Regular promotions make it good value, particularly during the week. Rate includes breakfast. ❺

MS Garden Lorong Gambut, off Jalan Beserah ℡ 09/511 8888, Ⓦ www.msgarden.com.my. From the palatial lobby on up, this really is the slickest hotel in the city centre, with spacious rooms, a coffee house, a fitness centre and a swimming pool complete with waterfall. ❼

Oriental Evergreen 157 Jalan Haji Abdul Rahman ℡ 09/513 0168, Ⓕ 513 0368. This 1980s five-storey hotel has a shabby exterior, as befits a place marooned in an area undergoing redevelopment. The rooms, however, are very serviceable, with a/c that's almost too effective, plus TV and en-suite facilities. Places that are only slightly better charge almost double the rates here, which exclude breakfast. ❷

Shahzan Inn Jalan Bukit Ubi ℡ 09/513 6688. A mundane tower block of a hotel, but with comfortable en-suite rooms, some with great views of the State Mosque across the padang, and its own swimming pool. Rate includes breakfast. ❺

Sungai Wang 96 Jalan Besar ℡ 09/514 8912. Well placed for the local bus station, this cheap hotel has tolerable en-suite rooms, though they are very plain and a little worn in places. Some a/c rooms available too. ❷

Suraya 55–57 Jalan Haji Abdul Aziz ℡ 09/516 4266, Ⓕ 516 2028. Not dissimilar in price and facilities to the *Classic*, and featuring slick modern bathrooms as part of a recent partial refit. No breakfast though. ❹

Teluk Chempedak

Hyatt Regency ℡ 09/518 1234, Ⓦ www .kuantan.regency.hyatt.com. A long-established beach retreat (though note that the sands aren't private) for well-heeled folks from KL and Singapore, and deservedly so. Emerging from the breezy reception pavilion, you find a complex that just seems to go on and on, with two swimming pools (one with a built-in bar), a gym, tennis and squash courts, childcare facilities, two restaurants and a bar in a converted ship that once carried Vietnamese boat people. Rates include breakfast and vary through the year; ask about promotional discounts. ❾

Tembeling Resort Jalan Padang Golf ℡ 09/567 6688, Ⓕ 567 9988. A huge condominium development on the wooded headland just south of Teluk Chempedak, popular with expats based in the industrial area around Kuantan's port. The one-bedroom apartments face landward, but two- and three-bed apartments have gorgeous views over the South China Sea. The only beach is a rocky bit of public sand below, but there's no point tramping down there when you can use the resort's great swimming pool. Facilities include a coffee house, billiard tables and a gym. RM30 discount outside weekends. Weekends ❻.

Balok Beach

Swiss Garden Resort 30km north of Kuantan ℡ 09/544 7333, Ⓦ www.swissgarden.com. Boasting balconied rooms overlooking either a landscaped garden or the South China Sea, plus a freeform swimming pool and a spa with a range of herbal and other massages and treatments. Balok beach can be reached by taxi (around RM30) or on a Cherating-bound bus from the local bus station (45min). ❽

The City

The old commercial part of Kuantan is relatively small, squeezed between the padang and the river. On the northeastern edge of the padang is the town's one real sight, the **Masjid Negeri**, built in 1991, with a pastel exterior – green for Islam, blue for peace and white for purity. It's distinctly Turkish in appearance, thanks to the pencil minarets at all four corners of the sturdy square prayer hall, topped with a looming central dome; non-Muslims can visit in the morning by permission of the caretaker. At night, the sound of prayer calls and sermons don't exactly contribute to the serenity of the padang, while the mosque itself – subtly lit – takes on a whole new complexion, as the minarets, tipped with red points of light, look for all the world like rockets primed for launch.

Down by the river, starting at the *Megaview Hotel*, a smart promenade feels slightly out of place clinging to the banks of Sungai Kuantan. Early evening is a good time to take a stroll here, to see fishing boats returning with the day's catch and perhaps the occasional red eagle swooping on its prey. The walkway continues south to a jetty from where the **Kuantan River Cruise** departs (daily except Fri 10am & 2pm, Fri 10am & 3pm, Sat & Sun also 8pm; 1hr–1hr 30min; RM10); it heads downstream alongside the town and under the Tanjung Lumpur bridge, before turning around and navigating back upstream past the fishing villages of Tanjung Lumpur and Peramu. The highlight (omitted on the evening outings) is a stop at Taman Bakau, a **mangrove forest reserve** where a 250-metre raised wooden walkway has been built for easy viewing. Commentary during the trip is a recorded retelling, in Malay, of the history of Kuantan, though you may be able to get some information in English if a tour guide is present. Tickets for the cruise are available at the MPK (town council) office near the jetty.

Teluk Chempedak

East of the centre, Jalan Besar becomes Jalan Teluk Sisek, which swings east, parallel to the coastline, and transforms into Jalan Teluk Chempedak. This terminates 5km from the centre, around the corner from a wooded headland, at an east-facing stretch of coast where **Teluk Chempedak** has long been a popular evening and weekend hangout for Kuantan families and young people alike. The sands of the bay are encouragingly white, and though undertows can render the sea off-limits for swimming (in which event, watch out for hoisted red flags), there is an appealing liveliness about the place, quite at variance from the langourous mood on the otherwise even better sands of rural Terengganu.

Moving on from Kuantan

It's straightforward to head up and down the east coast from Kuantan; there are regular express **buses** up to Kota Bharu via Kuala Terengganu, and down to Singapore via Mersing and Johor Bahru. There are also frequent buses to KL and a few services daily to west-coast destinations. For Jerantut, the closest large town to the main Taman Negara entrance at Kuala Tahan, you can elect for either an express bus or a service operated by Bee Huat (look for the black-and-white vehicles with the company name in red) from the local bus station (3–4 daily; RM12).

KL **flights** are operated by MAS, at the airport (☏09/538 5194) and AirAsia (no local office), while Penang flights are with Firefly, at the airport (no phone). Flight information is available on ☏09/531 2100.

The bus service here had been suspended at the time of writing, though it's worth asking the tourist office what the latest situation is. A taxi to the beach will cost around RM15; other than late at night, it's usually not hard to find a taxi back to town from the main road.

Among the stalls at the end of the main road is the open-air *Pattaya* **restaurant**, both doing good seafood for around RM12 a head. There are also upmarket restaurants at the *Hyatt*, one Italian, the other offering both local and Western fare. **Nightlife** revolves around a handful of bars interspersed between the souvenir and batik shops on the main road just before the beach; if you like karaoke bars, *Lips TC* is the place to head.

Eating and drinking

Kuantan's eating scene isn't bad for a provincial city, though it is vaguely schizophrenic: laid-back **kedai kopis** dot the streets west and south of the padang, while the area around Berjaya Megamall is packed with brash cafés and *mamak* joints, many open extended hours and some even offering free wi-fi. For inexpensive Malay food, try the places on and around the northern end of Jalan Haji Abdul Aziz or the stalls off Jalan Merdeka; a little way further east is a collection of Chinese stalls called Lot 66. At the other end of the scale, the better hotels have decent restaurants, with the *Swan* Chinese restaurant at the *Grand Continental* hotel, on Jalan Merdeka, as good a place for a blowout as any. Both the Berjaya Megamall and Kuantan Parade have reliable **food courts**.

The closest thing to a decent **bar** in Kuantan is the *Checkers Pub & Grill* just off Jalan Beserah (Mon–Sat 5pm till late); Saturday evenings are your best bet, when they show live European soccer matches on TV.

Akob Patin House By the river near the local bus station. Come to this humble place under a tented canopy for a Malay culinary experience, the signature dish being *patin* – the silver catfish, from the rivers of southern Pahang. It's part of the *nasi campur* spread at lunchtime, when it's cooked *asam pedas tempoyak* – with chilli, tamarind and fermented durian, actually not as strong as you might think; other unusual lunch fare include *pucuk ubi* (young tapioca greens) and *jantung pisang* (banana flowers). Breakfast features the likes of *lontong* and *mee rebung* (noodles with bamboo shoots), but they only do snacks and a few dishes in the evening. Mon–Sat 9am till late.

Cottage 63 Jalan Haji Abdul Aziz ☏ 09/552 4069. A touch smarter and more adventurous than most Chinese restaurants in Kuantan, serving fish-head curry (RM16), the odd steak and even (not on the menu) *petai bee hoon*, rice vermicelli fried with *sambal* and *petai* beans. Mains are around RM10; Carlsberg, Tiger and Anchor beers served. Daily 11am–2.30pm & 5pm till late (from 6pm on Sun).

Jelita Café Jalan Haji Abdul Aziz. Essentially a posh-looking metal hangar, this houses several food outlets, the star attraction among which is a branch of *Satay Zul*, Kuantan's best-loved satay house, offering beef, chicken and even *perut* (stomach) at around 60 sen a stick. Elsewhere are stalls offering rice and noodles, basic Western fare and dubious doner kebabs.

Kemaman Kopitiam Lorong Tun Ismail, off Jalan Tun Ismail. A breakaway from the long-established *Hai Peng* in Chukai (see p.312), and offering a very similar range of hot and cold coffees and shakes, light bites, pastries and decor that's meant to recall Chinese cafés of yesteryear. Nowhere near as proficient as the original, but a cut above the many imitators you'll see in the vicinity. Wi-fi available. Daily 7am till late.

Ming Teck On an unnamed lane between Jalan Tun Ismail and Jalan Gambut, this Chinese veggie *kedai kopi* puts a mock-meat spin on local street food – hence serving up meatless and fishless *nasi lemak*, fishball noodles (in soup or fried), *bee hoon* (vermicelli) and so forth. There's a good range of *pow* too. Daily 7.30am–6.30pm, though hours may be reduced at weekends.

Restoran Alif 91 Jalan Mahkota. Reliable a/c *mamak* establishment with a wide range of roti and *thosai* for breakfast and lunch, plus banana-leaf meals at lunch and in the evening, all complemented by noodle dishes, *rojak* and *murtabak*. Branches near the Berjaya Megamall (24hr) and on Jalan Bank. Daily 7.30am till late.

🏃 **Tjantek Art Bistro** 46 Jalan Besar ☏ 09/516 4144. With designer lighting and artwork plastering the walls, this is certainly the most interesting place to eat in downtown Kuantan. The pasta dishes, properly al dente (from RM12), are probably the best thing on the menu, though they also do sandwiches, soups and salads, plus desserts such as mango pudding and chocolate cake. There's no a/c; if you find the noise from Jalan Besar annoying, ask for a table deep inside the building, where one of the spaces includes a mock jungle area. Mon–Sat 6pm till late.

Listings

Banks Standard Chartered Bank and Maybank are situated around the intersection of the aptly named Jalan Bank and Jalan Besar; other banks are to be found on Jalan Mahkota and Jalan Tun Ismail.

Bookshops Hamed Bros on Jalan Haji Abdul Aziz, midway along the padang, has a limited range of English-language books, plus various maps of Malaysia. The Parkson Ria Mall on Jalan Tun Ismail has a branch of Popular Bookstore, while tucked away on level 1 of the Berjaya Megamall is the MBS Bookstore.

Car rental Avis (℡09/539 8768) and Mayflower (℡09/538 4490) are both at the airport; Orix is at the *Grand Continental hotel* (℡09/515 7488), Jalan Gambut.

Cinemas Golden Screen Cinemas Multiplex (℡09/508 8188) on the top floor of Berjaya Megamall shows some English-language films, as does the Lotus Five-Star cinema in the Terentum Complex (09/515 6881).

Hospital The Hospital Tengku Ampufan Afzan is at the western end of Jalan Besar (℡09/513 3333); next to the Berjaya Megamall is the private Kuantan Medical Centre (℡09/514 2828, ⓦwww .kmcsb.com.my).

Internet access Try CD Access on the top floor of the Kuantan Parade mall, or the street-level internet café in the Centrepoint Complex opposite.

Post The GPO, with poste restante, is on Jalan Haji Abdul Aziz.

Shopping Both the Berjaya Megamall on Jalan Tun Ismail, close to the intersection with Jalan Beserah, and Kuantan Parade, Jalan Penjara, have supermarkets, pharmacies and a range of other outlets. On Sat evenings there's a *pasar malam* in Jalan Gambut, close to the junction with Jalan Bukit Ubi.

Travel agents Ping Anchorage, the Kuala Terengganu-based travel agent, sells its extensive range of east-coast packages from its branch on Jalan Tun Ismail (℡09/514 2020, ⓦwww .pinganchorage.com.my). There's also Holiday Tours and Travel in the Wisma Pan Global, Jalan Teluk Sisek (℡09/516 4051, ⓦwww.holidaytours .com.my), which may be able to arrange for day-trips to the attractions in the vicinity.

Visa extensions The immigration office is just over 2km northwest of the centre in the state government's offices at Kompleks KHEDM, Bandar Indera Mahkota (Mon–Fri 8am–5pm, closed Fri 12.15–2.45pm; ℡09/573 2200); buses head out here from the local bus station.

Gua Charas

One of the great limestone outcrops surrounding Kuantan is home to **Gua Charas** (aka Gua Charah), 25km northwest of the town, lying on Route C4. A temple built into the cave, it can be seen as a leisurely day-trip, and in conjunction with Sungai Lembing (see below).

Kuantan buses bound for Sungai Lembing take around half an hour to reach **Panching** village, where a sign to the cave points you down a four-kilometre track through overgrown rubber plantations and row upon row of oil palms. It's a long, hot walk to the cave, so take plenty of water with you. Alternatively, charter a taxi (around RM100 there and back, including a wait) for a combined trip to the caves (the taxi can take you right up to the steps for the caves) and the nearby Sungai Pandan **waterfall**, where you can splash around in various pools, though there are few facilities other than the odd food stall.

Once you've reached the outcrop and paid your RM1 donation, you're faced with a steep climb to the Thai Buddhist **cave temple** itself. About halfway up, a rudimentary path strikes off to the right, leading to the entrance of the main cave. Descending into the eerie darkness is not for the faint-hearted, even though the damp mud path is dimly lit by fluorescent tubes. Inside the echoing cavern, with its algae-stained vaulted roof and squeaking bats, illuminated shrines gleam from gloomy corners, guiding you to the main shrine deep in the cave, where a nine-metre sleeping Buddha is almost dwarfed by its giant surroundings. Back through the cave, steps lead to another, lighter hollow. It's nothing special, but if you go as far as you can to the back, the wall opens out to give a great view of the surrounding countryside, stubby oil palms stretching towards the horizon.

Sungai Lembing

Around 15km up Route C4 from Panching, **SUNGAI LEMBING** is a classic rural Malaysian town, retaining an old-fangled and unhurried feel that's fading from the likes of Kuala Lipis and Pekan, and has all but been destroyed at once-rustic settlements such as Marang. The creation of a museum showcasing the area's involvement in tin mining indicates that at least some people in authority recognize the significance of the town's heritage, though sadly the track record elsewhere suggests that a half-baked plan to "modernize" or "beautify" the place will be pushed through eventually.

For now, you can still luxuriate in the feeling of stepping back into a rural idyll as you approach the town, the road snaking through a lush valley with steep forested hills on both sides, with a muddy river – not called Lembing but Kenau – on the right; it's spanned by the first of several narrow suspension bridges close to where the short main street begins. The town centre is dominated by Chinese businesses occupying a string of two-storey, mainly timber, shophouses. At the end of the main street is a **padang**, still flanked by the odd bungalow and so lush and well kept that it's as though the colonial era ended only yesterday. The two-storey timber building on the left at the start of the padang is now used by local government, but was once the **staff clubhouse** of the Pahang Consolidated Company Limited (PCCL), which ran the mines from 1906 until the tin price collapsed in the mid-1980s, taking the company with it; look out for the sign reading "Asian Employees' Recreation Room" high up on one exterior wall.

The history of the town and the PCCL are explored in the worthy **museum** crowning the hill beyond the padang (daily 9am–5pm, closed Fri 12.15–2.45pm; free; sign in at the gate with your passport or other ID). Here, in what was once a grand house for the PCCL's top managers, you can discover the tales claiming to explain the town's name (one legend has it that the town is where hunters threw a spear – *lembing* – at a deer down by the Kenau) and learn more about tin-mining techniques than you ever cared to. The artefacts – mallets, helmets, lamps and so forth – are rather dull, but the photos of the company's staff in the 1940s and 1960s put a human face on what must have been quite an unforgiving industry, as do excerpts of memoirs penned by one or two of the Brits who lived in the town.

Walks

Descending from the museum, turn left, heading away from the town centre, to start an excellent short **walk** taking in the outskirts of the town. After just a few minutes you come to a series of stone terraces built into a hillside, strewn with bits of metal and gradually being reclaimed by vegetation; it looks like it could just about be Khmer ruins, though it is in fact what's left of a major PCCL works (the Malay sign is no more specific than that). Continue on for several more minutes and a long **suspension bridge** of metal cables, planking and chicken wire, just like the one at the start of the town, will appear over the river on the right. Not too rickety, it's used by pedestrians and even people on scooters, and leads across to the homely Chinese kampung of **Kolong Pahat** – if you'd assumed that only Malays lived in kampungs, the sight of the pretty timber houses here with red shrines outside and the sound of Mando-pop or mahjong tiles emanating from within will set you straight. The villagers are friendly, though be discreet about taking pictures in what is essentially a residential area. From here you can head through the kampung back towards town; after ten minutes or so, you will come to another suspension bridge back across the river to a site close to the mining relics you saw earlier. Turn left here and continue up the slope to return to the main road into town.

A more challenging walk is that from the town centre up **Panorama Hill**, from where there are great views over the town and the river; some locals like to stay up here overnight to catch the sunrise. Heading up the town's main street towards the padang, turn left at the market and food centre (opposite the Hakka and Hainanese association buildings) and proceed up the lane for a couple of minutes to reach the base of the forested hill, where a small white Muslim shrine stands at the start of a series of steps leading to the summit. The walk can be done in under an hour if you push yourself.

Practicalities

Seng Heng **buses** (usually green and white, though newer vehicles are yellow; some are signed #48) leave Kuantan hourly by day for Sungai Lembing, taking an hour to reach the mining town (RM4). You can go either to the local bus station or wait on the west side of Jalan Bukit Ubi, for example at the bus stop just beyond the *Greenleaf* hotel. A **taxi** from Kuantan will cost around RM60.

The only place to **stay** in town is the *Sungai Lembing Rest House* (☎019/906 2193 or 012/900 9622; ❷), a fairly basic affair though large and quite well kept; it's close to the padang end of the main street. Staff here can organize excursions to the impressive **Rainbow Falls** nearby (RM20 per person). For **food**, there are several largely Chinese-run *kedai kopis* on the main street, and quite a good food court together with the market. To get **on line**, head to Green Internet (evenings only), housed in an appropriately green building diagonally opposite the *Rest House*.

Pekan

Nearly 50km south of Kuantan lies the unassuming royal town of **PEKAN**, whose name literally means "small town". The state capital of Pahang until 1898, Pekan used to be a charming, tranquil place but has recently seen its dull modern centre burgeon and its heritage buildings receive a rather mixed makeover, thanks in no small part – so locals say – to the fact that the town's MP is none other than the deputy prime minister Najib Tun Razak, potentially leader of the country once Abdullah Badawi steps down in 2009. Still, the

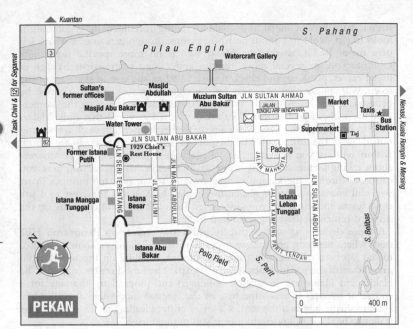

PEKAN

0   400 m

town is definitely a worthwhile day-trip from Kuantan: much of the place comprises unusually spruce, almost prim kampung houses with pretty gardens, and there are also a couple of museums and a few wooden former **royal residences** which deserve a look, even if they now feel somehow out of place and unloved.

The Town

At the edge of the commercial sector is Jalan Sultan Ahmad, facing the languid riverfront. Down the street, past a row of shophouses dating from the beginning of the twentieth century and shaded by huge rain trees, is the **Muzium Sultan Abu Bakar** (Tues–Sun 9.30am–5pm, closed Fri 12.15–2.45pm; RM1), the State Museum of Pahang. It's housed in a well-proportioned Straits colonial building that has been used for various purposes down the years: as the sultan's istana, as the centre of British administration and as the headquarters of the Japanese army during the occupation. Today it houses a collection which includes splendid Chinese ceramics salvaged from the wreck of a junk in the South China Sea, and an impressive display of royal regalia in the new east wing. There's also a collection of regional musical instruments including the xylophone-like *gambang kayu*, and a number of *kenong*s, large pot-shaped gongs set horizontally on a rack.

Opposite the museum, a footbridge leads to the **Watercraft Gallery** (same hours as State Museum; free), an innovatively designed museum of local boat-building, comprising four pavilions topped by pyramidal roofs of multicoloured glass on an island in the Pahang River. Besides a reconstruction of an ancient boat whose 1500-year-old hull was found submerged in murky water in 1926, you can also see some fine examples of the *perahu kulit kayu*, a boat fashioned from a single sheet of bark, favoured by the Orang Asli in the upper reaches of the Sungai Rompin and Sungai Endau, and a beautifully painted *perahu payang*, used for fishing.

Further west along Jalan Sultan Ahmad is the Moorish **Masjid Abdullah**, built during the reign of Sultan Abdullah (1917–32). No longer used for active worship, it is now home to the Pusat Dakwah Islamiah, the state centre for the administration of religious affairs. Next door, the current mosque, **Masjid Abu Bakar**, is more conventional, with bulbous golden domes.

The palaces

At the intersection of Jalan Sultan Abu Bakar and Jalan Sri Terentang, an archway built to resemble elephants' tusks marks the way to the royal quarter of the town. The timber building on the corner here, once the white **Istana Putih**, is now a gaudily painted centre for Koranic recitation. A few minutes' walk south is the squat **Istana Mangga Tunggal**, recently painted a dark Moroccan blue that would look marvellous against reddish desert peaks, but looks odd above lush green grass. Continue and turn left at the archway to reach the expansive walled grounds of the **Istana Abu Bakar**, where the royal family resides. Bits of military hardware can be glimpsed on display within, but the compound isn't open to the public. If you plod on following the walls, after nearly ten minutes you'll come to a vast **polo field**, still in regular use.

From here it's possible to head to the most impressive of Pekan's royal buildings, the **Istana Leban Tunggal** (Mon–Fri 10am–5pm, closed Fri 12.15–2.45pm, Sat 9am–1pm; free), though you'll have to use the winding lanes in the heart of the kampung area, and may well have to ask directions. More easily reached from the padang, the building is a refined wooden structure fronted by a pillared portico, with an unusual octagonal tower topped by a yellow dome.

Practicalities

From Kuantan, the black-and-white Bee Huat bus #31 leaves at least hourly from the local **bus station** for Pekan (RM4), an hour's journey, the last part of which involves crossing an impressively long bridge over the muddy Pahang River. The bus then turns left into Jalan Sultan Abu Bakar; if your main interest is the palaces and the museums, ask to be let off the bus when you see the "Daulat Tuanku" arch here, before the water tower. Arriving from the south by bus, you can ask the driver to drop you off in town – all buses pass through Pekan on their way to Kuantan. If you want to continue south from Pekan, you should be able to buy tickets at Pekan's **bus station**, which is in the modern centre taking up the area east of the padang.

Pekan has a characterful **place to stay**, the 1929 *Chief's Rest House* on Jalan Seri Terentang (℡09/422 6941; ❸). Occupying a spacious timber bungalow not unlike some of the istanas (and likewise now painted in gaudy colours), it has a few high-ceilinged rooms with suitably old-fangled four-poster beds and bamboo blinds, brought up to date only by air-conditioning and TV. As for **food**, there are Chinese *kedai kopis* on Jalan Sultan Ahmed and a decent *mamak* chain restaurant, the *Taj*, east of the padang close to the Mydin supermarket.

Travel details

Trains

The frequencies here combine express and local ("Mel") services, though the journey times are for express trains; local trains take roughly half as long again.

Kota Bharu (Wakaf Bharu station) to: Dabong (5 daily; 2hr); Gemas (3 daily; 8hr); Gua Musang (5 daily; 3hr 30min); Jerantut (3 daily; 6hr); Johor Bahru (2 daily; 13hr 30min); Kuala Lipis (3 daily; 5hr); Kuala Lumpur (1 daily; 13hr); Merapoh (3 daily; 4hr); Seremban (1 daily; 11hr 15min); Singapore (2 daily; 14hr 30min).

Buses

Kota Bharu to: Alor Star (2 daily; 8hr); Butterworth (2 daily; 8hr); Gua Musang (several daily; 4hr); Ipoh (2 daily; 7hr); Johor Bahru (3 daily; 12hr); Kuala Kangsar (2 daily; 6hr); Kuala Lumpur (at least 12 daily; 8hr); Kuala Terengganu (at least 8 daily; 3–4hr); Kuantan (at least 10 daily; 7hr); Melaka (1 daily; 10hr); Singapore (1 daily; 13hr). For details of buses into Thailand, see p.285.
Kuala Besut (for the Perhentians) to: Kuala Lumpur (1–2 daily; 8hr); Kuala Terengganu (3 daily; 3hr); Merang (3 daily; 1hr 30min).
Kuala Terengganu to: Alor Star (4 daily; 9hr 30min); Butterworth (2 daily; 12hr); Cherating (at least 12 daily; 3hr 30min); Ipoh (2 daily; 10hr); Johor Bahru (5 daily; 9hr); Kemaman/Chukai (at least 12 daily; 3hr); Kota Bharu (at least 8 daily; 3–4hr);

Kuala Besut (8 daily; 2hr 30min); Kuala Lumpur (every 1–2hr; 8hr 30min); Kuantan (at least 12 daily; 4–5hr); Marang (several daily; 30min); Melaka (3 daily; 9hr); Merang (3 daily; 1hr–1hr 30min); Mersing (5 daily; 7hr); Rantau Abang (several daily; 1hr 30min); Singapore (2 daily; 10hr 30min).
Kuantan to: Alor Star (2 daily; 10hr); Butterworth (2 daily; 9hr); Cherating (every 30min–1hr; 1hr–1hr 30min); Ipoh (2 daily; 6hr); Jerantut (7 daily; 3hr); Johor Bahru (at least 14 daily; 5hr 30min); Kota Bharu (at least 10 daily; 7hr); Kuala Lipis (2 daily; 5hr); Kuala Lumpur (at least hourly; 3hr); Kuala Terengganu (at least 12 daily; 4–5hr); Marang (several daily; 3hr 30min); Melaka (6 daily; 4hr); Mersing (6 daily; 3hr); Pekan (hourly; 1hr); Seremban (2 daily; 7hr); Singapore (4 daily; 6hr 30min).
Tasik Kenyir (Pangkalan Gawi) to: Kuala Lumpur (2 daily; 8hr).

Flights

Kerteh to: Kuala Lumpur (4 weekly; 45min).
Kota Bharu to: Kuala Lumpur (around 10 daily; 1hr); Penang (daily; 1hr).
Kuala Terengganu to: Kuala Lumpur (at least 7 daily; 45min); Penang (daily; 1hr).
Kuantan to: Kuala Lumpur (at least 6 daily; 40min); Penang (daily; 1hr).
Pulau Redang to: Kuala Lumpur (Subang airport; March–Oct 2 daily; 45min); Singapore (Seletar airport; March–Oct at least 4 weekly; 1hr).

The south

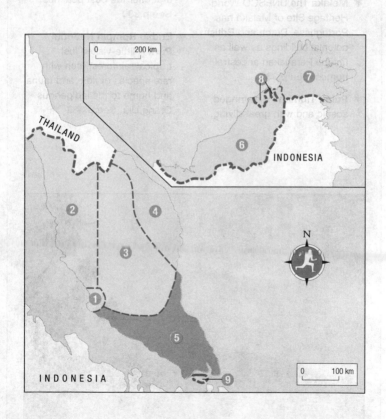

CHAPTER 5

Highlights

✳ **Minangkabau architecture**
The towns of Seremban
and Sri Menanti are home
to the spectacular and
distinctive architecture of the
Minangkabau, an ancient
Sumatran tribe. See p.335

✳ **Melaka** The UNESCO World
Heritage Site of Melaka has
Portuguese, Dutch and British
colonial buildings as well as
unique Peranakan ancestral
homes. See p.338

✳ **Pulau Tioman** Palm-fringed,
scenic and with great diving,
this has been named one of
the ten most beautiful islands
in the world. See p.369

✳ **Seribuat Archipelago** Tioman
may attract all the attention,
but it's the other islands of
the Seribuat Archipelago
that offer the best beaches.
See p.380

✳ **Endau Rompin National
Park** A little-visited lush
tropical rainforest, rich with
rare species of flora and fauna
and home to the indigenous
Orang Ulu. See p.383

▲ Beach at Air Batang village, Pulau Tioman

5

The south

The south of the Malay Peninsula, below Kuala Lumpur and Kuantan, has some of the most historically and culturally significant towns in the country. In the fifteenth century, the foundation of the west-coast city of **Melaka** led to a Malay "golden age" under the Muslim Melaka Sultanate. For all its influence, the sultanate was surprisingly short-lived, its fall in the early sixteenth century to the Portuguese marking the start of centuries of **colonial involvement** in Malaysia. The Dutch and British followed the Portuguese in Melaka; indeed, British colonial rule was an essential part of the eighteenth- and nineteenth-century development of the country. Melaka also boasts the unique culture of the Peranakan community (also called Baba-Nonya), a society that resulted from the intermarriage of early Chinese immigrant traders and Malay women.

Between KL and Melaka, the region that's now the state of Negeri Sembilan, is where the intrepid **Minangkabau** tribes from Sumatra settled, making their mark in the spectacular architecture of **Seremban** and **Sri Menanti**, both just over an hour south of the capital by road.

At the tip of the Peninsula, the town of **Johor Bahru** (or JB) dates back to only 1855, its origins in the establishment of a settlement, Tanjung Puteri, across the Johor Straits from Singapore. Visitors tend to travel along the east or west coasts, from KL and Kuantan to JB, avoiding the mountainous interior where the road network is poor. Along with the train line, the North–South Expressway (NSE) connects KL with Singapore via the west coast; its counterpart, the narrow Route 3 on the east coast, is a good deal more varied, winding for 300km through oil-palm country and past luxuriant beaches. The biggest draw of this region is Pulau Tioman and the other islands of the Seribuat Archipelago; a haven for divers and snorkellers as well as holiday-makers, because of their white sandy beaches, clear waters and tranquil atmosphere. The primeval Endau Rompin National Park is the southernmost tropical rainforest on the Peninsula and is a more rugged and less visited alternative to Taman Negara.

Negeri Sembilan

In the fifteenth century, the Minangkabau tribes from Sumatra established themselves in the Malay state of **Negeri Sembilan**, whose modern-day capital is the town of **Seremban**, 67km south of Kuala Lumpur. The cultural heart of the state though, is the royal town of **Sri Menanti**, 30km east of Seremban.

THE SOUTH

50 km

0

N

Pekan, Kuantan & Kuala Terengganu

Kuala Lipis

Kuala Lumpur

Ipoh & Butterworth

Dumai

Dumai

SOUTH CHINA SEA

Pulau Pemanggil

Pulau Aur

Pulau Tioman

Pulau Rawa

Pulau Besar

Pulau Tinggi

Pulau Sibu

Tanjung Leman

Telok Mahkota

Desaru

Kampung Pengerang

SINGAPORE

Nenasi

Kuala Rompin

S. Endau

Padang Endau

Mersing

S. Mersing

Jemaluang

Mawai

Kota Tinggi

92

Masai

Johor Bahru

Tanjung Piai

Kukup

Pontian Kecil

Kahang

Lombong

S. Johor

Kulai

Kluang

Keluang

Labis

Segamat

Gemas

Sagil Waterfall

Sagil

Gunung Ledang

Tangkak

S. Muat

Batu Pahat

Merlimau

Muar

Pulau Besar

Melaka

Tanjung Kling

Ayer Keroh

S. Melaka

Masjid Tanah

Tampin

Tanjong Bidara

Pantai Kemunting

Bahau

Kuala Pilah

Sri Menanti

Seremban

Port Dickson

Sepang

Morib

Kuala Lumpur International Airport

Formula One Circuit

PAHANG

JOHOR

MELAKA

NEGERI SEMBILAN

ENDAU ROMPIN NATIONAL PARK

Kinchin

G. Besar (1036m)

G. Tiong (1014m)

Kampung Peta

N-S EXPRESSWAY (NSE)

N-S EXPRESSWAY (NSE)

Straits of Melaka

E1

E6

12

11

10

23

5

5

5

5

5

1

1

2

2

3

3

3

50

50

E3

Centres of **Minangkabau** civilization (see box, p.336) since the early years of the Melaka Sultanate, both towns showcase traditional Minangkabau architecture, typified by distinctive, saddle-shaped roofs.

The modern state of Negeri Sembilan is based on an old confederacy of nine districts (hence its name – *sembilan* is Malay for "nine"). By the middle of the nineteenth century, the thriving **tin trade** and British control over the area were well established, with colonial authority administered from Sungai Ujong (today's Seremban). Wars between rival Malay and Minangkabau groups for control over the mining and transport of tin were commonplace, most notably between the Dato' Kelana, the chief of Sungai Ujong, and the Dato' Bandar, who controlled the middle part of Sungai Linggi, further to the south.

The heavy influx of Chinese immigrants – who numbered about half the total population of Negeri Sembilan by the time of the first official census in 1891 – only had the effect of prolonging the feuds, since their secret societies, or triads, attempted to manipulate the situation to gain local influence. The most significant figure to emerge from this period was **Yap Ah Loy**, a charismatic leader who helped orchestrate clan rivalry through a series of violent skirmishes, one of which resulted in the sacking of Sri Menanti. He later moved to the newly established tin-mining town of Kuala Lumpur, where he quickly became an influential figure (see p.80). In an attempt to control a situation that was rapidly sliding out of control, British Governor Jervois installed Abu Bakar of Johor as overlord, a man not only respected by the Malays but also apparently sympathetic to the colonists' aims. However, two prominent British officials, Frank Swettenham (later Resident in Selangor at the time of KL's early meteoric expansion) and Frederick Weld, weren't convinced about Abu Bakar's loyalty and bypassed his authority with the use of local British officials. Learning from their mistakes in Perak, where the hurried appointment of J.W.W. Birch as British advisor had caused local uproar and led eventually his being shot, the British adopted a cautious approach. A treaty was eventually signed in 1895, narrowing the divide between the British colonial authorities and the Minangkabaus that had been the cause of so much strife.

Seremban

An hour south of the capital and just twenty minutes from KL International Airport, the bustling town of **SEREMBAN** is often overlooked by passing tourists, having little in the way of specific sights. While not the place for long stays, it's worth stopping by in order to visit **Taman Seni Budaya Negeri**, a museum complex that celebrates the distinctive Minangkabu architectural style; it's located 3km northwest of the centre, close to the North–South Expressway.

Arrival and information

Seremban has regular train connections with Kuala Lumpur and is linked with both Melaka and KL by express buses. The **bus** and **taxi stations** are about five minutes' walk from the centre of town across the river, while the **train station** is just south of the centre. To get to town from KL, either take the bus from KL town (every 15min, 7am–10pm; RM6) or KLIA (twice daily; RM5) or get a Komuter train from KL Sentral. A taxi from KL Sentral is around RM60 during the day. Most **internet** cafés are in or around the giant Terminal One shopping centre (next to the bus station) which also has a **cinema** on the top floor.

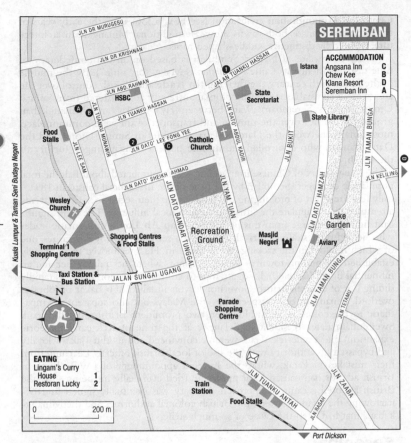

▼ Port Dickson

Accommodation

The town has a chronic shortage of decent, inexpensive **hotels** (indeed, many of the cheaper ones are brothels; the places we've listed below are all above board).

Angsana Inn 114 Jalan Dato' Bandar Tunggal ☎06/767 8777. Good-value, clean rooms in corner hotel. All rooms come with own bathrooms, TV and a/c. Free parking and handy location, but not much in terms of atmosphere. ❹

Chew Kee 41 Jalan Tuanku Munawir ☎06/762 2095. Hidden away on the first floor of a poorly signposted building, this place has cheap, uninspiring partitioned rooms with or without a/c and private bathrooms. It's clean enough and there's a reassuring note saying "Prostitution is prohibited here" above the door. ❷

Klana Resort Jalan Penghula Cantik ☎06/762 9600, ⓦwww.allsonklana.com.my. Set 500m east of the Lake Garden, this is *the* top spot in Seremban, with everything you'd expect from a high-class resort hotel, including a swimming pool, gym and restaurant. ❽

Seremban Inn 39 Jalan Tuanku Munawir ☎06/761 7777, ⓕ763 7777. Clean and good-value mid-range hotel in town with helpful staff and well-equipped rooms. ❹

The Town

Seremban's commercial centre is a mixture of decorative Chinese shophouses and faceless concrete structures, while further out, imposing colonial mansions line its streets. North of the river from the bus and taxi stations, past the **Wesley Church** of 1920, is the **business district** where most of the hotels, restaurants and banks are located. East along Jalan Dato' Sheikh Ahmad, a right turn leads to the recreation ground, across which the nine pillars supporting the scalloped roof of the grey concrete **Masjid Negeri** come into view. Each pillar, topped by a crescent and star (symbols of Muslim enlightenment) represents one of the nine districts of the state. Beyond this lies the artificial **Lake Garden**.

Head north along Jalan Dato' Hamzah beside the park and after a ten-minute walk you'll see the white-stuccoed Neoclassical **State Library** – once the centre of colonial administration – with its graceful columns and portico. Past the black-and-gilt wrought-iron gates of the Istana (closed to the public) just to the north, a left turn leads to the current **State Secretariat**, whose architecture reflects the Minangkabau tradition. Its hillside position ensures that the layered, buffalo-horn roof is one of the first sights you see in the town.

The **Taman Seni Budaya Negeri** (State Arts & Culture Park; daily 10am–6pm, Fri 10am–noon & 2.45–6pm; free) is the best introduction that you could have to the principles of Minangkabau architecture. The museum building is of traditional construction, and the grounds contain three original timber houses, reconstructed here in the 1950s. The first of these, the **Istana Ampang Tinggi**, built forty years before the palace at Sri Menanti (see p.337), was passed down through successive generations of royalty until 1930. The interior of the veranda, where male guests were entertained, displays a wealth of exuberant and intricate leaf carvings, with a pair of unusual heavy timber doors. The two other houses nearby are similar, though less elaborate, their gloomy interiors only relieved by shutters in the narrow front rooms. Inside the museum proper, the ground floor contains an exhibition of four human skeletons, unearthed in a recent archeological dig at Melaka Fort, and

▲ A Minangkabau house

The **Minangkabau people**, whose cultural heartland is in the mountainous region west of central Sumatra (Indonesia), established a community in Malaysia in the early fifteenth century. As they had no written language until the arrival of Islam, knowledge of their origins is somewhat sketchy; their own oral accounts trace their ancestry to Alexander the Great, while the *Sejarah Melayu* (see p.687) talks of a mysterious leader, Nila Pahlawan, who was pronounced king of the Palembang natives by a man who was magically transformed from the spittle of an ox. Oxen feature prominently, too, in the legend surrounding the origins of the name "Minangkabau". When their original home in Sumatra came under attack from the Javanese, the native people agreed to a contest whereby the outcome of a battle fought between a tiger (representing the Javanese) and a buffalo (representing the locals) would determine who controlled the land. Against all the odds, the buffalo killed the tiger, and henceforth the inhabitants called themselves Minangkabau, meaning "the victorious buffalo".

In early times the Minangkabau were ruled in Sumatra by their own overlords or rajahs, though political centralization never really rivalled the role of the strongly autonomous *nagari* (Sumatran for village). Each *nagari* consisted of numerous **matrilineal clans** (*suku*), each of which took the name of the mother and lived in the *adat* house, the ancestral home. The *adat* household was also in control of ancestral property, which was passed down the maternal line. The *sumando* (husband) stayed in his wife's house at night but was a constituent member of his mother's house, where most of his day was spent. Although the house and clan name belonged to the woman, and women dominated the domestic sphere, political and ceremonial power was in the hands of men; it was the *mamak* (mother's brother) who took responsibility for the continued prosperity of the lineage (he was the administrative figurehead and the authority for the proper distribution of ancestral property).

When and why the Minangkabau initially emigrated to what is now **Negeri Sembilan** in Malaysia is uncertain. Their subsequent history is closely bound up with that of Melaka and Johor, with the Minangkabau frequently called upon to supplement the armies of ambitious Malay princes and sultans. Little is known of their interaction with the native Malay population, although evidence of intermarriage with the region's predominant tribal group, the Sakai, indicates acceptance by the Malays of the matrilineal system. What is certain is that the Minangkabau were a political force to be reckoned with. Their dominance in domestic affairs was aided by their reputation for supernatural powers, rumours of which were widespread.

Although migration remained standard practice, after the mid-nineteenth century the drift was towards urban centres, and communal living in the *adat* house became relatively rare. Today, the Minangkabau are very much integrated with the Malays, and their dialect is almost indistinguishable from standard *Bahasa Melayu*.

---

believed to date from the fifteenth century. The only way to get here is to take a taxi from town (RM7).

Eating

There's no shortage of **places to eat**. *Lingam's Curry House*, on the corner of Jalan Dato' Abdul Kadir and Jalan Tuanku Hassan, serves reliable Indian dishes, including meat and veggie biriyanis; busy *Restoran Lucky* on Jalan Dato' Lee Fong Yee, does good *laksa* as well as claypots and a lunch buffet. There are **food stalls** along Jalan Tuanku Munawir, Jalan Dato' Lee Fong Yee, Jalan Lee Sam and close to the train station.

Sri Menanti

Thirty kilometres east of Seremban lies the former royal capital of Negeri Sembilan, **SRI MENANTI**, its palaces, ancient and modern, set in a lush, mountainous landscape. The only reason to visit this little town, however, is to see a jewel of Minangkabau architecture, the **Istana Lama** (daily 10am–6pm; free). A timber palace set in geometric gardens, it was the seat of the Minangkabau rulers, whose migration to the Malay Peninsula began in the fifteenth century during the early years of the Melaka Sultanate. The sacking of Sri Menanti during the Sungai Ujong tin wars destroyed the original palace; the four-storey version that stands here now was designed and built in 1902 by two Malay master craftsmen who, as the tradition dictates, used no nails or screws in its construction. Until 1931, the palace was used as a royal residence, with the ground floor functioning as a reception area, the second as family quarters, and the third as the sultan's private apartments. The tower, once used as the treasury and royal archives, offers a lovely view and can be reached by ladder from the sultan's private rooms. At its apex is a forked projection of a type known as "open scissors", now very rarely seen (though it's reproduced in the roof of the Muzium Negara in Kuala Lumpur).

The whole rectangular building is raised nearly 2m off the ground by 99 pillars, 26 of which have been carved in low relief with complex foliated designs. Though the main doors and windows are plain, a long external veranda is covered with a design of leaves and branches known as *awan larat*, or "driving clouds". Above the front porch is the most elaborate decoration, a pair of fantastic creatures with lions' heads, horses' legs and long feathery tails, its style suggesting that the craftsmen responsible were Chinese.

Reaching Sri Menanti is relatively straightforward, though there is nowhere to stay. From Seremban, take a United **bus** for the 45-minute journey to **Kuala Pilah**. There, you can either wait for an infrequent local bus to Sri Menanti, or take a shared taxi, a ten-minute ride costing no more than RM5 per person or around RM15 for the cab. A cab from Seremban is RM45. Tell the driver where you are going and he'll drop you off in front of the Istana Lama. Don't be misled by the sign for the Istana Besar, the rather imposing current royal palace, topped by a startling blue roof.

Port Dickson

The rather dismal strip of the **coast** stretching south of the capital to Melaka is a major draw for KL weekenders who, attracted by the populous resort of **PORT DICKSON**, turn a blind eye to its polluted sea. The town itself, 34km southwest of Seremban, is not much more than a few shops and banks, but there are luxury resorts aplenty. Port Dickson's beach, stretching as far as the Cape Rachado (Tanjung Tuan) lighthouse, 16km to the south, is marred by passing oil tankers, dishwater-grey sea and an enormous sewage pipe spilling out into the north of the bay.

There are no direct **bus** connections with KL or Melaka; you will have to change bus in Seremban, where buses leave every 20 minutes between 6am and 8pm for one-hour journey. The coastal road, Route 5, branches west off the North–South Expressway south of KL and reaches the west coast at Morib.

Buses from Seremban stop at the **bus station** in the commercial part of town, about 2km north of the beach. The best **places to stay** are strung out along Jalan Pantai (part of Route 5), which runs south of Port Dickson. Note that weekend and peak season rates soar. Locations along the road are usually specified according to milestones – the number of which are painted on lampposts along the way, prefaced by *batu* (stone). There are local buses serving the stretch, but they finish as the sun goes down and taxis can be hard to come by after dark and are expensive – a kilometre or two costs RM20 when booked through one of the resorts.

Practicalities

When it comes to **accommodation**, there are plenty of luxury resorts – Port Dickson is not a budget destination, though most hotels offer packages during off-peak times. The most upmarket resort is the *Selesa Beach Resort* (☎06/647 4090; ❽) near the five-mile marker, built in striking Minangkabau style with excellent facilities, including a pool. The best stretch of the beach is found near the *Bayu Beach Resort* (☎06/647 3703; ❻), halfway between the four- and five-mile marker. The only budget choice is south of the three-mile marker: the friendly *Rotary Sunshine Camp* (☎06/647 3798; ❷), which also has dorm beds at RM10.

Most hotels have their own **restaurants**; *The Regency* next door to *Selesa Beach Resort*, has a nice setting right on the beach. The **food stalls** around the four- and five-mile markers offer everything from burgers to freshly caught fish – a good selection is found just past the Petronas service station.

Melaka and around

When Penang was known only for its oysters and Singapore was just a fishing village, **MELAKA** (also spelt "Malacca") had already achieved worldwide fame. Under the auspices of the Melaka Sultanate, founded in the early fifteenth century, political and cultural life flourished, helping to define what it means to be Malay. Yet, beginning in 1511, Melaka suffered a series of takeovers and botched administrations involving the Portuguese, Dutch and British, causing the humiliating subjugation of the Malay people.

Because of its cultural legacy, Melaka achieved UNESCO World Heritage listing in July 2008 (jointly with Georgetown, Penang), a fact displayed proudly across most of the city and certainly reflected in the many new developments taking place. For the cynical eye, there's something about Melaka that smacks of over-preservation, all too easily apparent in the brick-red paint wash that covers everything in the so-called "historical centre". At its core lies the **Dutch Square**, with its many museums and historical buildings. For a more authentic encounter with the past, it's better to strike out into **Chinatown**, where the rich Baba-Nonya heritage is displayed in the opulent merchants' houses, elegant restaurants and relaxed bars lining the narrow thoroughfares. In the evening, Chinese lanterns illuminate the streets in this generally sleepy part of town – even the busy weekend market in **Jonker Walk** has an air of quiet bohemia about it.

There are reminders of the human costs of empire-building in the many churches and graveyards scattered around the town, where tombstones tell of whole families struck down by fever and of young men killed in battle. The **Portuguese Settlement** to the east of the centre has something of the synthetic colonial heritage that typifies Melaka, while land reclamation in the new town area, **Taman Melaka Raya**, southeast of the centre with most of the city's budget accommodation and close to the huge shopping malls, points to the urban regeneration also taking place. That Melaka is banking on tourists is only too evident in the newest developments, such as the **hydraulic**

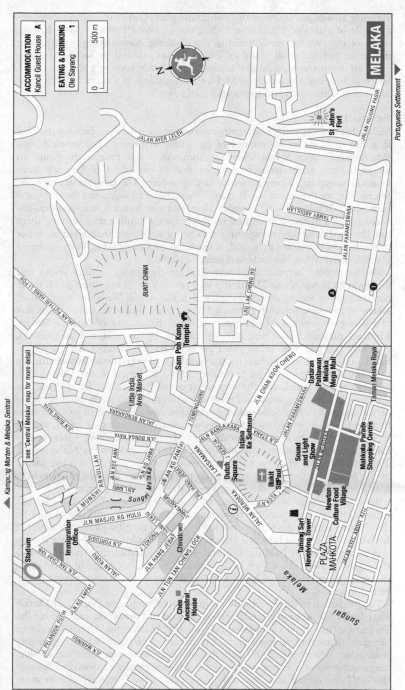

MELAKA

ACCOMMODATION
Kancil Guest House   A

EATING & DRINKING
Ole Sayang   1

0   500 m

N

Kampung Morten & Melaka Sentral ▲

▲ Masjid Tranquerah

Stadium

Immigration
Office

JLN TAN CHAY YAN

JLN KG EMPAT

PELANDUK PUTIH

JLN MARIMUNG

Chee
Ancestral
House

JLN TUN TAN CHENG LOCK

Chinatown

JALAN KUBU

JLN PORTUGIS

J MUNSHI AB'JULLAH

JLN MASJID KG HULU

JLN KEE ANN

JLN BUNGA RAYA

JLN KG PANTAI

JLN KG JAWA

JLN BARU

TIANG LEKIU

TIANG GAJAH

TUKANG BESI

TUKANG EMAS

JLN HANG JEBAT

JLN HANG LEKIR

JLN HANG KASTURI

JLN HANG LEKIU

Sungei Melaka

JLN BUNGA RAYA

Little India
Area Market

JALAN BENDAHARA

JLN BUNGA RAYA

JLN RING RAYA

see 'Central Melaka' map for more detail

JALAN AYER LELEH

BUKIT CHINA

Sam Poh Kong
Temple

JLN POTRI HANG LI POH

LRG LAK CHENG HO

J TAMBY ABDULLAH

JALAN PARAMESWARA

J TEMENGGONG

JLN BANDA KABA

GEREJA

JLN LAKSAMANA

Dutch
Square

Istana
Ke Sultanan

JLN CHAN KOON CHENG

JLN STANA

JALAN PARAMESWARA

Dataran
Pahlawan
Melaka
Mega Mall

Taman Melaka Raya

Bukit
St Paul

JLN KOTA

JALAN MERDEKA

Sound
and Light
Show

Mahkota Parade
Shopping Centre

JALAN SYED ABDUL AZIZ

Newton
Culture Food
Village

PLAZA
MAHKOTA

Taming Sari
Revolving Tower

Melaka

Sungai

St John's
Fort

JALAN HUJUNG PASIR

Portuguese Settlement ▶

viewing tower just south of the swimming pool. Out of the centre, there are a couple of places of interest, including the green-belt area of **Ayer Keroh**, north of the city, the turtle sanctuary at **Padang Kemunting**, north along the coast, and the small island of **Pulau Besar**, viewed by locals as a holy place. At a push you could get around the colonial core in a day; it's better, however, to spend three days in Melaka, taking things at a more leisurely pace and seeing Chinatown and the outskirts of town.

Some history

Melaka has its roots in the fourteenth-century struggles between Java and the Thai kingdom of Ayuthaya for control of the Malay Peninsula. The *Sejarah Melayu* (Malay Annals) records that when the Sumatran prince Paramesvara could no longer tolerate subservience to Java, he fled to the island of Temasek (later renamed Singapore), where he set himself up as ruler. The Javanese subsequently forced him to flee north to Bertam, where he was welcomed by the local community. While his son, Iskandar Shah, was out hunting near modern-day Melaka Hill, a mouse deer turned on the pursuing hunting dogs, driving them into the sea. Taking this courageous act to be a good omen, Shah asked his father to build a new settlement there and, in searching for a name for it, he remembered the *melaka* tree, which he had been sitting under.

Melaka rapidly became a cosmopolitan market town, trading spices and textiles with Indonesia and India; the levy exacted on all imported goods made Melaka one of the wealthiest kingdoms in the world. With the adoption of **Islam** in the early fifteenth century, Melaka consolidated its influence; it was said that to become a Muslim was to enter the society of Melaka Malays. Melaka's meteoric rise was initially assisted by its powerful neighbours, Ayuthaya and Java, who made good use of its trading facilities. But they soon had a serious rival, as Melaka started a campaign of **territorial expansion**. By the time of the reign of its last ruler, Sultan Mahmud Shah (1488–1530), Melaka's territory included the west coast of the Peninsula as far as Perak, the whole of Pahang, Singapore and most of east-coast Sumatra. By the beginning of the sixteenth century, Melaka's population had increased to one hundred thousand, and it would not have been unusual to count as many as two thousand ships in its port. **Culturally**, too, Melaka was supreme – its sophisticated language, literature and dances were all benchmarks in the Malay world. The establishment of a court structure (see box opposite) defined the nature of the Melaka state and the role of the individuals within it, a social system which remained virtually unchanged until the nineteenth century.

But a sea change was occurring in Europe which was to end Melaka's supremacy. The Portuguese were seeking to extend their influence in Asia by dominating ports in the region and, led by Alfonso de Albuquerque, conquered Melaka in 1511. Eight hundred officers were left to administer the new colony and maintained their hold for the next 130 years, introducing Catholicism to the region through the efforts of St Francis Xavier. Little tangible evidence of the Portuguese remains in Melaka today, bar the Eurasian community to the east of town.

The formation of the Vereenigde Oostindische Compagnie (VOC), or **Dutch East India Company**, in 1602 spelled the end of Portuguese rule. Where the Portuguese had tried to impose rule on the Malays, the Dutch sought to integrate them, finding them useful on matters of etiquette when negotiating with other Malay rulers; the primary objective here was trade rather than religious conversion. However, the settlement never really expanded in the way the VOC had hoped, and due to their high taxes, the Dutch relied ever more on force to maintain their position in the Straits – which lost them the respect of their Malay subjects.

The superior maritime skills and commercial adroitness of the **British East India Company** provided serious competition for the control of Melaka. Weakened by French threats to their posts in the Indies, the Dutch handed Melaka over to the British on August 15, 1795. But the colony continued to decline, and with the establishment of the free-trade port of Singapore in 1819, Melaka looked set to disintegrate. The British wanted Penang to be the main west-coast settlement but attempted to revitalize Melaka, introducing progressive agricultural and mining concerns, while the **Chinese** continued to flock to the town, taking over former Dutch mansions. However, investment in new hospitals, schools and a train line did little to improve Melaka's spiralling deficit. It wasn't until a Chinese entrepreneur, Tan Chay Yan, began to plant **rubber** that Melaka's problems were alleviated for a time. After World War I, though, even this commodity faced mixed fortunes – when the **Japanese occupied** Melaka in 1942, they found a town exhausted by the interwar depression.

Malay court structures

One of the most outstanding achievements of the Melaka Sultanate was to create a **court structure**, setting a pattern of government that was to last for the next five hundred years, and whose prominent figures are still reflected in the street names of most towns in the country. At the top of the hierarchy was the **sultan** who, by virtue of his ancestry (traced back to the mighty empire of Srivijaya), embodied the mystique which set Melaka apart from its rivals. He was far from being an autocratic tyrant: a form of social contract evolved whereby the ruler could expect undying loyalty from his subjects in return for a fair and wise dispensation of justice (this was the crux of the confrontation between Hang Tuah and Hang Jebat; see box, p.346). Nor were sultans remote ceremonial figures; many supervised the planting of new crops, for instance, or wandered freely in the streets among the people, a style of behaviour that may explain the relative humility of the palaces they occupied.

Below the ruler was a clutch of **ministers**, who undertook the day-to-day administration of government. The most important of these was the **Bendahara**, who dealt with disputes among traders and among the Malays themselves. In effect, he was the public face of the regime, wielding a great deal of power, backed by his closest subordinate, the **Penghulu Bendahari**, who supervised the *syahbandars* (harbour masters) and the sultan's domestic staff. Potential bendaharas were trained at the office of the **Temenggung**, who was responsible for law and order, working in close partnership with the **Laksamana**, the military commander, whose strongest armed force was the navy. Wide-ranging consultation regarding new measures took place in a **council of nobles**, who had earned their titles either through land ownership or from blood ties with royalty. Little is known of the **common people** of Melaka, though it is certain that they had no part in the decision-making process; the *Sejarah Melayu* nevertheless speaks of them with some respect: "Subjects are like roots and the ruler is like the tree; without roots the tree cannot stand upright."

To reinforce the status of the royal family, the colour yellow was only allowed to be used by royalty and no one but the ruler was permitted to wear gold – unless it was a royal gift. In addition, commoners could not have pillars or enclosed verandas in their houses, or windows and reception rooms in their boats. Despite these methods of distinction, threats to the throne were commonplace – particularly from the Bendahara.

Modern-day developments, such as the land reclamation in Taman Melaka Raya and the recently granted UNESCO World Heritage Site status, may help to reverse Melaka's long-term decline. Whatever damage was wrought during its centuries of colonial mismanagement, nothing can take away the enduring influence of Melaka's creation of a Malay language, court system and royal lineage – a powerful legacy established in a mere hundred years that was permanently to affect development in the Peninsula.

Arrival, information and city transport

There is only one **bus station** in Melaka (Melaka Sentral), located on the corner of Jalan Panglima Awang and Jalan Tun Razak, about 3km north of the town centre, operating buses to pretty much anywhere on the Peninsula. You will most likely arrive here and the #17 bus from the domestic part of the station takes you into town in 10–15 minutes (RM1). For details of the airport, train station and ferry terminal, see p.356. A taxi into town from here costs RM15–20; pay at the booth. There is a rather annoying commission system between the taxis and the guesthouses; if you already have a booking somewhere, or if you know where you want to go, don't necessarily believe the driver telling you that the place is full. Many of the streets are very narrow and the one-way system is awkward, so **drivers** should park their cars at the first possible opportunity and get around the city by foot, bus, trishaw or taxi.

The **tourist office** is on Jalan Kota (daily 9am–5pm; ℡06/283 6538), just by the bridge from the historical centre to Chinatown. An RM5 **ticket** can be purchased at any of the town's public museums, for entry to the cluster of **museums** on Bukit St Paul.

City transport

Most of the places of interest are located within the compact historical centre, and so are best visited **on foot**. For longer journeys, **taxis** or the colourful disco **trishaws** are the best bet, both costing roughly the same; a sightseeing tour by trishaw, covering all the major sights including the Portuguese Settlement, costs RM40–50 per hour for two people. You should be able to get a trishaw around the Dutch Square and outside the Mahkota Parade shopping centre. Taxis are quite hard to find on the street, but there is a **taxi rank** by the Mahkota Parade and another by the bridge into Chinatown.

The **town bus service** has several useful routes for visitors, departing from Melaka Sentral: #17 runs through the historical centre to Taman Melaka Raya and the Portuguese Settlement (RM1); the SKA Muar-bound bus goes to Anjung Batu for Pulau Besar (RM1.20); #19 goes out to Ayer Keroh (RM1.20).

Accommodation

Melaka has a huge selection of **hotels** and guesthouses. In general, most places are good value and well kept with higher standards than their Georgetown counterparts. Except where noted the places below appear on the map on p.347.

Aldy House 27 Jalan Kota ℡06/283 3232, ℗www.aldyhotel.com.my. With a rooftop terrace split between a small sunning area with a cold jacuzzi and a large BBQ restaurant (open Thurs), as well as the *Bamboo Hut Bistro* downstairs (open till 1am and with free wi-fi), this red block is the only hotel and bar in the historical centre.

Rooms have a/c, TVs and minibars and there are expensive apartment suites with all the trimmings. There is a sister hotel on Jalan Bunga Raya. ❻

Baba House 125 Jalan Tun Tan Cheng Lock ℡06/281 1216, ℗www.thebabahouse .com.my. These beautifully restored Peranakan houses have been turned into an atmospheric hotel, with most of the smallish rooms newly renovated. If you can't get a room, it is worth having a look around the hallways, with permission. ❶

Chong Hoe 26 Jalan Tukong Emas ☏06/282 6102. A well-looked-after, family-run hotel in Chinatown offering smallish rooms with a/c and shared or private showers, though the location – within earshot of the temple and mosque – can be noisy at times. ❷

🏃 **Emily's Traveller's Home** 71 Jalan Parameswara ☏012/301 6574. Lovingly created with imaginative use of recycled materials, this peaceful and friendly gem has two chalets (with own bathrooms) and rooms in the heritage house with shared bathrooms; there are a few dorm beds at RM16, too. The common area is stunning with entry past a fish pond into a small tropical garden. A small and cosy evening fire is lit to keep the mosquitoes away and there's even a pet rabbit, but no TV. ❷

Equatorial Bandar Hilir (Jalan Parameswara) ☏06/282 8333, ⓦ www.equatorial.com. With brightly decorated rooms boasting huge beds, and a wide range of restaurants, this comes a close second to the *Renaissance* in terms of grandeur. ❽

Fenix Inn 156 Jalan Merdaka, Taman Melaka Raya ☏06/281 5511, ⓔ reservation@fenixinn .com. Well-appointed rooms and friendly service, with hairdryers, in the heart of Taman Melaka Raya. It's the most upmarket choice in this area and has a business centre with several internet terminals. ❹–❺

Heeren House 1 Jalan Tun Tan Cheng Lock ☏06/281 4241, ⓔ info@heerenhouse.com. An ideal location in Chinatown and tasteful rooms – some with four-poster beds – make this a good choice for a small, upmarket hotel. Prices, which include English breakfast, are slightly higher at weekends. There is a small café and craft shop downstairs. Book ahead. ❺

Heeren Inn 23 Jalan Tun Tan Cheng Lock ☏&ⓕ06/288 3600. Though the location is superb, it's probably not a place you would stay for long as the management can be rather abrupt. The rooms have a/c and there is internet access. ❹

Hollitel 20-K Jalan PM5, Plaza Mahkota Bandar Hilir ☏06/286 0608 (see map, p.339). In a part of town relatively unvisited by travellers (but not short of restaurants, hairdressers, designer shops and bars), this is a good option if you want to get away from the main drag, but still be close enough to the centre. The rooms are clean and come with a/c and bathrooms. ❸

Hotel Johan 210 Jalan Melaka Raya 1, Taman Melaka Raya ☏06/286 5703, ⓔ travellodgemlk @yahoo.com. With the same management as the *Traveller's Lodge* next door, this smart hotel is excellent value with cheaper rooms on the top floor, closer to the small roof terrace. All rooms have own bathrooms and a/c. ❸

Hotel Puri Jalan Tun Tan Cheng Lock ☏06/282 5588, ⓦ www.hotelpuri.com. Set in a beautifully restored Peranakan shophouse, this place has all the mod cons, a slight air of superiority and a good restaurant. Rooms are decorated in a contemporary style and make good use of space. Breakfast is included in the rates, and its *Galeri Café* is a good spot for dinner with an excellent and varied menu. ❻

🏃 **Jalan-Jalan** 8 Jalan Tukang Emas ☏06/283 3937, ⓦ www .jalanjalanguesthouse.com. With a tiny sign above the door and a warm and friendly welcome, this is an excellent budget choice with a light and airy dorm at RM13 for a bed. The rooms are mainly cubicles with four-poster metal beds and mosquito nets. The shared bathrooms have hot showers and there's a good communal area with wi-fi and a terminal. ❷

Kancil Guest House 177 Jalan Parameswara ☏06/281 4044, ⓦ www.machinta.com.sg/kancil/. (see map, p.339). Lovely and spotless guesthouse in an old Chinese ancestral home with a small garden and terrace. Facilities include library, bicycles for hire, a small breakfast café, internet access and plenty of information. ❷

🏃 **Number Twenty** First floor, 20 Jalan Hang Jebat ☏06/281 9761, ⓔ reservations @selesalifestyle.com. All with spotlessly clean shared bathrooms, a/c and windows, this new and very friendly place is tastefully decorated, gay-friendly and has wi-fi. Breakfast is included. ❺

Renaissance Melaka Jalan Bendahara ☏06/284 8888, ⓦ www.renaissancehotels.com. The town's foremost luxury hotel, with an imposing lobby – complete with huge chandeliers – and elegant, well-furnished rooms. ❼

Sama Sama Guest House 26 Jalan Tukan Besi ☏012/305 1980. This excellent travellers' choice in a great location in Chinatown has rooms on the first floor around an atmospheric skylight. Shared bathrooms have cold showers and there is a good communal area. Dorm beds at RM12. ❷

Samudra Inn Guest House 348b Taman Melaka Raya ☏06/2827441. Homely and very friendly, this family-run guesthouse is spotlessly clean and some of the rooms share a balcony, making them excellent value. There is a toaster and kettle for guest use and a fridge with beers and soft drinks for sale. Favourable rates are given for longer stays. ❷

Shirah's Guest House Second floor, 207b Taman Melaka Raya 1 ☎014/644 6231. With only six rooms and a small roof terrace, this place is well looked after with brightly coloured murals on the walls. Two a/c rooms share a lovely balcony and all have shared showers. One room (RM65) sleeps five people. ❷

Sunny's Inn First floor, 270 Taman Melaka Raya 3 ☎019/337 6232, ✉sunny_prestige@hotmail.com. This increasingly popular place is a good budget option with a communal kitchen and free 10pm movies. The fan rooms are small cubicles; a few more ringgits will get you a/c and bathroom. Shared bathrooms have hot and cold showers and the place is generally kept clean. You'll need to bring your own top sheet. ❷

🏃 **Tang House** 80-1 Jalan Tokong ☎06/283 3969, ✉tanghouse@live.com.

Well-presented family-run guesthouse with a small café located opposite the *Temple Street Bistro* down the side street. There are free wi-fi and internet terminals, and the shared bathrooms have hot showers. A small kitchen on the first floor common area is available for guest use. ❸

Traveller's Lodge 214b Jalan Melaka Raya 1 ☎06/226 5709. Pleasant and spotlessly clean, this family-run place boasts a shady roof terrace, handy cafeteria and traditional Malay-style lounge area complete with books and board games. ❷

Voyage Guest House Jalan Tukan Besi ☎012/305 1980. With the same management as *Sama Sama*, this place has a huge dorm room (RM12) and a few fan rooms. There is also a roof room sleeping four or five. Free wi-fi and bicycle loan. The *Voyage Café* around the corner is a good hangout and has free (though limited) wi-fi. ❷

The City

The centre of Melaka is split in two by the murky **Sungai Melaka**, the western bank of which is occupied by **Chinatown** – charmingly lit up by hundreds of lanterns at night – and, 2km to the north, **Kampung Morten**, a small collection of stilt houses. On the eastern side of the river lies the colonial core – the main area of interest – with **Bukit St Paul** at its centre, encircled by Jalan Kota. Southeast of here is a section of reclaimed land known as **Taman Melaka Raya**, a new town that's home to a giant shopping centre and many of the budget hotels, restaurants and bars. There are a few sights further east of the centre, a little too far-flung to be comfortably covered on foot: the **Portuguese Settlement**, **St John's Fort** and **Bukit China**, the last of these being the Chinese community's ancestral burial ground and about a fifteen minute walk from the town centre. Bus #17 runs regularly to the Portuguese Settlement, 3km from town and stops at St John's Fort; you can take a taxi or trishaw from the latter to Bukit China (around RM15).

The Istana

On Jalan Kota, the **Istana ke Sultanan** (daily 9am–5pm, closed Fri 12.15–2.45pm; RM4), in the geographical centre of town, has played a central role in Malaysian history. The imposing dark-timber palace, set in neatly manicured gardens, is a contemporary reconstruction, based on a description in the *Sejarah Melayu*, of the original fifteenth-century istana. In the best Malay architectural tradition, its multilayered, sharply sloping roofs contain no nails. It was here that the administrative duties of the state were carried out, and also where the sultan resided when in the city (for the most part he lived further upriver at Bertam, safe from possible attacks on Melaka). Inside – remove your shoes to ascend the wide staircase to the verandaed first floor – is a cultural museum which houses an interesting and colourful display of life-sized re-creations of scenes from Malay court life, including the epic duel of Melaka's most famous warriors, Hang Tuah and Hang Jebat (see box, p.346), as well as costumes and local crafts. The building alone is worth the entrance fee.

▲ Porta de Santiago

At the time of their conquest of Melaka, the Portuguese used the forced labour of fifteen hundred slaves to construct the mighty **A Famosa** fort. All that's left of it today is a single gate, the crumbling whitewashed **Porta de Santiago**, just to the right as you leave the palace museum. When it defeated the Portuguese in 1641, the Dutch East India Company used the fort as its headquarters, later modifying it, adding the company crest and the date 1670 to the Porta de Santiago – features which are just about distinguishable today.

The fort stood steadfast for 296 years and probably would have survived, were it not for the arrival of the British in 1795. With their decision to relocate to Penang, orders were given in 1807 to destroy the fort and the task of demolition fell to Resident William Farquhar, who reluctantly set about doing so with gangs of labourers armed with spades and pickaxes and for more effect, gunpowder.

Independence Memorial Museum

Around 250m south of the Istana is the **Independence Memorial Museum** (Tues–Thurs, Sat & Sun 9am–5pm, Fri 9am–noon & 3–6pm; free). Built in 1912, this elegant mansion of classic white stucco, with two golden onion domes on either side of its portico, formerly housed the colonial **Malacca Club**, whose most famous guest was the novelist Somerset Maugham. This is where he was told the tale that formed the basis of his short story, *Footprints in the Jungle*, in which both the Club and Melaka itself (which he calls Tanah Merah) feature prominently. The museum depicts the fascinating events surrounding the run-up to independence in 1957 and showcases the proud achievements of modern Malaysia.

The Muzium Rakyat and the Islamic Museum

Skirting west around the base of the hill from Porta de Santiago brings you to the **Muzium Rakyat** (People's Museum; daily 9am–5pm, Fri closed 12.15–2.45pm;

Hang Tuah and Hang Jebat

Recounted in the seventeenth-century epic *Hikayat Hang Tuah*, the tale of the duel between two friends, **Hang Tuah** and **Hang Jebat**, symbolizes the conflict between absolute loyalty to the sovereign and the love of a friend. These two characters, together with Hang Kasturi, Hang Lekir and Hang Lekiu, formed a band known as "The Five Companions" (because of their close relationship since birth), and were highly trained in the martial arts. When they saved the life of Bendahara Paduka Raja, the highest official in the Malay court, Sultan Mansur Shah was so impressed by their skill that he appointed them court attendants. Hang Tuah rapidly became the sultan's favourite and was honoured with a beautiful *kris*, **Taming Sari**, which was said to have supernatural powers. This overt favouritism rankled with other long-serving officials who, in the absence from court of the rest of the companions, conspired to cast a slur on Hang Tuah's reputation by spreading the rumour that he had seduced one of the sultan's consorts. On hearing the accusation, the sultan was so enraged that he ordered the immediate execution of Hang Tuah. But the bendahara, knowing the charge to be false, hid Hang Tuah to repay his debt to him, reporting back to the sultan that the deed had been carried out.

When Hang Jebat returned to the palace, he was shocked to discover Hang Tuah's supposed death and ran amok through Melaka, killing everyone in sight as retribution for the life of his treasured friend. The sultan, in fear of his own life, soon began to regret his decision, at which point the bendahara revealed the truth and Hang Tuah was brought back to protect the sultan from Hang Jebat's fury and to exact justice for the murders committed. Hang Tuah wrestled hard with his conscience before deciding that the sultan had the absolute right to dispose of his subjects how he wished. So, with a heavy heart, Hang Tuah drew his *kris* against Hang Jebat and, after a protracted fight, killed him, a much-recounted tale whose moral – of deference to the sovereign – is seen by some as setting the seal on the Malay system of government.

RM2) on Jalan Kota. Its ground and first floors house exhibits showing the development and successes of Melaka during the last decade – fine if you're into housing policy and the structure of local government. The third floor contains the much more interesting – and at times gruesome – **Museum of Enduring Beauty** (covered by Muzium Rakyat ticket). Taking "endure" in the sense of "to suffer", the exhibits show how people have always sought to alter their appearance, no matter how painful the process might be: head deformation, dental mutilations, tattooing, scarification and foot-binding are just some of the "beautifying" processes on display. For some light relief, the top floor here has a display of **kites** from Malaysia and around the world.

Continuing north along Jalan Kota brings you to the **Islamic Museum** (daily 9am–5pm, Fri closed 12.15–2.45pm; RM2) housed in a renovated Dutch building. Billed as an introduction to Islam and the Muslim way of life, the displays focus on Islamic culture as is practised by ethnic Malays from Sumatra to Mindinao.

Bukit St Paul

If you double back through the Porta de Santiago and climb up the steps behind, past the trinket and picture sellers, you reach **Bukit St Paul**. On the summit stands the roofless shell of **St Paul's Church**, a ruin for almost as long as it was a functioning church. Constructed in 1521 by the Portuguese, who named it "Our Lady of the Mount", the church was visited by the Jesuit missionary **St Francis Xavier** between 1545 and 1552. On his death in 1553

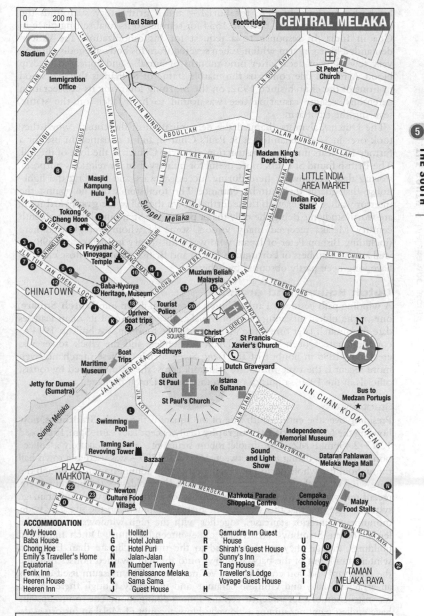

CENTRAL MELAKA

0   200 m

Taxi Stand   Footbridge

Stadium

Immigration Office

St Peter's Church

JLN TAN CHAY YAN

JLN HANG TUA

JALAN MUNSHI ABDULLAH

JALAN MUNSHI ABDULLAH

JLN KUBU

JLN PORTUGIS

JLN MASJID KG HULU

JLN L BARU

JLN KEE ANN

Madam King's Dept. Store

JALAN BUNGA RAYA

JLN BENDARARA

LITTLE INDIA AREA MARKET

Masjid Kampung Hulu

Indian Food Stalls

Tokong Cheng Hoon

J TOKONG

JLN KG JAWA

JLN HANG JEBAT

JLN HANG LEKIR

J HANG LEKIU

JLN TUKANG EMAS

HANG KASTURI

JALAN KG PANTAI

Sungei Melaka

JLN BT CHINA

Sri Poyyatha Vinoyagar Temple

JLN TUN TAN CHENG LOCK

Muzium Beliah Malaysia

J LAKSAMANA

J TEMENGGONG

ORONG HANG JEBAT

CHINATOWN

Baba-Nyonya Heritage, Museum

Tourist Police

JLN BANDA KAYA

J GEREJA

St Francis Xavier's Church

Upriver boat trips

DUTCH SQUARE

Christ Church

N

Boat Trips

Stadthuys

Dutch Graveyard

Maritime Museum

JALAN MERDEKA

Bukit St Paul

Istana Ke Sultanan

JLN CHAN KOON CHENG

Bus to Medzan Portugis

Jetty for Dumai (Sumatra)

JLN KOTA

St Paul's Church

JLN SIANA

Sungai Melaka

Swimming Pool

JALAN PARAMESWARA

Independence Memorial Museum

Taming Sari Revoving Tower

Bazaar

Sound and Light Show

Dataran Pahlawan Melaka Mega Mall

PLAZA MAHKOTA

JLN PM 2

JLN PM 8

JLN PM 3

JLN PM 1

JLN PM 4

Newton Culture Food Village

JALAN MERDEKA

Mahkota Parade Shopping Centre

Cempaka Technology

Malay Food Stalls

JLN TAMAN MELAKA RAYA

MELAKA RAYA

TAMAN MELAKA RAYA

ACCOMMODATION

Aldy Houoo		L	Hollitcl	O	Samudra Inn Quest
Baba House	G	Hotel Johan	R	House
Chong Hoe	C	Hotel Puri	F	Shirah's Guest House	Q
Emily's Traveller's Home	N	Jalan-Jalan	D	Sunny's Inn	S
Equatorial	M	Number Twenty	E	Tang House	B
Fenix Inn	P	Renaissance Melaka	A	Traveller's Lodge	T
Heeren House	K	Sama Sama		Voyage Guest House	I
Heeren Inn	J	Guest House	H		

| | | | | | | U |

EATING & DRINKING

Café 1511	9	Dutch Harbour	15	Limau-Limau Café	11	Riverside Kopitiam	20
Capitol Satay	19	Geographer Café	4	No. 1 Kopitiam	18	Sea Shell	1
Calanthé Art Cafe	13	Harper's		Madras Restoran	16	The Nest	7
Coconut House	3	Honky Tonk Haven Café	14	Nadeje Patisserie	22	The Baboon House	17
D'Arts Café	2	Kocik Kitchen	5	Ole Sayang	24	Tribe Chillout Bar	23
Discovery Café	6	Korean Café "To Be"	8	Peranakan Town House	12	Zheng He Tea House	10
			21				

his body was brought here for burial – and a grisly story surrounds the exhumation of the saint's body in 1554 for transfer to its final resting place in Goa in India. In response to a request for his canonization, the Vatican demanded his right arm which, when severed from his body, allegedly showed very few signs of decay after nine months of burial – and appeared to drip blood. A related tale concerns the marble statue of St Francis that has stood in front of the church since 1952: on the morning following its consecration ceremony, a large casuarina tree was found to have fallen on the statue, severing the right arm.

The Dutch Calvinists changed the denomination of the church when they took over in 1641, renaming it St Paul's Church, and it remained in use for a further 112 years until the construction of Christ Church at the foot of the hill. The British found St Paul's more useful for military than for religious purposes, storing their gunpowder here during successive wars, and building the lighthouse that guards the church's entrance. The tombstones that lie against the interior walls, together with those further down the hill in the **graveyard** itself, are worth studying. Being the only major port in the Straits until the nineteenth century, Melaka received many visitors, some of whom were buried here (including Bishop Peter of Japan, who was a missionary in Melaka in 1598), as well as large numbers of Portuguese, Dutch and British notables, whose epitaphs have long been partly obscured by lichen.

Dutch Square and around

A winding path beside St Paul's Church brings you down into **Dutch Square**, one of the oldest surviving parts of Melaka, although two of its main features date from much later times: the Victorian marble fountain was built in 1904 to commemorate Queen Victoria's Diamond Jubilee, and the clock tower was erected in 1886 in honour of Tan Beng Swee, a rich Chinese merchant. Even more recent is the twee miniature windmill across the road, installed by tourist officials in the 1980s, a quirky nod to the town's Dutch heritage.

Stadthuys

Presiding over the entire south side of the square is the sturdy **Stadthuys**, now housing the **Museum of Ethnography** (daily except Tues 9am–5pm, Fri closed 12.15–2.45pm; RM2). The simple, robust structure – more accurately a collection of buildings dating from between 1660 and 1700 – was used as a town hall throughout the whole period of Dutch and British administration. Although the long wing of warehouses projecting to the east is the oldest of the buildings here, recent renovations have revealed the remains of a Portuguese well and drainage system, suggesting that this was not the first development on the site. The wide, monumental interior staircases, together with the high windows that run the length of the Stadthuys, are typical of seventeenth-century Dutch municipal buildings, though they are less suited to the tropical climate than European winters. Look out of the back windows onto the whitewashed houses that line the courtyard and you could be in a Vermeer scene. The museum itself displays an array of Malay and Chinese ceramics and weaponry, though there's also a reconstruction of a seventeenth-century Dutch dining room. The rooms upstairs have endless paintings giving a blow-by-blow account of Melakan history as do most of the other smaller museums on the hill.

Christ Church and the Dutch Graveyard

Turn to the right as you leave the Stadthuys and you can't miss **Christ Church** (Mon–Sat 8.30am–5pm; free), also facing the fountain. Built in 1753 to commemorate the centenary of the Dutch occupation of Melaka, its simple design, with neither aisles nor chancel, is typically Dutch; its porch and vestry were nineteenth-century afterthoughts. The cool, whitewashed interior has decorative fanlights high up on the walls and elaborate, 200-year-old hand-carved pews, while the roof features heavy timber beams, each cut from a single tree. The plaques on the walls tell a sorry tale of early deaths in epidemics, and a wooden plaque to the rear of the western wall of the church commemorates local planters who were killed in World War II. There is a service in English every Sunday at 8.30am.

East of the church, along Jalan Kota, lies the overgrown **Dutch Graveyard**. This was first used in the late seventeenth century, when the VOC was still in control (hence the name), though British graves easily outnumber those of their predecessors. The tall column towards the centre of the tiny cemetery is a memorial to two of the many officers killed in the Naning War in 1831, a costly attempt to include the nearby Naning region as part of Melaka's territory in the new Straits Settlements.

North to St Peter's Church

Back at Christ Church, head north up Jalan Laksamana, moving quickly past the **Muzium Belia Malaysia** (Museum of Youth; Wed–Sun 9am–5.30pm, closed Fri 12.30–2.45pm; RM2), replete with pictures of smiling, wholesome youths shaking hands with Dr Mahathir, Malaysia's former strongman. Continuing north, the road leads to **St Francis Xavier's Church**, a twin-towered, nineteenth-century, Neo-Gothic structure. Further up from here, skirting the busy junction with Jalan Temenggong and taking Jalan Bendahara directly ahead, you're in the centre of Melaka's tumbledown **Little India**, a rather desultory line of incense and saree shops, interspersed with a few eating houses. After about five minutes' walk, you come to a sizeable crossroads with Jalan Munshi Abdullah, beyond which is **St Peter's Church**, set back from the road on the right. The oldest Roman Catholic church in Malaysia, built by a Dutch convert in 1710 as a gift to the Portuguese Catholics, it has an unusual barrel-vaulted ceiling. The church really comes into its own at Easter as the centre of the Catholic community's celebrations.

The river and docks

The **Maritime Museum** (daily 9am–5pm, Fri–Sun till 8.30pm, closed Fri 12.15–2.45pm; RM3) on the quayside is hard to miss – housed in a towering replica of the Portuguese cargo ship, the *Flor De La Mar*, which sank in Melaka's harbour in the sixteenth century. Inside its hull, lots of model ships and paintings chart Melaka's maritime history from the time of the Malay Sultanate to the arrival of the British in the eighteenth century. Next door, a small exhibition houses some of the recovered items from the wreck of the *Diana*, which sank in the Straits of Melaka while en route to Madras in 1817. Across the road, another section of the museum has a drab display about the Malaysian navy, complete with a gravy boat. The Royal Malaysian Navy patrol craft in the gardens is popular with the kids.

If you feel like a rest from pavement pounding, take one of the **boat trips** up Sungai Melaka. These leave from the small jetty behind the Maritime Museum (hourly 10am–11pm; 45min; RM10). The trip takes you past "Little Amsterdam", the old Dutch quarter of red-roofed godowns, which backs directly onto the water. The boat turns round without stopping at Kampung Morten (see p.352), opposite which, on the east bank, you can just make out a few columns and a crumbling aisle – all that remains of the late-sixteenth-century Portuguese church of **St Lawrence** – poking out from beneath the undergrowth.

Turning the corner on Jalan Quayside into Jalan Merdaka, you can't miss the eighty-metre-tall **Taming Sari Revolving Tower** (daily 10am–11pm; RM20), offering a great (and expensive) 360° view of the city and the sea.

Chinatown

Melaka owed a great deal of its nineteenth-century economic recovery to its Chinese community: it was one Tan Chay Yan who first planted rubber here, and a certain Tan Kim Seng who established a steamer company early on, which later became the basis of the region's great Straits Steam Ship Company. Most of these entrepreneurs settled in what became known as **Chinatown**, across Sungai Melaka from the colonial district. The elegant townhouses that line Jalan Tun Tan Cheng Lock, formerly Heeren Street, are the ancestral homes of the Baba-Nonya community (see box opposite). The wealthiest and most successful of these merchants built long, narrow-fronted houses, and minimized the "window tax" by incorporating several internal courtyards, designed for ventilation and the collection of rainwater. At no. 8, a **shophouse** dating back to the seventeenth century has been lovingly restored and includes an interpretation centre (Tues–Sat 11am–4pm; free).

At nos. 48–50, the **Baba-Nonya Heritage Museum** (daily 10am–12.30pm & 2–4pm; RM8) is an amalgam of three adjacent houses belonging to one family, and an excellent example of the Chinese Palladian style. Typically connected by a common covered footway, decorated with hand-painted tiles, each front entrance has an outer swing door of elaborately carved teak, while a heavier internal door provides extra security at night. Two red lanterns, one bearing the household name, the other messages of good luck, hang either side of the doorway, framed by heavy Greco-Roman columns. But the upper level of the building is the most eye-catching: a canopy of Chinese tiles over the porch frames the shuttered windows, almost Venetian in character, their glass protected by intricate wrought-iron grilles, with eaves and fascias covered in painted floral designs. Inside, the homes are filled with gold-leaf fittings, blackwood furniture inlaid with mother-of-pearl, delicately carved lacquer screens and Victorian chandeliers.

Further up the road, at no. 107, the **Restoran Peranakan Town House** is another former mansion, now a restaurant specializing in Nonya cuisine (see p.354). Beyond, at no. 117, you can't fail to notice the **Chee Ancestral House**, an imperious Dutch building of pale-green stucco topped by a gold dome, and home to one of Melaka's wealthiest families, who made their fortune from tapioca and rubber.

Jalan Hang Jebat – formerly named **Jonkers Street** – runs parallel to Jalan Tun Tan Cheng Lock and is Melaka's antiques centre, worth a wander even if you don't intend to buy. The street is closed to vehicular traffic on Friday and Saturday nights, when you'll find all the shops stay open late and the street is paved with vendors. Most of the antique shops are selling handicrafts these days – much of the stock from Bali – and what few antiques are left are almost insultingly expensive. Crammed between the Chinese temples and shophouses here is the small, whitewashed **tomb of Hang Kasturi**, one of the "Five Companions" (see box, p.346). A short way east up Jalan Tokong is **Tokong Cheng Hoon** (Merciful Cloud Temple), reputed to be the oldest Chinese temple in the country – though several others would dispute the title. Dedicated to the goddess of mercy, the main prayer hall has a heavy saddle roof and oppressive dark-timber beams, reminiscent of the Khoo Kongsi in Georgetown (see p.188). Smaller chambers devoted to ancestor worship are filled with small tablets bearing a photograph of the deceased and strewn with wads of fake money and papier-mâché models of luxury items, symbolizing creature comforts for the dead. The temple authorities here act as the trustees for Bukit China, the ancestral burial ground to the northeast of town.

A little further down the road is the 1748 **Masjid Kampung Kling**, displaying an unusual blend of styles: the minaret looks like a pagoda, there are English and Portuguese glazed tiles, and a Victorian chandelier hangs over a pulpit carved with Hindu and Chinese designs. Next door, the Hindu **Sri Poyyatha Vinayagar Temple** also has a minaret, decorated with red cows and dedicated to the elephant deity and dates back to the 1780s. From the temple, head north for Jalan Kampung Hulu and **Masjid Kampung Hulu**, thought to be the oldest mosque in Malaysia in its original location. Constructed around 1728 in typical Melakan style, it's a solid-looking structure, surmounted by a bell-shaped roof with red Chinese tiles and, again, has more than a hint of pagoda in its minaret. Such architecture has its origins in Sumatra, perhaps brought over by the Minangkabau (see box, p.336) who settled in nearby Negeri Sembilan.

From here, an alternative route back to the centre of town is to walk south down Jalan Kampung Hulu as it follows the river and merges into Jalan Kampung Pantai. At the junction with Jalan Hang Kasturi, a couple of minutes further on, you can pause for a moment at **Hang Jebat's Tomb**, another tiny mausoleum to one of the great warriors of the Malay "golden age".

Masjid Tranquerah

Continuing northwest from the Chee Ancestral House, up Jalan Tengkera, you pass through Melaka's suburbs of picturesque Peranakan mansions and come to the **Masjid Tranquerah**, about 2km from the town centre on the right. A pagoda-like Melakan mosque dating from the eighteenth century, it's where Sultan Hussein, who ceded Singapore to Stamford Raffles in 1819, is

The Baba-Nonyas

Tales of Melaka's burgeoning success brought vast numbers of merchants and entrepreneurs, eager to benefit from the city's status and wealth, to its shores. The Chinese, in particular, came to the Malay Peninsula in droves, to escape Manchu rule – a trend that began in the sixteenth century, but continued well into the nineteenth. Many Chinese married Malay women; descendants of these marriages were known as **Peranakan** or sometimes "Straits-born Chinese". While their European counterparts were content to while away their time until retirement, when they could return home, the expatriate Chinese merchants had no such option, becoming the principal wealth-generators of the thriving city. The **Babas** (male Sino-Malays) were not ashamed to flaunt their new-found prosperity in the lavish townhouses which they appropriated from the Dutch, transforming these homes into veritable palaces filled with Italian marble, mother-of-pearl inlay blackwood furniture, hand-painted tiles and Victorian lamps. The women, known as **Nonyas** (sometimes spelt Nyonya), held sway in the domestic realm and were responsible for Peranakan society's most lasting legacy – its **cuisine**. Taking the best of both Malay and Chinese traditions, its dishes rely heavily on sour sauces and coconut milk; traditionally, its eating etiquette is Malay – using fingers, not chopsticks.

buried. You can also get here on the local bus Patthup, which continues onto Tanjung Kling.

Kampung Morten

The village of **Kampung Morten**, named after the British district officer who donated RM10,000 to buy the land, is a surprising find in the heart of the city. The wooden stilt houses here are distinctively Melakan, with their long, rectangular living rooms and kitchens, and narrow verandas approached by ornamental steps. On the left as you cross the footbridge, the **Villa Sentosa** (daily 9am–6pm, Fri 2–6pm; voluntary donation), with its miniature kampung house and mini-lighthouse, is a 70-year-old family home that now functions as a museum. The warm and welcoming family will gladly show you artefacts and heirlooms handed down by the old patriarch, Tuan Haji Hashim Hadi Abdul Ghani, who died at the age of 98. It's easiest to explore this community on foot: take the footbridge down a small path off Jalan Bunga Raya, one of the principal roads leading north out of town.

The Portuguese Settlement and St John's Fort

The road east of Jalan Taman Melaka Raya leads, after about 3km, to Melaka's **Portuguese Settlement**; turn right into Jalan Albuquerque, clearly signposted off the main road, and you enter its heart. You can also get here on bus #17 from Jalan Merdaka, just outside Jalan Taman Melaka Raya or from the Dutch Square.

In 1933, the colonial administration, prompted by increasing levels of poverty and the depletion of the Portuguese community (which was barely any larger than the two thousand recorded in the first census in 1871), established this village on the historic site of their original community. Today you're likely to recognize the descendants of the original Portuguese settlers only by hearing their language, **Kristao**, a unique blend of Malay and old Portuguese, or by seeing their surnames – Fernandez, Rodriguez and Dominguez all feature as street names.

Medan Portugis (Portuguese Square), at the end of the road, is European to the hilt – you could be forgiven for thinking that this whitewashed edifice, worn by the salty winds, was a remnant from colonial times. Through the archway, the souvenir shop and tourist-oriented restaurants surrounding the central courtyard make it clear that this is a purpose-built "relic", dating only from 1985. That said, the square, cooled by the sea breeze, is a good place for a quiet beer at sunset, and the local restaurateurs make an effort to conjure up a Portuguese atmosphere, though the food is Malay in character. A three-day **fiesta** – the feast of St Pedro – is held in the square, commencing on June 29 every year, with traditional Portuguese food, live music and dancing.

Heading back into town, you can make a brief detour to **St John's Fort** (daily 8am–5pm, closed Fri 12.15–2.45pm; free) up Bukit Senjuang. The fort, a relic of the Dutch occupation with its cannon pointing inland rather than to the sea, offers good views over the town and the Straits of Melaka.

Bukit China

Northeast of the colonial heart of Melaka is **Bukit China**, the ancestral burial ground of the town's Chinese community, indeed the oldest and largest such graveyard outside China. Although Chinese contacts with the Malay Peninsula probably began in the first century BC, it wasn't until the Ming Emperor Yung-Lo sent his envoy Admiral Cheng Ho here in 1409 that commercial relations with Melaka were formally established, according the burgeoning settlement vassal status. At the foot of the hill, at the eastern end of Jalan Temenggong is the **Sam Poh Kong**, a working temple dedicated to Cheng Ho, upon whom the title of "Sam Poh" or "Three Jewels" was conferred in 1431. Accounts of the time are vague about the arrival of the first Chinese settlers, though it's said that on the marriage of Sultan Mansur Shah (1458–77) to the daughter of the emperor, Princess Hang Liu, the five hundred nobles accompanying her stayed to set up home on Bukit China. It was supposedly these early pioneers who dug the well behind the temple; also known as the **Sultan's Well**, it has been of such importance to the local inhabitants as a source of fresh water that successive invading armies all sought to poison it. The Dutch enclosed it in a protective wall, the ruins of which still remain.

At the top of Bukit China, horseshoe-shaped **graves** stretch as far as the eye can see. On the way up, you'll pass one of the oldest graves in the cemetery, belonging to Lee Kup who died in 1688. He was the first Chinese *kapitan*, a mediatory position created by the VOC, which made it possible for them to rule the various ethnic communities. In the 1980s, the burial ground was the subject of a bitter legal battle between its trustees and the civil authorities. Competing plans to develop the area into a cultural and sports centre provoked a claim by the government for a RM2 million bill for rent arrears, stating that the exemption over the previous centuries had been a "clerical error". This outraged the Chinese community, who flatly refused to pay. The controversy was only settled in the early 1990s when the decision was made to develop Melaka's waterfront area instead. Today, Bukit China is more an inner-city park than burial ground, where you're likely to encounter locals jogging, practising martial arts or simply admiring the view.

Eating and drinking

Melaka is an excellent place to dine unhurriedly on Nonya, Chinese, Malay, Indian and Western food. The best place for this is **Chinatown**, where new and established restaurants, bars and cafés compete for the hungry tourists and locals. **Taman Melaka Raya** is fast catching up; it is generally cheaper and some places stay open until well into the night. Budget meals are not as common as elsewhere in Malaysia – even the city's principal **food stalls** on Jalan Merdeka aren't particularly cheap; *Newton Culture Food Village* is pricier than elsewhere, but the food is good. Don't miss sampling **Nonya cuisine** at some stage during your stay; the emphasis is on spicy dishes, using sour herbs like tamarind, tempered by sweeter, creamy coconut milk.

Usual restaurant **opening hours** are daily 9am to 11pm, unless otherwise stated; phone numbers are given where it's necessary to book (usually only on Sat nights).

Cafés and restaurants

Café 1511 52 Jalan Tun Tan Cheng Lock. Reasonably priced snacks and mains for the address – with breakfasts at RM5 as well as curries, Western dishes and Nonya delicacies. Try the *pai tee*, little top hats made of rice flour filled with turnip, omelette and shallots and dipped in chili sauce. Free internet for 15min.

Calanthé Art Cafe 11 Jalan Hang Kasturi. Themed to represent the thirteen states of Malaysia, this art and coffee house serves a myriad coffees and teas and has a jewellery shop next door selling handmade accessories. The menu has daily specials, good *laksa* and a few Western dishes.

Capitol Satay Lorong Bukit China. Experience the Melaka version of fondue – *satay celup* – at this lively café, where you take your pick of assorted fish, meat and vegetables skewered on sticks and cook them in a spicy peanut sauce before eating. Each stick is around 70 sen; you'd be hard pressed to spend more than RM10 per person. Daily 7pm–midnight.

Coconut House 128 Jalan Tun Tan Cheng Lock. Art gallery, bookshop, art-film venue and woodfire pizzeria, all in a tastefully renovated Chinese townhouse. Mid-range prices, good atmosphere and great salads and pizzas amongst other, pricier dishes.

Discovery Café 3 Jalan Bunga Raya. Traveller-oriented café-bar with inexpensive local and Western cuisine, live music almost every night, internet and a library.

Dutch Harbour 39 Jalan Laksamana. With riverside tables and a nicely appointed restaurant, this place serves Dutch specialities, cheesecake and pizza (RM22). It's a good place for a quiet evening beer. There is free wi-fi, open 9am–midnight.

Geographer Café 83 Jalan Hang Jebat. This airy prewar shophouse on a busy corner in Chinatown is a good place to have a drink, meet fellow travellers and watch the world go by. The food is reliable and the service friendly. Curries from RM10.

Harper's 2 Lorong Jang Jebat. Upmarket and with a riverside location to die for, this place does fusion cuisine, predominately Western and with a wine list to match. The combo "tasters" are between RM40 and RM50 and give you a taste of four or five dishes from the main menu with a selection to satisfy every tastebud.

Honky Tonk Haven Café 68 Lorong Hang Jebat. One of the first bars on the Chinatown side with riverside tables and low-volume music. It opens in the afternoon and has reasonably priced local dishes, promotions on beers and decent house wine.

Kocik Kitchen 100 Jalan Tun Tan Cheng Lock. Not as atmospheric as *Café 1511*, but with similar dishes and prices on the menu – the Nonya *laksa* is excellent. Closed Mon.

🏃 **Korean Café "To Be"** 58 Jalan Tun Tan Cheng Lock. Each meal comes with an assortment of delicious Korean pickles and delicacies. The Korean omelettes are very tasty and the Kimchi Stew Pot has a good, spicy kick to it. You can enjoy a beer or one of their healthy teas (including red ginseng), while fish nibble your feet in a lovely courtyard with seating around a fish spa.

Limau-Limau Café 49 Jalan Hang Jebat. This is the place to come for fresh fruit juices, *lassis* and milk shakes; the coffee and banana one is particularly good. Fresh sandwiches, ciabattas and foccacia are also on the menu.

🏃 **Nadeje Patisserie** G23 Jalan PM4, Plaza Mahkota. See map, p.339. The best (western) coffee and cakes in town. Try their famous *mille crêpe* – layers of fine crepe alternated with fresh cream; there are four different variations, though the original is hard to improve on.

No. 1 Kopitiam 1 Jalan Hang Jebat. This is the place to go for *Nonya cendol*, a dessert prepared before your eyes using coconut milk, palm sugar syrup, fine short strings of green-bean flour dough

and topped with lots of shaved ice. There is usually a queue, but it moves quickly. Inside the *Kopitiam* is an Aladdin's cave of knick-knacks, antiques and random memorabilia.

🏃 **Madras Restoran** Corner of Lorong Bukit China and Jalan Temenggong. It may not look like much from the outside, but the rotis, in particular the *roti murtabak* or *roti pisang* are to die for and will cost you next to nothing. Most curries are potent with spice, except the dhal, which is deliciously delicate.

Ole Sayang 198–199 Jalan Taman Melaka Raya ☎06/283 4384. See map, p.339. A moderately priced Nonya restaurant with re-created Peranakan decor. Try the beef *goreng lada*, in a rich soya-based sauce, or the *ayam lemak pulut*, a spicy, creamy chicken dish (around RM15 each). Daily 11.30am–9.30pm.

Peranakan Town House 107 Jalan Tun Tan Cheng Lock ☎06/284 5001. Marble tables with white-lace tablecloths, and a reasonably priced Nonya menu in a picture-book Chinatown setting; try the hot *rendang* dishes or claypot *ayam*. Dishes average around RM18. Daily 11am–9pm.

Riverside Kopitiam 17 Jalan Laksamana. Predominately visited by travellers and tourists reading their guidebooks or playing cards on the riverside terrace, this café-bar has daily specials, the usual rice and noodles dishes and some Western food, including breakfasts.

Sea Shell Jalan Bunga Raya. Down a small alley next to Mama King's Department Store, these two hawker stalls specialize in shellfish and people flock from all over the area to sample it. Point at what you want and they'll cook it for you there and then.

The Baboon House 89 Jalan Tun Tan Cheng Lock. Arts and crafts shop with a courtyard café inside serving cheap local food, soft drinks and beers from a young and friendly crew. Open 9am–7pm.

The Nest 129 Jalan Tun Tan Cheng Lock. Right next to the *Baba House*, this place has loud music and beer promotions. Open 6pm–1am serving rice and noodle dishes in a beer garden just off the street.

🏃 **Zheng He Tea House** 17 Jalan Tukang Besi. Old residency of Melaka's second Chinese Kapitan, Li Jin Chang, and over 350 years old, this glorious house and museum (the latter not fully operational at the time of writing) is the place to come for a traditional Chinese tea ritual. Ms Pak, the friendly manager, will tell you anything you want to know about Melaka. The teas range from RM15 to RM30 for up to five people and you can bring snacks with you, but there is no restaurant. There's a "secret" entry on Jalan Hang Jebat through a long hallway of moneyplant creepers.

Nightlife and entertainment

Nightlife in Melaka is no great shakes; most places tend to shut at around 1am. Around **Chinatown**, the liveliest street is Jalan Hang Lekir with cafés and bars spilling into the street and more places opening up along the riverfront. Around **Taman Melaka Raya** there's no shortage of karaoke bars (usually 8pm–2am), though these are not recommended, due to their often seedy character. For the uber-chic, the *Tribe Chillout Bar* (see map, p.339)on the first floor of Jalan PM4, Plaza Mahkota has plush seating, chilled house music, cocktails and snacks – entertaining the pretty Chinese arts crowd. It's essential to book a table (℡012/601 3492; Tues–Sun 8pm–2am) and you need to press the door buzzer to get in. If you're aching to watch sports, *D'Arts Café* on 121 Jalan Hang Jebat has several large screens. Though it lacks atmosphere, the service is friendly.

Mahkota Parade includes a 24-lane bowling alley, an amusement arcade and a three-screen Cineplex; the **Dataran Pahlawan Melaka Megamall** has a cinema on the top floor as well as state of the art amusement games. Otherwise the only source of entertainment is the nightly **Sound and Light Show** on Padang Pahlawan. A must for fans of high drama, it drags a bit at an hour in length, but provides a one-stop introduction to the city's history. Shows are in English (daily 8.30pm; RM10) and you can buy tickets from the booths at each end of the padang.

Shopping

Melaka is famed for its **antiques**, but these days you'll find cheaper Asian antiques anywhere but in Asia. Among the handicraft outlets along Jalan Hang Jebat and Jalan Tun Tan Cheng Lock, you will find a handful of antiques – mostly Chinese – but the prices are nothing short of heartbreaking. If the item you're thinking of buying is a genuine antique (most shops fill their windows with colourful but inauthentic clutter), check that it can be exported legally and fill in an official clearance form; the dealer should provide you with this. Jalan Bunga Raya and Jalan Munshi Abdullah comprise the modern shopping centre, where you'll find a variety of Western and local goods.

Jehan Chan Art Gallery 10 Jalan Tun Tan Cheng Lock ℡06/286 1615. Jehan Chan, a former teacher, has achieved considerable fame nationally for his paintings in watercolour and oil. They can be viewed and purchased at his small gallery.

Joe's Design 6 Jalan Tun Tan Cheng Lock. Handmade artisan jewellery with one-of-a-kind designs.

Koo Fatt Hong 92 Jalan Tun Tan Cheng Lock. Specialists in "Asia Spiritual and Buddha images" – various deities carved in stone and wood.

Orang Utan 59 Lorong Hang Jebat. Here, local artist Charles Chan sells his paintings, and T-shirts printed with witty cartoons and sayings.

Ringo 12 Jalan Hang Jebat. British bikes and old biker artefacts, as well as unusual toys; pricey.

Tribal Arts Gallery 10 Jalan Hang Jebat. Specialists in Sarawakian crafts, including woodwork and weaving.

Wah Aik 103 Jalan Kubu. Renowned for making silk shoes for bound feet. With foot binding no longer practised, the shoes are now lined up in the window as souvenirs, at a mere RM75 per pair.

Listings

Banks and exchange Bank Bumiputra, Jalan Melaka Raya; Hong Kong Bank & Maybank, Jalan Hang Tuah. Often more convenient, with rates as good as the banks', are the moneychangers, including Malaccan Souvenir House and Trading, 22 Jalan Tokong; and SPAK, 31 Jalan Laksamana.

Bookshops MPH, on the ground floor of Mahkota Parade, has an excellent range of books, as does Tai Khuang upstairs on the second level.

Car rental Annah Car Rental, 27 Jalan Laksamana ℡06/283 5626; Hawk, Jalan Laksamana ℡06/283 7878.

Cinema The UBO in Mahkota Parade shows English-language films as does the Cineplex above the Carrefour; check in the newspapers for what's on when.

Hospital The Malacca Hospital is in the north of town on Jalan Mufti Hj Khalil (☎06/282 2344). The Budra Hospital is nearer the centre of town at 169 Jalan Bendahara (☎06/283 5888). The well-equipped Mahkota Medical Centre is at 3 Mahkota Melaka, Jalan Merdeka (☎06/281 3333).

Internet access There are plenty of places around town to get online, usually costing around RM3 per hr. Try the *Discovery Café* (see p.354), the *Fenix Hotel* (see p.343) or the east end of Jalan Merdeka.

Police The Tourist Police office (☎06/282 2222) on Jalan Laksamana is open 24hr.

Post office The GPO is inconveniently situated on the way to Ayer Keroh on Jalan Bukit Baru – take town bus #19 from Melaka Sentral. There is also a smaller branch on Jalan Laksamana by the Muzium Belia Malaysia.

Sport The Merlin Melaka sports centre on Jalan Munshi Abdullah offers ten-pin bowling, snooker, squash and roller-skating. There's a public swimming pool on Jalan Kota (daily 10am–1pm, 2–4.15pm & 6–8pm; RM5).

Telephones The Telekom building is on Jalan Kota (daily 8am–5pm). The quietest and most efficient place to make international calls, though, is the Cempaka Technology Shop at 155 Jalan Taman Melaka Raya.

Travel agents Try Atlas Travel at 5 Jalan Hang Jebat (☎06/282 0777) for plane tickets (nearest working airports being KL, JB or Singapore).

Visa extensions Visas can be extended on the spot at the immigration office on the second floor of the Wisma Persekutuan, Jalan Hang Tuah (☎06/282 4958).

Around Melaka

While there's more than enough to keep you occupied in Melaka itself, you may well fancy a break from sightseeing for more relaxed pleasures. Some 20km up the coastline is the tranquil coastal village of **Padang Kemunting**, a hatching site for the hawksbill turtle during the months of April to September, with a passable beach. The nearby town of **Ayer Keroh** is also a popular local

Moving on from Melaka

By air
The airport was, at the time of writing, undergoing renovation and is due to reopen in 2010 with some international flights as well as domestic, including AirAsia. There are six direct buses daily to KLIA/LCCT (2am–7.15pm; 2hr–2hr20 min; RM36) with A-Bus Tours and Travel at 125 Jalan SP1, Taman Semabok Perdana (☎06/281 7669). The office is 2km from Melaka Sentral and they can organize transport to get you there.

By bus
There are frequent departures from the Melaka Sentral express bus station to KL, Ipoh, Butterworth, Alor Star, Mersing, Singapore and other points on the Peninsula. There's rarely any need to book in advance unless in high season: just turn up before departure and buy a ticket from one of the booths at the bus station.

By ferry
There is one service daily to Dumai in Sumatra at 9am (RM119 one way) and one for Pekan baru on Tuesdays, Thursdays and Saturdays at 10am (RM159 one way); for tickets and information contact Tunas Rupat at 17a Jalan Merdeka (☎06/283 2506). The Shah Bandar jetty is by Jalan Quayside within easy walking distance of the historical centre, Chinatown and Taman Melaka Raya.

By train
From Tampin train station, 38km to the north of town (☎06/341 1034), there are three daily train services to Singapore via JB. There are regular buses between Tampin (40min) and Melaka Sentral; a taxi from there is RM50.

excursion, with recreation parks, tame wildlife and frequent cultural displays. Finally, the nearby island **Pulau Besar**, seen as a holy place by many locals, provides an opportunity to feel some sand between your toes – the sea is fairly polluted though.

Padang Kemunting Turtle Sanctuary

One of the last nesting areas of the hawksbill turtle and the painted terrapin in south Malaysia, Padang Kemunting is 24km up the coast from Melaka. Follow Coastal Road 5 through Tanjung Kling and a further 7km, turn left onto Route 143 and continue 6km until you reach the coast. Turning left on the small road following the coast line will take you to the Padang Kemunting Turtle Management Centre (℡06/384 6754; Tues–Sun 10am–4pm; free). By bus, Patthup #47 goes to Masjid Tanah, 8km inland, from where you will have to get a taxi. A taxi from Melaka Sentral costs RM50.

Though the **turtle sanctuary** itself is not worth a visit outside the hatchling months of April to September, it's a friendly place with lots of information, including an introductory video about the turtle population of Melaka. There are a few places to stay and the best is the Muslim *Ismah Beach Resort* (℡06/384 8141, ⓦwww.ismahresort.com; ❺), which has its own restaurant, and is just next door to the sanctuary. If the turtles appear at night, the sanctuary will contact you where you are staying. There are several seafood restaurants along the shore and a couple of convenience stores, but apart from the cars and motorbikes, there is not much going on in this friendly kampung.

Ayer Keroh

Fourteen kilometres north of Melaka city centre is **AYER KEROH** – which, despite its position adjacent to the North–South Expressway, is a leafy recreational area with lots of entertainment. Town buses #19 and #105 run here every thirty minutes from Melaka Sentral, from where a taxi costs RM25.

The major attractions are all within a few hundred metres or so of one another. Apart from the **Hutan Rekreasi** (daily 7am–6pm; free), an area of woodland set aside for walking and picnicking, all the attractions – the **Taman Buaya** (Crocodile Park; Mon–Fri 9am–5pm, Sat & Sun 9.30am–7pm; RM10); the **Melaka Zoo** (Mon–Fri 9am–5pm, Sat & Sun 9.30am–6.30pm, RM8; evening daily 8–11pm, RM10), purportedly the oldest and second largest in the country; and the **Taman Rama Rama** (Butterfly Park; daily 8.30am–5.30pm; RM8), with its walk-through aviary and small marine centre – are somewhat contrived. The only thing that demands more than fleeting attention is the **Taman Mini Malaysia** and **Mini ASEAN** (℡06/232 0422; daily 9am–8pm; RM10), a large park fifteen minutes' walk north of the Crocodile Park, with full-sized reconstructions of typical houses from all thirteen Malay states and the other members of the Association of Southeast Asian Nations, an economic alliance of the region's states. The specially constructed timber buildings are frequently used as sets for Malaysian films and soap operas, and cultural shows featuring local music and dance are staged at the park's open-air arena – ask at the ticket office for details.

The area around the lake, just off the main road, is where you'll find most of the **places to stay**, limited exclusively to upmarket resort accommodation. The best of the bunch is the *INB Resort* (℡06/553 3023, Ⓕ 553 3022; ❺–❻), with comfortable chalet-style accommodation and a swimming pool. Nearby, *D'Village Resort* (℡06/232 8000; ❺) is the least attractive option, with blue-roofed chalets crammed together, though it does have the cheapest rooms with off-season promotions on advance bookings. **Places to eat** are more or less limited to those in the resorts, save for a few tourist-oriented food stalls at the main attractions.

Pulau Besar

Long before it was turned into a failed exclusive beach resort, **PULAU BESAR** (literally "Big Island", though it covers just sixteen square kilometres), about 5km off the coast of Melaka, was known as the burial ground of passing Muslim traders and missionaries, tales of whom live on in distorted local legends; the island is considered mystical, if not spooky in character. Although its historic sites consist of little more than a few ancient graves, several wells and remnants of the Japanese occupation, locals see the island as a holy place and visitors are asked to behave accordingly. Though the island's beaches and hilly scenery are pleasant enough, the waters are still fairly polluted and Western-style sunbathing is frowned upon. Note that at the time of writing, reports were out that Pulau Besar was set to become the country's largest independent oil storage terminal by 2010.

Pulau Besar is easily reached by **ferry**, departing from the Anjung Batu jetty in Melaka (six daily starting 8.30am, last boat back 6.30pm; RM12 one way). You can also get there by fishing boat from the **Pengkalan Pernu jetty** in Umbai (on request; RM80 one way for up to eight people), 6km southeast of Melaka. Inconveniently, there are no direct buses to the jetties and a taxi costs RM25–30 each way. The only available **accommodation** on the island is the campsite (☎06/281 8007, ⓕ281 5941; RM20 per person including tent rental), next to a resort now only used for conventions. As for **eating**, there are a couple of local *kedai kopis* serving rice and noodle dishes.

From Melaka to Johor Bahru

The journey from Melaka southeast along **Route 5** to Johor Bahru covers a distance of 206km, the first 45km of which – to the Malay town of **Muar** – is through verdant countryside dotted with neatly kept timber stilt houses with double roofs. These houses, in some of the prettiest kampungs in Malaysia, are especially numerous along Route 5 and worth a stop if you have time. One of the best is the striking **Penghulu's House**; heading south, you find it to your right, just off the main road 2km south of the village of **Merlimau**. The house, built in 1894 for a local chieftain, has elaborate woodcarvings adorning the veranda and eaves, and the front steps are covered in colourful Art Nouveau hand-painted tiles. It's still inhabited by the chieftain's descendants, who will show you around for a voluntary donation (RM5). Further south, the towns of **Batu Pahat** and **Pontian Kecil** are of scant interest (the former, slightly inland, has a reputation as a red-light resort for Singaporeans). If you do want to stop anywhere else before Johor Bahru and Singapore, aim for **Kukup**, right at the southern end of the west coast, and terrific for seafood, whilst the view from mainland Asia's southernmost point at **Tanjung Piai** of the dense horizon of freight liners and oil tankers is a startling sight.

To get to Johor Bahru in a hurry, skip the scenery of Route 5 and use the North–South Expressway instead. From Melaka, you can head north to the expressway via Ayer Keroh; it's also straightforward to join the expressway from Muar (take the Bukit Pasir road for about 20km) and Batu Pahat (take Route 50 northeast off Route 5). On **public transport**, hourly express buses from Melaka (RM12) and Muar (RM6) are faster than the convoluted train journey south from Tampin.

Muar

The old port town of **MUAR** – also known as Bandar Maharani – is a calm and elegant town that attracts few tourists, perhaps because of its lack of any budget accommodation. Legend has it that Paramesvara, the fifteenth-century founder of Melaka, fled here from Singapore to establish his kingdom on the southern bank of Sungai Muar, before being persuaded to choose Melaka. Although rejected by the Sumatran prince, Muar later became an important port in the Johor empire (see p.361), as well as a centre for **ghazal music** (see p.727) and the place whose **dialect** is considered the purest Bahasa Malaysia in the Peninsula.

Today, Muar's commercial centre looks like any other, with Chinese shophouses and *kedai kopis* lining its parallel streets, Jalan Maharani, Jalan Abdullah and Jalan Meriam. But if you turn right out of the **bus station** on Jalan Maharani, following the river as the road turns into Jalan Petri, you'll see an altogether different part of town. Under the shade of huge rain trees, Muar's **Neoclassical colonial buildings** – the Custom House and Government Offices (Bangunan Sultan Abu Bakar) on your right, and the District Police Office and Courthouse on your left – still have an air of confidence and prosperity from the town's days as a British administrative centre. The graceful **Masjid Jamek Sultan Ibrahim**, completed in 1930, successfully combines Western and Moorish styles of architecture, in a design that was duplicated for the Masjid Jamek Kedua, built in 1999 on the opposite bank of the Sungai Muar. Further along Jalan Petri you'll pass a jetty on your right, from where irregular **river cruises** depart.

Practicalities

Bus #2 runs frequently here from Melaka's Sentral and most JB bound express buses will stop here, too. The local bus takes about 90 minutes, whilst the express bus takes about an hour to arrive in Muar at the **bus station** on Jalan Maharani. There is a distinct lack of decent **hotels** in town, but the reliable *Townview Hotel*, 60 Jalan Sisi (⏀06/951 1788; ❹) has comfortable rooms with air-conditioned and their own bathrooms. A little further down the street, on the corner with Jalan Meriam is the somewhat grubby *Hotel Kingdom*, 158 Jalan Meriam (⏀06/952 1921; ❷), the cheapest place in town. Aside from **eating** houses in the commercial centre of town, none of which can be particularly recommended, the *Medan Selera* near the bridge on Jalan Maharani serves Malay snacks, while the *Classic Hotel* has a good ground-floor restaurant with great Chinese food – to get there, head down Jalan Sulaiman, which leads away from the river from a point about 100m southwest of the bridge, and turn left into Jalan Ali.

Batu Pahat and Pontian Kecil

Continuing south, Route 5 hugs the palm-fringed coast as far as **BATU PAHAT** (also called Bandar Penggaram), where the Art Deco **Masjid Jamek** and Straits Chinese **Chamber of Commerce** are the only buildings of note. The town has a reputation as a venue for "dirty weekends", though a more noteworthy association is with a couple of important political events. The governing party, UMNO, initially a coalition of organizations opposed to the British-inspired Malayan Union, had its origins here in 1946. Years later, during the constitutional crisis of 1983, Prime Minister Dr Mahathir purposefully held a mass rally in the town to protest against the position taken by the sultans, urging the people to assert their constitutional rights and elect him, whilst reminding the rulers of how they were marginalized during the ill-fated Malayan Union many years before (see p.696).

Batu Pahat is a convenient point at which to cut across to the **east coast**: Route 50 links the town with Mersing, 140km away, and there are bus connections to all the major destinations on the peninsula, including Singapore (not directly to Mersing – you will have to go via Keluang). The next place of any consequence is the unassuming town of **PONTIAN KECIL**, 70km southeast of Batu Pahat. It's low on sights other than the fishing boats on the river and a lacklustre market, but *Hotel Kim Mah* 726 Jalan Taib (☎07/687 9907; ❷) can put you up if you get stuck. There are regular **bus** services from the bus station to JB (RM3.30; 1hr).

Kukup

The signs flanking the roadside at **KUKUP** feature giant king prawns waving their tentacles – in eager expectation, no doubt, at the money you're about to part with. This small fishing community, just 19km south along Route 5 from Pontian Kecil, has opened its doors to the Singapore package-tour trade, whose clients come to see the ancient, stilt houses built over the murky river and to sample Kukup's real attraction, the **seafood**: the town's single tumbledown street is packed with restaurants..

Kukup is a little-known exit point from Malaysia to Tanjung Balai in **Indonesia**, a 45-minute ferry ride from the jetty (daily except Fri; regular boats between 8.30am & 5.30pm; RM60 one way). The problem with **arriving** in Kukup from Indonesia is that onward travel connections are sketchy – you'll have to catch a taxi from Kukup to Pontian Kecil and then catch a bus on from there.

Practicalities

There's a **local bus** from Pontian Kecil to Kukup (hourly between 6am & 10pm; RM3); a **taxi** costs RM25. There are at least a dozen **places to eat** on the town's small street; a popular place is the enormous *Makanan Laut*, closest to the jetty, where you can sit on the large wooden waterfront deck and watch the fishermen and tourists floating around on the river. Immediately opposite is the more modest *Restoran Zaiton Hussin*, where the emphasis is on Malay rather than Chinese-style seafood. The influx of visitors has pushed prices up; expect to pay RM22 for fish, RM15 for prawns and RM12 for mussels.

A kilometre back towards Pontian Kecil from Kukup, you'll see a turn-off for **Tanjung Piai**. A gradually narrowing road through lush tropical fruit plantations takes you to the "southernmost tip of the mainland Asia continent" as the advertising for the *Tanjung Piai Resort* (☎&☎07/696 9000; ❸–❹) puts it. This string of large wooden bungalows and rooms, on concrete stilts at the edge of the mangrove swamps and connected by causeways, commands a dramatic vista of the ships coming to and from Singapore, clearly visible on the horizon; there's also a seafood restaurant, though the place generally is in need of repair.

Johor Bahru

The southernmost Malaysian city of any size, **JOHOR BAHRU** – or simply **JB** – is the main gateway into **Singapore**, linked to the city-state by a 1056-metre **causeway** carrying a road, a railway, and the pipes through which Singapore imports its fresh water. Around sixty thousand vehicles a day travel across the causeway (the newer **second crossing** from Geylang Patah, 20km west of JB, to Tuas in Singapore is much less used because of its tolls), and the ensuing traffic, noise and smog affects most of downtown Johor Bahru. Despite the lack of sights, JB does have the air of both a border town and a boomtown. This is where all of Singapore comes to shop for cheap everything, from shark's fin soup to sex. The past half-decade saw a burst of construction that begat huge indoor malls – keeping the unending stream of visitors from Singapore busy, and ensuring an impressive amount of food is on offer (the night food market is particularly worth a visit). By far the vast majority of visitors to the city are day-trippers and Johor Bahru's nightlife is aimed at Singaporean men, whose appetite for liquor, hostesses and karaoke is more than adequately provided for. Development plans for the region, known as Iskandar Malaysia, are taking form with the aim to rival neighbouring Singapore in terms of industry and tourism.

Besides the commercial scene, Johor Bahru's only real attraction is the royal **Istana Besar**; but for most, the city is merely a hurdle to jump on the way to the North–South Expressway and the more noteworthy sights of Melaka and Kuala Lumpur.

Some history

Historically, JB stands with Melaka as one of the most important sites in the country. Chased out of its seat of power by the Portuguese in 1511, the Melakan court decamped to the Riau Archipelago, south of modern-day Singapore, before upping sticks again in the 1530s and shifting to the upper reaches of the Johor River, followed by a century of offensives by both the Portuguese and the Acehnese of northern Sumatra. Stability was finally achieved by courting the friendship of the Dutch in the 1640s; the rest of the seventeenth century saw the kingdom of Johor blossom into a thriving trading **entrepôt**. By the end of the century, though, the rule of the tyrannical Sultan Mahmud had halted Johor's pre-eminence among the Malay kingdoms, and piracy was causing a decline in trade. In 1699, Sultan Mahmud was killed by his own nobles and, with the Melaka-Johor dynasty finally over, successive power struggles crippled the kingdom.

Immigration of the Bugis peoples to Johor eventually eclipsed the power of the sultans (see p.691), and though the Bugis were finally chased out by the Dutch in 1784, the kingdom was a shadow of its former self. The Johor-Riau empire – and the Malay world – was split in two, with the Melaka Straits forming the dividing line following the Anglo-Dutch Treaty of 1824. As links with the court in Riau faded, Sultan Ibrahim assumed power, amassing a fortune based upon hefty profits culled from plantations in Johor. The process was continued by his son Abu Bakar, named Sultan of Johor in 1885 and widely regarded as the father of modern Johor; it was he who, in 1866, named the new port across the Johor Straits Johor Bahru, or "New Johor".

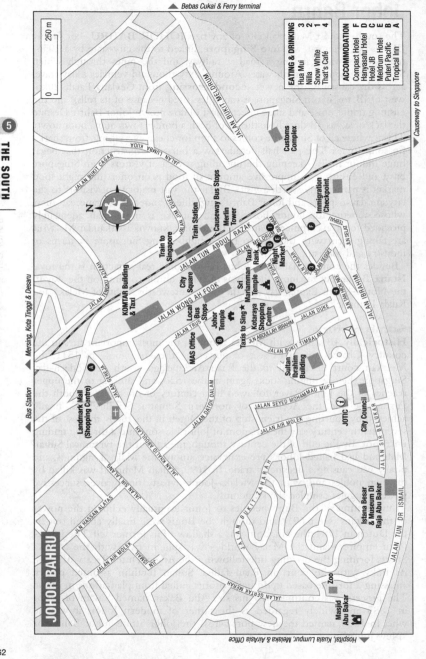

▲ Bebas Cukai & Ferry terminal

Causeway to Singapore ▶

▲ Hospital, Kuala Lumpur, Melaka & AirAsia Office

JOHOR BAHRU

EATING & DRINKING
Hua Mui   3
Nilla   2
Snow White   1
That's Café   4

ACCOMMODATION
Compact Hotel   F
Hanyasittu Hotel D
Hotel JB   C
Meldrum Hotel   E
Puteri Pacific   B
Tropical Inn   A

Customs
Complex

Immigration
Checkpoint

Causeway Bus Stops

Merlin
Tower

Train Station

Train to
Singapore

Night
Market

Taxi
Rank

City
Square

KOMTAR
Building
& Taxi

Sri
Mariamman
Temple

Local
Bus
Stops

Johor
Temple

Kotaraya
Shopping
Centre

MAS Office

Taxis to Sing ★

Sultan
Ibrahim
Building

Landmark
Mall
(Shopping Centre)

JOTIC

City Council

Istana Besar
& Museum Di
Raja Abu Baker

Masjid
Abu Bakar

Zoo

JALAN BUKIT MELDRUM

JALAN LUMBA KUDA

JALAN BUKIT CAGAR

JALAN JIM DUFF

JALAN TUN ABDUL RAZAK

JALAN MELDRUM

JALAN PASAR

UNGKU PUAN

JALAN SEGGET

JALAN WONG AH FOOK

JLN ABDULLAH IBRAHIM

JALAN DUKE

JALAN IBRAHIM

JALAN TRUS

JALAN BUKIT TIMBALAN

JALAN DATO DALAM

JALAN SISILAID ABDULLAH

JALAN SEYED MOHAMMAD MUFTI

JALAN AIR MOLEK

JALAN SIR BELUKAR

JALAN BUKIT ZAHARAH

JLN TUN ABU BAKAR

JALAN TENGKU PATALH

JLN ISMAIL

JALAN AIR MOLEK

JLN HASSAN ALATAS

JLN SIR LALANG

JALAN GERTAK MERAH

JALAN TUN DR ISMAIL

▲ Bus Station   ▲ Mersing, Kota Tinggi & Desaru

N

0   250 m

Arrival and information

The Larkin **bus station** is on Jalan Gcruda, 3km north from the centre of JB; the **train station** is to the east of the city centre, off Jalan Tun Abdul Razak. Flights to JB land at **Senai airport**, 28km north of the city, from where a regular bus service (RM4) runs to the bus station; alternatively, you can get a taxi to the city for about RM45. Heading out to the airport, there's a shuttle bus (RM8) from outside the Kotaraya Shopping Centre. The MAS office is directly opposite the *Puteri Pacific Hotel* on Jalan Abdullah Ibrahim (℡07/219 9999). AirAsia has an office (℡03/2171 9333 – central reservations) on Jalan Skudai in the Danga Festive Street Mall a few kilometres northwest of the centre. **Ferries** from Tanjung Pinang and Pulau Batam in Indonesia arrive at the terminal in the Bebas Cukai shopping centre, 2km east of the causeway; tickets for these services can be booked directly through the ferry company Tenggara Senandung (℡07/221 1677).

The main **tourist office** (JOTIC; Mon–Fri 8am–5pm; ℡07/222 3590, ⓦwww.tourismmalaysia.gov.my) is on Jalan Air Molek, above the TGI Fridays. There are moneychangers in the main shopping centres, or try Maybank, 11 Jalan Selat Tebrau; or OCBC, Jalan Ibrahim. A brace of ATMs can be found on the south side of the Merlin Tower. **Internet** access is available at many places along Jalan Meldrum and the internet terminals in the *Hanyasatu Hotel* are open 24 hour. You can **rent a car** by contacting either Avis at the *Tropical Inn* (℡07/224 4824), or Hertz at JOTIC, Jalan Ayer Molek (℡07/223 7570).

Accommodation

JB's manufacturing boom means the city attracts more businessmen than tourists, so **hotel** prices tend to be a little higher than elsewhere in mainland Malaysia. Moreover, since the city's nightlife continues to appeal to Singaporeans, some of its budget hotels double as brothels. The majority of JB's lower-priced hotels are on or around Jalan Meldrum, right in the centre of town, but most of them are extremely unappealing, so staying overnight in JB means paying a little more.

Compact Hotel 18 Jalan Wong Ah Fook ℡07/221 3000, ⓦwww.compacthotel.com.my. Stylish, although a little dated, hotel – all wooden floors, soft lighting and designer furniture – whose higher floors command good views across JB and Singapore. The rates include breakfast, but you can get a cheaper rate if you eat elsewhere in the morning. ❺

Hanyasatu Hotel 29 Jalan Meldrum ℡07/ 221 1118, ℮hotelhanya1@yahoo .com. In the lower end of this price range, this hotel has nicely appointed rooms with a/c and great bathrooms. Many rooms don't have windows as the building is not on a corner, so make sure you ask if you want one. ❹

Hotel JB 80a Jalan Wong Ah Fook ℡07/224 6625, ℮hoteljb8@gmail.com. Clean, and right in the hustle and bustle of the night market, this place could do with sprucing up its bathrooms and losing the musty smell, but the sheets are crisp and the rooms come with hot (own) showers and a/c. ❹

Meldrum Hotel 1 Jalan Sui Nam ℡07/ 227 8988. This mid-range hotel has been a reliable and well-run place in JB for years. All rooms have a/c, bathrooms and TV. Rather than a dorm, there are "double decker" beds for RM33 per bed and the room sleeps eight people in total. ❹

Puteri Pan Pacific Jalan Abdullah Ibrahim, ℡07/219 9999, ⓦwww.puteripacific.com. Central JB's most opulent address, with five hundred sumptuous rooms including huge corner suites, and five restaurants. Prices halve during the seemingly random promotions. ❼

Tropical Inn 15 Jalan Gereja ℡07/224 7888, ℮reservation@tropicalinn.com.my. Friendly hotel a 2min walk north from the train station, this is the best choice in this category with a couple of decent cafés, great views from the top floors, wi-fi and free parking. Breakfast is included. ❺

The City

JB is a sprawling city, with most places of interest located close to the causeway. Downtown JB is both scruffy and modern, a fact born out by a stroll through the claustrophobic alleys of the sprawling market, where machetes, silk and "one-thousand-year-old eggs" (actually preserved for a year in lime, ash and tea leaves) are sold and then, a few paces on, stepping into one of the several modern shopping malls with designer shops, hairdressers, cafes and restaurants. Although KOMTAR is an enduring favourite for cheap shopping, the retail epicentre is with the City Square, a huge, glitzy shopping and office complex. A little way further south, the **Sri Mariamman Temple** lends a welcome splash of primary colours to the cityscape. Underneath its *gopuram*, and beyond the two gatekeepers on horseback who guard the temple, is the usual collection of vividly depicted figures from the Hindu pantheon. Just west of the Sri Mariamman is JB's oldest temple, the nineteenth-century **Johor Temple** on Jalan Trus, its murals of Chinese life darkened by years of incense smoke.

From here, it's a short walk to the western seafront. Take Jalan Trus south, past weathered shophouses and the occasional ladyboy, turn right at the end of the street, and follow this feeder road as it leads on to Jalan Ibrahim. After the cramped streets of the city centre, the open waterfront comes as a great relief. There are good views of distant Singapore, and of the slow snake of traffic labouring across the causeway. Turning your back on Singapore and looking towards JB, the view is dominated by the austere, grey-bricked **Sultan Ibrahim Building** on Jalan Bukit Timbalan, which today houses the state government offices. Completed in 1940, it was used by the Japanese to command their assault on Singapore in February 1942.

Continuing west along the water, past the garlanded facade of the **City Council**, you soon reach the grey arch marking the entrance into the expansive gardens of the **Istana Besar** – the former residence of Johor's royal family. Ornate golden lamps line the path to the istana, a magnificent building with chalk-white walls and a low, blue roof, set on a hillock overlooking the Johor Straits. Nowadays, the royal family lives in the Istana Bukit Serene, a little further

Travel between JB and Singapore

Two frequent **bus** services run between JB and Singapore throughout the day from Larkin station: the air-conditioned Singapore–JB Express (daily 6.30am–11pm; every 15min; RM2.80) is the more comfortable, though the #170 is cheaper (RM2) and runs every ten minutes from 5.20am to 12.10am. It's also possible to board buses to Singapore at the causeway terminal or just outside the train station, both near the centre of JB. The buses drop passengers outside the immigration checkpoints at each end of the causeway; retain your bus ticket as you'll need it for the onward journey. Once you're through immigration (the formalities take about ten minutes to complete), you continue into Singapore on any bus of the same type as the one that you took to the causeway, though not necessarily on the very same vehicle; keep your luggage on you. There's also a bus service from JB's Senai airport to Singapore's *Novotel Orchid* on Dunearn Road.

The KTM **train** service to Singapore, with a modern station next to the domestic train station opposite the City Square Mall, has trains running solely between JB and Singapore between 6.30am and midnight; a one-way ticket costs RM5, and there are immigration checkpoints at either end. **Taxis** between JB and Singapore (RM40 per person) depart from Kotaraya Shopping Centre and leave only when they are full.

The sultans and the law

The antics of the British royal family are nothing compared to what some of the nine royal families in Malaysia get up to. Nepotism, meddling in state politics and flagrant breaches of their exemption from import duties are among their lesser misdemeanours, which generally go unreported in the circumspect local press. But the most notorious of them all is Johor's Sultan Iskandar ibni Al-Marhum Sultan Ismail – along with his son, the Tunku Ibrahim Ismail. The former is alleged to have beaten his golf caddy to death in the Cameron Highlands after the unfortunate man made the mistake of laughing at a bad shot. Tunku Ibrahim, for his part, was convicted of shooting dead a man in a JB nightclub, though the prince was immediately pardoned because of who his father was.

Such behaviour had long incensed former Prime Minister Dr Mahathir, who was itching to bring the lawless royals into line. He got his chance in 1993 when yet another beating incident involving the Sultan of Johor was brought up in the federal parliament along with 23 other similar assaults since 1972. As a result, the federal parliament voted in the Constitutional Amendment Bill, removing the sultans' personal immunity from prosecution. Naturally, the royal families were not too happy about this, but following a stand-off with Mahathir, they agreed to a compromise – no ruler would be taken to court without the attorney-general's approval. To underline his victory against the sultans, Mahathir introduced another constitutional amendment in 1994, to the effect that the sultans could only act on the advice of the government. Despite this, the Sultan of Johor retains considerable influence in the state and is the only one of the Malay royals to have a private army.

west of the city, and the Istana Besar is open to the public as the **Royal Abu Bakar Museum** (Mon–Fri 8am–5pm, last entry 4pm; RM7). The bulk of the pieces on show here are gifts – some exquisite, some tacky – from foreign dignitaries, including ceramics from Japan, crystal from France and furniture from England, as well as Southeast Asian items like stuffed tigers, ornate daggers and an umbrella stand crafted from an elephant's foot.

Five minutes' walk further west, the four rounded towers of the **Masjid Abu Bakar** make it the most elegant building in town. Completed in 1900, the mosque can accommodate two thousand worshippers; as at the istana, Sultan Abu Bakar himself laid the first stone, though he died before the mosque was completed.

Eating

There are scores of **restaurants** in JB, serving everything from Pakistani to Japanese dishes. The liveliest place to eat is the large **night market**, beside the Sri Mariamman Temple. A smaller night market takes place on the waterfront in front of the General Hospital on Jalan Skudai, about 500m west of the Abu Bakar Mosque.

Food markets and malls

City Square Jalan Wong Ah Fook. Popular top-floor food court plus various Western fast-food establishments in a huge shopping centre.

Kotaraya Shopping Centre Top floor, Jalan Trus. Several Western fast-food outlets and a good range of hawker stalls which stay open till 9.30pm.

Pasar Malam Jalan Wong Ah Fook. Colourful and vibrant night market with a mouthwatering array of goodies. Try the local speciality *mee rebus* – noodles in a thick sauce garnished with bean curd, sliced egg, green chillies and shallots.

Restaurants

Hua Mui 131 Jalan Trus. Western and Chinese dishes are on the menu in this two-storey restaurant. The first floor is a good place to escape the midday sun for lunch as the large windows facilitate a good breeze.

Nilla 109 Jalan Trus. "The best banana leaf food in town" boasts the sign and it's certainly tasty and inexpensive as well as friendly, with herbal chappathi on the menu along with the usual fare. Daily 7am–10pm.

Snow White 9a & 11a Jalan Siu Nam. Affordable, open-sided restaurant up above the thrum of JB's traffic; specializes in Cantonese seafood and steamboats, though it also serves Malay food. Daily 3pm–6am.

That's Café 55 Jalan Tan Hiok Nee. Chic and cheap set menu, though their specials can be pricier – with tables downstairs as well as in the upstairs clothes and shoe shop. There is also a stylish hairdresser at the back. Daily noon–midnight.

Up the east coast from Johor Bahru

Without the patronage of neighbouring Singapore, the area around Johor Bahru would have quietly nodded off into a peaceful slumber. Not that it's exactly a thrilling region even now: places like the seaside resort of **Desaru** on the east coast have flourished due to its close proximity to Singapore, but most people heading east beat a hasty path along Route 3 to **Mersing**, an attractive little town that is the departure point for boats to Pulau Tioman.

Desaru

As beaches in this part of Malaysia go, **DESARU**, isn't bad. With its sheltered, casuarina-fringed bay, it's the nearest major resort to Singapore and, as a result, it gets busy during weekends and holidays. The wide, well-kept but empty streets mean spending all your time on the beach or at the resort as there is nothing else to do. During the monsoon months, the current is dangerously strong; if the red flag is flying, do not go in the water and use caution at any time during these months; fatalities even at low depth are common. Despite Desaru's popularity, there are better places further up the coast.

With the road route here from JB covering nearly 100km (via Kota Tinggi, then southeast along Route 92), most visitors from Singapore come by sea from Changi Point (see p.589), arriving at the Malaysian port of **Kampung Pengerang**. Shuttle buses make the 45-minute journey from the port to Desaru itself. From JB, catch one of the four daily Mara Liner express buses from the Larkin bus station (RM9; 90min; last bus leaves Desaru at 5pm) or a local bus to Kota Tinggi, from where there are regular buses to Desaru.

The *Golden Beach Hotel* (see below) has a water-sports centre – and is also the place to find go-karts and quad bikes.

Accommodation

The five **places to stay** are all strung in a row along the beach, but be warned that room rates rise by about fifty percent at weekends and holidays.

Desaru Holiday Chalet ☎07/822 1211, ℻822 1245. Next to the *Desaru Leisure Camp*, 1km from the *Perdana* and *Impean*, with large and comfortable cabins set on the beach. There is a reasonably priced food court and bikes can be hired. **⑤**

Desaru Hostel ☎07/822 2333, ℻822 2188. A kilometre or so beyond the *Desaru Perdana*, this is the only budget option, with sixteen triple rooms, each containing three beds at RM25 per bed. There is a pantry, a shuttle service to the bus station and a common room; group dining can be organized as well as local tours. Though the place is a little run-down, it's only a 5min walk from the beach.

Desaru Impean Resort ☎07/838 9911, ℻838 9922. At the northern end of the beach, this is the largest of the hotels in town. Modern, though rather kitsch with a Disneyland feel, it comes complete with a miniature railway, theme park and well-kitted-out rooms. **⑥**

Golden Beach Hotel ☎07/822 1101, ℮hotel @desaruresort.com. At the southeastern end of the strip, this hotel has a nice swimming pool and golf course, and the lower-priced rooms are in the complex itself; better are the luxurious beachfront villas. ⑥–⑧

Pulai Desaru Beach Resort ☎07/822 2222, ℱ822 2223. A little less grand than the *Desaru Impean* next door, but more tasteful. ⑦

Eating

All the above hotels have **restaurants** – predominantly Chinese and Japanese – where a very average meal costs a bare minimum of RM22 a head. There are a handful of cheap **food stalls** on the beach near the car park just north of the *Golden Beach Hotel*.

Mersing and around

The fishing port of **MERSING**, 130km north of Johor Bahru, lies on the languid Sungai Mersing. You're unlikely to stay more than one night, if at all, in this industrious little town, which is the main gateway to **Pulau Tioman** and the smaller islands of the Seribuat Archipelago. It pays to work out exactly what you want to do before arriving in Mersing, or you may be swamped by the touts that hang around the jetty.

Arrival and information

Mersing is grouped around two main streets, Jalan Abu Bakar and Jalan Ismail, fanning out from a roundabout on Route 3. The **jetty** is about five minutes' walk east along Jalan Abu Bakar from the roundabout. **Express buses** drop you

MERSING

▲ Pulau Tioman

Kuantan, Pekan, Kuala Rompin, Endau, Ⓐ & Ⓑ

Government Rest House

ACCOMMODATION
Country Hotel	D
Fishing Bay Resort	B
Hotel Golden City	E
Kali's Guesthouse	A
Timotel	C

EATING
Al Arip	3
Loke Tien Yuan Restaurant	2
Mersing Seafood Restaurant	4
Sweet Story	1

Getting to the islands

Mersing is the main departure point for Tioman and the other islands of the **Seribuat Archipelago** (for details of departures from Tanjung Gemuk, see opposite). At the jetty there's a secure **car park** (RM7–10 per day, depending who owns the car-parking space) and a cluster of agency booths representing various islands, boats and resorts, known collectively as the **Tourist Centre**. For impartial information you're better off going to METIC. It's sensible to change money in Mersing before you head out to the islands, as the exchange rates there are lousy; the only ATM is in Tekek, opposite the airport.

Daily **express boats** operate **to Tioman** (Blue Water Ferries ℗ 07/799 4811; RM35 for the one-way trip); the journey takes two hours or more, depending on the tide. At the jetty, you'll find signboards giving details of the day's sailings and it is advised to buy a ticket here, rather than from an invariably more expensive tout or travel agent. Several ferry companies operate in high season; Blue Water operates throughout the year, depending on weather conditions.

Transport to the **other islands from Mersing** is organized by the resorts on the islands and accommodation is booked in their respective offices by the jetty – though it is possible to purchase just boat transport from some of the resorts if there is space available. For Pulau Besar, try the office for the *Mirage* (RM90 return); for Pulau Rawa, the Tioman-bound ferries will sometimes stop on prior request, but if you cannot find anywhere to stay and there are no boats back, you're stuck. About 30km south of Mersing is **Pulau Sibu**, where the resort ferries depart from Tanjung Lemak.

off just before the roundabout or take you to the main bus station on Jalan Jemaluang, unless they terminate at the R&R Plaza next to the jetty. The R&R Plaza is a concrete block awash with shops, food outlets, resort offices and tour operators. All are in easy walking distance of each other. **Taxis** can be picked up either at the main bus station or at the jetty.

Mersing's **tourist office** (METIC; Mon–Fri 8am–5pm; ℗ 07/799 1979) is on Jalan Abu Bakar opposite the **post office**, with helpful staff who offer advice on the many different island deals. Mersing is well supplied with **cyber-cafés**, most of which can be found along Jalan Abu Bakar. You can **change money** at the Maybank or Bank Bumiputra on Jalan Ismail.

It can be problematic **leaving Mersing** by bus in peak season as they often get full, so there can be a scramble for seats. Express-bus tickets can be bought in advance at the station or from most resorts and travel agencies, though beware these charge commission.

Accommodation

There are many **hotels** in Mersing, none particularly appealing, but all OK for one night. For longer stays, going a little out of town is a more pleasant option.

Country Hotel 11 Jalan Sulaiman ℗ 07/799 1799. The best budget place in town with a/c rooms with hot showers (❸), and fan rooms with shared bathrooms (❷). Some rooms have small balconies.

Fishing Bay Resort ℗ 07/799 6753, ⓦ www.fishingbayresort.com. Bungalows and rooms set around a beachside garden with a small pool, this place is good value and the restaurant does excellent local and Thai food. Take the local bus to Padang Endau and get off just before Air Papan and walk the 4km from the main road. A taxi from town is RM20 one way. ❹–❻

Hotel Golden City First Floor, 23 Jalan Abu Bakar ℗ 07/799 5028. Fan and a/c rooms with own bathrooms (cold showers) at affordable prices. There is no atmosphere to speak of, but the staff are friendly enough. Dorm beds RM15. ❷

Kali's Guesthouse ℗ 07/799 3613. 2km north of town with a peaceful garden and a choice of

A-frames, chalets or dearer cottages; charming, but a little run-down. Phone them to be picked up from town, or take the Padang Endau-bound bus. A taxi is RM8. ②–③
Timotel 839 Jalan Endau ⓣ07/799 5888, ⓦwww .timotel.com.my. Rather gloomy-looking, this is the

most expensive place in town, with huge double beds, well-equipped rooms and breakfast included in the rate; there's also an attached bar and a decent, though un-atmospheric, restaurant. ⑥

Eating

Mersing is a good place for **eating** out, with seafood topping the menu. The **food stalls** near the roundabout at the southern end of the bridge are good value, serving the usual rice and noodle dishes. The **market** is a good place for the popular local breakfast dish *nasi dagang*: glutinous rice cooked in coconut milk, served with *sambal* and fish curry.

Al Arlp Jalan Ismail. Opposite the Tops super-market, this Indian café serves good-quality food, including great roti and has some of the only vegetarian options in town.
Loke Tien Yuan Restaurant 55 Jalan Abu Bakar. The oldest and friendliest Chinese restaurant in town with a small, reliable menu. The sweet and sour pork is particularly good. Averages RM6 per dish, seafood around RM15.

Mersing Seafood Restaurant 56 Jalan Ismail. A variety of delicious seafood dishes though some can be pricey; steamed fish with delicate flavours is their speciality and the chilli crab is good.
Sweet Story 11 Jalan Abu Bakar. Only open during the day, this place does cheap, strong coffee and the usual rice dishes, including a few sandwiches and rounds of toast.

North of Mersing

About 35km north of Mersing along Route 3, past **Kampung Air Papan** (regarded as the best beach in the locality), is the village of **Padang Endau**, on the Johor side of the Sungai Endau. Across the bridge, in Pahang State, 3km from the village centre, is the **Tanjung Gemuk ferry terminal**, from where there are four daily services to Tioman (March–Nov; RM35 one way; ⓣ09/413 1997). The journey is slightly faster than from Mersing, taking just over an hour to reach the island. Heading further north up Route 3 brings you eventually to the former state capital of Pahang, Pekan, served by hourly buses from Mersing.

Pulau Tioman

Shaped like a giant apostrophe in the South China Sea, **PULAU TIOMAN**, 30km northeast of Mersing, has long been one of Malaysia's most popular holiday islands. Though Tioman itself falls under the state of Pahang, its entry point, Mersing, lies in Johor. At 38km in length and 19km at its widest point, Tioman is the largest of the 64 volcanic islands that form the **Seribuat Archipelago**. According to legend, the origins of Pulau Tioman lie in the flight of a dragon princess on her way to China. She fell in love with the surrounding waters and decided to settle here permanently by transforming her body into an island.

Ever since the 1970s, when Tioman was voted one of the ten most beautiful islands in the world by *Time* magazine, sun worshippers and divers have been flocking to its palm-fringed shores, in search of the mythical Bali H'ai (for which it was the chosen film location in the Hollywood musical, *South Pacific*). This, and the "**duty-free island**" status designated by Malaysian Customs, has helped destroy the sense of romantic isolation that once made the island so

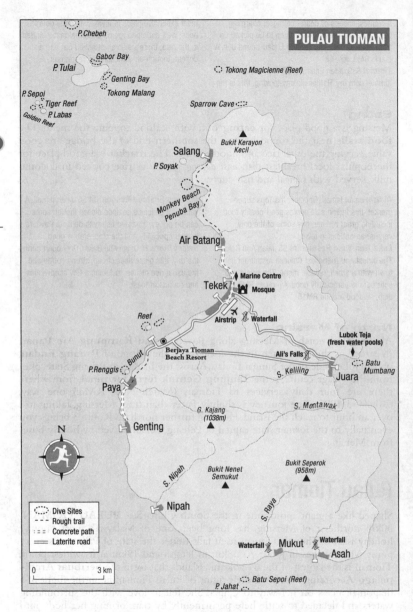

desirable. However, Pulau Tioman displays a remarkable resilience, and to fail to visit is to miss out – the greater part of the island has still not lost its intimate, village atmosphere, probably due to the lack of a decent road network; getting around the island is mainly done by water. Those in search of unspoilt beaches will on the whole be disappointed, though there are some superb exceptions.

As you approach, Tioman's mountains loom above you, shrouded in cloud; the two peculiar granite pinnacles of Bukit Nenek Semukut on the southern part of the island are known as *chula naga* (dragon's horns). The sheer size and inaccessibility of its mountainous spine has preserved its most valuable asset – the dense **jungle**; you can go **wildlife-spotting** on its few easy hikes, which afford a high chance of seeing mouse deer, tree snakes, eagles, fruit bats, flying lemur, long-tailed macaques and monitor lizards, some upwards of two metres long. There are also plenty of opportunities for **outdoor activities**, particularly diving and water sports. The island's ridge of mountains culminates in an impressive cluster of peaks in the south, of which the highest, **Gunung Kajang** (1038m), is inaccessible to all but the most experienced and well-equipped climbers.

Like the rest of the Peninsula's east coast, Tioman is affected by the **monsoon** from November to February/March, when the whole island winds down

Snorkelling and diving around Pulau Tioman

With such abundant **marine life** in the waters around Tioman, it's unlikely that you'll want to be island-bound the whole time. Many of the nearby islets provide excellent opportunities for **snorkelling**, and most of the chalet operations offer **day-trips** for the purpose, costing around RM50 (excluding equipment; to hire, add another RM25). The relatively untouched coral and huge bio-diversity in these temperate waters make for some world-class **dive sites**. Many dive centres on Tioman offer a full range of PADI certificates, from an intensive four-day "Open Water" course which includes three days of theory and eight dives (around RM1000), through to the fourteen-day "Dive Master" (RM3200); check that qualified English-speaking instructors are employed, and that the cost includes all the necessary equipment. For the already qualified, a daily dive costs around RM105 per person. Of the dive shops, B&J's in Air Batang is the best established (℡09/419 1218, ℮bjabc@divetioman.com) with a second shop in Salang (℡09/419 5555, ℮bjsalang@divetioman.com).

Golden Reef (typical depth 10–20m). Fifteen minutes off the northwestern coast; boulders provide a breeding ground for marine life, as well as producing many soft and hard corals.

Pulau Chebeh (15–25m). In the northwestern waters, this is a massive volcanic labyrinth of caves and channels. Napoleon fish, trigger fish and turtles are present in abundance.

Pulau Labas (5–15m). South of Pulau Tulai, tunnels and caves provide a home for puffer fish, moray eels and corals such as fan and sweet-lip nudibranch.

Pulau Renggis (5–13m). Near the *Berjaya Tioman*, this sheltered spot is suitable for training and night dives. Good for spotting stingray, angel fish and buffalo fish, as well as two resident black-tip reef sharks.

Tiger Reef (10–25m). Southwest of Pulau Tulai between Labas and Sepoi islands, and deservedly the most popular site, with yellow-tail snappers, trevally and tuna, spectacular soft coral and gorgonian fans.

Tokong Magicienne (10–25m). Due north of Pulau Tioman, this colourful, sponge-layered coral pinnacle is a feeding station for larger fish – silver snappers, golden-striped trevally, jacks and groupers.

Tokong Malang (5–15m). Just off the southeastern tip of Pulau Tulai, this shallow reef is well visited by blue-spotted rays as well as less frequent turtles, barracudas, large cuttlefish, yellow-spotted stingrays and black-tip reef sharks.

Soyak wrecks (22–30m). With two former Thai fishing boats lying by Soyak island, this is a great place for wreck diving.

dramatically and many places close. July and August are the busiest months, when prices increase and accommodation is best booked in advance.

Accommodation possibilities range from the island's one international-standard resort through to chalet developments and simple beachfront A-frames. The standard and pricing of each type of accommodation hardly varies from place to place on the same beach, so it's a good idea to pick your spot according to atmosphere and view as much as anything else. Most of the budget establishments on Tioman are in the bay of Air Batang, just north of the island's main village, Tekek. The east coast's sole settlement, Juara, is very quiet – you'll easily find a place to stay here or in Air Batang for under RM20 per head. Paya and Genting are home to more upmarket resorts though both also have budget outlets. Salang has many cheap places to stay as well, while on the southern coast, sleepy Nipah and Mukut have only a few basic accommodation options. **Nightlife** is a chilled affair, with most going on in Salang and Air Batang; beer is available everywhere on the island, though not in all restaurants.

Arrival and information

Arriving by express boat or speedboat **from Mersing**, it's important to decide in advance which bay or village you want to stay in, since the express boats generally make drops only at the major resorts of Genting, Paya, Tekek, Air Batang and Salang (in that order). There are only occasional express boats from Mersing to Juara on the east coast. The two daily ferries **from Tanjung Gemuk** stop first at Genting, too. There are small **tourist information huts** at each jetty.

Planes land at the airstrip in Tekek. To reach the other beaches, you will have to rent a boat, a jeep (to Juara only) or walk. There is a fee of RM5 to enter the island due to its designated marine park status.

Getting around the island

A two-metre-wide concrete path runs north from Tekek to the headland marking the end of the beach, a twenty-minute walk. The path continues up steps to the other side of the rocks for the length of Air Batang, another twenty-minute walk to the furthest end.

The road between Tekek and the *Berjaya Tioman Beach Resort*, is the only main road on the west coast of the island and branches off to a newer road just before the resort through the jungle to Juara – a trip by jeep will cost RM35 per person for four people or RM120 for the jeep.

The network of **trails** is limited, spanning the coastline wherever there are resorts, and it is also possible to cross the island on foot using the older dirt track to Juara from Tekek jetty (see p.378 for details of the route). Less obvious trails connect Genting with Paya, and Air Batang with Penuba Bay, Monkey Beach and Salang – details are given in the respective sections.

Transport around the shore of the island is via hired boats; these are very expensive by Malaysian standards, hops costing RM20–80 per person, depending on where you go and where you are coming from. To get from one side of the island to the other will cost around RM150–200 for up to ten people. Or, join the Mersing ferry for its scheduled stops for around RM10–15 per person. You could also jump onto one of the **round-the-island boat trips** (RM150) which run from the various chalets, but they tend to spend an hour or so in each spot. Since so much of the west coast is paved, **bicycle rental** – at RM5 an hour from several outlets in Tekek and Air Batang – seems a sensible

Leaving Tioman

Although many of the travel agencies in Mersing may try to sell you an open-return boat ticket to Tioman, tickets are readily available from outlets at any of the bays on the island. **Express boats** all leave at around 7 or 8am daily, making their pick-ups from each jetty. Slower boats usually leave before noon, picking up from every bay – check with your chalet-owner. The ferry to Tanjung Gemuk (noon & 4pm) leaves from Genting. If you are planning to leave Tioman during a full or new moon, ask ahead of time if the tidal conditions will affect departure times. There are also **flights** to Kuala Lumpur (RM230) and Singapore (RM300) with Berjaya Air (℡03/7846 8228, Ⓦwww .berjaya-air.com).

option, but you can't go far without having to carry the bike over the headlands at some point and the road to Juara is only for the resilient.

Tekek

The sprawling village of **TEKEK**, the main settlement on the island, isn't really a place you'd want to stay for long. The incessant stream of chugging ferries, the roar of aeroplanes and the churning of concrete mixers all combine to make Tekek the least inspiring part of Tioman.

The central beach now has concrete boardwalks making beach life obsolete, and the whole area suffers from an unpleasant litter problem, though things start to get better well south of the main jetty where, apart from a few high-end resorts, the shore is relatively unspoilt. For a break from the beach, pop into the **Tioman Island Museum** (daily 8am–5pm; RM2) on the first floor of the airstrip's terminal complex. Apart from displaying some twelfth- to fourteenth-century Chinese ceramics, which were lost overboard from early trading vessels, it also outlines the facts and myths concerning the island. North of the main jetty, at the very end of the bay, is the government-sponsored **Marine Centre** (daily 8am–5pm; free), its hefty concrete jetty and dazzlingly blue roofs making it hard to miss. Set up to protect the coral and marine life around the island, and to patrol the fishing taking place in its waters, the centre also contains an aquarium and displays of coral.

Practicalities

You'll find an **ATM**, moneychangers and duty-free shops in and around the terminal complex next to the airstrip. For **post**, drop items at the airport. The police station is a five-minute walk south from here.

There are lots of **places to stay** in Tekek, though most are dilapidated and located next to piles of rubbish and the ever-present building materials. With Air Batang just a little way north and transport to other areas easy to come by, it is best to keep moving. If do you decide to stay, however, try *Babura Seaview Resort* (℡09/419 1139), a large and friendly complex (❷), with chalets (❹–❺) and beachside terraced rooms (❺); there's a good restaurant and a nearby diving outfit. Alternatively, there's *Swiss Cottage Beach Resort* (℡09/419 1642; ❹), a pleasant resort in a shady garden right on the beach. There's also a dive shop and small restaurant. Situated about 15km south of Tekek is *Berjaya Tioman Beach, Golf & Spa Resort* (℡09/419 1000, Ⓦwww.berjayaresorts.com; ❾), a village-sized complex with its own private beach. There's everything from double rooms to deluxe apartments; other facilities include two pools, tennis courts, donkey riding, a large games room, water sports and a golf course. Occasional promotions offer good value.

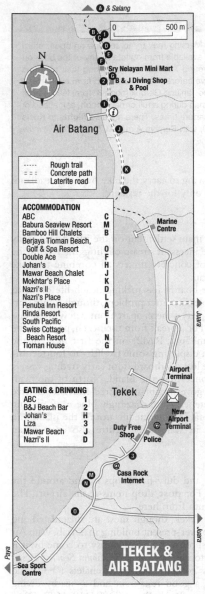

ACCOMMODATION
ABC	C
Babura Seaview Resort	M
Bamboo Hill Chalets	B
Berjaya Tioman Beach,	
Golf & Spa Resort	O
Double Ace	F
Johan's	H
Mawar Beach Chalet	J
Mokhtar's Place	K
Nazri's II	D
Nazri's Place	L
Penuba Inn Resort	A
Rinda Resort	E
South Pacific	I
Swiss Cottage	
Beach Resort	N
Tioman House	G

EATING & DRINKING
ABC	1
B&J Beach Bar	2
Johan's	H
Liza	3
Mawar Beach	J
Nazri's II	D

TEKEK & AIR BATANG

Most of the **places to eat** are attached to the chalet operations, and one of Tekek's nicest restaurants, *Liza*, is at the far southern end of the bay, with a wide-ranging menu specializing in seafood and Western snacks – the average meal here costs about RM20.

Air Batang and Penuba Bay

Despite its ever-increasing popularity, **AIR BATANG**, 2km north of Tekek from jetty to jetty, is still one of the best areas on Tioman, competing with Juara for the budget market, though having the inferior beach. Larger than Salang or Juara, far less developed than Tekek and well connected by boat services, Air Batang (or ABC as it's often called), is a happy medium as far as many visitors are concerned; what development there is here tends to be relatively tasteful and low-key.

A jetty divides the bay roughly in half; the beach is better at the southern end of the bay, where there are fewer rocks, though the shallow northern end is safer for children. The cement path that runs the length of the beach is interrupted by little wooden bridges over streams, overhung with greenery and soft evening lighting. A fifteen-minute **trail** leads over the headland to the north which, after an initial scramble, flattens out into an easy walk, ending up at **Penuba Bay**. This secluded cove is littered with dead coral right up to the sea's edge, which makes it hard to swim comfortably, though the snorkelling is good; many people prefer the peace and quiet here to the beach at Air Batang. From Penuba Bay, it's an hour's walk to Monkey Beach, beyond which is Salang.

Accommodation

As you get off the boat, a signpost helpfully lists the direction of the numerous **places to stay** in the bay. All but the most basic A-frames have fans and their own bathrooms, and mosquito nets are usually provided. The pricier options should have hot showers. **Internet** facilities are available at *Double Ace*, *Nazri's* and *Bamboo Hill*, but they're uniformly expensive (around RM10 an hr).

▲ Traditional-style beach bungalow

ABC ☎ 09/419 1154. At the far northern end of the bay, and therefore a little quieter than most, this long-established operation is still among the best in Air Batang, run by a local family. The pretty chalets are set in a well-tended garden with its own freshwater stream. In addition to basic huts (②–③) there are five newer, sturdier chalets (⑥).

Bamboo Hill Chalets ☎ 09/419 1339, ℮ bamboosu@tm.net.my. Six beautiful wooden chalets on stilts, perched on the northern headland of Air Batang, with stunning views. The rooms have bathrooms, kettles, mosquito screens and bedside lamps; the more expensive ones have a fridge and can sleep up to four people. ④–⑤

Double Ace ☎ 09/419 1184. Run by the internet café and shop of the same name, this friendly place has a few rooms with a/c and hot showers; the simpler options are good value as they are fairly new. ③–⑤

Johan's ☎ & ℱ 09/419 1359 A good choice, with well-spaced standard chalets and larger ones up the hill on a pleasant lawn, as well as a very good beachside restaurant. There's also a dorm (RM15); some rooms have a/c, all cold showers. ②–④

Mawar Beach Chalet ☎ 09/419 1153. Simple, well-run chalets with a good location right on the beach; rooms are smallish but have a veranda and fans. The service is very friendly and there's a resident monitor lizard. Bike rental available. ②

Mokhtar's Place ☎ 09/419 1148. South of the jetty, this place is more comfortable than most, though the chalets are a little close together and face inwards, rather than out to sea. ②

Nazri's II ☎ 09/419 1375, ℮ info@nazrisplace .com. At the northern end of Air Batang, this elaborate outfit boasts large, a/c cottages set in spacious grounds, as well as some ordinary chalets at the back. The lively restaurant offers a good selection of travellers' fare with a few local dishes and there is a lovely beach bar with a chilled vibe. ④–⑥

Nazri's Place ☎ 09/419 1329, ℮ info @nazrisplace.com. At the southern end of the bay, on the best bit of beach on the strip. Offers the same range of rooms as the affiliated *Nazri's II*, as well as massage and reflexology. The twelve new luxury rooms have a/c. ③–⑥

Penuba Inn Resort ☎ 07/419 1424, ℮ panuba @hotmail.com. The only accommodation at Penuba Bay. If you stay here, you're committed to eating here every night too, unless you fancy a scramble over the headland in the dark. Its chalets, on stilts and high up on the rocks, have fantastic views out to sea. ④–⑥

Rinda Resort ☎ 09/419 1157. A good spot in a neat, shaded setting at the northern end of Air Batang; this is a good place for long-term, cheap stays. One of the friendliest and lowest-priced hostels on Tioman, with simple en-suite huts. ❶

South Pacific ☎09/419 1176. Close to the jetty. Clean chalets with attached bathrooms and mozzie nets, some right on the beach (❷), making these

excellent value. There are also a few modern chalets with hot showers and a/c (❺) and there is a small café and laundry services. Strictly no alcohol.

Tioman House ☎019/704 5096. Next door to B&J Diving Centre, these brand-new brick chalets with a/c, fridge and hot showers are good value. ❷

Eating, drinking and nightlife

Air Batang keeps its **nightlife** low-key, unlike Salang, which can get rowdy during the season. Most of the chalets have their own **restaurants**, open to non-residents. Menus, which tend to reflect Western tastes, have fish as a staple feature. Many do not serve alcohol, which is left to the beachside bars.

ABC Good-quality food – chicken and fish dishes average RM12 – and fresh fruit juices.

B&J Beach Bar Run by the friendly Desmond, this place has beers, spirits and the occasional bottle of wine at good prices; this is where the dive crew mostly hang out.

Johan's The best omelette in Air Batang with Malay, Thai and Western dishes on the menu, too.

Mawar Beach Great seafood at reasonable prices as well as equally reliable curries and Chinese and Malay dishes. The fish curry is recommended.

Nazri's II The food is slightly more expensive than elsewhere – but there is pretty much everything on the menu and the beachside bar is great for a sunset beer.

Salang and Monkey Beach

Just over 4km north of Air Batang, **SALANG** is a smaller bay with a better beach at its southern end by the jetty. Nevertheless, there has been a lot of development and every suitable inch of land has been built on. The crowded accommodation here makes for a busy and vibrant atmosphere, and with a couple of lively bars, Salang is the only place on the island with much **nightlife** to speak of.

The southern end of the beach is the more scenic, while swimming is a bit of an ordeal at the northern end, where sharp rocks and coral make the water difficult to approach. Just off the southern headland is a small island, Pulau Soyak, with a pretty reef for snorkelling. There are two good **dive schools**, Fisherman Divers and B&J's Diving Centre, both of which run daily courses.

A rough trail takes you over the headland to the south for the 45-minute scramble to **Monkey Beach**. There are few monkeys around these days, but the well-hidden cove is more than adequate compensation. It's a popular spot for trainee divers because of its clear, calm waters.

SALANG

Dive Asia
Police
A-D Internet @ Service
Fishermen's Divers
Fours Bar
Ben's Diving Centre
Salang Complex

0   200 m

N

▼ Monkey Beach

EATING & DRINKING
Fours Café   2
Salang Dream   3
Sunset Boulevard   1

ACCOMMODATION

Ella's Place	A	Puteri Salang Inn	D
Nora's Chalet	F	Salang Indah	B
Pak Long Chalet	E	Salang Pusaka Resort	C
Pondok Sri Salang	G	Salang Sayang Resort	H

Accommodation

On the right (south) as you leave the jetty are a little cluster of budget **places to stay**.

Ella's Place ☎09/419 5004. Run by the friendly Ella, this place is a great option; chalets are with fan or a/c and all have cold showers. She also helps with bookings for the more run-down *Salang Huts*, next door. ②–④

Nora's Chalet ☎09/419 5003. A friendly family operation, whose well-kept chalets with bathroom, fan and mosquito nets make them great value. Set behind a little stream where the local monitor lizards are getting on for alligator size. ②

Pak Long Chalet ☎09/419 5000. Set in a shady garden with a range of chalets starting at RM60 for fan rooms sleeping up to three people. There are more expensive a/c options available, sleeping three to four people. ③–⑤

Pondok Sri Salang ☎019/720 2169. A little tricky to find in the gardens behind *Pak Long Chalet*, this place has clean fan chalets with mosquito nets (②) as well as nice a/c chalets with hot showers and fridges (⑤). Discounts are available for longer stays.

Puteri Salang Inn ☎09/799 3592. Nice fan and a/c chalets set in a beautifully landscaped garden, makes this the most peaceful spot in Salang. Their water-taxi prices are very reasonable. ③–④

Salang Indah ☎09/419 5015. The largest outfit in Salang, towards the centre of the bay. Well-appointed chalets to suit every budget, from run-of-the-mill box rooms (③) to sea-facing family chalets with a/c and hot shower (⑥). They also arrange snorkelling and diving trips.

Salang Pusaka Resort ☎09/419 5317, ✉salangpusaka@yahoo.com. With friendly management, this place is set back from the beach and some of the rooms have a/c and hot showers. There is a restaurant serving local and Western food. ③–⑤

Salang Sayang Resort ☎09/415 5020, ✉salangsayang@hotmail.com. At the southern end of the beach, where swimming is possible, this resort has comfortable, hillside chalets (③–④) and more expensive sea-facing ones (⑤). There are also some family rooms (⑥).

Eating, drinking and nightlife

Eating choices include the expensive restaurants at *Salang Dream* and *Salang Beach Resort*, where the emphasis is on Malay cuisine and seafood at around RM12 per dish, and the more informal cafés around town, which serve excellent Western and Malay dishes for no more than RM6. For **nightlife**, head to *Four's Bar* next to B&J Diving Centre, which boasts a large cocktail list and, further north, the *Sunset Boulevard* that has the best views of the bay.

Juara

As Tioman's western shore becomes more developed, many people are making their way to **JUARA**, the only settlement on the east coast. Life is simpler here; it is a quiet and peaceful kampung with two excellent beaches. Although Juara's seclusion may have saved it so far from the excesses all too apparent on the west coast, plenty of simple chalet resorts have already been built. For the time being, Juara has fewer speedboats and motorbikes buzzing around, while its lovely wide sweep of beach is far cleaner and less crowded than anywhere on the other side of the island. The constant sea breeze means that the water is always choppy and the waves can reach up to 4m in February on the southern beach, making it a popular time for surfers. The bay, facing out to the open sea, is the most susceptible on the island to bad weather.

There are a couple of very easy **walks** from Juara; a 45-minute walk

JUARA

Tekek

Jetty

Juara Mutiara
Shop

N

0   200 m

ACCOMMODATION
Beach Shack	H
Bushman's	G
Juara Beach	C
Mutiara	D
Paradise Point	B
Rainbow	F
Riverview	A
Sunrise	E

South Bay & ❸

to a small waterfall with a big freshwater pond good for swimming, starting at the south beach, clearly marked by red dots and bottoms of cans, painted yellow. There is also a slightly harder hour-long jungle trek to Lubok Teja, another good spot for a dip. Maps (RM2) are available at the **sea bus ticket counter** at the jetty.

Arrival

A road starting just before the *Berjaya Tioman Beach, Golf & Spa Resort* (see p.373) has enabled easy access to Juara by **4X4 vehicles**, costing RM120 per car or RM35 per person with four people in the car for the thirty-minute journey. The cheapest way to get to Juara is **on foot** through the jungle, a steep trek that takes about two hours from Tekek, not counting rest stops, suitable for a day-trip without luggage. The start of the trail (a 5min walk from the airstrip) is easy enough to identify, since it's the only concrete path that heads off in that direction. The path passes the local mosque but the paved section ends soon after. Continue in the same direction into the jungle; a rocky path and intermittent sections of concrete steps guide you uphill through the greenery, tapering off into a smooth, downhill path once you're over the ridge. After 45 minutes, there's a **waterfall**, where it's forbidden to bathe – it supplies Tekek with water. From this spot, it's another hour or so to Juara village, which consists of two bays; the path emerges at the northern one, opposite the **jetty**.

The southern bay has one chalet resort and there is a turtle sanctuary at the far end. Many accommodation options hire out **snorkelling** equipment.

Accommodation and eating

Most of the **accommodation** is on the northern bay, within a five-minute walk of the jetty, and have attached **restaurants**.

Beach Shack ☎012/696 1093. The only place to stay on the southern bay and a great place for surfing (boards are for hire) with a good communal area with regular BBQs and beach bonfires. The chalets are simple and clean and tents can be hired at RM15, too. ❷

🏃 **Bushman's** ☎09/419 3109. With only four chalets at the far end of the beach, this friendly place is easy-going and the restaurant serves delicious local food and great breakfast porridge. They will also do the Tekek trip for RM70 for the car; book in advance. ❷

Juara Beach ☎09/419 3188. The best place to stay for hot showers with new chalets and boasting an excellent Chinese restaurant. There is a little (independent) beach bar next door with great views over the ocean. ❺–❻

Mutiara ☎09/419 3159. The biggest operation here, close to the jetty and with a variety of rooms

and prices, including dorm beds at RM20. There is also a mini-market and they can arrange boat trips for fishing. ❸–❺

Paradise Point Standard, cheap chalets with attached bathrooms at a good stretch of the beach. ❷–❸

🏃 **Rainbow** Brightly painted, good-sized chalets, with own bathrooms and mosquito nets make these excellent value. The friendly owners sell teas and coffees. ❷–❸

Riverview ☎09/419 3168, ⊛www .riverview-tioman.com. At the north end of the bay with a good common area with a pool table and friendly owner, this place is nice, though a little pricey for a chalet with cold showers. ❷–❸

Sunrise ☎09/419 3102. With good chalets and a beachside restaurant, this place is also the only diving centre on the beach.

Asah

On the southeast corner of the island are the deserted remains of the village at **ASAH**; you can get here on the round-the-island boat trip, or take a sea taxi from Genting (RM70 per person), the nearest point of access. These days, the only signs of life are the trails of litter left by day-trippers dropping by to visit the famous **waterfall**, the setting for the "Happy Talk" sequence from the film version of *South Pacific*. A fifteen-minute walk from the ramshackle jetty, the twenty-metre-high cascade is barely recognizable as the one in the film, though certainly photogenic enough. Though the deep-plunge pool at the foot of the waterfall provides a refreshing dip, there's not much else to detain you in Asah, except for the stunning view of the dramatic, insurmountable twin peaks of **Bukit Nenet Semukut**, or "Dragon's Horns" as referred to by the locals.

Mukut

It's far better to spend time at nearby **MUKUT**, a tiny fishing village just five minutes from Asah by sea taxi, in the shadow of granite outcrops. Shrouded by dense forest, and connected to the outside world by a solitary cardphone, it's a wonderfully peaceful and friendly spot to unwind, though be warned that this is still a conservative place, unused to Western sunbathing habits, and open intake of alcohol is frowned upon.

The **accommodation** at *Sri Tanjung Inn Adventure* (☎013/376 5181; ❷), at the far western end of the cove, overlooks a patch of beach – book at the house in the village where the name is painted on a tyre. There is a small secluded beach bar, and **treks** to "Dragon's Horn" can be organized from here. *Mukut Harmony* (☎09/412 0326) just back from the beach by the trail, has various types of chalets with fans (❹) or a/c (❺) and has a restaurant nearer the beach. Otherwise, places to eat are cheap and offer local dishes.

South of Tekek

The western beaches south of Tekek are rarely frequented by foreign tourists, though they're popular with local holiday-makers. There seems to be more of a sense of local kampung life here, despite the concrete resorts.

Paya

Just 5km south of Tekek, the understated developments at **PAYA**, in contrast to those at Genting a little further south, seem relatively peaceful. Once again, package tours are the norm, and individual travellers turning up at this narrow stretch of pristine beach will find their options somewhat limited.

Jungle walks are worth exploring here, as the island's greenery is at its most lush. The thirty-minute trail north to Bunut ends up at a fantastic, deserted beach. From here it's a hot 45-minute walk through the golf course back to the *Berjaya Tioman Beach Resort* (see p.373) and a further half-hour to Tekek. You can also walk between Paya and Genting, a pretty thirty-minute route along a concrete coastal path.

The *Paya Holiday* (☎09/4197090; ❹), right in the centre of the small bay, is quite serviceable. A little further to the north, the *Paya Beach Resort* (☎07/799 1432, ⓦwww.payabeach.com; ❻) has comfortable chalets, and offers water sports and snooker. By far the best operation is the *Sri Paya Tioman Chalet* (☎012/310 2676, ⓦwww.sripayatiomanchalet.bravehost.com; ❺), set back in the woodland, with an open-air restaurant and barbecue facilities, though you would need to buy a full-board package. The best place **to eat** in Paya is the *Pantai Paya* in the centre of the beachfront, which has a good selection of tasty, hot Malay specials and some Chinese dishes.

Genting

Usually the first stop for boats from the mainland is **GENTING**, at the western extremity of the island, which looks the least inviting of the villages on the island. Genting's cramped developments cater largely for Singaporean tour groups, with discos and karaoke bars and prices can double during the weekends and peak times.

The southern end of the beach is the best, and it's here that you'll find the least costly **accommodation**. The *Idaman Beach Holiday* (☎07/419 7048; ❸), is a friendly place with a good restaurant and there are rooms for four people for RM100. *Sun Beach* (☎07/799 4918; ❸–❺), the largest enterprise just north of the jetty, has the widest variety of rooms and a large balcony restaurant. **Places to eat** are generally limited to big, open-plan restaurants attached to the resorts; the emphasis is on catering for large numbers rather than providing interesting, quality meals. Prices are predictably inflated, though the **food court** in front of the jetty has cheap noodle and rice dishes.

Nipah

For almost total isolation, head to **NIPAH** on Tioman's southwest coast. This is the closest you'll get to an idyllic beach hideaway on the island, comprising a clean, empty beach of white sand, and a landlocked lagoon with clear water. It has no village to speak of, though there is a **dive centre** with canoeing, and **snorkelling** at the nearby island is good. As there is no jetty, Nipah remains secluded and the only way to get here is by water taxi; the nearest ferry stop is Genting (water taxi from here is RM20 per person), where you would need to stock up on any essentials before heading over.

There's only one **place to stay**: the 🍴 *Nipah Chalets* (☎012/957 6001, ⓦwww.thenipah.com; ❷), offering basic chalets and more expensive A-frames, as well as a nicely designed restaurant; the food can get a little monotonous, but the owner is very friendly.

The other Seribuat islands

Though Pulau Tioman is the best known and most visited of the 64 volcanic islands which form the **SERIBUAT ARCHIPELAGO**, there are a handful of other accessible islands whose beaches and opportunities for seclusion outstrip those of their larger rival, though they do not enjoy the duty-free

---

Sandflies

Sandflies can be a real problem on all of the Seribuat islands. These little pests, looking like tiny fruit flies with black bodies and white wings, suck blood and so cause an extremely itchy lump, which can sometimes become a nasty blister if scratched. The effectiveness of various treatments and deterrents is much debated; the general feeling is that short of dousing yourself all over with insect repellent or hiding out in the sea all day long, there's not much you can do to avoid the insects, although using suntan oil rather than lotion or cream is supposed to help, as are vitamin B supplements. Urine (your own) is among the more esoteric remedies for the itching. The closest thing to a consensus, though, seems to be that Tiger Balm, available at any chemist, can reduce the maddening itch and help you get a night's sleep. If you are able to take them, anti-histamines provide some relief; speak with your doctor before travelling.

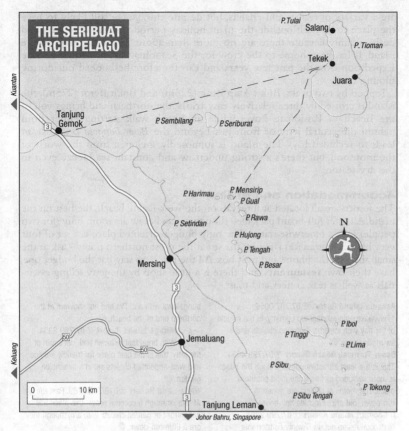

status. For archetypal azure waters and table-salt sand, three in particular stand out: Pulau Besar, Pulau Sibu and Pulau Rawa – though due to their desirability, they are largely occupied by upmarket resorts. All the islands are designated **marine parks**.

Pulau Rawa

The privately owned island of **Pulau Rawa** is only a thirty-minute boat ride from Mersing, with a small stretch of fine, sugary sanded beach and transparent waters. There are only two **accommodation** options: the deluxe *Rawa Safaris Island Resort* (℡07/799 1204, Ⓦwww.rawasfr.com; ➒) with full-board packages and deluxe chalets; and the old school *Le Club* (℡017/790 6076; ➏) next door; although it's not cheap, the beach adequately makes up for price and it has a decent restaurant. The only way to get to the island is by resort-owned speedboat, booked in advance, though the Tioman-bound ferry can make a stop (on request), depending on luck.

Pulau Besar

The long and narrow **PULAU BESAR**, 4km by 1km in size, is also known as Pulau Babi Besar, or "Big Pig Island" due to its wild boar inhabitants. There are a variety of resorts and chalets, but despite this, you're still likely to have the place to yourself outside the main holiday periods (when there are good deals), mainly because there are no more than about 25 locals living on the island. It has been home to the crew for the Scandinavian and Dutch Crusoe Expedition over the past few years and can therefore be booked out during filming times.

Topped by two peaks, Bukit Atap Zink (225m) and Bukit Berot (275m), the island is crossed by three relatively easy **trails**: the northern end brings you to the Beach of Passionate Love; while an hour's walk starting either from behind the central jetty or from just beyond the *Besar Formosa Beach Resort* leads to secluded bays. The island is supposedly sheltered from the worst of the monsoon, but there's a strong undertow and constant sea breeze even in the dry season.

Accommodation and eating
The resorts are all located at intervals on the west-facing beach, the best on the island. All offer full-board packages, though prices below are room only (for two people) unless otherwise stated. The only budget-oriented place is a set of four very basic A-frames (❷) right by the sea at the most northern point – ask at the small shop by the phone and post box. All the places to stay, bar the budget one, have their own **restaurants**, and there is a little shop by the jetty selling essentials as well as teas, coffees and toast.

Aseania Island Resort ☎07/797 0059, ⓦwww.aseaniaresortsgroup.com.my. In the middle of the bay with superbly designed chalets and a swimming pool. ❽

Besar Formosa Beach Resort ☎07/799 4831. This is the least attractive option, though the beach is more secluded as this is the most southern place. The rooms or chalets are generally run-down, but prices include half-board. ❻

D'Coconut Island Resort ☎07/799 2381, Ⓔdcoconut@tm.net.my. Twenty comfortable bungalows with a/c, TVs and hot showers at the northern end of the beach. ❻

Mirage Island Resort ☎07/799 2334. With breakfast included and just south of the jetty, this is the best place for friendly service and well-appointed chalets set in a beachside garden. ❻

White Sand Resort ☎019/772 2763. Past the *Mirage*, through a coconut grove, this place has beachfront or garden chalets with a/c, though they are a little run-down. ❺

Pulau Sibu
Closest to the mainland, **PULAU SIBU** is the most popular of the islands after Tioman. Though it's also the least scenically interesting, the huge monitor lizards and the butterflies here make up for the lack of mountains and jungle. The island's narrow waist can be crossed in only a few minutes, revealing a double bay known as Twin Beach. Like the rest of the islands, Sibu boasts fine beaches, though the sand is yellower and the current more turbulent here than at some others; most of the coves have good offshore coral.

Arrival and information
The majority of the resorts on Sibu operate their own boats from **Tanjung Leman**, a tiny mainland coastal village clearly signposted off Route 3, about 30km south of Mersing. These boats, which take twenty minutes to reach the island, need to be arranged in advance and it is not possible to get to the island without a booking or guarantee that you can get back.

Tanjung Leman is awkward to get to without your own transport. The cheapest way is getting the Kota Tinggi–Mersing bus and getting off at the Tenggaroh Junction (ask the driver); from there taxis are waiting for the RM26 ride to the jetty, one ringgit per mile. A taxi to the village from Mersing costs around RM70 and it can be tricky getting a taxi from Tanjung Leman back, so it is advisable to book beforehand with your place of accommodation.

Accommodation and eating

Most resorts are Western-run, making this the least culturally exciting place in the archipelago. All resorts operate on **all-inclusive package deals** (bar one listed below), which is just as well, seeing as there are no independent restaurants; all have water-sports facilities on offer.

Rimba Resort North coast ☎012/7106855, ⓦwww.resortmalaysia.com. Simply furnished, cosy two-bed cottages with an African theme. The communal areas are scattered with floor cushions. The beach isn't great for swimming due to its shallow water and many rocks, however. ❽

Sea Gypsy Village Resort East coast ☎07/222 8642, ⓦwww.siburesort.com. A well-run family resort with good diving facilities and a few "backpacker" chalets (RM50 per night excluding food) of superior quality. ❾

Sibu Island Cabanas ☎017/755 2690, ⓦwww .sibuislandcabanas.com. Next to *Sea Gypsy Village Resort*, this place has a variety of comfortable chalets with lovely sea views, and equipped with fans, large beds and ensuite showers with hot water. There's a fun bar, too. ❾

Twin Beach Resort Across the small ridge in the centre of the island ☎07/799 1268, ⓦwww .twinbeach.com. Its A-frames and pricier chalets are a little run-down, but it's the only place with views of both sunrise and sunset. ❽

Endau Rompin National Park

One of the few remaining areas of lowland tropical rainforest left in Peninsular Malaysia, the **ENDAU ROMPIN NATIONAL PARK** covers approximately 870 square kilometres – about one and a half times the area of Singapore. Despite being valued by conservationists for the richness of both **flora and fauna** (see box, p.384), the area was the site of damaging logging in the 1970s, and it wasn't until its designation as a national park in 1989 that adequate protective measures were finally put in place. This dense, lush habitat has nurtured several species new to science, including at least three trees, eight herbs and two mosses. There's plenty on offer for the less specialized nature-lover, from gentle **trekking** to more strenuous **mountain-climbing** and **rafting**; and for the time being at least, its trails remain refreshingly untrampled and the park abounds with **waterfalls**.

Surrounding the headwaters of the lengthy Sungai Endau and sitting astride the Johor–Pahang state border, the region was shaped by volcanic eruptions more than 150 million years ago. The force of the explosions sent up huge clouds of ash, creating the quartz crystal ignimbrite that's still very much in evidence along the park's trails and rivers, its glassy shards glinting in the light. Endau Rompin's steeply sloped mountains level out into sandstone plateaus, and the park is watered by three **river systems** based around the main tributaries of Sungai Marong, Sungai Jasin and Sungai Endau, reaching out to the south and east. The aboriginal people of the area are commonly referred to by the generic term **Orang Ulu**, meaning "upriver people"; their lives revolve around the rivers and you can still see them using dugouts made from a single tree trunk and canoes made of lengths of bark sewn together with twine. In recent years, these nomadic peoples, traditionally collectors of forest products such as resins, rattan and camphor wood, have become more settled, living in permanent villages such as Kampung Peta or just outside Bekok.

Flora and fauna in Endau Rompin

There are at least seven species of **hornbill** (see box, p.474) in the park; they are hard to miss, particularly in flight, when their oversized, white-tipped wings counterbalance their enormous curved orange bills. Early in the morning, the hooting of the male **gibbon** joins the dawn chorus of insects, cuckoos and babblers. This is the time of day when the wildlife is most active; by noon all the action has died down. The late afternoon cool heralds a second burst of activity, and is a particularly good time for birdwatching, and at night, owls, frogs, rats and pythons are about. If you're on a tour with a guide, you've a better chance of spotting tiger or elephant **footprints**, though wild pigs, mouse deer and colourful toads are far more usual sightings. The park is also the habitat of the increasingly rare **Sumatran rhinoceros**, though this hides out in the far western area of the park, off-limits to visitors.

At the upper levels of the jungle, **epiphytes** are common: these non-parasitic plants take advantage of their position on tree branches to get the light they need for photosynthesis. Massive palms are found here too, but it's mostly orchids and ferns that flourish. Lower down in the forest shade, moths and spiders camouflage themselves among the greyish brown lichen that covers the bark, and squirrels and lizards scurry up and down. Much closer to eye level, where most of the light is cut out by the virtually impenetrable canopy, are **birds** like babblers and woodpeckers. You'll also see **tree frogs**, whose expanded disc-like toes and fingertips, sticky with mucus, help them cling to leaves and branches. The forest floor is mostly covered by **ferns and mosses**, as well as tree seedlings struggling to find sunlight from a chink in the canopy.

Visiting the park

The **best time** to visit Endau Rompin is between March and October, while the paths are dry and the rivers calm. During the monsoon, however, the park is completely inaccessible, since many of its waterways are swollen and the trails are too boggy to use. For **information** on current conditions in the park call any of the park offices cited below. Take loose-fitting, lightweight cotton clothing that dries quickly – even in the dry season you're bound to get wet from crossing rivers – which helps to protect you from scratches and bites. Waterproofs will come in handy, and you'll need tons of insect repellent – plus a lighter to burn off leeches. Day-trips are available (guide mandatory) and the only way to stay in the park is to **book** with the respective park office (you need to call at least three days in advance to register, as walk-in visitors are not permitted entry). Of course, tour packages are available at travel agents, too, particularly in Mersing.

Arrival and information

There are three **entry points** to the park, one in Pahang via Kuala Rompin and two in Johor: Peta via Kahang and Selai via Bekok. From **Kuala Rompin** in Pahang, there's a road 24km to Selanding through paddy fields; and from there it is another 24km to **Kuala Kinchin**, on the park boundary, passing the Sri Mahkota Waterfall on the way. The park entrance office (℡09/414 5577) can organize tours, treks and kayaking with a guide and there are well-appointed chalets. There is no public transport to the park entrance; a taxi costs around RM80 from Kuala Rompin, which has bus connections with Kuantan. This entry is the most mundane of the three and easy packages are available at RM200–350 per person for two days and one night, excluding transport to the park.

Entering via the established Kahang entrance in **Kampung Peta** is preferable. Take the Ayer Hitam exit from the North–South Expressway if approaching from the south and continue straight through Kluang to Kahang. The park office (daily 8am–5pm, registration 8am–3pm; ☏07/788 2812, Ⓔpeta_er @yahoo.com) at **Taman Kahang Baru** is on the right-hand side, where you need to register and pay entry fees. Continue 5km east of Kahang, turn north at the park sign and continue for 48km along logging tracks (passable in an ordinary car unless it's very wet) until you reach the Orang Asli settlement of Kampung Peta, where the Visitor's Complex is located. From here, you will need to hire a 4X4 to get to the base camp at **Kuala Jasin**. The Taman Kahang Baru office can also advise on arranging **white-water-rafting** trips down the Sungai Endau. There are good chalets and dorms, as well as a cafeteria.

The **Selai** entry is reached via **Bekok**, from where you hire a 4X4 to get to the park. There is a train service to Bekok from KL Sentral as well as buses to **Segamat**, from where the Bekok train can be caught. By road from the west, exit the North–South Expressway at Yong Peng and follow Route 1 north for 30km, exiting onto Route J150 for another 11km. The Visitor Centre (daily 8am–5pm; ☏07/922 2875, Ⓔerseliajnpc@yahoo.com) can organize permits, **tubing**, fishing trips and guides as well as 4X4 transport to the base camp of **Lubuk Tapah**. Voluntary conservation work applications are also taken here.

Prices vary from site to site and depending on what you want to do. Guide prices are as follows: entrance fee RM5–10, guide for a day RM50–60, 4X4 transport in the park RM200–300 per vehicle, chalets RM60–120 and dorm beds RM10–15. Visiting the park is costly and to get the most out of your visit, it is probably best to stay for several days.

Travel details

Trains	Buses
Johor Bahru to: Butterworth (1 daily; 13hr 15min); Ipoh (2 daily; 9hr); Gemas (3 daily; 3hr 25min); Kuala Lipis (2 daily; 8hr); Kuala Lumpur (3 daily; 6hr); Segamat (3 daily; 3hr); Seremban (3 daily; 4hr 30min); Singapore (5 daily; 40min); Tumpat (1 daily; 12hr).	**Johor Bahru** to: Alor Star (7 daily; 12hr); Butterworth (at least 4 daily; 9hr); Desaru (4 daily; 1hr 30min); Ipoh (4 daily; 7hr); Kota Bharu (1 daily; 10hr); Kota Tinggi (hourly; 1hr); Kuala Lumpur (hourly; 4hr 30min); Kuala Perlis (1 daily; 12hr); Kuala Terengganu (1 daily; 9hr); Kuantan (4 daily; 6hr); Lumut (1 daily; 8hr); Melaka (hourly; 3hr); Mersing (at least 4 daily; 2hr 30min); Muar (2 daily; 2hr 30min); Seremban (10 daily; 3hr 30min); Singapore (every 10min; 1hr).
Segamat to: Butterworth (1 daily; 10hr 40min); Ipoh (1 daily; 6hr 40min); Kuala Lipis (2 daily; 5hr); Tumpat (1 daily; 10hr 30min); Kuala Lumpur (3 daily; 3hr 35min); Johor Bahru (3 daily; 4hr); Singapore (3 daily; 4hr).	**Melaka** to: Alor Star (5 daily; 12hr); Butterworth (14 daily; 9hr); Ipoh (14 daily; 4hr); Johor Bahru (10 daily; 3hr); Kluang (3 daily; 2hr); Kota Bharu (3 daily; 10hr); KLIA/LCCT (6 daily; 2hr–2hr 30min); Kuala Lumpur (hourly; 2hr); Kuala Terengganu (3 daily; 9hr); Kuantan (3 daily; 5hr); Mersing (3 daily; 5hr); Singapore (10 daily; 3hr 30min).
Seremban to: Gemas (3 daily; 1hr 30min); Johor Bahru (3 daily; 5hr); Kuala Lumpur (3 daily; 1hr 30min or regular Komuter trains); Singapore (3 daily; 5hr 30min).	**Mersing** to: Butterworth (daily; 9hr); Kuala Rompin (4 daily; 45min); Ipoh (daily; 7hr); Johor Bahru
Tampin to: Butterworth (1 daily; 9hr 20min); Gemas (3 daily; 1hr); Ipoh (1 daily; 5hr 15min); Johor Bahru (3 daily; 4hr); Kuala Lumpur (3 daily; 2hr); Singapore (3 daily; 5hr 15min).	

(at least 4 daily; 2hr 30min); Kota Bharu (3 daily; 10hr); Kluang (hourly; 2hr); Kuala Lumpur (5 daily; 6hr); Kuala Terengganu (2 daily; 10hr); Kuantan (1 daily; 3hr); Melaka (3 daily; 5hr); Muar (hourly; 1hr 30min); Seremban (hourly; 1hr 15min); Singapore (3 daily; 3hr 30min).

Seremban to: Alor Star (3 daily; 8hr); Butterworth (3 daily; 6hr); Ipoh (3 daily; 5hr); Johor Bahru (7 daily; 4hr); KLIA (2 daily; 1hr); Kota Bharu (3 daily; 10hr); Kuala Lumpur (every 15min; 1hr); Kuala Pilah (7 daily; 45min); Melaka (half-hourly; 1hr); Mersing (2 daily; 5hr); Port Dickson (half-hourly; 1hr).

Ferries

Kukup to: Tanjung Balai (Indonesia; 2 daily; 45min).

Melaka to: Dumai (Sumatra; 2 daily; 2hr); Pekanbaru (Sumatra; 3 weekly; 6hr).
Mersing to: Pulau Tioman (2–8 daily depending on season; 2–4hr).

Flights

Johor Bahru to: Kota Kinabalu (2 daily; 2hr 20min); Kuala Lumpur (8 daily; 45min); Kuching (4 daily; 1hr 25min); Miri (4 weekly; 2hr); Penang (2 daily; 1hr); Sandakan (6 weekly; 2hr 40min); Sibu (daily; 35min).
Pulau Tioman to: Kuala Lumpur (1–2 daily; 45min); Singapore (at least 4 weekly; 35min).

Sarawak

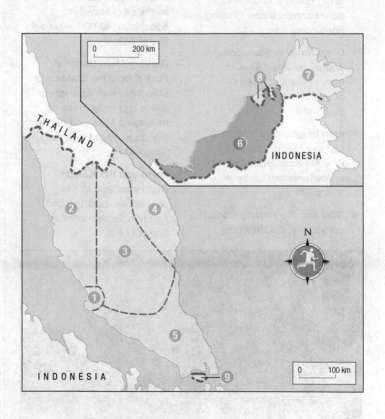

CHAPTER 6

Highlights

* **Kuching** A buzzing city, with tremendous cuisine and nightlife as well as captivating historic sites. See p.395

* **Santubong/Damai** Lovely beaches hosting chilled resort hotels and back-to-nature camps below Gunung Santubong. See p.412

* **Bako National Park** Beautiful and accessible park with easy trekking and plenty of proboscis monkeys. See p.415

* **Iban longhouses** Traditional communities dot the rivers near the Kalimantan border in southwestern Sarawak. See p.423

* **Sibu and the Rejang** Vibrant upriver city, the launching pad for meandering journeys along the Rejang, Katibas and Baleh rivers. See p.427

* **Niah National Park** Enormous cave chamber within a state park where archeologists have found evidence of human occupation 40,000 years ago. See p.449

* **Gunung Mulu National Park** Simply the State's top attraction, with astonishing caves and tough treks to mountains Mulu and Api, for the razor-sharp Pinnacles. See p.465

* **Bario and the Kelabit Highlands** Trek at this cool upland paradise and visit remote communities. See p.474

▲ Deer Cave in Gunung Mulu National Park

Sarawak

T he largest state in the federation, **SARAWAK** is a very different place from Peninsular Malaysia. Its 125,000 square kilometres border the Indonesian state of Kalimantan on its eastern and southern boundaries, and the Sultanate of Brunei to the north. Rivers spill down the jungle-covered mountains to become wide, muddy arteries nearer the sea, while surviving rainforest, highland plateaus and river communities combine to form one of the most complex and diverse ecosystems on earth. Sadly, the logging industry and indigenous farming have led to diminishing wildlife as well as impacting on indigenous communities. Even Sarawak's official state emblem, the eccentric-looking hornbill, whose beak has been used for centuries by tribespeople to carve images from the natural and supernatural worlds, is at risk as numbers have been substantially reduced as a result of logging practices. However, there are flora and fauna galore in the beautiful **national parks**, including the mountainous Gunung Mulu, the ornithologist's paradise Bako, the cave-riddled Niah and the littoral paradise, Tanjung Datu.

Another convincing reason for hopping across the sea to Sarawak is its culture. Visitors can't fail to meet members of the state's indigenous tribes – including the Iban and the Kelabit – while enjoying a drink in a lively Kuching nightspot or visiting the traditional upriver or highland communities. It will be harder to encounter the semi-nomadic Penan but it is nevertheless a possibility. Making up around half the state's population, the indigenes are known historically as Land Dyaks (who live up in the hills – the Bidayuh of southwestern Sarawak are the chief example), Sea Dyaks (such as the Iban and Melanau, who dwell along river valleys) and Orang Ulu (like the Berawan, Kenyah, Kelabit and Kayan, who live along rivers in the remote regions of the northern interior). The indigenous peoples have for centuries lived in multi-doored **longhouses**, visits to which are among the highlight of many travellers' trips to Sarawak. Unfortunately, as a result of government policies and economic changes, the number of traditional, hardwood longhouses is slowly decreasing as communities move into more conventional kampung-style housing. The majority of visits to longhouse communities in the southwest of the state are made close to the **Batang Ai National Park**, almost always through a tour operator (there are many excellent outfits to choose from in Kuching). However, the relatively unexplored, but still accessible, communities along the **Katibas and Baleh rivers**, off Batang Rejang near Kapit, offer promising possibilities for the independent-minded traveller.

Most people start their exploration of Sarawak in the busy and attractive capital **Kuching**, in the southwest of the state, a perfect base to explore **Bako National Park**. Often underestimated by travellers, this is one of Asia's most

SOUTH CHINA SEA

SARAWAK

N

Kampung
Tellian
Oya   Mukah   Tatau
S. Igan   S. Mukah
Dalat
Sibu
Bintangor
Sarikei   Kanowit   Batang Rajang
Song   Kapit
TANJUNG DATU
NATIONAL PARK   Kabong   Saratok
Teluk Melano   Santubong   S. Katibas   S. Bangkit
Sematan   GG. GADING   Peninsula   Kampung   Rumah
NATIONAL   Buntal   Pusa   Sereliau   Tambi
PARK   BAKO
Lundu   Kuching   NATIONAL PARK   Betong   S. Skrang
Wetlands   Kampung   S. Engkat   BATANG AI
KUBAH   KUCHING   Sereliau   NATIONAL PARK
NATIONAL   Simunjan   Betong   S. Lemanak   Nanga   G. Lawit
PARK   Bau   Sri Aman   Lupar   Sumpa   (1767m)
Serian   Nanga   S. Ulu Ai
G. Niut   Serubah
(1701m)   Kg. Anna Rais   Lubok
G. Penrissen   Tebedu   Antu   Putussibau
(1300m)   Entikong
Balaikaran
Semitau
Pontianak
S. Kapuas

perfect nature parks with a wild shoreline of mangrove swamp and a hinterland of *kerangas* bush bustling with proboscis monkeys and birdlife. Although Sarawak is not noted for its **beaches**, there are beautiful ones in Bako, and further west to the edge of the state's southwestern seaboard at the insanely remote **Tanjung Datu National Park**, only accessible by boat in the dry season (March–Sept).

A five-hour ferry ride northeast of Kuching, the city of **Sibu** marks the start of the popular route along **Batang Rejang**, Sarawak's longest river (*batang* means "big river" or "river system"). Upriver beyond Sibu, it's worth stopping at the bazaars of **Song** and **Kapit**, and using these busy little places as bases for

travel along the Katibas and Baleh tributaries. From Kapit, it is five hours by express boat, running the Pelagus Rapids, to **Belaga**, a remote settlement fronting the upper section of the Rejang. Tribal peoples still come to this bazaar to sell goods but the area is much changed by the devastation caused by the Bakun Dam development. One advantage of reaching Belaga, though, is that you can travel quickly by 4X4 to **Bintulu** on the coast, first along logging trails, and then paved road.

The road route north from Sibu to Bintulu makes for a quick, reasonably comfortable trip; increasingly, travellers are inclined to stop briefly at the riverside town of **Mukah**, itself rather nondescript but close to the Melenau

Flights from Peninsular Malaysia to Sarawak have in recent years become much more competitive with the advent of AirAsia, which competes on many routes with Malaysia Airlines (MAS). Accommodation and travel within the state still cost a little more than on the mainland. However, food and drinks are always a bargain (though beer is pricier than on the Peninsula), and ethnic artefacts bought along the way are excellent value too, as well as often being unique to the region. Note that Sarawak has different rules on **entry permits** from the rest of Malaysia (see p.65).

Getting there

Flights to **Kuching and Miri** are the most straightforward way into Sarawak. There are daily flights on MAS (ⓦ www.malaysiaairlines.com) and AirAsia (ⓦ www.airasia .com) to Kuching from Peninsular Malaysia's **KL**, **Penang** and **Johor Bahru** and the Sabah capital **Kota Kinabalu** as well as daily non-stop flights from KL to coastal cities, **Bintulu** and **Miri**, and the Rejang river town, **Sibu**. There are direct connections from Kuching to the Brunei capital, **Bandar Seri Begawan**, and to **Singapore** and **Macau**.

The main overland route into Sarawak is by bus from **Kuala Belait** in Brunei to Miri, though this can involve slow passage through border stations (avoid the weekend log jams if at all possible). A second crossing is via **Sipitang** in Sabah (see p.509) to **Lawas,** one of Sarawak's two northern divisions. The Lawas Express coach originates in Kota Kinabalu, and will get you to Lawas before nightfall. Lawas is connected by plane to Miri and by boat to the Sabah island, Labuan. More straightforward is the overland route in the south of the state, with daily buses leaving from Pontianak, the capital of Kalimantan, crossing from Entikong to **Tebedu** in southwestern Sarawak, 100km from Kuching.

Getting around

Boats nearly always run to a reliable timetable, and come in three main types: sea-going **launches**, which ply the busy stretch from Kuching to Sarikei, at the mouth of the Rejang and onwards to Sibu; express **boats**, which shoot up and down the Rejang; and smaller **longboats**, which provide transport along the tributaries. If you need to **rent a longboat** to get to remote longhouses, note that this can be prohibitively expensive if you're not travelling in a group. It's common to pay in excess of RM300 a day per person as diesel goes up in price substantially the further you are away from a filling station. In addition, although the distances travelled from one longhouse to another are often not great (around 2km on average), travelling upstream against the current, in shallow waters (in the dry season) and through rapids, can be hard going.

In northern Sarawak, an essential way of getting around is by small planes, a service run by MAS subsidiary, MASwings (ⓦ www.MASwings.com.my). Their Twin Otters seat either twelve or eighteen, while the Fokkers and ATRs each seat fifty plus people. These small aircraft service many remote communities, most significantly Bario and Ba' Kelalan in the Kelabit Highlands, Marudi and Gunung Mulu National Park. It's best to book a few weeks in advance for both legs of your journey, as planes can fill up fast. The standard baggage allowance is only 10/20kg per person on Twin Otters/Fokkers respectively, with excess baggage charged at RM1/5 per kilo.

base of **Kampung Tellian**, a colourful traditional community. Beyond Bintulu, the main route passes close to the national park, **Similajau**, famed for its crocodiles, before reaching **Niah National Park**, with its vast cave system and forest hikes. The road snakes north to the Brunei border via **Miri**, a vibrant town built on oil money, and noted for its excellent restaurants and high-end hotels.

From Kuala Baram express boats go along Batang Baram to **Marudi**, where a proud fort, housing a museum, overlooks the majestic river. Most travellers fly direct to the state's number one attraction, **Gunung Mulu National Park**, although the trip can be done by river, a picturesque ride deep into the forested interior. Mulu features the limestone Pinnacles and numerous extraordinary caves and passageways sequestered within its three mountains. The show caves can be seen easily in a day; others require adventure caving. A final, requisite stop is the northeast's forested plateau, the **Kelabit Highlands**. Flying into Bario or Ba' Kelalan opens the door to visiting the remote communities and longhouses of the indigenous Kelabit tribes, where paths in the jungle lead to ancient megaliths and where you may meet the shy, semi-nomadic Penan.

Some history

Sarawak's first inhabitants were cave-dwelling **hunter-gatherers** who lived here forty thousand years ago. The various tribes lived fairly isolated lives and there was little contact with the wider world until the first trading boats from Sumatra and Java arrived in around 3000 BC, exchanging cloth and pottery for jungle produce. By the thirteenth century Chinese merchants had become dominant, bartering beads and porcelain with the coastal Melenau people for bezoar stones (from the gall bladders of monkeys) and birds' nests, both considered aphrodisiacs by the Chinese. In time, the traders were forced to deal with the rising power of the Malay sultans including the Sultan of Brunei. Meanwhile, Sarawak was attracting interest from Europe; in the seventeenth century the Dutch and English established short-lived trading posts near Kuching in order to obtain pepper and other spices.

With the eventual decline in power of the Brunei Sultanate, the region became impossible to administrate. At the beginning of the eighteenth century civil war erupted as a result of feuding between various local sultans, while piracy threatened to destroy what was left of the trade in spices, animals and minerals. In addition, the indigenous groups' predilection for **head-hunting** had led to a number of deaths among the traders and the sultan's officials, and violent territorial confrontations involving the more powerful ethnic groups were increasing.

Matters were at their most explosive when the Englishman **James Brooke** took an interest in the area. A former soldier, Brooke helped the beleaguered Sultan of Brunei quell a rebellion by Dyak miners and, as a reward, demanded sovereignty over the area around Kuching. The sultan had little choice but to relinquish control of the difficult territory and in 1841 Brooke was installed as the first White Rajah of Sarawak, launching a dynastic rule which lasted for a century.

Brooke signed treaties with the sultan, tolerated the business dealings of the Chinese, built a network of **forts** to strengthen his rule and sent officials into the malarial swamps and mountainous interior to make contact with the Orang Ulu (upriver tribes). Despite these successes, Brooke's administration was not without its troubles. In one incident his men killed dozens of marauding Dyaks, while in 1857 Hakka Chinese **gold-miners**, based in the settlement of Bau on Sungai Sarawak, opposed Brooke's attempts to eliminate their trade in opium and suppress their secret societies. They attacked Kuching and killed a number of officials – Brooke got away by the skin of his teeth. His nephew, **Charles Brooke**, assembled a massive force of warrior Dyaks and followed the miners; in the ensuing battle over a thousand Chinese were killed.

In 1863 Charles Brooke took over and continued the acquisition of territory from the Sultan of Brunei. River valleys – known as **divisions** – were bought for a few thousand pounds, the Dyaks living there either persuaded to enter into deals or crushed if they resisted. Brunei itself had shrunk so much it was now surrounded on all three sides by Brooke's Sarawak, establishing the geographical parameters that still define the sultanate today.

The third and last rajah, **Vyner Brooke**, consolidated the gains of his father, Charles, but was less concerned with indigenous matters. The **Japanese invasion**, however, effectively put an end to his control. Brooke escaped, but most of his officials were interned and some subsequently executed. With the Japanese surrender in 1945, Australian forces temporarily ran the state; Vyner returned the next year and ceded Sarawak to the British government. Many Malays opposed this, believing that **British rule** was a backward step, and their protest reached its peak in 1949 when the British governor was murdered. With Malaysian independence in 1957, attempts were made to include Sarawak, Sabah and Brunei in the **Malaysian Federation**, inaugurated in 1963, but Brunei exited at the last minute. Sarawak's inclusion in the federation was opposed by Indonesia, and skirmishes broke out along the Sarawak–Kalimantan border, with Indonesia arming communist guerrillas inside Sarawak, who opposed both British and Malay rule. During this insurgency, known as the **Konfrontasi**, the small Sarawak army had to call upon British military aid to help defend the bazaar towns in the interior; the conflict continued for three years, but was eventually put down by Malaysian troops aided by the British.

Throughout the 1960s and 1970s, reconstruction programmes strengthened regional communities and provided housing, resources and jobs. Beyond the millennium Sarawak remains a peaceful, multiracial state, though social tensions, triggered by the government's economic strategy, sometimes rise to the surface. Over the last few years the question of **land rights** has become paramount, with small non-governmental organizations like Rengah Sarawak (ⓦwww .rengah.c2o.org) assisting rural communities and remote longhouse and Penan groups in conflicts with **oil-palm estates** and the timber industry, over encroachment on community lands. It is a social phenomenon which, despite state government promises to enforce laws protecting the poor, continues to spill over into localized demonstrations and even sporadic violence.

Southwestern Sarawak

Located upriver from the swamp-ridden coastline, state capital **Kuching** is on most people's itinerary, both as a captivating place in itself and as a starting point for travel around the southwest and onwards to Sibu, reachable by air, bus and boat. The city and environs certainly contain enough to occupy a few days' sightseeing: Kuching's **Sarawak Museum** holds the state's best collection of ethnic artefacts, while easy half-day trips can be made to **Semenggoh Wildlife Rehabilitation Centre** and the **Sarawak Cultural Village**, at Damai to the north. Although visitors do go to **Bako National Park** on a day-trip, it is better to allow more time – preferably a few days – to visit this delight. Some travellers also choose to overnight at either of two small parks to the west of Kuching: **Gunung Gading** and **Kubah**. With an early start, it is also possible to visit them in a single day. You need two days plus to visit to the **Bidayuh communities** near the Kalimantan border and the languid, coastal village of **Sematan**, access point for the spectacular and little-visited **Tanjung Datu Park** to the west. Experiencing the **Iban longhouses** east of the capital on the edges of Batang Ai National Park, especially on the Ai, Engkari and Lemanak rivers, is nearly always done as part of a tour over one to three nights, and is well worth the effort and relative expense.

Kuching

With its period attractions and zestful energy **KUCHING** is one of Malaysia's most pleasant cities. Occupying the southern bank of the Sarawak River, the centre is easy to traverse on foot and architecturally distinctive. But despite the prevalence of colonial architecture and the occasional echo of a bygone era, Kuching very much lives in the present: techno beats boom from boutiques, fashionable cafés serve health drinks and fusion food, while internet cafés provide hot-wiring to the world.

The heart of the old town is a warren of crowded lanes in which the city's Chinese community runs cafés, hotels, general stores and laundries. Main Bazaar, the city's oldest street, sports the remains of its original godowns – now converted into shops – overlooking the river, Kuching's main supply route since the city's earliest days for Iban war parties and White Rajahs alike. In recent years much of the city's highly visible youthful energy has moved to the eastern commercial quarter around Jalan Tunku Abdul Rahman and Jalan Padungan, where Western-style cafés, bars and restaurants have sprung up. All this adds up to a newfound confidence, imbued with an atmosphere that's at once exciting and laid-back. But then the city has always been an ethnic melting pot, its inhabitants divided between Chinese, Malays, Indians and the various Dyak and Orang Ulu groups (mainly Iban and Bidayuh, but also Melenau, Kayan and Kenyah) with no one group predominating.

The city is of cultural interest too, with attractions including the **Sarawak Museum**, one of the finest in Malaysia, and the **Textile Museum**, an insight into cultural history and dapper dress sense. Whenever there's an auspicious date in the Chinese calendar, keep an eye on China Street's **Chinese temple**, where there's often a frenzy of activity; and check for events like the annual Mooncake festival in September, when nearby Carpenter Street becomes a conduit for carnivalesque masquerades, food, music and much more.

Some history

In 1841, James Brooke came up the river, arriving at a village known as Sarawak, which lay on a small stream called Sungai Mata Kuching ("Cat's Eye"), adjoining the main river; it seems likely that the stream's name was shortened by Brooke and came to refer to the fast-expanding settlement. However, a much-repeated tale has it that the first rajah pointed to the village and asked its name. The locals, thinking Brooke was pointing to a cat, replied – reasonably enough – "kucing" ("cat"). Either way, it wasn't until 1872 that Charles Brooke officially changed the settlement's name from Sarawak to Kuching.

Until the 1920s, the capital was largely confined to the south bank of the Sarawak river, stretching only from the Chinese heartland around Jalan Temple east of today's centre, to the Malay kampung around the mosque to the west. On the north bank, activity revolved around the fort and a few

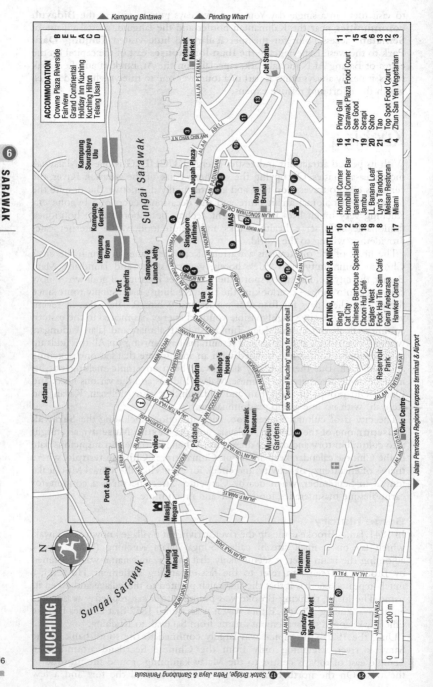

KUCHING

Sungai Sarawak

N

0 — 200 m

▲ Kampung Bintawa   ▲ Pending Wharf

SARAWAK

6

Sungai Sarawak

Kampung Sourabaya Ulu

Kampung Gersik

Kampung Boyan

Fort Margherita

Singapore Airlines

Sampan & Launch Jetty

Tua Pek Kong

Tun Jugah Plaza

JLN. CHAN CHIN ANN

JALAN ABELL

JALAN PADUNGAN

MAS

Royal Brunei

JALAN SONGTHIAN CHEOK

JALAN BUKIT MATA

JALAN BAN HOCK

JALAN TUNKU ABDUL RAHMAN

JLN. BORNEO

JALAN HAJI

JLN. MARKET

Astana

JLN WAYANG

JLN TABUAN

LEBUH TEMPLE

Bishop's House

Cathedral

JALAN TUN HAJI OPENG

JLN CARPENTER

MAIN BAZAAR

Sarawak Museum

Museum Gardens

JLN MCDOUGALL

JALAN P. RAMLEE

JLN COURTHOUSE

Padang

LEBUH JAWA

JLN NI MOSQUE

JLN MARKET

Police

JLN. INDIA

LEBUH INDIA

Port & Jetty

Masjid Negara

Kampung Masjid

Sungai Sarawak

JALAN DATUK AJIBAH ABOL

JALAN HAJI TAHA

JALAN PALM

Miramar Cinema

Sunday Night Market

JALAN BUBBER

JALAN SATOK

JALAN NANAS

Reservoir Park

Civic Centre

JALAN BUDAYA

JALAN CENTRAL BARAT

Cat Statue

Petanak Market

JALAN PETANAK

see 'Central Kuching' map for more detail

▼ Jalan Penrissen Regional express terminal & Airport

▼ Satok Bridge, Petra Jaya & Santubong Peninsula

ACCOMMODATION
Crowne Plaza Riverside	B
Fairview	E
Grand Continental	F
Holiday Inn Kuching	A
Kuching Hilton	C
Telang Usan	D

EATING, DRINKING & NIGHTLIFE
Bing!	10
Cat City	2
Chinese Barbecue Specialist	5
Choon Hui Café	18
Eagles' Nest	9
Fock Hai Tin Sam Café	8
Geral Anekarasa	21
Hawker Centre	17

Hornbill Corner	11
Hornbill Corner Bar	15
Ipanema	7
Jambu	19
LL Banana Leaf	6
Lyn's Tandoori	13
Meisan Restoran	12
Miami	3

Pinoy Grill	16
Sarawak Plaza Food Court	14
See Good	1
Serapi	A
Soho	20
Tao	21
Top Spot Food Court	12
Zhun San Yen Vegetarian	4

dozen houses reserved for British officials. It was the prewar **rubber boom** that financed the town's expansion, with the elegant tree-lined avenue Jalan Padungan, 1km east of the centre, becoming the smart place in which to live and work. The city escaped serious destruction during World War II, since Japanese bombing raids were mainly intent on destroying the oil wells in the north of Sarawak.

Since independence, business has boomed, and though many of the impressive nineteenth-century buildings have been restored, others have been destroyed to make way for new roads and office developments. However, the planners cast a sympathetic eye over perhaps the most important part of Kuching. Following large-scale renovation and the closure of Jalan Gambier's wet markets, a pedestrian riverside area, referred to now as the **waterfront**, once again integrates the city with the waters that have shaped its growth. Another sensible decision has been to close busy Jalan India to traffic, better highlighting its dense concentration of colourful shops.

Arrival and information

Kuching's modern international **airport** (☎082/457373) is 14km south of the city; the arrivals hall contains shops, cafés and a taxi kiosk. The airport shuttle bus, #8a, leaves from 8am to 7pm for the city centre (RM1.40); a taxi costs RM23. Buy a taxi coupon from the clearly marked kiosk. For buying or changing MAS or MASwings tickets use the office in the airport arrivals, or in central Kuching, at the large, glass-fronted MAS office on Jalan Song Thian Cheok (see p.409). AirAsia has a stand in airport arrivals and an office in the city (see p.409). For details of bus and boat terminals see p.409.

There is a small **Sarawak Tourist Association** (STA) desk in the airport (daily 8am–5pm; ☎082/456266), but the main place for tourism information and enquiries is the **Visitors' Information Centre** (VIC), located in the Old Courthouse, Jalan Tun Haji Openg, on the western edge of the waterfront (Mon–Fri 8am–6pm, Sat, Sun & public hols 9am–3pm; ☎082/410944, ⓦwww .sarawaktourism.com). Next door is the booking desk of the **National Parks and Wildlife Office** (☎082/248088, ⓦwww.forestry.sarawak.gov.my), where accommodation in the parks can be organized. The English-language *Borneo Post*, *Sarawak Gazette* and *The Star*, available at newsagents, contain small sections on cultural events in town and around the state.

City transport

You can **walk** around much of downtown Kuching with ease and so will have little use for the city buses. A few of the local **bus** routes are handy, however, including the blue-and-white buses run by the Chin Lian Long company that trundle out from Jalan Mosque to the Indonesian Consulate, the immigration office and Pending wharf (for the Sarikei/Sibu boat).

The main **taxi ranks** are in the old part of town, at the Jalan Gambier and Jalan India intersection. You can usually flag down a taxi in East Kuching's commercial district, in front of the hotels along the Jalan Tunku Abdul Rahman. Be aware though that the fixed price charged by these taxis is steeper than at other points, starting from RM12 for most places in the city rather than the RM10 charged at the taxi ranks or on the road.

Sampan boats (daily 6am–10pm; every 15min; RM1) depart from the jetty opposite the visitors' centre on the western end of the waterfront, taking only a few minutes to cross the Sarawak River. A slightly longer boat trip (RM3) takes you one kilometre upstream to the jetty at Kampung Bintawa, a small

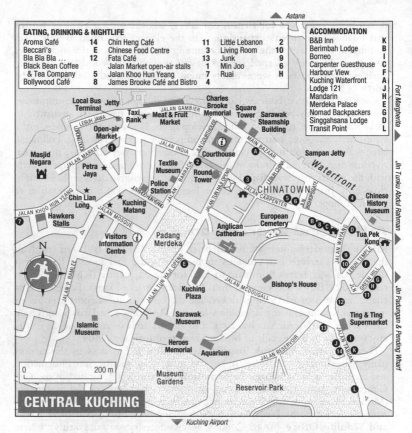

EATING, DRINKING & NIGHTLIFE

Aroma Café	14	Chin Heng Café	11	Little Lebanon	2
Beccari's	E	Chinese Food Centre	3	Living Room	10
Bla Bla Bla ...	12	Fata Café	13	Junk	9
Black Bean Coffee		Jalan Market open-air stalls	1	Min Joo	6
& Tea Company	5	Jalan Khoo Hun Yeang	7	Ruai	H
Bollywood Café	8	James Brooke Café and Bistro	4		

ACCOMMODATION

B&B Inn	K
Berimbah Lodge	B
Borneo	I
Carpenter Guesthouse	C
Harbour View	F
Kuching Waterfront	A
Lodge 121	J
Mandarin	H
Merdeka Palace	E
Nomad Backpackers	G
Singgahsana Lodge	D
Transit Point	L

Fort Margherita ▶

Jln Tunku Abdul Rahman ▶

Jln Padungan & Pending Wharf ▶

6

SARAWAK | Kuching

Local Bus Terminal · Jetty · Taxi Rank · Open-air Market · Meat & Fruit Market · Charles Brooke Memorial · Square Tower · Sarawak Steamship Building

LEBUH JAWA · JALAN GAMBIER · JALAN INDIA · JALAN MARKET

Masjid Negara · Petra Jaya · Chin Lian Long · Hawkers Stalls · Kuching Matang · Kuching Mosque · Visitors Information Centre

JALAN KHOO HUN YEANG · JALAN MOSQUE · JALAN P. RAMLEE

Textile Museum · Police Station · Round Tower · Courthouse · MAIN BAZAAR · Waterfront · Sampan Jetty

CHINATOWN · JLN CARPENTER · JLN BISHOPSGATE · JLN WAYANG · JLN GREEN HILL

European Cemetery · Chinese History Museum · Tua Pek Kong · LEBUH TEMPLE

Padang Merdeka · Anglican Cathedral

Kuching Plaza · JALAN McDOUGALL · Bishop's House · Ting & Ting Supermarket

Sarawak Museum · Heroes Memorial · Aquarium · JALAN RESERVOIR · JALAN TABUAN

Islamic Museum

0 ——— 200 m

Museum Gardens · Reservoir Park

CENTRAL KUCHING

Malay suburb few travellers visit. Should you wish to take in more of the river, go on a **river cruise** – the best are organized by CPH Travel (see p.408). You can choose between a morning cruise (9am) and a sunset one (5pm) – both costing around RM80. The journey usually takes two to three hours; it's not necessary to book ahead, just turn up at the jetty, mid-way along the waterfront, twenty minutes before departure.

Accommodation

Kuching has a wide range of **accommodation** but prices tend to be a little higher than elsewhere in Sarawak: be prepared to pay at least RM50 for a double room if the budget places are full. The big hotels, with swimming pools and 24-hour service, are mostly clustered on or near the waterfront, often offering great views. Promotional rates, which slash the published price are often available and are sometimes there for the asking, or by booking early online. The appealing guesthouses and mid-range hotels are mostly located back from the river, but are still close to the main restaurant and café areas.

As an alternative to staying in the city, head for Damai on the coast (see p.412). All the hotels below are marked on either the map of greater Kuching on p.396 or central Kuching above.

Guesthouses

B&B Inn First floor, 30–31 Jalan Tabuan ☎082/237366. Ever-popular backpacker spot with rather cramped dorms and a few bare but tidy private rooms, both ranges sharing common facilities. A basic but unlimited tea-and-toast breakfast is included. Dorm beds RM14, rooms ❶.

Berimbah Lodge 104 Jalan Carpenter ☎082/238589, ⓦwww.berimbah.com. Neat, homely spot with super-cheap dorm beds (RM20) and other rooms. ❷

Carpenter Guesthouse 94 Jalan Carpenter ☎082/256050, ⓦwww.carpenterguesthouse.com. Perfectly positioned, tiny, yet stylish establishment in old Kuching's sleeping options. Five-bed dorms are excellent value at RM28 and there are a small number of twin/family rooms too. ❷

Fairview 6 Jalan Taman Budaya (beside Reservoir Park) ☎082/240017, ⓔthefairview@gmail.com. Located 200m behind the Sarawak Museum, this heritage site is set in a lush, secluded garden. Eric's perfectly restored house includes two massive en-suite rooms with period touches, and a number of four-bed en-suite dorms (RM25). Guests can make their own meals in the house kitchen. ❸

Nomad Backpackers First floor, 3 Jalan Green Hill ☎082/237062, ⓦwww.borneobnb.com. Next door to the city's most happening bar, *Ruai*, *Nomad* is not for those who want to get an early night in. But this Kuching staple has the city's second cheapest backpacker beds (dorm RM26) as well as twins and doubles. ❸

Singgahsana Lodge 3 Lorong Temple ☎082/429277, ⓦwww.singgahsana.com. Stylishly renovated by young owners Donald and Marina Tan, and 30m from the waterfront, this boutique backpacker lodge packs in dozens of themed and tastefully decorated rooms, including some with dorm beds at RM30, set around a central sitting and eating area. It has rapidly become a popular spot for travellers visiting southwestern Sarawak and its attic bar (only open to residents) with an eclectic music soundtrack, snooker table and cut-price drinks, is quite simply one of the best places in town to while away an evening. Excellent value. ❹

Transit Point Roundabout at Jalan Tabuan/Jalan Ban Hok intersection ☎082/239961. Oddly perched on a roundabout and within an acre of garden, this new facility, aimed at student and budget travellers, has a long, functional, two-storey block with simple twin-bed rooms with external toilet and showers. ❷

Mid-range hotels and lodges

Borneo 30 Jalan Tabuan ☎082/244122, ⓔbidasbuan@yahoo.com. This comfortable hotel, one of Kuching's oldest, has lovely rooms with polished wooden floors, a/c, bath or shower and TVs. There's an excellent café/restaurant beside the foyer. ❺

Kuching Waterfront 15 Main Bazaar ☎082/231111. This gorgeously refurbished godown has small but stylish rooms; a simple, continental breakfast is included. ❺

Lodge 121 First floor, Section 33 KTD, Jalan Tabuan ☎082/428121. Mid-priced backpacker place on breezy first and second floors, opposite the *Borneo*. Rooms include singles, doubles and a large attic dorm (RM30) with common showers. ❸

Mandarin 6 Jalan Green Hill ☎082/418269. A good option in this cramped thoroughfare with full facilities including a/c, shower, toilet and TV, but the rooms are a little on the shabby side. ❸

Telang Usan off Jalan Ban Hock ☎082/415588, ⓦwww.telangusan.com. Friendly, Kayan-run place, an easy walk from the centre. Its wall and stairs are adorned with art by the late Kenyah artist Tusan Padan, and facilities include an excellent restaurant and veranda-style bar. Rooms range in size and shape but are generally cosy, comfortable and clean, and the bathrooms have tubs. ❺

Expensive hotels

Crowne Plaza Riverside Jalan Tunku Abdul Rahman ☎082/247777, ⓦwww.holidayinn-sarawak.com. One of Kuching's priciest and most opulent hotels, this ten-floor marble extravaganza offers all the comforts and amenities you could wish for: several classy restaurants and bars, full sporting facilities, a business centre and an adjoining shopping complex. The rooms aren't very large but are sumptuously appointed, and the views from those that face the river are breathtaking. Breakfast included. ❼–❽

Grand Continental 46 Jalan Ban Hock ☎082/230399, ⓦwww.ghihotels.com/malaysia. Slightly away from the centre, the *Grand* is a good deal, with regular promotional rates. Rooms are immaculate, as expected from a business-class hotel, and there's a swimming pool on the second floor. ❺

Harbour View Lebuh Temple ☎082/274666, ⓦwww.harbourview.com.my. Slick, business-oriented hotel in a lively location. The en-suite rooms are competitively priced – often promotional rates can get down close to RM120 – but smallish. ❺

Holiday Inn Kuching Jalan Tunku Abdul Rahman ☎082/423111, ⓦwww.ichotelsgroup.com.

Overlooking the river, with some of its superbly appointed rooms looking directly out across to the fort on the opposite bank (for an extra RM20), this hotel has an inviting pool to cool off in, restaurants, cafés and a well-stocked bookshop among its amenities. ⑦

Kuching Hilton Jalan Tunku Abdul Rahman ☎082/248200, ⓦ www.kuching.hilton.com. Another top-class hotel, whose front rooms have a great view of the river. There's a pool

and a mouthwatering range of food and drink outlets. ⑧

Merdeka Palace Jalan Tun Haji Openg ☎082/258000, ⓦ www.merdekapalace.com. This excellent place boasts large rooms with satellite TV and elegant bathrooms, plus a fine Italian restaurant with pizza to die for. The rooms at the front overlook the Padang; there are sometimes reductions on rooms at the back and for mid-week bookings. ⑤–⑦

The City Centre

The central area of the city, sandwiched between Jalan Courthouse to the west, Jalan Wayang to the east and Reservoir Park to the south, is usually referred to as **old Kuching**. The former Courthouse, the Post Office and the Sarawak Museum are the most impressive buildings here – aside from the museum, the buildings will occupy just a few hours of your time. Set within this small area is **Chinatown**, which incorporates the main shopping streets Main Bazaar and Jalan Carpenter. To the east of Jalan Wayang lie Jalan Green Hill, Jalan Tunku Abdul Rahman and Jalan Padungan, the principal entertainment districts. Further south from the old town's narrow, busy streets – yet only fifteen minutes' walk from the river – is **Reservoir Park**; bordering the colonial area, on the western edge of the centre, is the pedestrianized Jalan India, another shopping street. A short hop further west is **Kuching mosque** and main Malay residential area, dominated by detached kampung-style dwellings with sloping roofs and elevated verandas. Southwest of here, Satok Bridge leads to the suburb Satok, famed for its Saturday night market.

The waterfront and Old Courthouse

Fronting the city for almost a kilometre – from Jalan Gambier in the west to the Triangle's *Holiday Inn* – the **waterfront** is a pleasant spot to begin a city

▲ Kuching Mosque

tour, its manicured lawns enlivened by sculptures, seating areas and a dozen little soft-drink and snack stalls. Several of the godowns that once fronted onto the river were sacrificed during the development, but two fine buildings – the carefully restored **Sarawak Steamship Building**, which now houses a multi-media centre and a café, and the former Chinese General Chamber of Commerce – have survived. Early-morning strollers here may see enthusiasts going about their daily t'ai chi routines.

At the western end of the waterfront, at the junction of Main Bazaar and Jalan Tun Haji Openg, lies the renovated **Old Courthouse**, now housing the Visitors' Information Centre. Built in 1874, and sporting impressive Romanesque columns, the Courthouse is fronted by the **Charles Brooke Memorial**, a six-metre-high granite obelisk erected in 1924, at whose four corners are stone figures representing the four largest ethnic groups in Sarawak: the Chinese, Dyaks, Malays and Orang Ulu. Close by on the waterfront, the single-turreted **Square Tower** is all that's left of a fortress that was built in 1879. An earlier wooden construction was burnt down in the 1857 gold-miners' rebellion.

The Post Office, Textile Museum and south to the Bishop's House

Opposite the Courthouse, across Jalan Tun Haji Openg, is the excessively grand **Post Office**, whose massive ornamental columns, semicircular arches and decorative friezes were outmoded almost as soon as they were completed in 1931. Nearby, housed in the immaculately restored Pavilion Building, a lovely example of colonial baroque architecture on Jalan Barrack, lies the city's newest cultural attraction, the **Textile Museum** (daily 9am–5.30pm; free). The three-floor collection is a cornucopia of dazzling costume and artefacts from the region across the centuries. The first floor's photographic display covers all the state's races, including one mesmerizing shot of a young Iban couple, just married, in the early years of the century. On the second floor are headdresses, belts and traditional woven fabrics, known as *pua kumba*, from the upriver peoples, displayed alongside models of traditional Iban and Malay weddings.

Continuing south, skirt the well-groomed grassland known as **Padang Merdeka**, turn east onto Jalan McDougall and you'll see the modern Anglican **Cathedral**. A walk through its grounds leads to the oldest consecrated plot in Borneo, the European **cemetery**, now a rather unassuming patch of land. A few steps further east stands another Kuching landmark, the large, two-storey wooden **Bishop's House**, built in 1849, making it the oldest surviving building in the city.

The Sarawak Museum

Return to the padang, and head a little way south along Jalan Tun Haji Openg to reach the **Sarawak Museum** (daily 9am–6pm; free; free 1hr guided tour Fri 9.30am; ☎082/244232), set back from the road in deep gardens. Built in the 1890s, it's the largest colonial structure in Kuching. It was Charles Brooke who conceived the idea of a museum in Kuching, prompted by the nineteenth-century naturalist Alfred Russell Wallace, who spent two years in Sarawak in the 1850s. Wallace's natural history exhibits now form the basis of the collection on show. The museum's best-known curator was **Tom Harrisson** (1911–76), whose discovery of a 39,000-year-old skull in the caves at Niah in 1957 incited a radical reappraisal of the origins of early man in Southeast Asia. Under the museum's auspices, Harrisson frequently visited remote Orang Ulu tribes, bringing back the ceremonial artefacts that comprise some of the museum's greatest assets.

Sarawak's ceramic jars

The status and wealth of members of Sarawak's indigenous tribes depended on how many **ceramic jars** they possessed, and you can still see impressive models in longhouses, as well as in the Sarawak Museum, today. Ranging in size from tiny, elegantly detailed bowls to much larger vessels, over a metre in height, the jars were used for a range of purposes including storage, brewing rice wine and making payments – dowries and fines for adultery and divorce settlements. The most valuable jars were only used for ceremonies like the *Gawai Kenyalang* (the rite of passage for a mature, prosperous man, involving the recitation of stories by the longhouse bard), or for funerary purposes: when a member of northern Sarawak's Berawan died, the corpse was packed into a jar in a squatting position. As decomposition took place, the liquid from the body was drained away through a bamboo pipe, leaving the individual's bones or clothing, which would subsequently be removed, placed in a canister and hoisted onto an ossuary above the river bank. It's said that the jars can also be used to foretell the future, and can summon spirits through the sounds they emit when struck.

There's an information desk at the main entrance, beyond which is the **natural science** section, whose varied exhibits include a massive ball of dried hair from a crocodile's stomach and fairly pedestrian displays highlighting the diverse range of plant, animal and bird species in Borneo. The **ethnographic** section on the upper floor is much more interesting. Here you can walk into an authentic wooden Iban longhouse (for more on longhouses, see *Visiting a longhouse* colour section) and climb up into the rafters of the *sadau* (loft), which is used to store bamboo fish baskets, ironwork and sleeping mats; you're also free to finger the intricately glazed, sturdy Chinese ceramic jars and fine woven *pua kumbu* cloth. The Penan hut here is a much simpler affair, constructed of bamboo and rattan, within which are blowpipes and *parang*s (machetes), animal hides and coconut husks used as drinking vessels. At the other end of the floor, there's a collection of fearsome Iban war totems and woodcarvings from the Kayan and Kenyah ethnic groups who live in the headwaters of the Rejang, Baram and Balui rivers. Cabinets lining the walls close by showcase **musical instruments** used by the various tribes: the Bidayuh's heavy copper gongs, Iban drums and the Kayan *sape*, a stringed instrument looking a little like a lute.

To the right of the museum entrance is a small modern wing, the **Art Museum** (daily 9am–4.30pm; free). Worth a very quick tour, the museum houses contemporary concepts like figures of ostriches made in scrap metal.

From the Sarawak Museum to Reservoir Park

Ten minutes' walk west, on the other side of Jalan Tun Haji Openg, the **Islamic Museum** (daily except public hols: 9am–6pm; free) is housed in the Melayu Building, a former religious school painted in brilliant white and with a cool, tiled interior. The museum's seven galleries represent diverse aspects of Islamic culture, from architecture to weaponry, history to coinage and textiles to prayer.

Back across Jalan Tun Haji Openg, a path leads across the Sarawak Museum's sloping gardens to the **Heroes' Memorial**, commemorating the dead of World War II and the Konfrontasi, just five minutes' walk. You will pass the Kuching **aquarium** (daily 9am–6pm; free) on the way, which contains a small collection of marine life, including turtles from Sipadan in Sabah. Following the path past the memorial takes you to the corner of the museum gardens and out onto narrow Jalan Reservoir, across which lies **Reservoir Park**, a pretty, if artificial, tropical environment with many resident bird species and wildlife. There's a café (daily 8am–5pm), a drinks kiosk, boats for rent, a playground and stretching frames for workout enthusiasts.

Chinatown and East Kuching's commercial district

Back at Jalan Tun Haji Openg, the grid of streets behind the waterfront, running eastwards to the main Chinese temple, Tua Pek Kong, constitutes Kuching's **Chinatown**. On busy Main Bazaar and, one block south, on Jalan Carpenter, there are numerous cafés, restaurants, and stores operating out of two-storey shophouses, built by Hokkien and Teochew immigrants who arrived in the 1890s. Sandwiched between the western ends of Jalan Tunku Abdul Rahman and Jalan Padungan, overlooking the river, stands **Tua Pek Kong**, the oldest (it was built in 1876) Taoist temple in Sarawak. Supplicants burn paper money and joss sticks, and pray for good fortune to the temple deity, Tua Pek Kong. The temple maintains an immensely busy cultural life, especially during Chinese New Year when there are theatrical and musical performances.

Close by, on the waterfront, a cream-coloured edifice houses the **Chinese History Museum** (daily except Fri 9am–6pm; free), which makes use of paintings, black-and-white photographs and a modest selection of artefacts to chart the arrival and subsequent integration of Sarawak's Chinese community.

Jalan Tunku Abdul Rahman heads east from Tua Pek Kong temple, past several of the swankier hotels, and two plazas, Tun Jungan and Sarawak. Based in this commerical district are most of the city's banks with ATMs, Western-style cafés and boutiques. Also leading east from the temple, a little way south of Jalan Tunku Abdul Rahman, is **Jalan Padungan**, which runs eastwards out to the edge of the city. The one-kilometre walk along this tree-lined avenue takes you past bars and fusion restaurants, and ornate shophouses (whose elaborate decor was paid for by the rubber boom of the 1930s). At its eastern end, you can't fail to spot the **cat statue**, a 1.5-metre-high white-plaster effigy, her paw raised in welcome.

North across the Sarawak River

Cross the Sarawak River in a sampan to visit a number of interesting buildings. Sampans leave from a number of waterfront jetties, including the one opposite the Courthouse (daily 6am–10pm; every 15min). The first buildings constructed on the north side of the river here were small dwellings, part of the earlier Malay kampung, but following the arrival of the British in Kuching, Charles Brooke had two of the city's most important buildings constructed here. The **Astana**, built by Charles Brooke in 1869 and still the official home of Sarawak's governor, is the first of these, and accessible along a marked path from the jetty. An elegant, stately building with a distinctive shingle roof, it's set in a long, sloping garden with an excellent view of the Courthouse on the opposite bank. Various pieces of Brooke memorabilia and other relics are kept in one of the rooms, but unfortunately you can only visit the Astana on two days of the year, over the *Hari Raya Puasa* holiday at the end of Ramadan.

Along the river bank, 1km to the east, is **Fort Margherita**, one of the finest examples of the Brookes' system of fortifications; it's worth asking if it has re-opened to the public. There are around twenty other river forts of humbler construction throughout Sarawak, strategically placed to repel pirates and Dyak or Kayan war parties. If you do wish to walk around the periphery of the fort, take a rest in the nearby **Kuching Orchid Garden** (Tues–Sun 10am–6pm; free), which contains around one hundred orchid species.

From the fort, it's easy to thread your way eastwards and down to the Malay kampungs over which it stands guard: **Kampung Boyan** shades into **Kampung Gersik**, which in turn is assimilated by **Kampung Sourabaya Ulu**. All three feature pretty clapboard stilt houses, some in cheery pastel blues and greens, others somewhat dilapidated, teetering on knock-kneed stilts and accessed by bowed promenades. From this side of the fort, boats will deposit you near the *Crowne Plaza Riverside* hotel on the east side of the city centre.

In between the Astana and Fort Margherita but dominating both is the just-completed **State Assembly** building. This structure is an extraordinary sight – some kind of fusion between a postmodern mosque and a 1960s spaceship.

West Kuching

Back at the waterfront on the south bank, head one block back on Jalan Market, where there's a stream of open-air food stalls, focal point for the port workers, who tuck into noodle soups and stir fries, *roti canai* and dhal throughout the day and night. East of here, hopping over a concourse congested with taxis and through an arch leads into **Jalan India**, a busy pedestrian thoroughfare and a good place to buy shoes and cheap clothing. The street is named after the Indian coolies who arrived in the early part of the twentieth century to work at the docks.

About 100m west of the Jalan Market food stalls is the **Masjid Negara** (9am–3pm; closed Fri), standing on a steep hill, topped with gold cupolas. There's been a mosque on this site for around two hundred years, though this one only dates from the 1960s. Male visitors must wear long trousers and women skirts and a headscarf (provided by the mosque at the entrance).

From here, following the curve of the river southwest for 300m or so along Jalan Datuk Ajibah Abol, you reach the Malay enclave of **Kampung Masjid**. The area retains many well-preserved family houses, built at the start of the twentieth century by well-to-do government officials and boasting traditional features such as floor-level windows fronted by carved railings.

Satok

To the south of Kampung Masjid is the wide, traffic-clogged **Jalan Satok**. At its junction with Jalan Palm, opposite the Miramar Cinema, lies the site of Kuching's **Sunday night market**, which actually kicks off late Saturday afternoon; it continues until about midnight, picks up again at 7am on Sunday and finally ends around noon. Buses #4a and #4b get you there from the stop on Jalan P. Ramlee or from outside the post office, in around fifteen minutes, or it's about a 25-minute walk from the waterfront. Here dozens of stalls sell textiles, kitchen utensils and electrical paraphernalia, while others provide satay, *nasi campur* and sweets, washed down by watermelon and sugarcane juice, and *lycheesank*, a soft drink – Iban in origin – made from rice pellets and lychee fruit. Amid the congested confusion, look out for the alley where Dyaks sell fruit, vegetables and handicrafts – a good place to pick up inexpensive baskets and textiles. Lining the stalls are cheap cafés where you can rest for a plated meal and alcoholic drink.

Eating

Kuching is an excellent city to eat out in; it's a competitive environment where new places regularly open and shut. The culinary range is wide too: the mainstays – Malay, Chinese and Indian – still pull in the crowds but now Western-style cafés and bars have opened up, broadening to include a form of Malaysian/ Western fusion cuisine.

Local **specialities** such as wild boar and deer sometimes crop up on Chinese menus; seafood favourites include steamed pomfret fish and *umai*; jungle fern vegetables, *midin* and *paku*, are available throughout the city; and delicious rubbery little vegetables, *ambal* (known locally as "monkeys' penises"), are a delicacy, collected wild amongst the mangrove swamps lining the coast and rivers. In addition, Kuching has its own versions of *kuey teow* (thick rice "Shanghai" noodles, with meat and vegetables in a thick soy gravy), and *laksa*, the coconut-laced thick soup often slurped down by Sarawakians for breakfast, though some prefer *kolok mee*, an oily, tasty dish featuring dry noodles.

With such a rich range of dishes to sample, it's worth noting that many of the **cafés** and **hawker stalls**, especially those on Jalan Carpenter and around Jalan Khoo Hun Yean, close around sunset.

Hawkers and food courts

Chinese Food Centre Jalan Carpenter. Opposite the Chinese temple, this atmospheric centre offers a range of dishes, including owner Taniwah's superb *laksa* from RM2.

Gerai Anekarasa Hawker Centre Jalan Satok, under the bridge; you can take any Petra Jaya bus there. Famous for its barbecued chicken and steaks; a whole chicken plus rice and vegetables only costs around RM10 for two. Sun–Fri, from 6pm.

Jalan Khoo Hun Yeang 100m further west of the Mosque bus stand lies a favourite evening dining area with seating for a hundred plus, where half a dozen well-stocked hawkers serve fresh fish and Chinese dishes. Expect to pay RM30 a head, or up to RM50 for steamed fish.

Jalan Market open-air stalls Dozens of tiny stalls, very cheap and popular with dock workers, serving basic rice, noodle and curry dishes. A few sell seafood and beer into the early hours. Look out for the line of outlets selling fresh madeira cake and strong tea.

Sarawak Plaza Food Court Basement fast-food mall with an array of Malay and Chinese options, and very popular with Kuching youth; closes around 7pm.

Top Spot Food Court Jalan Bukit Mata Kuching. The top floor of the car park is devoted to seafood and fish, with claypot a speciality. The vegetables are very fresh too and other culinary styles, including Malay and Western, are available. Open daily 2pm–midnight.

Chinese

Black Bean Coffee and Tea Company 87 Jalan Carpenter. One of the few cafés in East Malaysia serving coffee made from locally harvested beans – *liberica* and *robustica* from Bau district. Daily except Wed 10.30am–11pm.

Chin Heng Café 5 Jalan Green Hill. Taxi drivers' haven and local café for those who stay at the nearby hotels. Breakfast is served until 11am, after which delicious chilled beans, sweet and

sour dishes and stir fries appear for around RM3–5 a portion.

Chinese Barbecue Specialist Jalan Padungan. Takeaway meals of barbecued duck, chicken and back cuts of pork are hacked up unceremoniously and laid on rice at the front of this bustling, rough-and-ready shophouse; a Cantonese kitchen with a sitting area operates at the back.

Choon Hui Café 34 Jalan Ban Hock. Fiery *laksa* and filling *kolok mee* make this stylish coffee shop, just beyond Kuching's Hindu temple, a huge breakfast-time hit with locals and visitors in the know.

Fata Café Jalan McDougall. Plain-looking place serving delicious Malaysian–Chinese home food. Daily except Sun 8am–2pm & 6–9pm.

Fock Hai Tin Sam Café 52 Jalan Padungan (Triangle end). Busy coffee shop with scrumptious noodles, a breakfast-size portion setting you back just RM3.

Hornbill Corner *Telang Usan* compound, off Jalan Ban Hock. Outdoor seafood restaurant well known for steamboat, where you grill stingray and marinated meats on a barbecue plate yourself.

Meisan Restoran Ground floor, *Holiday Inn Kuching*, Jalan Tunku Abdul Rahman. Spicy Szechuan food. Although the Sunday lunchtime dim sum is reasonably priced, evening meals are expensive – RM50 for two including beer – but worth splashing out for.

Min Joo Corner of Jalan Carpenter and Jalan Bishopsgate. Usually packed with Chinese-Malaysian locals and famous for the *kolok kosong* (plain noodles) that comes with a soup of pork, kidney and seaweed. Don't be put off by the gruff man taking the orders – it's worth the treatment and the wait.

See Good Jalan Ban Hock (in front of the *Telang Usan* hotel and beside the *Hornbill*). Don't be fooled by the house's inauspicious surrounds: standards of seafood dishes are the very highest here. Slipper lobster in pepper, bamboo clams, steamed pomfret, *ambal* and *midin* make for a fine (but not cheap) dinner with the cost coming in at RM60, including beer, or more if you make a selection from the extensive wine list. Evenings only; closed on the 14th and 18th of every month and for a long spell over Chinese New Year.

Malay, Indian and indigenous

Aroma Café Jalan Tabuan. Set back from the street in an office block, this outlet for Bidayuh cuisine is extremely good – classic Land Dyak food, with the spicy fish out of this world. The lunch buffet (11am–2pm) is particularly good value. Daily except Sun 6am–midnight.

Bollywood Café 66 Jalan Carpenter (Jalan Ewe Hai end). Super-friendly Naraindas and family serve up vegetarian and non-vegetarian savoury dishes, but excel with their Indian sweets. 8am–8pm.

LL Banana Leaf 7 Lorong Rubber 1, Jalan Rubber, off Jalan Satok. Lucy Lingam's simple and delicious traditional South Indian place with dosai, banana-leaf and vegetarian thali, plus meat and fish curries. A visit could be combined with one to nearby Satok Market (Sat night and Sun morning). Daily 9am–9pm.

Lyn's Tandoori Lot 62, Lorong 4, Jalan Nanas ℡082/234934. Tandoori specialist, a short taxi ride from the town centre (RM10), but worth seeking out for its excellent North Indian menu. Closed Sun.

Serapi *Holiday Inn*, Jalan Tunku Abdul Rahman. Top-drawer authentic North Indian food courtesy of an Indian chef. Lunch buffets offer a wide range of Western, Malay, Chinese and Indian dishes.

Western and global fusion

Beccari's *Merdeka Palace Hotel*. This is among the best Italian restaurants in East Malaysia with fine wines and great pizzas and lasagne – expect to pay RM60–80 per person. Daily noon–11pm.

Bing! 84 Jalan Padungan. Comfortable, Western-style coffee lounge with all the usual range of brews, plus delicious cakes. Mon–Thurs noon–midnight & Fri–Sun noon–1am.

Bla Bla Bla... 27 Jalan Tabuan, Jalan Wayang end ℡082/233944. Like *Tao*, a beautifully designed world of exotic water features, luscious art and Balinese wall hangings. The main dishes, especially

the prawn and chicken curries, are inventive, delicious and pricey (RM25–35). Daily except Tues 11am–11.30pm.

Jambu 32 Jalan Crookshank, a 15min walk from centre ℡082/235292. Wonderful addition to the city's inventive culinary landscape, with a constantly evolving menu combining Western and Malaysian elements and much else besides into "modern Borneo cuisine". Quite expensive at RM25–35 per main, but exceptional, with puddings like Moroccan date tart to die for. Also has a superb garden terrace bar out the back. Daily except Mon 6pm–12.30am.

The Junk 80 Jalan Wayang. An essential spot to visit, with its topsy-turvy decor of elegant multicultural bric-a-brac; house favourites include lamb with mashed potatoes and come in massive portions. Prices around RM30 for main courses.

James Brooke Café and Bistro Waterfront eastern end. Perfect part-open spot to sit back over a pot of tea and watch the waterfront's comings and goings with the Tua Pek Kong Temple at your back. The main dishes, although good, are quite pricey (RM20). Daily 10am–midnight; last order 10.30pm.

Little Lebanon Sarawak Tourism Complex (Jalan India end). You either love or hate this straight-ahead rendition of pan-Arab evergreens like falafel and kebab. Prices mid-range, at around RM20 for one.

Pinoy Grill and Restaurant 143 Padungan. Bracing and tasty Filipino dishes including tangin fish and crispy pata (pig knuckles), apparently a delicacy. Around RM35 for two.

Tao 175 Jalan Padungan. Called a lifestyle café and gallery, *Tao* is as stylish as they come, serving health and energy drinks, lattes, beer and wine, while the food covers Malaysian tapas and fusion. Global chillout and funky pop is played on the sound system and the Balinese decor, including lovely water features, is stunning. Daily 10am–midnight.

Vegetarian

Zhun San Yen Vegetarian Jalan Chan Chin Ann. Quite exceptional Chinese-run café with a dozen delicious, exclusively vegetarian and vegan dishes, sold from a buffet by weight. Also excellent juices, including watermelon and carrot. The overall cost hardly ever comes in at more than RM30 for two. Mon–Sat 8am–2.30pm & 5–8.30pm.

Drinking and nightlife

Although the city's nightlife scene is minor by Kuala Lumpur's standards, and some bars and clubs come and go with the seasons, Kuching has a standard set of great venues doing the biz. Expect an excitable but polite crowd and a music mix of international pop, R&B, hip-hop, house and the odd Cantonese tune, usually remixed with a techno throb. Aim straight for the

Triangle end of Jalan Padungan where most of the bars and nightclubs stay open until 4am Friday and Saturday nights, and up to 1am the rest of the week (Mon is "quiet night").

Bars

Cat City Taman Sri Sarawak Plaza (opposite *Kuching Hilton* hotel). Renovated pub-style bar with a balcony. Happy hour is 5.30–8.30pm, and there's karaoke, DJs and occasionally live music.

Eagles Nest 16 Jalan Bukit Mata. Also know as *The Cottage*, this prime watering hole serves almost-frozen beers and wines in a convivial atmosphere.

Ipanema Jalan Padungan, next to *Soho*. Narrow but stylish bar with cool music and cocktails. Fusion food is also available.

Junk Bar 82 Jalan Wayang. Kuching's most suave bar for the night-crowd; open 11pm–4am.

Living Room 84 Jalan Wayang. Next to *Junk Bar*, this is a very chilled, ultra-modern drinking haunt, open 7pm–midnight.

Miami Taman Sri Sarawak, opposite *Kuching Hilton*. Though the beer is often just Tiger and the music a touch kitsch, this is a classic, not-to-be-missed, very friendly watering hole – the kind of place where the Kuching hardcore go for their last drink (and one more). Open 6pm–3am.

Ruai Jalan Green Hill. Next door to *Nomad Backpackers*, this bar, owned by Iban singer and music producer, Peter Jaban, was, at least in late 2008, Kuching's best. Opening at 4.30pm daily and often staying open 12 hours at a stretch, it manages to be both laid-back and wild at the same time, with a mostly young crowd singing along to local hits and drinking with abandon. Also does delicious indigenous food.

Soho 64 Jalan Padungan. This ultra-fashionable two-floor bar absolutely heaves at weekends, when the DJ plays international funky pop and house. The veranda isn't quite Ibiza, but is pretty good nonetheless. Come early if you want to eat (local tapas-style small plates). 6pm–early hours.

Shopping

Kuching is the best place in Sarawak to buy just about anything, especially tribal textiles, pottery, Iban *pua kumbu* (hand-woven rugs), lovely rattan mats of various sizes and other handicrafts. However, if you are offered a locally made item that you like in a longhouse at a price that seems reasonable, snap it up and don't wait for Kuching, as some of the admittedly lovely-looking products on Main Bazaar, Jalan Temple and Jalan Wayang are produced in factories and aren't bespoke.

The city is known especially for its locally produced Chinese pottery, whose decoration bears local Dyak influences. There are some ceramics stalls on the road to the airport, but it's better to visit the **potteries** (daily 8am–noon & 2–6pm) themselves, where you can walk around and watch the potters in action at the wheel and firing kilns; each pottery also has a shop on site. They're clustered together on Jalan Penrissen, around 8km from town – take bus #3, #3a or #9a from the Mosque bus stand.

A-Ha Organic Jalan Tabuan. Organic shop stocking exotic products like unpolished red rice and black glutinous rice.

Artrageously Ramsey Ong 94 Main Bazaar. Ong is a leading modernist Malaysian painter, specializing in nature and rural culture. His gallery/shop includes work from other artists, including silk paintings.

Arts of Asia 68 Main Bazaar. One of the most comprehensive private galleries in town, it sells naturalistic paintings and sculpture, which tend to be expensive.

Atelier Galley 104 Main Bazaar. Collection of handicrafts, *objets d'art*, furniture and antiques.

Boonia 73 Jalan Padungan. Gallery displaying new work by mostly naturalistic Sarawakian artists which doubles as a picture-frame store.

Edric Ong 26 Main Bazaar. Lovely fabrics, textiles and sculpture.

Nelsons' Antiques and Jewellery 14 Main Bazaar. Cornucopia of Sarawakian crafts from mats to pottery, furniture to jewellery.

Ngee Tai Pottery Factory Eighth mile, Jalan Penrissen. Located on the right-hand side of the road as you head out of town, this is probably the best of the potteries. The master potter, Ng Hua Ann, shows visitors a wide range of ceramic wares ranging from huge pots to small souvenir items such as coffee mugs and flower vases.

Sarakraf 78 Jalan Tabuan. Decent stock of baskets, textiles and ironwork.

Sarawak House 67 Main Bazaar. Flashy and expensive but usually worth a look for textiles and longhouse artefacts.

Sarawak Plaza Jalan Tunku Abdul Rahman. This mall is the major focus for Western products – fashion accessories, shirts and designer shoes, and Malay and Western music – plus a few handicraft stores with a good range of bags, T-shirts and ethnic jewellery.

Spring Mall 3km from the centre, has outlets including Starbucks, clothes suppliers Roxy, Esprit and G2000, a global food court and a large supermarket, Ta Kiong.

Supermarket Ting & Ting Jalan Tabuan. Excellent store for a wide range of cut-price food stuffs – local, pan-Asian and Western (daily 9am–9pm).

Tan Brothers Jalan Padungan, close to the junction with Jalan Mathies. Baskets, carvings and bags.

Yeo Hing Chuan 46 Main Bazaar. Interesting carvings and other handicrafts; a quality 30cm carved hardwood figure costs about RM300.

Tour operators

Tour operators in Sarawak have grown into a vital resource for adventure travel in the state. Essential for **longhouse** visits, operators offer trips to national parks, tailor-made treks and even cities – particularly useful if you're not in town for long. Standards, particularly around the Ai, Lemanak and Skrang rivers, 300km east of Kuching, are usually high. The longhouse tours have changed over the years, evolving to show more sensitivity to this particular culture – for example, a tour will be postponed if there has been a death in the community as by custom, a private, grieving period must be respected.

Shop around to see what is on offer, although prices are largely uniform – the standard fee is around RM150 per person per day. All operators listed here have a proven record in quality, highly enjoyable trips.

Asian Overland First floor, 286a Westwood Park, Jalan Tubuan ☎ 082/251163, ✆ www .asianoverland.com.my. Provides quality longhouse trips on the Batang Ai river system. Also arranges tours north to Gunung Mulu National Park and on the "Head-hunters' Trail" from Mulu to Limbang.

Borneo Adventure 55 Main Bazaar ☎ 082/245175, ✆ www.borneoadventure.com. Award-winning operation running excellent trips throughout Sarawak and Sabah. Its jungle lodge (6), beside the Nanga Sumpa longhouse, along the Ulu Ai, is a fine example of best practice and a beacon for ecotourism in Malaysia. Owner Philip Yong is developing an even more remote, riverside "boutique camp" in the same area. The Rainforest Kayak Adventure, involves kayaking through gentle rapids not far from Semenggoh Wildlife Rehabilitation Centre.

Borneo Interland 63, first floor, Main Bazaar ☎ 082/426328, ✆ www.bitravel.com.my. Also has tour desk at *Merdeka Palace Hotel* (☎ 082/258000, ext. 8018). Specializes in local trips, including Gunung Gading Park, Bau's Fairy and Wind caves and the now over-commercialized Annah Rais longhouse.

Borneo Transverse 15 Jalan Green Hill ☎ 082/257784, ✆ www.borneotransverse.com.my.

Excellent, veteran outfit which offers culturally fascinating tours to Iban longhouses on Sungai Lemanak.

CPH Travel 70 Jalan Padungan ☎ 082/243708, ✆ www.cphtravel.com.my/cph. Water-bound experts offering Sarawak river city cruises (2 daily; 2hr; RM80 from the waterfront jetty) and, when the sea isn't too rough, cruises to the fascinating Kuching Wetlands National Park, close to Santubong, to view Irrawaddy dolphins, proboscis monkeys and birds (morning and evening; 4hr; from RM150/165). Also goes to Talang-Satang and Tanjung Datu parks for longer visits.

Diethelm Travel Second floor, Lot 168, Jalan Chan Chin Ann ☎ 082/412778, ✆ www.diethelmtravel .com. Directly opposite the restaurant *Zhun San Yen*, this experienced group has excellent contacts on the Lemanak River. Assistant Director Panch is a mine of information on the region's longhouse culture. Also organizes trips along Batang Rejang and northwards to Gunung Mulu National Park.

Interworld 161 Jalan Temple ☎ 082/252344, ✆ www.interworldborneo.com. Organizes expeditions up the Skrang and Batang Ai rivers. The three-day/two-night "Head-hunters of Borneo" trip costs RM500–600 per person; plus Niah and Gunung Mulu park trips too.

Listings

Airlines AirAsia, ground floor, Wisma Ho Ho Lim, 291, Lot 4, Jalan Abell (ⓣ082/283222, 24hr call centre ⓣ03/2171 9333); MAS, Lot 215, Jalan Song Thian Cheok (ⓣ082/246622 or 244144; Mon–Fri 8.30am–5pm, Sat 8.30am–1pm); Royal Brunei Airlines, first floor, Rugayah, Jalan Song Thian Cheok (ⓣ082/243344); SilkAir, Gateway Kuching, Jalan Bukit Mata ⓣ082/256772.

Airport Flight enquiries on ⓣ082/457373 or 454242.

Banks and exchange Reliable ATM at Maybank, 13 Jalan Tunku Abdul Rahman. Overseas Union Bank, Jalan Tun Haji Openg; Standard Chartered, Wisma Bukit Mata Kuching, Jalan Tunku Abdul Rahman. Moneychangers: Majid & Sons, 45 Jalan India; Mohamad Yahia & Sons, basement, Sarawak Plaza, Jalan Abell. Both offer OK rates.

Bookshops Popular Books, third floor, Tun Jegah Mall and Premier Books, first floor, Sarawak Plaza, both have a reasonable range of English-language books including travel, cookery and fiction. Mohamad Yahia & Sons – with branches in the *Holiday Inn* and the basement of the Sarawak Plaza – offers the best range of books in the city, and also stock the best maps of the state. Sky Book Store, 57 Jalan Padungan, and Star Books, 30 Main Bazaar, are good for geography, culture and anthropology and there's an MPH outlet at the new Spring mall (see opposite).

Car rental Expect to pay around RH140 for day hire, though this drops the longer you hire for. Borneo Interland, 63 Main Bazaar ⓣ082/413595 (24hr line ⓣ082/426328), ⓦwww.bitravel.com .my; Mayflower Car Rental, first floor, Wisma Bukit Mata Kuching, Jalan Tunku Abdul Rahman ⓣ082/410110 (evenings and weekends ⓣ019/8160553), ⓦwww.start.com.my/wiki/index .php/Car_rentals; Pronto Car Rental, first floor, 98 Jalan Padungan ⓣ082/237889, 24hr ⓣ013/811 6778.

Caving Kuching Caving (ⓣ012/2688675, ⓦwww .kuchingcaving.com) is run by Englishman James, and offers adventure-caving day-trips around Kuching division.

Consulates Australia ⓣ082/233350; Indonesia, 111 Jalan Tun Haji Openg ⓣ082/241734 (Mon–Thurs 8.30am–noon & 2–4pm); New Zealand ⓣ082/482177; UK & Ireland ⓣ082/250950.

Moving on from Kuching

By air

A taxi from the town centre to the airport is RM25 (airport information: ⓣ082/457373 or 454242). Alternatively, take either #12a (RM1.60) or #8a buses (RM1.40) from the Mosque bus stand on Jalan Datuk Ajibah Abol, just in front of the Kuching mosque, to the airport (6.30am–7.30pm; every 50min). There are daily flights on AirAsia and MAS to Peninsular cities, KL, Johor Bahru and Penang, to the Sabah capital KK and to domestic destinations, Sibu, Bintulu and Miri.

By boat

Express Bahagia, 50 Jalan Padungan (ⓣ082/410076 or 016/8966235), runs a daily service to **Sarikei** (RM35) and **Sibu** (RM45), departing at 8.30am from Pending wharf – get there at least 20min before the ferry departs. Note that if the weather's bad the vessel may well not leave and tickets will be held over for the next day's departure, or you can get a full refund. The wharf is 6km from the city centre: bus #1 (35min; RM1.50) leaves from the Mosque bus stand; a taxi from anywhere in the city centre costs RM20.

By bus

Long-distance **buses** to points north in Sarawak depart from the Express Bus Terminal on Jalan Penrissen, 5km southeast, and a RM20 taxi from the city centre. Transit buses leave (twice-hourly; 6am–7pm; RM1) from the Mosque bus stand, and Jalan Barrack behind the Courthouse. Although it is advisable to buy tickets for express buses in advance, it is impractical as there is nowhere in the centre where you can do this; plan to arrive at least 30min in advance. Local buses to destinations Annah Rais, Serian, Sri Aman and Lubok Antu depart from the Mosque bus stand, and to Bako park from Jalan Market close by.

Hospitals Sarawak General Hospital, Jalan Ong Kee Hui (☎082/276666). For private treatment, go to Normah Medical Centre, Jalan Tun Datuk Patinggi (☎082/440055). For holistic treatment try Akita Foot Reflexology, 51 Jalan Padungan (☎082/230239).

Internet Cyber City, Taman Sri Sarawak, off Jalan Borneo (☎082/257555, daily 10am–10pm), is the only internet café in town (RM3 per hr).

Laundry City Laundry, Jalan Padungan (close to junction with Jalan Bukit Mata); Easy Wash, corner of Jalan Ban Hock, and Mr Dobi, Jalan Abell (next block along from *Pizza Hut*). All excellent value as you pay by weight. Open Mon–Sat 7.30am–5.30pm.

Massage The Blind Health Massage Centre in the Timberland Medical Centre, Jalan Ong Tiang Swee, situated 2km from the city centre, offers excellent massage from blind people at very reasonable prices (RM40 for 1hr; 10am–7pm).

Motorbike rental Teck Hua Motor, 31 Jalan Tabuan ☎082/417068. The cost is RM30–50 per day, depending on the size of bike.

Pharmacy Apex Pharmacy, first floor, Sarawak Plaza.

Police Central Police Station (Tourist Police Unit), opposite Pandang Merdeka (☎082/241222). Come here to report stolen and lost property.

Post office The main post office is on Jalan Tun Haji Openg (Mon–Sat 8am–6pm, Sun 10am–1pm); poste restante/general delivery can be collected here – take your passport.

Swimming There's a pool at MBKS Building, Jalan Pending (Mon–Fri 2.30–9pm, Sat 6.45–8.45pm, Sun 9.30am–9pm; ☎082/426915; RM3 adults, RM1 children). Closed on public hols.

Taxi Contact the ever-reliable and reasonable Chris Khoo (☎013/822 0133) for taxi trips around the city and for the airport hop; 24hr services ☎082/480000 and 348898.

Visa extensions Immigration Office, first floor, Bangunan Sultan Iskandar, Jalan Simpang Tiga (Mon–Fri 8am–noon & 2–4.30pm; ☎082/245661); take Chin Lian Long bus #11. Get there by 3pm to have your application processed on the day.

Day-trips around Kuching

The area **around Kuching**, well served by road, has at least a few days' worth of interesting excursions easily reached by bus or car. Within an hour's minivan ride from the city are the beaches and resorts of the **Santubong Peninsula**, also known as **Damai**. Some people stay out at the peninsula's stylish accommodation or at *Camp Permai*, a more budget choice, near to which is the **Sarawak Cultural Village**, a showpiece community where model longhouses are staffed by guides from each of the ethnic groups. Other worthwhile activities are trekking in **Kubah National Park** and, if you're travelling outside the rainy season (March–Oct), going on a day tour to **Kuching Wetlands National Park**. Also enjoyable is a morning or afternoon in the **Semenggoh Wildlife Rehabilitation Centre**.

Semenggoh Wildlife Rehabilitation Centre

Sarawak's first forest reserve, set aside by Vyner Brooke in 1920, **Semenggoh Wildlife Rehabilitation Centre** (☎082/442180), is a success story which, akin to Sabah's more famous Sepilok, has numbers of rehabilitated orang-utans now roaming freely in the surrounding forest. All the primates have been orphaned as a result of logging activities in primary forest or seized after having been kept illegally as pets. At feeding times (9am & 3pm daily; RM3), the animals gather to munch on seasonal fruit like over-ripe bananas and watermelons, though note that during the fruit season (April–May) very few will bother to come to the feeding stands as they will find their food elsewhere in the forest. The Centre is 32km south of Kuching; as no bus goes directly there, you will require a private minivan (8am & 2pm departures from the Waterfront; RM25); taxi (RM40 one

SOUTH CHINA SEA

Maludam

Sebuyau

P. Burung

Batang Lupar

Simunjan

Batang Sadong

Serian

Tebedu

Entikong

▶ Pontianak

Kampung
Benuk

Kampung Abang

Anna Rais

Gunung
Penrissen
(1325m)

Muara Tebas

BAKO NATIONAL PARK

Kampung
Bako

Bako

Buntal

KUCHING

Kota
Padawan

Semenggoh
Rehabilitation Centre

Gunung
Santubong
(810m)

Santubong

Sarawak Cultural Village
Damai Beach

KUCHING
WETLANDS
NATIONAL PARK

Potteries

KUBAH NATIONAL PARK

Bau

Fairy Cave/
Wind Cave

INDONESIA

P. Satang Besar

P. Satang Kecil

Pandan
Beach

Siar Beach

Lundu

GUNUNG
GADING
NATIONAL PARK

Sematan

Sematan
Beach

TANJUNG DATU
NATIONAL PARK

Teluk Melano

N

AROUND KUCHING

25 km

0

411

way; waiting RM10 per hr); or tour, such as the one offered by CPH Travel (see p.408), for around RM80.

Kubah National Park

Located just 20km west of Kuching, the dipterocarp forest of **Kubah National Park** (T082/248088; RM10) offers a pleasing and manageable day-trip out of Kuching. Bus #11 leaves from Kuching's Mosque bus stand hourly from 6.30am to 4.30pm (RM2.20; 35min) and drops you a three-hundred-metre walk from the park entrance. (To get back to Kuching hail a bus on the other side of the road; the last one passes at 5pm.)

Situated on a sandstone plateau, the small park contains crystal-clear streams, waterfalls created out of hardened limestone and a wide selection of palms and orchids. Indeed Kubah is considered one of the richest sites for **palm** species in the world: 95 types have been found there, including coconut, sago and many rattans, with eighteen of these species endemic to the region (among Sarawak's other parks, only Mulu has more types of native palm).

Three modest mountains, **Selang**, **Sendok** and **Serapi**, emerge out of the lush forest; they're crisscrossed by trails, waterfalls and streams. Staff at the park headquarters will point you in the direction of Kubah's marked hikes, among them: the three-hour **Ulu Raya Trail**, a good walk to catch sight of the palms; the **Waterfall Trail**, a ninety-minute uphill hike to impressive, split-level falls; and the **Bukit Selang Trail**, less than an hour's walk from headquarters and boasting some grand views. Kubah's best views, however, are from the three-hour **Gunung Serapi (Summit) Trail** – from the mountain's summit, you can see Kuching and much of southwestern Sarawak. There's **accommodation** (RM15 for a dorm bed; RM150 for a four-bed lodge) but no canteen or places to eat nearby, so bring your own **provisions** – the main park building has a small kitchen for use. The parks desk at Kuching's Visitors' Information Centre (see p.397) handles bookings.

Kuching Wetlands National Park

Located just 15km from Kuching and 5km from Damai the estuarine **Kuching Wetlands National Park** contains a mangrove system interspersed by marine waterways. The site has value especially as a breeding and nursery ground for fish and prawn species – over forty families of fishes and eleven species of prawns have been found here – and is particularly well worth visiting for its marine wildlife, most notably **Irrawaddy dolphins**. It is only accessible on a tour and in a sturdy boat or launch; the main company accessing the region is Kuching-based CPH Travel (see p.408); trips leave at around 4pm, getting onto the water at 5pm, the best time to view the dolphins. Pick-up is usually by coach or minivan from your accommodation in Kuching, and then on to the Santubong Boat Club (30min from Kuching), where you board the launch.

Santubong (Damai) Peninsula

Located 25km north of Kuching and bordered by the Sarawak River to the south, the **Santubong Peninsula** (also called Damai) is dominated by the densely forested 810-metre Gunung Santubong. It is a fascinating area, its inhabitation going back to pre-history. During excavation in the 1960s and 1970s tens of thousands of objects, including digging implements, were found across six neighbouring sites here, and were dated back to 3000 BC when the

Indian/Javanese Empire reached this far, probably its furthest extent. Little can be seen today – a possible tantric shrine at **Bongkissah**, 2km from Kampung Santubong, is covered by grass and jungle ferns. In the eighth century, the peninsula was the location for a larger trading settlement. The region is also dotted with spectacular geological formations including strangely shaped rocks amongst the patches of thick forest.

Since the 1980s, stretches of the river and coastline have been rapidly developed as retreats for tourists, curious travellers and city-weary locals, though thankfully the spectacular **resorts**, *Damai Puri* and *Damai Beach*, hardly disturb the tranquil, almost lonesome, nature of the area. There are two pleasant fishing villages, **Buntal** – famed for its seafood restaurants – and **Kampung Santubong**. An added attraction, worth two to three hours, is the informative and entertaining **Sarawak Cultural Village**, a collection of traditionally built dwellings, which showcases the lifestyles of the state's indigenous peoples.

Arrival and accommodation

To get to the villages of Buntal and Kampung Santubong, take the #2b bus (daily 6.40am–6pm; hourly; 40min) from Kuching's Jalan Market. For the Damai beach resorts, hop on the bus shuttle service from outside the *Holiday Inn* and the *Crown Plaza* hotels in Kuching (7.15am–10pm; returning 10am–8pm; 8 times daily; RM10 one way); the drop-off point is *Holiday Inn Resort Damai Beach*. Note that the last bus back leaves promptly at 5pm, while later ones leave from the resorts. Most people stay at the resorts, though there are a couple of options near Kampung Santubong.

Damai Beach Teluk Bandung ☎082/846200, ⓦwww.damaibeachresort.com. Nestling in a natural hollow and fronted by a luscious swimming pool, an outdoor massage centre and a private palm-fringed, pebbled beach, *Damai Beach* is just one small step from paradise. Most rooms surround these facilities and are spacious and well appointed but for the most spectacular ones, consider the Bidayuh-style Baruk chalets (RM300 a night for two people), poised up on the hill among casuarina trees overlooking the beach. The hotel, which is just 100m from the Sarawak Cultural Village, lays on lavish buffets (breakfast included in room price). ⑤–⑦

Damai Puri Resort Teluk Penyuk ☎082/846900, ⓦwww.damaipuriresort-kuching.com. Right at the end of the Kuching road, the *Puri* is a gloriously isolated, high-end hotel featuring breezy, open-planned architecture, upscale rooms and a variety of exotic eating options, as well as a long stretch of fabulous beach. Opened in 2008, the Puri has yet to pull the crowds, so keep an eye on promotional offers which could slash the currently over-high room price. ⑨

Nanga Damai Kampung Santubong, 3km from the village on the main road towards Damai ☎019 & 010/887 1017. Beautifully designed, this tall house has a large, semi-open dining terrace with a bar

and large rooms, either en suite or with adjacent bathrooms, with an open feel and panoramic views. The owner, Polycarp Teo Sebom, will pick you up from Kuching given a bit of warning and can drive you in and out of the city some days. ④–⑤

Permai Rainforest Resort ☎082/846487, ⓦwww.permairainforest.com. The hard-to-find *Permai* is reached by crossing the car park just by the *Damai Puri Resort*'s front gate, and following a plank-walk into the forest – you are now on the lower reaches of Gunung Santubong. The resort/camp has a dozen en-suite tree houses (⑤), 30m from the water's edge, and two more functional longhouses (②) on either side of the plankwalk. Its *Rainforest café* (daily) offers excellent meals at reasonable prices and there's a lovely little beach at the end of the plank-walk where you can swim safely.

The Village House Kampung Santubong, 30m down the track to the Beach from Santubong crossroads ☎082/846166, ⓦwww.villagehouse .com.my. A beautiful development that sees a small number of traditional Malay-style stilted rooms and chill-out areas wrapping around a long, thin swimming pool. The à la carte menu contains Western, local and fusion, and the owners, keen travellers Donald and Marina Tan, are usually on hand to swap stories. ⑦

A forty-minute trip north from Kuching through the city's ever-expanding suburbs and small rubber and pepper plantations, leads to **BUNTAL**, a quiet riverside kampung off the main road, bordered by forest and possessing a small beach. Locals offer short boat trips along Sungai Sarawak, but there's no accommodation.

From Buntal, the bus returns to the main road and runs alongside Gunung Santubong, before turning east down a narrow road for 2km to **KAMPUNG SANTUBONG**, a pretty place set on an inlet with fishing boats hauled up onto the beach. Just visible in the hills above the kampung is a wooden bungalow where the famous scientist Alfred Russell Wallace lived on his arrival in Sarawak, at the invitation of Rajah James Brooke, in 1854. Wallace penned part of his theory on speciation and biogeography here. There are plans to restore the bungalow, currently a ruin and convert it into a museum and/or guesthouse.

Sarawak Cultural Village

Beside the entrance to the massive *Holiday Inn Resort Damai Beach* is the **Sarawak Cultural Village** (daily 9am–5.15pm, stage shows 11.30am & 4.30pm; RM60; ☎082/846411, ⓦwww.scv.com.my). It comprises seven authentically built traditional dwellings which stand in a dramatic setting, the sea to one side, a lake in the middle of the site and the jungle escarpment of Gunung Santubong looming behind. As well as Iban, Orang Ulu and Bidayuh longhouses, there's a Malay townhouse, a Chinese godown, a Melenau "tall house" (*rumah tinggi*), a Penan jungle settlement and, the latest addition, a Kenyah/Kayan longhouse where you can watch local craftsmen make the *sape*, the Sarawakian harp-cum-lute. A café offers light and full meals and a wide range of beverages.

When it was opened in the early 1990s, the village was a kind of theme park for the state's varied ethnic groups, though today the set-piece houses and facilities feel like a real community, and many of the people you come across in the houses, most notably the Iban and Bidayuh, live there a lot of the time. In the daytime, there are demonstrations of weaving, cooking and instrument-playing, along with more idiosyncratic pursuits like top-spinning (in the Malay townhouse), blowpipe-drilling (in the Penan settlement) and sago-processing (at the Melenau tall house). The shows put on twice daily are, although performed for tourists, enjoyable, entertaining and, to some degree, educational. For a brief overview of the costumes, traditions and daily lives of Sarawak's peoples, the Cultural Village is a worthwhile experience. A particularly good time to visit is July over the **Rainforest Music Festival** (see box opposite) when for three nights the Village soaks up excellent world music performances.

Trails

There's a **trail** that loops uphill from the entrance to the *Holiday Inn* and returns to the road close to the entrance of the Cultural Village, making for a pleasant thirty-minute forest stroll. The *Green Paradise Café*, along the main road towards Santubong, is the starting point for the much more demanding climb up **Gunung Santubong**. The trail takes four to five hours, is well marked and you don't need a guide.

The Rainforest Music Festival

Held annually at the Sarawak Cultural Village since 1998, the **Rainforest Music Festival** (day-tickets RM90; three-day pass RM250; see Ⓦ www.rainforestmusic-borneo.com or contact organizers, the Sarawak Tourist Board Ⓣ 082/423600, for line-up and festival pass details) takes place annually over a July weekend. There are seminars, workshops and small performances in the afternoons, and an outdoor stage provides the setting for the main performances in the evenings. Such a setting for a major world music event only adds to the evocative atmosphere, with the Village's beautiful tribal homes all around and the densely forested Gunung Santubong the perfect backdrop. While a variety of Western artists have performed over the years, the festival is especially worthwhile for the opportunity it affords to watch performers from across Malaysia, especially Sarawak, with its rich folk-music traditions (see p.728). Favourites have included the Sape Ulu Quartet (the *sape* being a traditional bamboo lute) from the upriver division of Belaga; Usun Apau, a Penan vocal group that sings **sinui** (ancestral) tunes; and the magnificent Tuku Kame, led by the head of the Cultural Village's Heritage Resource Centre and able flautist, Narawai Rashidi, and featuring the excellent electric *sape* player Jerry Kamit. With festival-goers numbering close to 20,000 over the three days, the RMF is now a major player on the world music stage. Beds are hard to come by in Damai and Kuching over the period, so book early.

Eating

You'd do best to eat at one of Buntang's celebrated **seafood restaurants**, which stand on stilts in the seaside shallows; *Lim Hok An* is the pick of the bunch. There's just one **café** in Kampung Santubong, with limited food options. On the main road out of Kampung Santubong towards Damai is the *Green Paradise Café* (daily 9.30am–11.30pm), which sells inexpensive, basic and tasty meals including grilled fish and Malay curries. Behind the café is the starting point for the Santubong mountain trail (see box opposite). Otherwise, check out the hotel restaurants.

Bako National Park

Though no further away from Kuching than the Santubong Peninsula, **BAKO NATIONAL PARK** (Ⓣ 082/248088; RM10) is too much of a gem to try to pack into one day, although many try to do just that. The park's ecology, wildlife, views and atmosphere make it feel like a place which time forgot where the enchanting proboscis monkey families swing from trees and beaches that are among the best in Sarawak can be reached on short hikes.

Bako is Sarawak's oldest national park, occupying the northern section of the Muara Tebas Peninsula at the mouth of the Bako River. The area was once part of a forest reserve – a region set aside for timber growing and extraction – but in 1957 was made a national park, fully protected from exploitation. Although relatively small, Bako is spectacular in its own way: its steep rocky cliffs, punctuated by deep bays and lovely sandy beaches, are thrillingly different from the rest of the predominantly flat and muddy Sarawak coastline. The peninsula is composed of sandstone which, over the years, has been worn down to produce delicate pink iron patterns on cliff faces, honeycomb weathering and contorted rock arches rising from the sea. Access to some of the beaches is difficult, requiring tricky descents down nearly vertical paths. Above, the forest contains various species of wildlife, and rivers and waterfalls for bathing. The hike to the

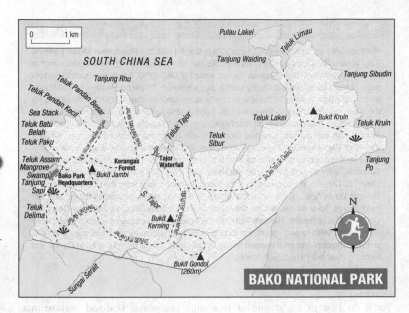

highest point, Bukit Gondol (260m), offering a wide view over the park to the South China Sea, is among the most popular of the trails that crisscross the park. Bako's **plant life** is varied and stunning, ranging from looming eighty-metre dipterocarp trees to dense mangrove forest, with pitcher plants easily visible on many of the trails.

Arrival and information

Many visitors get to the park by minivan, either on an organized tour or one arranged by their guesthouse/hotel. Public transport options are the #6 **bus** (hourly 6.30am–6pm; RM2.50; 45min) from Jalan Market, or a **minivan** (hourly 7am–6pm; RM4; 40min) from the same location, which leaves when full. Both run to the rather squalid **Bako Bazaar**, from where it's a short boat trip to the park's HQ; the jetty is close to the Bazaar. Note that if travelling from Kuching by **car**, you can safely leave your vehicle in a car park close to the jetty. Visitors should bring ID for the jetty authorities to inspect. The boat trip (RM8 per person; RM40 charter price) takes twenty-five minutes unless the water is choppy. Indeed, if conditions are rough, the boats may not go at all. If returning the same day, arrange a pick-up time with the boatman.

Once at the **park HQ** (RM10) the ranger will supply an informative **map** of the park and direct you to your accommodation if you are staying overnight. You may want some minutes to look around the excellent displays and exhibits at the **Information Centre**; these identify the flora and fauna in the park as well as describing in detail the park's history and unique characteristics. In the evening, films and slide shows on the park's ecology are shown in the Centre.

Accommodation and eating

Accommodation can be booked by phone or in person at the parks desk next door to the Visitors' Information Centre in Kuching (see p.397). Various types of accommodation have been built along the edge of the forest, divided from the beach 50m away by a row of coconut trees. For budget travellers, there's a **campsite** (RM5) and snug, four-bed dorms (RM15.75), with reasonably equipped shared kitchens, in the **forest hostel**. Going up the scale, there's also a range of **forest lodges**: two rooms with three beds in each (RM105 per room) and two en-suite rooms, each with two single beds (RM52.50 per room). Note that none of the accommodation is particularly well maintained.

The **café** (daily 8am–8pm) at park HQ has very simple fare, with a daily menu of rice with vegetables, meat or fish and egg dishes, all at budget prices. Although the park **shop** has a limited range of goods, it's advisable to bring some staples, or luxuries, from Kuching. An ever-present problem at park HQ are the macaque monkeys who are very brave (to put it mildly) and quite capable of rushing into the kitchen and sleeping areas in search of food. Visitors are warned to keep the kitchen and dormitory doors locked.

Inside the park

Given the easy access from Kuching and cheap accommodation within the park, many people stay a few days at Bako, taking picnics to one of the seven **beaches**, relaxing at the park HQ itself, or going slow on the trails to observe the flora and fauna. You'll come across seven different types of **vegetation**, including peat bog, scrub and mangrove; most of the sixteen trails run through an attractive mixture of primary dipterocarp forest and *kerangas* (in Iban, "poor soil"), a sparser type of forest characterized by much thinner tree cover, stubbier plants and more open pathways. On top of the low hill on the Lintang trail, the strange landscape is covered in rock plates, where, among the shrubs, you'll find **pitcher plants**, whose deep, mouth-shaped lids open to trap water and insects which are then digested in the soupy liquid below. On the cliffs, delicate plants cling to vertical rock faces or manage to eke out an existence in little pockets of soil, while closer to the HQ the coastline is thick with mangrove trees.

▲ Proboscis monkey

There's also the near-certainty that you will see **animals**, either while lazing at the chalets or out on the trails. Aside from monkeys, even the rare flying lemur has been sighted swinging from the trees around the park HQ. Although the best time to see wildlife on the trails is undoubtedly in the early morning and dusk – the proboscis monkeys as well as silver-leafs will make sure they are heard if not easily seen – even in the raw heat of the day, animal activity is usually assured. Snakes, wild boar, giant monitor lizards, squirrels, bearded pigs, otters and mouse deer can be sighted too, especially if you're quiet and observant.

The trails

The park map you receive when you first sign in clearly shows the **trails**, which all start from park HQ. The sixteen trails are all colour-coded, with splashes of paint, denoting the trail, clearly marked every 20m on trees and rocks. It's best to get an early start, taking rests at the strategically positioned viewpoint huts along the way. You'll need to carry a litre of water per person (you can safely refill your bottle from the streams), a light rainproof jacket, mosquito repellent and sunscreen. Wear comfortable shoes with a good grip (there's no need for heavy-duty walking boots), light clothing like a T-shirt and shorts, and take a sun hat. Don't forget your swimming gear either, as cool streams cut across the trails, and beaches and waterfalls are never far away.

Probably the most popular trail is the 3.5-kilometre hike to **Tajor Waterfall**, a hike lasting around two and a half hours, though it can easily be done in ninety minutes if you don't linger too long for rests or plant study. The initial half-hour climb from the jetty, on a steep and circuitous path up the forested cliff is the hardest section. At the top you move swiftly through scrub and into *kerangas*, where pitcher plants abound. The path leads to a simple wooden hut with a fine prospect of the peninsula. Moving on, you return to sun-shielded forest, where the dry, sandy path gives way to a muddy trail through peat bog, leading eventually to the waterfall itself, a lovely spot for swimming.

Leaving the Tajor trail at the wooden hut and viewpoint, a path descends west to two beautiful **beaches**, Teluk Pandan Kecil and Teluk Pandan Besar, each around a thirty-minute hike from the viewpoint, with Kecil in particular involving a steep, rugged descent down sandstone rocks to reach the refreshingly clean water. The other two main beaches at Bako – Teluk Sibur and Limau – are even harder to reach, but enjoyable once you've got there. To find **Teluk Sibur**, continue past Tajor Waterfall, following the main trail for around forty minutes, before turning west on the black-and-red trail. The demanding descent to the beach takes anything from twenty minutes to an hour to accomplish. It is at once stunningly beautiful and desolate, a perfect spot for swimming and relaxing.

The hike to **Teluk Limau**, estimated at seven hours, can be done in five at a push, especially if you get an early start. The terrain alternates between swampland and scrub, giving an exhilarating variety of environments on one trail, and provides fabulous views round the whole peninsula. It's not really feasible to get to the beach, which marks the most northerly point in the park, and return the same day; either bring a **tent** and **food** and camp on the beach – as perfect a spot to lay your head as you will ever find – or arrange with park HQ for a boat to pick you up for the trip back (around RM200). Once out at Limau you could detour on the way back along the marked trail to **Kruin**, at the eastern end of the park.

Far western Sarawak

Far western Sarawak has become an increasingly popular region on Sarawak's tourism trail largely due to the development of facilities in the national parks and other attractive locations. A visit to the region is best spread over a few days, visiting the caves near **Bau**; **Gunung Gading National Park**, located just north of the small town of Lundu; the beaches at **Sematan**; and the stunning **Tanjung Datu National Park**, further west along the coast, usually only accessible outside from November to February, when the seas are quieter.

Bau and the caves

To reach the small market town of **BAU**, take an STC #2 bus (every 30min 6.30am–6pm; 1hr; RM3.50) from Kuching's Mosque bus stand. Nineteenth-century prospectors were drawn here by the gold that veined the surrounding countryside, but modern-day Bau doesn't live up to its romantic past and it's only worth visiting really as a stepping stone to the nearby caves. There is no accommodation in Bau although there are a number of *kedai kopis* for food.

From Bau take the #3 bus (every 30min 6.30am–6pm; 20min) and ask to be let off at the junction, from where the route to the caves is marked. It is a 500-metre signposted walk to Wind Cave, and a 1.5-kilometre walk further to Fairy Cave. **Wind Cave** meanders through a rocky outcrop on the banks of the Sarawak River; a plankway makes it possible to wander from one side of the outcrop to the other. **Fairy Cave** is larger, with a flight of concrete steps leading up to a cave high in a limestone cliff. As at Wind Cave, plankways enable visitors to explore the passage. The cliff face also holds some outdoor adventure; **Batman Wall** is popular with rock climbers, with routes of varying degrees of difficulty.

Lundu and around

STC bus EP07 leaves Kuching's regional bus terminal on Jalan Penrissen for **LUNDU** (8am, 11am, 2pm & 4pm; 75min; RM10), clattering through a landscape that gradually transforms from plantation into forest, with jungle-clad hills close by. A dozy and enchanting place reaching out from the banks of the Lundu River, the town comprises a few blocks of shophouses, a large, new, two-storey market and some government buildings. Along the signposted road out towards Gunung Gading National Park lie attractive kampung houses within lush gardens where pineapples and papaya and mango trees compete for space. If you're merely waiting for an onward connection, take a walk around the small **market**, where you can buy fresh fruit, or go into one of the busy *kedai kopis* that border the town square, selling excellent *roti canai* and *nasi campur* throughout the day; the *Jouee* serves tasty noodles. For the best food though, go to *One and One Food Court*, opposite the Chinese temple, the town's most popular eatery, with a wide range of mostly Chinese dishes. There are a couple of **places to stay**: the *Lundu Gading Hotel*, Lot 174, Jalan Lundu (❸) and the *Cheng Hak Boarding House*, 51 Jalan Bazaar (☎082/735018; ❷) nearby.

Beyond the entrance for Gunung Gading National Park, the road from Lundu continues north until it reaches the coast, some 8km later, at **Pandan Beach**, which you can reach on the same bus that heads to the park. Considered by many locals to be the best in the area, Pandan is a half-kilometre-long stretch of white sand near a beachfront kampung. A campsite at Pandan has recently opened, with basic facilities including toilets, showers, lights and a canteen (❶). Two kilometres east of Pandan lies the smaller **Siar Beach**, another pleasing spot, where the *Siar Beach Resort* is located (Jalan Siar; ☏082/572300, ⊛www .siarbeachresort). Consisting of a modern longhouse with five rooms (RM65), and various bungalows (three rooms; RM260–360), the *Siar* is a relaxing spot on a nice stretch of beach, but to be avoided at weekends when it gets filled up with Kuching families. There is no public transport to Siar Beach – either walk from Pandan or get a taxi from Lundu (RM15).

Gunung Gading National Park

Gunung Gading National Park (RM10) is 2km north of Lundu; either hop on a minivan from the centre of Lundu or take a taxi (RM15) from beside the town's Chinese temple. The park, which mostly clings to the sides of four small mountains, was used solely as a conservation zone for the vast, parasitic **Rafflesia** plant until it received full national park status in 1994. The emphasis, however, is still on conservation, with visitors only allowed to view the spectacular plant, with its enormous, smelly blooms, from plankways that stop anyone treading on the young buds. If you call Kuching's National Parks and Wildlife Office (see p.397) first thing in the morning, you can find out if one is likely to be in bloom that day. When you arrive, a ranger may (if you are in luck) lead you to the plant.

It's possible to climb two of the park's small mountains, Gading and Perigi, on the colour-coded trails that thread the forest. Both are full-on hikes, not to be undertaken lightly; the first is a seven-hour round trip, the second, eight hours. It's best to aim to camp on the summit where you'll be rewarded with a sublime sunrise. From there you can follow a trail back to Batu Bakubu, a former communist camp during the insurgency. For lesser mortals, the two-hour round trip offered by the Waterfall Trail is a more sedate alternative. Waterfall 7, where it ends, offers good, refreshing swimming.

For **accommodation** the park has a campsite (RM5), a hostel (four rooms with dorm beds at RM15, or RM40 for a four-bed room) and a lodge (six-bed chalets for RM150). It's likely that during the week there'll be empty beds, though the usual form is to book at Kuching's Visitors' Information Centre.

Sematan and around

Some 40km west of Lundu, and at the end of the road from Kuching, lies the seaside town of **SEMATAN**. Unless you have your own transport the only way to reach Sematan from Lundu is by taxi (RM60 one way, RM80 return). The town has few facilities and no stand-out café; most people come to walk on the long, picturesque **beach** with its reasonably clean yellow sand backed by coconut palms. The only accommodation here is at the *Sematan Hotel*, 12 Sematan Bazaar (☏082/711162) with basic facilities (❶). However, there is a **homestay** programme in the area that's been running for a few years – contact Mohamad Abdullah (☏013/8041404) for details and vacancies in Trusan Jaya, Teluk Melano and Kilong River kampungs.

Jalan Sematan beaches

One of the main reasons for travelling this far west (the other being to visit Tanjung Datu National Park) is to stay at the *Sematan Palm Beach Resort* on Jalan Sematan (☏082/711808, ⊜spbr295@streamyx.com), a picturesque place, spread along a magnificent coastline, three kilometres west of the small town. Run by a charming, enterprising couple, Nicholas and Elizabeth Nor, this development offers two-room chalets (RM280 per chalet), quadruplex chalets (one room; RM153), two-bed terrace twins (RM153) and six-bed family terrace apartments (RM330), and is a perfect spot for total relaxation. Unfortunately, its café – the only place for miles around to eat – is not of a high standard.

Also on Jalan Sematan – 300km closer to the town – is *Holiday Chalet Sematan* (☎082/232255, ✆mobili@streamyx.com), which has small, basic chalets (RM 189; four beds) in a compound 30m from the beach. However, the canteen (8am–6pm) sells only basic meals and there is no jetty.

Teluk Melano

About 30km west from Sematan, the Malay fishing village **TELUK MELANO** – only accessible by water – is the best place to enjoy a **homestay** as it's picturesque and its jetty is well positioned for half-day river cruises (RM80), or fishing trips (RM150 for 2–4 persons), and access to the Tanjung Datu park. The kampung is a pretty place, home to around forty families who live in traditional wooden Malay houses. If you're on the homestay programme, you'll stay with one of these families.

There are two ways to get to Teluk Melano from Sematan: by speedboat (RM250; six passengers; 40min) or by a daily boat (RM25; 2hr) which normally leaves Sematan jetty around midday. Another option, if staying at the *Palm Beach Resort*, is owner Nicholas Nor's speedboat (check for price). From the kampung, the main place to visit is Tanjung Datu Park, but you'll have to ask around for speedboats (prices from RM200).

Tanjung Datu National Park

Further along the coast from Teluk Melano is **Tanjung Datu National Park** (RM10). The only way to get there is by boat from the jetties at Sematan (1hr; six passengers; RM450 total) and Teluk Melano (20min; RM200), though boats can only negotiate the large swell and difficult currents between March and October. Situated in a mountainous region around a coastal spur close to the Kalimantan border, with peaks towering above, the tiny park offers splendid rainforest, swift, clean rivers and isolated bays. The main draws though are its dazzling beaches, the best in East Malaysia, and shallow, unspoilt **coral reefs** perfect for snorkelling, only a short distance from the shore; further out there are a number of artificial reefs, begun in 1986 and now starting to take shape, with marine life establishing itself alongside. The park is also one of the few destinations in Sarawak where ocean turtles come to lay eggs. The park has four marked **trails**, the longest, the Belian trail, takes just two hours, leading to the highest point in the park, the peak of Gunung Melano (542m).

There are only the most rudimentary visitor facilities at the park, little beyond a basic **campsite** (RM5; bring all equipment and provisions). A number of Kuching-based tour operators, including CPH Travel (see p.408), can arrange trips to the park (from RM600 for two nights), as can the Nors at the *Palm Beach Resort*.

Talang-Satang National Park

Gazetted the state's first **marine park** in 1999 for the primary purpose of preserving sea turtles' eggs, the park consists of two pairs of islands, Satang Besar and Satang Kecil and Talang-Talang Kecil and Talang-Talang Besar. The first two, bigger islands are open to visitors who are patient enough to jump through all the necessary hoops. Permits can be applied for at Kuching's National Parks and Wildlife Office (see p.397). There is a team of forestry staff based year round on the island; you may be lucky enough to see small **turtles** being released and scampering into the sea or watch staff transport the eggs from under the sand to a hatchery. Ask too at the parks office about the Sea Turtle Volunteer programme which invites helpers for a short stay at Talang-Talang Besar's **conservation centre** between May and September. One Kuching operator, CPH Travel, runs tours to the islands (once permits have been granted) and the *Palm Beach Resort* – the closest accommodation – may ferry people out to the park in a speedboat for around RM250.

South of Kuching

One hundred kilometres south of Kuching, near the mountains straddling the **border** with Kalimantan, lies **ANNAH RAIS**, the largest Bidayuh settlement in the area and the only significant one easily accessible by road. Here in the south of Samarahan division, the **Bidayuh longhouses** offer insights into the culture of the only remaining Land Dyaks in Sarawak still living a semi-authentic lifestyle. The community is used to visitors so everybody is greeted warmly at any time of year.

From Kuching's Mosque bus stand, buses #6 or 3A (twice hourly 9am–5pm; 1hr) head to a small town, Kota Padawan, where the only transport onwards to Annah Rais is by minivan (RM6; 20min). The van weaves towards the cloud-enveloped mountains along a bumpy road which snakes towards the border with Kalimantan. When visitors arrive at Annah Rais, they are met in the car park and escorted around the settlement, which consists of two large longhouses on either side of the Penrissen River plus other, separate dwellings. As you wander around, you'll be offered food and drink, possibly even betel-nut to chew – a traditional way of making someone welcome – and maybe invited to watch and participate in craft demonstrations.

Gunung Penrissen

The most accessible of the mountains on the Sarawak/Kalimantan border is the spectacular 1300-metre-high **GUNUNG PENRISSEN**, located 5km west of Annah Rais. The Penrissen hike involves tough walking along narrow paths and crossing fast-flowing streams that descend from the source of the Sarawak River; vertical ladders help you on the last section. As the trails aren't easy to follow, you must hire a guide. Some climbers ask at Annah Rais – expect to pay RM80–100 for a group of four) – while others opt to go with a Kuching-based tour operator (see p.408) with an experienced guide included, although prices will be higher at around RM100 per day each. Gunung Penrissen was strategically important in the 1950s border skirmishes between the Malaysian and Indonesian armies, and there's still a partially manned Malaysian **military post** close to the summit, from where you can gaze over the rainforest into Kalimantan to the south and east, and to the South China Sea over the forests to the north.

Serian and the border crossing

Twenty kilometres southeast of Annah Rais is the **border crossing** at **Tebedu**, 120km from Kuching. Buses to Tebedu leave from **Serian**, a workaday town on the main Kuching–Sri Aman road, although most people get coaches direct from Kuching to Pontianak (7am, 8am, 10.30am & 12.30pm; RM60). If you're not on the through-coach then make sure you get to Tebedu in time to catch one of the local buses that go to the Indonesian town of **Entikong** and on to Pontianak; these stop running in the early afternoon. Tebedu is little more than an administrative centre, with a couple of dispiriting hotels. The border crossing at Entikong is open 6am–6pm; ask at the Indonesian Consulate in Kuching (see p.410) for information on **visas**.

East of Kuching

Sri Aman, 150km east of Kuching, is the closest sizeable town to the Iban longhouses of the Batang Ai region, though tour operators tend to bypass it, heading to the longhouses straight from Kuching. Taking a tour is an ideal way to visit the upriver longhouses, though check that the size of the tour group doesn't exceed twenty, and ideally it shouldn't be more than ten. Though nondescript, Sri Aman can be a useful base if you're travelling independently.

Many tours to the longhouses start from **Batang Ai river system** jetty, 50km east of Sri Aman, from where you can visit some of the few dozen **longhouses** on the Ai, Delok and Engkari rivers. There are also many popular longhouses on two other rivers, the Lemanak and Skrang – the jetty for the Lemanak longhouses is 20km northwest from the park jetty; that for Skrang 10km further north.

Sri Aman

SRI AMAN, the second biggest town in southwest Sarawak, is the administrative capital of this part of the state. It sits near the mouth of Batang Lupar, whose lower reaches are over 1500m wide, though the river narrows dramatically further up the flat alluvial plain. The town is famed for a tidal bore, which careers upstream from the river mouth fifty miles away.

Sri Aman has a central defensive fort, **Fort Alice**, more compact than the forts in the capital and the only one of its kind still to have its original turrets, drawbridge and parts of its period spiked fence. It was built by Charles Brooke in 1864, thus predating Fort Margherita in Kuching, and named after his wife, Ranee Margaret Alice Brooke. Charles Brooke based himself in this region for many years, heading a small force which repelled the advances of pirates and intervened in the upriver conflicts between warring Iban factions. Now the town sits astride an agricultural region, where oil palm, rubber, cocoa and pepper are the chief cash crops.

Practicalities

Buses to Sri Aman leave from the Kuching regional bus terminus (daily at 7.30am, 9.45am, noon, 3.15pm & 7.45pm; 3hr; RM22). There are several **hotels** in Sri Aman: the *Champion Inn*, 1248 Main Bazaar (☎083/320140; ❷), is the most central, with small, comfortable rooms; the *Hoover Hotel*, 139 Jalan Club (☎083/321985; ❸), is the best in town, with larger rooms than the *Champion Inn*. You can **eat** at the *Hoover's* **café**, or at *Chuan Hong*, a Chinese *kedai kopi* in the centre of town at 1 Jalan Council.

Batang Ai region and the longhouses

The **Batang Ai river system** consists of various rivers which feed into Batang Ai reservoir, creating a vast lake, 90 square kilometres in size. The Ai river was dammed in 1985 to develop the state's first hydroelectric operation, now providing a little less than ten percent of electricity needs.

The **Iban** – one of the ethnic groups categorized as Sea Dyaks – comprise around one-third of the population of Sarawak, making them easily the most numerous of Sarawak's indigenous peoples. They originated in the Kapuas River basin of west Kalimantan, on the other side of the mountains that separate Kalimantan and Sarawak, but having outgrown their lands they migrated to the Lupar River in southwest Sarawak in the sixteenth century.

Dyak wars

Once in Sarawak, the Iban clashed with the coastal Melenau, and by the eighteenth century they had moved up the Rejang into the interior, into areas that were tradition-ally Kayan. Inevitably, great battles were waged between these two powerful groups, with one contemporary source recording seeing "a mass of boats drifting along the stream, while the Dyaks were spearing and stabbing each other; decapitated trunks and heads without bodies, scattered about in ghastly profusion".

Although conflict between the various ethnic groups stopped as migration itself slowed down, heads were still being taken as recently as the 1960s during the Konfrontasi skirmishes, when Indonesian army units came up against Iban fighters in the Malaysian army.

The Iban, urbanization and economy

More than half of Sarawak's Iban are fully or partly urbanized, living in the main centres of Kuching, Sri Aman, Kapit and Sibu. These days they work in most sectors of the state's economy, from handicrafts and tour-guiding to manufacturing and white-collar positions in banking and law. Indeed, many Iban hold positions of power – some of Sarawak's best-known politicians have been drawn from their ranks. Even the bulk of the rural Iban, the vast majority of whom still live in longhouses, undertake seasonal work in the rubber and oil industries, and it is no small irony that logging – the business that most devastated their own customary lands – has in the past supplied much plentiful and lucrative work; these days oil-palm cultivation and production provide more employment. As a consequence, some longhouses have become occasional homes, with many families living close to their work for much of the year. You may visit one week and see few people, and return at the weekend to find the place is buzzing, though not at harvest time – June to August – when all hands are on deck. Traditionally, young men would have left the longhouse to go on **bejalai** (the activity of joining a warring party); nowadays though, youths on *bejalai* are more likely to be found pursuing ambitions in higher education, or working on oil rigs offshore in Brunei or in the burgeoning oil-palm sector. The idea behind *bejalai* is for a young man to establish his independence and social position before getting married. Further complicating the *bejalai* tradition, of course, is that young women are now more socially mobile, and able to leave the longhouse for school, university or other pursuits.

Iban community life

For the traditional Iban the longhouse *tuai* (headman) is more a figurehead than someone who wields great power. Women in these communities though have different duties from men; they never go hunting or work in logging, but are great weavers; indeed, traditionally it's been an Iban woman's weaving prowess that has determined her status in the community. The women are most renowned for their **pua**

Further along these rivers lie a few dozen longhouses, the main spots for travellers to experience traditional Iban life. The majority of the longhouses in the river system – including all the ones discussed below – are outside the boundaries of the nearby **Batang Ai National Park**, part of Lanjak Entimau

kumbu (blanket or coverlet) work, a cloth of intricate design and colour. The *pua kumbu* once played an integral part in Iban rituals, when they were hung up prominently during harvest festivals and weddings, or used to cover structures containing charms and offerings to the gods.

Of all the customs maintained by the Iban, perhaps the most singular is their style of **tattooing**, which is not just a form of ornamentation, but also an indication of personal wealth and other achievements. Many designs are used, from a simple circular outline for the shoulder, chest or outer side of the wrists, to more elaborate designs (dogs, scorpions or dragons) for the inner and outer thigh. The two most important places for tattoos are considered to be the hand and the throat. The tattooing process starts with a carved design on a block of wood which is smeared with ink and pressed to the skin; the resulting outline is then punctured with needles dipped in dark ink, made from a mixture of sugar-cane juice, water and soot. For the actual tattooing a hammer-like instrument with two or three needles protruding from its head is used. These are dipped in ink, the hammer placed against the skin and hit repeatedly with a wooden block, after which rice is smeared over the inflamed area to prevent infection.

Iban parties
The best time for visiting the Iban is during Gawai Dayak in early June (see also *Visiting a longhouse* colour section), though another festival, the Gawai Antu (festival for the departed souls), is sometimes celebrated in November or December; it's the Iban equivalent of the Christian All Souls' Day or the Taoist Hungry Ghost Festival.

▲ Iban woman weaving

Wildlife Sanctuary (LEWS), an region of pristine dipterocarp forest and rivers bordering Kalimantan. There are no facilities in the park and tourists only visit whilst staying at the longhouses below.

Practicalities

There is no direct public **transport** to the Batang Ai river system jetty from Sri Aman or Kuching, but buses do run from Sri Aman to Lubok Antu, a small town 10km from the jetty (twice daily; 1hr; RM12). Ask to be let off at the Batang Ai turn-off, from which you will have to walk the remaining two kilometres. The only **accommodation** on the reservoir is at the sprawling *Hilton Batang Ai* (☎082/248200, ⓦ www.batang.hilton.com; ❻). With small but luxurious rooms, housed in four longhouses, it's a relaxing place to while away your time and a good place to stay for a night before visiting the authentic longhouses upstream. There's also a large swimming pool, reasonably priced guided activities (such as fishing, trekking and longhouse visits) and high-quality local cuisine.

Batang Ai and the Delok River

After crossing the reservoir, the scenery becomes quite spectacular, the forest mass reaching down to the water's edge as the longboat snakes along dodging driftwood. The closest upriver longhouse to the Batang Ai jetty and the *Hilton* is **Rumah Ipang** on Sungai Delok (40min by motorized longboat), a traditional thirty-door structure, rebuilt in 1988 after a massive fire. It is home to thirty Iban families and is built largely from traditional materials.

Beyond Ipang, Batang Ai branches off from the Delok River. One hour upstream along the steadily narrowing Ai lies **Nanga Sumpa**, another lively and busy Iban community. The tour operator Borneo Adventure (see p.408) has built a lodge a few metres from the longhouse, where visitors regularly stay, allowing them to be independent but still able to join in longhouse culture. Though basic, the ten-bedroom lodge is large, and has a kitchen, hot showers and toilets. The Sumpa longhouse itself is a great place to visit: a traditionally built dwelling with an outer first-floor veranda, invariably covered by drying crops, and a communal inner space running the building's length, where people come and go all the time; beyond here are the private family rooms.

A local trek with Borneo Adventure takes visitors to a lovely waterfall (1hr), while other activities include trips further up the river, fishing and visiting the nearby communities. The evenings are usually spent in the longhouse, drinking, chatting and playing games with one of the families and perhaps the chief.

The Engkari River

Starting back from the reservoir, one hour upstream on the Engkari River, is **Nanga Spaya**, where 52 families inhabit two longhouses. Reputed to be a great place to visit at Gawai Dayak (harvest festival), Spaya is a lovely, authentic design combining local wood and bamboo with concrete and iron, longer-lasting materials.

The Lemanak and Skrang rivers

The jetty from which boats leave to visit the longhouses on the Lemanak River is at Kampung Sereliau, 15km northeast of the Batang Ai river system jetty on the road to Betong. Most tour operators however access the most popular and well-resourced longhouse on the river, **Nanga Serubah**, by a road that was opened a few years ago. With greater ease of access to the community has come a new building programme by the longhouse residents nearby, and Serubah also now has a small lodge where visitors can stay; these are frequently used by Diethelm Travel and Borneo Transverse (see p.408). The longhouse itself is a spectacular design, built in 1999 to authentic specifications: the roof is made from *belian* (ironwood) shingle, and locally sourced timber, including the *ankabang* tree, is used for the main structure. Elegantly engraved motifs adorn the bamboo hallway in the inner veranda. Twenty minutes further up the Lemanak is a smaller, more modern longhouse, Nanga Kesit, and beyond that, Nanga Ngemah.

There are also longhouses on the Skrang, some of which are regularly used by the tour operators. To reach the Skrang river jetty, continue on the road north to Betong from Kampung Sereliau to reach the kampung at Entaban.

Sibu and the Rejang Basin

At the very heart of Sarawak stretches the 560-kilometre-long **Rejang**, Malaysia's longest river. Already over two hundred metres across downstream at the inland bazaar town of Kapit, by the time the Rejang reaches **Sibu**, the largest town on the river, it is eight times as wide. At Sibu, your initial impressions of the river will be of a massive, messy channel, but in fact its soupy, brown appearance these days is caused by ecological erosion and landslides generated by forest clearance.

Although Sibu's importance in the timber trade has made it a prosperous, forward-looking place, in spirit it's changed little since the late nineteenth century, when Chinese and Malay adventurers took boats from its wharf to **Kapit** and beyond. Between Sibu and Kapit, the little town of **Song** is a jumping-off point for **Iban longhouses** along the Katibas tributary of the Rejang; there are also Iban communities along the Baleh tributary, east of Kapit. Beyond here, through the **Pelagus Rapids** and onwards to the remote settlement of **Belaga**, the Rejang becomes wild and unpredictable and the scenery spectacular. Upstream from Belaga is soon a no-go area for visitors as you close in towards the Bakun Dam (see p.441).

Some history

For centuries, the Rejang was rife with tribal conflict. In the fifteenth century, when the Malay sultanates were at their height, Malays living in the estuaries of southern Sarawak pushed the immigrant Iban up the rivers towards present-day Sibu. This antagonized the indigenous people of those regions, especially the Baleh and upper Rejang Kayan, and throughout the seventeenth and eighteenth centuries they and the Iban fought amongst themselves for territory and heads. Occasionally, when they felt threatened, the Malays and the Iban would form an uneasy alliance to attack inland Kayan tribes and carry out piratical raids on passing Indonesian and Chinese ships.

With the arrival of the British, it was clear that no serious opening up of the interior could go ahead until the region was made relatively safe – which meant controlling the land and subjugating, or displacing, many of the indigenous inhabitants. To this end, James Brooke bought a section of Batang Rejang from the Sultan of Brunei in 1853, while his successor, Charles, asserted his authority over the Iban and Kayan tribes, and encouraged **Chinese pioneers** to move into the interior. Some of the more intrepid among these started to trade upriver with the Iban and, with support from the Malay business community and Brooke's officials, built settlements at Kanowit and Sibu, hacking out farms in the jungle for rice, pepper and rubber cultivation. Indeed, Sibu's early growth was largely financed by the proceeds of rubber cultivation.

Sibu

SIBU began life in the 1850s as a tiny Melenau encampment, and has grown into Sarawak's third largest city, with a population of around 220,000, and its biggest port. Most of Sibu's population is Foochow Chinese (the town is known locally as New Foochow) – and the town's speedy modern growth is largely attributed to these industrious and enterprising immigrants. Sibu, unlike Kuching or Miri, never retained a large contingent of Brooke's officials, which means its Chinese character has never really been diluted. Following the success of the early rubber plantations, manufacturing industries (largely textiles and consumer items) were established here, while later, after independence, Chinese businessmen moved into the lucrative trade in **timber**. But it wasn't all unimpeded expansion: in 1889 a fire razed the embryonic town to ashes, and in 1928 the Chinese godowns along the wharf and many of the cramped lodging houses and cafés were destroyed by another fire. The town was devastated again in World War II by advancing Japanese forces, who occupied it for three years, during which time much of the Chinese population was forced into slave labour. Sibu recovered through the 1950s with the intensification of the logging industry. It became the centre for timber processing in Sarawak and large fortunes were made by investors, many of whom came from the old Chinese families who had proved so enterprising in earlier decades. Although the decline of the timber industry started in the 1990s, Sibu has retained its regional supremacy and energetic manner.

The town's most striking landmark is the towering, seven-storey Tua Pek Kong Temple. North of here is the old **Chinatown**, its warren of narrow streets home to hawker stalls and miscellany of retail stores. Beyond simply soaking up the town's vibrant atmosphere, there's little for visitors to do in Sibu, though you'll want to check out the bustling day market and **pasar malam**, and the small **museum** on the edge of town, which focuses on the Chinese migration and the displaced ethnic communities. Most people come here as a starting point for an expedition upriver but end up finding its unpretentious vibe highly appealing.

Arrival and information

The **airport** is 25km east of the city centre; to reach the city take a taxi (RM35) – buy a ticket from the taxi desk in arrivals – or wait for bus #20/21 (every 30min; 6.30am–4.30pm), which will take you to the town bus station (beside the ferry terminal).

Buses from Sarikei, Kuching and points north arrive at the long-distance **bus station**, 10km northwest of the centre and only reachable by taxi (RM10). The express boat terminal, **Terminal Penumpang**, is at the western end of the esplanade, Jalan Maju, where boats arrive from Kuching downriver and Kanowit, Song, Kapit and Belaga upriver.

Sibu's enthusiastically staffed **Visitors' Information Centre** is centrally located at 16 Jalan Tukang Besi (Mon–Fri 8am–5pm, Sat 8am–12.30pm; ☎084/340980). Another useful spot is at Sazhong Trading, Sibu's leading travel

SIBU

ACCOMMODATION

Bahagia	F
Kingwood	J
Li Hua	I
Malaysia	C
Phoenix	A
Premier	D
RH Hotel	B
River Park Hotel	H
Tanahmas	G
Villa Hotel	E

EATING & DRINKING

Bakis Islamic Café	1
Dung Fang Café	9
Hai Bing Coffee Shop	10
Hock Chu Leu	6
Hua Chao Coffee Shop	7
Kiaw Hin Café	11
Le Ark Café Gallery	3
Little Roadhouse	4
Manna Café and Gallery	2
Nur Islamic Café	G
Peppers Café	G
Sin Chuang Hua Coffee Shop	5

Airport

0 — 200 m

Kapit, Song & Karowit

Kuching

Batang Rejang

Rejang Esplanade

Local Bus Terminus and Taxis

Terminal Penumpang

SMC Market

Car Park

Jalan Lanang

Lorong Lanang

Jalan Maju

Jalan Tan Sri

Jalan Khoo Peng Loong

Jalan Mission

Sibu Gateway

Food Stalls

Palace Cinema

Pasar Malam

Hawker Stalls

Jln Bengkel

High St

Jalan Market

Jalan Channel

Jalan Central

Sazhong Trading

CHINATOWN

Jalan Wong Nai Siong

Police Station

Taxis

Jalan Hua Kiew

Persiaran Brooke

Jalan Tuanku Osman

Mr Dobi (Laundry)

Civic Centre, Long Distance Bus Station & Airport

MAS

N

Padang

Wisma Sanyan

Terazone

Jalan Causeway

Jalan Sukan

Jalan Pulau

Jalan Morshidi Sidek

Rajan Way

Jalan Wharf

Jalan Bank

Jalan Temple

Tua Pek Kong Temple

Jalan Tukang Besi

Jalan Lintang

Jalan Tiong Hua

Jalan Mui Hong

Jalan Emplam

Jalan Tai Chee

Jalan Foochow

Hardin Walk

Jalan Hoe Ping

Jalan Pedada

Jalan Tong Sang

Jalan Bukit Assek

agency, 4 Jalan Central (☎084/336017). Run by veteran tour operator, the ebullient Frankie Ting, Sazhong offers trips to longhouses close to Sibu.

Accommodation

It's usually easy to find good-quality, reasonably priced **accommodation** in Sibu, with most places located within a ten-minute walk of the boat terminal. There are few budget places, and no backpackers, but like elsewhere in Sarawak, keep a lookout for promotional cuts at some of the city's leading hotels.

Bahagia 21 Jalan Wong Nai Siong ☎084/331131. Located in a good central position close to the *pasar malam*, though the rooms are quite small and bathrooms cramped. ❸

Kingwood 12 Lorong Lanang ☎084/335888, Ⓔ kingwood@tm.net.my. Beside the new *RH*, this is biggest hotel in Sibu, with huge, lovely rooms overlooking the river. Check if they have any promotions on – these can slash the price by around RM70. ❻

Li Hua Hotel Jalan Maju (behind *Le Ark Café*) ☎084/324000. Sibu's best deal; perfectly located 20m from the river with small but comfortable en-suite rooms – try 703 for a king's view of the Rejang. Its on-site coffee house does fine breakfasts too. ❸

Malaysia Jalan Kampung Nyabor ☎084/332299. A popular, though fairly shabby place, located on a busy main road, with small rooms, shared toilet and shower; it's family-run and friendly. ❷

Phoenix 1–3 Jalan Ki Peng, off Jalan Kampung Nyabor ☎084/313877. Smart and friendly, this is one of the best upmarket hotels, with spacious modern rooms, some with bath and TV. It can be a little noisy. ❸

Premier Jalan Kampung Nyabor ☎084/323222. Large-scale hotel with high central atrium; rooms are spacious and smartly decorated. ❼

RH Hotel Jalan Kampung Nyabor ☎084/365888, Ⓦwww.rhhotels.com.my. Sumptuous recent addition, assertively located north of the centre. The *RH* has large, fully equipped rooms and a restaurant serving top-notch buffets. ❻

River Park Hotel 51 Jalan Maju ☎084/316688. Tucked away on the eastern part of the esplanade, and close to the riverside café, the *River Park* is a superb, mid-range hotel with comfortable beds, spacious bathrooms and friendly service. ❸

Tanahmas Lorong Bengkel ☎084/333188, Ⓦwww.tanahmas.com.my. A fine, top-quality hotel with a vast lobby and large, a/c rooms. The ground floor café, *Peppers*, has a wide-ranging menu and is often packed until midnight at weekends. ❻

Villa Hotel 2 Jalan Central ☎084/337833. Always busy, this Chinese-run, first-floor place is clean and friendly, with small rooms and communal bathrooms. ❷

The Town

Sibu has been engulfed since the millennium by a surge of civic pride, with a vast covered market, the Sibu Gateway, a futuristic-looking car park and various landscaping projects all helping to spruce up the town. For a century or more, the Rejang has been Sibu's commercial and industrial lifeline. Along the **wharf**, on Jalan Khoo Peng Loong, plankways lead to several points where cargo boats dock, while the stores lining the road sell everything you may ever need for a river journey. At the eastern edge of the harbour lies the express and ferry **terminal** and beyond that, the **Rejang Esplanade**, a lovely little waterfront park built on reclaimed land and a popular place to sit and enjoy the evening breeze. Occasionally cultural events like traditional dancing and Chinese firework displays are put on here, and the park is also host to an early-morning tai chi routine.

Head along to the other end of Jalan Khoo Peng Loong, and west along Jalan Channel to reach Jalan Temple and the **Tua Pek Kong Temple**. There was a small, wooden temple on this site as early as 1870, though soon afterwards it was rebuilt on a much grander scale, with a tiled roof, stone block floor and decorative fixtures imported from China. Two large concrete lions guard the entrance, while the fifteen-metre-wide main chamber is always busy with people paying respects to the deity, Tua Pek Kong, a prominent Confucian scholar. The statue of Tua Pek Kong, to the left of the front entrance, is the most important image in the temple and survived both the fire of 1928 and Japanese bombardment. Elsewhere, the roof and columns are decorated with traditional statues of dragons and birds, while emblazoned on the temple wall to the left of the entrance are murals depicting the signs of the Chinese zodiac. In 1987, the rear section of the temple was replaced by the RM1.5-million, seven-storey **pagoda**, from the top of which there's a splendid view of the immense Rejang snaking away below.

Across Jalan Pulau, in the network of streets around Jalan Market, Jalan Channel and Jalan Central is **Chinatown**, with its plethora of hardware shops, newspaper stalls, busy cafés, textile wholesalers, cassette sellers, food and fruit-juice vendors and hotels. The central artery, **Jalan Market**, is the hub of one of the most vibrant *pasar malam*s in Sarawak (nightly from dusk until midnight) with dozens of stalls offering a wide variety of foods and every imaginable household item.

A few streets to the south is the social heart of Sibu, the huge, three-storey **Central Market**, which opens before dawn and closes around 5pm. It stocks all food necessities on the ground floor and has clothing stalls and a food court above. Hawkers at the market's edges sell anything from edible delicacies like flying fox, squirrel, snake, turtle, snail, jungle ferns and exotic fruits to rattan baskets, beadwork, charm bracelets and leather belts.

The **Sibu Gateway**, on the southwestern side of Jalan Kampung Nyabor, comprises a large stage and lawn where civic performances of drama and music occasionally take place. Fifty metres southwest of the Gateway is a set of pleasant water features in front of the *Tanahmas* hotel, close to which is the teeming **Central Market** and the incongruously gleaming car park to its left.

The civic centre

On the outskirts of Sibu but well worth visiting is **Dewan Suarah Sibu** (☏084/322900), the modern **civic centre**, on Jalan Suarah, 2km north of the centre, which contains a small but high-quality collection in its **Cultural Exhibition Hall** (Tues–Sun 10.30am–5pm; free) on the ground floor. To get there, take bus #3 from the local bus station and ask for the civic centre. In a series of display chambers, the hall details the varied peoples of Rejang region by means of well-chosen photographs, artefacts and paraphernalia. Among the costumes, backpacks and instruments in the Orang Ulu chamber, look out for some evocative old snaps of headmen, and an amazing photograph of a peace-making ceremony between Kayan and Iban tribespeople on November 16, 1924, at which represent-atives from both tribes killed pigs to authenticate their truce. There are more atmospheric pictures – of tattooing and cockfighting – in the adjacent Iban chamber, plus a scale model of an Iban longhouse that was made using bark, ironwood and bamboo. There are also records of numerous cultural associations, the Chinese immigrants' first port of call when they disembarked; in exchange for voluntary labour, the associations would find the new arrivals paid work and lodgings and induct them into the business and cultural life of the city.

Eating

Throughout town there are Chinese **cafés** selling Sibu's most famous dish, **Foochow noodles** – steamed and then served in a soy and oyster sauce with spring onions, chilli, garlic and dried fish. Other local favourites include *midin* (a type of wild fern), *kang puan mee* (noodles cooked in lard) and *kong bian* (oriental bagels, sprinkled with sesame seed). Prawn and crab are of a high quality and, when in season, tropical fruit like star fruit, rambutan, durian, papaya and guava are available from market stalls. Many of the hotels offer competitively priced buffets where an assortment of Chinese, Malay/Indian and Western dishes is on offer.

Although Sibu has a few air-conditioned **restaurants**, most people prefer to be outside at the **hawker stalls** when the weather's good, or to head to one of many superior Chinese **coffee shops**. Busiest in the morning are those on the first floor of the **Central Market**, while in the evening everyone congregates at the **pasar malam** one hundred metres north, which serves up Sibu delicacies like stuffed dumplings, grilled fish in shrimp sauce and chicken wings in peanut oil, as well as a range of offal and pigs' and ducks' heads. The *pasar malam's* only drawback is that there's nowhere to sit and consume the delicacies – most people wander over to the esplanade to eat.

Cafés are **open** throughout the day, from around 7am to 8pm, with the Chinese coffee shops staying open until midnight. Restaurants open from around 11am until 11pm.

Balkis Islamic Café 69 Jalan Osman. Near the MAS office, this excellent-value café offers a buffet from RM3 per head, with very good North Indian staples like *roti canai*, *murtabak* and curries.

Dung Fang Café 37 Jalan Maju. Beside the *River Park Hotel*, this large café is a great place for lunch, usually a *nasi* buffet with an array of tasty meat, fish and vegetable dishes to choose from.

Hai Bing Coffee Shop 31 Jalan Maju. A stone's throw from the *River Park Hotel*, this is an atmospheric Chinese establishment with excellent seafood and typical pork and chicken dishes, and also serves beer. You can choose between a/c and pavement tables.

Hock Chu Leu 28 Jalan Tukang Besi. Renowned, licensed Foochow place with delicious baked fish and fresh vegetables. Around RM40 for two, including drinks.

Hua Chao Coffee Shop Jalan Market, 20m from the night market. A venerable establishment, the *Hua* is frequented by a colourful cross-section of Sibu locals – plus a few visitors coming by for a beer or tea. Food is tasty Chinese fare, quickly delivered, with the musical rhythms coming courtesy of the brightly-lit CD store across the road.

Kiaw Hin Café Jalan Pulau (near Jalan Tukang Besi intersection). A busy café run by the bubbly Irene Sew with high-quality staples like *nasi campur* and a variety of noodles dishes. Open all day but with less food available in the afternoon hours.

Le Ark Café Gallery Rejang Esplanade. Opposite the *Li Hua Hotel*, this café is about the most

comfortable and pleasant place to eat in town. Its fabulous interior, which doubles as an art gallery, has a number of rooms on the ground floor, while upstairs is more open-plan. The menu borrows from Malaysian and Western cuisine with curries, fresh fish and local vegetables available. Open from breakfast to late evening; licensed.

Little Roadhouse 4 Jalan Causeway. Atmospheric first-floor bar-restaurant with a comfortable balcony serving Malaysian staples and excellent green vegetables. Has a wide-screen TV for football et al.

Manna Café and Gallery Top floor, Wisma Sanyan. Large café in a new plaza selling soft drinks and a wide variety of local dishes. It's worth resting here for a while if only to admire the bird's-eye view of the city and Batang Rejang. Books and local artwork are also on show.

Nur Islamic Café Jalan Kampung Nyabor (Jalan Tuanku Osman end). Perfectly acceptable and inexpensive Malay and Indian curries, roti, rice and fried fish.

Peppers Café *Tanahmas Hotel*, Jalan Kampung Nyabor. The wide-ranging menu here – from Western dishes to Malay fish curries – is very popular but doesn't come cheap at around RM60 for two. The lunchtime menu is better priced.

Sin Chuang Hua Coffee Shop Jalan Market. Like the *Hua*, a very busy Chinese café where over a beer, noodles or rice, you can watch market life revolve.

Listings

Airlines The MAS office is a 30min walk northwest from the centre at 61 Jalan Tunku Osman (☏084/326166).

Airport For flight information call ☏084/307082.
Banks Bumiputra, Lot 6 & 7, Jalan Kampung Nyabor; Public Bank, 2–6 Jalan Tunku Osman.

By air

From Sibu's airport, there are daily flights on AirAsia to Kuala Lumpur, Johor Bahru and Kuching, and on MAS to Bintulu, Kuching, Miri, KK (3 daily) and KL. MASwings flies to Bintulu, KK, Kuching and Miri. Bus #3a runs out to the airport (RM2) from the local bus terminal, Jalan Maju.

By boat

Express launches depart from **Terminal Penumpang** up the Rejang to Kanowit, Song and Kapit, leaving half-hourly or hourly from 5.45am till around 4.30pm. Boats often leave a few minutes early so plan to arrive at least fifteen minutes before departure; it is not necessary to book ahead for these routes. To reach Belaga you must obtain a permit in Kapit (see p.435). You'll probably have to overnight in Kapit as the first express boat from Sibu doesn't always connect with the last service to Belaga.

By bus

There are numerous departures from the Regional Bus Terminal at Sungai Antu to Sarawak towns and cities: Kuching (8hr), Mukah (3hr 30min), Bintulu (3hr 30min) and Miri (7hr). Some of the Kuching-bound buses travel onwards to Pontianak, in Kalimantan.

Boat enquiries (Kuching) ☏ 082/410076.

Handicrafts There are stalls selling baskets where Jalan Channel hits the wharf. There are several ceramics factories close to Sibu: buses leave every hour from the local bus station to one, Toh Brothers, on Jalan Ulu Oya.

Hospital Jalan Ulu Oya ☏ 084/343333.

Internet access Terazone, fifth floor, Wisma Sanyan (10am–10pm; RM4 per hr).

Laundry Mr Dobi, 5 Jalan Bintang (Mon–Sat 7.30am–6pm).

Police Jalan Kampung Nyabor ☏ 084/336144.

Post office The main office is on Jalan Kampung Nyabor (Mon–Fri 8am–6pm, Sat 8am–noon).

Taxis Sibu Taxis ☏ 084/320773.

Tour operators Sazhong Reading and Travel, 4 Jalan Central ☏ 084/336107. Sibu expert Frankie Ting can offer one or two night trips to Iban longhouses, reached by 4X4 for around RM150 (1 night) or RM250 (2 nights).

Along the Rejang

From Sibu, express launches head up the Rejang, stopping at **Song**, from where it's possible to explore the **Katibas River**. Most then terminate at Kapit, a three-hour journey from Sibu; however, one boat a day goes beyond Kapit to Belaga, the last stop. As the river narrows, tiny Iban boats can be seen hugging the sides of the river to get as far away as possible from the swell the speeding launches create. Wood-reprocessing plants – a frequent sight on the stretch from Sarikei to Sibu – are thankfully less common as you head upriver, so the weight and mass of the jungle on either side becomes more apparent.

The first Sibu–Kapit boat sets off at dawn (5.45am), after which launches leave once or twice an hour until around 4.30pm. Although it is theoretically possible to make the 9.10 connection to Belaga, visitors are required to obtain a permit at Kapit's Residence Office and, given that there is no kiosk at the jetty to do this, by the time you have concluded this bureaucratic manoeuvre the boat would have left. Thus it is necessary to stay overnight in Kapit – not an unpleasant option – before onward travel northeast. Remember that if the water level is low boats don't go beyond the Pelagus Rapids, near Kapit, anyway – you can check at the jetty. Boats seldom sell any provisions, so bring your own water and food.

Song

The small Iban settlement of **SONG** is two hours upstream from Sibu, beyond sleepy Kanowit. It lies close to the junction of one of the Rejang's loveliest tributaries, the **Katibas**, which winds south towards the mountainous border region with Kalimantan. This is a breathtaking region of the state and well worth the visit, where longhouse communities retain a balance between the modern and traditional.

There's not much to Song, beyond a few blocks of waterfront shophouses, some of them 1920s wooden affairs, their shutters painted in cheery blues and greens, a jetty, a small Chinese temple and two waterfront **hotels**. However, the small town is readying itself for a major facelift, with a planned esplanade, which will bring stores, cafés and seating areas to the ordinarily scruffy riverside area.

Accommodation options are limited to the *Capital Hotel* (☎084/777264; ❷) which has dark corridors, small, stuffy rooms and shared bathrooms; the *Katibas Inn* (☎084/777323; ❷), with neat rooms and acceptable bathrooms; and the *Mesra Inn* (☎013/8280477; ❷), one block back from the river, with a pleasant lobby and airy, neatly decorated and clean rooms.

Along the riverside are the usual Chinese stores, plus several **coffee shops** serving simple noodle dishes. In addition, stalls on the upper floor of the market facing the *Capital* offer *nasi lemak* and other Malay staples; you have to head up to the nearby *Happy Garden Seafood Restaurant* for a meal of any sophistication.

The Katibas River

To explore the **Katibas River**, you need to catch the passenger longboat that leaves Song daily at 9.30am from the jetty. On the Katibas are several Iban longhouses well worth visiting.

It takes between two and three hours to reach **Rumah Tambi**, a small settlement comprising a longhouse and other houses, where the narrow Bangkit River branches away from the Katibas. This is the boat's final port of call, so most of your fellow passengers will get off here. The settlement's longhouse women here are excellent **weavers**, and you can buy a wall hanging or thin rug for around RM300. The boat back to Song leaves at 6am the next morning – note that it's impossible to visit Rumah Tambi as a day-trip.

Despite their proximity to big-town Sibu, these river communities still hold their customs dear. Along the banks of the Katibas and the Bangkit you may catch sight of small **burial houses** set back on the banks. For a good 100m either side of the burial spots, the jungle is left undisturbed; these areas are strictly out of bounds to locals from neighbouring longhouses and other visitors. The surrounding areas also remain uncultivated out of respect to the ancestors. In contrast to the longhouses in southwestern Sarawak, those here see few overseas visitors.

Kapit and around

The next town on the Rejang, **KAPIT** – around three hours east of Sibu – is the centre for buying and selling in the middle Rejang. It started life as a remote settlement for a small community of British officials and Chinese *towkays* trading with the region's indigenous population, but these days, the

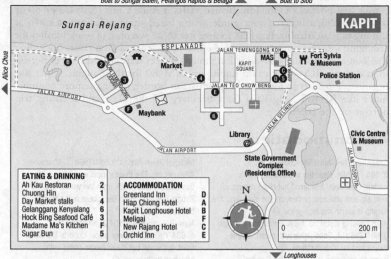

Boat to Sungai Baleh, Pelangos Rapids & Belaga ▲   ▲ Boat to Sibu

KAPIT

Sungai Rejang

Alice Chua

ESPLANADE

JALAN TEMENGGONG KOH

Market

KAPIT SQUARE

MAS

Fort Sylvia & Museum

Police Station

JALAN TEO CHOW BENG

JALAN AIRPORT

Maybank

JALAN AIRPORT

Library

JALAN SELINIK

State Government Complex (Residents Office)

Civic Centre & Museum

JALAN HOSPITAL

N

EATING & DRINKING	
Ah Kau Restoran	2
Chuong Hin	1
Day Market stalls	4
Gelanggang Kenyalang	6
Hock Bing Seafood Café	3
Madame Ma's Kitchen	F
Sugar Bun	5

ACCOMMODATION	
Greenland Inn	D
Hiap Chiong Hotel	A
Kapit Longhouse Hotel	B
Meligai	F
New Rajang Hotel	C
Orchid Inn	E

0   200 m

▼ Longhouses

SARAWAK | Kapit and around

signs of rapid expansion are easily visible: machine parts and provisions are unloaded from the tops of express boats while, as in Sibu, new municipal buildings are fast changing the character of the town. As well as its remote location and usefulness as a base for onward travel and longhouse visits, Kapit offers an opportunity to visit Fort Sylvia, one of the splendid wooden structures erected by the Brooke dynasty, now converted into an informative museum, redolent of the upriver colonial era. Although most travellers stay just one night in Kapit – waiting for boats either way along the Rejang – it's easy to develop a soft spot for the town. Though the place is little more than a compact grid hacked out from the luxuriant forest, there are lots of good cafés in which to while away the time.

Around the town, there's the nearby **Pelagus Rapids** and some Iban longhouses that welcome overnight visits. Kapit has a registered tour operator, Alice Chua (see p.436), who organizes trips on the Baleh and Gaat tributaries. Kapit's premier tourist activity is the annual Balleh/Kapit Rafting Safari, held in April; contact Sibu's Visitors Information Centre (see p.428) to find out exact dates. The day-long race features boatmen on locally made rafts traversing rapids on nearby rivers.

Arrival and information

Express **boats** dock at the town jetty, from where it is a few minutes' walk to anywhere in town. Three **banks** can change traveller's cheques: the Maybank, beside the *Hotel Meligai*, which also has an ATM; MBF, beside the *Kapit Longhouse Hotel*; and Bank Simpanan Nasional on the riverfront. The only **internet café** is in the town library on Jalan Selinik (Mon–Fri 9am–5pm, Sat 9am–12.30pm). There is no tourist office.

To travel beyond Kapit by river you need a **permit**, available from the Resident's Office (☎084/796963; Mon–Fri 8am–12.30pm & 2.15–4.15pm) on the first floor of the State Government Complex, 80m north of the jetty on Jalan Selinik. Take your **passport** with you; the process can take an hour to complete. Express boats leave from the jetty for Belaga once a day at 9.20am (5hr; RM25) and hourly from 6.30am to 3.30pm for the trip back to Sibu (3hr; RM20).

Your first port of call for **longhouse visits** is Alice Chua (℡084/340980 or 019/8593126), a licensed tour guide, who's based three miles out of town at Lorong 6, Jalan Airport. It is best to give her some warning (a week ideally) for arranging visits to communities on the nearby Baleh and Gaat rivers (including the Iban at Bundong, a 65-door longhouse). Prices start at RM290 per person for a day-trip, RM400 for two nights and RM480 for three nights. Chua also organizes longer trips towards the Kalimantan border, passing remote communities like Rumah Seng Kuai on a tributary off the Gaat, and a rafting trip upriver on the Baleh.

Accommodation

Greenland Inn Jalan Teo Chow Beng ℡084/796388. Near the waterfront, Kapit's second-best hotel has small but clean rooms, all with a/c and attached bathroom. The view over the Rejang is worth the high price. ❺

Hiap Chiong Hotel 33 Jalan Temenggong Jugah ℡084/796314. Good value with clean, simple rooms and small bathrooms. ❷

Kapit Longhouse Hotel 21 Jalan Berjaya ℡084/796415. Although a bit grubby, this budget place is popular with travellers. The rooms are small, with chugging fans; bathrooms are shared. ❷

Meligai Jalan Airport ℡084/796817, ℮aswee @tm.net.my. The town's most upmarket spot, this hotel is 5min walk from the waterfront. Rooms are large with tiled floors and attached bathrooms. ❹

New Rajang Hotel 104 Jalan Wharf ℡084/796600. Popular place, close to the waterfront. It's small but clean rooms come with attached bathrooms. ❶

Orchid Inn 64 Jalan Teo Chow Beng ℡084/796325. Adequate rooms with a/c, showers and TV. ❸

The Town

Close to the jetty is Kapit's main landmark, the imposing white **Fort Sylvia**. Renamed after Vyner Brooke's wife in 1925, it was built in 1880 in an attempt to prevent the warring Iban attacking smaller and more peaceable groups such as the upriver Ukit and Bukitan. The fort also served to limit Iban migration along the nearby Sungai Baleh, and confine them to the section of the Rejang below Kapit. Now the fort houses an intriguing **museum** (Tues–Sun 10am–noon and 2–5pm; free), spread over two floors. There are evocative photographs of great moments in the history of the upriver divisions, including the 1924 peacemaking ceremony in Kapit between Brooke officials and the warring Iban and Kayan tribal representatives. In addition, there are spectacular carvings, ceramic jars, *pua kumba* textiles, small cannons and precious stones on display.

Leading away from Fort Sylvia is Kapit's main street, **Jalan Temenggong Koh**, whose rows of simple shophouses that once nestled between patches of jungle are now giving way to stores and cafés housed in concrete buildings, which can better withstand the deluges of rain that regularly occur here. The **jetties** in front are a hive of activity, too, with longboats bobbing up and down and scores of people with bulky bundles of goods making their way back and forth between the express boats and smaller craft. Merchants, timber employers and visitors watch the goings-on from marble-topped tables in the *Chuong Hin* café, opposite the jetty.

Kapit's main square – simply called **Kapit Square** – is always busy in the middle of the day, full of stalls selling sweet and savoury snacks. It is surrounded by cafés and shops selling everything from electrical items to ubiquitous retail clothing. The walk westwards along Jalan Temenggong, which forms the square's northern edge, leads to the **day market** where tribespeople sell clusters of tropical fruit, and other traders supply boxes of wriggling eels and shrimps. There are textile and shoe stalls upstairs in the main building, and the stalls in front of the market sell fast food – prawn cakes, *pow*, curry puffs and sweet pastries.

Back from the jetty along Jalan Hospital, near the pond, is the **Civic Centre and Museum** (Mon–Thurs & Sat 9am–noon & 2–4pm; free), which has a collection of interesting exhibits on the tribes in the Rejang region, including a well-constructed longhouse and a mural painted by local Iban. The sketches and watercolours of Kapit, Belaga and Song by Timothy Chua on display there portray a life that is slowly disappearing. The museum also describes the lives of the Hokkien traders who were early pioneers in the region.

Eating

Kapit is a reasonable town for food although there is not much choice beyond regular Chinese and Malaysian fare. The food from the **hawker stalls** and **markets** is usually plentiful and tasty, and you can always get fresh meat and vegetables in the sit-down **coffee shops** and **restaurants**.

Ah Kau Restoran Jalan Temenggog Jugah. Specializes in local recipes: wild boar, steamed fish, jungle vegetables and as much rice as you can eat, with beer, at RM25 for two.

Chuong Hin Jalan Temenggong Koh. The best of the cafés in the morning – savoury cakes, curry puffs and hard-boiled eggs will set you up for the day. The staff are rather surly with travellers, but there's no better place to watch the comings and goings at the wharf.

Day Market stalls Jalan Teo Chow Beng. Sarawak fast-food like curry puffs, prawn cakes, cornmeal cake and tofu buns. Open 7am–5pm.

Gelanggang Kenyalang Two blocks back from Kapit Square, this covered market's dozen separate stalls serve Chinese, Malay and Dyak dishes, including *roti canai* and various noodle dishes with local vegetables, seafood and meat. The optimum time to eat here is between noon and 3pm, after which the food may not be so fresh.

Hock Bing Seafood Café Jalan Temenggong Jugah. With some pavement tables, this bustling café serves the best prawn, wild-boar and fern dishes in Kapit. Friendly, atmospheric and excellent value at around RM20 for two people, including beer.

Madame Ma's Kitchen *Meligai* hotel. This a/c hotel eatery is about the best Kapit has to offer with tasty dishes from all the Malaysian cuisines, albeit at prices higher than the cafés nearby.

Sugar Bun Jalan Teo Chow Beng. Not the town's finest food but a good place to watch Kapit's youth culture congregate.

Pelagus Rapids

Forty minutes' upriver from Kapit the **Pelagus Rapids** churn the Rejang's waters – an 800-metre-long, deceptively shallow stretch of the river where large, submerged stones make the through passage treacherous. According to local belief, the rapids' seven sections represent the seven segments of an enormous serpent which was chopped up and floated downriver by villagers to the north. It's only in the last fifteen years that running the rapids has become safe, thanks to the new express boats, which have reinforced steel hulls and immense thrust.

Tucked in between the rapids and the jungle-covered Bukit Pelagus is the *Regency Pelagus Rapids Resort* (T 084/799051, W www.theregencyhotel.com .my/Pelagus; ❼), a longhouse-shaped hideaway with a large number of double rooms, all with attached bathroom and a veranda. Its riverfront dining room serves three meals a day, the menu including local dishes like *pangsoh* (chicken baked in bamboo) and various exotic takes on steamed fish.

The resort's guide, Nyaring Bandar, leads day-trips (from RM100) for residents and non-residents to the nearby Iban longhouse where he was raised, as well as a two-hour boat trip to visit a **Punan** community (a small subgroup of the Orang Ulu). Also on offer are night-time hikes into the surrounding

▲ Punan tribesman

rainforest and a rewarding half-day trek (guide not required). The latter follows a trail up the hill behind the resort to an old forest track and back down towards the river, offering fabulous views of the surrounding undisturbed forest, accompanied by a cacophony of birdsong, before meandering back along a path running beside the river (a 3hr round trip).

In order to get to the resort, most people call it in advance to arrange a speedboat from Kapit (45min; RM60 return). Express boats to and from Belaga can use the landing bay 300m along the river from the resort's jetty, but you'll need to arrange for the resort's boat to drop you at this bay as there's no path there to or from the resort.

The Baleh

The **Baleh** River branches off from the Rejang east of Kapit, at the point where the main river twists north towards the Pelagus Rapids. If you want to explore the Baleh in any depth, you will need to charter a longboat from Kapit (around RM200 a day), or better yet, discuss a tailor-made tour with Alice Chua. The **Gaat**, a tributary of the Baleh, also has some fascinating longhouses along it.

If you have the time and money, it is worth making the effort to get to this inaccessible and seldom visited part of upland Borneo. Wherever you head, the **scenery** is magnificent – the land is covered in dense jungle, with the mountains on the Sarawak–Kalimantan border, to the south, peeping out of the morning mist. Occasionally you'll hear sounds of conversation or splashing as you round a corner and catch sight of an Iban family pulling their bamboo fish traps out of the water, or cooking their catch over an open fire. The river brims with fish, while the surrounding forest supports deer, buffalo and wild boar.

To Belaga

In the nineteenth century, the 150km trip from Kapit to **Belaga** (see below), on the furthest reaches of the Rejang, took two weeks in a longboat, a treacherous journey which involved negotiating rapids and dodging Iban raids on longhouses that belonged to the original inhabitants of the **upper Rejang** – the **Kenyah** and the **Kayan**. These days the trip takes up to six hours from Kapit, depending on the river level. If the water level is very low or conditions at Pegasus Rapids too hazardous – when the Rejang can become a raging torrent – the boat is cancelled. However, if the conditions are right, it's an excellent trip. Deep in the centre of Sarawak, wispy clouds cloak the hills and the screech of monkeys and birds can be heard.

Longhouses are dotted along the river bank. As far as **Long Pila**, ninety minutes from Kapit, the people are mostly Iban, though between here and Belaga there are many other tribes, including the Ukit, Kayan and Kenyah.

Belaga

BELAGA, which lies 40km west of the confluence of the Rejang and the Balui, is as remote as you can get in the Sarawak interior. However, it's not uncharted territory by any means. The town started life as a small bazaar, after Charles Brooke had purchased the region from the Sultan of Brunei in 1853. As early as 1900, pioneering Chinese *towkays* arrived to open up Belaga to trade and were supplying the tribespeople – both the Kayan and the nomadic Punan and Penan, who roamed over a wide swath of forest – with kerosene, cooking oil and cartridges, in exchange for beadwork and mats, beeswax, ebony and tree gums. The British presence in this region was nominal – officials would occasionally brave the trip from Kapit, but no fort was built this far up the river.

The Kayan and Kenyah

The **Kayan** and the **Kenyah** are the most numerous and powerful of the Orang Ulu groups who have been living for centuries in the upper Rejang, along the Batang Baram, the Balui and their tributaries. The Kayan are the more numerous, at around forty thousand, while the Kenyah population is around ten thousand (though there are substantially more Kenyah over the mountains in Kalimantan). Both groups migrated from East Kalimantan into Sarawak approximately six hundred years ago, although during the nineteenth century, when Iban migration led to clashes between the groups, they were pushed back to the lands they occupy today.

The Kayan and the Kenyah have a lot in common: their language, with Malay–Polynesian roots, is completely different from those of the other groups, and they have a well-defined social hierarchy (unlike the Iban or Penan). Traditionally, the **social order** was topped by the **tuai rumah** (chief) of the longhouse, followed by a group of three or four lesser aristocrats or **payin**, lay families and slaves (slavery no longer exists). Both groups take great pride in the construction of their **longhouses**, which are very impressive. Tom Harrisson, of the Sarawak Museum, learned in the 1950s of a longhouse on the upper Baleh which was nearly one kilometre long.

Kayan art

Artistic expression plays an important role in longhouse culture, the Kayan especially maintaining a wide range of **musical traditions** including the lute-like **sape**, which is used to accompany long voice epics. **Textiles** are woven by traditional techniques in the upriver longhouses, and Kayan and Kenyah **woodcarvings**, which are among the most spectacular in Southeast Asia, are produced both for sale and for ceremonial uses. One artist, Tusau Padan, originally from Kalimantan, became much revered as one of the finest Malaysian artists of his time. He used mixed media of vibrant colours to create the flowing motifs he applied to painting and textiles – adorning burial poles, longboats and the walls of many Ulu Sarawak chiefs' homes. Potent **rice wine** is still drunk by some Kayan, although nearly all the communities have now converted to Christianity, as a result of which alcohol is harder to come by.

Now, logging roads snake their way across the interior, with a well-maintained one linking Belaga with the main Bintulu–Miri road, 100km away.

The Town

Belaga is fairly compact, comprising a market, some shops selling provisions, a few nondescript houses and, beyond, a small track snaking towards the formidably dense forest, a few hundred metres away. Twenty minutes' walk along a riverside path there's a pretty kampung where the **Kejaman** (a small ethnic group related to the Kayan, and now almost extinct) burial pole that's on display outside the Sarawak Museum in Kuching was found in the early years of the twentieth century.

The chief activity in town is watching the comings and goings of the colourful characters that make up the area's wide ethnic mix. Occasionally Penan tribespeople, experts in metalwork, come by to sell their uniquely carved knives, which can be picked up here for far less than you would pay for them in Sibu. A seasonal appearance is also made by the **wild-honey collectors** from Kalimantan, who arrive in March and again in September to trade their jungle produce for supplies. Other faces on Belaga's small network of streets include Kayan and Kenyah, with their fantastic tattoos and elongated ear lobes,

Visiting a longhouse

One of the most resonant images of Sarawak, the longhouse is the centre of daily life for many communities. Despite the pressures of deforestation and the lure of the city it's estimated a few thousand survive, each housing up to hundred families and occasionally reaching up to a kilometre in length. Tourists are welcome to visit; participating in the daily routine of the people who live here is a captivating experience and one that will leave a lasting impression.

Longhouse at the Sarawak Cultural Village near Kuching ▲

Boys learning to weave rattan baskets ▼

The house

Longhouses are designed to sustain entire communities under a single roof. They are traditionally made of hardwoods and bamboo with ironwood shingles on the roof, and comprise three storeys. The house is often elevated on stilts so as to provide shelter for livestock.

On approach to the house, you will first see a long open veranda (*tanju*) where rice, pepper or rubber can be laid out to dry. Entrance to the longhouse is via a ladder to a roofed veranda (*ruai*), the area in which the community's social life is conducted. Here women weave pattered textiles and boys are taught to construct baskets and mats. On the opposite side of the *ruai* from the *tanju*, through closed doors, lies each family's apartment, or *bilik*. Directly above the *ruai* is the loft, where rattan baskets, sleeping mats, and the odd shrunken head, are kept.

Location, location, location

Longhouses are often found in truly spectacular settings – usually on the bends or at the confluences of rivers. While aesthetically pleasing, these locations were actually selected for strategic reasons, as a good defensive position was essential until well into the twentieth century when inter-tribal warfare died down. In keeping with their concerns about defence, longhouse tribes would also consider their combative strength when choosing a location. Larger groups might build big longhouses in open locations as a show of strength, while smaller ones might opt for more modest homesteads deeper in the forest.

Iban Longhouse ▼

Visiting the longhouse

Longhouses are working buildings where a traditional way of life continues to this day. Be mindful and **respectful** of the age-old practices and rituals practised by these tribes, who might be Christian, animist or Muslim in belief. The following is a rundown of what to expect when first arriving at a longhouse, and what your subsequent stay will entail. For further information see p.46.

▶ On arrival you will be introduced to the chief (*tuai*); smile and shake hands. Be sure to shake hands with everyone who wants to shake yours – neglecting to do this will cause offence.

▶ Don't ascend the longhouse ladder to the veranda until invited to do so.

▶ After the formalities, you'll be led onto the *ruai* and offered a glass of *tuak* (rice wine), or a non-alcoholic drink if you are visiting a Christian community.

▶ During your stay, you may be taught how to weave, cook traditional dishes and use a blow-pipe, or even hunt wild boar.

▶ You will eat with one of the families. Dishes on offer may include chicken stewed in aromatic herbs, glutinous rice, or, for special occasions, wild boar roasted on spit. Feel free to eat as much as you like – eating lots is considered a compliment to the chef.

▶ Following the meal there are often dancing and singing shows, in which visitors often participate. The *ngajat*, a dance traditionally performed by warriors on their return from battle, is sometimes performed, albeit in a milder, truncated form.

▶ Some of the larger longhouses have built lodges close by to house visitors; otherwise, you will sleep on a simple mattress set on the longhouse veranda.

▲ Iban elder with fighting cock

▼ Weaving a ceremonial rug

▼ Preparing for a feast

Gawai Dayak feast ▲

Traditional headhunter dance ▼

Party time

The **Iban** are the largest tribal group in Sarawak, and the most social time to visit them is when the **Gawai Dayak** (harvest festival; May–June) gets into full swing. It is a time for relaxing and merrymaking, and also the season for celebrations such as weddings and christenings. Proceedings can last for three full days and involve dancing, singing and storytelling; some participants wear traditional garments and heirlooms such as old *parangs* (swords) and beautifully woven fabrics are taken down from the rafters. To find out where and when one is being held, ask at the Visitor Information Centre in Kuching (see p.397). Visitors are welcome during *Gawai*, though it's customary to bring gifts.

Our favourites

Visits to longhouses in Sarawak are arranged by tour operators; see p.408 for a list.

▶▶ **Iban** (southwest). Most popular with tourists. Built on rivers near Kuching, Iban longhouses are lively places where musical ensembles often perform, and modern entertainment (radio, television, DVD) is encouraged and enjoyed. See p.424

▶▶ **Bidayuh** (southwest/Kalimantan border). Longhouses are located around Gunung Penrissen, mostly built away from rivers. The Bidayuh are a small, shy and seldom-visited tribe. See p.422

▶▶ **The Ulu Kayan and Kenyah** (north). Known for their spectacular longhouses and their prowess as fine weavers and woodcarvers. Expect to see lovely decorative touches and the odd dried skull, for old time's sake. See p.440

▶▶ **The Kelabit** (Kelabit Highlands; around Bario and Ba' Kelalan). Small longhouses often set beside streams. The Kelabit are gregarious people with a great sense of humour. See p.474

Dried skulls ▼

wandering through the bazaar and eating wild boar and fried ferns in the Chinese cafés.

Practicalities

Boats terminate at the jetty directly in front of the town's main street. Belaga's three basic **hotels** all offer similar rooms. *Belaga Hotel*, 14 Main Bazaar (℡086/461244; ❷), is most peoples' favourite, perhaps because the rooms have bathrooms and fans. Owner Andrew Tiong and his family run a **café** downstairs, which is a good place to eat in town. The *Bee Lian Hotel*, 11 Main Bazaar (℡086/461439; ❷), and *Sing Soon Huat Hotel*, 27 New Bazaar (℡086/461307; ❸), are the alternatives, both offering small, basic rooms with external bathrooms.

Note that a number of **unlicensed travel guides** operate in Belaga – names include Daniel Levoh and John Belarik – and it is best to **avoid** trips offered by these men as some travellers have complained about their behaviour. The Visitors' Information Centre in Sibu advises travellers to contact licensed operator Alice Chua (see p.436) who has an assistant contactable in Belaga, Hamdani Louis.

Moving on from Belaga, there are two boats daily downstream: the 6am express boat, via Kapit, goes all the way to Sibu (RM60), while the 7.30am one only travels as far as Kapit (RM30). Most days a 4X4 vehicle leaves for Bintulu in the mornings (3hr; around RM60) at around 8am. There is no obvious way of booking this trip in advance; see Andrew Tiong to help point you in the direction of whoever's driving the following day.

The Bakun Dam

The controversial **hydroelectric dam** at **Bakun** was given the go-ahead by Malaysian Prime Minister Dr Mahathir in 1993. It promised 2,400MW of electricity but in the process would flood 69,000 hectares of rainforest and river channels, displacing up to eleven thousand indigenous people, mostly Penan who for hundreds of years had lived off the jungle. The forest also included indigenous agricultural lands and many thriving longhouse communities. The 200-metre-high, concrete-faced dam, one hour upstream on Batang Rejang from Belaga, was designed to generate much more than just Sarawak's power needs, and environmentalists, already red in the face about the social displacement and inevitable ecological degradation, pointed out that the task of exporting power to Peninsular Malaysia was technically nigh on unfeasible. The massive project has been subject to delay after delay and many people are asking if it is on target to become a multi-billion-ringgit white elephant.

First, the economic crisis of 1997 put paid to the original plans for the dam, but they resurfaced in 2000. By then, the social damage had already been done: the vast majority of the local communities had already been displaced to Asap, two hours' drive along logging roads north from Belaga. Only small groups of Kayan and Kenyah families held on in the most isolated of the longhouses furthest along Sungai Balui.

Construction at Bakun may now be complete, but power generation will not commence until 2011. A further setback in 2008 saw the developers, Sime Darby, pull out from a key commitment to finance the RM6-billion submarine cable project that was to transport power from the dam to Peninsular Malaysia. The earliest this part of the project can now be completed is 2013. Critics continue to argue that the power the dam will generate will be as expensive as an oil or coal-fired plant. And, if the long-stated plan to export power to the Peninsula is to be shelved, they ask what will be done with all that excess electricity – power that Sarawak's population simply won't need.

The central coast from Sibu to Niah

The route along the western flank of Sarawak from Sibu towards the Bruneian border is one of the most travelled in the state. Although dense mangrove swamp deprives the 150km of inland road linking Sibu with Bintulu of a clear view of the South China Sea, a lone chink in the vegetation leads across to the busy riverside town of **Mukah**, close to which lies the charming Melenau village of Kampung Tellian, with its appealing museum-cum-guesthouse.

Further northeast, the Sibu–Brunei road offers diversions into a number of national parks. **Similajau National Park** 20km northeast of the industrial town of **Bintulu**, is a strip of forest with a long, isolated and windswept beach; the small forest enclave of **Lambir Hills National Park**, has easily covered trails and good accommodation; and Sarawak's most-visited natural wonder, **Niah National Park**, halfway between Bintulu and Miri, is noted for its formidable **limestone caves** – Deer Cave includes the largest chamber in the world. Niah was put on the map in the mid-1950s when the curator of the Sarawak Museum, Tom Harrisson, discovered human remains and rock graffiti inside the caves.

Northeast of Niah, it's another two hours to the vibrant city of **Miri**, Sarawak's second biggest city, and an important administrative centre. The town has benefited from the discovery of massive oil reserves in the vicinity, though in the energy stakes, Miri has recently been rivalled by Bintulu, which has specialized in the tapping of abundant pockets of natural gas on its doorstep. Both towns have a smaller percentage of indigenous inhabitants than Sarawak's other main settlements, and although some Iban and Melenau live in the area, there are very few longhouses to visit.

Northwards beyond Kuala Baram (the mouth of Batang Baram), the highway reaches Kuala Belait and the **Brunei border**. East of here, tucked into the folds of Brunei, are two small "divisions": finger-shaped **Limbang**, and **Lawas**, the most northerly strip of Sarawak, stretching north to meet Sabah.

Mukah and around

MUKAH, lying on the languid Mukah River a few kilometres inland from the South China Sea, is a three-hour bus journey from either Sibu or Bintulu. The last ninety kilometres of the trip, north from the Sibu–Bintulu highway, is a real bone-shaker, though the discomfort is somewhat alleviated by the views of the lush sago palms along the way.

Mukah comprises a congested but atmospheric **old town**, a simple grid of streets running roughly east–west along the south bank of the Mukah River, and a new section two kilometres away from the river. Old Mukah's most defining image is its casuarina-lined waterfront, which contains both new shophouses and older, more charismatic wooden versions, some of which are brightened by striped screens. The town's main sights are the **Sago Furnace**, a simple brick construction unobtrusively sited beside the waterfront and a reminder of the region's importance in the collection and processing of the vitamin-rich sago palm; and, close by, **Tua Pek Kong Chinese Temple**, from whose veranda you can view the river's stilt houses and boats. The bearded Tua Pek Kong, patron saint of businessmen, sits at the head of the temple's main hall, while on its walls are finely painted murals of Buddhist and Taoist deities.

Practicalities

Mukah's **airport** lies five kilometres west of town with MASwings flights to Kuching (1–2 daily; 1hr 10min) and Miri (1 daily; 50min). There are no buses from the airport into Mukah; a taxi costs around RM15. The **bus station** lies on the eastern edge of the old town on Jalan Sedia Raja, which is within walking distance of the centre. Tickets for outbound flights can be purchased at MA, on the waterfront at 6 Jalan Pasar, or in the departures hall of the airport itself.

Most of the **accommodation** in Mukah is found in the old town, either on or just south of Jalan Pasar. *Sri Umpang* (T084/872415; ❸), on the Main Bazaar, is the town's best choice, with a bright and appealing foyer and clean, air-conditioned rooms with sizeable bathrooms, while *King Ing Hotel* on Jalan Boyan (T084/871400); ❸) has tidy rooms with adequate bathrooms. A good alternative, if these two are full, is *Weiming Hotel*, positioned opposite the *Umpang* on the Main Bazaar (T084/872278; ❸), which has modern rooms with nice bathrooms. To **eat** during daytime head for the *Melenau Food Court* on the western edge of the market facing the river, close to the Chinese temple. All of the stalls here sell fresh local cuisine, including the area's speciality, *umai*, a delicious raw fish and lime dish. One block back from the river, on Jalan Oya, *Arwa Café*, another daytime place, sells excellent *nasi campur* and fresh noodles. In the evening, try *Nibong House*, a five-minute walk from the old town on Jalan Orang Kaya Sedia Raja for a wide choice of Chinese dishes.

Kampung Tellian

Three kilometres east of Mukah on the Misan, a tributary of the Mukah, lies the Melenau water village of **Kampung Tellian**. Buses here are few and far between; taxis from Mukah's bus terminus will charge RM8. The kampung is a veritable spaghetti junction of winding paths, precarious crisscrossing boardwalks and bridges. Some of the Melenau residents of its many stilt houses still work at processing sago the traditional way – by pulverizing the pith in large troughs and squeezing the pulp through a sieve, then leaving it to dry.

Aside from its picturesque appeal, Tellian's main attraction is its little museum and guesthouse, **Lamin Dana** (Mon–Sat 9am–5pm for non-residents; RM3 entry fee; T084/871543) centred around a traditional Melenau tall house, a thin form of a longhouse hoisted on a platform high off the ground. It is the first of its kind to have been built in over a hundred years. Exhibits include a collection of betel-nut jars, traditionally used to store heirlooms, finely woven textiles for ceremonial occasions, musical instruments including a medley of gongs, and handicrafts such as handwoven ratten baskets for which the Melenau are renowned across Sarawak. A short walk along the plankway to the front of the tall house reveals a Melenau burial ground, or *bakut*, amidst a clump of bare, ancient trees.

Lamin Dana also offers **accommodation**, in the form of eight variously sized, airy en-suite rooms (❹–❺) off a central corridor on the building's first floor. The views are lovely, overlooking the kampung's colourful stilt houses and the Misan. Directly outside the tall house is the kitchen and eating area – food is made to order and includes Melenau, Malay and Western dishes (RM20 per person). *Lamin Dana* can also arrange short **boat trips** along the river (RM65; 2hr), which include a visit to a sago-making house and birdwatching.

Bintulu and around

BINTULU is at the centre of Sarawak's fast-growing industrial area. Up until thirty years ago, the settlement was little more than an inevitable resting point on the route from Sibu to Miri, but when large **natural gas** reserves were discovered offshore in the 1960s, speedy expansion began. Since then Bintulu has followed in Miri's footsteps as a primary resources boom town, a far cry from its origins. The name Bintulu is, in fact, derived from the Malay *Menta Ulau* – "the place for gathering heads"; before Bintulu was bought by Charles Brooke from the Sultan of Brunei in 1853, Melenau pirates preyed on the local coast, attacking passing ships and decapitating their crews.

Modern Bintulu has developed into a flat, compact rectangle of streets bordered by the old airfield to the east and the wide Kemena River to the west, with dense lines of shops and cafés in between. It's a functional, unexciting place, visited by travellers heading for **Similajau National Park**, or by those waiting for travel connections between Kuching or Sibu to the south, and Niah or Miri, to the north. That said, inexpensive accommodation is easy to find, the restaurants and cafés are excellent, and the flourishing day and night markets, which sell local delicacies like fresh fish grilled with *belacan* (shrimp paste), are well worth a wander round.

Bintulu has an annual Kite Festival (@www.borneokite.com), held in August on the old airfield, which brings together kite fliers from around the world.

Arrival

The international **airport** is 25km from the town, a taxi ride that will set you back RM35 for the forty-minute journey; there are no buses. The **long-distance bus station** is, however, 5km out of town at Medan Jaya, from where you can get into the town centre on local bus #29 (RM1.50) or by taxi (RM15). Bintulu's main **taxi rank** is on Main Bazaar, just behind the day market. There is no tourist office.

Accommodation

There's quite a wide range of **accommodation** in Bintulu with the mid-priced choices offering particularly good value for money.

Fata Inn 113 Jalan Masjid ☎086/332998. Amiable staff and pleasant a/c rooms with attached bathrooms make the *Fata* an appealing choice; ask for a room with hot water. ❸
Hoover 92 Jalan Keppel ☎086/337166. Acceptable rooms equipped with a/c and shower. ❸
Kemena Inn 78 Jalan Keppel ☎086/331533. Excellent small-scale place with decent en-suite rooms, run by a friendly family. Ask for rooms at the back, away from the main road. ❸
Kintown Inn 93 Jalan Keppel ☎086/333666, @kintowninn@yahoo.com. Popular central hotel with tiny rooms and clean en-suite bathrooms. ❸

National Inn Jalan Keppel (intersection with Jalan Pedada) ☎086/337222. Small rooms with powerful a/c but showers and toilets are out in the passage. ❷
Park City Everly Bintulu Jalan Tun Razak (2km east of town centre) ☎086/318888, @www .pinganchorage.com.my/malaysia_hotel/bintulu _parkcity_everly_hotel.htm. The town's plushest hotel by far is a real bargain, with beautiful en-suite rooms, pool and restaurant. Don't forget to ask about promotional rates when booking. ❻
Regency Plaza Jalan Abang Galau ☎086/335111, @hotel@plazabintulu.com.my. Friendly,

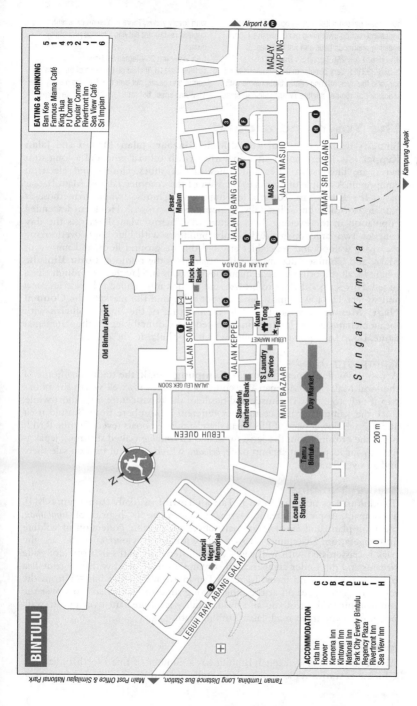

BINTULU

EATING & DRINKING

Ban Kee	5
Famous Mama Café	1
King Hua	4
PJ Corner	3
Popular Corner	2
Riverfront Inn	J
Sea View Café	1
Sri Impian	6

ACCOMMODATION

Fata Inn	G
Hoover	C
Kemena Inn	B
Kintown Inn	A
National Inn	D
Park City Everly Bintulu	E
Regency Plaza	F
Riverfront Inn	I
Sea View Inn	H

Airport & **E**

MALAY
KAMPUNG

SARAWAK

Kampung Jepak

6

Pasar
Malam

Hock Hua
Bank

Old Bintulu Airport

Jalan Somerville

JALAN KEPPEL

JALAN LEU GEK SOON

Standard
Chartered Bank

LEBUH QUEEN

TS Laundry
Service

MAIN BAZAAR

Kuan Yin
Tong

Taxis

LEBUH MARKET

JALAN PEDADA

JALAN ABANG GALAU

JALAN MASJID

MAS

TAMAN SRI DAGANG

Day Market

Tamu
Bintulu

Local Bus
Station

Council
Negri
Memorial

LEBUH RAYA ABANG GALAU

Sungai Kemena

N

0   200 m

Taman Tumbina, Long Distance Bus Station,   ▲ Main Post Office & Similajau National Park

445

business-oriented hotel with an opulent lobby, appealing rooftop swimming pool, massive rooms boasting enormous beds and full facilities. ⑤
Riverfront Inn 256 Taman Sri Dagang ☎086/333111. Very popular mid-range hotel bang opposite the river, offering comfortable rooms with spacious bathrooms, satellite TV and minibar; some

with lovely views. There is also an excellent, popular restaurant serving Chinese and Malay dishes. ❸
Sea View Inn 254 Taman Sri Dagang ☎086/339118. Tucked on the edge of the town centre and gazing out over the river, the friendly *Sea View* has small, but rather shabby en-suite rooms. ❷

The Town and around

Bintulu's main commercial streets, **Main Bazaar**, **Jalan Masjid** and **Jalan Keppel** (the latter named after an early British official who did a long stint here), are lined with cafés and stores full of shoes, clothes and electrical equipment. A couple of blocks to the west of the commercial hub, Main Bazaar passes the **Kuan Yin Tong**, a less impressive Chinese temple than those at Kuching or Sibu but still a rallying point for the town's Hokkien-descended population in the evening. Fifty metres west, across Main Bazaar, is the **day market**, two large, open-sided circular buildings with blue roofs overlooking the river; seafood and vegetables are sold on the ground floor, and numerous Malay and Chinese cafés are upstairs. Adjacent is the outdoor **Tamu Bintulu**, where locals still bring in small quantities of goods and lay them on rough tables to sell. This is a good place to browse, and to tuck into grilled fish, pastries, *umai* and sweets. The town's most historic spot is beyond the markets, the **Council Negri Memorial**, a monument to the meeting of the Brooke officials with local chieftains in 1867, which inaugurated the Council Negeri, the state legislature. Beside, is a good food court, which is popular in the evening.

Kampung Jepak

Across the wide Kemena River lies **Kampung Jepak**, the traditional home of the local Malay and Melenau-descended population. It's well worth the hour's trip, if only to escape the hustle and bustle of the town centre for a short while, since the kampung has a completely different atmosphere from Bintulu itself and a much slower pace of life. Small diesel-powered boats (every 20min; RM2) make the crossing from the jetty. As well as its *cencaluk* (salted shrimps), Jepak is famous for its pungent shrimp paste, *belacan*, which you will find on sale there and all over Sarawak.

Taman Tumbina

Two kilometres north of town is **Taman Tumbina** (daily 9am–6pm; RM4), a compact tropical recreation area, whose name (a hybrid of *tumbuhan*, meaning plant, and *binatang*, animal) reflects its sizeable collection of wildlife and vegetation. Extending across a hill, with lovely views over the sea, the park is crisscrossed with walkways, wooden steps and paths that run alongside streams and dip under creepers, and contains a small wood with bougainvillea plants, fruit trees and ferns. To reach Taman Tumbina, take bus #1 from the local bus station, get off at the Sing Kwong supermarket, then cross over the roundabout in front of you and head uphill – it's a pleasant five-minute walk north from the main road, Jalan Tanjung Batu.

Eating

Although no culinary capital, Bintulu has a number of fine North Indian and Chinese **restaurants** as well as **food stalls** at both the day market (closing at

By air

Bintulu is served by non-stop **flights** on MAS and AirAsia from KK, KL, Kuching, Miri, Mukah and Sibu.

By bus

More than a dozen daily coaches run the arterial route north from Bintulu to Miri, passing the Niah National Park junction (2hr). (Note you will have to hail a taxi or hitchhike the remaining 10km from here to Niah Park.) There are buses four times a day to Mukah, and many more to Sibu and Kuching. To reach the long-distance bus terminal in Medan Jaya, take a local bus from Lebuh Market (hourly 7am–9pm).

6

5pm) and the *pasar malam*, the latter in particular serving great fish. Unfortunately though there is nowhere to sit here.

Ban Kee Between Jalan Masjid and Jalan Abang Galau. Tucked away in a pedestrianized area, this daytime café transforms at night into one of Sarawak's top seafood restaurants. There's room for well over one hundred diners here to enjoy superb fish and vegetables from a long Chinese menu with prices slightly higher than other outdoor spots (RM20–30). A town institution not to be missed.

Famous Mama Café Jalan Somerville. This Indian café is a Bintulu legend with its vats of scrumptious curries, *biriyanis* and Malay specialities. Opens early evening and stays open into the early hours.

King Hua Jalan Abang Galau. High-quality Chinese café with lavish portions of *umai*, roast pork, chicken in chilli, seafood dishes and fresh vegetable options including *kalian* (baby spinach), *sayur masi* (aubergine), *midin* and long beans in garlic and *belacan*. Expect to spend RM30 per person including beer.

PJ Corner Jalan Abang Galau. Daytime Indian café with tasty inexpensive curries and *roti canai*.

Popular Corner Lebuh Raya Abang Galau. Several outlets under one roof selling claypot dishes, seafood, chicken rice and juices; out front is a capacious forecourt where you can sit.

Riverfront Inn Restaurant 256 Taman Sri Dagang. High-quality Chinese eatery with a/c and a menu covering local Bintulu favourites like shark-fin soup with scrambled egg, plus Western, Thai and Malay dishes. Expect to pay around RM20 per person.

Sea View Café 254 Taman Sri Dagang. Excellent Chinese coffee shop in a pleasant position overlooking Sungai Kemena and away from the traffic. Exquisite noodle dishes are served until mid-morning, after which equally good rice dishes take over.

Sri Impian Jalan Abang Galau. Café offering an expansive spread of Malay food at reasonable prices (RM5 per plate). There's also an in-house *murtabak* and *roti canai* stall.

Listings

Airlines MAS is at 129 Jalan Masjid (open Mon–Fri 8.30am–4.30pm, Sat 8.30am–12.30pm; ☎086/331554).

Airport Call ☎086/331073 for flight information.

Banks Standard Chartered Bank, 89 Jalan Keppel; Hock Hua Bank, Jalan Sommerville.

Hospital Lebuh Raya Abang Galau ☎086/331455.

Internet Fi Wee, Jalan Masjid (near *Fata Inn*).

Laundry TS Laundry Service, Lebuh Market. Same-day service costs around RM5.

Pharmacies There are two directly opposite the main jetty.

Police Branch on Jalan Sommerville ☎086/332113.

Post office Main office is on Jalan Tun Razak (☎086/339450), while a smaller branch is on Jalan Sommerville.

Taxis Thian Sek Chong ☎086/252133.

Visa extensions The Immigration Department (☎086/312211) is on Jalan Tun Razak, 3km north of the town centre.

Similajau National Park

Thirty kilometres northeast along the coast from Bintulu, **Similajau National Park** (T086/391284; RM10) is well worth a day-visit or, even better, an overnight stop. The seventy-square-kilometre park has a lot in common with Bako, near Kuching, with its long, unspoilt sandy beaches broken only by rocky headlands and freshwater streams. Unfortunately, the park suffers from being very inaccessible and poorly served by transport options.

Beach walks and short hikes are possible here, either along its 30km of coastline or following the **trails** which run alongside small rivers winding through the forest, down from the undulating hills that rise only a few hundred metres from the beach. Shrubs grow on the cliff faces, pitcher plants are found in the ridges and orchids hang from the trees and rocks. Two dozen or so species of mammal have been recorded in the park, including gibbons and long-tailed macaques, mouse deer, wild boar, porcupines, civets and squirrels. Most of all though, the park is famous for its saltwater crocodiles; notices along the river warn against swimming although there haven't been any recent cases of attack-by-croc.

The trails and beaches

By far the greatest attractions are the beaches, on which turtles occasionally nest in April and May. The two-and-a-half-hour walk north to the two **turtle beaches** starts from the park headquarters, the first stage involving crossing the Likau River in a motorized longboat. The trail ascends into the forest and soon reaches the turning to the **Viewpoint Trail** which, some forty minutes from the headquarters, delivers superb views of the South China Sea. Meanwhile the main trail follows the coastline to the turtle beaches, an hour beyond which is **Pasir Mas** ("Golden Beach"), noted for its fine sand. It is also the place where green turtles come ashore to lay their eggs August to October but numbers have been down in recent years. Walk north along Golden Beach for ten minutes, and you reach the trail that runs inland along the side of the Sebubong River. It is possible to reach this point by boat from headquarters (trips are offered by the park authorities) but the forest route is much more enjoyable. After fifteen minutes the trail reaches **Kolam Sebubong**, a freshwater pool whose waters are stained a ruby red by the (harmless) tannin from the nearby peat swamp.

The other worthwhile trail leads to the **Selansur Rapids**. Follow the Turtle Beach trail for one hour and look for a marked trail which heads into the forest parallel to the small Kabalak River. It passes through forests of sparse *kerangas* and towering dipterocarp trees before climbing the sides of hills, where you'll hear monkeys high up in the trees and the omnipresent chainsaw-like call of the cicadas. After around ninety minutes you reach the rapids, a pleasant place to rest and take a dip.

Though the trails aren't particularly arduous, it's best to **wear** light boots, a long-sleeved shirt and long trousers, as well as a hat to protect against the sun. It's also useful to have a water bottle, although the river water is quite drinkable.

Practicalities

The only feasible way to get to the park, as there are no buses, is by taxi from Bintulu (a one-way trip costs RM60; RM80 return for 3hr stop). The road to the park leaves the Bintulu–Miri highway after 15km and bears left, signposted to the small kampung of Kuala Likau, 3km further on. The park entrance is a few hundred metres beyond the village. In the dry season it is possible to access the park by speedboat from the jetty on Taman Sri Dagang in Bintulu, though this is likely to cost as much as RM300 each way. The park HQ, the starting point for the short trail north to the beach, is just by the jetty where you alight.

Accommodation at the park (☎086/391284) ranges from two forest hostels with a large quantity of dorm beds (RM15) and two-bed rooms (❷) with bathrooms outside, to four-bed, en-suite chalets (RM75) and a **campsite** (RM5) although camping equipment is not provided. The park HQ (where you pay the RM10 entrance fee) has a **canteen** serving simple rice and noodle dishes, and an **information centre** (both daily 8am–6pm), with a small display on the local flora and fauna.

Niah National Park

NIAH NATIONAL PARK (☎085/737454; RM10), 130km northeast of Bintulu, consists of 31 square kilometres of lowland forest and limestone massifs, the highest of which is the cave-riddled **Gunung Subis**, rising to nearly 400m. A visit to the park is a great experience – in less than a day you can explore a **cave** that's among the world's largest, see prehistoric rock paintings in the remarkable Painted Cave and hike along trails through primary forest. Although the region wasn't designated a national park until 1975, it has been a National Historic Monument since 1958, when Tom Harrisson discovered evidence that early man had been using Niah as a cemetery. Fragments of human skull, dated nearly 40,000 years ago, were found – the earliest examples of *homo sapiens* in southeast Asia. The **display room** (free), beside park HQ, offers a solid account of the history of the caves, as well as geological and archeological information.

The caves

To get to the caves take the path uphill from the park museum which continues along a wooden walkway through dense rainforest where you are likely to see monkeys, hornbills, bird-wing butterflies, tree squirrels and flying lizards. A clearly marked path on the left leaves the walkway after forty minutes, running to a small longhouse, **Rumah Chang**, where you can buy soft drinks and snacks.

Further along the main walkway, a rock- and creeper-encrusted jungle wall looms up ahead and the path takes you up through the **Trader's Cave** (so called because early nest-gatherers would congregate here to sell their harvests to merchants) to the mind-blowing, 60m by 250m, west mouth of the **Great Cave**. The smell of bat guano intensifies as the path leads around extraordinary rock formations, and the sounds – of your voice, of dripping water and of bat chatter – are magnified considerably. As the walkway worms deeper into the darkness, the light through the cave mouth ebbs and it gets increasingly hard to see around. As the planks are often slippery with guano, it's best to wear shoes with a grip and take a **torch**.

After a thirty-minute walk through the cave you exit briefly into the light before entering the **Painted Cave**, in which early Sarawak communities buried their dead in **boat-shaped coffins**, or "death ships", arranged around the cave walls; when Harrisson first entered, the cave had partially collapsed, and the contents were spilled all around. Subsequent dating proved that the

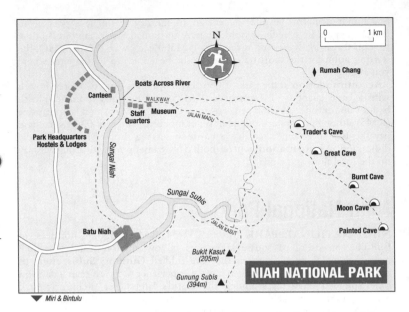

caves had been used as a cemetery for tens of thousands of years. One of these wooden coffins is still perched on an incline, as though beached after a monumental journey, its contents long since removed to the Sarawak Museum for safekeeping.

Despite the light streaming from an opening at the far end of the cave, it's hard to distinguish the **wall paintings** that give the cave its name (especially as they are now fenced off), but they stretch from the dark right-hand corner behind the coffin – a thirty-metre-long tableau depicting boats on a journey, the figures apparently either jumping on and off, or dancing. This image fits various Borneo mythologies where the dead undergo water-bound challenges on their way to the afterlife. The markings, although crude, can be made out, but the brown paint strokes are now extremely faded. The only way back to the entrance is by the route you came – try to be there at dusk to see the swiftlets return and the bats swarm out for the night.

The trails

There are two **trails** in the park which, after the claustrophobic darkness of the caves, offer a much-needed breath of fresh air. The first, **Jalan Madu**, splits off a little way along the caves walkway from the museum and cuts first east, then south, across a peat swamp forest, where you see wild orchids, mushrooms and *pandanus*. The trail crosses the Subis River and then follows its south bank to its confluence with Sungai Niah, from where you may find a passing boat to Batu Niah (RM5), 400m away. A three-kilometre trail leads back to park HQ, or you can pick up a boat en route; there is no trail on Batu Niah's eastern bank.

The other trail, **Jalan Kasut**, takes you to Bukit Kasut, winding through *kerangas* forest, round the foot of the hill and up to the summit. It is a hard one-hour slog, but at the end there's a fine view both of the impenetrable forest canopy and of Batu Niah.

Practicalities

Roughly halfway between Bintulu and Miri, the park is 11km off the main highway and 5km from the small town of **Batu Niah**. As there are no direct buses to Niah Park or Batu Niah, you need to get off the bus at Niah Junction and either hire a taxi or hitch the distance. From Batu Niah you can take a boat along the Niah River (20min; RM15), hitch-hike, or walk (1–2hr).

If you need to **stay** in Batu Niah, try the *Niah Cave Inn* (☎085/737333; ❸), a smartish, modern hotel with adequate, if overpriced, rooms. Below the inn is a good **café**, offering Chinese noodle and rice dishes. The park itself has a wide of accommodation at **Park HQ**, offering forest hostels with dorm beds (RM15); four-bed lodges with veranda, communal sitting area and shared bathrooms (RM105); two forest lodges each consisting of two simple but spacious en-suite double rooms (❸); and a campsite (RM5), for which you need to bring your own equipment. It must be said that the standard of the dorms has deteriorated, with some run-down and not regularly cleaned. If you are intending to visit on a weekend it's advisable to **book** accommodation in advance (by telephone or at the tourist office in Miri, see p.454). The park's **canteen** (daily 7am–8pm) is inexpensive, with a limited menu and shoddy service. Given these facilities most visitors just come to visit Niah Caves for the day, but to do this, you really need your own transport or to be on a tour.

To Miri and the border

The monotonous drive from Niah Junction north passes the exquisite Lambir Hills Park, before the ever-expanding Miri suburbs come into view. North of Miri, the route to **Brunei** is quite straightforward, passing close to oil installations at Lutong and crossing over the undignifiied, grubby river mouth at Kuala Baram, and onwards to the border just short of Brunei oil town, Kuala Belait. Getting to **Sabah** can take up to two days altogether from Miri; many people prefer either to fly direct to Kota Kinabalu (KK), or to take a flight to Labuan and a boat from there to KK. The only advantage of the overland route through Brunei is that you can visit the territorial divisions of **Limbang** and **Lawas**, which contrast greatly with the land around Miri as they are comparatively sparsely populated with an ethnic mix of Iban, Murut, Berawan and Kelabit. This is a difficult area to get around, though, as there are few boats and roads. Note that you can visit Limbang easily either from Brunei or Gunung Mulu National Park if you choose to leave the park by the adventurous Headhunters Trail (see p.473).

Lambir Hills National Park

Three-quarters of the way from Bintulu to Miri, and beside the highway, is **Lambir Hills National Park** (☎085/491030; RM10), which has some pleasant trails and is particularly popular with Miri day-trippers at weekends. Lambir Hills offers good accommodation, making an overnight stay a tempting option.

The contours of the region comprising the park were formed sixty million years ago, when a vast area of sedimentary rock was laid down, stretching from present-day western Sarawak to Sabah. There is limestone and clay at lower levels, and sandstone and shale closer to the surface. Subsequent upheavals created the hills and the rich soil substrata, and gave rise to the local rainforest, with its distinctive vegetation types. Mixed dipterocarp forest makes up over half the area with the vast hardwood trees – *meranti*, *kapur* and *keruing* – creating deep shadows on the forest floor; there is also *kerangas* forest, with its peat soils, low-lying vegetation and smaller trees.

The trails

Fourteen well-marked **trails** crisscross the south part of the park, several leading to **waterfalls**. The longest trail – the four-hour trek to the summit of **Bukit Lambir** – is tough but rewarding, with a wonderful view across the park, the sounds of insects and birds echoing below. The trail cuts across deceptively steep hills, where gnarled roots are often the only helping hand up an almost vertical incline – you may well catch sight of monkeys, lizards or snakes on the trail.

To reach the three **Latak waterfalls**, 1.5km from park headquarters, follow the trail marked "Latak", which branches off north from the Bukit Lambir trail. The furthest of the falls (Latak itself) is the best, its 25-metre cascade feeding an alluring pool, but given its proximity to park headquarters, it is inevitably overrun at the weekends. There are more spectacular falls further afield, past Latak; it takes two and a half hours to reach the **Pantu** and **Pancur** waterfalls – watch for the narrow paths which lead down to the rivers from the main Bukit Lambir trail. These are fine places to stop and eat, and take a deliciously cool swim. The most remote waterfall, **Tengkorong**, is a further thirty minutes' walk from Pancur.

Practicalities

Lambir Hills is clearly signposted from the Bintulu–Miri highway but make it clear to the bus driver that you want to be dropped there as the park is not a registered stop. All Bintulu–Miri and Miri–Bintulu coaches (hourly 6.30am–4.30pm from both towns) pass by the park, but when at the bus stop outside the gates you may have to gesticulate firmly to get them to stop given the speed they go.

As at other parks, to book **accommodation** it's best to call the park directly or book at the parks desk at the nearest Visitors' Information Centre (Sibu or Miri). At Lambir you can choose between the immaculately clean three-bed chalets (RM75) or the campsite (RM5), although for this you'll need to bring your own tent. A **canteen** (daily 7am–6pm) has a limited menu comprising simple Malay and Chinese dishes. Note that if you intend to go on the longer trails, bring hiking boots, water bottle, torch, sun hat and insect repellent.

Miri and around

With a population of over 320,000, **MIRI** has well and truly burst out of its early geographic confines – the narrow streets of the old town – and in recent years has seen major development eastwards including the sprouting of plazas crammed with stores and eateries, the reclamation of riverside land and the expansion of office space, car parks and so on. But despite historic links with

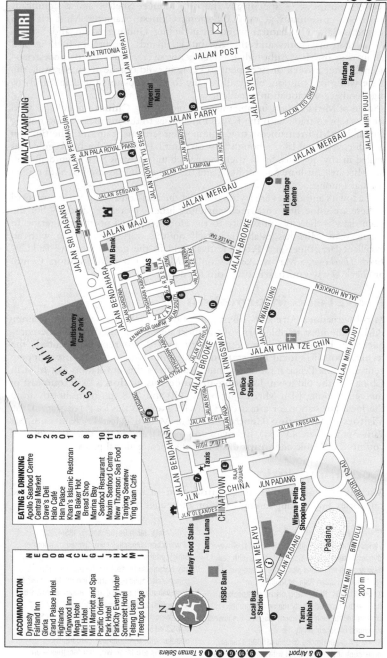

MIRI

MALAY KAMPUNG

JLN TRITONIA

JALAN MERPATI

JALAN POST

JALAN PERMAISURI

JLN PALA ROYAL PAKIS

JALAN PARRY

JALAN SYLVIA

JALAN TEO CHEW

Bintang Plaza

Imperial Mall

❷

❸

❹

JALAN NORTH YU SENG

JALAN HAJI LAMPAM

JALAN RICE MILL

JALAN MERBAU

JALAN MIRI PUJUT

JALAN SERDANG

JALAN MIMOSA

JALAN PERMAISURI

JALAN MAJU

Maybank

JALAN SRI DAGANG

AM Bank

JALAN BENDAHARA

❶

MAS

⑤

JLN INDIA

JALAN LEE TAK

JLN LEE TAK

JALAN MERBAU

Miri Heritage Centre

Ⓛ

JALAN BROOKE

Ⓖ

Multistorey Car Park

PERSIARAN KABOR

JALAN GARDENIA

JLN YU SENG

⑥

Ⓕ

Sungai Miri

JLN NAKHODA GAMPAR

JALAN SOUTH

Ⓓ

JALAN CYTHULA

JALAN KINGSWAY

JALAN KWANGTUNG

Ⓚ

JALAN HOKKIEN

JALAN MIRI PUJUT

Ⓝ

JALAN CHIA TZE CHIN

JALAN CYTHULA

PERSIARAN KABOR

JALAN BROOKE

Police Station

JLN SRI DAGANG

JALAN ENTIRA

JALAN BEGIA

JALAN RAJA

JALAN ANGSANA

❽

JALAN BENDAHARA

HIGH STREET

Taxis

⑦

★

Ⓔ

RAJA SQUARE

CHINATOWN

JALAN CHINA

JLN PADANG

JLN OLEANDES

Malay Food Stalls

Tamu Lama

HSBC Bank

Wisma Pelita Shopping Centre

Padang

JALAN MELAYU

JALAN PADANG

Local Bus Station

Ⓙ

ⓘ

Tamu Muhibbah

AIRPORT ROAD

JALAN MIRI

BINTULU

0   200 m

N

ACCOMMODATION	
Dynasty	N
Fairland Inn	E
Gloria	D
Grand Palace Hotel	O
Highlands	B
Khan's Islamic Restoran	A
Kingwood Inn	C
Mega Hotel	F
Miri Hotel	G
Miri Marriott and Spa	L
Pacific Orient	J
Park Hotel	H
ParkCity Everly Hotel	K
Somerset Hotel	M
Telang Usan	I
Treetops Lodge	

EATING & DRINKING	
Apollo Seafood Centre	6
Central Market	7
Dave's Deli	2
Halo Café	3
Han Palace	0
Ma Baker Hot Bread Shop	1
Marina Bay	8
Seafood Restaurant	10
Maxim Seafood Centre	11
New Thomson Sea Food	5
Tanjong Seaview	9
Ying Yuan Café	4

Western businesses – specifically the **oil** producer Shell – and a significant expatriate community, it retains a strong Chinese character. Most visits to northern Sarawak's natural wonders, including Gunung Mulu and Loagan Bunut national parks and the Kelabit Highlands, require re-fuelling and pampering in Miri. Although the city is not overly attractive or pedestrian-friendly, after a week or two spent trekking in wild northeastern Sarawak, the place will grow on you, especially as the food is top-notch and the mid- to high-end accommodation excellent.

Some of Miri's earliest inhabitants were pioneering **Chinese** merchants who set up shops to trade with the Kayan longhouses to the northeast along Batang Baram. But Miri remained a tiny, unimportant settlement up until the time oil was discovered in 1882, though it wasn't until 1910 that the black gold was drilled in any quantity. Since then, over six hundred wells have been drilled in the Miri area, onshore and offshore, and the main refineries are just 5km up the coast at Lutong.

The town's authorities are trying to boost the area's offshore tourism potential – there are some fine coral reefs currently little explored by divers – but the main draw is the city's proximity to the aforementioned northern interior. In recent years Miri has established itself on the world music map with an excellent Jazz, Blues and Roots festival held in the grounds of the *ParkCity Everly Hotel* over a May weekend. Contact Michael Liu at Miri Visitors' Centre or check ⓦ www.mirijazzfestival.com for details.

Arrival and information

Miri International Airport is 10km west of the town centre, with a taxi (15min; RM20) the most reliable form of transport into town. Alternatively, the infrequent #9 bus (daily 6.15am–8pm; every 1hr 10min) runs from outside the terminal to Miri's **local bus station**, located next to the town's first shopping centre, Wisma Pelita. It's a five-minute walk from this bus station east to Jalan China and the old town. The **long-distance bus station** is 4km southeast of the centre along Jalan Miri Pujut; buses #30 and #28 run there hourly from the local bus station, or a taxi costs RM17. Next to the local bus station, the **Visitors' Information Centre**, 452 Jalan Melayu (Mon–Fri 8am–6pm, Sat 9am–5pm; ☏085/434181), has maps and leaflets, and is also the place to go if you need to **book accommodation** at the local national parks.

Accommodation

Miri has a good array of **accommodation** in the mid-range and top-end categories, but a disappointing selection of budget options.

Centre of town

Dynasty Jalan Miri Pujut ☏085/421111, ⓦ www.dynastyhotelmiri.com. Beautiful rooms with sea view and full amenities plus large bathrooms. ❺

Fairland Inn Jalan Raja, at Raja Square ☏085/413981. Reasonably priced backpackers' place with cramped, stuffy rooms and grubby external toilets; only just about reaching the lowest standards of acceptability. ❶

Gloria 27 Jalan Brooke ☏085/416699. Friendly, large, centrally located hotel with compact rooms and neat bathrooms. ❹

Highlands

Highlands Jalan Sri Dagang ☏085/422327, ⓦ www.borneojungles.com. Owned by a former British pilot and his Sarawakian wife, this small, airy backpackers' spot on the top floor of a commercial building overlooking the Miri River, is good value with small dorms (RM25) and two-bed rooms (❷) with external bathroom.

Kingwood Inn Lot 826, Jalan North Yu Seng ☏085/415888. Upmarket place which is popular with the business community. The rooms are large with full facilities – a/c, showers and TV. ❹

It is only recently that the exquisite **reefs** off Miri's coastline have begun to be appreciated by divers who, for decades have been flocking to other East Malaysian dive sites like Sipidan and Mabul. Miri's **coral** can be viewed on reefs varying in depth from 10m to 30m, with an average visibility of 15m to 30m, making diving conditions very good indeed. The most visually exciting reefs are Batu Mass, Siwa and VHK, none of which is more than forty minutes by speedboat from the city. Marine wildlife includes anemones, while reef fish such as groupers, stingray and wrasses are also abundant. Diving is generally good all year round but busiest in the peak tourist season, between December and February. A number of specialist dive operators have begun to promote diving here; try Dive Borneo (ⓦwww.diveborneo.com) for trips ranging from half-day dives (RM150) to full three- or four-day packages (from RM1200, including accommodation). Miri-based operators include the ever-dependable Seridan Mulu (see p.458), who offers a one-day dive package for RM250, including dive equipment, transfers, two dives and lunch.

6

Mega Hotel 907 Jalan Merbau ☏085/432432, ⓦwww.megahotel.net. Highly popular with families. The rooms are faultless, the restaurant top class, and the a/c extremely efficient. **⑥**

Miri Hotel 47 Jalan Brooke ☏085/421212. This is a good choice with pleasant rooms and neat bathrooms; central for both parts of town. **④**

Pacific Orient Jalan Merbau ☏085/413333, ⓔpohotel@stramyx.com. A reliable, mid-range option. **④**

Park Hotel Jalan Raja (in front of bus station) ☏085/414555. Excellent value, perfectly positioned city hotel, with brisk service and adequate en-suite rooms. **③**

Somerset Hotel 12 Jalan Kwangtung ☏085/422777, ⓔsohotel@po.jaring.my. A discreet and stylish place, with small but perfectly formed rooms, and quite the most exquisite foyer of any Miri hotel. **⑤**

Outside the centre

Grand Palace Hotel 2km, Jalan Miri-Pujut, Pelita Commercial Centre ☏085/428888, ⓦwww.grandpalacehotel.com.my. Located in Miri's most up-and-coming suburb, Pelita, the *Palace* is a confidant, smart place with all the trimmings expected of a three-star city hotel. Its main claim to fame is the restaurant's mouthwatering dim sum on Sunday morning. **⑧**

Miri Marriott and Spa Jalan Temenggong Datuk Oyong Lawai ☏085/421121, ⓦwww.marriotthotels.com/myymc. Three kilometres along the coast road, this five-star resort is one of Malaysia's top hotels, with a few hundred sumptuous rooms, some with balconies facing the sea. The giant swimming pool is a joy, the spa options are plentiful, with massage, reflexology and aromatherapy all available, and there's a wide range of restaurants and bars. **⑧**

ParkCity Everly Hotel Jalan Temenggong Datuk Oyong Lawai ☏085/440288, ⓦwww.vhhotels.com. With immaculate rooms, first-class service and a snug, shaded swimming pool, this hotel is preferred over its neighbour, the *Marriott*; rates are far cheaper than next door, the in-house restaurant is better and the service friendlier, though the pool isn't quite in the same league. Ask for promotional rates. **⑥–⑦**

Telang Usan Block 1 ☏085/411433. Three kilometres from the centre, positioned on a large traffic island on the airport road and easily reachable on bus #28, this Miri institution is something of a fall-back option nowadays. Although the en-suite rooms are inexpensive and spacious, they are in serious need of renovation. **③**

Treetops Lodge Lot 210, Siwa Jaya Kampung, off Jalan Bakam ☏085/482449, ⓦwww.treetops-borneo.com. A lovely hideaway, run by an Englishman and his Kayan wife, *Treetops* is a comfortable house nestling on the edge of the jungle, 20km south of Miri. It features small, en-suite rooms built of locally sourced wood, a paddling pool and delicious Kayan food available on request. Just built, a thirty-metre longhouse on a small lake 50m away, offers more, funkier, rooms. Owner Mike is happy to pick up guests from Miri's airport or bus station as long as you give him plenty of notice; alternatively, catch bus #13 from Miri's local bus station, get out at the last stop, take the first turning on the left, walk up into the hills for 20min and it's on your left. **②–④**

The City

The **old town** around Jalan China teems with cafés and shops and remains Miri's social hub and the most enjoyable area of the town to wander around. Parallal to Jalan China on Jalan Oleandes, you'll come across the daily food and retail market, at the north end of which is the **Chinese temple**, a simple red-and-yellow building whose bottle-green roof is patrolled by fearsome dragons. The wide road running parallel to the river, **Jalan Bendahara**, is seeing significant development, which is rapidly transforming the old wet-fish and meat market into neat and, some argue, featureless, shopfronts. Turning east on Bendahara is the simplest route into the **new town** area, where you find most of Miri's mid-range hotels, tour operators and plazas. Many of the town's best restaurants can be found along **Jalan North Yu Seng**, one block south of Jalan Bendahara, and at **Imperial Mall**, where dozens of stalls and boutiques vie for trade. Four hundred metres further east, along Jalan Merpati, on the city's outskirts, is a vast open-air theatre, the under-used **Miri City Fan**, which has capacity for a few thousand people; walk southwards 300m and you'll get to the always crowded **Bintang Plaza**, with its collision of music retail stores and food courts.

Directly south of the local bus station next to Wisma Pelita is the padang, on the edge of which lies **Tamu Muhibbah** (daily 6am–2pm), the town's jungle-produce market, where locals sell rattan mats, tropical fruits, rice wine and even bush meat like mouse deer and squirrel. Just east of the bus station is the oldest of Miri's many shopping malls, **Wisma Pelita**, with a good range of stalls and boutiques and two reliable internet cafés.

Taman Selera, 4km west of town and just past the *ParkCity Everly* and *Marriott* hotels, has a tranquil **beach** one kilometre long; it's a fine place to watch the sun go down, eating satay from the hawker stalls. Buses #11 and #13 (RM1) head out here from the local bus station.

Eating and drinking

You can hardly go wrong for food in Miri. At the bottom of the Jalan Oleandes market there is a set of **Malay stalls** serving delicious *laksa* and Malay *nasi* buffets; vegetable dishes include *sayur kacang* (green beans) and *sayur nangaka* (a grey root vegetable) served in *sambal*. For breakfast, one block east of Jalan China, check out the Central Market **breakfast food court** (daily 6.30–11am) where you'll find the best wet noodles in town; vegetables and fruit are also sold here.

The **bar** scene has quietened down in recent years with many expats preferring to drink in hotel bars or at home. Most of the places listed below serve beer.

Apollo Seafood Centre 4 Jalan South Yu Seng. This is central Miri's most famous restaurant. It is a highly popular place, and with good reason – the grilled stingray and pineapple rice is exquisite, and just about any other seafood option excels – though meals are not cheap at around RM70 for two. Open daily 6–11pm, except public hols; no bookings so turn up before 9pm.

Central Market This rather dark, gloomy and dirty food court is actually a Miri legend; food is at pre-millennium prices, the noodles (especially in the morning) are delicious and the beer the cheapest around town.

Dave's Deli Jalan Merpati. Western-style deli with a wide range of pies, soups, roast chicken (RM10) and desserts.

Halo Café 751 Jalan Merpati. Large, modern café aimed at the young market with an extensive menu of Western and local dishes; bands play some evenings.

Han Palace First floor, *Grand Palace Hotel*, Pelita Commercial Centre. Crisp and smart traditional Chinese restaurant famed across North Sarawak for its Sunday morning dim sum; pricey but not exorbitant, at RM40 a head.

Khan's Islamic Restoran 233 Jalan Maju. This excellent eatery specializes in inexpensive buffet-style spicy North Indian and Malay dishes with *biriyani* rice.

Ma Baker Hot Bread Shop Ground floor, Lot 1286, Jalan Parry. Clean Western-style daytime café with naughty, super-sweet cakes as well as Malay staples.

Mae Nam Thai Restaurant *Dynasty Hotel*, Jalan Miri Pujut. Authentic but pricey Thai cuisine at around RM40 a head for a full meal.

Marina Bay Seafood Restaurant Marina Park, Jalan Temenggong Datuk Oyong Lawai Jau ☏085/730019. Handsome, longhouse-style top-of-the-range seafood mecca located 3km out of town (towards *Miri Marriott*) in the new reclaimed area, Marina Park. Call for opening times.

Maxim Seafood Centre Lot 342, Block 7, Jalan Miri Pujut. Three kilometres out of town but worth the RM10 taxi ride, *Maxim* is Miri's top restaurant, serving a superb array of grilled fish with *belacan*,

and delicious vegetable dishes with chilli, herbs and garlic; meals cost roughly RM80 for two, including beer. It's not possible to book, so it's best to arrive early – preferably before 8.30pm.

New Thomson Sea Food Lot 382, Jalan South Yu Seng. Close to *Apollo*, the *New Thompson* is less flashy but just as good, with tremendous fish, seafood and vegetable dishes served up in a trice by the friendly, harmonious team. Outstanding house specials include preserved green mustard and bean curd soup. Expect to pay around RM60 for two. Open daily 6pm–2am.

Tanjong Seaview Taman Selera Beach. Large food centre very popular with local families, offering superb satay at low prices.

Ying Yuan Café Jalan South Yu Seng (opposite *Apollo Seafood Centre*). Busy Chinese café noted for its *nasi campur*, which includes filling and delicious prawns, chicken, baby sweetcorn and okra at RM10 per portion.

Listings

Airlines AirAsia, first floor, Main Terminal Building, Miri Airport; also at Pelita Commercial Centre, next to *Grand Place Hotel* (call centre ☏03/2171 9333). MAS & MASwings, Lot 239, Taman Jade Manis (☏085/417315).

Airport For flight enquiries call ☏085/414242.

Banks and exchange Am Bank, Jalan Bendahara/Jalan Maju; HSBC, Jalan Bendaharda, Centrepoint Commercial Centre; Maybank, Jalan Sri Dagang. Moneychanger at Asia Gangsa, ground floor, Imperial Mall.

Books Popular Book Store, second floor, Bintang Plaza, Jalan Mir Pujut; Pelita Book Centre, first floor,

Wisma Pelita, has a wide selection of English-language books on Sarawak culture and geography.

Car rental Mega Services, 3 Lorong 1, Sungai Krokop ☏085/427436.

Handicrafts Borneo Arts, 548 Jalan Yu Seng Selatan (☏085/422373) for handicrafts, textiles and pottery; Dapher Gallery, Jalan Brooke, has well-made handicrafts; Miri Heritage Centre, Jalan Merbau, sells tourist-oriented crafts and textiles.

Hospital Miri General Hospital, Jalan Lopeng (☏085/420033).

Internet access Cyber Corner.biz and Cyberworld, first floor, Wisma Pelita (daily 9am–9pm); *Planet*

Moving on from Miri

By air
There are non-stop **flights** from Miri on MAS and AirAsia to Bintulu, KK, KL, Kuching, Labuan, Lawas, Limbang, Marudi, Mukah, Mulu and Sibu. The Kelabit Highland destinations covered include Bario, Ba' Kelalan and Long Akah.

By bus
All long-distance **buses** leading south to Lambir Hills National Park, Bintulu and beyond leave from the long-distance bus terminal, at Pujuk Padang Kerbau, 4km from the town centre on Jalan Padang. Buses #1 and #1A north to Kuala Baram and Kuala Belait (for Brunei) leave from the local bus station, Wisma Pelita. The last departure from Kuala Belait to Bandar Seri Begawan in Brunei is at 3.30pm, so it's best to leave Miri early, ideally on the 7.30am service, getting to station by 7am, if you want to be sure of getting to the Brunei capital the same day.

Café, first floor, Bintang Plaza (RM6 per hr; fast connection).

Laundry Tally Laundry Service, Lot 514, Jalan Merbau (daily 8am–6pm). Excellent deal as you pay by weight.

Pharmacy First floor, Wisma Pelita.

Police HQ Jalan Kingsway (℡085/433222).

Post office Jalan Kingsway.

Taxis Miri Taxis (℡019 8151093); Miri Taxi Association (℡085/432277)

Tour operators Tropical Adventure, ground floor, *Mega Hotel*, Jalan Merbau (℡085/419337, ⓦwww.borneotropicaladventure.com) specializes in treks to the Baram, Gunung Mulu National Park and the Kelabit Highlands; expect to pay around

RM800 for two people to go on a 3–5 day trek. Seridan Mulu, ground floor, Lot 273, Brighton Centre, Jalan Temenggong Datuk Oyong Lawai (beside *ParkCity Everly Hotel*, ℡085/415582, ⓦwww.seridanmulu.com) runs trips into the little-visited Loagan Bunut National Park as well as Gunung Mulu Park visits and Miri reef dives (ⓦwww.tropical-dives.com). Its five-day trip, incorporating both parks and a night in a longhouse, is excellent value at around RM450 per person. Also, SM arranges trips to West Malaysia, Thailand and Laos.

Visa extensions Tingkat Bawah, Wisma Persekutuan, 98000 Miri, Sarawak (℡085/442112).

To Kuala Baram and Brunei

The trunk road north of Miri runs a few kilometres in from the coast to **Kuala Baram**, 20km away, a small town situated at the mouth of Batang Baram – you can catch the express boat to Marudi from here. Buses #1 and #1A leave Miri's long-distance bus station regularly between 6am and 5pm for Kuala Baram (40min; RM2.20).

There are also direct buses from the long-distance bus station to the Bruneian border town of **Kuala Belait** (3hr; RM13.50), leaving at 7am, 10am, 1pm and 3.30pm; note, to reach Bandar Seri Begawan the same day you need to catch the first bus. The bus goes via **Kuala Baram** before arriving at Kuala Belait another 6km further on. From here you can catch a Bruneian bus to Seria, where you need to change again for BSB. The last bus from Seria to the Bruneian capital leaves at around 3.30pm. This is a relatively intricate route; many travellers prefer to go by charted minivan, arranged by the *Highlands* management, although the price is negotiable. Another route, but a more expensive one, is flying to the Sabah island of Labuan (around RM90) and then getting the speedboat to Brunei (RM35).

Limbang

To the south of Bandar Seri Begawan is **Limbang**, a strip of Sarawak roughly 30km wide and 50km deep, sandwiched between the two parts of Brunei. It's an inaccessible and thus seldom-visited district, though travel here is possible along Sungai Limbang, which snakes into the interior from the mangrove-cloaked coast, and provides access to Gunung Mulu National Park by the adventurous river trip along the Medalam, the Headhunters Trail. For centuries, Limbang Town was a trading centre run by Malays, who bartered the jungle produce collected by the Berawan, Kelabit, Besayak and Murut peoples with fellow Malay and Chinese merchants. Although the White Rajahs never actually bought Limbang from the Sultan of Brunei, as they did the areas to the south, Charles Brooke occupied the region in 1890, following demonstrations by the ethnic groups against the increasingly decadent rule of the sultan. However, Brooke's main reason for intevening was to acquire as large a slice of what was left of Brunei as possible, before his Sabah-based rivals in the British North Borneo Chartered Company overran it. Today Limbang Town is a thriving place, noted for its Friday produce market when tribespeoples bring vegetables, fruits and poultry to sell and barter.

The Town

The only building of note in the division's only settlement, **LIMBANG TOWN**, is the riverbank **fort**, the most northerly of Charles Brooke's defensive structures, which now houses a small museum (Tues–Sun; 9am–4.30pm; free). Constructed in 1897, it was renovated in 1966 when much of the woodwork was replaced by more durable materials like concrete and *belian* (ironwood). The fort was originally designed to serve as an administrative centre, but was instead used to monitor native insurgency in the early years of the twentieth century. The collection, on the fort's upper floor, comprises exhibits and photographs on the region's archeology and cultural life.

The rest of the small town is composed of a few busy streets set back from the river; the main street, Jalan Bangsiol, leads to the **tamu** (market), set in a pink building, which is at its best on Fridays, when fruit, animals and vegetables are brought in from the forest to be sold.

Practicalities

The **airport** is 4km south of the town; a taxi into the centre (there are no buses on this route) costs RM10. There are two daily flights to Miri. The jetty is located close to the market building. Here you can get **express boats** to Labuan in Sabah (leaves 8.30am; 2hr; RM25), Muara, Brunei's port (30min; RM20) and Lawas (one daily; 40min; RM25) which leaves when enough travellers arrive – but get there for 7.30am. The bus terminus is five minutes' walk along Jalan Bangkita from the Labuan/Brunei jetty; **buses** go to Nanga Medamit, first stop for the trip into Gunung Mulu National Park (see p.465), but there is no published schedule for the ninety-minute trip, so check at the bus station on Jalan Bangkita. There are also buses to the Bruneian border town of Kuala Lurah (RM5) but they are so irregular that most people get there by sharing minivans; find these at the bus terminus.

Many visitors to Limbang are Bruneian males, sometimes on the lookout for prostitutes, so many guesthouses here specialize in short-term bookings. Among the hotels – note that there's no budget **accommodation** – there are a couple of mid-range options that are preferable, including *Centre Point* (☎085/212922; ❹) on Jalan Tarap, with clean, en-suite rooms, and the *National Inn* (☎085/212922; ❸), close to the Lawas jetty with neat, functional air-conditioned rooms.

The hawker **stalls** on the first floor of the **tamu** offer the most affordable **food** in town, as well as good views of the water village across the river. There are more stalls in the covered building south of the bus station, and still more on the open ground below Jalan Merdeka. The pick of Limbang's **restaurants** are the Malay ones, the *Mesra* and the *Selera Muhibbah*, both good for *rotis* and *biriyanis* and the *Fortune*, serving quality Chinese food. All are located in the centre of town.

Lawas

Boxed in between Brunei's sparsely inhabited Temburong district and Sabah is Sarawak's most northwesterly district, **Lawas**. Bought by Charles Brooke from the Sultan of Brunei in 1905, the division is a little larger than Limbang, and has more coastline. From its origins as a remote bazaar and trading centre for

Berawan, Kelabit and Chinese pioneers, **LAWAS TOWN** – the only settlement of any size in the area – has grown into a bustling centre on the Lawas River. Above the river is a large **tamu** that has become the town's main focal point, selling fruits and vegetables, and with several food stalls on the first floor. On the other side of the street is another produce market situated underneath a massive *ara*, a tropical hardwood tree, providing much-needed shade for the traders. Saturdays are the busiest days at both markets, when traders from Sabah sometimes arrive to sell clothes and textiles. The only other diversion in town is the **Chinese temple** five minutes' north of the market on Jalan Bunga Teratai, remarkable only for the unusual fact that a large portion of it is open to the elements.

North of town, Jalan Punang leads, after around 7km, to **Punang**, the site of a reasonably attractive beach – minibuses (RM4) make the trip from the bus station. Lawas makes a good starting point to embark on the **Gunung Murud** trek in the Kelabit Highlands – a three-day, two-night hike involving first a five-hour 4X4 drive along logging tracks to the base of the mountain. For details on the Murud trail from the logging road, see p.481.

Practicalities

Lawas **airport** is 2km south of town, from where you will need to get a taxi (RM8) into town. There are four daily MASwings flights back and forth to Miri and two to Ba' Kelalan, a remote settlement in the Kelabit Highlands. **Boats** arrive and depart from the jetty beside the old mosque, 300m east of the town; the one to Limbang Town is daily (9am; 1hr; RM20) except on Thursday, and to Labuan daily (7.30am; 2hr; RM33) except Tuesday and Thursday. Tickets are sold at the jetty just before departure.

The *Hup Guan Lodging House* at 18 Jalan Dato Taie (☎085/285490; ❶) is the town's most inexpensive **place to stay**, with adequate rooms and communal bathrooms. Higher up the scale is the *Mega Inn*, 1 Jalan Muhibbah (☎085/283888; ❷), with modern air-conditioned, en-suite rooms, though they can be noisy in the mornings. The best choice though is the sizeable *Hotel Perdana*, 365 Jalan Punang (☎085/285888; ❸), fifteen minutes' walk north out of town, with large, en-suite rooms.

For inexpensive **food**, try the upper floor of the market, with the usual selection of Malay and Chinese stalls. There's no menu at the tidy *Soon Seng* **restaurant** below the hotel of the same name, but the Chinese food there is tasty.

The northern interior

The **northern interior**, loosely defined as the watershed of **Batang Baram** – the major river to the northeast of Miri – incorporates both some of the wildest, most untouched parts of Sarawak, and other patches which are among the most environmentally degraded. At the northernmost point of the White Rajahs' reach, Batang Baram had a number of imposing military fortifications, but the tribal groups living along the river's reaches were largely left to their own devices. From the 1960s, though, the Baram was the first part of Sarawak to be systematically logged, though now timber clearance has given way to wood- and oil-palm-processing plants, which operate at the edge of the wide, soupy artery, and to the proliferation of oil-palm plantations. Many of the **Kayan** and **Kenyah longhouses** in this beautiful part of the state have in fact gained economically from the new industries, though the ecological damage is obvious.

Despite the despoliation, the northern interior holds many of Sarawak's most renowned natural delights. Beyond the gateway town of **Marudi**, one of Batang Baram's tributaries, the **Tutoh**, branches off east to **Gunung Mulu National Park**, with its famous limestone Pinnacles and extensive caves. Further east still, straddling the border with Kalimantan and only accessible by plane, lies the lush and magnificent sparsely populated mountain plateau of the **Kelabit Highlands**. The pleasing climate and low humidity makes it the best place in the state for long treks in the rainforest. **Loagan Bunut National Park**, some distance off the Miri–Bintulu road, boasts an exquisite lake, the home to a large population of tropical birdlife, while beyond, on the banks of the Baram, it's possible to visit the fascinating Kenyah community at **Long San**.

Travel in the region is surprisingly efficient, thanks to the MASwings connections and reliable river travel. In a seven-day trip you could easily, for example, visit Gunung Mulu, the Kelabit Highlands and Marudi. Bear in mind, however, that it's difficult to get a seat on some of the small Twin Otter flights to Bario and Ba' Kelalan and on the larger Fokker and ATR 72s to Mulu, unless you book some weeks in advance.

Marudi and around

On Batang Baram 80km southeast of Miri, **MARUDI** is the only sizeable bazaar town in the whole Baram watershed, supplying the interior with consumer items, from packaged food to outboard engines. Round the small town's jetty, where the express boats dock, stalls and cafés do a brisk trade especially when the boats from Kuala Baram come in.

Marudi was acquired from the Sultan of Brunei by Charles Brooke in 1882. He renamed it Claudetown, after the first official sent by James Brooke to administer the area. Charles Brooke encouraged Iban tribespeople from the middle Rejang to migrate here, to act as a bulwark against Kayan war parties who, at their peak in the mid-nineteenth century, amassed up to three thousand warriors on expeditions downriver in search of human trophies.

The town is dominated by two features, the jetty and the hilltop **Fort Hose**, now a museum (Tues–Sun; 10am–4.30pm; free), which is reached by following Jalan Fort from the main Bazaar Square, west of the jetty, to the top of the hill. Built in 1901, the fort was named after the best known of Sarawak's colonial officials, the naturalist Charles Hose; its ironwood tiles are still in perfect condition, as are the ceremonial brass cannon at the front. The fort's exhibits include photographs of colonial officials and longhouse communities through the years, plus textiles and ceremonial handicrafts. Five minutes further along the hilltop road is the old **Resident's house** which, though sturdy and quite habitable, is abandoned and becoming increasingly tatty in the tropical climate.

Practicalities

It is a short walk from Marudi's **airport** into town; a taxi costs RM5. Flights arrive from and depart for Miri and Kelabit Highlands destinations. The **jetty**, where boats go back and forth to Kuala Baram and into the interior, is north of the centre and only five minutes' walk from the massive *Grand* (☎085/755711; ❷). Just off Jalan Cinema – the airport road – on Lorong Lima, it provides far and away the best **accommodation** in town, with clean, quiet rooms; the reception also has details of Mulu tours and visits to longhouses on tributaries off the Baram.

There are two good **restaurants**: the Indian *Restoran Koperselara* on Jalan Cinema, which sells *roti canai* and curries (a full meal here costs around RM5) and *Boon Kee Restoran*, set behind the main street in Jalan Newshop, which is best for dinner. A favourite meal here is sweet and sour prawns, greens in garlic, and rice – all for around RM15 a head, including beer. Otherwise, **cafés** beside the jetty and on the square do adequate rice and noodle dishes.

River trips from Marudi

The downriver express boat to Kuala Baram leaves hourly between 7.30am and 2.30pm (3hr; RM30). Upriver, boats leave daily at noon for **Long Terawan**, on Sungai Tutoh (5hr; RM20), where there's a connection for **Gunung Mulu National Park**, returning from the park the following day at 7.30am. The problem with this route to the park is that at Long Tutoh it is necessary to charter the longboat for the final part of the journey. This is very expensive, at around RM250 for the two to three hour trip. Travellers must be willing to pay the full price among themselves unless the boat has already been chartered by others whereupon the single pay will be around RM50 each. Although most people travel this route specifically to go to the park, on the way you pass a number of traditional Kayan longhouses.

Loagan Bunut National Park

Loagan Bunut National Park (☎085/779410; RM10) is a good spot for ornithologists, boasting many species of **birds**, including bitterns, stork-billed kingfishers and hornbills. Most of the birdwatching in the remote, hundred-square-kilometre park, occurs around the lake, **Tasik Bunut**, close to the park's main buildings and accommodation, and tucked away on the upper reaches of the **Teru River**, a tributary of the Tinjar. In the dry-spell months of February, May and June the water level drops drastically, and it's then that a peculiar form of fishing, which the local **Berawan** people call *selambau*, is carried out. Just prior to the whole lake becoming one expanse of dry cracked mud, the fish that haven't escaped down the lake's two watercourses are scooped up into giant spoon-shaped wooden frames in a spectacular action; they even jump into the boats in a lame attempt at escaping their fate. For birds, these months are a perfect time to feed too, and in May and June the surrounding peat-swamp forest supports breeding colonies of many avian species, particularly darters, egrets and herons. Initially the lake can appear huge, its edges hard to detect as the sunlight is often hazy; however, it's only around 500m in width and 1km in length. On the lake are a number of rafts with small cabins built on them, housing Berawan fishermen. Around these homes lie an intricate network of fishing plots, with underwater nets and lines tied to stakes pushed into the lake bed; boats move slowly and carefully around here so as not to get entangled with them.

The best times to drift by boat across the lake are **early morning** and **dusk** when the birds are at their most active. It's then that you may well see the lumbering gait of a **hornbill** and hear its characteristic, guttural squawk. You can also go **fishing** along Sungai Teru, just east of the lodge, when the river is high.

Practicalities

Most people get to the park on a **tour** from Miri or by their own transport. Operator Seridan Mulu in Miri (see p.458) is one company offering day and overnight visits (from RM150). To get to Loagan Bunut by **public transport**, take the Lapok bus (7am–midday; 2hr 30min; RM12) from Miri (see p.454). The bus terminates in **LAPOK**, a small bazaar town at the junction of the Tinjar and Teru rivers, 80km south of Miri; on the main street, where the bus drops you, there are a few cafés offering simple **meals** and drinks. From Lapok, the last bus back to Miri leaves at 2pm. Buy any provisions you need in Lapok, as there are no shops in the park; also bring mosquito repellent, as the mosquitoes at the lake are particularly voracious. The remaining 20km of the journey from Lapok to the park cannot be covered by public transport, and you must charter a motorbike or jeep; the one-way cost for the former is RM20, while four-wheel transport is around RM80 for up to four people. Alternatively, contact the park or the National Parks desk in Miri (☎085/434184) to try to arrange a pick-up in Lapok.

Once at the park there's just one type of **accommodation**, the forest hostel, which has dorm beds in four seven-bed rooms (RM15 with fan) and some smart doubles (❺) plus a small canteen serving basic meals and snacks. For reservations, contact the parks desk in Miri or call the park direct.

Long San and around

LONG SAN, 250km southeast of Miri, is home to one of the largest **Kenyah** tribal communities on the Baram. It was just sixty years ago that the settlement was established by the community, who moved here from Long Tikan, 20km upstream, when the agricultural lands there became exhausted. The Kenyah here are a strong and forward-looking community who are keen to develop a small, manageable tourist industry. With Lapok just three hours away by 4X4, making Marudi easily accessible, they now have a good clinic and an excellent school.

The region around Long San constitutes a further reason to travel so far upcountry. Only a few minutes away by longboat is the historic bazaar of **Long Akah** (where there is a tiny airport). Visitors here will be taken to the fort, a highly atmospheric ruin – it's as if colonial soldiers had only just left. Also nearby, the settled **Penan** community at **Long Beku** offers an insight into the world of Borneo's last hunter-gatherers.

The settlement

There are dozens of longhouse communities on the river, but Long San is in fact more of a small town, which can surprise those who believe Sarawak's indigenous peoples live either just in longhouses or have exchanged traditional life for the modernity and anonymity of the city. In fact, it's a busy, thriving community where you are just as likely to hear dance music blasting from a window as watch an old-timer deliver a long prose poem at a night's revelry. It has a variety of dwellings, including shops, an art gallery and a prominent Catholic church. The village, with around a thousand people, has two distinct sections, one on each side of a small river, Sungai San, a tributary of Batang Baram. Tragically, the community's main living area, a forty-door longhouse, was burnt to the ground, but will be replaced.

Practicalities

The most direct way to get to the settlement is a five- to six-hour drive by Land Cruiser (4X4) along rough logging roads; call the *Telang Usan* hotel in Miri for details (⊕085/411433; RM400 for the vehicle, RM80 per passenger). The MASwings weekly flight to Long Akah (Thurs) is an option, but then you will need to arrange onward boat travel from Long Akah to Long San. There is just one **place to stay** at Long San: an attractive wooden guesthouse close to the river, which serves inclusive meals (❷). Opposite is a shop where you can buy snacks, essential items, cold beer and local firewater. Staff at both the guesthouse and the shop speak some English and can help with arrangements.

Around Long San

A **day-trip** (RM150 per person), booked at the guesthouse in Long San, takes in a nearby **Kayan longhouse (**Long Liam), a **Penan community** at Long Beku and **Long Akah** and its **fort**, finishing with a **swim** in the rapids upstream. It's also possible to visit isolated longhouses further afield, though this is expensive (around RM250 per day), owing to the high cost of buying diesel upriver: the best ones to make for are **Long Mekaba**, a Kayan longhouse two hours upriver – where resident musicians play the lute-like *sape* and traditional dances are sometimes performed – and **Long Moh** and **Long Pallai** (4–5hr by boat), where the accoutrements of longhouse culture – firewood, chickens, pigs and longboats – are still housed underneath the traditional *belian* building.

Long Liam and Long Beku

Twenty minutes down Batang Baram from Long San is the thirty-door Kayan longhouse of **LONG LIAM**. Along the way, the longboat passes *laran* trees whose large white flowers drop into the water and are eaten by the fish which the Kenyah and Kayan net. The longhouse, which houses 150 people, is fifty years old; its inhabitants, many of whom originally came from the Akah River, near Long Akah, grow rice, tapioca, maize and sweetcorn in fields close by Long Liam. Their diet is supplemented with wild fruits from the jungle, and *kuman babi* (wild pig), which is plentiful in the forest. The only other building of note here is a small school staffed by three teachers giving lessons in Malay and Kayan.

Another two hours along the river is the **Penan** community at **LONG BEKU**. The Penan here – who are extremely poor, in stark contrast to the nearby Kayan and Kenyah – have been in the area for around fifty years, using Beku as a base while they hunt wild boar and cut sago. Some members of the community derive an income from making *parangs* (machetes), and you may well see them smelting the iron, then slotting the blade into a wooden handle before sharpening it on a lathe.

Long Akah

In the nineteenth century, **LONG AKAH** was a vital trading post supplying the whole of the upriver region. Sarawak's Resident was once based here, the settlement's fort was permanently garrisoned, and its pretty little cottages, with their well-tended gardens, were used by colonial officers and civil servants on missions into the territory. Now, Long Akah is decaying, the superb *belian* shingle roof of the vast barn-like centrepiece building – the former storehouse – seemingly collapsing a little more with every tropical storm. Still, the place is redolent of history: to walk along its overgrown concrete path alongside white, wooden bungalows is to revisit a tropical outpost of Empire. Nowadays employees of Sarawak's Agricultural Department reside here, supplying farmers with pesticides, fertilizers, seeds and know-how.

Accessible now only by a five-minute river trip is Long Akah's once-impressive **fort**, overlooking a spur on Batang Baram. Now dilapidated, this spacious building started life as the furthest outpost of the Brookes' security apparatus. Unless funds are put aside to preserve this magnificent, whitewashed wooden structure the place will soon collapse.

Gunung Mulu National Park

Located deep in the rainforest, **GUNUNG MULU** is Sarawak's premier **national park** and largest conservation zone, and is a listed UNESCO World Heritage Site. The region has been a magnet for explorers and scientists since the nineteenth century. Quite apart from the park's primary rainforest, which is characterized by clear rivers and exquisite belts of vegetation at various altitudes, there are three mountains dominated by dramatically eroded features, including dozens of fifty-metre-high razor-sharp limestone spikes – known as the **Pinnacles** – on Gunung Api.

The most popular overall draw though is the park's network of **caves**, constituting the largest limestone **cave system** in the world. This includes dramatic show caves, others accessible on "adventure" packages and more still being explored. The caves, which penetrate deep into the mountains, were formed by running water and are ancient: the oldest formed around five million years ago, the youngest during the last fifty thousand years. The surface water driving down the slopes of Mulu has eroded vast amounts of material, shaping the landscape outside, as well as carving cave passages within, dividing the great chunks of limestone into separate mountains.

Modern **explorers** have been coming to Mulu for a century and a half, starting in the 1850s with Spenser St John, who wrote inspiringly about the region in his book *Life in the Forests of the Far East*, though he didn't reach the summit of Gunung Mulu. A more successful bid was launched in 1932 when the explorer Lord Edward Shackleton got to the top during a research trip organized by Tom Harrisson, who would later become the curator of the Sarawak Museum. Over 250km of the caves have now been explored, yet experts believe this is only around thirty percent of the total.

Arrival and information

There are twice-daily MASwings **flights** to Mulu from Miri (around RM90 one way). It's essential to **book** ahead on the website or by phone ideally two weeks or more, as flights get full far in advance, especially for travel in and out of the park at weekends and public holidays. The **airstrip** is 500m east of the park HQ; vans ferry people either to the HQ or to the *Royal Mulu Resort* (RM5 one way).

Reaching Mulu by **boat from Marudi** involves a number of stages and takes much of the day. Getting to, or away from, the park by this route is not just more time-consuming but substantially more expensive. The reasons for doing so would be if flights were booked up far in advance or if you prefer the undeniably picturesque journey, especially along the Melinau tributary to Long Terawan. One option is to fly one way and do the boat trip on the other. From Marudi, the express boat leaves at noon for Long Terawan (RM20) on the Tutoh. When the river is low, this may only go as far as Long Panai, from where you may have to switch to another craft for Long Terawan. In all, it takes about three hours to reach Long Terawan, where you switch to a longboat (RM330 chartered for four persons, RM80 each extra person) for the final two-hour trip along the Tutoh tributary, the Melinau, and then on to the park HQ. Along the Melinau, the scenery becomes really breathtaking, the multiple greens of the forest deepening in the early-evening light and the peaks of Gunung Mulu and Api often peeping through a whirl of mist. The return trip requires an early start to get the boat to Long Terawan in time for the next stage on to Marudi at 7.30am. Give the park HQ ample warning (two days) if you aim to leave the park this way.

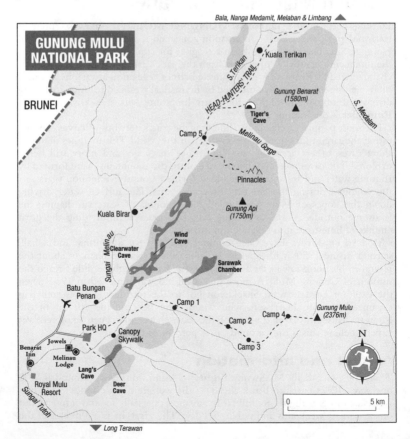

▲ Boat trip in Gunung Mulu National Park

Another way of accessing the park by boat is from the north, chiefly from Limbang in Sarawak, along the so-called **Headhunters Trail** (see p.473). The trail begins at **Nanga Medamit** in Limbang division, travels up the Medalan river into the park and requires a guide. The boat trip from Nanga Medamit costs around RM100 to **Kuala Terikan**, from which it's a five-hour hike to the park's Camp 5. Note that you will have to book accommodation well ahead at Camp 5 as it's the same lodge that trekkers on the Pinnacles trail use. For details of getting to Nanga Medamit from Limbang Town, see p.459.

Whether you're here independently or as part of a group, you won't be able to avoid shelling out for **boat travel** within the park. For a group of up to four people prices range from RM30 per person for the return trip from HQ to Clearwater and Wind caves; and RM90 (five persons or more) for the return trip to Kuala Litut, for the Pinnacles trek.

Many people visit Gunung Mulu National Park (RM10; ☏085/792301, ⓦwww.mulupark.com) as part of a package offered by **tour operators** such as Miri-based Tropical Adventure and Seridan Mulu (see p.458) or one of the Kuching-based companies (see p.408). These can be quite reasonable (RM500 for three days and two nights), but shop around as prices differ.

Upon arrival at the **Park HQ** (open daily 7am–8pm) you must sign in and pay the RM10 park fee.

Trekking

There are a variety of **treks** in the park, ranging from the gentle to the tough, for all of which you'll need the following equipment: comfortable walking shoes with a good tread; sun hat; swimming gear; a poncho/rain sheet; torch; mosquito repellent; headache pills; salt solution; and a basic first-aid kit and cotton gloves (available from the park shop) if you are to climb Gunung Api for the Pinnacles. Check with the park office if you'll need a sleeping bag and mat for any trek you intend to do. On the trails it's best to wear light clothing – shorts or loose trousers and T-shirts – rather than fully cover the body; this way,

Costs: guiding and transport

Although guide fees below look steep, it is important to note that quality guiding is essential as the park lies over a vast area and weather can change very quickly and dramatically. Guides can be picked up at the park HQ.

The minimum **guiding costs** for a group of up to five people (more for each extra person) are as follows:

The Pinnacles
3 days/2 nights; RM400 + RM25 per person at Camp 5

Mulu Summit
4 days/3 nights; RM1000

Garden of Eden
4 hours; RM200

Headhunters Trail
2 days/1 night (from Camp 5); RM220 (excluding boat from Kuala Terikan and van road transport from Medamit to Limbang)

Adventure caving
Lagang Cave RM200
Racer Cave RM200 (RM72 boat return)
Clearwater Cave RM300
Sarawak Chamber RM500

As well as the **park fee** (RM10), there is an extra charge of RM10 for staying at any of Camps 1, 3, and 4 and a RM15 transport fee for getting to Wind and Clearwater caves.

Canopy Skywalk RM30 per person
Night walk RM10 per person

if the conditions are wet, it'll be easier to see any leeches that might be clinging to you. **Two major hikes**, to the Pinnacles and to the summit of Gunung Mulu, are daunting, but the reward is stupendous views of the rainforest, stretching as far as Brunei: bring long trousers and long-sleeved shirts for the dusk insect assault, and for the occasional cool nights.

Join a group if you want to share guide costs for the longer treks; to do this, look the HQ's useful noticeboard and lodge your requirements with park staff. As a rule of thumb, if you visit independently as a group of two to four people, you will pay less than on an organized tour arranged through an operator, but the drawback here is that you may have to wait around at HQ before other trekkers are available to join your group and share costs. Certainly allow for an extra day at the beginning of the visit to explore options and prices. Note that if you are doing the main treks with an independent tour operator and not with park guides, your guide needs to bring the food to be cooked at base camp, Camp 5.

Accommodation and eating

If you are travelling to the park independently, remember that it is essential to **book accommodation** at the park HQ weeks, if not a month, ahead, either by email or phone. It is best to book directly with the parks management, but a second option is to make your reservation at the parks desks at the Visitors' Information Centres in Miri, Kuching, Sibu or Kota Kinabalu.

Opposite the park HQ's administrative block, on the other side of the verdant padang, you'll find various lodging: the hostel offering 21 dorm beds (RM37), the Rainforest lodge four-bed en-suite rooms (**4**) and the Longhouse lodges en-suite twin-shares (⑤). Also within the main building, with a large veranda sitting area, is *Café Mulu* (daily 8am–11pm), serving a wide range of **meals**, with good vegetarian options, fresh fish, rice and noodles. Breakfasts are particularly enticing with eggs and pancakes the standout options. Beside the café is a small **shop** selling just the sort of foodstuffs you'll want while trekking – nuts, chocolate, fruit and biscuits, plus bottled water.

Across the bridge connecting the park to the road, you'll find one budget sleeping option, *Melinau Lodge and Canteen* run by Nancy Juwing, which has a number of five-bed mini dorms (①). Close by is the unassuming but excellent café, *Jowels* (daily 7am–midnight), where you can order tasty local Berawan dishes including exotic jungle ferns, wild boar and riverine fish. The café also sells beer and *tuak* (rice wine).

Situated 2km further down the road from the airport is the other place to stay, the chic, lavish jungle hideaway, *Royal Mulu Resort* (℡085/790100, Ⓦwww.royalmuluresort.com; ⑧). From the park HQ it can be reached by a ten-minute boat ride. Elevated on stilts to protect it from flooding during the lashing monsoon rains, the sprawling resort has hundreds of self-contained chalets, each with balcony, large bathroom, TV and minibar. At its centre lies a stylish, longhouse-style entrance, a small swimming pool and the café, which serves up rather average Western and Malaysian food at inflated prices. Finally, close to the *Resort* is the *Benarat Inn* (℡012/8703541 or 085/419337) owned by Miri-based operator Tropical Adventure, mostly used by tour groups; it is possible to stay here if there's availability. The *Inn* has twin-bed rooms with fan (④) and others with air-conditioning (⑤) plus a café selling Malaysian and Western food, and beer.

The park

Everyone's itinerary at Mulu includes visits to the Canopy Skywalk and the **show caves**, and if you're fit and have time to stay for more than two days in the park, scaling the **Pinnacles** as well. More specialized are the four-day trek to **Gunung Mulu** itself and **adventure caving**, both of which will push up the cost significantly.

Canopy Skywalk

Mulu's Canopy Skywalk (RM30), at 480m long, is the longest tree-based walkway in the world and is a captivating, near-thrilling experience. Twenty metres away from a limestone cliff, the narrow 20m-high walkway laces around six broad hard wood *kasai, betang, meranti, peran* and *segera* trees, and takes around 30 minute to cover. The purpose of the walkway is to experience the eco-system's flora and fauna, the ferns and vines, bird and insect life from a vantage point half- way up from the forest floor to the treetops. It is compulsory to go on a guided tour, with no more than eight people traversing the skywalk at any one time. Walks depart from HQ five times a day, the first at 7am and the last at 2.15pm and it's essential to book the day before for the two morning tours, and on the day for the three afternoon ones. The skywalk can be found 30 minute along a plankway from HQ, on the way to Deer and Langs Caves and passing the trail to Paku Waterfall.

The show caves

Only four of the 25 caves so far explored in Mulu are open to visitors – Deer Cave, Lang's Cave, Wind Cave and Clearwater Cave. Deer Cave was only fully surveyed in 1961, as too were sections of Clearwater and Wind. As these so-called **show caves** are Mulu's most popular attractions, they can sometimes get quite crowded, and there's the occasional log jam along the plankway to the two closest to park HQ, Deer Cave and Lang's Cave. Over 90 percent of people at the park visit the show caves, the highest figure of any of the attractions.

Deer and Lang's caves

The most immediately impressive cave in the park is **Deer Cave**, the nearest to the HQ (1hr), which contains the largest cave passage in the world. It was once inhabited by deer, which used to shelter in its cavernous reaches. Inside, the cave passage is over 2km long and 174m high, while up above, hundreds of thousands of bats live in the cave's nooks and crannies. Also numerous are the cave's swiftlets, who navigate and identify their nests – cup-shaped homes made from threads of saliva – using the cave's echoes. Birds'-nest gatherers climb up the cave shafts to extract the nests, which sell in the outside world for the same price per kilogram as silver.

After an hour, the path through the cave leads to an area where a large hole in the roof allows light to penetrate. Here, in the so-called **Garden of Eden**, scientists of the 1976 Royal Geographical Society expedition discovered luxuriant vegetation that had been undisturbed for centuries; the leader, Robin Hanbury-Tenison, noted that "even the fish were tame and gathered in shoals around a hand dipped in the water". It's an incredible spot: plants battle for the light, birds and insects celebrate the warm air, giant ferns grow in clusters around rocks and families of grey-leaf monkeys scuttle about unafraid. Note that most trips to Deer Cave do NOT extend to Garden of Eden – you will have to discuss this option with the park officials.

The best – and the busiest – time to visit Deer Cave is in the late afternoon. Wait around the cave entrance at dusk and you'll usually see the vast swarms of bats – up to three million – streaming out in a protective doughnut-shaped formation into the darkening skies on food and plant-fertilizing missions.

Close to the Deer Cave entrance is the entrance to **Lang's Cave** (named after the local guide who first found it), the smallest of the show caves. It has weird and wonderful rock formations, most spectacularly the curtain stalactites and coral-like growths – helicites – gripping the curved walls.

Clearwater and Wind caves

Probing some 150km through Mulu's substratum, the **Clearwater Cave system**, thought to be the longest in Southeast Asia, is reached by a fifteen-minute longboat journey along the Melinau from the park HQ. The longboats moor at a small jungle pool, after which the cave is named, at the base of the two-hundred-step climb to the cave mouth. Discovered in 1988, the cave tunnels here weave deep into the mountain; ordinary visitors can only explore the small section close to the entrance, where lighting has been installed along a walkway leading 300m on to **Young Lady's Cave**, which ends abruptly in a fifty-metre-deep pothole. Deep inside the main body of the cave is the subterranean **Clearwater River**, which flows through a five-kilometre passage reaching heights and widths of as much as 90m. En route to Clearwater Cave, most visitors halt at the comparatively small **Wind Cave**, which contains a great variety of golden, contorted rock shapes, stalactites and stalagmites, best appreciated in the subtly illuminated King's Room. It's another five minutes from Wind Cave to Clearwater Cave, whether by boat or via the walkway joining them; the alternative is to indulge in some adventure-caving and trek between them, an exhausting and muddy five-hour trip involving lots of wading and swimming in the icy Clearwater River. Wind Cave and Clearwater Cave can be combined with a trip to or from the Pinnacles.

Adventure caving

Not discovered until the 1980s, eight of the park's subterranean caves are now open for adventure caving. Those categorized as appropriate for beginners are Turtle and Lagangs; intermediate Drunken Forest and Racer; and advanced Stonehorse, Clearwater Connection and Sarawak Chamber.

Although fewer than ten percent of park visitors opt for adventure caving it is gradually growing in popularity, especially with young visitors, with the recommended minimum age being 8 for beginners, 12 for intermediate-level caves and 16 for advanced. Most caving trips involve following the cave water passage, scrambling over boulders and observing cave formations, like straws and stalagmites. Prices (see p.468) include lights and helmet but it's important to bring a torch and good walking shoes (rubber shoes can be hired at the shop at HQ) and to wear durable, old clothes as in most instances you will get muddy.

Batu Bungan

Most tour operators' show cave itineraries include a stop at a nearby Penan settlement, **Batu Bungan**, where handicrafts are available. The first Penan here were workers helping in the construction of the park. They were joined by their families and now the camp has expanded into a thriving settlement. Tour groups stop during the mornings when the Penan women lay out artefacts for sale. Although some of the crafts are beautifully made, the short stop is unlikely to be a highlight of any trip to Mulu as the whole experience feels rather forced.

The Pinnacles and around

Five million years ago, a constant splatter of raindrops dissolved Gunung Api's limestone and carved out the **Pinnacles** – fifty-metre high shards, with the sharpness of samurai swords – from a solid block of rock. The erosion is still continuing and the entire region is pockmarked with deep shafts penetrating far into the heart of the mountain: one-third of Gunung Api has already been washed away and in perhaps another ten million years the whole of it will disappear. Getting a good view of the Pinnacles requires an almost masochistically demanding **ascent** up the south face of Gunung Api to a ridge 1200m up the mountain. Once there, it's impossible not to be over-awed by the sheer size and grandeur of the Pinnacles. At that height in such a volatile jungle climate, conditions can alter within minutes – piercing sun can be replaced by billowing clouds, and tumultuous rain can follow moments later. Most treks reach the top mid-morning as soon after that the weather is liable to change. Beware that the climb is tough and must not be underestimated. Some tour operators are being economical with the truth when they describe the climb as "moderate" – to the less than fully fit, climbing to the Pinnacles can be extraordinarily taxing, if not quite on a par with Mount Kinabalu in Sabah. Your guide will recommend that you bring at least two litres of water each; other than snacks, carry little else or you'll be too weighed down. Wear light clothing, waterproofs, a hat and shoes or boots with grip.

Day 1: To Camp 5

From the park HQ, the first part of the trip to the Pinnacles is an hour-long journey by longboat upstream along the Melinau River; you may have to help pull the boat through the rapids if the water level is very low. After mooring at Kuala Birar, there's a two-and-a-half-hour trek through lowland forest to reach **Camp 5**, which is beautifully situated on the edge of the river. The large, open-plan one-storey building has around half a dozen rooms with raised platforms for sleeping and a communal eating area at one end with a kitchen behind.

Here you're close to the Melinau Gorge, across which nearby **Gunung Api** (1750m) and **Gunung Benarat** (1580m) cast long shadows in the fading afternoon light. A bridge straddles the river here – the path that disappears into the jungle on the other side is the first stage of the Headhunters Trail (see opposite).

Day 2: The ascent

The next morning, trekkers retrace their steps 50m along the track and turn left onto a path at the base of the mountain which at times nearly disappears among tree roots and slippery limestone debris. The trail is honeycombed with holes and passages through which rainwater immediately disappears. After two hours' uphill climb, during which you will have rested on numerous occasions, a striking vista opens up: the rainforest stretches below as far as the eye can see, and wispy clouds drift along your line of vision. The climb gets even tougher as you scramble between sharp rocks at steeper gradients, but fatigue will give way to appreciation when the high trees give way to **moss forest**, where pitcher plants feed on insects, and ants and squirrels dart in and out among the roots of trees.

The last thirty minutes of the climb is almost a sheer vertical manoeuvre, painful and exhausting. Nineteen ladders, thick pegs and ropes help you on this final ascent; just when your limbs are finally giving way, you arrive at the top of the **ridge** that overlooks the Pinnacles. The ridge is itself a pinnacle, although sited across a ravine from the main cluster, and if you tap the rocks around you, they reverberate because of the large holes in the limestone underneath. The vegetation here is sparse, but includes the balsam plant, which has pale pink flowers, and pitcher plants. After taking in the stunning sight of the dozens of fifty-metre-high grey-limestone shapes, jutting out from their perch in an unreachable hollow on the side of the mountain, it's time for the return slog, which many people find harder on the legs and nerves – it takes three to four hours, or even longer when the route is particularly slippery. Once back at the camp, there's a chance to rest, swim, eat and sleep.

Days 3 and 4: Walks from Camp 5

Some people opt to leave early on day three for the return journey back to camp but others prefer to go on a few undemanding treks from Camp 5. From the camp, a two-hour round-trip takes you along the path that follows the river further upstream and ends below the **Melinau Gorge**, where two vertical walls of rock rise 100m above the river, which emerges from a crevice. There's nowhere other than slippery rocks to rest and admire this beautiful spot before you return to Camp 5.

Another short trail leads to the base of **Gunung Benarat** and to the lower shaft of **Tiger's Cave**, a return trip of around three hours.

The trek to Gunung Mulu

The route to the summit of **Gunung Mulu** (2376m) was first discovered in the 1920s by Tama Nilong, a Berawan rhinoceros-hunter. Earlier explorers hadn't been able to find a way around the huge surrounding cliffs, but Nilong discovered the southwest ridge trail by following rhinoceros tracks, enabling

Lord Shackleton in 1932 to become the first mountaineer to reach the summit. It's still an arduous climb, as much of the route is very steep, and few visitors to Mulu Park undertake it. Park guides will argue against setting out if the weather is very wet; **book** ahead by email or telephone if you are thinking of undertaking it.

Day 1: To Camp 1
The first stage is from park HQ to Camp 1, a straightforward, three-hour walk on a flat trail which crosses from the park's prevalent limestone plain to the sandstone terrain of Gunung Mulu. En route, hornbills fly low over the jungle canopy and, if you watch the trail carefully, you may see wild boar and mouse-deer tracks. The first night is usually spent at Camp 1, a hut which has been renovated, where after a meal prepared by your guide, you sleep on raised platforms.

Day 2: Into the moss forest
Day 2 comprises a hard, ten-hour, uphill slog; there are two resting places on the way where you can wash your tired limbs in small rock pools. From here onwards you're in a moss forest, where small openings in the canopy reveal lovely views of the park. The next part of the trail is along Nilong's southwest ridge, a series of small hills manoeuvred via a narrow, twisting path. When the rain has been heavy, there are lots of little swamps to negotiate; one known as "Rhino's Lake" because it was here that what was thought to be the last rhinoceros in the area was shot in the 1950s. You will stay the night at Camp 4's hut, 1800m up, which can be cool so you'll need a sleeping bag.

Days 3 and 4: To the summit and back to Camp 1
Most climbers set off well before dawn for the hard ninety-minute trek from Camp 4 to the **summit**, if possible timing their arrival to coincide with sunrise. At dawn itself, the forest wakes up, the insect and bird chorus reverberating in the thin, high-altitude air. After an hour's climb you pass an overgrown helicopter pad. On the final stretch there are big clumps of pitcher plants, though it's easy to miss them as by this point you are hauling yourself up by ropes onto the cold, windswept, craggy peak. From here, the view is exhilarating, looking down on Gunung Api and, on a clear day, far across the forest to Brunei Bay. The Melinau can also just be made out, a pencil-thin wavy light-brown line, bisecting the deep-green density of the forest carpet.

In good conditions it's just about possible to do the **return leg** from the summit to park HQ in one day, omitting a return night at Camp 3, but the trip, which can't be done in less than twelve hours, is exhausting. The red-and-white marks on the trees at least make the trail easier to follow in fading light.

The Headhunters Trail and beyond the park
The **Headhunters Trail** – so called as it corresponds to the route taken by warring parties of Kenyah and Kayan peoples as they traversed the Tutoh and Medalam rivers – runs between the park and Limbang, a town in the northernmost section of Sarawak. It's a particularly compelling excursion for travellers wanting to reach Brunei or Sabah as onward travel beyond Limbang is reasonably easy, either by bus, boat or plane. As with the park's other trekking, caving and climbing packages, at the first instance consult the park HQ for information and costs.

Hornbills

Hornbills are those bizarre, almost prehistoric-looking, inhabitants of tropical forests, whose presence (or absence) is an important ecological indicator of the health of the forest. You should have little difficulty in identifying hornbills: they are large, black-and-white birds with disproportionately huge bills (often bent downwards), topped with an ornamental **casque** – a generally hollow structure attached to the upper mandible. The function of the casque is unknown, though it's thought it may play a role in attracting a mate and in courtship ceremonies. Ten of the world's 46 species of hornbill are found in Malaysia, many of them endangered or present only in small, isolated populations. Two of the most commonly seen species are the pied hornbill and the black hornbill. The **pied hornbill** can be identified by its white abdomen and tail, and white wingtips in flight. Apparently more tolerant of forest degradation than other species, it's the smallest hornbill you're likely to see, reaching only 75cm in length. Outside breeding season, it gathers in noisy flocks which are generally heard well before they are seen. The **black hornbill** is only slightly larger and black, save for the white tips of the outer tail feathers (some individuals also show a white patch behind the eye). Among the larger species of hornbill are the **helmeted hornbill** and the **rhinoceros hornbill**, both over 120cm in length, mainly black, but with white tails and bellies. The rhinoceros hornbill has a bright orange rhino-horn-shaped casque (hence the name), whereas the helmeted hornbill has a bright red head, neck and helmet-shaped casque. The call of the helmeted hornbill is a remarkable series of "took" notes that start off slowly and then accelerate to reach a ringing crescendo of cackles.

Good places to spot hornbills in east Malaysia are Sarawak's Gunung Mulu National Park and Sabah's Danum Valley, Labuk Bay Proboscis Monkey Sanctuary and Gunung Kinabalu National Park.

You'll need to get an early start at Camp 5 for the trail's 11km (4–5hr) flat, but often boggy, trail to Kuala Terikan, where you board a longboat on the Medamit River for the three-hour journey downriver to overnight at a Berawan **longhouse**. Expect to sleep on mats and eat local food, which is likely to comprise rice, eggs, ferns and maybe chicken or wild boar. The next morning the boat continues for two hours to the small settlement, **Kuala Medamit**, where you catch a van or minibus for the one-hour ride to Limbang Town. Reaching Limbang by 1 or 2pm, it is possible to go by bus to Kuala Lurah on the Brunei border, and then travel onward to the capital, Bandar Sri Begawan. To get to Labuan, and for onward travel to Sabah, you will need to stay in Limbang, as the daily express boat leaves at 8.30am.

The Kelabit Highlands

Along the border with Kalimantan and 100km southeast of Gunung Mulu, the long, high plateau of the **Kelabit Highlands** has been the home of the Kelabit people for hundreds of years. Western explorers had no idea of the existence of this self-sufficient mountain community until the beginning of the twentieth century, when officials made a few brief visits. But the Highlands were (literally) not put on the map until World War II, when British and Australian commandos, led by Major Tom Harrisson, used a number of Kelabit settlements as bases for waging a guerrilla war against the occupying Japanese forces. Before Harrisson's men built an airstrip at Bario, trekking over the inhospitable terrain was the only way to get here – it was a two-week trek from Marudi to the west. After the war, missionaries arrived and converted the animist Kelabit to Christianity, with the consequence that many of their traditions, like burial rituals and wild parties called *iraus* (where Chinese jars full of rice wine were consumed) mostly disappeared. Many of the magnificent Kelabit **megaliths** associated with these traditions have been swallowed up by the jungle, but some dolmens, urns, rock carvings and ossuaries used in funeral processes are locatable, constituting one of the chief reasons why the region is a magnet for archaeologists and anthropologists worldwide.

Now, the four most populous Kelabit settlements – the central **Bario**, **Long Lellang** to the southwest, **Long Banga** to the south and **Ba' Kelalan** to the north – have regular air services using Twin Otter planes, giving the highland people the chance of daily contact with the world beyond, and curious tourists the opportunity to visit them with relative ease.

For all the recent contact, the Highlands remain a generally unspoilt region, with vivid flora, occasional animal sightings and a cool refreshing climate. Not surprisingly, these factors make it a popular target for walkers – as well as researchers – attracted by jungle **treks** and the prospect of encountering friendly local people, many of whom live in sturdy **longhouses** (a visit to which is an unmissable part of any trip here), surrounded by their livestock, fruit trees and wet paddy (rice) fields. The Kelabit aren't as concerned as the Iban or Kayan with formality; when you turn up at a longhouse you don't need to be too concerned with who is or isn't the *tuai* (chief).

It is essential to hire a **guide** (see p.477) for treks beyond day-trips around Bario; the routes are hard to follow, with many paths consumed by mud or foliage. Travellers usually hire guides from their guesthouse in the main settlements, Bario and Ba' Kelalan.

Bario and around

The centre of the Kelabit Highlands is the sprawling village of **BARIO**, approximately 15km west of the border with Indonesian Kalimantan, and a few days' hard hike from Long Lellang to the south or Ba' Kelalan to the north. It's a small, widely dispersed but busy community with a number of distinct sections set among the plateau's rolling hills and surrounding paddy fields. The village is arranged on either side of a long road, which snakes from the airport 4km west to the Bario Asal Longhouse, where a number of local families live. With no land-line telephone, very irregular mobile reception and few motorized vehicles, the pace of life is slow, with many people's schedule organized around the arriving planes which bring in people, provisions and the odd tourist. The isolated mountain region is on line, however – the E-Bario project, based in Bario's Telecentre block, receives its satellite connection from solar power; visit Ⓦ www.ebario.com or Ⓦ www.kelabit.net for information on Kelabit culture and the region. Also the Telecentre has an internet café (daily except Sun noon–5pm; RM10 per hr), although connection is haphazard.

Arrival and information

There are two daily MASwings **flights** from Miri and three weekly from Marudi (Mon, Wed, Sat). The planes can't fly when the weather's bad so it's easy to get stuck in Bario or at Miri or Marudi waiting for the flight in. In case of such eventualities, bring funds to stay a few days longer than you intended, as there are no banks. Trying to get on the flight from Miri in the first place can be hard, as Kelabits tend to book ahead and the eighteen-seater Twin Otter flights fill up quickly. If you can't get a seat, you can ask to be put on the reserve list and you will be notified when a seat comes up. If you're still unsuccessful, go to Miri or Marudi airport early in the day, and queue for standby. The same applies on leaving Bario.

Bario's **airport** is 2km away to the east of the village centre at **Padang Pasir**. Guesthouse owners congregate at arrivals to offer rooms to visitors, and then ferry them into the village. Also, motorbikes are usually available there, offering pillion travel (RM10). As well as the semi-paved airport road there are tracks to six nearby communities, though these are accessible only by motorbike or 4X4. The furthest village accessible by road is just six kilometres away; all the other arteries hacked out of the highland forest and shrub are jungle trails, used by locals, trekkers and buffalo alike. But times are changing in the region; a road built by a timber company is due to join Bario village with the spider's web of existing logging tracks.

Accommodation

The Bario region now has several places to stay, all cheap and mostly of a high standard. Many are in the settlement's centre, but others are some distance along narrow lanes. See also p.478 for the most isolated one of them all, *Gem's Lodge*. Prices include three meals a day unless otherwise stated.

Bariew Backpacker Lodge and Homestay (Reddish's Place) Jalan Bario ☏016/8853685, Ⓔreddisharan@hotmail.com. Fifty metres past the Telecentre block, local Kelabit Reddish has a spacious lodge with seven beautifully decorated little rooms, three sitting rooms and an out-house for meals. Reddish is the perfect host, helping travellers with various requirements such as finding an available guide for trekking. His wife, Julfiness, serves up tremendous meals specializing in local dishes combining exotic ferns, wild boar and locally reared fish. There's 24hr tea, milo and coffee. ❸

De Plateau Lodge Ⓔdeplateau@hotmail.com. Three kilometres east of Bario centre, on the way to Pa Umor, lies Douglas Munney Bala's tranquil and well-equipped compound which comprises comfortable rooms, and a sitting and dining area. Bala specializes in birdwatching trips nearby, and is a fount of knowledge on Kelabit culture and lands. His friend Rian John Lamulun (contactable via Bala) is first choice as a guide for treks further afield. ❸

JK View Lodge Run by Reddish's aunt, Rose, *JK's* is a homestay with neat rooms and clean bathrooms on the main road out towards Ulung Palang longhouse. ❸

Junglebluesdream Ulung Palang Longhouse, north Bario ⓔ junglebluesdream@gmail.com. This longhouse is getting steadily rebuilt after burning to the ground some years ago. Local artist Stephen Baya and partner Tine Hjetting's renovated rooms offer rustic conditions and a fabulous view – plus Tine's cooking is a treat. On the communal longhouse landing outside the three-bed rooms,

Baya's studio showcases his colourful naturalistic and abstract canvases. ❸

Labang's Longhouse ☎016/895 2102. One kilometre east of Bario centre, this seventeen-room longhouse was been built for use by visitors, instead of local Kelabits. It had recently fallen into disrepair, and should only be used as a fall-back if the other places are full. ❷

Tarawe's Jalan Bario ⓔ jtarawe@bario.net. Despite being at the centre of the village, this option will have you waking to the sounds of cockerels and pigs while gazing over paddy fields to the hills beyond. Its four rooms have three beds in each, with extra mats to accommodate bigger groups if necessary. Unfortunately, *Tarawe's* doesn't offer regular meals. Owner Lian is an experienced guide and, when available, can lead visitors on any of treks covered here. ❷

Eating

Most visitors eat in the guesthouses listed above, although there are two **cafés** beside Bario's Telecentre. One, *Café Batu Lawi*, sells acceptable noodle and rice dishes. There is also a small café in the airport at Padang Pasir which sells hot and soft drinks, biscuits and cakes; everyone ends up waiting in here for flights to arrive and leave.

Day-trips from Bario

Treks around Bario are varied, enjoyable and often quite challenging. An excellent way of getting acclimatized to the terrain is the half-day hike along unpaved roads to two longhouses, **Pa Umor** and **Pa Ukat**, both best visited at weekends when the maximum number of Kelabit are at home. A shorter but

Guides and trekking

Guides are usually arranged at guesthouses, but be aware that none can be fully relied upon to produce a free guide extra fast. Contacting ahead and trying to reserve a guide is vital but not foolproof. Sometimes visitors have to wait a day or more for a guide to become available. Reddish of the *Bariew Backpacker Lodge*, for example, is often too busy to take visitors away for more than a day. Another exceptional guide, Jaman Riboh, a former high-school teacher specializing in nature walks on which he'll point out plants and wildlife, runs a guesthouse (*Gem's Lodge*), situated on a river at Pa Umor. Jaman seldom comes to the airport to meet flights so, other than email (and that is less than reliable), the only way to find him is to walk to *Gem's* from Bario – a two-hour hike. Another, Florence Apu (ⓔ florenceapu @hotmail.com), is an expert in the Highlands' archeological heritage and is often away with researchers. Apu helps coordinate a group, Bario Nature Guides, who are contactable at ⓔ bbn_natureguides@yahoo.com.

Kelabit guides will estimate the fitness of those in the group and set the trekking pace accordingly. The trips often involve gathering wild vegetables, catching fish and cooking, Kelabit-style, on the campfire, as well as locating dolmens and visiting longhouses. The usual rate to hire a guide is from RM80 per day for one person, and RM100 a day plus overnight.

harder trek is the enjoyable three-hour hike up a steep hill to a cutting, **the Bario Gap**, from where there are spectacular views across the Highlands.

Bario Gap

An energetic four-and-a-half-hour round trip (around RM40 for the guide), the trek to the cutting in the forest, known as the **Bario Gap**, starts from central Bario where the first forty minutes follows the main road north to Bario Asal longhouse. Here, a path crosses a buffalo field before snaking steeply up a forested hill, running for some time alongside a pretty, fast-flowing stream. Soon you are in dense jungle – wear strong shoes as the path is slippery and strewn with creepers. The ascent takes around one hour before you reach the cutting, also known as the Millennium Gap, as it was constructed as part of Kelabit millennium celebrations. Aside from the mini-trek being good practice for the longer ones described below, the cutting offers magnificent views over the Bario plateau. This hill path is the start of the two-day hike to the Penan settlement of Pa Tik, and it's likely you will meet Penan family traffic on it.

Pa Umor

Another, less strenuous way to acclimatize to the Highlands, is the two-and-a-half hour stroll to the longhouse at Pa Umor. From central Bario take the fork uphill behind the Telecentre. A kilometre along here, at the point where the road snakes away downhill, take the track to your right. Two kilometres down the pretty route, which is likely to be caked in mud if it has been raining hard, look out to your right towards a gate. Beyond is *Gem's Lodge*, a seemingly magical hideaway tucked away in a small wood. The large wooden building, run by Jaman Riboh, has four double bedrooms and a chalet with an additional two en-suite bedrooms (℡019/8553546, ✉gems_lodge@yahoo.com; food included; ❸).

Just 100m past the *Gem's* turning you reach the settlement of **PA UMOR**. The village is centred on a longhouse with a neat, tiny church beside it. These days most visitors stay in *Gem's* rather than the longhouse, but it used to be a very popular stopover with a reputation for great food and parties. Another longhouse, **Pa Ukat**, is situated a pleasant forty-minute hike along the main track from Bario, after *not* turning right towards Pa Umor and soon passing *De Plateau Lodge*.

South of Bario

You can visit the three large longhouse communities at **Ramudu**, **Pa' Dali** and **Pa' Mada**, where it's possible to stay, via a demanding but very rewarding three- to five-day trek through secondary forest that starts and finishes in Bario. The cost shouldn't be more than RM400 for five days, but extra is tagged on for food and beverages. Check with your guide if there are extra costs for accommodation. Comfortable shoes with a good grip are essential, as are waterproofs and a light pack.

Kelapang River loop

Tracing the **Kelapang River trail** is an exemplary way to experience the natural beauty and attractive longhouses of the Kelabit Highlands, and is the most popular long-distance route in the region. This clockwise trek takes you in a rough oval through the nearby settlement of Kampung Baru, and then onwards to Pa' Mada, Pa' Dali and Ramudu. All walkers stop over in Pa' Mada, Ramudu and Pa'Dali, with the option of spending an extra night at Pa

Berang. Some guides arrange for trekkers to stay in the longhouses, others prefer using more private homestays which have opened up in recent years in these settlements.

Kampung Baru

The first leg is the eight-hour slog from Bario to Pa' Mada; first crossing the old Bario airfield and then along a wide, streamside track reaching the longhouse settlement of **Kampung Baru**, some 45 minutes later. One kilometre beyond the settlement, you follow a path to the left over a wobbly steel-and-bamboo bridge, which leads onto a narrow, undulating buffalo path. Four or five hours out of Kampung Baru, you'll pass through the area where the longhouse of **Pa' Main** used to stand, until its residents relocated to the Bario settlements of Pa Ramapuh and Ullong Pallang during the uncertain times of the Konfrontasi (see p.699).

Pa' Mada

Another three hours' walking through remote, beautiful countryside brings you to the first night's accommodation, the Kelabit longhouse community of Pa' Mada, which nestles in fields beside a small brook. Visitors spend most of their time on the communal bamboo veranda, from where you can see tiny apartments – one for each family. A room in the longhouse is usually reserved for walkers to sleep. Below the veranda are storerooms for stocks of rice and other grains. A Christian community, Pa' Mada incorporates a Methodist church and even a tiny shop. The settlement is surrounded by tended fields, the river nearby is full of fish, and game is abundant. Jobs like rice harvesting, mat-making and textile-weaving are dictated by the time of year – the rice-growing cycle starts in August with the clearing and planting of the fields and the crop is harvested in February. After the hard labour required in processing the rice, the Kelabit women turn their attention to crafts and the men to hunting or fishing, going on trips to other longhouses or to big towns like Miri and Marudi.

Pa' Dali

The track from Pa' Mada to **Pa' Dali** is quite easy, the journey taking just two hours. It's tempting to push on to Ramudu, but since this next leg is arguably the most exacting of the loop, you might want to catch your breath before the rigours of the tough four-hour hike ahead. Comprising three longhouses, a school and a football field, Pa' Dali is a springboard to several highland adventures, among them the half-day hike to see the village's huge stone drums, once used as caskets for the dead.

Ramudu

The journey from Pa' Dali to **Ramudu** kicks off by skirting paddy fields. Shortly afterwards you emerge into buffalo pasture, where to your left is a large rock in whose carved niches the remains of the village's dead were once left in jars; one collapsed example is still apparent. Four or five hours of steep rises and drops follow, before you reach the ten-door Ramudu longhouse, set behind groves of pineapple trees and sugar cane, vegetable gardens and a grassy airstrip. The people of Ramudu are famed for their skilfully woven rattan baskets, worn on the back, and they may have a surplus of stock and thus some on sale. They also make delicious *gula tapur*, or sugar-cane candy. Ten minutes before you reach Ramudu you'll pass a **carved boulder** with intriguing representations of a face, a buffalo and a human figure.

Back to Bario via Pa Berang

Most guides on this route will suggest returning from Ramadu in one day. This entails a 4X4 on a logging road to Pa Berang and a boat trip on the Kelapang River from Pa Berang to close to Bario; the final stretch is a one-hour easy hike. Expect to incur extra costs (RM80–100) for this shuttle. **Pa Berang** is home to some Penan families, who live in somewhat poorer conditions than those enjoyed by the residents of the loop's other longhouses.

North of Bario

The other main excursion from Bario is the three-day trail due north through the villages of Pa Lungan and Pa Rupai to the Kelabit settlement of **Ba' Kelalan**, from where it's possible to fly to Lawas and Miri. A side trip to climb **Gunung Murud** (2423m) is possible from Ba' Kelalan too, though there are no package trips to this peak, so ask at Ba' Kelalan's *Apple Lodge* about hiring guides. Particularly for this trek, bring a sleeping mat as some nights are spent in basic shelters and, if it's the rainy season, beware of heavy mud, leeches and mosquitoes.

To Ba' Kelalan via Pa Lungan

The route from Bario heads past the longhouse at Pa Ukat; watch out for the **trailside boulder** a few kilometres along the trail, on which human faces are carved. After four to five hours you reach **Pa' Lungan**, which consists of detached family units around a large rectangular field for pigs and buffalo. Visitors can stay at *Batu Ritung Lodge* (❶) a lovely homestay run by a local lady, Supang Galik, who provides simple, but delicious meals. Your guide, or Supang herself, can lead you to nearby dolmens.

On the second – very long – day, it takes from four to six hours to get to the abandoned village of **Long Rapung**. On the way, before the forest closes in around you, look out for Gunung Murud on your left, if it's not shrouded in mist. There is just a small shelter at Long Rapung – little more than an intersection of paths and a place to rest – but it's a very beautiful place nonetheless, with a small clean river running gently past, and most guides opt to spend the night here, allowing for a less strenuous third day. Four more hours on a hard and narrow trail – infamous for its wet-season leeches – is needed to reach **Pa Rupai**. The long downward slope passes through irrigated rice fields to the village. You're now in Kalimantan, although there are no signs to prove it. Two hours further and you pass through the village of **Long Medang** and on up a short, steep hill which marks the frontier with Kalimantan. After a short walk, the trail leads to Ba' Kelalan.

Ba' Kelalan and around

Ba' Kelalan is smaller and more compact than Bario, with a smattering of single dwellings, one large longhouse, two coffee shops, and a few shops selling basic provisions. It is renowned for its apples and other citrus fruits which grow well at this altitude. There is just one place to stay, *Apple Lodge*; the owners are contactable in Miri by phone (☎085/435736). The lodge is surprisingly large and well maintained, something of a magnet for people visiting with out-of-the-way place (❸, including meals). There are MASwings flights from the airport, close to the town centre, to Lawas, Monday and Saturday, and from Miri, Monday, Wednesday and Saturday. There is also a road from Ba' Kelalan to Lawas; it's a hard, six-hour trip by 4X4 on logging roads through largely deforested but sometimes quite spectacular scenery (RM150).

The trek to Gunung Murud

From Ba' Kelalan, **Gunung Murud** presents a quite challenging but highly rewarding trek with spectacular views across the Highlands. The two-day hike requires a guide; ask at *Apple Lodge* for guide availability and prices. The trip entails a thirty-minute drive along a logging road and onto a flat trail into primary jungle. After some distance, the path steepens up the mountainside; two more hours of steady walking gets you to Church Camp, buildings constructed by local Lun Bawang evangelical groups for a three-day Christian meeting held just once a year but deserted the rest of the time. Here you spend the night, leaving early in the morning for the two-hour haul onto the Murud ridge, where for some distance you intermittently follow a plankway. You follow this onto a large rock, dubbed the "Rock Garden" which, although not technically the summit, constitutes the most accessible high point on Murud. After returning to Church camp you can rest for a while before returning back down the trail, and then travel by 4X4 back to Ba' Kelalan.

Travel details

Buses

Bintulu to: Miri (hourly; 3hr); Mukah (3 daily; 3hr); Sibu (8 daily; 4hr).
Kuching to: Bako (12 daily; 1hr); Damai Beach (every 40min; 1hr); Lundu (4 daily; 2hr); Kota Paduwan (3 daily; 1hr); Pontianak; (Indonesia; 6 daily; 8–10hr); Sarikei (3 daily; 5–6hr); Serian (1 daily; 1hr); Sibu (10 daily; 8hr); Sri Aman (6 daily; 3hr); Tebedu (1 daily; 10hr).
Limbang to: Lawas (1 daily; 5hr); Miri (1 daily; 5hr).
Miri to: Bintulu (hourly; 3hr); Kuala Baram (every 15min; 45min); Kuala Belait (6 daily; 3hr); Lambir Hills (every 30min; 40min); Sibu (hourly; 7hr).
Mukah to: Bintulu (3 daily; 3hr); Sibu (3 daily; 3hr 30min).
Sarikei to: Bintulu (4 daily; 4hr); Kuching (3 daily; 5–6hr).
Sibu to: Bintulu (8 daily; 4hr); Kuching (hourly; 8hr); Miri (hourly; 7hr); Mukah (3 daily; 3hr 30min).

Boats

Belaga to: Kapit (1 daily; 6hr).
Kapit to: Belaga (1 daily; 6hr); Kanowit (12 daily; 1hr 30min); Sibu (12 daily; 3hr); Song (8 daily; 1hr).
Kuala Baram to: Marudi (7 daily; 3hr).
Kuching to: Sarikei (1 daily; 3hr); Sibu (1 daily; 5hr).
Limbang to: Labuan (1 daily; 2hr); Lawas (1 daily; 1hr).
Marudi to: Kuala Baram (7 daily; 3hr); Long Terewan (1 daily; 4hr).
Sarikei to: Kuching (2 daily; 2–3hr); Sibu (2 daily; 1–2hr).
Rumah Tambi to: Song (1 daily; 3hr).

Song to: Kapit (8 daily; 1 hr); Kanowit (8 daily; 2hr); Rumah Tambi (1 daily; 3hr); Sibu (8 daily; 2hr).
Sibu to: Kapit (12 daily; 3hr); Kuching (1 daily; 4hr); Song (8 daily; 2hr).

Flights

Ba Kelalan to: Bario (2 weekly; 40min); Lawas (2 weekly; 35min).
Bario to: Ba Kelalan (2 weekly; 40min); Marudi (1 daily; 40min); Miri (2 daily; 50min).
Bintulu to: Kota Kinabalu (2 daily; 1hr 15min); Kuala Lumpur (4 daily; 2hr 10min); Kuching (2 daily; 1hr); Miri (4 daily; 35min); Mukah (1 daily; 35min); Sibu (3 daily; 1hr).
Kuching to: Bintulu (1–2 daily; 1hr); Johor Bahru (4 daily; 1hr 20min); Kota Kinabalu (6 daily; 2hr 20min); Kuala Lumpur (17 daily; 1hr 40min); Miri (7 daily; 1hr); Mukah (2 daily; 1hr 10min); Cibu (10 daily; 40min).
Lawas to: Ba Kalalan (2 weekly; 35min); Limbang (2 weekly; 20min); Miri (5 daily; 45min).
Limbang to: Lawas (2 weekly; 20min); Miri (3 daily; 35min).
Long Banga to: Marudi (1 weekly; 50min); Miri (2 weekly; 1hr).
Long Lellang to: Marudi (1 weekly; 30min); Miri (2 weekly; 1hr).
Long Seridan to: Marudi (1 weekly; 30min); Miri (2 weekly; 1hr).
Marudi to: Bario (1 daily; 40min); Long Banga (1 weekly; 1hr); Long Lellang (1 weekly; 1hr); Long Seridan (1 weekly; 1hr); Miri (4 daily; 20min).
Miri to: Bintulu (4 daily; 35min); Johor Bahru (8 weekly; 2hr); Kota Kinabalu (6 daily; 1hr 40min); Kuala Lumpur (8 daily; 2hr 15min); Kuching

(5 daily; 1hr); Labuan (4 daily; 40min); Lawas
(5 daily; 45min); Limbang (3 daily; 35min); Long
Banga (2 weekly; 1hr); Long Lellang (2 weekly;
1hr); Long Seridan (2 weekly; 1hr); Marudi (4 daily;
20min); Mukah (1–2 daily; 1hr); Mulu (1–2 daily;
40min); Sibu (2 daily; 1hr).
Mukah to: Bintulu (1 daily; 35min); Kuching
(2 daily; 1hr 10min); Miri (1–2 daily, 1hr); Sibu
(1 daily; 25min).

Mulu to: Miri (1–2 daily; 40min).
Sibu to: Bintulu (4 daily; 35min); Johor Bahru
(6 weekly; 1hr 30min); Kota Kinabalu (2 daily;
1hr 40min); Kuala Lumpur (4 daily; 1hr 45min);
Kuching (10 daily; 40min); Miri (2 daily; 1hr);
Mukah (1 daily; 25min).

Sabah

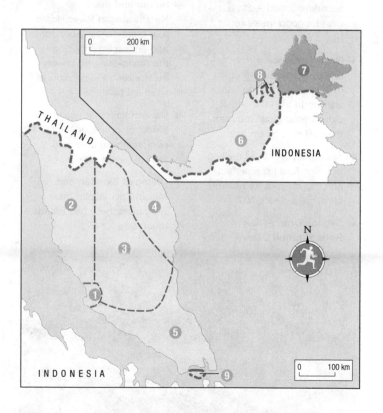

CHAPTER 7

Highlights

✱ **KK cuisine** You're never short of a new shrine to foodie bliss in Sabah's lively capital, Kota Kinabalu. **See p.497**

✱ **Pulau Tiga** "Survivor Island" is a veritable paradise with amazing beaches, stylish accommodation – and a mud bath for good measure. **See p.508**

✱ **Gunung Kinabalu** The arduous climb to see dawn over the South China Sea is well worth the effort – just expect aching calf muscles the next day. **See p.519**

✱ **Sandakan** An ethnic melting pot, Sandakan is a perfect jumping-off spot for nearby attractions. **See p.527**

✱ **Sepilok Orang-Utan Rehabilitation Centre** Orphaned and injured orang-utans are nursed back to health in this popular rainforest reserve; visitors get to observe scheduled feeding sessions. **See p.535**

✱ **Sukau and the Kinabatangan River** Home to a great diversity of bird and animal life including the orang-utan, proboscis monkey and the occasional elephant herd. **See p.538**

✱ **Danum Valley** Stunning stretches of untouched rainforest with treks and wildlife galore. **See p.542**

✱ **Diving at Sipadan and Mabul** Spectacular marine life makes these two islands a must. **See p.545**

▲ Snorkelling

Sabah

U ntil European powers began to gain a foothold here in the nineteenth century, **SABAH**, at the northern tip of Borneo, was inhabited by tribal peoples who had only minimal contact with the outside world, thus preserving their unique costumes, traditions and languages. But since joining the Malaysian Federation at its foundation in 1963, Sabah has undergone rapid modernization, its various peoples largely exchanging traditional indigenous ways for a collective Malaysian identity. As the state's cultural landscape has changed, so has its environment; the **logging** industry has decimated much of the state's natural forests, the cleared regions often used to plant thousands of acres of oil palm, a monoculture which has little truck with ecological diversity. This agro-industry, however, offers thousands work and generates much-needed income into the state coffers.

Thankfully, this bleak picture neglects the natural riches on view in a fertile region, whose name – according to some sources – goes back to biblical times and means "the land below the wind" (Sabah's 72,500 square kilometres lie just south of the typhoon belt). Within the state are a variety of **terrains**, from wild, swampy, mangrove-tangled coastal areas, through the dazzling greens of paddy fields and pristine rainforests to the dizzy heights of the Crocker Mountain Range – home to the highest mountain peak between the Himalayas and New Guinea, **Gunung Kinabalu** (Mount Kinabalu).

Many varieties of dialect are spoken by Sabah's ethnic groups, which number over a dozen. The peoples of the **Kadazan/Dusun** tribes constitute the largest indigenous racial group; then there are the **Murut** of the southwest, and Sabah's so-called "sea gypsies", the **Bajau**. More recently, Sabah, which has a popualtion of over three million, has seen a huge influx of Filipino and Indonesian immigrants, particularly on its east coast. **Tamus**, or market fairs, usually held weekly in towns and villages across the state, are a wonderful opportunity for visitors to take in the colourful mixture of cultures. Two such large fairs are held on Sundays, one at Jalan Gaya, in the capital Kota Kinabalu, the other in the small town of Kota Belud, two hours north by bus.

Sabah's **urban centres** are not very attractive or historically rich places: World War II bombs and hurried urban redevelopment have conspired to produce a capital city and a chain of towns devoid of much architectural worth. But what places like **Kota Kinabalu** (KK) and **Sandakan** lack in notable buildings they make for in atmosphere and energy. A walk through their streets is always an event; whether watching the day develop in Sandakan's gargantuan general market or choosing where to eat along KK's Jalan Pantai.

From KK, the trunk road north climbs into Bajau country and eastwards through **dipterocarp forest** onto the huge granite shelves of the awesome

SABAH

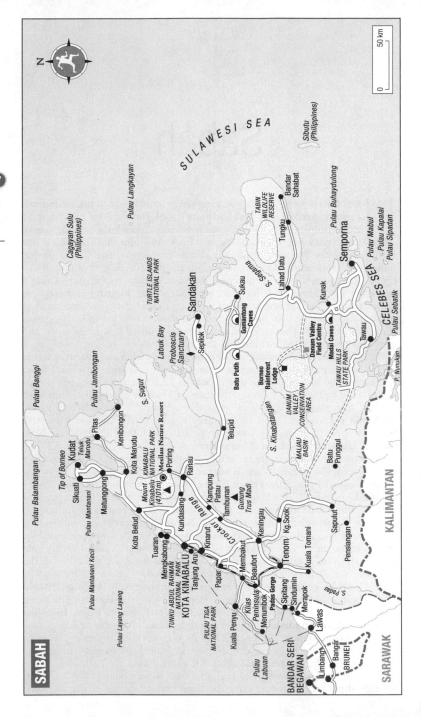

Gunung Kinabalu. Further north are the beaches and coconut groves of the small town of **Kudat**, where the few remaining longhouses of the Rungus tribe can be visited; the region north of here was recently coined the Tip of Borneo, and offers windy shorelines and splendid isolation. Eastwards is **Sandakan**, a rapidly modernizing town, mostly used as a jumping-off point for visits to offshore Pulau Selingan in the **Turtle Islands National Park**, where you're likely to see a turtle laying her eggs, and the nearby **Sepilok Orang-utan Rehabilitation Centre**, where you can view orang-utans at feeding times and walk on plankways in the rainforest reserve.

Deeper into the forests of east Sabah lies a small riverside kampung, **Sukau**. Visitors then travel the lower reaches of the **Kinabatangan River**, which supports families of proboscis monkeys, elephants and wild orang-utans. Further south from here, the **Danum Valley Conservation Area** has embarked on a programme of ecotourism, its *Borneo Rainforest Lodge* offering visitors a luxurious environment from which to enjoy a spectacular canopy walkway revealing the splendours of the rainforest. Also in this region, close to **Lahud Datu**, lies **Tabin Wildlife Reserve**, with a mud volcano and an often-spotted elephant colony.

Sabah practicalities

Sabah is 600km away from the Peninsula. Prices are on a par with Sarawak, but if you want to take advantage of the region's unique wildlife and nature, it can take a large chunk out of your budget.

Getting there

Kota Kinabalu (KK), almost certain to be your first port of call in Sabah, is particularly well served by **flights** from the mainland and from other Asian hubs. From the Peninsula, AirAsia flies from KL, Johor Bahru and Penang, and MAS from KL. AirAsia also goes to KK from Chenzhen in China, Jakarta in Indonesia, Manila in the Philippines and from Singapore. MAS also has international flights to KK from Bandar Seri Begawan, Cebu in the Philippines, Guangzhou and Hong Kong in China, Kaohsiung and Taipei in Taiwan, Seoul-Incheon in South Korea (shared with Korean Airlines), Singapore and Tokyo. As regards domestic services, MASwings flies into KK from Sarawak's Bintulu, Miri, Sibu and Kuching and from other Sabah locations: Labuan, Sandakan, Tawau and Lahad Datu.

A regular **boat** service runs from Muara in **Brunei**, and from **Lawas** in northern Sarawak, to Pulau Labuan, from where there are fast sea connections to KK. There's also a daily ferry from northeastern **Kalimantan** to Tawau and a weekly ferry from Zamboanga in the **Philippines** to Sandakan. The only **overland route** into Sabah is from Lawas, which is a short bus ride away from the border at Merapok, close to Sipitang (see p.509).

Getting around

The most common forms of public transport on both local and long-distance routes are **buses** and **minivans**. Minivans travel at all times but in contrast, **buses** are most plentiful early in the morning. Landcruisers, or **4X4s**, are the most comfortable, though appreciably more expensive than other options, and just used for travelling upcountry, for example from Keningau to Sapulut in the south or for the Tawau-Keningau loop. Taking **internal flights** makes sense and is inexpensive. For example, the route from KK to Lahad Datu – for onward travel to Semporna – costs around RM100 and takes just fifty minutes by plane compared to ten hours plus by bus. Sabah is crisscrossed by a good plane network, operated by **MASwings** and **AirAsia** with flights between KK, Kudat, Lahad Datu, Sandakan and Tawau.

7

SABAH

In the deep south, accessible via the boon town of Tawau, nestles the untouched forest sector, the **Maliau Basin**, now open for first-degree trekking. The trails here are particularly challenging: you need to have the kind of insurance cover that can pay for getting you out by helicopter, if need be.

For divers, the islands of **Sipadan**, Mabul and their northernly neighbours are the jewel in Sabah's crown. Sipadan offers superb deep diving off a coral wall; its neighbour Mabul is rated as one of the world's top muck dives; and on Kapalai, a snorkeller's paradise, shallow waters lap pure-white sand bars.

Some history

Little is known of Sabah's **early history**, though archeological finds in limestone caves in the east of the state indicate that the northern tip of Borneo has been inhabited for well over ten thousand years. Chinese merchants were trading with local settlements by 700 AD, and by the fourteenth century, the tract of land now known as Sabah came under the sway of the sultans of Brunei and Sulu, though its isolated communities of hunter-gatherers would generally have been unaware of this fact. Europe's superpowers first arrived in 1521, when the ships of the Portuguese navigator Ferdinand Magellan stopped off at Brunei and later sailed northwards. But it was to be nearly 250 years before any colonial settlement occurred, when – in 1763 – one Captain Cowley established a short-lived trading post on Pulau Balambangan, an island north of Kudat, on behalf of the **British East India Company**. Further colonial involvement came in 1846, when Pulau Labuan (at the mouth of Brunei Bay) was ceded to the British by the Sultan of Brunei, and by 1881 the **British North Borneo Chartered Company** had full sovereignty over northern Borneo.

First steps were then taken towards making the territory pay its way: rubber, tobacco and, after 1885, timber, were commercially harvested. By 1905 a **rail line** linked the coastal town of **Jesselton** (later called Kota Kinabalu) with the resource-rich interior. When the company introduced taxes, the locals were understandably displeased and native resistance followed – **Mat Salleh**, the son of a Bajau chief, and his followers sacked the company's settlement on Pulau Gaya in 1897. Another uprising, in **Rundum** in 1915, resulted in the slaughter of hundreds of Murut tribespeople by British forces.

No other major disturbances troubled the Chartered Company until New Year's Day, 1942, when the Japanese Imperial forces invaded Pulau Labuan; less than three weeks later Sandakan fell. The years of **World War II** were devastating ones for Japanese-occupied Sabah and by the time of the Japanese surrender on September 9, 1945, next to nothing of Jesselton and Sandakan remained standing. Even worse were the hardships that the captured Allied troops and civilians endured – culminating in the infamous Death March of 1945 (see p.526).

Unable to finance the rebuilding of North Borneo, the Chartered Company sold the territory to the British Crown in 1946, and Jesselton was declared the new capital of the **Crown Colony of North Borneo**. However, within fifteen years, plans had been laid for an independent federation consisting of Malaya, Singapore, Sarawak, North Borneo and Brunei. Although Brunei pulled out at the last minute, the **Federation** was still proclaimed at midnight on September 15, 1963, with North Borneo renamed Sabah.

Relations with federal Kuala Lumpur have seldom been smooth, but differences had seemed to narrow when, in 1985, the opposition **Parti Bersatu Sabah** (PBS), led by the Christian Joseph Pairin Kitingan, was returned to office in the state elections – the first time a non-Muslim had attained power in a Malaysian state. Anti-federal feelings were worsened by the fact that much of the profits from Sabah's flourishing **crude oil** exports were being siphoned off to KL. Pairin held power in the 1994 **state elections** but in recent years local BN-aligned parties have taken power across east Malaysia by 2008 only one seat was held by an opposition politician. Nowadays, central government is sticking by the policy of patching up long-running, cross-state disunity to further realize Malaysia's vision of a multi-ethnic, but Muslim-dominated, nation.

Kota Kinabalu and around

First impressions of **KOTA KINABALU**, which everyone calls KK, is of a rather utilitarian concrete sprawl, but it's not long before visitors are charmed by the friendliness of its citizens, the lively buzz which characterizes its bars, cafés and markets and its proximity to a clutch of idyllic islands. It also has excellent transport links whether by air, sea or road and is the headquarters of most of the main tour operators, which are a vital resource whether you are diving, visiting remote islands or capitalizing on the state's abundant natural wonders. The city has just a few specific sights, the best of which are its markets, the **State Museum** and – 3km north of the city centre at Likas Bay – the **Sabah Foundation (Yayasan Sabah) Complex** and close by, the **Bird Sanctuary**. Kampung Tanjung Aru – now really an extension of KK – is also worth visiting to eat seafood, look around the five-star *Shangri-La Tanjung Aru Resort* or just relax on the attractive beach. The highlight of any extended stay is, though, the offshore **Tunku Abdul Rahman Park**, whose five unspoilt islands (including the exquisite Pulau Gaya), are just a short trip away by boat. Three of the islands, Manukan, Sapi and Gaya are easy to visit on a day-trip, although you can choose to overnight on any of them.

Some history

Modern-day KK can trace its history back to 1882, the year the British North Borneo Chartered Company first established an outpost on nearby **Pulau Gaya**. After this was burned down by followers of the Bajau rebel, Mat Salleh, in 1897, the Company chose a mainland site for a new town which was known to locals as *Api Api*, or "Fire, Fire". One explanation for the name was that it referred to the firing of the original settlement; another, that it reflected the abundance of fireflies inhabiting its swamps. Renamed **Jesselton**, after Sir Charles Jessel, the vice-chairman of the Chartered Company, the town prospered. By 1905, the Trans-Borneo Railway reached from Jesselton to Beaufort, meaning that for the first time, rubber could be transported efficiently from the interior to the coast.

The Japanese invasion of North Borneo in 1942 marked the start of three and a half years of **military occupation**: of old Jesselton, only the Atkinson Clock Tower, the red-roofed Land and Surveys Building and the post office (today's tourist office) survived the resulting Allied bombing. In 1967 the name was changed to Kota Kinabalu and city planners set about expanding outwards into the sea. On the resulting tracts of reclaimed land, interconnecting concrete buildings have been constructed – the Sinsuran and Segama complexes and Asia

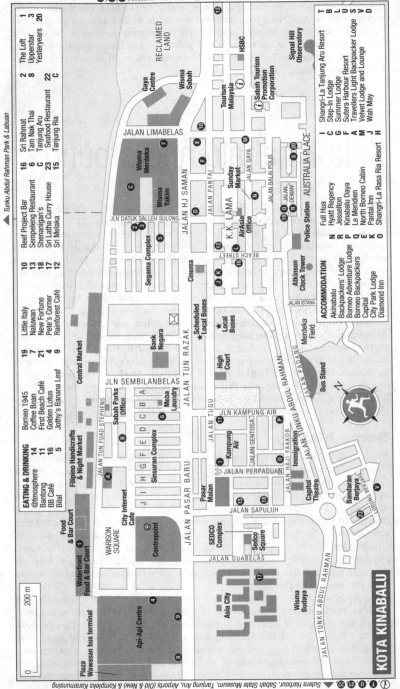

KOTA KINABALU

7 SABAH

Tunku Abdul Rahman Park & Labuan

490

▲ *Sutera Harbour, Sabah State Museum, Tanjung Aru, Airports (Old & New) & Kompleks Karamunsing*

EATING & DRINKING

@tmosphere	14
Bantong	11
BB Café	16
Bilal	5
Borneo 1945	19
Coffee Bean	21
First Beach Café	4
Golden Lotus	9
Jothy's Banana Leaf	5
Little Italy	10
Naluwan	13
New Fortune	18
Pete's Corner	12
Rainforest Café	9
Reef Project Bar	10
Sempeleng Restaurant	13
Shenanigan's	18
Sri Latha Curry House	17
Sri Melaka	12
Sri Rahmat	16
Tam Nak Thai	6
Tanjung Aru	C
Seafood Restaurant	23
Tanjung Ria	15
The Loft	1
Upperstar	3
Yesteryears	20

ACCOMMODATION

Akinabalu	N
Backpackers' Lodge	R
Borneo Adventure Lodge	P
Borneo Backpackers	Q
Capital	E
City Park Lodge	K
Diamond Inn	H
Full Hua	N
Hyatt Regency	R
Kinabalu Daya	P
Le Meridien	Q
North Borneo Cabin	E
Pantai Inn	K
Shangri-La Rasa Ria Resort	O
Shangri-La Tanjung Aru Resort	I
Step-In Lodge	C
Summer Lodge	G
Sutera Harbour Resort	F
Travellers Light Backpacker Lodge	A
Velvet Lodge and Lounge	M
Wah May	J

City in particular have developed their own identities. Progress has been startling, and today, with a population of over a quarter of a million, KK is a beehive of activity once again.

Arrival and information

KK International Airport (KKIA) has two terminals a few kilometres from each other. **Terminal 1**, 7km south of the centre, is a vast, gleaming affair covering international destinations, while **Terminal Two**, 5km from the centre and close to Kampung Tanjung Aru, is used exclusively by AirAsia for its international and domestic flights. Terminal 1 is served by City Bus 1 and terminal 2 by City Bus 2, both taking passengers to the city bus stand on Jalan Tugu (every 30min; daily 7am–7pm). Most travellers, though, opt for a **taxi** (RM20; coupon from taxi kiosk in arrivals; RM25 after 10pm).

Long-distance **buses** from Sandakan and elsewhere north of KK arrive at City Bus Terminal North (CBTN), 8km east of the city centre in the suburb of Inanam. Short-hop buses between CBTN and Jalan Tugu, run every twenty minutes (6am–8pm). Arriving at CBTN outside these hours requires a taxi (RM12) from directly outside the terminal. **Buses** from southern Sabah arrive at the Merdeka Field bus stand on Jalan Tunku Abdul Rahman, Kampung Air. **Ferries** from Labuan and the Tunku Abdul Rahman Islands arrive at the Jesselton Point Ferry Terminal, east of the centre, on Jalan Haji Sarnan.

The **Sabah Tourism Board** (STB; Mon–Fri 8am–5pm, Sat & Sun 9am-4pm; ☎088/212121, ⓦwww.sabahtourism.com) is in the old GPO at 51 Jalan Gaya. The friendly staff can help with just about anything – ask for the excellent free tourist **map** of KK. **Tourism Malaysia** (Mon–Fri 8.30am–4.30pm, Sat 8.30am–noon; ☎088/248698, ⓦwww.tourism.gov.my), ground floor, 107, Api-Api Centre, Jalan Pasar Baru, is also stocked with leaflets on Sabah, but better at answering questions about Peninsular Malaysia or Sarawak.

For information about the environment and ecology of Sabah's National Parks, visit the **Sabah Parks office** (Mon–Thurs 8am–1pm & 2–4.30pm, Fri 8–11.30am & 2–4.30pm, Sat 8am–12.50pm; ☎088/211881, ⓦwww.sabahparks.org.my), which faces the South China Sea at Block K of the Sinsuran Complex, Jalan Tun Fuad Stephens, opposite the Central Market. The website has an excellent overview of Sabah's protected areas, facilities and ecology.

What's on information is in relatively short supply in KK; the **noticeboards** at guesthouses, however, are invaluable sources of information on matters as diverse as learning about the Maliau Basin or checking the latest and tastiest hawker stalls to eat at in KK.

City transport

The city centre is compact enough to cover on foot inside an hour. **Taxis** are inexpensive – it costs no more than RM8 to travel right across the city centre. There are taxi ranks outside the *Hyatt* hotel on Jalan Datuk Salleh Sulong; at the GPO on Jalan Tun Razak; along Jalan Perpaduan (close to the spot used by the long-distance buses) in Kampung Air; and at Centre Point Mall on Jalan Pasar Baru.

There is not one specific local bus station; buses congregate at the Jalan Tugu bus stand for northern suburbs including Likas Bay and the CBTN at Inanam, and beside the Milimewa supermarket on Jalan Haji Saman for outlying southern locations, including Tanjung Aru and KKIA terminals. Minivans also draw up on Jalan Haji Saman for trips south.

Accommodation

KK is king when it comes to **accommodation** in east Malaysia; its backpackers ranking is among the best in Malaysia. In addition, the mid-range hotels are tremendous and – when you want to spoil yourself – the high-end ones, and resorts, are top-notch too. The bulk of the **backpacker hostels** and **hotels** are evenly spread across the city, with the most popular quarter around Jalan Pantai and Jalan Gaya and in nearby Australia Place. Note that most are set above shopfronts on the first, second and third floors.

For the resorts, you need to head out of the city – the *Shangri-La Tanjung Aru Resort*, for example, is 4km south of the centre near KKIA terminal 2 while *Sutera Harbour* is close to KKIA terminal 1.

Hostels

Akinabalu Floors 1–4, 133 Jalan Gaya ☏088/272188, ✉akinabaluyh@yahoo.com. Inexpensive backpackers' place with clean, fairly spacious four- to six-bed dorms, compact double rooms and an airy communal area. Dorm beds RM20, ❸.

Backpacker's Lodge Lot 25, Lorong Dewan, Australia Place ☏088/261495, ✉backpackerkk @yahoo.com. Also known as *Lucy's Homestay*, this homely, cluttered place with small four- and six-bed dorms, TV, library and washing facilities is a KK institution. Dorm beds RM18, ❸.

Borneo Adventure Lodge 2 Lorong 1, Kampung Air ☏088/241515, ✉borneoadventurecenter @yahoo.com. This labyrinthine complex has tidy doubles and small dorms. Located close to the minivans for Gunung Kinabalu Park, seldom crowded and run by a friendly staff, this is a good choice. Dorm beds RM21, ❸.

Borneo Backpackers Lorong Dewan ☏088/234009, ⓦwww.borneobackpackers.com. Set up by the man behind the excellent Borneo Eco Tours, and managed by the energetic Ali, this is an excellent place, tucked away on a side street in Australia Place, and backing onto the jungle. As well as one double room and a number of four- to ten-bed dorms, there is a communal area with TV and internet, plus an interesting museum/coffee shop downstairs. Dorm beds RM20, ❸.

North Borneo Cabin 74 Jalan Gaya ☏088/272800, ⓦwww.northborneocabin.com. In the main café and bar district, this backpacker hangout has a large open communal room, neat doubles and dorms, at RM20 per bed. ❸

Step-In Lodge Block L, Kompleks Sinsuran, ☏088/233519, ⓦwww.stepinlodge.com. Very popular addition to KK's backpacker action,

Step-In has info galore about trips, treks, guides and rides. Dorms (RM25 per bed) are a little pricier, and smaller, than elsewhere. ❸

Summer Lodge 120 Jalan Gaya ☏088/244499, ⓦwww.summerlodge.com. The *Summer* has prime position above the Beach Street action. A magnet for young travellers, this place has small, functional doubles, compact dorms (RM18) and free internet. ❸

Travellers Light Backpacker Lodge 19 Lorong Dewan, Australia Place ☏088/238877, ✉tvlodge @live.com. Small and very quiet place tucked up against the KK hill, with cosy doubles and adequate six-bed dorms (RM25). ❸

Velvet Lodge and Lounge First floor, 56 Lorong Berjaya 5, Bandan Berjaya ☏088/212196, ✉velvet@streamyx.com. Run by Joe and Crystal, this lodge is very much a family business with smart contemporary design and well-priced, lovely doubles. ❸

Hotels

Capital 23 Jalan Haji Saman ☏088/231999. Light and comfortable rooms with a/c and terrestrial TV, though the hotel has few other amenities. ❻

City Park Lodge 49 Jalan Pantai ☏088/257752, ✉cplodge@streamyx.com. Competing with the *Pantai* next door, the *City* has small rooms, cell-like windows and rather grubby bathrooms – problems somewhat offset by its reasonable rates, prime location and very friendly staff. ❹

Diamond Inn Block 37, Kampung Air ☏088/213222. Centrally placed, this comfortable and friendly hotel is not as clean as it once was, but is still a bargain. ❸

Full Hua 14 Jalan Tugu, Kampung Air ☏088/234950, ✉hotelfh@hotmail.com. Superbly

7

▲ Kampung Air, Kota Kinabalu

positioned for Kampung Air's vibrant atmosphere, this popular, friendly place has small, neat en-suite rooms with a/c and TV. ④

Hyatt Regency Jalan Dutuk Salleh Sulong ☎088/221234, ⓦkinabalu.regency.hyatt .com. The elegant, four-star *Hyatt* is quite simply one of Southeast Asia's best city-centre hotels. From its sprawling dining area, with three enormous buffet spreads three times a day, to the wonderful swimming pool and the perfectly appointed rooms with lovely bathrooms and satellite-TV with views towards the TAR Park islands, the *Hyatt* ticks all the boxes. ⑦

Jesselton 69 Jalan Gaya ☎088/223333, ⓦwww .jesseltonhotel.com. Lady Mountbatten and Muhammad Ali are just two of this KK's institution's most famous guests. Run by an ebullient Texan lady, the *Jesselton* is suavely positioned in between the busy commercial sector and more laid-back Australia Place. Near-perfect rooms and an excellent restaurant-coffee shop make this hard to beat and, like others in KK, promotional prices are often on offer. ⑥

Kinabalu Daya Lot 3, 9 Jalan Pantai ☎088/240000, ⓦwww.kinabaluhotel .com. Excellent mid-range establishment, perfectly placed in the busy northern section of town, opposite shoppers' paradise, Wisma Merdeka. The rooms are snug and en suite and there's a ground-floor café and an alfresco bar. ⑤

Le Meridien Kota Kinabalu Jalan Tun Fuad Stephens ☎088/322250, ⓦwww.kotakinabalu .lemeridien.com. What's quite bizarre about *Le Meridien* is that its sumptious facilties (including high spec rooms, bars, restaurants, pool and gym) are located opposite the lively – and edgy – Filipino night market, one of the chief centres of action in town. ⑧

Pantai Inn 56 Jalan Pantai ☎088/217095. Functional rooms to an adequate standard in this busy central spot popular with out-of-town locals. ④

Wah May 36 Jalan Haji Saman ☎088/266118, ⓦwww.wahmayhotel.com. This is a friendly place with compact rooms and neat bathrooms in a central location. ⑤

Resort hotels

Shangri-La Rasa Ria Resort Dalit Bay, Tuaran ☎088/792888, ⓦwww.shangri-la.com. This massive resort is set 30km north of KK on a gorgeous bay in an idyllic location. Swimming pools, excellent buffets and a relaxed atmosphere make it close to paradise. The grounds include a large forest nature reserve where monkeys can be spotted and there are even a few resident orang-utans. Shuttle bus to/from KK available (RM20). Although prices are high, good-value promotional rates are often available on enquiry. ⑧

Shangri-La Tanjung Aru Resort Tanjung Aru Beach ☎088/225800, ⓦwww.shangri-la.com.

Five kilometres southwest of the centre and set in rolling, landscaped grounds, this luxury hotel boasts two pools, water-sports and fitness centres, several food outlets and prices to match. Hourly shuttle buses ensure easy access to the city and the resort speedboats to TAR Park's Manukan Island promise a swift getaway when needed. ⑨ **Sutera Harbour Resort** (*Pacific* and *Magellan* hotels) 1 Sutera Harbour Blvd, Sutera Harbour ☎ 088/317777, ⓦ www.suteraharbour.com.

This spectacular shore-side development, 1km south of the centre, boasts two contrasting venues: *Pacific* (⑦) is more functional – designed with business and family needs to the fore – whereas *Magellan* (⑧) adopts a more luxurious longhouse design. There's a marina park squeezed between the two, massive golf course and no fewer than seventeen swimming pools in all. The hotels are often full, as travel agencies from China, Japan and South Korea block-book far in advance. ⑨

The City

There is little left of heritage KK, given the destruction caused in World War II. There are though a few surviving buildings worth taking a quick look at, namely the old General Post Office (now housing the Sabah Tourism Board) and on Signal Hill, **Atkinson's Clock Tower**. Down from the Clock Tower is **Australia Place**, and two blocks across from here is the northern part of commercial KK, **Jalan Gaya** and **Jalan Pantai**, where you will find many of the mid-range hotels, the entertainment hub around the *Hyatt* hotel and the refurbished plaza, **Wisma Merdeka**. Southwest along the city's central artery, Jalan Tun Razak, leads to **Kampung Air** and **Sinsuran**, two utilitarian blocks housing many of the city's best inexpensive cafés, backpacker places and hotels. Close by is the transport hub, the **Merdeka Fields bus stand** and the padang, where civic and cultural events frequently take place. Further west on Tun Razak's extension, Jalan Pasar Baru, you'll find the plazas **Centre Point** and **Warisan Square** and the restaurants in **Asia City**, on the south side of the road, and **Api-Api Centre** to the north. Crossing over Jalan Pasar Baru, along the side of Centre Point gets you to the **Waterfront**, where an esplanade leads back eastwards passing dozens of cafés and restaurants before reaching the night market, the handicrafts market and the two-storey **Central Market**. The water-front path ends at Wisma Merdeka, on Jalan Tun Fuad Stephens, and 200m further on, the Jesselton Point Ferry terminal.

Signal Hill and Australia Place

A ten-minute walk along Jalan Istana onto the lower reaches of Signal Hill is **Atkinson's Clock Tower**, built to commemorate the first district official of Jesselton, Francis George Atkinson, who contracted malaria and died in 1902. Although of little architectural importance, the robust wooden landmark occupies a lovely vantage point overlooking the padang and the city. A further twenty-minute walk up the hill on Jalan Bukit Bandera gets to the Signal Hill Observatory, with its dramatic view over the city, the South China Sea and the islands in the TAR park (best at sunset). Early photographs of the city show colonial officers playing cricket on the padang below. Retracing your steps on Jalan Istana and turning onto Jalan Dewan leads to Australia Place, a warren of lorongs and site of the original Chinese timber shophouses – stop at the elegant washboard building, the Community Hall. The area is so named because the Australian Liberation Army made camp here after landing in KK in 1945. *Borneo Backpackers* now houses a coffee shop-cum-museum, **Borneo 1945**, its walls displaying wartime photographs of Australian and British soldiers, local unsung heroes, as well as replicas of war memorial plaques in Sabah.

North KK

One block north of Australia Place, across the busy artery Jalan Belai Polis, lies **Jalan Gaya**, KK's most elegant street, lined with stylish Chinese *kedai kopis*; its chief landmarks are the city's oldest and most beautiful hotel, the *Jesselton*, and, a few metres away, the wood-boarded, *belian*-tiled, old **Post Office**, now housing the Sarawak Tourism Board. A lively street **market** is held along Jalan Gaya every Sunday, with stalls selling items as disparate as herbal teas, handicrafts, orchids and rabbits while nearby coffee shops do a roaring trade in dim sum and noodles. Connecting Jalan Gaya with Jalan Pantai is Beach Street, a pedestrianized area of cafés and fast-food outlets, which has become the nerve centre of backpacker KK. Across Jalan Pantai is the four-storey **Wisma Merdeka**, housing dozens of boutiques, cut-price retail stores, electrical outlets, coffee shops and on the top floor, an excellent food court, offering a wide array of Malay, Indian and Chinese dishes throughout the day. Beyond Wisma Merdeka is Wisma Sabah, where many of the **tour operators** specializing in nature tours and diving are based.

Mid-town and the waterfront

It's a ten-minute stroll from Jalan Gaya across town to the older commercial centres, **Kampung Air** and **Sinsuran**, functional blocks with clusters of cafés, restaurants, budget accommodation and markets. Although Kampung Air has at its centre a small evening market, of more interest are the markets lined along the waterfront one further block north, the most diverting of which is the Filipino Handicrafts Market, opposite the Sinsuran Complex. The warren of stalls are run by Indonesian and Filipino immigrants, who stock Sabahian ethnic wares beside their own baskets, shells and trinkets. Next door is the dark and labyrinthine Central Market (6am–6pm) – the first floor has dozens of daytime food stalls – and, behind that, the manic waterfront fish market – worth investigating if you can stomach the smell. At dusk, the **Handicrafts Market** area transforms into a gargantuan maze of food stalls, offering rice, noodle and vegetable dishes as well as barbecued meats and fish.

Sabah State Museum

The **Sabah State Museum** (℡088/253199; daily except Fri 9am–5pm; RM15) can be reached on the State Museum bus from Jalan Haji Saaman or by taxi (RM10); however, the twenty-minute walk there is interesting enough, taking you southwest along Jalan Tunku Abdul Rahman, past the pyramidal Catholic **Sacred Heart Cathedral**, turning left at a roundabout before the **Sabah State Mosque**, whose eye-catching dome sits, like a Fabergé egg, on top of the main body of the complex.

The museum buildings are styled after Murut and Rungus longhouses and set in exotic grounds that are home to several splendid steam engines. Its highlight is the **ethnographic collection** which features a *bangkaran*, or cluster of human skulls, dating from Sabah's head-hunting days; and a *sininggazanak*, a totemic wooden figurine which would have been placed in the field of a Kadazan man who had died leaving no heirs. Photographs in the history gallery trace the development of Kota Kinabalu – look out for an intriguing picture of

Jesselton at a time when Jalan Gaya still constituted the waterfront, lined with lean-tos thatched with *nipah*-palm leaves.

The **Science and Technology Centre** (same hours as museum; free), next door to the museum, houses less-than-gripping exhibitions on oil-drilling and broadcasting technology, so head upstairs to the **Art Gallery** (same hours) instead. Its centrepiece is a giant string of Rungus beads, created by Chee Sing Teck, hanging from the ceiling.

Fronting the museum is a **botanical garden** (daily 8am–5pm; free), whose range of tropical plants is best experienced on one of the free guided tours (daily except Fri at 9am & 2pm). Finely crafted traditional houses representing all Sabah's major tribes border the garden, in the Kampung Warisan, or Heritage Village.

Tanjung Aru

Past the museum, Jalan Tunku Abdul Rahman continues on for another 3km (becoming Jalan Mat Salleh) to the **beach** at Tanjung Aru, site of the swanky and sprawling *Shangri-La Tanjung Aru Resort* beyond. Bus #2 from the city centre's Jalan Haji Saman runs here. The long, narrow beach itself isn't spectacular, and given that there are so many beautiful islands just off the coast, there's no great incentive to visit other than at weekends, when large numbers of locals come for satay and barbecued seafood sold at the food and drink stalls. For better cuisine and a quieter setting, go back along the main road 100m, turning left into Kampung Tanjung Aru, a small grid of streets which manage to retain a village feel. Here there are a number of *kedai kopis* popular with locals, and seldom visited by the well-heeled visitors to the *Shangri-La* resort hotel, 200m away.

Likas Bay

Designated as a bird sanctuary in 1996, **Kota Kinabalu City Botanical Park**, Jalan Bukit Bendahara Upper (℡088/262420, ⓔlikaswetlands@hotmail.com; Tues–Sun 8am–6pm; RM10), comprises 24 hectares of mangrove forest, 3km north of the city centre; it's the only remaining patch of an extensive mangrove system that once covered this coastline. The site is an important refuge and feeding ground for many species of resident birds, as well as several migratory species from northern Asia.

There are a number of marked trails on **boardwalks** where you may catch sight of various herons, egrets, sandpipers, pigeons and doves, but come quite early in the morning or late in the afternoon for optimum viewing conditions. Other mangrove wildlife here includes fiddler crabs, mudskippers, monitor lizards, weaver ants, water snakes and mud lobsters.

To get there it's possible to take the Likas bus (half-hourly) from the Jalan Tugu bus stand. It won't go right into the park though; ask to be dropped at the turn-off before Likas where you must walk for twenty minutes to reach the park reception. Given this, it is clearly more convenient to get a taxi from the centre (RM15).

Also at Likas Bay is the extraordinary Menara Tun Mustapha, a 28-floor glass sculpture, which is the tallest building in east Malaysia. A powerful organization tasked with protecting and managing some of Sabah's most precious natural areas (including the Maliau Basin and Danum Valley), the Yayasan Sabah HQ houses the chief minister's office and the outstanding *@tmosphere* restaurant (see p.498), on the top floor. The only convenient way of getting out to the complex is by taxi (RM20).

Eating, drinking and nightlife

In recent years KK has moved up a notch, from being merely Sabah's food capital to now one of Malaysia's best cities to eat in. The standard is high; round-the-clock outlets cover breakfast, lunch, dinner and post-club snacks; and most important, the range is wide and inventive. From the ever-expanding, waterfront **night market**, where pan-South Asian food is as its most popular, to the fantastic buffets on offer in the resort and high-end hotels, KK suits all tastes and pockets. Sabahian cuisine is less on offer, unfortunately – rather a disappointment considering the state's indigenous peoples all have their own tasty dishes.

Bear in mind that locals tend to eat quite early and many restaurants require last orders by 9.30pm. There are a few good **bars**, listed below, but generally KK is not noted for its **nightlife**, with most of the top hotels having their own bar, and occasionally, a club space too.

Hawker stalls & food courts

Central Market Jalan Tun Fuad Stephens. The *nasi campur* stalls on the upper floor provide filling, good-value meals during the day but it all closes up around 6pm.

Jesselton Point Hawkers In the daytime these stalls are quiet but in the evening they roar to life with satay, fried fish and other popular dishes. There's even an Aussie steak house (RM18 per steak) and the seating is pleasantly alfresco, looking out over the harbour toward the islands.

Night market Jalan Tun Fuad Stephens. To the west of Central Market, the narrow stretch between the road and the South China Sea is transformed at sunset by hundreds of stalls selling vegetables, fruit, juices and fish as well as spicy barbecued meats, noodles, rice and vegetables. Some stalls have tables where you can sit and eat, or else you can walk east to the new esplanade and sit on benches overlooking the TAR Park islands. Open 6–11pm.

SEDCO Square SEDCO Centre (between Jalan Sepuluh and Jalan Duabelas). Cavernous indoor food court with half a dozen outlets and hundreds of tables; majors in Chinese seafood and steamboat, and is popular with local families and tour groups. Prices vary from RM5 for satay sticks to RM50 for king prawns and fresh red snapper.

Waterfront Food and Bar Court Jalan Tun Fuad Stephens. New development in the western corner of the city overlooking the South China Sea where two dozen restaurants and cafés compete for business; just walk along the communal boardwalk, choosing from outlets such as the *Cock and Bull Bistro* (Western), *Tandoori Kebab Naan* (Indian), *Abesha Corner* (Malay) and the excellent, *Oregano Café* (Malay fusion). Daily 6pm–2am.

Wisma Merdeka Food Court In 2008 the Merdeka Plaza got a major facelift, transforming its rather nondescript and weary stalls into a gleaming array of boutiques, electrical stores and fast-food points. Set on the top floor, the food court has a couple of fantastic, inexpensive Malaysian buffet outlets which choke with life from late afternoon.

Cafés

Bantong 1 Jalan Kampung Air. Cheap, cheerful and top-notch café. Cooks David and Ian churn out enticing *iyam goring* (lemon chicken), *nasi* and the KK speciality *bonga* – greens in shrimp sauce, ginger, garlic and soy. Daily 8am–11pm (dinner menu begins at 7pm).

Borneo 1945 24 Lorong Dewan, Australia Place ☏088/272945. This stylish coffee shop, located on the ground floor of *Borneo Backpackers*, doubles as a tiny World War II museum. Smoked chicken and beef stew – in memory of wartime ration packs – are the trademark dishes and are extremely tasty. Daily 7.30am–10pm.

Coffee Bean Ground floor, Wisma Merdeka ☏088/232333. Popular but pricey Western-style coffee shop with scrumptious cakes and excellent coffee. Daily 9am–9pm.

New Fortune Block 36, Jalan Laiman Diki, Kampung Air. A busy local favourite, housing several stalls, the best of which serves superb dim sum at breakfast and later if there are any left. Daily 7am–7pm.

Pete's Corner Block B, Asia City. Neatly tiled, open-fronted corner shop serving egg, sausage and baked-bean breakfasts, omelettes and sandwiches, as well as more substantial Western meals such as steaks and chops plus Malaysian favourites, all at very affordable prices (RM15 for lamb chops). Daily 8am–6pm.

Restaurants: Malay/ Indian

Bilal Block B, Segama Complex. A classic North Indian Muslim eating house with a buffet-style range of tasty and inexpensive curries. Daily 6am–9pm.

Golden Lotus 14 Block 1, Lorong Api-Api 2. Easy to spot, just into the Api-Api Centre opposite Centre Point's western edge, this is a favourite North Indian buffet. Scrumptious curries, *biriyanis* and fried fish make it an essential stopover; daily 10am–11pm.

Jothy's Banana Leaf 1/G9, Api-Api Centre. Excellent South Indian establishment with immaculate dosai and a variety of delicious curries including vegetarian banana leaf. Daily 11am–11pm.

Naluwan 16–17 Jalan Haji Saman. A huge, cavernous place, which for a modest outlay (RM12 lunch, RM20 dinner) buys you all you can eat from a buffet that's constantly replenished with all manner of tasty pan-Asian dishes. Daily 8am–10pm.

Sempeleng Restaurant Sinsuran Complex. Slap bang in an area of KK where, from 8pm, poor families settle down for a night's sleeping on the pavement, the *Sempeleng* is the kind of place Sabah travellers dream about: cheap fruit juices, an ample buffet and Western dishes à la carte. Open daily, 24hr.

Sri Latha Curry House 33 Jalan Bandaran Berjaya. The banana-leaf curry in this simple South Indian restaurant west of Kampung Ayer is one of the best deals in KK (RM3.50 for vegetarian, RM6 for meat), accompanied by an informed and friendly staff. There's chicken *biriyani* on a Saturday (RM2.50), and *masala dosai* on Sunday (RM1.50). Daily 8am–11pm.

Sri Melaka 9 Jalan Laiman Diki, Kampung Air. Popular spot, best for Malay and Nonya food; try the excellent *asam* fish-head (RM20 portion feeds two) and *ulang ulang*, the in-season vegetable platter, which at RM10 is enough for two. Daily 11am–10pm.

Sri Rahmat Lot 7, Block D, Segama Complex. A basic, no-frills Malay restaurant (though with a/c) that's worth frequenting for the delicious *laksa* alone. Mon–Sat 7am–9pm, Sun 7am–5pm.

Tanjung Aru Seafood Restaurant Aru Drive, Tanjung Aru. Popular with tour groups, this massive sea-food emporium is a KK institution. Quite expensive at RM40 per head, but worth the price for the King prawns alone; daily 11am–2am & 5–10.30pm.

Restaurants: Pan-Asian/ fusion/Western

@mosphere Eighteenth floor, Menara Tun Mustapha Likas Bay ☎088/425100 (for reservations). Situated at the top of the tallest building in Borneo, this ultra-modern and very classy restaurant and bar is well worth the five-mile trip out from the city centre. Prices are surprisingly fair given the high quality of the pan-Asian and fusion cuisine on offer in this amazing, revolving venue. Go at sunset. Open 11am–1am.

First Beach Café Aru Drive, Tanjung Aru Beach. The main draw at this mellow café, which just serves drinks and simple meals, is its prime beach-front position for KK's famous sunset.

Little Italy Jalan Pantai/Jalan Limabelas ☎088/232231. Although setting you back around RM80 plus for two, this is a most welcome addition to KK's culinary landscape; superb pizzas, fresh salads and acceptable house wine. Daily 10am–11pm.

Rainforest Café 47 Jalan Pantai (corner of Beach St). Chef Terry Herman's relaxed eatery is a wonderful place to head for. Service may be slow and the electronic ambient music on automatic replay, but the Malay and fusion food is nourishing, well-priced and beautifully presented. Expect to pay around RM20 per head; daily 7am–midnight.

Tam Nak Thai Y/G5, Api-Api Centre ☎088/257328. Fine Thai cuisine and a pleasing ambience. Best to book, especially if you to intend to eat after 8pm. Daily 11.30am–3pm & 6–10pm.

Yesteryears 9 Lorong Dewan, Australia Place ☎088/239257. Funky little pizza house frequented by locals, tucked away down a quiet street. Reasonable prices – RM8 for a margarita – and cheap beer make this a very casual, but top spot. Daily 10am–10.30pm.

Bars and clubs

BB Café Beach St. Below the *Reef Project*, the *BB* is the city-centre's top bar for meeting other travellers, many of whom will be nursing sore legs from climbing Mount Kinabalu. Serves excellent small plates and snacks as well as a full range of beverages. 11am–midnight.

The Loft Waterfront. Spacious and well-stocked Western-style bar run by energetic locals. A wide-screen TV jammed on the sport channels specializes in all things football.

Reef Project Dance Bar Beach St. First-floor club/bar with nightly live music and a funky terrace overlooking a busy pedestrianized street. The only downsides are the expensive beer and average food. Daily 6pm–2am; occasional entry charge.

Shenanigan's *Hyatt Regency* (entrance on Jalan Datuk Salleh Sulong). KK's top town-centre bar whose staff pull English pints as well as local lagers. Features live Filipino bands nightly and a rather good international music mix from 10pm onwards at weekends, including local hits, soul, R&B and hip-hop. Mon–Thurs 6pm–1am, Fri & Sat 6pm–3am, Sun 4pm–midnight. Free entry; dress code smart (no trainers, shorts or T-shirts).

🏃 **Upperstar Café & Bar** Jalan Datuk Salleh Sulong (opposite the *Hyatt*). Youthful bar with a cracking balcony on KK's hippest street; eclectic soundtrack, friendly service, competitively priced beers and tasty tapas-style dishes. Daily noon–2am. Free entry.

Tour operators

KK has plenty of reliable and reasonably priced **tour operators** offering an immense array of trekking, rafting, diving and wildlife-watching packages. Many are based in the Wisma Sabah plaza at the eastern end of the city centre. Note that many of the locations on offer are only possible on a tour and these are often tailor-made to travellers' requirements; for this reason it's best to contact operators as far **in advance** as possible. Expect to pay around RM75 for a half-day KK city tour, or RM80 for a half-day dive; RM120 for day-trips to Tunku Abdul Rahman; RM180 for a day's white-water rafting; RM300 upwards for extended tours into the forested interior and RM1000+ for two days diving off Semporna. For other diving specialists see also the sections on Semporna (p.544) and Tawau (p.547).

Borneo Divers and Sea Sports Ninth floor, Menara Jubili, 53 Jalan Gaya ☎ 088/222226, 🌐 www.borneodivers.info. Diving specialists with a high end resort on Mabul for Sipidan dives. RM1000 for two-night stay plus dives.

Borneo Eco Tours Lot 1, Pusat Perindustrian, Kolombong Jaya, mile 5.5, Jalan Kolombong ☎ 088/438300, 🌐 www.borneoecotours.com. Ecotourism pioneer running the superb *Sukau Rainforest Lodge* on the Kinabatangan River (see p.540), the very best place to view wildlife in Sabah.

🏃 **Borneo Nature Tours** Ground floor, Lot 10, Sadong Jaya Complex ☎ 088/267637, 🌐 www.borneonaturetours.com. BNT runs the luxurious *Borneo Rainforest Lodge* (RM250 a night) in Danum Valley (nearest town Lahud Datu); it's also the only operator with a licence to take groups into the inaccessible Maliau Basin, Sabah's "lost world".

Borneo Ultimate Ground floor, Lot G29, Wisma Sabah ☎ 088/225188, 🌐 www.borneoultimate .com.my. Offers a heart-racing day white-water rafting on the Padas River for RM180 including lunch.

River Junkie Tours Ground floor, G23, Wisma Sabah ☎ 019/6012145, 🌐 www.river-junkie.com /proboscis-monkey. Part of Semporna-based Scuba

Junkie, this sister team offers white-water rafting on the Padas and Kiulu rivers and a proboscis monkey river cruise; RM180 for day trip.

🏃 **Sabah Divers** Ground floor, G27, Wisma Sabah ☎ 088/256433, 🌐 www.sabahdivers .com. Diving outfit offering excellent SSI courses (as industry-acceptable as PADI) from RM488 for beginners, as well as specializing in dives off the Tunku Abdul Rahman islands.

Seaventures Tours and Travel Fourth floor, Wisma Sabah ☎ 088/422423, 🌐 www .seaventuresdive.com. Leading, well-resourced operator offering Sipadan and Mabul diving packages from around RM1200 for three nights with morning and afternoon dives, and owner of a lodge off Mabul island, housed on a former oil rig.

Sipadan Dive Centre Eleventh floor, A1103, Wisma Merdeka ☎ 088/240584, 🌐 www .sipadandivers.com. Offers a three-day diving trip to Sipadan for around RM1300; also runs the *Pulau Tiga Resort* where the TV series *Survivor* was shot.

Wildlife Expeditions Ground floor, Tanjung Wing, *Shangri-la Tanjung Aru Resort* ☎ 088/246000, 🌐 www.wildlife-expeditions.com. Wildlife specialists with a lodge near Sukau on the Kinabatangan River, where a two-day, one-night visit, plus transport from Sandakan, costs around RM400–500 (more if including flight from KK).

Listings

Airlines AirAsia, 94 Jalan Gaya (☎ 088/284669), Mon–Sat 8.30am–5pm; MAS, tenth floor, Karamunsing Complex, Jalan Tuaran

(☎ 088/213555 or 290600), Mon–Fri 8.30am–5pm, Sat 8.30am–noon (24hr no. ☎ 1300883000), and eleventh floor, Gaya Centre, beside Wisma Sabah

(☎088/213555); Mon–Fri 9am–5pm. British Airways; Jalan Haji Sam (☎088/428057); Royal Brunei (☎088/242193), SilkAir, Block B, Plaza Tanjung Aru, Jalan Mat Salleh (☎088/265770); and Thai Airways (☎088/232896) are both on the ground floor of Kuwasa Complex.
Airport information ☎088/238555.
American Express Third floor, Lot 3.50 and 3.51, Karamunsing Complex, Jalan Tuaran ☎088/241200 (Mon–Fri 8.30am–5.30pm).
Banks and exchange HSBC, 56 Jalan Gaya; Sabah Bank, Block K, Sinsuran Complex; Standard Chartered Bank, 20 Jalan Haji Saman. Money-changers (Mon–Sat 10am–7pm) include Ban Loong Money Changer and Travellers' Money Changer, both on the ground floor of Wisma Merdeka; there's also an office in the Taiping Goldsmith, Block A, Sinsuran Complex.
Bookshops Iwase Bookshop (Wisma Merdeka), Tung Nam, 129 Jalan Gaya, and the Yaohan bookstore (second floor, Centrepoint) have a few shelves of English-language novels. For an unparalleled array of books on Southeast Asia, head for Borneo Books, (ground floor and second floor Wisma Merdeka, ⊛www.borneobooks.com) and Borneo Crafts (first floor, Wisma Merdeka), or the latter's branch at the Sabah State Museum; the *Hyatt*'s bookshop stocks a modest range of international newspapers and magazines.
Car rental Kinabalu Rent-A-Car, third floor, Lot 3.60, Karamunsing Complex ☎088/232602, ⊜rentcar@po.jaring.my; Hertz, Level 1, Lot 39,

KK International Airport ☎088/317740, ⊜kk@hertz.simenet.com. Rates start from around RM150 per day, though 4X4 (from RM230) are advisable if you plan to get off the beaten track.
Cinemas The Poring and Kilan Cinema and the Capitol Theatre, below the SEDCO Centre at the western edge of downtown KK, both have regular screenings of English-language movies. Programme listings are in the *Borneo Mail* or *Daily Express*.
Consulates Konsulat Jenderal Indonesia, Jalan Kemajuan ☎088/218600, issues visas for Kalimantan. The nearest consular representation for most nationalities is in KL; see p.131.
Hospital Queen Elizabeth Hospital is beyond the Sabah State Museum, on Jalan Penampang ☎088/218166. In an emergency, dial ☎999.
Internet *The Net*, sixth floor, Wisma Merdeka, also branches at fourth floor, Lot D-50, Wisma Sabah and third floor, Centrepoint (1RM for 30min); *City Internet Café*, ground floor, Lot 41, City Parade, Jalan Centrepoint (3RM per hr).
Laundry Meba Laundry Services, Block B, Sinsuran Complex (daily 8.30am–7pm). Very reasonable prices.
Pharmacies Centrepoint Pharmacy, Centrepoint; Farmasi Gaya, 122 Jalan Gaya; Metropharm, Block A, Sinsuran Complex.
Police The main police station, Balai Polis KK ☎088/247111, is below Atkinson's Clock Tower on Jalan Padang.
Post office The GPO (Mon–Sat 8am–5pm, Sun 10am–1pm) lies between the Sinsuran and

Moving on from KK

By air
From KK's **airports** there are regular, non-stop MAS and AirAsia flights to points across Sabah (Labuan, Sandakan, Lahad Datu and Tawau), to Sarawak and the Peninsula. In addition, there are flights to Bandar Seri Begawan in Brunei.

By bus
Long-distance buses for destinations including **Sandakan, Lahad Datu, Semporna** and **Tawau** leave from the new City Bus Terminal North (CBTN) at Inanam, on the outskirts of KK. Buses and minivans heading to **Ranau** (for Gunung Kinabalu), and southwards to Tenom, Beaufort, Keningau and Kuala Penyu (for Pulau Tiga), or onwards to Brunei and Sarawak, leave from Merdeka Field Bus Station, Jalan Padang.

By ferry
There are two daily services to **Labuan** (RM31; 3hr; Mon–Sat 8am & 1.30pm, Sun 8am & 3pm). All tickets are sold at the Jesselton Point Ferry Terminal building on Jalan Haji Saman. It's worth booking at least a day ahead if you plan to travel at the weekend or over a public holiday. Speedboats go hourly to the **Tunku Abdul Rahman Park** islands a few kilometres offshore; prices from RM10. Note that all passengers pay a RM3 terminal fee for ferries leaving KK.

Segama complexes, on Jalan Tun Razak; poste restante/general delivery is just inside the front doors.

Shopping Borneo Handicraft, first floor, Wisma Merdeka, has a good choice of woodwork, basketry and gongs; Borneo Handicraft & Ceramic Shop, ground floor, Centrepoint, stocks ceramics, antiques and primitive sculptures. Also good are the souvenir shops at the Sabah State Museum and the STB, while the Filipino Market's scores of stalls sell both local and Filipino wares. Sri Pelancongan, ground floor, Lot 4, Block L, Sinsuran Complex (☎088/232121; located behind Sabah Parks) has a small but quality selection of baskets, artwork and textiles.

Spas and massage H.T. Reflexology Centre, ground floor, Lot 49, Shoplot 11, Block F, Raun inggah Mata 3, Asia City ☎5088/270273 (daily 8am–6.30pm); Ka'andaman Traditional Healing Garden, KM8, Hongkod Kolsam, Jalan Penampang (on the road to Donggongon from KK) ☎088/721008, ⊛www.kaandamanspa.com.my (daily 11am–11pm).

Taxis Book a taxi on either ☎088/252113 or 251863.

Telephones There are IDD facilities at Kedai Telekom (daily 8am–10pm), in Centrepoint. Phonecards, available at the GPO and any shops displaying the "Uniphone Kad" sign, can be used for international calls from orange public phone booths; yellow booths are for local calls only.

Visa extensions Immigration Department, fourth floor, Wisma Dana Na Bandang, Jalan Tunku Abdul Rahman (Mon–Thurs 8am–1pm & 2–4.30pm, Fri 8am–1pm & 2–3.30pm, Sat 8am–1pm; ☎088/216711). Visa extensions of up to one month are available.

Day-trips from KK

The main attraction around KK is undoubtedly the beaches and wildlife of **Tunku Abdul Rahman Park**. It's also worth considering a day-trip south to the **Monsopiad Cultural Village** and on to **Kinarut**, a village nestling below the Crocker Mountain Range.

Tunku Abdul Rahman Park

Named after Malaysia's first prime minister, and situated just a short boat trip from KK, the five islands of **Tunku Abdul Rahman Park** (sometimes written "TAR Park") represent the most westerly ripples of the undulating Crocker Mountain Range. The islands' forests, beaches and coral reefs lie within just an eight-kilometre radius from the city with park territory as close as 3km off the mainland. They constitute west Sabah's most-visited site and are well worth visiting; try to avoid the weekends and public holidays when facilities are often overstretched.

Pulau Gaya and Pulau Sapi

The site of the British North Borneo Chartered Company's first outpost in the region, **Pulau Gaya** is the closest of the islands to KK and also the largest, its name derived from *goyoh*, the Bajau word for "big". The island's premier trail starts on the southern side of the island at **Camp Bay**, which is adjacent to a mangrove forest where crabs and mudskippers can be seen from the boardwalk that intersects it. The easy-going three-hour jungle trail starts at quite a gradient and climbs to 1750m at its highest point, providing glimpses of the emerald sea through the trees. Lizards flicker across your path and there is abundant birdlife, depending on the time of day. The path drops back to the shoreline, close to the resort, where a boat can ferry you back (RM10), although plan to leave this no later than 6pm as boatmen are harder to catch after then. As the boatmen have a small office on the beach, there is no need to book their services earlier.

While Camp Bay offers pleasant enough swimming, a more secluded and alluring alternative is **Polis Beach**, 500m south. Boatmen demand extra for the trip but it's money well spent: the bay is idyllic, its white-sand beach, running gently down to the water, lined by trees. The wildlife on Gaya includes hornbills, wild pigs, lizards, snakes and macaques – which have been known to swim over to **Pulau Sapi** (Cow Island), an islet just 200m from Gaya. Though far smaller than its neighbour, Sapi too has trails and is home to macaques and hornbills; with the best beaches of any of the islands, it's popular with swimmers, snorkellers and picnickers. Sapi has simple facilities including toilets, a small stall and changing rooms; camping is possible (RM5) but you need to bring all the gear.

Pulau Manukan

Park HQ is situated on crescent-shaped **Pulau Manukan** – site of a former stone quarry and now the most developed of the islands. Manukan's sandy beaches and coral have led to the construction of chalets and restaurants. Just twenty minutes by speedboat from embarkation points at the *Sutera Harbour* and *Shangri-la Tanjung Aru* resort hotels, for their guests and from Jesselton Point Terminal for public access, Manukan has become something of a victim of its own success, drawing many hundreds on a busy day, and leading to over-congestion in its developed corner. That said, the beach is attractive, water-sports are good and an excellent – although pricey – buffet lunch is available most days. It is however easy to escape the crowds; the thirty-minute walk to Sunset Point is enjoyable and the point itself a tranquil spot to watch the sun setting.

The smaller islands

Across a narrow channel from Manukan is tiny **Pulau Mamutik**, a snorkeller's delight. The island is surrounded by coral gardens with the most exquisite stretch off the beach at the southwest, toward the back of where the boat drops you. Most swimmers won't be encouraged to venture to this spot as it is necessary to clamber over rocks to get to where the garden is, but with care, there's no real danger.

The last island of the group, **Pulau Sulug**, is the most remote and consequently the quietest, though its lovely coral makes it popular with divers.

Park practicalities

There are frequent **boat services** to Manukan from the Jesselton Point Ferry Terminal (9am–5pm; RM25 return) and less frequent ones to Mamutik and Sapi (check frequency and prices at terminal). It is possible to go on a day-trip island hop; again, check for details. Pulau Gaya is different – the only way to get there is to either charter a boat from the terminal (around RM200 per half-day) or travel as part of a package with *Gayana Eco Resort* (☎088/245158, ⊛www.gayana-resort.com; ❼), which runs the only accommodation. The resort has attractive chalets on either side of a plankway jutting out from the beach over the sea and has two fantastic little restaurants in the same, rustic complex. At one end of the plankway is a marine conservation centre with various tanks containing eels, lobsters and strange-looking flora and fauna. You can also sign up for a number of activities including kayaking and trekking.

In turn, *Manukan Island Resort*, run by the Sutera Pacific resort-based *Sutera Sanctuary Lodges*, or *SSL* (bookings ☎088/318888, ⊛www.suterasanctuarylodges.com.my) has the only accommodation on that island. The twenty or so units (❾; RM910), all two storey and some strung along a narrow plankway overlooking the island's nicest beach, are extremely well appointed, with TV, semi-outdoor bath, four-poster bed and veranda. To stay the night on Manukan is to enjoy it at its best; the crowds depart on the last boats, leaving at 5pm, with only the *SSL* and Parks staff, and chalet occupants left. Dinner, either buffet (RM60) or à la carte, is served in the only café by candlelight and sometimes "strummers" (buskers) are employed to add to the faux-romantic air. Granted, it's all a bit cheesy, but enjoyable nevertheless.

Donggongon and Monsopiad Cultural Village

Bus #13 leaves hourly from KK's Jalan Tugu bus stand for **Penampang suburb** (Donggongon town), around 10km to the south. From here catch a regular minivan to Kampung Kandazon for the three-kilometre trip to the Kadazan theme park, the **MONSOPIAD CULTURAL VILLAGE** (daily 9am–5pm; RM65; guided tours 10am, noon, 3pm & 5pm; cultural dance 11am, 2pm & 4pm; ⓦ www.monsopiad.com). It's arguable whether the village is really worth the effort given the high entrance price, although the interesting exhibits might just swing the balance.

Founded in memory of the Kadazan head-hunter Monsopiad, the village comprises a museum, handicraft workshop, granary and main hall, in which cultural performances and native feasts are held (the latter by prior arrangement). Monsopiad's grisly harvest of 42 skulls are displayed in a row along a rafter in his ancestral house and decked with *hisad* (palm) leaves signifying the victims' hair. Monsopiad eventually grew too fond of harvesting heads and constituted a public menace; killed by a group of friends, he was buried beneath a stone that still stands near the house, with his own head left intact out of respect.

Once you're out in Donggongon, take the opportunity to see Sabah's oldest church, **St Michael's Catholic Church**, only a twenty-minute walk (or short bus ride) beyond the bus terminus and along the main road. Built in 1897, the sturdy granite building stands on a hillock above peaceful Kampung Dabak, its red roof topped by a simple stone cross. Inside, the church is undecorated, save for a mural depicting the Last Supper and framed paintings of the Stations of the Cross.

On to Kinarut and Papar

Further down the main road south, KK's suburbs are interspersed by paddy fields that stretch away to the foothills of the Crocker Mountain Range. From Merdeka Field in KK there are frequent departures to the village of **KINARUT**, 20km away, the starting point for an enjoyable half-hour stroll along a quiet road to **Kampung Tampasak**, where there's a replica of the *sininggazanak* in the State Museum in KK. From the two faded old shophouses that form the centre of Kinarut, walk across the train line, cross the bridge to your left and turn right – the turning to the kampung is signposted by an overgrown tyre. On your way, you'll see two or three mysterious *menhirs*, upright stones thought to have been erected centuries ago either as status symbols or boundary stones, or to mark the burial places of shamans.

Two to three kilometres away at **KINARUT LAUT** (take a Papar minivan from Merdeka Field), the *Seaside Travellers' Inn* (ⓣ 088/750313, ⓦ www .infosabah.com.my/seaside; ❸) has become a popular retreat for KK weekenders, with neat, clean dorms (RM25) and airy, pleasant rooms with communal shower and toilet, and some detached en-suite chalets. A balcony off the dining room looks out to the nearby islands of Dinawan and Muntukat, and over the inn's own stretch of beach which, unfortunately, is extremely messy. Close to the inn is the equally appealing, small-scale beachfront resort, *Langkah Syabas* (T088/752000, Wwww.langkahsyabas.com,my; ⑥) managed by an environmentally focused couple. The fourteen small detached and semi-detached chalets are set in a nice garden and encircle a small swimming pool, but are a little overpriced. Activities on offer include boat trips to nearby islands, horseriding and short treks; shuttle bus available. With notice, you can get picked up from town or the Inanam coach terminal.

The one town of any size between KK and Beaufort, **PAPAR**, is another 20km or so further south; minivans run here all through the day from KK. Unless you're in Papar on Sunday for the decent weekly market, the only reason to break your journey here is to visit the nearby beach – **Pantai Manis** – reached by minivan (RM1.50), from the small town's centre.

Southwestern Sabah and the interior

Inland and south of KK the highway claws its way up onto the ridges of the **Crocker Mountain Range**, passing Gunung Alad (1964m). This **southern route** divides the state's west coast and the swampy Klias Peninsula from the area christened the **interior** in the days of the Chartered Company. At one time, this sparsely populated region was effectively isolated from the west coast by the mountains. This changed at the turn of the twentieth century, when a rail line was built between Jesselton (modern-day KK) and Tenom in order to transport the raw materials being produced by the region's thriving rubber industry. Today, oil-palm cultivation takes precedence, though the Kadazan/Dusun and Murut peoples still look to the interior's fertile soils for their living, cultivating rice, maize and cocoa. Despite the prevalence of oil palm there is a wild beauty to the region, traditionally only accessible to the most independent of visitors.

Travelling by bus, train or car/4X4, it is possible to circumnavigate the region from KK, starting with a drive southeast over the mountains to the Kadazan/Dusun town of **Tambunan**, which sits on a plain chequered with paddy fields. From Tambunan, the road continues further south to **Keningau** and **Tenom**, which marks the start of Murut territory, stretching down to the Brunei-Kalimantan border. This is one of the ways to the Maliau Basin – a route only negotiable by 4X4 vehicles – although most trekkers arrive via Tawau in eastern Sabah (see p.547).

From Tenom, the road west makes for Beaufort, a favourite outpost for colonial officials, arriving back at the coast at Kuala Penyu, from where boats travel to the tiny **Pulau Tiga National Park**, one of east Malaysia's loveliest spots.

The interior towns

Seventeen kilometres short of Tambunan, a kink in the road reveals the paddy fields of **Tambunan Plain** below. **Gunung Trus Madi**, Sabah's second highest mountain (2642m), towers above the plain's eastern flank; climbing it is an exciting alternative to ascending Gunung Kinabalu. The road weaves on to the bustling, but nondescript centre **Keningau**, and further south to **Tenom** where the **Agricultural Park** is worth a brief stop. This interior route then turns northwest to arrive at tranquil Beaufort, and beyond to the sea.

Tambunan and around

After such a riveting approach, the bustling little town of **TAMBUNAN**, centred on an ugly square of modern shophouses, is bound to disappoint. The best thing about the place (the administrative centre of Tambunan District) is its lively *tamu*, held on Thursday mornings close to the town centre.

Buses to and from KK, Ranau and Keningau stop in the main square, around which are a number of unremarkable cafés. The only reasonable **place to stay** is the *Tambunan Village Resort Centre (TVRC*; ☎087/774076), 2km north of town, with nine twin-bed chalets (RM130) and first-floor twin-bed rooms (③) close by a little lake. To get there, catch a minivan (RM1) from the town square going along the KK road and ask to be dropped at the *TVRC* turning to the right. The centre, in a lovely location beside a fast-running river, has a **café** serving basic Chinese and Malay dishes, as well as *lihing* – the rice wine for which Tambunan is locally renowned. Kayaking and buffalo-riding are available here too, though for residents only.

Mawar Waterfall and Gunung Trus Madi

The *Tambunan Village Resort Centre* arranges tours to the lovely **Mawar Waterfall**, located in dense forest at Kampung Patau, though it's possible to get there by catching the Ranau bus, for the 7km ride from Tambunan to **Kampung Patau** (hourly; RM4). Here there's a wide gravel trail leading to the waterfall, a two-hour hike away through an idyllic bowl of hills stepped with groves of fern and bamboo.

The centre also arranges treks up **Gunung Trus Madi**. It's renowned as a good place to catch sight of the rare insectivorous pitcher plant (*Nepenthes*) close to the summit, and also offers fabulous views across the Crocker Range towards Tambunan and Gunung Kinabalu. The climb, an exhausting day-trek, starts with a one-hour journey by van to **Kampung Kaingaran**, at the base of the mountain. The summit trail takes five hours up, and three hours down on rough, often steep paths, which shouldn't be attempted without a guide. To get an update on local **weather conditions** and to hire a **guide** contact the *TVRC* or a tour operator in KK.

Keningau

A fifty-kilometre bruising journey south from Tambunan on one of the poorest roads in the state brings you to the ugly town of **KENINGAU**. It's a hectic, noisy place with streets crammed with tooting buses and taxis and pavements lined with locals hawking all manner of goods. Keningau's single attraction is its **Chinese temple**, situated right beside the bus terminus. The brightly painted murals that cover its walls and ceilings are more reminiscent of those in a Hindu temple, while in the forecourt is a statue of a fat, smiling

Buddha, resplendent in red-and-yellow gown. If you're in town on a Thursday morning, check out Keningau's weekly *tamu*, a short walk up the main Keningau–Tambunan road.

Rather than moving on, to either Tenom or Tambunan, a more exciting alternative is to head for **Sapulut** to explore Sabah's Murut heartland. This remote region is effectively a dead end and accessible only from Keningau, to which you'll have to backtrack afterwards, although it's possible to take a 4X4 and strike east along the logging roads which connect the interior with Tawau, the largest town in southern Sabah. The trip will take longer than a day unless you ask around for a vehicle to leave no later than 7am.

Practicalities

There are **minivans** to Keningau from Tambunan (RM10; 90min) and from Tenom (RM12; 2hr), these vehicles terminating around the town's central square. It isn't possible to reserve a seat on a 4X4 to Tawau (RM100–150 depending on number of passengers). Turning up early (around 6.30am) is necessary if you want to head out this way.

You will find an adequate **hotel**, *Hotel Tai Wah* (℡087/3322092; ❷) on Jalan Besar, but the town's best hotel, the *Hotel Perkasa* (℡087/331045; ❹), with an in-house fitness centre and restaurants, is 1km out of town on the Tambunan road. Locals congregate at the *Wan Hing kedai kopi*, which serves tasty meals and is located beside Maybank. Nearby on the square is *Restoran Shahrizal*, which serves fine rotis and curries behind its bamboo facade; and Keningau's finest, the *Mandarin*, where one of the specialities is freshwater fish. For the most economical food, try the cluster of **food stalls** beside the bus stop, bearing in mind that most are closed by dusk, or the stalls at the Thursday market.

Tenom and around

After Keningau, the small town of **TENOM**, 42km to the southwest, comes as some relief. The heady days when Tenom was the bustling headquarters of the Interior District of British North Borneo are now long gone, and today it's a peaceful backwater with its fair share of simple hotels and good cafés. Lying within a mantle of forested hills, the town boasts a selection of tasteful wooden shophouses and a blue-domed mosque. The surroundings are extremely fertile, supporting maize, cocoa and soybean – predominantly cultivated by the indigenous Murut people.

The **Sabah Agricultural Park** (℡087/737952, ⓦwww.sabah.net.my /agripark), Tues–Sun 9am–4.30pm; RM25) is where the state's Agricultural Department carries out studies on a wide range of crops; it's a pleasant enough spot to spend an hour or two if you are in the area. The research station is renowned for its **Orchid Centre**, where a profusion of orchids cascade from trees and tree trunks. Less tempting, though actually much better than it sounds, is the nearby **Crop Museum** (free), where you can easily spend an hour strolling through the groves of exotic fruit trees and tropical plants. To get there from Tenom catch a minivan (RM3) from in front of the *Hotel Sri Perdana* and ask to be dropped off at Lagud Seberang, from where it's a one-kilometre walk signposted to Taman Pertaniam. Alternately, a round trip by taxi costs RM50, allowing for a two-hour wait.

A second attraction is the **Murut Cultural Village** (℡087/302421; daily 9am–5pm; free), a few miles out of Tenom on the KK road and accessible by Tenom minivans (RM3). This show village has a number of well-built wooden structures, reflecting Murut design, with its intricate carvings. At its centre is a gallery which displays artefacts including jars and gongs.

Practicalities

Minivans congregate on the town's main street, Jalan Padas, which runs along the north side of the padang. Minivans north to Keningau (RM6) circle around Tenom all day, looking for passengers; you can catch a bus up on the main street, at the western edge of the padang, which leaves four times daily (7am–4pm). Shared taxis to Keningau cost RM10 and leave from the main street whenever they've assembled enough passengers.

Accommodation here includes the reliable *Hotel Sri Perdana*, on Jalan Tun Mustapha (☎087/734001; ❷) and the *Hotel Kim San* (☎087/735485; ❷), one street north of Jalan Tun Mustapha, about 500m southwest of the padang. **Places to eat** are plentiful, with a clutch of coffee shops and restaurants in the area around the *Hotel Kim San*. For a tasty *mee* soup, try the *Restoran Double Happiness*, below the padang; or, for something a bit more lavish, head 2km south of town along Jalan Tomani to the cavernous *YNL Restaurant* (daily 6–11pm), where the speciality is fresh fish caught in the nearby Padas River.

Beaufort

Named after Leicester P. Beaufort, one of the early governors of British North Borneo, **BEAUFORT** is a quiet, uneventful town whose commercial significance has declined markedly since the laying of a sealed road from KK into the interior lessened the importance of its rail link with Tenom. The town's position on the banks of the Padas leaves it prone to flooding, which explains why its shophouses are raised on steps – early photographs show Beaufort looking like a sort of Southeast Asian Venice. But once you've poked around in the town market, inspected angular **St Paul's Church** at the top of town and taken a walk past the stilt houses on the river bank, you've exhausted its sights.

Practicalities

Beaufort's two **hotels** are the *Beaufort* (☎087/211911; ❸), east of the market, and the *Mandarin Inn* (☎087/212798; ❷), five minutes' walk across the river – they're practically identical, each with basic rooms. The *Beaufort* has en-suite bathrooms to its credit, though the *Mandarin* has the edge in terms of freshness. For **eating** try the *Loong Hing*, 250m over the bridge and out of town, though if it's curry and rotis you're after, the *Bismillah* in the town centre is hard to beat.

The bus rank is at the southern end of main street, Jalan Masjid; four daily buses go to KK (9am–5pm; RM10; 90min) and four go to Sipitang (9.10am–6.15pm; RM4.50; 90min). If heading for Lawas in Sarawak, note that the sole daily bus from KK arrives at around 3pm (RM13; 1hr 45min).

The Klias Peninsula

Thirty kilometres west of Beaufort, and served by regular minivans from the centre of town, is the **Klias Peninsula**, an area of flat marshland. The most westerly settlement is tiny **MENUMBOK**. There's no accommodation here, although there are a few cafés at the jetty. From Beaufort a minivan trip here costs RM8 and a taxi is RM60. Regular speedboats and two ferries depart daily for Menumbok from Pulau Labuan.

A jarring, hour-plus bus or minivan ride from Beaufort (RM5) northwest leads to **KUALA PENYU**, at the northern point of the peninsula, the departure point for **Pulau Tiga National Park**. There are also minivans here from Menumbok (RM6). Kuala Penyu is a simple grid of streets with little more than a few stores, filled with basic supplies, and a couple of *kedai kopis*. The only place to stay nearby is the ⚘ *Tempurung Seaside Lodge* (☏088/773066, ⓔinfo@borneoauthenticadventure.com; ➎) a few kilometres out of town, in Kampung Tempurung, plus another seven kilometres along little more than a bumpy track. The owners are happy to pick you up from Kuala Penyu, given some warning. Sitting atop a hill and overlooking the South China Sea, the charming chalets are snug and comfortable, and you can eat delicious food in the lovely dining room (food available on request). The lodge has a private beach too, a short trek down a cliff path.

Leaving Kuala Penyu, it takes just over two hours to travel by minivan to KK's Merdeka Field bus stand, or you can get a minivan to Beaufort (RM5). These vehicles leave from one block back from the jetty.

Pulau Tiga National Park

In the South China Sea, 12km north of Kuala Penyu, **Pulau Tiga National Park** (RM10) once comprised three islands, but wave erosion has reduced one of them, Pulau Kalampunian Besar, to a sand bar. The remaining two, Tiga and Kalampunian Damit, offer good **snorkelling** around the coral reef that surrounds Tiga and the chance to see some unusual **wildlife**. The islands are comparatively new arrivals, created in 1897 by activity from mud volcanoes bursting forth from the sea floor.

The island has acquired notoriety – and fame – as the location of the first 2001 *Survivor* reality TV series. Nowadays though, most visitors content themselves with relaxing on the perfect, sandy beaches (Pagong-Pagong on the north side is certainly one to write home about) and swimming in the azure-coloured sea.

A popular activity on the island is the easy thirty-minute walk to the centre where you'll find the only remaining reminder of the **mud volcanoes**. Here your guide will urge you to wade into the mud for an invigorating cleanse. The mud is a perfect lukewarm temperature and the wallow is indeed surprisingly recuperative. While walking the network of trails, keep an eye out for the island's most famous inhabitants, the *megapode* – a rotund incubator bird, so called because she lays her eggs in mounds of sand and leaves. A fifteen-minute walk beyond is fabulous **Pagong-Pagong** beach where mud immersers can clean up. **Pulau Kalampunian Damit**, 1km northeast of Pulau Tiga, is known locally as Pulau Ular, or Snake Island, as it attracts a species of sea snake called the yellow-lipped sea krait in huge numbers – on an average day, dozens of these metallic-grey and black creatures come ashore to rest, mate and lay their eggs. Though dozy in the heat of the day, the sea kraits are poisonous, and you can only visit them with a park ranger or guide from one of the resorts.

Practicalities

Boat transport from Kula Penyu jetty has to be chartered (RM120; 30min) as there are no scheduled departures. Most visitors come on a tour-operator package; however there is often room on these boats – run by local boatmen – and in this instance the price is negotiable – don't pay more than RM50 one way. The tour-group boats tend to leave around 10.30–11am & 3.30–4pm daily. From Pulau Tiga, expect to pay around RM30 or more for a boat visit to Snake Island.

There are three **accommodation** options on Tiga. The park authorities run a hostel (dorm beds RM30) and also twin-bed cabins (⑥) bookable through the KK Sabah Parks office (☏088/211881); note that there is no restaurant but you can use the kitchens provided to cook your own food. Alternatively, the ⚐ *Pulau Tiga Resort* (☏088/240584, ⓦ www.pulautiga.com.my; ⑥) run by the *Sipadan Dive Centre*, has dozens of twin-bed chalets and a longhouse attractively nestling on a short beach; there's also a shop, bar and a fine café-restaurant open to non-residents, with tasty buffets for all tastes (RM30). The resort's rates range from a twin-bed room in the longhouse (⑥) to standard and superior chalets (RM250–300) and include transport from and to Kuala Penyu. The resort can arrange a minibus connection to KK for RM120. The resort's dive store is equipped for shallow dives and snorkelling with prices from RM200 for a half-day dive plus equipment. Lastly, the *Borneo Survivor Resort* (☏088/230806, ⓦ www.borneosurvivor.com.my) offers lovely chalets (⑥) and six-bed dorms (RM30), plus a campsite nestling on a hill behind the beach. The resort offers a variety of two-day, one-night minimum packages from RM158 (camping) to RM338 (deluxe chalet) per night, which includes boat transfer and meals.

Sipitang

On the bumpy gravel road 45km southwest of Beaufort, **SIPITANG** is a sleepy seafront town worth bearing in mind if you need a place to stay en route to Sarawak. As you approach from the north, a bridge marks the start of town – look out for the pretty stilt houses to your left as you cross. Just over the bridge and a further 200m, is the **jetty** from where speedboats leave twice daily for Labuan (7.30am & 1pm; RM25).

The **four daily buses** from/to KK and one to Lawas congregate in the centre of town, right next door to which is the **shared taxi** stand, from where a seat in one to Beaufort costs RM6. Except for a minivan trip to Taman Negara – a beachside picnic spot a few kilometres south of town, and favoured by locals at the weekend – there's nothing especially to do in Sipitang. On the bright side there are a few decent **places to eat**. Across the main road, *Restoran Bismillah* does delicious curries and breakfast rotis; a minute or so further south, the *Asandong* puts on a good Malay buffet every night and the *Shangsan* café on Jalan Datuk Haji Mohd Yassin, does reasonable basic meals too. Also, a number of satay and fried-chicken sellers set up stalls on the waterfront at dusk. Of the **hotels** along the main road, the *Hotel Asanol* (☏087/821506; ②), Jalan Datuk Haji Mohd Yassin, is the friendliest and most affordable with compact, en-suite rooms, while the *SFI Motel* (☏087/802097; ⑤), 31 Jalan Jeti, is on a grander scale with spacious, en-suite rooms and facilities including a bar and Chinese restaurant.

Crossing into Sarawak

To travel to Lawas town in **Sarawak,** the daily bus from KK arrives at Sipitang at 10am and leaves at 10.15am. Once at the border, it stops first at Kampung Sindumin on the Sabah side, where you need to show your passport, before crossing the border, stopping 200m further on at Merapok, Lawas. This is where your passport's stamped, entitling you to remain in Sarawak for thirty days.

Pulau Labuan

A short distance west of the Klias Peninsula, **PULAU LABUAN** is a key transit point between KK and Brunei with an immensely busy ferry terminal, and airport. Its attractive centre is a clean harbour town with pleasant gardens, adequate eating and high-quality accommodation. Given that ferries from KK and Brunei interconnect at Labuan, you may well end up over-nighting here, wishing to benefit, perhaps, from the lower alcohol prices.

Some history

Labuan's fine anchorage and **coal deposits** – the northern tip is still called Tanjung Kubong, or Coal Point – made it a vital trading post and the island fell into the hands of the British in 1846, long before neighbouring Sabah was procured. The British administration made Labuan a free port in 1848, and by 1889 it had been incorporated into British North Borneo, a state of affairs that lasted until it joined the Straits Settlements a few years into the twentieth century.

World War II brought the focus of the world upon Labuan. Less than a month after the bombing of Pearl Harbour, the island was occupied by the invading **Japanese** army; it was through Labuan that the Japanese forces penetrated British North Borneo. In June 1945, the men of the Ninth Australian Infantry Division landed on the island and three and a half years of occupation came to an end. Labuan, along with Sabah, reverted to the British Crown in July 1946, though it was a further seventeen years before it actually became part of Sabah. Then, in 1984, the island was declared part of Malaysian Federal Territory, governed directly by Kuala Lumpur. Today, with a population of over eighty thousand, Labuan, is still a duty-free port, but has grown into a magnet for weekenders visiting from Sabah and Brunei. It has a steady expat population, with many working in the oil industry.

Arrival and information

Labuan's **airport** is 5km north of town; the only way into the centre is by taxi (RM10). **Ferries** from KK, Limbang and Lawas in Sarawak, and Muara, Brunei, dock at the **new ferry terminal** on Jalan Merdeka, which runs along the seafront below the town centre, forming the spine of Labuan Town. The **tourist Information Centre** (☎087/423445) is on Jalan Merkeka, 50m east from the Labuan museum, where you can pick up a copy of the excellent island and town map. The best places for **internet** access are Tawau Internet, next door to *Sugar Bun* on Jalan Tun Mustapha, and The Net (daily 10am–8pm; 3RM for 30min), on the first floor of the Wisma Ujana Kewangan Mall, 200m east on Jalan Merdeka, past the *Grand Dorsett Hotel*.

Accommodation

There are plenty of **places to stay** in Labuan, all mid-range or higher up the scale; there are no budget options. In town, most of the accommodation is within the grid between the east of the centre, Jalan Okk Abdullah and Jalan Bunga Tanjung on the western edge.

Global Hotel Jalan OKK Awang Besar ☎087/425201. Nicely sequestered in the northwest of the city centre, the *Global* is a great deal with friendly staff and clean, compact rooms. ❹

Grand Dorsett Jalan Merdeka ☎087/422000. Fine rooms plus three restaurants and a bar to keep you busy at this high-end hotel. Price includes breakfast and there's a discreet little pool to wallow in, too. ❼

Manikar Beach Resort ☎ 087/418700. You will have to find your own way to this waterfront resort, which is 20min by taxi (RM30) from the town centre. Set in fifteen acres of private beach and gardens up on the northern tip of the island, this 250-room complex constitutes a fine deal – especially if a promotional price is available. It has a lovely little pool, a fabulous beach, palm trees galore and a fine in-house restaurant serving Western and Asian dishes ❸

Mariner Jalan Tanjung Purun ☎ 087/418822, ✉ mhlabuan@tm.net.my. A tremendous deal, the *Mariner*'s rooms are small but first class, and the in-house breakfast in the ground-floor café is tasty and plentiful. Location is perfect – near the centre, but still in the town's greenest quarter. ❸

Melati Inn Jalan OKK Awang Besar ☎ 087/416307. Right opposite the ferry terminal, *Melati*'s double rooms come with TV, a/c and en-suite bathroom. ❸

Hotel Pulau Labuan 28 Jalan Muhibbah ☎ 087/416288. Comfortable but somewhat overpriced option, with large a/c, en-suite rooms. ❹

Victoria 360 Jalan Tun Mustapha ☎ 087/412411. Large hotel with neat, clean rooms and adequate, en-suite bathrooms. ❺

Waterfront Financial Hotel Jalan Wawasan ☎ 087/418111. Three hundred metres east of the padang, the *Waterfront* commands a superb position overlooking the South China Sea. The foyer is palatial, the rooms compact and perfectly appointed, and the service prompt. Non-business folk are welcome and promotional rates often available. ❻

Labuan Town

The centre of Labuan, previously known as Victoria but now referred to simply as **LABUAN TOWN**, lies on the southeastern side of the island. The *gerai*, or general **market**, at the western end of town, is small in comparison with other Sabah markets though its upper level affords good views of Kampung Patau Patau, the modest **water village** northwest of town. Replacing the cramped, chaotic bays of old, the town now has a gleaming ferry terminal on Jalan Merdeka that, along with the just completed international airport, attests to the island's relative prosperity and geographic importance. To find the duty-free shops, selling alcohol cheaper than elsewhere in Sabah, head for Jalan Merdeka, the main street adjacent to the sea, and Jalan Tun Mustapha, which leads off at right angles from Harrisons travel agency.

The town's chief attraction is the **Labuan Museum** (☎ 087/414135; 9am–5pm; free) situated behind the padang on Jalan Dewan in a colonial era, two-storey washboard building. In a maze of rooms, the photo- and caption-led exhibits document the island's history, notably the dramatic events of World War II, including the traumatic period of the Japanese occupation.

One kilometre east of here on Jalan Tanjun Purun, is the **Marine Museum** (☎ 087/425927; 9am–5pm daily; free), set within the Labuan International Sea Sports Complex, which also houses the Labuan Tourism Action Council (☎ 087/422622; Mon–Fri 8am–1pm & 2–5pm) a better promoter of things to do and events in Labuan than the Tourist Information Centre. There is little to detain you in the Marine Museum – beyond a plethora of fish tanks and, on the first floor, the carcass of an extremely dried-out fin whale.

Eating and drinking

Along Jalan Merdeka and Jalan OKK Awang Besar you'll find lots of adequate, no-frills, Chinese and Indian restaurants while a cluster of popular, and very good cafés can be found two blocks back on Jalan Bunga Mawar.

Choice Restaurant Jalan OKK Awang Besar. Tremendous, spacious café with a long à la carte menu, as well as the midday *nasi campur* buffet with a wide range of meat and fish curries.

Fah Fah Jalan Bunga Mawar. Relaxed café that's popular with expats and locals for/after a few beers. Daily 8am–midnight.

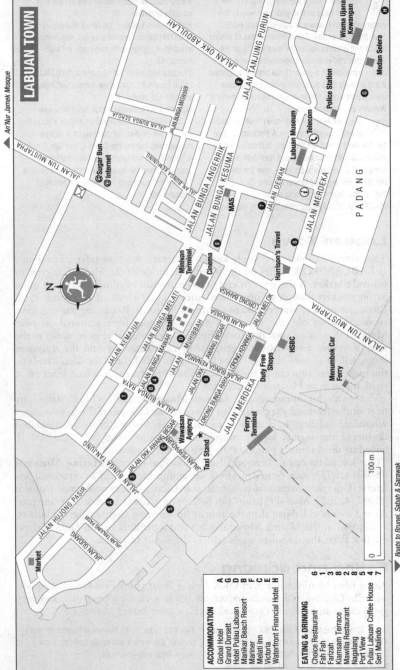

An'Nur Jamek Mosque ▲

❷ , Airport, War Cemetery, ▲ Labuan Bird Park & Labuan Chimney

Borneo Divers ▲

LABUAN TOWN

JALAN OKK ABDULLAH

JALAN TANJUNG PURUH

JALAN TUN MUSTAPHA

@ Sugar Bun
@ Internet

JALAN BUNGA SEROJA

JALAN BUNGA ANGERRIK

JALAN BUNGA KESUMA

JALAN BUNGA KEMUNING

MAS

PADANG

JALAN DEWAN

JALAN MERDEKA

Telecom

Labuan Museum

Police Station

Wisma Ujana Kewangan

Medan Selera

❻

❼

❽

Harrison's Travel

JALAN MELOK

LORONG BAHASA

JALAN BAHASA

Minivan Terminal

Cinema

Statis

JALAN BUNGA MELATI

JALAN KEMAJUA

JALAN BUNGA MAWAR

JALAN MUHIBBAH

JALAN BUNGA RAYA

❶

❹

❷

JALAN OKK AWANG BESAR

JALAN KENANGA

LORONG KENANGA

JALAN BUNGA RAYA

LORONG BUNGA RAYA

❻

HSBC

Duty Free Shops

Menumbok Car Ferry

JALAN TUN MUSTAPHA

JALAN OKK AWANG BESAR

Wawasan Agency

JALAN PERPADUAN

Taxi Stand ★

❸

❺

JALAN MERDEKA

Ferry Terminal

JALAN HUJUNG PASIR

JALAN GUDANG

JALAN TANJUNG PASIR

Market

100 m

0

Boats to Brunei, Sabah & Sarawak ▼

Farizah Jalan Bunga Tanjung. Good, very inexpensive choice for Indian rotis, *murtabaks* and curries. Daily 7.30am–9pm.

Kiamsam Terrace Jalan Merdeka. Small coffee shop beside the *Nagalang*. Daily 8am–6pm.

Mawilla Resturant & Labaun Beach stalls Jalan Tanjung Batu. Five hundred metres east of the town centre lie a number of excellent seafood outlets, including the pricey *Mawilla* (RM50 per head).

Nagalang Chinese & Japanese Jalan Merdeka. Situated in the *Hotel Labuan* this is an upmarket restaurant serving Chinese and Japanese staples. RM40 per person; daily noon–10pm.

Port View Jalan Merdeka ☏ 087/422999. Indoor and equipped with a/c, this is the top Chinese restaurant in town, with tasty dishes including greens in garlic and steamed fish. It's situated on the waterfront with harbour action all around. Around RM40 per person; daily 11am–11pm.

Pulau Labuan Coffee House Jalan Bunga Mawar ☏ 087/416288. A/c restaurant with a wide range of Malay and western Chinese dishes. RM30 per person; daily 7.30am–11pm.

Seri Malindo Jalan Dewan ☏ 087/416072. Busy, outdoor restaurant with a wide range including breakfast, Malay and Chinese buffets and set meals. RM10–15 per person; daily 8.30am–11.30pm.

Around Labuan Town

Three kilometres northeast from the centre along Jalan Tanjung Batu is the **World War II Cemetery**, Malaysia's largest war grave, and a serene, reflective spot. The graves are neatly laid out on perfectly manicured lawns, with a memorial to one side where the names of the nearly four thousand mostly Australian soldiers, but British and Indian as well, are listed. War veterans and relatives make special visits to this cemetery and some attend the annual Remembrance Day service. The cemetery is a pleasant thirty-minute walk from the town centre, or RM10 by taxi (RM16 return).

Near the northern tip of the island are a few sites of marginal interest, worth visiting if you have your own transport, or on a half-day tour. The **Labuan Bird Park**, Jalan Tanjung Kubong (daily 9am–6pm; free) is arranged around three aviaries where a large variety of tropical birds from around the region, such as hornbills, kingfishers, sharmas, mynas, herons, ostriches and peacocks, are housed. Close by is the **Labuan Chimney**, a red-brick stack believed to be linked to the coal-mining days of Labuan. Beside the chimney is a small building with exhibits on the Labuan coal industry. Five hundred metres north of here is the *Manikar Resort*, a beautiful hotel, superbly positioned on a lovely beach. The coast southeast of here, running back towards Labuan Town has mile on mile of gorgeous beaches but, sadly, no facilities whatsoever.

Scuba divers will find more to entertain them offshore: there are several World War II and postwar **shipwrecks** in the waters off Labuan's southern coast, among them the *USS Salute* (scuppered by a mine in 1945); a freighter which

Moving on from Labuan

By air
There are daily **flights** to KL, KK and Kuching operated by MAS and AirAsia. There are also daily flights to Miri on MASwings.

By boat
There are two departures per day to **KK** (Mon–Sat 8am & 1.30pm, Sun 10.30am & 3pm; 3hr; RM31) while numerous ferries go to **Brunei** (1hr 15min; RM35) and speedboats to **Limbang** (one daily at 2.30pm; 2hr; RM28) and **Lawas** (daily except Tues & Thurs 12.30pm; 2hr; RM33). For **Menumbok**, there are hourly speedboats (30min; RM10) and two daily car ferries (2hr; RM40), although foot passenger can travel for RM5. The car ferries go from a separate dock, 50m east.

was transporting cement to Brunei in the mid-1950s when it hit another ship; and the *Semerang*, a passenger steamer commandeered by the Japanese and sunk by the Australian air force in 1945. Borneo Divers (see p.499), charge around RM200 for one wreck dive (half-day), RM350 for two dives (full day), and RM100 for a reef dive off Pulau Kuraman, one of several islands off Labuan's southern coast.

Also of interest, **Labuan Marine Park** has its base on Kuraman where accommodation is available in chalets (❹) and at a camping ground (RM15), to the western end of the island. Beginners' courses in **diving** are on offer and other activities include snorkelling, sailing, fishing and short jungle walks as well as the opportunity to enjoy the island's unspoilt beaches. Contact the tourist office for boat transport times (RM50 return) and to arrange accommodation.

The **diving specialist**, Borneo Divers, is at 1 Jalan Wawasan, Waterfront Labuan (☎087/415867).

From KK north to Kudat

North of KK, Sabah's trunk highway hurries through the capital's suburbs to the more pastoral environs of **Tuaran**. From here, the *atap* houses of the Bajau water villages, **Mengkabong** and **Penambawang**, are both a stone's throw away. Just outside Tuaran, the main road forks, with the eastern branch heading towards Gunung Kinabalu National Park, Ranau and onwards to Sandakan. Continuing north the main road arrives at **Kota Belud**, a bustling town and the site of a weekly *tamu* that attracts tribespeople from all over the region. Beyond, the landscape becomes more colourful: jewel-bright paddy fields and stilted wooden houses line the road for much of the way up to the **Kudat Peninsula**, with Gunung Kinabalu dominating the far distance. Journey's end is signalled by the coconut groves and beaches beyond **Kudat**, a sleepy place nowadays but formerly the capital of British North Borneo, and nearby **Tip of Borneo**, a wind-lashed enclave, where you can gaze out over the ocean, and consider lavish plans on the drawing board to develop it into a self-styled Riviera.

Buses for Tuaran, Kota Belud and Kudat leave KK's CBTN through the day, with the first two destinations perfect for enjoyable day-trips out of the capital. Kudat requires an overnight stay; it's realistically a three-hour round trip to the Tip of Borneo; and another overnight is needed to explore Palau Banggi.

Tuaran and the water villages

It takes just under an hour to travel the 34km from Kota Kinabalu to **TUARAN**, from where it's possible to visit two water villages: **MENGKABONG**, ten minutes out of Tuaran on a local bus from the town centre, is the most accessible and a favourite destination with some KK tour operators. The sight of a village built out over the sea on stilts is usually a compelling one, but Mengkabong is a noisy, charmless example, and you'd do well to make the extra effort to reach **PENAMBAWANG**. Minivans to Kampung Surusup – the tiny settlement from where you can catch a boat to Penambawang – leave from the road west of Tuaran's brown clock tower; it's a twenty-minute drive (on a rough road) through idyllic paddy fields. Once in Surusup, you need to ask around at the jetty for a boat (RM20 return) – Penambawang is fifteen minutes northeast, across a wide bay skirted with mangroves. The Bajau people's houses are made of *atap*, bamboo and wood interconnected by labyrinthine boardwalks – called *jambatan* ("bridge") – along which fish are laid out to dry.

▲ Sunday market at Kota Belud

While **hotels** in Tuaran are nothing to write home about, the *Shangri-La Rasa Ria Resort* (see p.493), 5km west on Dalit Bay, is worth considering if you want to splash out. Several shuttle buses leave daily from the *Shangri-la Tanjung Aru Resort*, taking forty-five minutes to reach Dalit Bay, and there's also a bus service to the bay from Tuaran town centre (9am & 2pm), and back again.

Kota Belud

For six days of the week, **KOTA BELUD**, 75km northeast of KK, is a busy but undistinguished town. Early on a Sunday, however, it springs to life as hordes of villagers from the surrounding countryside congregate at its weekly **tamu**, undoubtedly the biggest in Sabah. The market, ten minutes' walk out of town along Jalan Hasbollah, fulfils a social as well as commercial role, and draws – among others – Rungus, Kadazan/Dusun and Bajau indigenous groups. Though Kota Belud's popularity among KK's tour operators means there are always tourists here, you're far more likely to see dried fish, chains of yeast beads (used to make rice wine), buffalo, betel-nut and *tudung saji* (colourful food covers used to keep flies at bay) for sale, than souvenirs. Arrive early – if heading here from KK, plan to leave the city by 8am at the latest.

At Kota Belud's annual *tamu besar*, or "big market", usually held in November, there are cultural performances, traditional horseback games and handicraft demonstrations in addition to the more typical stalls. For specific details each year, ask at the STB office in KK (see p.491).

Practicalities

Buses for Kota Belud (RM5) leave from KK's Merdeka Field bus stand – the same area as for Kudat-bound ones – for the ninety-minute trip. Buses from KK drop and pick up passengers at the district office in the centre of town, from where it's a twenty-minute walk to the *tamu*; it's a better bet to hail one of the minivans (RM1) which ply the stretch on market days.

There is only one place worth staying in town: the basic but clean and cheerful *Kota Belud Travelers' Lodge* (℡088/977228; dorms RM25; ❸) is at 6 Plaza Kong Guan, 200m southwest of the mosque. However, there is an abundance of decent **cafés**; the *Restoran Rahmat* below the district office has particularly varied and appetizing Malay meals, and of the many coffee shops over in the newer part of Kota Belud (to the west of the Kudat road), the *Restoran Zam Zam*, 50m north of the main street and on the edge of the old market, does good curries and fried chicken.

Kudat and around

The town of **Kudat** is located on the peninsula's northeastern coast, north from the little town of Kota Marudu, which travellers have no need to visit. Although a small town, Kudat has regional and political significance becoming, in 1881, the first administrative capital of the East India Company. Although this status was moved to Sandakan two years later, Kudat's strategic importance had been recognized. A short way north of Kudat lies an area recently named the **Tip of Borneo**. There is currently little here beyond a car park, a plaque, café and a set of chalets where you can stay. Northeast of here lies **Banggi Island**, an undeveloped, remote place, accessible by boat from Kudat, where it is possible to stay overnight.

The peninsula is home to the **Rungus people**, members of the wider Kadazan/Dusun ethnic group. Like most, the Rungus have gradually modernized, but many still hold their traditions dear. In the kampungs many of the older people still dress in black, and only two generations ago some Rungus wore coils of brass and copper on their bodies. The architectural style of the traditional longhouse is distinctive too, built with outwards leaning walls and decorated with motifs and imagery from farming and the world of nature.

Today though, most of the dwellings are made from sheets of corrugated zinc, whose durability makes it preferable to the traditional materials like timber, tree bark, rattan and *nipah* leaves. Set back from the main road, 37km short of Kudat, Kampung Tinanggol consists of three twenty-five-door longhouses and a quaint white church. The Sabah Tourism Board has helped construct a longhouse in the village, allowing visitors to stay in a traditional Rungus environment with locals cooking tasty, inexpensive meals when required (RM50 plus meals).

Arrival and information

Downtown Kudat centres on the intersection of Jalan Ibrahim Arshad and Jalan Lo Thien Chock – the latter is Kudat's main street, with most of its shops and a Standard Chartered Bank. **Shared taxis** to and from Kota Belud and KK arrive and leave from the car park opposite *Hotel Sunrise*; ask any of the drivers whose turn it is to leave next and at what time. For **ferries** to Pulau Banggi, head for the jetty at the southern end of Jalan Lo Thien Chock. Kudat's **airport**, for MASwings flights from KK and Sandakan, is 9km out of town (minivan RM5; taxi RM15).

Accommodation

Tourist traffic has ensured that Kudat has a few decent **accommodation** options.

Hotel Sunrise Jalan Lo Thien Chock ⊕088/611517. A reasonable choice. Its small, neat rooms have fans but the shared bathrooms are rather basic. ❸
Kudat Marina Resort 4km out of town ⊕088/212366, ⓦ www.kudatgolfmarinaresort .com. Airy, pleasant rooms, many overlooking the large pool and sea. There's a popular golf course here, too. ❻

Ria Hotel Jalan Marudu ⊕088/622794, ⓦ www.geocities.com/riahotel. The best place to stay in Kudat. Beyond Chinese owner Mr Soon's scrupulously clean foyer, lie 24 small and neat rooms, with en-suite bathrooms. ❹
Upper Deck Hotel Jalan Lintas. Located 5min west of the *Ria Hotel*, this place commands a fine view over Marudu Bay. ❹

The Town

Occupying a small grid of streets and overlooking Marudu Bay, **Kudat** is friendly, slow place, where there's little to do except perhaps visit Sabah's oldest **golf club**, opened in 1906 (⊕088/611002, non-members can play Mon–Thurs; RM50) or stay at the rather lovely *Kudat Marina Resort* nearby.

The town's main thoroughfare, Jalan Lo Thien Chock, is dominated by two-storey wooden shophouses, among the oldest in Sabah. During a visit, leave time to peek at the town centre's orange-hued **Chinese temple**, the **stilt**

village and the harbour, now significantly quieter than in the days when Kudat had an active fishing industry. There are a number of places to eat on the riverside promenade. Across the dual carriageway to the east of the centre is the late afternoon/evening market, *Sudi Sampir* – very good for fresh fruit, satay and rice dishes.

Kudat's only good nearby beach is **Bangau**, on the west coast, near the town of **Sikuati** – a shared taxi heading for KK can drop you at the turning. After that you'll need to wait for a Kudat-based minivan plying the last 6km stretch (RM4).

Eating

Kudat has little in the way of quality **places to eat** – even the restaurant at the *Kudat Marina Resort* is distinctly average. The best **restaurant** in town is probably the *Sungai Wang* on the promenade, which serves such delights as scallops in black-bean sauce and tofu with crabmeat for around RM12 each; it also serves beer. Adjoining the *Ria Hotel*, is *Selera Ria Coffee House*, a clean, modern place selling pastries and drinks, plus a cracking breakfast of toast, two fried eggs, beans and a chicken hotdog, all for RM3.80.

Fifty metres closer to the town centre, *Sri Mutiara* on Jalan Lo Thien Chock, opposite the *Sunrise Hotel*, serves tasty Malay food and fried chicken, while *Restoran Borneo*, also on Lo Thien, is a distinctive blue establishment, very popular with locals and serving inexpensive Malay dishes.

Pulau Banggi

Forty kilometres north of Kudat lies Pulau Banggi, off Sabah's north coast, accessible by twice-daily ferry. The island is mostly flat but has lovely beaches, one close to the jetty at Kampung Kalaki, the main settlement. There are no sights to speak of but it's arguably worth a visit just for the boat ride and amble on the beach. There is little need to stay over – you can catch the morning boat and return on the afternoon one – but if you choose to, there's a small government resthouse (☎088/612511; ❷) and the *Banggi Resort* (☎088/671495) with doubles (❸) and small chalets (❸). Take food and drink with you as there are no shops on the island; the resort has cooking facilities for guests to use. The Kudat Express leaves the town at 9am and 2.30pm and departs from Kalaki at 7am and 3pm. The journey takes 40min and costs RM15.

The Tip of Borneo

Anyone imagining the thin strip of promontory 13km north of Kudat, the **Tip of Borneo**, to have already been transformed by developers into some kind of attraction will be disappointed – or relieved. This beautiful area, where cliffs drop away to steep, forested hills and waves, buffeted by wind, crash onto the golden sandy beaches, remains almost completely unvisited. At Cape Keretang, Sabah Tourism has built a car park where steps lead down to a viewing area but that's about all. Local families visit, mostly at the weekend, and, as there are no buses or minivans out this way, you need to use your own transport, or a taxi. Two hundred metres round the cape on a paved main road, look for *Bay View Homestay* (☎013/5580801 or 13/5411339), where owner James Kadai has built a few basic, two-bed chalets (❸) in a cliff garden, overlooking the breathtakingly beautiful **Kalumpinian Beach**, accessible by a path. He also runs a café there offering simple meals.

Up ahead, but unlikely to affect the long coast's desolate beauty too much, is an ambitious project from the same people who run Sandakan's *English Tea House*

(see p.533). *Exquisite Borneo Villas* (☎088/249276, ⓦwww.exquisiteborneovillas
.com; ⑨), a forty-minute drive from Kudat and further around Cape Keretang
from the actual Tip, combines a type of lavish timeshare not seen before in east
Malaysia with a high-end hotel complex. Certainly such an enterprise – and other
such ones earmarked for the region – promise development for north Kudat, and
will push for upgrades in the region's tourism infrastructure.

Kinabalu National Park

Eighty-five kilometres northeast of KK and plainly visible from Sabah's west
coast, there's no more impressive sight than **Gunung Kinabalu** (Mount
Kinabalu), whether it's poking dramatically through the clouds or looming
serenely over the Crocker Range and valley below. At 4101m high, it totally

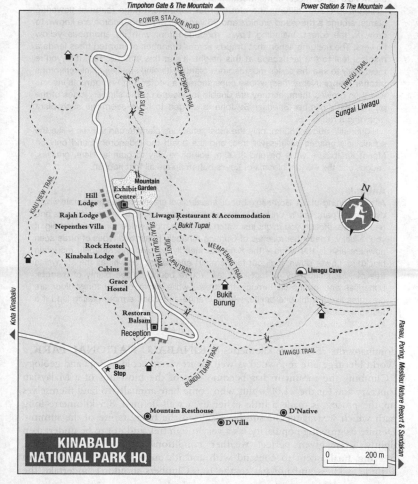

KINABALU
NATIONAL PARK HQ

0   200 m

If you dash headlong up and down Gunung Kinabalu and then depart, as some visitors do, you'll miss out on many of the region's natural riches. The national park's diverse terrains have spawned an incredible variety of **plants** and **animals**, and you are far more likely to glimpse some of them by walking its trails at a leisurely pace. Remember, you do not need to hire a guide to trek below Panar Laban so if you're able to stay in the park for a few more days you may wish to return to the mountain trails for a less hurried meander.

Plants

Around a third of the park's area is covered by **lowland dipterocarp forest**, characterized by massive, buttressed trees, allowing only sparse growth at ground level. The **world's largest flower**, the parasitic – and very elusive – *Rafflesia*, occasionally blooms in the lowland forest around Poring Hot Springs. Between 900m and 1800m, you'll come across the oaks, chestnuts, ferns and mosses (including the *Dawsonia* – the world's tallest moss) of the **montane forest**.

Higher up (1800–2600m), the **cloudforest** supports a huge range of flowering plants: around a thousand orchids and 26 varieties of rhododendron are known to grow in the forest, including Low's rhododendron, with its enormous yellow flowers. The hanging lichen that drapes across branches of stunted trees lends a magical feel to the landscape at this height. It's at this altitude, too, that you're most likely to see the park's most famous plants – its nine species of insectivorous **pitcher plants** (*Nepenthes*) whose cups secrete a nectar that first attracts insects and then drowns them, as they are unable to escape up the slippery sides of the pitcher. Early climber Spenser St John is alleged to have seen one such plant digesting a rat.

Higher still, above 2600m, only the most tenacious plantlife can survive – like the agonizingly gnarled *sayat-sayat* tree, and the heath rhododendron found only on Mount Kinabalu – while beyond 3300m, soil gives way to granite. Here, grasses, sedges and the elegant blooms of Low's buttercup are all that flourish.

Animals

Although orang-utans, Bornean gibbons and tarsiers are among the **mammals** which dwell in the park, you're unlikely to see anything more exotic than squirrels, rats and tree shrews, though you might just catch sight of a mouse deer or a bearded pig if you're lucky. The higher reaches of Gunung Kinabalu boast two types of **birds** seen nowhere else in the world – the Kinabalu friendly warbler and Kinabalu mountain blackbird. Lower down, look out for hornbills and eagles, as well as the Malaysian tree pie, identifiable by its foot-long tail. You're bound to see plenty of **insects**: butterflies and moths flit through the trees, while down on the forest floor are creatures like the trilobite beetle, whose orange-and-black armour-plating lend it a fearsome aspect.

---

dominates the 750 square kilometres of **KINABALU NATIONAL PARK**, a World Heritage Site renowned as well for its varied ecology, flora and geology.

Climbing the mountain has become one of the must-dos of a Malaysian itinerary and for the 24,000-plus who come here annually to haul themselves up, the process is made a little easier by a well-defined, 8.5-kilometre-long path which weaves up the southern side to the bare granite of the summit. Despite its growing popularity, it's a very tough trek and not to be undertaken lightly. Even given perfect weather conditions, there's the remorseless, freezing, final ascent to contend with and it's quite possible to suffer from altitude sickness and not get to the top. Climbers shouldn't undertake the challenge unless fully prepared with suitable clothing (see p.522) and in good general health; they should also keep close to their mandatory guide at all points in the trek. Although the park is equipped with a wide range of high-standard accommodation, prices are high and visitors often prefer to stay in guesthouses outside the park boundaries, or at **Mesilau** on the eastern edge of the park, which is quieter. You can also begin the Gunung Kinabalu climb from here. Increasingly too, climbers begin in KK, drive to the park and get on the trail by 10am. This option usually entails a night on the mountain and the descent the following day.

A third option is to accomplish the climb up and down in one day, which cuts the price considerably. This is only to be considered by the super-fit and, given that the authorities limit the number of people attempting it to just four per day, there is little chance of doing this unless you book some time in advance.

Traditionally, limbs weary from the climb will welcome the warm, sulphurous waters of the **Poring Hot Springs**, around 40km away, just outside the park's southeastern border. Between these two sites on the main trunk road to Sandakan is the small, unexciting town of **Ranau**, which has a couple of places to stay.

Some history

Conquering Gunung Kinabalu today is far easier than it was in 1858, when Spenser St John, British consul-general to the native states of Borneo, found his progress blocked by Kadazan "shaking their spears and giving us other hostile signs". Hugh Low, at the time British colonial secretary on Pulau Labuan, had made the first recorded ascent of the mountain seven years earlier, though he baulked at climbing its highest peak, considering it "inaccessible to any but winged animals". The peak – subsequently named after Low – was finally conquered in 1888 by John Whitehead.

The origin of the mountain's name is uncertain; one legend tells how a Chinese prince travelled to Borneo to seek out a huge pearl, guarded by a dragon at the summit of the mountain. Having slain the dragon and claimed the pearl, the prince married a Kadazan girl, only to desert her and return to China. His wife was left to mourn him on the slopes of the mountain – hence *Kina* (China) and *balu* (widow) – where she eventually turned to stone. Another idea is that the name derives from the Kadazan words *Aki Nabalu* – "the revered place of the dead". Nineteenth-century climbers had to take into account the superstitions of local porters, who believed the mountain to be a sacred ancestral home. When Low climbed it, his guides brought along charms, quartz crystals and human teeth to protect the party, and Kadazan porters still offer up chickens, eggs, cigars, betel-nut and rice to the mountain's spirits.

Getting there and arrival

Hourly **buses** leave KK's CBTN for Sandakan and Ranau from 7am and take around two hours (RM15) to get to the park entrance, but the preferred option for many is to catch a Ranau minivan (hourly; RM20) or to split a shared taxi (RM80); both leave from the Merdeka Field bus stand from 7am.

Buses and minivans drop you opposite the park gates (RM15 entrance fee) on the KK–Ranau road. Directly inside are an extended cluster of lodgings, restaurants and offices including park **reception** (daily 7am–7pm), where you confirm your accommodation with *Sutera Sanctuary Lodges* (see p.523). Next door, at the Sabah Parks office, is where you fix up the details of your climb.

Information sheets and a **map** are available at reception and, more specialist material on trekking and the park environment from the Sabah Parks office.

Information

Twenty kilometres of **trails**, including the two-hour Liwagu one, loop the montane forest around HQ, with a guided walk (RM3) leaving daily from the reception office at 11am. A ten-minute walk up the road from reception, the **Exhibit Centre** contains a number of facilities, including the *Liwagu* restaurant on the ground floor and, upstairs, an exhibition with photographs and mounted exhibits of park flora and fauna (look out, in particular, for the monster stick insect). There is also a video show daily at 2pm (RM2). There are more plants on show at the **Mountain Garden** (Mon–Fri 8am–4.30pm, Sat & Sun 9am–5pm; RM5) just to the rear of the Exhibit Centre.

There's no getting away from the fact that ascending and descending Gunung Kinabalu takes two days. It is technically possible for the super-fit to do it in a day, but park authorities tend to encourage walkers to take longer. Climbers have to spend a night two-thirds of the way up the mountain in huts at **Laban Rata**, allowing for a final dawn ascent – the time of the day when the mountain is least likely to be engulfed by mist or hit by lashing rain. After coming off the summit, you return to Laban Rata for breakfast and then go back down.

The Kinabalu trail does suffer these days from a sense of impatience, a kind of amateur machismo that leads people to want to accomplish the feat as quickly as possible. Despite these urges it's sensible, if time is on your side, to factor in an extra day or two as, in the event of cloud cover spoiling the view from the summit, you may decide to postpone the climb. (In the case of very poor weather conditions, the park officials stop people setting out from park HQ, full stop.)

A good ploy is to arrive in the early afternoon the previous day, giving you time to **acclimatize** on the short trails beginning from park HQ. For those arriving at the park for the climb on the same morning, it's essential to call ahead to **reserve** your place in a climbing group (the last group usually sets off by 11am).

Guides, porters and equipment

Unless you're starting the climb from the *Mesilau*, aim to be at the park reception by 8am, where, besides the **climbing permit** (RM100) and compulsory **insurance** (RM7), you must pay for a **guide** (RM70 per group of one to three people; RM74 for four to six; and RM80 for seven or eight). Some climbers opt to pay for a **porter**, costed by the weight he carries (maximum load 10kg). For one to three climbers the cost is RM60, four to six, RM80 and seven or eight, RM90. **Lockers** and a safe room are available at reception to deposit valuables or even your pack. Note that if you want to do the climb in just one day – an option only available from specialist tour operators based outside the park, like Scuba/River Junkie – a day-price of around RM400 substantially cuts the official all-in SSL price of RM700–800.

Essential items to take with you are a torch, headache tablets (for altitude sickness), suntan lotion, energy boosters like nuts, fruit and muesli bars and adequate drinking water. You should also wear waterproof shoes or hiking boots with a good tread and bring a few layers of warm clothing to combat the bracing cold on the summit. Also, most guides do not carry first-aid kits, so it might be worth investing in one.

Accommodation and eating

Park **accommodation** – and at Poring and Mesilau – is run by **Sutera Sanctuary Lodges** (SSL), based in the *Sutera Pacific Hotel* in KK (see p.494; ☎088/243629, ⓦwww.suterasanctuarylodges.com). It is essential to book on the website or by phone **before arriving** at the park, so contact SSL as far in advance as possible. Note that most climbers also book their climb through SSL, who encourage **all-in packages** – these are cheaper than the prices quoted on the website. SSL, it seems, want to move the "park experience" more upmarket; this is one reason, perhaps, why some climbers spend less time, and money, in the park environs, notwithstanding the inevitable costs incurred in the mandatory night at Laban Rata and the requisite climb costs.

There is a good choice of hostels and chalets/lodges around **park HQ** and further on up the mountain at the **Laban Rata complex**; a good cluster of hotels and resxthouses has also sprung up along the main road **outside the park** towards Ranau.

There are two **restaurants** around park HQ: the *Balsam* (daily 7am–10pm, Sat & Sun until 11pm) offering expensive, but wholesome, buffets with Chinese, Malay, Indian and Western dishes (RM25–50); and the equally priced, but à la carte *Liwagu* (daily 11am–11pm). There is also a basic restaurant at *Laban Rata* with buffet breakfast (7.30–10.30am) and dinner (4.30–8pm).

Inside the park

Park headquarters C/o Sutera Sanctuary Lodges. Accommodation ranges from basic, budget lodges with cooking facilities and communal sitting areas, such as *Grace* and *Rock* (dorm bed RM120) to the more comfortable *Hill Lodge*, *Liwagu Suite* in the Exhibit Centre and *Nepenthes Villa* (7–8); top of the scale are the luxurious eight-bed *Kinabalu Lodge* and ten-bed *Rajah Lodge* (⑨; from RM2500 per unit), which have TV, heated showers, kitchen facilities and snug bedrooms.

On the mountain

Laban Rata complex C/o Sutera Sanctuary Lodges. The complex is siuated at 3000m altitude, near the peak of Mount Kinabalu. The compound is made up of the main-site lodge, *Laban Rata Resthouse*, which has twin-share rooms (⑨; RM765 per room), the more basic, unheated huts, *Papar Laban* and *Waras*, suitable for groups, and the large, heated *Guntung Lagadan* (RM208).

🏃 **Mesilau Nature Resort** C/o Sutera Sanctuary Lodges. Seventeen kilometres east of HQ, located slightly higher up in the mountain's foothills. The advantage of being based at this resort is that it's a lot quieter, with far fewer people starting the climb from this point. Note that the climb takes a little longer from here – a narrow path curls up the slope before joining the main trail at Carson's Camp. There's just one rather average café to eat at here, but the place has a special atmosphere, with a gushing river running through the resort and abundant birdlife. Accommodation consists of various dorms (RM120 per bed) and numerous, spacious chalets and lodges, equipped with all mod cons (⑧). The only way to reach *Mesilau* is the minivan shuttle from park reception (RM85).

Outside the park

D'Native On the main road from the park ☎013/8923755. A pleasant two-storey lodge with one dorm (RM20) and neat, en-suite doubles. ❹
D'Villa On the main road from the park ☎088/889282. Twelve-bed dorms (RM20), standard rooms with balconies and lovely views over the Kinabalu valley. ❸
Kinabalu Pine Resort On the outskirts of Kundasang ☎088/889388, ⓔpatrvl@tm.net.my. Large and comfortable upmarket lodge. ❻
Mountain Resthouse 200m from the park, on the main road. Very basic, ramshackle place with a few rooms. ❷

The climb

The summit route begins with a minibus ride (RM18; 25min) to the beginning of the mountain path, Timpohon Gate. The climb to the mountain huts at

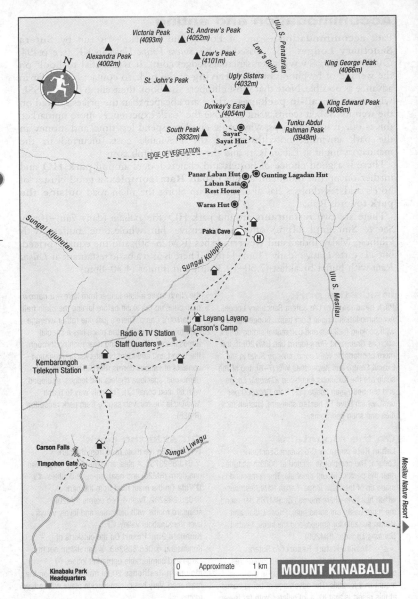

Victoria Peak
(4093m)

St. Andrew's Peak
(4052m)

Ulu S. Penataran

Alexandra Peak
(4002m)

Low's Peak
(4101m)

Low's Gully

King George Peak
(4066m)

N

St. John's Peak

Ugly Sisters
(4032m)

Donkey's Ears
(4054m)

King Edward Peak
(4086m)

South Peak
(3932m)

Sayat
Sayat Hut

Tunku Abdul
Rahman Peak
(3948m)

EDGE OF VEGETATION

Panar Laban Hut   Gunting Lagadan Hut
Laban Rata
Rest House

Waras Hut

Sungai Kijuhutan

Paka Cave

H

Sungai Kolopis

Ulu S. Mesilau

Layang Layang
Carson's Camp

Radio & TV Station
Staff Quarters

Kembarongoh
Telekom Station

Carson Falls

Sungai Liwagu

Timpohon Gate

Mesilau Nature Resort

Kinabalu Park
Headquarters

0   Approximate   1 km

MOUNT KINABALU

Laban Rata takes between five and seven hours, depending on your fitness and trail conditions. Roots and stones along the trail serve as steps, with wooden "ladders" laid up the muddier stretches. The air gets progressively cooler as you climb, but the walk is still a hard and sweaty one, and you'll be glad of the water tanks and rest point at **Layang Layang** (2621m) around three hours into the climb. At around this point, if the weather is kind, incredible views of the hills, sea and clouds below you start to unfold; higher up, at just above 3000m, a detour to the left brings you to **Pondok Paka**; Paka Cave is little more than a large overhanging rock, and was the site of overnight camps on early expeditions. It's a further 6km to Laban Rata, which lies at 3272m, the final 2km dominated by large boulders and steep slippery rock surfaces which, combined with lower oxygen levels, are demanding even for the fittest. The benefit as the first day draws to a close is witnessing the mighty granite slopes of the **Panar Laban rock face**, veined by trickling waterfalls, and the promise of reaching your accommodation.

To the summit

Most climbers get up at 2.30am for the final ascent, crossing the sheer **Panar Laban** rock face, past the **Sayat Sayat** hut and onwards to the summit at Low's Peak. Although ropes, handrails and wooden steps help in places, this is at the very least a stiff climb, in pitch darkness – head lamps are an advantage and a powerful torch a must. Vegetation is shrub height and offers little protection against the biting cold. Climbers should also be aware of the symptoms of altitude sickness – headaches, nausea and breathlessness – setting in. Some believe that it's fruitless leaving so early as you get to the summit as much as an hour before sunrise – you can always ask your guide if your group can leave a little later.

After the final push, the beautiful spectacle of sunrise at **Low's Peak** will rob you of any remaining breath. Remember that it'll be biting cold there, so bring very warm clothing for that brief stop at the summit. Then, after all that toil, it's back to Laban Rata for a hearty breakfast before the return journey to park HQ, usually covered in three to five hours. When you finally get back and start to feel the delayed rebellion of your leg muscles, reflect on the fact that the Nepalese Kusang Gurung, the winner of the annual **Kinabalu Climbathon** in 1991, ran up *and* down the mountain in a staggering two hours and forty–two minutes.

▲ The summit of Mount Kinabalu

Poring Hot Springs

Located 43km from park HQ, on the southeastern side of Kinabalu National Park, are the **Poring Hot Springs** (RM15 conservation fee). The springs were developed by the Japanese during World War II, though the wooden tubs they installed have since been replaced by outdoor cement versions, large enough to seat two people at a time.

After a few days' hiking up the mountain, a soak in Poring's hot (48–60°C), sulphurous waters is just the ticket. The baths (daily 7am–6pm; free) are a couple of minutes from the main gates, across a suspension bridge that spans the Mamut River; here there are two enclosed baths with jacuzzi and an adjacent plunge pool. Unfortunately many of the tubs are in poor condition, chipped and with a film of grime and the staff appear uninterested and generally unhelpful.

A fifteen-minute walk beyond the baths brings you to Poring's **canopy walkway**, affording a monkey's-eye view of the surrounding lowland rainforest. Another trail strikes off to the east of the baths, reaching the 150-metre-high **Langanan Waterfall** about an hour and a half later. On its way, the trail passes the smaller **Kepungit Waterfall** – whose icy pool is ideal for swimming – and a cave lined with squealing, fluttering bats, as well as groves of towering bamboo.

Practicalities

To get to Poring from park HQ you'll need to book a seat on the shuttle bus (RM85) for the one-hour trip (RM60 from *Mesilau Nature Resort*). For **accommodation**, there's a large campsite (RM10 per tent), the *Serindit* hostel (dorm beds RM120), twin share cabins (RM350) and lodges which sleep four up to six (RM420–2500). As at park HQ and at *Mesilau*, **book** accommodation in advance through SSL.

Besides the excellent *Rainforest Restaurant* (8am–10pm) by the hot tubs, there are two **eating** options outside the gates: the *Poring Restoran* (daily 8am–8pm), which serves average Chinese food, and the *Kedai Makanan Melayu* (daily 8am–6pm) next door, offering simple Malay dishes.

To Ranau

From Poring it's impossible to get direct transport to Sandakan or back to KK; instead take a minivan (RM10) from outside the gates to the small town of **RANAU**, where buses stop on trips across the state. En route to Ranau from the park, after 10km you come to **Kundasang**, little more than a junction with simple stalls selling fruit and vegetables. The only reason to stop is to see the **war memorial**, signposted 150m off the main road. It commemorates the victims of the "Death March" of September 1944, when Japanese troops marched 2400 POWs from Sandakan to Ranau (see p.532).

Ranau is based around a functional grid, with street names in short supply, though one exception is Jalan Kibarambang – the first turning on the right if you're coming from KK, and home to both a rickety old market and a new **Chinese temple**, its cream walls striped by red pillars. The first day of every month sees a lively *tamu*, around one kilometre out of town towards Sandakan.

Practicalities

Long-distance **buses** (Sandakan RM30; KK RM15), stop on the trunk road beside the turning into the town while **minivans** arrive at the eastern edge of town. There's **internet access** at Cyber City Centre, Lot 4, Wisma Budaya, right in the centre (daily 9am–9pm; RM2.50 per hr).

Ranau has quite a few **hotels**, the best of which is the *Kinabalu View Lodge* (℡088/879111; ❸) at first floor, Tokogaya Building, Lorong Kibarambang, with small, clean rooms. The less inspiring *Hotel Ranau* (℡088/875661; ❷), next to the Bank Bumiputra on the north side of the square, has box-like singles and spacious en-suite, a/c doubles. The *Kinabalu Hotel* (℡088/876028; ❸), south of the square in Block A, has cosy rooms and shared bathrooms.

Eating options include the cheerful *Restoran Muslim* (daily 8am–10pm), where you eat fried chicken to the strains of wrestling videos on the TV; the next-door *Yeong Hing* does good *pow*. Finally, *Restaurant Double Luck* on Jalan Kibarambang, has a good range of Chinese dishes, and is licensed.

East Sabah

East Sabah contains the greatest concentration of attractions in the state. Starting in the former capital **Sandakan** – infamous in military history as the location of the Death March of Allied soldiers under the Japanese – nearly all visitors make the half-day trip to **Sepilok Orang-Utan Rehabilitation Sanctuary** and some the overnight one to **Turtle Islands National Park**, to catch sight of greenback females laying their eggs. Next stop is the Kinabatangan River, where numerous lodges are bases for languid longboat journeys to view wildlife. Further into the interior, there is the option of visiting a primary rainforest area, **Danum** with its majestic canopy walkway, and **Tabin Wildlife Reserve**, home to interesting conservation projects. Back on the coast, divers especially are pulled to **Semporna**, the jumping-off point for the myriad flora and fauna hidden in the waters surrounding Palau **Sipidan**, Palau **Mabul** and other islands in the Marine Reserve. Trekkers keen to explore the **Maliau Basin**, referred to by some as "Sabah's Lost World" need to get to the frontier boom town, Tawau, from where the little-explored region is a six-hour drive away by 4X4.

Sandakan and around

Situated at the neck of Sandakan Bay and looking out to the Sulu Sea and onwards to the Philippines, the commandingly positioned **SANDAKAN**, like KK, was all but destroyed during World War II. Postwar reconstruction, much of it on reclaimed land, worked around an unimaginable grid system of indistinguishable concrete blocks, but without the sense of space you find in KK. Town life has for decades revolved around the harbour's teeming fish market, but the authorities have cleaned up recently, taking the fish industry into a new, massive concrete, harbourside General Market. An esplanade built on the waterfront and a five-star hotel – set to open in 2010 – adds a bracing sense of regeneration to this lively town.

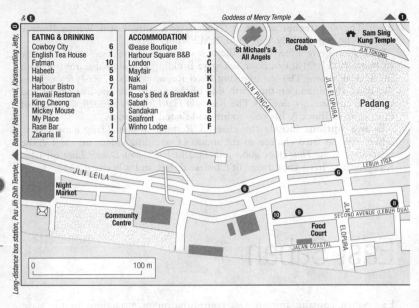

Sandakan's main visitor attractions, beyond the excellent range of accommodation and eating options, are away from the centre. The **Australian War Memorial** is 5km out of town in the suburb of Taman Rimba, whereas Sandakan's heritage is mostly concentrated 1km above the town on Bukit Berenda. Here you can find the Japanese War Memorial, the **Agnes Keith House** and the *English Tea House*, a café with croquet lawn in a restored colonial villa, with stupendous views of the bay beyond.

Outside the town environs, visitors often sign up for trips to **Turtle Islands National Park**, which involve an overnight stay on Pulau Selingan; the three-hour round trip to **Sepilok Orang-Utan Rehabilitation Centre**, 25km along the Labuk road; and the fascinating, and little-visited **Labuk Bay Proboscis Monkey Sanctuary**, a one hour twenty-minute drive east of the town.

Some history

Although there are eighteenth-century accounts of a trading outpost called Sandakan within the Sultanate of Sulu (whose centre was in what's now the Philippines), the town's modern history began in the late 1870s. The area of northeast Borneo between Brunei Bay and Sungai Kinabatangan had been leased by the Sultan of Brunei to the American Trading Company in 1865 but its attempt to establish a settlement here failed, and in 1877 an Anglo-American partnership took up the lease, naming Englishman **William Pryer** as the first Resident (the most senior administrative official) of the east coast.

By 1885 Sandakan was the **capital** of British North Borneo, its natural harbour and proximity to sources of timber, beeswax, rattan and edible birds' nests transforming it into a thriving commercial centre. Sabahian timber was used in the construction of Beijing's Temple of Heaven, and much of Sandakan's early trade was with Hong Kong; there's still a strong Cantonese influence in the town.

In January 1942 the Japanese army took control, establishing a POW camp from where the infamous Death March to Ranau commenced (see p.532).

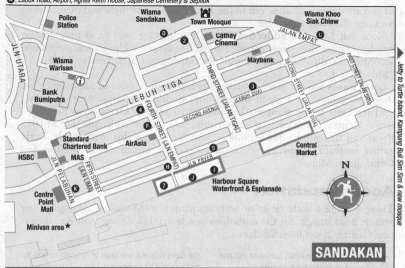

Map labels: Police Station · Wisma Sandakan · Town Mosque · Wisma Khoo Siak Chiew · Catnay Cinema · JALAN EMPAT · Maybank · JLN UTARA · Wisma Warisan · LEBUH TIGA · THIRD STREET (JALAN TIGA) · SECOND STREET (JALAN DUA) · FIRST STREET (JALAN SATU) · Bank Bumiputra · SECOND AVENUE · (LEBUH DUA) · FOURTH STREET (JLN EMPAT) · Standard Chartered Bank · AirAsia · HSBC · MAS · FIFTH STREET (JLN LIMA) · JLN PELABUHAN · JLN PRYER · Central Market · Centre Point Mall · Harbour Square Waterfront & Esplanade · Minivan area · N · **SANDAKAN**

What little of the town was left standing after intensive Allied bombing was burnt down by the Japanese, and the end of the war saw the administration of Sabah shift to KK. Nevertheless, by the 1950s a rebuilt Sandakan profited from the **timber** boom and by the 1970s had generated such wealth that the town was reputed to have the world's greatest concentration of millionaires. Once the region's decent timber had been exhausted in the early 1980s, Sandakan looked to **oil palm** and cocoa, crops which now dominate the surrounding landscape. Nowadays, these agro-industries face hard times; commercial suburbs on either side of Sandakan's Labuk Road have sprouted, reflecting an emphasis on small-scale, service and niche technology industries.

Arrival, information and transport

The **long-distance bus station** is 4km west of town; buses and minivans (RM1) pass by on the main road in front of the station. Taxis (RM10) often congregate in the station, or can be hailed on the main road. There are no buses into town from the **airport**, 11km north of Sandakan. Catch a minivan from arrivals (RM2); otherwise you're dependent on a taxi into the centre (RM22). The **ferry** from Zamboanga, in the Philippines, docks at **Karamunting Jetty**, 6km west of town – there are usually minivans (RM3) awaiting the new arrivals. A taxi from the docks into town costs around RM15.

Sandakan has an excellent **tourist office** (Mon–Fri 8am–12.30pm; ☏089/229751, ✉esong02@tm.net.my), housed in Wisma Warisan, the old government building of the British administration, reached by going up the steps from Lebuh Tiga and turning left at the top. The centre's coordinator is highly knowledgeable and has good local contacts.

It's best to contact Crystal Quest at Sabah Parks jetty, Jalan Buli Sim-Sim, 400m west of the town centre (☏089/212711, ✉cquest@tm.net.my) ahead of time if you are going to Turtle Islands National Park, for which you need to overnight in chalets on **Pulau Selingan**. Many visitors arrange the trip through another tour operator (see p.534), but Crystal Quest's prices, given that all you are doing is heading out to the island, staying the night and then coming back, are the most reasonable.

Note that Sandakan **addresses** take a little getting used to, as they rely on numbers rather than street names; indeed less central addresses are pinpointed according to their distances out of the downtown area, hence "Mile 1.5", "Mile 3" and so on.

Local **buses** vie for space on Jalan Pryer; the only ones of importance are the red-, yellow- and green-striped ones bound for points west, travelling up Jalan Leila to the night market and out to Sepilok Orang-utan Rehabilitation Centre. There are two bus termini, one on the esplanade side of Jalan Pryer and the other – for Sepilok – 50m further on this road, south. **Taxis** gather in front of the supermarket beside the esplanade bus station and Gentingmas Mall.

Accommodation

There is quite a wide range of accommodation in Sandakan, although many visitors head straight for the resthouses beside Sepilok Orang-utan Rehabilitation Centre, 20km from Sandakan.

@ease Boutique Hotel Sandakan Harbour Square ☎089/214888, ⓦwww.at -easehotels.com. Financed by the Miri-based *ParkCity Everly*, the *@ease* is far from a chain hotel. Its colourful, glass-dominated foyer leads one way to the esplanade's line of cafés and the other, out toward Sandakan's busiest street and bus station. Rooms are quite fantastic, with numerous, minimally elegant touches and the view – overlooking Sandakan Bay – is so sublime that it is worth begging for a front-side room. The *@ease* also has a mellow coffee lounge and a breakfast room in an annexe. ❹

Harbour Square B & B First floor, 100 Harbour Square ☎089/211113. Friendly backpackers' place with a pivotal location overlooking the bay; dorms, the cheapest in town (RM18) are, like the doubles, small and stuffy. There's a rooftop extension – perfect for drying clothes. ❷

London First floor, 10 Jalan Empat ☎089/216371, ⓦwww.hlondon.com.my. The refurbished *London's* most enticing feature is its rooftop area with fine views overlooking town and out towards the sea. Rooms are simple and clean. ❸

Mayfair First floor, 24 Jalan Pryer ☎089/219855. This is a treat of a place: a superbly positioned, wonderfully airy guesthouse which is the pride and joy of its Chinese owner. All rooms are equipped with DVD players (guests can borrow DVDs for free from the owner's huge collection) and the a/c is extremely cooling. ❷

Nak Jalan Pelahuban ☎089/272988, ⓔinfo @nakhotel.com. Close to the second bus terminus,

the *Nak's* rooms are in need of sprucing up and the bathrooms a bit grubby, but it's a solid place nevertheless. A nice roof garden café, too. ❹

Ramai Jalan Leila ☎089/273222. Real effort has been made in this excellent mid-range hotel, whose forty spacious rooms, complete with splendid bathrooms, TV and a/c, are 2km west of the city centre on the main drag into town. Minivans pass every few minutes (RM1) and taxis usually arrive in a jiffy (RM6). ❹

Rose's Bed and Breakfast second & third floors, Block C, Lot 6, Bandar Ramai Ramai ☎089/223582, ⓔrosebb@tm.net.my. Friendly and functional hostel (close to the *Ramai*), with a communal living room, internet access and kitchen. Dorm beds RM15; ❷.

Sabah Km 1, Jalan Utara ☎089/213299, ⓦwww .sabahhotel.com.my. Sandakan's five-star finest, located 2km north of town (taxi RM5), with swish restaurants, business centre, swimming pool and sports facilities. ❽

Sandakan Wisma Sandakan ☎089/221122, ⓦwww.hotelsandakan.com.my. The town's most popular hotel for business folk and visiting local families. It is quite good value, given the fine service, large rooms and excellent restaurant. ❺

Seafront Fourth lane, Jalan Leila ☎089/222233. At the corner with Jalan Elopura, this mid-range is a good choice, although the neat rooms can be small. ❸

Winho Lodge First floor, 19 Jalan Dua ☎089/212310. Backpackers with small dorms (RM22) and rooms with communal bathrooms. ❷

The Town

The grid of streets which constitutes the centre of the town is hemmed in by the Bukit Berenda (Trig Hill) to the west and Sandakan Bay to the east. The northern end of town is dominated by the massive three-storey **Central Market** (daily 6am–8pm) with fresh produce (fish, meat, fruit and vegetables) on the first floor, a variety of clothes and produce stalls on the second, and a range of cafés, best at breakfast, on the top. The ones offering Malay buffets and local coffee are of the highest quality. Back from the market are blocks of busy, but grubby, streets, lined with cafés and retail shops; along Lebuh Tiga you'll see a set of wide steps, which leads to the tourist office and, across a car park, up onto the hill, the fastest, pedestrianized route up to Trig Hill, and heritage Sandakan.

Immediately south of the market, circumnavigate the various building sites to hit the Waterfront, where an esplanade is backed by various excellent cafés and restaurants. From here the main street, Jalan Pryer, leads to the two bus stations and the small plaza, Centre Point. Two blocks west of here is the padang now, sadly, used just once a year on Merdeka Day.

A five-minute walk northwest of the padang, up Jalan Puncak gets you to the well-tended surroundings of Sandakan's colonial remnants, in particular the quintessentially English **St Michael's and All Angels Church**. A few minutes

The house on the hill

The house on the hill was where **Agnes Newton Keith** lived in the 1930s, writing evocative and descriptive books on Sabah including *Land Below the Wind* and *White Man Returns*. But her most famous novel, *Three Came Home*, was written during World War II while she and her infant son were interned at Pulau Berhala in terrible conditions, along with other European women. These works sold Sabah to the rest of the world long before detailed guidebooks came about. Now, after many years as a ruin, the house's restoration has been overseen in a joint project by the Museums and Antiquities Department in KL and the Sabah Museum in KK. In 2005 the house opened, largely to highlight Sabah's colonial heritage.

Downstairs, reproductions of colonial furniture decorate the rooms while the staircase landing is adorned with imitation skulls and other artefacts including Murut blowpipes; upstairs is a study room with a collection of guns and knives and ceramics from the Sung and Ming dynasties (on loan from the Sabah Museum collection). There is also an area displaying first editions of Agnes Keith's seven books, all in their original covers, and exhibits featuring photographs, quotations and texts of the Keith family. The end room has been converted into a small cinema where the movie version of *Three Came Home* and the documentary, *Sandakan 1950*, a vivid testimony to the era that's well worth watching, are both screened.

Keith was one of only twenty Caucasian women living in Sandakan on the eve of World War II but her writings indicate that she didn't identify much with the rest of the Europeans, preferring to describe the indigenous peoples – especially the servants she had regular dealings with – the country and local architecture. She loved Sandakan's friendly, inviting people and atmospheric warren of godowns. In *Barefoot in the Palace* she wrote, "We knew that we could walk into any ramshackle, threadbare, war-salvaged dwelling or shop of any pre-war Sandakan inhabitant, and ask, and receive, whatever we needed." It seems she was less enamoured of the lifestyle of the British of the time. "The significance attached to doing and saying the right thing irked me", she wrote, but she adapted to it because her husband, Harry, was an administrative officer.

further north up Jalan Singapura is Sandakan's oldest temple, the Taoist **Goddess of Mercy Temple**, set in a grove of magnificent palms; unfortunately modernization has robbed it of any character.

Heritage Sandakan

From the temple, a sweaty, twenty-minute walk north up Jalan Utara, across on the eastern side of the padang, brings you to the foot of Jalan Istana on Trig Hill, from where an **observation point** offers good views of the town, boats and islands below. It is also possible to reach the point a rather faster way – if you are in the centre – by climbing the hundred steps from behind the tourist office. This route leads you out onto Jalan Istana. To reach the **Japanese War Memorial**, financed and built by the families of the deceased, walk ten minutes north (to the right).

Directly ahead (on Jalan Istana) is the beautifully restored colonial building that's now the *English Tea House and Restaurant*, and next door is the **Agnes Keith House** (daily 9am–5pm; RM15), a museum based on the life and achievements of the World War II British novelist (see box, p.531).

Turn left down Jalan Istana, past the observation point, and you're at the half-Tudor, half-kampung-like **Astana**. Just past this grand building, is the huge town **cemetery**, its thousands of green and sky-blue gravestones banked impressively up a hillside.

Sandakan Memorial Park

Ten kilometres west of Sandakan, past the long-distance bus station on Jalan Rimba, is **Sandakan Memorial Park** (9am–5pm; free). The park marks the site of the World War II POW camp where the **Death March** of 1945 originated. In 1942, 2700 British and Australian soldiers were transported from Singapore to Sandakan and set to work building an airstrip. By early 1945 many had died, but the surviving 1800 Australians and 600 British troops were force-marched to Ranau, where they were to start work on a new project. Just six soldiers, all Australian, survived the 240-kilometre march through mud and jungle. Dominating the park is a simple white block dedicated to the Allies who fought in North Borneo, as well as the locals who helped POWs and those involved in the Sandakan underground movement. Remnants of the camp are scattered around the sadly neglected grounds of the park; notice the decaying, and surprisingly small, tank and odd shards of corroded piping sticking out of the forlorn shrub. To get there take bus #4 (Mile 8: RM1.30) from Jalan Pryer bus station 1 and asks for the Taman Rimba stop; then walk along Jalan Rimba for ten minutes – the park is on your right; a taxi costs RM25 from central Sandakan.

Eating, drinking and nightlife

Sandakan may not be able to match KK's variety of **restaurants**, but there's still enough choice here to suit most people, with Malay, Chinese, Indian and Western food all well represented. Most places are in the town centre or along Jalan Leila, where several popular **seafood** restaurants open every evening. A recent addition is the set of cafés along the Waterfront esplanade, which have proved very popular with independent travellers and tour groups.

Also, take time to visit the *English Tea House* which attracts anyone who's after a quality cup of tea, with optional toast and jam. The *Tea House* garden commands a wonderful view at sunset and has the added attractions of a croquet lawn and Pimms on request as well as more substantial fare.

For **hawker stalls**, head first for the Central Market, where stalls open early and are particularly good for breakfast, or the night market on Jalan Leila, ten minutes' walk west of the centre, where Malay *nasi*, including mango salad in lime dressing and *lanka* – bamboo shoots in curry sauce – as well as chicken wings and *pisang goreng* (fried bananas) are of the highest standard but at the customary low prices.

Beer is widely available in Chinese restaurants and coffee shops. Head for the esplanade's cafés and the bar in front of the *@ease Hotel*. Amid the town's grid of streets, **bars** include *Cowboy City* on Jalan Lelia, a big, bare, air-conditioned place which doesn't get started until after 10pm and *Fatman* and *Mickey Mouse* – close to the Rex Cinema at the western end of Second Avenue.

English Tea House Jalan Istana ☏089/222544, ⊛www.asiaextreme .biz/eth. British favourites including pies, both savoury and sweet, and baked potatoes are firm favourites although quality Malay and Indian food is also available. Most important perhaps – you can get the best pot of tea in Sabah here. Prices range from RM5 for tea, RM15 for the pies and RM25 for full meals. Daily 10am–midnight.

Habeeb Jalan Pryer. Fast and efficient two-floor canteen on Sandakan's busiest street serving no-frills favourites like *nasi campur* and *roti canai*.

Haji The fresh juices and rotis at this popular Muslim Indian place are memorable, as is the creamy chicken korma. There's an a/c dining room upstairs. Daily 8am–9pm.

Harbour Bistro 88 Harbour Square. One of a number of busy cafés on the esplanade overlooking the bay with a wide choice of meals from Western burgers to satay, *nasi campur* and seafood.

Hawaii Restoran *City View Hotel*, Lebuh Tiga. Trumping just about everywhere else for evening dining, this nondescript-looking evening café churns out delicious fare, from an extensive menu of Western, Chinese, Malay and Indian dishes.

King Cheong 34 Lebuh Dua. A Sandakan legend, this excellent café serves delicious dim sum in the mornings.

My Place 12 Harbour Square. This new café, fronting the *@ease Hotel*, has well-cooked Chinese dishes, plus beer; the TVs are usually tuned to global sports channels.

Zakaria III Corner of Jalan Buli Sim-Sim and Lebuh Tiga (opposite the *Sandakan* hotel). Inexpensive and highly popular locals' eatery specializing in fiery dhal and South Indian curries; softer Malay dishes are available too.

Moving on from Sandakan

By air

There are daily flights on AirAsia and MAS to KL and KK; MASwings also flies to KK, and to Tawau.

By boat

Two companies currently run passenger **ferries** to Zamboanga in the Philippines, each once a week. Velvet Success (☏089/212872) go via Bongao and Jolo, leaving at 6am (13hr; RM250) whereas Timarine (☏089/224009), leaves at 7pm (20hr; RM250). Take a Pasir Putih bus from the city bus station to the latter's office (RM1) at Batu 1.5, Jalan Leila. The ferries depart from the harbour, 5km west of town. Take the minivan from the minivan stand (RM3); a taxi costs RM15.

By bus

There are hourly **buses** every day to KK (first departure 6.30am, last departure 8pm; 6hr; RM50), passing the entrance to Gunung Kinabalu park (4hr 30min; RM40); five to Lahad Datu (3hr; RM25) and five to Tawau (6hr; RM50). It is necessary to book ahead with bus company Luyung-Luyung (☏019/8419879) for the Sandakan–KK coach as this is a particularly busy route. The best way to book ahead is by travelling to the long-distance bus station at Batu 2.5, 4km north of town, to buy your ticket. Buses from the local bus station travel there (RM1), or a taxi costs RM12.

Listings

Airlines MAS, main branch at airport
☏089/674813; town branch, Sabah Building, Jalan
Pelabuhan ☏089/273966 (Mon–Fri
8am–4.30pm, Sat 8am–3pm, Sun 8am–noon).

Banks and exchange CIMB, opposite Standard
Chartered Bank, Lebuh Tiga ☏089/213271;
Maybank, Lebuh Tiga ☏089/213918; HSBC, corner
of Third Ave and Jalan Pelabuhan; Maybank, Third
Ave ☏089/213122; Standard Chartered Bank,
Sabah Building, Jalan Pelabuhan ☏089/275723.

Buses for pre-booking seats to KK, call Tung Ma
☏089/210054 or Sida ☏019/8737808, although
it's best to book at the long-distance bus station,
4km north of town.

Car rental M.B. Permai Tours (☏089/219534 or
019/8014795, ✉mbpermaitours@yahoo.com), Lot 3,
Terminal Building, Sandakan Airport; *Sabah Hotel*
Cars (☏089/213299, ⓦwww.sabahhotel.com.my).

Hospital Duchess of Kent, Jalan Utara, 2km north
of the centre (☏089/212111).

Internet access Cyberjazz.net & Komputer Jazz,
lot 7, Centre Point mall; Internet Cybercafé, second
floor, room 219, Wisma Sandakan.

Pharmacy Borneo Dispensary, corner of Fifth St
and Second Ave.

Police The main police station is on Jalan Utara,
1.5 km from town (☏089/211222).

Post office Sandakan's GPO is 5min walk west of
town, on Jalan Leila (Mon–Sat 8am–4.30pm).

Telephones International calls can be made at the
Telekom office, A-6-G, Block A, Jalan Utara, Bandar
Maju (Mon–Fri 8.30am–5.30pm); IDD calls can only
be made on card phones.

Tour operators Borneo Eco Tours, c/o *Hotel
Hsiang Garden*, Jalan Leila, PO Box 82
☏089/220210, ✉info@borneoecotours.com for
Sukau Lodge, Gomantong Caves and Turtle
Islands; SI Tours, tenth floor, Lot 1002, Wisma
Khoo Siak Chiew ☏089/213502, ⓦwww
.sitoursborneo.com for Turtle Islands, Abai Lodge
on the Kinabatangan River, Sepilok and Labuk
Bay; Wildlife Expeditions, Room 903, ninth floor,
Wisma Khoo Siak Chew ☏089/219616, ⓦwww
.wildlife-expeditions.com.my for Sukau, Sepilok,
Turtle Islands and Labuk Bay Proboscis Monkey
Sanctuary. For *Sepilok Nature Resort* and accom-
modation at *Lankayan Island Dive Resort* contact
Pulau Sipadan Resort and Tours, first floor, Lot 7,
Block A, Bandar Pasaraya, Mile 4, North Rd
☏089/228081, ✉sepilok@po.jaring.my. To
arrange accommodation on Turtle Islands,
contact Crystal Quest (see p.529).

Visa extensions Immigration Office, Wisma Secretariat, Batu 7, Ranau Rd ☏089/666552.

Turtle Islands National Park

Peeping out of the Sulu Sea some 40km north of Sandakan, three tiny islands comprise Sabah's **TURTLE ISLANDS NATIONAL PARK**. They are the favoured egg-laying sites of the green and hawksbill turtles, varying numbers of which haul themselves laboriously above the high-tide mark to bury their clutches of eggs almost every night of the year. Malaysia's first turtle hatchery was established here to help protect them and, today, all three of the park's islands (Pulau Selingan, Pulau Bakkungan Kecil and Pulau Gulisaan) have hatcheries – though only **Selingan** can be visited by tourists. It's an extraordi-nary experience – as well as seeing a mother turtle laying her eggs, you can watch as the park wardens release newly hatched turtles, which waddle, Chaplin-like, into the sea to face an uncertain future.

Turtles of both species don't begin to come ashore until after 7pm – rangers scout the island after dark and alert you once a sighting has been made. Typically, it takes a few hours for a female to lurch up the sand, dig a nesting pit and lay her slimy, ping-pong-ball-sized eggs – an average clutch will contain between thirty and eighty. All the egg-laying turtles are tagged, to aid research into the size and distribution of Southeast Asia's turtle population; their eggs, meanwhile, are taken for reburial to the hatchery, where they are safeguarded from hungry rats and birds.

There's plenty of time for **swimming** and **sunbathing** on Selingan before the turtle-watching (but watch out for sandflies which can be voracious, especially when it rains); alternatively, you can go **snorkelling** off nearby Bakkungan Kecil (RM60 per person, minimum four people; details from reception).

Practicalities

You can only visit the park as part of a **tour** with island transfer and accommodation included in the package price (for example, RM230 with Crystal Quest, see p.529). Although you need a **permit** to visit the island, the tour group you are with will organize that for you. The package is pretty much the same whichever operator you go with – **boats** leave the Crystal Quest jetty, 300m east of Sandakan town centre at 8am to 9am (operators will pick you up from your hotel or hostel a little earlier) and arrive at the island an hour later. Note that the day is then yours to stroll around the tiny island, swim or chill out in your room before the turtle viewing. There are beds for around fifty visitors a night, all of whom are put up in the island's comfortable, although fairly basic, **chalets**. Everyone eats in the same **café** – the rather average buffet spreads are included in the package. Boats leave the next morning at 7am, after breakfast.

Sepilok Orang-utan Rehabilitation Centre

Orang-utans – tail-less, red-haired apes (their name means "man of the forest" in Malay) – can reach a height of around 1.65m, and can live to over 30 years old. Solitary but not aggressively territorial, these primates live a largely arboreal existence, eating fruit, leaves, bark and the occasional insect. One of only a few sanctuaries for these creatures in the world is the **Sepilok Orang-utan Rehabilitation Centre** (daily 9am–noon & 2–4pm; RM30, photographic pass RM10; ℡089/531180, ✆soutan@po.jaring.my) set up in 1964 and occupying a 43-square-kilometre patch of lowland rainforest 25km west of Sandakan. Sepilok is Sabah's most popular tourist site and on most days there are two hundred plus people crowding onto the viewing platform during feeding hours. So closely related to mankind, these wonderful creatures charm viewers as they swing and lope about, and gnaw at the ripe fruit tossed by the wardens. Recent research has established that orang-utans operate trading systems for food stuffs.

▲ Orang-utan

The orang-utans at the centre are mostly victims of forest clearance, with many orphaned and injured and (not surprisingly) traumatized in the process. Some have also been kept as pets (now prohibited by law) – when domesticated their survival instincts remain undeveloped. At Sepilok they're trained to fend for themselves in the wild. Although not always successful, the training process has so far seen more than a hundred reintroduced to their natural habitat.

At the **information centre** there's an exhibition on forest preservation and a useful video outlining the work carried out here is shown five times daily; check for times on arrival.

Feeding times

Close to **feeding time**, a warden leads the assembled group for the ten-minute walk along a plankway, passing the nursery, where baby orang-utans are taught elementary climbing skills on ropes and branches, to the feeding station (feeding times 10am & 3pm, daily). There are usually at least two orang-utans waiting for their meal, often the very young ones, and they immediately cluster round the warden as he sets out the fruit. Others may soon come along, swinging, shimmying and strolling towards their breakfast (or lunch), jealously watched by gangs of macaques that loiter around for scraps. The more cunning orang-utans take away enough bananas for a less public meal in the surrounding trees.

Getting there

The blue Sepilok Batu 14 **minibus** (30min; RM3.50) leaves from Jalan Pryer terminus 2 six times daily (8am–3.20pm) but the two most useful ones for visitors are the 9am and 2pm as they arrive in good time for the feeding sessions. These minivans aren't that regular; an alternative is to catch, from the same spot in Sandakan, a Batu 16 or 19 bus (50min; RM2.50), which drops you at Sepilok Junction, 3km from the Sanctuary, on Jalan Sepilok. Although taxis frequently ply this route (RM10), it's also generally easy to hitchhike the remaining distance. The last Batu 14 leaves from the centre at 4.30pm; any later and you'll need to hitch or walk to the main road and flag down a bus or minivan.

Accommodation & eating

Many visitors choose to stay in and around Sepilok as the **accommodation** is of quite a high standard – and good value for money; plus the location is particularly convenient for onward bus travel to Lahud Datu, for Danum or Tabin, and to Semporna for diving off Sipadan. The resorts and guesthouses below are on or just off the Sepilok Road which leads from the trunk road to the Orang-utan Rehabilitation Centre. Most offer food but there is also a café at the centre itself (9am–4pm) selling simple meals, cakes and drinks.

Labuk B & B Jalan Rambutan-Sepilok, Mile 14 ☎089/533190, ⓦwww .sepilokforestedge.com. The most isolated of the lodges, set 1km down a road which runs at right angles from the centre, this charming place has a tiny pool and funky chalets dotted around a landscaped garden. The owners have small dorms too (RM28). ❸

Paganakan Dii Tropical Retreat Mile 14, Jalan Labuk ☎089/532005. The furthest lodge from the centre, the *Paganakan* is located at Sepilok Junction, 4km away. Dorm beds at this tasteful retreat are RM28 and the stand-alone cabins extremely good value. ❷

Sepilok B&B Lorong Sepilok ☎089/532288. Rather more basic than the others with small, pleasant rooms and acceptable dorms (RM22). ❸

Sepilok Jungle Resort Lorong Sepilok ☎089/533031, ⓔsepilokjr@yahoo.com. Large set-up with a complex of dorms (RM28) and rustic cabins nestling under coconut trees. Its *Banana Café* serves good Malay cuisine and snacks. ❸

Sepilok Nature Resort Lorong Sepilok ☎89/765200, ⓦsepilok.com. Plush, eco-aware chalets nestling in lush jungle; the in-house restaurant serves the best food in Sepilok (around RM25 for a full meal). ➐

Sepilok Resthouse Lorong Sepilok ☎089/534900, ✉imejbs@tm.net.my. Located a little further down the lane but still only 5min walk from the centre, this resthouse has spacious en-suite rooms and internet access. ➌

🏃 **Uncle Tan's B&B** Jalan Sepilok ☎016/8244749, ⊛www.uncletan.com. A Sabah institution, this enormously popular backpackers' place has recently moved closer to the Orang-utan Rehabilitation Centre. Although this competitively priced place is a perfect stop for the centre, most visitors are on a package tour, which also includes a night or more at *Uncle Tan's Wildlife Camp* on the Kinabatangam River (RM320 for three days, two nights, including three meals a day and transport to/from Sandakan). To get to *Uncle Tan's B&B* take the Batu 16 bus from Sandakan's Jalan Pryer terminus 2 and get off at Sepilok Junction. The *B&B* (RM38 plus three meals a day) is 50m along Sepilok road, 3km from the centre. ➌

Wildlife Lodge Lorong Sepilok ☎089/533031. A welcoming, family-run operation set in delightful grounds. Dorm beds RM25, ➌.

Labuk Bay Proboscis Monkey Sanctuary

The **Labuk Bay Proboscis Monkey Sanctuary**, Mile 8, Jalan Lintas (☎089/672133, ⊛www.proboscis.cc), is 20km west of Sepilok near Kampung Samawang, Labuk Bay. The sanctuary, reached by a track through an oil palm plantation, is set in an area of mangrove forest teeming with wild proboscis monkeys (see box, p.724). A large observation platform at sanctuary HQ offers a perfect vantage point from which to view them (there are set feeding times at 10am and 3pm). Also at the HQ, the sanctuary's **Information Centre** shows a video on the monkeys, viewable on request, and a kiosk provides drinks and snacks. From the viewing platform you can watch other monkeys scavenge fruit left for the proboscis families, and some fantastic birdlife – including hornbills. The sanctuary is a great place to visit, a highlight of any trip to east Sabah.

Practicalities

As yet it is not possible to travel independently to the sanctuary – most visitors come on a half-day tour (RM150), or catch a taxi (RM60 one way; RM100 return with 2hr maximum waiting time). Given warning, the sanctuary's manager Sean Lee Vui Vun can arrange for a small group to be transported back and forth from Sandakan, particularly if guests want to stay at his *Nipah Lodge* (RM150 minimum two people, RM200 if alone).

Accommodation is in the *Nipah Lodge*, a mini-resort closer to the sea and set in a mangrove forest, around 5km from the Sanctuary HQ and observation platform. As well as a large communal area and café there are a few dozen lovely chalets amid the mangroves, reachable on plankway (➏), and a longer building where small dorms are available (RM30).

Pulau Lankayan

An hour-and-a-half's boat ride north of Sandakan in the Sulu Sea lies the **Sugud Islands Marine Conservation Area**, comprising three islands: Lankayan, Billiean and Tegaipil. Designated a protected area in December 2001, only **PULAU LANKAYAN** is open, following a deal struck between the eco-friendly Pulau Sipadan Tours and Resorts and the Sabah state government. Most of the other end of the island is taken up by a Malaysian navy base. Although the island itself is beautiful – at most points the lush tropical vegetation stretches down to the coastline's pure white sandy beaches – it's the diving which is the real pull. The dive sites compare well with the better-known Pulau Sipadan. The island is surrounded by hard and soft corals, which offer an array of macro fauna. From March through to May, sightings of whale sharks are frequent.

Pulau Lankayan itself can only be visited on a tour with Pulau Sipadan Tours and Resorts (ground floor, Block C, Lot 38 & 39, Mile 6, Bandar Tyng, off the Labuk Rd, Sandakan; ℡089/673999, Ⓦwww.lankayan-island.com) and although all packages include transport to the island (there is no other way of getting there), prices vary depending on the amount of diving you want to do. A two-day, one-night stay including transport from KK on a Russian Antonov plane and food costs, around RM1000 (not including dives).

Sungai Kinabatangan and Sukau

South of Sandakan Bay, Sabah's longest river, the 560km **Kinabatangan**, ends its northeasterly journey from the interior to the Sulu Sea. Whereas logging has had an adverse impact on the river's ecology upstream, the dual threats of piracy and flooding have kept its lower reaches, with its boundaries a narrow corridor of primary and secondary rainforest, largely free of development, and the area is therefore rich in **wildlife**. It is the largest forested flood plain in Malaysia, laden with oxbow lakes, mangrove and grass swamps and distinctive vegetation including massive fig trees overhanging the water's edge.

The best way to view the **Kinabatangan Wildlife Sanctuary** is on a tour, (see p.534) with each operator offering similar activities: boat trips along the river and its tributaries in the early morning, early evening or at night. Visitors can also go on short hikes away from the river on narrow paths in search of **orang-utan** nests – catching sight of a new nest usually means the orang-utan isn't far behind, as the solitary animal builds a different one each day.

Independent travellers head for **Sukau**, a quiet kampung near to the main tributaries. It is possible to stay here and charter boats at a much reduced cost. There are however reports that nature-watching at the lodges close to Sukau

▲ Boating down Sungai Kinabatangan

has become a frustrating experience, with dozens of boats converging along the same narrow tributaries at the same hour. It's worth heading here on Friday for Sukau's weekly *tamu*, when locally made sarongs are sold alongside chickens, kitchenware and jungle produce; there's also a smaller daily market.

Some travellers prefer the downstream areas of Bilat and Abai, which attract fewer tourist boats.

Arrival and information

Although tour operators arrange transport to their lodges and camps, it's relatively easy to get to Sukau (10km from the river mouth) by public transport. From Sandakan's terminus 2 take a Lahud Datu **minivan** (hourly; 3hr; RM10), get off at the Sukau junction, and wait for a Sukau minivan (hourly; 80min; RM10). For travel direct from Sandakan to Sukau call Nazim Siddek (℡019/8001956) or Haj Nordim (℡014/8508714), who run minivans on that route. However, both need to be contacted ahead, as they don't go every day. These vans usually leave Sandkan at 1pm and return from Sukau early the next day.

Accommodation

Most visitors stay in their tour operators' comfortable **jungle lodges** located on the Lower Kinabatangan flood plain. There are also quite a few **lodges** around the Sukau stretch of the river, all of which can only be visited on a pre-booked package: prices vary immensely; from RM300 to upwards of RM800 for overnight packages (including transport from Sandakan). The cheapest option is to stay in **Sukau** itself (most of the jungle lodges are only a few hundred metres upstream from here), from where you can hire a boat and guide to take you up to the Wildlife Sanctuary.

Lower Kinabatangan flood plain

🏃 **Abai Jungle Restaurant and Lodge** C/o as SI Tours (see p.534).
A spacious base situated 47km from the Kinabatangan River mouth, with easy access to tributaries, which are far less congested with tourist boats than those near Sukau. The lodge has eighteen en-suite doubles; a number of 500m trails snake out from the lodge into the jungle. Prices are around RM850 for a package including overnight stay, meals and transport from Sandakan.

Nature Lodge Kinabatangan ℡089/220299, ✉singmata@streamyx.com. This budget option, also downstream from Sukau, has the added advantage of trails in the surrounding forest. A one-night stay here (plus transport and meals) costs around RM350.

Uncle Tan's Wildlife Camp ℡089/531639, ⓦwww.uncletan.com. Located further downriver, away from the sometimes rather congested upriver waterways around Sukau, this lodge is twinned with *Uncle Tan's B&B* near Sepilok. Although the camp is more basic than the hostel, it has an excellent location, and has been a big hit with the backpacker market for many years. The standard three-night package (RM320) includes accommodation in four-to-six berth huts, three meals a day, river safaris and jungle treks.

Kampung Sukau

Sukau B&B 1km east of the village. ℡089/230269. Run by Esri Masri, this has a few twin-bed rooms with communal bathrooms in a homestay arrangement. Masri can provide lunch and dinner (RM30 per day). Hiring a boat (plus guide) costs from RM70 to RM100 a day depending on the intended destination. ❶

Temonggoh Riverview Lodge ℡089/235525. Located 2km along the river bank and run by the brothers Udik and Udin. They offer treks into the surrounding forest (RM50 for 3hr; minimum two people) and can arrange boat trips along the river (same prices as *Sukau B&B*). ❷

Around Sukau

Proboscis Lodge run by Sipadan Dive Centre ℡088/240584, ⓦwww.sipadandivers.com/pls. This lodge, which has two dozen en-suite doubles, a café and communal area, is close to the Sukau jetty, a little further away from the tributaries the boats snake down. Prices range from RM450 for overnight stay, meals and river cruise, with pick-up from Sukau jetty, to RM800 for overnight stay and transport from Sandakan.

🏃 **Sukau Rainforest Lodge** run by Borneo Eco Tours ☎ 088/438300, ⊛ www.sukau .com. Comprises twenty twin-bed chalets on stilts

just 200m upstream from the kampung. This lodge is a fine example of ecotourism, using only solar energy, and is well worth a visit. The three daily meals (included in the price) are of a superb standard and the guided trips at dawn and dusk organized by Joseph "Sumo" Chung are fascinating. RM750 two day, one night package includes transport, boat travel and food.

Kinabatangan Wildlife Sanctuary

Despite Sabah's rather haphazard approach to making the most of its superb natural resources, the designation of the Kinabatangan as a **wildlife sanctuary** in 1999 was a brilliant move. That said, sanctuary status is one level below that of a national park, and so villages and agricultural development have been allowed to crisscross the protected sections. The river's protected wildlife corridor makes it highly likely that over a number of boat rides and short treks, you will see Asian elephants, orang-utans, proboscis and macaque monkeys and gibbons, who all dwell in the forest flanking the river. The resident **birdlife** is equally impressive. With luck, visitors get glimpses of hornbills, brahminy kites, crested serpent eagles, egrets, exquisite blue-banded and stork-billed kingfishers, and oriental darters, which dive underwater to find food and then sit on the shore, their wings stretched out to dry. In the river itself are freshwater sharks, (small) crocodiles and rays, and a great variety of fish species.

River safaris

A usual river safari along the Kinabatangan tributary, the **Menanggul**, where you may catch sight of gibbons, proboscis monkeys and the occasional orang-utan, takes around three hours. A visit to Kelenanap and Kelandaun **oxbow lakes**, a most relaxing trip, good for birdwatching and perhaps for a sighting of a napping crocodile, usually takes four hours in total. Longer rides to kampungs of **Bilet** and **Abai**, close to quieter tributaries, are an adventurous alternative but will take all day and are likely to cost at least RM150. Note that there is no public transport to either Abai or Bilet – travellers either go from Sukau by boat or arrange transport with the lodge owners/operators mentioned on p.534.

Batu Putih and Gomantong Caves

Within the limestone outcrop of **Batu Putih** (known locally as Batu Tulug), 1km north of the Kinabatangan bridge on the road between Sandakan and Lahad Datu, small **caves**, visible from the road, contain wooden coffins well over a hundred years old. It was from here that the coffin lid with a buffalo's head carved into handles, displayed at the Sabah State Museum, was taken; other coffins are still in their original spots, though unless archeology is your passion, think twice about making the detour to see them. All buses running between Sandakan and Lahad Datu pass by the caves (no admission charge).

Gomantong Caves

Off the Sukau road, the **Gomantong Caves** are vast limestone cavities with a strange claim to fame: deep in the main cave, there is the largest pile of guano (bat's droppings) in the world. The bats, as at Deer Cave in Sarawak, vacate the caves at sundown to forage for food, before returning before morning. The caves' other chirpy residents are an equally large number of **swiftlets** whose nests are harvested for the bird's nest soup trade (see p.622). Outside the caves there's a picnic site and canteen, and an **information centre** (☎089/230189, Ⓦwww.sabah.gov.my /jhl; RM30), which adequately describes the caves' ecosystem.

It's easiest to visit the caves as part of a **tour**; *Uncle Tan's*, for example, will include a detour to the caves as part of their tours around Sungai Kinabatangan for an extra RM40 per person.

To get to the caves under your own steam **from Sandakan**, get a Sukau-bound minivan and ask to be dropped at the junction for Gomantong (RM15; 20km before Sukau), from where it's a five-kilometre hike to the caves. Alternatively, if you're on a bus to or from Lahad Datu (see p.542), get off at the turning for Sukau, and catch a minivan or motorbike taxi (both RM10) for the 20km to the Gomantong junction. It is best to bring ID with you to show to the park staff at the caves.

There is nowhere to stay or eat in and around Gomantong, so plan to leave the caves well before dark if you are not on a tour.

From Semporna to the Maliau Basin

Sabah's main trunk road southeast continues to the towns of **Lahad Datu** and **Tawau**; the central mountain ranges taper away, to be replaced by lowland – and sometimes swampy – coastal regions lapped by the **Sulu** and **Celebes** seas, and dominated by oil-palm plantations. Archeological finds around **Madai** – halfway between Lahad Datu and Tawau – indicate that this area of Borneo has been inhabited for over five thousand years. Nowadays, this is Sabah's "wild east": historically, pirates working out of islands in the nearby Filipino waters posed a real threat to fishermen, and the separatist Filipino organization Abu Sayyaf has operated from the Mindanao islands, only twenty minutes by speedboat from Semporna. There are estimates that around one million illegal immigrants from the Philippines and Indonesia now call Sabah home, eking out a living on the streets. The influx began in the 1960s, when they were drawn by the prospect of work on Sabah's plantations, and has risen sharply since the 1970s as a result of the civil unrest in Mindanao and higher living standards in Malaysian Borneo.

West of the Lahad Datu road lies the rainforest enclave, **Danum Valley Conservation Area**, while east is the mostly secondary-forested **Tabin Wildlife Reserve**. Closer to Kalimantan, and around the southern lip of wide **Darvel Bay**, the oceanic islands off Semporna, **Sipadan**, **Mabul** and **Kapalai**, are acclaimed **diving** spots, their reefs ablaze with exotic fishes and sea creatures.

From the busy, noisy town of **Tawau**, ferries depart for Indonesian Kalimantan and 4X4s daily for Keningau, bouncing along the rough roads that complete a **ring road** of sorts around Sabah. This is also the way to the **Maliau Basin**, a magnet for trekkers, although currently only accessible within almost prohibitively expensive tour packages.

Lahad Datu

LAHAD DATU, 175km south of Sandakan, has something of a frontier feel, the conspicuous consumption in the town resulting from the oil-palm and timber industry money which has underpinned its growth. In the 1990s, this boom town was flooded by immigrants – many of whom have found gainful, if illegal, employment on the plantations and in town. The town itself isn't particularly exciting, just a jumping-off point for the Danum Valley Conservation Area and Tabin Wildife Reserve.

Buses from Sandakan, Semporna and Tawau stop at the **bus terminus** on Jalan Bunga Raya, a couple of minutes' walk east of the town centre. From the **airport** north of town (for MASwings daily flights to KK) it's only a short taxi ride (RM5) into the centre (there are no buses on this route). If you are heading out to the *Borneo Rainforest Lodge* in Danum Valley your first port of call is likely to be the **Borneo Nature Tours office**, ground floor, Lot 20, Block 3 Fajar Centre (☎089/880207, ⓦwww.borneorainforestlodge.com).

The best **accommodation** option is *Tabin Lodge*, Jalan Urus Setia Kecil (☎089/889552; ❷), opposite the bus and minivan terminus, with small, functional rooms. There are also acceptable rooms at the *Ocean Hotel* (☎089/881700; ❸) with the *Executive* (☎089/881333; ❺) on Jalan Teratai, geared up for business folk, but nevertheless a welcoming place in an otherwise dull town. The *Executive* also has an excellent **restaurant** with a mostly Chinese menu.

Danum Valley Conservation Area

Spanning 438 square kilometres of primary dipterocarp rainforest 65km west of Lahad Datu, the **Danum Valley Conservation Area** (DVCA) is contained within a sprawling logging concession owned by the Sabah Foundation (☎088/422211, ⓦwww.ysnet.org.my). The logging work has helped fund the foundation's charitable works across the state. Established in 1981 for the purpose of rainforest-related "conservation, research, education and recreation", the DVCA is a meeting place for naturalists worldwide. The valley supports a wealth of wildlife including bearded pigs, orang-utans, elephants and proboscis monkeys, as well as 250 bird species, reptiles, fish and insects. Short hiking **trails** are limited to the eastern side, where the tourist accommodation is located. The remainder is pristine forest, out of bounds to all but researchers on well-resourced and long scientific expeditions.

Practicalities

The valley has two **places to stay**: the *Danum Valley Field Centre* and, nine kilometres further into the area, the *Borneo Rainforest Lodge*, sited on a bend on the Danum River – the latter can only be visited as part of a package tour with Borneo Nature Tours. For many years the **Field Centre** (☎089/881092, ⓦwww.ysnet.org.my/Maliau/Danum/location.htm) was used exclusively by scientists but it's now opened up for limited ecotourism. Facilities include twin-bed chalet accommodation (❸), an excellent café, a library of academic standards and internet access. There are two observation towers for wildlife-watching and **excursions** include treks to two waterfalls and a Dusun burial site, as well as night safaris by jeep (available on request, RM40 per person).

The 🦎 *Borneo Rainforest Lodge* (☎088/267637) is a luxurious network of hardwood **chalets** situated in a beautiful spot on the Danum with the multi-layered sound of the rainforest reverberating around. The lodge has a cavernous communal hall, a bar and a little library. The high prices (three-night, two-day packages from RM1300) include excellent buffet **meals** – usually a mix of

▲ Canopy walkway, Danum Valley Conservation Area

Western and Asian dishes. **Activities** include braving the sixty-metre-high canopy walkway (where, given patience and luck, you may glimpse orang-utans), guided night safaris (in an open-backed truck) and jungle walks.

Guests are picked up either from the airport or the Borneo Nature Tours office in Lahud Datu for the two-hour trip to the lodge by jeep or minivan. **Bookings** are taken at both their Lahad Datu and KK offices.

Tabin Wildlife Reserve

One-and-a-half hours' drive northeast of Lahad Datu lies **Tabin Wildlife Reserve** (Ⓦ www.tabinwildlife.com.my). Although just eleven percent primary dipterocarp forest – the rest is secondary forest – Tabin is yet another place to visit in east Sabah where you are very likely to see wildlife. Either by **trekking** or **night drives** along the edge of the nearby oil-palm plantation, there are opportunities to come across elephant, *bantering* (Asian cattle), *tembedau* (deer) or wild boar as they cross the tracks from the forest to the plantations in search of food. Endemic species like the red giant flying squirrel and birds including hornbills are easy to spot too. There are also several interesting **treks** inside Tabin including a one-hour walk to a splendid **waterfall** and lake for bathing in, and to a **mud volcano**, a conically shaped combination of mud, rock and sand. Under-visited at present, the reserve has excellent facilities, including stunning **chalets** overlooking the Lipad River and sleeping platforms to rent lower down the river valley.

Practicalities

From central Lahad Datu a **minivan** (daily noon–1pm; RM20) makes the one-hour fifteen-minute journey to the reserve, returning to the town at 8.30am the next day. That said, the reserve's managers, Intra Travel Services

(☎088/267266, ⓦwww.intra-travel.com.my), only offer all-inclusive packages combining travel, accommodation and activities. Packages are around RM700, including transfer from Lahud Datu, food and chalet occupancy. Food at the *Lipad Café* is excellent with wide range of Western, Malaysian and pan-Asian dishes.

Semporna and around

The chaotic, traffic-clogged town of **SEMPORNA** is usually only visited by travellers on their way to scuba dive and snorkel off Celebes islands **Sipadan**, **Mabul** and **Kapalai**. One of the brashest and dirtiest towns in the whole of Malaysia, Semporna is an incongruous place to have a thriving diver-backpacker scene but that's precisely what it now has, given that staying inexpensively here releases funds for that extra dive or two, which may entail swimming with a greenback turtle or hammerhead shark. and there are a few reasonable places to eat too. Transport connections have improved with morning buses to KK and Sandakan and minivans to Tawau; the nearest airport is Tawau, 30km away.

For generations Muslim Bajau and Suluk peoples have farmed the surrounding seas for fish, sea cucumbers, shells and other marine products. Often dubbed "sea gypsies", these people were originally nomads who lived aboard their intricately carved wooden boats, called *lipa-lipa*. Although they are now mostly settled in and around Semporna, their love of (and dependence upon) the sea remains strong today and the characteristic white sails of the Bajau boats can still be seen, billowing in the breeze across the bay and around the Celebes Sea's picture-postcard islands.

Arrival and information

Though not served by long-distance buses, Semporna is linked by hourly **minivans** with Lahad Datu (RM25), Sandakan (RM40) and Tawau (RM15). The terminus is towards the back of the old town's grid of dirty, congested streets. There is no official tourist office, though the Semporna Ocean Tourism Centre (SOTC; ☎089/769950, ⓦwww.northborneo.net), dangling out from the harbour, can provide some information on the area.

Accommodation

Semporna's accommodation facilities are just about adequate. Another option is to stay on Mabul or on Kapalai. Small-scale development, also aimed at the burgeoning diving market, is occurring on outlying islands Mataking, Maiga, Sibuan and Pom Pong. Note that accommodation has been banned on Sipidan for some years, with operators mostly moving to Mabul.

Damai Lodge One block back from Seafront ☎089/782011. Now rather run-down, with not-so-clean en-suite rooms and small dorms. Dorm beds RM20, ❸.

Dragon Inn Jalan Kastam ☎089/781088. Semporna staple with quite expensive doubles. Dorms RM15, ❻.

Scuba Junkie 45 Semporna Seafront ☎089/785372, ⓦwww.scuba-junkie.com.

Owned by dive-mad British marine biologist Rik Owen, this is a hectically busy, super-friendly place with doubles and dorms. The focal point for budget travellers, offering reasonably priced, professionally run dives (around RM200 a day). Dorm beds plus breakfast for divers RM20. ❸

Seafest Hotel Seafront ☎089/782333, ⓦwww .seafesthotel.com. Imposing concrete block with smart en-suite doubles. ❻

The Town

Semporna has three sections: **downtown**, where the buses and minivans collect, and where there are some places to eat as well as a few grubby hotels; the **new town**, Semporna Seafront, where the dive operators are based; and the jetty-lined **Jalan Kastan** where you can find more dive outfit kiosks, a few cafés and the town's main hotel, the *Seafest Inn*.

Of most interest is new town's main drag, Semporna Seafront, where at Block B, Lot 36, you will find specialist Scuba Junkie's dive school (℡089/785372, Ⓦwww.scuba-junkie.com), while opposite is their pizza lounge and backpackers' hostel. Also on this street are other dive schools, including Sipidan Scuba (℡089/919128, Ⓦwww.northborneo.net), places to eat and the *Mabul Internet Café* at first floor, Block G, Lot 39 (RM4 per hr).

Eating

Although Semporna has any number of mostly unappetising *kedai kopis*, most visitors prefer the excellent *Mabul Café and Seafood Restaurant*, 40 Semporna Seafront (daily 10am–11pm) or the *Scuba Junkie* pizza lounge (daily 2pm–midnight), a few doors down. Also, try the *Seafest Café*, Lorong Kastam (beside the *Seafest Inn*), with Chinese dishes at reasonable prices (RM25 plus beer).

Pulau Sipadan

For some years, visiting **Pulau Sipadan** – 30km south of Semporna in the Celebes Sea – has become de rigueur for the hardcore scuba-diving fraternity. Acclaimed by the late marine biologist Jacques Cousteau as "an untouched piece of art", Sipadan is a cornucopia of marine life, its waters teeming with turtles, moray eels, sharks, barracuda, vast schools of gaily coloured tropical fish, and a diversity of coral that's been compared to that at Australia's Great Barrier Reef. Tragically, a serious accident in May 2006, where a dredger ripped a large amount of the reef's coral away, seriously threatens the area's ecological riches.

Among the highlights for divers here is a network of **marine caves**, the most eerie of which is Turtle Cavern, a watery grave for the skeletal remains of turtles that have strayed in and become lost. There's also White-tip Avenue and Barracuda Point, frequented respectively by white-tip sharks and spiralling shoals of slender barracuda; and the Hanging Gardens, an extraordinarily elegant profusion of soft coral hanging from the underside of the reef ledge. Snorkellers can expect to see reef sharks, lion fish, barracuda and scores of turtles, without having to leave the surface, and from a point known as the Drop-off, large schools of jack fish, bump-head parrot fish and Napoleon wrasse (very rare elsewhere).

Pulau Mabul

Mabul is the largest island in the chain, now housing around ten accommodation options, many meeting just about anyone's criteria for paradise. The only part of the island not colonized by resorts is home to a community of Bajau fisherfolk, who live in homes perched on stilts above the waves. Kampung Bajau has shops, a school, a sports ground and a number of cafés, and is well worth a visit.

Although visibility is poor compared with Sipadan, the silted waters around Mabul are perfect for **muck dives**, popular perhaps for the shock element – you can't see the fish, or other marine life, until they suddenly loom up in front of you. Among the marine life close to the island are seahorses – including the pygmy seahorse, which is very rare everywhere else – frog fish, cuttlefish, mimic octopus, lion fish, stone fish and crocodile fish. Rays and turtles are common too. Apart from diving, there is little else to do on this tiny island except stroll between the resorts or visit the kampung.

Accommodation

The following resorts-cum-dive operators all have fully equipped dive centres. Room **prices** tend to be part of a package deal; expect to pay around RM1000–1500 for a two-night stay, including transport and food, but excluding dives. Below these are the budget options, with their own, much more reasonable pricing structures.

Resorts

Borneo Divers Mabul ℡088/222226, @www .borneodivers.info. Dozens of lovely two-room chalets and an excellent restaurant close to a lovely beach. **❼**

Mabul Beach Resort @www.scubajunkie.com. New location run by Semporna's Scuba Junkie intends to fill Mabul's mid-range gap, with 2–4-bed rooms, quality food and a kicking bar for post-dive socializing. Dorms plus meals RM50, **❹**.

Mabul Water Bungalows ℡088/230006, @www.mabulwaterbungalows.com. Owned by the *Sipidan-Mabul* resort these chalets, perched on stilts, along plankways stretching out into the azure sea, are compact but beautiful. **❾**

Sipadan Water Village ℡089/752996, @www .swvresort.com. Top-of-the-range kampung-style resort arranged around a stilted water village, built to Bajau architectural design. It includes a bar, reception area and a large circular restaurant. **❾**

🏃 **Sipadan-Mabul** (SMART) ℡088/230006, @www.sipadan-mabul.com.my. Located on the southeast side of the island overlooking nearby

Pulau Sipadan, this resort boasts over forty wooden en-suite chalets, an exquisite swimming pool and a top-class restaurant. **❾**

Guesthouses

Arung Hayat Resort Kampung Bajau ℡012/8614366 & 089/782846. Manager John's family stilt homestay has compact, neat rooms and can arrange dives from the jetty at the front. Daily rate includes meals. **❸**

Lai Homestay Kampung Bajau @kclai_268 @hotmail.com. Very basic homestay close to *Uncle Chang's*. No dive master in residence. **❸**

🏃 **Uncle Chang's Mabul Backpackers Lodge** Kampung Bajau ℡089/781002, @www.sipidanbackpackers.com. With a catch phrase "now everyone can stay at Mabul island", pony-tailed, dive-nut Chang provides a budget challenge to the reign of the resorts with this stilted backpackers' lodge perched over the sea. The daily rate (RM50) includes dorm bed and three meals. Transport from Semporna is RM50 each way and, with dives starting at a very competitive RM80 each, it's no wonder the place is heaving.

Pulau Kapalai

Little more than a sandbar, tiny **Kapalai** is exquisite and other-wordly – an ever-changing kaleidoscope of sand, sky and water. There is only room for one resort, the *Sipadan-Kapalai Resort* run by Pulau Sipadan Resort and Tours, 484 Bandar Sabindo, Tawau (℡089/765200, @www.sipadan-kapalai.com; **❾**). The two dozen chalets are spectacular, and appear to hover above the shallow azure water, which is perfect for snorkelling. The resort's boats can take divers to nearby Sipadan and Mabul.

The Tun Sakaran Marine Park

Sipadan and Mabul aside, there are a number of islands off Semporna, which are part of the **Tun Sakaran Marine Park**, and seldom visited despite their beauty. **Sibuon**, for example, on the edge of the chain and just over half an hour by boat from Semporna, has a breathtaking beach and shallow coral reefs, perfect for viewing turtles and rays, frog, cuttle, devil and ghost pipe fish, as well as nudibranches. **Sabangkat**, twenty minutes from Semporna, likewise has coral, as well as small villages and a seaweed farm.

On **Mantubuan**, where there's amazing pristine coral and very good visibility – divers can often see the very rare black coral, and swim through a forest of what appears to be underwater Christmas trees. Another tiny island, Boheyan, has strong currents and pristine coral. **Mataking** and **Boheian** have some coral too and are renowned for their turtles and magnificent rays. For terrestrial wildlife, the large island of **Timbun Mata** has a population of birds, deer, monkeys, wild boar and bats.

These jewels are often overlooked by visitors impatient to get out to Sipadan, Mabul and Kapalai. Most operators offer dive days out to them, with Scuba Junkie offering about the best rates (RM250 for three dives). There is no accommodation on any of these islands.

Tawau and around

The only town of any size in southeast Sabah, **TAWAU** is changing fast, with a large-scale civic modernization programme that's dwarfing the town's earlier Chinese character and architectural look. Most travellers rarely give the town a nod, as they are heading straight from the airport to Semporna, for Tun Sakaran Marine Park. That said, Tawau is an energetic and friendly place, has some excellent cafés and good accommodation and is, crucially, the only gateway into Kalimantan in Sabah, its port busy moving goods and people back and forth to Tarikan and Nunakan.

The town was originally a small Bajau settlement, until the British North Borneo Chartered Company, attracted by its fine harbour and rich volcanic soil, transformed it into a thriving commercial port, now a far less central part of Tawau's daily commercial life. However, the port is a key hub for onward travel to Indonesian Kalimantan with a trickle of travellers – and hundreds of Indonesians – using the daily ferries. While the town's prosperity relied at first upon the cultivation of cacao, then timber, nowadays oil-palm plantations are in the ascendancy (as in so many parts of Sabah), attracting many Filipino and Indonesian immigrants.

Central Tawau is a heady mixture of cars, polluting buses, people and shops. There are sprawling, chaotic **markets** too: the clothes and trinket stalls in the crowded building beside the *Soon Yee Hotel* and the produce market on the square of reclaimed land in front of Jalan Chen Fook are both worth a browse. The only attraction close by Tawau is **Tawau Hill State Park**, a charming park with lovely trails, one to a pretty little waterfall. More's the pity then that there's no public transport there – a taxi costs RM35 one way to cover the 25km.

Arrival and information

Tawau's **airport** is located 30km northwest of the town centre; MAS and AirAsia have ticketing offices on the first floor. Small buses run six times a day from outside the terminal (RM10), whereas a taxi into town costs RM38. **Long-distance buses** arrive at the **station** below the eastern end of Tawau's main street, Jalan Dunlop. **Ferries** from Kalimantan arrive at Customs Wharf, Jalan Pelabuhan, 150m south of Jalan Dunlop's Shell petrol station. The **local bus station** is on Jalan Stephen Tan, in the centre of town, while minivans to Semporna run from Sabindo Square.

As well as several **banks**, the commercial estate known as the Fajar Centre, east of Jalan Masjid, houses both the Telekom building in Block 35, and the MAS town

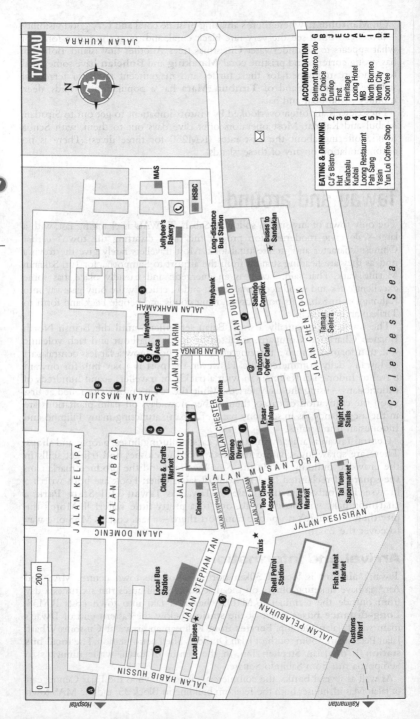

SABAH

7

548

TAWAU

JALAN KUHARA

Celebes Sea

Kalimantan

Hospital

ACCOMMODATION
Belmont Marco Polo	G
De Choice	B
Dunlop	J
First	E
Heritage	C
Kinabalu	A
Loong Hotel	F
MB	I
North Borneo	D
North City	H
Soon Yee	

EATING & DRINKING
CJ's Bistro	2
Hut	3
Kinabalu	6
Kublai	4
Loong Restaurant	A
Pah Sang	5
Yasin	7
Yun Loi Coffee Shop	1

MAS

HSBC

Jollybee's Bakery

Long-distance Bus Station

Buses to Sandakan

Maybank

JALAN MAKHAWHAW

Maybank

Air Asca

Sabindo Complex

Taman Selera

JALAN DUNLOP

JALAN HAJI KARIM

JALAN BUNGA

@ Datcom Cyber Café

JALAN CHEN FOOK

JALAN MASJID

Cinema

JALAN CHESTER

Pasar Malam

Night Food Stalls

JALAN CLINIC

Borneo Divers

JALAN KELAPA

JALAN ABACA

Cloths & Crafts Market

Cinema

JALAN STEPHAN TAN

JALAN COLE ADAM

Teo Chew Association

JALAN MUSANTORA

Central Market

Tai Yuen Supermarket

JALAN DOMENIC

JALAN PESISIRAN

Local Bus Station

Taxis

JALAN STEPHAN TAN

Shell Petrol Station

Fish & Meat Market

Local Buses

JALAN PELABUHAN

Customs Wharf

JALAN HABIB HUSSIN

200 m

0

office (℡089/761293) on Jalan Haji Sahabudin; AirAsia's office (℡089/761946) is on Jalan Bunga opposite *First Hotel*. You'll find the **post office** across the southern side of Jalan Dunlop. One of provincial Sabah's busiest **internet** cafés *Datcom Cyber Café*, is right in the centre of town on the second floor of Suhindo Plaza, Jalan Dunlop. Pulau Sipadan Resort and Tours (℡089/765200, ⓦwww.sipidan-resort .com), who run the resort on Pulau Kapalai (see p.546), have an office on the first floor of 484 Bandar Sabindo, while *Sipadan Water Village* (℡089/752996, ⓦwww .swvresort.com), who run dive trips and accommodation on Pulau Mabul, are on Jalan Bunga.

Accommodation

Although budget accommodation is non-existent, the town has plenty of good-value places to stay. A number of ultra-modern business hotels are expected to open in the near future.

Belmont Marco Polo Jalan Stephen Tan ℡089/777988. The classiest address in town, with large a/c rooms, a friendly bar equipped with piano and karaoke, a fitness centre and a reasonable restaurant (RM25 for Chinese dishes). ❻

De Choice Jalan Masjid ℡089/776655. Nice hotel offering lovely rooms with a/c and good showers. Café downstairs concentrates on Malay food. ❹

Dunlop Jalan Dunlop ℡089/770733. Average Chinese-run place with small, adequate rooms. ❷

First 208 Jalan Bunga ℡089/778989. Very good-value hotel, with neat rooms and compact bathrooms. ❸

Heritage 210 Jalan Bunga ℡089/766222. An attractive, classy place, this hotel picks up on images from Tawau's colonial history. Rooms are small but well fitted and the bathrooms acceptable. ❹

Loong Jalan Abaca ℡089/765308. Good choice with large, clean rooms that have small, neat bathrooms. ❹

MB 339 Jalan Masjid ℡089701333. Very modern addition aimed at the business sector with immaculate, although rather over priced, rooms. ❻

North Borneo Jalan Dunlop ℡089/763060. A mid-range establishment located behind Tawau's cinema, with neat en-suite rooms. ❺

North City 175 Jalan Belia Tawau ℡089/773100. Medium-sized functional place close to the local bus and minivan stands with acceptable clean rooms. ❸

Soon View 1362 Jalan Stephan Tan ℡089/772447. The best of the lower mid-range spots in town; most rooms share bathrooms but a few are en suite (RM50). ❷

Eating

As well as the cafés and restaurants listed below, Tawau has a **pasar malam** on Jalan Nusantaras selling good Malay and Indian food (daily 6–11pm). Many visitors head for the concentration of cafés in the Fajar Commercial District stretch of open-air restaurants and stalls collectively known as **Taman Selera** which sets up in the Sabindo Complex, south of Jalan Dunlop (daily 7.30am–6pm).

Moving on from Tawau

AirAsia **flies** daily from Tawau to KK, KL and Johor Bahru. MAS goes to KK, while MASwings flies to Sandakan. Tawau is also the stepping-stone for **boat travel** to Kalimantan, with daily departures to Pulau Nunukan (1hr; RM40) and onwards to Tarakan in Indonesia. There's also a Tarakan express, leaving every morning except Sunday (3hr 30min; RM75). **Long-distance buses** to KK leave from the express stand on Jalan Chen Fook, while minivans to Semporna and buses to Sandakan leave from close to the Sabindo Plaza on Jalan Dunlop; 4X4s **to Keningau** leave from beside the Jalan Chen Fook stand. 4X4s **to Maliau** pick trekkers up from the airport, bus terminus or their hotel.

CJ's Bistro Jalan Haji Karim. You'll find Western and Malaysian dishes at this spot, popular with Tawau's youth.

Hut Block 29, Fajar Centre. Among the many cafés in this commercial sector, the *Hut* serves Western set meals including decent steaks. Daily 6–11pm.

Kinabalu Jalan Kong Fah. Good Muslim restaurant with a buffet and set meals. Daily 10am–8pm.

Kublai *Belmont Marco Polo*, Jalan Stephen Tan. Popular, upmarket choice with Malaysian and Western cuisines; the signature steamboat buffet is every Saturday. Daily 6.30am–10pm.

Loong Hotel Restaurant Jalan Abaca. Serves good claypot dishes within an international menu. In the evenings there's a BBQ seafood stall out on the covered forecourt. Daily noon–10pm.

Pah Sang Jalan Cole Adam. Chinese café specializing in good noodle dishes. Daily 9am–8pm.

Yasin Jalan Dunlop. Indian café with curries, rotis and *murtabak*. Daily 8am–8pm.

Yun Loi Coffee Shop Jalan Masjid. Probably the best sit-down café in town with delicious noodles and dumplings. Also stocks beer and fruit juices. Daily 8am–10pm.

Tawau Hills State Park

Out of town, an hour's drive north, is the 270-square-kilometre, **Tawau Hills State Park** (T089/925719; RM10), a lovely stretch of lowland rainforest with the Tawau River cutting through its centre. Reaching the park, however, is tricky – no buses come here and most taxi drivers are often unfamiliar with the maze of roads crisscrossing the Borneo Abaca Ltd agricultural estate in which the park is situated (RM35). Jungle lodge **accommodation** (❷) is in a large block at park HQ and, like the food in the canteen, basic, but there also are more comfortable four-bed chalets to hire at RM200 each.

Trails

There is one main trail, a three-hour hike up **Gelas Hill** to a hot spring and waterfall. The path is open to begin with – the lower reaches of the park have been logged – but then the trail leads through thick, damp, mossy forest. The trail is worth the effort though when you arrive at small hot springs and, close by, the Gelas Waterfall on the Tawau River, a perfect spot for swimming. The park authorities have built shelters, toilets and changing rooms; expect to find energetic locals here at weekends and bank holidays arriving for swim and a picnic. The shorter, thirty-minute **Bombalai** trail leads up a hill from park HQ.

To Keningau

While certainly uncomfortable and not cheap, the route from Tawau to Keningau (see p.505) by **4X4** (departure by arrangement; 8hr; RM80–100) is quite an experience. The journey is comfortable enough as you leave Tawau's Jalan Chen Fook but at **Merotai**, some 20km out, the sealed road ends and the jolting ride begins, taking you past cocoa and palm plantations and vast timber mills. There are some sections that pass through lush forest but these forested interludes are growing sparser by the year. As long as you leave Tawau before 9am, you should reach Keningau by the early evening. The main reason for venturing into this section of the southern interior is to visit the **Maliau Basin**, dubbed Sabah's Lost World (see below).

Maliau Basin

Sabah's last wildlife wilderness, the **MALIAU BASIN CONSERVATION AREA** (W www.ysnet.org.my/maliau), was originally part of a one-million-hectare timber concession belonging to the Sabah Foundation, an organization that characterizes itself as ecologically sustainable. In 1981 the Foundation designated Maliau Basin – along with Danum Valley 50km to its east – a conservation area for the purposes of research, education and training, thus ensuring the protection of these two small and habitat-rich forests from further logging or oil-palm exploitation.

The area is still hardly explored, with most visitors scientists or researchers. The basin features various types of forest including lower montane, heath and dipterocarp and is known to be home to an impressive range of large mammals, notably the Asian elephant and the Malayan sun bear, while the variety of birds include rare species found otherwise only at Gunung Kinabalu and Gunung Trus Mardi. There are around 60km of **marked trails**, a 30m-high canopy and an **observation platform** at the Camel Trophy Camp. To visit you must be on a **tour** and, at the time of writing, Borneo Nature Tours (see p.542), owners of the *Borneo Rainforest Lodge* in Danum Valley, are the sole providers.

Arrival, information and accommodation

There is no public transport to the Maliau Basin Conservation Area; it's four hours by 4X4 from Keningau (see p.505) or the preferred route, five hours from Tawau, to the Security Gate. From there it's 25km to research base, **Maliau Basin Studies Centre**, and 20km along a rough and usually very muddy track to the base for trekkers, **Agathis Camp**, a timber and corrugated-iron building with adequate dormitory sleeping quarters, plus kitchen and eating area.

The only other spot where visitors stay is **Camel Trophy Camp**, 7km north, by trail. This is a timber house with a dining area; upstairs, the bedrooms are equipped with bunk beds. From *Camel Trophy Camp* it's a hard day's hike to the region's top draw – the Maliau Falls. There are no roads in the Maliau Basin Conservation Area.

Before booking with Borneo Nature Tours (BNT) visitors need to send copies of personal insurance covering emergency helicopter evacuation and a copy of a fitness certificate. Most people do the five-day, four-night trek, which, including transport from Tawau, accommodation, food and guides costs around RM3000 per person, unless in a big group when the price reduces to around RM1300.

Trekking practicalities

If you are considering taking on Sabah's most demanding, but arguably most rewarding, trekking challenge then this is what you'll need to take: water bladders; insect repellent and anti-perspirant stick; anti-malaria tablets; walking pole; lightweight waterproofs and clothing; anti-leech socks; sleeping bag liner; fleece; flip-flops; torch; small first-aid kit; compass (in case you get lost); toilet paper; sealable plastic bag; binoculars and camera (useful); trekking boots/trainers; hat. But remember, nevertheless, to travel as light as possible.

The trails

Most visitors start their exploration at *Agathis Camp* and, early the following day, take on the tough, mostly uphill, hike to *Camel Trophy Camp* (6–8hr). Using vertical ladders in places, you gradually climb to a height where the vista opens out to reveal magnificent views over dense, pristine rainforest. At the camp a huge *agathis* tree forms the basis of a 33-metre observation platform, climbed via a vertical steel ladder – worth the strain for the wonderful view from the top.

From *Camel Trophy*, the main route is to **Maliau Falls** (the third night can be spent at the third and last stopover, the spartan *Ginseng Camp*), which involves a 700m descent (3hr). The falls are a great natural wonder; it's possible to swim gingerly at the edge, but avoid being swept away by the current. Trekkers then retrace their steps, stopping at an abandoned camp, *Lobah*, before turning off on the trail to *Ginseng*.

Following a night at *Ginseng*, the circular trail loops back to *Agathis Camp*, an undulating, nine-kilometre, six-hour hike with steep ascents and downhill sections. This trek should not be tackled by anyone who isn't very fit and has had prior experience of tough rainforest conditions; it is mostly wet, with the trails muddy and slippery. On this hike you might well see: the ground kouckat; barking deer; macaque monkeys; civet cats; bronzeback tree snakes; various insects and bugs including the violin beetle; spiders galore; bats; flying lizards; and hornbills.

Maliau Basin Studies Centre

The **Studies Centre**, an impressively large building made of hardwood and steel is where scientists and researchers stay. A short walk from the centre is a canopy walkway, the **Maliau Sky Bridge**, an excellent viewing platform for seeing wildlife and birds.

Travel details

Buses

Beaufort to: KK (4 daily; 1hr 30min); Kuala Penyu (8 daily; 1hr); Menumbok (8 daily; 1hr 30min); Sipitang (4 daily; 1hr 30min); Tenom (hourly; 50min).

Keningau to: KK (hourly; 2hr 30min); Tambunan (hourly; 1hr); Tenom (3 daily; 1hr).

KK to: Beaufort (4 daily; 1hr 30min); Keningau (hourly; 2hr 30min); Lawas, Sarawak (1 daily; 4hr); Papar (hourly; 1hr); Ranau (10 daily; 2hr); Sandakan (hourly; 6hr); Tambunan (hourly; 1hr 30min); Tawau (6 daily; 10hr); Tenom (3 daily; 1hr 30min).

Kota Belud (every 30min; 1hr 30min).

Sandakan to: KK (hourly; 6hr); Lahad Datu (6 daily; 2hr 30min); Ranau (8 daily; 3hr 30min); Tawau (8 daily; 4hr 30min).

Sipitang to: Beaufort (4 daily; 1hr 30min).

Tawau to: KK (6 daily; 10hr); Lahad Datu (hourly; 2hr); Sandakan (8 daily; 4hr 30min); Semporna (twice hourly; 1hr 30min).

Tenom to: Beaufort (hourly; 50min); Keningau (3 daily; 1hr); KK (3 daily; 1hr 30min).

Ferries

KK to: Labuan (2 daily; 3hr).

Labuan to: Brunei (hourly; 1hr 30min); KK (2 daily; 3hr); Menumbok (hourly; 25min).

Tawau to: Nunakan (Indonesia; 2 daily; 1hr 30min); Tarakan (daily; 3hr 30min).

Flights

KK to: Bandar Seri Begawan (3 daily; 40min); Johor Bahru (2 daily; 2hr 15min); Kuala Lumpur (16 daily; 2hr 30min); Kuching (7 daily; 2hr); Labuan (4 daily; 30min); Lahad Datu (4 daily; 50min); Sandakan (7 daily; 50min); Singapore (2 daily; 2hr 15min); Tawau (4 daily; 45min).

Labuan to: KK (4 daily; 30min); Kuala Lumpur (5 daily; 2hr 25min); Kuching (1 daily; 2hr 15min); Miri (3 daily; 40min).

Lahad Datu to: KK (4 daily; 50min).

Sandakan to: Johor Bahru (6 weekly; 2hr 40min); KK (7 daily; 50min); Kuala Lumpur (3 daily; 2hr 45min); Tawau (1 daily; 30min).

Tawau to: KK (4 daily; 50min); Kuala Lumpur (4 daily; 2hr 45min); Sandakan (1 daily; 30min).

Brunei

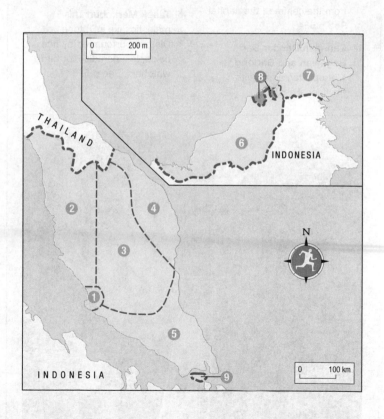

CHAPTER 8

Highlights

* **Omar Ali Saifuddien Mosque**
The centre of Brunei's
capital is dominated by
this magnificent mosque.
See p.564

* **Kampung Ayer** A fascinating
riverside village built out over
the water and easily reached
from the centre of the capital.
See p.564

* **Eating in Bandar Seri
Begawan and Gadong**
Metropolitan areas with
fresh local seafood

and international cuisine.
See p.568

* **Ulu Temburong National
Park** Brunei's premier park
with a heart-stopping canopy
walkway, exhilarating boat
rides and short treks.
See p.574

* **Tasek Merimbun** This
majestic lake in Tutong
District, surrounded by rice
fields, is a paradise for bird-
watchers. See p.576

▲ Canopy walkway, Ulu Temburong National Park

8

Brunei

he tiny Islamic sultanate of **BRUNEI** perches on the northwestern coast of Borneo, surrounded and split in two by the meandering border of Sarawak. It's officially titled Negara Brunei Darussalam, which translates as "Abode of Peace"; and tranquil it certainly is with virtually no crime and a general sense of calm bolstered by high employment levels and a high standard of living, comparable to anywhere else in Southeast Asia, all driven by its massive offshore oil and gas deposits which have produced an economy that is the envy of the region. Its 375,000 inhabitants (of which Malays account for seventy percent, the rest being Chinese, Indians, indigenous tribes and expatriates) enjoy a quality of life almost unparalleled in Southeast Asia – education and healthcare are free; houses, cars, and even pilgrimages to Mecca are subsidized.

Brunei, however, is virtually an absolute monarchy with **Sultan Hassanal Bolkiah** (see box, p.560), combining the dual roles of prime minister and defence minister, and his extended family, the Bolkiahs, in control of virtually all of the government departments and the vast majority of the nation's wealth; it's said that nothing of any real importance is done without the thumbs-up from a family member.

Geographically, Brunei lies on a slim coastal plain threaded by several substantial rivers. Most of the country is less than 150m above sea level, its rainforest, peat swamp and heath forest running down to sandy beaches and mangrove swamps. The country is divided into four districts: **Brunei Muara**, which contains the capital, **Bandar Seri Begawan** (known locally simply as BSB); agricultural **Tutong**; oil-rich **Belait**; and **Temburong**, a sparsely populated backwater severed from the rest of Brunei by Sarawak's Limbang district. Thanks to its oil, Brunei has never needed to exploit its forestry to any great degree, with the result that primary and secondary tropical forest still covers around seventy percent of the total land area.

An ambivalent approach characterizes tourism in Brunei – after some moves to open up the sultanate, things appear to have somewhat stalled: in 2008 the capital's central Tourist Information Centre closed, leaving just a slender kiosk at the airport to field any enquiries. Despite this, the sultanate is witnessing a steady increase in arrivals even if most visitors merely overnight between flights or linger just for one to three days. In that short time though you can cover three main attractions: the mellow capital Bandar Seri Begawan, pristine rainforest in **Ulu Temburong National Park** in the eastern section of the country, and the lovely lake, **Tasek Merimbun** in Tutong District.

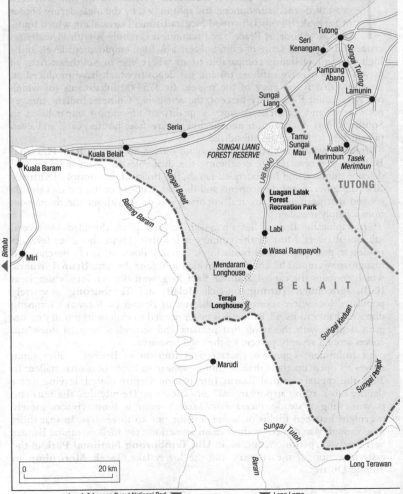

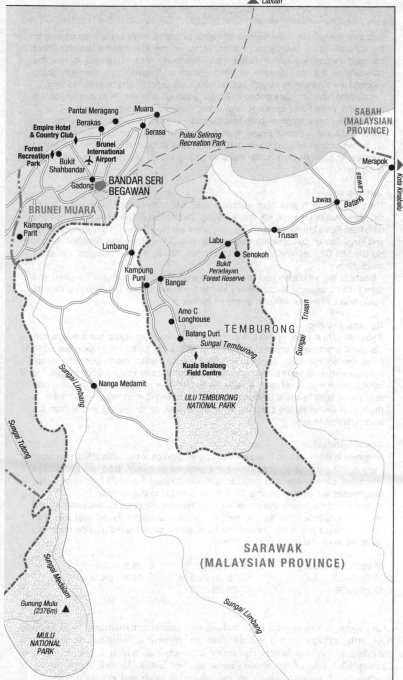

Following the growth in the number of **flights** to Brunei, more tourists are coming to the sultanate as a holiday destination. However, the international airport's most common visitors are transit passengers. Previously, visitors tended to use the sultanate as a stepping-stone to either Sabah or Sarawak, but numbers going overland are diminishing, largely because the route is fiddly and time-consuming.

Accommodation is quite pricey in Brunei, although of a very high quality; food is reasonably priced and excellent; and public transport is slowly improving. This all makes a few days' stopover both feasible and enjoyable. A further practical point to remember is that although Brunei is dry you are permitted to bring into the sultanate up to two bottles of hard liquor and twelve cans of beer. It is against the law to consume this alcohol in a public place so getting slightly pickled in your hotel room is the norm.

Getting there

There are regular **flights** from Malaysia to Brunei; both Royal Brunei and MAS fly daily from **Kuala Lumpur, KK** and **Kuching**. The budget airline AirAsia also has one daily from Kuala Lumpur. From Singapore, there are daily flights on Singapore Airlines and Royal Brunei. Direct flights also arrive from Auckland, Bangkok, Brisbane, Dubai, Ho Chi Min City, Hong Kong, Jakarta, London, Manila, Perth, Shanghai, Surabaya and Sydney.

Boats to Brunei depart daily from Lawas and Limbang in northern Sarawak, and from Pulau Labuan in Sabah. From Miri in Sarawak, several **buses** travel daily to Kuala Belait, in the far western corner of Brunei.

Getting around

If you intend to explore Brunei in some depth, you have little option but to **rent a car**. Car rental is not overly expensive, starting at B$80 a day (or B$350 a week; see p.570 for suggested agencies). Beyond a few main, mostly coastal, roads, **bus** services are non-existent, while **taxis** are expensive if you want to cover much ground outside the capital. Apart from short hops across the Brunei River in BSB's river taxis, the only time you're likely to use a **boat** is to get to Temburong District, which is cut off from the rest of Brunei by the Limbang area of Sarawak, or for leaving Brunei from the launch jetty at Muara.

Accommodation

All **hotels** in Brunei are up in the mid- to upper-range price brackets (B$60 upwards); there is little accommodation outside this price range, though BSB has two hostels which are quite cheap and popular with independent travellers. Although a few **longhouses** still exist in the interior, it is not possible to stay in them.

Throughout the Brunei chapter we've used the following **price codes** to denote the cheapest available room for two people. Single occupancy should cost less than double, though this is not always the case. Some guesthouses provide dormitory beds, for which the dollar price is given.

❶ B$25 and under	❹ B$76–100	❼ B$201–300
❷ B$26–50	❺ B$101–150	❽ B$301 and over
❸ B$51–75	❻ B$151–200	

City sights in and around BSB include two exquisite **mosques**, the Kampung Ayer **stilt village** and a steady flow of ambitious building developments including plazas and hotels, the most impressive of which is the *Empire and Country Club*, one of the world's most opulent hotels. As well, there are a few beaches worth visiting, which are popular with locals and expat families.

Some history

Contemporary Brunei's modest size belies its pivotal role in the formative centuries of Borneo's history. Little is known of the sultanate's **early history**, though trade was always the powerhouse behind the growth of its empire. Tang and Sung dynasty coins and ceramics, found in the Kota Batu area, a few kilometres from Bandar Seri Begawan, suggest that China was trading with Brunei as early as the seventh century. In subsequent centuries, Brunei benefited from its strategic position on the trade route between India, Melaka and China, and exercised a lucrative control over merchant traffic in the South China Sea. As well as being a staging post, where traders could stock up on supplies and offload some of their cargo, by the fourteenth century Brunei was commercially active in its own right; local produce such as beeswax, camphor, rattan and brassware was traded by the *nakhoda*, or Bruneian sea traders, for ceramics, spices, woods and fabrics.

Islam had begun to make inroads into Bruneian society by the mid-fifteenth century, as the sultanate courted the business of foreign Muslim merchants. The religion's presence was accelerated by the decamping to Brunei of wealthy Muslim merchant families after the fall of Melaka to the Portuguese in 1511. Brunei was certainly an Islamic sultanate by the time it received its first **European visitors** from Spain in 1521. This period is commonly acknowledged as the sultanate's golden age when its territory and influence stretched as far as the modern-day Philippines.

However, by the close of the sixteenth century, things were beginning to turn sour for the sultanate; following a sea battle in 1578, Spain took the capital, only to be chased out days later by a cholera epidemic. The threat of piracy caused more problems, scaring off passing trade. Worse still, at home the sultan's control waned with factional struggles loosening his grip.

With the arrival of **James Brooke** (see p.393) in 1839, the state was to shrink steadily as he siphoned off more and more of its territory to neighbouring Sarawak. This trend culminated in the cession of the Limbang region – a move which literally split Brunei in two. By 1888, the British had declared Brunei a **protected state**, which meant the responsibility for its foreign affairs lay with London.

The start of the twentieth century was marked by the **discovery of oil**: given what little remained of Bruneian territory, it could hardly have been altruism that spurred the British to set up a Residency here in 1906. By 1931 the **Seria Oil Field** was on stream and profits were soon such that, despite the British appropriating a hefty slice, the sultanate was able to pay off debts from the lean years of the late nineteenth century.

The Japanese invasion of December 1941 temporarily halted Brunei's path to recovery. As in Sabah, Allied bombing over the three and a half years of occupation that followed left much rebuilding to be done. While Sabah, Sarawak and Pulau Labuan became Crown Colonies in the early postwar years, Brunei remained a British protectorate and retained its British Resident. Only in 1959 was the Residency finally withdrawn and a new constitution established, with provisions for a democratically elected legislative council. At the same time, Sultan Omar Ali Saifuddien (the present sultan's father) was careful to retain British involvement in matters of defence and foreign affairs – a move whose sagacity was made apparent when, in 1962, an armed coup led by Sheik Azahari's pro-democratic **Brunei People's Party** was crushed by British Army Gurkhas. Ever since the attempted coup, which resulted from Sultan Omar's refusal to convene the first sitting of the legislative council, the sultan has ruled by decree in his role as non-elected prime minister, and emergency powers have

Brunei's head of state, **Sultan Hassanal Bolkiah** (whose full title is 31 words long), is the 29th in a line stretching back six hundred years. Educated in Malaysia and Britain, he was the world's richest man before high-tech moguls such as Bill Gates rapidly climbed the tree. Scandals involving a number of financial blunders – blamed on Hassanal's younger brother Jefri – also chipped away at the pot and eroded stock confidence. However, the sultan's wealth is still estimated at around US$20 billion and his nuanced extravagance is legendary: once, while playing polo with Britain's Prince Charles, he had his polo shoes delivered by the palace helicopter out to where they were playing in Jerudong. Interestingly, though, Hassanal is not quite out of touch with his people; perhaps like a ruler from a bygone era, anyone can meet him. For two days a year, on *Hari Raya Aidilfitri*, the populace – and any visitors in town – can queue at the palace for a handshake. During this, males only meet the male members of the family and females the corresponding female ones. Most people wait in line for up to ten hours and are rewarded with an envelope of money – around B$10 – and some food. Some – notably guest workers, who are on significantly lower wages than locals – queue up twice.

In 1991 the sultan introduced a conservative ideology called **Malay Muslim Monarchy**, which presented the monarchy as the defender of the faith. Apparently aimed at pre-empting calls for democratization, it is said to have somewhat alienated Brunei's large Chinese and expatriate communities. However, in September 2004 the sultan revived Brunei's **parliament**, two decades after it was suspended. With the constitution allowing up to fifteen elected MPs – although elections are still to take place – some observers feel that it was a tentative step towards giving some political power to the country's citizens, who may become more vocal as oil and gas reserves start to dwindle in 2015. Another intriguing move came in 2005 when the sultan sacked four members of his cabinet, replacing them with ministers with private-sector experience for the first time.

been in place. Despite showing interest in joining the planned Malaysian Federation in 1963, Brunei chose to opt out rather than risk losing its new-found oil wealth and compromising the pre-eminence of its monarchy; it remained a British protectorate until January 1984, when it attained full independence.

In 2009, apart from a growing anxiety over oil dependency, a chief concern is with the sultanate's high birthrate – Bruneians often have six children or more. This has helped generate unemployment, as there are not enough state-sponsored jobs to go around, and signs are there will be even fewer in future. A social stratum of bored – if not yet disaffected – teenagers has been generated, and no one seems to know what to do with them.

Bandar Seri Begawan

The capital of Brunei, **BANDAR SERI BEGAWAN (BSB)** is the sultanate's only settlement of any real size; first-time visitors tend to be pleasantly surprised by its sense of space and tranquillity – rare among Southeast Asia's leading cities. That contemporary BSB has become the clean and modern waterfront place it is today is due, inevitably, to oil. With the new-found wealth of the 1970s came a degree of urbanization north of the Brunei River, resulting in housing schemes, shopping centres and, more obviously, the magnificent **Omar Ali Saifuddien Mosque**, which dominates the city

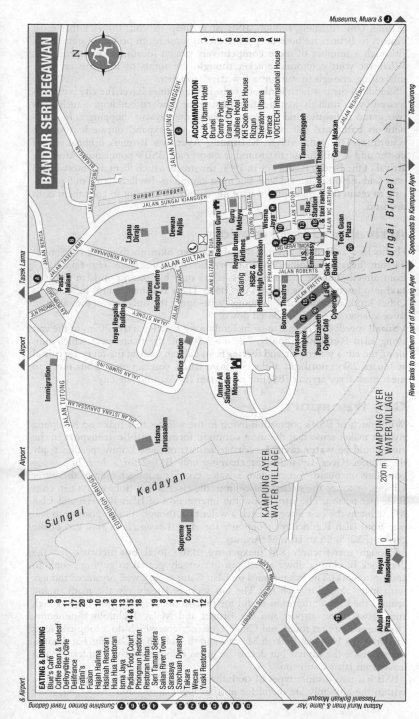

BANDAR SERI BEGAWAN

ACCOMMODATION

Apek Utama Hotel	J
Brunei	I
Centre Point	F
Grand City Hotel	G
Jubilee Hotel	C
KH Soon Rest House	H
Rizqun	D
Sheraton Utama	B
Terrace	A
VOCTECH International House	E

EATING & DRINKING

Blue's Café	5
Coffee Bean & Tealeaf	9
DeRoy@lle C@fe	11
Delifrance	17
Fratini's	20
Fusion	6
Hajah Halima	10
Hasinah Restoran	2
Hua Hua Restoran	16
Isma Jaya	13
Padian Food Court	14 & 15
Phongmun Restoran	18
Restoran Intan	19
Seri Taman Selera	8
Salian River Town	4
Sarasaya	1
Szechuan Dynasty	3
Takara	7
Wecan	12
Yuski Restoran	

Tasek Lama

Airport

Airport

Immigration

Supreme Court

Kedayan

Sungai

JALAN TUTONG

JALAN ISTANA DARUSSALAM

EDINBURGH BRIDGE

Istana Darussalem

Police Station

JALAN SUMBILING

Royal Regalia Building

Brunei History Centre

JALAN STONEY

JALAN JAMES PEARCE

JALAN SULTAN

JALAN BENDAHARA

JALAN TASEK LAMA

JLN PADANG

JLN BERTANI

JALAN BERITA

Pasar Malam

Lapau Diraja

Dewan Majlis

JALAN ELIZABETH DUA

JALAN KAMPONG

JALAN KAMPONG KIANGGEH

Sungai Kiangggeh

JALAN SUNGAI KIANGGEH

Omar Ali Saifuddien Mosque

Bangunan Guru

Guru

Royal Brunei Airlines

Padang

HSBC & British High Commission

JALAN ELIZABETH DUA

LORONG SWASTA

Wisma Jaya

Tamu Kiangggeh

Bokhiah Theatre

Geral Makan

JALAN CATOR

JALAN MC ARTHUR

Bus Station & taxi rank

Teck Guan Plaza

U.S. Embassy

Glok Tee Building

LRG GERAI TIMOR

JALAN PEMANCHA

JALAN ROBERTS

JALAN PRETTY

Borneo Theatre

Yayasan Complex

Paul Elizabeth@ Cyber Café

La@ Cybercafé

Sungai Brunei

Temburong

JALAN RESIDENCY

Speedboats to Kampung Ayer

River taxis to southern part of Kampung Ayer

River taxis to Kampung Ayer

Kampung Ayer Water Village

KAMPUNG AYER WATER VILLAGE

Royal Mausoleum

Abdul Razak Plaza

LEBUHRAYA SULTAN HASSANAL

JALAN KH KIM

N

0   200 m

▲ & Airport

▲ Astana Nurul Iman & Jame 'Asr Hassanil Bolkiah Mosque

Sunshine Borneo Travel Gadong ▲

◄ ❸ ❼ ❻ ❺ ❹ ▲ ❶ ❹ ❼ ❻ ❶ ▲

561

skyline. Unfortunately, though, BSB isn't cheap to visit; the fact that most visitors to Brunei are business people means most room prices are quite high, although a number of more competitively priced locations have sprung up. Whatever your economic bracket though, the sights of BSB are certainly interesting enough to warrant a few days' stopover.

Straddling the northern bank of a twist in the Brunei River, the city is characterized by its unlikely juxtaposition of striking modern buildings – such as its two grand **mosques** and the twin malls of the Yayasan shopping complex – with its traditional stilt houses, which hug and expand outwards from the waterfront. This water village, **Kampung Ayer**, was Brunei's original seat of power and is still home to around a quarter of BSB's population. After the arrival of the British Residency in 1906, the streets which form downtown BSB were laid out on reclaimed land, but most kampung-dwellers stayed put, preferring to retain their traditional way of life despite an attempt to coax them onto dry land.

Arrival and information

Flights land at **Brunei International Airport**, 8km north of the city; bus # 34 runs (departures coincide with international flight arrivals; 7am–6pm; B$1), from directly outside the terminal to BSB's only bus station on Jalan Cator. A **taxi** into town from the airport costs B$35. There is a small Visitor Information Office kiosk at the airport (no phone; 9am–8pm), the only one in the sultanate since a larger one in BSB closed down.

Small speedboats from Bangar in Temburong District arrive 200m to the east along Jalan Residency (hourly; 7.30am–3.30pm), the main street which runs along the city's waterfront, and **ferries** from Labuan dock at the **ferry terminal** at Muara, 25km northeast of the city, from where you can catch a bus, timed to meet most ferry arrivals (B$2) or take a taxi (B$35) into the city.

City transport

With much of BSB's population living in the villages that make up Kampung Ayer, it makes sense that the most common form of **public transport** in the city should be **water taxis**. A veritable armada of these skinny speedboats ply the Brunei River day and night, charging only B$1–2 for a short hop – pay your fare on board. You can hire a water taxi for a longer tour of the water villages, or to see the sultan's palace from the river; a half-hour round trip costs B$25 per person. The jetty below the intersection of Jalan Roberts and Jalan McArthur is the best place to catch a water taxi, though it's also possible to hail one from Jalan Residency or opposite the *Apek Utama Hotel*, 3km east of the centre (B$2; 5min to Jalan McArthur).

Though user-friendly and inexpensive, BSB's local **bus** network has the drawback of closing down at 6.30pm (it's largely geared to getting people to and from work). The bus terminal on Jalan Cator is very well organized though, with maps alongside each bay. The bus services largely ply the roads in and around the capital: the most useful for tourists are Central Line buses, which run between the airport and the Brunei and Malay Technology museums, crossing the city en route; and Circle Line services, which do a loop taking in the Jame 'Asr Hassanal Bolkiah Mosque and the suburb of Gadong. For destinations outside the capital, bus details are given throughout the chapter; services leave from Jalan Cator too.

BSB has two distinct types of **taxi**: the CTS service, whose purple cars run within the city only, are useful for districts like Gadong and Batu 1 but don't go as far as the museums or the airport. They charge a flat B$3 for a trip under 1km, with an extra B$1 tacked on for each kilometre after that. The rate goes up to B$4.50 after 9pm. The other type is the regular, metered, yellow taxis which congregate beside the bus station and outside shopping centres and hotels. Fares start from B$3, and a short journey – say, from the city centre to the Brunei Museum – costs B$5–7, with a B$2 surcharge between 9pm and 6am. For longer journeys, out to Seria or Kuala Belait for instance, you can haggle with drivers and fix a price.

Accommodation

Almost all options are concentrated in the city centre, with a few exceptions, in the suburb Gadong, and along the river, highlighted below. As well as a number of **budget places** there's a fair selection of comfortable mid-price **hotels** to choose from and a fair few top-bracket choices, with the *Empire* (see p.572) the most famously extravagant.

Downtown

Brunei 95 Jalan Pemancha ☎2242372, ⓦwww .bruneihotel.com.bn. Comfortable, with spacious, a/c, en-suite rooms, slap bang in the city centre. ④

Jubilee Hotel Jalan Kampung Kianggeh ☎2228070, ⓦhttp://www.jubileehotelbrunei.com East of Sungai Kianggeh, but still downtown, this mid-range hotel has large en-suite rooms with TV and a/c. It's set opposite a patch of traditional kampung houses, giving it a pleasant neighbourhood feel. ③

🏃 **KH Soon Rest House** First floor, Kiaw Lian Building, 140 Jalan Pemanacha ☎2222052, ⓦkhsoon-resthouse.tripod.com. BSB's only backpackers' place, the *Soon* is a friendly place, stocked with masses of information on Brunei, situated above *MonaFloraFauna Tours*. Five-bed dorms are excellent value at B$17 and doubles significantly cheaper than any other central spot. ②

Sheraton Utama Jalan Tasek Lama ☎2244272, ⓦwww.sheraton.com. Brunei's earliest international-standard hotel, this *Sheraton* is not well maintained and the service is rather slow and uninterested. It does though have a well-equipped business centre with internet access. ⑥

🏃 **Terrace** Jalan Tasek Lama ☎2243554, ⓦwww.terracebrunei.com. Well-positioned hotel within walking distance from the centre with small, comfortable rooms and adequate bathrooms. Ask for a room overlooking the lovely little swimming pool, set by a breakfast terrace and exquisite rockery. Has very good internet access (B$5 per 30min). ③

West of centre and Gadong

Centre Point Abdul Razak Complex ☎2430430, ⓦwww.arh.com. Gadong's oldest luxury hotel, now

offering cut-price deals; check website for latest offers. ④–⑦

Grand City Hotel Block G, Kampung Pengkalan Gadong ☎2452188, ⓔgrandcity@brunet.bn. Good-value modern hotel with large en-suite rooms. ⑤–⑥

Rizqun Abdul Razak Complex ☎2423000. ⓔreservation@rizquninternational.com. In a separate part of the complex to the *Centre Point*, this hotel has an exquisite dark marble foyer and sumptuous rooms. Again, deals are often available. ⑥–⑧

VOCTECH International House Jalan Pasar Baharu (take the Circle Line bus from the Jalan Cator terminal), ☎2447992, ⓦwww.voctech.org .bn. This large hostel ostensibly set up for international student groups, is now increasingly used by tour groups and independent travellers. Rooms are large and simply decorated, with balconies and attached bathrooms. It's got a well-priced café, a kitchen that can be used by guests and a library with internet access. 5min walk away is an excellent night market serving cheap, tasty food. ④

Along the river

🏃 **Apek Utama Hotel** Simpang 229, Kampung Pintu Malim, Jalan Kota Batu ☎2220808. Other than the *Soon*, *Apek* is BSB's main traveller haven with dozens of neat, light rooms (with communal bathrooms) spread over three floors, set in a modern complex 3km from town. Take the museum bus #39, which goes right by. An alternative way to get to and from the centre is to jump on a water taxi (B$1) from the jetty opposite the hotel entrance. ③

The City Centre

Downtown BSB's most obvious point of reference is the **Omar Ali Saifuddien Mosque**, which overlooks the city centre, sitting in a cradle formed by **Kampung Ayer** (Water Village), a collection of settlements protruding from the river. The city's commercial centre is formed around a simple layout of four main streets leading down to the river, with the mosque to the east. One, Jalan Sultan, is lined with daytime cafés and a number of Western coffee shops. Another, Jalan Sungai Kianggeh, leads to a daily produce market, and a third houses two plazas, jointly called the Yayasan Complex. Back from this grid lie the Brunei History Centre and the Royal Regalia Museum, the latter most certainly worth a visit.

The Omar Ali Saifuddien Mosque

At the very heart of both the city and the sultanate's Muslim faith is the magnificent **Omar Ali Saifuddien Mosque** (daily except Thurs & Fri 8am–noon, 1–3pm & 4.30–5.30pm, Thurs open to Muslims only, Fri 4.30–5.30pm). Built in classical Islamic style, and mirrored in the circular lagoon surrounding it, the mosque is a breathtaking sight. Commissioned by and named after the father of the present sultan, the mosque was completed in 1958 and makes splendid use of opulent yet tasteful fittings – Italian marble, granite from Shanghai, Arabian and Belgian carpets, and English chandeliers and stained glass. Topping the cream-coloured building is a 52-metre-high golden dome whose curved surface is adorned with a mosaic comprising over three million pieces of Venetian glass. In the lagoon is a replica of a sixteenth-century royal barge, or *mahligai*, used on special religious occasions. The usual dress codes – modest attire, and shoes to be left at the entrance – apply when entering the mosque.

Kampung Ayer

Stilt villages have occupied this stretch of the Brunei River for hundreds of years. Today, an estimated 25,000 people live in the scores of sprawling villages that compose **Kampung Ayer**, their dwellings connected by a maze of wooden promenades. These villages now feature their own clinics, mosques, schools, a fire brigade and even a police station; homes here have piped water, electricity and TV. There's a strong sense of community and all government attempts to move the inhabitants into modern housing schemes on dry land have met with little success.

The meandering plankways of Kampung Ayer make it an intriguing place to explore on foot, especially late on Friday afternoons when, following prayers, the fashion is to visit one another's homes. For a more panoramic impression of its dimensions though, it's best to charter one of the water taxis (B$20 per hr) that zip around the river. If you are going on a tour around the water village consider asking your boatmen to take you to Taman Persiaran Damuan, where you get an excellent view of the sultan's palace.

Jalan Sultan to the Royal Regalia Building

A short walk east of the Omar Ali Saifuddien Mosque, BSB's main drag, the broad **Jalan Sultan**, runs north past several of the city's lesser sights. First is the **Brunei History Centre** (℡ 2240166; Mon–Thurs & Sat 7.45am–12.15pm & 1.30–4.30pm; free), a research institution whose dull displays – maps showing Brunei's changing shape over the centuries, and tables outlining the genealogy of past sultans – will have you hurrying next door to the **Royal Regalia Building** (℡ 2228357; Sun–Thurs 8.30am–5pm, Fri 9–11.30am & 2.30–5pm), which is much more captivating. Opened in 1992 as part of the sultan's silver

▲ Kampung Ayer

jubilee celebrations, this magnificent semicircular building, fitted out with lavish carpets and marble, contains an exhibition charting the life of the present sultan. There's some interesting stuff here, including a surprisingly happy shot of the sultan taken during his circumcision ceremony, and one of him looking rather nervous at his installation ceremony in 1961. The **Constitutional Gallery** in the same building is inevitably drier, but its documents and treaties are worth a scan. Fronting the whole collection is the **coronation carriage**, or *usungan*, ringed by regalia from the coronation ceremony – which took place just across Jalan Sultan in the **Lapau Diraja** (Royal Ceremonial Hall). Quite fascinating are the numerous exhibits of presents other monarchs and leaders have given the sultan over the years, including a copper eagle atop a human fist (from Ukraine) and a silver sailboat courtesy of the Maldives.

Along Jalan Sungai Kianggeh

East of the **Lapau Diraja** and parallel to Jalan Sultan is **Jalan Sungai Kianggeh**, which runs south to the daily produce market, **Tamu Kianggeh** and to BSB's most central **Chinese temple**, and north to Jalan Tasek Lama, the turning to tranquil **Tasek Lama Park**, five minutes' walk east of the main road. Bear left and you pass through the pretty gardens to a small waterfall; bear right along the sealed road and right again at the fork and you end up at a bottle-green reservoir.

East to the Brunei Museum

On the eastern edge of the centre, **Jalan Residency** hugs the river bank on its way to the **Brunei Museum** and its neighbouring attractions. The Eastern Line #39 (every 15min) bus plies this route; only remember that the last one back is around 5.45pm. At its start, on the hillside to the left, is a Muslim cemetery whose scores of decrepit stones are shaded by an orchard of frangipani trees. After a little less than a kilometre, the road reaches the **Arts and Handicrafts Centre** (Ⓦ www.museums.gov.bn; Mon–Thurs 8am–5pm, Fri & Sat 8–11.30am & 2–5pm; free), an organization dedicated to perpetuating the sultanate's cultural heritage. Here, young Bruneians are taught traditional skills, such as weaving, basketry and bamboo-working, brass-casting and the crafting of the *kris* (traditional dagger). Apart from the occasional weaving demonstration though, you can't watch the proceedings unless you've sought permission to do so in advance. You'll probably have to make do with browsing through the **craft shop**'s decent selection of reasonably priced basketry, silverware and spinning tops (opening times as above).

Brunei Museum

From here it's a further 3km to the **Brunei Museum** (Ⓣ 2226495, Ⓦ www .museums.gov.bn; Mon–Sat 9.30am–5pm, Fri 9–11.30am & 2.30–5pm; free), shortly before which is the **tomb of Sultan Bolkiah** (1473–1521), Brunei's fifth sultan, who held sway at the very peak of the state's power. It's worth setting aside an hour or two for the museum, which has several outstanding galleries. In the inevitable Oil and Gas Gallery, set up by Brunei Shell Petroleum, exhibits, graphics and captions recount the story of Brunei's oil reserves, from the drilling of the first well in 1928, to current extraction and refining techniques. Also interesting, though tantalizingly sketchy, is the **Muslim Life Gallery**, whose dioramas allow glimpses of social traditions such as the sweetening of a newborn baby's mouth with honey or dates, and the disposal of its placenta in a *bayung*, a palm-leaf basket either hung on a tree or floated downriver. At the back of the gallery, a small collection of early photographs shows riverine hawkers trading from their boats in Kampung Ayer. The museum's undoubted highlight, though, is its superb **Islamic Art Gallery** (ground floor) where, among the riches on display are beautifully illuminated antique Korans from India, Iran, Egypt and Turkey, and exquisite prayer mats.

Malay Technology Museum

Steps around the back of the museum drop down to the riverside **Malay Technology Museum** (daily 9am–5pm except Fri 9–11.30am & 2.30–5pm, closed Tues; free), whose three galleries provide a mildly engaging insight into traditional Malay life. Of greatest interest is Gallery Three, whose exhibits include the *pelarik gasing*, a machine which evenly cuts spinning tops; the *lamin keleput*, used for boring blowpipes; and other devices worked from forest materials by Brunei's indigenous people. In the same gallery are authentic examples of Kedayan, Murut and Dusun dwellings, while elsewhere in the building you see dioramas highlighting stilt-house and *atap*-roof construction, boat-making and fishing methods. Also worth a look is the extensive betel box collection on the ground floor. The boxes, some shaped like boats and others representing animals including turtles, traditionally contain mixtures which avert bad spirits and witchcraft as well as more prosaic ointments to alleviate the irritation caused by mosquito bites and flatulence.

To catch the **bus** back to the city centre, return to the Brunei Museum, as there are no buses along the lower road where the Technology Museum is located.

Towards Gadong

Beyond the Royal Regalia Museum, Jalan Sultan north meets the Edinburgh Bridge, where **Jalan Tutong** runs westwards, past the Batu 1 area (a grid of shopping complexes and hotels), 3km later reaching the **Jame 'Asr Hassanal Bolkiah Mosque**. From there a number of roads lead north to the commercial suburb of **Gadong** and beyond to the airport, whereas going the other way gets you to the sultan's official residence, **Istana Nurul Iman**.

Circle Line buses #01 and #55 go from the bus terminal to Gadong and back, travelling westward along Jalan Tutong, over the Edinburgh Bridge and past the Istana (it's possible to walk there, however). En route you'll pass the city's **Batu 1** area, in the southwestern corner of which the **Royal Mausoleum and Graveyard** are tucked away. Brunei's sultans have been buried at this site since 1786, though only the last four were laid to rest in the mausoleum.

The Jame 'Asr Hassanal Bolkiah Mosque
Visiting the **Jame 'Asr Hassanal Bolkiah Mosque** (daily except Thurs & Fri 8am–noon, 1–3.30pm & 4.30–5.30pm; Thurs & Fri open to Muslims only), is a wonderfully serene experience. Constructed to commemorate the silver jubilee of the sultan's reign in 1992 and located northwest from the city centre in a large compound, the building has immense style and grandeur. Teams of Bangladeshi workers busily sweep outside, below the mosque's sea-blue roof, golden domes and slender minarets, while silk-clad Bruneians go about their prayers. The mosque, Brunei's largest, is referred to by locals as the Kiarong Mosque (after a neighbouring kampung), who find its full name rather a mouthful. Circle Line **buses** skirt the grounds of the mosque en route to Gadong. Directly across from the mosque in Kampung Kiarong is a useful **internet café** and a couple of cafés.

The Istana Nurul Iman
The **Istana Nurul Iman**, the official residence of the sultan, is sited at a superb riverside spot 4km west of the centre. Bigger than London's Buckingham Palace, the Istana is a monument to self-indulgence. Its design, by Filipino architect Leandro Locsin, is a sinuous blend of traditional and modern, with Islamic motifs such as arches and domes, and sloping roofs fashioned on traditional longhouse designs, combined with all the mod cons you'd expect of a house whose owner is estimated to earn millions of dollars a day. James

Bartholomew's book, *The Richest Man in the World*, lists some of the mind-boggling figures relating to the palace which, over half a kilometre long, contains a grand total of 1778 rooms, including 257 toilets. Illuminating these rooms requires 51,000 light bulbs, many of which are consumed by the palace's 564 chandeliers; simply getting around the rooms requires eighteen lifts and 44 staircases. The throne room is said to be particularly sumptuous: twelve one-tonne chandeliers hang from its ceiling, while its four grand thrones stand against the backdrop of an eighteen-metre arch, tiled in 22-carat gold. Inevitably, the palace is not open to the general public, apart from two days every year during Hari Raya Aidilfitri, at the end of Ramadan.

Gadong

The suburb of **Gadong**, 3km northwest of the centre of BSB, is worth visiting largely for shopping and eating. Gadong's Centre Point Plaza on the suburb's main street Jalan Kuilap, contains the *Centre Point Hotel* and a variety of outlets including jewellery, bargain clothing retailers, fast food and restaurants. The Mall, a much larger, five-floor plaza is next to Centre Point, boasting a vast, marble encrusted central atrium, lovely murals and elegant decorative touches. On the ground floor, there's a reasonable bookshop, *Best Eastern*, some expensive boutiques, a homeopathic store, Nature's Farm, and the pricey *Ringum Coffee House*.

Eating and drinking

BSB's **restaurants** are reasonably priced and there's an increasingly good range of places to eat, with numerous, excellent Indian and Malay cafés, as well as Chinese and Western options. If you're on a tight budget, it's worth heading to either of the **pasar malams**, one on Jalan Tasek Lama (opposite the *Terrace Hotel*; daily 6–10.30pm), the other situated in a car park across the road from *VOCTECH* (6–11.30pm). Here, Malay favourites are laid out buffet-style, but food has to be taken away as there are no tables and chairs. In the centre of town, on Jalan Sultan, try just about any of the Indian cafés for morning *roti canai* or midday curry buffet – note though that most close for Friday prayers.

Then there's Tamu Kianggeh, on the other side of Jalan Sultan, a large open market (daily 6am–5pm) with some food stalls and the small food court behind the Temburong jetty on Jalan Residency (daily 7am–6pm), which has good and cheap *soto ayam* (rice cubes served with shredded chicken and broth), *nasi campur* and other Malay staples. These stalls close in the early evening. Finally, follow the upmarket locals and go out in Gadong, where more adventurous cuisine is on offer.

Alcohol in Brunei

One thing you won't find in BSB, or for that matter in Brunei, is a bar. **Drinking alcohol** in public has been outlawed in Brunei since New Year's Day, 1991. The substantial expatriate community, though, is allowed to consume alcohol at home and at certain restaurants where beer or wine can be consumed with food. Expats and tourists do have an official **drinks allowance** of twelve cans of beer and two bottles of wine or spirits, to be cleared upon entry into Brunei. This can technically be done every 24 hours, so some expats find themselves visiting the closest off-licences in the small Sarawakian town of Kuala Lurah (see p.474) – a ninety-minute drive away – very frequently.

Downtown

Coffee Bean & Tealeaf Jalan Pemancha/Jalan Sultan. Western-style coffee shop with tasty cakes, great coffee and high prices. Also has an outlet in Gadong's Centre Point mall. Daily 8am–11.30pm.

DeRoy@lle C@fe Jalan Sultan. Next door to *Coffee Bean*, this is the only 24hr café in town. The food isn't exciting, but it's a good place to sit (inside or out) and watch sport on one of up to four large screens, or simply chat away the day or night.

Delifrance Ground floor, Yayasan Complex, Jalan Kumbang Pasang. Slick, French-style coffee and croissant joint. Very popular with Brunei's well-heeled youth. Daily 9am–9pm.

Fratini's Jalan McArthur. Quite expensive Western and Asian fare in a relaxing setting overlooking the harbour and Kampung Ayer. The pasta dishes and pizzas are tasty and filling but pricey, and the rice-based Malay and Chinese food is good as well. Daily happy hour 4–5pm when pizzas are half-price. Daily 11.30am–10pm. Also has a branch on the ground floor of Centre Point Mall in Gadong, 3km from BSB centre.

Hajah Halima Jalan Sultan. Friendly North Indian café with a *nasi campur*-style buffet with chicken and lamb options, prawn curry and vegetable side dishes. Daily 6am–9pm.

Hua Hua Restoran 48 Jalan Sultan. Steamed chicken with sausage is one of the highlights in this simple, no-frills Chinese establishment, where B$15 feeds two people. Daily 7am–9pm.

Isma Jaya 27 Jalan Sultan. One of several good Indian restaurants along Jalan Sultan; lip-smacking korma, *biriyani* and *roti canai* sell well here. Daily 6am–8pm.

Padian Food Court First floor, Yayasan Complex, Jalan Kumbang Pasang. Snow-bright, a/c food court whose spotless stalls serve Thai, Middle Eastern, Japanese and Indian fare plus several other regional cuisines. Daily 9am–10pm.

Phongmun Restoran Second floor, Teck Guan Plaza, Jalan Sultan. Classy and centrally located Cantonese restaurant serving dim sum, with wall panels depicting roses and dragons. Daily 6.30am–11pm; dim sum served 6.30am–4pm.

Restoran Intan Seri Taman Selera 1–2 Bangunan Mas Panchawarna, Batu 1, Jalan Tutong. Popular, buffet-style Malay restaurant with a satay stall outside at night. Daily 9am–9.30pm.

Sajian River Town (SRT) Jalan Pemancha. Opposite the padang and on a corner, SRT is an easy-going café serving quality local dishes at reasonable prices. Try the *assam udang dan nasi* (deep fried prawns with tamarind and rice). Daily 9am–11pm.

Yuski Restoran Jalan Sultan. Excellent Indian café renowned for its *biriyanis*, chicken and mutton curries.

Gadong

Blues Café 12 Yong Siong Hai Building, Jalan Gadong. At the end of block of shops (mostly DVD shops), next to Gadong Mall (entrance nearest river/VOCTEC), this lively café with quick service has inexpensive food from an extensive, mostly Asian menu. Very busy in the evenings with both locals and expats.

Fusion First floor, Unit 1.01 (near lift) Gadong Mall. Eclectic range of food (Thai, Malay, Western) at reasonable cost with outside seating, so all the better to watch the bustle of the main drag below. Weekends are buffet nights: all you can eat for B$12.

Hasinah Restoran Block 1, Unit 9, Abdul Razak Complex, Gadong. Excellent, inexpensive Malay and South Indian daytime café. With nine types of dosai and a mouth-watering *nasi campur* spread.

Sarasaya Block C, Abdul Razak Complex, Gadong. Top-drawer Japanese restaurant, owned by and popular with Japanese expatriates.

Szechuan Dynasty Centre Point, Abdul Razak Complex, Gadong. A truly elegant dining experience, though not necessarily to all tastes – the prevalence of chilli, pepper and ginger means the emphasis here is firmly on hot, spicy Chinese food. Daily noon–2.30pm & 6–10pm.

Takara Centre Point, Abdul Razak Complex, Gadong. Top-notch Japanese restaurant serving classics such as sashimi and teppanyaki; groups might consider dining the authentic Japanese way – cross-legged on the floor, in a tatami room. Daily 11.30am–2.30pm & 6–10pm.

Wecan Ground floor, N2 03 & 0, Block K, Wisma Siti Hamidah, Abdul Razak Complex, Gadong (street parallel to main drag in Gadong). New restaurant serving fusion cuisine in a colourful setting. Good value but with incredibly slow service. Evening only.

Tour operators

In the absence of the government developing and expanding tourism infrastructure, it has been left to **tour operators** to lead the way. Below is a short list of operators offering rewarding, well-priced trips in the sultanate, ranging from the enjoyable two-hour cruise in Brunei Bay's **mangrove area** (around B$65) to a two-day, one-night visit to **Ulu Temburong Park** including rafting (B$250). Note that although Brunei is more expensive to visit than Malaysia, tours are competitively priced when compared with equivalent ones in Sabah or Sarawak.

Freme Travel 403b Wisma Jaya, Jalan Pemancha ☎2234280, ⊛www.freme.com. Highly professional outfit with a good range of inbound tours, run by coordinator Jonathan Tuan, including a rafting day-trip along the Temburong River (B$135) and day, and overnight, trips to the park (B$220 overnight). Also offers the intriguing Cultural Experience Day Trip Tour (B$105) and half-day BSB city and Kumpung Ayer tour (B$35–50).

Mona Florafauna Tours First floor, Kiaw Lian Building, 140 Jalan Pemanacha ☎2230761/2, ⊛mft@brunet.bn. Run by Dave "Jungle" Coleman and specializing in nature tours, MFF has competitively priced trips ranging from the 2hr cruise along BSB's mangrove forests in search of playful proboscis monkeys (B$65), to the full-day visit to Tasek Merimbun (B$120) and its two-day Wildlife Adventure camping tour (B$180), where Dave goes

out into the primary rainforest in Tutong District. The outfit has excellent guides and provides top-of-the-range service.

Pulong Jungle Tours ☎7108408, ⊛touringtemburong@gmail.com. Contact Iban Bruneian Patrick Padan by phone or email for tailor-made visits to Iban longhouses, and little-visited areas in Temburong District. Prices are very fair – B$45 per person for a half-day tour; B$85 for a full day.

Sunshine Borneo No. 2, Simpang 146, Jalan Kiarong ☎2441791, ⊛www.sunshineborneo .com. This in- and out-bound veteran operator now runs the accommodation at Ulu Temburong national park, as well as running tours, from day trips to two-night stays, through it. Packages start from B$100 for a day-trip, rising to B$220 for a one-night stay. Sunshine also has day-trips in BSB and around.

Listings

Airlines British Airways, Lot 100, Jalan McArthur/Jalan Kianggeh ☎2225871; Garuda Indonesia, 49 Wisma Jaya, Jalan Pemancha ☎2235870; MAS, 144 Jalan Pemancha ☎2224141; Philippine Airlines, first floor, Wisma Haji Fatimah, Jalan Sultan ☎2244075; Royal Brunei Airlines, RBA Plaza, Jalan Sultan ☎2242222; Singapore Airlines, 49–50 Jalan Sultan ☎2244901; Thai Airways, fourth floor, Kompleks Jalan Sultan, 51–55 Jalan Sultan ☎2242991.

Airport For flight information call ☎2331747.

American Express Fourth floor, Unit 401–03, Shell Building, Jalan Sultan ☎2228314 (Mon–Fri 8.30am–5pm, Sat 8.30am–1pm).

Banks and exchange HSBC, Jalan Sultan; International Bank of Brunei, Jalan Roberts; Overseas Union Bank, RBA Plaza, Jalan Sultan; Standard Chartered Bank, Jalan Sultan. Banking hours are Mon–Fri 9am–3pm, Sat 9–11am.

Bookshops Best Eastern Books, first floor, The Mall, Gadong & G4 Teck Guan Plaza, Jalan Sultan, stocks a modest range of English-language books and magazines; Times Bookshop, first floor, Yayasan Complex, isn't bad either.

Car rental Ellis Jalan Kiarong ☎8117884; Hertz, counter 3, Arrival Hall, International airport & Lot Q33, Lambak Kanan Industrial Estate, Berakas Link BB1714 ☎2390300/239.

Cinemas Borneo Theatre, on Jalan Roberts, and Bolkiah Theatre, on Jalan Sungai Kiangggeh, both screen English-language movies; tickets around B$6.

Embassies and consulates Australia, Dar Takaful IBB Utama, Jalan Pemancha ☎2229435; Indonesia, Lot 4498, Simpang 528, Sungai Hanching Baru, Jalan Muara ☎2330180; Malaysia, 61 Simpang 336, Kampong Sungai Akar, Jalan Kebangsaan ☎2381095; Philippines, 17 Simpang 126, Mile 2, Jalan Tutong ☎2241465; Singapore, 8 Simpang 74, Jalan Subok ☎2262741; Thailand, 2 Simpang 682, Kampung Bunut, Jalan Tutong ☎2653108; UK, Unit 2.01, Block D, Complex Yayasan Sultan Hassanil Bolkiah ☎2222231; US, third floor, Teck Guan Plaza, Jalan Sultan ☎2225293.

Hospital The Raja Isteri Pengiran Anak Saleha Hospital (RIPAS) Jalan Tutong ☎2242424; or there's the 24hr Katong Clinic, first floor, Block B, Abdul Razak Complex, Jalan Gadong ☎2428715. For an ambulance, call ☎991.

Internet access *Kotitiam Internet Café*, second floor & *Paul and Elizabeth Cybercafé*, third floor, Yayasan Complex (Mon–Sat 9.30am–9.30pm, Sun 10am–6pm).

Pharmacies Khong Lin Dispensary, G3A, Wisma Jaya, Jalan Pemancha; Sentosa Dispensary, 42 Jalan Sultan.

By air

Central and Northern line buses (B$1) run to the airport from the bus station hourly between 6am and 6pm; you can also get a taxi there (B$25) from the bus station or most hotels. The **airport tax** is B$5 for flights to Malaysia and Singapore, B$12 for all other destinations. Note that if you are travelling Royal Brunei Airlines the tax is included in the ticket price.

By boat

Boats for **Labuan** leave from the **ferry terminal** at Muara, 25km northeast of BSB. To get there, take the Muara express bus from BSB's bus station (every 30min; 6.50am–4.50pm; 30min; B$2); B$35 for a taxi from the centre. Express boats leave for Labuan (regular daily departures 7.30am–4.40pm; 1hr; B$15) and Lawas (one daily at 11.30am; 2hr; B$10); tickets bought at the terminal. From Labuan, there are daily connections on to KK and Menumbok in Sabah, though to ensure you catch one, it's wise to leave BSB early in the day. Note that the schedule can change, so double-check departure times to all destinations at @ www.bruneibay.net.

Boats to **Bangar** in Temburong (hourly; 6.30am–4.30pm; 40min; B$7) depart from the Temburong jetty, 300m east of the centre on Jalan Residency; tickets are sold beside the jetty.

By bus

Given how skimpy the **bus network** is, if you want to make a day-trip out of BSB, you have to start early in the morning. Among the main routes from the bus station, are the buses north to Muara (B$2), and west to Tutong (B$4) and Seria (B$6) – here you can change for Kuala Belait, from where there are departures for Miri in Sarawak. If you're heading for Miri, it's best to catch the 7.15am BSB–Seria bus that connects with the 9.30am Seria–Kuala Belait service. This arrives in Kuala Belait in time to catch the 11am to the Sarawak border. It is necessary however to go through a small rigmarole at the bus station office where you buy the onward ticket to Miri as you need to show your passport. Buses #44, #48 and #49 (B$1; 40min) travel to Kuala Lurah on the Limbang border, from where you'll have to catch a minivan (RM5.50) or hire a taxi onward to Limbang Town (RM20). There is also one bus daily to Lawas in Sarawak, which leaves at 9.30am.

Police Central Police Station, Jalan Stoney ☏2222333, or call ☏993.
Post office The GPO (Mon–Thurs 8am–4.30pm & Sat 8am–12.30pm) is at the intersection of Jalan Elizabeth Dua and Jalan Sultan. Poste restante is at the Money Order counter.
Taxis ☏2394949; airport taxis ☏2343671.
Telephones Telekom (daily 8am–midnight) is next

to the GPO on Jalan Sultan; international calls can be made from here, or else buy a phone card (in B$5, B$10, B$20 or B$50 denominations) and use a public booth.
Visa extensions At the Immigration Office, Jalan Menteri Besar ☏2383106 (Mon–Thurs & Sat 7.45am–12.15pm & 1.45–4.30pm).

Muara District

As most of Brunei's nature attractions are in Temburong and Tutong there's little to detain you in the capital's district, **Brunei Muara**. However, no visit to Brunei would be complete without checking out the **Empire Hotel & Country Club**, although the size of your budget will most likely prevent you from actually checking in. Also worth a visit is **Muara Beach** and the **Bukit Shahbandar Forest Recreation Park**, a medium-sized nature reserve with just the most basic facilities for visitors. Although Muara Beach can be reached with some struggle by bus, the easiest way to get to all these places is by car, either rental or taxi, unless you are travelling on a day tour.

North to Muara

Northeast of BSB, beyond the Brunei Museum, Jalan Kota Batu stretches all the way up to **MUARA**, Brunei's main port for sea-based import and export and for transport links to Labuan in Sabah. While there's no other compelling reason to go to Muara itself, nearby **Muara Beach** boasts an adequate stretch of sand, although food stalls or cafés are thin on the ground outside the weekend when, in good weather, locals often descend.

At **Serasa Beach**, a few kilometres south of Muara, a water-sports complex has facilities for sailing, windsurfing, water-skiing and fishing. Again this beach can get popular at weekends with families – on Sundays a "snake man" usually arrives to display his collection of tame snakes. Opposite the water-sports centre is a turtle research base (daily 10am–5pm). **Buses** (B$2) to Muara from BSB's Jalan Cator pass along Jalan Kota Batu, skirting the Brunei River's north bank, but don't go to either beach. You will need to change in Muara town; the local bus to the beaches is, however, extremely infrequent – around every two hours (B$1).

The Empire Hotel & Country Club

A favourite stop on the global circuit for celebrities, the **Empire Hotel & Country Club** (℡2417788, Ⓦwww.theempirehotel.com; Ⓞ) at Jerudong BG3122, is situated on the Muara–Tutong highway, around 10km northwest of BSB. One of the world's few seven-star hotels, this opulent work of architecture cost US$1.1 billion to build and is understandably a top attraction for Bruneians and visitors alike.

Apart from the hotel itself the complex includes one of the world's top golf courses, a number of restaurants, a bowling alley, cinema, beach, three swimming pools and a vast semi-covered, air-conditioned café-bar-restaurant. (note the bar is "dry"). Visitors who aren't hotel guests can explore most of the complex, although there's a B$10 levy applied for pool use. The complex's water-sport centre offers banana boat rides, snorkelling, dive courses and parasailing (see website for prices). On Fridays (10–11am) the hotel offers a free buggy tour of the complex from the main entrance. Non-residents can eat throughout the complex; the food is superb, but prices are steep (B$50 for a main dish from the à la carte evening menu); this all makes, afternoon tea, taken in the atrium, a deal at just B$10.

A pet project of Prince Jefri, the sultan's discredited and ostracized brother, the hotel complex benefited from the skills of thousands of craftsmen from a variety of artistic traditions – the result is jaw-dropping. Just to walk in the 25-metre-high central atrium with its marble columns, covered with complex Islamic designs in shimmering gold leaf is striking enough. Then there's the lobby staircase's gold-plated balusters laden with 370 tiger's eye gemstones and the handrails coated with mother-of-pearl and semi-precious stones from the Philippines.

Practicalities

The *Empire* has over 300 opulently appointed rooms, as well as 63 suites and 16 secluded villas, the least expensive room hardly a pinch at over B$360. Promotions are sometimes on, especially for the villas, when prices can be cut substantially. Check through the website or contact directly by phone. There's no public transport serving the hotel so taxis (B$15) from BSB, or renting a car (see p.570), are the only options for getting here.

Bukit Shahbandar Park

Around 20km west of Muara, and a few kilometres form the *Empire*, is the **Bukit Shahbandar Forest Recreation Park** (daily 8am–6pm; free), a compact area of acacia, pine and heath forest equipped with trails, and dotted with *pondoks* (shelters), weaving around up a hill to lookout points over *Empire Hotel* complex, BSB and the South China Sea. Marking the entrance to the park is an information centre with displays on the surrounding terrain, and a few amenities including toilets and two stalls selling snacks and drinks. The trails are well signposted and popular with joggers, and people training for an ascent of Mount Kinabalu, but some of the more distant ones are badly eroded. Unfortunately, Bukit Shahbandar is tricky to reach; unless you're prepared to pay for a taxi, you'll have to take the bus to Berakas (B$2) and try to hitch-hike from there.

Selirong Recreation Park

A final attraction near BSB is Brunei Bay's **Selirong Recreation Park**, only approachable by a one-hour boat journey from the capital, where plankways have been built across swamp and mangrove forest. It is possible to see water-birds like storks, egrets, plovers, herons and kingfishers and, less frequently, mammals including monkeys, flying foxes, lemurs, snakes and turtles. The park currently lacks any facilities, and visitors can only go by arranging a visit through the Forestry Department (☏02/2381687, ✉jphq@brunet.bn).

Temburong District

Hilly **Temburong District** has been isolated from the rest of Brunei since 1884, when the strip of land to its west was ceded to Sarawak. Sparsely populated by Malay, Iban and Murut groups, this rainforest-dominated region is worth a visit, notably to see the 500-square-kilometre **Ulu Temburong National Park**, with its dense forest trails, canopy walkway and lovely river. The visit to the park starts in the district capital, Bangar, a small sleepy town. Less essential than the park is the Labi region of Temburong. However, equipped with your own transport and with a half-day to spare, it's worth visiting another tract of rainforest, **Bukit Peradayan Forest Reserve**, although there aren't any facilities there.

Bangar

The starting point for all the above trips in Temburong is the district's only town, **BANGAR**. The only way to get here is by speedboat from BSB (daily 6.30am–4.30pm; every 45min; 40min; B$6). The boats dart through narrow mangrove estuaries that are home to crocodiles and proboscis monkeys, swooping around corners and sometimes narrowly missing vessels travelling the opposite way, before shooting off into open expanses of water and then down the Temburong River. It is a gorgeous ride, given good weather. After all that, you'll find the town of Bangar is nothing much to write home about; its main street, which runs west from the jetty to the town mosque, has a handful of coffee shops and provisions stores. Also on the main road, across the bridge from the jetty, is Bangar's grandest building, the District Office, with a waterfront **café** in front.

The main street has a small **tourist office** (☎5221439; 9am–5pm daily except Fri 9am–12.30pm), where it may be possible to organize trips into Temburong Park for a lower price than those offered by the BSB-based operators. For **accommodation**, there is one option, the *Bangar Resthouse* (☎5221239; ●) on Jalan Batang Duri, a pretty, well-laid-out place two blocks behind the harbour across the main road. The *Resthouse* has six-bed rooms and communal bathrooms (B$20–30 per bed), or you can have a whole room for B$80 but note that it doesn't have a café.

Ulu Temburong National Park

Contained within the Batu Apoi Forest Reserve, which constitutes a tenth of the area of Brunei, the **Ulu Temburong National Park** (B$5 park fee inclusive in tour price), is a fine example of the sultanate's quite successful forest protection policy (although there have been reports that the border region, to the south of the park, suffers some illegal logging). The park is reached via longboat from the jetty at **Kampung Batang Duri**, 15km south of Bangar, but only visitors on tours run by registered operators (see p.569) can visit. Most trips begin in BSB although it is possible to join the tour group in Bangar.

The one-hour boat journey traverses mangrove forests on the way to the *nipah*-lined Temburong River and the park HQ. En route, dense jungle cloaks the hills on either side and birds and monkeys bustle around in the trees; it's an atmospheric journey that sets the tone for the park itself.

The main attraction of the park is the **canopy walkway**, reached by an hour-long trek taking in two hanging bridges and a plankway, followed by a giddying climb up the stairs around a near-vertical, sixty-metre-high aluminium structure. The view from the top, of Brunei Bay to the north and Sarawak's Gunung Mulu National Park to the south, is quite breathtaking. At this height (on a good day) you can see four types of hornbills and gibbons in the trees, as well as numerous squirrels and small birds. According to a University of Brunei Darussalam survey, fifty species of birds have been sighted on the netting around the walkway, and flying lizards, frogs and snakes feed regularly at ground level. Other activities in the park include chartering a small **longboat** (around B$50 return) to go further upstream to a tree house where a few trails weave for short distances into the surrounding jungle; and **night walks**, conducted from time to time by the park staff.

Practicalities

From Batang Duri, longboats take around ninety minutes to reach park **HQ** (daily 8am–6.30pm) set on a spit of land at the junction of the Temburong River and a tributary. Beside HQ is the park's recently upgraded **accommodation**. Now run by tour operator, Sunshine, the nineteen chalets (22 doubles in all) are well appointed with en-suite bathrooms, comfortable beds and veranda. Over-nighting though doesn't come cheap, at around B$220 (all transport to and from BSB and meals included). As a result, many travellers prefer to go for a day visit (with Sunshine, around B$100), which is all you really need anyway given that there are few trails into the jungle.

On to Labu

Twenty kilometres east of Bangar, on the road to Lawas in Sarawak, lies Temburong's **Labu** region. The area used largely to comprise rubber plantations until the bottom dropped out of the rubber market in the 1950s; today, paddy fields line the road on the north side, while the forest creeps down to the road on the other. Fifteen kilometres out of Bangar, you come to the **Bukit Peradayan Forest Reserve**, a small park featuring a strenuous three-hour trek along an uphill plankway to **Bukit Patoi** (310m), passing unusual rock formations and caves on the way. From the top of the hill there are great views across Brunei's spectacular and largely undisturbed rainforests, south towards Sarawak. There are no amenities in the park, so bring your own food and drink.

Five kilometres further east, a signposted road to the right leads to **SENOKOH**, a Malay and Murut village comprising a few dozen stilt dwellings. While there's little to do besides walking around the kampung, meeting people and having local fruit trees pointed out, a visit can offer a rare insight into the lifestyle of traditional, rural Bruneians; it's well worth making the effort to get here for that alone. There are no bus services in this area.

Tutong District

West of Brunei Muara District is wedge-shaped **Tutong District**, whose main settlement, **Tutong**, is a little over 40km west of BSB. Tutong is slowly becoming an agricultural zone as the government prepares for the eventual demise of the oil reserves. The district contains coffee, tapioca and cinnamon plantations and a research station, at **Birau**, which develops new strains of cereal crops. The main reason to come out here is to visit the sublime Tasek Merimbun, a lake teeming with wildlife.

Though a coastal highway connects Tutong with Muara District, buses (daily 8.30am–3pm; every 2hr; B$3) from BSB's Jalan Cator terminal only travel along the inland route along Jalan Tutong, which is skirted by scrublands and grasslands.

Tutong and around

The sleepy little town of **TUTONG** is an amiable enough place to break the trip between BSB and Sarawak. The one street of any size, Jalan Enche Awang (buses drop you at the end beside the river), is flanked by rows of shophouses on one side, and on the other by the broad Tutong River. Tutong has no places to stay, though it does have several **restaurants**: try the *Haji K-K-Koya* at Jalan Enche Awang 14, or the Chinese *Ho Yuen* at no. 12.

If you're in town on a Friday morning, you should visit the animated **Tamu Tutong**, a market which draws fruit and vegetable vendors from the interior of Brunei. The market takes place on a patch of land 1km south of central Tutong at Kampung Serambagaun, and is reached by walking out of town along Jalan Enche Awang and taking a left turn at the fork in the road. Ignoring this fork and continuing on across the coastal highway brings you, after fifteen minutes, to the best stretch of beach in the area, **Seri Kenangan**, whose yellow sands divide the Tutong River from the South China Sea. Its name translates as "Memorable Beach", and though this may be rather stretching the point, the beach is pleasant, with a sometimes open basic café.

Tasek Merimbun

Tutong District's most impressive geographical feature is an ASEAN National Heritage site, **Tasek Merimbun**, the largest lake in Brunei. It's home to a variety of flora and fauna and facilities include elevated plankways and basic chalet accommodation. The walkways run from the attractively landscaped lake shore across to Pulau Jelandung, a tiny wooded island which has a profusion of **birdlife** (ask the staff for boat availability), and pathways and picnic spots are to be found around the lake itself. Bird species easily spotted in the vicinity include egrets, falcons and eagles plus a host of smaller ones. Studies have identified over 180 species of moths and butterflies there.

Practicalities

Unfortunately, there's no public transport to the park, so you will have to rent a car or go on a **tour** (see p.569 for tour operators). To get there from BSB follow Jalan Tutong and after around 30km take the left turn to Lamunin. From there, signposts lead you to Tasek Merimbun, along roads that traverse glistening paddy fields. **Accommodation** is limited, consisting of a few huts (B$100 for one three-bed room) with basic toilets and shower, and a large chalet, which has a small number of two-bed rooms (◐). Camping in the chalet's communal room is also available for groups.

Belait District

The coastal section of **Belait District**, to the west of Tutong, is oil and gas country, and has been the economic heart of the sultanate ever since the Seria Oil Field was established in 1931. The oil boom led directly to the rise of the region's two main towns, **Seria** and **Kuala Belait**. Inland, though, it's a different story: down the fifty-kilometre-long **Labi Road**, a few Iban **longhouses** and tiny kampungs survive in the face of the tremendous changes brought about by the sultanate's wealth and the substantial population shift to the coast. Along with Temburong, this is the most serene and attractive part of Brunei to visit.

Along the coastal road 20km west of Tutong at Kampung Sungai Liang, a turning south marks the start of **Labi Road**, which offers the chance to explore the region's **Sungai Liang Forest Reserve**, **Luagan Lalak Forestry Recreation Park** and remote longhouses. Like most of Brunei's prettiest areas, there's no public transport here. The coast leads to **Seria** and **Kuala Belait**, unattractive towns with large expat communities mostly working in the energy sector.

The Labi Road

Just 500m from the northern end of Labi Road is the **Sungai Liang Forest Reserve**, whose thick lowland forest can be explored by following one of the walking trails leading from the lakes. A small information centre and a few picnic shelters cluster around the entrance. Twenty kilometres further along the road is the **Luagan Lalak Forestry Recreation Park**, whose freshwater swamp swells into a lake with the onset of the monsoon rains, flooding the area around it. A little further on and you reach **LABI** itself, a small agricultural settlement relying on harvests of durian and rambutan for its livelihood. Despite much speculative drilling, its surrounding hills have so far refused to yield any oil, though it was Labi's oil potential that led to the construction of the road here in the first place. There's nowhere to stay or eat in Labi. Shortly after Labi, the road turns into a laterite track; around 300m along, a trail off to the east leads, after two hours' walk, to **Wasai Rampayoh**, a large waterfall. Back on the track, continue south and you reach **Mendaram Longhouse**, the first of several Iban communities here, where a few dozen people live. Like most Iban architecture in Brunei, this is a modern structure with electricity and running water. The people here are very friendly and happy to guide you along the trail to **Wasai Mendaram**, a small waterfall twenty minutes' walk away with a rock pool perfect for swimming.

A few kilometres further on, and around half-an-hour's drive from Labi, there is another longhouse, **Teraja**, which marks the end of Labi Road, with only swamp forest beyond. The locals can point out a trail, which runs alongside a stream eastwards, to another small waterfall and on up to the largest hill in the region, Bukit Teraja, where there are spectacular **views** across Brunei and Sarawak; this route takes around 40 minute.

Seria

At the very centre of Brunei's oil and gas wealth is **SERIA**, 65km west of BSB. Until oil was first discovered here at the start of the twentieth century, the area where the town now stands was nothing more than a malarial swamp, known locally as Padang Berawa, or "Wild Pigeon's Field". It took until 1931 for S1, the sultanate's first oil well, to deliver commercially, after which Seria expanded rapidly, followed by offshore drilling in the 1950s. Despite its mineral wealth, Seria remained an isolated settlement for several decades, unlinked by road with the capital.

As you approach from Tutong, you see numbers of small oil wells called "nodding donkeys" because of their rocking motion, though they actually bear a closer resemblance to praying mantises. Around the town are green-roofed housing units and bungalows, constructed by Brunei Shell for their employees; while on the waterfront is the **Billionth Barrel Monument**, whose inter-locking arches celebrate the huge productivity of the first well.

Practicalities
Seria town centre is a busy, congested place, dominated by the Plaza Seria shopping mall, across from the **bus terminus** where the regular buses from BSB (hourly 7am–3pm) terminate. The only **place to stay**, *Hotel Koperasi* (⊕ 3227589; ❹), with simple, clean, en-suite rooms is on Jalan Sharif Ali Seria, 150m northwest of the bus station. Budget coffee shops abound though: on Jalan Sultan Omar Ali (left of the plaza when viewed from the bus station), you'll find the *Universal Café* at no. 11, a sleepy retreat that's good for coffee. Next door, the air-conditioned *Restoran Sayang Merah* sells Asian and Western dishes such as spaghetti, omelettes and steaks. For a more upmarket meal, try the *New China Restaurant* in Plaza Seria.

Kuala Belait

It's a little under 20km from Seria to the neighbouring oil town of **KUALA BELAIT**. There's nothing very enticing about the place, but with all buses to and from Miri in Sarawak stopping here, it's a spot you may have to visit, if only for an hour or two. The town is ringed by suburban development that caters for the expat community, while central Kuala Belait is characterized by the many workshops and businesses that the local oil industry has spawned.

Buses stop at the intersection of Jalan Bunga Raya and Jalan McKerron, across which is the town's **taxi** stand. There are just two **hotels**, one of which, *Hotel*

Sentosa (☎3334341, ⓦhttp://www.bruneisentosahotel.com; ④) at 93 Jalan McKerron, has thirty spacious, well-appointed and welcoming rooms. The alternative is the slightly less expensive *Seaview Hotel* (☎3332651; ④), 3–4km back along the coastal road towards Seria, which also has good-standard en-suite rooms. You can **change money** in town at HSBC (Mon–Fri 9am–3pm, Sat 9–11am).

Jalan McKerron houses several good **restaurants**, the best of which are the tastefully decorated *Buccaneer Steakhouse* at no. 94, whose mid-priced international food is aimed squarely at the expat market; and the *Akhbar Restaurant*, at no. 99, with a Malay and North Indian menu which includes good dosai. Of Kuala Belait's handful of other restaurants, two in particular, the first-floor *Healthy Way Tandoori* at 30 Jalan Pretty (the town's main drag, a block east of McKerron), and Jalan Bunga Raya's *Orchid Room*, are worth a visit – the former for its naans, tikka masalas and *lassis*, the latter for its good-value three-course Western set lunches (Mon–Fri; B\$5). There is also the Morning Market (6–11am) whose small stalls are ideal for breakfast options like Chinese soups and *roti canai*.

Travel details

Buses

BSB to: Berakas (5 daily; 20min); Jerudong (5 daily; 40min); Kuala Lurah, for connections to Limbang (every 30min; 1hr); Muara (every 30min until 4.30pm; 30min) with a connection to Muara Beach; Seria, for Kuala Belait, and the Sarawak border (hourly until 3pm; 2hr); Tutong (hourly until 3pm; 1hr).
Kuala Belait to: Miri (Sarawak; 5 daily; 2hr 30min); Seria (every 30min until 6.30pm; 45min).
Muara to: Berakas (5 daily; 20min); BSB (hourly 7.30am–430pm).

Seria to: BSB (every 45min until 3pm; 1hr 45min); Kuala Belait (every hour; 30min).

Boats and ferries

BSB to: Bangar (11 daily; 40min).
Muara to: Labuan (several daily; 1hr 30min).

Flights

BSB to: Kota Kinabalu (5 daily; 40min); Kuala Lumpur (2 daily; 2hr 30min); Kuching (2 daily; 1hr 15min); Singapore (3 daily; 2hr).

Singapore

CHAPTER 9

Highlights

✳ **The National Museum**
A slick showpiece, with artefacts, video and audio celebrating Singapore's history, culture and food.
See p.611

✳ **Chinatown Heritage Centre**
The colour and the slums of the Chinatown of old are brilliantly recreated at this museum. See p.620

✳ **Thian Hock Keng Temple**
Drink in the atmosphere of the gilt altars, chanting monks, praying worshippers and incense.
See p.626

✳ **The Baba House** At long last, Singapore can boast a showcase Peranakan residence comparable to those in Melaka and Penang.
See p.628

✳ **Little India** Old Singapore's most atmospheric district, a sensory overload of fortune-telling parrots, colourful sarees and aromatic spice-grinding shops. See p.631

✳ **The Botanic Gardens** A relaxed and distinguished park with an immaculate orchid collection and forest walks. See p.642

✳ **Bukit Timah Reserve** This pocket of primary rainforest offers a decent jungle experience, without the leeches. See p.644

✳ **Food** Not for nothing does Singapore market itself as a foodie paradise – hundreds of restaurants serve up every style of Chinese cuisine, sophisticated fusion fare and more. See p.658

▲ Singapore Slings

Singapore

Singapore is certainly the handiest city I ever saw, as well planned and carefully executed as though built entirely by one man. It is like a big desk, full of drawers and pigeon-holes, where everything has its place, and can always be found in it.

William Hornaday, 1885

Despite the immense changes the past century has wrought upon the tiny island of Singapore, natural historian William Hornaday's succinct appraisal is as valid today as it was in 1885. This absorbing city-state, just 1° north of the Equator and only 700 square kilometres in size – if you include all the outlying islands – has evolved from a colonial backwater into a slick shrine to wealth and consumerism, its downtown area dense with gleaming towers and shopping malls.

Lacking any noteworthy natural resources, Singapore initially acquired prosperity through a vigorous **free trade** policy, put in place in 1819 when Sir Stamford Raffles took advantage of the island's superb natural harbour and strategic position on the maritime route between China and India to set up a British trading post here. The port thrived from the word go, and remains one of the busiest in the world. The country's coffers were also boosted by **industrialization**, especially after independence, and when Singapore grew too successful to remain a cheap sweatshop for multinationals, it maintained its competitive edge and kept the money flowing in by developing a super-efficient infrastructure and work ethic, and diversifying into technology and finance.

With its dynamism and lack of a welfare system, Singapore today appears a paragon of capitalism, and enjoys a standard of living on a par with that in western Europe. Yet a huge slice of the economy is dominated by conglomerates which were set up by the state and in which it retains a controlling interest. At the core of the success story is **paternalism**, in which some personal freedoms have been sacrificed so that the government can engineer the economy and society to deliver affluence. It's this unwritten pact that has allowed kampungs and unsanitary slums to be cleared and the historic parts of the city remodelled, with much of the population being resettled in well-planned but bland new towns; such is the rate of churn even today that Singapore feels dogged by a feeling of impermanence, with modern complexes scarcely bedding down in the public's consciousness before being replaced by something more grandiose. If prosperity has been the carrot, there have also been sticks: regulations governing everything from flushing public toilets after use to jaywalking, and, less benignly, a low tolerance of **dissent**. Consequently, Singaporeans have acquired a reputation, partly deserved, for unquestioning subservience.

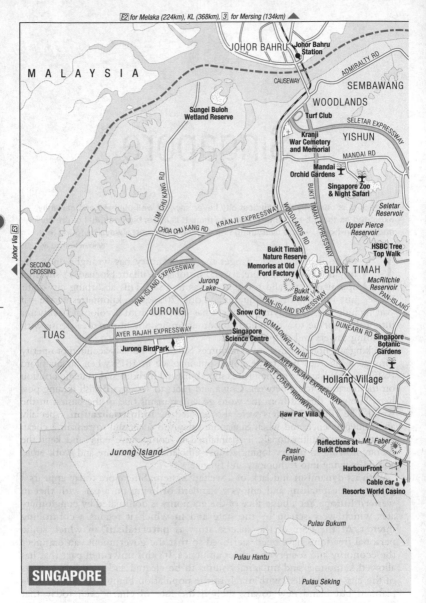

E2 for Melaka (224km), KL (368km), 3 for Mersing (134km) ▲

JOHOR BAHRU — Johor Bahru Station

M A L A Y S I A

CAUSEWAY

ADMIRALTY RD

SEMBAWANG

WOODLANDS

Turf Club

SELETAR EXPRESSWAY

Sungei Buloh
Wetland Reserve

Kranji
War Cemetery
and Memorial

YISHUN

MANDAI RD

Mandai
Orchid Gardens

Singapore Zoo
& Night Safari

Seletar
Reservoir

LIM CHU KANG RD

KRANJI EXPRESSWAY

CHOA CHU KANG RD

BUKIT TIMAH EXPRESSWAY

WOODLANDS RD

Upper Pierce
Reservoir

HSBC Tree
Top Walk

SECOND
CROSSING

PAN-ISLAND EXPRESSWAY

Jurong
Lake

Bukit Timah
Nature Reserve

Memories at Old
Ford Factory

BUKIT TIMAH

MacRitchie
Reservoir

PAN-ISLAND

JURONG

Bukit
Batok

PAN-ISLAND EXPRESSWAY

Snow City

COMMONWEALTH AV

DUNEARN RD

Singapore
Botanic
Gardens

TUAS

AYER RAJAH EXPRESSWAY

Singapore
Science Centre

Jurong BirdPark

AYER RAJAH EXPRESSWAY

WEST COAST HIGHWAY

Holland Village

Haw Par Villa

Pasir
Panjang

Reflections at
Bukit Chandu

Mt. Faber

Jurong Island

HarbourFront

Cable car
Resorts World Casino

Pulau Bukum

Pulau Hantu

Pulau Seking

SINGAPORE

582

Whatever the political ramifications of the state's economic success, visitors prepared to peer beneath the state's squeaky-clean surface will discover a profusion of colonial buildings, dusty temples and age-old values and traditions that have survived profound social and physical change. Singapore undoubtedly lacks the personality of some Southeast Asian cities, but to dismiss it as sterile is unfair. As with Malaysia, much of Singapore's fascination springs from its having

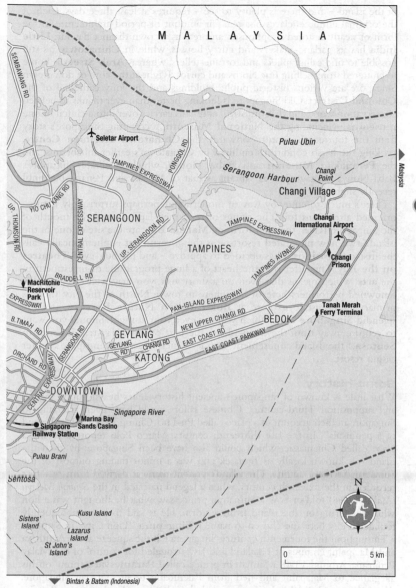

Bintan & Batam (Indonesia) ▼

a **multicultural population**, the main groups being the Chinese (75.6 percent), the Malays (13.6 percent) and the Indians (8.7 percent). This diverse ethnic mix can turn a ten-minute walk across town into what seems like a hop from one country to another.

Inevitably, Singapore is seen by most visitors simply as a pricey stopover en route to Malaysia or some other part of Southeast Asia, but getting a decent taste of the island – and there is plenty to see – requires at least three days. Each of the original ethnic enclaves boasts a fair amount of period architecture in the form of neatly restored shophouses, and retains its own distinct flavour: **Little India** has its garland-makers and curry houses, while in **Chinatown**, it's still possible to find calligraphers and fortune-tellers, whereas **Arab Street** is home to cluttered stores selling fine cloths and curios. Right at the core of downtown Singapore are various historic public buildings and the lofty cathedral of the **Colonial District**. Old Singapore is looking better than ever thanks to belated conservation work, and that historical emphasis carries over into a clutch of fine **museums** – including the **National Museum**, recounting Singapore's story from the fourteenth century onwards; the **Chinatown Heritage Centre**, evoking the harsh conditions endured by Chinatown's earlier inhabitants; and the **Peranakan Museum** and **Baba House**, which celebrate Singapore's Baba-Nonya heritage, just as vibrant as that of Melaka and Penang but until recently slighted.

There's much to enjoy by way of modern and, perhaps surprisingly, nature-oriented attractions too. The wings of reclaimed land around the mouth of the Singapore River, together forming **Marina Bay**, are the site of one of the island's two new integrated resorts – as the government euphemistically calls the first-ever **casinos** it has decided to approve – and the bug-eyed **Theatres on the Bay**. The latter is at the heart of a huge programme of investment in the **arts**, which means that even on a short visit, you may well catch world-renowned performers here or elsewhere in town. North of the city, there is primary rainforest to explore at **Bukit Timah Nature Reserve**, and the splendid **Singapore zoo**, which you can even tour at night. Should you want to venture away from the main island, the best offshore day-trip is south to **Sentosa**, the island amusement arcade which features Singapore's other casino resort.

Some history

What little is known of Singapore's ancient history relies heavily upon legend and supposition. Third-century Chinese sailors could have been referring to Singapore in their account of a place called Pu-Luo-Chung, or "island at the end of a peninsula". In the late thirteenth century, Marco Polo reported seeing a place called Chiamassie, which could also have been Singapore: by then the island was known locally as Temasek and was a minor trading outpost of the Sumatran Srivijaya empire. The island's present name is derived from one first recorded in the sixteenth century, when a legend narrated in the *Sejarah Melayu* (*Malay Annals*) told of how a Sumatran prince saw what he thought was a lion while sheltering on the island from a storm. He is said to have subsequently founded a city here and chosen to name it **Singapura**, "Lion City" in Sanskrit.

Throughout the fourteenth century, Singapura felt the squeeze as the Ayuthaya and Majapahit empires of Thailand and Java struggled for control of the Malay Peninsula. Around 1390, a Sumatran prince called **Paramesvara** threw off his allegiance to Majapahit and fled from Palembang to present-day Singapore. There, he murdered his host and ruled the island until a Javanese offensive forced him to flee up the Peninsula, where he and his son, **Iskandar Shah**, subsequently founded the Melaka Sultanate; meanwhile, Singapore faded away into an inconsequential fishing settlement.

The British colony

By the late eighteenth century, with China opening up for trade with the West, the British East India Company felt the need to establish outposts along the

Straits of Melaka. Penang was secured in 1786, but with the Dutch expanding their rule in the East Indies (Indonesia), a port was needed further south. Enter **Thomas Stamford Raffles** (see box, p.608), lieutenant-governor of Bencoolen in Sumatra, who was authorized in 1818 by the governor-general of India to establish a British colony at the southern tip of the Malay Peninsula. Early the following year, Raffles stepped ashore on the north bank of the Singapore River accompanied by Colonel William Farquhar, former Resident of Melaka and fluent in Malay. At the time, inhospitable swampland and tiger-infested jungle covered Singapore, and its population is thought to have been under a thousand. Raffles recognized the island's potential for providing a deep-water harbour, and immediately struck a treaty with **Abdul Rahman**, *temenggong* (chieftain) of Singapore and a subordinate of the Sultan of Johor, to establish a British trading station there.

The Dutch were furious at this British incursion into what they considered their territory. Raffles, realizing that the sultan's loyalties to the Dutch would make final approval of his deal impossible, approached the sultan's brother, **Hussein**, recognized him as His Highness the Sultan Hussein Mohammed Shah, and concluded a second treaty with both him and the *temenggong*. The Union Jack was raised, and Singapore's future as a trading post was set. With its duty-free stance and **strategic position** at the gateway to the South China Sea, Singapore experienced a meteoric expansion, as Chinese, Indians and Europeans arrived in search of work and commercial opportunities.

In 1822, Raffles set about drawing up the demarcation lines whose effects can still be seen in the layout of modern Singapore. The area south of the Singapore River was earmarked for the Chinese; a swamp at the mouth of the river was filled and the commercial district established there; while Muslims were settled around the sultan's palace in today's Arab Street area. In 1824, Hussein and the *temenggong* were bought out, and Singapore was ceded outright to the British. By now the population had reached ten thousand. Three years later, the new trading post was united with Penang and Melaka to form the **Straits Settlements**, which became a British Crown Colony in 1867. Singapore's *laissez-faire* economy boomed all this time, though life was chaotic and disease-ridden. By 1860 the population had reached eighty thousand; Arabs, Indians, Javanese and Bugis all came, but most numerous of all were southern Chinese immigrants, who settled quickly thanks partly to the clan societies (*kongsis*) which already had footholds on the island.

By the end of the century, the opening of the Suez Canal and the advent of the steamship had consolidated Singapore's position as the hub of international trade in the region. This status was further enhanced by the steady drawing of all of the Malay Peninsula into British clutches, allowing Singapore to gain further from its hinterland's tin- and rubber-based economy.

The twentieth century

By the 1920s, Singapore's various communities were beginning to find their political voice; in 1926, the Singapore Malay Union was established, and four years later, the Malayan Communist Party, backed by local Chinese. But grumblings of independence had risen to no more than a faint whisper before an altogether more immediate problem reared its head.

In December 1941, the **Japanese** bombed Pearl Harbour and invaded the Malay Peninsula; less than two months later they were at the Causeway between Johor and Singapore. "Fortress Singapore" had not been prepared for an attack from the north – Singapore's artillery were pointed south from what is now Sentosa Island. On February 15, 1942, the **fall of Singapore** was complete. Winston Churchill called the surrender "the worst disaster and the largest capitulation in British history"; ironically, it later transpired that the supply lines of the Japanese forces had been hopelessly stretched prior to the surrender. Three and a half years of brutal Japanese rule ensued, during which Europeans were either herded into **Changi Prison** or marched up the Peninsula to work on Thailand's infamous "Death Railway". Less well known is the vicious **Operation Sook Ching**, during which upwards of 25,000 Chinese men were shot dead at Punggol and Changi beaches as enemies of the Japanese.

In the war's aftermath, Singaporeans demanded a say in the island's administration, and in 1957 the British agreed to the establishment of an elected legislative assembly. Full internal self-government was achieved in May 1959, when the **People's Action Party** (PAP), led by Cambridge law graduate **Lee Kuan Yew**, emerged on top in elections. Lee became Singapore's first prime minister, and quickly looked for the security of a natural-looking merger with Malaya (now Peninsular Malaysia). This ensued in 1963 when Singapore combined with Malaya, Sarawak and British North Borneo (now Sabah) to form the **Federation of Malaysia**, but within two years Singapore was asked to leave (see p.699). One hundred and forty-six years after Sir Stamford Raffles had set Singapore on the world map, the tiny island with a marvellous harbour but no natural resources faced the prospect of being consigned to history's bottom drawer of crumbling colonial ports.

Instead, Lee's personal vision and drive transformed Singapore into an Asian economic heavyweight and enabled his party to utterly dominate Singapore politics to this day, though at a price. The media has been treated in a heavy-handed fashion, and even more disturbing was the government's attitude towards **political opposition**. When the Workers' Party won a by-election in 1981, the new MP, the late J.B. Jeyaretnam, found himself charged with several criminal offences, and chased through the Singapore courts for the next decade. In more recent times the few successful opposition candidates have found themselves similarly in court over apparent affronts to the government's probity.

Prospects

Upon Lee's retirement in 1990, **Goh Chok Tong** became prime minister, though many felt that Lee still called the shots in his new role as senior minister. In August 2004, Goh was succeeded by **Lee Hsien Loong**, Lee Kuan Yew's son, and on the same day the elder Lee was named "minister mentor", a newly created cabinet position that gave him an official high horse from which to influence affairs.

While the younger Lee has a sternness about him that is reminiscent of his father, Singapore has actually become a less uptight place in recent years. This new climate may be linked to government efforts to foster enterprise and creativity, or it may be part of a pitch to tempt back the many Singaporeans who have emigrated in search of more personal space. Whatever the reasons, one unexpected spin-off has been the appearance, unthinkable in the 1980s, of a smattering of shops selling sex aids; more positive has been a more relaxed attitude to artistic expression and gay life.

Any goodwill this more liberal atmosphere generates can only help as the island deals with one of its worst-ever **economic setbacks**, triggered by the downturn which swept the globe in 2008. The government's schemes had appeared to be going swimmingly beforehand, with property prices soaring and massive projects under way to turn Marina Bay into a **reservoir** (to help the island wean itself off Malaysian water supplies) and to build two daring **integrated resorts**, approved in the face of much public hand-wringing over the introduction of large-scale **gambling** to Singapore.

The island state has enormous cash reserves and can weather the storm. But for the man and woman in the street, even the years prior to the crisis had been tough, with inflation far outstripping the derisory rates of interest offered by Singapore banks, healthcare costs rising and many junior service-sector jobs going to foreign workers. In fact, **immigration** is concerning locals, though not out of racism, as many of the migrants hail from India and China, as Singapore's own citizens once did. It's the scale of immigration that grabs the attention: of the island's population of 4.8 million in 2008, over a million were migrants on short-term contracts. Having once advocated birth control to keep the population down to 3–4 million, the government now speaks of a staggering 6 or 7 million as necessary for Singapore to become the ultimate economic powerhouse for its size. Singaporeans mutter that the island seems more crowded than ever, that the MRT metro trains are getting even more packed and that mainland Chinese staff in restaurants speak minimal English and have little familiarity with local food. While neither immigration nor economic woes pose any threat to Singapore's social fabric, it will be interesting to see if these testing times finally prompt Singaporeans to take a more vocal interest in decisions affecting their lives.

Arrival

Shaped roughly like a diamond, the main island of Singapore is 42km from east to west at its widest, and 23km from north to south. The **downtown** area radiates out from the mouth of the **Singapore River** at the southern tip of the diamond, with all the historical quarters within 4km or so of the rivermouth. On the north bank are the **Colonial District** and, further afield, **Little India** and the **Arab Street** area, with the shopping mecca of **Orchard Road** also to the north though further inland; to the south lie **Chinatown** and the modern **Financial District**.

Most visitors arrive at Changi Airport, in the east of the island, or via the Causeway from Malaysia, at the northern tip of the diamond; downtown arrival points are shown on the map on p.604. Wherever you arrive, the well-oiled public transport system, including MRT metro **trains** and an elaborate **bus** network, means that you'll have no problem getting into the city centre.

By air

Most people's first glimpse of Singapore is of **Changi International Airport** (ⓦ www.changiairport.com) at the eastern tip of the island, 16km from downtown, and a telling glimpse it is too: modern, efficient and air-conditioned, the airport is Singapore in microcosm. There are three main terminals, connected by free Skytrains and shuttle buses, plus a separate **budget terminal** (at the time of writing, used mainly by Tiger Airways; ⓦ www.btsingapore.com) some 1500m southwest of the main terminals, with a free shuttle bus to terminal 2. The main terminals have every facility you could wish for, from **tourist offices** (daily 6am–2am) to short-stay hotel rooms. There are also accommodation booking counters representing members of the Singapore Hotel Association, which don't include some of the cheaper hotels and guesthouses.

If you're planning to travel overland into Malaysia, note that Singapore dollar ticket prices on buses and trains are massively inflated compared to what they would be in Malaysia; KTM actually adopts the pretence that the Singapore dollar is worth the same as the ringgit – an exchange rate that hasn't applied since the 1970s. If you're counting every cent, take advantage of ringgit fares by catching a bus to Johor Bahru and continuing your journey from the train station there or the Larkin terminal.

By train
Among the trains that head to **KL** are a sleeper service and another that continues on to Ipoh and Butterworth (though it's much faster to reach these destinations by bus). There's also a daily train to Wakaf Bharu (for **Kota Bharu**) via interior towns such as Jerantut (for **Taman Negara**) and Kuala Lipis. You can check current timetables and buy tickets on line on Ⓦ www.ktmb.com.my or at the train station (daily 8.30am–2.30pm & 3–7pm; Ⓣ6222 5165). It's also possible to ride the sumptuous **Eastern & Oriental Express** (see p.29; Ⓦ www.orient-express.com) all the way to **Bangkok**, a fairy-tale trip for which you will need a healthy wallet and to dress smartly or risk ostracism; bookings can be made in Singapore at E&O Services, #32-01/3 Shaw Towers, 100 Beach Rd (Ⓣ6395 0678).

By bus and taxi
To Johor Bahru: For JB, you can simply take the SBS **#170** JB-bound bus from the Ban San Terminal (every 10min; daily 5.30am–midnight; up to around S$1.90). Alternatively, there are two nonstop services, the **Singapore–Johor Express** (every 10min; 5.30am–11.30; S$2.40) and the **Causeway Link** CW2 service (same fare), both of which take around an hour (including border formalities) to reach their destination. If you're on the #170 bus, hang onto your ticket at immigration so you can use it to resume your journey (not necessarily on the same vehicle) once you're through. These buses terminate at JB's Larkin bus station, though if you want to reach the town centre, leave the bus at the Causeway. From the taxi stand (Ⓣ6296 7054) next to the Ban San Terminal, a shared four-person taxi to JB costs S$10 per person.

To the rest of Malaysia, and Thailand: From the Lavender Street Terminal, there are intercity buses to Malaysian cities operated by Transnasional (to KL and the east coast; Ⓣ6294 7034), Hasry Express (KL and the west coast; Ⓣ6294 9306, Ⓦ www .hasryexpress.com) and Malacca–Singapore Express (Meleka; Ⓣ6293 5915). Other bus companies serving not just Malaysia but also Hat Yai in Thailand, such as

The easiest way to get into the city centre is to get an **MRT** metro train (daily 5.30am–11.15pm). A single to the downtown City Hall interchange station is around S$1.70, and the trip shouldn't take more than half an hour. Alternatively, the #36 **bus** (daily 6am–midnight roughly every 10min; S$1.60, no change given) heads to the Orchard Road area via Suntec City, the Capitol Building (for Beach Road and North Bridge Road) and the *YMCA* on Stamford Road (for the Bras Basah Road/Bencoolen Street area). Regular **taxis** from the airport levy a S$3 surcharge on top of the regular fare, rising to S$5 at the weekend; the ride into downtown costs at least S$18 and takes up to half an hour. Another option is to take a **MaxiCab** limousine taxi (S$45 to any destination in Singapore).

The only flights that don't land at Changi are Berjaya Air services from Pulau Tioman and Pulau Redang. These set down at the tiny **Seletar airport**, part of a former British military base in the north of the island. From here, bus #103M runs to the Serangoon MRT station, while a taxi into town will cost

Konsortium (☎6392 3911, ⓦwww.konsortium.com.sg), use the Golden Mile Complex; one company to try for Hat Yai is Grassland Express (☎6293 1166, ⓦwww.grassland .com.sg). Sample **fares** for regular buses are around S$20 to Melaka, S$35 to KL and S$55 to Kota Bharu or Hat Yai. There are also a few luxury-bus companies operating from various locations around Singapore, notably Transtar (KL and the west coast; ☎6295 9009, ⓦwww.transtar.com.sg); most of its departures go from its own terminal at 114 Lavender St, though a few leave from the Golden Mile Complex. It also operates regular buses, which leave from its office at Lavender Street MRT (☎6292 9009).

By boat

To Malaysia: From Changi Point (☎6542 7944; bus #2 to Changi Village), bumboats leave when full for **Kampung Pengerang**, on the southeastern tip of Johor (for Desaru, see p.366; daily 7am–4pm; S$9 one way).

To Indonesia: Ferries serve Batam, Bintan and Karimun islands in the Riau archipelago. **Batam** boats mostly depart from the HarbourFront Centre (S$16–18 one way excluding taxes and fuel surcharges), though a few sail from the Tanah Merah Ferry Terminal. All boats to **Bintan** Island (S$20–28) use the Tanah Merah Ferry Terminal, while services to Tanjung Balai on **Karimun** depart from the HarbourFront Centre (S$24). Details of these ferries are summarized on the website ⓦwww.singaporecruise .com; for tickets and schedules, contact the ferry operators, among them BatamFast (☎6270 0311 or 6542 6310, ⓦwww.batamfast.com), Bintan Resort Ferries (☎6542 4369, ⓦwww.brf.com.sg), Indofalcon (☎6270 6778, ⓦwww.indofalcon.com.sg) and Penguin Ferry Services (☎6377 6335, ⓦwww.penguin.com.sg).

By air

There are direct **flights** from Changi airport to KL, Penang, Langkawi, Kota Kinabalu, Kuching and Bandar Seri Begawan; live flight information for these and other destinations is available on ⓦwww.changiairport.com. There are also flights from Seletar airport to Redang and Tioman islands with Berjaya Air (☎6227 3688, ⓦwww.berjaya-air.com).

If you're planning to head for either Malaysia or Indonesia, it's often quite a bit cheaper to fly from, respectively, Senai **airport** beyond JB or **Batam** (the nearest Indonesian island). If you're on Causeway Link's CW2 bus, you can transfer for free to their CW1 service from the Causeway to JB's Kotaraya shopping centre, from where there are buses on to the airport (every 20min; RM8).

at least S$15, excluding the S$3 airport surcharge, with an additional booking fee to pay if you end up having to phone for a taxi.

By bus and train

A few luxury buses from Malaysia use the **Second Crossing** from Johor, arriving along the Ayer Rajah Expressway in the Tuas district of western Singapore. But trains and most road traffic from Malaysia use the old one-kilometre **Causeway** from Johor Bahru into Woodlands town in the north.

Local buses from JB arrive at the **Ban San Terminal** at the junction of Queen and Arab streets (see map, p.615), a stone's throw from Bugis MRT station. Buses from elsewhere in **Malaysia** and **from Thailand** mostly terminate either at Lavender Street Terminal or the Golden Mile Complex (see map, p.632). The **Lavender Street Terminal**, a mere bus park at the corner of Lavender Street and Kallang Bahru, is around five minutes' walk from Lavender

MRT; bus #145 passes the terminal on its way into Chinatown down North Bridge Road and South Bridge Road, while nearby on Jalan Besar, bus #65 heads to the Orchard Road area via Bencoolen Street. Any westbound bus from outside the **Golden Mile Complex** will take you to the City Hall MRT station at Raffles City. The only intercity services that don't use these two terminals are **luxury buses** operated by various companies, for example Plusliner, which uses the *Copthorne Orchid* hotel just outside downtown on Dunearn Road, from where buses #66 and #170 head to Little India and #171 goes to Orchard Road via the Newton MRT station.

Trains from Malaysia end their journey at the **Singapore Railway Station** on Keppel Road, southwest of Chinatown. Oddly, you haven't officially arrived in Singapore until you step out of the station – as a sign saying "Welcome to Malaysia" above the main station entrance testifies. The grounds of Singapore's railway system were sold lock, stock and barrel to the Federated Malay States in 1918, and the Singapore government has been unable to reach a deal with the Malaysians on buying back this prime land. From Keppel Road, bus #80 heads to Chinatown MRT station, while bus #131 travels past Tanjong Pagar, Raffles Place and City Hall MRT stations en route to Little India.

By sea

Boats from Indonesia's Riau archipelago dock either at the **HarbourFront Centre**, off Telok Blangah Road at the southern tip of Singapore, or at the **Tanah Merah Ferry Terminal** in the east of the island. The former is the southern terminus of the MRT's North East line, while the latter is linked by bus #35 to Tanah Merah and Bedok MRT stations. Most ferries from the resort island of **Batam** end up at HarbourFront Centre, though a few of these boats plus all services from the other Riau resort island, **Bintan**, use the Tanah Merah terminal.

The only ferry service **from Malaysia** comprises humble bumboats from Kampung Pengerang just east of Singapore in the Straits of Johor. These moor at Changi Point, beyond the airport, from where bus #2 travels to Tanah Merah MRT station and on to Geylang, Victoria Street and New Bridge Road in Chinatown.

Information, transport and tours

Much of the information a traveller to Singapore would need is online, but away from the virtual world your main port of call for information will be the tourist offices run by the Singapore Tourism Board (**STB**; 24hr information line ☎1800/736 2000, ⓦwww.visitsingapore.com) and billed as **Visitor Centres**. The main downtown location is smack in the middle of Orchard Road, at the junction with Cairnhill Road (daily 9.30am–10.30pm); there are also offices at #01-35 Suntec City Mall (daily 10am–6pm), close to Beach Road and the Colonial District, and at 73 Dunlop St in Little India (daily 10am–10pm). It's worth dropping in to pick up their free hand-outs and **maps**, though if you want a detailed street atlas, head to a bookshop to buy the *Singapore Street Directory* (S$13, or check the online version at ⓦwww.streetdirectory.com) – invaluable if you're going to rent a car.

A number of publications offer listings of entertainment **events** plus restaurant reviews and so forth. The best of these are the weeklies *I-S* (free) and *8 Days* (S$1.50) and the monthly *Time Out* (S$4; ⓦwww.timeoutsingapore.com.sg).

Other freebie publications available from Visitor Centres and hotels contain similar information, and the "Life!" section of the *Straits Times* also has a decent listings section. Geared towards the large **expat** community (though with some information of interest to tourists) are *The Finder*, a free monthly magazine available at some downtown bars and restaurants, and the website ⓦwww .expatsingapore.com.

Transport

Singapore's public transport network is operated by two companies, namely **SBS Transit** (ⓣ1800/225 5663, ⓦwww.sbstransit.com.sg) – historically a bus company, though it's now responsible for one of the MRT metro lines – and **SMRT** (ⓣ1800/336 8900, ⓦwww.smrt.com.sg), which was set up to run the MRT system, though it now has quite a few bus services of its own. All parts of the island are accessible by bus or MRT and fares are eminently reasonable, though note that there can be quite a lot overcrowding during rush hour (8–9.30am & 5–7pm). Taxis are also affordable and usually easy to find.

Most Singaporeans avoid the rigmarole of buying tickets for each bus or MRT ride by purchasing a stored-value **ez-link card** (ⓦwww.ezlink.com.sg) available at MRT stations and bus interchanges. Besides offering convenience, the card shaves a few cents off the cost of each trip, and a journey involving up to three transfers – from MRT to bus or vice versa or from one bus to another – is treated as one extended trip if you use the card, again resulting in a slight saving. Cards start at S$15, comprising S$7 credit, a S$3 deposit (refunded along with any remaining credit if you return the card) and S$5 covering the cost of the card itself (not refundable). The cost of each journey you make is automatically deducted from the card when you hold it over a reader as you exit an MRT barrier or step off a bus. Cards can be topped up with additional credit at ticket offices or using ticket machines, and are worth hanging onto if you're likely to be revisiting Singapore, as they stay valid for at least five years.

Alternatively, you can buy the **Singapore Tourist Pass**, costing S$8 per day (plus a S$10 deposit, refunded along with remaining credit when you return the card) and valid for up to three days' travel. Used in the same way as ez-link cards, the passes are sold at Visitor Centres and a few downtown MRT stations, and can be topped up at MRT ticket offices for additional days' travel.

The MRT

Singapore's MRT (Mass Rapid Transit) metro network is a marvel of engineering – the island's remarkably soft subsoil made it a real challenge to

---

Singapore addresses

Addresses pertaining to high-rise towers, shopping complexes and other buildings are generally written using a system containing two numbers usually preceded by #, as in #xx-yy. Here xx refers to the floor (ground level is 01, the next floor up 02, and so on) while yy refers to the unit number – hence a restaurant whose address includes #04-08 can be found in unit 8 on the building's fourth storey. It's also worth noting that all buildings within municipal housing estates have a **block number**, displayed prominently on the side, rather than a number relating to their position on the street on which they're located.

If you want to look up an address on a map, note that you can enter the street, building name or six-digit postal code into ⓦwww.streetdirectory.com and will usually get a fairly precise fix on the location.

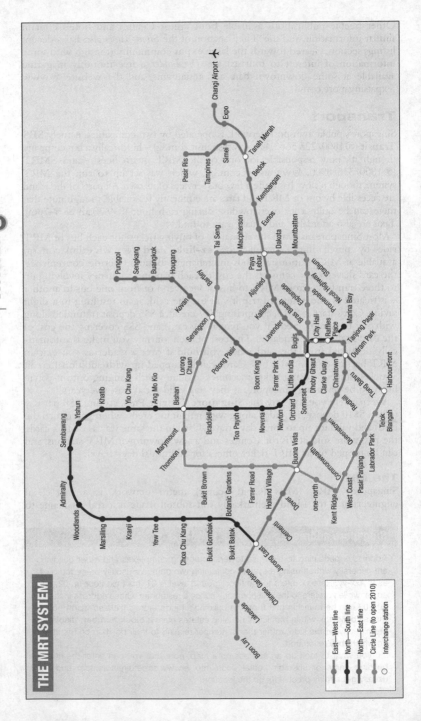

THE MRT SYSTEM

East—West line
North—South line
North—East line
Circle Line (to open 2010)
Interchange station

drill train tunnels while avoiding cave-ins – and of cleanliness, efficiency and value for money. That said, with Singapore's population having been swelled by immigration in recent years, the network is often packed, particularly downtown, and trains could arguably run more frequently.

The system has three lines. SMRT operates the **North South Line**, which runs a vaguely horseshoe-shaped route from Marina Bay up to the north of the island and then southwest to Jurong; and the **East West Line**, connecting Boon Lay in the west to Pasir Ris and Changi airport in the east. The **North East Line**, linking the HarbourFront Centre in the south with Punggol in the northeast, is operated by SBS Transit (W www.sbstransit.com.sg). A fourth line, the **Circle Line**, is being built and may open in 2010; to be run by SMRT, it will run from Bras Basah Road downtown out to the Marina Bay area and then make a long arc through suburbs all around the city centre, eventually returning along the west coast to HarbourFront Centre. Circle Line stations are shown on maps in this chapter, though some of the locations and names are provisional.

Trains run every five minutes on average from 6am until midnight downtown. **Tickets** cost between S$1.10 and S$2 per journey (S$0.75–1.80 with an ez-link card). You need coins for the ticket machines, found inside the main hall at each station; adjacent change machines break S$1 and S$2 notes, while larger notes can be changed at the station control room. Eating, drinking and smoking are not permitted on trains. Signs in the ticket concourse appear to ban hedgehogs from the MRT; in fact, they signify "no durians". For detailed timetables, fares and other information on the MRT, consult the SMRT and SBS Transit websites or call their helplines, or enquire at the control room on station concourses.

There are also three **LRT** (Light Rail Transit) networks that connect suburban estates with the MRT. As a tourist, you're unlikely to make use of any of them.

Buses

Singapore's **bus** network is incredibly comprehensive and thus initially daunting to use, as there seem to be so many routes available throughout downtown. Thankfully, detailed lists of destinations which each bus serves are displayed at many central bus stops, and both the SBS Transit and SMRT websites contain full route information and rather complicated journey planners – though unfortunately they don't tell you about potential connections involving each other's buses. If you intend to use buses a lot, you might want to buy the *Singapore Bus Guide and Bus-Stop Directory* (S$4), sold at bookstores.

Most buses are air-conditioned and slick. On most buses **fares** ascend in small steps according to the distance travelled. Cash fares on air-conditioned buses start at S$1 (slightly less on buses without a/c), rising to a maximum of S$1.90; the corresponding ez-link fares lie in the S$0.70–1.70 range. Some buses charge a flat fare while a few don't take cash at all – check signage at the front of the bus. Paying cash, tell the driver where you want to go, then drop the sum asked for into the adjacent metal chute and collect the tiny paper ticket. **Change** isn't given, so have coins to hand if you don't want the bus company to pocket the difference. If you have an ez-link card, note that you must tap the card on the card reader upon entering the bus *and* at the exit door when you get off so that the correct fare is deducted.

Buses start running around 6am and wind down from 11.30pm, with the very last regular buses leaving downtown around 12.30am. Between midnight and 2am a few **Night-Rider** (run by SMRT and with route numbers prefixed "NR"; S$3.50) and **Nite Owl** (SBS Transit, with route numbers suffixed "N"; S$4) buses

Below is a selection of handy **bus routes**. Note that one-way systems downtown mean that services that use Orchard Road and Bras Basah Road in one direction return via Stamford Road, Penang Road, Somerset Road and Orchard Boulevard; buses up Selegie and Serangoon roads return via Jalan Besar and Bencoolen Street; and services along North and South Bridge roads return via Eu Tong Sen Street and Hill Street.

#2 From Eu Tong Sen Street in Chinatown all the way to Changi Prison and Changi Beach, via the Arab Quarter and Geylang Serai.

#7 From the restaurants of Holland Village to the Botanic Gardens and on to Orchard Road, Bras Basah Road and Victoria Street (for the Arab Quarter), then on to Geylang Serai.

#36 A loop service between Orchard Road and Changi airport via Suntec City and the Singapore Flyer.

#65 Orchard Road to Little India and on up Serangoon Road.

#170 From the Ban San Terminal at the northern end of Queen Street to JB in Malaysia, passing Little India, the Newton Circus food court, the northern end of the Botanic Gardens, Bukit Timah Nature Reserve and Kranji War Cemetery on the way.

#174 Runs between the Botanic Gardens and the Baba House in Neil Road, via Orchard Road, the Colonial District, Boat Quay and Chinatown.

are available; they can be useful for travel within the city centre, but then operate as express services between the downtown area and their ultimate destinations, the outlying new towns.

Taxis

There are thousands of **taxis** on the streets of Singapore, so you'll hardly ever have trouble hailing a cab, day or night – unless a tropical downpour is in progress, in which case demand for taxis soars. They come in various colours and styles, but are always clearly marked "TAXI"; On the whole, the drivers are a friendly enough bunch, but their English isn't always good, so if you're heading off the beaten track, it's a good idea to have your destination written down or to be aware of a landmark nearby that they can aim for.

Unlike in KL, all drivers do use their meters, the fare starting at S$2.80 for the first kilometre, after which it rises 20¢ for every third of a kilometre or so (classier limousine taxis are only slightly more expensive). Note that you have to pay a third extra on top of the metered fare for journeys undertaken Monday to Friday between 7am and 9.30am and Monday to Saturday between 5pm and 8pm, and fifty percent extra is added between midnight and 6am. Journeys from airports incur a S$3 surcharge (S$5 Fri–Sun 5pm–midnight) and there's a fee of S$3.50–5 if you **book** a taxi over the phone (try any of the following companies for this: Comfort/CityCab ☏6552 1111, ⓦwww.cdgtaxi.com.sg; Silvercab ☏6363 6888, ⓦwww.premiertaxis.com.sg; SMRT Taxis ☏6555 8888, ⓦwww.smrt.com.sg). Tolls levied on journeys along expressways and within the CBD (see below) are also factored into fares.

Driving

Given the efficiency of public transport, there's hardly any reason to **rent a car** in Singapore, especially when it's a pricey business. Major disincentives to driving are in place in order to combat traffic congestion, including a large fee for a permit just to own a car and the creation way back in the 1970s of a restricted zone around the Central Business District (**CBD**) – encompassing Chinatown, Orchard Road and the Financial District. You have to pay **tolls** to drive into and within the CBD and to use many of the island's expressways, and this being Singapore, it's all done in the most hi-tech way using Electronic Road Pricing (**ERP**). All Singapore cars have a gizmo installed that reads a stored-value **CashCard** (in the near future, a new generation of ez-link cards will become usable too) from which the toll is deducted as you drive past an ERP gantry. **Parking** can be expensive, though at least many car parks offer the convenience of taking the fee off your CashCard, failing which you will have to purchase coupons from a licence booth, post office or shop. The only sensible reason to rent a car in Singapore is to travel up into Malaysia – and even then it's far cheaper to rent in JB. If you are still keen to rent in Singapore itself, you can contact Avis (Ⓦwww.avis.com.sg) or Hertz (Ⓦwww.hertz.com), both of which have offices at Changi airport.

If you want to drive a **Malaysian car** into Singapore, you will need to buy a stored-value **Autopass card** at the Causeway or Second Crossing. The card magically records any ERP tolls you incur without requiring a card reader on board; the total charge is deducted from the card when you return to Johor. The website Ⓦwww.lta.gov.sg has more details on this and other matters to do with driving in Singapore.

Cycling

Though largely flat, Singapore is hardly ideal cycling country. There are few bike lanes along main roads, where you'll have to brave furious traffic, though this doesn't put off the few dedicated locals and expats whom you'll see pedalling equally furiously along suburban thoroughfares such as Bukit Timah Road. Cycling downtown isn't such a great idea though, and bicycles aren't allowed at all on expressways.

Where bikes come into their own is in out-of-town recreational areas and nature parks, which are linked by a **park connector network** that it's possible to cycle; for more on this, check the Visitors' Guide section of the National Parks Board website Ⓦwww.nparks.gov.sg. The East Coast Park, on the southeast shore of the island, has a popular cycle track with rental outlets along the way (expect to pay S$5–8 per hr for a mountain bike, and have some form of ID handy). It's also possible to cycle at Bukit Timah Nature Reserve (see p.644). Wherever you cycle, you'll need a high tolerance for getting very hot and sweaty – or drenched if you're caught in a downpour.

Organized tours

If you're pushed for time, consider taking a **sightseeing tour**. Four-hour city tours typically take in Orchard Road, Chinatown and Little India, and cost around S$40; specialist tours are also available – on such themes as Singapore by night, World War II sights and Peranakan culture. For details of current offerings, contact the STB or check their website. It's also possible to arrange a tour with one of the country's **registered tourist guides** (see the directory at Ⓦwww .visit-singapore.com/guides-online), each of whom will have their own fees and specializations.

Among the more popular tours are **boat trips** along the Singapore River (see p.603) and **harbour cruises** (2hr; information and bookings on ☎6533 9811 or Ⓦwww.watertours.com.sg). The latter offer views of the Financial District and the Singapore Flyer, and supposedly evoke the spirit of journeys made by the fifteenth-century Chinese mariner Cheng Ho, though the boats used look not so much like a traditional junk as a miniature Chinese palace stuck on top of a floating platform. Boats depart daily from the Marina South Pier, 1500m southeast of Marina Bay MRT station, with prices starting at S$27 including light refreshments and free pick-up from the station or a few downtown hotels; there are also pricier, longer trips with tea or dinner thrown in.

Finally, **trishaws** – three-wheeled cycle rickshaws – were once a practical transport option in Singapore, though these days they provide a sort of novelty sightseeing ride to tourists lasting 45 minutes or so. Many drivers congregate in Chinatown behind the Buddha Tooth Relic Temple, and here an official charge applies of S$36; the trishaws on the stretch of Queen Street between Middle Road and Rochor Road (near Bugis MRT station) may well charge fifty percent more.

Accommodation

Room rates in Singapore have soared in recent years, and for a time the island republic was looking distinctly poor value as regards accommodation. While rates have since plateaued, they remain much higher than in KL – mid-range hotel rooms hardly ever come cheaper than S$90 a night. The good news is that, as in Malaysia, hotels often have **promotional rates** or online discounts much of the year, while budget travellers can choose from plenty of **hostels** and **guesthouses**, mostly situated in Little India and the surrounding area and usually well managed (though seldom with en-suite rooms). Most hotels are blandly modern, but there has also been a new wave of **boutique hotels**, usually characterful affairs in refurbished shophouses, especially in Chinatown.

Note that some **budget hotels** offer hourly or "transit" rates – a sign that they are to some extent used by locals for illicit liaisons. A few of these places have a obvious seedy underside, notably in Little India, though even members of the ubiquitous and well-run chains *Hotel 81* and *Fragrance* may have hourly rates. The establishments reviewed here are largely untainted by this, but should you encounter it, be assured that the goings-on are usually discreet. At the other end of the scale, **five-star** and some four-star hotels have a pricing quirk of their own, namely that they continuously adjust their rates depending on demand. The reviews here reflect what are meant to be typical prices, while the hotel website will list whatever their current rate is for the dates when you want to stay. Besides contacting places directly, you can also book and find discounts through sites such as ⓦwww.asiatravel.com and www.singaporehotelbooking .com or, if you're after a guesthouse, ⓦwww.hostelworld.com.

Accommodation price codes

Throughout this chapter, the following price codes are used in accommodation reviews to denote the price (inclusive of any ten-percent **service charge** and seven-percent **tax** that may apply) of the cheapest room for two people. Single occupancy can cost up to a third less than double, though a few places don't offer such discounts. Some guesthouses provide dormitory beds, for which actual prices are given in the text.

❶ S$30 and under	❹ S$91–120	❼ S$221–300
❷ S$31–60	❺ S$121–160	❽ S$301–400
❸ S$61–90	❻ S$161–220	❾ S$401 and over

You'd have to be extremely hard up to want to **camp** in Singapore, but it is possible to do so for free within National Parks sites, which mostly comprise designated recreational areas dotted around the island. The most sensible locations to try are Changi Beach (see p.651) and, more centrally, the East Coast Park (reachable on bus #401 from Bedok MRT); maps of both are available at ⓦ www.nparks.gov.sg. Note that park rangers do register campers on weekdays, so have ID available. Finally, it is possible to stay "offshore" on **Sentosa** island, but having to change for Sentosa transport at the HarbourFront Centre makes nipping back to your hotel a bit of a pain; for more on this, see p.656.

Little India, Arab Street and Lavender Street

Little India is very much the centre for budget accommodation in Singapore, and easily accessible thanks to the Little India station; the area around **Arab Street** also has a few good places to stay and is convenient for Bugis MRT station. Both are atmospheric districts and packed with inexpensive restaurants. There are also quite a few decent budget and mid-range places to stay beyond Little India proper, in the zone extending up to **Lavender Street**, reachable via Farrer Park or Lavender stations, and with an excellent public swimming pool close by (see p.683). All the places reviewed here are marked on the map on p.632.

Hostels and guesthouses

Ali's Nest 23 Roberts Lane ⓣ6291 2938, ⓔalisnest@yahoo.com.sg. Simple accommodation in an old Chinese shophouse, a bit spartan and shabby but the more appealing for that. Some rooms have a/c; amenities are limited to a kitchen, small sitting area and internet access. Rate includes a self-service breakfast. If you have difficulty finding the place, look out for the "Shanghai Kotat Trading" sign outside. Dorm beds S$12, ❶.

Dragon Inn 1 Kelantan Rd ⓣ6296 0776, ⓦwww .dragoninnhostel.blog.com. A laid-back a/c hostel in a little shophouse well away from the hubbub of Little India proper. There's no breakfast, but they do have free internet access (including wi fi) plus self-service laundry facilities. Get here by walking down Kitchener Road from Farrer Park station and then taking any bus down Jalan Besar. Dorm beds S$18, ❷.

Fragrance Hostel 63 Dunlop St ⓣ6295 6888, ⓦwww.fragrancebackpackers.com.sg. Owned by the budget hotel chain, this competently run but rather sterile establishment offers only single-sex dorms, each with six beds. Facilities include a lounge with TV and terminals for internet access. Dorm beds S$22.

Inn Crowd Hostel 73 Dunlop St (reception) & 35 Campbell Lane ⓣ6296 9169, ⓦwww.the -inncrowd.com. Endearing hostel with dorms plus four double rooms with TV and a/c. Shared showers and toilets are kept spotless, and there's a pool table, cheap beer and internet access

(30min free per day). Breakfast is included in the rate. Dorm beds S$20, ❷.

Prince of Wales Backpackers Hostel 101 Dunlop St ⓣ6299 0130, ⓦwww.pow.com.sg. Justifiably popular place done out in primary colours, with a/c dorms, a couple of double rooms and a 24hr bar/beer garden. Breakfast and wi-fi access (you'll need your own laptop) are included in the rate. Dorm beds S$18, ❷.

🏃 **Sleepy Sam's** 55 Bussorah St ⓣ9277 4988, ⓦwww.sleepysams.com. A welcoming and surprisingly stylish hostel, superbly placed in the heart of the Arab Street area and around the corner from the Sultan Mosque. Besides mixed and women-only dorms, there's a shared triple room plus a single and a double; amenities include a kitchen, a small café, laundry service and free internet access. Dorm beds S$28, ❸.

Tresor Tavern 243 Jalan Besar ⓣ6293 6005, ⓦwww.tresortavern.com. It's dorms and more dorms here, each of which has a/c and four, six or eight beds. Things can be bit cramped, though there is some compensation in the unusually swish decor, with designer lounge sofas and bathrooms fittings, and fancy lighting throughout. Rate includes breakfast and internet access (including wi-fi). Dorm beds from S$25.

🏃 **Welcome Inn Backpackers Hostel** 259a Jalan Besar ⓣ6296 3259, ⓦwelcomeinn .com.sg. The pastel lilac exterior is a muted prelude to bright bed linen and snazzy murals on gaudy interior walls. It's all pretty inviting, featuring a spacious lounge with TV and DVD, plus free internet access (including wi-fi), a kitchen and a free self-service breakfast. The mixed-sex dorm is huge, sleeping twenty in bunk beds, though the women's dorm sleeps a more typical six. There are also single and double rooms. Dorm beds from S$25, ③.

Hotels

Aliwal Park 77 Aliwal St ☎6293 9022, ⓔaliwal @pacific.net.sg. The rooms, equipped with TV and kettle, are small and rather gloomy, but they are en suite. The hotel is well placed for Arab Street and rates are keen. Room only. ③

Cityhub 270 Jalan Besar ☎6499 8999, ⓦwww .cityhubhotel.com. The yellow, green and black striped exterior of this new hotel is practically a capital offence, but inside is a better-than-average mid-range set-up with gratifyingly muted modern decor. Rates include breakfast – and are slashed by almost half most of the time. ⑤

Fortuna 2 Owen Rd ☎6295 3577, ⓦwww .fortunahotel.com.sg. Some of the otherwise unremarkable en-suite rooms in this modern establishment have good views over Serangoon Road, though you might prefer a room facing away from the road as noise can be a problem. ⑤

Fragrance Imperial 28 Penhas Rd ☎6297 9888, ⓦwww.fragrancehotel.com. A short walk from Lavender MRT, this is a cut above fellow members of the budget chain, with slick though smallish rooms, a café (breakfast is included in the rate) and a rooftop swimming pool. It's overpriced if the rack rate applies, but frequent promotional deals shave a quarter off that. ⑤

Golden Landmark 390 Victoria St ☎6297 2828, ⓦwww.goldenlandmark.com.sg. Beyond the dated

shopping centre downstairs is this modern, well-appointed hotel with its own pool and restaurants, and frequent promotional rates. ⑥

Haising 37 Jalan Besar ☎6298 1223, ⓦwww .haising.com.sg. Friendly Chinese-run cheapie offering simple, a/c en-suite rooms, rather boxy but not bad for the price. ②

Kerbau 54–62 Kerbau Rd ☎6297 6668, ⓔkerbauinn@pacific.net.sg. In a row of restored shophouses, the *Kerbau* is a compact place with en-suite rooms boasting a/c and TV, and a good location near Tekka Market and Little India MRT. ③

Madras 28–32 Madras St ☎6392 7889, ⓦwww .madrassingapore.com. Smallish, slightly tatty rooms with the standard mod cons and the bonus of a DVD player in each room, just in case the usual TV channels don't thrill you. ④

Parkroyal 181 Kitchener Rd ☎6428 3000, ⓦwww.parkroyalhotels.com. The classiest place to stay in the Little India area, boasting a recently redesigned marbled lobby, spacious and tasteful rooms, a pool and a couple of restaurants. If you're heading here by taxi rather than via the nearby Farrer Park MRT, make sure you mention the address as there's a sister hotel of the same name on Beach Road. ⑦

Perak 12 Perak Rd ☎6299 7733, ⓦwww .peraklodge.net. This hotel is housed in a nicely restored shophouse and is somewhat sedate, probably not a bad thing given the hullaballoo of Little India outside. It's slightly overpriced but makes partial amends with friendly staff, comfy if unremarkable rooms and a pleasant residents-only rest area on the ground floor with old-fashioned *kopitiam*-type tables. Rate includes breakfast. ⑥

Bras Basah Road to Rochor Road

The grid of streets between **Bras Basah Road** and **Rochor Road** (see map, p.615), also boxed in by **Beach Road** to the east and **Selegie Road** and the **Istana grounds** to the west, has been rendered a bit sterile by redevelopment – though a sprinkling of old shophouses, temples and churches still lend character – and has eliminated most of the cheap accommodation that once packed Bencoolen Street. What remains is mostly modern mid-range establishments with the notable exception of the *Raffles* which, with its colonial connections, is reviewed on p.601. The area remains a good choice if you can afford it, as it's within walking distance of the Singapore River, Little India, Arab Street and the southern end of Orchard Road.

Hostels and guesthouses

🏃 **G4 Station** 11 Mackenzie Rd ☎6334 5644, ⓦg4station.com. "A hostel by a group of businessmen" is how they bill themselves, so it's

perhaps no surprise that the place is short on atmosphere but impeccably run. Accommodation comprises dorms of various sizes plus double rooms, all with a/c and plenty of modern fittings (including chunky lockers), and sharing immaculate bathrooms and showers. Free wired and wi-fi internet access are available, plus a Wii console and a small café; rates include breakfast. Dorm beds from S$30, rooms ❸.

🏃 **Hangout @ Mount Emily** 10a Upper Wilkie Rd ☎6438 5588, ⊛www.hangouthotels .com. Owned by the company behind the historic Cathay cinema at the foot of Mount Emily – this being Singapore, it's really a hill – the *Hangout* is an impressive cross between a hostel and a designer guesthouse, with smart dorms and en-suite rooms, including two singles, plus a breezy rooftop terrace that's great for chilling out in the evening. The only drawback is that it's a 10min walk uphill from Selegie Rd. Best to book on-line, both because the place is popular and so you can get lower rates (all of which include a buffet breakfast and free internet use) than if you simply turn up. Dorm beds S$40, ❸.

Hawaii Hostel Second floor, 171a Bencoolen St ☎6338 4187, ⊛www.hawaiihostel.com.sg. Plain, slightly faded a/c rooms (some have a tiny shower for a few dollars extra), plus dorms. Rate includes breakfast (not on Sun though). Dorm beds S$15, rooms ❷.

Waterloo Hostel Fourth floor, Catholic Centre Building, 55 Waterloo St ☎6336 6555, ⊛www .waterloohostel.com.sg. A tidy Catholic-run hostel offering a/c rooms with TV and the option of en-suite facilities though you'll pay at least twenty percent extra for these. Breakfast is included; promotional rates sometimes available. ❹

Hotels

Albert Court 180 Albert St ☎63393939, ⊛www .albertcourt.com.sg. This self-styled boutique hotel benefits from preserved shophouse facades and amenities such as gym, jacuzzi and sauna. The superior and deluxe rooms boast old-fashioned ceiling fans – which you're unlikely to use as there's a/c – while the pricier executive rooms are ultra-modern. ❻

🏃 **Carlton** 76 Bras Basah Rd ☎6338 8333, ⊛www.carltonhotel.sg. Plastic palm trees in the lobby sound the wrong note, but this multi-storey tower of a four-star hotel boasts elegant rooms, restaurants, a pool and gym – and great promotional rates most of the time. ❼

Hotel 81 Selegie 161 Selegie Rd ☎6332 8181, ⊛www.hotel81.com.sg. One of the better branches

of this budget franchise, featuring modern if rather small and simply furnished rooms with a/c, flatscreen TV and a fairly slick attached bathroom. Surcharges at weekends. ❹

Intercontinental 80 Middle Rd ☎6338 7600, ⊛www.intercontinental.com. Like the adjoining Bugis Junction mall, the *Intercontinental* incorporates some of the area's original shophouses, here converted into so-called "shophouse rooms" with supposedly Peranakan decor, though this merely amounts to oriental-looking vases and paintings of tropical fruit. Regular rooms are S$50 cheaper and attempt to evoke a Victorian English flavour, unconvincingly. Still, the hotel is luxurious and has all the amenities you could want, and rates can fall by a quarter at weekends. ❽

Naumi 41 Seah St ☎6403 6000, ⊛www .naumihotel.com. The slate grey exterior with what look like vines crawling up the building behind netting doesn't inspire, but inside is a stunning boutique hotel where every room is kitted out like a luxury apartment and boasts an iPod dock, a kitchenette and free access to the hotel's wi-fi network. Accommodation on one floor is for women only. There's also a rooftop pool and a couple of bars. Online discounts usually available. ❽

Rendezvous 9 Bras Basah Rd ☎6336 0220, ⊛www.rendezvoushotels.com. Unmissable at the start of Bras Basah Rd, this comfortable four-star hotel blends the original shophouses on the corner into a huge modern extension beyond. Amenities include a pool, jacuzzi and some good restaurants, mostly famous the *Rendezvous* curry house (see p.665). ❼

🏃 **South East Asia Hotel** 190 Waterloo St ☎6338 2394, ⊛www.seahotel.com.sg. Behind the yellow and white 1950s facade is a modern hotel with spotless doubles, some en suite and all featuring the usual mod cons. Downstairs is a vegetarian restaurant serving continental and Asian breakfasts, and right next door is a lively Buddhist temple. ❹

Victoria 87 Victoria St ☎6622 0909, ⊛www .santagrandhotels.com. This compact hotel is dwarfed by the buildings around, but punches above its weight with modern en-suite rooms equipped with flatscreen TV and fridge. No breakfast though, and rooms with twin beds cost quite a bit more than standard doubles. ❺

Chinatown and around

There aren't that many places to stay south of the Singapore River or in Chinatown, and the accommodation in the Financial District is unexciting – the

Fullerton excepted – but there is something here for most budgets. The area has a couple of guesthouses and quite a number of hotels, including a few chic designer establishments, and Chinatown itself is certainly a lot more rewarding to stay in than Orchard Road. The following places are shown on the map on pp.618–619.

Hostels and guesthouses

Service World Backpackers Hostel Block 5, #02-82, Banda St ☎6226 3886, ⓦwww .serviceworld.com.sg. By far the better of two hostels in this block but the harder to find – it's on the far side of the building relative to the nearby Buddha Tooth Relic Temple (the confusing numbering means it's easier to look out for the adjoining unit #02-70). The place is hardly exciting, but it does have a/c and is kept spotless throughout. Residents are put up in four mixed-sex dorms with up to fourteen beds, with a self-service breakfast and 15min of internet access a day as part of the deal – not bad for S$20 per bed per night.

Summer Tavern 31 Carpenter St ☎6535 6601, ⓦwww.summertavern.com. Justifiably popular hostel whose best feature is the relaxed ground-floor lounge stuffed with leatherette sofas and serving beer, but the dorms are comfy and there are several double rooms too. They have more rooms diagonally across the road at no. 16 in a new and stylish hotel-style set-up. Free internet access; prices include breakfast. Dorm beds S$40, ❹ in original building, ❺ new building.

Hotels

Fullerton 1 Fullerton Square ☎6733 8388, ⓦwww .fullertonhotel.com. As impressive as the *Raffles*, with a stunning atrium whose massive columns are like something out of an Egyptian temple; amenities include a gym, spa and pool. The rack rates start at around S$900 a night, but promotions can bring prices down by almost a half – great value for such a historic and brilliantly sited building. ❾
Hotel 1929 50 Keong Saik Rd ☎62223377, ⓦwww.hotel1929.com. Less pricey than its sister hotel, the *New Majestic*, this shophouse building looks genuinely 1929 on the outside, but the interior has been renovated to look like a twenty-first-century version of the early 1960s, all very retro chic. The highly rated *Ember* restaurant is a bonus, as is the breakfast included in the rate. ❼
Hotel Dragon 18 Mosque St ☎6323 1611, ℉6224 1661. Compact, well-located cheapie with an entrance fronted by smartish wood and glass panels, giving on to corridors painted in primary colours. En-suite rooms, small, spartan and a bit gloomy thanks to wooden window shutters, which have the fringe benefit of helping to keep noise levels down. ❸
Keong Saik 69 Keong Saik Rd ☎6223 0660, ⓦwww.keongsaikhotel.com.sg. Something of a

plain Jane for a place that dares call itself a boutique hotel, featuring simply furnished, slightly faded rooms in an oldish building that's doesn't exactly stick in the memory. Reasonable rates, which include breakfast, are the main attraction. ❹
New Majestic 31–37 Bukit Pasoh Rd ☎6222 3377, ⓦwww.newmajestichotel .com. If money is no object, this is the boutique hotel to make a beeline for. In a country whose buildings aspire to arctic levels of air-conditioning, the open-air lobby here and its shabby ceiling (highlighting the vintage status of the building) offer the first of many surprises. Every room has been eccentrically decorated by different local designers – one room has arty seaweed simulations growing out of the wall, for example. Other quirks include separate bath and toilet cubicles in every room, surrounded by partly frosted glass, and a pool with floor portholes that allow you to look down into the restaurant – just as diners can look up at you swimming by. ❾
Royal Peacock 55 Keong Saik Rd ☎6223 3522, ⓦwww.royalpeacockhotel.com. Occupying a series of adjoining shophouses, this boutique hotel has an impressive facade with plenty of dark wood, though the rooms within aren't as lavishly decorated as elsewhere. Still, it offers some of the best value in its class, especially as breakfast is included and discounts often knock a tenth off rack rates. ❻
Swissôtel Merchant Court 20 Merchant Rd ☎6337 2288, ⓦwww.singapore-merchantcourt .swissotel.com. One of the best located of all downtown hotels, smack in the thick of the action on the south side of the Singapore River, with part of its *Ellenborough Market Café* encroaching on the promenade itself. Discounts can shave a third off rates. ❼
The Inn at Temple Street 36 Temple St ☎6221 5333, ⓦwww.theinn.com.sg. Sculpted out of a row of Chinatown shophouses, this boutique hotel is filled with old-fangled furniture for that period feel, while rooms do boast more mod cons than usual, including fridge and safe. Service could be a touch friendlier though. ❻
The Scarlet 33 Erskine Rd ☎6511 3333, ⓦwww .thescarlethotel.com. Another impressive shophouse refurbishment houses the *Scarlet*, with one of the most extravagant lobbies of all the boutique hotels, though here and in the rooms the opulence of the decor seems to lack a unifying theme. Amenities include free internet access (wired and wireless), a gym and an outdoor jacuzzi. ❼

The Colonial District and Marina Centre

Between the **north bank** of the Singapore River and Bras Basah Road (including the area around **Fort Canning Park**) are a handful of mid-range and pricey hotels, though none owes anything to the area's colonial heritage. East of here are several swanky hotels on the rather soulless triangle of reclaimed land called **Marina Centre**, forming the northern jaw of Marina Bay. See the map on p.604.

Novotel Clarke Quay 177a River Valley Rd ☏6338 3333, ⓦwww.novotel.com. This dull tower block might appear just another bland business-oriented hotel, but the elegant wood-panelled lobby and tasteful contemporary furnishings make clear this is all about giving the boutique hotels a run for their money. Comes with the usual four-star amenities, including pool and jacuzzi. ❽

Peninsula Excelsior 5 Coleman St ☏63372200, ⓦwww.ytchotels.com.sg/sp-ytcexcel. Really two hotels merged together – as hinted at by the presence of two swimming pools at either end, one of which abuts the current lobby – and nicely modernized, unlike the 1970s shopping arcades below. Decent value. ❼

Raffles 1 Beach Rd ☏63371886, ⓦwww.raffleshotel.com. Though the modern extension is a mixed bag, the *Raffles* remains refreshingly low-rise and still has colonial-era charm in spades, especially evident in the opulent lobby and the courtyards fringed by frangipani trees and palms, though muzak does spoil the atmosphere. Amenities include a dozen restaurants and bars, a rooftop pool and a spa. You'll need deep pockets to stay, of course: even though online discounts knock a third off the rack rate, prices for suites – as all rooms here are – start at around S$900 a night. ❾

Ritz-Carlton Millenia 7 Raffles Ave ☏6337 8888, ⓦwww.ritz-carlton.com. Arguably king of the pricey hotels in Marina Centre, with magnificent views across to the towers of the Financial Centre – even from the bathrooms, where butlers will fill your bath for you. Rooms start at around S$470. ❾

Robertson Quay 15 Merbau Rd ☏6735 3333, ⓦwww.robertsonquayhotel.com.sg. A circular riverside tower whose compact but inviting rooms yield great views of the river and city skyline. There's a cute round pool with slide and waterfall on the third-floor terrace. Great value (with online discounts), and not too far from Clarke Quay MRT on the south bank. ❺

Swissôtel The Stamford 2 Stamford Rd ☏6338 8585, ⓦwww.singapore-stamford.swissotel.com. Upper-floor rooms – and the restaurants and bars on the 70th to 72nd floors – aren't for those with vertigo, though the views are as splendid as you'd expect from the second tallest hotel in the world, with over a thousand rooms. Facilities include a pool, spa and tennis courts, though the biggest plus is the location above the Raffles City mall and City Hall MRT. Expect to pay at least S$420 even with a discount. ❾

YMCA International House 1 Orchard Rd ☏6336 6000, ⓦwww.ymcaih.com.sg. Nominally on Orchard Road but really part of the Colonial District, this is essentially a rather staid hotel with its own café and comfortable if slightly institutional rooms, all with a/c, fridge and modern bathroom. More exciting are the rooftop pool and the buffet breakfast (included in the rate). ❻

YWCA Fort Canning Lodge 6 Fort Canning Rd ☏6338 4222, ⓦwww.ywcafclodge.org.sg. In the same vein as the *YMCA*, offering decent mid-range rooms – and not to women only as you might assume. Amenities include a café, pool and tennis courts. The dorms are unlikely to tempt though, at a staggering S$120 per bed. The rate includes breakfast, though even with online discounts, you can do better elsewhere. ❻

Orchard Road and around

Orchard Road still packs the highest concentration of hotels, mostly upmarket affairs, in downtown Singapore, but it's hardly the most interesting place to stay. The chief attractions used to be the excellent shopping and restaurants, but now that many stores and eating places have branches across town, it's only the sheer modernity of the area that gives some sort of edge. Though prices are on the high side, at least it's hard to go wrong here; the places reviewed below are shown on the map on pp.640–641.

Goodwood Park 22 Scotts Rd ☏6737 7411, ⓦwww.goodwoodparkhotel.com. Designed by the architect responsible for the *Raffles* and likewise a genuine landmark in a cityspace characterized by transience. Redolent of the refinements of a bygone era and set on a leafy hillock, the hotel boasts a variety of rooms and suites, several highly rated restaurants and two pools, and isn't as steeply priced as some of its competitors. ❾

Hotel Supreme 15 Kramat Rd ☏ 6737 8333, ⓦ www.supremeh.com.sg. A 1970s concrete box of a hotel with rather tired en-suite rooms, though they are spacious. Small discounts often available on line. ❻

Lloyd's Inn 2 Lloyd Rd ☏ 6737 7309, ⓦ www .lloydinn.com. Less than a 10min walk from Orchard Road is this motel-like building with large if rather bland and dated rooms, equipped with TV, kettle and attached bathroom with actual bathtub. Free wi-fi too, though no breakfast. ❹

🏃 **Meritus Mandarin** 333 Orchard Rd ☏ 6737 4411, ⓦ www.mandarin-singapore.com. Female staff at this long-established favourite wear kitsch scarlet quasi-oriental uniforms, but don't let that put you off; the hotel is still at the top of its game, luxurious to a fault, and also still one of the tallest buildings in the area – which makes the 39th-floor *Chatterbox* coffee house all the more worthwhile. It's right in the middle of Orchard Rd too. ❽

Orchard Parade 1 Tanglin Rd ☏ 6737 1133, ⓦ www.orchardparade.com.sg. It's hard to discern much that's Mediterranean – their description – about the decor, though to the management's credit everything is shipshape, not a small feat in what is a refurbished 1970s hotel. Good rates too. ❼

Shangri-La 22 Orange Grove Rd ☏ 6737 3644, ⓦ www.shangri-la.com. An old faithful which still epitomizes elegance, and whose seven hundred-plus rooms are set in oodles of landscaped greenery. Facilities include a pitch-and-putt golf, tennis courts and a climbing wall. It's a 10min walk from Orchard Road, with free shuttle buses laid on too. Recommended, if you can afford doubles costing at least S$450 a night. ❾

Singapore Marriott 320 Orchard Rd ☏ 6735 5800, ⓦ www.marriott.com. This minor icon of a hotel, occupying a pagoda-style tower rising above Tangs department store, is among the plushest in Orchard Road, featuring a hot tub in every room plus the obligatory pool, spa and gym and plenty of restaurants. ❾

Traders 1a Cuscaden Rd ☏ 6738 2222, ⓦ www .shangri-la.com. Top-flight hotel with tastefully restrained contemporary decor, an immaculate freeform pool, a spa and gym – and some attractive discounts available on line. Unusually for a hotel in this class, there's free use of wi-fi in the lobby, too. ❼

Geylang (Joo Chiat Road)

With such a huge range of accommodation available in the city centre, there are few compelling reasons to stay further out. **Geylang**, a few MRT stops east of downtown, is the one district you might consider for its relative tranquillity and Malay character, though it's also worth noting that parts of it are red-light areas – thankfully not where the accommodation is located in the old shophouses of **Joo Chiat Road**, which runs 2km south to the adjacent Katong district. While the northern end of Joo Chiat Road is not more than ten minutes' walk from Paya Lebar MRT, anywhere numbered 180 and up is more easily reached using bus #33 from Kallang MRT (see p.648 for locations).

Betel Box 200 Joo Chiat Rd ☏ 6247 7340, ⓦ www.betelbox.com. This friendly hostel has a good vibe and is well set up, offering regular trips and tours. Besides a few doubles, they have two sixteen- and twenty-bed mixed dorms with toilets and showers inside, and two cosier dorms (eight-bed female-only and six-bed mixed) with facilities outside. Rate includes breakfast, free use of a gym down the road and 30min internet use per day; on the down side, there could be more shared facilities. Dorm beds from S$20, ❷.

Fragrance Hotel 219 Joo Chiat Rd ☏ 6344 9888, ⓦ www.fragrancehotel.com. Among the more characterful members of this chain with a chocolate-box exterior and modern rooms with TV and fridge. ❸

Gateway Hotel 60 Joo Chiat Rd ☏ 6342 0988, ⓦ www.gatewayhotel.com.sg. Bland modern en-suite rooms with TV and safe; most bathrooms have bathtubs too. ❹

Hotel 81 12 Joo Chiat Rd ☏ 6346 8181; 181 Joo Chiat Rd ☏ 6247 8181; 305 Joo Chiat Rd ☏ 6348 8181; ⓦ www.hotel81.com.sg. The branch at no. 12 (which they call *Classic*) is easily reached from Paya Lebar MRT and so charges a bit more; the ones at no. 181 (*Sakura*) and no. 305 (*Joo Chiat*) are both housed in restored properties, especially attractively so at the latter. ❹–❺

Downtown Singapore

Downtown Singapore is a convenient place to tour given its compactness and the excellent transport network, though individual districts are best explored on foot. You need at least two days to do some kind of justice to the main areas, namely the **Colonial District**, **Chinatown**, **Little India** and the **Arab Quarter**, though three days would be more sensible, especially if you want to have a quick look around the **Financial District** or the **Marina Bay integrated resort**, or shop in **Orchard Road**. Getting around on foot is the best way to do justice to the central areas.

The Colonial District

North of the Singapore River, the Padang is the nexus of the **Colonial District** (see map, p.606), flanked by dignified reminders of British rule. The view from here is a panorama that defines Singapore's past and present. On the Padang's southern edge is the Singapore Cricket Club, epitomizing colonial man's stubborn refusal to adapt to his surroundings. Behind that are clustered yet more colonial edifices, including the former Parliament House and what is now the Asian Civilizations Museum, and behind them is the river, snaking inland past the last few godowns from Singapore's original trade boom, all converted into trendy nightspots. West of the Padang are City Hall and the former Supreme Court, screening **Fort Canning Hill** from view, while to the north are the grand old *Raffles Hotel* and a string of nineteenth- and early twentieth-century churches. This being Singapore, modernity is hardly absent amid all these echoes of the past: to the north is the towering *Swissôtel* on Stamford Road; to the south loom the spires of the **financial district** (see p.629); while to the east in the

The Singapore River

Nothing more than a creek, in the nineteenth century the **Singapore River** became the main artery of Singapore's growing trade, and was clogged with **bumboats** – traditional cargo boats with eyes painted on their prows as if looking where they are going. The boat pilots ferried coffee, sugar and rice to warehouses called **godowns**, where coolies loaded and unloaded sacks. In the 1880s the river itself was so busy it was practically possible to walk from one side of it to the other without getting your feet wet. Of course a series of **bridges** were built across it as well, mostly endearingly compact and old-fangled, with the exception of the massive new Esplanade Bridge at the mouth of the river.

Walk along at the river today, all sanitized and packed with trendy restaurants and bars, some occupying the few surviving godowns, and it's hard to imagine that as recently as the 1970s this was still a working river. It was also filthy, and the river's current status as one of *the* nightlife centres of Singapore ultimately originates in a massive clean-up campaign launched back then. Several of Singapore's museums have sections exploring the commercial role played by the river and the pros and cons of its transformation, with a particularly good discussion at the Asian Civilizations Museum (see p.605).

You can get a view of the city from river level on trips in tarted-up versions of traditional bumboats (daily 9am–11pm; every 15min; ☎6336 6111, ⊛www.rivercruise .com.sg): the **Singapore River Experience** (S$13), which takes in Clarke Quay, Boat Quay and Marina Bay, and the **New River Experience** (S$18), which adds Robertson Quay. There are several ticket booths along the final stretch of the river, and you can board the boats at any of them.

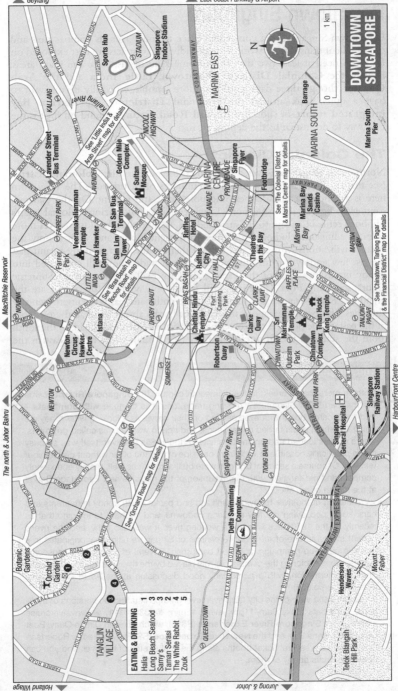

▲ Geylang   ▲ East Coast Parkway & Airport

◄ The north & Johor Bahru

◄ MacRitchie Reservoir

DOWNTOWN SINGAPORE

N

0   1 km

EATING & DRINKING
Halia   1
Long Beach Seafood   3
Samy's   3
Taman Serasi   2
The White Rabbit   4
Zouk   5

Sports Hub
STADIUM
Singapore Indoor Stadium

Lavender Street Bus Terminal

Golden Mile Complex

See 'Little India & Arab Street' map for details

Sultan Mosque

Veeramakaliamman Temple

Sim Lim Ban San Bus Terminal
Tekka Hawker Centre
Tower

Raffles Hotel

Raffles City

See Bras Basah to Rochor Road map for details

City Hall

Theatres on the Bay

Singapore Flyer

Footbridge

ESPLANADE

MARINA CENTRE

PROMENADE

MARINA EAST

MARINA SOUTH

Marina South Pier

Barrage

See The Colonial District & Marina Centre map for details

Marina Bay Sands Casino

Marina Bay

MARINA BAY

Farrer Park

LITTLE INDIA

Chettiar Hindu Temple

Fort Canning Park

Clarke Quay

Sri Mariamman Temple

RAFFLES PLACE

See 'Chinatown, Tanjong Pagar & the Financial District' map for details

Istana

Newton Circus Hawker Centre

NEWTON

Robertson Quay

Chinatown Complex
Outram Park
Thian Hock Keng Temple

Chinatown

TANJONG PAGAR

See 'Orchard Road' map for details

ORCHARD

SOMERSET

Singapore River

Delta Swimming Complex

Singapore General Hospital

Singapore Railway Station

► HarbourFront Centre

Botanic Gardens
Orchid Garden

TANGLIN VILLAGE

Henderson Waves
Mount Faber

Telok Blangah Hill Park

◄ Holland Village   ◄ Jurong & Johor

Marina Centre area (see p.638) sit the ultramodern Theatres on the Bay arts complex and the glorified ferris wheel that is the Singapore Flyer.

Cavenagh Bridge

Cavenagh Bridge, with its elegant suspension struts, is a good place to start a tour of Singapore's colonial centre. It's easily reached from the Raffles Place MRT station, the walk here taking you past the former GPO on the south bank, now the beautiful *Fullerton* hotel (see p.600). Named after Major General Orfeur Cavenagh, governor of the Straits Settlements from 1859 to 1867, the bridge was constructed in 1869 by Indian convict labourers using imported Glasgow steel. Times change, but not necessarily on the bridge, where a police sign still maintains: "The use of this bridge is prohibited to any vehicle of which the laden weight exceeds 3cwt and to all cattle and horses." The bridge takes only pedestrians nowadays.

The Asian Civilizations Museum

On the north side of Cavenagh Bridge is the **Empress Place Building**, a robust Neoclassical structure named after Queen Victoria and completed in 1865. It served for ten years as a courthouse before the Registry of Births and Deaths and the Immigration Department moved in. Today it houses the fine **Asian Civilizations Museum** (daily 9am–7pm except Mon from 1pm, Fri until 9pm; S$5, or S$10 for joint ticket with the Peranakan Museum – see p.611; Ⓦ www.acm.org.sg lists special exhibitions and free guided tours), tracing the origins and growth of Asia's many and varied cultures, from the Middle East through to China. In the small Malay World section, look out for a spectacular Kelantan *makara*, a huge goggle-eyed mongrel creature once used in rituals, while elsewhere there are Dayak masks from Borneo, *kerises* from Indonesia, Hmong garments from Laos and so forth.

A bit of a misfit here – though most apt, given the museum's location – is the excellent **Singapore River gallery**. There are displays of sampans and other river craft, and a diorama of a timber dwelling for coolies that recalls the grim lodging houses that once featured in London's docklands, but best of all are fascinating oral history clips featuring people who once worked on and lived by the river. The museum is frank about the side effects of the successful Clean River Project launched in 1977, which saw commercial traffic on the river moved west to Pasir Panjang within the space of a few years: "[the project] also washed away…[the river's] thriving vibrant history as a trade waterway. Its newly cleaned waters now appeared characterless and sterile." At least the river is now enjoying a renaissance as a major area for wining and dining – and housed in the same building as the museum are several posh riverside restaurants (see p.663).

The Victoria Concert Hall and Victoria Theatre

Next door to the Empress Place Building stand two fine examples of colonial architecture, the **Victoria Concert Hall** and adjoining **Victoria Theatre**, still in use. The theatre was completed in 1862 as Singapore's town hall, while the concert hall was added in 1905 as a tribute to the monarch's reign. During the Japanese occupation, the statue of Raffles that once stood in front of the tower only narrowly escaped being melted down. The newly installed Japanese curator of the National Museum (where the statue was sent) valued it sufficiently to hide it and report it destroyed. A copy of the statue nearby marks the **landing site** where, in January 1819, the great man apparently took his first steps on Singaporean soil. Sir Stamford now stares contemplatively across the river towards the business district.

THE COLONIAL DISTRICT & MARINA CENTRE

ACCOMMODATION

Novotel Clarke Quay	F
Peninsula Excelsior	E
Raffles	C
Ritz-Carlton Millenia	H
Robertson Quay	G
Swissôtel The Stamford	D
YMCA International House	B
YWCA Fort Canning Lodge	A

EATING & DRINKING

Balaclava	5
Bar Opiume	14
Colours By The Bay	11
Dbl-O	7
Doc Cheng's	8
Hai Tien Lo	13
Indochine	3
The Long Bar	9
Paulaner Bräuhaus	1
Seah Street Deli	6
Spinelli's	10
Swensen's	4 & 12
Timbre	2

0 — 200 m

Kallang & Indoor Stadium

Arab Street

Little India

Financial District

N

The parliament buildings

Just upriver of the Victoria Concert Hall is **Old Parliament House**, a dignified white Victorian building that was originally the private dwelling of a rich merchant and designed by Singapore's pre-eminent colonial architect, the Irishman George Drumgould Coleman, who was named the settlement's superintendent of public works in 1833. Relieved of its legislative role in 1999, the building is now home to a contemporary arts centre called **The Arts House** (Ⓦ www.theartshouse.com.sg), including a shop stocking literature, DVDs and so forth by home-grown talent. The bronze elephant in front of Parliament House was a gift to Singapore from King Rama V of Thailand (upon whose father *The King and I* was based) after his trip to the island in 1871 – the first foreign visit ever made by a Thai monarch.

Just across the road from here is the back of the rather soulless new **Parliament House**, whose front facade can be viewed from North Bridge Road and across the river. The public is allowed to view parliamentary sessions, arrangements for which appear on Ⓦ www.parliament.gov.sg.

The Padang

The **Padang**, earmarked by Raffles as a recreation ground shortly after his arrival, is the very essence of colonial Singapore. Its borders have never been encroached upon by speculators and so it remains much as it was in 1907, when G.M. Reith wrote in his *Handbook to Singapore*, "Cricket, tennis, hockey, football and bowls are played on the plain...beyond the carriage drive on the other side, is a strip of green along the sea-wall, with a footpath, which affords a cool and pleasant walk in the early morning and afternoon." Once the last over of the day had been bowled, the Padang assumed a more social role: the image of Singapore's European community hastening to the corner once known as Scandal Point to catch up on the latest gossip is pure Somerset Maugham.

The brown-tiled roof, whitewashed walls and green blinds of the **Singapore Cricket Club**, at the southwestern end of the Padang, have a nostalgic charm. Founded in the 1850s, the club was the hub of colonial British society and still operates a "members only" rule. Eurasians, formerly ineligible for membership, founded their own establishment instead in 1883: the **Singapore Recreation Club**, which lies at the opposite end of the Padang. The current grandiose, colonnaded clubhouse dates back to an overhaul, completed in 1997.

The old Supreme Court and City Hall

West of the cricket club and on the opposite side of St Andrew's Road is Singapore's erstwhile **Supreme Court**, built in Neoclassical style between 1937 and 1939 and sporting a domed roof of green lead and a splendid, wood-panelled entrance hall. Occupying a site once home to the exclusive *Hotel de L'Europe*, whose drawing rooms allegedly provided Somerset Maugham with inspiration for many of his Southeast Asian short stories, the building was itself usurped early in the new millennium by the Sir Norman Forster-designed **New Supreme Court**, behind it on North Bridge Road – and unmistakable with its flying-saucer-like upper tier.

Next door to the former Supreme Court is the older **City Hall**, which has likewise been vacated. Its grandiose Corinthian columns lend it the austere air of a mausoleum and reflect its role in recent Singaporean history: it was on the steps of this building that Lord Louis Mountbatten (then supreme allied commander in Southeast Asia) announced Japan's surrender to the British in

1945. Fourteen years later, Lee Kuan Yew chose the same spot from which to address his electorate at a victory rally celebrating self-government for Singapore. For now, newlyweds line up to have their big day captured in front of one of Singapore's most imposing buildings, but both City Hall and the old Supreme Court are being renovated as they will jointly comprise the prestigious new **National Art Gallery of Singapore** (Ⓦ www.nationalartgallery.sg), to be launched in 2013.

St Andrew's Cathedral

In its own expansive grounds next to Coleman Street, west of the Padang, **St Andrew's Cathedral** is the third church on this site. It was built in high-vaulted Neo-Gothic style, using Indian convict labour, and consecrated by Bishop Cotton of Calcutta on January 25, 1862. The exterior walls were plastered using Madras *chunam* – an unlikely composite of eggs, lime, sugar and shredded coconut husks which shines brightly when smoothed – while the small cross behind the pulpit, a later addition, was crafted from two fourteenth-century nails salvaged from the ruins of England's Coventry Cathedral after it was razed to the ground during World War II. Closed-circuit TVs allow the whole congregation to view proceedings up at the altar – a reflection of the Asian fascination with things hi-tech, since the cathedral's size hardly requires it.

Sir Stamford Raffles

Let it still be the boast of Britain
to write her name in characters of light;
let her not be remembered as the tempest
whose course was desolation,
but as the gale of spring reviving
the slumbering seeds of mind and
calling them to life
from the winter of ignorance and oppression.
If the time shall come
when her empire shall have passed away,
these monuments will endure when her triumphs
shall have become an empty name.

This verse, written by **Sir Stamford Raffles** himself, speaks volumes about the man whom history remembers as the founder of modern Singapore. Despite living and working in a period of imperial arrogance and land-grabbing, Raffles maintained an unfailing concern for the welfare of the people under his governorship, and a conviction that his country was, as Jan Morris says in her introduction to Maurice Collis's biography, *Raffles*, "the chief agent of human progress...the example of fair Government."

Fittingly for a man who was to spend his life roaming the globe, Thomas Stamford Raffles was born at sea on July 6, 1781, on the *Ann*, whose master was his father Captain Benjamin Raffles. By his fourteenth birthday, the young Raffles was working as a clerk for the **East India Company** in London, his schooling curtailed because of his father's debts. Even then, Raffles' ambition and self-motivation were evident as he stayed up through the night to study and developed a hunger for knowledge which would later spur him to learn Malay, amass a treasure trove of natural history artefacts and write his two-volume *History of Java*.

Raffles' diligence showed through in 1805, when he was chosen to join a team going out to Penang, then being developed as a British entrepôt; overnight, his

Raffles City and the War Memorial

North of the cathedral and Padang is **Raffles City**, a huge development that sits beside the intersection of Bras Basah and North Bridge roads and comprises two hotels – one of which is the 73-storey **Swissôtel** – as well as floor upon floor of offices and shops. Completed in 1985, the complex was designed by Chinese-American architect I.M. Pei – the man behind the glass pyramid which fronts the Louvre in Paris – and required the controversial demolition of the Raffles Institution, a school established by Raffles himself and built in 1835 by George Drumgould Coleman. Once a year, athletes take part in a contest to run all the way up to the top floor (Ⓦ www.swissotelverticalmarathon.com); the current record stands at under seven minutes. The open plot east of Raffles City is home to four seventy-metre-high white columns, nicknamed "the chopsticks"; it's actually the **Civilian War Memorial**, commemorating those who died during the Japanese occupation (beneath are remains reinterred from unmarked wartime graves around the island).

Raffles Hotel

Across the way from what was, for a time, the world's tallest hotel is one of the world's most famous. The lofty halls and peaceful gardens of the legendary **Raffles Hotel**, almost a byword for colonialism, prompted Somerset Maugham to remark that it "stood for all the fables of the exotic East". Oddly, this inherently

annual salary leapt from £70 to £1500. Once in Southeast Asia, Raffles enjoyed a meteoric rise: by 1807 he was named chief secretary to Penang's governor. Upon meeting Lord Minto, the governor-general of the East India Company in India, in 1810, Raffles was appointed secretary to the governor-general in Malaya; this was quickly followed by his appointment as **governor of Java** in 1811. Raffles' rule of Java was libertarian and compassionate, his economic, judicial and social reforms transforming an island bowed by Dutch rule.

Post-Waterloo European rebuilding saw Java returned to the Dutch in 1816 – to the chagrin of Raffles. He was transferred to the governorship of **Bencoolen** in Sumatra, but not before he had returned home for a break. While there he met his second wife, Sophia Hull (his first, Olivia, died in 1814), and was knighted.

Raffles and Sophia sailed to Bencoolen in 1818. Once in Sumatra, Raffles found time to study its flora and fauna, discovering the incredible *Rafflesia arnoldii* (see p.420) on a jungle trip. By now, Raffles strongly believed that Britain should establish a base in the Straits of Melaka; meeting Hastings – Minto's successor – in late 1818, he was given leave to pursue this possibility and in 1819 duly sailed to the southern tip of the Malay Peninsula, where his securing of Singapore early that year was a daring masterstroke of diplomacy.

For a man inextricably linked with Singapore, Raffles spent remarkably little time there. His last visit was in 1822; by August 1824, he was back in England. Awaiting a possible pension from the East India Company, Raffles spent his free time founding the **London Zoo** and setting up a farm in Hendon.

But the new life he had planned for Sophia and himself never materialized. Days after he heard that a Calcutta bank holding £16,000 of his capital had folded, his pension application was refused; worse still, the company was demanding £22,000 for overpayment. Three months later, on July 4, 1826, the brain tumour that had caused him headaches for several years took his life. He was buried in Hendon with no memorial tablet – the vicar had investments in West Indian slave plantations and was unimpressed by Raffles' friendship with the abolitionist William Wilberforce. Only in 1832 was Raffles commemorated, by a statue in Westminster Abbey.

British hotel started life as a modest seafront bungalow belonging to an Arab trader, Mohamed Alsagoff. After a spell as a tiffin house run by an Englishman, one Captain Dare, the property was bought in 1886 by the Sarkies brothers, enterprising Armenians who eventually controlled a triumvirate of quintessentially colonial lodgings: the *Raffles* in Singapore, the *Eastern & Oriental* in Penang (see p.184), and the *Strand* in Rangoon.

Raffles Hotel opened for business on December 1, 1887, and quickly attracted an impressive list of guests. Despite a guest list heavy with politicians and film stars over the years, the hotel is proudest of its **literary connections**. Hermann Hesse, Somerset Maugham, Rudyard Kipling, Noël Coward and Günter Grass all stayed here, and Maugham is said to have written many of his Asian tales under a frangipani tree in the garden.

The hotel's heyday was during the first three decades of the twentieth century, when it firmly established its reputation for luxury and elegance – it was the first building in Singapore with electric lights and fans. In 1902, a little piece of Singaporean history was made at the hotel, according to an apocryphal tale, when the last tiger to be killed on the island was shot inside the building. Thirteen years later, bartender Ngiam Tong Boon created another *Raffles* legend, the **Singapore Sling** cocktail.

In 1942, British expatriates who had gathered in *Raffles* as the Japanese swept through the island were quickly made POWs, and the hotel became a Japanese officers' quarters. After the Japanese surrender in 1945, *Raffles* became a transit camp for liberated Allied prisoners. Postwar deterioration earned it the affectionate but melancholy soubriquet, "grand old lady of the East", and the hotel was little more than a shabby tourist diversion when the government finally declared it a national monument in 1987. A hugely expensive facelift and extension followed, and the hotel reopened in 1991. Though much of the revamped hotel still oozes colonial grace, the modern arcade on North Bridge Road is relatively mundane. If you do pop in, as most tourists do, there is a memorabilia-crammed **museum** (daily 10am–7pm; free) upstairs at the back of the hotel complex, and you can partake of a Singapore Sling in the *Long Bar* for around S$20.

Hill and Coleman streets

A couple of blocks west of the Padang, **Hill Street** heads south along the eastern side of Fort Canning Park to the river. The brash building at no. 47 with a striking pagoda roof is the **Singapore Chinese Chamber of Commerce**, dating from 1964 though remodelled since. Along its facade are two large panels, each depicting nine intricately crafted porcelain dragons flying from the sea up to the sky. By way of contrast, the tiny Armenian **Church of St Gregory the Illuminator** across the road was designed by George Drumgould Coleman in 1835 (which makes it one of the oldest buildings in Singapore). Inside is a single circular chamber, fronted by a marble altar and a painting of the Last Supper. Among the white gravestones and statues in the church's frangipani-scented gardens is the tombstone of Agnes Joaquim, a nineteenth-century Armenian resident of Singapore, after whom the national flower, the delicate, purple Vanda Miss Joaquim orchid is named; she discovered it in her garden and had it registered at the Botanic Gardens.

A stone's throw away at the junction with **Coleman Street** is the splendid red-and-white striped **Central Fire Station**. When it was built in 1908, the watchtower was the tallest building in the area and made it easy for firemen to scan the downtown area for fires. Though the station remains operational, part of it is now taken up by the Civil Defence Heritage Galleries (Tues–Sun

10am–5pm; free), tracing the history of fire fighting in Singapore from the formation of the first Voluntary Fire Brigade in 1869. The galleries display extinguishers, hand–drawn escape ladders and steam fire engines, all beautifully restored and buffed up; upstairs there are explanations of current equipment and practices. Of more interest, though, is the account of the Bukit Ho Swee fire of 1961, which claimed four lives and sixteen thousand homes when it ripped through a district of *atap*-thatched huts and timber yards. This led directly to a public housing scheme that spawned Singapore's many new towns.

Continue along Hill Street from here and you come to the MICA Building (see p.614), before which is a set of steps up Fort Canning Hill (see p.613). Up Coleman Street itself directly behind the Central Fire Station is Singapore's **Masonic Lodge**, with its colonial facade of moulded garlands and protractors.

The Peranakan Museum

Dating from 1910, the beautifully ornamented three-storey building at 39 Armenian St, just west of Hill Street, was once the Tao Nan School, the first school in Singapore to cater for new arrivals from China's Fujian province. Today it houses the worthy **Peranakan Museum** (daily 9.30am–7pm except Mon from 1pm, Fri until 9pm; S$6, or S$10 joint ticket with Asian Civilizations Museum – see p.605; ⓦ www.peranakanmuseum.sg for details of special exhibitions and free guided tours), honouring a culture which, in its own way, is to Singapore, Malaysia and Indonesia what Creole culture is to Louisiana. But while the museum boasts that the island's Peranakans are "fully integrated into Singapore's globalized society", in reality they are at best keeping a low profile, and in a country where ethnicity is stated on everyone's ID, "Peranakan" isn't recognized as a valid category – meaning they are inevitably lumped together with the wider Chinese community. At least the launch of the museum and the Baba House (see p.628) in 2008 indicates recognition that the culture represents a distinctive tourist draw for Singapore (and one which Malaysia, with its ethnic fault lines, has not fully exploited). Such considerations aside, the museum should whet your appetite for not only the Baba House but also the Peranakan heritage of the Katong area (see p.649).

The diversity of the Peranakans in the widest sense of that term comes through in the first gallery, which includes video interviews with members of Melaka's small **Chitty** community, a blend of Tamil, Chinese and Malay. Thereafter the galleries concentrate on the **Baba-Nonyas** who comprise Singapore's Peranakans, and on their customs (in particular the traditional twelve-day **wedding**, which gets four galleries to itself) and possessions (theirs was always largely a material culture). Early on you reach one of the most memorable displays, showing the classic entrance into a Peranakan home, overhung with lanterns and with a pair of *pintu pagar* – tall swing doors – across the doorway; you'll see something similar if you visit the Baba House. Elsewhere, look out for artefacts such as the ornate, tiered "pagoda trays" used in the wedding ceremony, furniture inlaid with mother-of-pearl, and beautiful repoussé silverware, including betel-nut sets and "pillow ends", coaster-like objects which for some reason were used as end-caps for bolsters.

The National Museum

On Stamford Road just around the corner from Armenian Street is the eye-catching dome, seemingly coated with silvery fish scales, of the **National Museum of Singapore** (daily 10am–8pm, History Gallery until 6pm; S$10; ⓦ www .nationalmuseum.sg), to give it its full title. Its forerunner, the Raffles Museum and

Library, opened in 1887 and soon acquired a reputation for its natural history collection. In the 1960s, following independence, the place was renamed the National Museum and subsequently altered its focus to local history and culture, an emphasis retained after a recent overhaul that saw the original Neoclassical building gain a hangar-like rear extension larger than itself. That extension houses the mainstay of the new-look museum, the **History Gallery**, while the old building is home to the **Living Galleries** focusing on various aspects of Singapore culture and society. If you have no interest in seeing the History Gallery, note that after it shuts there's free admission to the rest of the museum.

The History Gallery

The History Gallery requires at least a couple of hours to see, thanks to the novel presentation with hardly any labelling; instead, textual descriptions and audio clips of extended commentaries or oral history are all stored on the **Companion**, a device like a jumbo iPod which every visitor is given on entry. The sound clips do enliven a collection of artefacts that is in part mundane, but they also take a frustrating amount of time to get through.

Things begin unpromisingly with a two-storey rotunda through which you descend on a spiral ramp while watching a 360° film projection of Singapore scenes accompanied by a bombastic choral soundtrack. Thankfully you're soon into the first gallery proper, focusing on **Temasek** (as the Malays called Singapore) before the colonial era. Pride of place here goes to the mysterious Singapore Stone, all that survives of an inscribed monolith that once stood near where the *Fullerton* hotel is today, though more memorable is beautiful gold jewellery excavated at Fort Canning in 1926 and thought to date from the fourteenth century. There's another dubious film installation here, a cryptic affair depicting fourteenth-century conflict in Temasek.

From here onwards the displays are split into a chronological **Events Path** and a human-interest-driven **Personal Path**, covering the same developments in parallel; you can switch from one to the other as you please. The Personal Path is often more entertaining, featuring, for example, a video reminiscence by a revue performer from Shanghai who arrived to perform in postwar Singapore and ended up staying. It's also worth keeping an eye out for the few items the museum designates **national treasures**, some of which are truly worthy of the label, such as some gorgeous **Chinese watercolours** depicting hornbills and tropical fruit, acquired by William Farquhar.

Two aspects of the twentieth-century coverage are worthy of special attention: the dimly lit, claustrophobic area dealing with the **Japanese occupation** and the horrors of Operation Sook Ching (see p.586), and the sections on **postwar politics** in Singapore – even if most of the cast of characters is unfamiliar. From today's perspective it seems hard to believe that up until the early 1970s perhaps, much was still up for grabs in Singapore politics. A glimpse of the times emerges in the interview with Fong Swee Suan who, along with his late colleague Lim Chin Siong, had been a PAP member before becoming part of the opposition in the 1960s. Fong speaks movingly of Lim being exiled to London and of meeting him years later – though at no point is any reason given as to why Lim was exiled (he left after being released from six years of detention without trial). It's through such an imperfect prism that postwar Singapore is often glimpsed here, though the museum deserves credit for tackling this tumultuous period.

The Living Galleries

The most accessible of the museum's four **Living Galleries** focuses on **street food**, covering the history of and variations in local favourites such as *laksa* and *char kuay teow*, displaying soft drinks and kitchenware that generations of Singaporeans remember from their childhood, and offering an explanation as to why Singapore uses the term *roti prata* for what everyone in Malaysia calls *roti canai*. Also appealing is the **photography** gallery that, under the banner of "Framing the Family", displays many Singapore family portraits made over the past hundred years, enriched with yet more oral history clips. It includes some interesting commentary on the prevalence of polygamy – not as you might assume in Muslim families but among the Chinese. The most edifying gallery tackles **film and wayang** and includes plenty of memorabilia of the Malay-language film industry which took off in Singapore in the middle of the last century; it's a sign of how the times have changed since the divorce from Malaysia that this cinematic flowering is news to many non-Malay Singaporeans today. Finally, there's the **fashion** gallery, using trends in women's clothing over the years as an indicator of the changing status of Singapore women.

Fort Canning Park

When Raffles first caught sight of Singapore, **Fort Canning Park** was known locally as Bukit Larangan (Forbidden Hill). Malay annals tell of the five ancient kings of Singapura said to have ruled the island from here six hundred years ago, and artefacts unearthed here prove it was inhabited as early as the fourteenth century. The last of the kings, Sultan Iskandar Shah, reputedly lies here, and it was out of respect for – and fear of – his spirit that the Malays decreed the hill forbidden. Singapore's first Resident, William Farquhar, displayed typical colonial tact by promptly having what the British called Government Hill cleared and building a bungalow, Government House, on the summit. It was replaced in 1859 by a fort named after Viscount George Canning, governor-general of India, but only a gateway, guardhouse and adjoining wall remain today.

History apart, Fort Canning Park is spacious, offers respite from Singapore's crowded streets and is packed with mature trees (which do, unfortunately, often put paid to panoramas over town). The most obvious of several routes up the hill starts by the National Museum, but there's a popular alternative involving a long flight of steps beside the MICA Building on Hill Street. If you use the museum route, you enter the park down the slope from the grandiose and slightly incongruous **Fort Canning Centre**, a former British barracks now home to a dance company, a culinary school and other organizations; there is also an information point here with **maps** of the park. Turn left to reach a *keramat* (auspicious place), the supposed site of Iskandar Shah's grave, which attracts a trickle of local Muslims. Continue round the hill and you meet the staircase from Hill Street at **Raffles Terrace**, where there are replicas of a colonial flagstaff and a lighthouse. From here the paths swing northwest, with River Valley Road and the Singapore River below, to the far side of the hill from Raffles Terrace. Here there is yet another grand former British military building, now called **Legends** and home to a couple of restaurants and a private club.

Just uphill from Legends and behind the Fort Canning Centre are **Fort Gate** – the surviving gateway to Canning's fort – and the 1939 underground operations bunkers from which the Allied war effort in Singapore was master-minded. The latter, now restored and called the **Battle Box** (daily 10am–6pm, last admission 4.50pm; S$8), holds an animatronics-based exhibition which brings to life the events leading up to the British surrender of Singapore in February 1942.

Fort Canning Park's southwest boundary is defined by **River Valley Road**, at whose eastern end is the **MICA Building** – formerly the Hill Street Police Station, but now home to the Ministry of Information, Communications and the Arts, with shuttered windows in bright colours; its central atrium houses several galleries majoring in Asian artworks. Next to the Coleman Bridge here is **GMAX** (Mon–Thurs 1pm–1am, Fri 1pm–2am, Sat noon–2am, Sun noon–1am; S$45; Ⓦwww.gmax.com.sg), billed as a "reverse bungy" but more like an enclosed metal cradle suspended from several cables, allowing it and screaming passengers within to be tossed around in the air for several minutes at a time. The ride is better attempted before rather than after you settle into a bar or restaurant at **Clarke Quay**, just up River Valley Road. This assembly of nineteenth-century godowns, now shielded from the elements by rather ugly circular canopies, consists of nothing but eating and nightlife venues – and remains nowhere close to nearby Boat Quay (see p.627) in terms of atmosphere. Further up the road is **Robertson Quay**, rather quieter than either of these, though it boasts a few entertainment venues of its own.

Northeast of Robertson Quay, reached by turning right into Tank Road off River Valley Road (or on bus #143 from Orchard Road or Chinatown), is what many still refer to as the **Chettiar Temple** (officially the Sri Thendayuthapani Temple; daily roughly 8.30am–12.30pm & 5.30–8.30pm; Ⓦwww.sttemple .com). The shrine, boasting a large, attractive *gopuram,* was built in 1984 to replace a nineteenth-century temple constructed by *chettiars* (Indian money-lenders), and is the destination of every participant in Singapore's annual Thaipusam festival (see p.634).

Bras Basah Road to Rochor Road

The zone between **Bras Basah Road** – the main thoroughfare between Orchard Road and what would have been the seafront – and **Rochor Road** at the edge of Little India has a transitional sort of feel, sitting as it does between the Colonial District and what were intended to be "ethnic" enclaves to the northeast; in fact the aptly named Middle Road, running smack through the centre of the grid, was originally meant to be the boundary between the two. Despite modernization, the area still boasts some long-established places of worship and spruced-up shophouses, and has been transforming into a nexus for the visual and performing **arts**. City planners have turned over many distin-guished old properties on and around **Waterloo Street** to arts organizations, including the **Singapore Art Museum**, and lured the country's leading insti-tutes in the field here, among them the Nanyang Academy of Fine Arts (**NAFA**) on Bencoolen Street; the **Lasalle College of the Arts**, whose futuristic glass buildings under a translucent canopy between McNally Street and Albert Street deserve a look; and the **School of the Arts**, whose grand building next to the Cathay cinema should be open by the time you read this.

CHIJMES and the Cathedral of the Good Shepherd

Just up Bras Basah Road from the *Raffles* hotel is **CHIJMES** (pronounced "chimes"; Ⓦwww.chijmes.com.sg), a complex of shops, bars and restaurants, based in the restored Neo-Gothic husk of the former Convent of the Holy Infant Jesus – from which name the acronym for the complex is derived. Its lawns, courtyards, waterfalls, fountains and sunken forecourt give a sense of spatial dynamics that is rare in Singapore. For some locals, however, it sticks in the craw that planners allowed what had been one of several historic schools in the area to assume its present role; if the arts-district idea had matured earlier,

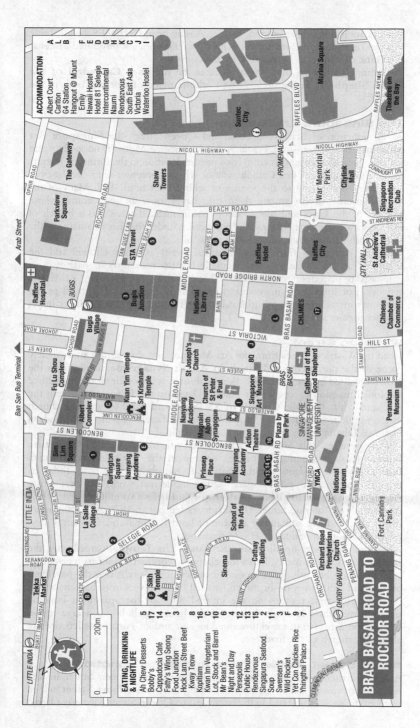

BRAS BASAH ROAD TO ROCHOR ROAD

ACCOMMODATION
Albert Court	A
Carlton	L
G4 Station	B
Hangout @ Mount Emily	F
Hawaii Hostel	E
Hotel 81 Selegie	D
Intercontinental	G
Naumi	H
Rendezvous	K
South East Asia	C
Victoria	J
Waterloo Hostel	I

EATING, DRINKING & NIGHTLIFE
Ah Chew Desserts	5
Bobby's	17
Cappadocia Café	14
Fatty's Wing Seong	1
Food Junction	3
Hock Lam Street Beef	8
Kway Teow	
Kopitiam	16
Kwan Im Vegetarian	10
Lot, Stock and Barrel	6
Mr Bean's	4
Night and Day	12
Persepolis	13
Public House	15
Rendezvous	2
Singapura Seafood Soup	11
Swensen's	3
Wild Rocket	F
Yet Con Chicken Rice	9
Yhingthai Palace	7

chances are it might have evaded that fate. A relic from CHIJMES' original role survives on its Victoria Street flank, where local families left unwanted babies at the **Gate of Hope**, to be taken in by the convent.

A minute's walk up Bras Basah Road is the dignified **Cathedral of the Good Shepherd**, Singapore's oldest Catholic place of worship, built in the 1840s.

The Singapore Art Museum

At the junction of Bras Basah Road and Queen Street, the **Singapore Art Museum** (daily 10am–7pm, Fri till 9pm; S$8, but free Mon–Fri noon–2pm and Fri after 6pm; ⓦwww.singart.com) has a peerless location in the former St Joseph's Institution, Singapore's first Catholic school, whose impressive semi-circular front and silvery dome rang to the sounds of school bells until 1987. Many of the original rooms survive, among them the chapel (now an auditorium), whose Stations of the Cross and mosaic floor remain intact. There's also a branch of the *Dôme* café chain, where you can have a drink under the gaze of a statue of the seventeenth-century saint, John Baptist de la Salle.

Visiting collections from such acclaimed artists as Marc Chagall and the sculptor Carl Milles are on show regularly, but the museum's strength is in its emphasis is placed on contemporary local and Southeast Asian artists and artwork. For more experimental and community-themed work, head to the museum's impressive new offshoot called **8Q**, housed at 8 Queen Street in yet another former school.

Waterloo Street

Head up Waterloo Street from the Art Museum and you almost immediately come to the peach-coloured **Maghain Aboth Synagogue**, dating from the 1870s. Dwarfed by the modern buildings around, it looks for all the world like a colonial mansion except for the Stars of David on the facade. Opposite is the blue-and-white Catholic **Church of SS Peter and Paul** (ⓦwww.sppchurch .org.sg) built around the same time and likewise dwarfed by the hypermodern National Library tower a couple of blocks behind.

A few minutes' walk on, at the intersection with Middle Road, is **Sculpture Square** (ⓦwww.sculpturesq.com.sg), erected in the 1870s as the Christian Institute, where residents could debate and read about their faith. Today, its grounds and interior gallery space feature modernist works by local artists. Across the way is the **Sri Krishnan Temple**, just before you hit the pedestrianized stretch of Waterloo Street. The shrine started out in 1870 as nothing more than a thatched hut containing a statue of Lord Krishna under a banyan tree; today it's a popular venue for Hindu weddings.

A couple of doors up the road, the **Kuan Yin Temple**, named after the Buddhist goddess of mercy, looks too classy for comfort thanks to renovations over the years, but still draws thousands of devotees daily. Along the pavement outside, old ladies in wide-brimmed hats sell fresh flowers from baskets; one of the religious-artefact shops on the ground floor of the apartment building opposite specializes in small shrines for the house, including a deluxe model with an extractor fan to expel unwanted incense smoke. Fortune-tellers operate along this stretch of the road, too.

Albert Street, Bugis Village and Bugis Junction

A little further northeast along Waterloo Street and Queen Street lie the remnants of two of old Singapore's most famous streets. **Albert Street**, which once ran from Selegie Road in the northwest to Queen Street, formerly offered street eating approaching what you still find on Jalan Alor in KL. Today it's been so remodelled that much of it isn't even shown on some maps; it is worth a stroll, however, if only to gaze at the zigzagging glass facades of the Lasalle College of the Arts near the street's northern end.

Albert Street continued on the other side of Queen Street as **Bugis** (pronounced "boogis") **Street**, which once crawled with rowdy sailors, transvestites and prostitutes by night. The street was duly cleared, partly because it was anathema to the government and partly so that the Bugis MRT station could be built. In its place today is **Bugis Village**, a bunch of market stalls and snack vendors lining two covered alleyways. It's hardly the Bugis Street of old, though it does recapture something of the bazaar feel that some Singapore markets once had. Amid the T-shirt sellers is at least one outlet selling sex toys – about the only obvious link to the area's seedy past.

Across Victoria Street from here is another throwback to the past, the **Bugis Junction** development, in which whole streets of shophouses have been gutted, scrubbed clean and then encased under glass roofs as part of a modern shopping mall and hotel, the *Intercontinental*. The mall itself has some good places to eat, particularly *Food Junction* on level 3 (see p.664).

Chinatown

The two square kilometres of **Chinatown**, bounded roughly by Eu Tong Sen Street to the northwest, Neil and Maxwell roads to the south, Cecil Street to the southeast and the Singapore River to the north, once constituted the focal point of Chinese life and culture in Singapore. The area was first earmarked for Chinese settlement by Sir Stamford Raffles himself, who decided in June 1819, on his second visit to the island, that Singapore's communities should be segregated. As immigrants poured in, the land southwest of the river took shape as a place where new arrivals from China, mostly from Guangdong (Canton) and Fujian (Hokkien) provinces and to a lesser extent Hainan island, would have found temples, shops with familiar products and, most importantly, *kongsis* – clan associations which helped them to find lodgings and work as small traders and coolies.

This was one of the most colourful districts of old Singapore, but after independence the government chose to grapple with its tumbledown slums by embarking upon a **redevelopment** campaign that saw whole streets razed. Someone with an unimpeachable insight into those times, one Lee Kuan Yew is quoted thus in the URA Gallery (see p.625): "In our rush to rebuild Singapore, we knocked down many old and quaint Singapore buildings. Then we realized that we were destroying a valuable part of our cultural heritage, that we were demolishing what tourists found attractive." It wasn't until the 1980s that the remaining shophouses and other period buildings began to be conserved, though restoration has often rendered them improbably perfect. Furthermore, few retain their original function: clan houses and religious and martial-arts associations have been driven out by spiralling rents, while boutique hotels, art galleries, new-media companies and upmarket (or sometimes not so respectable) bars have moved in. Ironically, getting a taste of the old ways of Chinatown now often means heading off the main streets into the surrounding housing estates.

Even so, the area still holds many engaging shrines – not just Chinese – in particular the **Thian Hock Keng**, **Buddha Tooth Relic** and **Sri Mariamman** temples. The **Chinatown Heritage Centre** museum is also a must-see, and there's enough worthwhile shophouse architecture to justify a leisurely wander

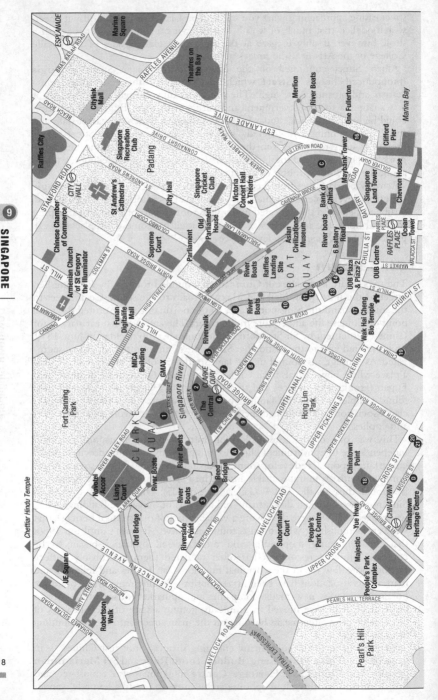

◄ Chettiar Hindu Temple

MOHAMED SULTAN ROAD

UNITY STREET

UE Square

Robertson Walk

MERBAU ROAD

CLEMENCEAU AVENUE

Ord Bridge

Riverside Point

Liang Court

Novotel Accor

River Boats

CLARKE QUAY

RIVER VALLEY ROAD

Fort Canning Park

Singapore River

The Central

CLARKE QUAY

GMAX

MICA Building

Funan Digitalife Mall

HILL ST

CANNING RISE

ARMENIAN ST

Armenian Church of St Gregory the Illuminator

Chinese Chamber of Commerce

COLEMAN ST

HILL ST

Supreme Court

Parliament

Old Parliament House

St Andrew's Cathedral

CITY HALL

STAMFORD ROAD

ST ANDREW'S ROAD

City Hall

Singapore Cricket Club

Victoria Concert Hall & Theatre

Padang

Singapore Recreation Club

CONNAUGHT DRIVE

QUEEN ELIZABETH WALK

ESPLANADE DRIVE

Raffles City

Citylink Mall

Marina Square

RAFFLES AVENUE

Theatres on the Bay

BRAS BASAH ROAD

BEACH ROAD

ESPLANADE

Merlion

River Boats

One Fullerton

Clifford Pier

16

Maybank Tower

Singapore Land Tower

Chevron House

Ocean Tower

COLLYER QUAY

FULLERTON ROAD

BATTERY ROAD

Bank of China

Asian Civilizations Museum

River boats

6 Battery Road

CAVENAGH BRIDGE

PARLIAMENT LANE

Raffles Landing Site

River Boats

NORTH BRIDGE ROAD

HIGH STREET

NORTH BRIDGE ROAD

ELGIN BRIDGE

CIRCULAR ROAD

8

10

12

13

15

14

B O A T   Q U A Y

RAFFLES PLACE

OUB Centre

CHULIA ST

MARKET ST

MALACCA ST

PHILIP ST

UOB Plaza & Plaza 2

17

Wak Hai Cheng Bio Temple

CHURCH ST

19

GEORGE ST

PICKERING ST

SOUTH CANAL RD

Riverwalk

5

NEW BRIDGE ROAD

SOUTH BRIDGE ROAD

CARPENTER ST

7

B

9

NEW CHOW ST

2

6

1

Reed Bridge

3

4

River Boats

River Boats

MERCHANT RD

MAGAZINE ROAD

Subordinate Court

People's Park Centre

HAVELOCK ROAD

UPPER PICKERING ST

Hong Lim Park

UPPER HOKKIEN ST

UPPER CROSS ST

NORTH CANAL RD

HONG KONG ST

A

Chinatown Point

18

Yue Hwa

Majestic

People's Park Complex

CROSS ST

MOSQUE ST

20

21

Chinatown Heritage Centre

NEW BRIDGE ROAD

CHINATOWN

SOUTH BRIDGE ROAD

People's Park Centre

PEARLS HILL TERRACE

Pearl's Hill Park

HAVELOCK ROAD

CENTRAL EXPRESSWAY

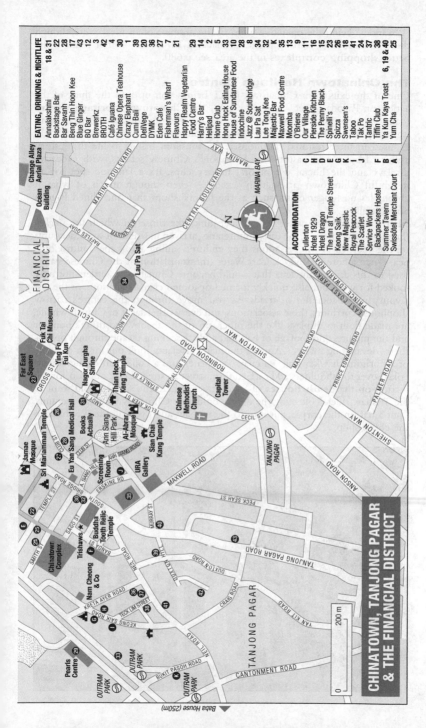

CHINATOWN, TANJONG PAGAR & THE FINANCIAL DISTRICT

ACCOMMODATION	
Fullerton	C
Hotel 1929	H
Hotel Dragon	D
The Inn at Temple Street	E
Keong Saik	G
New Majestic	K
Royal Peacock	I
The Scarlet	J
Service World Backpackers Hostel	F
Summer Tavern	B
Swissôtel Merchant Court	A

EATING, DRINKING & NIGHTLIFE	
Annalakshmi	18 & 31
Backstage Bar	22
Bar Savanh	28
Beng Thin Hoon Kee	17
Blue Ginger	43
BQ Bar	12
Brewerkz	3
BROTH	42
Café Iguana	4
Chinese Opera Teahouse	30
Crazy Elephant	1
Cumi Bali	39
DeliVege	20
DYMK	36
Eden Café	27
Fisherman's Wharf	7
Flavours	21
Happy Realm Vegetarian Food Centre	29
Harry's Bar	14
Helipad	2
Home Club	5
Hong Hock Eating House	33
House of Sundanese Food	10
Indochine	28
Jazz @ Southbridge	8
Lau Pa Sat	34
Lee Tong Kee	32
Majestic Bar	K
Maxwell Food Centre	35
Moomba	13
O'Briens	9
Our Village	11
Pierside Kitchen	16
The Penny Black	15
Spinelli's	23
Spizza	26
Swensen's	18
Taboo	41
Tak Po	24
Tantric	37
Tiffin Club	38
Ya Kun Kaya Toast	6, 19 & 40
Yum Cha	25

Baba House (250m)

– "wander" being the operative word in the absence of an ideal route, though there is an obvious starting point, Chinatown MRT station. For a list of the better **shopping complexes** in the area, see p.680.

The Chinatown Heritage Centre

One of the exits from Chinatown MRT brings you up into the thick of the action on Pagoda Street where, at no. 48, the **Chinatown Heritage Centre** (daily 9am–8pm, last admission 7pm; S$9.80; ⓦ www.chinatownheritage.com .sg) stands in marked contrast to the tacky souvenir stalls and touts hereabouts. Housed in three restored shophouses, the museum brings to life the history, culture, labours and pastimes of Singapore's Chinese settlers, with evocative displays and the liberal use of oral history clips. It's a fantastic spot for an insightful Chinatown orientation session – even though much of what it chronicles no longer exists, such as the tailors' shops that once lined Pagoda Street itself.

Early on, the scene is set by a model junk, like those on which the *singkeh* (literally "new guests"), the early immigrants, arrived in search of work; accounts on the wall tell of the privations they endured sailing across the South China Sea. Once ashore at Bullock Cart Water (the translation of the Chinese name, used to this day, for the area that would become Chinatown), settlers not only looked for work but also quickly formed or joined clan associations, or the less savoury secret societies or triads. As you move through the centre's narrow shophouse corridors, these associations, and every other facet of Chinatown life, are made flesh in displays like the mock-up of the shabby prostitute's boudoir and the pictures and footage of haunted addicts seeking escape through opium, their "devastating master". Among the many artefacts, look out for an example of an original hawker stall – a charcoal burner and a collection of ingredients yoked over the shoulders and carried from street to street. Look out, too, for the section on the **death houses** of Sago Street, where the sick and old went to die. Trishaw riders collecting the dead would, one Chinatown veteran recounts, "put a hat on the corpse, put it onto the trishaw, and cycle all the way back to the coffin shop".

▲ Shophouses in Chinatown

The tour climaxes with a recreation of the conditions that settlers endured in Chinatown's shophouses. Landlords were known to shoehorn as many as forty tenants into a single floor, and their cramped cubicles, cooking and bathing facilities are reproduced in all their squalor, enhanced by the absence of air-conditioning in this section. If you think it couldn't possibly happen today, spare a thought for the thousands of mainly Indian and Bangladeshi migrant workers who toil on building sites all over Singapore; most live in basic dormitories, and in 2008 a journalist documented 54 workers crammed into triple-decker beds in an eight-by-six-metre room.

Along South Bridge Road

Continue down Pagoda Street from the Chinatown Heritage Centre and you come to **South Bridge Road**, one of Chinatown's main thoroughfares, taking southbound traffic. Here at no. 218, on the corner of Mosque Street, is the pastel green **Jamae Mosque** (also called the Chulia Mosque), established by south Indian Muslims in the 1820s. Its twin minarets appear to contain miniature windows while above the entrance stands what looks like a miniature doorway, all of which makes the upper part of the facade look strangely like a scale model of a much larger building.

One street northeast is the junction with **Upper Cross Street** where, during the Japanese occupation, roadblocks were set up and Singaporeans vetted for signs of anti-Japanese sentiment in the infamous **Sook Ching** campaign (see p.586). That tragic episode is commemorated by a simple, signposted monument here in the **Hong Lim Complex**, a housing estate which also happens to boast walkways lined with medical halls, makers of *chops* (rubber stamps), stores selling dried foodstuffs and so forth – much more representative of the area's original character than more recent arrivals.

The Sri Mariamman Temple

In the opposite direction and practically next door to the mosque is Singapore's oldest Hindu shrine, the **Sri Mariamman Temple**, with a superb entrance *gopuram* bristling with brightly coloured deities. A wood and *atap* hut was first erected here in 1827 on land belonging to Naraina Pillay, a government clerk who arrived on the same ship as Stamford Raffles when he first came ashore at Singapore; the present temple was completed around 1843. Once inside, look up at the roof and you'll see splendid friezes depicting a host of Hindu deities, including the three manifestations of the supreme being: Brahma the creator (with three of his four heads showing), Vishnu the preserver, and Shiva the destroyer (holding one of his sons). The main sanctum, facing you as you walk inside the temple, is devoted to Mariamman, a goddess worshipped for her healing powers. Smaller sanctums dotted about the walkway circumnavigating the temple honour a host of other deities. In the one dedicated to the goddess Periachi Amman, a sculpture portrays her with a queen lying on her lap, whose evil child she has ripped from her womb; it's odd, then, that the Periachi Amman is the protector of children, to whom babies are brought when one month old. Sri Aravan, with his bushy moustache and big ears, is far less intimidating; his sanctum is at the back on the right-hand side of the complex.

To the left of the main sanctum is an unassuming patch of sand which, a year during the festival of **Thimithi** (Oct or Nov), is covered in red-hot coals that male Hindus run across to prove the strength of their faith. The participants, who line up all the way along South Bridge Road waiting for their turn, are supposedly protected from the heat of the coals by the power of prayer.

Across the road from the Hindu temple is the beautifully renovated **Eu Yan Sang Medical Hall** (Mon–Sat 8.30am–6pm), at 267–271 South Bridge Road. The smell is the first thing you'll notice (a little like a compost heap on a hot day), the second, the weird assortment of ingredients on the shelves, which to the uninitiated look more likely to kill than cure. Besides the usual herbs and roots favoured by the Chinese, there are various dubious remedies derived from exotic and endangered species. Blood circulation problems and wounds are eased with centipedes and insects, crushed into a "rubbing liquor"; the ground-up gall bladders of snakes or bears apparently work wonders on pimples; while deer penis is supposed to provide a lift to any sexual problem.

Above the hall is the small but engaging **Birds' Nest Gallery** (Mon–Sat 10am–5.30pm; S$5), which casts light on this most famous of Chinese delicacies. Produced by swiftlets, the nests are a mixture of saliva, moss and grass, and emerged as a prized supplement among China's royal and noble classes during the Ming Dynasty. Today they are still valued for their supposed efficacy in boosting the immune system and curing bronchial ailments. The swiftlets live high up in the caves of Southeast Asia, and you may be shown a video of men scaling long bamboo poles to get at the nests. The high prices the nests command have in the past been down to the difficulty of harvesting them, though these days some Malaysians are getting round the problem with the dubious practice of using disused town-centre properties as "caves", around which swiftlets can be seen wheeling at dawn and dusk.

Just a few doors down at no. 285, the egg tarts, walnut cookies, buns and other Chinese cakes at the **Tong Heng pastry shop** (daily 9am–10pm) offer a great way to top up your blood-sugar level before pressing on to other sights.

The Buddha Tooth Relic Temple

Just after Sago Street, and just before South Bridge Road becomes Neil Road, is the most startling addition to Chinatown's shrines in many a year, the imposing **Buddha Tooth Relic Temple** (daily 7am–7pm; free; no shorts, vests or non-vegetarian food; ⊛ www.btrts.org.sg). This is a place that simply clobbers you with its opulence – even the elevators have brocaded walls – and the thousands upon thousands of Buddhist figurines plastered up and down various interior surfaces. It also boasts its own museum and a gallery of Buddhist art.

The temple has its origins in the discovery, in 1980, of what was thought to be a tooth of Buddha inside a collapsed stupa at a Burmese monastery. The monastery's chief abbot visited Singapore in 2002 and decided the island would make a suitable sanctuary for the relic, to be housed in its own temple if there were a chance of building one. A prime site in Chinatown was duly secured, construction began in 2005 and the temple was opened in 2007.

The main entrance on South Bridge Road, flanked by two bare-torsoed, ripply guardian statues, leads directly to the main hall, where the focus is **Maitreya**, a Buddha who is yet to appear on Earth. Carved from juniper wood said to be 1000 years old, his statue has a yellow flame-like halo around it. But what really captures the attention here are the Buddhas covering the entire side walls. There are a hundred main statuettes, individually crafted, interspersed with thousands more tiny figurines embedded in a vast array of shelving, every one with its own serial number displayed. Signage soon makes you aware that many things in the temple are up for "**adoption**" – figurines and fittings can be the object of sponsorship, presumably winning donors good karma while recouping the S$62 million construction bill and helping the temple keep up with its outgoings. Behind the main hall is another large hall, centred on the **Avalokitesvara** bodhisattva, with smaller statuettes of Ruri Kwan Yin – yours to adopt for S$88 – to the sides.

The **mezzanine** floor affords great views over proceedings and chanting ceremonies in the main hall, while **level 2** contains the temple's own **teahouse**. On **level 3** are some seriously impressive examples of Buddhist **statuary** in brass, wood and stone, plus other artworks, many up for adoption

▲ Guardian statue at Buddha Tooth Relic Temple

– just S\$250,000 will link you with the Lotus sutra stele, brought here from China. They're all part of the **Buddhist Culture Museum** (daily 8am–6pm), with panels telling the story of Gautama Buddha in the first person. At the back is the relic chamber, displaying what are said to be the cremated remains of Buddha's nose, brain, liver etc, all looking like fish roe in different colours.

On **level 4** you finally encounter what all the fuss is ultimately about – the **Sacred Buddah Tooth Relic Stupa**. Some 3m in diameter, it sits in its own chamber behind glass panels (unveiled daily 9am–noon & 3–6pm) and can't be inspected close up, though there is an accurate scale model at the front which can be viewed at any time. The Maitreya Buddha is depicted at the front of the stupa, guarded by four lions, with a ring of 35 more Buddhas below; floor tiles around the stupa – a S\$5000 adoption – are "made of pure gold".

Above is the temple's lovely **roof garden**, its walls lined with twelve thousand 5cm figurines of the Amitayus Buddha (a bargain to adopt, at S\$68). But the centrepiece is "the largest cloisonné **prayer wheel** in the world", around 5m tall. Each rotation of it (clockwise, in case you have a go) dings a bell and represents the recitation of one sutra. Curiously, the ten thousand Buddhas in the chamber housing it don't seem to be up for adoption.

Sago Street and Trengganu Street

Today, the tight knot of streets west of South Bridge Road between Sago Street and Pagoda Street is Chinatown at its most touristy, packed with souvenir sellers and foreigner-friendly restaurants. But in bygone days these streets formed Chinatown's nucleus, teeming with trishaws and food hawkers, while opium dens and brothels lurked within the shophouses. Until as recently as the 1950s, **Sago Street** was home to several death houses – rudimentary hospices where skeletal citizens saw out their final hours on rattan camp beds. Sago, Smith, Temple and Pagoda streets only really recapture something of the best of their original atmosphere around Chinese New Year, when they're crammed with stalls selling festive branches of blossom, oranges, sausages and waxed chickens – which look as if they have melted to reveal a handful of bones inside. The ugly concrete **Chinatown Complex** at the end of the street is a workaday place housing outlets selling silk, kimonos, rattan, leather and, at unit #01-K3, Buddhist amulets.

Sago Street skirts to the right of the Chinatown Complex and becomes **Trengganu Street**. Despite the hordes of tourists here, there are occasional glimpses of Chinatown's **old trades** and industries, such as Nam's Supplies at 22 Smith St, producing shirts, watches, mobile phones and laptops – all made out of paper so that they can be burnt at Chinese funerals to ensure the deceased aren't lacking creature comforts in the next life.

Keong Saik Road and Bukit Pasoh Road

In the southernmost corner of Chinatown, west of Kreta Ayer Road and accessible from Outram Park MRT, is a pocket of streets lined with **restored shophouses**, worth a look not only for their beautifully painted facades, shuttered windows and tilework but also because the area is the evolving new Chinatown in microcosm. Already in situ are boutique hotels like the *New Majestic* on Bukit Pasoh Road and *Hotel 1929* on Keong Saik Road; at 16 Bukit Pasoh Road, the erstwhile Gan Clan Association is now home to karaoke bars. Glimpses of the old Chinatown survive, for example, at 5 Bukit Pasoh Road, where you'll find a Taoist shrine, admittedly too pristine for its own good; and even in modern residential towers like Block 334, Keong Saik Rd, where in unit #01-04 Nam Cheong and Co produces houses and near-life-size safes, servants and Mercedes cars out of paper for funerary use.

New Bridge Road and Eu Tong Sen Street

Chinatown's main shopping drag comprises southbound **New Bridge Road** and northbound **Eu Tong Sen Street**, along which are a handful of shopping malls. Try to pop into one of the barbecued-pork vendors around the intersection of Smith, Temple and Pagoda streets with New Bridge Road – the thin, flat, red squares of *bak kwa*, coated with a sweet marinade, produce a rich, smoky odour that is pure Chinatown as they're cooked. As you chew on your *bak kwa*, check out two striking buildings across the road. Nearest is the flat-fronted **Majestic Opera House**, which no longer hosts performances but still boasts five images of Chinese opera stars over its doors. Just beside it, the Yue Hwa Chinese Products Emporium occupies the former **Great Southern Hotel**, which was built in 1927 by the son of Eu Yan Sang, Eu Tong Sen. In its fifth-floor nightclub, wealthy locals would drink liquor, smoke opium and pay to dance with so-called local "taxi girls".

Ann Siang Hill and Club Street

Ann Siang Hill is both the name of a little mound and that of a lane that leads off South Bridge Road up a slope, where it forks into Club Street on the left and Ann Siang Road, which veers gently right. Despite being only a few paces removed from the hubbub of the main road, the hill is somehow a different realm, a little collection of gentrified shophouses with a distinct villagey feel. It's an area that typifies the new Chinatown, packed with swanky restaurants, cafés and bars, plus the odd boutique. The temple-carving shops on **Club Street** have long since gone, and just a handful remain of the **clan associations** and **guilds** whose presence gave the street its name. They're easy to spot: black-and-white photos of old members cover the walls, and old men sit and chat behind the screens which almost invariably span the doorway. Most notable of all is the **Chinese Weekly Entertainment Club** at no. 76, on a side street also called Club Street. Flanked by roaring lion heads, it's an imposing mansion that was built by a Peranakan millionaire in 1891. This offshoot of Club Street ends at **Ann Siang Hill Park**, a sliver of generic hilltop greenery whose only attraction for visitors is that there are steps down the far side offering a **shortcut** to Amoy Street.

The URA Gallery

Town planning may not sound the most fascinating premise for a gallery, but then again, no nation remodels with such ambition as Singapore, whose planners are constantly erasing roads here and replacing one ultramodern complex with an even more souped-up development there. The latest grand designs for the island are exhibited west of Ann Siang Hill at the surprisingly absorbing **URA Gallery** (Mon–Sat 9am–5pm; free; Ⓦ www.ura.gov.sg/gallery), within the Urban Redevelopment Authority's headquarters on Maxwell Road, close to Ann Siang Hill and easily reached from Tanjong Pagar MRT.

The URA has rightly been criticized in the past for slighting Singapore's architectural heritage, so it is heartening to see displays on the first and second floors making reassuring noises about the value of the venerable shophouses and colonial villas that remain. But the gallery's emphasis is more upon the future than the past, amply illustrated by the vast and incredibly intricate **scale model** of downtown Singapore on the ground floor, every row of shophouses, every roof of every building – including some not yet built – fashioned out of plywood; it's best scrutinized through one of the telescopes set up on the floor above. This and other scale models are turned out by a dedicated team whose first-floor workshop is sadly not open to the public, though you might catch a glimpse of them at work through the glass.

Amoy Street

Amoy Street, together with Telok Ayer Street, was designated a Hokkien enclave in the colony's early days (Amoy being the old name of Xiamen city in China's Fujian province). Long terraces of smartly refurbished shophouses flank the street, all featuring characteristic **five-foot ways**, or covered verandas, so called because they jut five feet out from the house. If you descend here from Ann Siang Hill, you'll emerge by the small **Sian Chai Kang Temple** at no. 66. With the customary dragons on the roof, it's dominated by huge urns, full to the brim with ash from untold numbers of burned incense sticks. Guarding the temple are two carved stone lions whose fancy red neck ribbons are said to attract good fortune and prosperity.

Telok Ayer Street

One street removed from Amoy Street is **Telok Ayer Street**, whose southern end starts near Tanjong Pagar MRT. The name Telok Ayer, meaning "Watery Bay" in Malay, recalls a time when the street would have run along the shoreline. Nowadays, thanks to land reclamation, it's no closer to a beach than is Beach Road, but alongside the shops and stores are still a number of temples and mosques that have survived from the time when immigrants and sailors stepping ashore wanted to thank the gods for their safe passage.

The first building of note you come to if you walk up from the station is the square 1889 **Chinese Methodist Church**, whose design – portholes and windows adorned with white crosses and capped by a Chinese pagoda-style roof – is a pleasing blend of East and West. Just beyond McCallum Street, the blue-and-white **Al-Abrar Mosque** marks the spot where Chulia worshippers from the coast of southern India first set up a thatched *kuchu palli* (in Tamil, small mosque), in 1827.

A couple of minutes' walk further on is the substantial **Thian Hock Keng Temple** (daily 7.30am–5.30pm; free; ⓦ www.thianhockkeng.com.sg), an impressively restored Hokkien building. Its construction began in 1839 using materials imported from China, and took place on the site of a small joss house where immigrants made offerings to Ma Chu Por (also known as Tian Hou), the queen of heaven. A statue of the goddess, shipped in from southern China in time for the temple's completion in 1842, still stands in the centre of the main hall, flanked by the god of war on the right and the protector of life on the left. From the street, the temple looks spectacular: dragons stalk its broad roofs, while the entrance to the temple compound bristles with ceramic flowers, foliage and figures. Two stone lions stand guard at the entrance, and door gods, painted on the front doors, prevent evil spirits from entering. Look out, too, for the huge ovens, always lit, in which offerings to either gods or ancestors are burnt.

It's a testament to Singapore's multicultural nature that Thian Hock Keng's next-door neighbour is the charming brown-and-white **Nagore Durgha Shrine**. A shrine to the ascetic, Shahul Hamid of Nagore, it was built in the 1820s by Chulias from southern India, as was the Jamae Mosque (see p.621), so it's not surprising that the buildings appear cut from the same cloth, so to speak. **Telok Ayer Green**, a paved garden dotted with life-sized metal statues depicting the early settlers, separates temple and shrine.

At no. 98, beyond the junction with Cross Street, is **Ying Fo Fui Kun**, one of Chinatown's surviving clan houses (daily 10am–10pm; free), in this case established in 1822 by Hakkas from Guangdong province. The place has been rebuilt and refurbished several times, most recently in the 1990s, and has narrowly avoided being swallowed up by the adjacent Far East Square complex, but in its present orderly state, with an immaculate altar boasting gilt calligraphy and carvings, it's hard to imagine it having been the social hub of an entire community. The clan association which runs it has been undertaking membership drives to stop itself decaying into a senior citizens' club, which is a real danger in a country where provincial dialects – traditionally used as a marker of identity among the Chinese – have been on the decline since the 1970s after a sometimes aggressive state campaign to standardize on Mandarin.

Far East Square

Far East Square is a sort of heritage development which incorporates the northernmost section of Amoy Street into what is otherwise a rather mundane collection of shops, restaurants and offices on Cross Street. Also co-opted into the complex is the **Fuk Tak Chi Street Museum** at 76 Telok Ayer Street (daily 10am–10pm; free). This was once Singapore's oldest surviving temple, having been established by the Hakka and Cantonese communities in 1824; today it's a mere "street museum", its altar holding a model junk crewed by sailors in blue shorts. There's also a diorama depicting how Telok Ayer Street would have appeared in its waterfront heyday, with pigtailed labourers taking part in a procession to the temple, which is depicted with a stage set up in front where opera performers are getting ready to strut their stuff.

Boat Quay and the Wak Hai Cheng Bio Temple

Reachable from Clarke Quay or Raffles Place stations, the pedestrianized row of riverside shophouses known as **Boat Quay** is an example of successful urban regeneration, since it was derelict in the early 1990s. Today it's one of Singapore's most fashionable hangouts, sporting a huge collection of thriving restaurants and bars.

Just to the south on Philip Street, the **Wak Hai Cheng Bio Temple** (also called the Yueh Hai Ching Temple) completes Chinatown's string of former waterfront temples. Its name means "Temple of the Calm Sea", which made it a logical choice for early worshippers who had arrived safely in Singapore; an effigy of Tian Hou, the queen of heaven and protector of seafarers, is housed in the temple's right-hand chamber. This temple, too, has an incredibly ornate roof, crammed with tiny models of Chinese village scenes.

Tanjong Pagar

The district of **Tanjong Pagar**, south of Chinatown and between Neil and Tanjong Pagar roads, was once a veritable sewer of brothels and opium dens. Then it became earmarked for regeneration as a conservation area, following which over two hundred shophouses were painstakingly restored and converted into bars, restaurants and shops. The main attraction here is the **Baba House**, but it's also worth making time to stop at one of the traditional **teahouses** elsewhere on Neil Road. At *Tea Chapter* at no. 9a–11a (daily 11am–11pm), you can have tea in the very chair in which Queen Elizabeth sat when she visited in 1989; the shop is plastered with photographs of the occasion. Buy a bag of tea here and one of the staff will teach you the rituals associated with its

If you're in need of a quick, thirst-quenching drink, avoid **Chinese teahouses**: the art of tea-making is heavily bound up in ritual, and the unhurried preparation time is crucial to the production of a pleasing brew. What's more, when you do get a cup, it's barely more than a mouthful and then the whole process kicks off again.

The basic procedure is as follows: the server places a towel in front of himself and his guest, with the folded edge facing the guest, and stuffs leaves into the pot with a bamboo scoop. Water, boiled over a flame, has to reach an optimum temperature, depending on which type of tea is being made; experts can tell its heat by the size of the bubbles rising, which are described variously, and rather confusingly, as "sand eyes", "prawn eyes", "fish eyes", etc. Once the pot has been warmed inside and out, the first pot of tea is made, transferred into the pouring jar and then, frustratingly, poured back over the pot – the thinking being that over a period of time, the porous clay of the pot becomes infused with the fragrance of the tea. Once a second pot is ready, a draught is poured into the sniffing cup, from which the aroma of the brew is savoured. Only now is it time to actually drink the tea; if you want a second cup, the procedure starts all over again.

consumption; 100g bags cost anything from just a few dollars to over S$60 and tea sets are also on sale, though they don't come cheap.

The Baba House

Since being acquired by the National University of Singapore's Centre for the Arts, the property at 157 Neil Road has been painstakingly dissected, studied and restored before being opened to the public in 2008 as the **Baba House** (compulsory guided tours Wed & Thurs only; S$10; book at least two weeks in advance on ⊤6227 5731 or email ⓔbabahouse@edu.nus.sg). This is one of the most impressive museums you can visit in Singapore, because it is and isn't a museum. There are no displays as such; what you see is simply a Peranakan house dating from around the late nineteenth or early twentieth century and which has been returned to its appearance in the late 1920s, a particularly prosperous time in its history. It's easy to get here from Outram Park MRT (use the Cantonment Road exit and turn right at the end of the slight slope into Neil Rd) or by riding bus #174 from Orchard Road or Bras Basah Rd right to its terminus.

Just like the Cheong Fatt Tze Mansion in Penang, the place is easily spotted as it's painted a vivid blue. Note the **phoenixes** and **peonies** on the eaves above the entrance, signifying longevity and wealth and, together, marital bliss. Even more eye-catching is the **pintu pagar**, the pair of swing doors with beautiful gilt and mother-of-pearl inlays. The Chinese characters above the windows to either side are the names of the golden osmanthus (on the left), a shrub symbolizing prosperity, and the bauhinia (on the right), a pink-blossomed tree representing family harmony (there's a street lined with bauhinias just to the east at Duxton Hill).

Beyond the *pintu pagar*, yet more exquisite inlay work is in evidence on the antique chairs in the **main hall**, used for entertaining guests. The altar here, one of the last of its kind in Singapore, is backed by an exquisitely carved wood screen behind which the women of the household could eavesdrop on proceedings.

Behind is the **family hall**, with an air well, open to the sky, in its midst. Note the original tilework here depicting roses and tulips, indicating a European influence, and the gilt bats on the walls; the Mandarin term for bats is *bianfu*, and the *fu* in question is a homonym for the Chinese character meaning "good fortune" – hence the bat motifs.

Upstairs at the front end of the house is the **main bedroom**, its centrepiece an ornate wooden four-poster bed with gilt and red lacquer decorations, and bearing carved motifs such as musical instruments and yet more bats. Your guide will almost certainly open up the **peephole** in the floor, exposing a small shaft down to the main hall. The **third storey**, a later addition to the house, is used as a space used for temporary exhibitions.

The Financial District and Marina South

The patch of land south of the mouth of the Singapore River was swampland until an early exercise in land reclamation in the mid-1820s rendered the zone fit for building. Within just a few years, Commercial Square here had become the colony's busiest business address, boasting the banks, ships' chandlers and warehouses of a burgeoning trading port. The square was later Singapore's main shopping area until superseded by Orchard Road in the late 1960s; today the square, now called Raffles Place, forms the nucleus of Singapore's **Financial District** (see map, pp.618–619). Until recently, if the area figured in the popular imagination at all, it would have been because of the rogue trader Nick Leeson, whose antics here brought about the **Barings Bank collapse** of 1995, though his transgressions seem like small beer when set against the global financial improprieties of recent years. East of here, the southern jaw of Marina Bay, **Marina South**, will be home to risk-taking in a different vein as the site of the *Marina Bay Sands* hotel and casino.

Raffles Place

Raffles Place makes a good prelude to a stroll along the south bank of the river to Boat Quay (see p.627) or across Cavenagh Bridge to the Colonial District (see p.603), but the main reason to visit the Financial District itself is to feel like ants in a canyon of skyscrapers. Surfacing from Raffles Place MRT, follow the signs for Raffles Place itself out of the station to be confronted by a veritable grove of gleaming towers. To the left is the soaring metallic triangle of the **OUB Centre** (home to the Overseas Union Bank), and to its right, the twin towers of the rocket-shaped **UOB Plaza** and the slightly older **UOB Plaza 2** (United Overseas Bank); in front are the rich brown walls of **6 Battery Road**; and to the right rise sturdy **Singapore Land Tower** and the almost Art Deco **Chevron House**. The three roads that run southwest from Raffles Place – Cecil Street, Robinson Road and Shenton Way – are all chock-a-block with more high-rise banks and financial houses.

You can get an idea of how the skyline would have looked in the late 1980s by peering at the large art installation, entitled *Progress and Advancement*, at the northern end of Raffles Place. It was erected in 1988 and inevitably, it wasn't long before the depiction of the city it carries was out of date.

The south bank

Heading towards the river, you come to **Battery Road**, whose name recalls the days when Fort Fullerton (named after Robert Fullerton, first governor of the Straits Settlements) and its attendant battery of guns used to stand to the east on the site of the *Fullerton* hotel. From here Bonham Street, to the right of the UOB Plaza, leads to the riverside promenade, with Cavenagh Bridge (see p.605) just a short distance away to the right. If you're not heading on to the Colonial District, it is still worth darting across the bridge for a look back at the quintet of towers right on the south bank: from left to right, the grey-and-blue metallic sliver of the Maybank Tower, the clean, white Bank of China, 6 Battery Road and finally the two UOB Plaza towers.

The main attraction here, Boat Quay aside, is the elegant **Fullerton Building**, worth viewing from Collyer Quay to the east for its facade fronted by sturdy pillars. In keeping with the rest of the area, this was one of Singapore's tallest buildings when it was constructed in 1928 as the headquarters for the General Post Office (a role it fulfilled until the mid-1990s). These days, the building is the luxury *Fullerton* hotel, whose atrium is worth a peek if only to admire the enormous columns within; the lighthouse that used to flash up on the roof is now a swanky restaurant.

Collyer Quay and Raffles Quay

Collyer Quay runs south along what is now the western shore of Marina Bay, linking the Colonial District with Raffles Quay and Shenton Way further south, both of which mark the old position of the seafront. Just east of Collyer Quay is the Merlion Park, home to the **One Fullerton** development, whose bars and restaurants and nightclub boasts views out over the bay, and to a cement statue of Singapore's national symbol, the **Merlion**. Half-lion, half-fish and wholly ugly, the creature reflects the island's maritime connections and the old tale concerning the derivation of its present name, derived from the Sanskrit "Singapura", meaning "Lion City" (see p.584).

South of the park is the Art Deco **Clifford Pier** building, long the departure point for boat trips out to Singapore's southern islands, but defunct now that Marina Bay is enclosed by a barrage; in line with the redevelopment at Marina South, the building will be transformed into yet another leisure complex. From here it's just a short walk along Raffles Quay to the octagonal cast-iron **Lau Pa Sat**, literally "old market". Built in 1894 and also called Telok Ayer Market, it's a great place for refreshments as it houses a 24-hour food court, part of the *Kopitiam* chain (see p.662).

Marina South

For years, **Marina South** had all the makings of a folly, a huge chunk of reclaimed land that seemed to have little purpose other than to carry the East Coast Parkway on its journey west and to house the so-so Marina City Park. But by the time you read this the area should have been transformed by the emergence of the enormous **Marina Bay Sands** hotel and casino on the western, bay-facing side of the area, to be run by Las Vegas Sands, which had previously ventured beyond Nevada to run a hotel/casino complex in Macau. Their Singapore undertaking, to open in 2010 or even late 2009, will be one of their most audacious yet.

The centrepiece of the development is a three-towered hotel topped by a vast roof platform that will not just link the towers but also house a so-called Sky Park that could literally be one of the hottest stretches of greenery in town, when the cruel tropical sun beats down. The casino will be situated between the towers and the bay, along with the ArtScience Museum – "devoted to the exploration of art and science and the connections between them" – and yet more entertainment, conference and shopping facilities, as if Singapore wasn't already drowning in these. Potentially the most interesting feature is the glass-and-steel **footbridge** encased in a DNA-like double-helix design; it will start near the museum and run for almost 300m to end up close to the Singapore Flyer across the bay.

Marina South is also the site of what's being billed as a **new financial centre** taking shape just north of Marina Bay MRT, though it will comprise just a few towers to begin with and is so close to the existing banking district that it's hard to think of it as a separate entity.

Little India

Of all the districts of old Singapore, the most charismatic has to be **Little India**, just fifteen minutes' walk from the Colonial District. The area retains more cultural and physical integrity than Chinatown: Indian pop music blares out from speakers outside cassette shops; the air is perfumed with incense, curry powder and jasmine garlands; Hindu women parade in bright sarees; and a wealth of restaurants (see p.665 for recommendations) serve up excellent, inexpensive curries. Though the remaining shophouses are fast being touched up from the same pastel paintbox as that which has "restored" Chinatown to its present doll's-house cuteness, the results seem to work better in an Indian context.

The original occupants of this downtown niche were Europeans and Eurasians who established country houses here, and for whom a racecourse was built (on the site of modern-day Farrer Park) in the 1840s. Only when Indian-run brick kilns began to operate here did an Indian community start to take shape. Since then Indians have featured prominently in the development of Singapore, though not always out of choice: from 1825 onwards, **convicts** were transported from the subcontinent and by the 1840s there were over a thousand Indian prisoners slaving away on buildings such as St Andrew's Cathedral and the Istana. Today migrant Tamil and Bangladeshi men labour on the island republic's MRT stations, shopping malls and private villas, and on Sundays they descend on Little India in their tens of thousands, making the place look like downtown Calcutta or Chennai after a major cricket match. Thankfully it's all very good-natured; swarms of workers gather to chat on every street corner, while mobile-phone operators set up simple fairground-type games to entice new arrivals into buying their SIM cards.

The district's backbone is **Serangoon Road**, one of the island's oldest roadways, dating from 1822. It's a kaleidoscopic whirl of Indian life, its shops selling everything from nose studs to *kum kum* powder (used to make the red dot Hindus wear on their foreheads). Look out here and elsewhere for parrot-wielding **fortune-tellers** – you tell the man your name, which he passes on to his feathered partner, and the bird picks out a card with your fortune on it.

As with Chinatown, there is no ideal route through the area, so exploring means doing some backtracking, which is no ordeal as there are always interesting pickings to be had. The account below starts from Tekka Market, conveniently next to Little India MRT, and then covers the side roads off Serangoon Road in stretches. The best time of year to visit is in the run-up to **Deepavali** (Oct or Nov) when much of Serangoon Road is festooned with festive lighting and special markets are set up in the open space beyond the Angullia Mosque (opposite Syed Alwi Road) and on Campbell Lane, selling decorations, garlands, traditional confectionery and clothes.

Tekka Market to Klang Road

At the southwestern end of Serangoon Road, **Tekka Market** combines many of Little India's ventures under one roof. After major renovations to the building, the wet market is more sanitary than before but hardly sanitized – traders push around trolleys piled high with goats' heads while live crabs shuffle in buckets, their claws tied together. There's also a mouthwatering range of tropical fruit on sale, while elsewhere you'll find an excellent food centre and shops selling Indian fabrics, leather, shoes and watches.

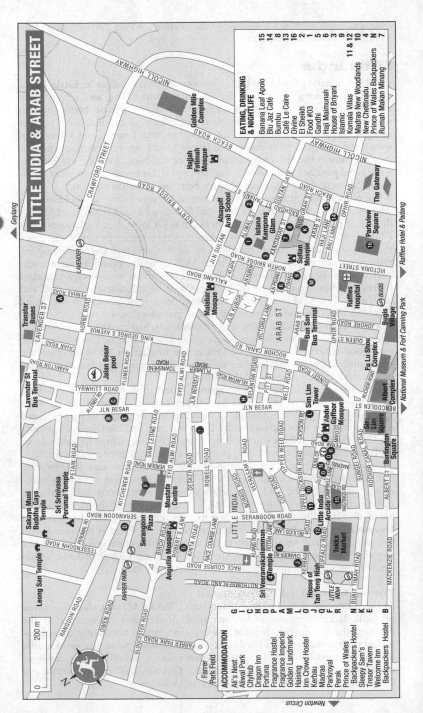

LITTLE INDIA & ARAB STREET

EATING, DRINKING & NIGHTLIFE

Banana Leaf Apolo	15
Blu Jaz Café	14
Bumbu	8
Café Le Caire	13
Divine	16
El Sheikh	2
Food #03	1
Gandhi	5
Haji Maimunah	6
House of Briyani	3
Islamic	9
Komala Villas	11 & 12
Madras New Woodlands	10
New Chettinadu	4
Prince of Wales Backpackers	N
Rumah Makan Minang	7

ACCOMMODATION

Ali's Nest	G
Aliwal Park	I
Cityhub	C
Dragon Inn	H
Fortuna	D
Fragrance Hostel	P
Fragrance Imperial	A
Golden Landmark	M
Haising	L
Inn Crowd Hostel	O
Kerbau	J
Madras	Q
Parkroyal	F
Perak	R
Prince of Wales Backpackers Hostel	N
Sleepy Sam's	K
Tresor Tavern	E
Welcome Inn	W
Backpackers Hostel	B

Buffalo Road, along the northern side of the market, sports a few provisions stores with sacks of spices and fresh coconut, ground using primitive machines. Its name, and that of neighbouring Kerbau ("buffalo" in Malay) Road, recall the the latter half of the nineteenth century when a number of **cattle and buffalo yards** opened in the area, causing the enclave to grow as more Indians were lured here in search of work. **Kerbau Road** is notable for its meticulously renovated shophouses and for being, like Waterloo Street 1km to the south, a designated "arts belt", home to several creative organizations. Curiously, the road itself been split into two parts with a pedestrianized bit of greenery in the middle. Here, at no. 37, you can't miss the restored **Chinese villa**, its window shutters and fretwork eave ornamentations painted in garish colours. Now used as commercial premises, the shophouse-style property was built by a confectionery magnate, Tan Teng Niah, in 1900. Look out also for the traditional picture framer's at no. 29, packed with images of Hindu deities.

Back on Serangoon Road and around 100m short of Klang Road is the eye-catching *gopuram* of the **Sri Veeramakaliamman Temple** (Ⓦwww .sriveeramakaliamman.com), dedicated to the Hindu goddess, Kali. Worshippers ring the bells hanging on the temple doors as they enter, in the hope that their prayers will be answered. Inside, the *mandapam*, or worship hall, holds a ferocious image of Kali, the goddess of power and incarnation of Lord Shiva's wife. Flanking her are her sons, Ganesh (left) and Murugan (right).

Hastings Road to Cuff Road

Across Serangoon Road from the Tekka Market is the **Little India Arcade**, a lovingly restored block of shophouses bounded by Hastings Road and Campbell Lane. It's a sort of Little India in microcosm: behind pastel-coloured walls and green shutters you can purchase textiles and tapestries, bangles, religious statuary, Indian sweets, tapes and CDs, and even traditional ayurvedic herbal medicines.

Exiting the arcade onto **Campbell Lane** brings you opposite the riot of colours of the Jothi flower shop, where staff thread jasmine, roses and marigolds into garlands, or *jothi*, for prayer offerings. The next street along, **Dunlop Street**, has become something of a backpacker enclave in the past few years, but it remains defined by beautiful **Abdul Gaffoor Mosque** at no. 41 (daily 8.30am–noon & 2.30–4pm), whose green dome and bristling minarets have enjoyed a comprehensive and sympathetic renovation in the last few years. Set amid gardens of palms and bougainvillea and within cream walls decorated with stars and crescent moons, the mosque features an unusual sundial whose face is ringed by elaborate Arabic script denoting the names of 25 Islamic prophets. Renovated shophouses to the left of the mosque as you enter the grounds have been converted into a madrasah, or Islamic school. One more street along are **Dickson Road** and, back towards Serangoon Road, **Upper Dickson Road** where a shop at no. 15 sells cooling *kulfi*, Indian ice cream. Next along is **Cuff Road**, where a traditional spice grinder can still be seen at no. 2.

Rowell and Desker roads

It might seem odd to spend any time at all on two roads long synonymous in Singapore with **vice**, but there's something about the openness of goings-on on Rowell and Desker roads that seems almost radical on this straitlaced island. Between the two roads, running along the backs of two rows of shophouses, is an alleyway punctuated by open doorways which are illuminated at night by pink-tinted fluorescent lighting. Here gaggles of bored-looking prostitutes sitting around inside watching TV, seemingly oblivious to the men – usually poor migrant labourers – gathered outside, often not so much to gawp as simply to observe as though it's all a kind of free entertainment. Occasionally someone finds the courage and the funds to step out from the crowd and venture in, whereupon the madam might shut the door for a while. This being Singapore, there's nothing edgy or threatening about any of this, though women visitors will probably want to give it a wide berth. Even if you give it a miss, it's hard not to notice the few dodgy-looking massage parlours that have sprung up all over Little India.

Backing onto the alley and a totally different proposition is **Post-Museum**, a proudly independent experimental art space at 109 Rowell Rd (ⓦwww .post-museum.org), complete with a great vegetarian café (see p.665).

Syed Alwi Road to Petain Road

Syed Alwi Road, the next side street along from Desker Road, is notable for being the hub of the shopping phenomenon that is **Mustafa**, an agglomeration of department store, moneychanger, travel agent, jeweller and supermarket, much of it actually open 24/7. The business started modestly and somehow carried on growing till it became the behemoth that it is today, occupying two interlinked buildings of its own as well as part of the Serangoon Plaza at the junction of Serangoon and Syed Alwi roads. Visit and you'll probably find it more appealing than most places on Orchard Road as you rub shoulders with Indian families seeking airflown confectionery from Delhi, and Chinese and Malay shoppers wanting durians, luggage or pots and pans.

One street to the north is Sam Leong road, home to some surviving **Peranakan shophouses** decorated with depictions of stags, lotuses and egrets. There's more Peranakan architecture a few blocks north on **Petain Road**, where the shophouses have elegant ceramic tiles reminiscent of Portuguese *azulejos*, and on **Jalan Besar** – turn left into it near the southern end of Petain Road.

North of Rangoon Road

Little India more or less comes to an end at Rangoon and Kitchener roads, close to Farrer Park MRT, but it's worth heading on up Serangoon Road to see two very different temples. At 397 Serangoon Rd, the **Sri Srinivasa Perumal Temple** has an attractive five-tiered *gopuram* with sculptures of the various manifestations of Lord Vishnu the preserver. On the wall to the right of the front gate, a sculpted elephant, its leg caught in a crocodile's mouth, trumpets silently. But the temple's main claim to fame is that it is the starting point for the annual Thaipusam festival in late January, at which time the temple courtyard witnesses a gruesome melee as Hindu devotees don huge metal frames (*kavadi*) which are fastened to their flesh with hooks and prongs. The devotees leave the temple in procession, pausing only while a coconut is smashed at their feet for good luck, and parade all the way to the Chettiar Temple on Tank Road (see p.614).

Just beyond the Sri Srinivasa Temple complex, a small path leads northwest to Race Course Road where the **Sakaya Muni Buddha Gaya Temple** (also called the Temple of the Thousand Lights; daily 8am–4.45pm) sits at no. 366. The temple betrays a strong Thai influence – which isn't surprising as it was built by a Thai monk, Vutthisasala. On the left as you enter is a massive replica of Buddha's footprint, inlaid with mother-of-pearl; beyond sits a huge Buddha ringed by the thousand electric lights from which the temple takes its alternative name, while 25 scenes from the Buddha's life decorate the pedestal on which he sits. It is possible to walk inside the Buddha, through a door in his back; inside is a smaller Buddha, reclining. The left wall of the temple features a sort of wheel of fortune – to discover your fortune, spin it (for a small donation) and take the sheet of paper bearing the number corresponding to that at which the wheel stops.

Arab Street and around

Before the arrival of Raffles, the area of Singapore south of the Rochor River (see map, p.632) housed a Malay village known as Kampong Glam, after the Gelam tribe of sea gypsies who lived there. After signing a dubious treaty with the newly installed "Sultan" Hussein Mohammed Shah (see p.585), Raffles allotted the area to him and designated the land around it as a Muslim settlement. Soon the zone was attracting Malays, Sumatrans and Javanese, as well as Hadhrami Arab traders from the region of Arabia that is now eastern Yemen, as the road names in the area today – **Arab Street**, Baghdad Street, Bali Lane and so on – suggest. Today Singapore's Arab community, comprising the descendants of those Yemeni traders, is thought to number around 15,000, though they don't stand out visually or geographically, having intermarried with the rest of Singapore society and being resident in no particular area.

Like Little India, the Arab Street district remains one of the most atmospheric pockets of old Singapore, its lanes home to many a bright, refurbished shophouse; the golden-domed **Sultan Mosque**; the **Istana Kampong Glam**, now a Malay heritage museum; and plenty of great curry houses and Arabic restaurants (see p.666). It couldn't be easier to get here, with Bugis MRT just a stone's throw away.

Arab Street, Haji Lane and Bali Lane

While Little India is memorable for its fragrances, it's the vibrant colours of the shops of **Arab Street** and its environs that stick in the memory. Textile and carpet stores are most prominent, but you'll also see leather, basketware, gold, gemstones and jewellery for sale; the pavements of Arab Street in particular are an obstacle course of merchandise. Most of the shops here have been modernized, though one or two (like Bamadhaj Brothers at no. 97 and Aik Bee at no. 69) still retain their original dark wood and glass cabinets, and wide wooden benches where the shopkeepers sit. There's also a good range of basketware and rattan work – fans, hats and walking sticks – at Rishi Handicrafts, at no. 58. It's easy to spend a couple of hours weaving in and out of the stores, but you won't always enjoy a quiet browse; some traders are masters of persuasion and will have you loaded with sarongs and whatnot before you know it.

South of Arab Street, **Haji Lane** and tiny **Bali Lane** have both seen a fair amount of gentrification in recent years and now have a distinctly alternative feel in places, their restored shophouses home to several trendy boutiques and, on Bali Lane, the excellent *Blu Jaz Café* (see p.666).

Sultan Mosque

Along the eastern side of North Bridge Road (though the best initial views of its golden domes are from palm-tree-lined, pedestrianized Bussorah Street to the east) is the **Sultan Mosque** or Masjid Sultan (Mon–Sat 9am–4pm outside prayer times, Fri closed 11.30am–2.30pm), the beating heart of the Muslim faith in Singapore. An earlier mosque stood on this site, finished in 1825 and constructed with the help of a S$3000 donation from the East India Company. The present building was completed a century later to a design by colonial architects Swan and MacLaren. Steps at the top of Bussorah Street lead past

▲ Sultan Mosque

papaya and palm trees into a wide lobby, where a digital display lists current prayer times. Beyond, and out of bounds to non-Muslims, is the main prayer hall, a large, bare chamber fronted by two more digital clocks which enable the faithful to time their prayers to the exact second.

During the Muslim fasting month of **Ramadan**, neighbouring **Kandahar Street** is awash with stalls of the Ramadan bazaar from 2pm onwards, selling *biriyani*, *murtabak*, dates and cakes for consumption by the faithful after dusk. South of the mosque, **Bussorah Street** is now home to some smart restaurants and worthwhile souvenir outlets.

Istana Kampong Glam

Squatting between Kandahar and Aliwal streets, the **Istana Kampong Glam** was built as the royal palace of Sultan Ali Iskandar Shah, son of Sultan Hussein who negotiated with Raffles to hand over Singapore to the British. The sultan's descendants lived here until just a few years ago when it was transformed from a tumbledown colonial-era building, thought to have been the handiwork of George Drumgould Coleman, into the over-smart **Malay Heritage Centre** (Mon 1–6.30pm, Tues–Sun 10am–6.30pm; ⓦwww.malayheritage.org.sg). Its mainstay is a museum (S$4) spanning maps, model boats, cannon, ceremonial drums and daggers from around the Malay archipelago. The most engaging exhibits are upstairs, where touchscreens cast light on Malay community life in the prewar years, and where you can peek inside a mock-up of a kampung house. The centre also puts on occasional cultural shows and has its own **art workshops** where courses in pottery and batik design are taught by leading local practitioners; you can pop in and have a look around if they're not busy.

North of Sultan Mosque

The stretch of **North Bridge Road** around the Sultan Mosque has, not entirely surprisingly, a conservative feel. Here, men sport Abe Lincoln beards, and the women fantastically colourful shawls and robes, while some shops are geared more towards locals than tourists: Kazura Aromatics at no. 705, for instance, sells alcohol-free perfumes, while neighbouring stores stock prayer beads, the *songkok* hats worn by Malay men, *miswak* sticks – twigs the width of a finger used to clean teeth – and even swimwear for Muslim women.

A little way east of the mosque is Jalan Kubor (Grave Street), leading north off North Bridge Road and across Victoria Street to an unkempt Muslim **cemetery** where, it is said, Malay royalty are buried. A block northeast of here, at the junction of Kallang Road and Jalan Sultan, stands the attractive blue **Malabar Mosque** topped with its own golden domes – a little cousin of the Sultan Mosque.

Along Beach Road

The **Hajjah Fatimah Mosque** on **Beach Road**, a few minutes' walk east from Arab Street, is named after a wealthy businesswoman from Melaka who amassed a fortune through her mercantile vessels, and whose family home formerly stood here. She moved elsewhere after two break-ins and an arson attack on her home, then underwrote the construction of a mosque on the site, finished in 1846. The minaret, looking strangely like a church steeple (perhaps because its architect was European), has a six-degree slant – locals call it Singapore's Leaning Tower of Pisa. Across from the mosque, the modern **Golden Mile Complex** at 5001 Beach Rd is a major social focus for Singapore's Thai community; bus journeys to Thailand begin here, and shops inside sell Thai foodstuffs and Singha beer.

It's worth taking the time to head southwest along Beach Road from here to see the two logic-defying office buildings that together comprise **The Gateway**. Designed by I.M. Pei, they rise magnificently into the air like vast razor blades, appearing two-dimensional from certain angles. When the huge, Gotham-esque tower of **Parkview Square** was built across on North Bridge Road, much care was taken to site it dead between The Gateway's sharp points for *feng shui* considerations. To be on the safe side its developers placed four giant figures carrying good-luck pearls along the top of the tower. Elsewhere on Beach Road, you'll still find a few shops – ships' chandlers and fishing-tackle specialists – betraying its former proximity to the sea.

Marina Centre

Marina Centre (see map, p.606) is the name generally applied to the large tract of reclaimed land east of the Padang and the *Raffles* hotel, forming the northern arc of Marina Bay and robbing Beach Road of its beach. The area still has a somewhat artificial feel, boasting no residential areas or traditional places of worship, and is instead dominated by malls, conference centres and expensive offices and hotels. Visitors who come here mostly do so to enjoy views of the Singapore cityscape from either the southern end of Marina Centre or the Singapore Flyer – or both. You can easily walk here from City Hall MRT via the subterranean CityLink Mall, and when the Circle Line opens it will be possible to use Esplanade and Promenade stations as well.

Esplanade – Theatres on the Bay

Singapore's skyline changes almost by the day, but rarely has a building here caused such ripples as the **Esplanade – Theatres on the Bay** project (Ⓦwww .esplanade.com), just east of the Padang. Opinion is split on whether the two huge, spiked shells that roof the complex are peerless modernistic architecture or indulgent kitsch. They have variously been compared to kitchen sieves, hedgehogs, even durians (the preferred description among locals), though they are perhaps best likened to two giant insect eyes.

Opened in 2002, Esplanade boasts a concert hall, theatres, a recital studio, gallery space and, on the third floor, **library@esplanade**, a performing arts library with a wide range of arts-related resources. It's possible to take a self-guided **iTour** of the building (daily 10am–6pm; S$10) based around audiovisual content stored on a handheld gizmo, but what lures most casual visitors are the excellent **views** across the bay to the Financial District from the south side of the complex, which has the additional attraction of being packed with restaurants and bars.

▲ Esplanade – Theatres on the Bay

The Singapore Flyer

Some ten minutes' walk east of the Theatres on the Bay, the **Singapore Flyer** (Ⓦwww.singaporeflyer.com) stands a lofty 165m tall – the same as the summit of Bukit Timah, the island's highest point, and about 30m taller than the London Eye. While not lacking in altitude, the Flyer does fall slightly flat as a tourist attraction because of its location at the southeastern end of Marina Centre. From here the most atmospheric areas of old Singapore, including the remaining rows of shophouses in Chinatown and Little India, are largely obscured by a forest of jagged and somewhat interchangeable towers; better views can be had from various high-rise hotels. If you do shell out for the half-hour "flight" (daily 8.30am–10pm; every 30min; S$29.50), you'll be photographed individually on the way in – not apparently for security reasons but so that when you leave, you can buy prints of yourself looking expectant on the way in.

The flight initially has you looking east over the **Kallang** district, where Singapore's grand new Sports Hub stadium complex is due to be completed in 2012. Also visible is the golf course of mundane **Marina East**, the lobe of land east of Marina Bay, south of which lies the narrow **barrage** allowing the bay to be used as a reservoir. In the distance beyond the shipping lanes is Indonesia's **Riau archipelago**, so close and yet somehow in a different realm, thanks to the 1824 Anglo-Dutch treaty under which the British let the islands south of Singapore slip into the Dutch sphere of influence. Looking north, it's much more exciting to pick out the golden domes of the Sultan Mosque and the shophouses of **Arab Street** beyond the twin **Gateway** buildings on Beach Road. As your capsule reaches maximum height, you might just make out the low hump of **Bukit Timah**, topped with a couple of radio masts, on the horizon beyond Theatres on the Bay.

The descent affords great views of **Marina South** (see p.630) and the **Financial District**. Originally the latter could be seen on the ascent, but *feng shui* concerns ensured the wheel's direction of rotation had to be reversed (apparently having the capsules ascend pointing towards the banks' towers was channelling good luck up and away from the area). The floating rectangle you see close by on the north side of the bay is a sports ground, large enough for soccer matches.

Orchard Road and around

It would be hard to conjure an image more at odds with the present reality of **Orchard Road** than C.M. Turnbull's depiction, during early colonial times, of "a country lane lined with bamboo hedges and shrubbery, with trees meeting overhead". In the early part of the last century, merchants here for their daily constitutionals would have strolled past rows of nutmeg trees, followed at a discreet distance by their manservants. Today, Orchard Road is synonymous with **shopping** – huge, often glitzy malls selling everything you can imagine line the road (for a list of the best, see p.679). But with malls all over downtown and in every new town on the island, Orchard Road has not been totally untouched by the malaise afflicting other city-centre shopping areas the world over. Perhaps with this in mind, Singapore's planners have put Orchard Road through a costly makeover in recent years, revamping walkways and adding two lavish new malls – the larger of which, **Ion Orchard**, is located right above Orchard MRT and vaguely resembles a smaller version of Theatres on the Bay, with a soaring tower block of luxury apartments behind. If you're not staying in one of the area's sleek hotels or into shopping, the main reason to come here

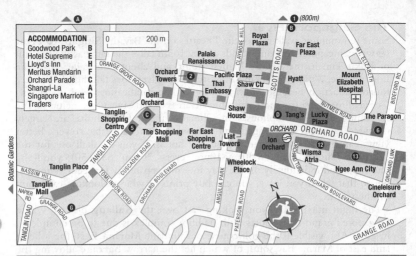

ACCOMMODATION
Goodwood Park	B
Hotel Supreme	E
Lloyd's Inn	H
Meritus Mandarin	F
Orchard Parade	C
Shangri-La	A
Singapore Marriott	D
Traders	G

EATING, DRINKING & NIGHTLIFE
Akashi	5	Crystal Jade La Mian Xiao Long Bao	13	Howl At The Moon	10
Bar None	D	The Dubliner	14	Ice Cold Beer	8
Breeks! Café	13	Food Republic	12	Lao Beijing	7
Cafe l'Espresso	B	Harry's Bar	2	Magic of Chongqing Hotpot	5

is to partake of a good selection of restaurants and bars (see p.667 & p.673) – though again, many of these have branches elsewhere in town.

Orchard Road begins as the continuation of Tanglin Road and channels traffic east for nearly 3km to Bras Basah and Selegie roads, near the Colonial District. The bucolic allure of the Orchard Road of old survives 1500m west of the start of the road, for it's here that you'll find Singapore's excellent **Botanic Gardens**.

Dhoby Ghaut to the Istana

In the **Dhoby Ghaut** area, at the eastern end of Orchard Road, Indian *dhobies* (laundrymen) used to wash clothes in the Stamford Canal, which once ran along Orchard and Stamford roads. Those days are long gone, though something of the past survives in the **Cathay Building** (ⓦ www.cathay.org.sg), home to the company behind one of Singapore's and Malaysia's oldest cinema chains. The building's 1939 Art Deco facade looks better than ever today after a three-year remodelling which, unusually, saw the original tower behind torn down and replaced by a *smaller* complex. It houses a multiplex cinema, a shopping mall and, on level 2, the **Cathay Gallery** (Mon–Sat noon–8pm; free), offering another window into the past by displaying memorabilia of the Cathay Organization's eight decades in the movie business, including the nostagic 1950s and 1960s, when the company made its own Chinese- and Malay-language films.

A three-minute walk west along Orchard Road from Dhoby Ghaut MRT takes you past the **Plaza Singapura** mall, beyond which stern-looking soldiers guard the main gate of Singapore's **Istana**, built in 1869. With ornate cornices, elegant louvred shutters and a high mansard roof, the building was originally the official residence of Singapore's British governors; now it is the residence of Singapore's president, a ceremonial role though also one which for elections are contested. The first Sunday of the month sees a **changing of the guard**

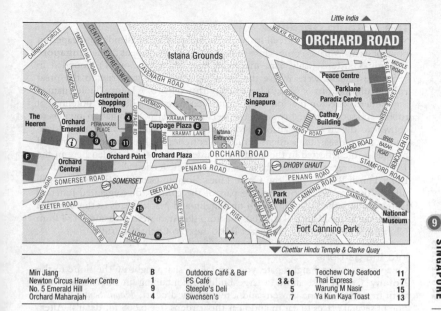

Min Jiang	B	Outdoors Café & Bar	10	Teochew City Seafood	11
Newton Circus Hawker Centre	1	PS Café	3 & 6	Thai Express	7
No. 5 Emerald Hill	9	Steeple's Deli	5	Warung M Nasir	15
Orchard Maharajah	4	Swensen's	7	Ya Kun Kaya Toast	13

ceremony take place at the main gate at 5.45pm, but the istana and grounds are only open to visitors five days a year (details on Ⓦ www.istana.gov.sg; S$1).

Emerald Hill

Not ten minutes' walk west of the istana, a number of architecturally notable houses have survived the bulldozers at **Emerald Hill**, behind the Centrepoint mall. The hill was granted to Englishman William Cuppage in 1845 and for some years afterwards was the site of a large nutmeg plantation. After his death in 1872, the land was subdivided and sold off, much of it to members of the Peranakan community. Walk up Emerald Hill Road today and you'll see a number of exquisite houses dating from this period in the so-called Chinese Baroque style, typified by the use of coloured ceramic tiles, carved swing doors, shuttered windows and pastel-shaded walls with fine plaster mouldings. Unsurprisingly, quite a few of these houses now host trendy restaurants and bars, with a few more to be found in a less distinguished row of restored shophouses called **Cuppage Terrace**, on the east side of the Centrepoint mall.

The Goodwood Park Hotel

A few minutes' walk north up Scotts Road from Orchard MRT brings you to the impressive **Goodwood Park Hotel**, with gleaming walls and a distinctive squat, steeple-like tower. The hotel started life in 1900 as the Teutonia Club for German expats, but with the outbreak of war across Europe in 1914, it was commandeered by the British Custodian of Enemy Property and didn't open again until 1918, after which it served for several years as a function hall. In 1929, it became a hotel, though by 1942 it and the *Raffles*, which incidentally was designed by the same architect, were lodging Japanese officers; fittingly, the *Goodwood Park* was later used for war-crimes trials. Today the hotel remains one of the classiest in town and is a well-regarded venue for a British-style tea.

The Botanic Gardens

Singapore has long made green space an integral part of the island's landscape, but none of its many parks comes close to matching the refinement of the **Singapore Botanic Gardens** (daily 5am–midnight; free; ⓦwww.sbg.org.sg). Founded in 1859, the gardens were where the Brazilian seeds that gave rise to the great **rubber plantations** of Malaya were first nurtured in 1877. Henry Ridley, named the gardens' director the following year, recognized the financial potential of rubber and spent the next twenty years persuading Malayan plantation-owners to convert to this new crop, an obsession which earned him the nickname "Mad" Ridley. In later years the gardens became a centre for the breeding of new **orchid** hybrids, a role reflected in the creation of a dedicated orchid garden here in the 1990s. More recent additions have seen the park extended all the way north to Bukit Timah Road, where the Circle Line's Botanic Gardens MRT station will offer a route to the least interesting part of the gardens; the suggested itinerary below assumes the classic approach up Tanglin and Napier roads to the **Tanglin gate** at the start of Cluny Road (bus #7 from the Arab Street area and #174 from Chinatown come here via Somerset Road, next to Orchard Road).

Into the gardens

Once through the Tanglin gate, you can take a sharp right up the slope to the **Botany Centre** just ahead, a large building containing an information desk with free **maps** of the gardens and a terrific food court, *Taman Serasi*; it's only one of several places to eat in and near the gardens (see p.668 for details). Alternatively, continue straight down the path from the gate, lined with frangipanis, casuarinas and the odd majestic banyan tree, for five minutes to reach the tranquil main **lake**, which is nearly as old as the gardens themselves. At the lake's far end is a small tract of surviving **rainforest**. Paths run through it to the **ginger garden**, packed with flowering gingers as exotic and gaudy as anything you could hope to see in the tropics, and home to the fine *Halia* restaurant.

▲ Bandstand, Botanic Gardens

The gingers are outdone only by the feast of blooms of almost every hue at the **National Orchid Garden** a little further on (daily 8.30am–7pm, last admission at 6pm; S$5). Most orchids anchor themselves on trees in the wild, so it's initially odd to see them thriving here at ground level in specially adapted beds, all the better for photographing. There's an entire section of orchids named after visiting dignitaries and celebrities; *Dendrobium Margaret Thatcher* turns out to be a severe pink with two of its petals looking like twisted ribbons, while *Vandaenopsis Nelson Mandela* is a reassuring warm yellowy-brown. In the attached gift shop you can buy orchids encased in glass paperweights or plated with 24-carat gold (or even silvery rhodium for extra snob value).

Back to Tanglin gate
By now you've seen the best of what the gardens have to offer, and there's not that much to be gained by continuing north. An alternative route back from the orchid garden involves proceeding up the Maranta Avenue path to one of the most stunning trees in the park, a 47-metre *jelawai*; this and several other exceptionally tall trees are actually fitted with lightning conductors. Close by, to the right, is one of the loveliest spots in the gardens, a grassy area with a gazebo-like 1930s **bandstand** in the middle, and encircled by eighteen rain trees for shade. From here you can either go straight on to arrive eventually at the Botany Centre, or head downhill through the **sundial garden** to end up back at the lake.

North to Bukit Timah Road
Exiting the orchid garden, head up the boardwalk to enter a second patch of **rainforest** with a trail past numbered highlights, including a spectacular banyan tree (#8) which is just a mass of aerial roots. The trail and forest end above **Symphony Lake**, to one side of which is an impressive colonial-era house with more than a hint of mock Tudor about it; the gardens' assistant director would once have lived here. Nearby, marooned in the middle of the gardens, is the **Visitor Centre** with its own gift shop and café. Next comes the rather dreary **Evolution Garden**, where cycads and fake petrified trees are part of an illustration of how plant life has evolved over the millennia. From here, it's several minutes' walk, skirting the back of the National University of Singapore's Bukit Timah campus, to the mundane **Eco Garden** dominating the northern end of the park, with the new MRT station to the left. To reach the main road, head generally right (northeast) past the enclosed **Jacob Ballas Children's Garden**, containing a water play area (kids will need swimming gear and buckets), treehouse and maze; beyond is Bukit Timah Road, where you can cross to **Dunearn Road** on the far side of the canal to catch bus #66 or #170 to Little India or #171 to Orchard Road.

The central nature reserve

For a taste of Singapore's wilder side, the **Central Catchment Nature Reserve** – to give it its formal title – is not a bad place to head. A glance at the map shows that the centre of the island is indeed dominated by **rainforest** and several **reservoirs**; here there are opportunities for **hikes** up **Bukit Timah**, the island's tallest hill, or around **MacRitchie reservoir**. The interest isn't limited to the jungle though: close to Bukit Timah is **Memories at Old Ford Factory**, a museum housed in the building where the British surrendered to the Japanese during World War II; while at the northern end of the nature reserve are Singapore's highly regarded **zoo**, with a separate **Night Safari** section open from dusk, and the **Mandai Orchid Gardens**.

Bukit Timah

Bukit Timah Road shoots northwest from Little India, passing some of the island's leafiest suburbs en route to Johor Bahru (it was the main road to the Causeway until superseded by the Bukit Timah Expressway). Some 9km on from Little India, the road becomes Upper Bukit Timah Road and arrives at **Bukit Timah** itself, often called "Bukit Timah Hill" by locals – a deliberate tautology as the surrounding district is also known as Bukit Timah. Blanketing the hill is one of Singapore's last pockets of primary rainforest, comprising the excellent **Bukit Timah Nature Reserve** (daily 6.30am–7.30pm; free), established in 1883 by Nathaniel Cantley, then superintendent of the Botanic Gardens. **Bus #171** passes along Somerset and Scotts roads en route to the reserve, while #170 heads here from Little India MRT; ask to be let off opposite Bukit Timah Shopping Centre, then walk on to the Courts furniture store. Here an overhead footbridge takes you across to **Hindhede Road**, which leads under the KTM railway bridge to the foot of the hill and the **Visitor Centre** (daily 6am–7pm; ☎1800/468 5736), offering **maps** of the reserve (also downloadable from the "nature reserves" section of Ⓦ www.nparks.gov.sg) and displays on forest ecology.

Wildlife abounded in this part of Singapore in the mid-nineteenth century, when the natural historian Alfred Russel Wallace did field work here; he later observed that "in all my subsequent travels in the East I rarely if ever met with so productive a spot". Wallace also noted the presence of tiger traps here, but by the 1930s the tiger had met its end in Singapore (the Visitor Centre displays a photo of the last specimen to be shot on the island). **Long-tailed macaques** haven't dwindled away though – in fact you'll see hordes of them, some even wandering around the houses off Hindhede Road looking in bins for discarded food. Otherwise, what really impresses is the rainforest itself, with its towering **emergents** – trees that have reached the top of the jungle canopy as a result of a lucky break, a fallen tree allowing enough light through to the forest floor to nurture saplings to maturity.

Four colour-coded **trails** head up the hill from the Visitor Centre, all requiring only a moderate level of fitness, though note that three share a very steep start up a metalled road (the exception, the green trail, meanders along the side of the hill before rejoining the others). Most people tackle the red trail (30min), which heads fairly directly to the summit at a paltry 164m, with a flight of narrow steps halfway along – the Summit Path – offering a shortcut to the top. There are also **cycle trails** which circuit the reserve, though the nearest bike rental outfit, Bikehaus (☎6468 3908, Ⓦ www.bikehaus.com.sg), is nearly 5km away at 553 Bukit Timah Rd, just after the junction with Farrer Road; they charge S$35 to rent a mountain bike for the day.

A great place for **refreshments** after your exertions is *Al-Ameen*, serving *murtabak*, *roti prata* and other local favourites; if you arrived by bus, you'll spot it in the row of shophouses where the bus dropped you. For buses back to town, turn left out of Hindhede Road, head past the church and continue uphill to the bus stop.

Memories at Old Ford Factory

Nearly 1500m further up from Hindhede Road at 351 Upper Bukit Timah Rd is the old Ford car factory, which was the first plant of its type in

Southeast Asia when it opened in October 1941. But by February 1942 the Japanese had shown up, and on February 15 Lt Gen Percival, head of the Allied forces in Singapore, surrendered to Japan's General Yamashita in the factory's board room. Today the Art Deco building houses a little wartime museum, **Memories at Old Ford Factory** (Mon–Fri 9am–5.30pm, Sat 9am–1.30pm; S\$3, or S\$4 for a joint ticket with Reflections at Bukit Chandu – see p.652; Ⓦwww.s1942.org.sg), making good use of military artefacts, period newspapers and oral history recordings. The site is on the left (west) side of the road just after the Hillside apartment complex, and can be reached on bus #170 or #171.

While the surrenders that bookended the Japanese occupation obviously get some attention, as does the life of British POWs (covered in detail at Changi Museum; see p.650), it's with its coverage of the **civilian experience** of the war that the museum really scores. Predictably, the occupiers mounted cultural indoctrination campaigns, and displays recall how locals were urged to celebrate Japanese imperial birthdays, and how Japanese shows were put on at Victoria Memorial Hall. This was not a benign intellectual sort of occupation, however. Stung by local Chinese efforts to raise funds for China's defence against Japan, the Japanese launched **Sook Ching**, a brutal purge of thousands (the exact number is unknown) of Singapore Chinese thought to hold anti-Japanese sentiment. These violent events are illustrated by, among other items, some moving sketches by Chia Chew Soo, who witnessed members of his own family being killed in 1942. Not least among the privations of occupation were **food shortages**, as recalled by displays on wartime crops – speak to any Singaporean above a certain age today, and chances are they can tell you of having to survive on stuff like tapioca during those dark years.

The MacRitchie Trails

East of Bukit Timah, the shoreline and environs of MacRitchie Reservoir play host to the **MacRitchie Trails** (daily 6.30am–7.30pm; free), a network of colour-coded tracks and boardwalks. Traversing lush forest and skirting the reservoir's waters, the trails offer the chance to see macaques, monitor lizards, terrapins, squirrels, eagles and kingfishers in the wild. There's also the **HSBC TreeTop Walk** (Tues–Fri 9am–5pm, Sat & Sun 8.30am–5pm; free), a 250-metre-long suspension bridge that gives you a monkey's-eye view of the forest canopy. As long as there are no noisy school parties bustling across it, you've a pretty good chance of spotting birdlife.

The trails mostly start at MacRitchie Reservoir Park, just south of the reservoir, where there are toilets, a café and information boards; you can get here on **bus** #132 from Scotts Road or #166 from Clarke Quay, Little India or Novena MRT stations. The TreeTop Walk is tucked away in the far north of the area, however, a 2.5-kilometre trek from Upper Thomson Road (also served by bus #132 and #166; ask to be left at the Island Club turning) via Venus Drive and Island Club Road. On the second Sunday of the month, there's a free **nature appreciation walk** that starts from the head of the Prunus Trail in the reservoir park at 9.30am (booking required on Ⓣ6554 5127).

The zoo and the Mandai Orchid Garden

Both the **Singapore Zoo** (daily 8.30am–6pm; S\$18, or S\$30 with Night Safari or BirdPark, or S\$40 with Night Safari and BirdPark; Ⓦwww.zoo.com.sg) and its **Night Safari** offshoot (daily 7.30pm–midnight, with shops/restaurants from 6pm and last admission at 11pm; S\$22; Ⓦwww.nightsafari.com.sg) have an "open" philosophy, preferring to confine animals in naturalistic enclosures behind moats, though creatures such as big cats still have to be caged. Both parts of the zoo are on a promontory jutting into peaceful Seletar Reservoir, reached via Mandai Road and then Mandai Lake Road, off the Bukit Timah Expressway; **bus** #138 comes here from Ang Mo Kio MRT, while #927 heads here from Woodlands Road (site of the Kranji War Memorial; see opposite), which is served by #170 from downtown. There's also a privately run service from BusHub (☎6753 0506, ⓦwww.bushub.com.sg; S$4), which, if you can't be bothered with regular buses, is most useful for its departures from the Night Safari back to town (every 30min 9.30–11.30pm), though they also have one morning and one evening service to the zoo from downtown.

The zoo could easily occupy you for half a day if not longer. A **tram** (S$5) does a one-way circuit of the grounds, but as it won't always be going your way, be prepared for a lot of legwork. Highlights include orang-utans, komodo dragons, polar bears (which you view underwater from a gallery), and the **Fragile Forest** biodome, a magical zone where you can actually walk among ring-tailed lemurs, tree kangeroos, sloths and fruit bats. Also worth seeing are the **white tigers**, which aren't white but resemble Siamese cats in the colour of their hair and eyes, and the **Primate Kingdom**, packed with unusual monkeys such as red-ruffed lemurs. Various **animal shows** and **feeding shows** run throughout the day, including the excellent Splash Safari, featuring penguins, sea lions and manatees. There are also elephant (S$8) and pony (S$6) rides, and at 9am daily, the **Jungle Breakfast – with Wildlife** programme affords you the privilege of having your first meal of the day in the company of some of the zoo's orang-utans (S$29).

The Night Safari

Many animals are nocturnal, so why not run a nighttime zoo? The Night Safari section of the zoo addresses this simple question so competently that you wonder why similar establishments aren't more common. The Borneo-style tribal show at the entrance is admittedly somewhat tacky, and there can be lengthy queues for the **trams** (45min; S$10), but these are just niggles. It's enjoyable to forgo the tram rides altogether and simply walk around the leafy grounds, an atmospheric experience in the muted lighting, but the paths allow you to see only about a third of the enclosures. From the tram, you'll additionally see large mammals like elephants, hippos and the Greater Asian rhino.

For those who walk it, the obvious first port of call is the so-called Bridge of Suspense, a slightly rickety affair reached on the short **Forest Giants Trail** through actual rainforest, starting at the tram departure point. Close by on the far side of the bridge is the **Malayan tiger** enclosure, one of the most exciting and yet sad experiences here, given that the population of these creatures has sunk so low there's virtually no chance of seeing any from a hide in Taman Negara. From here you continue past spotted hyenas, bat-eared foxes and eventually zebras, then turn back to explore the **Leopard Trail**, where your eyes may strain to spot the clouded leopard and the slow loris. The path now heads back towards the entrance, passing the **Fishing Cat Trail**, where highlights include the Indian gharial – a kind of crocodile, disarmingly log-like in the water – and the *binturong*, sometimes called the bearcat (you'll understand why when you see it).

Mandai Orchid Garden

It's only a ten-minute walk from the zoo back up Mandai Lake Road to the **Mandai Orchid Garden** (daily 8am–7pm except Mon till 6pm; S$3.50;

@www.mandai.com.sg), or you can take the #138 bus. A colourful detour, the site boasts several gardens packed with not only orchids but also other tropical plants and fruit trees, plus areas where you can view orchids being grown commercially. There's a shop where you can buy orchid bouquets and sprays.

Kranji War Memorial and Sungai Buloh

While land reclamation has radically altered the east coast and industrialization the west, the **northern** expanses of the island up to the Straits of Johor still retain pockets of the **rainforest** and mangrove swamp which blanketed Singapore on Raffles' arrival in 1819. Though thickets of state housing blocks are never far away, something of Singapore's agricultural past also clings on tenaciously here by way of the odd prawn or poultry farm, or vegetable garden.

For visitors, there are two attractions worth considering coming this far from town to see. One of these, in the **Kranji** area, dominated by a reservoir, is the **Kranji War Cemetery and Memorial** (daily 7am–6pm; free), the resting place of the many Allied troops who died in the defence of Singapore. The cemetery is on Woodlands Road, a ten-minute walk west and south from Kranji MRT station; you can be dropped right outside if you arrive from downtown on bus #170, or from the zoo on bus #927. If you're heading here by taxi and the driver doesn't know the way, try mentioning the adjacent Turf Club.

As you enter the cemetery, row upon row of graves slope up the landscaped hill in front of you, some identified only as "known unto God". Above the simple stone cross which stands over the cemetery is the **memorial**, around which are recorded the names of more than twenty thousand soldiers (including personnel from Britain, Canada, Australia, New Zealand, Malaya and South Asia) who died in this region during World War II. Two unassuming **tombs** stand on the wide lawns below the cemetery, belonging to Yusof bin Ishak and Dr B.H. Sheares, independent Singapore's first two presidents.

Sungai Buloh Wetland Reserve

The other tourist draw on the far northern fringes of Singapore is the **Sungai Buloh Wetland Reserve** (daily 7.30am–7pm, Sun from 7am; Sat & Sun S$1, otherwise free; @www.sbwr.org.sg), the island's only wetland nature park, on the coast 4km northwest of the cemetery. Beyond its Visitor Centre, café and video theatre (shows Mon–Sat 9am, 11am, 1pm, 3pm & 5pm, Sun hourly 9am–5pm) are trails and walkways through and over an expanse of mangrove, mudflats and grassland, home to kingfishers, herons, sandpipers, kites and sea eagles and, in the waters, archerfish – which squirt water into the air to knock insects into devouring range. Between September and March, you may catch sight of migratory birds from around Asia roosting and feeding, especially in the early morning.

The five-hundred-metre **mangrove boardwalk** offers an easy means of getting a sense of the shoreline environment, and tortoises, crabs and mudskippers can often be seen. From here you can graduate to walks ranging from three to seven kilometres into the guts of the reserve. Time your visit right on a Saturday and you can join a free **guided tour** of the mangrove boardwalk or one of the trails (9.30am & 3.30pm).

To reach the park, take the MRT to Kranji station, then transfer to **bus** #925, which will take you right to the park on Sundays and public holidays. On other days it's easier to use the special **Kranji Express** bus service from Kranji MRT, which leaves every 90 minutes between 9am and 4.30pm for the fifteen-minute ride to the reserve (S$2); otherwise you can ride bus #925 as far as Kranji Reservoir car park, then walk a short distance west along Kranji Way and turn right into Neo Tiew Road for the reserve entrance.

Geylang and Katong

Malay culture has held sway in and around the eastern suburbs of Geylang and Katong since the mid-nineteenth century, when Malays and Indonesians first arrived to work in the local *copra* (dried coconut kernel) processing factory and later on its *serai* (lemon grass) farms. **Geylang** retains quite a strong Malay feel today, and the shops, markets and restaurants are worth checking out for Malay fare or merchandise, though there are no specific sights. **Katong**, on the other hand, has been through rather more of a transformation. In prewar times, the wealthy, including many of Peranakan ancestry, built their villas here in what was then a beachfront district. The area has remained a mainly residential affair, though the beach has long since gone – pushed further south by the creation of the East Coast Park, with its leisure facilities and restaurants, on several kilometres of reclaimed land. Thankfully, the area's **Peranakan heritage** lives on to some degree, and provides the main lure for visitors to head to Katong. You can sample a bit of what both districts have to offer by heading south from the **Geylang Serai** area, in the east of Geylang, to Katong via **Joo Chiat Road**, as described below; for a list of interesting eating places you'll encounter along the way, see p.670.

Geylang Serai

Paya Lebar **MRT** is just a short walk north of Geylang Serai, while **buses** will drop you right on Sims Avenue, the main eastbound drag in Geylang; it's served

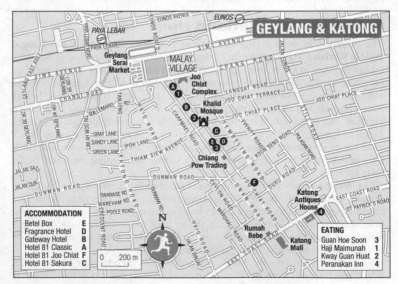

by bus #2 (from Chinatown), #7 (from the Botanic Gardens and Orchard Rd) and #51, all of which pass through Victoria Street. If you do arrive by bus, you'll spot numerous numbered lorongs (lanes) on the way, mainly on the right side of Sims Avenue. These lorongs have accrued a certain notoriety as they house not a few brothels, recognizable by the coloured lights outside – unfortunately Geylang has been identified with prostitution for quite a few years.

The chief attraction, such as it is, in Geylang Serai is the **market** on the left of Sims Avenue, with a large Malay presence; stalls sell Malay textiles, *kuih* and snacks such as *rempeyek*, fried flour rounds with spices or peanuts. Opposite is a collection of incongruous kampung houses, genuine in style but not substance – they're not actual residences but comprise the so-called **Malay Village**, set up years ago as a sort of right-on heritage showcase, and now on its last legs. At the time of writing some were being converted into retail space, a sad irony for the few examples of kampung architecture left on Singapore's main island.

Joo Chiat Road

Just beyond the Malay village is a lane actually called Geylang Serai, which leads south to the start of **Joo Chiat Road**. It's worth popping into the **Joo Chiat Complex** here, on the left, looking like a drab suburban mall from the outside but more market than modern shopping precinct inside. With a notable Malay/ Islamic feel, this is a good place to buy silk, batik or rugs, and you'll also find shops selling Malay music CDs and *jamu* – herbal remedies.

After the bustle of Singapore's downtown streets, Joo Chiat Road can seem almost languid, and this laid-back air, along with several distractions en route, makes walking the 1500m southeast to East Coast Road in Katong hardly a chore. At no. 95, look out for Kway Guan Huat, one of several cottage-industry set-ups along the road; they manufacture spring-roll wrappers and even have a small restaurant serving up *popiah* (see p.670). A little further on is the low-key **Khalid Mosque**, its red-tiled roof and green walls an appetizer for much more eye-catching architecture elsewhere in the vicinity; Fatimah Trading nearby at no. 140 has more Malay medicines for sale. At no. 252, Chiang Pow Joss Paper Trading produces funerary paraphernalia in a nicely restored shophouse, one of several on the road, while at no. 267 is an outlet making mackeral *otah* – *otah* being a kind of dumpling. Just beyond, the immaculate **Peranakan shophouses** on Koon Seng Road (on the left) are the architectural highlight of the area, with their restored multicoloured facades, French windows, eaves and mouldings.

Katong

From the Koon Seng Road intersection, Joo Chiat Road runs another 600m on to **East Coast Road**, home to a pocket of outlets celebrating the area's Peranakan traditions. If you turn left out of Joo Chiat Road, you soon come to the **Katong Antiques House** at 208 East Coast Rd (closed Mon; ☎6345 8544), just after the Holy Family Church. Owner Peter Wee, a veteran spokesman for the Peranakan community, has amassed a treasure trove of artefacts from wedding costumes to vintage furniture, and can give you a tour of the upstairs gallery of the shophouse (45min; S$15 per person) if contacted in advance. Turn right out of Joo Chiat Road and just a few doors down is no. 113, where you'll find **Rumah Bebe** (closed Mon; ⓦwww.rumahbebe.com), a delightful shop that sells beaded shoes and handbags, costume jewellery and the traditional garb – *kebaya* and *sarong* – of Nonya women. They also offer courses in beading and Nonya cookery – and with food being as important it is in Peranakan culture, both these shops also sell some Nonya confections.

You can get to this stretch of East Coast Road directly from Chinatown, Victoria Street and Lavender MRT on bus #12, or from Orchard Road on bus #14; both buses call at the new Mountbatten MRT en route.

Changi

Even in the 1970s, eastern Singapore still looked the way the outskirts of some Malaysian towns do today, dotted with kampungs, low-rise housing estates and tracts of wooded land or stands of coconut palms. It's hard to visualize that landscape as you head out through areas like Bedok – a quiet seaside suburb until the arrival of state housing projects and the reclamation of land for the East Coast Park – on the way to **Changi**, right at the eastern tip of the island. The main reason to head this far east is to see **Changi Museum**, commemorating the internment of Allied troops and civilians by the Japanese during World War II. But in the Singaporean popular consciousness, the Changi district has long embodied a beachside idyll rather than runways able to take Airbus A380s, and just a bit further afield from the museum is the **beach**, all right for a dip or bask on a hot day.

The quickest way to get to Changi is to take the MRT to **Tanah Merah** and pick up the #2 bus, which takes around twenty minutes to reach the museum, then continues to **Changi Village**, close to the beach and ferry terminal. You could also hop on the #2 from its starting point in Chinatown or elsewhere downtown, but the ride takes ages.

Changi Museum

The infamous Changi Prison was the site of a World War II POW camp in which Japanese jailers subjected Allied prisoners to the harshest of treatment, brutalities which are movingly remembered in the **Changi Museum** at 1000 Upper Changi Rd North (daily 9.30am–5pm; audio guides or guided tours S$8 per person, otherwise free; ⓦ www.changimuseum.com). The museum used to be housed within the prison itself, which is still in use – drug offenders are periodically executed here – but an expansion of the prison a few years ago prompted the museum to be moved just up the road to its current site.

Early on in the museum, sketches, photographs and information boards plot the Japanese occupation of Singapore and the fate of soldiers and civilians subsequently incarcerated in camps around Changi. Most moving here, though, is the board of remembrance where relatives and compatriots have pinned messages to the dead.

Novelist **James Clavell** drew on his experience of Changi in writing *King Rat*, never forgetting that in the cells "the stench was nauseating…stench from a generation of confined human bodies." You can get the merest sense of what he meant by entering the **Changi Cell**, a dark, stuffy alleyway just outside the building that approximates the POW's cramped confinement, and in which the voices of former POWs recall the "howling, crying, shouting" of fellow inmates being tortured.

The museum's **gallery** section showcases the work of various prison artists, among them W.R.M. Haxworth. During his internment he produced over four hundred paintings and sketches revealing the stiff upper lip that sustained internees in the face of adversity; one sketch, in which a character holds up two shirts, one white and one black, is entitled *White and Changi white*.

Pride of place in the centre of the museum is given over to a simple wooden **chapel**, typical of those erected in Singapore's wartime camps; the brass cross on its altar was crafted from spent ammunition casings. The museum's final section, focusing on the war's end, includes a recreation of an improvised **theatre** where the internees put on entertainments to amuse fellow inmates, though the museum's version only has a TV screen showing wartime footage.

Changi Village and the beach

Beyond the prison, the tower blocks finally thin out and the landscape becomes a patchwork of rolling green fields, often a relic of colonial-era military bases still used by Singapore's forces. Ten minutes on via the #2 bus is **Changi Village**, a cluster of eating places and shops mainly serving the beachgoing public. To reach the **beach** from the bus terminus, head on past the market and food court and bear left to the *Ubin First Stop* seafood restaurant, where you'll see a canalized inlet from the sea. A footbridge leads over it to a stretch of manicured grass and trees, the prelude to a narrow strip of brownish sand fronting greenish-blue water. As a beach, it wins few prizes but is actually not uninviting (unless you were expecting something out of coastal Terengganu), and you'll soon get used to the sight of aircraft rumbling in low every few minutes on the Changi flight path. Facilities include showers, toilets and a camping area, all shown on a map of the so-called Changi Beach Park available from ⓦ www.nparks.gov.sg, while for **food** there's ample choice in Changi Village itself – the food court isn't at all bad and the restaurants on the main road do everything from pizzas to *murtabak*. The only other reason you might end up here is to use the **Changi Point ferry terminal**, which lies just beyond the footbridge.

The Southern Ridges and Pasir Panjang

While no less endowed with new towns and industrial estates than the east of the island, western Singapore has retained a leafier, more open feel to this day, the urban sprawl here tending to be interspersed with ribbons of woodland. An unusually green example of this is at the **Southern Ridges**, an umbrella term recently dreamt up for the coastal ridge that begins at the southern tip of the island and continues some 9km northwest, under various names, to a site just beyond the main campus of the National University of Singapore. The ridge is lined by a chain of parks and general greenery, and it's now possible to do an extended walk through these areas thanks to a series of ingenious **footbridges** and elevated **walkways**. The main attractions en route are **Reflections at Bukit Chandu**, a museum commemorating the defence of the hill of that name by Singapore's Malay Regiment; and **Mount Faber**, with views over downtown Singapore and cable-car rides across to Sentosa island (see p.656). In between the Southern Ridges and the sea is **Pasir Panjang**, once a sleepy district of kampungs and still a relatively quiet residential area today; it's home to just one sight, the tacky but amusing Buddhist theme park of **Haw Par Villa**.

Harbourfront **MRT** is right at the foot of Mount Faber, at the start of the Southern Ridges. From here, **buses** #10, #30, #143 and #188 run west along Pasir Panjang road to Haw Par Villa, passing close to Reflections at Bukit Chandu en route. However, the account below takes the Southern Ridges walk in an *easterly* direction, ending at Harbourfront – a sensible choice as this avoids a steep climb up Mount Faber and allows you to end the walk at the massive **VivoCity** mall, where you can assuage the appetite and thirst you worked up along the way. Haw Par Villa, the furthest site west covered here, is really an optional extra. One more practical point: the links between parks on the walk often offer little shade, so be assiduous about **sun protection** and bring a reasonable supply of water.

Haw Par Villa

As an entertaining exercise in bad taste, **Haw Par Villa** at 262 Pasir Panjang Rd (daily 9am–7pm; free) has few equals. It describes itself as a "historical theme park founded on Chinese legends and values", for which read a gaudy parade of over a thousand grotesque statues. The site is 5km northwest of Harbourfront, and can be reached on bus #200 from Buona Vista MRT or #51 from Chinatown MRT, in addition to the routes mentioned earlier.

Previously known as Tiger Balm Gardens, the park was once a zoo owned by the Aw brothers, Boon Haw and Boon Par, who made a fortune early last century selling Tiger Balm – a cure-all unguent created by their father. When the British began licensing the ownership of large animals, the brothers closed their zoo and replaced it with statuary; subsequently the park acquired a new appellation, a mishmash of the brothers' names.

The statues featured are of characters and creatures from Chinese legend and religion, as well as a fantastical menagerie of snakes, dragons, elephants, kissing locusts, monkeys and crabs with women's heads. The best, and most gruesome, statues lie in the **Ten Courts of Hell** exhibit (daily 9am–5pm; S$2), whose explanation of the Buddhist belief in punishment for sins and reincarnation is not for the faint-hearted. Accessed through the gaping mouth of a huge dragon, the displays depict deceased sinners undergoing a ghastly range of tortures meted out by leering demons: prostitutes are drowned in pools of blood, thieves and gamblers frozen into blocks of ice and loan sharks thrown onto a hill of knives. Finally, the dead have their memories wiped in the Pavilion of Forgetfulness before being sent back to earth to have another stab at godliness.

Reflections at Bukit Chandu

The defence of Pasir Panjang against the Japanese by the 1st and 2nd Battalion of the Malay Regiment is remembered at the tiny **Reflections at Bukit Chandu** museum (Tues–Sun 9am–5pm; S$3, or S$4 with Memories at Old Ford Factory; ⓦwww.1942.org.sg). It's a ten-minute walk up the slopes of the ridge: head north on Pepys Road, which leads off Pasir Panjang Road 3km from Harbourfront, until you see the lone surviving colonial house at no. 31k, built as officer accommodation, though it became a food and munitions store during the war. It was here that 'C' company of the Malay Regiment's second battalion made a brave stand against the Japanese on February 13, 1942 – two days before the British capitulation – and sustained heavy casualties in the process.

There's nothing special about the museum's small collection of artefacts focusing on this event, and indeed you can glean a lot of the salient information by perusing the museum's website. The displays do, however, get across the human toll of the conflict, as well as highlighting British ambivalence about working with the Malays: the Malay Regiment was only begun as an experiment in Negeri Sembilan to see "how the Malays would react to military discipline", and it was only when they began to prove themselves that the regiment was taken seriously, with members increasingly sent to Singapore for training. This supposed slighting of the Malay community is still cited in Malaysia today as one reason for maintaining the controversial "bumiputra policy" (see p.701).

The canopy walk and Hort Park

Leaving the museum, bear left along the ridge for your first taste of the Southern Ridges trail – and a wonderful introduction it is too, for this is where the **canopy walk** begins. Soaring above the actual trail, the walkway takes you east through the treetops, with signage pointing out common Singapore trees such as cinnamon and *tembusu*, and views north across rolling grassy landscapes, the odd mansion poking out from within clumps of mature trees. After just a few minutes, the walkway rejoins the trail leading downhill to some mundane nurseries and the west gate of **Hort Park** (daily 6am–10pm; free). A hybrid of garden and gardening resource centre, it's sadly dull, with barely a proper tree for shade. At the eastern end of the park is the Visitor Centre, including a restaurant or two and drinks machines, but you'll probably want to exit promptly to Alexandra Road.

From Alexandra Arch to Mount Faber

The Alexandra Road end of Hort Park is very close to one of the huge, purpose-built footbridges on the Southern Ridges trail, the white **Alexandra Arch**, meant to resemble a leaf but looking more like North Bridge Road's Elgin Bridge on steroids. Not a bad point to begin a Southern Ridges walk, it can be reached on bus #166 from HarbourFront MRT or #51 from Chinatown MRT.

On the east side of Alexandra Arch, a long, elevated metal walkway zigzags off into the distance; it's called the **forest walk** though it passes through nothing denser than mature woodland on its kilometre-long journey east. The walkway zigzags even more severely as it rises steeply to the top of **Telok Blangah Hill** (you can leave before the last few bends and use a flight of steps up to the summit), whose park offers views of the usual residential tower blocks to the north and east, and of Mount Faber and Sentosa to the southeast.

Proceed downhill and east, following signage for **Henderson Waves**, and after 700m or so you come to a vast footbridge of wooden slats over metal. Way up in the air over broad Henderson Road, the bridge has high undulating parapets – Henderson Waves indeed – boasting built-in shelters against the sun or rain.

On the far side, the bridge deposits you on the road to the top of leafy **Mount Faber** (Ⓦ www.mountfaber.com.sg), named in 1845 after government engineer Captain Charles Edward Faber. In bygone years this was a favourite recreation spot for its superb **views** over downtown, but these days you'll have to look out for breaks in the dense foliage (the odd gap does offer vistas over Bukit Merah new town to Chinatown and the Financial District), or head to the **Jewel Box**, a smart bar and restaurant complex at the very apex of the summit. The *Jewel Box* is also the departure point for **cable cars** to the HarbourFront Centre and on to Sentosa island (daily 8.30am–11pm; one ride between any two points S$12, two rides S$13).

To descend from Mount Faber, follow signs for the **Marang Trail**, which eventually leads down a steep flight of steps on the south side of the hill to HarbourFront MRT and Vivocity, with the HarbourFront Centre just next door.

HarbourFront Centre

On Telok Blangah Road, the **HarbourFront Centre** is nothing more than a glorified ferry terminal from where boats set off for Indonesia's Riau archipelago (see p.589), as well as the departure point for **cable cars** heading to

Mount Faber and Sentosa island. Much more interesting is the **Vivocity** mall, with a curious fretted white facade that looks like it was cut out of a set of giant false teeth, and housing three good food courts (in particular *Food Republic* on level 3), a slew of restaurants, a cinema and other amenities. The red-brick box of a building with the huge chimney east of the mall, and connected to it by an elevated walkway, is **St James Power Station**, a clubbing mecca housed in, surprise surprise, a converted power plant.

Jurong

Occupying a sizeable slab of southwestern Singapore, sprawling **Jurong** was notoriously dubbed "Goh's folly" in the 1960s when, with the island on the road to independence, Goh Keng Swee, then Singapore's finance minister, decided it was vital to create a major industrial town here on unpromising swampy terrain. To the surprise of not just avowed sceptics, the new town took off, and today Jurong boasts a diverse portfolio of industries, including pharmaceuticals and oil refining – in which Singapore is a world leader despite having nary a drop of black gold of its own. Jurong also has sizeable residential quarters and various leisure attractions, though only two constitute a serious temptation to make a trip here: the extensive avian zoo that is the **Jurong BirdPark**, and the **Singapore Science Centre**, genuinely ahead of the curve as such museums go, with an entertaining emphasis on interactivity.

Jurong BirdPark

The **Jurong BirdPark** (daily 8.30am–6pm; S$18, or S$30 with zoo or Night Safari, or S$40 with zoo and Night Safari; ⓦ www.birdpark.com.sg) on Jalan Ahmad Ibrahim is home to one of the world's biggest bird collections, with more than six hundred species. You'll need at least a couple of hours to have a good look around the grounds, which are large enough for the management to have installed a circular **Panorail** (S$5), like an airport transit train, with commentary describing the main attractions.

One of the big draws, just inside the entrance, is the **Penguin Expedition** (feeding times 10.30am & 3.30pm), a glass enclosure with a pool where the water level is at head height, affording great views of the birds diving and swimming. Another highlight is the **Southeast Asian Birds** section, a far easier way to see local birdlife than overnighting in a hide in Taman Negara; here'll you see fairy bluebirds and other small but delightful birds feasting on papaya slices, with a simulated thunderstorm at midday. Close by is the **Lory Loft**, a giant aviary under netting, its foliage meant to simulate the Australian bush. Its denizens are dozens of multicoloured lories and lorikeets, which have no qualms about perching at the viewing balcony or perhaps even on your arm, hoping for a bit of food (you can buy suitable feed here for S$2). At the far end of the park from the main entrance is the **African Waterfall Aviary**, another large space under netting and long the park's pride, with a tract of "rainforest" that includes a thirty-metre-high waterfall. The aviary's design not only allows visitors to enter on foot but also lets the Panorail chug in without providing an escape route for the 1500 winged inhabitants – including carmine bee-eaters and South African crowned cranes.

For something a bit different, head to **World of Darkness**, a fascinating owl showcase which swaps day for night using specially designed lighting. There are also a variety of **bird shows** throughout the day, the best of which involve birds of prey such as vultures and brahminy kites being fed; check the park's website for details of the current programme.

To reach the park, take either bus #194 or #251 from Boon Lay MRT station (10min). Heading back, note that you pick up the #194 from the same stop where you arrived, while for the #251 you should cross to the other side of the road.

Singapore Science Centre

At the **Singapore Science Centre** (Tues–Sun 10am–6pm; S$6; ⓦwww .science.edu.sg), on the eastern edge of the parkland around the artificial Jurong Lake, a range of galleries hold hundreds of hands-on displays designed to inject interest into even the most impenetrable scientific principles. The majority of the visitors are seemingly hyper schoolchildren, who sweep around in deafening waves trying out every interactive display. Exhibitions focusing on genetics, space science, marine ecology and other disciplines allow you to experience sight through an insect's eyes, write in Braille and see a thermal heat reflection of yourself. At the northern end of the site is the **Omni-Theatre** (Tues–Sun 10am–8pm; S$10 or S$13 joint ticket with Science Centre; ⓦwww.omnitheatre .com.sg), showing hourly IMAX movies about the natural world and housing an **observatory** which the public can access (Fri 7.50–10pm; free).

Bus #335 comes here from Jurong East MRT, though you could walk as it only takes ten minutes from the station. Alternatively, there's bus #66 all the way from Little India. If you're here with kids in tow, you might want to extend your visit to check out the winter-themed **Snow City** next to the Omni-Theatre, featuring tobogganing and opportunities to explore an igloo or build snowmen (Tues–Sun 9.45am–5.15pm; S$16 per hr including loan of jackets and boots, or S$16 for a joint ticket with the Science Centre including 1hr at Snow City).

Sentosa

Given the rampant development over the past thirty years that has transformed **Sentosa** (ⓦwww.sentosa.com.sg) into the most built-up of Singapore's southern islands (with the possible exception of one or two that are home to petrochemical installations), it's ironic that its name means "tranquil" in Malay. The island has certainly come a long way since World War II, when it was a British military base known as Pulau Blakang Mati ("Island of Death Behind"). Contrived but enjoyable in parts, the Sentosa of today is a hybrid of so-so resort island and out-of-town theme park, promoted for its rides, passable beaches, hotels and its massive new integrated resort on the northern shore. Besides the mandatory casino, *Resorts World at Sentosa* (ⓦwww.rwsentosa.com), as it will be known, will feature a **Universal Studios** theme park, a **Marine Life Park** claimed to be "the world's largest oceanarium", a hi-tech **maritime museum** – and six new hotels, doubling the amount of accommodation on the island.

Note that the launch of *Resorts World* in 2010 could well cause a shake-out of the facilities and attractions described here; the Singapore Tourism Board and the websites above should provide the latest picture. And just in case you'd like to visit for a bit of seaside peace and quiet, be aware that the island is very busy at weekends; even at other times you may have to hunt around for a corner of beach without a student party or a huddle of work colleagues undergoing a bonding session.

Travel practicalities

Despite Sentosa being linked to Telok Blangah Road by bridge, you can't get any closer to the island by MRT or ordinary bus than the HarbourFront centre. From here, orange Sentosa **buses** (daily 7am–11pm, later at weekends) set off for Beach Station on the southern shore of the island, and you can get off anywhere en route. Beach Station is also served by the convenient Sentosa Express (daily 7am–midnight), a **light rail** system with its northern terminus on level 3 of the Vivocity mall. Trains call at a station on Sentosa's northern shore (yet to be named at the time of writing) for the integrated resort, then at the central Imbiah Station close to the Merlion replica, and finally at Beach Station. **Tickets** on both the trains and buses are valid for either service and cost S$3 for a day's travel to and around the island and back; once you return, however, you will need to buy another ticket if you have to go to Sentosa again that day. The most spectacular approach to Sentosa, however, is by **cable car** from either Mount Faber or the HarbourFront Centre (see p.653). **Taxi** rides to the island incur a S$2 surcharge per person.

The island also has three colour-coded internal buses which run on loop routes, plus a so-called **beach tram** running the length of the southern beaches; both are free to use. **Renting a bike** (S$5–10 per day) isn't a bad idea; there are a couple of rental outfits behind the beaches, though note that it's not possible to return a bike to any location other than where it was rented. **Maps** of the island are available at various points or from ⓦ www.sentosa.com.sg.

The attractions

Until the integrated resort is up and running, your first sight of anything vaguely interesting at Sentosa, assuming you arrive by bus or the light rail system, will be at Imbiah Station, which has a clump of attractions just to the west. You're greeted by the 37-metre-tall **Merlion**, somehow even uglier than the original at the mouth of the Singapore River. It's possible to walk up through it to viewing decks (daily 10am–8pm; S$8) for vistas of the mainland skyline. There are more views nearby at the **Tiger Sky Tower** (daily 9am–9pm; S$12), basically a ring-shaped glass cabin which glides up a very tall pole and then back down again. But the star attraction in this cluster is **Images of Singapore** (daily 9am–7pm; S$10), using life-sized dioramas to present Singapore's history and heritage from the fourteenth century through to 1945. Though the scene-setting presentation is contrived and some of the wax dummies look like they came from clothes-shop windows, the overall effect is fascinating. Iconic images from Singapore's past – Raffles forging a treaty with the island's Malay rulers, rubber tappers at the Botanic Gardens, coolies at the Singapore River – spring to life, and actors dressed as labourers and kampung dwellers are on hand to provide further insight.

From the Merlion, it's a short downhill stroll along the **Merlion Walk**, with abstract mosaics supposedly inspired by Gaudí and "ethnic" piped music, to Beach Station; turn right here for Siloso Beach and left for Palawan and Tanjong beaches. One ride nearby on the right is worth considering, the **Luge** (it rhymes with "rouge") **and Skyride** (daily 10am–9.30pm; S$10; ⓦ www.hg.sg /sentosa/luge); the Skyride, akin to a ski lift, takes you up a leafy slope, after which you ride your luge – like a small unmotorized go-kart – and coast down a long, curving track back to the starting point. (If you prefer to do the luge first, use the entry point near the Tiger Sky Tower.)

Another highlight is **Fort Siloso** (daily 10am–6pm; S$8; ⓦ www.fortsiloso .com), on the far western tip of the island beyond Siloso Beach. The fort guarded Singapore's western approaches from the 1880s until 1956, but its obsolescence was shown up when the Japanese marched in. Today, the recorded voice of Battery Sergeant Major Cooper talks you through a mock-up of a nineteenth-century barracks, complete with a laundry and an assault course. Be sure to check out the Surrender Chambers where life-sized figures re-enact the British and Japanese capitulations of 1942 and 1945, respectively. After that, you can explore the complex's hefty gun emplacements and tunnels.

Also at the far end of Siloso Beach is **Underwater World** (daily 9am–9pm; S$23; Ⓦwww.underwaterworld.com.sg), where a moving walkway in a hundred-metre tunnel takes you through two large tanks: sharks lurk menacingly on all sides, huge stingrays drape themselves languidly above, and immense shoals of gaily coloured fish dart to and fro. A **touchpool** by the entrance allows you to pick up starfish and sea cucumbers – the latter rather like socks filled with wet sand. It's also possible to dive with the sharks and dugongs (from S$90) or swim with the dolphins (S$150), and if you prefer to get close up to marine creatures while staying dry, have a go on their user-controlled video camera system, the Ocean Invader. One part of the park is separate from the rest, namely the **Dolphin Lagoon** on Palawan Beach (daily 10.30am–6pm), where the marine acrobatics of its Indo-Pacific humpback dolphins are best viewed during a "Meet the Dolphins" session (daily 11.30am, 1.30pm, 3.30pm & 5.30pm).

Finally, if your Sentosa visit extends into the evening, you might well want to catch **Songs of the Sea** (daily 7.40pm & 8.40pm; 25min; S$8), a lavish sound-and-light show whose canvas is not ancient monuments but screens of water; seating for the show is right at the seafront just off Beach Station.

The beaches

The best that can be said about Sentosa's three beaches, created with vast quantities of imported yellowish sand, is that they're decent enough, with bluey-green waters, the odd lagoon and facilities for renting canoes, surfboards and aqua bikes. For tranquillity, however, you'd do a lot better at Changi Beach (see p.651), whereas at Sentosa you have to deal with not only crowds but also the view of one of the world's busiest shipping lanes – expect a parade of container ships and other vessels all day.

Siloso Beach, which extends 1500m northwest of Beach Station, is the busiest of the three, with well-established resorts and facilities, including some good restaurants. **Palawan Beach**, just southeast of Beach Station, is nearly as popular and, unusually, features a suspension bridge leading out to an islet billed as the "Southernmost Point of Continental Asia" – though it's conceded that this is so only by virtue of three manmade links, namely the suspension bridge itself, the bridge from HarbourFront to Sentosa, and the Causeway. Beyond Palawan is **Tanjong Beach**, which tends to be slightly quieter than the other two as it starts a full kilometre from Beach Station.

Accommodation, eating and drinking

One of the best of the pre-integrated-resort-era **hotels** is the *Rasa Sentosa Resort* (Ⓣ6275 0100, Ⓦwww.shangri-la.com; ❾), in leafy grounds at the far end of Siloso Beach. Good for families, it boasts a large freeform pool with water slides for kids, plus its own stretch of beach and a spa. Not nearly as slick is the *Siloso Beach Resort* halfway along the beach (Ⓣ6722 3333, Ⓦwww.shangri-la .com; ❼), though note that reception is right at the back of the complex. Its best feature is the swimming pool, its curvy fringes planted with lush vegetation and featuring a waterfall and slides. In secluded grounds above Tanjong Beach, the *Sentosa Resort and Spa* (Ⓣ6275 0331, Ⓦwww.thesentosa.com; ❽) is a swanky affair, with a spa featuring outdoor pools and imported mud from New Zealand that's said to be great for your skin.

Of the **eating** places on Siloso Beach, *Trapizza* (daily 11am–10.30pm, food noon–9.30pm) stands out for its excellent pizzas and pasta dishes, at reasonable prices, with drinks served after the kitchen closes for the evening. Also here, opposite the *Siloso Beach Resort*, is *Café del Mar* (daily 11am–1am, later at weekends; ⓦwww.cafedelmar.com.sg), an offshoot of the Ibiza original, with a poolside bar, Mediterranean-influenced cuisine, diverse sounds ranging from reggae to electronica, and themed beach parties on the last Saturday of the month (from 5pm; no cover charge). On Palawan Beach, there's the *Koufu*, a decent food court with indoor and outdoor sections; and the cheery *Bora-Bora Beach Bar*, which has a huge menu featuring everything from vegetarian platters to banana-and-Kahlua freezes.

⑨ Eating

Along with shopping, **eating** ranks as Singapore's national pastime. Walk along any street downtown and you'll be astonished at how just about every other building seems to be overflowing with food outlets, from proper restaurants to corner kiosks serving snacks, all kept afloat by the island's incredibly high density of population. As in Malaysia, food is both a widespread passion and a unifier across ethnic divides. And just as there's regional culinary variation across the Causeway, so there are foods that are largely or uniquely Singaporean: chilli crab, a sweet-spicy dish pioneered at long-gone rural seaside restaurants and now served all over the island; and *mee rebus*, a Malay dish of egg noodles served in a thick, spicy gravy based on yellow-bean sauce, with tofu, boiled egg and beansprouts as accompaniments – to name but two.

By far the cheapest and most fun places to eat are the ubiquitous **hawker centres**, also called **food courts**, particularly when they're housed within shopping malls. Old-fangled **kopitiams** (the same as *kedai kopi* in Malaysia) are also inexpensive, though not that common downtown; the best places to find them are Chinatown, Little India and the Arab Street area.

Naturally, food stalls and *kopitiams* mainly serve up local cuisines. For the full range of Asian and international fare, there are numerous **restaurants**, some specialist, others with menus that are a patchwork of Western cuisines. Costs can be steep though: while there are plenty of no-frills, open-fronted establishments where you can eat well for S$15 a head, there are just as many more sophisticated places where you'll pay three or four times that. There's also the matter of the ten-percent **service charge** and seven-percent **tax,** which all but the

Markets and supermarkets

The most entertaining places to buy fresh food are **wet markets**, so called because puddles often cover the floor, which is hosed down to keep it clean. Market traders are usually helpful even if you don't know a mango from a mangosteen. Downtown, the best wet market to head for is the Tekka Centre in Little India (see p.631).

Plenty of malls have a **supermarket** carrying plenty of familiar brands, including foreign beers, and with a deli counter. For more obscure imported fare, try **Market Place** (Level B1, Tanglin Mall, 163 Tanglin Rd; Level B1, Paragon, 290 Orchard Rd, near Orchard MRT), which is popular with expats for its specialist Western and Japanese fare, including organic produce.

cheapest restaurants and cafés add to the bill (price indications in our reviews include these surcharges).

If you're in Singapore in July, you can take advantage of events around the annual **Singapore Food Festival** (Ⓦ www.singaporefoodfestival.com), featuring everything from cookery classes to food-themed guided walks and appearances by international celebrity chefs.

Cafés and high-tea venues

Western-style **café chains**, including *Starbucks*, aren't hard to find in downtown Singapore, though they are thin on the ground in Little India. The places reviewed here have only a limited selection of food, typically pastries, muffins, sandwiches and so forth, but are inexpensive spots for a **Western breakfast** nonetheless; establishments with more extensive food offerings are reviewed under restaurants. Opening times aren't given here as they do vary from one member of the chain to the next, but are typically something like 9am to 9.30pm, with places outside shopping malls tending to shut on Sundays.

Also reviewed here are a couple of hotel venues renowned for that most colonial of traditions, **high tea**. It doesn't come cheap but it's a good excuse for a blowout – you get a lot more than just tea and scones for your money.

Café l'Espresso *Goodwood Park Hotel*, 22 Scotts Rd (see map, pp.640–641) ☏ 6730 1743. A legendary array of English cakes, pastries and speciality coffees for high tea (daily 2–5pm), not to mention chocolate fondue and even pasta. Around S$40 per person. Daily 2–5pm.

Dôme #01-02 UOB Plaza 1, 80 Raffles Place (see map, pp.618–619); Singapore Art Museum, Bras Basah Rd (see map, p.615). Slick Australian chain café boasting an impressive list of coffees and teas, plus better-than-average sandwiches and, at Boat Quay, good river views.

Spinelli's Branches include: #01-45 Raffles City Shopping Centre, Colonial District (see map, p.606); #01-02 Far East Square, Chinatown (see map, pp.618–619); Raffles Hospital, 585 North Bridge Rd, near Arab St (see map, p.632); Ⓦ www .spinellicoffee.com. Serves most of what you'd get in *Starbucks*, plus ice-blended coffees and some teas and smoothies. Croissants, muffins, bagels and a few sandwiches available too. The Raffles City branch is nicely placed, looking across to St Andrew's Cathedral.

Tiffin Room *Raffles Hotel*, 1 Beach Rd ☏ 6337 1886 (see map, p.604). High tea here (daily 3.30–5.30pm) is a buffet of local dishes plus servings of English scones, pastries, cakes and sandwiches – a real treat at S$46.

Ya Kun Kaya Toast Branches include: #01-01 Far East Sq, 18 China St; #01-31 The Central, 6 Eu Tong Sen St; 21 Tanjong Pagar Rd (see map, pp.618–619, for all of these); #B1-18 Raffles City Shopping Centre; #01-16 Funan DigitaLife Mall, 109 North Bridge Rd (see map, p.606); Level B1 Food Court, Bugis Junction, 230 Victoria St (see map, p.632); Basement 2 Food Hall, Takashimaya, Ngee Ann City, 391a Orchard Rd (see map, pp.640–641); Ⓦ www.yakun.com. Ubiquitous chain which started out as a Chinatown stall in the prewar years, offering classic *kopitiam* breakfast fare – *kaya* toast (the same as *roti kahwin* in Malaysia) plus optional soft-boiled eggs eaten with white pepper and soy sauce. Of course there's strong local coffee too, normally drunk with condensed or evaporated milk.

Restaurants, hawker centres and food courts

While Singapore's pricey hotels all have reliable restaurants, it's usually more interesting to check out the many great independent establishments, some of which have evolved into chains. If you're after an unhurried meal in tranquil surroundings, note that cuisine is no guide to ambience: some Western restaurants emphasize bustle and chatter just as would any self-respecting Chinese restaurant. In the reviews that follow, phone numbers are included where reservations can be advisable, particularly for Saturday evenings or lunch on Sunday.

▲ Lau Pa Sat food court

Having started out as faceless, cooked-food markets, created as a more orderly and hygienic way of organizing the stalls that once lined the island's streets, food courts are moving up in the world these days, not just in terms of having much-needed air-conditioning in some cases. Singapore now boasts several **food-court chains**, including *Food Junction*, *Food Republic* and *Kopitiam* (ⓦ www.kopitiam.biz), all featuring snazzy decor and, in some cases, even a "curated" selection of stalls, with every tenant chosen for their catering pedigree rather than their ability to keep up with the rent.

Chinatown

Chinatown in Singapore is, of course, no Chinese ghetto and its eating places are thus pretty diverse, though Chinese food retains a high profile in the heart of the area, on and around South Bridge Road. A few touts on touristy Sago, Smith, Terengganu and Pagoda streets will try to lure you into the clutch of foreigner-friendly restaurants here, all decent enough if not the best in their class. The places reviewed below are shown on the map on pp.618–619.

Annalakshmi #B1-02 Chinatown Point, 133 New Bridge Rd ☏ 6339 9993; 104 Amoy St ☏ 6223 0809, ⓦ www.annalakshmi.com.sg. Come here for amazing Indian vegetarian dishes served up by volunteers, with no prices specified; you pay what you feel the meal was worth. Be generous as profits go to Kala Mandhir, an association promoting South Indian culture. It's best to turn up for their incredible buffets (all the time at Amoy St and Fri–Sun at Chinatown Point), though don't help yourself to more than you can finish. Chinatown Point daily 11am–3pm & 6–9.30pm; Amoy St Mon–Fri 11am–3pm.

Beng Thin Hoon Kee #05-02 OCBC Centre, 65 Chulia St ☏ 6533 2818. Despite the unpromising location, tucked away on a floor that's largely taken up a car park, this restaurant offers a great introduction to Hokkien cuisine. They're well regarded for dishes like *hae cho*, rissole-like lumps of pork served with a sweet dip; cold duck salad with plum sauce; and steamed pomfret. Servings are generous and prices reasonable. Daily 11.30am–3pm & 6–10pm.
Chinese Opera Teahouse See p.677. Shows Fri & Sat.

DeliVege 200 South Bridge Rd ⓦ www.delivege
.com.sg. Inexpensive but surprisingly slick
vegetarian café, one wall of which is covered with
images of famous veggies. The menu advises that
"chewing between 25 and 100 times" is needed
for good digestion, though thankfully their own food
– a mixture of tasty local favourites such as *laksa*
or (mock) duck rice, plus some Western and
Japanese options – goes down with no such
bother. Combo deals, comprising a rice or noodle
dish plus a soup or drink, are great value at S$8.
Daily 11am–11pm.

Eden Café 54 Club St ⓦ www.edencafe.com.sg. A
plush little haven on villagey Ann Siang Hill, with an
unusual floral twist to some items – they serve
ginseng blossom tea and (quite decent) hibiscus
cheesecake, for example. There are more orthodox
soups, salads and sandwiches too, plus pasta
dishes and other light meals on weekday evenings.
Mon–Thurs 11.30am–3pm & 4.30–10pm (Fri until
11.30pm), Sat 11.30am–11.30pm, Sun
11.30am–10pm.

Fisherman's Wharf 27 & 29 South Bridge Rd.
Fish and chips is on many a hotel restaurant menu
in Singapore, but this simple place does it better
than most. Prices are reasonable – dory and chips
costs S$7.50, or you can have lemon sole instead
for S$16. Battered oysters and kalamari are also
available. Mon–Thurs & Sun 11.30am–10.30pm,
Fri & Sat 11.30am–11pm.

Flavours Corner of Mosque St and South Bridge
Rd. Excellent food court with a variety of stalls,
serving favourites like *roti prata* and *char siew* rice,
plus "scissors-cut" curry rice – basically a *nasi
campur* spread from which you select what you
want as usual, and then the server uses scissors to
cut up any large pieces of meat you've ordered into
bite-sized pieces. Open round the clock, too.

Happy Realm Vegetarian Food Centre #03-16
Pearls Centre, 100 Eu Tong Sen St ⓣ 6222 6141. In
an ageing mall, this unprepossessing restaurant
has basic furniture and plastic tablecloths, but
consistently delivers hearty, tasty Chinese veggie
food – not just greens but also tofu dishes and
excellent veggie satay – at low prices. Daily
11am–8.30pm.

🏃 **Hong Hock Eating House** 325 New Bridge
Rd. Less than 1min walk from the New
Bridge Rd exit of Outram Park MRT is this excellent
kopitiam with a multicultural approach, like all the
best old-time joints. Chinese fare includes claypot
curry fish and oyster omelette, while there's also
an Indian Muslim stall serving *murtabak* and tissue
prata – a sweet *roti* artfully folded up like a napkin.
A great place to head after partying into the small
hours. Daily 5pm–9am.

Indochine 49b Club St ⓣ 6323 0503, ⓦ www
.indochine.com.sg. One of Singapore's most
elegant restaurants, with beautiful fixtures complemented by a great menu embracing Vietnamese,
Lao and Cambodian cuisine. The Vietnamese *chao
tom* (minced prawn wrapped round sugarcane) and
deep-fried Vietnamese spring rolls (in veggie and
non-veggie versions) are mouthwatering starters,
while the Lao *larb kai* (spicy chicken salad) is just
one of many excellent main courses. Mon–Fri
noon–3pm & 6.30–11pm, Sat 6.30pm–midnight.

🏃 **Lee Tong Kee** 278 South Bridge Rd ⓣ 6226
0417, ⓦ www.ipohhorfun.com. For years the
speciality of this retro-styled restaurant, with
old-fashioned fans and marble tables, has been
Ipoh-style *hor fun*, supposedly smoother than regular
tagliatelle-type rice noodles. Though you may have
trouble discerning that difference, their many *hor fun*
offerings are undeniably good whether served dryish
or in soup (all around S$5). Also available are a
variety of dumplings and more substantial dishes,
plus their signature lime juice served with a pinch of
salt (it can be left out if requested) as per Chinese
taste. Get there early for lunch, when it gets packed
out. Daily except Tues 10am–9pm.

Maxwell Food Centre Corner of South Bridge Rd
& Maxwell Rd. One of Singapore's first hawker
centres and home to a clutch of venerated stalls,
including *Tian Tian* for Hainanese chicken rice.

Spizza 29 Club St ⓣ 6224 2525, ⓦ www.spizza
.sg. Homely and affordable pizzeria with a menu
boasting a tempting A–Z of thin-crust pizzas
cooked in a traditional wood oven. They deliver all
over the island, too (order on ⓣ 6377 7773). Mon–
Fri noon–3pm & 6–11pm, Sat & Sun noon–11pm.

Swensen's #01-02/03/04 Chinatown Point, 133
New Bridge Rd ⓦ www.swensens.com.sg. See
review on p.668. Mon–Fri 10.30am–10.30pm, Sat
& Sun 8am–10.30pm.

Tak Po 42 Smith St ⓣ 6225 0302. Compact,
competent and inexpensive Cantonese restaurant,
refreshingly untouristy considering the location,
with a/c inside and some tables out on the street.
They do all the usual dim sum favourites, including
siu mai dumplings, yam cake and excellent pork
ribs with black beans, and there's a wide range of
congees (savoury rice porridges) too. For afters, try
the baked egg tarts, which are spot on – the pastry
isn't too flaky and the custard filling isn't
oversweet. Daily 7am–10.30pm.

Tiffin Club 16 Jiak Chuan Rd ⓣ 6323 3189. Inside
a nicely restored, gleaming white shophouse, this
café-restaurant offers an eclectic range of mains
and snacks. In the morning they serve omelettes,
French toast and the cooked Tiffin breakfast
(S$10); lunchtime brings sandwiches (around

S$12) and stews (S$18); and there's some all-day fare like Turkish *köfte* (meatballs) and duck salad. Mon & Tues 8am–5pm, Wed–Sat 8am–10pm.

Yum Cha #02-01 20 Trengganu St (entry via Temple St) ☎6372 1717, ⊛www.yumcha.com.sg. Another dim sum restaurant but on a far grander scale than *Tak Po*, with several dining rooms and a wide-ranging menu, including plenty of main dishes at moderate prices. Mon–Fri 11am–11pm, Sat & Sun 9am–11pm.

Tanjong Pagar and the Financial District

You're unlikely to head to either of these areas bordering Chinatown (see map, pp.618–619) just for the food, but both districts do boast some excellent, if sometimes pricey, independent restaurants.

Blue Ginger 97 Tanjong Pagar Rd ☎6222 3928, ⊛www.theblueginger.com. Housed in a renovated shophouse, this trendy Nonya restaurant is proving a yuppie favourite thanks to such dishes as *ikan masal asam gulai* (mackerel in a tamarind and lemon-grass gravy), and that benchmark of Nonya cuisine, *ayam buah keluak* – chicken braised in soy sauce together with Indonesian black nuts, which have a savoury flavour and a rather pasty texture. Daily noon–2.30pm & 6–10.30pm.

BROTH 21 Duxton Hill ☎6323 3353, ⊛www.broth.com.sg. In a restored shophouse on a delightfully quiet Tanjong Pagar lane, the "Bar Restaurant On The Hill" serves beautifully presented Aussie-influenced fusion cuisine, including an exquisite spinach and portobello mushroom salad, and their trademark lamb loin in a "green coat" – a marinade of herbs, including mint. Not cheap though, with appetizers starting at S$25 and main courses at S$35. Mon–Fri noon–2.30pm & 6–10.30pm, Sat 7–10.30pm.

Cumi Bali 20 Duxton Rd ☎6220 6619. Bamboo sieves, flutes and xylophone-like *angklungs* line the walls at this compact, informal *nasi padang* joint. The beef *rendang* and *ikan bakar* both hit the spot, and they have generous set lunches too (S$7). Mon–Sat 11am–3pm & 5–10pm.

Lau Pa Sat 18 Raffles Quay ⊛www.laupasat.biz. This historic market building is home to an excellent *Kopitiam*-franchised food court. Foods to try include Hokkien *mee* (stall #81), *yong tau foo* (#17) and Indian veg fare offered by *Annalakshmi* (#93), with the same pay-as-you-see-fit philosophy as their restaurants (see p.660). There are also some pricier outlets offering cooked-to-order seafood such as chilli crab. Open 24hr.

Pierside Kitchen #01-01 One Fullerton, 1 Fullerton Rd ☎6438 0400, ⊛www.piersidekitchen.com. A well-established restaurant serving modern European fare with plenty of fusion influences: expect the likes of hazelnut-encrusted king prawns in a lemongrass and oyster sauce, for example. The menu changes regularly, though not quite as fast as the Singapore skyline, which you get great views of here. Reckon on at least S$50 per head for two courses, excluding drinks. Mon–Fri 11.30am–2.30pm & 6.30–10.30pm, Sat 5–11pm.

Boat Quay to Riverside Point

The south bank of the Singapore River is packed with busy restaurants and bars, at their most atmospheric in the restored shophouses of boisterous **Boat Quay**, though even the modern complexes on this side of the river can be a more enticing prospect than jaded Clarke Quay on the north bank. The places reviewed here (see map, pp.618–619) are all in riverside buildings or no more than a couple of streets back from the river.

Brewerkz #01-05/06 Riverside Point, 30 Merchant Rd ☎6438 7438, ⊛www.brewerkz.com. This buzzing restaurant is popular for its highly rated beers, brewed on site, and American fare, including a wide range of excellent burgers and sandwiches, plus barbecued ribs, pizzas, nachos, grilled potato skins and the like. It's all slightly overpriced though, with burgers starting at S$25. Busy at weekends. Mon–Thurs noon–midnight, Fri & Sat noon–1am, Sun 11am–midnight.

Café Iguana #01-03 Riverside Point, 30 Merchant Rd ☎6236 1275, ⊛www.cafeiguana.com. One wall of this open-fronted restaurant is taken up by a huge painting of Frida Kahlo along with other assorted Mexicana. The menu features tortillas, tacos, burritos and all the other standards, with plenty for veggies; mains cost around S$20. The avocado ice cream makes a great dessert, though it would be even better without the corn chips at the bottom of the bowl. Great as a drinking venue too (see p.671), and can get crowded in the evenings. Mon–Thurs 6pm–1am, Fri 6pm–3am, Sat noon–3am, Sun noon–1am.

House of Sundanese Food 55 Boat Quay ☎6534 3775, ⓦwww.sundanesefood.com. Cuisine from the Sunda region of western Java, served in simple yet tasteful surroundings. There are plenty of interesting seafood dishes, including barbecued squid and sea bass, both with a sweet marinade, plus Sundanese takes on beef *rendang*, *sayur lodeh* and the like. Mon–Fri 11am–2.30pm & 5–10pm, Sat & Sun 5–10pm.

Moomba 52 Circular Rd ☎6438 0141, ⓦwww .themoomba.com. With snazzy Aboriginal-influenced murals, this place has maintained great reputation for its Australian fusion cuisine, including a dish or two of kangaroo and more conventional

steaks. Most items on the menu have wine recommendations drawn from the stock at their own wine shop on site. Mon–Fri 11am–2.30pm & 6.30–10pm, Sat 6.30–10pm.

🏃 **O'Briens** #01-58/59 The Central, 6 Eu Tong Sen St. Housed in the mall above Clarke Quay MRT is one of the nicest sandwich shops in Singapore, with a great range of fillings – everything from hummus with sundried tomato to spicy Chinese chicken with mixed peppers and leaves. Breads include wrappos, which are basically wraps, and shambos, flattish ciabattas shaped like a clover leaf. Good range of coffees, smoothies and flapjacks too. Most sandwiches cost S$8–10. Daily 9am–10pm, Fri & Sat until 11pm.

Our Village Fifth floor, 46 Boat Quay ☎6538 3092. A hidden gem, with fine North Indian and Sri Lankan food, and peachy views of the river, city and Colonial District from its charming, lamplit roof terrace. Mon–Fri noon–1.45pm & 6–11pm, Sat & Sun 6–11pm.

The Colonial District and Marina Centre

It's shopping malls rather than heritage buildings that house most of the restaurants in the Colonial District, with the notable exception of the Empress Place complex on the north bank of the Singapore River and, more obviously, the *Raffles Hotel*. Marina Centre, nothing but malls and hotels, is not the most atmospheric place for a meal, though it compensates with some good offerings. The places reviewed here appear on the map on p.606.

Colours By The Bay Esplanade – Theatres By The Bay. Like a very posh food court with restaurants rather than stalls as tenants. You can't go wrong here with *Thai Express* (☎6533 6766; see p.668) or the Italian *Al Dente* (☎6341 9188), both mid-priced chain restaurants.

Doc Cheng's *Raffles Hotel*, 328 North Bridge Rd ☎6412 1816, ⓦwww.raffles.com. East meets West in the decor and fusion-influenced menu of ✦ this ice-cool *Raffles* joint, themed around the global travels of imaginary local bon viveur, Doc Cheng. Pricey, though three-course set lunches (S$45) and dinners (S$85) are available. Mon–Fri noon–2pm & 7–10pm, Sat & Sun 7–10pm.

Hai Tien Lo 37th floor, *Pan Pacific Hotel*, 7 Raffles Blvd, Marina Sq ☎6826 8338. If you have money enough for just one blowout, come here for exquisitely presented Cantonese food and stunning views of downtown Singapore. Extravagant set meals are available, while Sunday lunchtimes are set aside for an oriental buffet brunch (11.30am–2.30pm; S$70 excluding drinks). Daily noon–2.30pm & 6.30–9.30pm.

Indochine Asian Civilizations Museum, Empress Place ☎6339 1720 (café ☎6338 7596), ⓦwww .indochine.com.sg. *Indochine* just about monopolizes the museum's river frontage with a restaurant, café and bar (see p.672). The restaurant has great views of Boat Quay and the Financial District, and both it and the café have somewhat different menus from the original Club Street premises, with the café's *pho bo* (beef noodle soup) particularly highly rated. Restaurant open for lunch Mon–Fri noon–3pm, dinner Mon–Fri & Sun 6.30–11.30pm, Fri & Sat 6.30pm–12.30am; café daily 11am–11pm.

Paulaner Bräuhaus Millenia Walk, 9 Raffles Blvd ☎6883 2572, ⓦwww.paulaner.com.sg. The cavernous ceiling with a maypole sticking up into it is impressive, as is the menu of Bavarian delights such as the bitty pasta called *spätzle*, but the best reason to come here is the terrific Sunday brunch spread, including superb pork knuckle, a range of sausages and salads, and desserts like strudel and cheesecake. It's great value at S$39 with unlimited soft drinks, or S$51 with unlimited beer from their own microbrewery. Daily 6.30–10.30pm, Mon–Fri also noon–2.30pm, Sun brunch 11.30am–2.30pm.

Seah Street Deli *Raffles Hotel*, 1 Beach Rd (entrance on North Bridge Rd) ☎6412 1110, ⓦwww.raffles.com. The soda and root beer signs, jukebox and outsized Americana on the walls make this the most un-colonial establishment in *Raffles Hotel*. A great place for burgers, pizzas,

mountainous sandwiches and barbecued ribs; most mains are in the S$15–25 range. Daily 11am–10pm (Fri & Sat till 11pm).

Swensen's #03-05/06 Funan DigitaLife Mall, 109 North Bridge Rd ⓦwww.swensens.com.sg. See review on p.668, though note this branch doesn't serve breakfast. Daily 10.30am–10.30pm.

Bras Basah Road to Rochor Road

Sandwiched between the Colonial District and Little India (see map, p.615), this part of town features plenty of well-established restaurants, including a good cluster close to *Raffles Hotel*. There are also three great **food courts** worth checking out, two of which are in the Bugis Junction mall near Bugis MRT. On level 3 here, the plush *Food Junction* features an excellent range of local fare, including beef noodles and *yong tau foo*, while level B1 is dominated by Japanese food outlets, complete with plastic models of *yakitori* and even ice cream. Elsewhere, there's a *Kopitiam* food court at Plaza On The Park, 51 Bras Basah Rd, open round-the-clock and popular with revellers wanting munchies in the middle of the night.

Ah Chew Desserts #01-11, 1 Liang Seah St. A pleasant place, taking up two restored shophouses, where you're confronted with nothing but strange local desserts containing beans or other unexpected ingredients. The cashew-nut paste is not bad if you like the sound of a broth made of peanut butter; also available are the likes of *pulot hitam*, made with black sticky rice and better warm than with the optional ice cream. Order the small portions to cautiously sample a few items; hardly anything costs more than S$4 a bowl. Mon–Thurs 12.30–11.30pm, Fri 12.30pm–12.30am, Sat 1.30pm–12.30am, Sun 1.30–11.30am.

Bobby's #B1-03, CHIJMES, 30 Victoria St ☎6337 5477, ⓦwww.bobbys.com.sg. With an atmospheric setting around the basement fountain courtyard, *Bobby's* specializes in barbecued beef rib and other meaty delights, including steaks and burgers, though veggie burgers, pizzas and pasta dishes are also available. Mains from S$25. Mon–Wed & Sun noon–1am, Thurs–Sat noon–2am.

Cappadocia Café Ground floor, *Hotel Rendezvous*, 9 Bras Basah Rd ☎6337 9982. A great range of reasonable Turkish fare here, including *izgara köfte*, cigar-shaped skewerless kebabs; and the pizza-like *pide* and *lahmacun*. There's cherry juice and the buttermilk-like *ayran* to wash it all down with. Main courses around S$15. Daily noon–11pm.

Fatty's Wing Seong #01-31 Burlington Square, 175 Bencoolen St ☎6338 1087. Run by an avuncular chubby cook, *Fatty's* was an institution on the now-vanished foodie paradise that was Albert Street. Today this restaurant maintains the original's "*zi char*" approach, cooking Chinese food

to order without frills. Around S$20 a head. Daily noon–2.30pm & 5.15–10.15pm.

Hock Lam Street Popular Beef Kway Teow 27 Purvis St. The name says it all: for decades this was a highly regarded stall on the now-vanished Hock Lam St, which ran where Funan DigitaLife Mall now stands. The stall has survived, albeit as a little shophouse restaurant, serving the same *kuay teow* noodles with beef slices or beefball dumplings, dry or with soup; a serving costs around S$6. Daily 10.30am–8pm.

Kwan Im Vegetarian Restaurant *South East Asia Hotel*, 190 Waterloo St ☎6338 2394. This place may be bland to look at compared to the Kwan Im temple next door, but does serve a great range of classic Chinese fare made with the usual mock meats. Most dishes are under S$15. Daily 8am–8.30pm.

Mr Bean's 30 Selegie Rd. Not to be confused with the *Mr Bean* chain of soya-milk outlets, this café-restaurant offers decent sandwiches, pizzas and steaks, plus good-value two-course lunches (S$11) and dinners (S$16) on weekdays. Breakfasts also available for S$8. Don't be put off if the service isn't that great – it's a lot slicker than Mr Bean, whose visage has been stuck over a print of the Mona Lisa above the cake counter, would have managed. Open 24hr, too.

Persepolis Prinsep St ☎6238 1151. The strip of restored shophouses at the start of Prinsep St, known as Prinsep Place, is attractive at night with tables under illuminated trees, but the restaurants and bars here are no great shakes. This is arguably the most reliable of the bunch, cooking up not only

Iranian kebabs and stews served with nan bread or pilau rice, but also pizzas, pasta dishes and steaks. Around S$25 per person, excluding drinks. Daily 4.30pm till late.

Rendezvous #02-02 *Hotel Rendezvous*, 9 Dras Basah Rd ☎ 6339 7508, ⓦ rendezvous-hkl.com.sg. The spicy *nasi padang* here was once served out of a revered *kopitiam* on the very spot now occupied by the hotel. Thankfully the curries have stayed the course over the decades, in particular the superb chicken korma, which is unlike any you might have tasted: theirs is akin to a curried stew of just the right amount of richness, derived from coconut milk rather than cream or yoghurt. Daily 11am–9pm.

Singapura Seafood #01-31 Selegie House, Block 9, Selegie Rd ☎ 6336 3255. The seafood isn't bad, but it's the Foochow fare – from the capital of Fujian (Hokkien) province in China – that really hits the spot. At lunchtime they do a good-value set meal for S$49, enough to feed two or three, which includes their signature honey pork ribs, prawn rolls and Foochow fried noodles, done with bits of seafood and a dark savoury sauce. Daily 11am–2.30pm & 6–10.30pm.

Soup 39 Seah St ☎ 6333 9388. So-called *samsui* women once sailed from China's Canton province in droves, incredibly, to work on Singapore building sites. This fine little restaurant celebrates the cuisine of these redoubtable women, most famously their ginger chicken; similar to the steamed chicken in chicken rice, it comes with a gingery dip and iceberg-lettuce leaves to roll it up

in. Reckon on S$20 per head. Daily 11.30am–10.30pm.

Swensen's Level 1, Bugis Junction, 200 Victoria St ⓦ www.swensens.com.sg. See review on p.668. Mon–Fri 10.30am–10.30pm, Sat & Sun 8am–10.30pm.

Wild Rocket 10a Upper Wilkie Rd ☎ 6339 9448, ⓦ www.wildrocket.com.sg. At the *Hangout @ Mount Emily* hotel, this sleek restaurant is run by a lawyer-turned-chef who hates being associated with fusion food, though that is pretty much what he does; expect some delightful combinations of Western and local ingredients. Three-course set lunches (from S$32) and dinners (from S$48) are a reasonable deal, but going à la carte is pricey, and service could be sharper. Better to take a taxi here than trek uphill. Tues–Sat noon–3pm & 6.30–11pm, Sun 11.30am–3pm & 6.30–10.30pm.

Yet Con Chicken Rice Restaurant 25 Purvis St ☎ 6337 6819. Cheap and cheerful old-time restaurant known not just for chicken rice but also for its roast pork with pickled cabbage and radish. Around S$15 for two people. Daily 11am–9.30pm.

Yhingthai Palace #01-04, 36 Purvis St ☎ 6337 1161, ⓦ www.yhingthai.com. A smartly turned-out Chinese-influenced Thai restaurant, where you can't go wrong with their deep-fried pomfret served with Thai-style dressing, fried chicken wings with prawn filling and Thai fishcakes. Around S$40 per head, excluding drinks. Daily 11.30am–2pm & 6–10pm.

Little India

Little India (see map, p.632) is paradise if you're after maximum flavour for minimum outlay; the first part of **Serangoon Road** and its side streets, as well as **Race Course Road**, are packed with inexpensive, excellent curry houses naturally specializing in South Indian food, often dished out onto banana leaves and with plenty of **vegetarian** options; some places offer North Indian and Nepali dishes too. Among the South Indian establishments, particularly on or near Race Course Road, you may notice several outlets advertising Chettinad cuisine – food from the district of that name in Tamilnadu, though nobody seems to agree on exactly what distinguishes it from other Tamil fare (it hardly matters when it's all very tasty).

The only drawback to eating here is that there isn't a lot that isn't Indian, except on Kitchener Road where there are Chinese restaurants on the street and some smart venues in the *Parkroyal* hotel. For hawker stalls, try Tekka Market or the food centre on Jalan Besar where Rowell Road ends.

Banana Leaf Apolo 54 Race Course Rd & Little India Arcade ⓦ www .thebananaleafapolo.com. Pioneering banana-leaf-type restaurant with a wide selection of Indian dishes, including fish-head curry (S$18–25 depending on size of serving) plus chicken, mutton and prawn curries. Daily 10am–10pm.

Food #03 107 & 109 Rowell Rd ☎ 6396 7980, ⓦ www.food03.sg. Associated with the independent art gallery next door, this small veggie café shares its neighbour's offbeat approach, as is clear from menu items like pizza topped with *pak choy* and *petai*, that jungle legume much beloved of Malays. What's more, they bake their own wholemeal bread and sell ethically sourced coffee and other products. Ever so cool, despite the lack of a/c and the brothels nearby. Around S$20 per head for two courses, without drinks. Tues–Thurs 5–10pm, Fri 5pm–midnight, Sat noon–midnight, Sun noon–10pm.

Gandhi 29 & 31 Chander Rd, Little India. Many locals reckon this open-fronted banana-leaf place off Race Course Rd knocks out the best chicken curries in Little India. Daily 11am–11pm.

Komala Villas 76–78 Serangoon Rd & 12–14 Buffalo Rd. A cramped, popular vegetarian establishment specializing in fifteen varieties of *thosai*. The "South Indian Meal", served upstairs on a banana leaf, is good value at S$12. Daily:

Serangoon Rd 7am–10pm; Buffalo Rd 8am–10.30pm.

Madras New Woodlands 12–14 Upper Dickson Rd. Canteen-style place serving up decent vegetarian food at bargain prices. House specialities are the thali set meals (around S$7); samosas, bhajis and other snacks are available after 3pm, and there's a big selection of sweets, too. Recommended. Daily 7.30am–11.30pm.

New Chettinadu 41 Chander Rd. This tiny Chettinad place scores with its superb range of curries, displayed like a *nasi campur* spread. *Idlis*, *thosais* and so forth are available in addition to plain and *biriyani* rice. Daily 8am till late.

Arab Street and around

It seems quite natural that Arab Street (see map, p.632) should boast a couple of Middle Eastern café-restaurants with mezes to nibble at and *shishas* to puff on, but in fact these places have only been around for a few years; the mainstay of dining in the area has long been Malay and Indonesian food. Whatever you end up eating, it's hard to go wrong as regards atmosphere, as many of the restaurants are housed in cosy refurbished shophouses.

Blu Jaz Café 11 Bali Lane ☎6292 3800, ⓦwww.blujaz.net. Chilled-out café-restaurant stretching between Bali and Haji lanes, and easily spotted with its gaudy decor. They do reliable local and Western food – everything from fried rice with prawn and squid to fish and chips – and at affordable prices; a steak will set you back around S$18. Live jazz Mon, Fri & Sat evenings. Daily 11am–11pm (Fri & Sat until 1am).

Bumbu 44 Kandahar St ☎6392 8628. Boasting fine Peranakan artefacts amassed by owner, Robert Tan, *Bumbu* is as much a social history document as a restaurant. Happily, the furnishings don't outshine the fine Thai cuisine, with a few Indonesian offerings too. Tues–Sun 11am–3pm & 6–10pm.

Café Le Caire 39 Arab St ⓦwww.cafelecaire.com. This relaxed diner spearheaded the arrival of Arab cuisine in the area and is a good inexpensive bet for Lebanese and Egyptian specialities. Plenty for veggies, including veggie kebabs alongside the usual dips and falafel. If you're into hubble-bubbles, take advantage of the huge range of tobaccos – they do over a dozen. Daily 11am–2.30am, Fri & Sat until 5.30am.

El Sheikh 18 Pahang St ☎6296 9116, ⓦwww.elsheikhrestaurant.com. Slicker than *Café Le Caire*, with seating on three levels. The menu runs the usual gamut of Lebanese specialities, from meze to main courses such as *shish taouk*, filleted chicken done on a skewer (S$14). There's a great selection of juices and desserts too. Daily 11am–midnight.

Haji Maimunah 11 & 15 Jalan Pisang ⓦwww.hjmaimunah.com. See review p.670. Mon–Sat 7am–9pm (closed during Ramadan).

House of Briyani 742 North Bridge Rd. Ordering is child's play at this friendly, open-fronted place. Step 1 is to pick one of three basmati-rice *biriyanis*, which they name Afghan (yellow-grained), Turkish "dum" (yellow/orange) and Iranian (with flecks of colour); step 2 is to select a curry or stew made from fish, chicken or mutton. Your choices are then heaped on your plate along with *achar* (pickle) for the princely sum of S$7 or so. Daily 11am–8pm.

Islamic Restaurant 745 North Bridge Rd. Only the photos of functions this restaurant catered for in the 1920s give away its pedigree – certainly not the bland, modernized shophouse premises with a few 1970s album covers on the wall. *Biriyanis* are their trademark offering (S$6) though they also do a huge range of North Indian chicken, mutton, prawn, squid and veg curries, with good-value set meals at S$8. Daily 10am–10pm (closed Fri 1–2pm).

Rumah Makan Minang 18 & 18a Kandahar St. A street-corner place serving a superb range of *nasi padang*, including the mildly spiced chicken *balado* and more unusual curries made with *tempeh* (fermented soybean cakes) or offal. For dessert there are freshly made sweet pancakes stuffed with peanuts and corn – much better than they sound. Just S$5 per head for a good feed. Daily 8am–8pm.

SINGAPORE | Eating

Orchard Road and around

Eating in the heart of Singapore's shopping nexus – Orchard Road, Tanglin Road and Scotts Road (see map, pp.640–641) – is almost completely about restaurants in malls and hotels, though a few venues are housed in two rows of refurbished shophouses on **Emerald Hill Road** and at **Cuppage Terrace** next to the Centrepoint mall; both are near Somerset MRT. Almost every mall has a food court, with a particularly worthwhile one being *Food Republic* in Wisma Atria, near Orchard MRT.

Akashi Japanese Restaurant #B1-09 Tanglin Shopping Centre, 19 Tanglin Rd ⓣ6732 8662; *Orchard Parade Hotel*, 1 Tanglin Rd ⓣ6732 4438. Chain of understated, classical Japanese restaurants, where the *sake teriyaki* and the *tempura* are both good and there's a decent range of sakes. Daily noon–3pm & 6.30–10.30pm.

Breeks! Café #05-29 Ngee Ann City, 391a Orchard Rd ⓦ www.zingrill.com.sg. A cut above the other café-restaurant chains, with a surprisingly sophisticated range of main courses (from S$18), including several seafood and grilled chicken options, plus nice sandwiches and salads. Smoothies and sundaes too. Daily 11.30am–10.30pm.

Crystal Jade La Mian Xiao Long Bao #04-27, Ngee Ann City ⓣ6238 1661, ⓦ www.crystaljade.com. *Crystal Jade* is an umbrella for several Chinese restaurant chains, each with a different emphasis. Their mid-priced *La Mian Xiao Long Bao* outlets focus on Shanghai and northern Chinese cuisine, as exemplified by their signature dishes – *xiao long bao*, succulent Shanghai pork dumplings, and the northwestern speciality *la mian*, literally "pulled noodles", the strands of dough being stretched and worked by hand. Not fantastic for veggies though. Daily 11am–10pm.

Lao Beijing #03-01 Plaza Singapura, 68 Orchard Rd ⓣ6738 7207, ⓦ www .laobeijing.com.sg. Styled like a classy, oldfangled

Chinese teahouse, this restaurant specializes in northern Chinese fare, including Peking duck and "Chairman Mao's Favourite Braised Pork" – suitably red in colour – plus dishes from elsewhere in China. There's also a high-tea buffet featuring not scones and cream but plenty more Chinese specialities (3–5pm; S$15 weekdays, S$20 weekends). Daily 11.30am–5pm & 6–10pm.

Magic of Chongqing Hotpot Fourth floor, Tanglin Shopping Centre, 19 Tanglin Rd ⓣ6734 8135. Hotpots are Chinese savoury fondues, akin to the "steamboats" you may have encountered elsewhere in Singapore and Malaysia. There's a choice of two stocks, either a plain chicken one or the Szechuan *mala tang*, literally "numbing spicy soup", the least fiery grade of which still sears the mouth. As for what you cook in the soup, you can either order that individually or go with their buffet deal (lunch S$23, dinner S$36), which allows you to replenish the ingredients at no charge and includes some dim sum starters. Daily noon–3pm & 6–11pm.

Min Jiang *Goodwood Park Hotel*, 22 Scotts Rd ⓣ6730 1704. This plush restaurant serves dim sum and other Cantonese fare, though it's their Szechuan specialities that are the most interesting. Good choices include the chicken or prawn fried with dried chillies, Szechuan smoked duck and long beans fried with minced pork. Reasonably priced, considering it's at one of Singapore's best

---

Street ice cream

A couple of generations ago, ice cream in Singapore (and Malaysia) often meant stuff sold by hawkers from pushcarts, in exotic flavours like sweetcorn, red (aduki) bean and yam. This was so-called *potong* ("cut" in Malay) ice cream because it came in bricks and the seller would use a cleaver to slice it into slabs, to be served either rolled up in white bread or between wafers.

The large-scale manufacture of ice cream and the general elimination of street stalls put paid to that trade to Singapore, but in recent years the ice-cream vendors have made a comeback. They're often to be seen at Cavenagh Bridge (see p.605), on Orchard Road near Somerset MRT and outside Bugis MRT. The wafer option is hardly different from having a cone, while the bread compliments the ice cream surprisingly well, serving as a sort of neutral sponge cake. As for the weird flavours, they're all more than palatable; you can also find red-bean ice cream on a stick in supermarkets and convenience stores, sold under the name "Potong".

hotels. Daily 11am–2.15pm & 6–10.30pm, plus dim sum breakfast buffet Sun 8–10.30am, and dim sum and high-tea buffet Sat & Sun 3.30–5.30pm.
Newton Circus Hawker Centre Corner of Clemenceau Ave North and Bukit Timah Rd, near Newton MRT. A venerable open-air place with a good range of fare (if you find the variety bewildering, look out for signs pointing out the better-known stalls). It's noted for its seafood, though you can end up paying through the nose for this; prices are on the high side for stalls anyway, as the place is very much on the tourist trail. Only really gets going in the late afternoon and stays open till the small hours.
Orchard Maharajah 39 Cuppage Terrace ☎6732 6331, ⓦ www.maharajah.com.sg. This splendid North Indian restaurant has a large terrace and a tempting menu that includes the sublime fish *mumtaz* – fillet of fish stuffed with minced mutton, almonds, eggs, cashews and raisins. Daily 11am–11pm.
PS Café Level 2, Palais Renaissance, 390 Orchard Rd ☎9834 8232; Level 3, The Paragon, 290 Orchard Rd ☎6735 6765; ⓦ www .pscafe.sg. Marvellous if pricey restaurant (mains from S$25) offering an inventive, constantly revised menu; at the time of writing, you could have the likes of tandoori crab with Turkish bread and spicy coleslaw. Great desserts too. The original café in the Paragon is part of the Project Shop interior-furnishings store (daily 9.30am–11.30pm, with breakfast served until 11.30am), but the Palais Renaissance venue, resembling a huge glasshouse, is more attractive (Mon–Thurs 11.30am–11pm, Fri 11am–1am, Sat 9.30am–1am, Sun 9.30–11pm).
Steeple's Deli #02-25 Tanglin Shopping Centre, 19 Tanglin Rd. Singapore's original deli, *Steeple's*

has been knocking out high-quality home-made sandwiches, soups, cakes and savouries for over two decades now. Not a bad choice for breakfast. Mon–Sat 9am–7pm.
Swensen's #03-23 Plaza Singapura, 68 Orchard Rd ⓦ www.swensens.com.sg. Wins no prizes for trendiness, but for what is essentially a chain of ice-cream parlours, the food menu is extensive – salads, pasta dishes, jumbo-sausage subs, etc. Prices are reasonable, with soups and many of the huge range of ice-cream concoctions weighing in at around S$8. Breakfasts served at weekends. Mon–Fri 10.30am–10.30pm, Sat & Sun 8am–10.30pm.
Teochew City Seafood Restaurant #05-16 Centrepoint, 176 Orchard Rd ☎6733 3338, ⓦ www.pfs.com.sg. Despite the name, seafood isn't the only focus at this reasonably priced restaurant; it's also known for its classic Teochew-style goose, braised in soy sauce and served on a bed of tofu which soaks up the juices. They also do a mean cold crab with lemon sauce. Daily 10.30am–3pm & 6–10.30pm.
Thai Express #03-24 Plaza Singapura, 68 Orchard Rd ☎6339 5442; #B1-45/46 The Paragon, 290 Orchard Rd ☎6836 8417; ⓦ www.thaiexpress .com.sg. A modern chain with plenty of wood and chrome fittings and where everything is chop-chop. The menu is packed with Thai rice and noodle standards (from S$11) plus a good range of desserts. Daily 11.30am–10pm.
Warung M Nasir 69 Killiney Rd ☎6734 6228. Respected *nasi padang* joint offering standards such as the fried chicken *balado*, beef and chicken *rendang* and tofu or beans fried with *sambal*. Daily 10am–10pm.

Tanglin Village and the Botanic Gardens

Surprisingly, the so-called **Tanglin Village** (ⓦ www.tanglinvillage.com.sg), south of Holland Road and a couple of kilometres west of the start of Orchard Road, looks almost like something out of rural England. In fact, this sprawling collection of lawns and fields dotted with bungalows was originally a British military camp and later housed Singapore's Ministry of Defence; nowadays it's home to a jumble of sophisticated restaurants and bars, plus health spas, antique shops and so forth. The venues reviewed here (see map, p.604) can be reached on foot as they're not far from the main road, but in general it's better to arrive by taxi and let the driver hunt down the relevant bungalow. Opposite the village is the **Botanic Gardens**, itself home to a couple of good places to eat. Buses #7 and #174 head along this stretch of Holland Road from Orchard Boulevard.

Halia Botanic Gardens, near the Burkill gate on Tyersall Ave ☎6476 6711, ⓦ www.halia.com.sg. The East-meets-West menu here spans sandwiches and pasta at lunchtime plus more

substantial meals in the evening, when the magical candlelit veranda setting whisks you a world away from downtown Singapore. The restaurant is next to the ginger garden; if you're arriving by taxi, ask the driver to drop you on Tyersall Ave rather than at Tanglin gate. Daily noon–5.30pm & 6.30–10.15pm, Sat & Sun from 9am for brunch.

Long Beach Seafood Block 25, Dempsey Rd ⓣ 6323 2222, ⓦ www.longbeachseafood.com.sg. Once you had to trek to the beaches to find Singapore's finest Chinese-style seafood, but no longer, now that this beachside stalwart has set up here. The best dishes really are magic, including treacly crisp baby squid, chunky Alaska crab in a white pepper sauce, steamed *soon hock* (goby) and, of course, chilli crab. An expensive but worthwhile blowout. Dempsey Rd is a 10min walk west of the Botanic Gardens' Tanglin gate. Daily 11am–3pm & 5.30pm–1.30am.

Samy's Block 25, Dempsey Rd ⓣ 6472 2080, ⓦ www.samyscurry.com. Housed in a colonial-era hall with ceiling fans whirring overhead, *Samy's* is an institution that's been serving superb banana-leaf meals for decades. Choose from curries of jumbo prawn, fish-head, crab or mutton, and either plain rice or the delicate, fluffy *biriyani*. There's excellent freshly squeezed lemonade or *teh tarik* – made the old-fashioned way with much extravagant pouring of fluid – to wash it all down with. You'll eat well for S$15 a head excluding drinks. Daily 11am–3pm & 6–10pm.

Taman Serasi Botany Centre, Botanic Gardens, Cluny Rd. Just a couple of minutes' walk from the Tanglin gate is this excellent food court serving some top-notch local favourites, including fried oyster omelette, Indian *rojak* and *roti john* (omelette and sweet chilli sauce on French bread).

The White Rabbit 39c Harding Rd (reached along Minden Rd, a few minutes beyond the Botanic Gardens' Tanglin gate) ⓣ 6473 9965, ⓦ www .thewhiterabbit.com.sg. A beautifully refurbished church with a high ceiling and stained-glass windows is the setting for this restaurant serving fine modern European cuisine. Main courses start at S$35; weekday set lunches are good value (two courses S$35, three courses S$45). Tues–Fri noon– 2.30pm & 6.30–10.30pm, Sat & Sun 11am–3.30pm & 6.30–10.30pm.

Holland Village

A couple of kilometres west of the Botanic Gardens, **Holland Village** is nothing like Tanglin Village, being an area of residential terraces surrounded by high-rise public housing. The tenuous link between the two is that Holland Village was once home to some of the British soldiers based in Singapore; to this day it remains an expat stronghold, with a plethora of Western restaurants and shops. You can get here on bus #7 from the Botanic Gardens, Orchard

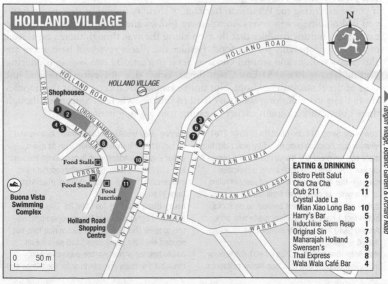

EATING & DRINKING

Bistro Petit Salut	6
Cha Cha Cha	2
Club 211	11
Crystal Jade La Mian Xiao Long Bao	10
Harry's Bar	5
Indochine Siem Reap	1
Original Sin	7
Maharajah Holland	3
Swensen's	9
Thai Express	8
Wala Wala Café Bar	4

Boulevard and the Colonial District, or using the Circle Line's Holland Village MRT, which will only be a few stops from HarbourFront (but note that it's a circuitous journey if you start from Dhoby Ghaut).

Bistro Petit Salut 44 Jalan Merah Saga #01-54 ☎6474 9788, ⓦwww.aupetitsalut.com/bps. Classic French fare and wines, in a nutshell. Most people take advantage of the two-course set lunches (S$30) or three-course dinners (S$45), featuring cassoulet, Provençale-style braised pork ribs, baked *escargots* and so on, though there are also a few à la carte selections. Mon–Sat 11.30am–2.30pm & 6.30–10.30pm.

Cha Cha Cha 32 Lorong Mambong, Holland Village ☎6462 1650. Classic Mexican dishes in this vibrantly coloured restaurant start at around S$15. Outside are a few open-air patio tables, ideal for posing with a bottle of Dos Equis beer, but book ahead for these. Daily 11am–11pm.

🏃 **Club 211** #04-01, Holland Road Shopping Centre ☎6462 6194. The "hidden gem" cliché has to be applied to this rooftop café-restaurant, serving a great range of decent pizza and pasta dishes, snacks and cakes. In the cool of evening you can sit out in their lovely garden to take in surreal views of residential tower blocks looming all around. Cooked breakfasts available too, accompanied by wholemeal or ciabatta bread. Daily 9am–10.45pm.

🏃 **Crystal Jade La Mian Xiao Long Bao** 241 Holland Ave ☎6463 0968, ⓦwww.crystaljade .com. See review p.667. Daily 11am till late.

Indochine Siem Reap I 44 Lorong Mambong ☎6468 5798, ⓦwww.indochine.com.sg. Another swanky representative of the *Indochine* empire, with a slightly different menu from its venues in Chinatown and Empress Place. The rice vermicelli dishes with beef and the Lao *laksa* are among many dishes that hit the spot. Daily 1pm–1am.

Maharajah Holland #01-52, 44 Jalan Merah Saga ☎6474 0096, ⓦwww.maharajah.com.sg. See review of its sister restaurant, *Orchard Maharajah*, on p.668. Daily 11am–3pm & 6–11pm.

Original Sin #01-62 Block 43, Jalan Merah Saga ☎6475 5605, ⓦwww.originalsin.com.sg. Quality vegetarian Mediterranean and Asian fare, everything from mixed veg green curry to mushroom and asparagus polenta with truffle oil. Pricey for what it is though, with mains from S$25. Mon 6–10.30pm, Tues–Sun 11.30am–2.30pm & 6–10.30pm.

Swensen's 251/253 Holland Ave ⓦwww .swensens.com.sg. See review on p.668. Open 24hr.

Thai Express 16 Lorong Mambong ☎6466 6766, ⓦwww.thaiexpress.com.sg. See review on p.668. Daily 11.30am–10.30pm, slightly later at weekends.

Geylang and Katong

If you're exploring the Peranakan heritage of these two suburbs (see map, p.648), you'll also come across several inexpensive Nonya and Malay restaurants to take care of any tummy rumbles that develop along the way, though there's no reason to come here specially for the food. Besides the places reviewed here, there are also Malay stalls in and around Geylang Serai market, and two *kopitiams* offering Katong *laksa* at 49 and 51 East Coast Road (either side of Ceylon Road and just west of the Rumah Bebe shop). Not unlike regular *laksa* except that the noodles are in short strips, Katong *laksa* isn't hard to find elsewhere in Singapore, though there's obviously a certain cachet in eating it in Katong itself.

Guan Hoe Soon 214 Joo Chiat Rd ☎6344 2761, ⓦwww.guanhoesoon.com. Over fifty years old, this place still turns out fine Nonya cuisine in a home-cooked style, including *ngoh hiang*, a delicious sausage-like item in which minced meat is rolled up in a wrapper made from bean curd, and *satay babi* – not satay as in meat barbecued on sticks, but in fact a sweetish red curry made with pork. Around S$40 for two. Daily except Tues 10.30am–3pm & 6–9pm.

Haji Maimunah 20 Joo Chiat Rd #01-02 ⓦwww .hjmaimunah.com. Unpretentious Malay restaurant

serving good breakfasts (*nasi lemak*, *lontong* and so forth) and interesting dishes such as *ayam bakar sunda* (Sundanese-style barbecued chicken) and *siput lemak sedut* (snails with coconut milk). Inexpensive. Tues–Sun 7am–9.30pm (Ramadan from 11am).

Kway Guan Huat 95 Joo Chiat Rd. Tiny *kopitiam*-style joint serving up only Nonya *popiah* (unfried spring rolls) and *kuey pie tee* (like spring rolls but shaped like little cups). Here S$16 pays for an ample helping of ready-made *popiah* for two, though it's actually cheaper to order the fillings and "skins" and do the rolling yourself at the table, as would be done if eating this in someone's home; staff can show you how. Tues–Sun 11am–8pm. **Peranakan Inn** 210 East Coast Rd ☎ 6440 6195. As much effort goes into the food as went into the renovation of this immaculate, bright green shophouse restaurant, which offers a great range of authentic Nonya favourites at reasonable prices; around S$10 a dish. Daily 11am–3pm & 6–9.30pm.

Drinking and nightlife

With its affluence and large expat community, Singapore supports a huge range of drinking holes, from slick cocktail joints through elegant colonial chambers to slightly tacky joints featuring karaoke or middling covers bands. There's also a bunch of glitzy and vibrant clubs which spin cutting-edge sounds, and one or two regularly manage to lure the world's leading DJs to play.

While the boom in the island's nightlife over the past decade will undoubtedly be checked by global economic woes, there are bound to be more venues coming on stream as the two integrated resorts get off the ground in 2010. All this means that the scene may be in a greater state of flux than usual; the usual listings magazines (see p.590) should give you a feel for current happenings.

Bars

Singapore's best bars cluster mainly in the Colonial District, along the Singapore River and on Orchard Road. At the time of writing, Boat Quay was continuing to thrive whereas Clarke Quay and nearby Mohamed Sultan Road, as well as CHIJMES on Bras Basah Road, all once favoured by the city's bright young things, had been off the boil for some while.

Bars tend to open in the late afternoon, closing anywhere between midnight and 3am, an hour or two later on Friday and Saturday, and are often shut on Sunday; a few places are also open at lunchtime. A pint of Tiger beer starts at around S$10, but prices can be double that in fancier venues or for imported brews. A glass of house wine usually costs much the same as a beer, and spirits a dollar or two more. Most bars offer snacks and quite a few serve more substantial fare. For venues with a strong emphasis on live music, see p.678.

Boat Quay to Riverside Point, and Chinatown
The venues here appear on the map on pp.618–619.

🏃 **Bar Savanh** 49 Club St ⓦ www.indochine .com.sg. Candlelit, and crammed with Buddha effigies, scatter cushions and plants, the *Savanh* (the name means "Heaven" in Lao) is a mellow bar if ever there was one. Mon–Sat 5pm–2am (Fri until 3am); happy hour until 8pm.
BQ Bar 39 Boat Quay ⓦ www.bqbar.com. One of Boat Quay's cooler venues, thanks to the friendly staff, memorable views of the river from upstairs and diverse sounds, anything from dance to rock. Kebabs available too from a nearby outlet run by the same management. Daily 11am till late; happy hour until 8pm.
Brewerkz/Café Iguana Riverside Point, 30 Merchant Rd. Owned by the same company, *Brewerkz* serves up a range of beers from its own microbrewery, while *Café Iguana* offers a huge selection of tequilas and margaritas, and also has access to its neighbour's beers. *Brewerkz* Mon–Thurs noon–midnight, Fri & Sat noon–1am, Sun 11am–midnight (special deals on drinks noon–3pm); *Café Iguana* Mon–Thurs 6pm–1am, Fri 6pm–3am, Sat noon–3am, Sun noon–1am (special deals on drinks until 9pm and after midnight).
Harry's Bar 28 Boat Quay ⓦ www.harrys.com.sg. House band ChromaZone provide live jazz and blues nightly except Mon at this well-established joint with branches all over downtown. There's a range of light meals and snacks; drinks, including six beers and ciders on draught, are 25 percent cheaper until 8pm. Mon–Thurs 11am–1am, Fri 11am–2am, Sat 6pm–midnight.

Helipad #05-22 The Central, 6 Eu Tong Sen St ⓦwww.helipad.com.sg. A superb venue in the rather dull Central mall atop Clarke Quay MRT. It's not encouraging that the entrance is via the fifth-floor car park, but you're immediately into a tunnel like something in a spaceship, leading into a circular bar with a terrace offering good views over the river. Staff can point out a staircase giving access to the actual helipad, where you can sit out on the "H" symbol while your drinks are brought up to a collection point. Daily 6pm–2am (Fri & Sat until 3pm); happy hour until 9pm.

Majestic Bar 41 Bukit Pasoh Rd. The *New Majestic* hotel's bar offers a good range of cocktails and beers, including Hoegaarden and Stella on draught, and amazing bar food from the hotel's innovative Chinese restaurant, including dim sum and some morsels with a Western twist, like burgers in Chinese *mantou* buns. The tables out by the road, which gets quiet in the evening, are a good choice for a relaxing drink in the relatively cool night air. Daily 5pm–1am (Fri & Sat till 3pm).

The Penny Black 26/27 Boat Quay ⓦwww .pennyblack.com.sg. Not a convincing evocation of a "Victorian London pub", but pleasant enough, with one table built around a red pillar box, cider and Old Speckled Hen on draught, plenty of pub grub – cottage pie, ploughman's lunches and so on – and live UK football matches on TV. Mon–Thurs 11.30am–1am, Fri & Sat 11.30am–2am.

The Colonial District and Marina Centre

The venues here appear on the map on p.606.

Balaclava #01-01b Suntec City, 1 Raffles Blvd ⓣ6339 1600, ⓦwww.imaginings.com.sg. Homage to G-Plan or nod to 1960s James Bond movies? Both could be said of this retro jazz bar, whose leather chairs, sassy red lamps and dark wood veneers may make the ambience too oppressive for some tastes. There's live music most nights; happy hour is 4–8pm. Mon–Thurs 4pm–1am, Fri 4pm–2am, Sat 6pm–2am.

Bar Opiume Asian Civilizations Museum, Empress Place ⓣ6339 2876, ⓦwww .indochine.com. Cool-as-ice cocktail bar, graced by huge chandeliers, modish, square-cut leather furniture and lordly Buddha statues. There are great Vietnamese spring rolls and other Indochinese snacks too, courtesy of its sibling establishments, the *Indochine* restaurant and café next door. Good views across to Boat Quay at night, too. Daily from 5pm: Mon–Thurs until 2am, Fri & Sat till 3am, Sun till 1am.

The Long Bar *Raffles Hotel*, 1 Beach Rd ⓣ6337 1886. It's practically mandatory to have a Singapore Sling amid the old-fashioned elegance of the bar where Ngiam Tong Boon invented it in 1915. [Rubber] tappers' time, as they call their happy hour, is 5–9pm (Mon–Wed & Sun). Daily 11am–12.30am.

Bras Basah Road to Little India

There aren't many worthwhile bars in this area (see map, p.615, except where noted), but those that do that exist tend to be friendlier and more relaxed than elsewhere.

Divine Parkview Sq, 600 North Bridge Rd ⓣ6396 4466; see map, p.632. All the decadence and excess of 1920s café society comes outrageously to life at *Divine*, a venue whose adoption of a wine angel (a waitress, kitted out in wings and harness, who is winched up and down the 12m wine rack) might just be the most politically incorrect thing you'll ever see. Elsewhere, Art Deco murals of prancing deer line the walls and vast brass lamps hang from the lofty ceiling. Heineken on draught; no happy hour though. Daily 11am–1am.

Lot, Stock and Barrel Pub 29 Seah St. Cheerful, unpretentious venue frequented by a post-work crowd in the early part of the evening, with some backpackers making their presence felt later on, drawn partly by the great jukebox which features everything from Sinatra to Beyonce. Daily 4pm–midnight; happy hour daily 4–8pm.

Night and Day 139a/c Selegie Rd ⓦwww .nightandday.sg. Tucked away upstairs in a restored 1950s building with a touch of Art Deco about the facade. The funky cartoons strewn across the walls inside hint at the fact that this is not just a bar but also an independent gallery, though there's nothing self-important about the place, which is more down-to-earth than much of the competition. Happy hour until 9pm. Mon–Sat 6pm–3am.

Prince of Wales Backpackers Hostel 101 Dunlop St ⓦwww.pow.com.sg; see map, p.632. Below the hostel is a buzzing travellers' bar with live acoustic music or bands most nights, plus an

Australian Pilsner-style microbrewery beer and pale ale on tap at keen prices. Daily 9am–1am (Fri & Sat 2am).

🏃 **Public House** 9 Bras Basah Rd. Part of the *Rendezvous Hotel* but with its own entrance on the main road, this small, agreeable bar attracts a mix of business types, tourists and academics from the various institutes in the area. There's Stella on draught and a great range of snacks, including satay, baby squid and burgers. Major discounts on drinks till mid-afternoon, with smaller discounts between then and 9pm. Mon–Thurs noon–midnight, Fri noon–3am, Sat 4pm–2am, Sun 1pm–midnight.

Orchard Road and around

Quite a few of Orchard Road's most interesting drinking venues occupy restored Peranakan shophouses at the start of Emerald Hill Road, close to Somerset MRT. The places reviewed here appear on the map on pp.640–641.

🏃 **The Dubliner** 165 Penang Rd ⓦwww .dublinersingapore.com. Set up in a colonial-era mansion, this is hardly your typical ersatz Irish pub. The grub – fish and chips, Irish stew and various burgers – is a notch above as well, and there are live bands every Fri. Daily 11.30am till late.

Harry's Bar @ Orchard #01-05 Orchard Towers, 1 Claymore Dr ⓣ6736 7330, ⓦwww.harrys.com. sg. Home to the doyens of Singapore's covers band circuit, Tania, playing various Seventies rock faves most nights. Mon–Fri 3pm–2am, Sat noon–3am, Sun noon–1am; happy hour 4–8pm.

Ice Cold Beer 9 Emerald Hill Rd ⓦwww .emerald-hill.com. Noisy, happening place where the beers are kept in ice tanks under the glass-topped bar. Shares a kitchen with *No. 5 Emerald Hill*. Daily 5pm–2am (Fri & Sat till 3am); happy hour daily 5–9pm.

🏃 **No. 5 Emerald Hill** 5 Emerald Hill Rd ⓦwww.emerald-hill.com. Set in one of Emerald Hill Rd's restored Peranakan houses, *No. 5* is not only a feast for the eyes with its opulence, but also offers various speciality cocktails plus great chicken wings and thin-crust pizzas, plus Carlsberg and Tetley's on tap and a good range of bottled beers. There's some outdoor seating and a pool table upstairs. Daily noon–2am (Fri & Sat till 3am); happy hours noon–9pm.

Outdoors Café & Bar Peranakan Place, corner of Orchard Rd and Emerald Hill Rd ⓣ6738 8898, ⓦwww.peranakanplace.com/outdoors.html. Pleasant alfresco place right at the start of Emerald Hill Rd, with a canopy for shade and an extensive menu of Western and Asian mains and light meals. It's a great spot to watch the passing trade on Orchard Rd, if you enjoy the sight of people struggling with full carrier bags from the area's designer outlets. Tiger and Erdinger on draught, plus other beers and a range of cocktails. Daily 11am–2am (Fri & Sat until 3am); happy hour till 7pm.

Tanglin Village and Holland Village

For transport information, see the sections on these areas on p.668 and p.669.

Harry's Bar @ Holland Village 27 Lorong Mambong, Holland Village ⓣ6467 4222, ⓦwww .harrys.com.sg. A relaxing venue to retire to after a meal elsewhere in the area. Live music Thurs & Fri. Daily noon–1am.

Wala Wala Café Bar 31 Lorong Mambong, Holland Village. Rocking joint, now into its second decade, with Beck's, Tetley's, Warsteiner and other beers on draught, and featuring a generous happy hour (until 9pm). Acoustic and electric acts play upstairs nightly. Mon–Thurs 4pm–1am, Fri 4pm–2am, Sat 3pm–2am, Sun 3pm–1am.

The White Rabbit 39c Harding Rd, Tanglin Village ⓣ6473 9965, ⓦwww.thewhiterabbit.com.sg. This refined restaurant housed in a restored church has a marvellous open-air bar at the back that buzzes after 10pm at weekends. There's Erdinger and Tiger on draught, though no happy hour, and loungey sounds; if you want a chilled-out drink away from the hubbub of downtown, this is the spot. Daily 6pm–1am (Fri & Sat until 2am).

Clubs

European and American dance music dominates in Singapore's best Western-style clubs, though some venues feature bands playing cover versions of current hits and pop classics. There are also more Asian-oriented places playing Chinese pop, and some of these can be seedy, with hostesses on commission trying to hassle you into buying them a drink. Fortunately, venues of this sort are easy to spot: even if you manage to get beyond the heavy wooden front door flanked by brandy adverts, the pitch darkness inside gives the game away.

Most clubs have a **cover charge**, if not all week then at least on Friday and Saturday; the charge fluctuates between S$15 and S$30 (weekends are pricier) and what sex you are (men pay slightly more than women), and almost invariably includes the cost of your first drink.

Bar None *Marriott Hotel*, 320 Orchard Rd ☎6831 4656; see map, pp.640–641. Draws a 30-something crowd with a mixture of Latin, top 40 sounds and classic hits, plus two cover bands a night, one playing oldies and the other dancier stuff. Cover charge S$10/12 for women/men on weekdays, S$20/25 at weekends. Mon–Thurs 5pm–4am, Fri & Sat 5pm–5am; happy hour until 9pm.

DBL-O #01-24 Robertson Walk, 11 Unity St Ⓦ www.emerald-hill.com; see map, p.606. With its massive dancefloor, sassy *DBL-O* can pack in the punters; expect queues outside when it's busy. House, garage and R&B are the favoured musical styles. Wed night is free for women; on other nights, cover charges range from S$15–S$25. Tues–Thurs 8pm–3am, Fri & Sat 8pm–4am.

Home Club #B01-06 The Riverwalk, 20 Upper Circular Rd Ⓦ www.homeclub.com.sg; see map, pp.618–618. This cosy venue makes the best of the riverside location with a chilled-out patio area outside; inside DJs spin a range of sounds, from R&B to 1980s synth-pop. Friday nights see a switch to indie, however, as a bunch of local bands play original material that wouldn't sound out of place on US college radio. Cover charge of around S$15 Fri & Sat. Tues–Thurs 9pm–3am, Fri & Sat 10pm–6am.

Powerhouse St James Power Station, Sentosa Gateway (next to Vivocity) Ⓦ www.powerhouse.sg. Arguably the best of the venues at this renovated power station, *Powerhouse* spins R&B on Wed & Sat and house on Fri. Cover charge from 10pm: women S$15, men S$20. Harbourfront MRT. Wed, Fri & Sat 9pm–4am.

🏃 **Zouk/Phuture/Velvet Underground** 17 Jiak Kim St Ⓦ www.zoukclub.com.sg; see map, p.604. Got up like some kind of alien hideout in a desert cave, *Zouk* is Singapore's oldest and still best club, having been launched in the early 1990s. House remains the mainstay, though there's also the popular retro night Mambo Jambo (Wed), and you can expect guest sets from world-renowned DJs from time to time. The place is also home to two smaller clubs, *Phuture*, majoring in hip-hop and R&B; and *Velvet Underground*, with a more organic mix of everything from Afrobeat to jazz. Each venue has its own cover charge (around S$28/23 for men/women at *Zouk*). Bus #51 or #186 from Chinatown MRT or bus #16 from Somerset/Orchard MRT; ask to be let off close to the *Grand Copthorne Waterfront* hotel, next door. *Zouk* Wed, Fri & Sat 10pm–4am; *Phuture* Wed, Fri & Sat 9pm–4am; *Velvet Underground* Tues–Sat 9pm–4am.

Gay venues

Singapore's more liberal climate means that gay bars and clubs thrive largely unhindered and in return keep a lowish profile (the word "gay" is hardly used in promotional material, for example). Many of the island's handful of gay bars and clubs are located in Tanjong Pagar. Singapore's own gay lifestyle website Ⓦ www.fridae.com lists new venues as they appear, though it's not always kept up-to-date as regards older ones. Note that the bars (see map, pp. 618–619) only really get busy at weekends, and even then only after 10pm. For more on the social backdrop to local gay life, see p.67.

Backstage Bar 13a Trengganu St Ⓦ www .backstagebar.moonfruit.com. Entered through a side door in Temple St (look out for the rainbow flag placed discreetly at the street corner amid the lanterns), this tiny bar offers a view over the souvenir stalls of Trengganu St. Daily 7pm–2am (Fri & Sat till 3pm).

DYMK 9 Kreta Ayer Rd Ⓦ www.dymk.sg. Probably the friendliest gay bar in town, though it can be a tad cliquey. There's a relaxed lounge area downstairs with a standing area upstairs, and the music generally isn't too loud. Easy to find – just look for the bright orange and yellow shophouse. Tues–Sun 8pm–midnight (Fri till 1am, Sat till 2am).

Tantric 78 Neil Rd ⓦwww.backstagebar
.moonfruit.com. Pleasant enough shophouse bar
with interior decor that wouldn't look amiss in a
gay venue on London's Old Compton St, and a few
tables outside. The clientele is possibly a little more
reflective of Singapore's multi-ethnic make-up than
the largely Chinese crowds you find in other
venues. Daily 8pm–3am (Sat until 4am).
Taboo 65/67 Neil Rd ⓦwww.taboo97.com. Small
club spinning the usual mix of house, trance and
other pulsating sounds. Wed & Thurs 10pm–2am,
Fri 10pm–3am, Sat 10pm–4am.

Entertainment

Even on a brief visit, it's hard not to notice how much money has been
poured into developing an **arts** community and infrastructure: prime
downtown property has been turned over to arts organizations in areas like
the Waterloo Street and Little India "arts belts", and prestige venues like
Theatres on the Bay attract a stream of world-class performers. Cynics might
say this cultural push is mainly about keeping Singapore attractive to skilled
expats, while others say a more important issue is whether world-class art can
bloom where **censorship** still lingers, if not as overtly as in the 1970s and
1980s, then in terms of there being well-established red lines concerning
party politics, ethnicity and religion which nobody dare cross. Even if
pushing the boundaries is now tolerated provided projects make money, as
some claim, it's hard to see how this can happen reliably when the Singapore
audience is relatively small.

Whatever the truth of the situation, Singapore does offer an excellent range
of cultural events in all genres, drawing on both Asian and Western traditions.
There are two major international arts festivals annually: the **Singapore Arts
Festival** (over four weeks in May & June; ⓦwww.singaporeartsfest.com),
running the gamut from theatre through dance and film to concerts; and the
Singapore Fringe Festival (Jan; ⓦwww.singaporefringe.com), concentrating on
theatre, dance and the visual arts. **Tickets** for concerts, plays and dance
performances in general are usually sold at the venues themselves, though it can
be easier to use ticketing agencies such as SISTIC (the largest; ☎6348 5555,
ⓦwww.sistic.com.sg), Tickets.com (☎6296 2929, ⓦwww.tdc.sg) and Gatecrash
(☎6100 2005, ⓦwww.gatecrash.com.sg).

Arts centres and general-purpose theatres

The Arts House 1 Old Parliament Lane ☎6332
6919 (tickets), ⓦwww.theartshouse.com.sg. Plays,
concerts, films and art exhibitions.
DBS Arts Centre 20 Merbau Rd, Robertson Quay
☎6221 5585, ⓦwww.srt.com.sg. Plays and
concerts.
Drama Centre Level 3, National Library, 100
Victoria St ☎6837 8400. Mainly plays by local
companies.
Esplanade – Theatres on the Bay 1 Esplanade
Drive ☎6828 8222, ⓦwww.esplanade.com.sg.
Sucks up all the biggest events to hit Singapore's
shores.
Jubilee Hall *Raffles Hotel*, 1 Beach Rd. Plays and
other performances are occasionally staged here;
check the press for details.

NAFA Lee Foundation Theatre Campus 3,
Nanyang Academy of Fine Arts, 151 Bencoolen St
Plays and other performances.
Singapore Indoor Stadium 2 Stadium Walk,
Kallang ⓦwww.sis.gov.sg. The usual venue for
big-name bands in town. The Circle Line's Stadium
MRT will be close by. Tickets through SISTIC.
Substation 45 Armenian St ☎6337 7800,
ⓦwww.substation.org. Self-styled "home for
the arts" with a multipurpose hall that presents
drama and dance, as well as art, sculpture and
photography exhibitions in its gallery.
Victoria Concert Hall and Theatre 11 Empress
Place ☎6338 8283, ⓦwww.vch.com.sg. Concerts
and plays; details in listings magazines.

Film

As well as the latest Hollywood blockbusters, Singapore's **cinemas** show a wide range of Chinese, Malay and Indian movies, all with English subtitles; Western movies in languages other than English also pop up occasionally. Cinema-going is popular in Singapore, so turn up early (or book in advance) to secure tickets (seldom more than S$10) if the film is newly released. Be prepared, also, for a lot of noise during shows: Singaporeans are great ones for chattering through the movie.

The annual **Singapore International Film Festival** (ⓦwww.filmfest.org .sg) takes place in April and screens over 150 films and shorts – mostly by Asian directors – over two weeks. If you intend to be in Singapore for a while, you might want to sign up to the **Singapore Film Society** (ⓦwww.sfs.org.sg), which puts on its own monthly screenings of films (members–only) and mounts occasional film festivals (with discounts for members).

Multiplex chains

Cathay Cinemas include: Cineleisure Orchard, 8 Grange Rd (near Somerset MRT); Cathay Cineplex, 2 Handy Rd (near Dhoby Ghaut MRT); bookings ☏6235 1155, ⓦwww.cathay.com.sg.

Eng Wah Downtown cinema at #03-51 Suntec City Mall, 3 Temasek Blvd, Marina Centre ☏6836 9074.

Golden Village Cinemas include: Level 7, Plaza Singapura, 68 Orchard Rd; Levels 2 & 3, Vivocity, Harbourfront; #03/04-01 Marina Leisureplex, 5a Raffles Ave, Marina Centre; ⓦwww.gv.com.sg.

Shaw Cinemas include: Lido 8 Cineplex, levels 5 & 6, Shaw House, 350 Orchard Rd; Bugis Cineplex, Bugis Junction, 200 Victoria St; bookings ☏6738 0555, ⓦwww.shaw.sg.

Independent venues

Alliance Française 1 Sarkies Rd ⓦwww .alliancefrancaise.org.sg/cineclub.html. Weekly French-language films with English subtitles; tickets through SISTIC. A 10min walk from Newton MRT.

National Museum Cinematheque National Museum, 93 Stamford Rd ⓦwww .nationalmuseum.sg. The museum mounts its own laudable programme of films from around the world. When Peter Bogdanovich's film of the Paul Theroux novel *Saint Jack*, shot in Singapore (where the story is set) in the late 1970s, was finally shown here after being banned by the government for more than 25 years, the place was crammed to the gills. Tickets from the museum itself.

Omni-Theatre See p.655. Singapore's IMAX cinema.

The Picturehouse Cathay Building, 2 Handy Rd; bookings ☏6235 1155, ⓦwww.thepicturehouse .com.sg. Part of the Cathay empire but, unlike its multiplexes, devoted to art-house films from Asia and the rest of the world.

The Screening Room 12 Ann Siang Hill ☏6221 1694, ⓦwww.screeningroom.com.sg. "Where art meets film" is the motto of this complex, incorporating a basement lounge, restaurant, gallery space, rooftop terrace with views over Chinatown and a cinema screening the relatively intellectual end of Hollywood's output plus the odd Asian flick, though nothing radical.

Sinema #B1-12 Old School, 11b Mount Sophia ☏6336 9707, ⓦwww.sinema.sg. Marvellous 130-seater venue screening work by home-grown talent plus some foreign art-house flicks, and hosting forums involving local actors and directors, with a shop selling DVDs of their work. This is one of many arts organizations housed within Old School, a rather confusing complex that was once the Methodist Girls' School; best to get here by taxi, though you can use the long flight of steps up from Handy Rd near the back of Plaza Singapura.

Theatre, dance and classical music

Singapore's arts scene is probably at its best when it comes to **drama**: a surprising number of small theatre companies have sprung up over the years, performing works by local playwrights which dare to include a certain amount of social commentary. Themes that have been tackled range from gay issues to the notorious "en bloc" craze, fuelled by Singapore's recent property-market bubble, which saw developers buying up whole apartment blocks just so they could tear them down and build something grander in their place. Foreign

Street theatre

If you walk around Singapore long enough, you're likely to stumble upon some sort of streetside cultural event, most usually a *wayang*, a Malay word used in Singapore to denote **Chinese opera**. Played out on outdoor stages that spring up next to temples and markets, or in open spaces in the new towns, *wayangs* are highly dramatic and stylized affairs, in which garishly made-up and costumed characters enact popular Chinese legends to the accompaniment of the crashing of cymbals and gongs. They're staged throughout the year, but the best time to catch one is during the Festival of the Hungry Ghosts, when they are held to entertain passing spooks (late Aug). Another fascinating traditional performance, **lion dancing**, takes to the streets during Chinese New Year, and **puppet theatres** appear around then, as well. The Singapore Tourism Board may be able to help you track down examples of all these events.

theatre companies tour regularly too, and lavish Western musicals are staged from time to time. Performances of **dance** are also common, involving local and foreign artistes.

At the heart of Singapore's **Western** classical music scene is the **Singapore Symphony Orchestra**, whose concerts often feature guest soloists, conductors and choirs from around the world; occasional **Chinese** classical music shows are included in the programme.

Companies and orchestras

Action Theatre 42 Waterloo St ⓣ6837 0842, ⓦwww.action.org.sg. Stages work by Singaporean playwrights as well as the standard repetoire, with its own hundred-seater venue on site.
Chinese Opera Teahouse 5 Smith St ⓣ6323 4862, ⓦwww.ctcopera.com.sg. For an interesting culinary and musical experience, come here for the Sights and Sounds of Chinese Opera Show (7pm), a set dinner followed by performances of excerpts from Chinese operas. The package costs S$35, though you can watch the opera selections alone for S$20 (includes tea and snacks; admission at 7.50pm).
Nanyang Academy of Fine Arts City Chinese Orchestra ⓦwww.cityco.com.sg. Chinese classical and folk music recitals, at various venues.
Singapore Chinese Orchestra Singapore Conference Hall, 7 Shenton Way, Financial District ⓣ64403839, ⓦwww.sco.com.sg. Performances of traditional Chinese music through the year, plus occasional free concerts.

Singapore Dance Theatre ⓣ6338 0611, ⓦwww.singaporedancetheatre.com. Contemporary and classical works at various venues, sometimes by moonlight at Fort Canning Park.
Singapore Lyric Opera ⓦwww.singaporeopera .com.sg. Western opera and operetta, at various venues.
Singapore Repertory Theatre DBS Arts Centre (see p.675). English-language theatre, and not just the most obvious British and American plays.
Singapore Symphony Orchestra ⓦwww.sso .org.sg. Performances throughout the year at Esplanade – Theatres on the Bay and, when it comes to chamber-music recitals by orchestra members, at the Victoria Concert Hall. Occasional free concerts at the Botanic Gardens and elsewhere.
Temple of Fine Arts ⓣ6535 0509, ⓦwww .templeoffinearts.org. This Indian cultural organiza-tion is dedicated to perpetuating traditional music and dance, and puts on occasional concerts and exhibitions.

Pop, rock, blues and jazz

Singapore has a thriving live music scene, attracting both Western stadium-rock outfits as well as indie bands, though some gigs can be marred by a rather staid atmosphere as locals are often still uncomfortable about letting their hair down. Rivalling Western music in terms of popularity in Singapore is **Canto-pop**, a bland hybrid of Cantonese lyrics and Western disco beats; Hong Kong Canto-pop superstars visit periodically, and the rapturous welcomes they receive make their shows quite an experience. The best music festival is **Mosaic** (March; ⓦwww .mosaicmusicfestival.com), showcasing an excellent range of jazz and rock acts at Theatres on the Bay; also worthwhile is **Singfest** (Aug; ⓦwww.singfest.com.sg), held in the open air at Fort Canning Park, where you can catch concerts throughout the year.

Small venues

Blu Jaz Café See p.666. Live torch song and jazz sets nightly.

Crazy Elephant #01-03 Block E, Clarke Quay ☎6337 7859, ⓦwww.crazyelephant.com; see map, p.606. Of the hotchpotch of brash venues along Clarke Quay, this bar has more street cred than most, with live music – blues and rock – practically every night and an open-mike jam session on Sun. Some tables are by the water's edge. Sun–Thurs 5pm–2am, Fri & Sat 5pm–3am. Happy hour is daily 5–9pm.

Jazz @ Southbridge 82b Boat Quay ☎6327 4671, ⓦwww.southbridgejazz.com.sg; see map, pp.618–619. The crowd at this shophouse venue, just next to Elgin Bridge, can be rather self-consciously jazzy, but there's no faulting the quality of the nightly live music sessions, often featuring foreign musicians and with a jam session on Sun. Plenty of light bites too, from goulash to springs rolls. Daily 11am–1am (Fri & Sat until 2am).

Home Club See p.674. Local indie bands play original material on Friday nights.

Howl At The Moon Second floor, Peranakan Place, corner of Orchard Rd and Emerald Hill Rd ☎6838 0281, ⓦwww.howlatthemoon.com.sg; see map, pp.640–641. This one-of-a-kind establishment in Singapore features "duelling piano" sessions every other night, at which two of the venue's resident team of pianists compete to play audience requests, with spontaneous outbreaks of singing. Best of all, on the last weekend (Thurs–Sat) of the month they do stand-up – quite a challenge in traditionally strait-laced Singapore – usually featuring British comedians (S\$40 in advance from agencies, S\$50 on the door). Stella, Hoegaarden and London Pride on tap. Tues–Sun 6pm till late; happy hour until 9pm.

Timbre Substation, 45 Armenian St and at The Arts House, 1 Old Parliament Lane; ⓦwww .timbre.com.sg; see map, p.606. Open-air venues with local bands and singer-songwriters serving up original material, though it can be a little derivative. Daily from 6pm (Arts House venue closed Sun).

Shopping

Choice and convenience make the Singapore **shopping** experience a rewarding one. While the scores of malls and department stores may appear uniform at first sight, housing various local and international chains, they all feature a fair number of independent retailers too. Prices aren't necessarily cheaper than in Western cities, however, thanks to the strong Singapore dollar and the island's affluence; Kuala Lumpur or Penang can be better hunting grounds for bargains, though Singapore boasts the best range of wares. If you're around during the **Great Singapore Sale** (late May to late July; ⓦwww.greatsingaporesale.com .sg), you'll find prices seriously marked down in many stores.

    Orchard Road, of course, offers the biggest cluster of malls, which between them stock more or less anything you could possibly want: clothes (by either Western or local designers), bespoke suits, sports equipment, electronic goods, antiques, and so on. There's a smaller peppering of malls in **Chinatown**, the most interesting of which are little more than multistorey markets, home to a few more traditional outlets stocking Chinese foodstuffs, medicines, instruments and porcelain. Chinatown also has a few antique and curio shops along South Bridge Road, and there are more knick-knacks on sale around **Arab Street**, where you'll also find textiles and batiks, robust basketware and some good deals on jewellery. **Little India** has various silk stores and goldsmiths as well as

Mustafa, a department store that's known all over the island for being open 24/7. South of Little India, the grid of streets between **Rochor Road** and the Singapore River is home to a few malls specializing in electrical and computer products. Elsewhere downtown, there are more malls at **Marina Centre** and **HarbourFront**, and there will be yet more shops at the two new integrated resorts; just outside downtown, **Holland Village** is another place to head for if you want to buy Asian art, crafts or textiles.

Typical **shopping hours** are daily from 10am to 9pm (10pm in some malls, especially along Orchard Rd). Tourists flying out of Singapore can claim a refund of the island's goods and services **tax** (GST; seven percent at the time of writing) on purchases over a certain amount (at least S$100, though some retailers require a larger outlay) at stores displaying a **Premier Tax Free** or **Tax Free Shopping** sticker. It's a fairly complicated process, and some stores deduct an administration fee; for detailed information, have a look at the "For consumers" section of ⓦ www.iras.gov.sg. Should you have a **complaint** with a particular store that can't be resolved, you can report it to the Singapore Tourism Board on ⓣ 1800/736 2000 or even go to the Small Claims Tribunal at the Subordinate Courts at 1 Havelock Square (on Upper Cross St near Chinatown MRT; ⓣ 6435 5946, ⓦ www.smallclaims.gov.sg), which has a fast-track system for tourists; it costs S$10 to have your case heard.

Shopping complexes and department stores

The best shopping opportunities in each part of town are listed below. Note that Orchard Road will soon boast two spanking new malls, **IonOrchard** above Orchard MRT, and **Orchard Central** next to Somerset MRT.

Orchard Road and around

See the map on pp.640–641 for locations.

Centrepoint 176 Orchard Rd (close to Somerset MRT) ⓦ www.fraserscentrepointmalls.com. Dependable all-round complex, whose seven floors of shops include Robinsons, Singapore's oldest department store.

Forum the Shopping Mall 583 Orchard Rd (near the *Orchard Parade* hotel) ⓦ www.forumtheshopping mall.com. Plenty of items to please the pampered brat – upmarket kids' clothes, toys and so forth.

The Heeren 260 Orchard Rd (next to the Visitor Centre) ⓦ www.theheeren.com.sg. Home to HMV for recorded music, plus quite a few shops selling trendy T-shirts to a young crowd.

Ngee Ann City 391a Orchard Rd ⓦ www .ngeeanncity.com.sg. A brooding twin-towered complex, home to the Japanese Takashimaya department store and the excellent Kinokuniya bookstore.

Palais Renaissance 390 Orchard Rd. A classy complex housing Prada, DKNY and other heavyweights.

Paragon Opposite Ngee Ann City ⓦ www.paragon .sg. Calvin Klein, Hugo Boss, Versace and many more at this swanky mall.

Plaza Singapura 68 Orchard Rd ⓦ www .plazasingapura.com.sg. Veteran mall with a bit of everything: Marks & Spencer, the Singapore department store chain John Little, sportswear and sports equipment, musical instruments, audio, video and general electrical equipment.

Tanglin Shopping Centre 19 Tanglin Rd (next to the *Orchard Parade* hotel) ⓦ www.tanglinsc.com. Good for art, antiques and curios.

Tangs Comer of Orchard and Scotts Rd ⓦ www .tangs.com. One of Singapore's most famous department stores, whose pagoda-style construction provides Orchard Rd with one of its most recognizable landmarks.

Wheelock Place 501 Orchard Rd, close to Orchard MRT. This impressive pyramid of a building boasts a well-stocked Borders bookshop and a Marks & Spencer.

Wisma Atria 435 Orchard Rd (opposite Tangs) ⓦ www.wismaonline.com. Hosts a good range of middle-market local and international fashion shops, plus the Japanese department store Isetan.

Chinatown

See the map on pp.618–619 for locations.

Chinatown Point 133 New Bridge Rd. One of the two buildings here is a handicraft centre with scores of tourist-oriented businesses.

Hong Lim Complex 531–531a Upper Cross St. Several Chinese provisions stores, fronted by sackfuls of dried mushrooms, cuttlefish, chillies, garlic cloves, onions, fritters and crackers. Other shops sell products ranging from acupuncture accessories to birds' nests.

Lucky Chinatown 211 New Bridge Rd, between Pagoda and Temple streets. Fairly upmarket place with lots of jewellery shops.

Pearl's Centre 100 Eu Tong Sen St. Home to some Chinese medicine clinics, where set-ups such as TCM Chinese Medicines at #02-20 will offer you a consultation for a few dollars, plus a few shops selling Buddhist paraphernalia.

People's Park Centre 101 Upper Cross St. Stall-like shop units selling Chinese handicrafts, CDs, electronics, silk, jade and gold.

People's Park Complex 1 Park Rd. A venerable shopping centre that, like the Hong Lim Complex and adjacent People's Park Centre, is among the most entertaining places to browse in Chinatown because it's so workaday, a place for ordinary folk to buy day-to-day needs. Also here is the Overseas Emporium on level 4, selling Chinese musical instruments, calligraphy pens, lacquer-work and jade.

The Colonial District and Marina Centre

See the map on p.606 for locations.

Funan DigitaLife Mall 109 North Bridge Rd Ⓦwww.funan.com.sg. A variety of stores here sell computer and electronics equipment.

Marina Square 6 Raffles Blvd Ⓦwww .marinasquare.com.sg. Nowhere near as large as its sprawling neighbour, Suntec City, but better laid out and with a very diverse range of outlets. If

you've time for just one Marina Centre mall, this is probably it.

Raffles City 252 North Bridge Rd (above City Hall MRT) Ⓦwww.rafflescity.com. Home to a branch of Robinsons department store with a Marks & Spencer within it, plus numerous fashion chains.

Bras Basah Road to Rochor Road

See the map on p.615 for locations.

Bugis Junction Junction Victoria St and Rochor Rd (above Bugis MRT) Ⓦwww.bugisjunction-mall .com.sg. Mall encasing several streets of restored shophouses, and featuring the Japanese/Chinese department store BHG and a number of fashion outlets.

Sim Lim Square 1 Rochor Canal Rd Ⓦwww .simlimsquare.com.sg. Electronics and computer equipment.

Little India

Mustafa Syed Alwi Rd Ⓦwww.mustafa.com.sg; see map, p.632. Totally different in feel to the malls of Orchard Rd, Mustafa is a phenomenon, selling electronics, fresh food, luggage, you name it – and never closes. See p.634 for more.

Elsewhere in Singapore

Holland Road Shopping Centre 211 Holland Ave, Holland Village. The shops above the supermarket are good places to browse for curios; you can buy anything from an Indian pram to a Chinese opium pipe here.

Vivocity Next to HarbourFront Centre and above HarbourFront MRT Ⓦwww.vivocity.com.sg. A humdinger of a mall, containing a branch of Tangs department store, the Page One bookstore, a cinema, zillions of fashion and other outlets, three food courts (*Food Republic* is exceptionally good) and several restaurants.

Things to buy

For addresses of malls and buildings not given below, consult the preceding directory.

Art, antiques, curios and souvenirs

Besides the outlets listed here, it's also worth calling in at the **MICA Building**, 140 Hill St, which houses as good a selection of art galleries as you'll find in Singapore; and the **Singapore Handicraft Centre** in Chinatown Point, which collects a few dozen souvenir shops under one roof.

Antiques of the Orient #02-40 Tanglin Shopping Centre ℡6734 9351. Antiquarian books, maps and prints.

Eng Tiang Huat 284 River Valley Rd ℡6734 3738. Oriental musical instruments, *wayang* costumes and props.

Jasmine Fine Arts #05-29 Paragon ☎ 6734 5688. Appealing artwork from all over the world.

Katong Antiques House 208 East Coast Rd, Katong ☎ 6345 8544. Peranakan artefacts and Chinese porcelain; see p.649.

Kwok Gallery #03-01 Far East Shopping Centre, 545 Orchard Rd ☎ 6235 2516. A broad, impressive inventory of antique Chinese artwork.

Lim's Arts & Living #02-01 Holland Rd Shopping Centre ☎ 6732 6486; #02-154 Vivocity ☎ 6376 9468. A sort of Asian Conran Shop, packed with bamboo pipes, dainty teapots, cherrywood furniture and lamps crafted from old tea jars.

Little Shophouse 43 Bussorah St, near Sultan Mosque ☎ 6295 2328. Well named, this little outlet boasts some beautiful examples of Peranakan beaded slippers (from S$180), plus replica Peranakan crockery.

Malay Art Gallery 31 Bussorah St ☎ 6294 8051. Stocks *songket* and *kerises* from Malaysia, Indonesia and even the Philippines.

Melor's Curios 39 Bussorah St ☎ 6292 3934. Aladdin's cave probably had fewer treasures than this shop, which sells Javanese and other Asian furniture, hangers made of bamboo for displaying fabrics, plus an assortment of batik, silk and *congkak* (mancala) sets. Daily 10am–5pm.

One Price Store 3 Emerald Hill Rd, off Orchard Rd ☎ 6734 1680. Everything from carved camphor-wood chests to Chinese snuff bottles.

Red Peach 68 Pagoda St, Chinatown ☎ 6222 2215. A repository of Asian art, incense sticks, tea sets, fabrics and chopsticks.

Rumah Bebe 113 East Coast Rd, Katong ⓦ www .rumahbebe.com. Peranakan products; see p.649 for more.

TeaJoy #01-05 North Bridge Centre, North Bridge Rd ☎ 6339 3739. Close to the National Library, this sells Chinese tea sets with special attention paid to oolong accoutrements.

Zhen Lacquer Gallery 1 Trengganu St, Chinatown ☎ 6222 2718. Specializes in lacquerware boxes and bowls.

Fabrics, silk and jewellery

C.T. Hoo #01-22 Tanglin Shopping Centre ☎ 6737 5447. Specializes in pearls.

Dakshaini Silks 65 Serangoon Rd, Little India ☎ 6291 9969. Premier Indian embroidered silks.

Flower Diamond #03-02 Ngee Ann City ☎ 6734 1221. Contemporary designs as well as more traditionally styled bling, at sensible prices.

Goodwill Trading Co 56 Arab St ☎ 6298 3205. Indonesian batik sarongs heaped on varnished wood shelves.

One George Street 95 South Bridge Rd, Chinatown. The entire first floor of this building is a jewellery market.

Risis National Orchid Garden (see p.643). Gold-plated orchids, either a classic Singapore souvenir or an utter cliché, depending on your viewpoint, are available here as well as at a few malls and at Changi airport.

Wong's Jewellery 62 Temple St, Chinatown ☎ 6323 0236. Chinese-style outlet, good for jade and gold items.

Books

Singapore bookshops are as well stocked as many in the West; all the larger ones carry a good selection of Western and local fiction, plus books on Singapore, Malaysia and the rest of East Asia, and a range of magazines.

BooksActually 5 Ann Siang Rd ⓦ www .booksactually.com. In a tidy restored shophouse, this small independent retailer takes pride in its literary selection and its central display devoted to the shop's cat.

Borders Ground floor, Wheelock Place ⓦ www .borders.com.sg. Always reliable. Open till 11pm most nights, Fri & Sat till midnight.

Earshot See listing under "CDs and DVDs".

Kinokuniya Level 3, Ngee Ann City; branch at Bugis Junction ⓦ www.kinokuniya.com.sg. The main outlet is simply one of Singapore's largest and best bookshops, with titles on every

conceivable subject and some foreign-language literature too.

MPH Level B1, Raffles City ⓦ www.mph.com.sg. Veteran of the local book trade, though not as comprehensive these days as it could be.

Page One Level 2, Vivocity ⓦ www .pageonegroup.com. Similar in feel to Kinokuniya, Page One started out as a publisher of art and architecture books and stocks plenty of titles on these areas, along with books on most other subjects.

Select Books #03-15 Tanglin Shopping Centre ⓦ www.selectbooks.com.sg. Tiny shop packing in a huge range of books on Malaysia and Singapore, plus literature on Southeast Asia in general. A great resource.

Times Bookstores Level 4, Centrepoint; Level 4, Plaza Singapura; ⓦ www.timesbookstores.com.sg. A well-stocked local chain.

CDs and DVDs

Plenty of Western CDs and DVDs are available in Singapore. If you want to buy Asian material, you'll find Chinese music and DVDs widely available; for Indian releases, there are several outlets in Little India, including Jothi Music Corner in the Little India Arcade at the start of Serangoon Road; and for Malay music, head to the Joo Chiat Complex, Geylang (see p.649).

Borders Wheelock Place. Carries the customary selection of pop and classical CDs, though it's not as comprehensive as HMV.

Earshot Arts House, 1 Old Parliament Lane ☎ 6334 0130, ⓦ www.earshot.com.sg. Nothing but CDs, DVDs and books by Singaporean artistes and writers.

Gramophone Cathay Building, 2 Handy Rd (where Orchard Rd becomes Bras Basah Rd). Largely mainstream CD releases.

HMV #01-11 The Heeren. A substantial store, your best bet for mainstream releases and with dedicated jazz and classical music sections.

Roxy Records #02-15 Excelsior Shopping Centre (at the Hill St end of the *Peninsula Excelsior Hotel*) ☎ 6337 7783. A range of imported indie and other hard-to-find releases, and even secondhand vinyl.

Sembawang Music Centre Level 3, Plaza Singapura; level 1, Funan DigitaLife Mall ⓦ www .sembawangmusic.com. Unadventurous chain.

That CD Level B1, Raffles City; Level B1, Paragon. More chart CDs.

Listings

Airlines Aeroflot, #05-02, 114 Middle Rd ☎ 6339 5500; AirAsia, at Changi airport (terminal 1) ☎ 6307 7688; Air China, #49-02 Republic Plaza, 9 Raffles Place ☎ 6225 2177; Air France, #14-05 Orchard Towers, 400 Orchard Rd ☎ 6415 5111; Air India #B1-10 UIC Building, 5 Shenton Way ☎ 6225 9411; American Airlines #25-06 Ocean Towers, 20 Raffles Place ☎ 6837 8577; ANA, #18-01, 80 Robinson Rd ☎ 6323 4333; Austrian Airlines, #09-01, 100 Tras St ☎ 6220 9047; Berjaya Air, 67 Tanjong Pagar Rd ☎ 6227 3688; British Airways, #06-05A, 15 Cairnhill Rd ☎ 6622 1747; Cathay Pacific #25-07 Ocean Towers, 20 Raffles Place ☎ 6533 1333; China Airlines, #14-00, 302 Orchard Rd ☎ 6737 2211; Emirates, #11-01 Parkview Sq, 600 North Bridge Rd ☎ 6735 3535; Etihad, #15-01 Suntec City Tower Two, 9 Temasek Blvd ☎ 6854 9788; Garuda #12-03 United Sq, 101 Thompson Rd ☎ 6250 5666; Japan Airlines, #03-01 Hong Leong Bldg, 16 Raffles Quay ☎ 1800/852 3688; Jetstar, no walk-in office ☎ 800/616 1977 or 6822 2288; KLM, #06-01, 79 Anson Rd ☎ 6823 2220; Korean Airlines, #26-01/05 Ocean Towers, 20 Raffles Place ☎ 6796 2048; Lufthansa #05-01 Palais Renaissance, 390 Orchard Rd ☎ 6835 5933; MAS #02-09 Singapore Shopping Centre, 190 Clemenceau Ave ☎ 6336 6777 (24hr); Philippine Airlines #10-02 Parklane Shopping Mall, 35 Selegie Rd ☎ 63361611; Qantas, #06-05A, 15 Cairnhill Rd #06-05/08 ☎ 6415 7373; Qatar Airways, #18-07 Paragon, 290 Orchard Rd ☎ 6732 9277; Royal Brunei #03-11 UE Shopping Mall, 81 Clemenceau Ave ☎ 6235 4672; SAS, #14-04, Shaw House, 350 Orchard Rd ☎ 6235 2488; SilkAir #17-08 Keypoint, 371 Beach Rd ☎ 6225 4488; Singapore Airlines #02-26 The Paragon, 290 Orchard Rd ☎ 6223 8888 (24hr); South African Airways, #13-01, 100 Tras St ☎ 6227 7911; SriLankan Airlines #13-02 Keck Seng Tower, 133 Cecil St ☎ 62257233; Swiss Airlines, #05-01 Palais Renaissance, 390 Orchard Rd ☎ 6823 2010; Tiger Airways, no walk-in office ☎ 6538 4437; Thai Airways, #03-00 The Globe, 100 Cecil St ☎ 6227 9391; Turkish Airlines, #15-04 Gateway West, 150 Beach Rd ☎ 6732 4556; United Airlines, #44-02 Hong Leong Bldg, 16 Raffles Quay ☎ 6873 3533.

Banks and exchange The banks with the most branches include DBS, HSBC, Standard Chartered, UOB and OUB, though as an international financial centre, Singapore is home to offices of many other major international banks. Normal banking hours are Mon–Fri 9.30am–3pm & Sat 9.30am–12.30pm. Licensed moneychangers, offering slightly more favourable exchange rates than the bank, aren't hard to find – particularly in Little India (eg at Mustafa, see p.634) and on Orchard Rd.

Embassies and consulates Australia, 25 Napier Rd ☎ 6836 4100; Brunei, 325 Tanglin Rd ☎ 6733

9055; Cambodia, #10-03 Orchard Towers, 400 Orchard Rd ☏ 6341 9785; Canada, #11-01 One George St, 95 South Bridge Rd ☏ 6854 5900; China, 150 Tanglin Rd ☏ 6479 3250; Denmark, #13-01 United Square, 101 Thomson Rd ☏ 6355 5010; India, 31 Grange Rd ☏ 6737 6777; Indonesia, 7 Chatsworth Rd ☏ 6737 7422; Ireland, #08-02 Liat Towers, 541 Orchard Rd ☏ 6238 7616; Japan, 16 Nassim Rd ☏ 6235 8855; Laos, #13-04 Goldhill Plaza, 51 Goldhill Plaza ☏ 6250 6044; Malaysia, 301 Jervois Rd ☏ 6235 0111; The Netherlands, #13-01 Liat Towers, 541 Orchard Rd ☏ 6737 1155; New Zealand, #15-06/10 Ngee Ann City, 391a Orchard Rd ☏ 6235 9966; Philippines, 20 Nassim Rd ☏ 67373977; South Africa, #15-00 Odeon Towers, 331 North Bridge Rd ☏ 6339 6948; Sweden, #05-01, 111 Somerset Rd ☏ 6415 9720; Thailand, 370 Orchard Rd ☏ 67372644; UK, 100 Tanglin Rd ☏ 6424 4200; US, 27 Napier Rd ☏ 6476 9100; Vietnam 10 Leedon Park Rd ☏ 6462 4519.

Emergencies See p.65.

Gyms California Fitness (⊕ www.californiafitness .com), Truc Fitness (⊕ www.truefitness.com.sg) and Fitness First (⊕ www.fitnessfirst.com.sg) all operate downtown gyms, though you will need to take out membership to use them.

Hospitals The state-run Singapore General Hospital, Outram Rd (SGH; ☏ 6222 3322, ⊕ www .sgh.com.sg), is near Outram Park MRT and has a 24hr casualty/emergency department, as do the privately run Raffles Hospital, 585 North Bridge Rd (☏ 6311 1111, ⊕ www.rafflesmedicalgroup.com); and Mount Elizabeth Hospital off Orchard Rd (☏ 6737 2666, ⊕ www.parkwayhealth.com).

Internet access Little India is the best place to look for internet cafés, which are fairly numerous here and cheap, charging as little as S$2.50 per hr. Orchard Rd and Chinatown have some internet cafés too, though Orchard Rd rates are high at S$5–6 per hr.

Pharmacies Both Guardian and Watson's are ubiquitous downtown, with branches in shopping malls and even in a few MRT stations.

Phones See p.71.

Police In an emergency, dial ☏ 999; otherwise call the police hotline ☏ 6225 0000.

Post offices The island has dozens of post offices (generally open Mon–Fri 8.30am–5pm & Sat 8.30am–1pm), with the one at 1 Killiney Rd (near Somerset MRT) keeping extended hours (Mon–Fri until 9pm, Sat until 4pm, plus Sun 10am–4pm). Poste restante/general delivery (bring proof of ID) is at the Singapore Post Centre, 10 Eunos Rd (near Paya Lebar MRT; Mon–Fri 8am–6pm, Sat 8am–2pm). For more on the mail system, contact SingPost (☏ 1605, ⊕ www .singpost.com).

Swimming Singapore arguably has the best state-run swimming pools in the world; just about every new town has a well-maintained 50m open-air pool, open from the early morning until well into the evening. Convenient venues include the Jalan Besar Swimming Complex on Tyrwhitt Rd, near Lavender and Farrer Park MRT stations; Buona Vista Swimming Complex in Holland Village; and Delta Swimming Complex at 900 Tiong Bahru Rd, near Redhill MRT. Charges are a mere S$1–1.50; have coins available for the ticket gates and lockers.

Travel agents The following are good for discounted airfares and packages: Airpower Travel, 131b Bencoolen St ☏ 6334 6571, ⊕ www .airpowertravel.com; STA Travel, 534a North Bridge Rd ☏ 67377188, ⊕ www.statravel.com.sg; Sunny Holidays, #01-70 Parco Bugis Junction, 200 Victoria St ☏ 6767 6868, ⊕ www.sunnyholidays .com.sg; and Zuji ⊕ www.zuji.com.sg.

Vaccinations Tan Tock Seng Hospital, across the road from Novena MRT, has a Travellers' Health & Vaccination Centre (☏ 6357 2233, ⊕ www.ttsh .com.sg).

Women's helpline AWARE ☏ 1-800/774 5935, ⊕ www.aware.org.sg.

Travel details

Trains

Singapore Railway Station to: Butterworth (1 daily; 14hr); Gua Musang (2 daily; 12hr); Ipoh (1 daily; 10hr); Jerantut (2 daily; 9hr); Johor Bahru (3 daily; 40min); Kota Bharu (2 daily; 14hr 30min); Kuala Lumpur (3 daily; 8hr); Seremban (3 daily; 5hr 30min); Taiping (1 daily; 11hr).

Buses

Ban San Terminal to: Johor Bahru (frequent; 1hr). **Golden Mile Complex** to: Alor Star (daily; 12hr 30min); Butterworth (daily; 10hr); Cameron Highlands (daily; 10hr); Hat Yai (at least 2 daily; 14hr); Kuala Lumpur (at least 10 daily; 6hr); Melaka (at least 2 daily; 3hr 30min); Mersing (March–Oct;

1 daily; 4hr); Penang (at least 3 daily; 11hr); Kuala Terengganu (2 daily; 10hr 30min).

Lavender MRT to: Ipoh (daily; 6hr 30min); Kuala Kangsar (daily; 7hr); Penang (daily; 10hr 30min); Taiping (daily; 7hr 30min).

Lavender Street Terminal to: Butterworth (at least 2 daily; 10hr); Ipoh (2 daily; 6hr 30min); Kota Bharu (1 daily; 12hr); Kuala Lumpur (6 daily; 6hr); Kuala Terengganu (2 daily; 10hr); Kuantan (3 daily; 6hr 30min); Melaka (10 daily; 3hr 30min); Mersing (3 daily; 4hr); Penang (2 daily; 10hr 30min); Seremban (2 daily; 5hr).

Ferries

Indonesia ferry schedules are available at ⓦ www .singaporecruise.com.

Changi Point to: Kampung Pengerang (for Desaru; no fixed times; 45min); Pulau Ubin (no fixed times; 25min).

HarbourFront Centre to: Batam (Indonesia; frequent; 40min); Karimun (several daily; 40min).

Tanah Merah Ferry Terminal to: Batam (Indonesia; hourly; 40min); Bintan (Indonesia; every 1–2hr; 1hr).

Flights

Changi airport to: Bandar Seri Begawan (2 daily; 2hr); Kota Kinabalu (2–3 daily; 2hr 30min); Kuala Lumpur (hourly; 55min); Kuching (3–4 daily; 1hr 20min); Langkawi (daily; 1hr 30min); Penang (4 daily; 1hr 15min).

Seletar airport to: Pulau Redang (March–Oct at least 4 weekly; 1hr 30min); Pulau Tioman (at least 4 weekly; 35min).

Contexts

Contexts

History

The modern-day nations of **Malaysia**, **Singapore** and **Brunei** only acquired independent status in 1963, 1965 and 1984 respectively. Before that, the history of these countries was inextricably linked with events in the larger Malay archipelago, from Sumatra across Borneo to the Philippines.

Unfortunately, there is little hard archeological evidence pertaining to the prehistoric period in the region, while the events prior to the foundation of Melaka are known only from unreliable written accounts by Chinese and Arab traders. For an understanding of events in the formative fourteenth and fifteenth centuries, there are two vital sources: the **Suma Oriental** (Treatise of the Orient), by Tomé Pires, a Portuguese emissary who came to Melaka in 1512 and used his observations to write a history of the region, and the **Sejarah Melayu**, the seventeenth-century "Malay Annals", which recount oral historical tales in a poetic style. Portuguese and Dutch **colonists** who arrived in the sixteenth and seventeenth centuries supplied written records, though these tended to concern commercial rather than political or social matters. At least there is a wealth of information from **British colonial** times which, despite an imperialistic bias, does give detailed insights into Malay affairs.

Beginnings

The oldest remains of *Homo sapiens* in the region were discovered in the Niah Caves in Sarawak and are thought to be those of hunter-gatherers, between 35,000 and 40,000 years old; other finds in the Peninsular state of Kedah are only 10,000 years old. The variety of **ethnic groups** found in both east and west Malaysia – from small, dark-skinned Negritos through to paler Austronesian Malays – has led to the theory of a slow filtration of peoples through the Malay archipelago from southern Indochina – a theory backed by an almost universal belief in animism, celebration of fertility and ancestor worship among the various peoples.

The Malay archipelago acquired a strategic significance thanks largely to the **shipping trade**, which flourished as early as the first century AD. This was engendered by the two major markets of the early world – India and China – and by the richness of its own resources. From the dense jungle of the Peninsula and northern Borneo came aromatic woods, timber and *nipah* palm thatch, traded by the forest-dwelling Orang Asli with the coastal Malays, who then bartered or sold it on to Arab and Chinese merchants. The region was also rumoured to be rich in **gold**, leading to its description by Greek explorers as "The Golden Chersonese" (*chersonese* meaning "peninsula"). Although gold was never found in the quantities supposed to exist, ornaments made of the metal helped to develop decorative traditions among craftsmen, and survive today. More significant, however, were the **tin fields** of the Malay Peninsula, mined in early times to provide an alloy used for temple sculptures. Chinese traders were also attracted by the medicinal properties of various sea products, such as sea slugs, collected by the Orang Laut (sea people), as well as by pearls and tortoise shells.

In return, the indigenous peoples acquired cloth, pottery, glass and new beliefs from foreign traders. From as early as 200 AD, **Indian traders** brought with them their Hindu and Buddhist practices, and archeological evidence from later periods, such as the tenth-century temples at Lembah Bujang (p.202), suggests that the local population not only tolerated these new belief systems, but adapted them to suit their own experiences. Perhaps the most striking contemporary example of such cultural interchange is the traditional entertainment of *wayang kulit* (shadow plays), whose stories are drawn from the Hindu *Ramayana*.

While trade with India developed very early, contact with **China** was initially less pronounced due to the pre-eminence of the Silk Road, further to the north. It wasn't until the eighth and ninth centuries that Chinese ships ventured into the archipelago. By the time Srivijaya appeared on the scene, a number of states – particularly in the Kelantan and Terengganu areas of the Peninsula – were sending envoys to China.

Srivijaya

The inhabitants of the western Peninsula and eastern Sumatra were quick to realize the geographical advantage afforded by the Melaka Straits, which provided a refuge where ships could wait for several months for a change in the monsoon winds. From the fifth century onwards a succession of **entrepôts** (storage ports) were created here to cater for the needs of passing vessels. One entrepôt eventually became the mighty empire of **Srivijaya**, eminent from the beginning of the seventh century until the end of the thirteenth, and encompassing all the shores and islands surrounding the Straits of Melaka. The exact location of Srivijaya is still a matter for debate, although most sources point to **Palembang** in southern Sumatra. The entrepôt's stable administration attracted commerce when insurrection elsewhere frightened traders away, while its wealth was boosted by extracting tolls and taxes from passing ships. Srivijaya also became an important centre for **Mahayana Buddhism** and learning. When the respected Chinese monk I Ching arrived in 671 AD, he found more than a thousand monks studying the Buddhist scriptures.

Political concepts developed during Srivijayan rule were to form the basis of Malay government in future centuries. Unquestioning **loyalty** among subjects was underpinned by the notion of *daulat*, the divine force of the ruler (who was called the Maharajah), which would strike down anyone guilty of *derhaka* (treason) – a powerful means of control over a deeply superstitious people.

The decision made around 1080 to shift the capital, for reasons unknown, from Palembang north to a place called **Melayu** seems to have marked the start of Srivijaya's decline. Piracy became almost uncontrollable, with even the Orang Laut, who had previously helped keep it in check, turning against the Srivijayan rulers. Soon both local and foreign traders began to seek safer ports, with the area that is now Kedah one of the main beneficiaries. Other regions were soon able to compete by replicating the peaceable conditions and efficient administration that had allowed Srivijaya to thrive.

Srivijaya's fate was sealed when it attracted the eye of foreign rivals. In 1275, the Majapahit empire of Java invaded Melayu and made inroads into many of Srivijaya's peninsular territories. Sumatra and Kedah were raided by the Cholas of India, while the Thai kingdom of Ligor was able to extract **tributes** of gold from Malay vassals, a practice that continued until the nineteenth century. Moreover, trading restrictions in China were relaxed from the late twelfth century onwards, making it more lucrative for traders to bypass the once mighty entrepôt and go directly to the source of their desired products.

Around the early fourteenth century Srivijaya's name disappears from the record books.

The Melaka Sultanate

With the collapse of Srivijaya came the establishment of the **Melaka Sultanate**, the Malay Peninsula's most significant historical period. Both the *Sejarah Melayu* and the *Suma Oriental* document the tale of a Palembang prince named **Paramesvara**, who fled the collapsing empire of Srivijaya to set up his own kingdom, finally settling on the site of present-day Melaka.

As well placed as its Sumatran predecessor, with a deep, sheltered harbour and good riverine access to lucrative jungle produce, Melaka set about establishing itself as an international marketplace. The securing of a special agreement in 1405 with the new Chinese emperor, Yung-lo, guaranteed trade to Melaka and protected it from its main rivals. To further ensure its prosperity, Melaka's second ruler, Paramesvara's son **Iskandar Shah** (1414–24), took the precaution of acknowledging the neighbouring kingdoms of Ayuthaya and Majapahit as overlords. In return Melaka received vital supplies and much-needed immigrants, which bolstered the expansion of the settlement.

To meet the needs of passing traders, port taxes and market regulations were managed by four **shahbandars** (harbour masters), each in charge of trade with certain territories. Hand in hand with the trade in commodities went the exchange of ideas. By the thirteenth century, Arab merchants had begun to frequent Melaka's shores, bringing with them **Islam**, which their Muslim Indian counterparts helped to propagate among the Malays. Melaka's prestige was enhanced both by its conversion to Islam, making it part of a worldwide community with profitable trade links, and by territorial expansion which, by the reign of its last ruler **Sultan Mahmud Shah** (1488–1528), included the west coast of the Peninsula as far as Perak, Pahang, Singapore, and most of east-coast Sumatra.

The legacy of **Melaka's golden age** reaches far beyond its material wealth. One of the most significant developments was the establishment of a **court structure** (see p.341), which was to lay the foundations for a system of government lasting until the nineteenth century. According to Malay royal tradition, the **sultan**, as head of state, traced his ancestry back through Paramesvara to the maharajahs of ancient Srivijaya; in turn Paramesvara was believed to be descended from Alexander the Great. The sultan also claimed divinity, a claim strengthened by the sultanate's conversion to Islam, which held Muslim rulers to be Allah's representatives on earth. To further secure his power, which was always under threat from the overzealous nobility, the sultan embarked on a series of measures to emphasize his "otherness": no one but he could wear gold unless it was a royal gift, and yellow garments were forbidden among the general population.

The Melaka Sultanate also allowed the **arts** to flourish; the principal features of the courtly dances and music of this period can still be distinguished in traditional entertainments today. Much more significant, however, was the refinement of **language**, adapting the primitive Malay that had been used in the kingdom of Srivijaya into a language of the elite. Such was Melaka's prestige that all who passed through the entrepôt sought to imitate it, and by the sixteenth century, Malay was the most widely used language in the archipelago. Tellingly, the word *bahasa*, although literally meaning "language", came to signify Malay culture in general.

The Portuguese conquest of Melaka

With a fortune as tempting as Melaka's, it wasn't long before Europe set its sights on the sultanate. At the beginning of the sixteenth century, the **Portuguese** began to take issue with Venetian control of the Eastern market. They planned instead to establish direct contacts with the commodity brokers of the East by gaining control of crucial regional ports. The key player in the subsequent conquest of Melaka was Portuguese viceroy **Alfonso de Albuquerque**, who led the assault on the entrepôt in 1511, forcing its surrender after less than a month's siege. Aloof and somewhat effete in their high-necked ruffs and stockings, the Portuguese were not well liked, but despite the almost constant attacks from upriver Malays, they controlled Melaka for the next 130 years.

There are few physical reminders of the Portuguese in Melaka, apart from the gateway to their fort, A Famosa, and the small **Eurasian** community, descendants of intermarriage between the Portuguese and local Malay women. The colonizers had more success with religion, however, converting large numbers of locals to **Catholicism**; their churches still dominate the city.

The Dutch in Melaka

Portuguese control over Melaka lasted for well over a century, until it was challenged by the Vereenigde Oostindische Compagnie (VOC), or **Dutch East India Company**, who were already the masters of Indonesia's valuable spice trade. Melaka was the VOC's most potent rival, and the company mounted a bid to seize the colony, succeeding in 1641 when, after a five-month siege, the Dutch flag was hoisted over Melaka.

Instead of ruling from above as the Portuguese had tried to do, the Dutch cleverly wove their subjects into the fabric of government: each racial group was represented by a *kapitan*, a respected figure from the community who mediated between his own people and the new administrators – often becoming a wealthy and powerful person in his own right. The Dutch were also responsible for the rebuilding of Melaka, much of which had been turned to rubble during the protracted takeover of the city; many of these structures, in their distinctive Northern European style, still survive today.

By the mid-eighteenth century, the conditions for Melaka's trade with China were at their peak: the relaxation of maritime restrictions in China itself had opened up the Straits for their merchants, while Europeans were eager to satisfy the growing demand for tea. The Chinese came to Melaka in droves and soon established themselves as the city's foremost entrepreneurs. Chinese settlement in the area and, in some cases, intermarriage with local Malay women, created a new cultural blend, known as **Peranakan** or Baba-Nonya – the legacies of which are the opulent mansions and unique cuisine of Melaka, Penang and Singapore (see p.712).

But a number of factors prevented Dutch Melaka from fulfilling its potential. Since their VOC salary was hardly bountiful, Dutch administrators found it more lucrative to trade on the black market, taking backhanders from grateful merchants, a situation which severely damaged Melaka's commercial standing. High taxes forced traders to more economical locations such as the newly established British port of **Penang**, whose foundation in 1786 heralded the awakening of British interest in the Straits. In the end,

Melaka never stood a chance: the company's attention was distracted by other centres such as Batavia (modern-day Jakarta), the VOC "capital", and by the kingdom of Johor.

Johor and Brunei

When Melaka fell to the Portuguese, the deposed sultan, Mahmud Shah, made for Pulau Bintan in the Riau archipelago, just south of Singapore, where he established the first **court of Johor**. When, in 1526, the Portuguese attacked and razed the settlement, Mahmud fled once again, this time to Sumatra, where he died in 1528. It was left to his son, Alauddin Riayat Shah, to found a new court on the upper reaches of the Johor River, though the capital of the kingdom then shifted repeatedly during a century of assaults on Johor territory by Portugal and the Sumatran Sultanate of Aceh.

The **arrival of the Dutch** in Southeast Asia marked a distinct upturn in Johor's fortunes. Hoping for protection from its local enemies, the court aligned itself firmly with the Dutch and was instrumental in their successful siege of Portuguese Melaka. Such loyalty was rewarded by trading privileges and by assistance in securing a treaty with Aceh, which at last gave Johor the breathing space to develop. Johor was the supreme Malay kingdom for much of the seventeenth century, but by the 1690s its empire was fraying under the despotic rule of another Sultan Mahmud. Lacking strong leadership, Johor's Orang Laut turned to piracy, scaring off trade, while wars with the Sumatran kingdom of Jambi, one of which resulted in the total destruction of Johor's capital, weakened it still further. No longer able to tolerate his cruel regime, Mahmud's nobles stabbed him to death in 1699. Not only did this change the nature of power in Malay government – previously, law deemed that the sultan could only be punished by Allah – but it also marked the end of the Melaka dynasty.

During Melaka's meteoric rise, **Brunei** had been busily establishing itself as a trading port of some renown. The Brunei Sultanate's conversion to **Islam**, no doubt precipitated by the arrival of wealthy Muslim merchants fleeing from the Portuguese in Melaka, also helped to increase its international prestige. When geographer **Antonio Pigafetta** visited Brunei with **Ferdinand Magellan**'s expedition of 1521, he found the court brimming with visitors from all over the world. This, indeed, was Brunei's "golden age", with its borders embracing land as far south as present-day Kuching in Sarawak, and as far north as the lower islands of the modern-day Philippines. Brunei's efforts, however, were soon curtailed by Spanish colonization in 1578, which, although lasting only a matter of weeks, enabled the Philippine kingdom of Sulu to gain a hold in the area – a fact which put paid to Brunei's early expansionist aims.

The Bugis and Minangkabau

Through the second half of the seventeenth century, a new ethnic group, the **Bugis** – renowned for their martial and commercial skills – had been trickling into the Peninsula, seeking refuge from the civil wars which wracked their homeland of Sulawesi (in the mid-eastern Indonesian archipelago). By the beginning of the eighteenth century, there were enough of them to constitute a powerful court lobby, and in 1721 they took advantage of factional struggles to capture the kingdom of Johor – now based in Riau. Installing a Malay puppet sultan, the Bugis ruled for over sixty years, making Riau an essential port of call on the eastern trade route; they even almost succeeded in capturing Melaka in 1756. But when Riau-Johor made another bid for Melaka in 1784, the Dutch held on with renewed vigour and finally forced a treaty placing all Bugis territory in Dutch hands.

In spiritual terms, the **Minangkabau** (see p.691), hailing from western Sumatra, had what the Bugis lacked, being able to claim cultural affinity with ancient Srivijaya. Although this migrant group had been present in the Negeri Sembilan region since the fifteenth century, it was in the second half of the seventeenth century that they arrived in the Malay Peninsula in larger numbers. Despite professing allegiance to their Sumatran ruler, the Minangkabau were prepared to accept Malay overlordship, which in practice gave them a great deal of autonomy. The warrior Minangkabau were not natural allies of the Bugis or the Malays, although they did occasionally join forces in order to defeat a common enemy. In fact, over time the distinction between various migrant groups became less obvious as intermarriage blurred clan demarcations, and Malay influence, such as the adoption of Malay titles, became more pronounced.

The arrival of the British

At the end of the eighteenth century, Dutch control in Southeast Asia was more widespread than ever, and the VOC empire should have been at its height. Instead, its coffers were bare and it faced the superior trading and maritime skills of the British. The disastrous defeat of the Dutch in the Fourth Anglo-Dutch War (1781–83) lowered their morale still further, and when the British, in the form of the **East India Company** (EIC), moved in on Melaka and the rest of the Dutch Asian domain in 1795, the VOC barely demurred.

Initially, the British agreed to a caretaker administration whereby they would assume sovereignty over the entrepôt to prevent it falling under French control, now that Napoleon had conquered Holland. The end of the Napoleonic wars in Europe put the Dutch in a position to retake Melaka between 1818 and 1825, but in the meantime, the EIC had established the stable port of **Penang** and – under the supervision of **Sir Thomas Stamford Raffles** – founded the new settlement of **Singapore**. The strategic position and free-trade policy of Singapore – backed by the impressive industrial developments of the British at home – threatened the viability of both Melaka and Penang, forcing the Dutch finally to relinquish their hold on the former to the British, and leaving the latter to dwindle to a backwater. In the face of such stiff competition, smaller Malay rivals inevitably linked their fortunes to the British.

The British assumption of power was sealed by the **Anglo–Dutch Treaty of 1824**, which apportioned territories between the two powers using the Straits of Melaka and the equator as the dividing lines, thereby splitting the Riau-Johor kingdom as well as ending centuries of cultural interchange with Sumatra. This was followed in 1826 by the unification of Melaka, Penang and Singapore into one administration, known as the **Straits Settlements**, with Singapore replacing Penang as its capital in 1832.

Raffles had at first hoped that **Singapore** would act as a market to sell British goods to traders from all over Southeast Asia, but it soon became clear that **Chinese** merchants, the linchpin of Singapore's trade, were interested only in

Malay products such as birds' nests, seaweed and camphor. But passing traders were not the only Chinese to come to the Straits. Although settlers had trickled into the Peninsula since the early days of Melaka, new **plantations** of pepper and gambier (an astringent used in tanning and dyeing), and the rapidly expanding **tin mines**, attracted floods of workers eager to escape a life of poverty in China. By 1845, half of Singapore's population was Chinese, and likewise principal towns along the Peninsula's west coast (site of the world's largest tin field) and, for that matter, Kuching, became predominantly Chinese.

The Pangkor Treaty

Allowed a large degree of commercial independence by both the British and the Malay chiefs, the Chinese formed **kongsis** (clan associations) and secret societies (triads). Struggles between clan groups were rife, sometimes resulting in large-scale riots such as those in Penang in 1867, where the triads allied themselves with Malay groups in a bloody street battle lasting several days. The **Malays**, too, were hardly immune from factional conflicts, which frequently became intertwined with Chinese squabbles, causing a string of **civil conflicts**.

Lawlessness like this was detrimental to commerce, giving the British an excuse to increase their involvement in local affairs. A meeting involving the chiefs of the Perak Malays was arranged by the new Straits Governor, Andrew Clarke, on Pulau Pangkor, just off the west coast of the Peninsula. In the meantime, Rajah Abdullah, the man most likely to succeed to the Perak throne, had written to Clarke asking for his position as sultan to be guaranteed; in return, he offered the British the chance to appoint a **Resident**, a senior British civil servant whose main function would be to act as adviser to the local sultan, and who would also oversee the collecting of local taxes. On January 20, 1874, the **Pangkor Treaty** (see also p.693) was signed, formalizing British intervention in Malay political affairs.

Perak's first Resident, J.W.W. Birch, was not sympathetic to the ways of the Malays; his centralizing tendencies were opposed by Abdullah when he became sultan. Senior British officials, fearful of a Malay rebellion, announced that judicial decisions would from now on be in the hands of the British. This went against the Pangkor Treaty, and furious Malays soon found a vent for their frustration: on November 2, 1875, Birch was killed on an upriver visit. It wasn't until the appointment of the third Resident of Perak, the respected Hugh Low, that the system began working far more smoothly.

Each state soon saw the arrival of a Resident, and agreements along the lines of the Pangkor Treaty were drawn up with Selangor, Negeri Sembilan and Pahang in the 1880s. In 1896, these three became bracketed together under the title of the **Federated Malay States**, with the increasingly important town of Kuala Lumpur made the regional capital.

British Malaya

By 1888 the name **British Malaya** had been brought into use – a term which reflected the intention to extend British control over the whole Peninsula. Over subsequent decades, the Malay sultans' economic and administrative powers were gradually eroded, while the introduction of rubber estates during the first half of the twentieth century made British Malaya one of the most productive colonies in the world. The rapidity and extent of the British takeover was unprecedented in the Peninsula, the process being aided by new technology that improved communications.

The gradual extension of British power brought further unrest, particularly in the east-coast states, where the Malays proved just as resentful of British control as in Perak. In Pahang a set of skirmishes took place in the early 1890s, when Malay chiefs protested about the reduction of their former privileges. One powerful chief, Dato' Bahaman, was stripped of his title by Pahang's Resident, Hugh Clifford, as a result of which the Dato' led a small rebellion which – though never a serious military threat to the British – soon became the stuff of legends. One fighter, **Mat Kilau**, gained a place in folklore as a heroic figure who stood up to the British in the name of Malay nationalism. From this time onwards, Malays would interpret the uprisings as a valiant attempt to safeguard Malay traditions and autonomy.

By 1909, the northern Malay states of Kedah and Perlis had been brought into the colonial fold. In 1910, Johor accepted a British general-adviser; a 1914 treaty between Britain and Johor made his powers equal to those of Residents elsewhere. Terengganu, which was under Thai control, was the last state to accept a British adviser, in 1919. These four states, together with Kelantan, were sometimes collectively referred to as the **Unfederated Malay States**, though they shared no common administration.

By the outbreak of World War I, British political control was more or less complete. The Peninsula was subdivided into groups of states and regions with the seat of power split between Singapore and Kuala Lumpur.

The expansion of British interests in Borneo

The Anglo-Dutch Treaty did not include **Borneo**, where official expansion was discouraged by the EIC, which preferred to concentrate on expanding its trading contacts rather than geographical control. The benefits of Borneo did not, however, elude the sights of one British explorer, **James Brooke** (1803–68). Finding lawlessness throughout the island, Brooke persuaded the Sultan of Brunei to award him his own area – **Sarawak** – in 1841, becoming the first of a line of "**White Rajahs**" that ruled the state until the start of World War II. Brooke quickly managed to assert his authority by involving formerly rebellious Malay chiefs in government, although the interior's Iban tribes proved more of a problem. Subsequently Brooke and his successors were to prove adept at siphoning more land into the familial fiefdom.

Though the association between the British and James Brooke was informal (Brooke was careful not to encourage European contacts that might compromise his hold on his territory), trade between Singapore and Sarawak flourished. By the mid-nineteenth century, however, the British attitude had altered; they chose Brooke as their agent in Brunei, and found him a useful deterrent against French and Dutch aspirations towards the valuable trade routes. Then in 1888, Sarawak, North Borneo (Sabah) and Brunei were transformed into **protectorates**, a status which entailed responsibility for their foreign policy being handed over to the British.

The legacy of James Brooke was furthered by his nephew Charles in the closing years of the nineteenth century. Like his uncle before him, **Charles Brooke** ruled Sarawak in a paternalistic fashion, recruiting soldiers, lowly officials and boatmen from the ranks of the tribal groups and leaving the Chinese to get on with running commercial enterprises and opening up the interior. The rule of the last White Rajah, **Vyner Brooke**, Charles's eldest son (1916–41), saw no new territorial acquisitions, though there was a steady development in rubber, pepper and palm-oil production. The tribal peoples mostly continued living a traditional lifestyle in longhouses along the river and, with the end of their practice of head-hunting, there was some degree of integration among the area's varied racial groups.

By way of contrast, the **British North Borneo Chartered Company**'s writ in what became Sabah encountered some early obstacles. The company's plans for economic expansion involved clearing the rainforest, planting **rubber** and **tobacco** over large areas, and levying taxes on the ethnic groups. Resistance ensued, with the most vigorous action, in 1897, led by a Bajau chief, **Mat Salleh**, whose men rampaged through the company's outstation on Pulau Gaya. Another rebellion by the Murut tribespeople in 1915 resulted in a heavy-handed response from British forces, who killed hundreds.

By the start of the twentieth century, the majority of the lands of the once-powerful **Sultanate of Brunei** had been dismembered – the sultanate was now surrounded by Sarawak. But the sultan's fortunes had not completely disappeared and with the discovery of oil in 1929, the British thought it prudent to appoint a Resident. Exploitation of the small state's oil fields picked up pace in the 1930s following investment from British companies.

Development and ethnic rivalries

In the first quarter of the twentieth century, the British encouraged hundreds of thousands of **immigrants** from China and India to come to Peninsular Malaysia, Sarawak, North Borneo and Singapore. They arrived to work as tin miners or plantation labourers, and Malaya's population in this period doubled to four million. This bred increasing resentment among the Malays, who believed that they were being denied the economic opportunities advanced to others. The British barely noticed the growing disparities between the communities – a factor which contributed to racial violence in later years.

A further deterioration in Malay–Chinese relations followed the success of the mainland Chinese revolutionary groups in Malaya. Chinese-educated Chinese joined the **Malayan Communist Party** (MCP) from 1930 onwards and also formed the backbone of postwar Chinese movements which demanded an end to British rule and to what they perceived as special privileges extended to the Malays. At the same time, Malay nationalism was gathering its own head of steam. The **Singapore Malay Union**, which held its first conference in 1939, advocated a Malay supremacist line. A year earlier, the first All-Malaya Malays Conference, organized by the Selangor Malays Association, had been held in KL.

The Japanese occupation

The **surrender** of the British forces in Singapore in February, 1942 ushered in a Japanese regime which proceeded to brutalize the Chinese, largely because of Japan's history of conflict with China; at least 25,000 people were tortured and killed in the two weeks immediately after the surrender of the island by the British military command. Allied POWs were rounded up into prison camps; many of the troops were subsequently sent to build the infamous "Death Railway" in Burma.

In **Malaya**, towns and buildings were destroyed as the Allies attempted to bomb strategic targets. But with the Japanese firmly in control, the occupiers ingratiated themselves with some of the Malay elite by suggesting that after the war the country would be given independence. Predictably, it was the Chinese activists in the MCP, more so than the Malays, who organized resistance during wartime; in the chaotic period directly after the war it was the MCP's armed wing, the **Malayan People's Anti-Japanese Army** (MPAJA), who maintained order in many areas.

The Japanese invasion of **Sarawak** in late 1941 began with the capture of the Miri oil field and spread south with little resistance. Although the Japanese never penetrated the interior, they quickly established control over the populated towns along the coast. The Chinese in Miri, Sibu and Kuching were the main targets: the Japanese put down rebellions against their rule brutally, and there was no organized guerrilla activity until late in the occupation. What resistance there was arose from the presence of Major **Tom Harrisson** and his team of British and Australian commandos, who parachuted into the remote Kelabit Highlands to build a resistance movement.

In **North Borneo**, the Japanese invaded Pulau Labuan on New Year's Day, 1942. Over the next three years the main suburban areas were bombed by the Allies, and by the time of the Japanese surrender in September 1945, most of Jesselton (modern-day KK) and Sandakan had been destroyed. Captured troops and civilians suffered enormously – the worst single outrage being the "Death March" in September 1944 when 2400 POWs were forced to walk from Sandakan to Ranau (see p.526).

In September 1945, just prior to a planned Allied invasion to retake Singapore, the **Japanese surrendered** following the dropping of atom bombs on Nagasaki and Hiroshima. The surrender led to a power vacuum in the region, with the British initially having to work with the MPAJA to exert political control. Violence occurred between the MPAJA and Malays, particularly against those accused of collaborating with the Japanese.

Postwar developments

Immediately after the war, the British introduced the **Malayan Union**, in effect turning the Malay States from a protectorate into a colony, as part of which the Malay rulers had their sovereignty removed. One impact of these changes was to give the Chinese and Indian inhabitants citizenship and equal rights with the Malays. This quickly aroused opposition from the Malays, the nationalists among whom formed the **United Malays National Organization** (UMNO) in 1946. Its main tenet was that Malays should retain special privileges, largely because they were the first inhabitants, and that the uniquely powerful position of the sultans should not be tampered with.

UMNO's resistance led to the Malayan Union idea being replaced by the **Federation of Malaya**. Established in 1948, this upheld the sultans' power and privileges and brought all of the Peninsula's territories together under one government, with the exception of Chinese-dominated Singapore, whose inclusion would have led to the Malays being in a minority overall. Protests erupted in Singapore at its exclusion, with the **Malayan Democratic Union** (MDU), a multiracial party, calling for integration with Malaya – a position that commanded little support among the Chinese population.

After the Japanese surrender in **Borneo**, the Colonial Office in London made Sarawak and North Borneo **Crown Colonies**, with Vyner Brooke offering no objection. Britain also signed a Treaty of Protection with the Sultan of Brunei, making Sarawak's high commissioner the governor of Brunei – a purely decorative position, as the sultan remained the chief power in the state.

Although Sarawak's ruling body, the Council Negeri (composed of Malays, Chinese, Iban and British) had voted to transfer power to Britain, some Malays and prominent Iban in Kuching opposed their country's new status. Protests reached a peak with the assassination in Sibu in 1949 of the senior official in the new administration, Governor Duncan Stewart. But on the whole, resentment at the passing of the Brooke era was short-lived as the economy expanded and infrastructure improved.

The Emergency

Many Chinese in the Peninsula were angered by the change of the status of the country from a colony to a federation, in which they effectively became second-class citizens. According to the new laws, non-Malays could only qualify as citizens if they had lived in the country for fifteen out of the last twenty-five years, and they also had to prove they spoke Malay or English.

After the communists took control of China in 1949, most of the Malayan Chinese ceased to look to China and the more political among them founded a new political party, the **Malayan Chinese Association** (MCA) in KL. But

---

The Emergency and the Orang Asli

The impact of the Emergency on the **Orang Asli** of the interior was dramatic. All but the most remote tribes were subject to intimidation and brutality, from guerrillas on one side and government forces on the other. In effect, the Orang Asli's centuries-old invisibility had ended; the population of Malaysia was now aware of their presence, and the government of their strategic importance.

The Orang Asli had no choice but to grow food and act as porters for the guerrillas, as well as – most important of all – provide intelligence, warning them of the approach of the enemy. In response, the government implemented a disastrous policy of removing thousands of Orang Asli from the jungle and relocating them in new model villages in the interior, which were no more than dressed-up prison camps. Hundreds died in captivity before the government dismantled these settlements. By then, not surprisingly, active support for the insurgents among the Orang Asli had risen – though allegiances were switched to the security forces when it was clear the guerrillas were heading for defeat. Government attempts to control the Orang Asli during the Emergency turned out to be the precursor to initiatives that persist to the present day, drawing the Orang Asli away from their traditional lifestyle and into the embrace of the Malaysian nation-state.

some local Chinese identified with the MCP, which, under its new leader, **Chin Peng**, declared its intention of setting up a Malayan republic. Peng fused the MCP with the remains of the MPAJA, and, using the arms supplies which the latter had dumped in the forests, from June 1948 he launched sporadic attacks on rubber estates, killing planters and employees as well as spreading fear among rural communities. At the peak of the conflict, around ten thousand of his guerrillas were hiding out in dozens of camouflaged jungle camps. For a long time they milked a support network of Chinese-dominated towns and villages in the interior, in many cases cowing the inhabitants into submission by means of public executions – although in some areas many of the poor rural workers identified with the insurgents' struggle. It was only when the government successfully planted informers that the security services started to get wind of guerrilla operations.

The period of unrest (1948–60) was undoubtedly a civil war but was euphemistically called **the Emergency**. This was mainly for insurance purposes – planters would have had their policies cancelled if war had been officially declared. Although the Emergency was never fully felt in the main urban areas, the British rubber estate owners would arrive at the *Coliseum Hotel* in KL with harrowing stories of how the "communist terrorists" had hacked off the arms of rural Chinese workers who had refused to support the cause, and of armed attacks on plantations.

The British were slow to respond to the threat, but once Lieutenant-General Sir Harold Briggs was put in command of police and army forces, Malaya was on a war footing. The most controversial policy Briggs enacted was the **resettlement** of 400,000 rural Chinese – mostly squatters who had moved to the jungle fringes to avoid the Japanese during the war – as well as thousands of Orang Asli (see box, p.697). Although these forced migrations were successful in breaking down many of the guerrillas' supply networks, they had the effect of making both Chinese and Orang Asli more sympathetic to the idea of a communist republic.

The violence peaked in 1950 with ambushes and attacks on plantations near Ipoh, Kuala Kangsar, Kuala Lipis and Raub. The most notorious incident occurred in 1951 on the road to Fraser's Hill, when the British high commissioner to Malaya, **Sir Henry Gurney**, was assassinated. Under his replacement, Sir Gerald Templer, a new policy was introduced to win hearts and minds. "White Areas", regions perceived as free of guerrilla activity, were established; communities in these areas had food restrictions and curfews lifted, a policy which began to dissipate guerrilla activity over the next three years. The leaders were offered an amnesty in 1956, which was refused, and Chin Peng and most of the remaining cell members fled over the border to Thailand where they received sanctuary.

Towards independence

The Emergency had the effect of speeding up political change prior to independence. UMNO stuck to its "Malays first" policy, though its president, **Tunku Abdul Rahman** (also the chief minister of Malaya), won the 1955 election by co-operating with the MCA and the Malayan Indian Association. The resulting bloc, the **UMNO Alliance**, swept into power under the rallying cry of **Merdeka** (Freedom). The hope was that ethnic divisions would no longer be a major factor if **independence** was granted, though those divisions still hadn't been eradicated.

With British backing, *merdeka* was proclaimed on August 31, 1957 in a ceremony in Kuala Lumpur's padang – promptly renamed Merdeka Square.

The British high commissioner signed a treaty which decreed that the Federation of Malaya was now independent of the Crown, with Tunku Abdul Rahman the first prime minister. The new **constitution** allowed for the nine Malay sultans to alternate as king, and established a two-tier **parliament**, comprising a house of elected representatives and a senate with delegates from each of the states. Under Rahman, the country was fully committed to economic expansion, with foreign investment actively encouraged – a stance which has survived to the present.

Similarly, in **Singapore** the process of gaining independence gained momentum throughout the 1950s. In 1957, the British gave the go-ahead for the setting up of an elected 51-member assembly, and full **self-government** was attained in 1959, when the People's Action Party (PAP) under **Lee Kuan Yew** won most of the seats. Lee immediately entered into talks with Tunku Abdul Rahman over the notion that Singapore and Malaya should be joined administratively. Tunku initially agreed, although he feared the influence of pro-communist extremists in the PAP.

In 1961, Tunku Abdul Rahman proposed that Sarawak and North Borneo should join Malaya and Singapore in a revised federation. Many in Borneo would have preferred the idea of a separate Borneo Federation, but the Konfrontasi (see below) made clear how vulnerable such a federation would be to attack from Indonesia. Rahman's suggestion was, however, not fuelled by security concerns but by **demographics**: if Singapore were to join the existing federation, the country would become one with a Chinese majority. This made the two Borneo colonies useful as a demographic counterweight to Singapore's Chinese.

Although Abdul Rahman had wanted **Brunei** to join the Malaysian Federation, Sultan Omar refused when he realized Rahman's price – a substantial proportion of Brunei's oil and gas revenues. Brunei remained under nominal British jurisdiction until its **independence** on December 31, 1983. For more on Brunei's history, in particular recent developments, see p.559.

Federation and the Konfrontasi

In September 1963, North Borneo (quickly renamed Sabah), Sarawak and Singapore joined Malaya in the **Federation of Malaysia** – "Malaysia" being a term coined by the British in the 1950s when the notion of a Greater Malaya had been propounded. Both Indonesia, which laid claim to Sarawak, and the Philippines, which argued it had jurisdiction over Sabah as it had originally been part of the Sulu Sultanate, reacted angrily to the new federation. Border skirmishes with Indonesia known as the **Konfrontasi** ensued, and a wider war was only just averted when Indonesian President Sukarno backed down from taking on British and Gurkha troops brought in to bolster Sarawak's small armed forces.

Within the federation, further differences surfaced in Singapore in this period between Lee Kuan Yew and the Malay-dominated Alliance over the lack of egalitarian policies; many Chinese were concerned that UMNO's overall influence in the federation was too great. Tensions rose on the island and ugly racial incidents developed into full-scale **riots** in 1964, in which several people were killed.

These developments were viewed with great concern by Tunku Abdul Rahman in Kuala Lumpur, and when the PAP subsequently attempted to enter

Peninsular politics, he decided it would be best if Singapore left the federation. This was emphatically not in Singapore's best interests, since it was an island without any obvious natural resources; Lee cried on TV when the expulsion was announced and Singapore acquired full **independence** on August 9, 1965. The severing of the bond between Malaysia and Singapore has led to a kind of sibling rivalry between the two nations ever since (see box, p.702).

Racial issues and riots

Singapore's exit from the Malaysian Federation was not enough to quell ethnic tensions. Resentment built among the Malaysian Chinese over the principle that Malay be the main language taught in schools and over the privileged employment opportunities offered to Malays. In May 1969, the UMNO Alliance lost ground in elections, and Malays in major cities reacted angrily to a perceived increase in power of the Chinese, who had commemorated their breakthrough with festivities in the streets. Hundreds of people, mostly Chinese, were killed and injured in the **riots** which followed; KL in particular became a war zone where large crowds of youths went on the rampage. Rahman kept the country under a state of emergency for nearly two years, during which the draconian **Internal Security Act** (ISA) was used to arrest and imprison activists, as well as many writers and artists, setting a sombre precedent for authoritarian practices still followed today.

Rahman never recovered full political command after the riots and resigned in 1970. In September that year, the new prime minister, **Tun Abdul Razak**, took up the reins with a less authoritarian stance. He brought the parties in Sarawak and Sabah into the political process and initiated a form of state-orchestrated positive discrimination called the **New Economic Policy** (NEP; see box opposite), which gives ethnic Malays and members of Borneo's tribes favoured positions in business and other professions. It was also under Razak that a crucial step was taken towards Malaysia's current political map with the formation of the **Barisan Nasional** ("National Front", usually abbreviated to **BN**) in 1974, comprising UMNO plus the main Chinese and Indian parties and – since the 1990s – parties representing indigenous groups in Sabah and Sarawak. This multi-ethnic coalition has governed the country ever since.

The Mahathir era

Arguably the most dominant figure in Malaysian politics since independence has been **Dr Mahathir Mohamad**, prime minister from 1981 until 2003. Even Malaysians not generally favourably disposed towards the BN credit him with helping the country attain economic lift-off; under Mahathir, industrialization changed the landscape of regions like the Klang Valley and Johor, manufacturing output eclipsed agriculture in importance, and huge **prestige projects** like the Petronas Towers and KLIA were completed. Mahathir meanwhile kept his supporters happy with a raft of populist pronouncements, including railing against the West for criticizing Malaysia's human-rights record (he claimed that in what he termed "Asian values", prosperity was valued more highly than civil liberties). Less well remembered is the fact that Mahathir's tenure also saw one of the most extensive uses of the ISA in what became known as **Operation Lalang** when, in 1987, more than a hundred politicians and activists were detained following tensions between UMNO and Chinese

Provisions in the New Economic Policy (NEP), introduced in the wake of the 1969 race riots, became known as the **bumiputra policy** as they were intended to provide a more level economic playing field for Malays, Orang Asli and the indigenous peoples of east Malaysia (*bumiputra* means something like "sons of the soil" in Malay). In terms of wealth, these communities (as well the Indians) were lagging far behind the Chinese. This was partly the result of colonial policy: the immigrant Chinese made strides as businesspeople in the towns, while the Malays were either employed as administrators or left to get on with farming and fishing in rural areas, and the Indians toiled on the rail lines and the plantations.

The policy has been moderated over the years, but basically awards *bumiputras*, in particular the Malays, privileges such as subsidized housing and easier access to higher education and civil-service jobs. The *bumiputra* policy has undoubtedly achieved a reasonable degree of **wealth redistribution**, though a less laudable consequence has been the creation of a super-rich Malay elite. What's more, the policy is deeply resented by the non-beneficiaries. The Indians are especially aggrieved, having never been wealthy and receiving no favours from the state; the Chinese have continued to rely on their own devices in business while shunning the public sector, where they feel the odds have been stacked against them.

Despite the policy's undoubted popularity among Malays, both Mahathir and Abdullah Badawi have questioned the wisdom of allowing the present system to continue indefinitely, fearing that it has fostered complacency in the very communities it is meant to help. The difficulty for all UMNO leaders is that any meaningful retreat from the policy requires much political daring. Only the opposition, which generally wants to reform Malaysian politics in a nonracial mould, has attempted to make progress in this regard, though it is just as risky an enterprise for them. In 2008, when a leading opposition figure suggested that the publically funded MARA Technology University should at last be open to non-Malay students, Malays in the opposition's own grassroots were unsettled. They had not quite realized that they, too, would be called upon to make sacrifices in the cause of a more transparent and equitable country.

political parties over matters to do with Chinese-language education. These arrests were bad enough, but more durable in its effects was state action to curb press freedom. Especially notable was the government's closure of the pro-MCA English-language *Star* newspaper for several months; when it reopened, many of its senior managers had been replaced.

In 1997, it was the economy that suffered a major setback when Malaysia was sucked into the **Asian economic crisis**, which began in Thailand and Korea. Mahathir took personal charge of getting the economy back on track, sacking his deputy and finance minister **Anwar Ibrahim** in September 1998. A former student leader and once an espouser of progressive Islamic policies, Anwar had enjoyed a meteoric rise after joining UMNO and had been groomed to succeed Mahathir, though relations between the two subsequently grew strained. Within a week of his dismissal, Anwar stunned the nation by being arrested on corruption and sexual misconduct charges – a succession of mass demonstrations in his support ensued. Anwar's treatment in detention became the subject of much concern when he appeared in court on the corruption charge sporting a black eye. He was eventually found guilty – leading many observers to question the independence of the judiciary – and sentenced to six years in jail. In August 2000, he was also found guilty of sodomizing his driver and sentenced to nine years in prison.

Meanwhile, Anwar's wife, Wan Azizah Wan Ismail, formed a new party, **Keadilan** ("Justice"), which contested the November 1999 elections in alliance with other opposition parties, including the Chinese-dominated Democratic Action Party (**DAP**) and the Islamist **PAS**. Though the BN retained a comfortable majority, PAS made significant gains at UMNO's expense and took control of the state government of Terengganu, while Keadilan achieved a creditable six seats in parliament.

Malaysia under Abdullah Badawi

Momentously, in 2003, Mahathir resigned and handed power to Anwar's replacement as deputy prime minister, **Abdullah Badawi**. Hailing from Penang, Abdullah (often referred to as Pak Lah) is a genial man, in marked contrast to his abrasive predecessor, and he asserted himself effectively, winning a landslide general election victory in 2004 in which the BN recaptured the Terengganu state assembly from PAS and ran them surprisingly close in their stronghold of Kelantan. Meanwhile, in mid-2003, Anwar lost an appeal against his sodomy conviction and returned to prison. He was released in September 2004 but remained barred from standing for parliament until April 2008, as his convictions had not been quashed.

As a relatively new broom, Abdullah enjoyed much goodwill early on; it was hoped he would make good on his promises of sweeping cronyism and corruption

Neighbourly spats: the case of Malaysia and Singapore

Ever since 1965, when Singapore left the Federation of Malaysia after just two bitter years of membership, relations between the governments of the two countries have been characterized by constant **bickering**. Early on, tiny Singapore attempted to bolster its security by establishing close ties with Indonesia and military links with Israel, moves which could only annoy Malaysia. Subsequent decades have seen a series of issues souring relations, ranging from arguments over how to administer the **train line** in Singapore – the line itself, plus Singapore's station, which sits on prime land in Tanjong Pagar, remain in Malaysian ownership – to recriminations over unguarded remarks made by various politicians, including an episode several years ago when Singapore's ex-prime minister, Lee Kuan Yew, appeared to intimate that Johor Bahru was a hotbed of crime. The terms under which Singapore receives mains **water** from Malaysia have long been a bone of contention, to the point that the crowded island has built an ambitious freshwater lagoon to wean itself off reliance on Malaysian supplies. There have also been tensions over Malaysia's creation of a port at **Tanjung Pelepas** in southern Johor, which Singapore sees as a threat to its historic *raison d'être* in shipping. Furthermore, Malaysia for a time threatened to build a bizarre **"crooked bridge"** replacing the portion of the causeway within its waters, in order, so it argued, to improve access to ports on its side.

Ironically, all this belies the fact that the two countries are like a pair of squabbling twins, unable to get along despite having a vast amount in common. Each has significant **investments** on the opposite side of the causeway: for example, the Malaysian company behind the Genting Highlands casino near KL has been awarded the contract to run one of Singapore's new casino-resorts. Furthermore, many Malaysians come to Singapore to work or to attend university courses. At least there has been a thaw in relations, with the two countries' prime ministers, Abdullah Badawi and Lee Hsien Loong, starting off on a fresh footing after coming to office within a year of each other.

out of Malaysian politics, and his wife's death from cancer in 2005 generated an additional wave of support for him. But as time wore on, authority seemed to ebb away from his government in the face of various crises and scandals.

The first and most sensational of these was the affair of **Altantuya Shaaribuu**, a Mongolian woman who went missing in the KL area in October 2006. Her remains, which had been blown to bits with explosives, were soon discovered, and it transpired that she was an associate of **Abdul Razak Baginda**, a defence analyst with links to **Najib Tun Razak** (no relation), Abdullah's deputy. Two policemen were later charged with her murder, while Abdul Razak was charged with abetting the crime. Revelations before and after their cases came to trial created a stink around the government, as did the release in October 2007 by Anwar Ibrahim of a video showing prominent lawyer, V.K. Lingam talking on the phone with, it was claimed, the country's then chief justice. If authentic, the clip, captured in 2002 on a mobile phone (and available on YouTube), had laid bare the extent of political skulduggery behind the appointment of the country's most senior judges.

Potentially more damaging to the government than either of these affairs was the appearance of **HINDRAF**, the Hindu Rights Action Force, in 2007. An umbrella organization for a number of groups representing Malaysia's Hindu Indian community, HINDRAF was aggrieved over dubious conversions of Hindus to Islam, the demolitions of several Hindu shrines which the government said had been built without proper approval and the fact that Hindu Indians continue to languish close to the bottom of the economic pile in Malaysia, without the benefits that Muslim Indians can claim. In August that year, HINDRAF attempted to file a lawsuit in the UK claiming reparations for the transport of Tamil indentured labourers to Malaya during colonial times, and then in November it tried to deliver a petition on the matter to the British High Commission in KL. A nasty stand-off between police and thousands of marchers ensued nearby in KLCC, during which tear gas and water cannon were used to disperse demonstrators. What could not be so readily dispelled was the damage to the BN's reputation for protecting the rights and livelihoods of all of Malaysia's ethnic groups.

The 2008 elections

In February 2008, Abdullah called a **snap general election** for the following month – when Anwar Ibrahim was still barred from standing. If the timing was maximally convenient for Abdullah, the result was anything but: the BN was duly returned to power, but on its **worst showing** since the UMNO Alliance slump in 1969. This time, the BN failed to win more than two-thirds of seats in parliament, which would have afforded it the right to tinker with the constitution. The HINDRAF debacle had made Indian voters view the Malaysian Indian Congress (MIC) – the BN's main Indian member party – as supine, and the MIC's veteran leader and deputy leader both lost their seats. To make matters worse, the opposition alliance unseated the BN in an unprecedented number of **state assemblies**, not just in largely Malay Kedah, where voters had previously flirted with PAS, but also in cosmopolitan, prosperous Selangor, Penang and Perak.

In the election's wake, amid euphoria and recrimination, it seemed that everything in Malaysian politics was up for grabs. A more clinical assessment would be that a large number of voters, not necessarily comprehending the opposition's platform but galvanized by issues such as cronyism, social and racial inequalities, rising crime and the soaring cost of fuel, were intent on firing a warning shot across the BN's bows. Perhaps the worst news for Abdullah was in how badly the BN fared in the Peninsula, home to three-quarters of the population: its majority there was wafer-thin, and it took just one out of eleven seats in KL. Only thumping victories by the BN-allied parties of Sabah and Sarawak had secured the coalition a working majority. The question now was whether the BN under Abdullah Badawi would recover its footing.

Testing times

Unfortunately for Abdullah, things got no better for the BN in the aftermath of the polls, as the various affairs that had come to light beforehand continued to play themselves out like a tragicomic drama. A couple of months after the elections, a commission of enquiry declared the **V.K. Lingam video** to be genuine, though no prosecutions had resulted at the time of writing. The **Altantuya Shaariibuu murder** was continuing to generate incredible claims, both inside and outside the courtroom. One version of events alleged that she was killed while visiting Malaysia to demand a commission from Abdul Razak Baginda for helping him broker an arms deal earlier on, and he had called on friends in high places for help in dealing with her; it was also alleged that she had previously been romantically linked with Abdullah's deputy. One source of these claims was a deposition from a detective engaged by Abdul Razak Baginda, but he mysteriously withdrew his statement just 24 hours after issuing it and then vanished; he had still not surfaced at the time of writing. Even more startling was the claim by the prominent blogging journalist **Raja Petra Kamaruddin** that the deputy prime minister's wife had been at the scene when the woman's body was blown up. He was later detained without trial under the ISA and, though set free by a judge after two months, still faces charges of sedition at the time of writing.

It was against this turbulent backdrop that, in August 2008, **Anwar Ibrahim** made a triumphant return to parliament, his wife resigning her seat so that he could take it in a by-election. Just prior to all this, however, Anwar was sensationally arrested once again on a charge of sodomy, this time involving a young aide of his. Allowed bail, Anwar took up his new role as leader of the opposition while having to make appearances in court. A couple of months later, Abdullah Badawi bowed to ongoing pressure and announced that he would step down in 2009.

Looking to the future, it's clear that Malaysia faces continued uncertainty, with the global economic downturn biting and all the main actors in the political sphere somewhat compromised and unable to seize the initiative. Abdullah's successor, **Najib Tun Razak**, lacks the common touch with voters (perhaps because his father was Tun Abdul Razak, Malaysia's second prime minister). He is also to some degree tainted by association with the Altantuya affair, which was grinding through the courts at the time of writing, though Abdul Razak Baginda had been acquitted. More seriously, Najib's leeway for reform – assuming he wishes to go down that road – is constrained by UMNO nationalists who stridently oppose any compromises they feel would affect the Malays' special status in the country's constitution, specifically any weakening of the *bumiputra* policy. As for **Anwar**, his acumen was called into question when he bragged in September 2008 that there would be mass defections by BN MPs, allowing him to form a new government; his grand takeover kept being postponed and eventually was quietly shelved. To keep making headway, Anwar has to better articulate the opposition's vision and, of course, be cleared of the new sodomy charge. **PAS**, despite winning over some non-Muslim voters with a more pragmatic approach, has not achieved a breakthrough, and made far fewer gains in the 2008 elections than its partners in opposition.

If there is a ray of hope amid the murk, it is that Malaysian democracy seems to be enjoying a little renaissance. Now that there are so many more elected opposition politicians, the press is less cowed about reporting their activities; meanwhile, thorny issues surrounding race and religion, long swept under the carpet of economic progress, are being debated with some rancour, but also more thoroughly and purposefully.

Religion

slam is a significant force in Malaysia, given that virtually all Malays, who comprise just over half the population, are Muslim; in Singapore, where three-quarters of the population are Chinese, **Buddhism** is the main religion. There's a smaller, but no less significant, **Hindu** Indian presence in both countries, while the other chief belief system is **animism**, adhered to by many of the indigenous peoples of Malaysia. The colonial period inevitably drew **Christian missionaries** to the region, but the British, in a bid to avoid unrest among the Malays, were restrained in their evangelical efforts. Christian missionaries had more success in Borneo than on the Peninsula; indeed, the main tribal group in Sabah, the Kadazan, is Christian, as are the Kelabit in Sarawak. That said, Christianity is a significant minority religion in Peninsular Malaysia and Singapore, with a notable following among middle-class Chinese and Indians.

One striking feature of religion in the region is that it can be **syncretic** – featuring a blend of beliefs and influences. In a region where fusion is noticeable in everything from food to language, it's not hard to come across individuals who profess one faith, yet pray or make offerings to deities of another, in the warm-hearted and woolly belief that all religions contain some truth and that it therefore makes sense not to put all your spiritual eggs in one devotional basket.

Animism

Although many of Malaysia's indigenous groups are now nominally Christian or Muslim, many of their old animist beliefs and rites still survive. In the animist world-view, everything in nature – mountains, trees, rocks and lakes – has a controlling soul or spirit (**semangat** in Malay) that has to be mollified. For the Orang Asli groups in the interior of the Peninsula, their remaining animist beliefs often centre on healing and funereal ceremonies. A sick person, particularly a child, is believed to be invaded by a bad spirit, and drums are played and incantations performed to persuade the spirit to depart. The death of a member of the family is followed by a complex process of burial and reburial – a procedure which, it is hoped, ensures an easy passage for the person's spirit.

In Sarawak, birds, especially the hornbill, are of particular significance to the Iban and Kelabit peoples. Many Kelabit depend upon the arrival of migrating flocks to decide when to plant their rice crop, while Iban hunters still interpret sightings of the hornbill and other birds as good or bad omens. In the Iban male rite-of-passage ceremony, a headdress made of hornbill feathers adorns the young man's head.

Hinduism

Hinduism arrived in Malaysia long before Islam, brought by Indian traders more than a thousand years ago. The earliest Hindu archeological remains in Malaysia are in Kedah (see p.202) and date from the tenth century, although the temples found here indicate a synthesis of Hindu and Buddhist imagery. While almost all of Malaysia's ancient Hindu past has been obliterated, elements live on in the popular arts like *wayang kulit* (shadow plays), for which sacred texts like the *Ramayana* form the basis of the plots.

The central tenet of Hinduism is the belief that life is a series of rebirths and reincarnations that eventually leads to spiritual release. A whole variety of deities are worshipped, which on the surface makes Hinduism appear complex; however, a loose understanding of the *Vedas* – the religion's holy books – is enough for the characters and roles of the main gods to become apparent. The deities you'll come across most often are the three manifestations of the faith's supreme divine being: **Brahma** the creator, **Vishnu** the preserver and **Shiva** the destroyer.

Hinduism returned to the Peninsula in the late nineteenth century when immigrants from southern India arrived to work on the Malayan rubber and oil-palm plantations. The Hindu celebration of Rama's victory – the central theme of the *Ramayana* – in time became the national holiday of **Deepavali** (or *Divali*; the festival of lights), while another Hindu festival, **Thaipusam**, when Lord Subramaniam and elephant-headed Ganesh, the sons of Shiva, are worshipped, is the occasion for some of the most prominent religious gatherings in the region.

Step over the threshold of a **Hindu temple** in Malaysia or Singapore and you enter a kaleidoscope world of gods and fanciful creatures. The style is typically Dravidian (South Indian), as befits the largely Tamil population, with a soaring **gopuram**, or entrance tower, teeming with sculptures and a central courtyard leading to an inner sanctum housing the presiding deity. In the temple precinct, you'll invariably witness incense being burnt, the application of sandalwood paste to the forehead, and *puja* (ritualistic acts of worship).

Islam

The first firm foothold Islam made in the Malay Peninsula was the conversion of Paramesvara, the ruler of **Melaka**, in the early fifteenth century. The commercial success of Melaka accelerated the spread of Islam and, one after another, the powerful Malay court rulers took to the religion, adopting the Arabic title sultan ("ruler"), either because of sincere conversion or because they took a shrewd view of the advantages that could be gained by embracing this international faith. On a cultural level, too, Islam had its attractions – its concepts of equality before Allah freed people from the Hindu caste system that had dominated parts of the region. Even after the Melaka Sultanate fell in 1511, the hold of Islam in the region was strengthened by the migration of Muslim merchants to Brunei.

The first wave of Islamic missionaries were mostly **Sufis**, representing the mystical and generally more liberal wing of Islam. Sufism in the region absorbed some animist and Hindu beliefs, including the tradition of pluralist deity worship. However, Sufism's influence declined in the early nineteenth century when a puritanical sect within mainstream **Sunni** Islam, the Wahhabis, captured Mecca. The return to the Koran's basic teachings became identified with a more militant approach, leading to jihads in Kedah, Kelantan and Terengganu against the Malay rulers' Siamese overlords and, subsequently, the British.

Islam in Malaysia and Singapore today is a mixture of Sunni and Sufi elements, and its adherents are still largely comprised of Malays, though a minority of the

Indian community is Muslim, too. While Islam as practised locally is relatively liberal, the trend that has swept the Muslim world in the last two or three decades, away from tacit secularism towards a more devout approach, has not left the two countries untouched. There's now a better understanding of Islam's tenets – and thus better compliance with those principles – among Muslims in both countries.

Of course, this drift has its social and political dimensions. In Malaysia, with its history of sometimes awkward race relations, Islam is something of a badge of identity for the Malays; it's significant that the Malaysian **constitution** practically regards being Malay as equivalent to being Muslim. Thus Malaysia has seen an increase in religious programming on TV and in state spending on often ostentatious new mosques, while even in consumerist Singapore, the Malay minority is becoming more actively engaged in religion. Malaysia's religious establishment has also become more vocal, making proclamations to discourage Muslims from practising yoga (because of its supposed Hindu origins) and Muslim women from wearing short hair and trousers (because this would apparently encourage lesbianism), though such decrees have no legal weight unless states of the federation adopt them into their law. All of this said, for most Muslims in Malaysia and Singapore, Islam remains not a matter of dogma but about blending a personal interpretation of the religion with living in a multifaith community and exploiting the opportunities for personal development that economic growth has brought.

Islam and the law

One striking way in which Islam influences day-to-day affairs is the fact that in certain areas, Muslim and non-Muslim citizens are subject to different **laws**. In Malaysia, for example, a Muslim man may avail himself of the Islamic provision for a man to take up to four wives, if certain criteria are met, but non-Muslim men are subject to the usual injunctions against bigamy and polygamy. Likewise, while it would be acceptable for an unmarried couple to share a hotel room if neither person is Muslim, it would be illegal (an act known as **khalwat**) if both were Muslim (and if only one of them were Muslim, only that person would be committing an illegal act). This legal divide is reflected in the judicial systems of both Malaysia and Singapore, in which **syariah** (sharia) courts interpreting Islamic law exist alongside courts and laws derived from the British legal system.

Both Malaysia and Singapore limit Islamic jurisprudence to matters concerning the family and certain types of behaviour deemed transgressions against Islam, such as *khalwat*, or for a Muslim to consume alcohol in public. In this regard, the *syariah* courts are in many ways subservient to the secular legal framework. This also means the harsher aspects of Islamic justice, such as stoning or the cutting off of a thief's hand, are not deemed permissible; an attempt in the 1990s by the state government of Kelantan, run by the Islamist opposition PAS party, to introduce them within the state was thwarted by Malaysia's federal government. The Islamic standard of proof in a case concerning rape – requiring the victim to be able to produce four witnesses – also does not apply, since rape cases are tried within the secular system.

However, there has been one key area where the two juridical systems are experiencing a sort of territorial dispute: that of **religious conversion**. It's very difficult for Malaysian Muslims to convert out of Islam as the secular courts are unwilling to uphold their choice without the involvement of the *syariah* court, which might refuse permission or, worse, wish to punish them as apostates. In this Catch-22 situation, any Muslims who become atheists or wish to take up a new faith can never make their choice official, and for the most part simply keep mum. Controversy has also arisen when one person in a marriage converts to Islam and then wants to use Islamic law to divorce the spouse or change the registered religion of their children, for example. The roles of the two legal systems in these situations ought to be clarified as a matter of urgency, but this looks a distant prospect. When, in 2008, the Malaysian Bar Council held a meeting in KL on these matters, the event had to be called off after an angry crowd of Muslim demonstrators accused them of trying to undermine the status of Islam, and few Malay politicians were willing to back the idea of resolving the legal impasse through rational debate.

The bomoh

An important link between animism and the Islam of today is provided by the Malay **bomoh**, a kind of shaman. While *bomohs* keep a low profile in these times of greater Islamic orthodoxy – no *bomoh* operates out of an office, and there are no college courses to train *bomohs* or listings of practitioners in the telephone directory – the fact is that every Malay community can still summon a *bomoh* when it's felt one is needed to cure disease, bring rain during droughts, exorcize spirits from a newly cleared plot before building work starts or rein in the behaviour of a wayward spouse. A central part of the *bomoh*'s trade is recitation, often of sections of the Koran, while – like his Orang Asli counterparts – he uses techniques such as burning herbs to cure or ease pain and disease.

Mosques

In Malaysia, every town, village and hamlet has its mosque, while the capital city of each state hosts a grandiose **Masjid Negeri** (state mosque). You'll rarely see contemporary mosques varying from the standard square building topped by onion domes and minarets, though the oldest mosques reveal unusual Sumatran or other Southeast Asian influences. Two additional standard features can be found inside the prayer hall, namely the **mihrab**, a niche indicating the direction of Mecca, towards which believers face during prayers (the green *kiblat* arrow on the ceiling of most Malaysian hotel rooms fulfils the same function), and the **mimbar** (pulpit), used by the imam.

One of the five **pillars of Islam** is that the faithful should pray five times a day – at dawn (called the *subuh* prayer in Malay), midday (*zuhur*, or *jumaat* on a Fri), mid-afternoon (*asar*), dusk (*maghrib*) and mid-evening (*isyak*). Travellers soon become familiar with the sound – sometimes recorded – of the **muezzin** calling the faithful to prayer at these times; loudspeakers strapped to the minaret amplify his summons, though a few mosques have their own distinctive methods for summoning the faithful, such as at the Masjid Langgar in Kota Bharu, where traditionally a giant **drum** is banged before prayer time. On **Friday** – the day of communal prayer – Muslims converge on their nearest mosque around noon, to hear the imam lead prayers and deliver a *khutbah* (sermon). All employers allow Muslim staff a three-hour break for *jumaat* prayers and the attendant socializing.

Chinese religions

The three different strands in Chinese religion ostensibly point in very different directions: **Confucianism** began as a philosophy based on piety, loyalty, humanitarianism and familial devotion, and has transmuted into a set of principles that permeate every aspect of Chinese life; **Buddhism** is primarily concerned with the attainment of a state of personal enlightenment, nirvana; and **Taoism** propounds unity with nature as its chief tenet. When Chinese pioneers opened up the rivers of Sarawak to trade, they could identify with many of the animist practices of the Iban and Melenau tribesmen they dealt with, thanks to the Taoist emphasis on harmony with nature.

Malaysian and Singaporean Chinese who consider themselves Buddhist, Taoist or Confucianist may in practice be a mixture of all three. This blend is first and foremost pragmatic: the Chinese use their religion to ease their passage through life, whether in the spheres of work or family, while temples double as social centres for people to meet and exchange views.

Most visitors are more aware of the region's Chinese religious celebrations than the Muslim or Hindu ones, largely because the Chinese festivities are particularly welcoming of tourists and often exciting too. Most are organized by *kongsis*, or clan associations, which were once the cornerstone of the immigrant Chinese communities in Malaysia and Singapore and traditionally provided housing, employment and a social structure for the newly arrived.

Chinese temples

The rules of **feng shui** are rigorously applied to the construction of Chinese temples, so that each building has a layout and orientation rendering it free from evil influences. Visitors wishing to cross the threshold of a temple have to step over a kerb intended to trip up evil spirits, and walk through doors flanked by fearsome door gods; fronting the doors may be two stone lions, providing yet another defence.

Temples are normally constructed around a framework of huge, lacquered timber beams, adorned with intricately carved warriors, animals and flowers. More figures are moulded onto outer walls, which are dotted with octagonal, hexagonal or round grille-worked windows. Larger temples typically consist of a front entrance hall opening onto a walled-in courtyard, beyond which is the hall of worship, where joss sticks are burned below images of the deities. The most striking element of a Chinese temple is often its **roof** – a grand, multi-tiered affair with low, overhanging eaves, the ridges alive with auspicious creatures such as dragons and phoenixes and, less often, with miniature scenes from traditional Chinese life and legend. In the temple grounds you'll see sizeable ovens, stuffed constantly with paper money, prayer books and other offerings; and possibly a **pagoda** – the presence of which is, once again, a defence against evil spirits.

Peoples

argely because of their pivotal position on the maritime trade routes between the Middle East, India and China, the present-day countries of Malaysia, Singapore and Brunei have always been a cultural melting-pot. During the first millennium, Malays arrived from Sumatra and Indians from India and Sri Lanka, while later the Chinese migrated from mainland China and Hainan Island. But all these traders and settlers arrived to find that the region already contained a gamut of indigenous tribes, thought to have migrated here around 50,000 years ago from the Philippines, which were then connected by a land bridge to Borneo and Southeast Asia. The indigenous tribes still existing on the Peninsula are known there as the Orang Asli, Malay for "the original people".

Original people they may have been, but the descendants of the various indigenous groups now form a minority of the overall populations of the three countries. Over the last 150 years a massive influx of Chinese and Indian immigrants, escaping poverty, war and revolution, has swelled the population of **Malaysia**, which now stands at over 25 million. Just over half are Malays, while the Chinese make up nearly a quarter of the population, the Indians eight percent, and the various indigenous groups just over a tenth.

Brunei's population of around 380,000 is heavily dominated by Malays, with minorities of Chinese, Indians and indigenous peoples. In **Singapore**, there were only tiny numbers of indigenes left on the island by the time of the arrival of Raffles. They have no modern-day presence in the state, where around three-quarters of the 4.6-million strong population are of Chinese extraction, while around fourteen percent are Malay and nearly nine percent Indian.

The Malays

The **Malays**, a Mongoloid people believed to have originated from the meeting of Central Asians with Pacific islanders, first moved to the west coast of the Malay Peninsula from Sumatra in early times. Then known as Orang Laut (sea people), they sustained an economy built around fishing, boat-building and, in some communities, piracy. It was the growth in power of the Malay sultanates from the fifteenth century onwards – coinciding with the arrival of Islam – that established Malays as a force to be reckoned with in the Malay Peninsula and Borneo. They developed an aristocratic tradition, courtly rituals and a social hierarchy (see p.341), which have a continued influence today. The rulers of Malaysia's states still wield great influence, reflected in the fact that they elect one of their number to hold the post of Yang di-Pertuan Agong, a pre-eminent sultan who holds the title for a five-year term. Although a purely ceremonial position, the *agong* is seen as the ultimate guardian of Malay Muslim culture and, despite recent legislation to reduce his powers, is still considered to be above the law. The situation is even more pronounced in **Brunei**, to which many Muslim Malay traders fled after the fall of Melaka to the Portuguese in 1511. There, the sultan is still the supreme ruler (as his descendants have been, on and off, for over five hundred years).

Even though Malays have been Muslims since the fifteenth century, the region as a whole is not fundamentalist in character. Only in Brunei is alcohol banned, for instance. Perhaps the most significant recent development affecting Malays in Malaysia has been the introduction of the **bumiputra** policy (see p.701).

The Chinese and Straits Chinese

Chinese traders began visiting the region in the seventh century, but it was in Melaka in the fifteenth century that the first significant community established itself. However, the ancestors of the majority of Chinese now living in Peninsular Malaysia emigrated from southeastern China in the nineteenth century to work in the burgeoning tin-mining industry. In Sarawak, Foochow, Teochew and Hokkien Chinese played an important part in opening up the interior, establishing pepper and rubber plantations along Batang Rejang; while in Sabah, Hakka Chinese labourers were recruited by the British North Borneo Chartered Company to plant rubber, and many stayed on, forming the core of the Chinese business community there.

Although a large number of Chinese in the Peninsula came as labourers, they graduated quickly to shopkeeping and business ventures, both in established towns like Melaka and fast-expanding centres like KL, Penang and Kuching. Chinatowns developed throughout the region, even in Malay strongholds like Kota Bharu and Kuala Terengganu, while **Chinese traditions**, religious festivities, theatre and music became an integral part of a wider Malayan, and later Malaysian, multiracial culture. On the political level, the Malaysian Chinese are well represented in parliament and occupy around a quarter of the current ministerial positions. By way of contrast, **Chinese Bruneians** are not automatically classed as citizens and suffer a fair amount of discrimination at the hands of the majority Malay population.

Singapore's nineteenth-century trade boom drew many Cantonese, Teochew, Hokkien and Hakka Chinese traders and labourers, who quickly established a Chinatown on the south bank of the Singapore River. Today, the Chinese are the most economically successful racial group in Singapore.

One of the few examples of regional intermarrying is displayed in the **Peranakan** or "Straits-born Chinese" heritage of Melaka, Singapore and, to a lesser extent, Penang. When male Chinese immigrants settled in these places from the sixteenth century onwards to work as miners or commercial entrepreneurs, they often married local Malay women; the male offspring of such unions were termed "Baba" and the females "Nonya". **Baba-Nonya** society, as it became known, adapted elements from both cultures to create its own unique culinary and architectural style (see p.351), and even had its own dialect of Malay. During the colonial era, many of the Baba-Nonyas acquired an excellent command of English and so prospered, but after the British departed they came under pressure to assimilate into the mainstream Chinese community. It's partly as a result of this that many of their traditions have since gone into serious decline.

The Indians

The second-largest non-*bumiputra* group in Malaysia, the **Indians**, first arrived as traders more than two thousand years ago, although few settled and it wasn't until the early fifteenth century that a small community of Indians (from present-day Tamil Nadu and Sri Lanka) was based in Melaka. But, like the majority of Chinese, the first large wave of Indians – Tamil labourers – arrived in the nineteenth century as indentured workers, to build the roads and rail lines and to work on the European-run rubber estates. An embryonic entrepreneurial class from North India soon followed and set up businesses in Penang and Singapore; these merchants and traders, most of whom were Muslim, found it easier to assimilate themselves within the existing Malay community than the Hindu Tamils did.

Although Indians comprise under a tenth of the populations of Malaysia and Singapore, their impact is widely felt. The Hindu festival of *Thaipusam* is celebrated annually at KL's Batu Caves by upwards of a million people (with a smaller but still significant celebration in Singapore); the festival of *Deepavali* is a national holiday; and Indians dominate certain professional areas like medicine and law. And then, of course, there is the area of food – very few Malaysians these days could do without a daily dose of *roti canai*, so much so that this Indian snack has been virtually appropriated by Malay and Chinese cafés and hawkers.

Indigenous peoples

The **Orang Asli** – the indigenous peoples of Peninsular Malaysia – mostly belong to three distinct groups, within which various tribes are related by geography, language or physiological features.

The largest of the groups is the **Senoi** (the Asli word for "person"), who number about forty thousand. They live in the large, still predominantly forested interior, within the states of Perak, Pahang and Kelantan, and divide into two main tribes, the Semiar and the Temiar, which still adhere to a traditional lifestyle, following animist customs in their marriage ceremonies and burial rites. On the whole they follow the practice of shifting cultivation (a regular rotation of jungle clearance and crop planting), although government resettlement drives have successfully persuaded many to settle and farm just one area.

The **Semang** (or Negritos), of whom there are around two thousand, live in the northern areas of the Peninsula. They comprise six distinct, if small, tribes, related to each other in appearance – they are mostly dark-skinned and curly haired – and share a traditional nomadic, hunter-gatherer lifestyle. However, most Semang nowadays live in settled communities and work within the cash economy, either as labourers or selling jungle produce in markets. Perhaps the most frequently seen Semang tribe are the Batek, who live in and around Taman Negara.

The third group, the so-called **Aboriginal Malays**, live in an area roughly south of the Kuala Lumpur–Kuantan road. Some of the tribes in this category, like the Jakun and the Semelais who live around the lakes of the southern interior, have vigorously retained their animist religion and artistic traditions despite living in permanent villages near Malay communities and working within the regular economy.

These three main groupings do not represent all the Orang Asli tribes in Malaysia. One, the Lanoh in Perak, are sometimes regarded as Negritos, but their language is closer to that of the Temiar. Another group, the semi-nomadic Che Wong, of whom just a few hundred still survive on the slopes of Gunung Benom in central Pahang, are still dependent on foraging to survive and live in temporary huts made from bamboo and rattan. Two more groups, the Jah Hut of Pahang and the Mah Meri of Selangor, are particularly fine carvers, and it's possible to buy their sculptures at regional craft shops.

It's difficult to visit most Orang Asli communities as they largely live off the beaten track. To learn more about the disappearing Asli culture, the best stop is KL's Orang Asli Museum (see p.137).

Sarawak

In direct contrast to the Peninsula, indigenous groups make up a larger chunk of the population in **Sarawak**, which currently stands at two million. Although the Chinese comprise 29 percent of the state's population and the Malays and Indians around 24 percent together, the remaining 47 percent are made up of various indigenous **Dyak** groups – a word derived from the Malay for "upcountry".

The largest Dyak groups are the Iban, Bidayuh, Melenau, Kayan, Kenyah, Kelabit and Penan tribes. These groups have very distinct cultures as well as a few commonalities. Many live in **longhouses** along the rivers or on the sides of hills in the mountainous interior, and maintain a proud cultural legacy that draws on animist religion (see p.706 and the *Visiting a longhouse* colour section), arts and crafts production and jungle skills.

The **Iban** (see p.424) make up nearly one-third of Sarawak's population. Originating hundreds of miles south of present-day Sarawak, in the Kapuas Valley in Kalimantan, the Iban migrated north in the sixteenth century, coming into conflict over the next two hundred years with the Kayan and Kenyah tribes and, later, the British. Nowadays, Iban longhouse communities are found in the Batang Ai river system in the southwest and along Batang Rejang and tributaries. These communities are quite accessible, their inhabitants always hospitable and keen to illustrate aspects of their culture like traditional dance and textile-weaving. In their time, the Iban were infamous head-hunters – some longhouses are still decorated with authentic shrunken heads.

The most southern of Sarawak's indigenous groups are the **Bidayuh**, who – unlike most Dyak groups – traditionally lived away from the rivers, building their longhouse on the sides of hills. Culturally, they are similar to the Iban, although in temperament they are much milder and less gregarious, keeping themselves to themselves in their inaccessible homes on Sarawak's mountainous southern border with Kalimantan.

The **Melenau** are a coastal people, living north of Kuching in a region dominated by mangrove swamps. Many Melenau, however, now live in towns, preferring the kampung-style houses of the Malays to the elegant longhouses of the past. They are expert fishermen and cultivate sago as an alternative to rice.

The **Kelabit** people live on the highland plateau separating north Sarawak from Kalimantan. Like the Iban, they live in longhouses and maintain a traditional lifestyle, but differ from some of the other groups in that they are Christian.

The last main group is the semi-nomadic **Penan**, who live in the upper Rejang and Limbang areas of Sarawak in temporary lean-tos or small huts. They rely, like some of the Orang Asli groups in the Peninsula, on hunting and gathering and collecting jungle produce for sale in local markets. In recent years, however, the state government has tried to resettle the Penan in small villages, rehousing them in concrete blocks – a controversial policy not entirely unconnected with the advance of logging in traditional Penan land.

Most of the other groups in Sarawak fall into the all-embracing ethnic classification of **Orang Ulu** (people of the interior), who inhabit the more remote inland parts of the state, further north than the Iban, along the upper Rejang,

Balui and Linau rivers. The most numerous, the **Kayan** and the **Kenyah**, are closely related and in the past often teamed up to defend their lands from the invading Iban. But they also have much in common with their traditional enemy, since they are longhouse-dwellers, animists and shifting cultivators.

Sabah

Sabah has a population of around 2.6 million, made up of more than thirty distinct racial groups, between them speaking over eighty different dialects. Most populous of these groups are the **Dusun**, who account for around a third of Sabah's population. Traditionally agriculturists (the word *Dusun* means "orchard"), the Dusun are divided into subgroups that inhabit the western coastal plains and the interior of the state. These days they are known generically as **Kadazan/Dusun**, although strictly speaking "Kadazan" refers only to the Dusun of Penampang. Other branches of the Dusun include the **Lotud** of Tuaran and the **Rungus** of the Kudat Peninsula, whose convex longhouses are all that remain of the Dusun's longhouse tradition. Although most Dusun are now Christians, remnants of their animist past are still evident in their culture, most obviously in the harvest festival, or *pesta kaamatan*, when their *bobohizans*, or priestesses, perform rituals to honour the *bambaazon*, or rice spirit.

The mainly Muslim **Bajau** tribe drifted over from the southern Philippines some two hundred years ago, and now constitute Sabah's second largest ethnic group, accounting for around ten percent of the population. Their penchant for piracy quickly earned them the sobriquet "sea gypsies", though nowadays they are agriculturalists and fishermen, noted for their horsemanship and their rearing of buffalo. The Bajau live in the northwest of Sabah and annually appear on horseback at Kota Belud's market (see p.515).

Sabah's third sizeable tribe is the **Murut**, which inhabits the area between Keningau and the Sarawak border, in the southwest. Their name means "hill people", though they prefer to be known by their individual tribal names, such as Timugon, Tagal and Nabai. The Murut farm rice and cassava by a system of shifting cultivation; through their head-hunting days are over, they retain other cultural traditions, such as the construction of brightly adorned grave huts to house the graves and belongings of the dead.

Development and the environment

M alaysia is gradually becoming more environmentally friendly, largely as a result of well-organized and scientifically persuasive organizations within the country, rather than pressures from outside, but the pace of change is slow and huge problems remain. Logging and large-scale development projects, like dams, hog the spotlight, and are still a prime focus for NGOs, but just as pressing are concerns over oil-palm cultivation and wetlands erosion, as well as the impact of environmental degradation on the lifestyles of indigenous groups.

As a small, highly built-up island, **Singapore** has few wild areas left to spoil; nevertheless the country maintains an area of rainforest around its central reservoirs as well as other nature reserves, such the wetland area at Sungai Buloh. Singapore's very compactness dictates that it has to be vigilant on matters of pollution, and thus the island has strict laws on waste emissions and even an island, Pulau Semakau, created entirely out of ash from incinerated refuse.

The tiny kingdom of **Brunei** is perhaps the most enlightened of all. With a small, wealthy population, there is no rampant commercial exploitation of natural resources as in Malaysia. Forest protection is successfully applied and the state's small percentage of indigenous peoples treated respectfully.

Logging and deforestation

The **sustainable exploitation** of forest products by the indigenous population has always played a vital part in the domestic and export economy of the region – for almost two thousand years, the ethnic tribes have bartered products like rattan, wild rubber and forest plants with foreign traders.

Although blamed for much of the deforestation in Sarawak and Sabah, the bulk of indigenous agricultural activity occurs in secondary rather than primary (untouched) forest. Indeed, environmental groups believe that only around one hundred square kilometres of primary forest – a tiny proportion compared to the haul by commercial timber companies – is cleared by the indigenous groups annually. **Logging**, despite having slowed, is still a cause of huge grievances among the indigenous peoples of east Malaysia.

The Peninsula

Peninsular Malaysia's pre-independence economy was not as reliant on timber revenues as those of Sabah and Sarawak. Although one-sixth of the region's 120,000 square kilometres of forest, predominantly in Johor, Perak and Negeri Sembilan states, had been cut down by 1957, most of the logging had been done gradually and on a small, localized scale. As in Sabah, it was the demand for rail sleepers – for the expansion of the Malayan train network in the 1920s – which had first attracted the commercial logging companies, but wide-scale clearing and conversion to rubber and oil-palm plantations in the more remote areas of Pahang, Perlis, Kedah and Terengganu didn't intensify until the 1960s. By the end of the 1970s, more efficient extraction methods, coupled with a massive increase in foreign investment in the logging industry, had led to over forty percent of the Peninsula's remaining forests being either cleared for plantation purposes or partially logged.

Only in the last twenty years has logging in west Malaysia slowed significantly, with more stringent assessments of the environmental impact being carried out before logging is allowed to proceed. Legislation enacted by the government has provided more protection for the environment. One particularly positive piece of legislation is the creation, more than a century ago, of Permanent Forest Reserves, which ensures that more land will be preserved in permanent reserves under the various Malaysia Plans. But unfortunately while this sounds good, it doesn't involve a watertight system: even if a parcel of land is labelled a reserve, it can still be partially logged. But at least now the work must be carried out in a sustainable manner integrating checks and impact assessments.

Sabah

Commercial logging started in **Sabah** (then North Borneo) in the late nineteenth century, when the British Borneo Trading and Planting Company began to extract large trees from the area around Sandakan to satisfy the demand for timber sleepers for the expanding rail network in China. By 1930 the larger **British Borneo Timber Company** (BBTC) was primarily responsible for the extraction of 178,000 cubic metres of timber, rising to nearly five million cubic metres by the outbreak of World War II, and Sandakan became one of the world's main timber ports. Most areas were logged indiscriminately, and the indigenous tribal groups who lived there were brought into the economic system to work on North Borneo's rubber, tobacco and, later, oil-palm plantations. The process intensified as the main players in Sabah tapped the lucrative Japanese market, where postwar reconstruction costing billions of dollars was under way.

By the early 1960s, timber had accelerated past rubber as the region's chief export, and by 1970 nearly thirty percent of Sabah had been extensively logged, with oil-palm and other plantation crops replacing around a quarter of the degraded forest. Timber exports had accounted for less than ten percent of all exports from Sabah in 1950; by the 1970s, this had rocketed to over seventy percent. Nowadays much of the logged land is used for oil-palm cultivation (see box, p.718) with powerful companies continuing to pressure the state government for access to more of the remaining forests to expand further this lucrative, but arguably ecologically suffocating monoculture.

Sarawak

A much larger share of contemporary logging takes place in **Sarawak** than in any other region in Malaysia. Timber extraction accelerated in northern Sarawak in the 1930s when Vyner Brooke proved less opposed to large foreign-run plantations than the earlier White Rajahs. Timber was viewed as a vital commercial resource to be utilized in the massive reconstruction of the state following the devastating Japanese occupation. During its short postwar period as a Crown Colony and, after 1963, as a Malaysian state, logging in Sarawak grew to become one of its chief revenue earners, alongside oil extraction. Today, most of the Baram basin in the north of the state has been logged – the river is now a soupy brown sludge due to the run-off of earth and silt caused by the extraction process – and attention has switched to the remote Balui River and its tributaries in the east of the state, where the Bakun Dam project (see p.441), nearly shelved due to financial constraints, is now back on course.

Accurate figures as to the current state of Sarawak's forests are, however, notoriously hard to come by with the most dramatic estimation being that Sarawak's primary forest has been depleted by nearly ninety percent.

Government initiatives

The Malaysian government is naturally keen to deflect attention away from the accusation that the timber concessions it grants are solely responsible for unsustainable timber production. Reforestation schemes within the **Permanent Forest Estates** – government-run tracts of land given over to tree cultivation – are on the increase. And organizations like the Forest Resource Institute of Malaysia (FRIM), which sustains an area of secondary forest on the edge of Kuala Lumpur, prove how rainforest habitats can be renewed. However, FRIM is the exception rather than the rule, and most environmentalists within Malaysia don't believe that renewable forestry can offset the damage caused by current timber-extraction techniques, which seldom aid regrowth.

In east Malaysia various initiatives aim to protect the remaining forests. In early 2006, WWF Malaysia announced The Heart of Borneo project, an international agreement between the governments of Malaysia, Indonesia and Brunei to protect 220,000 square kilometres of forest straddling the Bornean foothills and highlands, where the three nations' borders meet.

Dam construction

Massive **dam construction** is another issue often on the environmental agenda. The prime example is the **Bakun** Dam project in Sarawak in Belaga district. In preparation for construction, over ten thousand ethnic

Oil-palm cultivation in Malaysia

Malaysia is the world's biggest producer of **oil palm**, a valuable economic crop that's used as a biofuel and in food products. The industry has been a massive stimulus for employment – over half a million people are now involved in its production, and many more in its various subsidiary industries. Sabah, the poorest state in Malaysia, is benefiting in particular. Furthermore, land surrounding the cultivation areas has been subject to improved infrastructure: public services such as schools and hospitals have been developed, while roads are built and telecommunication networks established.

Yet for all those positives, there are negatives. The speedy proliferation of the industry has had a harmful impact on the environment: critics say the land cleared for the agro-crop contributes significantly to global warming, notably greenhouse gas emissions. Palm trees are increasingly replacing native tropical rainforest and thus threatening the survival of many animal species, including the orang-utan. Communities may also have their food and water supplies cut off or contaminated, while their cash-crop farms – fruit trees and rubber plantations – are wiped out. Meanwhile, social conflict is also brought about between the planters and local residents who are forced off their land.

And the industry keeps on growing: the oil's use as an alternative, "clean" biofuel has meant that demand is kept stable. While the negative impacts are ongoing, at least on some level there's increased awareness, fuelled by organizations like Friends of the Earth, of the substantial environmental impact and a growing recognition that there needs to be a stronger sustainability policy in order to safeguard Malaysia's rainforests and all who depend on them.

peoples were moved from their longhouses along the Balui River to a dry location, Asap. Environmentalists opposed to the scheme say it ignored scientific evidence indicating the adverse effects of flooding an area the size of Singapore. It isn't simply the uprooting of ethnic peoples, but also the eradication of the region's unique biodiversity, that has caused such controversy.

The international funding of such projects was highlighted in 1994 when it became clear that £1.3 billion's worth of defence contracts awarded to British companies had been linked to £234 million of British aid money for the building of a hydroelectric dam at **Pergau** in northern Kelantan. British civil servants declared the dam "a bad buy", but the British government went ahead, it was suggested, because the Malaysians had made the arms purchases conditional on the aid money to underwrite the dam. A parliamentary committee in Britain launched an inquiry, but the issue was firmly swept under the carpet in Malaysia where the press stood right behind former prime minister, Mahathir Mohamad.

Air pollution

For the inhabitants of Peninsular Malaysia and Singapore, the environmental issue that has affected them most has not been forest depletion or land rights, but **air pollution**, particularly dust and smoke caused by forest fires – dubbed "the haze" by the local media. Although such events had occurred sporadically during the 1990s, in 1997/8 the region suffered a severe, prolonged episode, when the haze was so bad that motorists were warned to keep their distance from one another and there was an alarming rise in respiratory illnesses. Visibility in the Straits of Melaka, one of the world's busiest shipping routes, also dropped dramatically.

The Malaysian government originally suggested that the agricultural methods of the indigenous peoples – which involve the burning of excess vegetation at the end of growing cycles – were to blame. However, further research indicated that small longhouse communities could not have caused such extensive fires. It's now thought that the haze is caused by Indonesian plantation companies using fire to clear large areas of forest to facilitate the planting of crops such as oil palm and acacia. The Indonesian government does not appear to have been able to change the habits of its forest developers, given that the 1997 catastrophe was repeated, albeit to a lesser extent, in 2000, 2002 and 2005. The 2005 event – cause by forest fires in Sumatra – prompted a state of emergency to be declared and crisis talks with Indonesia. Thankfully there has been no recurrence of the haze at the time of writing, though it must be regarded as a problem waiting to recur unless there is a marked improvement in the way Indonesia polices the plantation owners.

The threat to traditional lifestyles

Although large-scale projects such as the Bakun Dam are the most prevalent threat to indigenous tribes' way of life, illegal logging still threatens to undermine the gains made over the last fifteen years. In the case of Sarawak, customary land tenure, or *adat*, which was enshrined in law throughout the White Rajah period and forms the basis of the 1958 Sarawak Land Code, should protect the land claimed by the state's tribal groups. In practice, much commercial logging has ignored this. The forest-dependent people of northern Sarawak have responded to logging encroachment with spontaneous actions (such as destruction of machinery) through the 1960s and 1970s and developing collective actions (blockades) in the late 1980s and 1990s. Protests still sporadically take place today, achieving small mentions in the local press. The failure to respect *adat* has led to the desecration of locations of special importance – burial places, access routes and sections of rivers used for fishing – as it is hard for indigenous people to prove conclusively that they have lived and farmed there for generations.

The forests around Bintulu, Belaga and Limbang have suffered in this way, although the Iban in southwest Sarawak have had more success. A historic court case in 2001, Rumah Nor v. Borneo Pulp and Paper, should have proved a milestone in shifting the goalposts more the indigenes' way. Here the court ruled in favour of the longhouse community, after the community's map was accepted as court evidence for ownership of land. Emboldened by this ruling, a growing number of communities filed complaints but in many cases the courts have not been able to stand up to the powerful timber companies. However, severe criticism of timber company actions continues.

The Penan

The **Penan**, hunter-gatherers from northern Sarawak, have arguably been the worst hit by industrial logging. The particular ways in which they utilize the land make it harder for their land rights to be defined and recognized. An additional factor in the case of the Penan has been that since the mid-1980s the Sarawak state government's avowed policy has been to bring them into what it views as the development process (as has been applied to the more settled Dyak and Orang Ulu groups for many decades), urging them to move to permanent longhouses, work in the cash economy and send their children to school.

The Penan have proved resilient to these attempts to assimilate them into the wider Malaysian social system, largely because the government diktats seem to go suspiciously hand in hand with an expansion of logging in their customary land areas. Very often, there's been no warning that Penan land has been earmarked for logging until the extraction actually begins – examples in remote areas of the Belaga district have been well documented by the environmental group **Sahabat Alam Malaysia**. A recent report from one of the remaining semi-nomadic Penan communities situated in Sarawak's Batang Baram district reveals that loggers continue to penetrate their last reserves illegally: the timber company Interhill has reputedly destroyed the area's fruit trees and dumped toxic waste in the village's drinking water supply, while in July 2008, a gravesite was supposedly destroyed by the loggers.

Wildlife

There's an extraordinary tropical biodiversity in the Malay Peninsula and in Borneo, with over six hundred species of birds; more than two hundred kinds of mammals; many thousands of flowering plant species, among them the insectivorous pitcher plant and scores of others of known medicinal value; and over one thousand species of brightly coloured butterflies. This enormous variety of bird, plant and animal life makes any trip to a tropical rainforest a memorable experience.

Despite being separated by the South China Sea, the wildlife and plant communities of Peninsular and east Malaysia are very similar, since the island of Borneo was joined to the Asian mainland by a land bridge until after the last Ice Age. Nonetheless, there are some specific differences. The forests of the Peninsula support populations of several large mammal species, such as tiger, tapir and gaur (forest-dwelling wild cattle), which are absent from Borneo. Other large mammals, for example the Asian elephant, and birds such as the hornbill, occur both on Borneo and on the Peninsula; while Borneo features the orang-utan (the "man of the forest") and the proboscis monkey.

Below we feature two of the most exciting – and accessible – areas in Peninsular Malaysia in which to view wildlife, namely **Taman Negara** and **Fraser's Hill**. East Malaysia and Brunei also offer many opportunities for observing wildlife. It's easy to spot proboscis monkeys along **Sungai Kinabatangan** in Sabah and at **Bako National Park** in Sarawak, the former is also a good place to watch orang-utans. Those with an interest in birdlife should head for Sarawak's **Loagan Bunut National Park**, whose shallow lake is home to many different bird species, or to Brunei's **Ulu Temburong National Park**.

Even though it's now predominantly urban, without much plant or animal life, **Singapore** still has several remnants of its verdant tropical past, particularly at **Bukit Timah Nature Reserve**, the splendidly manicured Botanic Gardens and the **Sungai Buloh Nature Wetland Reserve** in the far north of the island. Day-trippers to Pulau Ubin, just off Singapore and easily accessible by boat from the Changi Point ferry terminal, can also see the mangrove flats of **Chek Jawa**.

Poaching and habitation loss due to deforestation mean that the future of the region's wildlife is far from assured. Fortunately, many **not-for-profit organizations**, such as WWF Malaysia (®www.wwfmalaysia.org), are campaigning to preserve the species and terrains most under threat.

For **books** on the wildlife of Malaysia, Singapore and Brunei, see p.736.

Taman Negara

The vast expanse (4343 square kilometres) of **Taman Negara** contains one of the world's oldest tropical rainforests, and is generally regarded as one of Asia's finest national parks. It has an **equatorial climate**, with rainfall throughout the year and no distinct dry season. Temperatures can reach 35°C during the day, with the air often feeling very muggy. Most rain falls as heavy convectional showers in the afternoon, following a hot and sunny morning – from November to February, heavy rains may cause flooding in low-lying areas.

Forest trees

The natural richness of the habitat is reflected in the range of forest types found within the park. Only a small proportion of Taman Negara is true **lowland forest**, though it's here that most of the trails and hides are located. The lowlands support **dipterocarp** (meaning "two-winged fruit") evergreen forest, featuring tall tropical hardwood species and thick-stemmed lianas. There are more than four hundred dipterocarp species in Malaysia, and it's not uncommon to find up to forty in just one small area of forest. Among other trees here are the majestic fifty-metre-tall *tualang*, Southeast Asia's tallest tree; many others have broad, snaking buttress roots and leaves the size of dinner plates. Several species of **fruit trees**, such as durian, mango, guava and rambutan, also grow wild here.

Montane forest predominates above 1000m, mainly oak and native conifers with a shrub layer of rattan and dwarf palm. Above 1500m on Gunung Tahan is **cloudforest**, where trees are often cloaked by swirling mist, and the damp boughs bear thick growths of mosses and ferns; at elevations of over 1700m, you'll find miniature montane forest of rhododendron and fan palms.

Mammals

The best method of trying to see some of the larger herbivorous (grazing) **mammals** is to spend the night in one of the park's six **hides** overlooking a salt lick. Animals commonly encountered include the Malayan **tapir**, a species related to horses and rhinos, though pig-like in appearance with a short, fat body, a long snout and black-and-white colouring. The **gaur** (wild cattle) is dark in colour apart from its white leg patches, which look like ankle socks. There are also several species of **deer**: the larger *sambar*; the *kijang* or barking deer, the size of a roe deer; and the lesser and greater mouse deer.

Primates (monkeys and gibbons) are found throughout the park, although they are quite shy since they have traditionally been hunted for food by indigenous groups. The dawn chorus of a white-handed **gibbon** troupe – making a plaintive whooping noise – is not a sound that's quickly forgotten. Other primates include the long-tailed and pig-tailed **macaques**, which come to the ground to feed, the latter identified by its shorter tail, brown fur and pinkish-brown face. There are dusky (or spectacled – with white patches around the eyes) and banded **leaf monkeys**, too, recognized by their long, drooping tails (gibbons are tailless) and their habit of keeping their bodies hidden among the foliage.

Other mammals you might encounter by – admittedly fairly remote – chance are the Asian **elephant**, with smaller ears and a more humped back than the African; **tigers**, now thought to number no more than five hundred in the Peninsula; and **sun bears**. The bears are an interesting species: standing about 70cm high on all fours, and around 1.5m in length. Their behaviour towards humans can be unpredictable, particularly if there are cubs nearby.

Clouded leopards – a beautifully marked cat species with a pattern of cloud-like markings on the sides of the body – also live here, mostly in the trees, crossing from bough to bough in their search for food, eating monkeys, squirrels and birds, which they swat with their claws; they're most active at twilight. Smaller predators include the **leopard cat** (around the size of a large domestic cat) and several species of nocturnal **civet**, some of which have been known to enter the hides at night in search of tourists' food.

Birds

Over 250 species of birds – including some of the most spectacular forest-dwelling birds in the world – have been recorded in Taman Negara, though many species are shy or present only in small numbers. Birds are at their most active from early to mid-morning, and again in the late afternoon and evening periods; the areas around Kuala Keniam, and the Kumbang and Tabing hides are particularly worth visiting.

Resident forest birds include several species of **green pigeon**, which feed on the fruiting trees; **bulbuls**, vocal, fruit-eating birds that often flock to feed; **minivets**, slender, colourful birds with long, graduated tails, white, yellow or red bands in the wings and outer tail feathers of the same colour; and **babblers**, various short-tailed, round-winged, often ground-dwelling species. The period from September to March is when the visitor can hope to encounter the greatest diversity of birds, with resident species joined by **wintering birds** from elsewhere in Asia, such as warblers and thrushes.

Pittas, brilliantly coloured in hues of red, yellow, blue and black, are ground-dwelling birds generally occurring singly or in pairs, though they are notoriously shy and difficult to approach. The resident species are the giant, garnet and banded pittas, with blue-winged and hooded pittas being winter visitors.

In addition, several species of pheasant may be seen along the trails, including the **Malaysian peacock pheasant**, a shy bird with a blue-green crest and a patch of bare, orange facial skin; the feathers of the back and tail have green *ocelli* (eye-spots). The crested and crestless **fireback** are similar species of pheasant, differing in the crested fireback's black crest, white tail-plumes, blue-sheen upper parts and white-streaked (rather than plain black) belly. The **great argus** is the largest pheasant species present in the area, with the male birds reaching a maximum of 1.7m in length. Finally, the mountain **peacock pheasant** – very similar in plumage to the Malaysian peacock pheasant and endemic to Malaysia – lives high on Gunung Tahan.

You may also see birds of prey, with two of the most common species, the **crested serpent eagle** and the **changeable hawk eagle**, often spotted soaring over gaps in the forest canopy. The crested serpent eagle (with a 75cm wingspan – about the size of a buzzard) can be identified by the black and white bands on the trailing edge of the wings and on the tail.

Other species confined to tropical forests are **trogons** (brightly coloured, mid-storey birds), of which five species are present at Taman Negara; and several species of **hornbill** – large, broad-winged, long-tailed forest birds, some species of which have huge, almost outlandish bills.

Reptiles and amphibians

Reptiles and amphibians are well represented in the area. **Monitor lizards** (which can grow to be over 2m long) can be found close to the park headquarters, as can **skinks** (rather short-legged types of lizard which wriggle as much as run among the leaf litter).

Several species of snakes are present, too, including the reticulated **python** (which feeds on small mammals and birds and can grow to a staggering 9m in length), and the king and common **cobras**; king cobras, the largest venomous snake in the world, grow up to 5m long. These are all pretty rare in Taman Negara, though, and you're more likely to come across **whip snakes** (which eat insects and lizards) and – most common of all – harmless green **tree snakes**.

For many, a trip to Borneo would not be complete without an encounter with a **proboscis monkey**, a shy animal found only in the riverine forests and mangrove swamps of the Bornean coast. The monkey derives its name from the enlarged, drooping, red nose of the adult male monkey; females and young animals are snub-nosed. The role of the drooping nose, which seems to straighten out when the animal is issuing its curious honking call, is unclear, although it is likely that it helps in attracting a mate.

The monkeys are reddish-brown in colour, with a dark red cap, long, thick, white tails and white rumps; in addition, the adult males have a cream-white collar and large bellies, giving them a rather portly appearance. The monkeys live in loose groups, spending their days in trees close to the water, though they will walk across open areas when necessary, and can swim proficiently, aided by their partly webbed feet. The creatures are most active at dawn and dusk, when moving to and from feeding sites. Feeding on young leaves, shoots and fruit, they are quite choosy eaters, preferring the leaves of the *Sonneraita* mangrove tree, a rather specialist diet which means that large areas of forest need to be protected to provide groups of monkeys with sufficient food.

Visitors can hope to see proboscis monkeys in several of the national parks in Sabah and Sarawak, most notably in the Kinabatangan area, the Labuk Bay Proboscis Monkey Sanctuary and in Sarawak's Bako National Park.

Fraser's Hill

At **Fraser's Hill**, visitors can escape the stultifying tropical heat of the lowlands and venture into the cool breezes and fogs of the mountain forests, where ferns and pitcher plants cling to damp, moss-covered branches. It's a noted area for birdwatching, with the hill itself harbouring several montane species of birds, while mammals represented in the area include those normally restricted to more mountainous regions, in addition to some lowland species.

Much of the **forest** at Fraser's Hill is in pristine condition and the route there takes you from lowland forest through sub-montane to montane forest. Higher up on the hill, there are more evergreen tree species present, while the very nature of the vegetation changes: the trees are more gnarled and stunted, and the boughs heavily laden with dripping mosses and colourful epiphytic orchids (ie, orchids that grow on other plants and trees).

Mammals

The more strictly montane mammal species at Fraser's Hill include the **siamang gibbon**, a large, all-black gibbon that spends its time exclusively in trees. There are also several species of **bat**, such as the montane form of the Malayan fruit bat and the grey fruit bat; and several **squirrel** species like the mountain red-bellied squirrel and the tiny Himalayan striped squirrel, the latter species having a pattern of black-and-yellow stripes running along the length of its back. Lowland mammal species here include the tiger, clouded leopard, sun bear and leaf monkeys (see p.722). However, most of these are scarce, and you can realistically expect to encounter only monkeys, squirrels and, possibly, siamangs.

Birds

A feature of montane forest bird flocks is the **mixed feeding flock**, which may contain many different species. These pass rapidly through an area of forest searching for insects as they go, and it's quite likely that different observers will see entirely different species in one flock. Species commonly occurring within these flocks are the **lesser racket-tailed drongo**, a black crow-like bird with long tail streamers; the **speckled piculet**, a small spotted woodpecker; and the **blue nuthatch**, a small species – blue-black in colour with a white throat and pale eye ring – which runs up and down tree trunks. Several species of brightly coloured **laughing thrushes**, small thrush-sized birds that spend time foraging on the ground or in the understorey, also occur in these flocks. One sound to listen out for is the distinctive cackling "took" call of the **helmeted hornbill** echoing up from the lowlands.

Fraser's Hill itself peaks at 1310m at the High Pines, where a ridge trail begins. Here, there's the possibility of encountering rare species unlikely to be seen at lower altitudes, including the brown bullfinch and the **cutia** – a striking bird, with blue cap, black eyeline and tail, white underparts barred black and a chestnut-coloured back.

Music

M alaysia's contemporary sounds encompass everything from Malay rock to English-language indie (also a notable feature of Singapore's scene), heavy metal, Chinese grunge, singer-songwriter initiatives and Tamil hip-hop. And despite Malaysia's rapid modernization, traditional sounds are clinging on, including music to accompany folk dances, as well as the largely hidden delights of the indigenous music and the interconnected bold fusions found in Sarawak.

A brief survey can't hope to cover this diversity, and thus here the focus is on Malay sounds, both traditional and modern, plus the folk and tribal music of east Malaysia. For a broader exploration of Malaysian music, consult the *Encyclopedia of Malaysia* series (published by Editions Didier Millet in Kuala Lumpur and Singapore; Volume 8 covers the performing arts in general, and has some useful sections on music) or the excellent musicological monograph *The Music of Malaysia*, by Patricia Matursky and Tan Sooi Beng (Ashgate Publishing). Websites such as Malaysia's ⓦwww.ricecooker.kerbau.com and Singapore's ⓦwww.audioreload.com offer a glimpse of the alternative scene.

Influences

Malaysia's music reflects a wide range of influences. The peoples of Malaysia share in the wider heritage of Indonesia and the Philippines, the cultures of the three nations having borrowed and adapted elements from one another from pre-Islamic times down to the present day. Furthermore, Malaysia lies at the hub of global trade routes that have brought a rich mixture of influences, most significantly Islam from the Middle East. Much of this can be seen in the instruments used in Malay music: the bronze gong is thought to be part of the Chinese influence, the Indonesian gamelan ensemble being one of its most refined derivatives; the skin drum in its many forms was first brought in by seafaring Arabs, who also introduced the three-string spiked fiddle (*rebab*), lute (*gambus*) and the choral tradition of *hadrah* (religious songs accompanied by tambourines); a species of oboe (*serunai*) is thought to be of Indian origin. To this mix, the aboriginal inhabitants of the Peninsula and Borneo contributed strong rhythms, reed flutes, the four and six-stringed *sape* and a wooden xylophone to the modern-day "national music". The policy of borrowing and adapting has continued, and today, traditional styles are still played on violins, accordions and hand drums, though electric guitars and electronic keyboards also feature.

Traditional styles

Authentic traditional Malaysian music still exists these days but has only a small presence on the CD racks in Malaysian music stores. You're more likely to come across live performances, particularly **asli** (literally "original"), a slow traditional music played by small ensembles. These also play the faster **joget** and **zapin** dances, the former with Portuguese roots, the latter considered typically

Malay (and popular throughout the Peninsula), though actually of Arabic origin. In their traditional form, both *asli* and *zapin* dances or songs are accompanied by the *gambus* and a couple of two-headed frame drums beating out an interlocking rhythm. These are often supplemented by violin and harmonium (or accordion), flute, keyboards and guitars. The traditional *joget* ensemble is not dissimilar to those for *asli*, but in Terengganu there's also *joget*-gamelan, featuring an assembly of ten gongs and metallophones, which originally came from the Riau islands of Indonesia.

Ghazal, associated particularly with Kuala Lumpur and Johor, is a sentimental form of folk pop derived from the poetic love songs of Indian light classical music. The great star of the genre remains the late Kamariah Noor, whose recordings are still available. Her voice, both intense and languid, enabled her to bend and hold notes, milking them for every last drop of emotion. Kamariah often sang with her husband Hamzah Dolmat, Malaysia's greatest **rebab** player, famous for his slow, rather mournful style combined with a wonderful melodic creativity.

The six-stringed Arabic lute, known as *gambus* in Malay, is used as an accompanying instrument for singers of *ghazal* and *asli* music as well as in ensembles for dance music. Malaysia's recognized master of the *gambus* was the late Fadzil Ahmad, who started performing in the 1950s and later assisted in the formation of several cultural groups dedicated to preserving traditional Malay-Arabic music.

Melaka

Like its buildings, a strange mix of Portuguese, Dutch and Chinese architecture, **Melaka's** music is a confluence and compromise between styles. Modern Malaysia accepts the Malaccan *ronggeng* as its own "folk music" – music played on the violin and the button accordion, accompanied by frame drums, hand drums and sometimes a brass gong. The melodies speak of their Portuguese origin, with faint echoes of Moorish intervals and motifs. The fiddle holds the floor until the singers join in, when it recedes to a plaintive accompaniment.

Another musical genre associated with Melaka is **dondang sayang**, a slow, intense, majestic form led by sharp percussive drum rolls which trigger a shift in melody or a change in the pace of rhythm. This is a typically Malaysian style, in fact an amalgam of Hindu, Arabic, Chinese and Portuguese instruments and musical styles. *Tabla* and harmonium, double-headed *gendang* drum and tambourine create the rhythm, while the violin (and sometimes the accordion) carries the melody.

The east coast

Kelantan, Terengganu and southeastern Thailand share a distinctive Malay culture, seaborne traffic having linked this region more to the cultures of the South China Sea and less to Western influence than is the case with the west coast of the Peninsula.

A Kelantan performance of *silat*, the Malay martial art, is accompanied by a small ensemble of long drums, Indian oboes and gongs, which generate a loose set of cross rhythms. The music rises to a crescendo as the *silat* intensifies, the *serunai* screeching atonally while the drums and gongs quicken their loose rhythm. **Kertok**, a form of music, which originated with the Orang Asli, is played by a very different sort of ensemble, in which six to twelve men play pentatonically tuned wooden xylophones.

Wayang kulit (shadow puppetry), an ancient artistic tradition of Southeast Asia, serves as a good example of the meeting and intermingling of cultures in the Malay Peninsula: the *wayang*'s roots are in the Hindu epic, the *Ramayana*; the craftsmanship of the puppets is Indonesian/Malay; while the music is produced by something similar to a *silat* ensemble, enhanced by the wooden xylophone and sometimes small hand drums.

The popular traditional music of the east coast is **dikir barat**, probably based on *zikir*, an Islamic (particularly Sufi) style of singing, featuring verses in praise of Allah sung to the beat of a single tambourine, sometimes accompanied by hand-clapping.

East Malaysia

The music of the various tribal groups of **Borneo** has been preserved in a relatively pure form, but in recent years a number of exciting fusions of traditional and modern music have taken place, fuelled by the tremendous success of the Rainforest Music Festival.

The true "folk" music in both Sarawak and Sabaha emanates from the artistic culture of the **longhouse**. Here, everybody and their grandmother can play the **gongs**, on which traditional **Iban** music is played to accompany dances. The lead instruments – the "melody gongs" – are heirloom pieces in sets of six or eight, laid in a wooden frame over a bed of string and played with two beaters. Rhythm is kept by the larger gongs, which are suspended singly.

The principal Orang Ulu instrument, the lute-like **sapé**, has seen a conscious attempt at a revival, and is one of the real joys of Sarawak music when played by a master. The *sapé* has a body hollowed out from a single block of wood, and is often painted with traditional geometric designs. There are three or four strings, of which the lowest is the melody string and the others drones. *Sapés* are commonly played in pairs, or even larger groups, possibly because they sound rather soft despite their large size. In an ensemble, *sapés* may be joined by a wooden xylophone, whose top end can be fastened to an upright support (in a longhouse, one of the house pillars) while the lower end is tied to the performer's waist. Currently a crop of new, young *sapé* players are emerging: Boboy, for example, plays traditional tunes but augments them with electronic accompaniment, while already established players like **Jerry Kamit** have fitted their instruments with electric-guitar pick-ups.

In the Orang Ulu longhouses you often see old "mouth-organs", called *keluré* or *kediri*, made from a gourd into which are fixed bamboo pipes; these instruments were once used to accompany dances or processions, though nowadays you really have to hunt to find anyone who can play one. There are also many types of **mouth and nose flute** found across Borneo. The **Lun Bawang** people are particularly active players and have formed "bamboo bands" incorporating every flute known to man, including a "bass flute" that looks more like a bamboo tuba than anything else. Schools and villages of east Sarawak and west Sabah have resounding bamboo bands, playing anything from *Onward Christian Soldiers* to the patriotic march *Malaysia Berjaya*.

Another Sarawakian folk style revived in recent years is **a capella** singing. A fine example is the **Voices of Bario**, a women's choir from the Kelabit Highlands, who now perform across Southeast Asia.

Another example of the new direction is the riveting dance ensemble, **Tuku Kame**, led by flautist Narawi Rashidi, who is also the musical co-ordinator at Damai's **Sarawak Cultural Village** (see p.414). Along with other local fusion groups, they perform at the Village's annual international world music festival, the Rainforest World Music Festival (see p.415). You can also catch the ethnic music of Sarawak and Sabah during harvest festivals in June.

Contemporary music

Modern music in Malay was almost entirely Indonesian, of the sentimental **kroncong** variety, until **P. Ramlee's** mellifluous baritone sang its way into Malaya's heart in the 1950s. Penang-born, Ramlee (1929–73) started crooning and writing songs during his teens, landing himself an invitation to become involved in the Malay film industry, then centred in Singapore. He soon became one of the biggest Malay stars of the era, appearing in (and later also directing) dozens of films, for which he composed and performed some gorgeous melodies. Musically, he steered Malay singing along a new course, personalizing the songs, adapting the folk instrument repertoire and also often recording with a dance-hall orchestra, reflecting the popularity of Latin ballroom music in the postwar period. Ramlee's great duets with his wife, Saloma, are regarded as Malaysian pop's glorious dawn.

Prominent among performers of "modern classical" Malay songs is **Sharifah Aini**, whose strong, sweet voice seems to improve with the years. In the popularity stakes, however, it's **Siti Nurhaliza** who is right at the front of the pack. Equally at home with both contemporary and traditional styles, she is regarded by her many fans as having genuine international appeal, but has yet to make a breakthrough abroad. **Sheila Majid** is also among Malaysia's best-known pop stars and was the first Malaysian to penetrate the Asian market, particularly in Indonesia. Her foundation in classical music has stood her in good stead as she sings her way from soft rock towards jazz – mostly in the Malay *balada* genre, though she is equally at home in English.

For one reason or another, Malay audiences have a particular affinity with rock, often 1970s-style pop-rock or straightforward heavy metal, though grunge has also had a big impact. Long-established rockers M. Nasir and Ramli Sarip, both Singapore-born though based in KL, retain a major following. Arguably the greatest pop musician Singapore has ever produced, singer-artist-actor **M. Nasir** remains, sadly, relatively unknown in the country of his birth. **Ramli Sarip** is nearly as iconic, a kind of Malaysian Neil Young, with a voice that makes Rod Stewart's sound positively velvety.

Among a number of disparate trends in recent years has been the advent of Malay rap and hip-hop, spearheaded by groups such as **KRU**, **Too Phat** and the more politically conscious **Ahlifiqir**. These groups have been no strangers to controversy in their lyrics, something that could not be less true of groups allied to the other major vogue of recent years, the style known as **nasyid** – the Muslim equivalent of gospel pop. Reflecting the more conservative bent of the last couple of decades, *nasyid* is performed by all-male or all-female groups to the accompaniment of drums and tambourines. Foremost in this vein is the group **Raihan**, whose debut album *Puji-Pujian* sold an unprecedented 600,000 copies in the late 1990s. Lately, there has been an intensification of "underground", hardcore rock music, with a rise in popularity of bands such as Second Combat and The Padangs.

Sarawak, with its large population of Dyaks, has a small, but very active, local rock industry where occasionally some absorbing fusions of indigenous and Western elements emerge. A case in point are the early albums by **Peter Jaban**, who runs Kuching's *Ruai* bar (see p.407). His *Joget To The Moon*, although essentially a pop song over a *joget* beat, is an evergreen Iban classic from the 1990s. Kuching FM station (KATS) champions original music whenever possible.

Discography

Very few recordings of Malaysian music see the light of day abroad, so shop around at Tower Records in KL for mainstream releases, or try the various outlets in the Campbell Shopping Centre in KL (on Jalan Dang Wangi, not far from Little India) or the Queensway Shopping Centre in Singapore (at the junction of Queensway and Alexandra Rd). East Malaysian cities have an abundance of CD retailers too.

Traditional

Fadzil Ahmad *Raja Gambus Malaysia* (Ahas Productions). Featuring instrumentals as well as songs, this is a great illustration of the art of Fadzil Ahmad, "Malaysia's king of the *gambus*", as the album's title has it.

Siti Nurhaliza *Cindai* (SRC, Malaysia). In a roots style, the band featuring *rebana* (drums), *tabla* and bamboo flutes, *Cindai* achieved sales of 200,000 copies, all the more staggering considering its release during the economic woes of the late 1990s.

Tuku Kame *Rhythms of the Rainforest / Gadong*. Second and third releases from the excellent folk and jazz fusion ensemble based in the Sarawak Cultural Village near Kuching.

Tusau Padan *Masters of the Sarawakian Sapé, featuring Tusau Padan* (Pan, Netherlands). Tusau Padan, who died in 1996, was an acknowledged exponent of the *sapé*, but no recordings of his survive other than these, featuring traditional dances plus a couple of duets with younger players.

Various *Muzik Tarian Malaysia* (Life Records). Two-CD set of *joget*, *zapin* and other traditional dances played by a small instrumental ensemble. Classical and refined.

Various *The Rough Guide to the Music of Malaysia* (World Music Network). A largely traditional compilation with a couple of excellent tracks, notably the S.M. Salim/Rosiah Chik duet *Berdendang Sayang*, plus Siti Nurhaliza's *Cindai*.

Contemporary

Ahlifiqir *Hari Ini Dalam Sejarah* (Powder/Warner Music, Malaysia). An audacious debut in which Ahlifiqir rail against the Malay establishment – a fact which appears all the more daring when you consider that three of the four members come from Singapore, not a place noted for encouraging outspokenness among its citizens. As a blend of hip-hop and Malay melodic influences, it's totally listenable even if you don't understand the language. Sadly nothing they've done since has lived up to this album's promise.

Alleycats *No. 1s* (Universal). Since the 1970s Penang's Alleycats, led by two Tamil brothers, David and Loga

Arumugam, have been seen as Malaysia's answer to the Bee Gees, having chalked up a string of easy-listening hits, both uptempo tunes and ballads. If you ever get to sample a Malay karaoke bar, expect some tune or other from this twenty-song compilation (half of which was written by M. Nasir) to crop up at some point.

Butterfingers *Selamat Tinggal Dunia* (Butterworld/EMI). After releasing a slew of albums in English, grungers Butterfingers hit their creative peak with this, their first Malay-language CD, using northern slang (from Kedahan to Kelantanese) to convey their disenchantment with the new Malay middle class and the Malay mass media. A terrific slice of angst-ridden Malay rock.

Joe Flizzow *President* (Kartel). There's a touch of Kanye West about this excellent solo release, in Malay and English, from one half of Too Phat.

Kembara *No. 1s* (Universal). A collection of Kembara's work from the early 1980s, when the group's singer-songwriters – A. Ali, S. Amin Shahab and M. Nasir – created something of a folk rock sensibility, building up barbed tunes from acoustic settings and tackling in their lyrics issues such as youth unrest, urban migration and the plight of rice farmers.

Sheila Majid *Ratu* (Warner Music, Malaysia). Easy-listening Malaysian-style, and superbly produced, justifying her claim to being one of Malaysia's few jazz singers.

M. Nasir *No. 1 "Dulu Dan Kini"* (Sony BMG). A whole bunch of Malay pop-rock standards on one album, including *Ekspres Rakyat*, *Mentera Semerah Padi* and *Keroncong Untuk Ana*. Indispensable.

M. Nasir *Phoenix Bangkit* (Warner Music, Malaysia). The rootsiest, most ambitious record by this veteran musician, bringing together his top-drawer songwriting and a lush production that makes traditional and modern instruments sound completely at home with each other.

Raihan *Puji-pujian* (Warner Music, Malaysia). Fresh young voices and sophisticated percussion characterize this huge-selling debut from *nasyid* pioneers Raihan, still worth picking up ten years on even though the genre has come off the boil of late.

P. Ramlee *Sri Kenangan Abadi Vols I–III* (EMI, Malaysia). Any of these three CDs are recommended as an introduction to P. Ramlee's most popular tunes.

S.M. Salim *Raja Irama Malaysia* (Warner Music, Malaysia). With a career stretching back to the days of Merdeka, S.M. Salim is one of the Malay music scene's great icons. This 26-track compilation ranges from much-loved *asli* and *joget* songs to hit-or-miss collaborations with the likes of M. Nasir, Siti Nurhaliza, Ramli Sarip, Raihan and the Malaysian Philharmonic Orchestra. File under "National Treasure".

Search *Terunggul* (Sony BMG). The story of Johor hard-rock outfit Search is one of good old rock 'n' roll excess, with a Malaysian spin. Back in the 1980s they were busted for drugs and – once a big issue, given domestic sensibilities – long hair, but they've survived to become one of the most respected local bands. This 28-track retrospective, focusing on the band's chart-busting back catalogue has enough decent faux glam-rock numbers and ballads here to make it worth investigating.

Books

T here's no shortage of **books** about Malaysia, Singapore and Brunei. In the past, the majority tended to be penned by Western visitors to the region, but in the last couple of decades local writing and publishing in English has really gathered momentum. Among the more interesting independent **publishers** are Select Books (ⓦwww.selectbooks.com.sg), Editions Didier Millet (ⓦwww.edmbooks.com), Pelanduk (ⓦwww.pelanduk .com), Media Masters (ⓦwww.mediamasters.com.sg), Silverfish Books (ⓦwww .silverfishbooks.com) and Natural History Publications, Borneo (ⓦwww .nhpborneo.com). It's obviously easiest to buy locally published material while you're travelling around the countries concerned, though a few titles are available internationally, while Select Books and MPH (ⓦwww.mph.com.my) have online mail-order services.

In the reviews that follow, books published outside the UK and US have the publisher listed. Books marked 🏃 are especially recommended, while o/p signifies that a book is out of print. Note that, as per Chinese custom, surnames are given first for those Chinese authors who don't have Christian names.

Travel and general interest

🏃 *Encyclopedia of Malaysia* (Editions Didier Millet). A brilliantly produced series of tomes on different aspects of Malaysia, all beautifully illustrated and – not always the case with locally published material – competently edited. The volumes on the performing arts and architecture are particularly recommended. Available to buy as individual volumes or as a set.

Isabella Bird *The Golden Chersonese*. Delightful epistolary romp through old Southeast Asia, penned by the intrepid Bird, whose adventures in the Malay states in 1879 ranged from strolls through Singapore's streets to elephant-back rides. A free download from various online libraries.

Margaret Brooke *My Life in Sarawak* (o/p). This engaging account of nineteenth-century Sarawak by the wife of White Rajah Charles Brooke reveals a sympathetic attitude to her subjects (which extended to rubbing eau de cologne into a Dyak warrior's forehead). Her

eye for detail conveys the wonder of an unprejudiced colonial embracing an alien culture.

Harry Foster *A Beachcomber in the Orient*. Recently reissued, this is a hilarious first-person account of a proto-backpacker who travelled through Malaya and other parts of Southeast Asia in the 1920s.

Eric Hansen *Orchid Fever*. Hansen's epic search for the world's most elusive strain of orchid took him from the Bornean jungle to Kew Gardens and from the Orinoco River to the peat bogs of Minnesota. The resulting account is a funny and compelling tale of orchids and obsession.

Judith M. Heimann *The Most Offending Soul Alive: Tom Harrisson and His Remarkable Life*. From his first expedition there in 1932 onwards, Tom Harrisson's life was inextricably linked with Sarawak. Heimann's biography tracks Harrisson's many dealings with Borneo, from his wartime exploits raising a head-hunter army against the Japanese, to his subsequent work as curator of the Sarawak Museum.

🏃 **Agnes Keith** *Land Below the Wind*. Bornean memories galore, in this charming account of expat life in prewar Sabah; Keith's true eye and assured voice produce a heart-warming picture of a way of life now long gone. Her naive sketches complement perfectly the childlike wonder of the prose.

Victor T. King *Moving Pictures: More Borneo Travel*. An anthology collecting accounts of Western encounters with the natural and cultural landscapes of Borneo.

Redmond O'Hanlon *Into The Heart of Borneo*. A hugely entertaining yarn recounting O'Hanlon's refreshingly amateurish romp through the jungle to a remote summit on the Sarawak/Kalimantan border, partnered by the English poet James Fenton.

Robert Twigger *Big Snake*. His hunt for the world's longest python takes Twigger on an entertaining and eventful jaunt from the sewers of KL to the forests of Sabah.

History and politics

🏃 **Munshi Abdullah** *The Hikayat Abdullah*. Raffles' one-time clerk, Melaka-born Abdullah became diarist of some of the most formative years of Southeast Asian history; his first-hand account is crammed with illuminating vignettes and character portraits.

Charles Allen *Plain Tales from the British Empire*. Memoirs of the last generation of British colonists, in which predictable Raj attitudes prevail, though some of the drama of everyday lives, often in inhospitable conditions, is evinced with considerable pathos.

🏃 **Barbara Watson Andaya and Leonard Andaya** *The History of Malaysia*. Unlike more paternalistic histories penned by former colonists, this standard text on the region takes a more even-handed view of Malaysia, and finds time for cultural coverage, too.

Noel Barber *War of the Running Dogs*. Illuminates the Malayan Emergency with a novelist's eye for mood.

Nigel Barley *White Rajah*. A highly readable biography of Sir James Brooke, focusing particularly on letters and other primary sources.

Jim Baker *The Eagle In The Lion City* (Landmark). About so much more than its declared theme, Singapore–American relations, this entertaining book tells of how British influence faded in the post-colonial era, allowing common interests in trade and defence to bring the US and Singapore ever closer – hence the somewhat "Californized" city-state you see today.

David Brazil *Insider's Singapore*. An Aladdin's cave of Singaporean history and trivia that remains fascinating throughout.

Maurice Collis *Raffles* (o/p). The most accessible and enjoyable biography of Sir Stamford Raffles.

Roy Follows *The Jungle Beat*. The Malaysian jungle proved as unforgiving an enemy as the Malayan communist insurgents when Follows joined the Malay police in the 1950s. His story engages from beginning to end.

Mary Somers Heidhues *Southeast Asia: A Concise History*. A Thames &

Hudson text packed with photographs and sketches reflecting the history of the region described within its readable prose.

Images of Asia series Maya Jayapal's *Old Singapore* and Sarnia Hayes Hoyt's *Old Malacca* and *Old Penang* chart the growth of three of the region's most important outposts, drawing on contemporary maps, sketches and photographs to engrossing effect.

Patrick Keith *Ousted* (Media Masters). Most of the largely young population of Malaysia and Singapore know little of the events that saw Singapore leaving the federation in 1965. And yet, as this excellent memoir by a former Malaysian government adviser demonstrates, many of the issues which led to the rift continue to shape both countries and their mutual ties today – Malaysia is still laden with ethnically based politics, while Singapore remains the fiefdom of the PAP.

Wendy Khadijah-Moore *Malaysia: A Pictorial History 1400–2003* (Editions Didier Millet). If you're going to do coffee-table books on Malaysia's history, you could come up with a lot worse than this well-illustrated portable museum. Don't come to it expecting trenchant commentary, though: Anwar's arrest in the late 1990s, for instance, gets a mere couple of lines.

Eric Lomax *The Railway Man*. Such is the power of Lomax's artless,

redemptive and moving story of capture during the fall of Singapore, torture by the Japanese and reconciliation with his tormentor after fifty years, that many reviewers were moved to tears.

James Minchin *No Man Is An Island* (o/p). A well-researched, and at times critical, study of Lee Kuan Yew, which refuses to kowtow to Singapore's ex-prime minister and is hence unavailable in Singapore itself.

Amir Muhammad *Malaysian Politicians Say The Darndest* (sic) *Things Vols 1 & 2* (Matahari). Incredibly crass utterances from the mouths of top public figures, ranging from the thought that only unattractive women should get state-sector jobs (as the pretty ones can find rich husbands) to the strange contention that Singapore, being small, lacks opportunities for corruption, "unlike in our country". Read them and weep.

Bob Reece *The White Rajahs of Sarawak* (Editions Didier Millet). A handsome coffee-table book about the extraordinary Brooke dynasty.

Carl A. Trocki *Singapore: Wealth, Power and the Culture of Control*. Highly readable dissection of how the PAP, after co-opting and marginalizing Singapore's Left in the 1960s and then allying "with international capital to create a workers' paradise", acquired its present grip on all aspects of life in Singapore.

World War II

Noel Barber *Sinister Twilight*. Documents the fall of Singapore to the Japanese, by re-imagining the crucial events of the period.

Russell Braddon *The Naked Island*. Southeast Asia under the

Japanese: Braddon's disturbing yet moving first-hand account of the POW camps of Malaya, Singapore and Siam displays courage in the face of appalling conditions and treatment; worth scouring second-hand stores for.

Spencer Chapman *The Jungle is Neutral.* This riveting first-hand account of being lost, and surviving, in the Malay jungle during World War II reads like a breathless novel.

Agnes Keith *Three Came Home.* Pieced together from scraps of paper secreted in latrines and teddy bears, this is a remarkable story of survival in the face of Japanese attempts to eradicate the "proudery and arrogance" of the West in the World War II prison camps of Borneo.

Lucy Lum *The Thorn of Lion City.* You might think a memoir of a wartime childhood in Singapore might be dominated by the savagery of Japanese, but that's nothing compared to the torment inflicted on the author at the hands of her manipulative and violent mother and grandmother. It's all told with zero artifice, which only makes it more compelling.

Colin Smith *Singapore Burning: Heroism and Surrender in World War II.* Highly detailed, definitive account of the fall of Singapore, written with a journalist's instinct for excitement.

Culture and society

James Harding and Ahmad Sarji *P. Ramlee: The Bright Star* (Pelanduk). An uncritical but enjoyable biography of the Malay singer, actor and director sometimes likened to Malaysia's Harry Belafonte. More importantly, it's a window onto what seems like a different era – though only half a century ago – when Singapore was the centre of the Malay entertainment universe, and when Malay life was, frankly, more carefree than today.

Gerrie Lim *Invisible Trade: High-Class Sex for Sale in Singapore* (Monsoon Books). This exposé of the escort industry in Singapore makes for an entertaining but somewhat unsatisfying read, its basic but revelatory flaw being that it shows Singapore to be much less squeaky clean than it may appear.

Andro Linklater *Wild People* (o/p). As telling and entertaining a glimpse into the lifestyle of the Iban as you could find, depicting their age-old traditions surviving amid the T-shirts, baseball caps and rock posters of Western influence.

Heidi Munan *Culture Shock! Malaysia.* Cultural do's and don'ts for the leisure and business traveller to the region, spanning subjects as diverse as handing over business cards and belching after a fine meal.

Heidi Munan *Music Without Borders: The Rainforest World Music Festival in Sarawak.* This coffee-table book makes a great festival memento, with informative text by ethnomusicologist Munan.

Colin Nicholas *The Orang Asli and the Contest for Resources* (International Workgroup for Indigenous Affairs). Puts into context the way in which the Orang Asli have been both drawn into mainstream society and yet marginalized over the years.

James Ritchie *Who Gives A DAM! The Bakun Odyssey* (Wisma Printing). Engaging, balanced account of the social and political consequences of the controversial Bakun Dam in Sarawak where over 10,000 indigenous peoples were moved from their lands to make way for a massive development project.

Bernard Sellato *Innermost Borneo: Studies in Dayak Cultures* (Seven Orients). Anthropologist Sellato

735

spent much of the 1990s with the indigenous Borneo tribes of Kalimantan, who are related to the Sea Dyaks of Sarawak. This excellent ethnographic work contains ravishing images of a traditional, isolated world that will eventually be subsumed into greater Indonesia.

Tan Kok Seng *Son Of Singapore*. Tan Kok Seng's candid and sobering autobiography on the underside of

the Singaporean success story, telling of hard times spent as a coolie.

🏃 **Dina Zaman** *I Am Muslim* (Silverfish). A well-observed set of wry essays, with more candour than would have been appropriate in this guidebook, on Islam as practised in Malaysia; form without enough substance is, sadly, often the verdict. The section on sexual attitudes is particularly recommended.

Cookbooks

Aziza Ali *Aziza's Creative Malay Cuisine* (PEN). A posh take on Malay food, by the woman who, for years, ran one of the best Malay restaurants in Singapore – a fact which means you won't find northern fare like *nasi kerabu* or *laksam* in here, but then, many of the recipes are intended more to impress at dinner parties than to reflect what's served on the street.

🏃 **Betty Saw** *Rasa Malaysia* (Marshall Cavendish). A nicely illustrated cookbook that covers dozens of the standard dishes you'll find served at food courts and in homes around the country, including various Chinese and Nonya recipes, though very little South Indian fare. It's all organized by state, which helps give a feel for regional cuisine, though annoyingly there's no index.

Natural history and ecology

G.W.H. Davison and Chew Yen Fook *A Photographic Guide to Birds of Borneo*; **M. Strange and A. Jeyarajasingam** *A Photographic Guide to Birds of Peninsular Malaysia and Singapore*; **Charles M. Francis** *A Photographic Guide to the Mammals of Southeast Asia*. Well-keyed and user-friendly, these slender volumes carry oodles of glossy plates that make positive identifying a breeze.

Robin Hanbury-Tenison *Mulu: The Rain Forest* (o/p). Hanbury-Tenison's overview of the flora, fauna and ecology of the rainforest, the result of a 1977 Royal Geographical Society field trip into Sarawak's Gunung Mulu National Park; makes enlightening reading.

Jeffrey McNeely and Paul Spencer Sochaczewski *Soul of the Tiger*. Offers insights into the wide-ranging importance of wildlife for Southeast Asia's indigenous peoples. Particularly fascinating is the chapter on Borneo, which suggests that birds are viewed as "messengers from the gods" in local culture.

Junaida Payne *Wild Malaysia: The Wildlife and Landscapes of Peninsular Malaysia, Sarawak and Sabah*. Coffee-table book, recently reissued, capturing forest and beach vistas of the kind that linger in the mind long after you've left Malaysia.

Ivan Polunin *Plants and Flowers of Malaysia* (Times Editions). A single volume simply can't do justice to the vast quantity of flora packed into tropical rainforest, and this doesn't attempt to try, instead providing a handy illustrated survey of plants in a variety of environments, from sandy beach to upland forest.

Morten Strange and Dennis Yong *Birds of Taman Negara* (Draco). Features colour photos of nearly a hundred birds seen in Taman

Negara, from Asian fairy bluebirds to grey-breasted spiderhunters; invaluable for twitchers.

🐾 **Alfred Russel Wallace** *The Malay Archipelago*. Wallace's peerless account of the flora and fauna of Borneo, based on travels made between 1854 and 1862 – during which time he collected over one hundred thousand specimens. Still required reading for nature lovers.

Art and architecture

Julian Davison and Luca Invernizzi Tettoni *Black & White: The Singapore House* (Talisman); **Peter and Waveney Jenkins** *The Planter's Bungalow* (Editions Didier Millet). Two tomes dealing with colonial "Anglo-Malay" residences, often strange hybrids of mock Tudor and Southeast Asian elements, and sometimes raised off the ground on posts like a kampung house. Both volumes also examine the lives of those who occupied these houses, not always as wealthy as you might assume; the photos of Singapore mansions in Davison and Tettoni's book are particularly impressive.

M. Heppell *Iban Art: Sexual Selection and Severed Heads* (KIT Publishers). Impressive illustrated volume exploring how Iban betrothals were crucially influenced by the prowess of the prospective partners at producing artwork and artefacts, as well as head-hunting.

Khoo Su Nin *Streets of George Town Penang* (Janus Print). This photograph-driven guide to Penang's traditional architecture is the perfect companion while strolling the lanes of Georgetown. Try the Cheong Fatt Tze Mansion in Georgetown or Select Books in Singapore for a copy.

Peter Lee and Jennifer Chen *The Straits Chinese House* (Editions Didier Millet). A beautifully illustrated volume exploring Peranakan domestic artefacts and their now largely vanished traditions; an excellent memento to a visit to the Baba-Nonya museusm of Penang, Melaka and Singapore.

🐾 **Lim Huck Chin and Fernando Jorge** *Malacca: Voices From the Street* (self-published; ⓦwww .malaccavoices.com). By the architects responsible for the restoration of 8 Heeren Street (see p.350), this labour of love chronicles the evolution of Melaka over the generations, street by street. The book also documents the decline of traditional trades and pastimes, and the degeneration of some areas into a crass modernity – a fate mirroring what has happened to parts of Penang, KL and Singapore. Printed on heavy-duty paper and illustrated with the authors' own colour photographs.

🐾 **Farish A. Noor and Eddin Khoo** *The Spirit of Wood: The Art of Malay Woodcarving* (Periplus). Much weightier in tone than your average coffee-table book, this deals not only with the superb woodcarving produced on the east coast of the Peninsula and in southern Thailand, but also with the whole pre-Islamic consciousness that subtly imbues the woodcarver's art. Packed with great photos, too, of gorgeous timber mosques, incredibly detailed *kris* hilts and the like.

Anthony Ratos and H. Berber *Orang Asli and their Wood Art*. One of few accessible explorations of Orang Asli lifestyles and cultures, though note that only a third of this

picture-heavy volume is devoted to their fantastical carvings; the rest of the photos are of Asli settlements and generic, if pretty, jungle scenes.

Robert Winzeler *The Architecture of Life and Death in Borneo*. Highly readable, illustrated study of the traditional architecture of Borneo, looking at the evolution of longhouses over the years and symbolism in building design.

Fiction

Anthony Burgess *The Long Day Wanes* (o/p). Burgess's Malayan trilogy (*Time for a Tiger*, *The Enemy in the Blanket* and *Beds in the East*), published in one volume, provides a witty and acutely observed vision of 1950s Malaya, underscoring the racial prejudices of the period. *Time for a Tiger* is worth reading for the Falstaffian Nabby Adams alone.

James Clavell *King Rat*. Set in Japanese-occupied Singapore, a gripping tale of survival in the notorious Changi Prison.

Joseph Conrad *Lord Jim*. Southeast Asia provides the backdrop to the story of Jim's desertion of an apparently sinking ship and subsequent efforts to redeem himself; modelled upon the sailor, A.P. Williams, Jim's character also yields echoes of Rajah Brooke of Sarawak.

J.G. Farrell *The Singapore Grip*. Lengthy novel – Farrell's last – of World War II Singapore in which real and fictitious characters flit from tennis to dinner party as the countdown to the Japanese occupation begins.

Henri Fauconnier *The Soul of Malaya*. Fauconnier's semi-autobiographical novel is a lyrical, sensory tour of the plantations,

jungle and beaches of early twentieth-century Malaya, and pierces deeply into the underside of the country.

Lloyd Fernando *Green is the Colour* (Silverfish). A remarkable novel, exploring the deep-seated racial tensions brought to light by the Kuala Lumpur demonstrations of May 1969.

K.S. Maniam *In A Far Country*; *Haunting the Tiger*. The purgative writings of this Tamil-descended Malaysian author are strong, highly descriptive and humorous – essential reading.

Preeta Samarasan *Evening Is The Whole Day*. Set mostly in the Ipoh of forty years ago, this ambitious debut novel ruthlessly dissects the lives of a dysfunctional upper-middle-class Indian family, though there are precious few *Simpsons*-style laughs to be had in a tale of infidelity, class disparities and violence behind closed doors, and the magical-realistic trappings just get in the way of the plot.

W. Somerset Maugham *Short Stories Volume 4*. Peopled by hoary sailors, bored plantation-dwellers and colonials wearing mutton-chop whiskers and topees, Maugham's short stories resuscitate

Malaya c.1900; quintessential colonial literature graced by an easy style and a steady eye for a story.

Tan Twan Eng *The Gift Of Rain*. This debut novel centres on the Eurasian scion of a wealthy family in prewar Penang. Despite some awkward patches, including a ludicrous episode set in Beijing's Forbidden City, it becomes a real page-turner as the main character's life is gravely compromised by his intense relationship with his father's Japanese tenant, who turns out to be a key figure during the war.

Paul Theroux *Saint Jack*; *The Consul's File* (o/p). *Saint Jack* tells the compulsively bawdy tale of Jack Flowers, an ageing American who supplements his earnings at a Singapore ship's chandlers by pimping for Westerners; Jack's jaundiced eye and Theroux's rich prose open windows on Singapore's past. In *The Consul's File*, the fictitious American consul to interior Malaya recounts a series of short stories.

Leslie Thomas *The Virgin Soldiers*. The bawdy exploits of teenage British Army conscripts snatching all the enjoyment they can, before being sent to fight in troubled 1950s Malaya.

Beth Yahp *The Crocodile Fury*. Described by one reviewer as a "spicy Malaysian curry" to Amy Tan's "lightly seasoned Chinese soup", Yahp has produced a garlicky, rambunctious storytelling treat that shadows the lives of three women – grandmother, mother and daughter – in colonial and post-colonial Malaysia.

Language

Language

Language

Malay, officially referred to as Bahasa Melayu (literally "Malay language"), is the national language of Malaysia, Singapore and Brunei. Part of the Austronesian language family, it's an old tongue, which became a language of prestige and a regional lingua franca through its use in the ancient kingdom of Srivijaya and during the fifteenth-century Melaka Sultanate. Native speakers of Malay are not just in Peninsular Malaysia and northern Borneo but also in pockets of Indonesia, where a version of Malay has been adopted as the official language.

Of course, Malay is only one of many languages used in the three countries covered in this book. In Singapore, English, Mandarin and Tamil are also official tongues, with English pre-eminent as the language of government and business, while Hokkien is the most used regional Chinese dialect. In Malaysia itself, English retains an important position in business, law and government, Tamil is widely spoken among the Indian community, while Mandarin is much used by the Chinese, as are Chinese dialects such as Cantonese (especially in KL and Ipoh) and Hokkien (in Penang and on the east coast).

In practice, you can get by with **English** except in rural areas and in the Malay-dominated east coast and the north of the Peninsula, where it really does pay to pick up a few words of Malay, especially since the basics are simple enough to learn. Besides, it's entertaining to get to grips with a tongue that, like English, is clearly a ready absorber of loan words. The influence of English on modern Malay is readily apparent to most travellers, and with an awareness of Asian languages, it's not hard to discern the infusion of words from Sanskrit (thanks to the ancient impact of Hinduism on Southeast Asia), such as *jaya* ("success") and *negara* ("country"), as well as from Arabic, which has contributed words like *maaf* ("sorry") and many terms to do with Islam.

To pick up the language, it's best to buy a coursebook that focuses on **vernacular** Malay, as our vocabulary section does, rather than the formal language used in print and broadcasting. The most recommendable book is *A Course in Conversational Malay* by Malcolm W. Mintz (SNP Publishing, Singapore).

Pronunciation

Malay was once written in Arabic script, but over the years this has been almost completely supplanted by a Romanized form. However, the Romanized **spellings** are prone to inconsistencies: for example, *baru*, "new", crops up in variant forms in place names like Johor Bahru and Kota Bharu, while new and old spellings of certain common words still coexist, for example *sungai/sungei, kampung/kampong*, and so forth.

Spelling quirks aside, Bahasa Malaysia is one of the more straightforward languages to pronounce, once you get your head round a few rules. One basic point to remember is that the consonants **k, p, t** have slightly less force in Malay than in English (to be precise, they aren't aspirated in Malay); if you emulate the

As diverting and as incomprehensible as Jamaican patois, Manglish and Singlish are aberrant forms of English widely spoken in Malaysia and Singapore respectively. They're really two sides of the same coin: in both, conventional English syntax gives way to a word order that's more akin to that of Malay or Chinese, and tenses and pronouns are discarded. Ask someone if they've ever been abroad, and you might be answered "I ever", while enquiring whether they've just been shopping might yield "Go, come back already". Pronunciation is so staccato that many words are rendered almost unrecognizable – "traffic light", for example, might be rendered "traffy-lie". Responses are almost invariably distilled down to single-word replies, often repeated for stress. Request something in a shop and you'll hear "have, have", or "got, got". Other stock manglings of English include:

aidontch-main	"I don't mind"
baiwanfriwan	"Buy one and you'll get one free", a sales ploy
betayudon(lah)	"You'd better not do that!"
debladigarmen	A contraction of "the bloody government"
is it?	(pronounced *eezeet*?) "Really?"
tingwat	"What do you think?"
watudu	"What can we do?", a rhetorical question
yusobadwan	"You're such a bad one!" meaning "that's not very nice!"

Suffixes and **exclamations** drawn from Malay and Hokkien complete this patois, the most ubiquitous being the Malay intensifier "lah", which seems to finish off just about every other utterance. In Malaysia you may hear the Malay question marker "kah" at the ends of queries, while Chinese on both sides of the Causeway might apply the suffix "ah", as in "so cheap one ah", which translates as "is it really that cheap?" or "wow, that's cheap" depending on the intonation; "ah" on its own can also mean "yes", especially if accompanied by a nod of the head. If Manglish and Singlish have you baffled, you might try raising your eyes to the heavens and crying either "ayoh" (with a drop of tone on the second syllable) or "alamak", both expressions denoting exasperation or regret.

Amusing though all this linguistic deviation is, concerns have been expressed in both countries as to how an apparent decline in **English standards** could affect their standing in global commerce. During the colonial era, the minority who could speak English tended to have a fair facility for the language. Today virtually everyone learns some English in school (in Singapore, English-language schools actually dominate) but too often students emerge with a weak grasp of the language. In Malaysia, former prime minister Mahathir Mohammed recognized the problem when, at the end of his career, he introduced a requirement that school mathematics and science classes be taught in English, thus back-pedalling on his own longstanding policy of emphasizing Malay in state education. For its part, Singapore, a country with a history of preachy state campaigns, has seen the creation of a government-backed Speak Good English movement (ⓦ www.goodenglish.org.sg).

sounds at the start of the Spanish words *cuatro*, *pero* and *toro*, you'd be in the right ball park. Other points of difference are listed below.

Syllable stress isn't that complicated in Malay. As a general rule, the stress lands on the **penultimate syllable** of a word (or, with words of two syllables, on the first syllable), a pattern that can lead to a few counterintuitive stress placements (eg SaRAwak, TerengGAnu). The chief exception to this rule concerns two-syllable words whose first syllable contains a short vowel (usually denoted by an "e"); in such cases, the stress sometimes falls on the second syllable – as in be*SAR* (big), le*KAS* (fast), and so forth, though unfortunately this isn't predictable.

Vowels and diphthongs

a somewhere in between the vowels of carp and cup, but changes to a short indeterminate vowel if at the end of a word, as in banana

aa like two "a" vowels separated by the merest pause; thus *maaf* (forgiveness) is rendered *ma + af*

ai as in fine (written "ei" in older spellings)

au as in how

e as in her, though in many instances (not predictable) it is like the é of sauté, as in *kereta* (car), pronounced *keréta*; in yet others it denotes a short indeterminate vowel (schwa)

i somewhere between the i of tin and the ee of teen

o as in stone, though shorter and not as rounded as in English

u sometimes short as in pull, sometimes long (eg, if at the end of a word) as in pool

ua as in doer

Consonants

c as in chip (and written "ch" in older spellings), though slightly gentler than in English

d becomes t when at the end of a word

g hard, as in girl

h can drop out when flanked by vowels; thus *tahu*, "know", is usually pronounced as though spelt *tau*

k drops out if at the end of the word or if followed by another consonant, becoming a glottal stop (a brief pause); thus *rakyat* (people) is pronounced *ra + yat*

kh as in the Scottish loch; found in loan words from Arabic

l unlike in English, l is not swallowed if it occurs at the end of a word

ng as in tang (the "g" is never hard – thus *telinga*, "ear", is te-ling-a and not te-lin-ga); can occur at the start of a word

ngg as in tango

ny as in canyon; can occur at the start of a word

r is lightly trilled (though in some accents it can be rendered like the French r of Paris); drops out at the ends of words when preceded by a vowel

sy as in shut

Grammar

Word order in Malay is similar to that in English, though note that adjectives usually follow nouns. **Nouns** have no genders and don't require an article, while the **plural** form is constructed either by saying the word twice, if the number of objects is unspecified (thus "book" is *buku*, "books" *buku-buku*, sometimes written *buku2*), or by specifying the number of objects before the singular noun ("three books" is thus *tiga buku*). **Verbs** have no tenses either, the time of the action being indicated either by the context, or by the use of words such as *akan* (functioning like "will") and *sudah* ("already") for the future and past. The verb "to be" seldom appears explicitly, so, for example, *saya lapar* literally means "I [am] hungry". There are two words for **negation**: *bukan*, used before nouns (for example *saya bukan doktor*, "I'm not a doctor"), and *tak* (formally *tidak*), used before verbs and adjectives (as in *saya tak lapar*, "I'm not hungry"; *saya tak makan*, "I've not eaten"). Possessive constructions are achieved simply by putting the "owner" after the thing that's "owned"; thus *kampung saya*, literally "village [of] I", is "my village".

Malay words and phrases

One point to note regarding **pronouns** is that Malay lacks a convenient word for "you", all the options being either too formal or informal. In fact, the normal way to address someone is to use their name to their face, which can seem strange to English-speakers. If you don't know someone's name, then you can use *abang* (brother) or *kak* (sister) to address a person of roughly the same age as you, or *adik* to a child, or *pak cik* or *mak cik* to a much older man or woman respectively.

You'll often see the word Dato' (or Datuk) or Tun placed before the name of a government official or some other worthy. Both are honorific titles of distinction roughly equivalent to the British "Sir". Royalty are always addressed as Tuanku.

Personal pronouns

I/my	saya	you (formal)	anda
we (excludes the	kami	(informal)	awak
person being		he/she	dia
spoken to) or		they	mereka
(includes the	kita	Mr	Encik *or* Tuan
person being		Mrs	Puan
spoken to)		Miss	Cik

Greetings and other basics

"Selamat" is the all-purpose greeting derived from Arabic, which communicates a general goodwill.

good morning	selamat pagi	never mind, no matter	tak apalah
good afternoon	selamat petang	yes	ya (sometimes
good midday (used	selamat tengah hari		pronounced a
around noon)			bit like "year")
good evening	selamat malam	no	tidak
good night (literally	selamat tidur	this/that	ini/itu
"peaceful sleep")		here	sini
goodbye (literally	selamat tinggal	there (very nearby),	situ
"peaceful stay";		(further away)	sana
used by someone		what is your name?	siapa nama awak?
leaving)		my name is…	nama saya…
safe journey	selamat jalan	where are you from?	dari mana?
welcome	selamat datang	I come from…	saya dari…
bon appetit	selamat makan	…England	…England
how are you?	apa khabar?	…America	…Amerika
fine	baik or bagus	…Australia	…Australia
see you again	jumpa lagi	…Canada	…Kanada
please	tolong	…New Zealand	…Zealandia Baru (or
thank you	terima kasih		just "New Zeelan")
you're welcome	sama-sama	…Ireland	…Irlandia
sorry/excuse me	maaf	…Scotland	…Skotlandia

husband	suami		to have, there is/are	ada
wife	isteri		what?	apa?
friend	kawan		what is this/that?	apa ini/itu?
person	orang		when?	bila?
do you speak English?	boleh cakap bahasa inggeris?		where?	di mana?
I (don't) understand	saya (tak) faham		who?	siapa?
that's fine/allowed	boleh		why?	mengapa? or kenapa?
can you help me?	boleh tolong saya?		how?	bagaimana?
can I...?	boleh saya...?		how much/many?	berapa?

Useful adjectives

good	bagus		enough	cukup
a lot	banyak		open/closed	buka/tutup
a little	sikit or sedikit		hungry	lapar
cheap/expensive	murah/mahal		thirsty	haus
hot/cold	panas/sejuk		tired	letih
big/small	besar/kecil		ill	sakit

Useful verbs

come/go	datang/pergi		know (someone)	kenal
do	buat		like	suka
eat/drink	makan/minum		push/pull	tolak/tarik
enter, go in	masuk		see	tengok
give/take	beri/ambil		sit	duduk
have, possess	punya or ada		sleep	tidur
hear	dengar		want	mahu
help	tolong		wish to, intend to	nak
know (something)	tahu			

Getting around and directions

where is...?	di mana...?		wait	tunggu
I want to go to...	saya mahu pergi ke...		turn	belok
how do I get there?	bagaimanakah saya boleh ke sana?		left	kiri
how far?	berapa jauh?		right	kanan
how long will it take?	berapa lama?		straight on	terus
when will the bus leave?	bila bas berangkat?		in front	di depan or di hadapan
what time does the train arrive?	jam berapa keretapi sampai?		behind	di belakang
			north	utara
go up, ride	naik		south	selatan
get down, disembark	turun		east	timur
nearby/far away	dekat/jauh		west	barat
stop	berhenti		street	jalan
			airport	lapangan terbang

bus station	stesen bas *or some-times* hentian bas	fare (adults/children)	tambang (dewasa/kanak-kanak)
train station	stesen keretapi	house	rumah
jetty	jeti *or* pangkalan	post office	pejabat pos
bicycle	baisikal	restaurant	restoran
boat	bot *or* bot penambang (the latter is used of small passenger-carrying craft)	church	gereja
		mosque	masjid
		Chinese temple	tokong
		museum	muzium
car	kereta	park, reserve	taman
motorcycle	motosikal	toilet (men/women)	tandas (lelaki/perempuan)
plane	kapal terbang		
taxi	teksi	entrance	masuk
trishaw	beca	exit	keluar
ticket	tiket		

Accommodation

hotel	hotel	I need a room	saya perlu satu bilik
guesthouse	rumah tumpangan *or* rumah rehat	I'm staying for... nights	saya mahu tinggal... malam
dorm	asrama	please clean my room	tolong bersih-kan bilik saya
room (double/single)	bilik (untuk dua/satu)		
bed (double/single)	katil (kelamin/bujang)	can I store my luggage here?	boleh titip barang?
fan	kipas		
air-conditioned	berhawa dingin	I want to pay	saya nak bayar
bath, shower	mandi		

Banking and shopping

how much is...?	berapa harga...?	shop	kedai
I want to buy...	saya mahu beli...	market	pasar
can you reduce the price?	boleh kurang?	night market	pasar malam
		supermarket	pasaraya
I'll give you no more than...	saya bayar tidak lebih dari...	bank	bank
		money	wang *or* duit
I'm just looking	saya hanya lihat-lihat	moneychanger	pengurup wang

Numbers

0	kosong	5	lima
1	satu (sometimes shortened to the prefix "se-" when used with a noun)	6	enam
		7	tujuh
		8	lapan
		9	sembilan
2	dua	10	sepuluh
3	tiga	11	sebelas
4	empat	12	duabelas

20	duapuluh	1000	seribu
21	duapuluh satu	2000	duaribu
100	seratus	1 million	sejuta
121	seratus duapuluh satu	a half	setengah
200	duaratus		

Time and days of the week

what time is it?	pukul jam berapa?	today	hari ini
time is...	pukul...	tomorrow	esok *or* besok
three o'clock	tiga	yesterday	semalam *or on the*
ten past four	empat sepuluh		*east coast* kelmarin
quarter past five	lima suku	now	sekarang
quarter to six ("five	lima tiga suku	later	nanti
three-quarters")		next...	...depan
six-thirty ("six half")	enam setengah	last...	....yang lalu, ...lepas
7am	tujuh pagi	not yet	belum lagi
8pm	lapan malam	never	tak pernah
hour	jam	Monday	hari Isnin
minute	minit	Tuesday	hari Selasa
second	detik	Wednesday	hari Rabu
day	hari	Thursday	hari Kamis
week	minggu	Friday	hari Jumaat
month	bulan	Saturday	hari Sabtu
year	tahun	Sunday	hari Ahad *or* Minggu

Food and drink glossary

The list below concentrates on Malay terminology, though a few Chinese and Indian terms appear (unfortunately, transliteration of these varies widely), as well as definitions of some culinary words used in local English.

Basics, including cooking methods

Deciphering menus and ordering is sometimes a matter of matching ingredients and cooking methods – for example, to get an approximation of chips or French fries, you'd ask for *kentang goreng*, literally "fried potatoes". If you don't want your food spicy, say *jangan taruh cili* ("don't add chilli") or *saya tak suka pedas* ("I don't like spicy [food]").

bakar baked
bubur porridge
garpu fork
goreng fried
istimewa special (as in "today's special")
kari curry
kedai kek bakery ("cake shop")

kedai kopi a diner ("coffee shop") concentrating on inexpensive rice spreads, noodles and other dishes, while serving some beverages
kering dried
kopitiam Hokkien Chinese term for a *kedai kopi*; commonly used in Singapore
kuah gravy

kukus steamed

layan diri self-service

lemak "fatty"; often denotes use of coconut
   milk

makanan/minuman food/drink

mangkuk bowl

manis sweet

masam sour

masin salty

medan selera food court

panggang grilled

pedas spicy

pinggan plate

pisau knife

rebus boiled

restoran restaurant

sedap tasty

sudu spoon

sup/sop soup

tumis stir-fried, sautéed

warung stall

Meat (daging) and poultry

ayam chicken

babi pork

burong puyuh quail

char siew Cantonese honey roast pork

daging lembu beef

itek duck

kambing mutton

lap cheong sweetish, fatty pork sausage
   (Cantonese)

Fish (ikan) and other seafood

ambal bamboo clams, a Sarawak delicacy

fishball spherical fish dumpling, rubbery in
   texture, often added to noodles and soups

fishcake fish dumpling in slices, often added
   to noodles

ikan bawal pomfret

lian bilis anchovy

ikan keli catfish

ikan kembong mackerel

ikan kerapu grouper

ikan kurau threadfin

ikan merah red snapper

ikan pari skate

ikan siakap sea bass

ikan tongkol tuna

ikan yu or jerung shark

kepiting or ketam crab

kerang cockles

keropok lekor tubular fish dumplings (an
   east-coast speciality)

sotong squid, cuttlefish

udang prawn

udang galah lobster

Vegetables (sayur)

bangkwang a radish-like root (also called
   jicama), used in Chinese rojak and in popiah
   fillings

bawang onion

bawang putih garlic

bayam spinach or spinach-like greens

bendi okra, ladies' fingers

bunga kobis cauliflower

bendawan mushroom

chye sim or choy sum brassica greens, similar to pak choy

cili chilli

halia ginger

jagung corn

kacang beans, pulses or nuts

kangkung convolvulus greens with narrow
   leaves and hollow stems; aka water spinach
   or morning glory

keladi yam

keledek sweet potato

kentang potatoes

kobis cabbage

lada chilli
lobak radish
lobak merah carrot
midin jungle fern, native to Sarawak
pak choy or pek chye soft-leaved brassica greens with broad stalks
petai beans in large pods from a tree, often sold in bunches

pucuk paku fern shoots, eaten as greens
rebung bamboo shoots
tauge beansprouts
terung aubergine
timun cucumber
ubi kayu tapioca

Other ingredients

asam tamarind; also used to indicate a dish flavoured with tamarind
belacan pungent fermented shrimp paste
daun pandan pandanus (screwpine) leaf, imparting a sweet bouquet to foods with which it's cooked; used not only in desserts but also in some rice dishes
garam salt
gula sugar
gula Melaka palm-sugar molasses, used to sweeten *cendol* and other desserts

kaya orange or green curd jam made with egg and coconut; delicious on toast
kicap soy sauce
kicap manis sweet dark soy sauce
mentega butter
minyak oil
tahu tofu (beancurd)
telur egg
tempeh fermented soybean cakes, nutty and slightly sour

Noodles and noodle dishes

The three most common types of noodle are *mee* (or *mi*), yellow egg noodles made from wheat flour; *bee hoon* (or *bihun* or *mee hoon*), like vermicelli; and *kuay teow* (or *hor fun*), like tagliatelle.

char kuay teow Chinese fried *kuay teow*, often seasoned with *kicap manis*, and featuring any combination of prawns, Chinese sausage, fishcake, egg, vegetables and chilli
Foochow noodles steamed and served in soy and oyster sauce with spring onions and dried fish
Hokkien fried mee *mee* and *bee hoon* fried with pieces of pork, prawn and vegetables; a variant in KL has the noodles cooked in soy sauce with *tempeh*
kang puan (or kampua) mee a rich Sibu speciality – noodles cooked in lard
kolok mee *mee* served dryish, accompanied by *char siew* slices
laksa basically noodles in a curried soup featuring some seafood and flavoured with the *laksa*-leaf herb (*daun kesom*); variations include Nonya *laksa* (featuring coconut milk),

asam laksa (Penang-style, with tamarind) and *laksa Johor* (made with spaghetti)
laksam *kuay teow* rice noodles in a fish sauce made with coconut milk and served with *ulam* (salad); an east-coast speciality
mee bandung *mee* served in thickish gravy flavoured with beef and prawn (both of which garnish the dish)
mee goreng Indian or Malay fried noodles; Indian versions are particularly spicy
mee hailam *mee* in an oyster-sauce-based gravy
mee kari noodles in a curried soup
mee pok Teochew dish using ribbon-like yellow noodles, served with fishballs and a chilli dressing
mee rebus boiled *mee*; varies regionally, but one of the best is that sold in Singapore, featuring *mee* in a sweetish sauce made

with yellow bean paste, and garnished with boiled egg and tofu

mee siam *bee hoon* cooked in tangy-sweet soup flavoured with tamarind, and garnished with slices of hard-boiled egg and beancurd

mee suah like *bee hoon* but even more threadlike and soft; can be made crispy if fried

sar hor fun flat rice noodles served in a chicken-stock soup, to which prawns, fried shallots and beansprouts are added; a speciality in Ipoh

wan ton mee roast pork, noodles and vegetables, accompanied by pork dumplings

Rice (nasi) dishes and spreads

char siew fan common one-plate meal, featuring *char siew* and gravy on a bed of steamed rice

claypot rice Chinese dish of rice topped with meat (such as *lap cheong*), cooked in an earthenware pot over a fire to create a smoky taste

daun pisang Malay term for banana-leaf curry, a Southern Indian meal with chutneys and curries, served on a mound of rice, and presented on a banana leaf with poppadums

Hainanese chicken rice Singapore's unofficial national rice dish: steamed or boiled chicken slices served on rice cooked in chicken stock, and accompanied by chicken broth, and a chilli and ginger dip

lemang glutinous rice stuffed into lengths of bamboo

nasi ayam Malay version of Hainanese chicken rice

nasi berlauk simply "rice with dishes"

nasi biryani saffron-flavoured rice cooked with chicken, beef or fish; a North Indian speciality

nasi campur standard term for a rice spread, served with an array of meat, fish and vegetable dishes to choose from

nasi dagang east-coast speciality; a slightly glutinous rice steamed with coconut milk, and often brownish in appearance, usually served with fish curry

nasi goreng rice fried with diced meat and vegetables and sometimes a little spice

nasi kandar a spread of rice and curries originating with Indian Muslim caterers in Penang; the rice is often stored in a container made of wood, which is said to give it a distinctive flavour

nasi kerabu blue or green rice traditionally coloured with flower pigments, though these days food colourings may be used; found particularly in Kelantan, it's usually served with a fish curry

nasi kunyit rice given a bright yellow colour by turmeric

nasi lemak a Malay classic, rice cooked with a little coconut milk and served with *ikan bilis*, cucumber, fried peanuts, fried or hard-boiled egg slices and *sambal*

nasi Minang rice spread featuring dishes cooked in the style of the Minang Highlands of western Sumatra; similar to *nasi Padang*

nasi minyak rice cooked with *ghee*

nasi Padang rice spread with the dishes cooked in the style of Padang, Sumatra

nasi putih plain boiled rice

nasi ulam rice containing blanched herbs and greens

pulut glutinous rice

Roti (bread) dishes

The word *roti* refers both to griddle breads and to Western bread, depending on the context.

murtabak thick griddle bread, usually savoury stuffed with onion, egg and chicken or mutton

murtabak pisang a sweet version of *murtabak*, stuffed with banana.

roti bakar toast, usually served with butter and *kaya*

roti bom an especially greasy *roti canai*, containing a cheesy-tasting margarine

roti canai light, layered griddle bread served with a thin curry sauce

roti John simple Indian dish, a French loaf split and stuffed with an egg, onion and sweet chilli sauce mixture; versions containing meat are occasionally seen

roti kahwin toast spread with butter and *kaya*

roti prata Singapore name for *roti canai*

roti telur *roti canai* with an egg mixed into the dough

roti telur bawang *roti canai* with an egg and chopped onion mixed into the dough

Other specialities

ayam goreng Malay-style fried chicken

ayam percik barbecued chicken with a creamy coconut sauce; a Kota Bharu speciality

bak kut teh literally "meat bone tea", a Chinese soup made by boiling up pork ribs with soy sauce, ginger, herbs and spices

chap chye a Nonya stew of mixed vegetables, fungi and sometimes also glass noodles (aka *tang hoon*, a rather elastic vermicelli)

chee cheong fun Cantonese speciality, vaguely like ravioli, featuring minced shrimp rolled up in rice-flour sheets, steamed and dredged in a sweet-salty red sauce

chye tow kuay also known as "carrot cake", comprising a rice flour/white radish mixture formed into cubes and fried with egg and garlic; a savoury-sweet version with added *kicap manis* is also worth trying

congee watery rice gruel eaten with slices of meat or fish or omelette; sometimes listed on menus as "porridge"

dim sum Chinese meal of titbits – dumplings, pork ribs, etc – steamed or fried and served in bamboo baskets

dosa/dosai/thosai Southern Indian pancake, made from ground rice and lentils, and served with dhal (lentils); *masala dosa* features a potato stuffing, while *rava dosa* has grated carrot in the batter

fish-head curry the head of a red snapper (usually), cooked in a spicy curry sauce with tomatoes and okra

gado-gado Malay/Indonesian salad of lightly cooked vegetables, boiled egg, slices of rice cake and a crunchy peanut sauce

idli South Indian rice and lentil cakes, steamed

kari kepala ikan *see* fish-head curry

kongbian Chinese-style bagels, found only in Sibu

kuih pai tee Nonya dish vaguely resembling fried spring rolls, except that the *pai tee* are shaped like cup cakes; filling is like that for *popiah*

lontong a pairing of a *sayur lodeh*-like curry with rice cakes similar to *ketupat*

oothapam rice-and-lentil pancakes; South Indian

otak-otak mashed fish mixed with coconut milk and chilli paste, then steamed in strips wrapped in banana leaf; a Nonya dish

popiah spring rolls, consisting of a steamed dough wrapper filled with peanuts, egg, bean shoots, vegetables and a sweet sauce; sometimes known as *lumpia*

rendang dry, highly spiced coconut curry with beef, chicken or mutton

rojak The Chinese version is a salad of greens, beansprouts, pineapple and cucumber in a peanut and prawn-paste sauce; quite different is Indian *rojak*, a variety of fritters with sweet chilli dips

satar similar to *otak-otak* but made in triangular shapes; found on the east coast

satay marinated pieces of meat, skewered on small sticks and cooked over charcoal; served with peanut sauce, cucumber, raw onion and *ketupat* (rice cake)

sayur lodeh mixed vegetables stewed in a curry sauce containing coconut milk

sop ekor Malay oxtail soup

sop kambing spicy Malay mutton soup

sop tulang Malay beef-bone soup

steamboat Chinese fondue: raw meat, fish, veggies and other titbits dunked into a steaming broth until cooked

umai raw fish salad, mixed with shallots and lime, found in east Malaysia and Brunei

umbut kelapa masak lemak young coconut shoots, cooked in coconut milk

vadai South Indian fried lentil patty

yam basket Sarawak speciality: meat, vegetables and soya bean curd in a fried yam crust

yong tau foo bean curd, fishballs and assorted vegetables, poached and served with broth and sweet dipping sauces

Snacks and accompaniments

acar pickle, often sweet and spicy

bak kwa Chinese-style sweet barbecued pork slices, eaten as a snack

budu fermented fish sauce

cempedak goreng *Cempedak* (see opposite) fried in batter, allowing not just the flesh but also the floury stones to be eaten

curry puff also called *karipap* in Malay; a semicircular pastry parcel stuffed with curried meat and vegetables

kerabu not to be confused with *nasi kerabu*, this is a salad of grated unripe fruit, mixed with chilli, grated coconut, cucumber and other ingredients

keropok (goreng) deep-fried prawn or fish crackers, derived from a dough like that used to make *keropok lekor* (see p.750)

ketupat unseasoned rice cubes boiled in packets of woven coconut-leaf strips, served as an accompaniment to satay

pau or **pow** Chinese stuffed bun made with a sweetish dough and steamed; *char siew pau* contains Cantonese honey-roast pork, *kai pau* chicken and egg, while there are also *pau* with sweet fillings include bean paste, dried coconut or *kaya*

rasam sour-spicy South Indian soup flavoured with tamarind and tomato

sambal dip made with pounded or ground chilli; *sambal belacan* is augmented with a little *belacan* for extra depth of flavour

sambar watery South Indian curry served with *dosa*

tempoyak fermented durian paste, a Malay condiment

ulam Malay salad of raw vegetables and herbs

yew char kuay Chinese fried dough sticks, good dunked in coffee; not unlike Spanish *churros* in flavour and texture

Drinks

When ordering beverages in a *kedai kopi*, there are various standard terms to bear in mind. *Kosong* ("zero") after the name of the drink means you want it black and unsugared; the suffix -*o* (pronounced "oh") means black with sugar, *susu* means with milk (invariably of the sweetened condensed variety), *ais* or *peng* means iced, *tarik* ("pulled") denotes the popular practice of frothing a drink by pouring it repeatedly from one mug to another and back, and *kurang manis* ("lacking sweetness") means to go easy on the sugar or condensed milk. A few places also allow you to order your drink *see* or *si*, meaning with unsweetened evaporated milk. It's quite possible to combine these terms, so in theory you could order *kopi susu tarik kurang manis peng*, which would be a frothy milky coffee, iced and not too sweet. Note that condensed milk is often assumed to be wanted even if you don't say *susu*.

air botol a bottled drink (usually refers to soft drinks)

air kelapa coconut water

air laici tinned lychee juice, very sweet, usually with a couple of lychees in the glass

air minum drinking water

air tebu sugar-cane juice

bandung or **air sirap bandung** a sweet drink, bright pink in colour, made with rose essence and a little milk

bir beer

chrysanthemum tea delicately fragrant tea made from chrysanthemum blossom, and served slightly sweet, either hot or cold

cincau or **chinchow** sweet drink, the colour of cola or stout, made with strips of jelly-like seaweed

jus juice (the word *jus* is usually followed by the name of the fruit in question)

kopi coffee; some *kedai kopis* offer it freshly brewed, others serve instant

kopi jantan coffee that's claimed to be a male tonic, often advertised with posters showing avuncular Malay men apparently endorsing the drink

kopi tongkat Ali similar to *kopi jantan* (*tongkat Ali* is a herb that Malays believe has aphrodisiac qualities for men)

lassi Indian sweet or salty yoghurt drink

susu milk

teh tea

teh bunga kekwa chrysanthemum

teh limau ais iced lemon tea

tuak rice wine (Borneo)

Fruit (buah)

belimbing starfruit

betik papaya

cempedak similar to jackfruit

duku, duku langsat small round fruits containing bittersweet segments

durian famously stinky large fruit containing rows of seeds coated in sweet creamy flesh

durian belanda soursop

epal apple

jambu batu guava

kelapa coconut

laici lychee

limau lime or lemon

limau bali pomelo

mangga mango

manggis mangosteen

nanas pineapple

nangka jackfruit

nyiur alternative term for coconut

oren orange

pisang banana

rambutan hairy-skinned stone fruit with sweet white flesh

salak teardrop-shaped fruit with scaly brown skin and bitter flesh

tembikai watermelon

Desserts

agar-agar seaweed-derived jelly served in squares or diamonds, and often with coconut milk for richness

air batu campur ("ABC") another name for *ais kacang*

ais kacang ice flakes with red beans, cubes of jelly, sweetcorn, rose syrup and evaporated milk

bubur cha cha sweetened coconut milk with pieces of sweet potato, yam and tapioca

cendol coconut milk, palm sugar syrup and pea-flour noodles poured over shaved ice

cheng tng clear, sweet Chinese broth containing fungi and dried fruit

kuih or **kuih-muih** Malay/Nonya sweetmeats, ranging from something like a Western cake to fudge-like morsels made of mung bean or rice flour

kuih lapis layer cake; either a simple rice-flour confection, or an elaborate wheat-flour sponge comprising numerous very thin layers and unusually rich in egg

pisang goreng bananas or plantains coated in a thin batter and fried

Glossary

adat customary or traditional law

air water

air panas hot springs

air terjun waterfall

atap/attap palm thatch

Baba Straits-born Chinese (male)

bandar town

bandaraya city

bangunan building

banjaran mountain range

batang river system

batik wax and dye technique of cloth decoration

batu rock/stone

bejalai period in an Iban youth's life when he ventures out from the longhouse to experience life in the towns

belian a hardwood traditionally used to construct Sarawak longhouses

belukar secondary rainforest, essentially woodland that regrows in areas where primary forest has been disturbed or cut down

bomoh traditional spiritualist healer

bukit hill

bumbun hide

bumiputra person deemed indigenous to Malaysia ("son of the soil")

bungalow in local English, any detached house

candi temple

Cantonese pertaining to the Guangdong province of southeast China

daerah an administrative district

daulat divine force possessed by a ruler that commands unquestioning loyalty

dipterocarp the predominant family of trees in the rainforest, comprising many types of exceptionally tall trees reaching up to the top of the forest canopy

ekspres express (used of boats and buses)

empangan dam

Foochow pertaining to Fuzhou, a city in Fujian province, southeast China

gasing spinning top

gawai annual festivals celebrated by indigenous groups in Sarawak

gelanggang seni cultural centre

gereja church

godown warehouse

gongsi Chinese clan-house

gopuram sculpted deities over the entrance to a Hindu temple

gua cave

gunung mountain

Hainanese pertaining to Hainan Island, southeast China

halal something permissible in Islam

hill station a settlement or resort at relatively high altitude usually founded in colonial times as an escape from the heat of the lowlands

Hokkien pertaining to the Fujian province of southeast China, the dialect of which is more formally called *minnan*

hutan forest

ikat woven fabric

istana palace

jalan road, street

jambatan bridge

kampung village

kelong a kind of fishing platform that extends out to sea from some beaches; it comprises two rows of vertical poles in the sea bed with a net at the far end, to which the fish are lured by a light hung over the water

kerangas sparse forest ("poor soil")

khalwat an offence under Islamic law, typically involving an unmarried Muslim couple being together in private

kongsi Chinese clan-house/temple; has entered Malay as a word meaning "share"

kota fort

kris wavy-bladed dagger

kuala river confluence or estuary

labu gourd; also used of the gourd-like ceramic bottles made as souvenirs in some parts of the Peninsula

lata waterfall

laut sea

lebuh avenue

lebuhraya highway/expressway

lorong lane

mak yong courtly dance-drama

makam grave or tomb

Malaya old name for the area now called Peninsular Malaysia

amak Indian Muslim; used particularly of restaurants run by Indian Muslims

mandi Asian method of showering by dousing with water from a tank using a small bucket or dipper

masjid mosque

mat Salleh Malaysian colloquial term for a foreigner, usually a white person

Melayu Malay

menara minaret or tower

merdeka freedom, in general; can specifically refer to Malaysian independence

Minangkabau matriarchal people from Sumatra

negara national

nipah a type of palm tree

Nonya Straits-born Chinese (female)

Orang Asli Peninsular Malaysia aborigines ("original people"); also Orang Ulu (upriver people) and Orang Laut (sea people)

padang field/square; usually the main town square

pangkalan jetty or port (literally "base")

pantai beach

parang machete

pasar market

pasar malam night market

pasir sand

pejabat Daerah district office

pejabat Pos post office

pekan town

pelabuhan port/harbour

penghulu chieftain, leader

Peranakan Straits-born Chinese

perigi well

persekutuan federal

pintu arch/gate/door

pondok hut or shelter

pulau island

rajah prince

Ramadan Muslim fasting month

rebana drum

rotan rattan cane; used in the infliction of corporal punishment

rumah persinggahan lodging house

rumah rehat older guesthouse (literally "rest house"), now mainly privately run, though once state-owned

rumah tumpangan boarding house

samping songket worn by a man as a short sarong over loose trousers

saree traditional Indian woman's garment, worn in conjunction with a choli (short-sleeved blouse)

sarung/sarong cloth worn as a wrap around the lower body

sekolah school

Semenanjung Peninsula

seni art or skill

shophouse a two-storey terraced building found mainly in town centres, and often featuring a facade that is recessed at street level, providing a shaded walkway that serves as a pavement

silat Malay art of self-defence

songket brocade

songkok Malay male headgear, a little like a flattish fez, made of black velvet over cardboard

storm corridor an exterior pathway with an overhead shelter throughout its length

sultan ruler

sungai/sungei river

t'ai chi Chinese martial art; commonly performed as an early-morning exercise

taman park

tamu market/fair

tanjung/tanjong cape, headland

tasik/tasek lake

telaga freshwater spring or well

teluk/telok bay or inlet

Teochew pertaining to Chaozhou, a city in Fujian province, southeast China

tokong Chinese temple

towkay Chinese merchant

tuai tribal headman (Sarawak)

wau kite

wayang show, ranging from a film screening to Chinese opera

wayang kulit shadow-puppet play (literally "skin show", after the fact that the puppets are made of hide)

wisma house (used of commercial buildings rather than residences)

Acronyms

ASEAN Association of Southeast Asian Nations, an economic and political grouping of ten regional states, including Malaysia, Singapore and Brunei

BN Barisan Nasional or National Front – the coalition, dominated by UMNO, which has governed Malaysia since 1974

KTM Keretapi Tanah Melayu, the Malaysian national railway company

MAS Malaysia Airlines

MCA Malaysian Chinese Association, the Chinese wing of the governing BN

MCP Malayan Communist Party

MRT Singapore's Mass Rapid Transit system

PAP Singaporean People's Action Party

PAS Parti Islam SeMalaysia, the Pan-Malaysian Islamic Party

PKR Parti Keadilan Rakyat, the Malaysian opposition People's Justice Party (usually called simply Keadilan)

SIA Singapore Airlines

UMNO United Malays National Organization

Small print and Index

A Rough Guide to Rough Guides

Published in 1982, the first Rough Guide – to Greece – was a student scheme that became a publishing phenomenon. Mark Ellingham, a recent graduate in English from Bristol University, had been travelling in Greece the previous summer and couldn't find the right guidebook. With a small group of friends he wrote his own guide, combining a highly contemporary, journalistic style with a thoroughly practical approach to travellers' needs.

The immediate success of the book spawned a series that rapidly covered dozens of destinations. And, in addition to impecunious backpackers, Rough Guides soon acquired a much broader and older readership that relished the guides' wit and inquisitiveness as much as their enthusiastic, critical approach and value-for-money ethos.

These days, Rough Guides include recommendations from shoestring to luxury and cover more than 200 destinations around the globe, including almost every country in the Americas and Europe, more than half of Africa and most of Asia and Australasia. Our ever-growing team of authors and photographers is spread all over the world, particularly in Europe, the US and Australia.

SMALL PRINT

In the early 1990s, Rough Guides branched out of travel, with the publication of Rough Guides to World Music, Classical Music and the Internet. All three have become benchmark titles in their fields, spearheading the publication of a wide range of books under the Rough Guide name.

Including the travel series, Rough Guides now number more than 350 titles, covering: phrasebooks, waterproof maps, music guides from Opera to Heavy Metal, reference works as diverse as Conspiracy Theories and Shakespeare, and popular culture books from iPods to Poker. Rough Guides also produce a series of more than 120 World Music CDs in partnership with World Music Network.

Visit www.roughguides.com to see our latest publications.

Rough Guide travel images are available for commercial licensing at www.roughguidespictures.com

Rough Guide credits

Text editor: Lucy White and Sarah Eno
Layout: Ajay Verma
Cartography: Alakananda Bhattacharya and Swati Handoo
Picture editor: Mark Thomas
Production: Rebecca Short
Proofreader: Jennifer Speake
Cover design: Chloë Roberts
Editorial: Ruth Blackmore, Andy Turner, Keith Drew, Edward Aves, Alice Park, Jo Kirby, James Smart, Natasha Foges, Róisín Cameron, Emma Traynor, Emma Gibbs, Kathryn Lane, Christina Valhouli, Monica Woods, Mani Ramaswamy, Harry Wilson, Lucy Cowie, Helen Ochyra, Amanda Howard, Lara Kavanagh, Alison Roberts, Joe Staines, Peter Buckley, Matthew Milton, Tracy Hopkins, Ruth Tidball; **Delhi** Madhavi Singh, Karen D'Souza, Lubna Shaheen
Design & Pictures: London Scott Stickland, Dan May, Diana Jarvis, Nicole Newman, Sarah Cummins, Emily Taylor; **Delhi** Umesh Aggarwal, Jessica Subramanian, Ankur Guha, Pradeep Thapliyal, Sachin Tanwar, Anita Singh, Nikhil Agarwal, Sachin Gupta
Production: Vicky Baldwin

Cartography: London Maxine Repath, Ed Wright, Katie Lloyd-Jones; **Delhi** Rajesh Chhibber, Ashutosh Bharti, Rajesh Mishra, Animesh Pathak, Jasbir Sandhu, Karobi Gogoi, Deshpal Dabas
Online: London George Atwell, Faye Hellon, Jeanette Angell, Fergus Day, Justine Bright, Clare Bryson, Aine Fearon, Adrian Low, Ezgi Celebi, Amber Bloomfield; **Delhi** Amit Verma, Rahul Kumar, Narender Kumar, Ravi Yadav, Debojit Borah, Rakesh Kumar, Ganesh Sharma, Shisir Basumatari
Marketing & Publicity: London Liz Statham, Niki Hanmer, Louise Maher, Jess Carter, Vanessa Godden, Vivienne Watton, Anna Paynton, Rachel Sprackett, Libby Jellie, Laura Vipond, Vanessa McDonald; **New York** Katy Ball, Judi Powers, Nancy Lambert; **Delhi** Ragini Govind
Manager India: Punita Singh
Reference Director: Andrew Lockett
Operations Manager: Helen Phillips
PA to Publishing Director: Nicola Henderson
Publishing Director: Martin Dunford
Commercial Manager: Gino Magnotta
Managing Director: John Duhigg

Publishing information

This sixth edition published September 2009 by
Rough Guides Ltd,
80 Strand, London WC2R 0RL
14 Local Shopping Centre, Panchsheel Park, New Delhi 110017, India
Distributed by the Penguin Group
Penguin Books Ltd,
80 Strand, London WC2R 0RL
Penguin Group (US)
375 Hudson Street, NY 10014, USA
Penguin Group (Australia)
250 Camberwell Road, Camberwell, Victoria 3124, Australia
Penguin Group (Canada)
195 Harry Walker Parkway N, Newmarket, ON, L3Y 7B3 Canada
Penguin Group (NZ)
67 Apollo Drive, Mairangi Bay, Auckland 1310, New Zealand
Cover concept by Peter Dyer.

Typeset in Bembo and Helvetica to an original design by Henry Iles.

Printed in Europe

© Charles de Ledesma, Mark Lewis, Richard Lim

No part of this book may be reproduced in any form without permission from the publisher except for the quotation of brief passages in reviews.

776pp includes index

A catalogue record for this book is available from the British Library

ISBN: 978-1-84836-059-4

The publishers and authors have done their best to ensure the accuracy and currency of all the information in **The Rough Guide to Malaysia, Singapore and Brunei,** however, they can accept no responsibility for any loss, injury, or inconvenience sustained by any traveller as a result of information or advice contained in the guide.

1 3 5 7 9 8 6 4 2

Help us update

We've gone to a lot of effort to ensure that the sixth edition of **The Rough Guide to Malaysia, Singapore and Brunei** is accurate and up-to-date. However, things change – places get "discovered", opening hours are notoriously fickle, restaurants and rooms raise prices or lower standards. If you feel we've got it wrong or left something out, we'd like to know, and if you can remember the address, the price, the hours, the phone number, so much the better.

Please send your comments with the subject line **"Rough Guide Malaysia, Singapore and Brunei Update"** to ©mail@roughguides.com. We'll credit all contributions and send a copy of the next edition (or any other Rough Guide if you prefer) for the very best emails.

Have your questions answered and tell others about your trip at
⊛community.roughguides.com

Acknowledgements

Charles de Ledesma In Brunei, Charles would like to thank Kay Williams for lifts, help and beers. And in Kota Kinabalu, Robin Chin from Sabah Tourism for quick responses to all queries great and small, and Rory, Howard and Victoria for being great scouts and promoters; and in Sandakan, Elvina Susanna Ong, for being such a superb facilitator and James Chan from *Ease Boutique* for a great view. Also in Sabah, thanks too to Jim and Sue Lynch who reported on the Maliau Basin and Ric Owen and team at the marvellous Scuba Junkie in Semporna. Over the border in Sarawak's Kelabit Highlands, thanks to Florence Apu and Reddish Aran for kindness, contacts and friendship, and in Kuching to the welcoming team, Wayne Taman, Mike Reid, Donald and Marina, and to Grace Geikie, who heads Sarawak Tourism with such panache and spirit. Finally thanks to brother David, sister-in-law Fiona, and niece Catherine who got to Agnes Keith's house before me.

Richard Lim thanks: Alex Au; Arnold Barkhordarian; Angelina Fernandez at Firefly; Dillon; Isa in Rhu Muda; Iskandar at PHK; Kamaruddin; Khalil Abo Al Thinin; M. Fazil Ismail at KTM; David Leffman; Harry Mulder; Murali; Nik Nora; Roselan and Azahar; Rosmawati; Alex Soh; Simon in Kuantan; Cik Tawfik and other Jabatan Perhilitan staff; Matthew Teller; Eddy Teo and Vijay Mohan at Pearson; Pauline Wee and Raphael Lee at the STB; Yati; Zack

in Marang; Zack in Merapoh; Wan Zawawi; and Zawi Ahmad. Special thanks to Azam and Ardiana; Ameen Talib; Amelia, Tricia and Firdaus; Appu; Azman; Mr Bob; Brian K; Peter Caron; Hani; Joe and Finola; Kamal Yasin; Ulrich Kratz; Alex Lee and Maslina at Ping Anchorage; Lim Ee Lin and Elizabeth Cardosa at Badan Warisan; Lim Huck Chin and Fernando Jorge; Nik Maseri; Ian M; Moni and Sanadure Durei; Pawi; Rahayu and Sharifah for the turtle drama; Reza Azam; Surin Suksawan; Janet T; and Peter Wee. Extra-special mentions to: John Gee; Martin aka Terry; Mazlena; Joe Ng; Ooi Kee Beng; Daya aka Dina Das for rolling back the years in Serangoon Road; Diego V, the wrong key for the wrong lock; Son of Colin Goh; and to my family in Singapore (the biggest unseen helpers in chapter 9).

Anette dal Jensen thanks: Matt Brooks; Bill Sillery; Lynn Torfason & Mike Allen; Lone Anker & Dan Johnson; Ron Rahmani; Malik and Jay; Neal Nrimal; Hymeir; Anne & Kua Kia Soong; Natasha Betts; Alexander Constantine; Annaafiz Jamaludin; Cedryyc; Pete Lawrence; Anthony McGeever; Emily and Azam; Betty Wallace; Sam-Anna Pering; Emily Cumming; Jane-Claire Bulmer; Trish Durkin; the family at Intan Beach Resort on Pangkor; and all the wonderful people of Malaysia who helped and made me laugh along with way, particularly the two random blokes at Kota Tinggi bus station, who will never read this. Thank you.

Readers' letters

Thanks to all the readers who have taken the time to write in with comments and suggestions (and apologies if we've inadvertently omitted or misspelt anyone's name):

Dominic Al-Badri; Kathie-Louise Black; Stephen P. Cahill; Emma Carew; John Chong; George Elliston; Valerie A. Ferguson; Naoise Gaffney; Angeline Goh; Mireille Helle; Steven Hogg; Merilyn Hywel-Vines; William F. Lamack; David Lennon; J.C. McIlwaine; Vincent Megaw; Ruaraidh Melvin; Senay Oakley; Caroline Porter; Allan Rickman; Nicholas Tan; Kirsten Wendt; Flavia Woodwark.

Photo credits

All photos © Rough Guides except the following:

Title page
Shadow puppet © Pat Behnke/Alamy

Full page
Rainforest and mist © Roine Magnusson/Getty Images

Introduction
Dragon fruits and carambola © Ludovic Maisant/ Getty Images
Market scene © Andrea Pistplesi/Getty Images
Shophouse © Richard Lim
Longhouse © Stephen Lloyd Malaysia/Alamy

Beach huts and palms © Naki Kouyioumtzis/ Getty Images
Caves in Mulu National Park © Robbie Stine/ Getty Images
Singapore at night © Tom Bonaventure/Getty Images
Wildlife sanctuary © Tim Laman/Getty Images
Perhentian Islands © Richard Lim

Things not to miss
01 Perhentian Islands © Jill Gocher/Jupiter Images
04 Painting batik © Ahmad Faizal Yahya/Alamy

05 Ulu Temburong Park © Tim Graham/Alamy
06 Omar Ali Saifuddien Mosque © David Kirkland/Photolibrary
07 Taman Negara © Marc Anderson/Alamy
08 Sungai Kinabatangan © Jochem D Wijnands/Getty Images
09 Shopping in Kuala Lumpa © Jon Hicks/Alamy
10 Georgetown © M Winch/Axiom
11 Kuching © Getty Images
12 Theatre performance © Stock connection/Alamy
13 Proboscis monkey © Chris Fredriksson/Alamy
14 Rainforest Music Festival © The Rainforest Music Festival
15 Top-spinning © Andrew Woodley/Alamy
16 Melaka © Jon Arnold/Alamy
17 Cameron Highlands © Walter Bibikow/Photolibrary
18 Mount Kinabalu © Banana Pancake/Alamy
19 Gunung Lulu National Park © Ian Cook/Axiom
20 Kampung Ayer © Stefano Paterna/Alamy
21 Langkawi © Dana Hoff/Getty Images
22 Lelabit Highlands © SDBAsia/Alamy
23 The Petronas Towers © Peter Adams/Getty Images
24 Street food © John Oates/Alamy
25 Pulau Sipadan © Reinhard Dirscherl/Photolibrary
26 Longhouses in Sarawak © Chris Hellier/Corbis

Malay Life colour section
Man with kite © Hugh Sitton/Getty Images
Kite-maker © Gavin Hellier/Getty Images
Man spinning top © Tibor Bognar/Alamy
Street vendor © Andrew Newey/Alamy
Traditional drums © Myimagefiles/Alamy
Man with shadow puppets © Richard Lim
Kampung House © Richard Lim
Men wearing the baju Melayu and samping © Tibor Bognar/Alamy

Visiting a longhouse colour section
Traditional Iban longhouse © dbimages/Alamy
Sarawak Cultural Village © Nigel Hicks/Alamy
Iban Longhouse © MARKA/Alamy
Longhouse on the Batang River © dbimage/Alamy
Elderly headhunter with fighting cock © MARKA/Alamy
Woman weaving © dbimage/Alamy
Typical longhouse scene © Nick Haslan/Alamy
Gawai picnic © jamehj/Alamy
Man performing Sarawak dance © Rolf Richardson/Alamy
Skulls © dbimage/Alamy

Black and whites
p.78 Petronas Towers, Kuala Lumpur © Rolf Richardson/Alamy

p.100 Jamek Mosque © Henry Westheim Photography/Alamy
p.102 Petaling Street Market © Richard Lim/Alamy
p.110 Stall in Chinatown © Richard Lim/Alamy
p.135 Batu Caves © Robert Harding Picture Library/Alamy
p.141 Pulau Ketam © Thomas Cockrem/Alamy
p.144 Kellie's Castle © Bare Essence/Alamy
p.152 Cameron Highlands © David Bowman/Alamy
p.167 Paulau Pangkor beach © JTB Photo Communications/Alamy
p.175 Taiping Lake Gardens © Bare Essence/Alamy
p.191 Cheong Fatt Tze Mansion © Rob Walls/Alamy
p.207 Tapir © Arco Images/Alamy
p.224 Ride down Kuala Koh, Taman Negara © Richard Lim
p.237 Taman Negara Resort © Richard Lim/Alamy
p.242 Bamboo on the Bukit Teresek trail © Richard Lim
p.259 Lipis administration building © Richard Lim
p.268 Pulau Perhentian beach © Richard Lim
p.281 Batik printing © Richard Lim
p.303 Boat building year, Palau Duyong © Richard Lim
p.317 East-coast market © Richard Lim
p.330 Beach at Batang Village © photograph/Alamy
p.335 Minangkabau House © Beaconstox/Alamy
p.345 Porta de Santiago © David Ball/Alamy
p.375 Beach bungalow © Andrew Woodley/Alamy
p.388 Deer Cave, Gunung Mulu National Park © Robert Harding Photo Library/Alamy
p.400 Kuching Mosque © dbimages/Alamy
p.417 Proboscis monkey © Image & Stories/Alamy
p.439 Punan tribesman © Toby AdamsonAxiom
p.467 Boat ride in Gunung Mulu National Park © Robert Harding Photo Library/Alamy
p.484 Snorkelling © Reinhard Dircherl/Alamy
p.493 Kota Kinabalu © Robert Harding Photo Library/Alamy
p.515 Market at Kota Belud © Iain Farley/Alamy
p.525 Mount Kinabalu © Panana Pancake/Alamy
p.535 Orang-utan © Reinhard Dircherl/Alamy
p.538 Sungai Kinabatanga © Ian Trower/Alamy
p.543 The Danum Valley Conservation Area © Neil McAllister/Alamy
p.554 Ulu Temburong National Park © Jeremy Horner/Alamy
p.565 Kampung Ayer © Reuter/Corbis
p.620 Shophouses in Chinatown © Richard Lim
p.623 Buddha Tooth Relic Statue at Temple © Richard Lim

Index

Map entries are indicated in colour. For a list of map symbols used in this book, see p.776. In this index, islands should in general be looked up under the word "Pulau", rivers under "Sungai" or sometimes "Batang", lakes under "Tasik" and mountains under "Gunung". When looking up names, bear in mind that both Chinese and Malay names are indexed according to the first word of the name.

Map symbols

maps are listed in the full index using coloured text

---	International borders	⊤	Public gardens
— ··	Malaysian state boundary	♦	Point of interest
---	Chapter division boundary	@	Internet access
═══	Highway	ⓘ	Tourist office
═══	Major roads	⊠	Post office
═══	Minor roads	⊞	Hospital
▥▥▥	Steps	P	Parking
-----	Path	©	Telephone
▬▬	Railway	⚐	Golf course
▥▥▥	Funicular	∩	Arch
— —	Ferry route	☺	Swimming pool
▬▬	Wall	⅄	Campsite
▭▭	Waterway	⬥	Hut/hide
⊠—⊠	Gate	◉	Accommodation
▲	Peak	▣	Restaurant/café
⁒	Rock	✡	Synagogue
/ı\	Hill shading	⳻	Church (regional maps)
⌒	Cave	+	Church (town maps)
⸮	Marshland	♜	Mosque
⅋	Waterfall	♠	Buddhist temple
⚶	Viewpoint	♣	Hindu/Sikh temple
⚲	Lighthouse	♣	Chinese temple
✈	Airport	▭	Market
✗	Airport (regional)	◯	Stadium
⊖	MRT station (Singapore)	▬	Building
★	Bus stop	+⊤+	Christian cemetery
∴	Ruin	ᵧᵧᵧ	Muslim cemetery
♙	Castle/fort		Park
⚑	Museum		Beach
🏛	Monument		Pedestrianized area